Praise from Reviewers

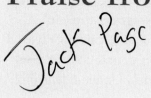

"I have taught this course for nine years and had not found a book this engaging. When I started reading the chapters, I wanted to continue reading. The material is presented in a balanced and fair manner, without the usual bias or slanted presentations common to marriage and family introductory texts. . . . This text includes a balance of theory, research, and practical applications. Students will have a much richer understanding of the contemporary family after reading this text."

—Bill C. Greenvalt, Western Kentucky University

"[T]he reading material was enjoyable, thorough, and academic. I work in an environment in which the majority of my students are either minority students or students who do not have English as a first language. I believe that the materials . . . presented in the text would not only be understandable to my students but would also be an asset to their understanding of my own lectures and presentation material."

—Richard Fraser, California State University,
Los Angeles

"I liked very much the Popular Culture and the Media input. I think this will be eye-catching and appeal very much to students. Students [who] are very media savvy will relate well to this. The Practical Action boxes seemed also to be very effective. Students like 'how-to' and self-study quizzes and materials, and will enjoy using these things. . . . The use of global comparisons, multi-ethnic, multi-class [examples] is useful for critical thinking applications. I think this book is very current and very useful."

—Linda Green, Normandale Community College

"[My students] find it interesting and easy to read. . . . They really liked the references to today's pop culture. Several of them commented they planned on keeping this text for future reference and to share with family and friends. I will be looking forward to the second edition."

—Bobbie Brannon, Catawba Valley
Community College

"I have found that the text is very readable and does engage the student in the subject matter. Students do find the Self-Assessments useful. Also, the textbook works well for a number of teaching and learning styles. I have used the book in both a lecture/discussion course and in a self-paced mastery-based course using the Keller model of student learning."

—*C. Stephen Glennon, Iowa Western Community College*

"The text is written in a manner that is easy for students to understand without being condescending. The material presented in the text is engaging, and the plethora of side projects (like the Practical Action boxes and the Learning Lab section) help generate interest in the subject. . . . It is a text I would use in future family classes."

—*Vondora Wilson-Corzen, Suffolk Community College*

Marriages, Families, & Intimate Relationships

A PRACTICAL INTRODUCTION

SECOND EDITION

BRIAN K. WILLIAMS

STACEY C. SAWYER

CARL M. WAHLSTROM

Genesee Community College
and
State University of New York at Geneseo

PEARSON

Boston   New York   San Francisco

Mexico City   Montreal   Toronto   London   Madrid   Munich   Paris

Hong Kong   Singapore   Tokyo   Cape Town   Sydney

Executive Editor: Jeff Lasser
Senior Development Editor: Leah Strauss
Supplements Editor: Lauren Houlihan
Senior Marketing Manager: Kelly May
Senior Production Administrator: Donna Simons
Composition Buyer: Linda Cox
Manufacturing Buyer: Debbie Rossi
Cover Administrator and Designer: Elena Sidorova
Text Designer: Ellen Pettengell
Project Manager: Lynda Griffiths
Editorial Production Services: Publishers' Design and Production Services, Inc.
Electronic Composition: Publishers' Design and Production Services, Inc.
Photo Research: Katharine S. Cebik

For related titles and support materials, visit our online catalog at www.ablongman.com.

Between the time website information is gathered and then published, it is not unusual for some sites to have closed. Also, the transcription of URLs can result in typographical errors. The publisher would appreciate notification where these errors occur so that they may be corrrected in subsequent editions.

Library of Congress Cataloging-in-Publication Data were not available at the time of publication.

ISBN-13: 978-0-205-52145-6
ISBN-10: 0-205-52145-2

Photo Credits appear on page PC1 (at the end of this book), which constitutes an extension of the copyright page.

Printed in the United States of America

10 9 8 7 6 5 4   CKV   12 11 10

To the precious memory of my father and mother, Harry A. Williams and Gertrude S. Williams. Also dedicated to my children and their spouses and their children—Sylvia, Scott, Atticus and Kirk, Julia, Nicholas, and Lily—who I hope can learn from this.

—B.K.W.

To Peter—my family for too short a time.

—S.C.S.

To my partner for eternity; and to the wonderful and special memory of my father and mother, Gustav C. Wahlstrom and Marie Elizabeth Wahlstrom.

—C.M.W.

Brief Contents

Contents

3 GENDER The Meanings of Masculinity & Femininity 88

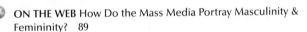

4 LOVE The Many Faces 118

5 INVOLVEMENT Dating, Pairing, Courtship, & Cohabitation 146

9 VARIATIONS Nonmarital Families & Households   286

10 REPRODUCTION Decisions about Having or Not Having Children   332

11 PARENTING Children, Families, & Generations   368

12 WORK Economics, Jobs, & Balancing Family Demands   412

13 CRISES Managing Stress, Disaster, Violence, & Abuse   446

14 UNCOUPLING Separation & Divorce   494

15 REMARRIAGE Reinvented, Renewed, & Blended Families   546

APPENDICES

Panels

Preface

Happiness: Can people still find it in intimate relationships in the complex world we now live in? With all the influences imposed on modern life and our expectations by globalization, computerization, the all-pervasive media, and so on, are there lessons we could pass along that would help our students negotiate the dangerous shoals and make lasting personal connections?

Marriages, Families, & Intimate Relationships: A Practical Introduction, Second Edition, discusses fundamental concepts and insights from across the social sciences. It also attempts to engage students with high-interest, useful information and to answer the questions that matter greatly to them. By blending our strengths—teaching, consulting, counseling, researching, and publishing—we have tried to create a research-based yet highly readable and practical text on intimacy, family, and personal happiness that appeals to today's visually oriented students.

A glance at the table of contents will show that the text covers the topics and principles that most instructors have come to expect: gender, love, marriage, sexuality, parenting, and so on. In addition, we cover issues that today's students need to know about: nonmarital families and households; the effect of work on intimate relationships; managing stresses, crises, and violence; and dealing with divorce and remarriage.

Beyond these, however, we believe our book has **four key features that make it unique:**

- An emphasis on practicality
- An emphasis on readability
- A student-centered approach to learning
- An emphasis on currentness

Major Theme & Features: Emphasis on Practicality

We want this book to be as **useful and meaningful as possible for students.** Accordingly, we cover not only basic concepts and the latest research but also offer a great deal of **practical advice,** of the kind students look for in magazines and newspapers, on the Internet, and from their friends and teachers.

This advice is expressed not only in the main narrative but also in the following features.

■ **Popular Culture & the Media** chapter introductions **help students separate fact from myth** by showing examples of the often misleading messages we receive about intimate relationships from TV, popular music, the Internet, advertising, and the like. Examples: "The Varieties of Gender Stereotypes," "What Is This Thing Called Love?," "How Do We Learn about Sex?," "Is Money the Measure of Love?"

■ **Numbers That Matter** boxes provide **provocative statistics** that will **stimulate class discussion** and help students focus on important data about marriages, families, and relationships. Many of the statistics used point out significant variations by race, ethnicity, gender, social class, and age.

■ **Practical Action** boxes, which usually appear at least once in every chapter, **offer concrete advice that students will find beneficial** in their personal and work lives. Examples: "Happiness: Is It within Your Grasp?," "Love on the Internet: Can You Find the Perfect Partner Online?," "Before Moving in Together: Setting Ground Rules for Understanding," "Legal & Financial Considerations for Unmarried Couples, Straight or Gay."

PRACTICAL ACTION
Tools for Reasoning

The way to break through the closed habits of thought called mind-sets is to use reasoning. *Reasoning—giving reasons in favor of this assertion or that*—is essential to critical thinking and solving life's problems.

How to Reason

Reasoning is put in the form of what philosophers call arguments. *Arguments consist of one or more premises, or reasons, logically supporting a result or outcome called a conclusion.*

An example of an argument is as follows:

The two main kinds of correct or valid arguments are *inductive* and *deductive*.

■ **Inductive argument: An *inductive argument* is defined as follows: If the premises are true, the conclusion is PROBABLY true, but the truth is not guaranteed.** An inductive argument is sometimes known as a "probability argument."

An example of an *inductive* argument is as follows (Rasool et al. 1993: 132):

Premise 1: Stress can cause illness.
Premise 2: Reuben experiences

An example of a *deduc* ment is as follows (Rasoc 1993: 132):

Premise 1: All students ex stress in their lives.
Premise 2: Reuben is a st
Conclusion: Therefore, R experiences stress in h

This argument is dedu conclusion is definitely t premises are definitely tr

Some Types of Incorrect Re

Patterns of incorrect reas

EXAMPLE OF
Being Childless in a Child-Oriented Society
A Woman's View, a Man's View

How do people who have never had children feel about their status? Here are two views, taken from the *Child-Free Zone: Why More People Are Choosing NOT to Be Parents*, at *www.childfree.net*:

were tal
had don
want on
'I'd rath
be a zoo

"My l
thought
having l
ever he
them. S
the sam
good wi
made a

glad that we don't have them. So I would say that we are equal in our decision. I'm glad that I didn't fall for someone who desperately wanted kids. I think that when I was younger, I may have changed my mind just to please them and it would have been a disaster. Now that I'm older, I know

started a business) in the of our marriage. Both my worked in the business, ar to travel a lot for a period five years. . . . I also think social and environmental are not conducive to havi Do we really want to brin

■ **Example of** boxes use **real-world situations** to illustrate key points made in the text. Among them are "Example of an Expression of Love: The Kiss" and "Example of Being Childless in a Child-Oriented Society: A Woman's View, a Man's View."

Readability: Helping Students Retain Information

Research shows that textbooks **written in an imaginative and accessible style significantly improve students' ability to retain information.** We make use of **frequent headings** as signposts to help readers along, **numbered and bulleted lists,** and **advanced organizers.** Besides presenting information in bite-size form, we have employed a number of journalistic devices—plenty of examples, colorful facts, short biographical sketches, apt direct quotes—to make the material as interesting as possible.

In addition, to help readers be clear on what important terms mean, we **print each key term in *italic boldface* AND its definition in boldface.** (The Glossary offers a pronunciation guide for some terms to help non-native speakers.) Finally, the names of **important theorists and scholars are boldfaced,** so that readers will know they should pay attention to these names for possible testing purposes.

CHAPTER 8

MARRIAGE
The Ultimate Commitment?

POPULAR CULTURE & THE MEDIA

What Kind of Marriage & Family Is Really Real?

"The way the whole issue of family life in America is framed politically and culturally is dependent on utopian images of the family that come out of '50s television," says Robert Thompson (quoted in Jayson 2006), professor of media and popular culture at Syracuse University.

Even if you never watched reruns of Father Knows Best, Leave It to Beaver, or The Adventures of

Ozzie and Harriet—*all 1950s-era shows featuring nuclear families that were "unnaturally wholesome," as* USA Today called them *("Dysfunction rules, man!" 2003)—your beliefs about families may have been influenced by these outmoded images, Thompson believes. Traditional TV families of the 1950s and 1960s (and even those that came later, such as* The Brady Bunch, The Waltons, The Cosby Show's Huxtables, and The Simpsons) *did not actually reflect the American family, says Thompson; rather, they established the notion of what a perfect American family is supposed to be.*

Since the 1990s, the dynamics, values, and humor of the television-family show have become increasingly edgy, if not downright dysfunctional. Ozzie and Harriet, for instance, yielded to a newer generation's Ozzy and Sharon of the MTV comedy The Osbournes (2002–2005), the real-life adventures of Beverly Hills oddballs—"an eccentric but loving family coping with dog poo on the rug, misplaced cats, and sibling rivalry," in one description. "Oh, and son Jack's pot use, daughter Kelly's vagina monologue, dad's Viagra habit, and mom's egg-throwing retaliation against noisy neighbors" (Gunderson 2002: 2E). Fox's animated series Family Guy (created in 1999)—described as "a traditional domestic sitcom soaked in battery acid" (Gordon 2005: 50)—has exhibited surprising longevity. Yet, says cultural observer Michael Medved (2002), even though we realize that the images of pop culture are "just TV" or "just a movie," they still inform what we think about marriage and families.

■ **Television:** Besides the shows just mentioned, television has also brought us the unorthodox family values of New Jersey gangster Tony Soprano in The Sopranos (1998–2007). Although he murders people, "he is a surprisingly good father," says one account (Teachout 2002), "at once sternly moralistic and unambivalently loving." (Some might disagree this constitutes a "good father," though he might be a great godfather.)

One critic, Robert Bianco (2006: 2E), observes that, outside of CW's Everybody Hates Chris (created in 2005), loosely based on the experiences of comedian Chris Rock, "children have almost vanished from the sitcom sphere. And when they do appear, they're on comedies aimed at a much older audience, such as Christine and Two and a Half Men." Or they are pushed into the background, as in Everybody Loves Raymond (1996–2005) or turned into "a target of prepubescent jokes, as on [Two and a Half] Men or The War at Home." Bianco also points out that life on TV is, with rare exceptions, usually one of ceaseless prosperity. "How many people," he asks, "do you know who hold jobs that leave them struggling to pay current bills and worrying about their futures? How many of those do you see on TV?" Except for Everybody Hates Chris—and perhaps My Name Is Earl, Friday Night Lights, and The Wire—few shows examine the economic insecurities of working-class families.

So-called reality television has also given us Who Wants to Marry a Multi-Millionaire, in which we could watch two strangers tie the knot and then follow their breakup days later, as well as Joe Millionaire, The Bachelor, and The Bachelorette—all of which portray marriage not as sacred institutions but "exploitable, instantly disposable commodities," says one critic (Laurence 2003).

■ **Films:** The dysfunctional family has long been the subject of Hollywood films, ranging from The Godfather trilogy, through Long Day's Journey into Night, to American Beauty. Against these are more lighthearted family comedies such as the Ben Stiller films Flirting with Disaster (with Patricia Arquette) and Meet the Parents (with Robert De Niro) or the surprise 2002 hit, My Big Fat Greek Wedding.

■ **Books:** Can people cure their dysfunctionality by reading self-help advice books? If so, there is a never-ending supply, beginning with The Complete Idiot's Guide to Being a Groom and Making Marriage Work for Dummies. Seekers of a "happy marriage" may choose from Seven Secrets of a Happy Marriage, 1008 Secrets of a Happy Marriage, and And They Lived Happily Ever After.

Getting married and staying married: Clearly, this is a complex subject. Let us begin to explore it.

ON THE WEB The Marriage Surprise

www.google.com

One way to get into the subject of marriage is to use an Internet search engine to search for interesting topics:

1. Go to Google.
2. Click on *News.*
3. At the top of the screen, type in the keyword *Marriage.*
4. Click on *Search news.*
5. Scroll down until you see an interesting topic. Click on it and read. What startling things did you learn?

WHAT'S AHEAD IN THIS CHAPTER

We first discuss good and bad reasons for getting married, the expectations people have for marriage, and different marriage contracts. We then describe four phases in a family life cycle: beginning, child rearing, middle age, and aging. In the third section, we discuss three classifications for marriage relationships. Finally, we cover what makes for successful marriages.

MAJOR QUESTIONS
you should be able to answer

What are good and bad reasons for getting married, and what expectations do people have?

What four phases might a marriage go through, and how do they relate to marital satisfaction?

What are two ways in which I might classify marriage relationships?

What are the characteristics of successful marriages, and how could I achieve success in my own marriage?

251

Pedagogy: A Student-Centered Approach to Learning

The strategy of this text is to use a visually appealing, **magazine-like layout** that couples design format with pedagogy **to help students read with purpose.** Accordingly, we have attempted **to arrange topics into constituent parts for easily manageable units of study,** chunking material into smaller, bite-size sections and making innovative use of boxes, photographs, and other graphics for reinforcement.

After a motivational chapter-opening discussion on Popular Culture & the Media (which we hope will inspire lively class discussion), we proceed with the following pedagogical approach:

■ **Major Questions** designed to be provocative, motivational, and **of high student interest** are given at the opening of each chapter and repeated at the beginning of each section. Examples: "How could an intimate relationship make me happy?"; "How did I learn to think what I think about sex?", and "What kind of alternative household structure might I consider good for me?"

■ **On the Web** directs students to a website where they will get **a close-up look** at one of the topics discussed in the chapter, encouraging them to think and talk about the topic right away. Example: In one chapter, we direct readers to the famous Gottman "Love Lab" website, where they can take a quiz about communication in their relationships.

THE LEARNING LAB

8.3 Different Kinds of Marriage Relationships

MAJOR QUESTION What are three ways in which I might classify marriage relationships?

PREVIEW We consider two different kinds of marriage relationships: (1) five types of enduring marriages and (2) four types of "good marriages" and their built-in "antimarriages."

Many social scientists have attempted to classify the different marriage relationships, although none of their studies has been based on representative samples of married couples. We will consider the following: (1) enduring marriages, studied by Cuber and Harroff, and (2) so-called "good marriages," studied by Wallerstein and Blakeslee.

1. Five Types of Enduring Marriages: Cuber & Harroff's Research

In their book *Sex and the Significant Americans*, **John Cuber and Peggy Harroff** (1965) proposed, on the basis of their interviews with 400 upper-middle-class couples in the 35 to 55 age range (not representative of most families, of course), that enduring marital relationships could be classified as five types divided between *utilitarian marriages* and *intrinsic marriages*. Although not all marriages were happy, all were enduring.

Utilitarian Marriages: Three Types of Unions Based on Convenience

A *utilitarian marriage* is one that is based on convenience. About 75 to 80% of the marriages in Cuber and Harroff's sample were in this category. There are three types of such marriages: *conflict-habituated*, *devitalized*, and *passive-congenial*.

■ Conflict-Habituated Marriages—"We thrive on conflict": **A** *conflict-habituated marriage* **is characterized by ongoing tension and unresolved**

DIFFERENT KINDS OF MARRIAGE RELATIONSHIPS

Self-Assessment: Homophobia Scale

In 1996, as part of his study on homophobia, Dr. Henry Adams and his colleagues at the University of Georgia developed a 25-item homophobia scale "designed to measure your thoughts, feelings and behaviors with regards to homosexuality." What came to be known as the Wright, Adams, and Bernat Homophobia Scale appears on the website for PBS Online and WGBH Frontline. The instructions stress that this scale "is not a perfect measure of anti-gay feelings or ideas, and is not a predictor of potential for anti-gay violence." Nevertheless, the website says, "the scale can be used as a rough but worthwhile measure of heterosexual attitudes toward homosexuals."

To do this self-assessment, go to *www.pbs.org/wgbh/pages/frontline/shows/assault/etc/quiz.html.*

Source: Wright, Adams, and Bernat Homophobia Scale. © 2000 PBS Online and WGBH Frontline. Based on Adams, Henry E., Lester W. Wright, Jr., and Bethany A. Lohr. 1996. Is homophobia associated with homosexual arousal? *Journal of Abnormal Psychology* 105(2):440–45; Wright, Lester W., Henry E. Adams, and Jeffrey Bernat. 1999. Development and validation of the homophobia scale. *Journal of Psychopathology and Behavioral Assessment* 21(4):337–47.

Key Terms Used in This Chapter

accommodationist single, p. 301
adoption, p. 318
adultolescents 291
anti-gay prejudice, p. 310
artificial insemination, p. 319
bisexuality, p. 305
civil union, p. 316
closed-couple single, p. 300
"come out," p. 309
committed single, p. 300
commune, p. 325
commuter marriage, p. 290
discrimination, p. 310
domestic partners, p. 316
domestic partnership movement, p. 316
erotic feelings, p. 309
family, p. 292

foster parent, p. 318
free-floating single, p. 300
gay male, p. 305
group marriage, p. 325
heterosexuality, p. 305
homoeroticism, p. 309
homophobia, p. 310
homosexuality, p. 305
involuntary stable singles, p. 300
involuntary temporary singles, p. 300
lesbian, p. 305
LGBT, p. 305
lifestyle, p. 293
living-a part-together (LAT) couples, p. 290
mutaa, 324
nonfamily household, p. 292
open-couple single, p. 300

open marriage, p. 327
prejudice, p. 309
procreation, p. 304
second-parent adoptions, p. 318
sex ratio, p. 297
sexual orientation, p. 304
sexuality, p. 304
sexually open marriage, p. 327
single, p. 296
sperm bank, p. 320
sperm donor, p. 320
surrogate mother, p. 319
swinging, p. 327
transnational marriages, p. 290
voluntary stable singles, p. 299
voluntary temporary singles, p. 299

Summary

9.1 Different Family & Household Relationships

■ Besides the more common nuclear and extended family structures, a number of new family structures have emerged. Four new variations are (1) platonic "roommate marriages"; (2) commuter, living-apart-together and transnational marriages; (3) grandparents raising children alone; and (4) adultolescents.
■ In platonic or "roommate marriages," there is no sexual bond, but the roommates develop a deep emotional attachment for each other. A commuter

marriage is a dual-career marriage in which each partner lives in a different location yet both of them still maintain their commitment to their family. Living-apart-together couples live in separate quarters. Transnational marriages are those in which one partner is in the United States and the other (and perhaps the children) is in another country.
■ Skipped-generation households are family structures in which grandparents raise grandchildren. According to the 2000 census, more than 2.4 million grandparents are primary caregivers to a grandchild,

Take It to the Net

Among the Internet resources on parenting and families are the following:

■ **Child Care Aware.** A nonprofit initiative committed to helping parents find the best information on locating high-quality child care and child-care resources in their community.
www.childcareaware.org
■ **Common Sense Media Guide.** A nonpartisan, non-profit organization whose purpose is to give parents, educators, and children a choice and a voice about the media they consume. By creating a grassroots movement of concerned citizens, the organization hopes to make media producers present programming that serves the interests of our kids.
www.commonsensemedia.org/mediaguide

■ **iVillage.** Child-rearing advice and connections to parent discussion groups.
http://parenting.ivillage.com
■ **National Child Care Information Center.** Offers links to other child-care resources.
www.nccic.org
■ **National Fatherhood Initiative.** Tips on effective parenting for fathers.
www.fatherhood.org
■ **Parenthood.** Tips on general parenting.
www.parenthoodweb.com
■ **Teenage Parent Demonstration.** Demonstration programs associated with welfare reform to help teenage parents be better parents.
www.aspe.dhhs.gov/hsp/isp/tpd/synthes/lessons.htm

■ **What's Ahead in This Chapter** provides an **overview of the material to come** in the chapter.

■ **Preview** appears at the beginning of each section, following a repeat of the "Major Question," to give students a **brief overview** of the section they are about to read.

■ **Critical-thinking questions** are **integrated throughout,** appearing in all photo captions, at the end of the "Example" boxes, and within the "Numbers That Matter" boxes, to help encourage student involvement and class discussion.

■ **The Learning Lab** that concludes each chapter offers tools to further motivate readers and to reinforce learning, including the following:

■ **Self-Assessments** enable students to explore their feelings about the chapter topic and to see themselves as active players who have choices in what they do in relationships and family life and how they respond to what happens to them. Among the assessments are "What's Your Gender Communications Quotient?," "How Compatible Are You & Your Prospective Partner?," and "Test Your Knowledge of Sexuality."
■ **Key Terms** defined within each chapter are repeated at the end of the chapter, along with page numbers for ready reference to the definitions.
■ **Summaries** provide a useful reprise of the most important concepts, not merely a once-over-lightly review.
■ **Take It to the Net** listings offer website addresses that students can use to investigate chapter topics further.

Emphasis on Currentness

We have updated this edition to include new coverage of many important issues that have entered the world of marriage and families in recent years. This second edition includes **more than 500 new references covering the years 2004 to 2007,** including more than 150 for the year 2007 and more than 180 for the year 2006.

Among the new topics discussed in this edition are:

Abstinence education controversy
Adultolescents
Alienation of affection laws
Assisted reproductive technology and ethical issues
Children and the effects of TV watching
Co-housing
Controlled separation
Divorce rent-a-judges
Elder abuse (expanded coverage)
Forced marriage
Foster children
Gender variance
Green-card marriage
Infant mortality rates
International adoptions
Latchkey children
Lesbian, gay, bisexual, and transgender people (LGBT)
Living-apart-together (LAT) couples

Living wage laws
Macro- and micro-level orientations
Magical thinking
Mutaa (or *Mut'a*) marriage
Neonaticide
Parenting coordinators
Post-adoption blues
Premature birth
Raw numbers
Reliability
Safe-haven laws
Same-sex civil unions and marriage trends worldwide
Secondary analysis
Social networking and social networking websites
State abortion law updates
Validity
Virtual visitation
Web 2.0

What's New in the Second Edition

In addition to the topics previously mentioned, this edition includes the following new features:

1. *We show how to apply a sociological perspective to the topics of gender, sexuality, marriage, and divorce.* We want to make the point to students that in this course they can't approach the subject by simply relying on their general knowledge in an "I feel" way. Thus, we present a complete discussion of the eight principal sociological perspectives in Chapter 2. We then show how to apply three of these perspectives—**structural-functional, conflict,** and **symbolic interaction**—to four important topics: *gender, sexuality, marriage,* and *divorce.*

2. *The "Communication" chapter is now presented earlier in the book.* Responding to instructors' suggestions, we now present "Communication: Realizing Effective Intimacy" as Chapter 6 instead of as Chapter 9.

3. *Details about sex have been moved from the text into appendices.* Because this is not a health book, we decided to move many of the more

biological and health kinds of topics (human sexual response, sexually transmitted diseases, contraception, abortion procedures) to the back of the book, as is done with most other marriage and family texts.

A Note from the Publisher on Supplements

Instructor's Supplements

■ **Instructor's Manual:** Each chapter includes learning objectives, chapter summaries and outlines, key terms with definitions, discussion topics and student activities, as well as diversity resources. The Instructor's Manual also includes a teaching guide for the **RELATE** and **READY** relationship inventories (see description on the next page). Available in print and electronically.

■ **Test Bank:** The Test Bank contains a multitude of questions in multiple-choice, true/false, short answer, and essay formats. Available in print and electronically.

■ **Computerized Test Bank:** The printed Test Bank is also available through Allyn & Bacon's computerized testing system, TestGen EQ. This fully networkable test-generating software is available on a CD-ROM for Windows and Macintosh. The user-friendly interface allows you to view, edit, and add questions, transfer questions to tests, and print tests in a variety of fonts. Search-and-sort features allow you to locate questions quickly and to arrange them in whatever order you prefer.

■ **PowerPoint® Presentation:** A PowerPoint presentation created for this text provides dozens of ready-to-use lecture outlines with graphics from the text. The presentation is available on a CD-ROM and electronically for Macintosh or Windows. PowerPoint software is not required to use this program; a PowerPoint Viewer is included to access the images.

■ **Allyn & Bacon Transparencies for Marriage and Family:** Seventy-five color acetates featuring illustrations from this text and other current Allyn & Bacon titles are available.

■ **Allyn & Bacon Marriage & Family Classroom Video, Second Edition:** This exclusive, 60-minute video is available only from Allyn & Bacon. It combines relevant TV news stories with interviews featuring students, young adults, and older adults from different family backgrounds and situations. Topics include gender and sexuality; dating and contemplating marriage; cohabitation; pregnancy, labor, and childbirth; raising children; single parenting; adoption; divorce; and family violence and abuse.

Student Supplements

■ **Student Workbook with Practice Tests and PowerPoint® Lecture Outlines:** This workbook contains practice tests for every chapter to help students prepare for quizzes and exams. It also includes learning objectives, key terms, and printouts of the PowerPoint lecture outlines prepared for this text, with space for notetaking.

■ **RELATE and READY Online Relationship Inventories:** RELATE and READY are comprehensive self-assessment inventories developed by a team of marriage and family professionals and researchers. RELATE is for those who are married, living together, or in a serious dating relationship. READY is for anyone who wants to learn more about how prepared he or she is to enter into a serious relationship. Either inventory can be completed online at the same website (*www.relate-institute.org*); students who complete one or the other instantly receive an extensive report analyzing their responses. It is free to students when the *RELATE and READY User's Guide* is packaged upon request with this text.

■ **Themes of the Times for Marriage & Family:** This collection of articles from the *New York Times*, all related to the study of marriage, family, and intimate relationships, can be packaged upon request at no additional charge with any Allyn & Bacon sociology text.

Online Course Management

PEARSON
myfamilylab

■ **MyFamilyLab—CourseCompass Version:** This state-of-the art interactive and instructive solution for your Marriage and Family course is designed to be used as a supplement to a traditional lecture course, or completely administered in an online course. MyFamilyLab includes a multimedia e-book, tutorials, videos, self-assessments, related news articles, interviews with experts in the field, and tests and quizzes. Customize your course or use the materials as presented. It is available at no additional cost to students when the text is packaged with a MyFamilyLab CourseCompass Student Access Code Card.

■ **MyFamilyLab—Website Version:** This website provides virtually the same online content and interactivity as the CourseCompass MyFamilyLab without any of the course management features or requirements. It is available at no additional cost to students when the text is packaged with a MyFamilyLab Student Access Code.

■ **WebCT and Blackboard Test Banks:** For colleges and universities with WebCT™ and Blackboard™ licenses, we have converted the complete Test Bank into these popular course management platforms. Adopters can request a copy on CD or download the electronic file by logging in to our Instructor Resource Center.

Acknowledgments

The authors thank the following reviewers for their contributions to the second edition: Bobbie Brannon, Catawba Valley Community College; Deva Chopyak, Cosumnes River College; C. Stephen Glennon, Iowa Western Community College; Dan Muhwezi, Butler Community College; Jacqueline Oertel, State University of New York, Plattsburg; and Vondora Wilson-Corzen, Suffolk Community College.

We also offer our gratitude to the following reviewers for their contributions to the first edition: Phyliss Bartram, California State University, Stanislaus; A. Therese Botz, Cuyamaca College; Katherine Clifton, Edison Community College; Diana Gay Cutchin, Virginia Commonwealth University; Gayle D'Andrea, J. Sergeant Reynolds Community College; Lisa Deneen, Portland State University; Charlotte Dunham, Texas Tech University; Frieda Fowler, University of Nebraska-Lincoln; Rick Fraser, California State University, Los Angeles; Phil Gillette, LA Pierce College; George W. Glann, Jr., Fayetteville Technical Community College; Linda L. Green, Normandale Community College; Bill C. Greenwalt, Western Kentucky University; Chad Hanson, Casper College; Sara Horsfall, Texas Wesleyan University; Gene House, Santa Fe Community College; Wanda Kaluza, Camden County College; Jean-Louis Marchand, Chesapeake College; Liz Matthews, Ellsworth Community College; Trent Maurer,Georgia Southern University; Pyong Gap Min, Queens College; Patricia A. Missad, Grand Rapids Community College; Christine A. Monnier, College of DuPage; James E. Polo, Nassau Community College; Margaret E. Preble, Thomas Nelson Community College; John C. Pulver, Community College of South Nevada; Patricia Sawyer, Middlesex Community College; Kenneth L. Smylie, Santa Fe Community College; Renee S. Torain, St. Philip's College; and Naihua Zhang, Florida Atlantic University.

There are only three names on the front of this book, but scores of others have been important contributors to its development. First, we wish to thank our sponsoring editor, Jeff Lasser, Executive Editor, Sociology, for his tremendous encouragement and patience, especially at the most difficult times. Donna Simons, Senior Production Administrator, ably kept the book moving through the production cycle. Lauren Houlihan coordinated the supplements that support this book. Thanks go to Leah Strauss for her fine developmental work. Outside of Allyn & Bacon, Katharine Cebik researched the photos within the text. We were fortunate to have the assistance of Lynda Griffiths as the project manager; Ellen Pettengell, interior designer; Karen Winget, indexer; and Publishers' Design and Production Services, illustrator.

Special thanks go to Rifat Salam, who provided great research assistance. Additional kudos go to Nancy J. Wahlstrom and Genesee Community College reference librarians Nichola Lerczak, Melissa Peterson, Vicki Lukhaup, Tracy Paradis, Michele Asmus, and Cindy Hagelberger for their help in gathering research for this text.

About the Authors

BRIAN K. WILLIAMS is married to Stacey Sawyer, and they live near Lake Tahoe, Nevada, and share an avid interest in seeing college students become well educated. Over the past two decades, they have individually or together **authored more than 25 books,** in such subjects as health, college success, and computers and information technology. Brian, for instance, has coauthored three introductory textbooks in health; several books in computing; and, with Carl Wahlstrom, six books in college success.

He has been Managing Editor for college textbook publisher Harper & Row/Canfield Press in San Francisco; Editor in Chief for trade book publisher J. P. Tarcher in Los Angeles; Publications & Communications Manager for the University of California, Systemwide Administration, in Berkeley; and an independent writer and book producer based in the San Francisco and Lake Tahoe areas. He has a B.A. in English and an M.A. in Communication from Stanford University.

STACEY C. SAWYER, formerly Director of Founder's Clinic, a women's reproductive health and family planning clinic in Columbus, Ohio, is an independent writer and book producer who has been based in the San Francisco and Lake Tahoe areas.

She has taught at Ohio State University and been a manager for Brooks/Cole Publishing Company in Monterey, California. She has a B.A. from Ohio Wesleyan and the University of Freiburg, Germany, and an M.A. from Middlebury College and the University of Mainz, Germany.

Stacey is coauthor of *Computers, Communications, & Information*, a college textbook in print for 15 years. She and husband Brian Williams also cowrote *Using Information Technology*, now in its seventh edition.

CARL M. WAHLSTROM is Professor of Intermediate Studies and Sociology at Genesee Community College, Batavia, New York, and is also an Adjunct Lecturer in Sociology at the State University of New York at Geneseo. He has taught courses in marriage and the family, human development, learning strategies, sociology, psychology, human relations, and college success.

In 2007, he was designated a State University of New York Distinguished Service Professor (the highest recognition SUNY can bestow on its faculty). He has also been the recipient of the SUNY Chancellor's Award for Excellence in Teaching, the Chancellor's Award for Excellence in Scholarship and Creativity, the National Freshman Advocate Award, and several other teaching honors. Carl has a B.S. in Sociology and an M.S. Ed. in Counselor Education from SUNY Brockport and an M.A. in Sociology from the University of Bridgeport. He is an active presenter and educational consultant.

With Brian Williams he is coauthor of *Learning Success, The Practical Student, The Urban Student, The Commuter Student, The Successful Distance Learning Student*, and *College to Career*. He lives with his wife, Nancy, an employee benefits consultant, in the Finger Lakes area of New York.

CHAPTER 1

SEEKING

Finding Happiness in Relationships in a Complex World

What Is It That We Seek?

"Sarah, my love for you is deathless, it seems to bind me with mighty cables that nothing but Omnipotence can break; and yet my love of country comes over me like a strong wind and bears me irresistibly with all those chains to the battle field.

"The memories of the blissful moments I have spent with you come crowding over me, and I feel most gratified to God and to you that I have enjoyed them so long. And hard it is for me to give them up and burn to ashes the hopes of future years, when, God willing, we might still have lived and loved together, and seen our sons grow up to honorable manhood, around us.*

"I have, I know, but few and small claims upon Divine Providence but something whispers to me . . . that I shall return to my loved ones unharmed. If I do not my dear Sarah, never forget how much I love you, and when my last breath escapes me on the battle field, it will whisper your name."*

This tender, passionate letter to his wife was composed by Sullivan Ballou, a Union Army major from Rhode Island, a week before he was killed at the first battle of Bull Run on July 21, 1861, during the Civil War (Ballou, quoted in Ward et al. 1990: 82–83). The letter expresses qualities we all seem to seek: Love. Devotion. Loyalty. Happiness. Isn't that what intimacy, marriage, and family are all about? Isn't this what we wish for ourselves—and to give to another?

■ *Vitalized versus devitalized marriages:* We live in supposedly cynical times, but there are many marriages today in which the partners might express similar devotion to each other. Presumably, such couples

🔍 WHAT'S AHEAD IN THIS CHAPTER

All of us seek happiness, the subject of the first section. We then consider the components of intimacy, marriage, and family. We describe the benefits of families and the economic and demographic trends that are changing today's families.

would be those whose marriages, as one 12-year study of 8,383 couples found (Lavee and Olson 1992), could be described as "vitalized" (9% of cases), "harmonious" (8%), or "balanced" (8%).

Unfortunately, they are almost overshadowed by the 40% that fall into the lowest category—"devitalized," which is characterized by "dissatisfaction with all dimensions of the marital relationship." The study is an assessment of nine dimensions of relationships: personality issues, communication, conflict resolution, leisure, parenthood, family and friends, religion, finances, and sexuality.

■ *Why not study relationships as you would for a career?* Perhaps, suggests David Olson, one of the study authors, so many marriages are mostly unhappy partly because society does little to help the institution of marriage. "We assume that if people are going to do well in a career, they're going to have to invest time and money in education," he says. "But we don't assume that with marriage." Thus, when marriages become unsatisfactory, "we shouldn't be surprised—if you don't invest anything, what can you expect?" (Olson, quoted in Kochakian 1992). With that in mind, we are going to ask you to invest your time and energies in this book and

this course with all the seriousness and attentiveness you would invest in preparing for a career.

■ *What do popular culture and the mass media tell us?* Our perceptions of love and family are affected not only by our own life experiences but also by *popular culture and the mass media,* as we discuss at the start of every chapter. Television, movies, music, magazines, the Internet, and most certainly advertising convey certain images, stereotypes, and myths, including these:

■ Somewhere there is a soul mate for each of us.
■ If we love each other enough, we can overcome all problems.
■ A marriage partner should be everything: best friend, terrific sex partner, sympathetic confidante, and good provider.
■ A normal family is a close-knit unit consisting of father, mother, and children plus close relatives.
■ Perfect families are "always there for us," providing love and solidarity, nurturing and support.
■ The main source of social problems is family breakdown.

Belonging, unity, and continuity are strong human needs. What kind of relationships will fulfill our desires? That is the subject of this book.

How could an intimate relationship make me happy?

What are the principal components of intimacy, marriage, and family?

What are the benefits of the family, and what economic and demographic trends are affecting it?

1.1 Seeking Happiness through Love & Intimacy

MAJOR QUESTION How could an intimate relationship make me happy?

PREVIEW Many people think that they will be happy if they can find the right relationship. In fact, among the happiest people are those who are married. It's possible that you can manage your emotions for happiness just as you manage other things in your life. Happy couples have common strengths in at least five areas.

"Human beings want to have meaning. They want not to wake up in the morning with a gnawing realization that they are fidgeting until they die."

So says University of Pennsylvania psychologist Martin Seligman (quoted in Corliss 2003: 72), former president of the American Psychological Association. Seligman has also become well known as the director of the Positive Psychology Network and author of *Authentic Happiness* (Seligman 2002a). He has urged that psychology be a discipline not only for studying mental illness and pathology but also for promoting positive traits and emotions—in a word, happiness (Max 2007).

Happiness. It is enshrined in the American Declaration of Independence ("life, liberty, and the pursuit of . . ."), in the words of popular songs ("what my life's about"—Vanessa Williams), in the titles of self-help books (*Eight Steps to Happiness*). Aristotle (384–322 B.C.E.) believed that happiness, as a form of excellence, was the supreme good, so much so that everything else was the means to its attainment. Philosopher-psychologist William James (1842–1910) thought happiness was so important that "how to gain, how to keep, how to recover happiness is in fact for most [people] at all times the secret motive of all they do" (quoted in Myers 1992: 19). Another psychologist, Abraham Maslow, proposed a hierarchy of five needs—physiological, safety, belongingness, esteem, and self-actualization—the last one representing self-fulfillment, the need to develop one's fullest potential. Indeed, when Seligman says that we "want to have meaning" in our lives, he is expressing one category of happiness—the third and ultimate level—as our discussion in the Practical Action box on page 6 shows.

And what is it—for the purposes of this book—about intimacy, marriage, and family that relates to happiness? According to the evidence, scholars say, the two factors that matter most in happiness are (1) marriage and (2) religious belief. "Married people are happier than any other configuration of people," says Seligman (quoted in Corliss 2003: 74). "And religious people are usually happier than nonreligious people."

Does this mean that happiness is not available to you if you're single and atheistic or gay and agnostic? (Atheists don't believe God exists; agnostics neither believe nor disbelieve.) Not at all. But let us see what the present facts show about love and happiness.

Love, Marriage, & Happiness

Q: "I know you believe there's no 'recipe' for happiness, but if you had to name one condition, what would it be?"
A: "The happiest people all seem to have good friends."

So stated University of Illinois at Urbana-Champaign psychologist Ed Diener, a serious researcher of happiness, in a newspaper interview (Elias 2002c). The happiest people seem to spend the least time alone, instead surrounding themselves with friends and family. Loneliness, in fact, may be hazardous to one's health, having been found to be a major risk factor in increasing blood pressure in older people (Hawkley et al. 2006). However, in this respect, singles may be better off, since some research shows that marriage actually reduces social ties, with less parental contact, including financial and emotional support, being found among married offspring (Gerstel and Sarkisian 2007). Some people think of a close group of friends as their "chosen family."

Marriage & Well-Being

In addition, as Seligman suggested, among the happiest people are those who are married. According to University of Chicago sociologist Linda Waite

NUMBERS THAT MATTER

Marriage, Families, & Happiness

- **Who is happy?** 40% of married people say they are happy compared with 22% of never-married people.[a]

- **What helps happiness?** 75% of happy couples agree on the high quality of their communication; only 11% of unhappy couples do.[b]

- **Can people change?** About two-thirds of couples who were unhappily married at the outset said they were happy five years later.[c]

- **Are people marrying later?** In 1970, the median age of first marriage was 23.2 years for men and 20.8 years for women. In 2005, it was 27.1 for men and 25.3 for women.[d]

- **Are married-couple families declining?** The percentage of married-couple families declined from 70.6% of all families in 1970 to 58.6% in 2005.[e] From 1990 to 2003, the percentage of unmarried-partner households increased from about 3.5% to 4.2%.[f]

[a]Waite and Gallagher 2000. [b]Olson 2000. [c]Waite and Gallagher 2000. [d]U.S. Census Bureau 2006a. [e]U.S. Census Bureau 2006b. [f]Fields 2004.

(Waite and Gallagher 2000), surveys show that those who say they are "very happy" include

- 40% of those married
- 24% of those living together
- 22% of those who have never married
- 18% of those previously married

Although there is evidence that people who marry are happier to begin with, "there's much stronger research showing that once adults marry, their well-being improves," Waite says (quoted in Elias 2002b).

Love, Appreciation, & Happiness

Psychologist Dan Baker, director of the Life Enhancement Program at Canyon Ranch in Tucson, Arizona, and author of *What Happy People Know* (Baker and Stauth 2002), believes that you can manage your emotions—grief, agony, sadness, or whatever—for happiness just as you can manage your physical health through diet and exercise. Specifically, he says, being happy is "the ability to practice appreciation or love" (Baker, quoted in Corliss 2003: 74).

John Gottman, co-author of *Ten Lessons to Transform Your Marriage* (Gottman et al. 2006), would agree. Gottman and his wife, Julie Schwartz Gottman, direct Seattle's Gottman Institute ("the Love Lab"), which specializes in marital stability and divorce prediction. "The best single predictor of whether a couple is going to divorce is contempt," he says, as when one corrects the other's grammar while they're arguing. The best antidote to contempt, he says is to cultivate "a culture of appreciation," constantly looking for "things to appreciate and moments to communicate respect" (Gottman, quoted in Cole 2007).

How Happy Are You in a Relationship?

What do happy couples know or do that unhappy ones don't? Are you currently in a happy relationship?

In the opening of this chapter, we mentioned pioneering University of Minnesota family researcher **David Olson** (2000). (Note: In this book we **boldface** the names of people who have made particularly distinctive contributions to the field.) Olson found that happy couples built at least five key areas of their relationship into solid strengths: (1) they communicate well, (2) they are flexible as a couple, (3) they are emotionally close, (4) they have compatible personalities, and (5) they agree on how to handle conflict. (For example, 75% of happy couples agree on the high quality of their communication; only 11% of unhappy couples do.)

The death of his infant son could certainly have been reason enough for Dan Baker to become depressed, as it would most people. However, he was able to use the results of his research to put his own personal tragedy in perspective. He draws comparisons with the aftermath of the September 11, 2001, terrorist hijackings. "We know that [now] many people have a greater sense of what's truly important, a greater awareness of their relationships and values" (Baker, quoted in Corliss 2003: 74).

The September 11 attack brought personal tragedy to Jacqueline Gavagan, who lost her husband, Donald, a bond broker, in the collapse of the World Trade Center. While continuing to grieve, she began asking people to contribute to a Donald Richard Gavagan fund to sponsor a life-saving operation for a child whose family could not afford it (Cowley 2002). By raising $35,000, she was able to help a 7-year-old boy from Kosovo undergo heart surgery. "I feel like if I'm doing something positive, and if my kids see me doing something positive, then they'll turn out to be positive people," she says. She also wants Donald to be remembered not just for how he died but for how he lived. "I want him to know that, you know, with all the people that loved him, we raised enough

money to pay for this child" (Gavagan, quoted in The Donald Richard Gavagan Fund 2003).

Tierney and Gregory Fairchild learned through prenatal tests that the child they were expecting would need heart surgery—and that the child also had Down syndrome (Zuckoff 2002). Since then, incidentally, doctors have recommended that *all* pregnant women be screened for Down syndrome (American College of Obstetricians and Gynecologists, cited in Rabin 2007). Although pro-choice, the Fairchilds decided to draw on their signature strengths of being an interracial couple who had faced many tough choices and go ahead and have the child. Naia walked late, talked late, and is potty-training late—just as her parents expected. "And so what?" asks Tierney (quoted in Elias 2002a: 2A).

EXAMPLE OF
Practicing Appreciation & Love
Finding Meaning & Joy amid Sorrow

"She's brought us a huge amount of joy because she's such a happy child."

WHAT DO YOU THINK? Do you know anyone who has triumphed over a similarly devastating event? How did this person do it?

A HAPPY CHOICE. Tierney and Gregory Fairchild learned during pregnancy that their first child would have Down syndrome and had a heart defect. Although pro-choice, they explored all the angles—medical, practical, and emotional—and decided to go ahead and have the girl they would name Naia, shown here at age 4. What choice would you have made if you had been in their circumstances? (Both Fairchilds are employed professionals with Ph.D.s) Do you think making the same decision would bring you happiness? ◀

PRACTICAL ACTION

Happiness: Is It within Your Grasp?

Are we meant to be happy? Perhaps not. "We aren't built to be happy," goes one view. "Rather, we are built to survive and reproduce. . . . Working hard and raising children may not make us happier. But these beliefs keep society functioning" (Clements 2006). We're also not very good at forecasting what will make us happy. Two groups of college students, one in the Midwest and one in southern California, who were asked where they thought someone like themselves would be happier both picked California; yet when asked how satisfied they were with their own lives, both groups declared themselves equally happy (Schkade and Kahneman 1998).

What's going on here? Nature or nurture, your genes or your environment—which more influences your mood? Do you feel the way you do because you're hardwired that way biologically? Or because something happened to you (say, you got an A— or an F—on a test) that makes you elated or depressed?

The Happiness "Set Point"

Scientists suggest that a person's happiness level is about half influenced by genetics. Each of us has a "set point" or baseline for moods, just as we do for weight, says Martin Seligman (2002a). Research by Richard Davidson and his colleagues (2002, 2003) and other scholars (Lyubomirsky et al.

2005) has identified an index for this set point. A few unlucky people, they found, had clinical depression or anxiety disorder, and another lucky few were happy and enthusiastic and rarely troubled by bad moods. Most people, of course, were in the middle, with a mix of good and bad moods.

Although the set point can change over the years (Lucas et al. 2004), what's interesting is that in general the set point keeps our our emotional ups and down from being lasting or extreme. Win the lottery? Suffer a horrible accident? Either way, most people's moods generally return to their established set points within a year. This phenomenon is sometimes called the "hedonic treadmill" or "hedonic adaptation"—the idea that we rapidly adapt to improvements in our lives and thus can end up feeling not much better off (Brickman and Campbell 1971).

Indeed, according to studies by social psychologist Daniel Gilbert, people expect that events will have a larger and more enduring impact on them—for good or ill—than they really do (Wilson et al. 2001; Gilbert and Ebert 2002; Gilbert 2006). But Gilbert theorizes that we have a "psychological immune system" that goes into effect in response to a big negative event such as the loss of a job or the death of a spouse but not in response to small negative events such as a car breakdown. This suggests, as one reviewer (Stossel 2006) put it, that "our day-to-day happiness may be predicated more strongly on little events than on big ones."

Will Money Make You Happy?

A country's wealth does not always dictate the happiness of its people. According to the World Values Survey, a project under way since 1995, inhabitants of many countries, particularly those in Latin America, had higher

marks for happiness than their economic situation would predict (Inglehart et al. 2004; see also Revkin 2005). People living in extreme poverty are, on average, not as happy as those whose basic needs have been met. Beyond that, however, wealth doesn't lead to a richer life (Diener and Oishi 2000). "Once you're safe and warm and fed," says management professor David Schkade (quoted in Clements 2006: D1), "it makes surprisingly little difference." In fact, the more money people earn, the more likely they are to spend their time working, commuting, and doing other compulsory activities that bring little pleasure (Kahneman et al. 2006).

In addition, beyond a certain threshold of wealth, people redefine their happiness to focus on their relative position in society instead of their material status. For instance, one study found that, given a choice of earning $50,000 in a world where the average salary was $25,000, half the subjects surveyed preferred that option to earning $100,000 where the average yearly salary was $200,000 (Solnick and Hemenway 1998).

Money does not buy happiness. "Money can buy *pleasure,* but pleasure isn't happiness," suggests *Star Wars* director George Lucas (quoted in Wilson 2004: 2D). "Happiness is a feeling that goes beyond pleasure." Because desire can be infinite, "materialism is toxic for happiness," says University of Illinois psychologist Ed Diener (quoted in Elias 2002a). Being happy means managing the natural yearning for more. "Evolution hasn't set us up for the attainment of happiness," suggests biological psychologist Daniel Nettle (2005), "merely its pursuit."

Cultural Well-Being

Happiness is influenced not only by genetic heritage but also by one's ethnic culture. Psychology professor Jeanne

Tsai, head of Stanford University's Culture and Emotion Lab, has found, for instance, that European Americans aspire to more high-energy elation, whereas Asian Americans tend to fall in between the Eastern idea of calm and the Western preference for elation. "Everybody wants to feel good," Tsai says, "but people want to feel good in different ways" (Tsai, quoted in Platoni 2006). However, in America today, according to scholar Christina Kotchemidova (2005), the main emotional norm is what she calls "the culture of cheerfulness."

Happiness can also depend on where you live. Dutch sociologist Ruut Veenhoven (2007), editor of the *Journal of Happiness Studies*, who launched a "World Database of Happiness" in the 1990s, finds that the happiest people on earth live in Denmark (followed by Switzerland, Austria, Iceland, and Finland—the United States ranks 17th; Zimbabwe ranks last at 94th). Analytic social psychologist Adrian White (2007) of the University of Leicester, who created a World Map of Happiness, also finds that Denmark ranks first out of 178 countries (followed by Switzerland, Austria, Iceland, the Bahamas, and Finland), with the United States ranking 23rd and the least happy countries being Zimbabwe and Burundi. "A nation's level of happiness was closely associated with health levels," declares White (quoted in Wagner 2006), "followed by wealth . . . and then provision of education." Another possible reason the Danes are on top (Christensen et al. 2006): They live in a culture of low expectations and thus aren't terribly disappointed when things don't go well. Incidentally, in the United States, a Pew Research Center (2006a) poll of 3,000 Americans found that 84% described themselves as being "very" or "pretty" happy.

Three Kinds of Happiness

Seligman (2002a) describes three categories or levels of happiness:

- **"The pleasant life"—good feelings from genetic predisposition:** This is "the Goldie Hawn, Hollywood happiness—smiling, feeling good, being ebullient," says Seligman (quoted in Corliss 2003: 74). However, because this is a matter of genetic disposition (as we just described), perhaps only half of us get to experience this.

- **"The good life"—knowing and using your strengths:** This kind of happiness "consists first in knowing what your strengths are and then recrafting your life to use them—in work, love, friendship, leisure, parenting. It's about being absorbed, immersed, one with the music," says Seligman. This is the kind of life satisfaction that occurs when you are engaged in absorbing activities that cause you to forget yourself, lose track of time, and stop worrying—what psychologist Mihaly Csikszentmihalyi (1990) has called *flow*. Being in a state of flow means you are doing an activity that stretches you pleasurably but not beyond your capacity.

- **"The meaningful life"—using your signature strengths for a higher purpose:** The third and ultimate level, Seligman says, consists of "identifying your strengths and then using them in the service of something you believe is better than you are." You need not be happy in the conventional sense to do this. "Churchill and Lincoln were two profound depressives who dealt with it by having good and meaningful lives," says Seligman (quoted in Corliss 2003: 74).

What Can You Do?

Moving beyond pleasure ("the pleasant life") to gratification ("the meaningful life") shows that your actions matter, though not as you might have thought. Following are some other contributors to "authentic" happiness:

- **Gratitude:** Examine your negative assumptions and savor positive experiences. Writing about what you're grateful for can help emphasize happiness.

- **Forgiveness:** This is "the queen of all virtues, and probably the hardest to come by," says University of Michigan psychologist Christopher Peterson (quoted in Elias 2002a: 2A). Yet it is, he says, the most strongly linked to happiness (Peterson and Seligman 2004).

- **Altruism:** Helping other people in need boosts happiness in the giver (Myers 1992: 21).

- **Time use:** Leisure is better than work, and cutting back on the hours you work will probably leave you happier (Kahneman et al. 2004; Kahneman and Krueger 2006). Keep your commute short, if you can. "You can't adapt to commuting because it's entirely unpredictable," says Daniel Gilbert (quoted in Clements 2006). "Driving in traffic is a different kind of hell every day."

- **Marriage:** Even if it's not great, marriage tends to improve well-being (Waite and Gallagher 2000). Indeed, 43% of married people describe themselves as being "very happy" compared with only 24% of unmarried people (Pew Research Center 2006a).

We describe other aspects of happiness in relation to our subject throughout the book.

Other areas that affect a couple's happiness are (6) their sexual relationship, (7) their choice of leisure activities, (8) the influence of family and friends, (9) the ability to manage finances, and (10) an agreement on spiritual beliefs.

We explore these matters in the coming chapters. At the end of this chapter, in the Self-Assessment, we present the RELATE and READY Questionnaire to help you determine what you and your partner, if any, bring to the relationship and how you feel about it.

The Challenges of Love, Work, & Raising Children

"Shortcuts to happiness often turn out to be detours," says Seligman (2002b: 48). "For most people, lasting satisfaction comes not from money, status, or fleeting pleasures but from rising to the challenges of love, work, and raising children."

Not everyone reading this book will marry or raise children (although the majority of people do). Probably everyone reading this, however, hopes to find love (a subject we explore in detail in Chapter 4, "Love"). Love begins with intimacy, as we discuss in the next section.

1.2 Intimacy, Marriage, & Family

MAJOR QUESTION What are the principal components of intimacy, marriage, and family?

PREVIEW Intimacy can be considered according to three dimensions—breadth, openness, and depth—shared across intellectual, physical, and emotional sectors of life. Marriage has five components: emotional, ceremonial, legal, sexual faithfulness, and parenting. Family may be a traditional "modern" or nuclear family. Or today it may be a "postmodern" family, such as a two-household (binuclear) or blended family (stepfamily), or even one consisting of "affiliated kin" who are family by reason of emotional closeness.

"A growing number of hotels," reports a newspaper story (Clark 2003), "are discovering that the surest way to create warm and fuzzy memories is by providing warm and fuzzy amenities. As in dogs, cats, and other creatures." For instance, like many other lodgings that are trying to differentiate themselves from their competitors, the St. Regis Aspen in the Colorado Rockies offers "loaner" dogs from a local animal shelter to provide guests with canine company during their stay, and this program has proved to be a huge success (Finn 2004). A survey by international travel agency Thomas Cook (cited in Harper 2001) found that 35% of the respondents admitted to missing their pets more than anyone or anything when away, and 11% actually phone home to speak to the pined-for animal.

A San Francisco prostitute, Michelle, who began working the streets at age 11, said that she always turned her earnings over to her pimp in return for being taken care of. "It was always about the guy," she said later. "You do it for love, comfort, support. It's a man to say 'I love you' to and sometimes he says it back" (quoted in Ryan 2003).

Both these examples show the powerful need that human beings have for *intimacy*. Many people attempt to find it in having pets—especially if their human relationships are less than fulfilling (Stallones et al. 1990). Indeed, 85% of dog owners and 78% of cat owners say they consider their pet to be a member of the family (Pew Research Center 2006b), and one study found that pets can be more supportive in times of stress than friends or spouses (Allen et al. 2002). Other people, such as Michelle, try to find it in partners who don't even treat them well—especially if they were abused early in life.

Let us begin to explore this fascinating subject.

What Is the Expression of Intimacy? The Three Dimensions of Breadth, Openness, & Depth

Intimacy is intense affection for, commitment to, and sharing of intellectual, physical, and emotional connections with another person. Intimacy is the opposite of emotional isolation, which has been linked to higher risks of physical and emotional disorders (Brown 1995; Ladbrook 2000). It is the deepest kind of social tie, the kind that helps us survive in our demanding, speeded-up society.

Bruce J. Biddle (1979) suggests that intimacy between you and another person—close friend, lover, spouse—should be considered according to three dimensions: (1) *breadth*, (2) *openness*, and (3) *depth*. These dimensions express the *intensity* of the relationship, which may be shared across *intellectual*, *physical*, and *emotional* sectors of life (Kieffer 1977).

1. Breadth: "What Is the Range of Our Shared Activities?"

Breadth considers the range of activities you and the other person share with each other. As Biddle says, broad (intense) relationships "are ones in which the partners characteristically spend a good deal of time together and in which they solve a majority of life's problems collectively" (1979: 309). In narrow relationships, interaction is confined to some restricted areas of the partners' lives. For example, you might ask yourself the following questions (after Kieffer 1977: 273):

■ **Intellectual Activity:** How much do I and the other person share news of our daily activities? How do we decide about managing the household? Do we participate in the same political activities?

■ **Physical Activity:** How much do we share such activities as dancing, athletics, shopping, gardening, caressing, and sex?

■ **Emotional Activity:** How well do we resolve conflict? Do we phone each other when we're not together to lend emotional support? Do we share pride at a child's graduation?

2. Openness: "How Trusting Are We in Making Self-Disclosures to Each Other?"

Openness describes the extent to which you and the other person feel able to make meaningful self-disclosures to each other—that is, how trusting you are in each other's honesty and acceptance. In open (intense) relationships, says Biddle, the partners "characteristically discuss a wide range of topics, whereas in closed ones their discussion is confined to limited effort or few topics of conversation" (1979: 309). For example, some questions you might ask are these (after Kieffer, p. 273):

■ **Intellectual Activity:** How trusting do I feel about sharing my secrets with the other, and how careful am I about sharing the other's secrets? Do I feel the need to lie to the other? Can I discuss controversial matters in politics, religion, ethics, and so on?

■ **Physical Activity:** How comfortable am I about sharing possessions, being nude, grooming myself, or bathroom behavior around the other? To what extent do I limit exploration of my body by the other?

■ **Emotional Activity:** How free do I feel to express anger and resentments with the other? How emotionally honest am I about resolving conflicts? How comfortable am I describing my emotional involvement with other intimates?

3. Depth: "How Deeply Do We Share Core Aspects of Ourselves?"

Openness, as we just described, is about trust. *Depth* is more difficult to achieve, taking trust to a more profound level and indicating the extent to which two people share the truest, more central cores of themselves. That is, depth is about the two of you transcending your own personal self-interests and achieving a near-spiritual connection with each other. "Within a shallow love," says Biddle, "the central identities and expectations of the partners are not affected, nor are their self-concepts greatly challenged. Within a deep (intense) love, however, central identities and expectations are challenged, reworked, and reinvested" (1979: 310). The extent of such depth is indicated by how you might answer the following kinds of questions (after Kieffer, p. 273):

■ **Intellectual Activity:** How deep is my faith in the other's love and reliability? How strongly do I feel I can work cooperatively or collectively with this person to change some of my core characteristics? Can we ever blend each other's selves in transcendental union?

■ **Physical Activity:** How physically relaxed am I in the other's presence? How deep are my feelings of contentment and well-being with this person?

■ **Emotional Activity:** Do I care as much about the other as I do about myself? Can I be supportive in a nonjealous way toward the other intimate relationships of this person?

Deep love, says Biddle, is probably a rare event, since it demands that a person be capable of self-analysis and "be willing to face even neurotic fears" (1979: 310). Those who love deeply, therefore, are more vulnerable to the illness or death of their partners than those in less intense relationships.

Is Deep Intimacy Really Attainable?

Achieving intellectual "transcendental union" or complete nonjealous emotional intimacy might not seem to be in the cards for most ordinary mortals. Indeed, many of us might be content simply to be in a long-term partnership that's reasonably free of problems and conflict. Is that possible?

Here's an interesting pair of facts to absorb as we begin our study of intimacy, marriage, and happiness. In surveys of thousands of married couples taken over five years, sociologist Linda Waite (2005) found the following:

THE INTIMACY IDEAL. If you were going to write an ad promoting the benefits of intimacy, what would you say? And how obtainable do you think true intimacy—in terms of breadth, openness, and depth—is for most people? ▼

- *The unhappy who stayed married:* About two-thirds of couples who were unhappily married at the outset *said they were happy* five years later.
- *The unhappy who got divorced:* Those who were unhappily married who had divorced five years later *were found to be no happier* than those who stayed with their original spouse. "There's a certain plasticity in marriage, an up-and-down," says Waite (quoted in Elias 2002b). "A lot of problems resolve over time, and married people tend to get happier. It's a message some people disbelieve, but they have unrealistic ideas about marriage."

What Is Marriage?

***Marriage* can be defined as a socially approved mating relationship.** We are referring to heterosexual marriages here (reserving discussion of homosexual unions to Chapter 8, "Variations"). Marriage has five components: (1) *emotional,* (2) *ceremonial,* (3) *legal,* (4) *sexual faithfulness,* and (5) *parenting.*

1. The Emotional Component: Is Love Necessary?

In most parts of the United States, people marry for love. In fact, only 3.5% of American college students in one survey said they would marry for reasons other than love (Levine et al. 1995). This contrasts with, for example, 10.2% of comparable students in Mexico and 49% in Italy.

That's not the case in many parts of the world or even in certain cultures within the United States and Canada, where the choice of spouse is arranged by the parents. Even in these marriages, however, love is often expected to develop as the spouses come to know each other. (We discuss arranged marriages in Chapter 4, "Love.")

2. The Ceremonial Component: Church, State, or Other?

Every culture has some sort of ceremony (what sociologists call "cultural universals") cementing the union. In the United States, you need to obtain a governmental marriage license for the jurisdiction in which you will be married, have an authorized person perform the ceremony (generally with two witnesses present), and return the necessary documentation to the government.

You might choose to be married in a civil ceremony—by a judge, marriage magistrate, justice of the peace, or courthouse clerk. Or you might be married in a church, synagogue, or mosque—or have a religious ceremony in a nonreligious setting. Or you can arrange to be married in a secular ceremony, for which there are many options. Sometimes couples will be married by a civil servant and then be married again in a more meaningful (to them) religious or other ceremonial occasion. In France, a couple living in the countryside may have three ceremonies: civil (performed by the mayor at the town hall); religious (performed by a priest in church); and village, with a 10-course banquet, singing, toasts, and banging of pots and pans by the villagers to remind the couple of the possible difficulties of marriage ("Marriage Today" 2007).

3. The Legal Component: Does the State Have to Be Involved?

In most states, it is no longer illegal (or laws against it are no longer enforced) for a boyfriend and girlfriend age 18 or over to live together without being married. But once a marriage license exists, then the state has an interest.

WATER WEDDING. Being legally married requires a piece of paper from the state, but the ceremony itself can be anything. Most couples prefer religious ceremonies, but others take their matrimonial vows, whether religious or civil, under circumstances meaningful to them, such as on ice skates, skydiving, or even under water. What form would your fantasy wedding take—and why? ◄

Generally, to get a license to marry *without* parental consent, bride and groom must be at least 18 years old (Mississippi and Nebraska are exceptions), must not already be married to someone else, and may have to pass a blood test (to detect for sexually transmitted diseases, among other things). Waiting periods may also be required between applying for and receiving a marriage license. State laws vary as to the minimum age at which people may marry *with* parental consent. *(See ■ Panel 1.1.)*

With a license, the marriage has legal standing that affects matters of property, children, debts, and inheritance. People who are married share property with each other, become heirs to their spouse's estate in event of death, become equally responsible for rearing children, and, in most states, are responsible for each other's debts.

One kind of marriage-without-a-license that is recognized in certain states is **common-law marriage, a type of living arrangement in which a man and a woman living together present themselves as being married and are legally recognized as such.** The states are Alabama, Colorado, Iowa, Kansas, Montana, Rhode Island, South Carolina, Texas, and Utah, plus the District of Columbia. (We consider this topic further in Chapter 8, "Variations.")

4. The Sexual-Faithfulness Component: Are Monogamy & Exclusivity Required?

For most people, marriage is based on sexual exclusivity: A partner is expected to be sexually faithful to his or her spouse. Yet there are variations. A marriage can be of three types: *monogamy*, the only legal form of marriage in North America, and two forms of *polygamy—polygyny* and *polyandry*.

■ PANEL 1.1   State Marriage Laws. Forty-eight states allow people 18 years or older to marry without parental consent, although in Nebraska the age is 19; in Mississippi, males may marry at age 17 and females at age 15 without parental consent. Forty-three states allow both males and females to marry with parental consent at age 16 or older; the exceptions are given below.

STATE	MINIMUM AGE MAY MARRY WITH PARENTAL CONSENT
Arkansas	Male 17, female 16
California	No limits
Delaware	Male 18, female 16
Hawaii	15
Indiana	17
Kentucky	18
Louisiana	18
Massachusetts	Male 14, female 12
Mississippi	No limits
Missouri	15
Nebraska	17
New Hampshire	Male 14, female 13
Ohio	Male 18, female 16
Oregon	17
Rhode Island	Male 18, female 16
Washington	17
West Virginia	18

Source: Adapted from *Marriage laws of the fifty states, District of Columbia, and Puerto Rico.* 2007. Legal Information Institute, Cornell Law School, www.law.cornell.edu/topics/Table_marriage.htm (accessed May 11, 2007).

■ **Monogamy—One Spouse Only:** ***Monogamy* is a marital or sexual relationship in which a person is committed exclusively to one partner.** In the past, breaking this marital rule (unfaithfulness, infidelity, adultery, "cheating") was legal grounds for divorce.

■ **Polygamy as Polygyny—More than One Wife:** ***Polygamy* is a form of marriage in which one person has several spouses.** One type, ***polygyny,* is a marriage in which one husband has more than one wife.** This describes the kind of marriages found among offshoots of the Church of Latter-Day Saints (LDS), also known as the Mormon Church, in parts of the American West, Canada, and Mexico. (These marriages are considered illegal by the state and are even grounds for excommunication by the LDS church.)

■ **Polygamy as Polyandry—More than One Husband:** ***Polyandry* is a marriage in which one wife has more than one husband.** This is a much rarer form of polygamy, although it has been found among certain Buddhists in Tibet and in parts of India and Polynesia (Crook and Crook 1988). It, too, is illegal in North America.

5. The Parenting Component: Are Children the Main Reason for Marriage?

If you decide to get married, it may be for love, companionship, and happiness. The idea of having children may be something you think the two of you might do "eventually"—or not at all.

From the standpoint of society, however, having children is probably *the* principal reason for the institution of marriage. That is, the main purpose of marriage is to provide a stable framework for the bearing, nurturing, socializing, rearing, and protection of children—tasks that the state cannot do as well or even at all. Thus, despite the great number of children currently being born to unmarried parents in the United States, there is a lot of pressure for fathers and mothers to be married. Indeed, even with unmarried parents, the state will insist, where possible, that they continue to be responsible for their offspring, as is seen in instances in which the state tries to get unmarried fathers (and occasionally mothers) to pay child support.

In Chapter 2, "Understanding," we present a short history of marriage.

What Is a Family?

Once a married couple has a child, does that mean that they are a family? Actually, they might be a family already—if, for example, as U.S. tax laws define it, they are supporting dependent parents. Moreover, it's clear that an unmarried couple with children also constitutes a family, which goes to show that defining "family" is more difficult than defining "marriage."

Traditionally, however, a ***family* has been defined as a unit of two or more people who are related by blood, marriage, or adoption and who live together.** This definition thus excludes foster families, couples who live together (cohabit), homosexual couples, and communal arrangements in which a child is reared by several people other than the parents. Let us try to sort this out.

The Formerly "Modern" Family: The Nuclear Family

The family into which you may have been born and the family that you will begin if and when you marry and have children are both nuclear families. **The *nuclear family*—also once thought of as the *modern family*—consists**

FAMILY MATTERS. If the word *family* describes only a married male and female couple with children, what should we call an unmarried couple with children, whether or not they're heterosexual? ◄

of father, mother, and children living in one household. The nuclear family, a term coined by anthropologist George Murdock in 1949, is the idealized version of what most people think of when they think of "family." In the past, the nuclear family has also often been thought of as the **traditional family, in which the man's role is primarily husband, father, and income earner and the woman's role is wife, mother, and homemaker.**

A nuclear family can be one of two types—*family of origin* or *family of procreation*:

■ Family of Origin: **The *family of origin*, also called the *family of orientation*, is the family into which you were born or in which you grew up.** As you might expect, this kind of family had an important influence on you and on your views about marriage and family in general.

■ Family of Procreation: **The *family of procreation*, also called the *family of cohabitation*, is the family you begin if and when you get married and have children.** In the United States in 2000, about 24% of black households and 36% of white households consisted of married couples with their own children under age 18, about 28% consisted of married couples without children (U.S. Census Bureau 2000).

Today's "Postmodern" Family: Binuclear & Blended Families

The old definition of what a family is—the modern or nuclear family—no longer seems adequate to cover the wide diversity of household arrangements we see today, according to many social scientists (Edwards 1991; Stacey 1996). Thus has arisen the term **postmodern family, which is meant to describe the great variability in family forms,** including *single-parent families* and *child-free couples*, as we discuss in detail in Chapter 9, "Variations," and Chapter 11, "Parenting."

Two common examples of the postmodern family are *binuclear families* and *blended families*:

■ Binuclear Family: When children talk about going to "Mom's house this week and Dad's house next week," they are talking about a binuclear family. **A *binuclear family* is a family in which members live in two different households,** usually the result of parents being divorced and their children spending time with both.

■ Blended Family: **A *blended family*, or *stepfamily*, is created when two people marry and one or both brings into the household a child or children from a previous marriage or relationship.** Clearly, children can find themselves not only in binuclear households but also in blended families if one or both their parents remarries someone who has children from a previous marriage or relationship.

The Extended Family: Kin & Affiliated Kin

No doubt many people think of their families as including more than just those in their nuclear family. These are members of their **extended family, which includes not only the nuclear family but others as well**—uncles and aunts, nieces and nephews, cousins, grandparents, even great-grandparents.

In addition, a postmodern family might consist not only of kin but also of *affiliated kin*.

■ **Kin: The *kin* in your family are your relatives by blood, marriage, remarriage, or adoption, ranging from grandparents to nieces to brothers-in-law.** Of course, some kin don't usually live in the same household with you, but here, too, there are many variations. For instance, it is not unusual to see grandparents raising their grandchildren because the generation in between is unable to do so (because they are incapacitated by drug abuse, for example).

■ **Affiliated Kin: *Affiliated Kin* are unrelated individuals who are treated as if they are related.** For example, godparents or the boyfriend of a divorced mother may be considered affiliated kin. The primary indicator seems to be *emotional closeness* rather than relationship through marriage, remarriage, descent, or adoption. One scholar, who has identified 23 different types of family structures, says that some include only friends or group-home members (Wu 1996).

Beyond the Household: Extended Families & Patterns of Residence

In many countries and cultures, members of extended families live in close proximity to one another; indeed, there are three common ways in which families establish residence—*neolocal, patrilocal,* and *matrilocal:*

■ **Neolocal—In Their Own Home:** This tends to be the pattern in North America. **A *neolocal residence* describes the situation in which newly married partners set up their own household,** not connected with the bride or groom's parents.

■ **Patrilocal—With the Husband's Family:** This is the most common pattern around the world. **A *patrilocal residence* describes the situation in which newly married partners live with the husband's family.**

■ **Matrilocal—With the Wife's Family:** This pattern is not as common. **A *matrilocal residence* describes the situation in which newly married partners reside with the wife's family.** This arrangement occurs, for example, among some groups in the Pacific Islands and Africa, and among some Native Americans.

Because housing in many industrialized countries today is so expensive, many young couples initially live with the bride or groom's parents or grandparents (Savage and Fronczek 1993). In addition, in the United States, often the newly divorced (and their children), unable to afford their own residences, will move in with parents or grandparents. Middle-aged couples may also have their own parents living with them.

We present a short history of the family in Chapter 2, "Understanding."

1.3 The Challenges to Relationships & Families Today

MAJOR QUESTION What are the benefits of the family, and what economic and demographic trends are affecting it?

PREVIEW The traditional family has four benefits: economic benefits, proximity, familiarity, and continuity. But traditional families are being radically influenced by economic and demographic trends. Economically, the family has been and is being affected by the Industrial Revolution, technological change, globalization, and the mass media and popular culture. Two overall demographic trends are (1) those affecting the postmodern family and (2) changes in ethnic and racial diversity.

"When it comes to Us versus Them, it's all about who your relatives are," writes Stanford University neurologist Robert M. Sapolsky (2003). "Kin— cooperate with them, defend them in a tough situation. Unrelated stranger— start growling menacingly."

Growling? Sapolsky is talking about animals: dogs, muskrats, deer mice. And animals instinctively are able to distinguish kin from nonkin by their smell, since every deer mouse, say, has a distinctive, genetically based odor— and if you were a deer mouse, the closer your relatives, the more similar they would smell to you.

Humans, however, can't do it instinctively. We have to figure out Us versus Them by using our brains. "This is where the trouble can begin," says Sapolsky, "because our thinking isn't perfect and can be manipulated. When social cues make you feel more cooperatively related to someone than you actually are, it is termed 'pseudokinship.' On a fairly trivial level, you have bunches of guys pseudokinshipping each other with 'Yo, bro' or secret handshakes in their Fraternal Order of Something." On a more serious level, feelings of pseudokinship can be exploited during wartime (or even during political elections) so that we can be made to think of everyone on our side as being a friend and everyone on the enemy's side as barely being human.

Why Have Families at All? Four Benefits

Since the feelings of kinship (or pseudokinship) can be duplicated so widely, you might wonder why families are even needed at all. However, the great family sociologist **William Goode** (1982) theorized that living in a traditional family offers four benefits: (1) *economic benefits*, (2) *proximity*, (3) *familiarity*, and (4) *continuity*.

1. Economic Benefits: Economies of Scale

Families offer economic benefits. It's easier to buy a house if both husband and wife are bringing in incomes. It's almost as easy for one person to clean house, do laundry, or buy groceries for three or four people as for one. Such savings in time and money result from what are called *economies of scale*—a reduction in the cost per unit because of the increased size of the "household production facilities." In other words, if the cost of providing for one person is spread over three or four people, the cost of those services per person (per unit) is reduced.

Indeed, most of the tasks of running a household (feeding babies, mowing lawns, and so on) don't require much training, so that nearly anyone can do them, whether you're a laborer or a neurosurgeon. Recently, however, a growing field of economic study known as *household production* has begun to look at household time use to examine when it's worthwhile for a family member to do domestic chores. Do you mow the lawn yourself? If you make more than $44,000 a year, it is recommended that you hire a lawn service (Spencer 2003).

2. Proximity: Convenience

If you're a single parent and need someone to watch your child, or if you feel like sitting down with a friend for conversation, you might have to travel some distance. A second benefit of a family, therefore, is—or at least can be—that members are in *close proximity*, and so it is more convenient to obtain help or company.

If you're a single working parent with no resources, an ill child is a crisis. Do you insist that the child go to school anyway (even though you know you shouldn't)? Or do you leave the child home alone while you are at work (a frequent occurrence, although most parents who do this have great misgivings)? Or do you telephone your boss and pretend that you're sick and can't come in (a frequent ploy)? By contrast, if you're fortunate enough to live close to a cooperative, nonworking relative—your own parents, say, or one of your siblings—who can agree to watch the child, such problems become easier to handle.

3. Familiarity: At Your Best & at Your Worst

Fellow family members are generally more apt than anyone else to know who you really are, and vice versa. That is, a family offers *familiarity*, because you and others in the family have seen one another under good and bad circumstances. Yes, they have observed you acting selfishly and irrationally, but they have also seen you behaving kindly and courageously. Most people's friends probably don't know them that well.

"AS YOU ARE, SO ONCE WAS I." At one time, the older woman may well have looked much like the younger one. What is the tradition in your family about caring for older members, and does it extend outside the immediate household to aunts, uncles, and others? What kind of connections do you hope to have with family members when you are elderly? ▲

4. Continuity: People Who Are Always There for You

Is your home the place in which, in poet Robert Frost's words, "when you have to go there, they have to take you in"? Although friends may offer you emotional comfort, bankers may lend you money, and hired contractors may fix your plumbing, it is home and family that can offer the possibility, at least, of *continuity*—long-time emotional support, attachments, and assistance.

Are the benefits that a traditional family offers being lost to us? Certainly, the family in the last hundred years has radically changed in character from that of earlier times. Does this mean that the family is weaker, stronger, or just different? To address this question, let us consider the economic and demographic trends affecting families.

Today's Changing Families: Economic Trends

Every few hundred years in Western history, according to acclaimed management theorist Peter Drucker, there occurs a sharp transformation in which, within a few decades, "society rearranges itself—its world view; its basic values; its social and political structure; its arts; its key institutions" (Drucker 1993: 3). We are living through such a transformation today. We consider the effects on intimacy, marriage, and family life posed by (1) *the Industrial Revolution*, (2) *technological change*, (3) *globalization*, and (4) *the mass media and popular culture*.

1. The Effect of the Industrial Revolution: From Familism to Individualism

In the past century and a half, powerful economic forces caused families to move from a philosophy of familism to a philosophy of individualism.

▪ **Familism:** Before the Industrial Revolution, which in the United States occurred mainly during the middle and late 1800s, human (and animal) labor, rather than machinery, was the dominant means of producing goods. In those times, families lived mainly on farms or in villages and produced goods and services principally for themselves. "The traditional family," points out sociological theorist **Anthony Giddens** (2003: 18), "was above all an economic unit."

Family decision making therefore followed the philosophy of *familism—* **that is, when decisions are made, family collective concerns take priority over individual concerns.** Familism is still a guiding principle of families in China, Mexico, and many other parts of the world.

▪ **Individualism:** As the United States became industrialized, families lost their self-sufficiency. Men were forced to leave home to work in mills and factories, while women were expected to tend to households and children. As a result, men became less actively involved in child rearing, and large numbers of children were no longer valued as contributors of labor to the family enterprise but instead were considered a drain on family resources.

To support their children, both parents then became obliged to work outside the home, giving rise to the two-income family, and families moved to cities to have access to factory jobs. With both parents out of the house a great deal, children had less adult direction (Zaretsky 1976). Increasingly, family decision making switched to the philosophy of *individualism—* **that is, when decisions are made, individual concerns take priority over family collective concerns.** Individualism led to a search for personal fulfillment and less focus on children that, it has been suggested, may have contributed to less nurturing and more absent parents, with a consequent rise in juvenile delinquency, violence, and divorce (Hewlett 1992).

2. Technological Change: More Complexity or More Choices?

The hallmark of great civilizations has been their effective systems of communications. In the beginning, communications was based on transportation—the Roman Empire's network of roads, the far-flung navies of the European powers, the unification of the North American continent by transcontinental railroads and later airplanes and interstate highways.

▪ **From Transportation to Communication:** Transportation began to yield to the electronic exchange of information. The amplifying vacuum tube, invented in 1906, led to commercial radio. Television came into being in England in 1925.

During the 1950s and 1960s, as television exploded throughout the world, communications philosopher Marshall McLuhan (1951, 1960, 1964, 1967) posed the notion of a "global village," the "shrinking" of time and space as air travel and the electronic media made it easier for the people of the globe to communicate with one another. Then, with the invention of cell phones, pagers, fax machines, and voice mail, the world became even faster and smaller.

■ **Computers, the Net, and the Web:** The microprocessor "is the most important invention of the 20th century," says Michael Malone (1995). This "silicon chip," used in all computers, enabled the revolution in consumer electronics, massive databases, and most certainly the Internet (the Net), that worldwide computer-linked "network of networks."

The Net might have remained the province of academicians had it not been for the contributions of Tim Berners-Lee, who came up with the system that debuted in 1991 as the World Wide Web. His work expanded the Internet into a worldwide mass medium.

Now we are well into the Internet's second generation, what is known as ***Web 2.0*, which, besides communication tools and wikis (websites that allow visitors to edit content), also includes social networking websites.** Of particular relevance to the subject of this book, ***social networking websites* are online communities of Internet users who share a common bond** (Wilson 2007). Well-known examples are MySpace and Facebook, as we describe elsewhere.

■ **Developments in Biology:** The discovery in 1953 of DNA, the "living thread" that is the genetic basis of evolution and inheritance, gave researchers insights into the molecule that makes and maintains all life. Now scientists are learning to redefine medicine from a discipline that tries to treat disease symptoms to one that finds out and fixes exactly what's wrong.

Discoveries in biology are already being used to treat fertility problems. It is expected that as gene therapy becomes available it will help spare prospective parents of having to deal with such heartbreakers as mental retardation, cystic fibrosis, and spina bifida in their children.

Technology can have both bad and good effects on relationships. Air travel may take breadwinners away from their families, for instance, but email, cell phones, and videoconferencing may keep them connected. Improved forms of birth control allow people to be physically intimate and pursue their educations and careers, yet they also can have the effect of pulling people away from extended family ties that revolve around child care.

3. Globalization

We are living in a world being rapidly changed by ***globalization*—the trend of the world economy toward becoming a more interdependent system.** In the late 1980s, the Berlin Wall came down, signaling the beginning of the end of communism in Eastern Europe; the countries of the Pacific Rim began to open their economies to foreign investors; and governments around the globe began deregulating their economies. These three events set up conditions by which goods, people, and money could move more freely throughout the world—a global economy. The global economy is the increasing tendency of the economies of the world to interact with one another as one market instead of many national markets.

Is globalization good or bad? There are opposing arguments:

■ **Argument for Globalization:** Some think the global connections among U.S. exports, international trade, and U.S. workers are a good thing. "As consumers in other regions of the world see their income go up, they are going to be more interested in U.S. products," says Nancy Birdsall, executive vice president of the Inter-American Development Bank in Washington, DC. "The

GLOBALIZATION. Easier cross-border trade may bring many benefits to the United States, such as chapter products and services. But how will you and the relationships within your family be affected if traditional good-paying American jobs are transferred to low-wage countries such as India, which hosts hundreds of customer call centers like this one? How should you prepare for this possibility? ◄

bottom line is that growth of jobs and income in other countries will mean growth of jobs and income in [the United States]. It's a win-win situation" (Birdsall, quoted in Kleiman, 1995).

■ **Argument against Globalization:** Economist Frederic L. Pryor (2002), an authority on the comparative study of economic systems, believes that globalization limits the ability of the United States to protect particular sectors of its economy and makes it more vulnerable to external shocks. Globalization can also lead to reduction in good-paying, low-skill manufacturing jobs in the United States as these jobs are moved to low-wage countries. In addition, multinational corporations may decide to redirect investments and businesses offshore instead of in the United States.

One result of globalization is that the U.S. economy is no longer dominated by manufacturing and the production of goods but rather by the performance of services, such as those in business, health, and social services. Service-providing industries are expected to account for approximately 18.7 million of the 18.9 million new wage and salary jobs generated between 2004 and 2014 (U.S. Department of Labor 2005a).

Some jobs in services require college educations and pay well (general managers, nurses, postsecondary teachers). Unfortunately, most of the growing service jobs don't require much education and do not pay well (food service personnel, retail salespeople, cashiers, clerks, security guards, truck drivers, nursing aides, and janitors, for example). Because the stability and happiness of relationships and families depend so much on good-paying jobs, globalization has meant trouble for some families.

4. The Mass Media & Popular Culture: Relief from Boredom & Other Effects

Therapists often blame adultery and divorce on communication breakdowns and other problems, but could the main threat be pure, simple boredom? That's what psychologist and attorney Rex Julian Beaber thinks. "No ongoing marriage," he says, "can ever compete with the arousal level, uncertainty, and novelty of a new relationship" (Beaber, quoted in Rivenburg 2003: 1D). We discuss the causes of infidelity elsewhere in this book, but here let us consider that huge empire built to fight boredom in modern life—the mass media, the entertainment industry, all those companies trying to sell new cars, clothes, music, and magazines with tips for spicing up your sex life.

The mass media and their sidekick—popular culture—are a major source of much of the information, both accurate and inaccurate, we have about *roles*, *beliefs*, and *values* in our lives.

■ **Roles:** **A *role* is the pattern of behaviors expected of a person who occupies a certain social position within a certain group or culture.** Spouses are expected to play one role, parents another, and sometimes the two collide, which is called *role conflict*. Popular magazines might encourage you to be wild and sexy for your mate, for example, but sober and responsible for your kids.

■ **Beliefs:** *Beliefs* **refer to the definitions and explanations people have about what is true.** The mass media perpetuate and reinforce many beliefs—for instance, that long-term marriages are "successful" and short-term marriages are "failures." Or that people who are handsome or beautiful are better than those who are not.

■ **Values:** *Values* **are deeply held beliefs and attitudes about what is right and wrong, desirable and undesirable.** The media encourage conflicting values: Being "swept away" in a romantic relationship is considered good, for instance, yet so is "standing by your man."

As was mentioned, because the mass media and popular culture can have such an impact on our roles, beliefs, and values in relation to intimacy, marriage, and family, we begin each chapter with examples and discussion of these powerful influences.

Today's Changing Families: Demographic Trends

Demography **is the study of population and population characteristics—called *demographics*—such as family size, marriage and divorce rates, and ethnicity and race.** Here let us consider two general kinds of demographic changes: (1) changes in ethnic and racial diversity and (2) changes in the postmodern family.

1. Changes in Ethnic & Racial Diversity

Much past research on American marriage and families was based on non-Hispanic whites. But research findings about whites should not be generalized to nonwhites. This conclusion becomes all the more important when we consider that the percentage of non-Hispanic whites is fast declining in the United States. *(See ■ Panel 1.2.)*

Let's consider the major racial and ethnic groups. *Race* **describes inherited physical characteristics that distinguish one group from another.** *Ethnicity* **describes cultural characteristics that distinguish one group from another.** *(See ■ Panel 1.3.)*

■ **Non-Hispanic Whites—66.9% of Americans in 2005:** The largest number of whites is of European descent, and most are not discriminated against racially because most white ethnic groups are not physically distinguishable from

■ **PANEL 1.2** Diversity Data: Declining U.S. Population That Is Non-Hispanic White—Actual and Projected

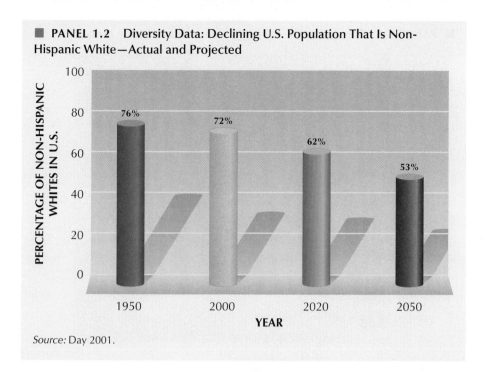

Source: Day 2001.

other whites (Lieberson and Waters 1988). The top three European ancestry groups in the United States are German, Irish, and English, followed by Italian, Polish, French, Scottish, Dutch, Norwegian, Scotch-Irish, and Swedish (Brittingham and de la Cruz 2004). *(See ■ Panel 1.4.)* People of Jewish ethnicity are also generally of European descent.

Whereas earlier in U.S. history members of European ethnic groups preferred to drop their ethnic identifications and take on the beliefs and values of the majority culture, now many descendants like to practice ethnic identi-

■ **PANEL 1.3** Diversity Data: Major Racial and Ethnic Groups in the United States, 2005

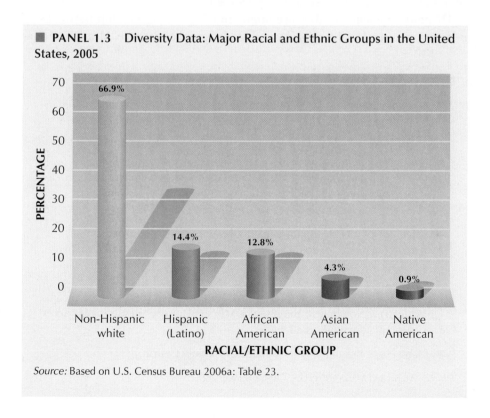

Source: Based on U.S. Census Bureau 2006a: Table 23.

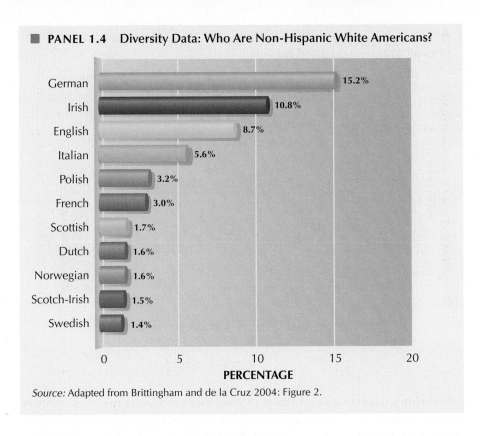

PANEL 1.4   Diversity Data: Who Are Non-Hispanic White Americans?

German — 15.2%
Irish — 10.8%
English — 8.7%
Italian — 5.6%
Polish — 3.2%
French — 3.0%
Scottish — 1.7%
Dutch — 1.6%
Norwegian — 1.6%
Scotch-Irish — 1.5%
Swedish — 1.4%

PERCENTAGE

Source: Adapted from Brittingham and de la Cruz 2004: Figure 2.

fication, especially during major holidays such as St. Patrick's Day (Irish), Columbus Day (Italian), and Hanukkah (Jewish).

■ **Hispanic (Latinos)—14.4% in 2005:** Members of ethnic groups calling themselves Hispanic or Latino—who might identify themselves racially as white, black, or Native American—make up the largest minority group in the United States as well as the fastest growing. *(See* ■ *Panel 1.5.)*

Hispanic nuclear families are augmented by strong kinship networks of relatives who tend to live close by and lend mutual assistance. More than one-

PANEL 1.5   Diversity Data: Who Are Hispanics?

■ Hispanics represent the largest minority in the United States. In 2005, there were far more Hispanics in the United States (42 million) than there were Canadians in Canada (32 million).

■ "Hispanics" and "Latinos" are the terms used by the Census Bureau, although Mexicans may use the term "Chicanos." Most people of Spanish descent identify with a particular country—Puerto Ricans, Dominicans, Cubans, and so on. (In this book, we use the term "Hispanics.")

■ There are 17 major Hispanic subcultures: Californians (divided among immigrant Mexicans, middle-class Mexicans, barrio dwellers, and Central Americans); Tejanos (South Texans, Houston Mexicans, Texas Guatemalans); Chicago Latinos (Chicago Mexicans, Chicago Puerto Ricans); Miamians (Cubans, Nicaraguans, South Americans); New York Hispanics (Puerto Ricans, Dominicans, Colombians); and elsewhere in the United States (New Mexico's Hispanos, migrant workers all over).

■ Many Hispanics in the United States speak only English.

Sources: Marin and Marin 1991; U.S. Census Bureau 2006b.

third of Hispanic families have five or more children. Hispanics are more likely to separate or divorce compared to non-Hispanic whites, though less so than African Americans.

■ **African Americans—12.8% in 2005:** Today one in three black families has an income over $35,000 a year, and middle-class black families are as stable as comparable white families. In two-parent black families, both parents often work, resulting in more egalitarian div ision of domestic responsibilities. Children are valued, family loyalty is prized, and many African Americans have extended families to lend economic and emotional support.

On the other hand, African Americans also have three times the poverty rate of whites and average only 61% of income compared to non-Hispanic whites (DeNavas-Walt et al. 2006). Because there is a high correlation between poverty and broken families, poor African Americans have high rates of divorce, of births to unwed mothers, and of households headed by a single parent.

Unlike many Hispanics and Asian Americans, most African Americans are not able to identify their country of origin.

■ **Asian Americans—4.3% in 2005:** As with Hispanics, Asian Americans trace their roots to many different countries of origin. *(See* ■ *Panel 1.6.)* Asian Americans are the most economically well off racial category in the United States. For instance, Chinese Americans tend to be among the best educated, have the highest incomes, and suffer lowest unemployment compared with other Americans.

How much Asian Americans tend to be culturally distinct depends on whether they are American-born or foreign-born, members of older immigrant groups or more recent ones. The newer they are to the United States, the more apt they are to emphasize familism, strong parental control, kinship ties, conservative sexual values, large families, and motivation to achieve (Lin and Fu 1990; Ishii-Kuntz 1997; Kitano and Kitano 1998).

■ **Native Americans—0.9% in 2005:** Native Americans include Eskimos and Aleuts as well as members of the Navajo, Hopi, Lakota, Cherokee, Tingit, Washoe, and other Indian tribes in the continental United States. More than half the 2.8 million Americans of Indian descent live outside tribal lands, mostly in cities.

Among married Native Americans, more than half have married non-Indians, which may ultimately affect their ethnic identity. Native American families often have extended kinship networks, which derive from clan membership rather than birth or marriage.

■ **PANEL 1.6   Diversity Data: Who Are Asian Americans?**

■ Asian Americans are the second fastest-growing minority in the United States, after Hispanics.

■ There are 28 separate groups of Asian Americans. In terms of ethnic origin, the largest groups are Chinese (22.9%), Filipino (17.4%), Asian Indian (15.8%), Vietnamese (10.6%), Korean (10.1%), and Japanese (7.5%).

■ The fastest-growing Asian American groups in recent years have been those from Vietnam, India, Korea, Cambodia (Kampuchea), and Laos.

■ Most Asian Americans (56%) live in the West. The three largest groups are found mainly in California (35%), New York (11%), and Hawaii (5%).

Sources: Barringer 1991; U.S. Census Bureau 2000: Table 26; Barnes and Barnett 2002.

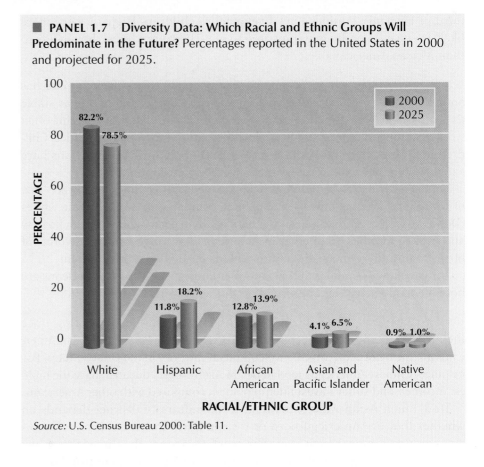

■ **PANEL 1.7   Diversity Data: Which Racial and Ethnic Groups Will Predominate in the Future?** Percentages reported in the United States in 2000 and projected for 2025.

Source: U.S. Census Bureau 2000: Table 11.

The changing racial-ethnic mix, fueled by immigration both legal and illegal as well as high birth rates, is one of the most significant events in the United States. *(See* ■ *Panel 1.7)* We will revisit its influence on marriage and families throughout the book.

2. Changes in the Postmodern Family

Since the 1800s in the United States, there have been two significant demographic trends.

■ Trend #1—People Are Living Longer and Marrying Later: The *median age* of the U.S. population was 36 in 2005—up from 17 in the mid-1800s. (*Median* means that half the people in the United States today are over 36 years of age and half are under it.) More adults are remaining single longer. The median age at first marriage has been rising since the 1950s: In 1970, it was 23.2 years for men and 20.8 years for women; in 2005, it was 27.1 for men and 25.3 for women (U.S. Census Bureau 2006a).

■ Trend #2—Women Are Having Fewer Children: Compared with the late 1800s, women in the United States are having fewer children, and they finish raising them earlier in life, which means that children grow up and leave home sooner. The birth rate was 14 per 1,000 persons in 2005, down from 16.7 in 1990 (Hamilton et al. 2006).

Also, women are having their first child at a later age: The mean age of the American woman at the birth of her first baby rose from 21.4 years in 1970 to 25.2 in 2003 (National Center for Health Statistics 2005). *(See* ■ *Panel 1.8.)*

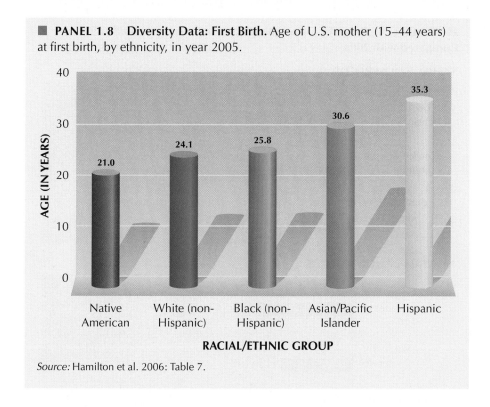

■ PANEL 1.8   Diversity Data: First Birth. Age of U.S. mother (15–44 years) at first birth, by ethnicity, in year 2005.

Source: Hamilton et al. 2006: Table 7.

Not surprisingly, U.S. households are getting smaller: The average household size fell from 3.35 in 1960 to 2.57 in 2003 (Fields 2004).

These two trends have had a major effect on the family, accelerating the pace with which the modern (nuclear) family has given way to the postmodern (many-faceted) family. Indeed, today *fewer than 25% of families can be considered nuclear or modern* (Fields 2004). *(See ■ Panel 1.9, next page.)* As Giddens (2003: 20) says, "Marriage is no longer the chief defining basis of coupledom."

■ More Unmarrieds: It is not unusual for people to live alone or with a partner in an unmarried relationship. In 2005, the number of never-married men and women was 28.2% and 21.6%, respectively. The percentage of married-couple families declined from 70.6% of all families in 1970 to 58.6% in 2005 (U.S. Census Bureau 2006b). From 1990 to 2003, the percentage of unmarried-partner households went from about 3.5% to 4.2% (Fields 2004). (We discuss unmarrieds in Chapter 9, "Variations.")

■ More Single-Parent Families: From 1970 to 2003, single-mother families grew from 12% to 26% and single-father families from 1% to 6% (Fields 2004). In 1970, 11% of all births were to unmarried women; in 2005, that figure rose to 36.8% (Hamilton 2006). More and more children are also being raised by single-parent fathers. (We discuss single-parent families in Chapter 9, "Variations," and Chapter 11, "Parenting.")

■ More Working Parents: In 1998, only 23% of all families with a child under the age of 6 had one parent working and the other parent staying at home. Families in which both parents are working doubled from 1976 to 1998—from 31% to 62%. Between 1970 and 2003, the percentage of married women with children under age 6 who were in the labor force went from 30% to 64%.

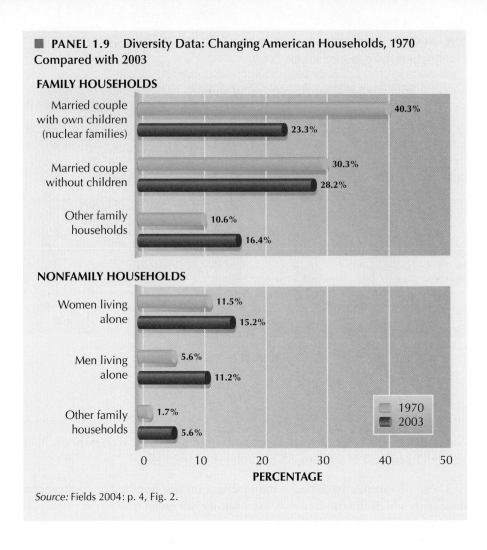

■ **PANEL 1.9** Diversity Data: Changing American Households, 1970 Compared with 2003

FAMILY HOUSEHOLDS

Married couple with own children (nuclear families): 40.3% (1970), 23.3% (2003)

Married couple without children: 30.3% (1970), 28.2% (2003)

Other family households: 10.6% (1970), 16.4% (2003)

NONFAMILY HOUSEHOLDS

Women living alone: 11.5% (1970), 15.2% (2003)

Men living alone: 5.6% (1970), 11.2% (2003)

Other family households: 1.7% (1970), 5.6% (2003)

1970
2003

PERCENTAGE

Source: Fields 2004: p. 4, Fig. 2.

From 1975 to 2004, the labor force participation rate of mothers with children under age 18 rose from 47% to 71% (U.S. Department of Labor 2005b). (We discuss this topic further in Chapter 11, "Parenting," and Chapter 12, "Work.")

■ **More Divorces, Remarriages, and Blended Families:** Between 1970 and 2005, the number of divorced persons rose from 4.3 million to 22.1 million (U.S. Census Bureau 2006b). If all marriages are considered, about 2% to 3% end in divorce in any particular year. However, anywhere from 40% to 60% of *new* marriages will eventually end in divorce at some point—about 1 out of 2. Divorces set the pattern for many of the postmodern families: single-parent families, remarriages, and blended families. In 2001, 10.6 million, or 15%, of children under age 18 lived in blended families; about half of these, 5.1 million, lived with at least one stepparent (Kreider and Fields 2005). (We discuss divorce in Chapter 14, "Uncoupling," and remarriage and blended families in Chapter 15, "Remarriage.")

Your Personal Exploration

Look at magazine ads from the 1950s and 1960s, and you'll see pictures of a family, usually white, with Dad in a suit and tie going off to work while waving to stay-at-home Mom flanked by Junior and Sis. Clearly, this racially uniform nuclear family is no longer the principal reality today. Besides the increase in single-parent families and the divorced and remarried, there are more people in live-together unmarried relationships (some as lovers, some not), more households without children, more gay and lesbian households, and other varieties of "families."

Myths, however, often die hard. As we have seen, all kinds of factors raise our expectations about what intimacy and happiness ought to be. This is why we open each chapter with a lengthy discussion of the influences of the media and why we try to address various other factors, including race, ethnicity, and economics, throughout the book.

This book is the study of intimacy from an academic point of view. But it is also meant to assist you in your personal exploration to find happiness with another person. This is one of the most important journeys you will ever take. We hope that you will be able to realize happiness by, as Dan Baker said, learning "to practice appreciation or love."

Self-Assessment: The RELATE and READY Relationship Questionnaires

A Self-Assessment appears at the end of every chapter to help you ascertain your own feelings and beliefs about marriage, family, and intimate relationships. This first one, RELATE and READY, is a pair of comprehensive questionnaires developed by a team of marriage and family professionals. RELATE is an assessment with 276 questions that you can use to build strengths and unearth challenges in an existing intimate relationship, such as marriage, engagement, or a serious dating relationship. It can be taken individually, or with a partner. READY is an assessment with 172 questions to help you determine how prepared you might be to enter into a serious long-term relationship. Either assessment can be completed online at the same website, and you will receive an immediate report electronically with all of your answers, and a summary illustrated with graphs.

There is a charge for taking RELATE or READY. If you received a new copy of the *RELATE and READY User's Guide* with this text, you have already paid for either assessment; look for the Personal Identification Number (PIN) that allows you to receive your report when you are finished. If not, you can pay for RELATE and READY online with a credit card. The RELATE questionnaire is $10 per individual and $20 per couple. The READY questionnaire is $10 per individual.

Instructions for Online RELATE and READY:

1. Go to the RELATE and READY website at www.relate-institute.org.

2. Click on the "New Users sign up" link toward the bottom of the page, or click on the "New Users" tab on the left side of the page. Click on **"Create a new account."**

3. On the New Account Registration screen type in your desired **username** in the box.

4. Type in your **password** in the "Desired password" box and repeat your password a second time in the "Confirm Password" box.

5. Type in your **email address** and then click the **"Finish"** button. At this point if your username has already been used by someone in the past you will receive a message such as the following **"This username is not available. Choose another one."** If you receive this message select a different username until you get one that hasn't been previously selected by someone else.

6. Once you select a username that is unique and you put in your password with your email address you will be taken to a new screen where you will need to type in your password one more time. Type in your password and click on the "Sign In" button. (If you are taking RELATE as a couple, write down your username and password to share with your partner later, and ask for your partner's username and password so you can select her or him when appropriate to get a couple report.)

7. You will now arrive at a page that says "Completed Evaluations" with a variety of tabs you can select. Follow the instructions on the page by:

8. Click on the tab that says "New Evaluation."

9. Answer the question "Are you currently in a relationship with someone special? (e.g., seriously dating, engaged or married)" by clicking on the yes or no button.

10. Click on the "Proceed to Evaluation" button. This will automatically take you to the RELATE instrument for couples, or the READY instrument for those who are not in a relationship yet.

11. Follow the directions on each page and at the end of each page click the "Next" button. (If you are taking RELATE as a couple, you cannot receive your Report until both partners complete the questionnaire and provide each other their username and password, and the PIN or credit card number is entered.)

Source: Vicki L. Loyer-Carlson and Dean M. Busy, *RELATE and READY User's Guide*, 2nd ed. (Boston: Allyn and Bacon, 2006).

Key Terms Used in This Chapter

Summary

1.1 Seeking Happiness through Love & Intimacy

- One way people seek happiness is through an intimate relationship with another person. Research suggests that the achievement of happiness is influenced by both one's genetic makeup and one's social environment. Happy people tend to spend the majority of their time with friends and family and relatively little time alone. Married people tend to be among the happiest of people and tend to have higher levels of emotional well-being.

- Happy couples exhibit five key traits in their relationships: (1) good communication, (2) flexibility as a couple, (3) emotional closeness to each other, (4) compatible personalities, and (5) agreement on how to handle conflict. The couple's (6) sexual relationship, (7) choice of leisure activities, (8) influence of friends and family, (9) ability to manage money, and (10) agreement on spiritual beliefs also affect their happiness.

1.2 Intimacy, Marriage, & Family

- Intimacy is the experiencing of the essence of one's self in intense intellectual, physical, and/or emotional communion with another human being across the three dimensions of (1) breadth, (2) openness, and (3) depth.

- Compared to unmarried people, married people tend to get happier over time. Unrealistic expectations about marriage may prevent the achievement of happiness in a marriage. Many people wonder whether deep intimacy is really attainable.

- Heterosexual marriage can be defined as a socially approved mating relationship involving five components: (1) emotional, (2) ceremonial, (3) legal, (4) sexual faithfulness, and (5) parenting.

- Although most people in North America marry for love, some other cultures favor arranged marriages. Universal to all cultures is some type of ceremony, ranging from the very secular to the very sacred, that cements or bonds the union of a couple.

- Cohabitation, or living together, requires no license, but marrying does, which has legal implications that affect property, children, debts, and inheritance. States may set minimum age for marriage and establish other requirements such as blood tests and waiting periods.

- Common-law marriage, in which a couple living together presents themselves as being married, is legally recognized in several states.

- For many people, a marriage or sexual relationship involves monogamy, with a person committed exclusively to one partner. However, other marital forms exist throughout the world, such as polygamy, or marriages involving several spouses. They include polygyny (a husband has more than one wife) and polyandry (a wife has more than one husband).

- From a societal point of view, the main function of marriage is to provide a stable framework for bearing, nurturing, socializing, rearing, and protecting children. Unmarried parents are still expected, where possible, to be responsible for their children, as is evident in the issue of child support.

- In the traditional definition, a family is defined as a unit made up of two or more people who are related by blood, marriage, or adoption. The concept of family outside of marriage can be subjective, with an unmarried couple with children being viewed as a family as much as a married couple with children.

- The nature and structure of a family can vary. The nuclear family, once thought of as the modern family, consists of a father, mother, and children living in one household. The nuclear family was once considered the traditional family or a family in which the man's role is primarily husband, father, and income earner and the wife's role is primarily wife, mother, and homemaker. The nuclear family can be either a family of orientation (the family in which a person is born and grows up) or a family of procreation or cohabitation (the family a person begins after getting married and having children).

- As a result of a variety of social forces, family structure has evolved beyond the nuclear family into new forms called the postmodern family, two examples being the binuclear family (a family in which members live in two different households) and the blended family or stepfamily (created when two people marry and one or both brings into the household a child or children from a previous marriage or relationship).

- The term *extended family* further expands the definition of family to include uncles, aunts, nieces, nephews, cousins, grandparents, and great-grandparents. Postmodern families may consist of kin that are defined as one's relatives by blood, marriage, or relationship. They also may consist of affiliated kin—unrelated individuals who are treated as if they are related.

- Members of an extended family may live in close proximity to one another and even in the same household. The arrangements may be neolocal (a newly married couple sets up their own household, which is not connected with the bride or groom's parents), patrilocal (a newly married couple lives with the husband's family), or matrilocal (a newly married couple lives with the wife's family).

1.3 The Challenges to Relationships & Families Today

- Traditional family structure has been and continues to be influenced by both economic and demographic trends: the Industrial Revolution, technological changes, mass media, popular culture, and globalization. Demographically the family is also experiencing changes in ethnic and racial diversity.

- Despite the changes, living in a family still offers four benefits: (1), economic benefits, reflected in the economies of scale (reduction in costs per unit) because of the increased size of the household; (2) proximity, when family members live close to one another and so obtaining help or company is more convenient; (3) familiarity—family members know an individual's characteristics during good times and bad; and (4) continuity—family members are available to offer long-time emotional support, attachments, and assistance.

- Economic forces have compelled families to change from a philosophy of familism (collective family concerns take priority) to a philosophy of individualism (individual concerns take priority).

- Technological changes in transportation (cars, air travel) and communications (cell phones, the Internet, biotechnology) have had good and bad effects on the family, as when mobility pulls people apart yet electronic technology also keeps people in touch.

- Globalization—the trend toward a more interdependent world economic system—affects the U.S. economy, as in reducing well-paying manufacturing jobs and increasing lesser-paying service jobs, which in turn affect the stability and happiness of relationships and families.

- The mass media are a major source of information and misinformation about success and happiness, resulting in a social construction of reality that can shape people's values, beliefs, and ideas about social roles. At the same time that the media convey images of success, they also create uncertainties and conflicting messages.

- Demography, the study of population and population characteristics, is concerned with such matters as family size, marriage and divorce rates, and ethnic and racial composition. Race describes inherited physical characteristics that distinguish one group from another. Ethnicity describes cultural characteristics that distinguish one group from another. Most past research about marriage and family has been based on whites; generalizations to minority groups may be inaccurate.

- Ethnic and racial diversity in the United States is changing, with the number of non-Hispanic whites decreasing while other minorities are increasing. Because different groups have different beliefs and values about the nature of family, their interaction with other segments of the population may lead to changes in family, divorce, and childbirth.

- Other significant demographic trends—that people are living longer and marrying later and that women are having fewer children—are accelerating the change from the nuclear family to the postmodern family. There are now more unmarried people, more single parents, more working parents, and more divorces, remarriages, and blended families.

Take It to the Net

Among the Internet resources on seeking happiness and intimacy are the following:

- **Authentic Happiness.** By the author of *Authentic Happiness*, Martin E. P. Seligman.
  www.authentichappiness.org

- **Intimacy/Success.** How to achieve intimacy and happiness.
  www.csulb.edu/~tstevens/c13-love.htm

- **LoveShack.org.** An "interpersonal relationship assistance center." Click on "Friends and Lovers."
  www.loveshack.org

CHAPTER 2

UNDERSTANDING
Learning about Intimate Behavior

"Advertising Doesn't Affect Me"

*"**Advertisers like to tell parents** that they can always turn off the TV to protect their kids from any negative impact of advertising. This is like telling us that we can protect our children from air pollution by making sure they never breathe. Advertising is our environment. We swim in it as*

fish swim in water. We cannot escape it. . . .

"Of course, we don't pay direct attention to very many of these ads, but we are powerfully influenced, mostly on an unconscious level, by the experience of being immersed in an advertising culture, a market-driven culture. . . . According to Rance Crain, editor-in-chief of Advertising Age, the major publication of the advertising industry, 'Only 8% of an ad's message is received by the conscious mind; the rest is worked and reworked deep within the recesses of the brain.'"

The foregoing was written by Jean Kilbourne (1999: 57, 58–59), an authority on the image of women in advertising, in *Can't Buy My*

Love: How Advertising Changes the Way We Think and Feel. As a young woman, Kilbourne had found herself unconsciously going along with advertisers' cynical equation of rebellion with smoking, drinking, and impulsive sex. Eventually, she came to realize she couldn't handle alcohol and tobacco. She then began studying the influence of advertising on addiction and on women, and in 1979, she made her first film, *Killing Us Softly: Advertising's Image of Women.*

■ *Are you immune to ads?* In 2007, Americans were expected to spend nearly half their waking lives, 3,518 hours, consuming media, 1,555 hours in front of the TV, according to the U.S. Census Bureau (2007: Table 1110). Young people view more than 40,000 ads a year on television alone, as well as others on the Internet, in magazines, and in schools, according to the American Academy of Pediatrics (2006).

You might think, of course, that *you* are not affected, that *you* are no

🔮 WHAT'S AHEAD IN THIS CHAPTER

We start by showing how marriage and family have differed over time. We then discuss mind-sets and uncritical thinking and explore ways to be more open-minded. We discuss how to evaluate research results. We conclude with theoretical perspectives on the family.

mindless robot. Rather, you are worldly, alert, skeptical, incapable of being influenced by such obvious hype and commercialism.

But you would probably be wrong.

"Almost everyone holds the misguided belief that advertisements don't affect *them*, don't shape their attitudes, don't help define their dreams," says Kilbourne (1999: 27). "What I hear more than anything else, as I lecture throughout the country, is 'I don't pay attention to ads . . . I just tune them out . . . they have no effect on me.' . . . In truth, we are all influenced by advertising. There is no way to tune out this much information, especially when it is carefully designed to break through the 'tuning out' process."

If advertising really did *not* have any influence on us, why would companies spend $300 billion a year on it? If no one pays attention to their ads, why would Grey Goose vodka go from selling 300,000 cases to 2.3 million cases in five years (Ball 2007)? As scholar Sut Jhally (quoted in Kilbourne 1999: 64) says, "To not be influenced by advertising would be to live outside of culture. No human being lives outside of culture."

■ *Does advertising lead to throwaway marriages?* Regarding advertising and intimacy, Kilbourne writes (1999: 25): "I believe there is a connection between the throwaway world of advertising and today's throwaway approach to marriage. All too often our market-driven culture locks people into adolescent fantasies of sex and relationships. And there is a connection between the constant images of instant sexual gratification and passion and the increasing burden on marriage and long-term lovers."

Perhaps you think advertising doesn't deserve that much attention— that it's "fun, sexy, often silly but certainly not anything to take seriously," as Kilbourne (1999: 26) says. Nearly everyone believes that advertisements don't affect them—even as they wear Tommy Hilfiger shirts or Guess jeans. Indeed, they might make a point of showing that they are supposedly not influenced by advertising—by deliberately drinking low-status Pabst Blue Ribbon beer, for example, or smoking hand-rolled cigarettes.

For the purposes of your study of intimacy, it's important to be aware how much advertising exploits our yearning for intimate and committed relationships. "We are surrounded by hundreds, thousands, of messages every day that link our deepest emotions to products, that objectify people and trivialize our most heartfelt moments and relationships," says Kilbourne (1999: 77). "Every emotion is used to sell us something. Our wish to protect our children is leveraged to make us buy an expensive car. A long marriage simply provides the opportunity for a diamond necklace. A painful reunion between a father and his estranged daughter is drawn out and dramatized to sell us a phone system."

In this chapter, we will give you the tools to help you look beyond the world of media images and popular culture and find what's important about intimacy and relationships: the truth.

How have the families of today been influenced by the past?

Is there a more beneficial way to approach the world and ideas than I might be taking now?

What are five principal kinds of scientific research?

What are eight perspectives for looking at the family and relationships?

🌐 **ON THE WEB** Understanding Advertising

www.mediaed.org/about

www.jeankilbourne.com

Do you really know how advertising works? See if you can find out one thing about ads that makes you realize how they influence you. To start you might go to the Media Educational Foundation's website, or go to Jean Kilbourne's website and click on "Get Active." What did you learn?

2.1 A Short History of Marriage

MAJOR QUESTION How have the families of today been influenced by the past?

PREVIEW This section presents the history of the American family during three eras: the early American era, the 19th and early 20th centuries, and the modern era. We describe variations for different ethnic and racial groups.

Seeking happiness, we've said, is a major motivation for why people seek intimate relationships. But is happiness itself enough? Deloy Bateman (cited in Krakauer 2003: 331), a high school science teacher in remote Colorado City, Utah, certainly found happiness in his large family of 17 children (all by one wife). But he is no longer a member of the extremely fundamentalist church he grew up in. "I think people within the religion—people who live here in Colorado City—are probably happier, on the whole, than people on the outside," he said. "But some things in life are more important than being happy. Like being free to think for yourself."

The purpose of this chapter is to depart from our theme of happiness to discuss ways to be free to think for yourself. As a way of beginning, we present a history of the American family to show how it differed from, yet led to, today's modern family. We begin by considering three eras in the history of the American family: (1) the early American era, (2) the 19th and early 20th centuries, and (3) the modern era.

American Families in the Colonial Era

The family in early America, during the 1600s through the mid-1800s, may be considered according to four groups: (1) Native American families, (2) white colonial families, (3) African American families, and (4) Hispanic (Latino) families.

Native American Families

At the time of the English settlement in North America in the early 17th century, there were possibly as many as 2 million Native Americans (north of

- **The good old days?** Black slaves in the 18th century at first were prohibited from legally marrying, although they had their own rituals for legitimizing unions.[a] Among whites, infant and child mortality rates were so high that up to a third of children didn't live through the first year. Among native-born whites in the middle and upper classes, women began to emphasize child rearing over childbearing, and the number of children per woman dropped from an average of 7 in 1800 to 3.5 in 1900.[b]

- **Who's the minority?** In 1950, the dominant racial-ethnic group in the United States, at 76%, consisted of white Europeans (non-Hispanic whites). In 2000, this group had declined to 72%—and is projected to slip to 53% by 2050.

- **What's the new immigration like?** A century ago, 90% of immigrants to the United States were European; in 2000, about 81% were from non-European countries. Today, 11.5% of the U.S. population is foreign born.[c]

- **How does family size vary?** The family size of Hispanics averages 3.95 people per family, compared to 3.2 people for non-Hispanic whites. Americans of Asian descent average 3.8 people per family.[d]

- **How does social science research work?** In observational research, researchers collect data by observing people in their usual surroundings, but this method is not often used, accounting for fewer than 5% of recent research articles.[e]

[a]Gutman 1976. [b]Demos 1970. [c]Sahlman 2002. [d]Collins 1997. [e]Nye 1988.

NUMBERS THAT MATTER
How Times Have Changed

Mexico) already there, living in more than 240 groups and speaking around 300 languages (John 1988; Mintz and Kellogg 1988). Family and kinship systems were amazingly diverse. Some, such as the Pueblo, were **matrilineal, meaning that children traced their descent, and perhaps rights and property, through the mother's line.** Others, such as the Cheyenne, were **patrilineal—descent and ownership of property came down through the father's line** (Mintz and Kellogg 1988).

■ **Marriage and Sex:** Most Native Americans married at young ages—usually 12–15 for females and 15–20 for males. In some families, young people were allowed to choose their own marital partners; in other families, such as those in California tribes, marriages were arranged by the parents. Some groups allowed men to take more than one wife (polygyny, described in Chapter 1, "Seeking"), although most were monogamous. Marriages were generally for a lifetime, but divorce was also allowed, practices varying according to tribes. "In many societies, divorce was easy," write Stephen Mintz and Susan Kellogg (1988: 30), "and either a husband or wife could dissolve a marriage." Some tribes also allowed men to have sex outside of marriage when their wives were pregnant or nursing.

■ **Families:** In general, children were welcomed. Most families were small because of high infant and child mortality, because mothers breast-fed their children for two or more years, and because the mothers abstained from sexual intercourse during that period. Children were treated with great kindness, and physical discipline was uncommon, although public shaming might be employed if they misbehaved. Children were taught by example, and

NATIVE AMERICANS: SOME MATRILINEAL.
In some Native American cultures, such as the Hopi and the Zuni, family systems were matrilineal—children traced their descent through their mother's line. Can you think of any other instances in world culture systems that are not based on the male line of descent? ▶

politeness and gentleness were emphasized. Among some tribes, mothers or grandmothers did the child raising, but among others, male relatives, such as uncles and grandfathers, were active mentors.

■ **Transitions:** Children began playing with dolls or hunting as preparation for the transition to adulthood. Later, during **_puberty_, the period during which one develops secondary sex characteristics (such as breasts or facial hair),** there would be ceremonies and rites of passage, as when a girl experienced her first menstruation or a boy killed his first game animal. "Among many tribes," say Mintz and Kellogg (1988: 30), "when a boy approached adolescence, he went alone to a mountaintop or into a forest to fast and seek a vision from a guardian spirit. On his return, he assumed adult status."

White Colonial Families

The European colonists—British, French, Spanish, and Portuguese—who arrived in the New World in the 1500s and 1600s brought with them the Christian-influenced model of the so-called _godly family_, a family ruled by the father much as the Christian God the Father was supposed to have ruled his children. Such a family is called a **_patriarchal family_, one in which the father holds the power,** as opposed to the less common **_matriarchal family_, in which the mother holds the power.**

■ **Marriage and Sex:** In the New England colonial family, the selection of mates for children of marriageable age was usually arranged by the parents, although the partners were usually known to the children. The notion of marrying for love was not a consideration. It was believed that love would come after marriage and that it was a duty for a person to love his or her spouse.

A committed couple was considered married, in others' views, even if a ceremony had not occurred. "If they could not restrain their sexual impulses," says one account, "they were forgiven more readily than couples who were not spouses (and the number of cases in which couples confessed to fornication during the period of their espousals suggest that Puritans possessed no more restraint than other human beings)" (Morgan 1966: 33). In one practice, known as *bundling,* parents would allow a visiting young male suitor to sleep in the same bed as their daughter, but the suitor (and sometimes the daughter) would be sewn into a sack up to his neck, and the couple would be inspected the next morning to ensure that sack and stitching were as they had been the night before. (Alternatively, young men and women slept together in the same bed fully clothed but separated by a wooden board.) Young women who were indentured servants (under contract for a number of years) were more at risk for sexual exploitation, with resulting unwanted sex and pregnancy (Mintz and Kellogg 1988; Harari and Vinovskis 1993).

■ **Families:** In colonial New England, the family was considered principally an economic unit for producing goods and a social unit for taking care of family members, including those who were widowed, orphaned, aged, or sick (Demos 1970). Wives, who were subordinate to their husbands and economically dependent on them, had 6 children on average. Infant and child mortality rates were so high that up to a third of children didn't live through the first year.

Although most women worked as homemakers—preparing food, cooking, washing, sewing, caring for children, and the like—their roles might also include working in the fields while men, older family members, or siblings took care of the children. However, women generally were limited in their ability to own property, collect debts, or obtain credit, even while (particularly as unmarried women) they might be running such businesses as inns, laundries, schools, and grocery stores or working as midwives.

■ **Transitions:** Boys—and usually only boys from fairly wealthy families—were given instruction in reading, writing, arithmetic, and religion at home; girls were generally given only minimal education. Puritans believed that children were inherently evil, being born with original sin, and therefore were thought to be corrupt, stubborn, and in need of frequent discipline.

The notion of *adolescence*—**a separate social and psychological stage of development coinciding with puberty and characterized by rebellion and crises**—did not exist in colonial times (Mintz and Kellogg 1988). In fact, children were set to some kind of useful work by age 7 (Morgan 1966). After that, they worked in households, fields, and shops for their own families. At age 10, they might be sent out to live with other families as indentured servants or as apprentices to learn a trade or a "calling," a process that might take seven years. The term *adolescence* was first used in 1903, probably in response to the greater amount of free time made possible by the Industrial Revolution.

African American Families

The first African Americans to appear in North America were not slaves but indentured servants. After fulfilling their years of service, they were then free to spend their energy on their own domestic interests. However, by the mid-17th century, this agreement between master and servant had dissolved; most blacks, who were largely brought from West Africa, were enslaved.

■ **Marriage and Sex:** As slaves, blacks were prohibited from legally marrying. Nevertheless, slaves themselves legitimized their unions by such rituals as "jumping over a broomstick." "The partner jumping over first, highest, or

AFRICAN AMERICANS: KINSHIP. Before and during the Civil War, blacks had strong kinship networks that often included slaves who were not blood related. Do you know of any families today, regardless of race or ethnicity, in which there is someone not related by blood, marriage, or adoption who is treated as if he or she were a family member? ▶

without falling," says one account, "was recognized by the wedding party as the one who would 'wear the pants' or rule the family" (Blassingame 1979: 166). At least where the slavery system did not break up marriages and families, the wedding was followed by permanent attachment.

A great problem during colonial times, however, was that it was difficult for an African American to find a spouse because either slaves were not allowed to associate with other blacks or they lived on plantations with few other slaves and at some distance from other plantations. When slave marriages did occur, they were often cut short by death from overwork or disease (Blassingame 1979; Mintz and Kellogg 1988). Moreover, prior to the 1800s, there was a great disparity in the ratio of men to women. Still, many slave owners realized that monogamy was conducive to discipline. Later, when slave imports were abolished, many owners recognized the importance of encouraging slave breeding and large families, although many marriages were disrupted by the selling of slaves (Gutman 1976; Blassingame 1979).

Although the black culture discouraged casual sexual relationships, female slaves were vulnerable to sexual exploitation by their white owners. Still, many resisted bearing or raising children by using various contraception and abortion techniques and even murdering their infants (Mullings 1997).

■ **Families:** Slave families were actually far stronger than was once believed. Historian Herbert Gutman (1976, 1983) has shown that—contrary to beliefs that slavery emasculated black men and made black women heads of their families—most black households had two parents or a single father. (Two-parent families were also characteristic of free blacks.) In fact, the adversity of slavery made many fathers and mothers exceptionally strong. "The family, while it had no legal existence in slavery, was in actuality one of the most important survival mechanisms for the slave," says historian John Blassingame (1979: 151), for it offered companionship, sympathetic understanding, lessons in avoiding punishment, and cooperation. "However frequently the family was broken, it was primarily responsible for the slave's ability to survive on the plantation without becoming totally dependent on and submissive to his master."

Black men acted as father figures to many children, became small-time entrepreneurs (hunting, cultivating vegetables, making furniture, and the like), and even tried to save females from being sexually exploited by slave masters (Genovese 1981; Jones 1985). Black women cared not only for their own children but also for those of the master, in addition to working in the fields or doing all the domestic chores required by the slave owner's family (Matthaei 1982; Jones 1985). Blassingame (1979) points out that slave parents could help cushion the shock of bondage for their children, teach them values different from those their master tried to instill in them, and give them a source of self-esteem other than the master.

Whenever possible, African Americans established strong kinship networks, which often included slaves who were unrelated. Children were named after aunts, uncles, grandparents, and other blood kin. After Emancipation, many former slaves preserved the kinship networks.

Hispanic (Latino) Families

Spanish-speaking people appeared in what is now Florida as well as Texas, New Mexico, Arizona, and California even before the Pilgrims arrived in New England. In 1848, at the end of the Mexican War, the Southwest became the territory of the United States. Most of the 80,000–100,000 Mexicans living there lost their land through confiscation or fraud, and as ranching, agriculture, railroads, and mining developed in the region, the benefits went mainly to whites of non-Mexican descent. Mexicans and their descendants became the laborers on whose backs economic development flourished.

■ **Marriage and Sex:** Much of Mexican family life was influenced by Catholic religious teachings. Rites of passage were important: baptism, first communion, confirmation, quinceañera (celebrating a girl's fifteenth birthday when, traditionally, she became a woman), marriage. Also important were ceremonial aspects of Mexican culture: saints' days, birthdays, and other occasions. Children in middle-class and well-off families were protected through adolescence, living at home until they were adults, although working-class children were obliged to go to work early.

As part of their training to become "good wives and mothers," girls were closely chaperoned and limited in their social lives outside the home. Women were expected to remain virgins until marriage and faithful to their husbands afterward. Men, by contrast, in accordance with the notion of *machismo*—a concept of masculinity that emphasizes dominance and sexual prowess—could engage in premarital and extramarital sexual adventures.

■ **Families:** Latino families were strongly influenced by familism (described in Chapter 1, "Seeking"), the well-being of the family being emphasized over the well-being of individuals. In accordance with the practice of *compadrazgo*—establishing a system of godparents and others as a way of expanding family ties—families consisted of a network of not only grandparents, aunts and uncles, and in-laws but also godparents (*padrinos*),

LATINOS: TRADITION OF FAMILISM. Traditionally many Latino families emphasized the welfare of the family over the welfare of the individual, with family networks including godparents who served as co-parents. How would you characterize the family you grew up in—more family oriented or individual oriented? ▼

who acted as co-parents (*compadres*). All these extended family members provided affection and perhaps financial support as well as discipline, and in turn children were expected to show obedience, affection, and respect (Ramirez and Arce 1981).

The father held all the authority in a Mexican family, and women were expected to be mainly mothers and homemakers (Williams 1990). However, in poorer families, in which men were forced to migrate to find jobs, many families were headed by women, even though the two-parent family was always held to be the most desirable type (Griswold del Castillo 1984). Often, when men became unemployed, the mother became the principal wage earner as well, usually working in agriculture or domestic services (Camarillo 1979).

Families in the 19th & Early 20th Centuries

In the 19th century, the United States was disrupted by upheavals that transformed the American family and set it on the road to becoming the modern family we see today.

Industrialization, Urbanization, & Immigration

Three kinds of social and economic forces occurred during the early and mid-1800s: (1) industrialization, (2) urbanization, and (3) immigration.

■ **Industrialization—From Self-Sufficient to Wage-Earning Families:** The *Industrial Revolution*, you'll recall, brought great economic and social changes during the 19th century, when the production of goods shifted from home-based human labor to machines and factories. Before the Industrial Revolution, families produced goods and services for their own consumption. But as factories began to churn out agricultural machines such as tractors and harvesters, less farm labor was needed, and people began to migrate to cities to sell their labor working in factories.

■ **Urbanization—The Movement to the Cities:** As families moved to the cities and as factories were built, the cities began to expand. Housing became scarce and more expensive, which affected birth rates. Transportation systems increased mobility, so husbands and fathers were able to travel far from their families. As a result, men became identified as the principal providers, contact with extended families was reduced, and children had less supervision and became more engaged in delinquency and crime.

■ **Immigration—Two Waves of Newcomers:** Immigration to America is commonly divided into two eras of old and new immigrants. (1) During the period 1830–1882, "old" immigrants came mostly from western and northern Europe (primarily English, Irish, German, and Scandinavian), although large numbers of Chinese also came to the West Coast. (2) In the period 1882–1930, "new" immigrants came mostly from eastern Europe (Russian, Polish, Hungarian, Slavic, Austrian) and southern Europe (Italian, Greek), although Japanese also came to Hawaii and the West Coast. Most new immigrants were poor and joined the low-wage old immigrants in dilapidated housing in crowded cities competing for bottom-rung jobs.

The Importance of Kinship Networks

For immigrants, kinship networks were important to survival. Most new-comers came from small villages and settled in ethnic neighborhoods of big cities, where mutual cooperation helped them overcome economic hardship and resist the hostility and prejudice directed at them by the dominant culture, as represented in such signs as "English speakers only" and "No Irish need apply." Kinship networks also helped former slaves in the aftermath of the Civil War, when they continued to suffer poverty and exploitation.

Indeed, it's particularly noteworthy that kinship systems enabled many immigrants and blacks to survive conditions such as slavery, poverty, and new beginnings in a new country that were probably far more difficult than some challenges of the modern era, such as unemployment, which often seem to be followed by family disintegration and violence (Newman 1988). As you might expect, however, the harsh conditions did lead many immigrant families to suffer family breakdown, demoralization, and delinquency among their children.

The Changing Family & Changing Roles

Among native-born whites in the middle and upper classes, the role of husbands and fathers became mainly economic, and they went off to work as the family breadwinners. Wives stayed home and spent their time in unpaid work—caring for and nurturing husbands and children, maintaining the home, socializing, and keeping up appearances. Their most important roles, of course, were in raising children and in keeping the household running, which served to make the home the center of their lives.

As social forces made the family less important as a work unit, women felt more free to choose marriage partners on the basis of compatibility and affection—in a word, *love*. In addition, as children became less important as contributors of labor to the family's economic well-being, women began to emphasize child rearing over childbearing. Indeed, the number of children per woman dropped from an average of 7 in 1800 to 3.5 in 1900.

Because fathers went off to work, they no longer exerted the same authority over their children's behavior. Because they usually had less land, fathers also had less importance in the distribution of property to their heirs, and so children became less dependent on fathers economically. In addition, children were no longer regarded as miniature adults, and they were allowed to spend more time playing than working. Adolescence came to be recognized as a separate stage of development.

All these benefits did not extend to the poor and to the working classes, however. In these groups, men, women, and children all had to work outside the home to survive economically.

Families in the Modern Era

With the arrival of the 20th century, many economic, educational, and social welfare activities had shifted from the family to outside agencies, and the main function of the family became one of taking care of its members' intimacy, sexual, and psychological needs. With this shift also came an emphasis on individualism over familism: Individual concerns began to take priority over collective family concerns.

ASIANS: IMMIGRATION AND DISCRIMINA-TION. Asians have experienced a long history of discrimination in the United States. In 1924, an immigration law banned further Asian immigration. During the 1930s, Chinese already in this country, such as those shown here, many of whom lived in urban "Chinatowns" or ghettos, suffered as much as anyone during the catastrophe of the Great Depression. If you're non-Asian, do you think about Chinese, Japanese, Filipinos, and other Asians in a way different from the way you think about other racial and ethnic minorities? Why? ▶

Rise of a New Form: The Companionate Family

Previously, families were based on patriarchal authority, sexual repression, and hierarchical organization. In the 1900s, sexual attraction and compatibility began to become the basis for middle-class marriage and family relationships. **Steven Mintz** and **Susan Kellogg** have written extensively about the history of the American family. They point out that in a ***companionate family*, the marriage was supposed to provide "romance, emotional growth, and sexual fulfillment"; wives were no longer supposed to exercise sexual restraint; spouses shared decisions and tasks equally; and adolescent children were allowed greater freedom from parental supervision** (Mintz and Kellogg 1988: 114).

The Effect of the World Wars & the Great Depression

World War I (1914–1917), the Great Depression (1929–1939), and World War II (1939–1945) all brought tremendous changes to American society and families.

■ **The Great Depression—Out-of-Work Men Blame Themselves:** In the Great Depression of the 1930s, unemployment rates reached 23.6% (in 1932) at a time when most of the workforce was male. Although families in the upper-middle classes survived with only a few adjustments, in many middle-class households, women took jobs such as clerical and white-collar government jobs that enabled their families to continue their standard of living.

The impact was greatest, as might be expected, on working-class agricultural and urban families. Husbands left in search of work (or sometimes deserted their families), farm families lost their land, young adults moved to the cities, and children dropped out of school to take menial jobs. Accustomed to being primary breadwinners, many men blamed themselves instead of the countrywide (indeed worldwide) economic conditions (Filene 1986).

■ **World Wars I and II—Women Take "Male-Only" Jobs:** The two world wars also affected gender roles. During World War I, as millions of men went off to war, 1.5 million women took many of their places in both civilian jobs and wartime production jobs. The same massive change in the workforce happened in World War II, when government patriotic campaigns induced millions of women to work in shipyards (giving rise to the famous Rosie the Riveter) and ammunition factories as well as civilian jobs. Many were middle-class married women, but working-class women, white and black, particularly benefited (Filene 1986; Mintz and Kellogg 1988).

When male war veterans returned home, many women found it difficult to leave the greater wages and freedoms associated with traditional male jobs. Participation of women in the workforce continued to increase after the war, even as the popular culture and mass media once again stressed the importance of women's roles as wives, mothers, and homemakers.

Families in the 1950s

When promoters of family stability wring their hands over today's family breakdowns, out-of-wedlock births, unmarried live-together couples, and two-income families, they often hark back to a highly unusual time: the 1950s, marked by a stable, suburban nuclear family consisting of a working Dad, a homemaker Mom, and their two children. Such a Golden Age of family life, as **Stephanie Coontz** (1992, 1997, 2005) points out, was not always so golden. Many of people's perceptions of the 1950s are based on the families portrayed in such TV sitcoms as *Ozzie and Harriet, Father Knows Best,* and *Leave It to Beaver.* Even at the time these series were on the air, "People didn't watch these shows to see their own lives reflected back at them," says Coontz (1997: 38). "They watched them to see how families were *supposed* to live."

What made the 1950s unusual were some singular events (Mintz and Kellogg 1988; Coontz 1997):

■ **The Baby Boom—The Swelling Population:** The Baby Boom, consisting of the group of people born in the United States between 1946 and 1964, who now make up about 26% of the entire U.S. population, had a major impact on society, economics, and family practices. More children were produced during this period than ever before—or since.

■ **Suburbanization—The Move to the Suburbs:** Buoyed by unprecedented prosperity, government support for home building and highway construction, low-interest mortgages, and other inducements, families began a huge migration from the cities to the suburbs to realize dreams of home ownership.

■ **The Child-Centered Culture:** Mothers, following the advice in Dr. Benjamin Spock's influential book on how to raise healthy children, *Baby and Child Care,* tended to communicate with their children rather than use physical discipline. Dr. Spock was unjustly blamed for the permissiveness that was alleged to be the cause of many subsequent social problems, including the hippie culture of the 1960s, juvenile delinquency, and divorce.

Despite the glowing pictures painted by the mass media, suburbia, a focus on child rearing, and frequent career-related moves didn't always make for happiness. Indeed, they often made for isolation and loneliness rather than personal fulfillment.

The Family in the 1960s–2000s: In Decline?

"Almost everyone who lives out an average life span enters the married state," wrote family sociologist William Goode a quarter century ago. "Most will eventually have children, who will later do the same" (Goode 1982: 1).

Is this still true? In 1960, nearly half of American households consisted of a married couple with at least one child under age 18. By 2003, however, less than one-fourth of households corresponded to this family model. Contributing to the decline were the decisions of the Baby Boomers in the 1970s, who postponed marriage and childbearing and who divorced at higher rates. Also contributing were longer-living seniors, who had more years as empty nesters (Frey 2003).

The changes in traditional family households has resulted in two points of view, as follows:

■ **"The American Family Is in Decline":** Some sociologists, such as **David Popenoe** (1993) of Rutgers University, believe that the changes between 1960 and today represent real, and steep, family decline, with serious consequences. He argues that families have lost power and authority, that familism has diminished as a cultural value, and that people have become less willing to invest time, money, and energy in family life, instead turning to investments in themselves. The breakup of the nuclear family, he suggests, leaves two essential functions at risk that cannot be performed better anywhere else: child rearing and the provision to its members of affection and companionship.

■ **"The American Family Still Matters":** Other sociologists, as represented by **Vern Bengtson** and his colleagues Timothy Biblarz and Robert Roberts (2002), who drew from one of the longest-running studies in sociology, the Longitudinal Study of Generations, say that Generation X youth, who came of age in the 1990s, actually were more ambitious, principled, and grounded than their Baby Boomer parents were 30 years earlier. The scholars also found that high rates of divorce, "fatherlessness," and working mothers had little or no negative effect. "The conventional wisdom that today's family is in decline implies that moms who work or choose to divorce are robbing their children in some way," said Biblarz (quoted in Silsby 2003). "Our study shows that single motherhood and working moms have not produced any dire consequences." The researchers hypothesized three reasons why Gen Xers had not become the "generation at risk" after all: (1) Extended kin relations, particularly the role of grandparents, were more important than ever. (2) Today's two-parent families were more successful than ever before. (3) Most parents seemed to continue to find ways to take good care of their children despite ups and downs.

Although the traditional married-with-children family accounts for just 23.3% of all households, its decline slowed considerably in the 1990s. One reason for this stronger-than-expected showing of traditional families is the population growth of immigrant Asians and Hispanics, who are more likely to form this family type (Frey 2003). We consider these and other immigrant groups next.

Recent History: Late 20th-Century Immigration

In Chapter 1, "Seeking," we mentioned that the racial and ethnic composition of the United States is changing in significant ways. The domination of the white European majority (non-Hispanic whites) has declined from 76% in 1950 to 72% in 2000 and is projected to slip to 53% by 2050. A big contributor to this demographic upheaval is the new immigration: In 2002, 11.5% of the U.S. population was foreign born. Whereas a century ago, 90% of immigrants to the United States were European, in 2000, about 81% were from non-European countries, Asian-born immigrants outnumbering European-born, and Latin American-born immigrants outnumbering both. *(See ■ Panel 2.1.)* In 2000, over 50% of legal immigrants arrived from North, Central, and South America and the Caribbean, and half of these immigrants migrated from Mexico. Also in 2000, Asia accounted for 26% of legal immigration into the United States; Europe accounted for 15%, and Africa accounted for 3%.

In addition, there were, and are, illegal immigrants—perhaps as many as 12 million (Escobar 2006). With a known almost 6.2 million illegal immigrants in the United States, Mexico is the largest contributor, followed by El Salvador, Guatemala, India, and China with a combined contribution of 1.4 million unauthorized immigrants (Gamboa 2006). Although more than 10% of Mexico's 116 million citizens now live in the United States as legal or illegal

■ **PANEL 2.1   Diversity Data: Recent Immigration.** U.S. legal immigrants by region of origin, 1991–2000.

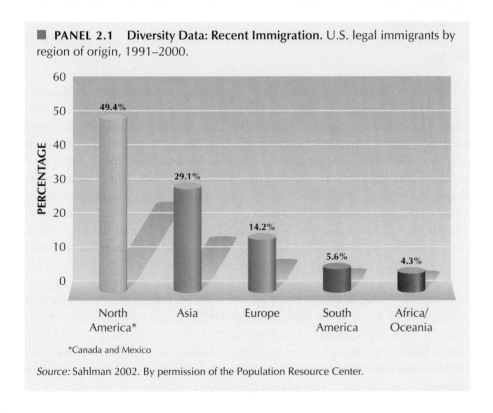

Source: Sahlman 2002. By permission of the Population Resource Center.

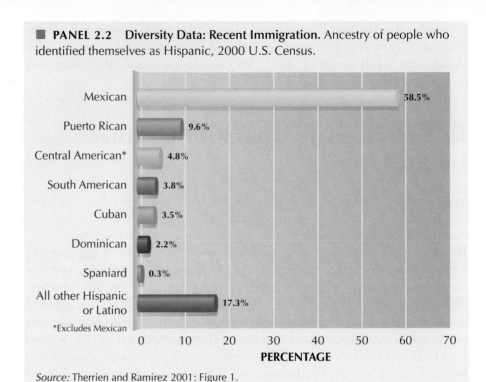

■ **PANEL 2.2 Diversity Data: Recent Immigration.** Ancestry of people who identified themselves as Hispanic, 2000 U.S. Census.

Source: Therrien and Ramirez 2001: Figure 1.

immigrants, traditionally many have returned home (Alvarez 2006). However, as border security has increased and as more immigrants have moved out of agricultural jobs and away from the border states of the southwest, the average probability of return for illegal immigrants has dropped, from 47% during 1979–1984 to 27% during 1997–2003 (Mexican Migration Project, cited in Navarro 2006).

Let's consider the composition and characteristics of the two largest groups:

■ **Hispanics:** As the chart shows, more than 58% of Hispanics are of Mexican origin. *(See ■ Panel 2.2.)* Hispanic families are particularly affected by economic upheavals occasioned by such forces as the increase in globalization, the rise of new computer-based technologies, the dominance of information and service sectors of the economy over manufacturing, and the movement of capital between countries (Baca Zinn and Wells 1999), which affect their employment. As a result, Hispanic families tend to be poorer than non-Hispanic whites, are more likely than whites or blacks to have a family household, and are more likely than blacks to have a married couple in the household. Family size is larger than that of non-Hispanics, with 3.95 people compared to 3.2 people in the average family (Collins 1997).

Interestingly, the notion of *machismo*, or male dominance, that we described as being associated with earlier Latino families seems to be less common than it was in the past, although husbands, particularly in working-class families, seem to have more power than their spouses. In most cases, Latino families seem to show more egalitarianism than male dominance, with men helping with child care and spending more time with their families than with other men (Staples and Mirande 1980).

■ **Asian Americans:** In 1882, Congress initiated a policy of prohibiting Chinese laborers from immigrating to the United States (who had earlier been encouraged to immigrate because of the need for cheap labor). The 1924 immigration law excluded in effect all Asians. The law was loosened in 1943, but discriminatory immigration quotas against Asians prevailed until 1965. Whereas most of the Asian immigrants before World War II were peasants, the ones who have arrived in recent times have been either college educated professionals (such as many Asian Indian, Filipino, and Chinese men) or poor, uneducated, refugees displaced by war (such as many Cambodians, Hmong, and Laotians) (Waters and Eschbach 1995). Asian Indians (people from India), or Indo-Americans, for example, have access to technologies that make communication with families in India more practical, which helps to sustain families ties but also maintain multigenerational conflicts (Pettys and Balgopal 1998).

The largest Asian groups are Chinese, Filipinos, and Asian Indians. *(See* ■ *Panel 2.3.)* Older immigrants, such as Chinese, Japanese, and Koreans, have become absorbed into the American culture and have taken on "typical American" behavior and traits. These immigrants generally have the highest family incomes (Asian Indians are highest). More recent ones tend to be poor. Although there is a considerable range of behavior among Asians, in general families are male dominated, extended family obligations are emphasized, education levels are high, family size is higher than that of whites (3.8 persons compared to 3.2 for non-Hispanic whites), divorce rates are lower than the average, and fertility rates are the lowest. Traditional families emphasize familism over individualism, so children are apt to be raised with the values of loyalty, obedience, emotional restraint, and respect for education (Hamilton 1996; Kao et al. 1997; Blair and Qian 1998).

■ **PANEL 2.3   Diversity Data: Ancestry of People Who Identified Themselves as Asian or Pacific Islander Descent, 2000 U.S. Census**

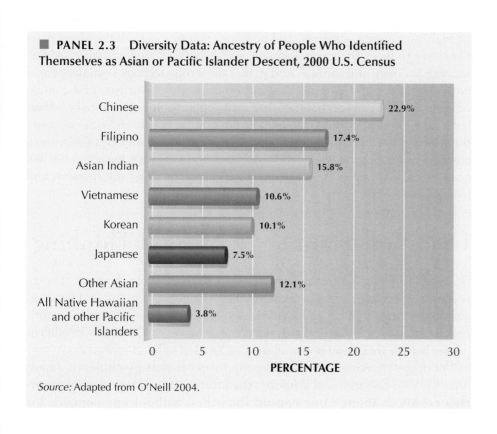

Source: Adapted from O'Neill 2004.

2.2 Learning How to Think: Keys to Being Open-Minded

MAJOR QUESTION Is there a more beneficial way to approach the world and ideas than I might be taking now?

PREVIEW We discuss how our mind-sets and uncritical thinking can hinder our approach to the truth. We then describe four steps in critical thinking. Finally, we show how to replace the unproductive attitude of mind-lessness with mindfulness as a vigorous approach to ideas.

Although marriages and families have taken many forms in many times and places, it can be hard to step outside the familiarity of our own culture and analyze how our own relationships work. In addition, love and intimacy can be highly emotional subjects, and at some time in most relationships partners have to work their way through such emotions as dominance, power sharing, jealousy, and the like. Add to that the strong feelings so many people have about such intimate matters as homosexuality, abortion, and contraception, and you can see that there are many opportunities for more heat than light. Often the temptation is to hold fast to our old beliefs and ways of doing things—to rely on one's general knowledge in an "I feel" way. But we live in a complex world—one in which such uncritical thinking is no longer viable. We need to learn to approach such important questions using the research and tools of sociology.

Uncritical Thinking & Magical Thinking

Uncritical thinking is all around us. People run their lives on the basis of horoscopes, numerology, and similar nonsense. They believe in "crystal healing" and "color therapy." They think cranks and quacks can cure cancer with apricot-pit extract or alleviate arthritis with copper bracelets. Otherwise intelligent people believe that mind power alone can be used to bend spoons.

Uncritical thinking can also take the form of what psychologist James Alcock (1995) calls **magical thinking, the interpreting of two closely occurring events as though one caused the other, without any concern for causal link.** "I hadn't thought about my old girlfriend in months, and then I

■ PANEL 2.4   Examples of Magical Thinking

- ■ I won't change my clothes if the team's winning.
- ■ I read my daily horoscope to help avoid trouble.
- ■ Crime and violence are linked to the breakdown of the traditional family.
- ■ I knock on wood when talking about future possibilities.
- ■ Vitamin C can head off or cure the common cold.
- ■ I stay away from the number 8.
- ■ I know some people can communicate with others by mental telepathy.
- ■ Visualization or prayer can destroy cancer cells.
- ■ Certain people can help solve crimes using their psychic abilities.
- ■ Wishing someone harm can make them sick.

Sources: Adapted from Alcock 1995; Carey 2007.

did, and she suddenly called." "When I get a cold, I take lots of vitamin C and visualize my immune system destroying the germs." "On game day, I always suit up in the exact same way." *(See ■ Panel 2.4.)* Magical thinking, which seems to be rooted in the circuitry of the brain, is quite common. Even people "who fashion themselves skeptics cling to odd rituals that seem to make no sense," points out one writer (Carey 2007). "On athletic fields, at the craps table, or out sailing in the open ocean, magical thinking is a way of life. Elaborate, entirely nonsensical rituals are performed with solemn deliberation." Students, too, engage in magical thinking ("I always wear my 'lucky shirt' to my final exam").

But magical thinking, uncritical thinking, can be dangerous. "We live in a society that is enlarging the boundaries of knowledge at an unprecedented rate," says James Randi (1992), a debunker of claims made by supporters of the paranormal, "and we cannot keep up with more than a small portion of what is made available to us. To mix our data input with childish notions of magic and fantasy is to cripple our perception of the world around us. We must reach for the truth, not for the ghosts of dead absurdities."

The Enemy: Our Mind-Sets

The enemy of clear thinking is our *mind-sets*. By the time we are grown, our minds have become set in patterns of thinking that affect how we respond to new ideas. These mind-sets are the result of our personal experiences and the various social environments in which we grew up. Such mind-sets determine what ideas we think are important and, conversely, what ideas we ignore. As one book on clear thinking points out, we can't pay attention to all the events that occur around us. Consequently, "our minds filter out some observations and facts and let others through to our conscious awareness" (Ruchlis and Oddo 1990: 109). Herein lies the danger: "As a result we see and hear what we subconsciously want to and pay little attention to facts or observations that have already been rejected as unimportant."

Having mind-sets makes life comfortable. However, as the foregoing writers point out, "Familiar relationships and events become so commonplace that we expect them to continue forever. Then we find ourselves completely unprepared to accept changes that are necessary, even when they stare us in the face" (Ruchlis and Oddo 1990: 110).

Critical Thinking

The way to deal with mind-sets is through critical thinking. **Critical thinking means clear thinking, skeptical thinking, active thinking. It is actively seeking to understand, analyze, and evaluate information in order to solve specific problems.** You need to exercise critical thinking, for example, when you're trying to analyze the correctness of someone's point of view—or of your own point of view. Unlike passive thinking, in which you unquestioningly accept the information given to you, critical thinking means that you constantly question everything.

The Steps in Critical Thinking*

Fortunately, critical thinking can be learned just as you can learn, say, how to explore the Internet or learn how to communicate better.

The four steps in critical thinking are these:

1. Get an understanding of the problem.
2. Gather information and interpret it.
3. Develop a solution plan and carry it out.
4. Evaluate the plan's effectiveness.

Do these four steps seem rather obvious? Perhaps so, but it's amazing how often we try to solve or fix something by simply stumbling around, hoping everything will work out. Let's consider these steps.

1. Get an Understanding of the Problem

How many times have you been told, as for a test, to read the directions? How often, when looking at a manual on how to operate a new appliance or assemble a child's toy, have you found yourself rereading the instructions? In both cases, you're taking the necessary first step: making sure you understand the problem. This is basic.

Impulsiveness hurts. If you don't take the trouble to make sure you comprehend the problem, you can waste a great deal of time trying to solve it and never do so. Getting an understanding might require you to read over the problem two or more times (as in math), ask someone for clarification (as an instructor), or seek alternative explanations (as in looking at a city road map instead of a state road map).

Often you can get a better understanding of a problem just by talking about it, as in a discussion in a study group with other students.

---

* Material in "The Steps in Critical Thinking," "Mindfulness: Taking Active Control," and "Tools for Reasoning" are from *Learning Success: Being Your Best at College and Life*, Media Edition (Non-InfoTrac Version), 3rd edition, by Wahlstrom/Williams, 2002. Reprinted with permission of Wadsworth, a division of Thomson Learning: www.thomsonrights.com. Fax 800-730-2215.

2. Gather Information & Interpret It

Sometimes just by making sure you understand a problem, you can see a solution to it. At other times, however, you might need to get additional information and interpret it. That is, you'll need to list resources that can give you help or identify areas that are preventing your solving the problem.

For instance, if your problem is that you are required to write a paper on better couples communication for a marriage and family course, you'll need to search the Internet and/or get books and other information on the subject from the library. Then you'll need to interpret the information to make sure you know the difference between, say, assertiveness and aggressiveness in communication.

CRITICAL THINKING? Students doing research for term papers are engaging in the third step of critical thinking. Do you think the critical-thinking approach has practical application outside school? Why or why not? ▲

3. Develop a Solution Plan & Carry It Out

Developing a plan is sometimes the most difficult step. The reason: You might have to choose between several alternatives. For example, in writing about couples communication, you'll have to decide between several possible outlines and draw on a variety of examples.

Finally, you'll need to carry out the plan, which might or might not turn out to be workable. Maybe the direction of your paper can't be supported by the research you did, and you'll have to rethink your approach.

4. Evaluate the Plan's Effectiveness

So you completed the paper on couples communication. Maybe your experience was a disaster, in which case you'll want to know how to do it right next time. Maybe your plan worked out okay, but there were things that might have been handled better.

Drawing lessons from your experience is part and parcel of critical thinking, and it's a step that should not be neglected. If the experience was successful, can it be applied to other, similar problems? If it was only partly successful, can you see ways to change the information-gathering step or the solution-planning step to make it work better? If the experience was a disaster, is there a slogan you can draw from it that you can post over your desk? (Example: "LOOK FOR RECENT ARTICLES WHEN RESEARCHING PAPERS.")

Critical Thinking: Skills versus Disposition

What we have just described are critical thinking skills. "Most research shows you can teach these skills," says cognitive psychologist D. Alan Bensley (quoted in Begley 2006). "But critical-thinking skills are different from critical-thinking dispositions, or a willingness to deploy these skills." He goes on: "Critical-thinking skills have to do with the cognitive ability of reasoning. Critical-thinking dispositions are more related to traits that determine whether you choose to use those skills." In other words, being curious, open-minded, and receptive to new experiences and having a preference for rational data (the head) over intuition (the gut) are the dispositions needed to make critical-thinking skills work.

This brings us to mindlessness versus mindfulness.

Mindfulness: Taking Active Control

We have all experienced mindlessness. We write checks in January using the previous year's date. We misplace our keys. We find ourselves standing in a room unable to recall why we are there. Among college students, mindlessness can take the form of scribbling page after page of lecture notes without really paying attention. Or underlining while reading a text with no particular strat-

PRACTICAL ACTION
Tools for Reasoning

The way to break through the closed habits of thought called mind-sets is to use reasoning. **Reasoning—giving reasons in favor of this assertion or that—**is essential to critical thinking and solving life's problems.

How to Reason

Reasoning is put in the form of what philosophers call arguments. **Arguments consist of one or more premises, or reasons, logically supporting a result or outcome called a conclusion.**

An example of an argument is as follows:

Premise 1: All instructors must grade students.
Premise 2: I am an instructor.
Conclusion: Therefore, I must grade students.

Note the tip-off word *therefore*, which signals that a conclusion is coming. In real life, such as arguments on TV or in newspapers, the premises and conclusions are not so neatly labeled.

Still, there are clues: The words *because* and *for* usually signal premises. The words *therefore, hence,* and *so* signal conclusions. Not all groups of sentences form arguments. Often they may form anecdotes or other types of exposition or explanation (Kahane 1988).

The two main kinds of correct or valid arguments are *inductive* and *deductive*.

■ **Inductive argument: An *inductive argument* is defined as follows: If the premises are true, the conclusion is PROBABLY true, but the truth is not guaranteed.** An inductive argument is sometimes known as a "probability argument."

An example of an *inductive* argument is as follows (Rasool et al. 1993: 132):

Premise 1: Stress can cause illness.
Premise 2: Reuben experiences stress in his life.
Premise 3: Reuben is ill.
Conclusion: Therefore, stress may be the cause of Reuben's illness.

Note the word *may* in the conclusion. This argument is inductive. The conclusion is not stated with absolute certainty; rather, it suggests only that stress *may* be the cause. The link between premises and conclusion is not definite because there might be other reasons for Reuben's illness (such as a virus).

■ **Deductive argument: A *deductive argument* is defined as follows: If its premises are true, then its conclusion is true also.** In other words, if the premises are true, the conclusion cannot be false.

An example of a *deductive* argument is as follows (Rasool et al. 1993: 132):

Premise 1: All students experience stress in their lives.
Premise 2: Reuben is a student.
Conclusion: Therefore, Reuben experiences stress in his life.

This argument is deductive—the conclusion is definitely true if the premises are definitely true.

Some Types of Incorrect Reasoning

Patterns of incorrect reasoning are known as *fallacies*. Fallacies such as these are used every day in promotional pitches, legal arguments, news analyses, and appeals for money. Clearly, then, being aware of them will serve you well throughout your life.

Some principal types of incorrect reasoning are as follows:

■ **Jumping to conclusions:** Also known as *hasty generalization,* the fallacy called **jumping to conclusions means that a conclusion has been reached when not all the facts are available.**

Example: Cab drivers might (illegally) refuse to take certain passengers to what they regard as dangerous neighborhoods merely on the basis of their skin color or looks, jumping to the conclusion

egy in mind. This kind of "automaticity," or automatic behavior, occurs because we are operating from preconceptions or mind-sets. Mindfulness, by contrast, is a form of active engagement.

Ellen J. Langer, the first woman to become a tenured professor of psychology at Harvard University, has become well known for her studies of "mindlessness" versus "mindfulness," described in her two books *Mindfulness* and *The Power of Mindful Learning* (Langer 1989, 1997). Mindlessless, says Langer, "is like being on automatic pilot" (Langer, quoted in Hilts 1997: B9).

that they are dangerous people. But what if such a person turns out to be a city councilman, as happened in Boston a few years ago?

- **False cause or irrelevant reason:** The faulty reasoning known as *non sequitur* (Latin for "it does not follow"), which might be better called *false cause* or *irrelevant reason,* **means that the conclusion does not follow logically from the supposed reasons stated earlier.** There is no *causal* relationship.

  Example: You receive an A on a test. However, because you felt you hadn't been well prepared, you attribute your success to your friendliness with the instructor or to your horoscope. Neither of these "reasons" has anything to do with the result.

- **Appeal to authority:** Known in Latin as *argumentum ad verecundiam*, the **appeal to authority argument uses an authority in one area to pretend to validate claims in another area in which the person is not an expert.**

  Example: You see the appeal to authority argument used all the time in advertising. But what does a champion golfer, for instance, really know about real-estate developments?

- **Circular reasoning:** The *circular reasoning* **argument rephrases the statement to be proved true. It then uses the new, similar**

statement as supposed proof that the original statement is in fact true.

  Examples: You declare that you can drive safely at high speeds with only inches separating you from the car ahead. After all, you have driven this way for years without an accident. Or you say that paying student-body fees is for the common good because in the long run paying student-body fees benefits everyone.

- **Irrelevant attack on opponent:** Known as an *ad hominem* argument (Latin for "to the person"), **the *irrelevant attack on an opponent* attacks a person's reputation or beliefs rather than his or her argument.**

  Example: Politicians frequently try to attack an adversary's reputation. Someone running for student-body president might attack an opponent's "character" or intelligence rather than the opponent's stand on the issues.

- **Straw man argument:** In the *straw man argument*, **you misrepresent your opponent's position to make it easier to attack, or you attack a weaker position while ignoring a stronger one.** In other words, you sidetrack the argument from the main discussion.

  Example: A politician might attack an opponent as a "socialist" for supporting aid to mothers with dependent children but not for sup-

porting aid to tobacco growers. (This is because the first politician favors supporting tobacco growers.)

- **Slippery slope:** The *slippery slope* **is a failure to see that the first step in a possible series of steps does not lead inevitably to the rest.**

  Example: The "domino theory," under which the United States waged wars against communism, was a slippery slope argument. It assumed that if communism triumphed in Nicaragua, say, it would inevitably spread to the rest of Central America and finally to the United States.

- **Appeal to pity:** The *appeal to pity* **argument appeals to emotion rather than arguing the merits of the case itself.**

  Example: Begging the dean not to expel you for cheating because your impoverished parents made sacrifices to send you to college exemplifies this fallacy.

- **Questionable statistics:** Statistics can be misused in many ways as supporting evidence. The statistics may be unknowable, drawn from an unrepresentative sample, or otherwise suspect.

  Example: Stating that people were less happy 2,000 years ago than today is an example of unknowable or undefined use of statistics.

More specifically, ***mindlessness* is characterized by three features: (1) entrapment in old categories, (2) automatic behavior, and (3) acting from a single perspective.**

The key qualities of mindfulness are the opposite. ***Mindfulness* is characterized by (1) creation of new categories, (2) openness to new information, and (3) awareness of more than one perspective.**

Let's examine these three qualities.

1. Entrapment in Old Categories versus Creation of New Ones

This quality has to do with inflexibility versus flexibility.

An avid tennis player, Langer says that at tennis camp, she was taught exactly how to hold her racquet and toss the ball when making a serve. Indeed, all other students in the camp were taught to serve the ball the same way. Later, she said, when she watched a top tennis championship, the U.S. Open, "I noticed that none of the top players served the way I was taught, and, more importantly, each of them served slightly differently" (Langer 1997: 4).

The significance of this: Because each person has different height, hand size, and muscle development, there can be no one right way of serving. Therefore, Langer says, it is important to teach everything conditionally. For example, she says, an instructor can teach "Here is one way of serving," or "If an incoming ball has backspin, here is one way that you can use to return it."

In this conditional way of teaching—the mindful way of teaching—the instructor doesn't say "This is THE answer" but rather "This is ONE answer." The method takes account of the fact that each case is different and a person's responses must change from day to day and from moment to moment.

In college, you might well encounter instructors who will teach as though there is just one right answer. Nevertheless, as a student, you should practice mindfulness by receiving the information as though it is *conditionally* true, not unconditionally (or absolutely) true. Even in the hard sciences, mathematics, and such subjects as grammar, in which it may seem as though there is just one correct answer, you should regard such information with open-mindedness, since there may be exceptions.

2. Automatic Behavior versus Openness to New Information

In automatic behavior, says Langer, we take in and use limited signals from the world around us without letting other signals penetrate as well. We are passive instead of active learners.

As an example of automatic behavior, Langer tells a story of using a new credit card in a department store. Noticing that Langer hadn't signed the card yet, the cashier returned it to her to sign the back. After passing the credit card through the imprinting machine, the clerk handed her the credit card receipt to sign, which Langer did. Then, says Langer, the cashier "held the form next to the newly signed card to see if the signatures matched" (Langer 1989: 12–13).

Mindfulness, then, is being open to new information—including information that has not been specifically assigned to you. Langer (1989: 26–27) reports a study in which novice piano players were recruited to learn simple fingering exercises. The first group was taught to practice in a traditional memorization-through-repetition style. Members of the second group, the

MINDLESS BEHAVIOR? Have you ever had a retail clerk ask you to sign the back of your newly acquired credit card, then compare your freshly signed card with the credit card receipt you also just signed (to see if you're the authorized user)? Or do you frequently sign credit card receipts without checking the amount? Or do you put away the returned card without checking to see if its yours or someone else's? All are examples of "automaticity," one form of mindlessness. What are some other examples of mindless behavior that you've found yourself (or others) doing? ◀

mindful instruction group, were instructed to be creative and vary their playing as much as possible. When independent evaluators (graduate students in music) listened to tapes of the students, without knowing which were assigned to which group, they rated the mindful students as more competent and creative; these students also expressed more enjoyment of the activity.

As a college student, you can see that mindfulness requires that you engage more fully with whatever it is you're studying. But, as with the mindful piano students, this can have the benefit of *making the material more enjoyable for you.*

3. Single Perspective versus Several Perspectives

The third feature of mindfulness is being open not only to new information but also to new perspectives—what Langer calls having "a limber state of mind."

Mindlessness is acting from a single perspective. Langer (1989: 16–17) reports an experiment she conducted to examine the effectiveness of different requests for help. A fellow investigator stood on a busy sidewalk and told passersby that she had sprained her knee and needed help. When someone stopped, he or she was asked to get an Ace bandage from the nearby drugstore, where the pharmacist had been enlisted to say he was out of Ace bandages. Not one person out of the 25 studied thought to ask the pharmacist whether he could recommend something else, and the helpful passersby all returned to the "victim" empty-handed. This seems to suggest that the request for help operated from a narrow perspective: A sprained knee needs an Ace bandage. Had the "victim" asked for less specific help, the passersby might have tried to find other kinds of assistance.

To a student, particularly one studying marriage, family, and intimate relationships, there are many benefits in trying out different perspectives. First, this gives you more choices in how to respond, whereas a single perspective that produces an automatic reaction reduces your options. Second, by applying an open-minded perspective to your own behavior, personal change becomes more possible.

2.3 How Do You Know What's True? Learning to Evaluate Research Results

MAJOR QUESTION What are five principal kinds of scientific research?

PREVIEW Five principal kinds of scientific research are survey, clinical, observational, experimental, and other—cross-cultural, historical, and longitudinal. When looking at research findings, be aware of the blinders of your own experience and the flaws that can affect research studies.

Most of us put some sort of faith in our intuition as a guiding light to making decisions. Intuition—unconscious, automatic, out-of-sight thinking that is often expressed in insights and impulses "like website pop-up ads," in the words of psychologist David Myers (quoted in Peterson 2003)—can be valuable. This "effortless, immediate, unreasoned [not thought about] sense of

INTUITION. If you meet someone in a bar, how much do you count on your intuition in making an assessment of that person? What factors go into your judgment? How well do you think your analysis would hold up one year later? ▶

truth" shapes our fears, our impressions of people, our hunches, our workplace decisions.

But there's a downside to going with your gut. "Smart thinkers will also want to check their intuitions against available evidence," says Myers. Adds Connecticut College psychologist Stuart Vyse (quoted in Peterson 2003), "It has been shown over and over again that gut reactions are not accurate. It is a mistake to base a decision on gut feeling."

Because intuition readily leads to distortions in perception and judgment, social scientists studying marriage, family, and intimate relationships (and other subjects) use the scientific method to avoid, to the extent possible, bias in their knowledge.

Five principal kinds of scientific research are (1) *survey,* (2) *clinical,* (3) *observational,* (4) *experimental,* and (5) *other—cross-cultural, historical, longitudinal,* and *content analysis.*

1. Survey Research: Collecting Data by Questionnaire or Interview from Representative Samples

Survey research uses questionnaires or interviews to collect data from small representative groups (samples), which are then used to generalize conclusions valid for larger groups (populations). An example of a survey (the leading source of information about marriage and family matters) is the U.S. Census, taken every 10 years. Another is the polls conducted by the famous Gallup and Roper organizations. These are based on surveys conducted by written questionnaires or by interviews done face to face or over the phone.

Survey research is a three-step process.

Step 1: Decide on the Population & the Sample

Social scientists use the word **population to describe any well-known group of people they want to study,** such as teenagers who have had sex before age 18. The first step is to find a **sample, or small group of the population to be studied.**

Samples may be *representative* or *nonrepresentative.*

■ **Representative (Random) Sample:** To be scientific, the sample should be a **representative sample or random sample—everyone in your population has the same chance of being included.** For example, you might interview every fifth person from every fifth house on every fifth block in every fifth census tract.

■ **Nonrepresentative Sample:** Not scientifically valid, in a **nonrepresentative sample, researchers pick people for convenience or availability** (such as professors using students in their classes, magazines inviting their readers to answer a questionnaire, or TV programs asking viewers to respond via the Internet).

One form of representative or random sample is the **stratified random sample, a sample of specific subgroups of your population in which everyone in the subgroups has an equal chance of being included in the**

study. For example, if you were comparing the attitudes about sex of married women with those of single men, you would first identify members of both groups, then use random numbers (every fifth person, for example) to choose subsamples from each group.

Step 2: Gather the Data: Using Questionnaires or Interviews

Data may be gathered in two ways: by *questionnaire* or by *interview*.

■ **Survey by Questionnaire:** The benefits of using questionnaires are that they are inexpensive, are easy and quick to administer, and allow both survey takers and survey respondents to be anonymous. The questions asked (such as "Do you have sex every week?") are often *close-ended questions*, which means that respondents choose among the same kinds of answers (such as "Always. Frequently. Sometimes. Seldom. Never") and so are easier to tabulate and quantify.

The drawbacks of questionnaires are that respondents aren't able to reply in depth, and many issues in social science are too complicated to be explored so simplistically.

■ **Survey by Interview:** The benefits of using interview questions (asked over the phone or in person, either one-to-one or one-to-many) are that interviewers are able to explore answers in greater depth, ask respondents follow-up questions, and get a picture of reality that corresponds more to the respondents' view than to preconceived choices thought up by the survey designers. Although the questions asked can be close-ended, they can also be *open-ended* (such as "Tell me about having sex before your 18th birthday"), so that respondents can tell how they really feel.

One drawback of interviews is possible ***interviewer bias**—interviewers allow their own preconceptions to influence how they ask questions.*

Step 3: Analyze & Generalize the Results

Once the answers are in, survey researchers tally the responses and, using a computer, analyze the results. At this point, they need to determine whether the survey results can be ***generalized**—that is, whether the results of the sample can be said to apply to the population, the larger group.* For instance, can the results of a survey about teen sex taken among upper-middle-class non-Hispanic white adolescents in Beverly Hills, California, be said to apply to teens of other ethnicities and income levels elsewhere in the Los Angeles area? (Answer: probably not.)

2. Clinical Research: In-Depth Examination of Individuals or Groups in Counseling

***Clinical research** entails in-depth study of individuals or small groups who have sought counseling for psychological, relationship, or marital/family problems from mental health professionals,* such as a psychol-

ogist, psychiatrist, social worker, or licensed marriage counselor (Miller and Crabtree 1994). Most clinical research involves use of the ***case study method***, **which consists of clinical practitioners working directly with individuals or families using interviews, observation, and analysis of records.**

Like other research methods, clinical research has benefits and drawbacks:

■ **Benefits—Host of Insights:** Clinical research can yield a host of insights from in-depth, long-term study. In addition, the description of the counseling techniques and their results can be useful for counseling or therapy.

■ **Drawbacks—Results Can't be Generalized:** Because patients in counseling or psychotherapy are not representative of the general population, the data obtained from the study can't be generalized to average individuals or families (even ones in distress).

3. Observational Research: Observing People in Their Usual Surroundings

In *observational research*, researchers obtain information data by observing people in their usual surroundings.

Two Kinds of Observation

There are two kinds of observation research:

■ **Participant Observation—Interact Anonymously with Subjects:** **In *participant observation*, researchers interact with the subjects they are**

observing but do not reveal that they are researchers. An example would be if you did observation research of teen dating behavior while you were working as a teacher's aide at a local high school.

▪ **Nonparticipant Observation—Just Observe Subjects: In *nonparticipant observation*, researchers observe their subjects without interacting with them.** An example would be if you observed a high school club through a videotape camera or a one-way mirror.

Observation research has both pros and cons:

▪ **Benefits:** Nonparticipant observation is considered valuable because the observer's presence does not interfere with a natural situation, so subjects are not as apt to alter their behavior. In addition, this method allows subjects to be studied over a long period time, unlike the "snapshot" methods of survey research. Finally, researchers can follow up on the data from their observations by using other research methods, such as interviews.

▪ **Drawbacks:** With participant observer research, subjects might try to hide socially unacceptable behavior. Indeed, sociologists use the term ***Hawthorne effect* to refer to the situation in which subjects of research change from their typical behavior because they realize they are under observation.** In addition, there are ethical concerns: The researcher might find it difficult to refrain from being a participant instead of an observer (as when a subject tries to harm another person). Another drawback concerns the ethics of doing research on people without revealing to them that one is doing the research. Finally, there is always the problem of researchers reporting their own biases because observation is so subjective.

The observation method is not often used, accounting for fewer than 5% of recent research articles, according to one study (Nye 1988).

4. Experimental Research: Measuring Behavior under Controlled Conditions

In an *experiment*, factors or behaviors are measured or monitored under closely controlled circumstances. In *experimental research*, researchers try to isolate a single factor or behavior under controlled conditions to determine its effect.

Two Kinds of Variables

What we have called a "factor" or "behavior" is what scientists call a ***variable*—a factor that can be varied or manipulated in the experiment.** If you were a faculty researcher interested in what improves people's self-esteem, for example, you could ask some of your students to take a test to measure their self-confidence. You could then expose the students to a certain variable—getting more exercise, for instance—then test them to see whether their self-confidence improved. The variable being manipulated here is the exercise (or lack of).

Variables are of two types: *independent* and *dependent*.

■ **Independent Variables:** *Independent variables* **are factors or behaviors that can be controlled or manipulated by the experimenter.** In our example, this is the amount of (or lack of) exercise the students are required to get.

■ **Dependent Variables:** *Dependent variables* **are factors or behaviors that are affected by changes in the independent variable.** In our example, this is the increase or decrease in self-confidence that occurs depending on the exercise performed.

Experimental Group versus Control Group

In the traditional method of conducting an experiment, two groups of people are selected and are matched for similar characteristics, such as age, gender, and education. The subjects are then assigned to one of two groups: experimental or control.

■ **Experimental Group:** **In an** *experimental group***, subjects are exposed to an independent variable introduced by the researcher.**

■ **Control Group:** **In a** *control group***, subjects are not introduced to the independent variable by the researcher.**

Experimental research has its advantages and disadvantages.

■ **Benefits:** One advantage of experimental research is that experimenters can observe behavior directly, so they are not dependent (as in survey research) on what respondents say (or lie) about their behavior.

A second advantage is that researchers have control over many of the factors in the experiment, so they can isolate variables.

■ **Drawbacks:** One disadvantage is that the behavior being observed takes place in an artificial, not actual, environment. Therefore, subjects might not behave in the same way they would in the complexity of the real world.

Another disadvantage is that subjects are often college students or paid volunteers and so might not be representative of the population at large.

5. Other Kinds of Research

Five other kinds of research that deserve mention are as follows:

Cross-Cultural

In *cross-cultural studies***, social scientists compare data on family life among different kinds of societies.** Much of this has been anthropological, as in the case of studies in the 1930s in Polynesia by Margaret Mead.

Historical

In *historical studies***, researchers compare census, social agency, or demographic data to ascertain changing patterns of family life.** An example is use of social agency data to show how women coped with domestic violence (Gordon 1988).

Longitudinal

In *longitudinal studies*, researchers use questionnaires or interviews over a number of years to follow up on earlier investigations. An example might be a study of married couples to see what factors affected the quality and duration of their marriages.

Content Analysis

***Content analysis* is the systematic examination of cultural artifacts or various forms of communication to extract thematic data and draw conclusions about social life.** For example, you might look at several magazine ads for cultural patterns of feminine beauty.

Secondary Analysis

***Secondary analysis* is the analysis of data collected by other researchers.** For example, if you were to analyze the original data from a study of divorce, you would be doing secondary analysis. Your reasons for undertaking secondary analysis might be because you lack funds to do an original study or because the existing data contain information that wasn't the focus of the original researchers. A drawback, however, is that the data might be incorrect or collected incorrectly.

Trying to Be Objective: How Do You Know What's True?

Most of us have personal views, some perhaps strongly held, about marriage, family, and intimate relationships—the results of our own family background, religious upbringing, media images, and similar experience. But considering all the effort you'll probably put into at least some of your relationships—in terms of time, energy, money, and intense feelings—it's clearly worthwhile trying to be objective whenever possible.

In looking at research findings, two considerations to be aware of that affect objectivity are (1) your mind-sets and (2) the flaws that can affect research studies.

Your Mind-Sets: The Possible Filters

Three examples of the ways our personal experience affects our mind-sets are discussed next.

■ **Ethnocentrism—"My Country or Culture Is Best":** Do you believe that other people's family lives are much like your own? If so, this view represents *ethnocentrism*, **the belief that one's native country, culture, language, abilities, or behavior are superior to those of another culture.** An example is embodied in the title of the classic Wesley Snipes/Woody Harrelson movie about urban basketball hustlers, *White Men Can't Jump.*

■ **Heterosexism—"The Only Legitimate Family Is Heterosexual":** *Heterosexism* **is the belief that the standard family is heterosexual, with homosexual families—lesbians and gays—not being viewed as true families.** The 1996 movie *The Birdcage* with Robin Williams pokes fun at this mind-set. As we discussed earlier in this chapter and as we will see in Chapter 9, "Variations," there are several variations on the standard heterosexual family.

■ **Bias against Not Having Children—"Children Are the Ultimate Reason":** Many people who get married assume that the ultimate purpose of their union is to have children. However, many couples discover that they like the freedom—and additional discretionary income—that being child-free gives them, even though they might have to put up with criticism from disappointed nongrandparents.

Possible Flaws in Research Studies

The most popular edible terms of endearment are "Honey" (65%), "Sweetie" (30%), "Sugar" (11%), and "Cookie" (6%), according to a survey done by International Communications Research (2003) for kitchenware maker Sur La Table. How many times have your heard or read the results of a survey something like this? Are they true?

Consumer research firms are often hired to bias their survey results in favor of their clients. However, even academic sociological research can have flaws. Some examples:

■ **Researcher Is Biased:** Our values, our mind-sets, can creep into research. A heterosexual researcher might make certain unconscious assumptions about the behavior of gays that are inaccurate.

CHILDLESS BIAS? Taking a self-portrait, this couple may hope that in the future their children will enjoy the photographic record—but what if they have no children? If you were studying this pair over many years, would you tend to think theirs are not lives well lived because they opted not to have kids? Would you think they are "selfish"? ◄

■ **Sample Is Biased:** People in a sample should be randomly chosen, or the results will be biased. Interviewing unemployed people, for example, will produce different results from interviewing employed people.

■ **No Control Group:** To study the independent variable of a group, you must also study a control group—one that is not exposed to that variable. Are frequent TV watchers anxious? You need also to look at normal TV watchers to see if they're anxious, too.

■ **Questions Not Neutrally Worded:** Are the meanings of survey questions clear? After all, what does "living together" really mean? Does it imply sex? Seniors, for example, might live together—share a household—for economic reasons.

■ **Time and Other Distortions:** Data might be time sensitive, or research subjects might distort their answers. Are 1990 survey results still applicable in 2009? Will 65-year-olds accurately remember their honeymoon four decades earlier?

■ **Questions of Reliability and Validity:** ***Reliability* is the degree to which a measurement method produces the same results when repeated by the same or other researchers.** A test that measures your intelligence should produce pretty much the same score over time, which means that it's reliable. ***Validity* is the degree to which a measurement method actually measures what it claims to measure and is free of bias.** If, for instance, a test is supposed to predict performance, then the individual's actual performance should reflect his or her score on that test.

2.4 Theoretical Perspectives on the Family

MAJOR QUESTION What are eight perspectives for looking at the family and relationships?

PREVIEW Theories offer perspectives explaining why processes and events occur. Eight perspectives for viewing marriage and family are structural-functional, conflict, symbolic interaction, family systems, social exchange, feminist/male studies, ecological, and family development.

Surveys can provide understanding, but to better understand marriage and family phenomena, we need a *theory*—**a perspective or a set of statements that explains why processes and events occur.** Theories can help analyze research findings and perhaps suggest solutions that can be made into policies and laws.

Although textbooks discussing family theory may cover as many as 16 perspectives, we will describe just the following eight: (1) structural-functional, (2) conflict, (3) symbolic interaction—which we will treat as the most important perspectives—followed by (4) family systems, (5) social exchange, (6) feminist, (7) ecological, and (8) family development. These are summarized in the following chart. *(See ■ Panel 2.5, next page.)* Note: *The first three theoretical perspectives are the most important.* From time to time we will show how these three could be applied to particular subjects (such as gender and sexuality) discussed in the book.

Two Types of Theories: Macro-Level versus Micro-Level Orientations

Sociologists divide the theoretical perspectives into two types—those with *macro-level orientation* and those with *micro-level orientation.*

Macro-Level Orientation: The Top-Down View

A theory representing **a *macro-level orientation* focuses on large-scale patterns of society.** The structural-functional perspective and the conflict per-

PANEL 2.5 The Eight Theoretical Perspectives Compared

	1. STRUCTURAL-FUNCTIONAL	2. CONFLICT	3. SYMBOLIC INTERACTION	4. FAMILY SYSTEMS	5. SOCIAL EXCHANGE	6. FEMINIST	7. ECOLOGICAL	8. FAMILY DEVELOPMENT
Type of orientation	Macro	Macro	Micro	Micro	Micro	Macro and micro	Macro and micro	Macro and micro
Principal features	Stability, consensus, instrumental and expressive roles; manifest and latent functions	Conflict, competition over scarce resources, lack of consensus, social inequality	Ongoing internal family interaction; actions and reactions of family members to each other	Family members act as interconnected parts in which changes in one part create changes in other parts; all parts work toward equilibrium	People's interactions in relationships represent the efforts of each person to maximize benefits and minimize costs	Inequality in women's roles is the result of male dominance in the family and society	Family is influenced by its immediate and distant environments	Family members accomplish tasks as they move through age-related stages
Illustrative questions	What functions does the family serve? How does the family contribute to societal stability?	Who benefits from the existing social arrangement?	How do family interactions create reality for the family? How is the family experienced by its members?	How do family members experience crises in the family (illness, economic changes, substance abuse)?	How does one partner react to a lack of affection from another?	How do men benefit from traditional gender roles? How are women oppressed by the traditional definition of family?	How do individuals grow and adapt through interactions with their environment?	How do family roles change based on absence or presence of children or father or mother figure?

spective are two examples. They take a top-down view, looking at such sweeping influences on marriage and family as economic forces, social movements, technological innovations, and popular culture.

Micro-Level Orientation: The Bottom-Up View

A theory representing **a *micro-level orientation* focuses on small-scale patterns of society, concentrating on individual interactions in specific settings.** The symbolic-interaction perspective is an example of a micro-level orientation. It takes a bottom-up view, assuming that society is the product of countless everyday interactions of individuals, whose perceptions of reality are variable and changing.

Now let us consider the theories themselves.

1. The Structural-Functional Perspective: The Family Is a Social Institution Performing Essential Functions

Representing a macro-level orientation, the ***structural-functional perspective* views the family as a social institution that performs essential functions for society to ensure its stability.** Just as your body is made up of parts that work together to enable you to function as a human being, society is viewed as being made up of institutions—family, school, workplace, and so on—that enable the larger society to function and have stability. Structural functionalists look not only at the functions that the family provides for society but also at the functions the family provides for its members and that its members provide for it.

The leading proponent of the structural-functional perspective was sociologist **Talcott Parsons** in the 1950s and 1960s, who held that families functioned best when husbands and fathers carried out instrumental roles and wives and mothers carried out expressive roles. **In his *instrumental role*, the male was the breadwinner and was hard-working, self-confident, and competitive. In her *expressive role*, the female was the homemaker and was nurturing and supportive** (Parsons and Bales 1955).

Structural-functionalists say there are two kinds of functions: manifest (intended) and latent (unintended).

■ **Manifest Functions—Intended:** *Manifest functions* **are open, stated, and conscious functions.** Manifest functions are intended. For example, the manifest functions of industrialization were to build things faster and better. The manifest function of an automobile is to provide transportation from one place to another.

■ **Latent Functions—Unintended:** *Latent functions* **are unconscious or unintended functions; they have hidden purposes.** Latent functions are unintended, accidental, or even covert. For example, some latent functions of industrialization were to loosen family control over children because they no longer worked within the home. A latent function of a car was to change the nature of dating (and some people were unintentionally conceived in cars).

Applying the Perspective

In the structural-functional view, today's families have three primary functions, all designed to lend stability to the larger society:

■ **To Ensure That Society Has an Ongoing Supply of New Members and to Be a Source of Socialization:** By bearing and raising children, families continue to supply the larger society with new members to help promote its stability. The members can't just be new warm bodies, however. They must be raised to speak the language of the society and understand its norms and roles. That is, the family is a source of *socialization*—**the process by which offspring learn attitudes, beliefs, and values appropriate to their society and culture so they can function effectively in society.** Many countries have different cultures within them (as Turkey, for instance, has Kurds) whose language and norms are sufficiently different that they represent a threat to the stability of the larger society.

■ **To Provide Economic Support for Family Members:** Until recent times, families mainly served an economic rather than emotional purpose. Even in early 20th century America, the family was largely an economic unit intended to provide food, shelter, and the like for its members. The importance of this function is still seen among poor families in countries without strong social safety nets. It is also apparent in the ways husbands and wives in the United States help each other during times of economic distress, as when a husband loses his job and the wife becomes the important source of support.

■ **To Provide Emotional Support for Family Members:** Recall poet Robert Frost's line from Chapter 1 that home is the place in which "when you have to go there, they have to take you in." This implies that a family gives not only economic but also emotional support to its members. Of course, not all families are so supportive. Indeed, some can cause considerable stress, as we discuss elsewhere in this book. Even so, a family considered in its broadest sense— not only immediate family members but also grandparents, aunts, and uncles—can be a source of emotional support that one cannot always find with friends or counselors.

NEW MEMBERS. One function of the family, according to the structural-functional theoretical perspective, is to ensure an ongoing supply of new members and to socialize them to the appropriate values of the society. Do you think the socialization process starts here, with different-colored identification cards or blankets—blue for boys, pink for girls? ▶

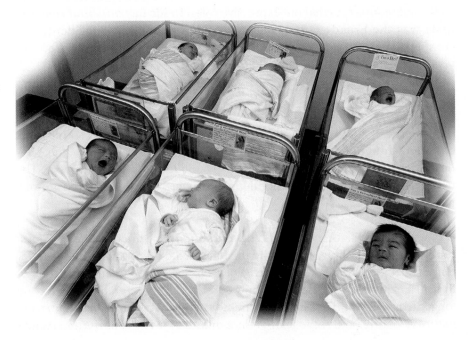

2. The Conflict Perspective: Conflict & Change, Not Harmony, Is the Normal State of the Family

Also representing a macro-level orientation, the **conflict perspective views individuals and groups as being basically in conflict with each other for power and scarce resources.** Indeed, unlike structural functionalists, adherents of the conflict perspective consider competition and struggle within the family and among groups in society at large to be natural and often desirable. We see this embodied in the views of different groups on such subjects as sex education, stem cell research, abortion, and right-to-die issues. Not everything that a family does is harmonious, and not everything that its members do is good for one another. Spouses conflict with each other about division of labor, with their children about homework and dating practices, and with relatives about holiday rituals. Although family differences can lead to positive changes and patterns of resolution, they can also lead to escalations in conflict, such as domestic violence.

Applying the Perspective

Family difficulties, according to conflict adherents, may result from societal problems, such as downturns in the economy. For example, although national statistics may lag by several years, localized surveys and court records showed that divorce filings were up in many parts of the United States during the poor economy and tense times following the September 11, 2001, terrorist attacks (Zaslow 2003).

Conflict perspective proponents believe that differences appear for two reasons:

■ **Conflict over Power:** All of us wish for autonomy and free choice. Living in a relationship or family, however, means that we must deal with the desires of others. Many relationships, therefore, consist of power struggles—over chores, over child care, over how to spend vacation time.

■ **Conflict over Resources:** Parents and children struggle over who gets to use the family computer, who gets to watch which TV programs, who can use the car, and so on. Most households never have quite enough time, money, or possessions to go around, and conflict ensues.

3. The Symbolic Interaction Perspective: People's Interactions Ultimately Determine Their Behavior

Herbert Blumer (1969) adopted the term *symbolic interaction* to refer to the process of interpersonal interaction. His work is based on that of **Charles Horton Cooley** (1909) and **George Herbert Mead** (1934), influential sociologists during the 1920s and 1930s.

Representing the micro-level (not macro-level) orientation, the *symbolic interaction perspective* **focuses on internal family interactions, the ongo-**

ing action and the response of family members to one another. In this perspective, a family is not considered to be a standard structure (as the structural functionalists thought) but rather the creation of its members as they spontaneously interact with one another. That is, a family takes on a reality of its own based on the interchanges of its members. As sociologist **William I. Thomas** said, in what became known as the ***Thomas theorem*, "If people define situations as real, they are real in their consequences"** (Thomas and Thomas 1928: 572).

For an *interaction*, or reciprocal act, to occur, there must be two people who are acting and responding to each other. The interactions are conducted by means of *symbols*—gestures or words that we interpret or define as we observe them in other people.

Applying the Perspective

The symbolic interaction perspective rests on three mechanisms, as follows:

■ **Definition of the Situation:** *Definition of the situation* means that when people define a situation as real, it has real consequences. For instance, how you interpret the glances and words your date is exchanging with others at a party (politeness? flirting?) determines the reality that follows (which could be simply innocuous or could be harmful if it makes you jealous).

■ **Self-Image Based on Others' Interactions:** Your self-image is a response to how others interact with you. For instance, you might interpret your date's animated conversation with others at the party as meaning that he or she does not consider you very important. If this were to happen frequently, it could contribute to your having a negative self-image.

■ **Predictability of Behavior:** Once you have defined the situation and determined how you think you ought to behave, you and the other person can act in predictable ways, both in the present and in the future. For instance, if you decide that your date is flirting, you might be jealous not only throughout the party, but also about that same person at future parties.

4. The Family Systems Perspective: Family Members Are Interconnected, & Changes in One Affect Others

Representing a micro-level orientation, the ***family systems perspective* suggests that family members make up a system of interconnected parts of a whole and that changes in one part change the other parts.** What interests proponents of this perspective, which represents a some what Traditional model, is not the individual family members as much as how members interact with each other to make decisions and solve problems so as to achieve the system's collective goals (Day 1995).

Applying the Perspective

A key concept in the family systems perspective is the notion of *equilibrium*. That is, a change in one part makes the family try to make adjustments that will help it go back to the way it was before—to attain equilibrium. An obvi-

CHANGING CLOTHES—OR EQUILIBRIUM?
According to the family systems perspective, when changes occur in a family—as when a new child comes along—the family members make adjustments to achieve equilibrium—that is, to keep the family functioning as it had before. Can you think of emergencies or drastic changes that forced your family to make radical adjustments? How did family members behave? ▲

ous example: When the major income earner becomes unemployed, everyone else in the household makes adjustments so that the family can keep going. That is, the other spouse might look for a job, the children's allowances are cut, and so on.

More interestingly, families have emotional equilibriums—ways of expression and behavior—that can be threatened by a change in any one part of the family. A common example is when the first child comes into a formerly childless relationship, altering the dynamics of interaction between husband and wife. "I'm convinced that this is one of the major reasons why so many divorces happen when the kids are young," says Armin Brott (quoted in Curiel 2001: C7), author of books about fatherhood. "You're focusing on the kids. You're tired as hell. You don't go out on dates anymore. You don't spend time nurturing your relationship. You don't spend time nurturing each other very much."

To keep the original equilibrium, new parents might try not allowing the relationship with their partner to focus solely on the child, to share responsibilities such as shopping and cooking, to eat dinner together (without the distraction of television), and to go to bed together at the same time (Curiel 2001).

5. The Social Exchange Perspective: Individuals Seek the Most Benefits & the Least Costs in a Relationship

An offshoot of the symbolic interaction perspective (and therefore representing a micro-level orientation), **the *social exchange perspective* proposes that people's interactions represent the efforts of each person to maximize his or her benefits and minimize costs** (Homans 1958; Blau 1964). The *benefits* (or rewards) you might seek from a relationship could include any or all of the following: wealth, security, affection, attractiveness, status, youth, power, fame, or intellectual gratification. The *costs* could be the loss of such things. If a relationship costs you more than it rewards you, you are apt to not continue it.

Applying the Perspective

The social exchange perspective follow an economicslike model of rationality, in which couples in a relationship trade off obvious costs for obvious benefits (for example, she gets security and he gets fertility). But there are many relationships in which, when observed from the outside, it's not obvious what benefits the couple gets ("What does she see in *him?*").

Indeed, it might not even be obvious to one partner that the other partner is not getting benefits. Michele Weiner-Davis (1993), author of *Divorce Busting*, coined the term "walkaway wives" to describe the phenomenon of women who start out being the caretakers of marriage but end up withdrawing from their husbands who don't pay attention to them and don't respond to their nagging. The wives then shut down emotionally (because the benefits don't exceed the costs) and start quietly preparing to leave—to walk away. The husbands, who were relieved at the lack of nagging (more benefits, fewer costs), are then stunned when told that their marriage is over. Weiner-Davis's advice to husbands: "Spending time talking and doing enjoyable things together for women is not the icing on the case. It *is* the cake" (quoted in Peterson 2000: 6D).

6. The Feminist Perspective: Inequality between Men & Women Results from Male Dominance

There are several feminist perspectives; indeed, one scholar (Lorber 1998) identified eleven variations. Nevertheless, we may summarize the *feminist perspective* (a subset of the conflict perspective, which embodies a macro-level orientation) **as being the view that inequality in women's roles is the result of male dominance in the family and in society.** That is, what the various views have in common are the twin ideas of inequality and oppression.

Applying the Perspective

A long-standing feminist belief is that marriage makes men much happier but makes women more miserable. This was a view postulated by feminist scholar **Jessie Bernard** (1972), which fueled the feminist belief that the institution of marriage oppressed women.

Subsequent investigation, however, has found that Bernard's studies were flawed, and recent research of 10,641 Australian adults (De Vaus 2002) has contradicted her conclusions altogether. Whereas Bernard found that married women were more depressed than married men or single women and married men were less depressed than bachelors, the Australian study found that mental illness was equal—16% for men and 16% for women—but that the disorders were different. (Depression and anxiety were more common among women, whereas drug and alcohol abuse tended to affect men.)

WALKAWAY WIFE. In the social exchange perspective, partners in a marriage trade off costs for benefits. When husbands stop paying attention to their wives, the wives may stop nagging them, begin to withdraw emotionally, and make plans to walk away (they decide the benefits of the marriage don't exceed the costs). The husbands, who may have been relieved at the reduced nagging (more benefits, fewer costs), are then surprised when the wife walks out the door. Have you seen this kind of behavior happen in marriages that to all appearances seemed to be stable relationships? ◄

Even so, the feminist perspective has had some important cultural and political consequences. Just three of many are the following:

■ **Emphasis on Inequality:** Feminists have insisted that spouses should be equal partners, that wives should not have to do more household and child-care tasks than their husbands, and that family leave should be available for both partners. They have also promoted the view that fathers have a great impact on the rearing of children. They have insisted on more equality in divorce laws. They have worked to secure reproductive rights.

■ **No One Kind of Family:** Challenging the view (especially of the structural functionalists) that husbands should be breadwinners and wives should be homemakers, feminists have pushed for an expanded definition of the family, including single parents, same-sex unions, stepfamilies, and grandparents and grandchildren, all representing various races and ethnicities.

■ **Reduction in Harassment and Violence:** A critical feminist contribution has been the insistence that society needs to pay close attention to eliminating sexual harassment, domestic violence, and assaults against children. This has led to changing policies in police handling of domestic disturbances, the issuing of restraining orders by courts, and medical scrutiny of women and children who are treated for bruises and beatings.

THE FEMINIST PERSPECTIVE. If this woman is unaware of the men ogling her legs, does that make their behavior acceptable? What would scholars holding the feminist perspective probably say about this picture? ▶

Men's Studies

Before feminist studies emerged, social scientists mistakenly tended to generalize the results of research involving just males to be applicable to *both* males and females. The contribution of feminist scholars, therefore, was to point up that women's experiences were different in many social areas—voting, crime, education, and so on.

However, in one field of study, that of the family, it was the reverse: Often the *men* were overlooked. That is, traditional scholars had studied the family as though men were not significant parts of it and studied men as though their family lives were not important. Recently, there has begun to be increased attention to studying how men's experiences are influenced by societal ideas about what a man is supposed to be. In addition, men are being studied for their roles within the family—as husbands, fathers, sons, ex-spouses, and so on.

Although men's studies is a relatively new discipline, it already has its own scholarly institutions, such as the American Psychological Association's Division 51, the Society for the Psychological Study of Men and Masculinity. The Men's Studies Press publishes three journals: *Fathering, International Journal of Men's Health,* and *The Journal of Men's Studies.*

7. The Ecological Perspective: The Family Is Influenced by & Influences Its Environment

The *ecological perspective* examines how a family (or individual) is influenced by and influences its environment. The ecological perspective, which is one of the newer perspectives in sociology and psychology and which embodies *both* macro-level and micro-level orientations, believes that human behavior is influenced by immediate and distant environments, ranging from, say, the family and child-care arrangements up to school, government, and church, then all the way to the earth's physical-biological environment (Bronfenbrenner 1979; Bubolz and Sontag 1993).

Applying the Perspective

The influence of emotional messages delivered through a television screen on infant behavior can be observed in babies as young as 12 months old (Mumme and Fernald 2003). After babies watched a short videotape of an adult actress reacting to a toy with a show of either positive or negative emotion, 1-year-old infants displayed similar emotions in interacting with the toy. "They are able to pick up where a person is looking, and, of course, they pick up the emotion," said Donna L. Mumme, the lead author on the study. "It was quite striking to us that 1-year-olds were able to gather that much information from a 20-second television clip" (Mumme, quoted in Goode 2003: D5). A more recent study (Christakis et al. 2004) of 1,300 infants and toddlers suggests that the more TV young children watch, the more they are apt to have trouble paying attention and concentrating during their early school years.

Adherents of the ecological perspective might say that these experiments demonstrate how individuals grow and adapt through interchanges with their surroundings, whether that of their parents (immediate environment) or that of the mass media (more remote environment).

8. The Family Development Perspective: Individuals & Families Change through Stages of Life

Embodying both macro- and micro-level orientations, the **family development perspective** **proposes that family members accomplish developmental tasks as they move through stages in the family life cycle.** There are several variations on the family life cycle, but the best known is that of **Evelyn Duvall** (1957), author of *Family Development,* who proposed eight stages. *(See ■ Panel 2.6.)* Another important researcher is Monica McGoldrick, who proposes a five-stage life family life cycle (McGoldrick et al. 1993). **In a**

■ **PANEL 2.6**   Eight Stages in the Family Life Cycle

1. Married couple: no children

2. Child-bearing family—lasts about $2^1/_2$ years: oldest child younger than 30 months old

3. Family with preschoolers—lasts about $3^1/_2$ years: oldest child $2^1/_2$–6 years old

4. Family with school children—lasts about 7 years: oldest child 6–13 years old

5. Family with adolescents—lasts about 7 years: oldest child 13–20 years old

6. Family as launching center—lasts about 8 years: oldest child an adult and has been "launched" into independence

7. Middle-age family: empty nest—no children

8. Aging family: from retirement to death of one or both spouses

Source: Adapted from Duvall 1957.

family life cycle, **members' roles and relationships change, largely depending on how they have to adapt to the absence or presence of child-rearing responsibilities.**

Applying the Perspective

A key contribution of the family development perspective is that family members have to accomplish *developmental tasks*—**fulfill specific role expectations and responsibilities as they move through the life cycle** (Duvall and Miller 1985). For example, in stage 1, you and your partner must establish a mutually satisfying marriage, fit into the kinship network, and adjust to pregnancy and the promise of parenthood. During stage 3, you must fit into the community of school-age families and encourage children's educational achievement. In stage 5, you must help teenagers mature and emancipate themselves as well as establish postparental careers and interests. In stage 7, middle age, you must rebuild the marriage relationship and maintain kinship ties with older and younger generations.

Of course, you can probably see that there are many facts of life that don't fit neatly into this life cycle. How, for example, do you apply this perspective to single-parent families, childless couples, and grandparent-grandchild families? How does the fact of divorce change the developmental tasks? We consider these matters elsewhere.

Is Any Perspective Better Than Any Other?

If you are confronted with a relationship or a family that is clearly not doing well, which perspective would you be inclined to take—or to take first? All of these have their value, but all also have drawbacks.

Pluses & Minuses

There are many critiques we might make here, but let us describe just the most important ones:

■ **Structural Functional:** The structural-functional perspective held sway in the 1950s and 1960s and helped to formulate ideas about order and stability in families as well as how politics, law, and economics affect the family structure.

This perspective has been faulted, however, for viewing the family narrowly as a harmonious unit with shared values and in regarding divorce as disintegration rather than as indicating possible positive change (Mann et al. 1997). It also has been criticized for not focusing enough on everyday interactions of individuals.

■ **Conflict:** The conflict perspective offers a refreshing alternative to the structural-functionalist view that existing family structures benefit society. That is, conflict theorists ask us to look at who, in fact, benefits from these structures.

Yet this view has also been faulted for stressing conflict over order and for holding that differences lead to conflict rather than (as often happens) to acceptance and cooperation.

■ **Symbolic Interactionist:** In contrast to the preceding perspectives, the symbolic interactionist view focuses attention on the daily interactions of members of a family.

For this reason, however, it has also been faulted for ignoring larger social influences on the family such as economic and political forces. Critics also complain that, despite its close-up view, it doesn't focus enough on personality, temperament, and power. Finally, it appears to emphasize individual happiness over familial values such as duty and stability (Schvaneveldt 1981).

■ **Family System:** The family system perspective focuses on interconnectedness and emphasizes the importance of the pieces (family members) to the whole (the family). It also stresses the dynamic aspects of a family, in which a change sets in motion an attempt to restore equilibrium.

However, many scholars have trouble even agreeing on what the family systems perspective is (Melito 1985). This viewpoint also grew out of therapeutic and clinical work with dysfunctional families, so there is some debate as to whether those results can be applied to functional families. Finally, it does not draw greatly on the effects of wider social, economic, and political forces on a given family.

■ **Social Exchange:** The social exchange perspective allows family relationships to be evaluated in terms of benefits and costs, thereby stressing the importance of individual choice and the notion that group phenomena and the social structure derive from individual actions.

However, this perspective has been criticized for assuming that people always act in rational, calculating ways. It also has been faulted for emphasizing individual self-serving over altruism and family values.

■ **Feminist:** The feminist perspective, which embraces a variety of viewpoints, brought needed attention to the fact that family roles and male and female roles are constructs of society—roles often created by men to maintain their own power.

On the other hand, this perspective has been criticized for stressing personal feelings over objectivity and emphasizing observation and interviewing instead of quantitative (statistical) research (Maynard 1994).

■ **Ecological:** The ecological perspective is valuable because it stresses the interaction of families and their political and societal environments.

However, it is not always easy to tell how environments exert such changes on families, especially alternative family groups such as stepfamilies or same-sex family groups (Ganong et al. 1995; Klein and White 1996).

■ **Family Development:** The family development perspective focuses on the family rather than on the individuals in it and emphasizes the importance of successful completion of developmental tasks. The viewpoint has been useful in providing insights about the two-parents-with-children nuclear family.

The perspective has been criticized because the processes of life do not always unfold in such clearly marked stages (Winton 1995). It has also been tilted toward white, middle-class families (Hogan and Astone 1986). In addition, the concept of a family life cycle has ignored other kinds of families, such as single parents, divorced parents, and same-sex households (Laird 1993; Rodgers and White 1993; Slater 1995).

Different Folks, Different Families

Today, as we mentioned, the family is no longer just the nuclear family of one breadwinner, one homemaker, and one or more children. North America has become a region of different varieties of families: Both intact, enduring families and serial-marriage families. One-earner families and two-earner families. Childless households and multigenerational households. Dual parents and single parents. Biological parents and adoptive parents. Young families and second- (or third-) time-around families. Heterosexual parents and gay and lesbian parents. Parents who are intimately involved with their children and parents who can't handle the responsibility. Singles and couples who live in isolation and individuals and families who open their homes and hearts to all comers. In the rest of this book, we apply the tools of scientific research and the theoretical perspectives just described to these fascinating subjects.

Self-Assessment: Gaining Self-Knowledge from the Harvard Project Implicit Website

Many of us state that we are not prejudiced, that we keep an open mind. What about unconscious prejudices, especially those that could negatively affect our chances for having satisfying intimate relationships?

Harvard University, the University of Virginia, and the University of Washington are conducting an online survey called Project Implicit to examine thoughts and feelings that exist either outside conscious awareness or outside conscious control. This project is for educational and research purposes only. The range of topics that you will be questioned about at their website should provide you with a great variety of experiences and an opportunity to think about topics that are very important to you or about issues that you have not yet had the occasion to consider.

To participate in Project Implicit, go to *https://implicit.harvard.edu/implicit/research/index.jsp*. You will be asked to register, which is free and requires only that you fill out a brief, confidential form and that you have an email address, which becomes your sign-in ID for subsequent sessions. Then you can begin. Each ques-

tion session lasts about 10 minutes and requires you to assign a positive or a negative value to each of two topics. The topics appear randomly, and you can skip any that you do not like or that you are not interested in. Examples are *married/unmarried, male/female, religious/atheist, geek/nerd, books/television, feminism/tradition, conservative/liberal, young/old, rich/poor*. After you have finished each session, you will receive feedback about your preferences and/or prejudices—and you might be surprised!

You will also be providing useful information for research about personal preferences on a large variety of topics.

After you finish each of the remaining chapters in this book, take a few minutes to return to the Harvard Project Implicit site and find out more about yourself. As you proceed through this course, print out your results or take a few notes, and then recheck them after the course is finished. Perhaps you will discover that some of your preferences and/or prejudices have changed.

Key Terms Used in This Chapter

adolescence, p. 41
appeal to authority, p. 57
appeal to pity, p. 57
arguments, p. 56
case study method, p. 63
circular reasoning, p. 57
clinical research, p. 62
companionate family, p. 46
conclusion, p. 56
conflict perspective, p. 73
content analysis, p. 66
control group, p. 65
critical thinking, p. 54
cross-cultural study, p. 65
deductive argument, p. 56
dependent variable, p. 65
developmental tasks, p. 80
ecological perspective, p. 78
ethnocentrism, p. 66
experiment, p. 64
experimental group, p. 65
experimental research, p. 64

expressive role, p. 71
fallacy, p. 56
false cause, p. 57
family development perspective, p. 79
family life cycle, p. 80
family systems perspective, p. 74
feminist perspective, p. 76
generalized, p. 62
Hawthorne effect, p. 64
heterosexism, p. 67
historical study, p. 65
independent variable, p. 65
inductive argument, p. 56
instrumental role, p. 71
interviewer bias, p. 62
irrelevant attack on an opponent, p. 57
irrelevant reason, p. 57
jumping to conclusions, p. 56
latent functions, p. 71
longitudinal study, p. 66

macro-level orientation, p. 69
magical thinking, p. 52
manifest functions, p. 71
matriarchal family, p. 40
matrilineal, p. 39
micro-level orientation, p. 71
mindfulness, p. 58
mindlessness, p. 58
nonparticipant observation, p. 64
nonrepresentative sample, p. 61
observational research, p. 63
participant observation, p. 64
patriarchal family, p. 40
patrilineal, p. 39
population, p. 61
premises, p. 56
puberty, p. 40
random sample, p. 61
reasoning, p. 56
reliability, p. 68
representative sample, p. 61
sample, p. 61

Summary

2.1 A Short History of Marriage

- Family in America can be viewed from the perspective of (1) the early American era, (2) the 19th and early 20th centuries, and (3) the modern era.

- The early American family can be considered according to four groups: (1) Native American families, (2) white colonial families, (3) African American families, and (4) Hispanic (Latino) families.

- Native American families included both family structures: matrilineal (children traced their descent through their mother's line) and patrilineal (descent traced through the father's line). Females were usually married at ages 12–15, males at ages 15–20, and couples chose their partners, although marriages were also arranged by parents. High infant mortality rates kept families small, but children were welcomed and participated in many rites of passage while growing up.

- White colonial families, who were primarily of British, French, Spanish, and Portuguese origin, adhered to a Christian-influenced family model that emphasized sexual restraint, a patriarchal structure in which the father held power, and mate selection by parental arrangement rather than by love. The family was considered primarily an economic unit for producing goods and a social unit for taking care of family members, including the widowed, orphaned, aged, and sick. Some middle-class boys were given instruction in writing, arithmetic, reading, and religion; girls were given only minimal education. Adolescence as a stage of social and psychological development did not exist. Instead, children were viewed as miniature adults whose labor was to be exploited.

- The first African families to appear in North America were not slaves but indentured servants who, after fulfilling their years of service, could own land, marry, and hire out their labor. By the mid-17th century, however, the majority of black immigrants were slaves brought primarily from West Africa. Though prohibited from marrying, slaves found rituals to legitimize marriage among themselves. Slave families were stronger than was once believed; adversity produced strong attachments between fathers and mothers and healthy kinship networks.

- Although Hispanic (Latino) families appeared in North America even before the New England Pilgrims, they lost most of their land through confiscation and fraud and became laborers exploited in the economic development of the Southwest. Influenced by Catholic teaching, family life stressed many rites of passage of religious significance, such as baptism, first communion, confirmation, and quinceañera as well as marriage. Socialization of children was very traditional, girls being taught to be wives and mothers and boys being brought up according to the concept of machismo, which emphasized male dominance, pride, and sexual prowess. The Latino family structure was also strongly influenced by familism.

- Families in the 19th and early 20th centuries were dramatically influenced by social and economic forces, including industrialization, urbanization, and immigration. The main impact of industrialization was to shift the production of goods from the home and human labor to machines and factories located mostly in urban areas, which prompted population movement to the cities, which resulted in a housing shortage that produced a decreasing birth rate. The growth of mass transit gave working husbands and fathers more mobility, but it also reduced their close connection to and supervision of their children. Kinship networks enabled many immigrants and blacks to survive the adverse conditions of slavery, poverty, and unemployment.

- As more people began working outside the home, the view of the family as a work unit began to decline, women felt more free to choose marriage partners for compatibility and affection, and children became less important as economic contributors. Therefore, women began emphasizing child rearing over childbearing, resulting in a declining birth rate.

- In the 20th century, many economic, educational, and social welfare functions began to be provided by outside agencies instead of families, and family members became more attentive to taking care of one another's emotional needs. Familism was replaced by individualism, and sexual attraction and compatibility became more important as the basis for middle-class marriage and family relationships. This led to the so-called companionate family, in which the purpose of marriage was to provide emotional growth, romance, and sexual fulfillment.

- In the last 100 years, the family has been changed by several social forces. During the Great Depression of the 1930s, formerly stay-at-home mothers were forced to seek employment, a trend that had begun during World War I, when able-bodied men were called to serve in the military, and that was reinforced during World War II. The shift of women into formerly male-oriented jobs helped to change traditional views of women as being mainly wives and mothers.

- The 1950s marked a return to traditional family values, as a booming economy impelled families to seek the good life in the suburbs and a stable household with a working father and stay-at-home mother. The Baby Boom years, 1946–1964, witnessed a massive population explosion that now constitutes approximately one-third of the U.S. population.

- Immigration continues to be a major factor shaping the nature of the American family. There has been a significant shift in the composition of the immigrant population from primarily European to Asian and Latin American–born groups.

2.2 Learning How to Think: Keys to Being Open-Minded

- Being raised in a particular culture makes it difficult for us to step outside and objectively analyze how our family and other relationships work. The emotional nature of love and intimacy also makes it hard to have a clear understanding. Our socialization and individual life experiences result in a mind-set that affects our perceptions.

- Open-mindedness requires avoiding magical thinking and developing critical thinking skills. Critical thinking means clear thinking, skeptical thinking, and active thinking. It is actively seeking to understand, analyze, and evaluate information in order to solve problems. Critical thinking skills can be learned. They involve four steps: (1) getting an understanding of the problem, (2) gathering information

and interpreting it, (3) developing a solution plan and carrying it out, and (4) evaluating the plan's effectiveness.

- The best way to break through the closed habits of thought or mind-sets is to use reasoning, which involves the use of arguments. Arguments consist of one or more premises, or reasons, logically supporting a result or outcome called a conclusion. The two main types of correct or valid arguments are inductive and deductive.

- Objectivity is further prevented by mindlessness—entrapment in old categories, automatic behavior, and acting from a single perspective. The opposite, mindful thinking, is characterized by the creation of new categories, being open to new information, and awareness of the existence of more than one perspective.

2.3 How Do You Know What's True? Learning to Evaluate Research Results

- To further enhance one's objectivity, it's important to understand the basic types of scientific research and the flaws that can affect them, as well as the blinders of one's own experiences. The five principal types of scientific research are (1) survey, (2) clinical, (3) observational, (4) experimental, and (5) cross-cultural, historical, longitudinal, and content analysis.

- Survey research uses questionnaires or interviews to collect data from small representative groups (samples); the questionnaires are then used to generalize conclusions that are valid for larger groups (populations). Samples may be representative, nonrepresentative, or stratified random samples. Information may be collected through questionnaires or interviews. In conducting interviews, researchers need to be aware that their own preconceptions can cause interviewer bias.

- Clinical research entails in-depth study of individuals or small groups who have sought counseling for psychological or relationship problems from mental health professionals. A significant amount of clinical research involves the use of case studies, reports derived from clinical practitioners working one on one with individuals or families using interviews, direct observations, and analysis of records.

- In observational research, researchers collect data by observing people in their natural surroundings. Observational research may be either participant observation (researchers interact naturally with the subjects they are observing but do not reveal that they are researchers) or nonparticipant observation (researchers observe subjects without interacting with them). A drawback to observational research is the possible occurrence of the Hawthorne effect—subjects of research change their typical behavior because they realize they are being observed.

- In an experiment, factors or behaviors are measured or monitored under closely controlled circumstances. In experimental research, researchers try to isolate a single factor or behavior under controlled conditions to determine its influence. Experimenters employ the use of variables—factors or behaviors that can be manipulated and measured. Variables may be independent variables (factors that can be controlled or manipulated by the experimenter) or dependent variables (factors or behaviors that are affected by changes in the independent variables). To determine whether the dependent variable was truly affected by the independent variable, researchers use experimental groups that are exposed to the independent variable and control groups that are not exposed to the independent variable.

- Additional research methods include cross-cultural studies (social scientists compare data on family life from different cultures), historical studies (researchers compare census, social agency, or demographic data to ascertain changing patterns of family life), longitudinal studies (researchers use questionnaires or interviews over a number of years to follow up on earlier research), content analysis (systematic examination of cultural artifacts or various forms of communication to extract thematic data and draw conclusions about social life), and secondary analysis.

- Objectivity in research may be hindered or prevented through ethnocentrism, heterosexism, and bias against childlessness. Possible research flaws also occur when a researcher is biased, the sample is biased, no control group is used, questions are not neutrally worded, data are time sensitive, there are distortions on the part of the research subjects, and there are problems of reliability and validify.

2.4 Theoretical Perspectives on the Family

- Theories are perspectives that explain why processes and events occur. Eight perspectives for viewing marriage and the family are (1) structural-functional, (2) conflict, (3) symbolic interaction, (4) family systems, (5) social exchange, (6) feminist/male studies, (7) ecological, and (8) family development.

- The structural-functional perspective views the family as a social institution that performs essential functions for society to ensure its stability. That is, the family is a source of socialization—the process by which offspring learn attitudes, beliefs, and values appropriate to their society and culture so they can function effectively in society. Traditional structural-functionalism views the male as being responsible for instrumental roles (he is the breadwinner, tough, hard-working, and competitive) and the female for expressive roles (homemaker and nurturer). Structural-functionalists identify manifest functions (those that are open, stated, and conscious) and latent functions (those that are unconscious or unintended).

- Conflict theory views individuals and groups as being basically in conflict with each other for power and scarce resources.

- The symbolic interaction perspective focuses on internal family interaction and the ongoing action and response of family members to one another.

- The family systems perspective suggests that family members make up a system of interconnected parts of a whole and that changes in one part change the other parts.

- The feminist perspective views the inequality in women's roles as the result of male dominance in the family and in society.

- The ecological perspective examines how a family (or individual) is influenced by and influences its environment.

- The social exchange perspective proposes that people's interactions represent the efforts of each person to maximize benefits and minimize costs.

- The family development perspective proposes that family members accomplish developmental tasks as they move through stages in the family life cycle, in which the roles and the relationships of family members change primarily according to how they have to adapt to the absence or presence of child-rearing responsibilities.

Take It to the Net

Among the Internet resources on understanding the topics discussed in this chapter are the following:

- **Allyn & Bacon Sociology Links.** Research methods and statistics.
  www.fsu.edu/~crimdo/soclinks/research.html
  www.fsu.edu/~crimdo/soclinks/soclinks.html#spot
- **Intute.** Connection to thousands of social science websites.
  www.intute.ac.uk
- **National Center for Health Statistics (NCHS).** As the nation's principal health statistics agency, NCHS is a great source of information about America's health.
  www.cdc.gov/nchs

- **Migration Information Source.** Offers tools and data on movement of people worldwide.
  www.migrationinformation.org
- **Population Resource Center.** Promotes use of accurate population data and sound analysis.
  www.prcdc.org
- **SocioSite.** Social science information. Links to home pages on social theory.
  www.pscw.uva.nl/sociosite/TOPICS/theory.html
- **Tiger Census.** Variety of illustrated maps powered by U.S. Census data.
  http://tiger.census.gov
- **U.S. Census Bureau.** Excellent website of the Census Bureau.
  www.census.gov

CHAPTER 3

GENDER

The Meanings of Masculinity & Femininity

The Varieties of Gender Stereotypes

In 1993, a group of artists *calling itself the Barbie Liberation Organization purchased several hundred of two of the most popular children's dolls— "Teen Talk" Barbie and Talking G.I. Joe Electronic Battle Command Duke. After switching the dolls' voice boxes, the group then sneaked the dolls back onto toy-store shelves, reports writer Ed Liebowitz (2002).*

The result: Children brushing the long blonde

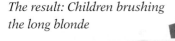

hair of the altered Barbies would hear them cry out, "Eat lead, Cobra!" Or, "Attack, with heavy fire-power!"

The G.I. Joes would say, in Barbie's soprano voice, "I love to try on clothes" and "Let's plan our dream wedding."

Is there a more dramatic way of showing how our popular culture stereotypes differences between the sexes? *Stereotypes* are, by definition, exaggerated expectations about a category of people, which can be completely inaccurate when applied to individuals.

Consider some sources of these exaggerated portraits:

■ ***Film roles:*** Although 42% of the women in the United States are 40 years of age or older, 78% of the actresses appearing in Hollywood movies in 2001 were 39 or younger (August et al. 2002). In addition, women play only 34% of the roles and—superstar Julia Roberts aside— earn a third less than males in comparable industry jobs (Rapping 1994). In addition, in G-rated films, according to one study (Smith 2006a), 77% of primary characters were male. That is, for every speaking female character there are three male characters. Moreover, G-rated movies (even animated ones) are dominated by physically

WHAT'S AHEAD IN THIS CHAPTER

This chapter considers the vocabulary needed to be able to discuss gender intelligently. We also describe the four principal theories offered to account for gender differences. We then consider the key influences that, in addition to the media, influence our gender behavior: parents, peers, teachers, and the workplace. Finally, we consider the benefits and drawbacks of traditional gender roles and how gender roles are changing.

aggressive white male characters, whereas women and minorities are relegated to the sidelines. G-rated movie men are seldom good models: Only about 35% are parents, versus 66% of female characters, and only about 32% of men are married or in a committed relationship (Smith 2006b).

■ *Television:* On TV, women represent just 36% of all prime-time characters (Children Now 2002). Men are often shown to be aggressive problem solvers—pilots, doctors, scientists—who rescue others from dangerous situations. Women on TV traditionally have been housewives, reporters, nurses, and sex objects, although recently they have been featured in more active roles (Vande Berg and Strekfuss 1992). On the influential Sunday morning political talk shows, only 14% of the guests are women and 56% of the episodes include no women at all (The White House Project 2005). In terms of televised sports, less than 10% of sports news was found to cover female athletes, and less than 2% of the time is used to cover women athletes in sports categorized as masculine (Koivula 1999). On music videos, such as MTV, women are often shown as sex objects or trying to get a man's attention or even experiencing some sort of violence; men are shown acting aggressively (Carter 1991; Kalof 1993).

■ *Newspapers:* Even though women make up more than half the popula-tion, in a survey of 20 newspapers, females appeared only 13% of the time in front-page stories (Overholser 1996). In newspaper coverage of political candidates, women were more apt to be described in terms of dress, hair color, and family data than men were (Devitt 1999; Noveck 2006; Fuextes 2007).

■ *Magazines:* In women's magazines, roles such as homemaker and mother predominate, although in recent years, more attention has been paid to career roles (Demarest and Garner 1992).

■ *Comic strips:* According to a study of six months of comic strips, women in the strips spend more time in such gender-stereotypical activities as domestic chores, child raising, and helping the spouse compared to men. Males spend more time in leisure activities (Berglund and Inman 2000; LaRossa et al. 2000).

According to the U.S. Census Bureau (2006), people were projected to spend nearly half their lives (3,518 hours in 2007) engaged with TV, radio, the Internet, and newspapers and listening to personal music devices. Every day the mass media and the popular culture give us a picture of how men and women are supposed to be and are supposed to behave. But are men really more aggressive, adventurous, and domineering than women? are women generally more dependent, fearful, and affectionate than men? Let us take a look at the backdrop to these questions.

What are the principal terms anyone needs to know to discuss gender differences intelligently?

What are some possible explanations for gender differences?

Who has influenced how I feel about being a man or a woman?

Is there more than one way to be masculine or feminine?

🌐 **ON THE WEB** How Do the Mass Media Portray Masculinity & Femininity?

www.seejane.org

How accurate do you think the mass media are in portraying men and women? Here's an opportunity to go on the World Wide Web and find out.

Dads & Daughters' See Jane program, founded by actor and producer Geena Davis, is concerned with looking at gender portrayals in media, for children ages 11 and under.

1. Go to the website.
2. Click on *Publications* at left.
3. Click on one of the three research briefs shown that interests you. Do you think the gender portrayals are correct?

3.1 Understanding Gender & Gender Roles

MAJOR QUESTION What are the principal terms anyone needs to know to discuss gender differences intelligently?

PREVIEW To talk about gender, you need to know the meaning of sex versus gender, of gender roles and sex roles, and of socialization and gender identity. It helps to understand the distinctions among cross-dressers, transvestites, transsexuals, transgenderists, and hermaphrodites. Finally, you should know the vocabulary of sexism—patriarchal and matriarchal, sexism and sexual harassment.

When you think of horse wranglers, race-car drivers, corporate raiders, and Navy SEALs, do you think of men or women? When you imagine baby-sitters, elementary school teachers, cosmetics sellers, and cheerleaders for NFL football teams, which sex comes to mind? Yes, we're all aware by now that many careers are not so rigidly gender-identified, but still the old habits of thinking die hard. And what of people who, at first glance, seem to be somewhat indefinite in their gender identity, such as men who like to dress up in women's clothes or women who become surgically altered to have men's physical characteristics? Are they "masculine" or "feminine"?

How to Talk about Gender: The Vocabulary

When you fill out a form for a driver's license, you're asked to specify your sex—male or female. Is "sex" the same as "gender"? The answer is: No, it's not.

Although social scientists have sometimes been accused of complicating their disciplines by inventing unnecessarily specialized terms (to put themselves on a par with physical scientists, say critics), that is not the case here. To keep our discussion clear, let us consider terms we will use in this book.

Sex

***Sex* refers to the biological characteristics with which we were born that determine whether we are male or female.** Sex, of course, includes anatomical differences (genitals, breasts, and the like) and whether your biology allows you to bear children. It also includes differences in sex chromosomes, hormones, and physiology. Women, for instance, have the X chromosome (XX); men have the Y chromosome (XY).

Males and females have the same sex hormones, but men usually have more testosterone and women more estrogen and progesterone.

Gender

Gender **refers to the socially learned attitudes and behaviors associated with being male or female.** We derive these from the social and cultural expectations placed on us while we are growing up. Sociologist Talcott Parsons, proponent of a structural-functionalist view of the family (discussed in Chapter 2, "Understanding"), held that the husband or father played the *instrumental* role of breadwinner and was hard-working, tough, and competitive. The wife or mother played the *expressive role* of homemaker and was nurturing and supportive (Parsons and Bales 1955). In the popular mind, male and female traits are often thought of as being opposites. (*See* ■ *Panel 3.1.*) However, gender differences may be viewed as appearing along a range or continuum of so-called masculine traits and feminine traits.

Roles, Gender Roles, & Sex Roles

A *role* **is the behavior expected of someone who holds a particular status.** The key word here is *expected.* A role consists of the expectations that are defined for a particular person in a particular situation in a particular culture. Thus, the role of an emergency medical technician called to a traffic accident is to save lives.

A *gender role* **is the behavior expected of a female or a male in a particular culture,** the attitudes and activities that a society expects of each sex. In the United States, for example, females are often expected to be sensitive and caring (except when they are competing in tennis). Males are generally expected to be competitive and ambitious (except when they are holding kittens or puppies). However, among certain New Guinea tribes studied in the 1930s by anthropologist Margaret Mead (1935), women were expected to be dominant, and men were expected to be submissive. Even today, on Orango Island in Guinea-Bissau, women are the ones who make the marriage proposals—and once they are asked, men are powerless to say "no" (Callimachi 2007).

■ **PANEL 3.1   Gender Opposites?** Many Americans think the following traits differentiate males and females. What do you think?

SUPPOSED MALE TRAITS	SUPPOSED FEMALE TRAITS
Active	Passive
Ambitious	Content
Analytical	Intuitive
Assertive	Receptive
Attractiveness derived from achievement	Attractiveness derived from physical appearance
Brave	Timid
Competitive	Cooperative
Dominant	Submissive
Independent	Dependent
Insensitive	Sensitive
Intelligent and competent	Unintelligent and incapable
Rational	Emotional
Sexually aggressive	Sex object
Strong	Weak

Source: Adapted from Macionis 2001: 330.

People often use the term *sex role* to mean gender role, but technically that's incorrect. **A *sex role* is the behavior defined by biological constraints.** For example, only women can give birth, and only men can be sperm donors.

Socialization & Gender Identity

How do we know what gender role is expected of us? We do it through learning, or *socialization,* **the process by which people learn the characteristics of their group—the attitudes, values, and actions that are thought appropriate for them.** Learning is what creates our sense of who we are as a man or woman—our gender identity.

Gender identity **is a person's psychological sense of whether he or she is male or female,** which may or may not correspond with their anatomy. *Gender variance* **is an intense psychological discomfort with one's sex.** This is also called *gender identity disorder (GID),* the American Psychiatric Association's diagnosis for people who repeatedly show, or feel, a strong desire to be the other sex. Much like sexual orientation, the biological basis for gender identity is somewhat of a mystery, although some researchers suspect it is linked with hormone exposure in the developing fetus (Brown 2006).

Cross-Dressers & Transvestites

Some people enjoy taking on, or feel compelled occasionally to take on, aspects of the roles of the other gender. You see this in the case of *cross-dressers,* **when a member of one gender dresses up in clothes, wigs, and so on to appear to be a member of the other gender.** It needs to be pointed out, however, that women have gained more fashion freedom than men have, so women can wear slacks without raising eyebrows, whereas a man generally cannot wear a dress without causing talk.

A different kind of cross-dresser is the *transvestite,* **usually a male who dresses provocatively in order to appeal to men.** Sometimes transvestites are simply entertainers, such as the drag queen character "Bernadette" played by Terence Stamp in the 1994 movie *The Adventures of Priscilla, Queen of the Desert.* Often, however, they are homosexual men acting as prostitutes who dress to lure male customers to engage in sex.

TRANSVESTITES. *Left:* In the 2005 movie *Transamerica,* Felicity Huffman plays a pre-op male-to-female transsexual who is forced to take a cross-country road trip with the son she never knew she had. *Right:* In *To Wong Foo, Thanks for Everything! Julie Newmar,* John Leguizamo, Wesley Snipes, and Patrick Swayze star as three "girls" going from New York City to Hollywood for a drag queen contest. Do you see anything peculiar about men dressing up as women?

Transsexuals & Transgenderists

A more complicated question of gender identity arises with the person who says, "I'm a woman trapped in a man's body" or "I'm a man trapped in a woman's body." This is a ***transsexual*, a person with the biological sex of one gender who has the identity or self-concept of the other gender and undergoes medical procedures to change to that sex.** A person born female who has the gender identity of a male spends on average $30,000 to $70,000 on "transitioning" medical measures: taking hormones to grow facial hair and having breast and genital surgery, although many do not have both surgeries (Buchanan 2007). Male-to-female transsexuals pay $50,000 to $67,000 for breast augmentation and surgery to create a vagina, along with facial feminization and laser hair removal. Some municipalities and big companies—General Motors, IBM, Eastman Kodak, and Hallmark Cards—now include transition-related coverage as an employee benefit (Buchanan 2007). The most famous transsexual to change surgically was Christine Jorgensen (1967), who underwent a series of operations in Denmark in 1953.

EXAMPLE OF

A Transgenderist?
Jazz Musician Billy Tipton

Billy Tipton was a saxophone and piano player who appeared with popular dance bands in the 1940s and early 1950s, traveling the jazz circuits of the American Southwest and Northwest. He had lots of friends and was married several times. But at the height of his glamorous life, he rejected a career-boosting opportunity to share the stage with famous entertainer Liberace at a Nevada hotel. As jazz began to go out of fashion, Tipton moved to Spokane, Washington, where he became an entertainment agent, married a former stripper named Kitty, and adopted three sons. He spent his last years alone in a trailer park with little money.

In 1989, at age 74, he developed a hemorrhaging ulcer, and his youngest son called an ambulance. The son watched in astonishment as the paramedics who tried to revive his dying father discovered that the elder Tipton was a woman, a fact that was later verified by the coroner. It developed that Billy Tipton had been born Dorothy Tipton in Oklahoma in 1914 but at the age of 19, in the year 1933, took the name Billy, and for the next 50 years lived life as a man.

All this has been described in *Suits Me: The Double Life of Billy Tipton*, a book by Stanford University English professor Diane Wood Middlebrook (1997). However, there is some dispute about the biographer's interpretation. Middlebrook thinks that Tipton, dealing with the difficulty of women jazz musicians getting jobs during the Great Depression, at first adopted the male identity for economic reasons, but then her sexual identity became an exquisite act. "I think the Tipton story is about the indeterminacy of gender identity," Middlebrook says. "You can understand her as someone

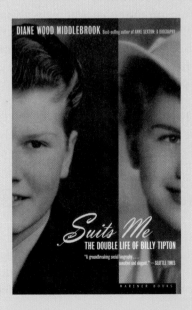

who chooses her self-presentation in the face of options. You can't draw a bottom line with her about identity. I believe Billy's relationship to herself was female. She was the actor; he was the role" (Middlebrook, quoted in Lehrman 1997).

It needs to be pointed out, however, that Tipton took pains to leave few legal documents that revealed a female identity, that he obtained new legal documents listing himself as male, and that he had many opportunities to reject his life as a man, which he never did. The people who know him report that he was a man in almost every psychological sense.

WHAT DO YOU THINK? At a time when hormones and surgery weren't available, is there a chance that Billy Tipton was a transgendered man?

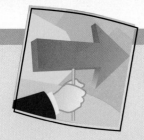

In the workplace, sexual harassment includes suggestive remarks, unwanted touching, sexual advances, requests for sexual favors, sexually oriented posters and graffiti, and similar verbal or physical actions of a sexual nature.

Most such behavior is harassment of women by men, but the reverse may also occur, or it may occur between people of the same gender (Abelson 2001). The inappropriate action may be between manager and employee, between co-workers, or between people outside with contacts with employees.

If the harasser is a manager or agent of the organization, the organization itself can be sued, even if it had no knowledge of the situation (Lavelle 1998).

There are two types of sexual harassment, according to the U.S. Supreme Court:

- **Quid pro quo—tangible economic injury:** In this type of harassment, the person receiving unwanted sexual attention is put in the position of jeopardizing being hired for a job or obtaining job benefits or opportunities unless he or she implicitly or explicitly acquiesces.
- **Hostile environment—offensive work environment:** In this type of harassment, the person being sexually harassed doesn't risk economic harm but experiences an offensive or intimidating work environment, as might be the case when one has to put up with lewd jokes or sexually oriented graffiti.

Some guidelines follow.

Preventing Sexual Harassment

- Don't laugh at sexually offensive comments, jokes, or gestures about other people.

- Don't make such remarks or gestures toward others.
- Don't touch others inappropriately — or touch at all, if they don't like it.
- Don't make sexual suggestions, requests, or advances.
- Try to identify with the other person's feelings.

Stopping Sexual Harassment

- Tell the offender in clear terms what the offensive behavior is and that you expect it to stop.
- If a face-to-face confrontation is impossible, write a letter. Ask the offender to stop. Give exact details of the offensive behavior. Explain how you feel.
- Don't be afraid of embarrassing the harasser. It's your rights that have been violated.
- If the harasser doesn't stop the offensive behavior, contact an appropriate authority.

A *transgenderist* **is a person with the biological sex of one gender who has the identity of the other gender, lives the full-time life of that gender but does not undergo medical procedures to change to that gender.**

While on the subject of transsexuals and transgenderists, we should mention the hermaphrodite. **A *hermaphrodite*, or *intersexual*, is a person who has both male and female sexual organs, or organs that are not distinct, as when a female's sex organ (the clitoris) resembles a male's sex organ (the penis).** In such cases, the organs are not fully developed. It has been suggested that perhaps one in 2,000 babies are born with genitals that aren't clearly male or female (Torassa 2002).

We discuss homosexuality, which deserves more extensive coverage, in Chapter 9, "Variations."

The Vocabulary of Sexism

The terms we used to describe gender roles and the like lead naturally to a consideration of another, more value-laden vocabulary that arises because people have certain expectations about gender-role behavior. Let's consider the words *patriarchal* and *matriarchal* and the terms *sexism* and *sexual harassment*.

Patriarchal & Matriarchal

Most societies are *patriarchal*, **meaning male-dominated, male-identified, and male-centered** (Johnson 1997). That is, males dominate economic and political institutions, core ideas are identified as being associated with men, and the focus of attention is mainly on men. In extremely patriarchal societies, women have few rights, as was the case in pre-2002 Afghanistan under Taliban rule.

Matriarchal **means female-dominated, female-identified, and female-centered.** Matriarchal societies don't seem to be much in evidence. However, there are institutions, such as some families and organizations, that are dominated by females.

Sexism & Sexual Harassment

Sexism **is unjust discrimination based on a person's sex or the belief that one sex is innately superior to the other.** It is expressed in attitudes, actions, or institutional arrangements in which people are discriminated against because of their sex. An example is the favoritism shown in China toward boys, which leads prospective parents to use technology (such as ultrasound) to determine the sex of the forthcoming child during pregnancy and then abort the fetus if it is shown to be a girl.

Sexual harassment **is the abuse of one's position of authority to force unwanted sexual attention on another person.** It is expressed through unwelcome and repeated comments, gestures, or physical contact of a sexual nature (although there is no objective standard for determining what is offensive, which makes sexual harassment difficult to define and prosecute).

NUMBERS THAT MATTER
Gender Differences

- **Do beauty and money matter?** Among 37 different groups of men and women in 37 different societies, heterosexual males were found to be drawn to physically attractive young women, and heterosexual women were found to be drawn to men with economic ambitions.[a] In 2004, women earned a median income ($17,629) that was only about 58% that of men ($30,513).[b] Women make up more than 90% of people with eating disorders.[c]

- **Why do more males fail?** Males get 70% of the D and F grades, account for 80% of high school dropouts and attention deficit disorders, in 2006 made up only 42% of college students, and are the suspected perpetrators in four out of five crimes.[d]

- **Women's work?** Females make up 97.6% of preschool and kindergarten teachers; 97.3% of secretaries and administrative assistants; 94.8% of child-care workers; 92.4% of receptionists and information clerks; 92.3% of registered nurses; 91.3% of bookkeeping, accounting, and auditing clerks; 90.9% of teacher assistants; 89.5% of maids and housekeeping cleaners; 88.7% of nursing, psychiatric, and home health aides; and 82.2% of elementary and middle school teachers.[e]

- **Men's work?** Males make up 97.5% of construction workers; 89% of engineers; 79% of workers in farming, forestry, and fishing; 71% of lawyers and judges; 70% of medical doctors; 69% of mathematical and computer scientists; 57% of college professors; and 54% of company managers.[f]

[a]Buss 1989. [b]*Statistical Abstract of the United States* 2007: Table 682. [c]National Women's Health Information Center 2002. [d]Mulrine 2001; Garofoli 2002. [e]U.S. Department of Labor Women's Bureau 2005. [f] U.S. Department of Labor 2002.

3.2 Why Do Gender Roles Differ? Some Theories

MAJOR QUESTION What are some possible explanations for gender differences?

PREVIEW Four theories that have been offered to account for gender differences are sociobiology, social learning theory, cognitive development theory, and gender schema theory.

Beauty in women is much valued in our society—indeed, in many societies—and heterosexual males everywhere seem to be drawn to physically attractive young women (although the standards of beauty may vary). Conversely, heterosexual women have been found in some research to be drawn to men with economic ambitions. In fact, both these characteristics have been found among groups of men and women in 37 different societies (Buss 1989).

Why do men and women show these and other gender differences? Several theories have been advanced as explanations. Let's consider the theories of (1) *sociobiology,* (2) *social learning,* (3) *cognitive development,* and (4) *gender schema*. We don't suggest that one perspective is better than any other; in fact, often they are used together. Indeed, we must point out that the theories have limited value because they often grew out of studies based on inadequate samples, so they can't be said to apply to all social groups.

1. Sociobiology: Does Biology Determine Our Gender Differences?

Does biology shape gender behavior? Every one of us begins life with a "female brain," suggests neuropsychiatrist Louann Brizendine (2006), who reviewed hundreds of studies on fundamental differences between the sexes. But about eight weeks after conception, testosterone floods male brains, diminishing connections in the communication centers, while estrogen enhances those connections, as well as those regions responsible for language and for expressing emotion and observing it in others. These differences, Brizendine proposes, "make women better negotiators and conciliators and men better fighters and lone wolves" (Henig 2006).

Sociobiology **suggests that our social behavior—and gender behavior—results from biological differences.** Although males and females have the same sex *hormones* —**chemical substances secreted into the bloodstream by the endocrine glands**—men usually have more *testosterone* (produced by the testes), and women usually have more *estrogen* and *progesterone* (produced by the ovaries). These hormones and the different sex chromosomes underlying them are certainly what produce different physical characteristics—for example, facial hair on men and breasts on women.

But sociobiologists suggest that these biological underpinnings may also explain differences in gender behavior—such as the observations mentioned previously about heterosexual men seeking attractive women and heterosexual women seeking economically secure men. In terms of the evolutionary goal of perpetuating the species, these theorists say, men seek mates who are more apt to be *fertile* and hence more likely to provide them with children; women seek mates who are more apt to guarantee the *security* of their offspring (Symons 1987; Symons and Ellis 1989; Ellis and Symons 1990).

RICH AND BEAUTIFUL. Would you agree with the sociobiologists' suggestion that biology explains the gender behavior of heterosexual men seeking attractive women for their apparent fertility and heterosexual women seeking economically successful men for their apparent security? ▲

2. Social Learning Theory: Does the Environment Determine Our Gender Differences?

Social learning theory **suggests that we learn attitudes and behaviors through our interaction with the environment.** Social learning theory is based on behavioral psychology, which stresses observable behavior rather than internal feelings, which cannot be observed.

Two Kinds of Learning

Learning, according to behaviorists, occurs in two ways: through *reinforcement* and through *modeling*.

■ **Learning by Reinforcement—Rewards and Punishment:** Are boys encouraged to play with dolls? Are girls urged to defend themselves through fistfights? The answers, for most children, suggest that we learn through reinforcement: desirable behavior is rewarded, and undesirable behavior is punished. That is, as children, we are more apt to repeat acts that are regularly followed by rewards ("You're taking good care of dolly") and not to repeat acts that are regularly followed by punishment ("Don't let those boys push you around").

■ **Learning by Modeling—Imitation:** While growing up, we all imitated the same-sex characteristics of parents, other children, other adults, and even characters we saw in the mass media, such as TV or music stars. In social learning theory, the kind of **learning through imitation of others is called modeling.** In general, children seem to imitate adults who are nurturing, powerful, or both, such as their parents.

The games in which boys and girls involve themselves early in school, points out Barrie Thorne in *Gender Play* (1993), have specific gender qualities. Boys' games are competitive, rule-based, open to many players, hierarchical in leadership, and fairly aggressive. Girls' games are cooperative, verbal, fairly small in nature, high in intimacy, and flexible in their goals and rules. These are ways of playing that we learn through reinforcement and modeling.

3. Cognitive Development Theory: Does Our Age Determine Our Gender Differences?

Social learning theory suggests that children and adults learn in the same way. By contrast, cognitive development theory suggests that the way we learn depends on our age. According to *cognitive development theory*, **how children think, understand, and reason changes as they grow older, the result of biological maturation and increasing social experience.** This perspective is based on the findings of Swiss psychologist **Jean Piaget** (1950, 1954) and was later reinforced by **Lawrence Kohlberg** (1966, 1969), who showed that children of different developmental stages handle gender identity differently. Consider the following timeline.

- *Two-year-olds:* As a 2-year-old, you might have become aware that two genders exist and decided, correctly, that you are either a boy or a girl. However, at this age, you wouldn't think of gender as being permanent. Rather, you would decide who was who based on changeable attributes such as hair length (short for boys and long for girls) and types of clothing (pants for boys and dresses for girls). Older children and adults identify sex on the basis of genitalia, but a 2-year-old does not yet think in these terms.
- *Five-year-olds:* By age 5, you would have developed a sense of gender identity and you probably identified yourself as wanting to do girl things or boy things simply because that was what was comfortable for you.
- *Six- and seven-year-olds:* By age 6 or 7, you probably began to understand your and others' gender as being permanent, unlike hair and clothing styles, which can be different every day.

4. Gender Schema Theory: Do We Develop Mental Categories for Organizing Our Gender Perceptions?

Some of cognitive development theory has been incorporated into gender schema theory. *Gender schema theory* **suggests that as children, we develop a framework of knowledge—a gender schema—about what we think males and females typically do, and we then use that framework to interpret new information about gender.** A *schema* consists of mental categories for organizing our perceptions of cultural stimuli (Bem 1981).

Thus, when as boys we realized that cultural expectations of being male were that we were supposed to be independent, courageous, and tough, we incorporated those views into our male gender schema. As girls, we did the same with such female gender schema as being affectionate, nurturing, and understanding. Once we developed these schemas, they influenced how we processed information about gender, so that we were apt to associate baking cookies, for instance, with girls and throwing a football with boys.

Clearly, this is a way in which gender stereotypes can become established; indeed, such stereotypes tend to become more rigid during adolescence. A *gender stereotype* **is the belief that men and women each display traditional gender-role characteristics.** Later, in adulthood, many people become less rigid in their beliefs about their expectations about gender characteristics.

3.3 Gender Socialization: Who Teaches Us How to Act Male or Female?

MAJOR QUESTION Who has influenced how I feel about being a man or a woman?

PREVIEW Besides the mass media, principal environmental influences on gender behavior are parents, peers, teachers, and the workplace.

Sociobiology stresses that gender differences are based on biology. However, the other three theories suggest that we learn gender behavior mainly from our environment. The principal environmental influences are (1) parents, (2) other children, (3) teachers, and (4) the workplace. A fifth, discussed at the beginning of the chapter, are the popular culture and mass media. Many would suggest that religion is also a major influence.

1. How Our Parents May Have Influenced Us

Who was your primary caretaker when you were young: a parent or parents, perhaps a grandparent or grandparents? Whoever they were, they probably had the most influence on how you learned your gender role, especially during your infancy and childhood.

If you're not a parent yourself, you might not realize how much work goes into parenting—feeding babies, changing diapers, giving baths, tending to illness, buying clothes and toys, providing schooling, transporting to doctors and play dates, and so on. Yet while all this was going on, your parents, like most, might not have been aware how much of what they said and did influenced your views of masculinity and femininity (Culp et al. 1983).

Most especially, they probably weren't aware that they treated girls and boys differently, often in subtle ways (Fagot and Leinbach 1987; Shapiro 1990). Or if they did, they simply thought they were adjusting their behavior to reflect the children's different personalities or supposedly inherent differences.

Let's consider some aspects of these.

How Fathers & Mothers Treat Their Children Differently

Parents tend to socialize their children differently according to what their own gender is (Fagot and Leinbach 1987).

■ What Fathers Do: Fathers tend to spend more time with sons than with daughters, and their attention may take the form of giving gifts or money (Starrels et al. 1994). Yet fathers are also important playmates to their children, particularly when it comes to rough-and-tumble play. Fathers set higher standards of accomplishment for their sons than they do for their daughters and are more aggressive in play and more goal directed. With daughters, fathers tend to stress emotions and feelings in their relationships. Children who are raised fatherless often have the same characteristics as children who are raised in permissive families.

■ What Mothers Do: Mothers tend to express affection and give verbal praise to daughters and sons equally. However, like fathers, they tend to stress emotions and feelings in their relationships with their daughters. In households headed by a single parent (whether father or mother), it has been found that in mother-headed households, children had less traditional-gender rearing than those in father-headed households (Leve and Fagot 1997; Wright and Young 1998).

AVOIDING GENDER STEREOTYPING. If you're male, did your father or mother discourage you from helping in the kitchen because it is "woman's work"? If you're female, did your parents also try to push you into gender-stereotyped activity? How do you feel about these activities now? ▲

Four Ways Parents Socialize Their Children

There are four subtle ways in which parents socialize their children from infancy to adulthood (Oakley 1985):

■ Uses Different Physical and Verbal Manipulations: If you're male, did your parents handle you somewhat more physically (roughly) than they did your sister, tell you not to cry, admire you for being "such a strong boy"? If you're female, did they treat you more gently than your brother, hold you, and tell you, "Let the boys take care of that job"? Physical and verbal manipulation is a big part of how parents influence the gender roles of children.

■ Directs Attention toward Certain Stereotypical Gender-Identified Objects: Did your parents direct you toward such toys as dolls and baby carriages? Or toward race cars and footballs? Certain toys, clothing, sports equipment, and other objects are often culturally identified more with one gender than the other. Boys' toys tend to encourage physical activity, whereas girls' toys tend to stress physical proximity and mother-child talk (Caldera et al. 1989).

■ Applies Different Verbal Descriptions to the Same Behavior: Even years later, working in professional careers, women might find that they have to deal with different standards for the same behavior, being called "pushy," for example, for behavior at work that in men is admired for being "aggressive." The same thing happens in childhood: A boy is encouraged for being "active," whereas a girl is rebuked for being "too rough." Or a girl is complimented for being "gentle," but a boy is criticized for not being "competitive enough."

■ **Encourages or Discourages Certain Stereotypical Gender-Identified Activities:** As a boy, were you asked to help mother with sewing, cooking, ironing, and the like? As a girl, were you made to help dad do yard work, shovel snow, take out the trash, and so on? For most children, it's often the reverse. Note that the identification of girls with *indoor* domestic chores and boys with *outdoor* chores becomes training for stereotypical gender roles (McHale et al. 1990; Blair 1992; Leaper 2002; Shellenbarger 2006).

Differences in Class, Ethnicity, & Religion

How you feel about gender matters may also depend on your social-class, ethnic, and religious background.

If you're white and come from a middle-class background, you might have had a less traditional gender upbringing than if you come from a white working-class background, particularly if you're female.

If you're a young female from a working-class Latino background, your parents might worry about your living away from home and perhaps expect you to come home often to help with chores and child care—an expectation that's generally not applied to Latino males (Zinn 1994; Reisberg 1999).

If you're African American, you probably were raised with fewer traditional ideas about gender (Taylor 1994). In fact, if you're a black female, you probably were raised to be more independent than if you had been brought up in a white family, perhaps because your mother worked as well as ran the household (Burns and Homel 1989; Lips 1997). If you're a black male, you might have been raised to act cool, wearing a mask intended to project an aura of control and inner strength (Majors and Billson 1992).

Although more women than men attend church, religion can reinforce gender stereotypes since many religions have a patriarchal basis, and some, such as Catholicism, have no female clergy (Basow 1992). One pair of scholars suggest that people who are regular churchgoers are more likely than irregular churchgoers to have traditional ideas about gender roles (Willets-Bloom and Nock 1994).

2. How Our Peers May Have Influenced Us

Your parents were probably the first ones to influence you as to your gender role, but once you entered school, other children—your *peers*, **or those of equal status in age, class,** and the like—became important. Although your parents might have had some misgivings about some of them, your peers probably had some positive effects, such as perhaps helping you develop intimate relationships in adolescence (Gecas and Seff 1991).

Among children, play is often divided by gender, with peers using their approval or disapproval to influence our choices of toys, games, food, music, TV programs, and so on (Carter 1987). Children actively socialize each other to conform to certain styles of interaction with members of their own sex. Girls have been found to encourage other girls to behave in a feminine or "communal" style that is connection oriented and focuses on maintaining personal relationships, cooperation, and support. As might be expected, boys sometimes encourage other boys to adopt a masculine or "agentic" style that is status oriented and focuses on goals of dominance. However, boys have

also been found to act counter to gender norms and to encourage communal styles and discourage agentic styles among other boys (Hibbard and Buhrmester 1998).

How Girls Are Influenced

Girls usually influence other girls to play with dolls—indeed, the average girl owns eight dolls (Greenwald 1996). Such dolls as Barbie often set unrealistic standards for female attractiveness by being molded with big busts and tiny waists—and recently with thongs, high heels, and bare midriffs, as in the Bratz line (Kluger 2006). An interesting new exception is the small-breasted Muslim doll, Fulla, which wears a long, flowing gown and comes with her own prayer rug (Al-Jadda 2005). By and large, however, a visit to any toy store will show that girl-appropriate toys include dollhouses and clothes, kitchen utensils, cosmetics, and sewing and crafts kits. Girls' toys tend to emphasize domesticity, nurturing, passivity, imagination, and emotional expression (Morse 1995).

In addition, girls take cues from boys, who regard appearance as the most important indicator of girls' popularity. Girls often put down other girls they regard as being overweight, underdeveloped or overdeveloped physically, or otherwise unattractive (Eder et al. 1995). Intelligent girls are often teased or put down by boys.

How Boys Are Influenced

Boys expect other boys to play with their own kind of dolls, although they're called "action figures," such as the weapon-toting Power Rangers, G.I. Joe, and *Star Wars* toys. Other supposedly boy-appropriate toys include plastic guns and swords, Batman and Spider-Man costumes, carpentry kits, race cars, Tanko construction equipment, toy footballs and baseball bats, and warlike

"Maybe because men enjoy so much power and prestige in society, there is a tendency to see boys as shoo-ins for success," says Michael Thompson, a child psychologist who coauthored *Raising Cain* (Kindlon and Thompson 1998). "So people see in boys signs of strength where there are none, and they ignore all the evidence that they are in trouble" (Mulrine 2001).

And in trouble they might well be. Males make up two-thirds of students labeled "learning disabled." They get 70% of the D and F grades. They account for 80% of high school dropouts and attention deficit disorders. They are less likely to go to college, and in 2006 they made up only 42% of college students. They are the suspected perpetrators in 4 out of 5 crimes. They are arrested for 9 out of 10 alcohol and drug violations (Mulrine 2001; Garofoli 2002; Lewin 2006).

But American girls are also behaving more like boys—and the picture isn't pretty. Girls might not be as violent as boys, but they are increasingly becoming as apt to smoke, drink, and do drugs as boys their age are and to get in trouble with the law (Phillips 1998).

WHAT DO YOU THINK? Why the differences?

EXAMPLE OF

Gender Differences

Who's Stronger, Boys or Girls?

video games. Boys' toys tend to emphasize logic, following rules, competition, and aggressiveness (Cargan 1991; Morse 1995).

Boys promote gender stereotyping by focusing not only on attractiveness as the most desirable feature of girls but on toughness as the most desirable feature of boys, using words such as *wimp* to put down boys not considered assertive enough (Eder et al. 1995).

3. How Teachers May Have Influenced Us

Once you started school—nursery school, kindergarten, elementary school—not only your peers but also teachers began to influence your ideas about appropriate gender behavior. Because most teachers in your early years were probably female, you might have tended to think of adult interactions as mainly being with women.

Teachers also subtly influence how boys and girls are more different than they are similar.

How Teachers Influence Boys

At least among white children, boys tend to get more attention from teachers than girls do, at all levels from nursery school to college (Lips 1995). Compared to girls, boys are more likely to be called on in class, to be given more time to talk, and to receive praise but also to be disciplined harshly (Sadker and Sadker 1995; Kindlon and Thompson 1998; Pollack 1998). Boys also tend to be louder and more demanding. Perhaps as a result, they are expected to work harder at finding answers to problems on their own.

NONTRADITIONAL ROLES. Female auto mechanics, male nurses: if you encounter people performing nontraditional gender roles, are you surprised? ▲

How Teachers Influence Girls

Girls do better than boys academically through elementary school. But by middle school, boys have caught up and surpassed girls in such subjects as science, math, and reading. Girls are not only less likely to be called on than boys but also, if their answers are incorrect, not to be helped to discover the error and correct it; instead, teachers are more apt to simply call on another student (Sadker and Sadker 1995). Except in all-girl schools, girls are also more apt to be praised for their appearance and for being neat in their work.

4. How Work May Influence Us

The gender gap in the workplace might be slowly narrowing. But while you were growing up, your sense of gender roles might have been influenced by which occupations you saw dominated by females and which by males. We discuss the effect of work on family and intimate relationships in Chapter 12, "Work," but here let us suggest how work roles have tended to follow gender stereotypes.

Occupations Dominated by Females

According to the U.S. Department of Labor, the ten occupations with the highest concentration of women in 2005 were preschool and kindergarten teachers (97.6%); secretaries and administrative assistants (97.3%); child-care workers (94.8%); receptionists and information clerks (92.4%); registered nurses (92.3%); bookkeeping, accounting, and auditing clerks (91.3%); teacher assistants (90.9%); maids and housekeeping cleaners (89.5%); nursing, psychiatric, and home health aides (88.7%); and elementary and middle school teachers (82.2%) (U.S. Department of Labor Women's Bureau 2005). In general, about half of working women are found in one of two types of occupations: administrative support and service support.

Occupations Dominated by Males

Again according to the U.S. Department of Labor, men are dominant in construction: 97.5% of construction workers are male. Eighty-nine percent of engineers are male, as are 79% of people in farming/forestry/fishing occupations, 71% of lawyers and judges, 70% of medical doctors, 69% of mathematical and computer scientists, 57% of college professors, and 54% of company managers (U.S. Department of Labor 2002). In politics, most U.S. senators and Congressional representatives are men (though this situation is changing; in 2007, there were 16 women in the Senate and 71 in the House, and Nancy Pelosi became the first female Speaker of the House). Most religions, including Catholicism, evangelical Protestantism, and fundamentalist Islam, are dominated by male leadership, with women representing about 20% of clergy in mainline Protestant religions (Rodgers 2007). In the military, only about 20% are women.

3.4 Gender Roles in Transition: Multiple Masculinities & Femininities

MAJOR QUESTION Is there more than one way to be masculine or feminine?

PREVIEW A man and a woman following traditional gender roles may derive certain benefits from their relationship but also experience certain drawbacks. More and more, however, gender roles are in transition.

Traditional gender roles were once based on biological differences. In preindustrial societies, men's greater physical size and strength were highly valued for bringing in food and providing for defense—hence the patriarchal role. Women had little choice about reproduction and pregnancy—hence the matriarchal role. In industrial societies today, these biological differences are no longer as important.

The Benefits of Traditional Gender Roles

Traditional gender roles promote stability because they are predictable—both people in a relationship know their rights and responsibilities. Therefore, traditional gender roles have continued to exist because, as long as both partners can tolerate the costs and are comfortable with the rewards, they provide some benefits. Let's see what these are.

Benefits to Males

The central feature of the traditional male role, as we've seen, is instrumental—the focus is on *work identity*. That is, for traditional males, the most important function is to be good providers and protectors for their families.

Aggression, dominance, and power orientation, then, are harnessed in the service of excelling in the workplace. This has resulted in certain benefits:

■ **Higher Income and Other Job-Related Advantages:** In 1998, according to a study by the Internal Revenue Service (2002), at annual wages of less than $25,000, women outnumbered men, accounting for 57% in that category. In the $25,000 to $30,000 range, men and women were roughly equal. Above that, however, men were dominant, and the higher the pay, the more men outnumbered women. For example, in the $200,000 to $500,000 range, men outnumbered women 9 to 1; in the $500,000 to $1 million range, it was 10 to 1; and in the over $1 million category, it was 13 to 1.

■ **Less Domestic Work and Marital Stress:** Not only do males make more money—polls show that both men and women think males have more opportunities and choices in jobs and quicker promotions (Roper Starch World-Wide, Inc. 1996). And, of course, the understood trade-off of traditional gender roles is that men are relieved of the tedium and stresses of typically female domestic chores—housework, food preparation, diaper changing, child care, and so on.

Benefits to Females

The central feature of the traditional female role is expressive—the focus is on expressing tender feelings and being concerned with others' needs. Thus, for traditional females, the most important function is home and hearth—taking care of the house, cooking, raising children, being emotionally supportive of the husband. This has the following benefits:

■ **Identity Tied to Relationships Rather than Work:** Women seem to gain more satisfaction from relationships, whether with spouses, children, or friends (Jones et al. 1990; Cherry 1998; Roy et al. 2000). They often also spend more time keeping in touch with family members, organizing family gatherings with grandparents and in-laws, and stage-managing special events such as birthdays and anniversaries.

■ **Closer Attachments with Children:** Traditional women who are mothers not only are able to spend more time with their children but also are able to help shape and enrich their children's development (Harris 1994). Traditional fathers, by contrast, often in later years regret their lack of closeness with their children. (A cemetery worker told one of the authors that Mother's Day is a bigger occasion for visits to family graves than is Father's Day.)

The Drawbacks of Traditional Gender Roles

If two people in a relationship have agreed to the division of effort represented by traditional roles—he is the breadwinner, she is the wife and mother—they may find fulfillment. Nevertheless, each is giving up something. Let us see what the negative side of traditional roles is.

TRADITIONAL MALE ROLE. What do men climbing the organizational ladder to the top executive's office get besides more income and a big office? What do they miss out on? How about women who do the same? ▶

Drawbacks for Males

If, as a male, the central feature of your identity is your job and career, it can deprive you of a whole valuable set of experiences and even have a negative effect on your health. Consider the following:

■ **Personal Self-Worth Being Tied to Job Position and Income:** The stars in their field stand at the summit of a pyramid. But the nature of a pyramid is that the farther you climb, the less space remains. Thus, the majority of pyramid climbers never make it to the top (Falvey 1986). Therefore, men who fall short—or work part time or are unemployed—are more apt to feel unmanly and even to experience depression or mental illness (Goodwin 1990; Gaylin 1992).

■ **Job-Related Stress:** It hardly needs to be pointed out that work for pay can be extremely stressful. This can result from tyrannical supervisors, unpleasant customers or co-workers, physical strains, boredom, constant deadlines, and other difficulties. It can also result because many working Americans are in the wrong job. Only 41% hold jobs that they had planned on, according to one survey (Gallup Organization 1990).

■ **Less Time for Family Life:** If most of the time what you do is work, necessarily there will be less time to spend with your family, including children. Many children have found their fathers to be distant figures because they were often away at work. Men who try to juggle work and family life often experience role overload (Gerson 1993).

■ **Limited Emotional Expression, Resulting in Loneliness and Fear of Intimacy:** The strong, competitive, but unemotional male is not just a creature of the movies; it has been a standard of traditional malehood. But the inability to share feelings can result in loneliness as well as anger, depression, and fear of intimacy (Derlega et al. 1993; Thelen et al. 2000).

■ **Limitations on Child Custody When Divorced:** Because traditional, career-oriented men often haven't spent much time with their children, and because of some societal messages that "real men don't take care of children," men might find themselves at a disadvantage when pressing for child custody if they become divorced. Indeed, some legal experts believe that if the "treatment fathers receive in the family court occurred in the workplace, an affirmative action plan would likely be implemented" to correct the situation (McNeely 1998).

Drawbacks for Females

Women might seem to have the better half of the bargain in a traditional relationship, because they are able to avoid work stresses and focus on family life. But this gender role too has its problems:

■ **Reduced Income and Career Fulfillment:** In part because traditional women value motherhood over career building, they tend not to go as far in school and to earn fewer advanced degrees (Ross and Van Willigen 1997). The result is that women in the United States earn a median income ($17,629 in 2004) that is only about 58% of men's ($30,513) (*Statistical Abstract of the United States* 2007, Table 682).

For a while, women at all economic levels steadily gained ground on their male worker counterparts, and in the mid-1990s they were earning more than 75 cents for every dollar in hourly pay that men did, up from 65 cents 15 years earlier. Since then, some groups of women have actually lost ground, with highly educated women faring less well than a decade ago (Leonhardt 2006).

This is an especially unfortunate consequence for traditional women who become divorced. Indeed, women of traditional backgrounds who are living alone or are single mothers are more apt to risk poverty, which has given rise to the phrase the "feminization of poverty," as we discuss in Chapter 12, "Work." Economic inequality is also the norm in many other countries, including Canada (Baxter and Kane 1995). It is certainly the case in most developing countries, such as those in Latin America, Asia, and Africa.

■ **Dependence on the Spouse, Resulting in Unhappiness:** Being a traditional wife and mother means that a woman is dependent on her husband for financial support. Whereas men seem to be happier married than unmarried, it is the reverse with traditional women, who might find household and child-raising tasks boring, exhausting, and never ending. Wives in traditional marriages report more symptoms of stress, more unhappiness about life, and more frustration, along with marital problems and wish for divorce, than do unmarried women (Rettig and Bubolz 1983; Spence and Sawin 1985). The dependency might make some women reluctant to leave abusive relationships.

■ **The Beauty Problem:** The emphasis on attractiveness means that some young women are apt to be drawn into weight-losing eating disorders (anorexia and bulimia) and other unhealthy habits in order to remain slim. Indeed, women make up more than 90% of people with eating disorders (National Women's Health Information Center 2002). As attractive women get older, they are apt to be less valued, especially if they have not taken steps to develop a career or other dimension to their lives. (As men age, they may be said to look "distinguished." Women are said to "lose their looks.")

■ **Less Personal Self-Worth:** Women in general are apt to have fewer feelings of positive self-worth than men are—lower self-esteem, less social self-confidence, and a diminished belief in their own intelligence (Smith 1995; Furham and Gasson 1998).

Changing Gender Roles

Despite some benefits of traditional gender roles, people do abandon them, perhaps out of necessity, as when a wife and mother must go to work to bring in a second family paycheck or when a father loses his job and becomes an inadvertent househusband. More and more, however, people are *voluntarily* opting to abandon traditional gender roles (Gerson 1985, 1993). In this, they have been offered guidance by the women's movement and the men's movement.

The Women's Movement

Historically *feminism*, **the view that women should have the same economic, social, and political rights as men have,** grew out of the 19th-century movement to abolish slavery, which made women sensitive to their own disadvantage, such as prohibitions on owning property or serving on juries. The first women's rights convention was held in 1848 in Seneca Falls, New York. In 1919, women won the right to vote, after which the women's movement basically dissolved for 40 years (Chafetz and Dworkin 1986; Renzetti and Curran 1995).

Feminism began to reassert itself again in the 1960s and 1970s in the wake of black civil rights and other political activism and following publication of Betty Friedan's *The Feminine Mystique* (1963). The National Organization for Women (NOW), a reform-minded group that eventually grew to half a million members, was established in 1966. The women's movement has generally endorsed such moves as the passage of an Equal Rights Amendment to the U.S. Constitution, affirmative action for women and minorities, abolition of sex discrimination in the workplace, the right to legal abortion, government-subsidized child care, ending violence against women, and the acceptance of females in nontraditional gender roles.

However, feminism does not speak with one unified voice. Indeed, there are several viewpoints in modern feminism (Renzetti and Curran 1995; Whittier 1995; Lindsey 1997).

■ **Liberal Feminism—Inequality Rooted in Sexism:** Liberal feminism, or "equal rights feminism," is principally concerned with promoting individual rights and achieving equal opportunities for women through legal and social reforms. It assumes that the cause of women's inequality is learned customs of gender inequality.

■ **Socialist Feminism—Sexual Division of Labor Rooted in Class Conflict:** Socialist feminism, which is rooted in classical Marxism, maintains that the sexual division of labor and gender inequality is an expression of class conflict. This view advocates government supports for parental leave and child care to enable women to achieve a better quality of life.

■ **Radical Feminism—Inequality Rooted in Patriarchy:** Radical feminism considers male oppression, or patriarchy, to be the cause of female inequality and sometimes advocates separatist roles for women from the existing social system. ***Patriarchy*** **describes social arrangements in which positions of power and authority are mostly held by men.** A key emphasis of radical feminism is violence, both physical and psychological, as perpetrated by male-dominated institutions against females.

■ **Lesbian Feminism—Oppression Rooted in Dominance of Heterosexuality:** Lesbian feminism focuses on the dominance of heterosexuality, particularly as an expression of patriarchy.

■ **Conservative Feminism:** Conservative feminism, at least in its most radical form, promotes a return to traditional gender and family roles. Phyllis Schlafly and the Council of Women for America are examples of leaders of this viewpoint.

This list is not exhaustive. Other views are psychoanalytical (Chodorow 1978), global, women of color, and ecofeminism, to mention a few.

The Men's Movement

The women's movement encouraged men to reconsider their own gender roles by embracing a movement of their own. The first meeting of the National Conference on Men and Masculinity took place in 1975 and has met every year since then.

Like feminism, the men's movement has divisions, which some have identified as follows (Kimmel 1995a, 1995b; Renzetti and Curran 1995):

■ **Profeminists:** The liberal branch of the men's movement, profeminists agree with feminist women that patriarchy benefits white heterosexual males but obliges all men, including minorities and gays, to follow rigid gender roles. This branch is represented by the National Organization for Men Against Sexism (NOMAS).

■ **Antifeminists:** The conservative branch of the men's movement, antifeminists believe that male dominance is natural and therefore women's attempts to attain gender equality must be resisted. This branch is represented by the National Organization for Men (NOM), which views feminism as encouraging the downfall of the family and the undermining of men's self-interest, especially in divorce settlements. The Promise Keepers, a Christian movement of men's rights advocates, stresses the traditional gender roles of men being responsible to and for their families.

■ **Masculinists:** A more recent variant of the men's movement is the masculinists, who agree that the patriarchal system causes oppression and isolation but are more concerned with males' attempts to achieve self-realization and self-expression. This is represented by the ideas discussed in poet Robert Bly's *Iron John* (1990), which led to men's campfire gatherings in which men were encouraged to share feelings and release their inner "wild man."

Not all men in the men's movement fit neatly into one of these three groups. For instance, there are those who believe that men, like women, are oppressed by social conditioning that limits their experiences and range of expression and skills (Franklin 1988). There are many males who take a gender-neutral approach and advocate equal rights and responsibilities for all men and women, without blaming one gender or the other for current inequalities.

Role Conflict, Androgyny, & Postgender Relationships

The awakening of consciousness about traditional gender roles brought about by the women's and men's movements has led to a lot of anxiety and confusion. Yet it also suggests hope for transcending these roles.

Anxiety & Confusion: The Effects of Role Conflict

Being in a traditional gender role has its discomforts, but so does finding one's way into new forms of gender behavior—especially when many of the old expectations remain. **Role conflict occurs when the expectations of two or more roles are incompatible.** For example, women who hold full-time jobs might find that they can't also be good mothers—look after sick children, go to school events, and the like. Men who assume housework or child-care duties might feel inadequate for not doing them as well as their spouses might. Role conflicts can produce stress-related problems, including anxiety attacks, insomnia, headaches, and various tensions (Weber et al. 1997). Is there hope for moving beyond such problems?

Androgyny: Achieving Flexibility

Whether you're a man or a woman, isn't it possible that you could be, for example, *both* competitive and achievement oriented *and* tender and nurturing? That is, you could have both the instrumental characteristics associated with traditional masculinity and the expressive characteristics associated with traditional femininity.

If so, you would be considered *androgynous*. **Androgyny is the quality of having in one person the characteristics, as culturally defined, of both males and females.** (In ancient Greek, *andros* means "man," and *gyne* means "woman.") Clearly, the benefit of being androgynous is that you would be a more *flexible* person, being logical in one kind of situation and emotional in another, for example, or being competitive at certain times and nurturing at other times (Bem 1975; Vonk and Ashmore 1993).

ANDROGYNY. Do you think the quality of having in one person the characteristics, as culturally defined, of both males and females can make one a more flexible person? *Left:* Jacquie Frazier and Laila Ali met June 2001 in a worldwide pay-per-view professional match in which Ali prevailed. Both are daughters of famous male boxers, Joe Frazier and Muhammad Ali, respectively. *Right:* Certainly men are known to cry, though usually not to the extent that women permit themselves. Do you see anything inappropriate about these photos? ▲

Postgender Transcendence: Beyond Gender

Some male-female couples have abandoned notions that gender is destiny—that, for example, being a breadwinner is the definition of male success and that being good at home and hearth is the definition of female success (Risman and Johnson-Sumerford 1998). In these couples, both partners have careers, both do the nurturing in the relationship, and both reject gender as an ideological justification for inequality. In other words, their relationship can be characterized as postgender—beyond gender. As one sociologist writes, compared to 150 years ago, "women are well on the way to becoming men's equals. Now, few say that gender equality is impossible or undesirable" (Jackson 1998: 95). Even so, a great barrier to achieving autonomy and equality at both home and work is, as sociologist Kathleen Gerson (2001) points out, effective social, institutional, or political solutions, whether employers or government, that can help people resolve these dilemmas.

What Do You Want?

What kind of role do you see for yourself in a relationship? In an egalitarian relationship, both partners pursue careers but also take care of the house and any children—on an equal basis. Not only do the different kinds of work get shared equally, but each partner is able to empathize with the other's experience. On the other hand, as a man, you would lose power in the relationship and have less time to devote to your career compared to men in traditional marriages. And as a woman, you would find yourself engaging with children less closely and having to make the necessary compromises that come with pursuing a career.

The accompanying table shows how the topic of gender is viewed from three principal theoretical perspectives: structural-functional, conflict, and symbolic interaction. *(See ■ Panel 3.2.)*

STRUCTURAL-FUNCTIONAL (MACRO ORIENTATION)	CONFLICT (MACRO ORIENTATION)	SYMBOLIC INTERACTION (MICRO ORIENTATION)
■ Clearly defined gender roles for men (instrumental/breadwinner) and for women (expressive/child care and homemaker) create stability for society.	■ Gender roles are no longer clearly defined or fully accepted.	■ The meanings attached to gender roles are socially constructed through day-to-day social interactions.
■ There is consensus and agreement about the clearly defined roles.	■ Social forces (such as the need for education beyond high school, the increased cost of living, and the necessity for dual-income families) work to influence gender redefinition through the competition for and redistribution of scarce resources.	■ Early patterns of socialization with significant others establish expectations that influence adult gender roles.
■ Gender roles are reinforced through social institutions such as religion and media.	■ Rigidly defined gender roles are viewed as limiting potential for both men and women.	■ People develop their own definitions of masculinity and femininity, and these social constructions affect one's perceptions.
■ Blending of roles or adoption of opposite gender roles are met with strong social sanctions to maintain the status quo.	■ Women are victimized as a result of rigidly defined roles and this is reflected in lower incomes and fewer women in leadership positions. This victimization results from societal definitions that keep women "in their place" and includes definitions of what constitutes rape and domestic violence. The roles are reinforced through the media, as in popular song lyrics.	■ Ideas as to what are considered desirable, beautiful, and handsome change over time and affect choice of partners.

Self-Assessment: What's Your Gender Communications Quotient?

How much do you know about how men and women communicate with one another? The 15 items in this questionnaire are based on research conducted in classrooms, private homes, businesses, offices, hospitals—the places where people commonly work and socialize. The answers are at the end of this quiz.

	True	False
1. Men talk more than women do.	____	____
2. Men are more likely to interrupt women than they are to interrupt other men.	____	____
3. There are approximately 10 times as many sexual terms for males as for females in the English language.	____	____
4. During conversations, women spend more time gazing at their partner than men do.	____	____
5. Nonverbal messages carry more weight than do verbal messages.	____	____
6. Female managers communicate with more emotional openness and drama than male managers do.	____	____
7. Men not only control the content of conversations, but they also work harder in keeping conversations going.	____	____
8. When people hear generic words such as "mankind" and "he," they respond inclusively, indicating that the terms apply to both sexes.	____	____
9. Women are more likely to touch others than men are.	____	____
10. In classroom communications, male students receive more reprimands and criticism than are female students.	____	____
11. Women are more likely than are men to disclose information on intimate personal concerns.	____	____
12. Female speakers are more animated in their conversational style than are male speakers.	____	____
13. Women use less personal space than men do.	____	____
14. When a male speaks, he is listened to more carefully than is a female speaker, even when she makes the identical presentation.	____	____
15. In general, women speak in a more tentative style than do men.	____	____

Answers: 1. T; 2. T; 3. F; 4. T; 5. T; 6–9. F; 10–15. T

Source: Hazel R. Rozema, Ph.D., University of Illinois at Springfield, and John W. Gray, Ph.D., Emeritus, University of Arkansas at Little Rock. Used by permission.

Key Terms Used in This Chapter

androgyny, p. 112
cognitive development theory, p. 98
cross-dresser, p. 92
feminism, p. 110
gender, p. 91
gender identity, p. 92
gender role, p. 91
gender schema theory, p. 98
gender stereotype, p. 98
gender variance, p. 92

hermaphrodite, p. 94
hormones, p. 97
intersexual, p. 94
matriarchal, p. 95
modeling, p. 97
patriarchal, p. 95
patriarchy, p. 111
peer, p. 101
role, p. 91
role conflict, p. 112

sex, p. 90
sex role, p. 92
sexism, p. 95
sexual harassment, p. 95
social learning theory, p. 97
socialization, p. 92
sociobiology, p. 97
transgenderist, p. 94
transsexual, p. 93
transvestite, p. 92

Summary

3.1 Understanding Gender & Gender Roles

- To talk about gender, you must first learn the correct vocabulary. *Sex* refers to the biological characteristics with which we were born that determine whether we are male or female. *Gender* refers to the socially learned attitudes and behaviors associated with being male or female.

- You should also understand distinctions between a *role*, which is the behavior expected of someone who holds a particular status; a *gender role*, which is the behavior expected of a female or male in a particular culture; and a *sex role*, which is behavior defined by biological constraints. We learn gender roles through socialization, the process by which people learn the characteristics of their group—the attitudes, values, and actions that are thought appropriate for them. This learning creates people's gender identity, a person's psychological sense of whether he or she is male or female.

- Some people take on aspects of the roles of the other gender. Examples are cross-dressers, members of one sex or gender who dress in clothes in the appearance of the other gender, and transvestites, who are people, usually male, who dress provocatively in order to appeal to men.

- A more complicated question of gender identity arises with a transsexual, a person with the biological sex of one gender who has the identity of the other gender and undergoes medical procedures to change to that gender. Another example is the transgenderist, a person with the biological sex of one gender who has the identity of the other gender, lives the full-time life of that gender, but does not undergo medical procedures to change to that gender. A hermaphrodite (intersexual) is a person who has both male and female sexual organs or organs that are not distinct.

- The vocabulary of gender leads to the vocabulary of sexism. Most societies are patriarchal, meaning that they are male dominated, male identified, and male centered. Matriarchal means female dominated, female identified, and female centered.

- Sexism is the belief that one sex is innately superior to the other. Sexual harassment is the abuse of one's position of authority to force unwanted sexual attention on someone.

3.2 Why Do Gender Roles Differ? Some Theories

- Several theories have been advanced to explain gender differences, and we considered four of them.

- Sociobiology suggests that our social behavior—and gender behavior—results from biological differences. For example, hormones—the chemical substances secreted into the bloodstream by the endocrine glands—differ, men usually having more testosterone and women more estrogen and progesterone. These hormones and the sex chromosomes underlying them produce different physical characteristics.

- Social learning theory suggests that we learn attitudes and behaviors through our interaction with the environment. Learning is said to occur in two ways. The first is learning by reinforcement—desirable behavior is rewarded and undesirable behavior is punished. The second is learning through imitation, which is called *modeling*.

- Blending biological and cognitive perspectives, cognitive development theory suggests that when we are children, our biological readiness in terms of our cognitive development—our thinking, understanding, and reasoning processes—influences how we respond to cues in the environment about gender differences. Two proponents of learning theory are Jean Piaget and Lawrence Kohlberg.

- Some of cognitive development theory has been incorporated into gender schema theory, which suggests that as children we develop a framework of knowledge—a gender schema—about what we think males and females typically do, and we then use that framework to interpret new information about gender. Cultural expectations can lead to gender stereotypes, the beliefs that men and women each display traditional gender-role characteristics.

3.2 Gender Socialization: Who Teaches Us How to Act Male or Female?

- Sociobiology stresses that gender differences are based on biology. However, the other three theories suggest that we learn gender behavior mainly from our environment. Besides the popular culture and mass media, four other influences were described.

- We are influenced by our parents, with fathers and mothers socializing their children differently according to what their own gender is. Four ways in which parents socialize their children are (1) by using different physical and verbal manipulations, (2) by directing attention toward certain stereotypical gender-identified objects, (3) by applying different verbal descriptions to the same behavior, and (4) by encouraging or discouraging certain stereotypical gender-identified activities. How you feel about gender matters also may vary according to your social-class, ethnic, and religious background.

- We are influenced by our peers, or those of equal status in age, class, and the like. Play and entertainment are often divided by gender.
- We are influenced by our teachers, who may subtly influence how boys and girls are more different than they are similar.
- We are influenced by the world of work, observing which occupations are dominated by males and which by females.

3.4 Gender Roles in Transition: Multiple Masculinities & Femininities

- Traditional gender roles have some benefits. The central feature of the traditional male role is instrumental—the focus is on work identity—which leads to higher income and other job-related advantages and less domestic work and marital stress.
- The central feature of the traditional female role is expressive—the focus is on expressing tender feelings and being concerned with others' needs. The benefits are that women's identity is tied to relationships rather than work and that they are able to develop closer attachments with their children.
- There are also drawbacks to traditional gender roles. For males, the drawbacks are that their personal self-worth is tied to job position and income; they suffer job-related stress; they have less time for family life; they are permitted only limited emotional expression, which results in loneliness and fear of intimacy; and there are limitations on their having child custody in the event of divorce.
- For females, the drawbacks of the traditional gender roles are that they have reduced income and career

fulfillment; they are dependent on their spouses, which can result in unhappiness; they are valued too much by standards of attractiveness; and they feel less personal self-worth.

- Gender roles are changing as a result of the influence of the women's movement and the men's movement. The women's movement reflected feminism, the view that women should have the same economic, social, and political rights as men. However, feminism has several branches. Liberal feminism ("equal rights" feminism) is principally concerned with achieving equal opportunities for women through legal and social reforms; it assumes that the cause of women's inequality is sexism. Radical feminism considers patriarchy—social arrangements whereby positions of power and authority are mostly held by men—to be the cause of female inequality. Socialist feminism, which is rooted in classical Marxism, maintains that the sexual division of labor is an expression of class conflict. Lesbian feminism focuses on the dominance of heterosexuality as a "compulsory" expression of patriarchy.
- The men's movement has its own divisions. Profeminists, the liberal branch, believe that a system of patriarchy forces all males into restrictive roles. Antifeminists, the conservative branch, believe that male dominance is natural. Masculinists agree the patriarchal system causes oppression but are concerned about males achieving self-realization.
- Trying to achieve a new gender role can lead to role conflict, the anxiety and confusion that occur when the expectations of two or more roles are incompatible. Some flexibility may be offered by androgyny, the quality of having in one person the cultural defined characteristics, of both males and females. Some male-female couples have abandoned the notion that gender is destiny—they are striving for postgender transcendence.

Take It to the Net

Among the Internet resources on gender are the following:

- **Eagle Forum.** Conservative women's issues.
  www.eagleforum.org
- **The Feminist Majority Foundation Online.** A liberal women's group.
  www.feminist.org
- **International Labour Organization.** Issues of gender equality in the workplace.
  www.ilo.org/public/english/bureau/gender

- **The Men's Bibliography.** Introduction to material on men.
  http://mensbiblio.xyonline.net
- **Men's Issues—Home Page.**
  http://home.vicnet.net.au/~mensissu
- **National Organization for Women (NOW).** A liberal women's organization.
  www.now.org
- **Women's Resources on the NET.**
  http://www.wic.org/misc/resource.htm

CHAPTER 4

LOVE

The Many Faces

What Is This Thing Called Love?

What is love—really?

Consider Debbie and Chris, who have been a couple for 10 years. When Chris first laid eyes on Debbie, "I thought, my God, that's the most beautiful woman I've ever seen," he said later. Today they live in Massachusetts with their young daughter.

An ordinary couple? Not quite. Debbie is a lesbian, with no interest in men.

The woman she fell in love with, born Christina, is a transgendered person, who always felt she was a man trapped in a woman's body. After a few years (following Debbie's pregnancy by an anonymous sperm donor), Chris began exploring having surgical and hormonal gender reassignment—from female to male—a move Debbie at first resisted.

Debbie said her decision to stay with Chris "was a total leap of faith." She added, "just realizing I had to be with her—with him, this person—was a big turning point. I needed to at least give it a try."

Said Chris: "I challenge anyone to look at their partner and think about what it would be like if he were a she, or she was a he. It's an enormous thing to even consider" (Corbett 2001).

This indeed raises an interesting question: Would you still love your lover if he or she changed gender?

But there's more to this story than its unusual partners. Underlying it are some assumptions about love that are reinforced by the popular culture and the mass media for more conventional relationships: Love at first sight. One true love. Love is blind. Love conquers all. All these are expressions of what's known as "romantic love."

◉ WHAT'S AHEAD IN THIS CHAPTER

In this chapter, we consider the concept of soul mate and different definitions of love—particularly romantic love and companionate love. We describe five theories of love: biochemical, attachment, wheel, triangular, and love styles. We also look at what happens when love goes awry—jealousy, unrequited love, and attempts to control.

Romantic love is, of course, the premise of many movies, songs, television programs, books, and, of course, Valentine's Day cards:

■ *Films:* Ain't love grand? This is the theme expressed in numerous celluloid romances—from *Crazy Love* (2007) and *A Lot Like Love* (2005) all the way back through *Love and Basketball* (2000), *Love Jones* (1997), *Love with a Perfect Stranger* (1988), *Love Story* (1970), *Love in the Afternoon* (1957), to *Love Affair* (1939).

Love is also the main topic of relatively recent films such as *Save the Last Dance, Something New, Someone Like You, Sweet November, She's All That, Serendipity, Sweet Home Alabama*—and probably several other titles beginning with "S."

■ *Popular songs:* Love and romance are frequent themes in contemporary music, from hip-hop to country and western: "I Do Cherish You" by Mark Wills, "I Melt" by Rascal Flatts, "I Swear" by John Michael Montgomery, "It's Your Love" by Tim McGraw and Faith Hill, "It's Your Song" by Garth Brooks, "Love You More" by Genuine, and "You're Still the One" by Shania Twain express both the emotional highs as well as the emotional lows of love.

■ *Television:* TV sitcoms wouldn't be able to keep viewers interested for long in weekly portrayals of the dramatic and painful ups and downs of a real love relationship, but so-called reality shows do focus on the roller coaster of love and the drive to find a partner—for example, *Blind Date*, (which debuted in 1999), *The Bachelor* (2002), *The Bachelorette* (2003), and *Who Wants to Marry My Dad?* (2004). Romance also develops in such TV shows as *Sex and the City* (1998), *The O.C.* (2003), and *Grey's Anatomy* (2005).

■ *Books:* Would you buy *A Relationship for a Lifetime: Everything You Need to Know to Create a Love That Lasts*? What about *Love Tune-Ups: 52 Fun Ways to Open Your Heart & Make Sparks Fly*? Or perhaps *The Seven Stories of Love: And How to Choose Your Happy Ending*. These are just three of a never-ending stream of books on the subject of romantic love.

For modern Americans, says anthropologist Charles Lindholm (2002), "romantic love is the highest attainment: We celebrate it in song, our poets and novelists chronicle its pains and pleasures, our movies present love stories that ordinary people attempt to emulate. . . . It 'makes the world go 'round.' It is seen as an essential human need."

Let us examine the workings of love.

What is love, and what are its two principal forms?

What are the five principal theories on the origins of love?

What are three ways in which love can go awry?

What distinguishes immature love from mature love?

4.1 Can We Define Love?

MAJOR QUESTION What is love, and what are its two principal forms?

PREVIEW Love is intimacy with, caring for, and commitment to another person. Many people think love is about finding a soul mate—a best friend, confidant, and romantic partner. In other times, places, and cultures, marriages have been made not on the basis of romantic love—intense, passionate love—but according to other customs, such as arranged marriages. Romantic love, which may spring out of sexual desire, can later turn to companionate love, which emphasizes intimacy with, affection for, and commitment to another person.

The lengths to which people will go for love never cease to surprise.

Consider this multicultural case: Sean Blackwell, age 27, was a sergeant in the Florida National Guard who had been serving in Iraq since April 2003. On August 17 of that year, with Corporal Brett Dagan, age 37, another Florida guardsman, Blackwell participated in a double ceremony in Baghdad in which the soldiers married two Iraqi women (both physicians). Both men were Christians who converted to Islam before they married.

For this triumph of love over culture and religion, Blackwell was given a written reprimand and, narrowly avoiding a court martial, was discharged from the army for dereliction of duty and disobeying orders. The reason: He had taken a break from a foot patrol to marry the woman and had divulged the time and location of the patrol to his future bride and to the Iraqi judge who presided over the ceremony (Associated Press 2003).

Is Love All about Finding a Soul Mate?

When you think about love, what you may well think about—especially if you are in your twenties—is the idea of a *soul mate*, the companion of your dreams. **A *soul mate* is a person who is temperamentally suited to another—one's best friend, confidant, and romantic partner.** According to

- **Is passionate love a worldwide phenomenon?** Evidence of passionate love has been found in 89% of 166 societies studied.[a]

- **When does romantic love die?** Six to 30 months into a relationship, romantic love tends to yield to a less passionate form of love known as companionate love.[b]

- **Does jealousy happen more in some cultures than others?** Cultures that value individual property rights, such as the United States, tend to engender more jealousy.[c] Sexually liberal countries such as Germany and the Netherlands experience less jealousy.[d]

- **How often do people love without being loved in return?** About 75% of respondents in one survey said they had not had their love returned, and about 20% said they were currently experiencing unrequited (unreturned) love.[e]

- **Are only men stalkers?** Most victims of stalking—repeated pursuit and frequent harassment, often by a rejected lover—are women. One in 12 women has been stalked at some point in her life, and the majority of stalking cases involve men. Still, one out of 45 men has been stalked at some time as well.[f]

[a]Jankowiak and Fischer 1992. [b]Hyde 1986. [c]Hupka et al. 1985. [d]Buunk et al. 1996. [e]Aron et al. 1998. [f]Tjaden and Thoennes 1998.

NUMBERS THAT MATTER
Love Bites

an online survey conducted by the religious website Beliefnet (cited in Rossi 2006), 61% of women and 50% of men believe there is one perfect soul mate out there for everyone. In another survey, 94% of never-marrieds from ages 20 to 29 agreed with the statement "When you marry, you want your spouse to be your soul mate first and foremost" (National Marriage Project, cited in Watters 2001: 25).

Is this what love is really all about—finding a soul mate?

Love Actually

Look up the word *love* in the glossary of a marriage and family textbook. The chances are that you won't find it. Is this because love is so overarching as to defy definition? After all, love can be many things—or even "a many-splendored thing," as an old song goes. For example, it can be passionate love—intense, exciting, and all-consuming. Or it can be companionate love—comfortable, calm, and reassuring. It can vary depending on whether it is directed toward, or shared with, lovers, family, or friends. We would try to define it as follows: **_Love_ is intimacy with, caring for, and commitment to another person.** It arises from need satisfaction, sexual attraction, and/or personal or kinship ties.

In one study of 184 college students (Knox et al. 1999a), 94% said they had been in love, and over one-third (36%) reported three or more love relationships. Younger students (those age 19 and under) were apt to believe in "love at first sight," with over half subscribing to this belief as opposed to a third of older students. Nearly two-thirds of younger students were also apt to agree that "love conquers all," compared with 43% of older students. The study found that men and women were more similar than different in their beliefs about love.

We explore this present-day concept further later in the chapter, but first let's take a look at how other cultures consider love.

Love in Other Times & Places

Love has had, and still has, various meanings and forms of expression in other times, places, and cultures. And passionate love has not always been considered a sound basis for marriage. Consider the following:

■ **Ancient Greece and Rome:** The ancient Greeks, and the Romans who followed them, viewed passionate love "as a kind of dangerous illness," says anthropologist Lindholm (2002). "It could tear respectable young people away from their families and draw them into disadvantageous affairs with inappropriate mates; it could make adults act like fools. Such passions had to be rigorously guarded against."

Passionate love was sexual love, or *eros*. More important to the Greeks were altruistic love (*agape*) and friendship love (*phileo*). Because Greek social organization was based on patriarchal (patrilineal) descent—a system by which men could make claims to property or assert leadership and by which women could rely on protection and honor—marriage based on passion was viewed as being too unreliable. Therefore, marriages were **arranged marriages, with partners determined not by the bride and the groom themselves but by their families.** "Marriage arrangements," says Lindholm, "were negotiated by elders, with an eye to advancing the interests of the clan."

If passion was removed from the marriage bed, men directed it elsewhere—to women who were slaves or courtesans in the business of providing pleasure and often to young men, both slaves and free men. Sex outside marriage preserved the stability of the family, although it could be disastrous when lust turned to love—for example, when a man sacrificed his honor for the sake of a pursuing a prostitute. (Wives of the propertied classes generally channeled their passions by lavishing attention on their sons.)

■ **Europe in the Middle Ages and Renaissance:** The Greek and Roman attitudes about love—and about marriage as a business and social arrangement—influenced Europe in the Middle Ages. Because land and wealth were controlled by kings—occasionally by queens or by other aristocrats—great care was taken to make sure marriages would produce strong alliances of wealth and power. Therefore, kings and princes took their marriage partners from the prominent royal families of other European countries, and merchants and other propertied men "sold" their daughters in arranged marriages to men who paid a bride price.

Between the 7th and the 12th centuries, however, the Roman Catholic church promoted marriage as "a sacrament, administered by the prospective spouses through individual consent" (Goody 1983: 7, in Edlund and Lagerlöf 2002). Then, during the 12th century, there emerged the notion of "courtly love"—a preoccupation with and longing for union with a beloved. This idea of passionate love led to a great deal of art and literature that celebrated the adoration of physical and spiritual beauty, as between a knight or a shepherd and his beloved. Courtly love is what we now call **romantic love, an emotionally intense, passionate love in which a person believes that there is love at first sight, that there is only one true love, and that love conquers all.** Later, as the revolutions of the 17th and 18th centuries reduced the power of the European aristocracy and the consequent importance of marriage as a political arrangement, romantic love became the preferred basis for binding men and women together for marriage.

■ **Other Countries Today—Arranged Marriages:** Many countries in parts of Asia, Africa, and the Middle East and in some parts of Eastern Europe practice arranged marriage. *(See* ■ *Panel 4.1.)* Such marriages, in which young people are introduced to their prospective mates in a 15-minute meeting or even through just a photo and a phone conversation, operate on the assumption that marriage is primarily an economic union and a means to having children.

In India, although women in the middle and upper classes are free to marry whomever they choose, many have their marriages arranged by their parents because they believe that arranged marriages are more stable than love-based marriages. Love? It evolves, supposedly. "All my family members had arranged marriages, no complaints," says one Indian woman, Geeta Rani (quoted in Jones 2006). "They are very happy. You fall in love and get married, or you get married and fall in love."

For centuries, China had a history of arranged marriages. After the communist revolution in 1949, however, people were encouraged to choose their own marriage partners—but with the permission of their bosses. In 2003, the Chinese government loosened marriage requirements, although arranged marriages are often still the norm. In Japan, arranged marriages were common until recently.

■ **PANEL 4.1 Countries in Which Arranged Marriage Is Common.** The practice has diminished in China, Japan, and South Korea.

Afghanistan
Bangladesh
India
Indonesia
Iran
Iraq
Nepal
Nigeria
Pakistan
Somalia
Sri Lanka
Sudan

Romantic Love & Companionate Love

Arranged marriages have not been a prominent feature of marital unions in America, although in the 18th and 19th centuries, parents had much more involvement in decisions about their children's future spouses. This kind of control may still exist to some extent among American upper-class families, in which wealth and social status are at stake and parents are in a position to deny a child a considerable inheritance (Goode 1982). However, with the expansion in individual economic opportunity, middle-class children became less dependent on their parents, and choosing a marriage partner shifted from having an economic basis to having an emotional one (Murstein 1986; Mintz and Kellogg 1988).

But emotional or romantic love is not confined to the United States and Western culture. Two anthropologists found evidence of passionate love in 147 of 166 societies they studied. They concluded that romantic love is "a human, universal, or at the least a near-universal phenomenon" (Jankowiak and Fisher 1992: 154). Other accounts (Jones 2006) suggest love marriages are superceding arranged marriages in parts of India, China, and Japan.

Romantic Love: More Than Lust?

Romantic or passionate love is represented by the frenzied, head-over-heels state of attraction portrayed in Hollywood movies and known as "falling in love"—or is it really "falling in lust"? Lust is *sexual arousal*, the physical state of getting "turned on." Lust is distinguished from *sexual desire*, which is a *psychological state*. Sexual desire is defined as wanting to obtain a sexual object to engage in sexual activity not previously available (Regan and Berscheid 1999: 17). Sexual desire, it is hypothesized, is the essential ingredient of romantic or passionate love.

BY ARRANGEMENT. A Japanese bride and groom (front row center) pose for wedding pictures with family and friends at Meiji Park, Tokyo. The men wear western clothing, while the women are dressed in kimonos and traditional costumes. Most marriages today in Japan are love marriages, like those in North America—a couple meets independently, without benefit of an "arranger" or matchmaker. However, 25% to 30% of Japanese unions are still arranged marriages. The woman's parents prepare an information packet about her and inquire among friends and acquaintances if they know of a suitable candidate for a husband. The packet is passed to a potential male, who, if interested, provides a packet about himself. A meeting is arranged for the couple and their families, which takes place at a restaurant or hotel. If the man and woman are interested, they then begin dating, with a view toward possibly, but not inevitably, getting married. Interestingly, the divorce rate for arranged marriages is lower in Japan than it is for love marriages. Why do you think this is? ▲

Companionate Love: Intimacy, Affection, & Commitment

The white-hot feelings of romantic or passionate love cannot last. Between 6 and 30 months into a relationship, companionate love begins to become the more dominant emotion (Hyde 1986). ***Companionate love*, calmer than romantic love, emphasizes intimacy with, affection for, and commitment to another person.** Of course, companionate love also is present during the romantic/passionate stage. And some passionate love, although reduced in intensity, can still be present during the later stages of a relationship (Tucker and Aron 1993).

With companionate love, lovers notice each other's imperfections. They also experience annoyances, boredom, and disappointment ("Is this all there is?"). They may even consider ending the relationship ("I might still find my real soul mate"). But they are also building the reality-based stability and friendship necessary for meaningful, lasting love.

Friendship & Love

Can you distinguish between liking and loving somebody? Is it necessary to be friends before you become lovers with someone? ***Friendship* is defined as an attachment between people. It is the basis for a strong love relationship.** Still, there are differences between friends and lovers.

The kiss is what the ancient Greek poet Ovid romanticized as "the blossom of love." But just how good are most people at kissing?

"Recent sex surveys indicate that modern lovers believe kissing is one of the most essential aspects of a relationship," says Michael Christian (quoted in Peterson 2002: 1D), who wrote *The Art of Kissing* under the pen name William Crane, "yet men and women are increasingly reporting that there is not enough kissing in their love lives."

Writers Laurence Roy Stains and Stefan Bechtal (quoted in Peterson 2002: 2D) did a national survey of 2,102 women for their book *What Women Want: What Every Man Needs to Know*. "All women said that guys—especially married guys—don't kiss them enough," they say. "One of the major differences between men and women is that women like kissing more and find it more intimate than intercourse," Stains says. "I wouldn't say guys don't find kissing intimate. But they look on kissing as a step to something else"—that is, sexual intercourse.

Cherie Byrd (2005), who founded The Kissing School in Seattle, suggests that the biggest mistake people make in kissing is "not being present" (Byrd, quoted in Wilson 2005). The good male kisser, says writer Lynn Snowden (1995), "sees the kiss as the destination itself. He kisses as if he will never do anything else with this woman." Because women are turned off by overpowering kisses, she advises, "The first thing to remember: When in Doubt Go Slowly. Make that first kiss slow and gentle and easy. . . . The second thing to remember while kissing is to make sure she can still breathe through her nose."

Snowden also suggests that men need to avoid dry, repeated kisses accompanied by loud smacky sounds. As for French kisses, which involve the tongue, men should avoid the tongue-rapidly-inserted-in-and-out kiss and the thorough tongue exploration of a woman's mouth. "Any tongue action should involve a give-and-take," she writes, "with both parties allowed the opportunity for interaction." French kisses should not be done on the first date.

Many of these same suggestions, of course, apply to women. A turnoff for both sexes is bad breath, as from smoking. Men are also turned off by too much lipstick. People who wear glasses should take them off before kissing. If one person wears braces, the other should avoid pressing too hard against the lips.

WHAT DO YOU THINK? Did you learn anything you didn't know? Is it possible to have a romantic relationship without much kissing?

EXAMPLE OF

An Expression of Romantic Love

The Kiss

Among other characteristics, friends enjoy each other's company, are willing to support and help each other, share feelings and experiences, and feel free to be themselves rather than something they are not (Davis and Todd 1985). Although love relationships are based on friendship, there is more: love involves emotional highs and lows, instability, passion, exclusiveness, and sexual desire—all qualities that are unstable.

Love on the Internet: Can You Find the Perfect Partner Online?

Match.com, eHarmony, American Singles, and nearly 1,000 other online dating sites are now a $700 million business (Stone 2007). Internet users are also meeting people through social networks such as Facebook, Friendster, and MySpace. Some use search engines such as Yahoo! and Google to research particular names for specific results (Heslin 2005).

But how effective is the Internet as a means of finding the perfect mate? Many Internet users—44% according to one Pew Research Center survey—say that online dating is a "good way to meet people," although 44% also disagree (Madden and Lenhart 2006). On the other hand, "When it comes to the search for lasting love," says another report, "psychologists are finding that chat rooms, message boards, and especially online dating services may have built-in mechanisms that make any offscreen romance very likely to fail" (Cohen 2001).

Although some happily married couples have found their mates online, there are reasons why online connections have their risks:

- **People lie online:** Women lie by subtracting years from their ages and pounds from their weights. Men lie by adding inches to their heights and dollars to their incomes (Hitsch et al. 2005; Vitzthum 2007).

- **Online sites stress superficialities:** The most important variable people look for in online dating sites is looks—hence the importance of posting a photo. Women who post photos receive about twice as many email messages as those who do not. Men who say they are "hoping to start a long-term relationship" receive much more email than those who are "just looking" or, worse, "seeking a casual relationship" (Hitsch et al. 2005). Other superficial attributes are income level and hair color.

- **Online life and real life aren't the same:** Psychologists say there is little similarity between "disembodied email consciousness" and a real-life encounter (Cohen 2001). Feelings can bloom quickly in an online relationship, leading people to have idealized expectations. But it's impossible to say whether two people who get along well online will get along in the real world.

- **Our culture of infinite choice makes people avoid "settling":** Comparing online dating to use of an iPod, Laura Vanderkam (2006) speculates that, just as your iPod allows you to have any song imaginable, customize the playlist any way you want, and skip to the next song whenever you feel like it, dating sites similarly give you infinite choices from 40 million singles, enable you to specify the "must-have" qualities you want to see in a mate, and allow you to keep your options open rather than "settle" on someone. Along this line, San Diego State University psychology professor Jean Twenge (2006) suggests that the amount of narcissism—"it's all about me"—has substantially increased among college students between 1982 and 2006, as measured by a jump in scores on the Narcissistic Personality Inventory. Narcissists tend to favor short-term relationships over close ones.

Still, the Internet does allow the *possibility* that a couple may develop real rather than false intimacy. "In real life," says psychologist Storm King (quoted in Cohen 2001: D9), "you don't talk to strangers. Online, you are encouraged to talk to strangers. The Internet lets people have relationships they could not have any other way."

We return to a discussion of online connections in Chapter 5, "Involvement."

Same-Sex Love

Although same-sex couples experience love with the same intimacy and intensity as any heterosexual couple, gays and lesbians often feel compelled to hide their true feelings because of perceptions of public disapproval of homosexual relationships. Basically, however, the ways men and women express love as genders are more different than are relationships between heterosexual and homosexual couples. One difference is that lesbian relationships tend to be more enduring and stable than gay relationships (Loewenstein 1985).

SLOW IS BETTER. How well, in general, do you think men kiss? How well do you kiss? ▲

4.2 The Origins of Love: Some Theories

MAJOR QUESTION What are the five principal theories on the origins of love?

PREVIEW Five theories to explain the origins of love are (1) biochemical theory, (2) attachment theory, (3) wheel theory, (4) triangular theory, and (5) styles of love. We also describe the importance of intimacy.

Does love have a reason, a purpose? Why do we like or love some people more than others? Here we consider five theories of love.

1. Biochemical Theory: "Love Is a Natural High"

When you think about "the chemistry of love," the following is probably not what you had in mind.

In a recent study, T-shirts worn by men for two consecutive days were placed in boxes. Forty-nine unmarried women were then asked to sniff the boxes and tell which T-shirt they preferred "if they had to smell it all the time." The results: Women were found to be attracted to the smell of a man who was genetically similar—but not too similar—to their fathers (Jacob et al. 2002). The study's authors believe that there's an evolutionary explanation for this. "Mating with someone too similar might lead to inbreeding," said Martha McClintock (quoted in Gupta 2002). Mating with someone too different "leads to the loss of desirable gene combinations."

The *biochemical theory* of love suggests that love results from our biological, chemical, and hormonal origins. Romantic attachments, biologists suggest, are nature's or evolution's way of bringing males and females together for the purpose of reproduction and child rearing. It's noteworthy, incidentally, that the same region of the brain (the caudate nucleus) is activated both for feelings of trust and for feelings of love (Bartels and Zeki 2000; King-Casas et al. 2005).

Today, the "natural high" of being newly in love—the feeling of being swept away—is as powerful a stimulant as amphetamines and cocaine, researchers assert (Walsh 1991; Fisher 1992). This is because, they contend, the brains of passionate lovers release a substance into the bloodstream called PEA (phenylethylamine), a natural amphetamine, or stimulant. Others believe the relevant substances are dopamine and norepinephrine (Fisher 2004; Flora 2004). This is why being engaged in passionate love is to feel such tremendous exhilaration and energy: Our bodies are awash in chemicals.

As with any stimulant, however, the feelings of euphoria resulting from these chemicals do not last, and as tolerance builds up, more and more PEA is needed to produce the same effect. Thus, some "love-addicted" people may well go from one passionate relationship to another to repeat the exhilaration (Peele and Brodsky 1976).

As evidence to support biochemical theory, Rutgers University anthropologist Helen Fisher (2004), who has conducted brain studies on love, has found that antidepressants may blunt emotions. Antidepressants "can jeopardize your feelings," she says. "You are tampering with the mechanisms that can help sustain feelings of romantic love and deep feelings of attachment" (Davis, quoted in Parker-Pope 2006).

Research has also shown that women looking for a long-term relationship like men who like children, and they can tell which males might be interested in becoming fathers just by looking at their faces and figuring out which of them have the highest testosterone levels (Roney et al. 2006). The evolutionary explanation is that women are apparently programmed to recognize men who might be interested in propagating the species by raising a family. "What this study illustrates," says neuroscientist Daniel Alkon (quoted in Babwin 2006), "is that there are genetic programs that increase survival of the species because there are hormones in women that are cuing their reactions to the hormones of the men." It's not clear, however, exactly what about the men's visages tipped off the women about their interest in children, whether the expressions on the men's faces or perhaps a rounded or gentler face.

Critics say that biochemistry alone cannot produce feelings of love, that a sociological-psychological component is also important. This brings us to the other four theories.

2. Attachment Theory: "Closeness Is a Survival Need"

The *attachment theory* of love suggests that our primary motivation in life "is to be connected with other people—because it is the only security we ever have. Maintaining closeness is a [genuine] survival need" (Johnson and Marano 1994: 34).

Attachment theory grows out of observations about infants' emotional attachments to their caretakers. "All important love relationships—especially the first ones with parents and later ones with lovers and spouses—are attachments," say one set of writers (Shaver and Hazan 1988). Studies by Mary Ainsworth and colleagues (1978) suggested that infants have three styles of attachment: *secure, avoidant,* and *anxious/ambivalent.* Other researchers (Hazan and Shaver 1987; Shaver and Hazan 1988; Brennan and Shaver 1995) found that these styles are reflected in adult love.

Secure

Secure adults find it not difficult to become friendly or intimate with others. They don't resist being dependent on others or having others depend on them, and they often don't worry about being either neglected (or abandoned) or being emotionally crowded by another person.

Avoidant

Avoidant adults are uneasy with being close to other people and with trusting and being dependent on them. They are nervous when others become too friendly or intimate, and their lovers often want more intimacy than they do.

Anxious/Ambivalent

These adults feel that others aren't as intimate as they would like. They are anxious that their partners don't really love them or that they won't stay. They want more close connection with their lovers, which sometimes has the opposite effect and scares them away.

For secure adults, relationships lasted an average of 10 years; for avoidant adults, 6 years; and for anxious/ambivalent adults, 5 years. Critics say that the studies on which attachment theory is based suffered from flaws in methodology, using samples that were too small, were not random enough, and involved dysfunctional families.

More recently, research has found that uneven attachment needs are common—that the idea of feeling "too close" varies not only with the individual but also with the couple (Mashek and Aron 2004; Aron et al. 2005). "The basic issue about being too close is being closer than you're comfortable with," says psychology professor Arthur Aron (quoted in Jayson 2006). "For some people, even slightly close is too much, and for other people being enormously close is great." Although in some cases dependent urges can undermine a relationship because of its annoying clinginess, they can also cement romantic relationships in times of stress (Bornstein and Languirand 2003. Carey 2007).

3. Wheel Theory: The Four Stages of Love

The *wheel theory* **of love suggests that love develops and is maintained through four stages: (1) rapport, (2) self-revelation, (3) mutual dependency, and (4) intimacy need fulfillment.** The wheel theory, which was proposed by sociologist **Ira Reiss** (1960; Reiss and Lee 1988), is represented in the accompanying illustration. *(See ■ Panel 4.2.)* Like a rolling wheel, these stages may be repeated many times, producing a deepening relationship, or the wheel may stop, as in a short relationship.

Let us consider the four stages.

Stage 1: Rapport—Feeling at Ease

When you first meet someone, you may quickly establish *rapport*, the feeling of ease that makes you comfortable with each other. Feelings of rapport are enhanced by similarities in social, cultural, and educational background and upbringing. Generally, we are able to communicate better and are more at ease with people of similar background and experience, who share our ideas about what constitutes appropriate social roles for men and women.

What about the notion that opposites attract? It's suggested that some people with different—but complementary—personalities are attracted to each other (Winch et al. 1954). Also, as with the Florida National Guardsmen marrying Iraqi women, described at the beginning of this chapter, people from all kinds of ethnic, racial, religious, age, and socioeconomic groups fall in love with each other. Even so, some researchers believe that for such basic differences to be overcome, a couple must share similar social values (Murstein 1971).

Stage 2: Self-Revelation—Disclosing Personal Feelings

Rapport leads to *self-revelation*, the disclosure of personal feelings—the discussion of your hopes, fears, and ambitions. Obviously, people who communicate easily and feel comfortable with each other will want to know about each other. Personal disclosures may also lead to sexual activities.

Here again, similarities in social, ethnic, racial, and age background may affect our willingness to disclose personal information, since we tend to distrust people different from ourselves. In fact, people often make quick assessments of another person's possibility as a lover on the basis of such differences (Newman 1995).

Stage 3: Mutual Dependency—Sharing with Each Other

Self-revelation leads to **mutual dependency, the sharing of pleasures, ideas, humor, and sexual desires.** That is, you and your partner become a couple. The two of you begin to do activities together that you don't want to do alone, such as taking walks, going to the movies, going to sleep, and taking a weekend trip. Your social and cultural backgrounds, age, values, and the like are important here, since they affect the kind of mutual behaviors you agree are acceptable.

Stage 4: Intimacy Need Fulfillment—Reinforcing Each Other

In this final stage, you and your partner make mutual decisions, reinforce each other's goals, offer sympathy and support, and help each other satisfy deeper needs. That is, the relationship now has developed into a consistent pattern of mutual dependence and exchange of needs. As rapport increases, self-revelation and mutual dependence deepen.

As long as the wheel rolls forward, Reiss suggests, love continues to develop. However, if one or more of the processes diminish, the wheel may roll backward—love no longer develops, or it is reduced.

4. Triangular Theory: Toward Consummate Love

The *triangular theory* of love emphasizes three important elements of love that interact with one another: intimacy, passion, and decision/commitment. This theory was developed by **Robert Sternberg** (1986, 1988) and others.

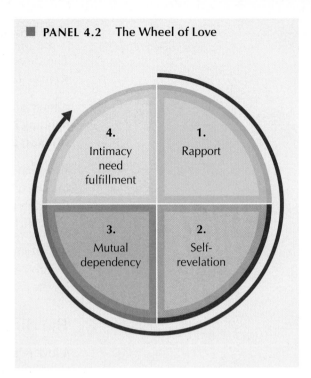

■ **PANEL 4.2**   The Wheel of Love

The Three Components of the Triangle

The three components can be thought of as the corners of a triangle. *(See ■ Panel 4.3.)*

■ **Intimacy:** This includes feelings that create the experience of warmth and bonding in a loving relationship, such as sharing one's self, giving emotional support, and being able to communicate with one's partner.

■ **Passion:** This includes romance, physical attraction, and sexuality. Passion may be driven by the desire to be sexually fulfilled, but it may also stem from the wish to increase one's self-esteem and to dominate or be subordinate to one's partner.

■ **Decision/Commitment:** In the short term, this component embodies one's *decision* (perhaps unconsciously) to love someone. In the long term, it embodies the *commitment* to love that person over time.

The Different Combinations of Love

A love relationship can vary in its combinations of intimacy, passion, and decision/commitment, Sternberg suggests. At one end is *nonlove*, when all elements are missing from a relationship between two people. The combination everyone dreams about, of course, is the perfect relationship known as ***consummate love*, when you and your partner's intimacy, passion, and decision/commitment are of the same intensity.** Although it's possible to achieve a state of consummate love in the short term, this state is difficult to sustain in the long run, since the components change over time, and each element must be nourished separately.

In between nonlove and consummate love are six other possible combinations, as follows. As you might guess, the more mismatched a couple is on the three elements previously listed, the more dissatisfied both will be with their relationship.

■ **Liking—Intimacy Only:** This is the love of good friends. There is no passion or commitment.

■ **Romantic Love—Intimacy with Passion:** This is love without commitment, although the commitment can develop over time.

■ **Infatuation—Passion Only:** This is "love at first sight," with overwhelming emotional involvement. Rarely are both people infatuated at the same time.

■ **Fatuous Love—Passion and Commitment:** This is foolish love, which may go from meeting to marriage, say, with blinding speed but without intimate involvement.

■ **Empty Love—Commitment Only:** This is love in which passion may have faded so that only commitment remains, although usually not for long if there is no intimacy.

■ **Companionate Love—Intimacy and Commitment:** This is love in which passion has diminished. Dissatisfied partners may seek passion in an affair with a third person.

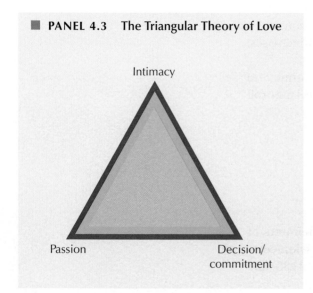

■ **PANEL 4.3   The Triangular Theory of Love**

Intimacy

Passion

Decision/
commitment

The triangular theory of love has been criticized for its methodology and on the grounds that passion, intimacy, and commitment often overlap. One study, for example, found that the triangular theory classification "is meaningfully related to individuals' similarity judgments" but that data did not provide strong support for the triangular theory (Hassebrauck and Buhl 1996).

5. Styles of Love: Lee's Six Kinds of Relationships

Although not really considered a theory, **Lee's six styles of love suggests there are six basic styles of loving: (1) love of beauty and the physical, or eros; (2) obsessive love, or mania; (3) playful love, or ludus; (4) companionate love, or storge; (5) altruistic love, or agape; and (6) practical love, or pragma.** This approach was formed by Canadian sociologist **John Alan Lee** (1973, 1988), who compiled 4,000 statements about love from several hundred works of fiction and nonfiction, then used them to create a questionnaire that he administered to people in Canada and Great Britain. From their responses, he constructed his six styles of love. Let's consider these.

Love of Beauty & the Physical: Eros

Pronounced "*air*-ros," **eros is the love of beauty; this love style is characterized by intense emotional attachment and powerful sexual feelings.** Lovers of this type are attracted to beauty or to powerful physical attraction and so are inclined to feel "love at first sight." Examples of this white-hot kind of love abound in romance novels and in other literature (as in Shakespeare's *Romeo and Juliet*).

Obsessive Love: Mania

Pronounced "*may*-nee-uh," the Greek word for "madness," **mania is obsessive love; this love style consists of strong sexual attraction and emotional intensity, extreme jealousy, and mood swings alternating between ecstasy and despair.** Roller-coaster manic love may stem from low self-esteem. When such a relationship ends, it sometimes leads to crimes of passion or suicide.

Playful Love: Ludus

Pronounced "*lewd*-us," **ludus is casual and carefree. This love style focuses on sex as recreation, the enjoyment of many sexual partners rather than concentrating on one serious relationship.** This is perhaps the kind of love endorsed by such magazines as *Playboy*.

Companionate Love: Storge

Pronounced "*stor*-gay," **storge is an affectionate, peaceful, and companionate kind of love.** It is sometimes called *conjugal love*. This kind of love frequently begins with shared activities and friendship and then gradually, over time, develops into love. Because of mutual trust, lovers of this type usually don't go through great swings of euphoria and depression, and they enjoy regular domestic activity.

OBSESSIVE LOVE. The style of love known as mania is characterized by emotional intensity and extreme jealousy. After a relationship ends, the partner's despair over the loss of the lover is so extreme that he or she may begin stalking the other partner—following or spying on the former partner and trying to win him or her back. Have you ever found yourself in an obsessive love relationship?

▲

Altruistic Love: Agape

Pronounced "ah-*gah*-pay," **agape is altruistic love—unselfish, self-sacrificing love. This love style describes those who attempt to fulfill others' needs even at the expense of their own.** Taken to extremes, this love style can be masochistic, as when one is a long-suffering partner of someone who is addicted or is a criminal.

Practical Love: Pragma

Pronounced "*prag*-ma," **pragma is practical love, the type of love that makes a rational assessment of a potential partner's positives and negatives.** A practical lover looks for compatibility in such things as educational and religious backgrounds. Practical partners look out for each other, but they are also practical about separating, remaining friendly, for example, for the sake of children.

Trying to Quantify Love: Is Intimacy the Foundation of Loving Relationships?

How realistic are theoretical constructs such as Lee's unidimensional six styles and Sternberg's multidimensional triangle? Many such theories represent attempts to clarify and measure love, in part to aid in relationship therapy.

In one study (Hook et al. 2003), researchers focused on one aspect—the concept of intimacy—as representing the crux, or essence, of loving relationships and as something that might be quantified. In defining intimacy (from a Western, heterosexual love viewpoint), the researchers identified it as consisting of (1) the presence of love and affection, (2) the knowledge that someone loves and approves of us (that is, personal validation), (3) being secure in the belief that one can disclose personal secrets (that is, trust), and (4) willingness to reveal one's self (self-disclosure).

Using three popular scales (Miller Social Intimacy Scale, Personal Assessment of Intimacy in Relationships Scale, and the Fear of Intimacy Scale) in a study of 360 undergraduate students, the scholars found that women scored higher than men did on intimacy factors (2) and (3) (Hook et al. 2003). In other words, compared with men, women "place more emphasis on love, affection, the expression of warm feelings, . . . and emotional sharing" in relationships. This does not mean that men do not experience or value intimacy, only, perhaps, that "researchers may not be accurately hearing or measuring the male voice of intimacy." Clearly, more investigation is required.

4.3 The Dark Face of Love: Jealousy, Unrequited Love, & Attempts to Control

MAJOR QUESTION What are three ways in which love can go awry?

PREVIEW Love, particularly passionate love, can take negative forms. One threat is jealousy, which may be either suspicious or reactive. Another is unrequited love—love that is not returned. A third threat is when one person tries to control the behavior of another, as through manipulation, stalking, or violence.

You go to a party with your lover, who then spends a lot of time talking to someone else. Afterward, you have a big fight about it. What's going on here?

Basically, you feel that something is threatening your relationship—that is, you're *jealous*. But jealousy is not the only way in which love can go awry; others are unrequited love and various attempts to control the partner's behavior.

Jealousy: The Green-Eyed Monster

Jealousy **may be defined as a usually intolerant or even hostile emotional response to a real or imagined threat to a love relationship.** The feeling of jealousy (what Shakespeare called the "green-eyed monster") can range from uncertainty, sadness, and resentment all the way up to great emotional pain and murderous rage—the stuff behind newspaper headlines, movies, and great literature. Astronaut Lisa Nowak became a media sensation in 2007, for instance, when she drove 900 miles (reportedly wearing an astronaut diaper to avoid bathroom stops) and allegedly pepper-sprayed her romantic rival for the affections of a space shuttle pilot (Schneider 2007). According to one nationwide study, marriage therapists identified jealousy as a problem in one-third of the couples they met with in the course of therapy (Pines 1992).

Jealousy: How It Works

It's important to understand jealousy not only because its pain can make us feel out of control and even lead to violence (Burcky et al. 1988; Laner 1990;

Riggs 1993). We also need to understand it so that we learn how it can either solidify or destroy a relationship. Consider two aspects:

■ **Jealousy Sets Boundaries for a Relationship:** If jealousy has a purpose, it's been suggested, that purpose is to set boundaries to what one feels is an important relationship (Reiss 1980). It determines the extent to which outsiders are permitted to enter the relationship. If a line is crossed, this can evoke the painful feelings of jealousy, such as anxiety and anger. Each couple determines its own boundaries. Jealousy is most intense in committed, sexually exclusive relationships, such as marriages.

■ **Jealousy May Be Either Suspicious or Reactive:** Jealousy may be *suspicious jealousy,* **occurring when there is no evidence or only ambiguous evidence for suspecting a partner is involved with someone else** (Bringle and Buunk 1991). This tends to occur when a relationship is in its early phase. ("Just dropping by to see if you're okay" might actually be an excuse for spying.) Or it might be *reactive jealousy,* **when evidence is revealed of a past, present, or anticipated relationship with another person.** This kind usually causes the most intense kind of jealousy because it reveals the breach of trust. (It can cause one to endlessly question the partner about the circumstances of past errands or trips.)

Characteristics of Jealousy

Research has turned up some interesting characteristics of jealousy:

■ **Men Are Jealous about Sex, Women about Intimacy:** Men are more apt to be jealous when they fear their partner is sexually involved with someone else. Women are more apt to be jealous when their partners become involved in an emotional relationship (Buss et al. 1992; Harris and Christenfeld 1996). Women are most jealous when they think their man is involved both emotionally and physically with someone else (White 1981).

■ **Men and Women Generally Have Different Reactions:** Both genders respond to jealousy with anger, but men are more apt to express it. Indeed, men may act out violently by injuring or even killing their partners. Women are more apt to suppress anger and be depressed. This may have to do with women having less power than men, with cultural prohibitions on women expressing anger, and with men's being allowed greater sexual freedom (Reiss 1980). Instead of acting violently by trying to hurt their lovers, women are more likely to do damage to property, such as vandalizing their partner's car (Tuller 1994).

■ **Jealous People Are More Apt to Be Insecure People:** People who are insecure in their love relationship—who depend on the partner for self-esteem and feel they have few alternatives—are more likely to feel jealous (Hansen 1985; Radecki Bush et al. 1988). People with low self-esteem are also more apt to have a problem with jealousy (Salovey and Rodin 1985; Buunk 1991; Cano and O'Leary 1997). Even if they aren't happy, jealous people feel strongly bound to their mates. Relationships of short duration (under a year) are more vulnerable to jealousy than those of long duration (over a year), according to a study of 185 college students (Knox et al. 1999b). The study also found that talking to or about a previous partner were the conditions most likely to elicit jealousy.

■ Jealousy Isn't Always Just about Sex, But It Often Is: Some jealous people are upset when their partners spend time not just with suspected lovers but also with family or when they devote time to special interests (Brehm 1992). Interestingly, however, people who are very jealous often themselves have been unfaithful (Salovey and Rodin 1985; White and Mullen 1989).

■ Jealousy Is More Prevalent in Some Cultures than in Others: Cultures that value individual property rights, such as the United States, tend to engender more jealousy (Hupka et al. 1985). Sexually liberal countries such as Germany and the Netherlands foster less jealousy (Buunk et al. 1996).

Unrequited Love: When Love Is Not Returned

Unrequited love, **love that is not returned,** is a common experience, and it can be as upsetting for the person doing the rejecting as it is for the one rejected (Baumeister et al. 1993). One survey found that about 75% of the respondents had experienced unrequited love and about 20% were then currently experiencing it (Aron et al. 1998). Two reasons for unrequited love are discussed next (Baumeister and Wotman 1992).

More Attractive Rejects Less Attractive

Because people who date and marry tend to be of similar attractiveness (Kipnis 2003), the unrequited lover may be rejected because of physical appearance. This can be especially painful to the rejected person because it is something that cannot be changed. People in this situation might try to insist that they have much more to offer than just good looks, but to no avail.

Less Serious Rejects More Serious

One person might want to "take the relationship to the next level," a more serious one, when the other person is not ready. This can be distressful not only for the rejected but also for the rejecter, who is faced with somehow ending the relationship tactfully.

Controlling: Trying to Control the Love Object

A third way in which love goes awry is when one person tries to control the behavior of the other, using tactics ranging from the manipulative to the violent.

HANDLING JEALOUSY. Jealousy can be *irrational*—suspicions and resentments that are actually based on personal feelings of inadequacy. Jealousy can also be *rational*—resentments and anger based on a discovery of a violation of the relationship's boundaries, as the woman here (standing) feels when finding her lover being intimate with another person. What would you do in this situation? ▲

Manipulation: From Charm to Threats

Controllers have a whole bag of tricks, ranging from charm, flattery, coaxing, and cajoling to sulking, guilt-tripping, humiliating, insulting, and threatening (Clarke 1990). Using love with guilt is a very common technique, as in "If you really loved me, you would . . ." (have sex now, stop seeing friends, quit school to take care of the kids, and so on).

Stalking: Unwanted Following

***Stalking* is repeatedly pursuing and frequently harassing another person.** Most objects of stalking are women—one in 12 has been stalked at some point—and most stalkers are men (Tjaden and Thoennes 1998). Nevertheless, one out of 45 men has been stalked at some time as well. Half the states have enacted antistalking laws, although their effectiveness is debatable.

Violence: Emotional or Physical Abuse

We devote another chapter (Chapter 13, "Crises") to the subject of violence. Here, let us simply say that the worst kind of misguided love is that which uses love to rationalize emotional and physical abuse. This may range from sarcasm, sexual jokes, insults, and withholding of affection to shoving, hitting, and outright beatings (often said to be "for your own good").

4.4 How Can You Tell Whether It's Meaningful Love?

MAJOR QUESTION What distinguishes immature love from mature love?

PREVIEW Love may be immature, characterized by passionate thinking, feeling, and behavior. Or it may be mature, consisting of energy, self-esteem, kindness, and the like.

In considering whether you are an ideal candidate for another person's love, you might fret about how you *look*. That is certainly something to consider. What most adults between ages 30 and 54, for example, say they look for in a mate, beyond first impressions, are good grooming, good health, and similar age.

But Sol Gordon, who is a North Carolina psychologist and sex educator and the author of 22 books, suggests that there are other qualities you need to consider about yourself to determine whether you're a good candidate for love (Gordon, reported in Ganahl 2002a, 2002b):

■ **Energy:** You're not tired. You have energy for the things you want to do. (Passionate love is exhausting.)

■ **Meaning:** You're not searching for the meaning of life. You're finding meaning in everyday occurrences.

■ **Self-Esteem:** You appreciate your own worth. You don't need affirmation from others to feel valued.

■ **No Ghosts:** Bad thoughts don't trouble you unduly. You don't allow "ghosts" of the past to haunt you.

■ **Kindness:** You're kind to everyone, not just to your partner. (In Buddhism, kindness is the most important part of marriage.)

All these qualities can be summarized in a single word: *maturity*. With maturity, one becomes a candidate for the kind of love—mature love—that, Gordon suggests, is what one should strive for.

IMMATURE VERSUS MATURE LOVE. Which is more desirable: The white-hot, "can't get you out of my mind" kind of love often found at the beginning of a love relationship? Or the comfort and predictability of a not-so-passionate but enduring union over a lifetime? ▲

Immature versus Mature Love

"If people think they're in love, they probably are," says Gordon (quoted in Ganahl 2002a). "But there's love suitable for a long-term relationship, and love that isn't." Since many people mistake one for the other, that can lead to disaster (as measured by the sky-high divorce rate in the United States—two-thirds of all first marriages). ***Immature love* is passionate or romantic love. *Mature love* resembles companionate love.** Let's consider these.

Immature Love

"People should not decide to get married based only on love or sex," Gordon emphasizes. Love and sex are what immature love is mainly about, the kind of passionate or romantic love seen in teenage relationships, although many adults also fall into this trap. It is love characterized by passionate ways of thinking, feeling, and behaving, as follows (Hatfield and Sprecher 1986):

■ **Passionate Thinking:** You persistently think about the beloved, have trouble concentrating on other matters, and idealize the other's qualities, such as looks. As the cliché goes, "I can't get you out of my mind!"

■ **Passionate Feeling:** You are physically aroused by the beloved, always want to be with him or her, and are upset when your relationship is not going smoothly. In another cliché, "I can't live without you!"

■ **Passionate Behavior:** You become obsessed, studying your beloved's behavior, trying to be a servant to him or her, striving to learn what your beloved thinks of you. Clichés include "I would do anything for you" and "Are you thinking about me?"

Immature lovers have unrealistic expectations about a new relationship. They don't allow a friendship to develop first. They are attracted to their partner's energy or personality without determining whether he or she is a caring and responsible person. They may equate jealousy and torment with love, even allow physical abuse ("I know he beats me up, but I love him!"). If they break up, they may feel unworthy.

Mature Love

With mature love, people no longer believe the clichés that tell us "love is blind" and "love conquers all." You have determined how important romantic images of love or torrid images of sex are to you. You possess the qualities mentioned earlier—energy, self-esteem, kindness, and the like. You have learned much about who you are and have traveled far on your voyage of self-discovery and the search for the meaning of life. You have found your own voice and your own values, even perhaps discovered that you prefer to remain single or to have nonsexual companionship. You realize that there are many ways to perceive love.

And if you are seeking a permanent union with someone else, you should also have taken a realistic look at your partner. You have asked whether he or she is . . .

■ **Trustworthy and Stable:** Is your partner loyal, able to handle conflicts maturely, not violently angry or frequently moody, and good parent material (if having children is important to you)?

■ **Caring and Kind:** Does your lover show love and respect for you? Do you like yourself more—that is, have more self-esteem—when you're with this person?

■ **Someone You Actually LIKE:** Do you enjoy your partner? Can you be friends and work through inevitable disappointments and unmet expectations about love and sex?

The Concept of Soul Mate Revisited

"Nothing has produced more unhappiness than the concept of soul mate," says Atlanta psychiatrist Frank Pittman (quoted in Shulman 2004: 34). The reason: Subscribing to the idea that there is a perfect match, that there is someone out there who will, as one writer put it, "counter our weaknesses, amplify our strengths, and provide . . . unflagging support and respect," means that while we are in our current relationship we always "have an eye open for a better deal or something on the side, choose someone impossible or far away" (Shulman 2004: 34–35). That is, we avoid the decision to commit or commit only partly to our partner, not relinquishing the right to keep looking.

But once the emotional high of the initial passion is past, the greatest rewards of love come from approaching it rationally—that is, from taking the steps we described to achieve mature love. And once mature love is realized, says Gordon (in Ganahl 2002b), "amazing things can happen." Both of you will experience high levels of energy for everything you want to do. Your work and important tasks will not be neglected. You will feel kindly toward each other and almost everyone else in your sphere. You will discover your life's priorities. You are committed to working out your differences.

Self-Assessment: How Capable Are You of Being Intimate?

Determine how closely each statement describes your feelings. Circle the number in the appropriate column.

Agree or Disagree

Strongly disagree	Mildly disagree	Disagree equally	Mildly agree	Strongly agree
1	2	3	4	5

1. I like to share my feelings with others. 1 2 3 4 5
2. I like to feel close to other people. 1 2 3 4 5
3. I like to listen to other people talk about their feelings. 1 2 3 4 5
4. I am concerned with rejection in my expression of feelings to others. 5 4 3 2 1
5. I'm concerned with being dominated in a close relationship with another. 5 4 3 2 1
6. I'm often anxious about my own acceptance in a close relationship. 5 4 3 2 1
7. I'm concerned that I trust other people too much. 5 4 3 2 1
8. Expression of emotion makes me feel close to another person. 1 2 3 4 5
9. I do not want to express feelings that would hurt another person. 5 4 3 2 1
10. I am overly critical of people in a close relationship. 5 4 3 2 1
11. I want to feel close to people to whom I am attracted. 1 2 3 4 5
12. I tend to reveal my deepest feelings to other people. 1 2 3 4 5
13. I'm afraid to talk about my sexual feelings with a person in whom I'm very interested. 5 4 3 2 1
14. I want to be close to a person who is attracted to me. 1 2 3 4 5
15. I would not become too close because it involves conflict. 5 4 3 2 1
16. I seek out close relationships with people to whom I am attracted. 1 2 3 4 5
17. When people become close, they tend not to listen to each other. 5 4 3 2 1
18. Intimate relationships bring me great satisfaction. 1 2 3 4 5
19. I search for close intimate relationships. 1 2 3 4 5
20. It is important to me to form close relationships. 1 2 3 4 5
21. I do not need to share my feelings and thoughts with others. 5 4 3 2 1
22. When I become very close to another person, I am likely to see things that are hard for me to accept. 5 4 3 2 1
23. I tend to accept most things about people with whom I share a close relationship. 1 2 3 4 5
24. I defend my personal space so others do not come too close. 5 4 3 2 1
25. I tend to distrust people who are concerned with closeness and intimacy. 5 4 3 2 1
26. I have concerns about losing my individuality in close relationships. 5 4 3 2 1
27. I have concerns about giving up control if I enter into a really intimate relationship. 5 4 3 2 1
28. Being honest and open with another person makes me feel closer to that person. 1 2 3 4 5
29. If I were another person, I would be interested in getting to know me. 1 2 3 4 5
30. I become close only to people with whom I share common interests. 5 4 3 2 1
31. Revealing secrets about my sex life makes me feel close to others. 1 2 3 4 5
32. Generally, I can feel just as close to someone of the same sex as to someone of the other sex. 1 2 3 4 5
33. When another person is physically attracted to me, I usually want to become more intimate. 1 2 3 4 5
34. I have difficulty being intimate with more than one person. 5 4 3 2 1
35. Being open and intimate with another person usually makes me feel good. 1 2 3 4 5
36. I usually can see another person's point of view. 1 2 3 4 5
37. I want to be sure that I am in good control of myself before I attempt to become intimate with another person. 5 4 3 2 1
38. I resist intimacy. 5 4 3 2 1
39. Stories of interpersonal relationships tend to affect me. 1 2 3 4 5

40. Undressing with members of a group increases my feelings of intimacy.　　5 4 3 2 1

41. I try to trust and be close to others.　　1 2 3 4 5

42. I think that people who want to become intimate have hidden reasons for wanting closeness.　　5 4 3 2 1

43. When I become intimate with another person, the possibility of my being manipulated is increased.　　5 4 3 2 1

44. I am generally a secretive person.　　5 4 3 2 1

45. I feel that sex and intimacy are the same, and one cannot exist without the other.　　5 4 3 2 1

46. I can be intimate only in a physical relationship.　　5 4 3 2 1

47. The demands placed on me by those with whom I have intimate relationships often inhibit my own satisfaction.　　5 4 3 2 1

48. I would compromise to maintain an intimate relationship.　　1 2 3 4 5

49. When I am physically attracted to another, I usually want to become intimate with the person.　　1 2 3 4 5

50. I understand and accept that intimacy leads to bad feelings as well as good feelings.　　1 2 3 4 5

Scoring

To calculate your total score, add up the items you circled. Find the score on the table below that is closest to your total score.

150	Significantly below average
161	Somewhat below average
172	Average
183	Somewhat above average
194	Significantly above average

Sources: Treadwell, T. 1981. Intimacy attitude scale: Its structures, reliability and validity. Doctoral dissertation, Temple University. *Dissertation Abstracts International* 42:837; and Amidon, E., V. K. Kumar, and T. Treadwell. 1983. Measurement of intimacy attitudes: The intimacy attitude scale—revised. *Journal of Personality Assessment* 47(6):635–639. Used by permission of Lawrence Erlbaum Associates and the author, Thomas Treadwell.

Key Terms Used in This Chapter

Summary

4.1 Can We Define Love?

■ Love can be defined as intimacy with, caring for, and commitment to another person. People hope to find their soul mate, or person who is temperamentally suited to them as well as their best friend, confidant, and romantic partner. The portrayal of love in films, popular songs, television, and books helps define and influence one's ideas about love.

■ The meaning of love is subjective and can vary according to time, place, and culture. In ancient Greece and Rome, love was believed to have a negative impact on people's behavior. This passionate or sexual love had to be controlled and guarded against.

■ More important to the Greeks were altruistic love (agape) and friendship love (phileo). Passionate love was seen as unreliable; and as a result, marriages were arranged marriages with partners determined not by the bride and groom themselves but by their families.

■ These views on arranged marriage influenced Europe in the Middle Ages, where great care was taken to make sure marriages would produce strong alliances of wealth and power.

- Between the 7th and 12th centuries, the Roman Catholic Church promoted marriage as a sacrament. The notion of courtly love became more and more accepted in society. By the end of the 18th century, romantic love became the preferred basis for binding men and women together in marriage.

- Arranged marriages still exist in many parts of the world. Cultures vary greatly in their views on affection and how it should or should not be shown.

- As the United States became further industrialized, jobs were created outside of the home, and children became less economically dependent and controlled by their parents' wishes. Choosing a marriage partner shifted from having an economic basis to an emotional one.

- Love can have both a physical state, referred to as lust or sexual arousal, and a psychological state, or sexual desire. Romantic or passionate love may evolve into companionate love, which is seen as calmer than romantic love, with a greater emphasis on intimacy, affection, and commitment to another person.

- Friendship, an attachment between people, is the foundation for a strong love relationship. Still, there are differences between friends and lovers. Friends enjoy each other's company, are willing to support and help each other, share feelings and experiences, and feel free to be themselves rather than something they are not. Love involves emotional highs and lows, instability, passion, exclusiveness, and sexual desire—all qualities that are unstable.

- Although same-sex couples experience love with the same intimacy and intensity as any heterosexual couple, the ways men and women express love as genders are more different than relationships between heterosexual and homosexual couples. One difference is that lesbian relationships tend to be more enduring and stable than those in gay relationships.

4.2 The Origins of Love: Some Theories

- Theories on the origin of love include the following: The biochemical theory suggests that love results from our biological, chemical, and hormonal makeup. The attachment theory suggests our primary motivation in life is to be connected with other people for security. The wheel theory of love suggests that love develops and is maintained through four stages: (1) rapport, (2) self-revelation, (3) mutual dependency, and (4) intimacy need fulfillment. The triangular theory of love emphasizes three important elements of love that interact with one another: intimacy, passion, and decision/commitment. Another approach by Lee suggests that there are six styles of loving: eros, or love of beauty and the physical; mania, or obsessive love; ludus, or playful love; storge, or companionate love; agape, or altruistic love; and pragma, or practical love.

4.3 The Dark Face of Love: Jealousy, Unrequited Love, & Attempts to Control

- Although love is normally seen as a positive thing, it can take negative forms. Jealousy occurs when you feel that something is threatening your relationship; it is a negative response to a real or imagined threat to a love relationship. It also serves to establish boundaries for the relationship. Men tend to be jealous about sex, women about intimacy. Men may react in a violent way; women are more apt to suppress their anger and become depressed. Jealous people tend to be insecure people. Jealousy may frequently be about sex. Jealously tends to be more common in cultures that value individual property rights.

- Unrequited love, love that is not returned, is also a common negative aspect of love. It may occur because the more attractive person rejects the less attractive person or because the less serious person rejects the more serious person.

- Love can also go awry as a result of one person trying to control the behavior of the other. The attempts to control can include manipulation, stalking, and emotional and physical abuse.

4.4 How Can You Tell Whether It's Meaningful Love?

- Maturity in a love relationship is characterized by energy, meaning, self-esteem, no ghosts, and kindness. Mature love resembles companionate love, whereas immature love is passionate or romantic love. Immature lovers tend to have unrealistic expectations about a new relationship and frequently don't allow a friendship to develop first.

- In meaningful love, partners tend to be trustworthy and stable, caring and kind, and likeable.

Take It to the Net

Among the Internet resources on love are the following:

- **Heartchoice.com.** Website run by sociologists David Knox and Carolyn Schacht; offers the "Rightmate Relationship Checkup" survey. *http://heartchoice.com*
- **Love Shack.** An "interpersonal relationship assistance center." Click on "Friends and Lovers" and categories under *romantic*. *www.loveshack.org*
- **The Loving Center.** Information on tantric and conscious loving. Click on "Conscious Loving." *www.consciouslovingtlc.com*
- **Trinity University's Family Page.** Various categories of information on love, marriage, and family. *www.trinity.edu/~mkearl/family.html*

CHAPTER 5

INVOLVEMENT

Dating, Pairing, Courtship, & Cohabitation

Meeting & Mating

The idea was simple: *Maria Dahvana Headley (2007), a 20-year-old New York University undergraduate searching for love, decided she would start accepting dates from anyone who asked—anyone, that is, except for men who were married, underage, crazy, drunk, high, or who introduced themselves "by grabbing me." It was an act of desperation, triggered by her frustration with intellectual, literary types. The ensuing 150 dates, described in* The Year of Yes, *included a subway conductor who brought along his pet iguana, a homeless man, a millionaire who still lived with his mother, several non-English speakers, ten taxi drivers, two lesbians, and a mime.*

Headley is socially awkward and far from glamorous, but she is approachable and friendly, with a midwestern trait of smiling at everyone she meets. "Lots of women are pretty set in what they think they have to have to be happy, but it doesn't hurt to date people who are not that," she told an interviewer (McGinn 2006). To stay safe, she made it a rule not to get into anyone's car or tell her dates where she lived.

How well did it all work? During her "dating spree," she met a playwright who was 25 years older, divorced, with two children. He turned out to be Robert Schenkkan, Pulitzer-winning writer of The Kentucky Cycle *plays. They are now married and live in Seattle.*

Do you really have to date 150 people in order to find the partner who's right for you? Some people, of course, become involved with just one person and stay with that partner lifelong. What's interesting, however, is that most young singles in the United States do not seem to be actively looking for romantic partners at all, according to a Pew Internet & American Life Project survey (Rainie and Madden 2006). In fact, even those who are seeking relationships are not dating frequently, with only half (49%) having been on no more than one date in the preceding three months.

But even if young singles aren't dating much, there has been an explosion of interest in information *about* dating

⬤ WHAT'S AHEAD IN THIS CHAPTER

We first consider courtship, both closed and open systems; six functions of dating; and how dating can operate as a filtering process. Next, we describe four ways of meeting people and variations in dating. We then discuss cohabitation and why people live together, their characteristics, why living together has increased, and how it differs from marriage. Finally, we discuss aspects of a deteriorating relationship and breaking up.

and relationships—on websites and in the media, as well as in books, movies about finding romance, and "reality" dating shows such as *The Bachelor, Blind Date, ElimiDate,* and *The 5th Wheel.* "Clearly, there is popular interest in dating, and evidence of great frustration with the challenge of finding a suitable partner," says social historian Barbara Dafoe Whitehead, codirector of the National Marriage Project at Rutgers University (quoted in Peterson 2003). "We are in the middle of [a] massive transition . . . a contemporary crisis in dating and mating."

At one time, becoming "involved" with another person was an understood ritual known as courtship, the slow progression of wooing a partner according to an accepted set of rules from dating to "going steady" to getting married (Bailey 1989). Today, rules about dating are confused and uncertain. "We have lost the ability to slow down the process of becoming intimate and choosing a partner," says Johns Hopkins University sociologist Andrew Cherlin (quoted in Peterson 2000b). "We have lost the assistance of parents and elders in the community, who were sometimes helpful and sometimes not."

Some examples of the changes:

■ *Assertive females:* After decades during which generations of young women were never even supposed to call a boy on the telephone, it is now girls—perhaps because of the gains of feminism—who not only do the calling but also often initiate romantic and even sexual activity. One New York City psychologist thinks that the habits of cable TV shows have perhaps trickled down to teenagers. "The popular culture saturates their mentality," says Linda Carter (quoted in Kuczynski 2002: 12). "It started among young single adults with *Sex and the City,* and there has been so much talk and thinking about female sexual assertiveness that it has finally come to influence adolescents."

■ *Workplace romances:* Another barrier that seems to be falling is the prohibition of romance in the workplace. Reasons for this change include longer work hours, more women in the labor force, and relaxed taboos about such relationships (Armour 2003; Hymowitz and Lublin 2005). However, some employers, fearing sexual harassment lawsuits, may insist that intraoffice couples protect them by signing "love contracts" (Klaff 2001).

■ *Speed dating and online meetings:* Finally, as we discuss at length, many people are using what were once considered unconventional means, such as speed dating and Internet-relationship websites, chat rooms, and email, to try to meet others.

Why date? What functions can it serve for me?

How can I find someone to love?

Why might I live together with someone, and what would it be like?

How do people react to a deteriorating relationship, and how can I handle a breakup?

ON THE WEB Learning about Commitment & Cohabitation

http://pewresearch.org/pubs/1/not-looking-for-love

http://marriage.rutgers.edu/publications/SWLT2%20TEXT.htm

Here's how to find some nonsectarian, nonpartisan information on some contemporary issues associated with this chapter on involvement—(1) the status of dating in America and (2) living together (cohabitation).

• Go to the website of Not Looking for Love: The State of Romance in America by the Pew Internet & American Life Project.

• Go to the website of Should We Live Together? What Young Adults Need to Know about Cohabitation before Marriage from the National Marriage Project at Rutgers University.

5.1 The Dating Game

MAJOR QUESTION Why date? What functions can it serve for me?

PREVIEW We first describe the concept of courtship, both closed systems (arranged marriages) and open systems (the relationship marketplace). We then describe the six functions of dating. Finally, we consider dating as a filtering process or as a relationship-driven or event-driven commitment.

Human connection: Why should it be so hard?

For some people, it's not, of course. Perhaps they are the ones who write books such as *The Fine Art of Small Talk* (Fine 2005) and *The Game: Penetrating the Secret Society of Pickup Artists* (Strauss 2005). Or work at places like Charisma Arts, which gives seminars on how to meet women. Or become dating coaches, such as Ohio psychologist David Coleman, "The Dating Doctor," and Seattle's Alma Rubenstein, a former actress who is now "The Professional Dater" (Jayson 2005a; Kugiya 2007). Or help clients provide professional-looking photos or enticing descriptions of themselves to post on dating websites (Wallack 2005).

To many people, the energy and time required to connect with others is so exhausting and difficult, it's no wonder that dating has declined. Of unattached singles interviewed in a 2006 Pew Research Center study, only 16% said they were looking for a partner; 55% reported no interest in a relationship (Rainie and Madden 2006). Of singles in the dating market, 36% said they hadn't had a date in the past three months; 13% had one date; 22% had two to four dates; and 25% had five or more.

Clearly, there are a lot of uncertainties surrounding the whole matter of match making. Let us take a look at this.

- **Are third-party introductions common?** Between one-third and one-half of dating relationships begin with a personal introduction.[a]

- **Is "hooking up"—sex without commitment—popular?** A study of the heterosexual dating culture of 1,000 college women at 11 four-year American colleges found that about 40% of the women respondents reported having had at least one hookup, and 10% had had more than six.[b]

- **Is there a lot of on-the-job dating?** Almost 40% of adults have dated a co-worker.[c]

- **What are people who live together without marriage like?** About 80% of living-together (cohabiting) couples are under age 45, and 19% are under age 25. Compared to married couples, cohabiting couples are more likely to be interracial.[d]

- **How likely are live-togethers to split?** The probability of a split within 5 years for people in a live-in relationship is 49% versus only 20% for those in a marriage.[e]

- **How likely are live-together partners to marry?** In the 1970s, two-thirds of cohabiting couples married within 3 years. Today, only half as many women marry their live-in mates.[f]

- **Why do couples break up?** One study found that the reasons college students break up are "too many differences/different values" (43%), "got tired of each other" (27%), "cheating" (18%), and "dishonesty" (18%).[g]

[a]Sprecher and McKinney 1993. [b]Glenn and Marquardt 2001. [c]Roper Starch, reported in Jackson 1999. [d]Glick and Spanier 1980. [e]National Center for Health Statistics, cited in Peterson 2002. [f]Manning and Smock 2002. [g]Knox et al. 1997.

NUMBERS THAT MATTER
Linking Up

Courtship: From Parental Decisions to the Relationship Marketplace

The general subject of this chapter is involvement: meeting and finding a partner. Before serial dating and living together in lieu of marriage became so popular, involvement was known as *courtship*, **the process by which a commitment to marriage is developed.** Let's consider the background to courtship.

The Closed Courtship System: Arranged Marriages

In times past, and in many cultures still, courtship was a closed system: Children's marital destiny was decided by their parents. This leads to *arranged marriage*, as we discussed in Chapter 4, "Love." Some consequences of arranged marriages are the following:

■ **Blind Marriage:** Whatever their feelings, the bridal partners in an arranged marriage usually do not have much influence on their parents' calculations

(Hatfield and Rapson 1996). Perhaps the most extreme variation was the sort that used to be found in China known as **blind marriage, in which neither partner saw the other until the day of their wedding.**

■ **Bride Price and Dowry:** In some non-Western nations, an arranged marriage involves a **bride price—a man must pay money or property to the future bride's family for the right to marry her.** Alternatively, a bride is required to provide a **dowry, the money, property, or goods a woman brings to the marriage.** A woman with a high-value dowry is more sought after than is one with a lesser dowry (Gaulin and Boster 1990).

■ **Elopement:** In some traditional societies, couples may try to marry for love but seek the parents' blessing or approval. If permission is not forthcoming, the couple might then **elope—run away and be married somewhere else.** On return, the groom might ask the bride's parents' forgiveness (Cherlin and Chamratrithirong 1993).

■ **Forced Marriage:** An extreme form of arranged marriage is **the *forced marriage*, in which the bride, groom, or both are coerced to marry against their will and under duress that includes both physical and emotional pressure** (Soriano 2006). Sometimes such involuntary marriage is forced on children. In India, for instance, Savita Chaudhry was married at the age of 3 to a boy two years older than she, then sent home to grow up, after which she was expected to move in with her husband (Lancaster 2005). Or a child may be given to an adult in repayment for a loan, as Mapendo Simbey's father did with her in the African country of Malawi (LaFraniere 2005).

In Kyrgyzstan, more than half the married women are reported to have been forced into wedlock after being snatched from the street by their husbands, in a custom known as *ala kachuu*, which translates roughly as "grab and run" (Smith 2005). In England, young women of Pakistani descent return to their parents' homeland for a vacation, then find themselves promised in marriage to relatives they have never met (Garwood 2006; Walsh 2006). Turkish girls who grew up in Austria may find themselves forced into marriage during a visit to Turkey, and young women in Turkey may be sold to Turkish men living in Germany who want wives (Geiger 2005; Schneider 2005). If the wives attempt to seek divorce, they may be disowned by their parents and community and condemned to a life of poverty.

■ **The Green-Card Fraudulent Marriage:** A final form of loveless marriage, although it may not be "arranged" by parents, is the sham marriage known as the **green-card marriage, in which an American marries, or pretends to marry, usually in exchange for money, an immigrant for the purpose of giving him or her a green card that grants permanent U.S. residency.** One government official near Atlanta said she had witnessed green-card couples who couldn't converse with each other because of a language barrier, who were "married" to more than one supposed spouse, and who did not know their spouse's last name or place of birth (Dell'Orto 2006).

The Open Courtship System: The Relationship Marketplace

Today in North America and in Western nations, we have an **open courtship system, in which most of us generally make our own decisions about**

RELATIONSHIP MARKET. Unlike couples in cultures whose marriages are arranged for them (as by their parents), partner-seeking men and women in North America generally participate in a "marriage market," in which they compare resources and then bargain for the best that they can get. Do you feel this is the best way to find a mate? ▶

choosing our partners. The result is a system that resembles the eBay auction website—**a *relationship market*, or marriage market, in which prospective partners compare the personal, social, and financial resources of eligible mates and then bargain for the best they can get** (Coltrane 1998). The market metaphor shows up in the descriptions of singles bars, where people go to seek sexual or dating partners, which are referred to as "meat markets." This system certainly fits in with the social exchange perspective (discussed in Chapter 2, "Understanding"), which proposes that people's interactions represent the efforts of each to maximize their benefits (wealth, affection, status, and the like) and minimize their costs.

In the relationship market, people have a so-called market value based on their assets and liabilities, which they use to "bargain" or "trade" with prospective partners. Participants in this marketplace may stress different objectives, as follows:

■ **People Seeking a Traditional Partnership:** Among people seeking traditional marriage partners, men might use their superior position in the economic system to offer financial security and status as bargaining chips. Women have traditionally offered cooking and other domestic skills, attractiveness, child-raising abilities, emotional support, and sexual accessibility (Sprecher et al. 1994).

■ **People Seeking an Egalitarian Partnership:** Men and women seeking a more egalitarian arrangement—in which both partners play similar roles—might play up similar assets. These include income potential, educational and social status, emotional support, sexual accessibility, and mutual willingness to share child-care and domestic responsibilities.

In the United States, the courtship mechanism for achieving these objectives is the activity known as *dating*.

The Functions of Dating

Dating is the process of meeting people socially for the purpose of possibly forming an exclusive long-term relationship. In North America, dating emerged at the beginning of the twentieth century and has waxed and waned in popularity since then. For instance, dating lost popularity in the 1960s and 1970s but enjoyed a resurgence in the 1980s and 1990s. However, today, as we'll explain, dating might have been replaced on college campuses by "hooking up" and "being joined at the hip," according to one study (Glenn and Marquardt 2001).

Dating has at least six functions. Four are easy to understand: (1) *recreation*, (2) *companionship*, (3) *intimacy and sex*, and (4) *mate selection*. Two are less obvious: (5) *socialization* and (6) *status achievement*. Let's consider these.

1. Recreation

Dating can be, or is supposed to be, *fun*. Whether a date is a meeting to have dinner, see a movie, go dancing, or simply hang out together, a principal reason is recreational. In this respect, two people dating is no different from three or four people getting together simply to amuse themselves.

2. Companionship

Whether you are a single college-age student at a large university, a recently divorced single parent, or a retired person living alone, dating is a way of maintaining a friendship or friendships and of avoiding isolation.

3. Intimacy & Sex

Depending on age, according to one study (Roscoe et al. 1987), a person may date to find romantic intimacy (sixth to eleventh grades) or sexual intimacy (college age). Indeed, many teenagers discover sex and sexuality in the course of dating.

4. Mate Selection

Clearly, for many (but not all) people, an important goal of dating is finding a mate, someone with whom to form a lasting relationship, especially marriage. Indeed, the more both partners in a dating relationship believe that it might lead to marriage, the more stable that relationship is (Lloyd et al. 1984).

5. Socialization

Socialization is the process by which we learn the skills we need to survive as individuals and as members of society. In the earlier years of our lives, we tend to interact primarily with other children of the same sex. When we reach puberty, dating helps socialize us to get along with members of the opposite sex.

6. Status Achievement

Status **is social ranking, or the prestige attached to a particular position in society.** For people who are coming into adolescence, dating enhances a person's status by showing others that he or she is more acceptable, more desirable, more grown up. This is especially so if one dates someone who is particularly popular, athletic, or attractive.

Throughout the "dating game," a sorting-out process may be going on. Let's consider this process.

Is Dating a Filtering Process?

Some scholars believe that dating is a process of filtering out possible partners for the purpose of achieving *homogamy*—**that is, marriage between partners of similar education, ethnicity, race, religion, age, and social class.**

Types of Filtering: Propinquity, Endogamy, Exogamy

Among the ways in which people are filtered are on the basis of *propinquity, endogamy,* and *exogamy.*

■ **Propinquity—People Who Are Nearby:** You might filter people on the basis of *propinquity*—**their nearness to you in place and time.** This means mainly geographic proximity—meeting people locally at school, work, or church or through social networks.

■ **Endogamy—People of the Same Social Group:** You would probably feel pressure to filter people on the basis of *endogamy*, **the cultural expectation that a person marries within his or own social group in terms of race, religion, and social class.** Although there are plenty of stories about "the prince and the showgirl," "the cowboy and the heiress," and the like, parents have traditionally encouraged their offspring to seek mates within their own social group.

■ **Exogamy—People Outside the Family Group:** The culture also encourages you to practice *exogamy*, **to marry outside your family group and not practice sex with a sibling.** That is, because of incest taboos, sisters and brothers are not allowed to marry one another because of the fear that such marriages might produce offspring with genetic defects.

Factors Affecting Availability: Race, Class, Age, Religion

The principal characteristics by which people seek out each other are shown in the accompanying figure (Kerchoff and Davis 1962). *(See ■ Panel 5.1, next page.)* Let us consider some of the homogamous factors that operate in the selection of mates.

Besides personality characteristics, the most important elements encouraging partners to seek each other out and marry (homogamy) are residential propinquity, physical attractiveness (Berscheid et al. 1982), race and ethnicity, religion, socioeconomic status, and age.

PANEL 5.1   Finding a Partner: The Likely Eligibles. Besides personality characteristics, the most important elements encouraging partners to seek each other out and marry (homogamy) are residential propinquity, physical attractiveness, race and ethnicity, religion, socioeconomic status, and age.

PHYSICAL ATTRACTIVENESS

Beauty and the Beast?

People tend to select partners whose physical attractiveness resembles their own. Physically attractive people are assumed to have other beneficial characteristics, such as sensitivity and

RESIDENTIAL PROPINQUITY

New York and New Mexico?

Most of us choose partners from a limited geographical area—"residential propinquity." That is, you are less likely to meet people who live far away from you.

RACE & ETHNICITY

Asian and Cajun?

About 97% of marriages are of partners from the same race, although interracial marriages are increasing. Intermarriage between ethnic groups is also increasing.

RELIGION

Baptist and Buddhist?

Despite opposition from most traditional religions, interreligious dating and marriage has increased—for example, 40% of Jews and about 50% of Catholics marry outside their faith.

SOCIOECONOMIC STATUS

Prince and Pauper?

Most people choose partners from within their social class who share similar educational background and attitudes. However, women sometimes "marry up" and men sometimes "marry down."

AGE

16 and 60?

Americans tend to marry partners within the same age range, the man generally being two to three years older than the woman. With large age differences, there are apt to be generational differences, such as preferences about music, child rearing, and values.

■ **Race:** Traditionally, race has been a strong factor in influencing dating, living-together, and marriage patterns (Blackwell and Lichter 2000). However, interracial dating seems to be becoming more acceptable. According to a 2005 Gallup poll (cited in Jayson 2006a; Mixed Media Watch 2005), 95% of 18- to 29-year-olds approve of blacks and whites dating. About 48% of that age group said they have dated someone of a different race. (*See* ■ *Panel 5.2.*)

Americans between the ages of 14 and 24 seem to be more tolerant and open-minded than previous generations. For instance, when asked in 2000 if they would favor a ban on interracial marriage, only 4% of younger Americans and 10% of those over age 26 said they favored such a ban—compared to 20% and 43%, respectively, in 1972 (Olander et al. 2005). Perhaps, speculates one writer (Jayson 2006a), "the media fuel this colorblindness as movies, TV, and advertising portray interracial friendship and romance." This is seen in *Grey's Anatomy,* in the relationship between doctors Cristina Yang, who is Asian, and Preston Burke (now gone), who is black, and in *Lost* with the married couple Rose, who is black, and Bernard, who is white (Oldenburg 2005).

Even so, as of a decade ago, interracial couples were still subject to stares and comments, even hostility, and were upsetting to parents and families (Nelson 1992). As late as 2004, one white woman, a Stanford University student who dates Asian men, complained that "while my parents have tried to be accepting, they've said they don't know how to talk to my Chinese boyfriends" (Ricketts 2004).

■ **Social Class:** Dating behavior varies with social class, and people tend to date and mate with people from their own social class. This is especially true in middle-class and upper-class families, who have more control over their children's dating behavior—and who might have more to lose if their children "marry down" or outside their economic and educational class (Ramu 1989; Whyte 1990).

One aspect of social class is the **mating gradient, or** *marriage gradient,* **which refers to the tendency for men to marry downward in class and women to marry upward with respect to age, education, and occupational success.** (The tendency to marry upward is referred to as *hypergamy;* the tendency to marry downward as *hypogamy.*)

■ Age: No legislation requires us to marry within our own age range (assuming that we have reached adulthood), but age is still an important factor in the dating/mating game. This is especially the case in what's known as the "marriage squeeze" for women. **In the *marriage squeeze,* one sex has a more limited pool of eligible marriage candidates than the other.** Because women tend to marry men who are somewhat older than themselves, there are more available women than there are men. The imbalance increases as people age, with many fewer unmarried men available over age 65. Indeed, when the never-married, the divorced, and the widowed are counted, unmarried women begin to outnumber men by the age of 35 (Fowlkes 1994).

■ PANEL 5.2 **Diversity Data: Who Dates Interracially?** Gallup Poll of 1,116 adults.

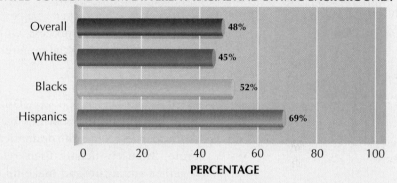

Source: Adapted from Gallup Poll, findings from 2005 Minority Rights and Relations poll, cited in Jayson 2006a and Mixed Media Watch 2005.

■ Religion: As many as 90% of people who get married do so with people who have similar religious values (Murstein 1986). Even so, over the past several years, the number of interfaith marriages, as between Protestants and Catholics or Jews and Protestants, seems to have been increasing (Mahoney 1986; Mindel et al. 1988; Adler 1997). Still, divorce rates are higher for couples with different religions: During the first five years of marriage, the divorce rate for a couple with the same religion is about 24%, but for a Protestant and a Catholic it jumps to 38% and for a marriage between a Jew and a Christian it is 42% (Lehrer and Chiswick 1993).

One Dating Model: A Three-Stage Filtering Process

It has been suggested that dating couples go through a three-stage filtering process known as *stimulus-values-roles* (Murstein 1986):

■ Filtering Stage 1—Stimulus: The first stage involves physical attraction. People come together because they are attracted to each other physically. If they are not attracted, this is the first filtering stage.

■ Filtering Stage 2—Values: In the second stage, the two people compare their individual values to determine whether they are compatible—for example, to find out whether they are in agreement on personal ambition, child raising, political views, and so on. This is another filtering stage.

■ **Filtering Stage 3—Roles:** In the third stage, the two negotiate role compatibility—for example, how they will handle work, housekeeping, and leisure arrangements. If they cannot agree, this represents a third filtering stage.

Another Dating Model: Is Commitment Relationship Driven or Event Driven?

Two scholars (Surra and Hughes 1997) have suggested an alternative to the filtering process.

■ **The Relationship-Driven Couple:** Some dating couples go through a filtering or *relationship-driven* process, with the two growing in their commitment as they sort out their mutual preferences, values, goals, and roles, as previously described.

■ **The Event-Driven Couple:** Other couples go through an *event-driven* process—the partners swing back and forth between commitment and ambivalence, often quite dramatically. They may have fights, temporarily separate, intensely debate their relationship with their friends, then come together and again and make up. In the long run, this sort of process may lead to a less positive outcome for the relationship.

Close Dating Relationships & Personal Growth

Does dating contribute to one's personal growth? One longitudinal study of partners from 301 dating couples found that it does (Ruvolo and Brennan 1997).

Using the definition that growth is an individual's perception of becoming closer to his or her ideals (Rogers 1954), the study authors hypothesized that the more the partner loves an individual, the more growth the individual will subsequently experience. The study then examined the growth that occurred during dating relationships over a 5-month period, on the assumption that dating relationships may be influential to an individual's life.

"If such short-term, relatively casual relationships can demonstrate individual growth and development," wrote the study authors, "the potential that more serious and long-term relationships have for fostering growth may be even stronger." The study concluded that the supportive assistance that individuals received from their dating partners and the love the partners reported for them indeed predict the growth that the individuals later experienced.

5.2 Pairing Up: Finding & Choosing a Partner

MAJOR QUESTION How can I find someone to love?

PREVIEW Four ways of meeting people are personal introductions, classified ads, meeting online, and introduction services. Among the variations in dating are traditional courtship; hanging out, hooking up, and being joined at the hip; dating in the workplace; and second-time-around dating.

Romantic movie plots are built around clichés of accidental meetings: the leashes of the two dog walkers that become ensnared, the package dropped by one person and picked up by the other, the vehicle breakdown, and so on. But how do real-life people usually meet?

Finding a Partner amid Masses of People

If you live in a big city or attend college on a big campus, you might see masses of people every day. And, by the way, if you are now in college, it is important to realize that campuses provide the opportunity to meet hundreds of people who are similar to you (in age range, social class, and life goals) in ways that will be difficult to match later, such as in the workplace. From this sea of humanity, how do you single out those who might make romantic partners? How do they become available to you? One way to analyze this is to distinguish between open and closed fields (Murstein 1976, 1987).

Open Fields: Interaction Unlikely

If you go to school on a large university campus, that setting is an open field. **Open fields are settings in which people do not normally interact and so potential partners are not likely to meet.** Other examples of open fields are shopping malls, airports, big athletic events, amusement parks, ski resorts, and public beaches. Because such pools of people are so large and anonymous, they discourage potential partners from meeting.

Closed Fields: Interaction Likely

Regardless of the size of your university or college, if you are in small classes, you are in what are known as closed fields. **Closed fields are settings in which people are likely to interact and so potential partners may meet.** Other examples are parties, church groups, dormitories, friends' homes, and small workplace settings. Clearly, such environments encourage you to meet people, whether or not they are possible romantic partners.

Meeting People

People meet people in all kinds of ways, of course. However, today they might rely less on chance and more on rational means of meeting prospective partners—as in using newspaper ads, the Internet, and introduction services—with a view toward reducing negative outcomes such as breakups and divorce (Bulcroft et al. 2000). Here, we will discuss four methods: (1) personal introductions, (2) classified ads, (3) meeting online, and (4) introduction services (video dating, marriage bureaus, mail-order bride services).

1. Personal Introductions

There are many closed-field settings in which to find a prospective partner: college classes, church groups, clubs, and recreational activities such as bicycling, hiking, and singing groups. Some 1980s studies found that the most common settings in which young adults meet are parties, followed by classes, work, bars, clubs, sports settings, and activities centered on recreation, such as hiking (Simenauer and Carroll 1982; Shostak 1987).

A 2005 survey questioned the dating habits of 3,400 people, 58% were men and 42% were women. Findings (multiple answers allowed) showed that the most favored methods for meeting a potential date were through friends at 53%, at pubs or clubs at 53%, and by going online at 33%, with traditional dating agencies, classified ads, and speed-dating events following in popularity (Online Dating Survey from Nielsen/Netratings, reported in "Internet Now Third Most Popular Way to Get a Date" 2005). Another 2005 nationwide telephone survey asked 1,503 people age 18 and older how they met the person they married, but the results show no use of Internet dating at all, possibly because the technology is so recent (*With This Ring . . .* 2005). *(See ■ Panel 5.3.)*

Between one-third and one-half of dating relationships begin with a personal introduction (Sprecher and McKinney 1993). Although men often introduce themselves directly, women are more apt to wait for the other person to make the first move or to be introduced by someone else (Berger 1987). Indeed, a third-person introduction might be considered best because it suggests that someone already finds the pair perhaps compatible.

A classic form of personal introduction is the **blind date, also known as the setup, in which a common friend or relative introduces two singles who are unknown to each other.** Even in the era of Internet dating, or perhaps because of it, blind dating has reportedly enjoyed a resurgence. With the traditional blind date, says one writer, dates "are vetted and vouched for" by the match-making friend or relative; thus, the dater is less likely to experience the rudeness that the anonymity of Internet dating can breed, in which

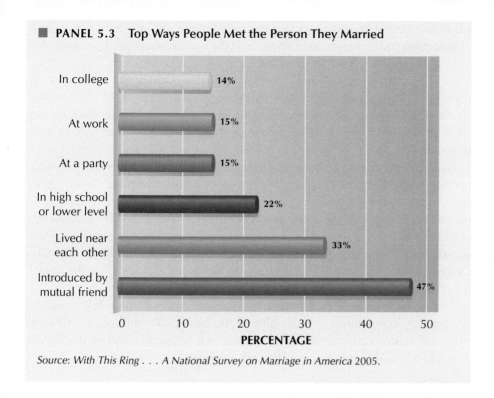

■ PANEL 5.3   Top Ways People Met the Person They Married

In college **14%**

At work **15%**

At a party **15%**

In high school or lower level **22%**

Lived near each other **33%**

Introduced by mutual friend **47%**

0   10   20   30   40   50

PERCENTAGE

Source: With This Ring . . . A National Survey on Marriage in America 2005.

people feel less compunction about not showing up for a prearranged meeting (Barker 2005).

2. Classified Ads

Personal classified ads started out in the 1960s in countercultural or hippie newspapers, such as New York's *East Village Other* and California's *Berkeley Barb*. Now they appear in all kinds of periodicals, including such upstanding publications as *The New York Review of Books* ("COOL, WISE WIDOW: shapely, fit, Harvard graduate, loves English literature, Bach, Eastern philosophy. Hopes to meet a man mid-fifties to mid-sixties, Boston area . . ."). Besides permitting anonymity, the benefits of such ads are that they save time and can expose one to numerous possible partners.

Personal classified ads have at least two important characteristics (Davis 1990; Cicerello and Sheehan 1995; Dunbar 1995; Raybeck et al. 1996):

■ Women as Sex Objects: Men, who are twice as apt as women to place personal ads, tend to emphasize appearance and attractiveness in the women they seek ("good-looking," "trim," "takes care of herself," and so on). Women will also describe themselves as attractive and feminine in ads about themselves ("Annette Bening with a touch of younger Stockard Channing. Considered 'extremely cute . . .'").

Women's personal ads drew an average of 15 replies in one study (Ahuvia and Adelman 1992). Those who received the most replies stressed physical attractiveness, youth, physical fitness, interest in sports, and allusions to sex.

■ Men as Success Objects: Women are more apt to say that they are looking for men who are "intelligent," "professional," "college-educated," and so on, while also stressing sensitivity and caring. Men are apt to use the same kinds of adjectives in their own ads ("Divorced white male, successful professional, 55+, world traveler. Kind, humorous, communicative").

In the study we just cited, men's personal ads drew an average of 11 responses (Ahuvia and Adelman 1992). Those who received the most replies stressed being older and taller, having received a higher education, having more professional status, and desiring an attractive woman but with no mention of sex.

Even so, a content analysis of singles ads in four different types of publications found that personality characteristics ("sense of humor," "kind," "honest," "warm," "intelligent") are extremely important in the search by both males and females. Indeed, personality characteristics were more frequently cited than either attractiveness or professional/educational background characteristics. "This analysis," says the study author, "suggests that the women's movement and changing gender roles are having an influence on the search for potential heterosexual partners" (Lance 1998).

Incidentally, because personal ads are big on clichés ("moonlight walks on the beach"; "companion to share all that life has to offer"), there are services that will help you create a successful ad, examples being Personals Trainer.com and E-cyrano.com (Bounds 2004a).

3. Meeting Online

Relationship websites take personal classified ads to another level by offering an opportunity to meet friends or partners online (St. John 2002; Egan 2003; Kornblum 2004a; Nussbaum 2004). There are perhaps three types of relationship or dating websites—*online dating websites, social networking websites,* and *online newsgroups.*

■ **Online Dating Websites:** *Online dating websites* provide electronic forums that people may join in hopes of meeting compatible potential mates. Five of the biggest and best-known sites are AmericanSingles, eHarmony, Match.com, True, and Yahoo! Personals (Romance.com 2006), although the list keeps changing. *(See ■ Panel 5.4.)* Most dating sites charge a fee, but PlentyofFish, OKCupid, MatchDoctor, VietSingle, and BookofMatches are free.

Most of the 1,000 dating sites are niche or specialty sites, as for people of different political persuasions (*loveinwar.com* versus *conservativematch.com,* or *single republican.com* versus *democraticsingles.net,* or *catholicmatch.com* versus *actforlove.org*); religious beliefs (*ChristianCafe.com, bigchurch.com,*

■ **PANEL 5.4** The Most Visited Internet Dating Sites, February 2007

1. Yahoo! Personals	6. eHarmony
2. True	7. Mate 1
3. Match.com	8. AmericanSingles
4. MSN Dating (Match.com)	9. PlentyofFish
5. Singlesnet.com	10. eCrush

Source: Based on Brooks 2007.

Soulmatch.com, Jdate.com for Jewish daters); gays *(Adam4Adam.com, Man Hunt.net, Gay.com)*; African Americans *(BlackPeopleMeet.com, OnlineBooty Call.com, BlackSingles.com)*; Asians *(LoveFromIndia.com, Shaadi.com, Asi-aFriendFinder.com)*; farmers *(OnlyFarmers.com, FarmersOnly.com)*; and mature adults *(SeniorFriendFinder.com, 50yearsplus.com, SeniorsCircle.com)*. There are also adult dating sites that purport to help users find one-night stands, swinger parties, and the like (Kesmodel 2006). Then there are all the niche dating sites for smokers, vegetarians, dog lovers, and so on.

■ **Social Networking Websites:** *Social networking websites* are not specifically designed for finding dates, but that is how they are being used. Sites such as MySpace, Facebook, Friendster, Xanga, and others let people build personal webpages to express their interests and display their personality. In February 2007, MySpace had a market share of 80.74% and Facebook 10.32%, with all other social networking sites at 1% or less, including Friendster (0.34%), once a dominant force (O'Hear 2007). *(See* ■ *Panel 5.5.)*

■ **Online Newsgroups:** *Online newsgroups* are for people who want to become members of online communities devoted to their neighborhoods, using free services offered by Yahoo Groups *(groups.yahoo.com)*, Google Groups *(www.groups.google.com)*, or the Freecycle Network *(www.freecycle.org)*. For instance, in Sebastapol, California, two dozen people have joined a group devoted to maintaining the rural and farming character of a street called Coffee Lane (Sullivan 2007). This and other groups use newsgroups to post meeting reminders, crime reports, and general announcements.

Eventually two people who meet online may decided to talk on the phone, and then to meet face to face. We gave some tips about relationship websites in Chapter 4, "Love," in the Practical Action box, "Love on the Internet: Can You Find the Perfect Partner Online?" Some more are given in the box on pages 164–165.

There are advantages and disadvantages to Internet romances:

■ **Advantages:** Relationship websites can expose you to a wider variety of potential partners than is possible in more conventional ways, as through school, church, or club activities. Indeed, for people who live in somewhat isolated circumstances, the Internet is especially a boon.

■ **PANEL 5.5** The Most Visited Social Networking Websites, February 2007

1. MySpace	9. hi5
2. Facebook	10. Tagged
3. Bebo	11. LiveJournal
4. BlackPlanet.com	12. Gaiaonline.com
5. Xanga	13. Friendster
6. iMeem	14. Orkut
7. Yahoo! 360	15. Live Spaces
8. Classmates	

Source: O'Hear 2007.

DIGITAL DATING. Online matchmaking sites have become tremendously popular, being visited by over a quarter of Internet users, according to some statistics. There are scores of such dating sites, open to people of all kinds of races, ethnicities, religions, political views, and sexual orientations. What do you think are the benefits and risks of Web dating? ▶

In addition, the initial investment of time and energy via email or chat room discussion can also be fairly minimal before you and the other person need to decide whether to continue communicating or not.

Finally, you can also get to know someone for qualities other than looks or physical attractiveness—the very qualities (such as intellectual interests) that might help to support a relationship over the long term.

■ **Disadvantages:** One immediate disadvantage of meeting someone on the Internet is that—unless both of you have webcam or video-phone setups and can observe each other—you do not have the nonverbal communication that can tell you a lot about a person.

Another disadvantage is that you might hit it off with someone who lives quite far away, even on another continent, which can complicate any physical meeting and certainly any long-term relationship.

Finally, there is always the possibility that when you finally do meet face to face, you will discover the other person is disturbed or even dangerous. You need, therefore, to know how to protect yourself.

4. Introduction Services

Introduction services do much the same thing as print and Internet dating ads, the services offering (for a fee) to introduce people to each other. Some examples are Eight at Eight, The Right One, Together Dating, Great Expectations, It's Just Lunch, Soulmates introduction service, Jewish Matchmaking Company, Single Colombian Latin Ladies Introduction Service, and *Filipina Ladies.com* (Bounds 2004b, Cullen 2004).

Variants are video dating, marriage bureau, and mail-order bride services.

■ **Video Dating Services:** When you sign up for a ***video dating service*** **, you are allowed to watch videotapes of others talking and in various activities in return for allowing others to watch your tape.** If you see someone you favor, the company contacts that person and invites him or her to watch your tape. Examples of video dating services are Great Expectations; Planet Intro, Inc.; ABC Search; and Apple Love. A variant on the video dating service is the video-on-demand service called Dating On Demand, in which Comcast cable television presents videos (shot either by clients or by Comcast) of people looking for relationships (Lieberman 2005).

■ **Marriage Bureaus:** ***Marriage bureaus*** **arrange introductions for a fee.** Such bureaus are most popular in other countries, such as India and Asia. Examples in the United Kingdom, for instance, are LAJ Marriage Bureau International, Farmers and Country Friendship and Marriage Bureau, and Muslim Marriage Service. An example in New York is the Meet the Elite dating service. One in Boston is Internet Matrimonials (Jana 2000).

■ **Mail-Order Brides:** Agencies specializing in so-called ***mail-order brides*** **publish profiles and photos of women mainly for the benefit of American men seeking wives** (Chang 2002). Most such services feature women from Asia, Latin America, and Russia. Examples are the Mail Order Bride Warehouse, Russian Mail Order Bride Directory, ACebuBride (Philippines), A Korean Bride, and My Thai Bride. Because of the traditional preference for sons in South Korea, China, India, and other Asian nations, a disproportionate number of men are now competing for a smaller number of women. This imbalance has created a rise in "marriage tour" brokers to serve these men, particularly in Vietnam (Onishi 2007).

Variations in Dating

Eight minutes, then—ding!—a bell rings. The couples in the New York nightclub quickly cease their conversation and rush off to other tables in search of new partners. Afterward, they turn in pencil-and-paper score sheets rating their eight 8-minute "dates" (to the company that is known, naturally, as 8minuteDating) and later will learn via email whether there's a match—or two or three—that they might follow up on (Barker 2002, 2003).

Is this your idea of dating? It's certainly efficient—eight dates in 64 minutes. The concept has also been extended by groups of college alumni, in which eight or so tables of eight singles are rotated during a three-course meal. Commercial companies have jumped in, some with operations in several cities, among them SpeedDating, 8minuteDating, FastDater, HurryDate, Nanodate, InstadateNY, 10-Minute Match, and Brief Encounters (Kurlantzick 2001). Says Paul Raman, a 37-year-old New Jersey mutual-fund manager, "It's a numbers game, like pulling the slots. Sooner or later, you'll hit the jackpot." Jenny Hust, age 29, who works in human resources, might agree. After 29 minidates, she hit it off with a man she met on HurryDate in Atlanta. He proposed five months later.

Clearly, the quick date is only one in a number of different kinds of dating or courtship practices. We discuss four others here.

1. Traditional Courtship: From Dating to Engagement

Traditional dating prevailed from the 1950s through the 1970s, at least among the American middle class. A boy would ask a girl out, arrive at her home to pick her up, perhaps chat with her parents, then take her to a certain event, such as dinner and a movie. The boy would pay for the date, and the girl was expected to reciprocate by, at the least, allowing a good-night kiss but also perhaps some amorous embracing and fondling ("making out") and even sexual intercourse. Sometimes the date would be highly formal, such as a coming-out party (with young women of the upper classes being introduced to society at a debutante ball or cotillion), a high school prom (formal dance), or a college homecoming party.

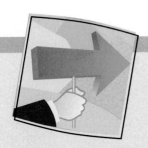

PRACTICAL ACTION

Dealing with Print & Online Relationship Ads: Anonymity, Intimacy, & Safety

The greatest examples of what we mean by the "relationship marketplace" are probably embodied in the dating ads that are found in some newspapers and magazines and on the Internet.

We mentioned in the Practical Action box in Chapter 4, "Love," that the Internet might not be the most effective means of finding someone with whom to have an enduring relationship. Nevertheless, because print and Internet ads have become so popular, you might be inclined to try either posting or responding to them.

Suggestions for Dealing with Ads

The following are some suggestions for advertising or answering personal ads (Booth and Jung 1998; Gwinnell 1998; Hafner 2002; McDermott 2002; Egan 2003):

- **Protect your identity until you're ready to reveal it:** If you run an ad about yourself in a newspaper or magazine, people answering it will

be asked to respond to a box number at the periodical, which then forwards you your mail, probably on a weekly basis. Online dating services have a similar "double-blind" system—respondents reply to an email mailbox at the organization—so that your identity remains anonymous until you are ready to give out your direct contact information.

When writing an ad about yourself, be careful not to give out any identifying information that could be used to trace you, particularly if you live in a small town. Don't indicate your college or workplace. Don't state your income. (If the dating service requests it in your profile, simply write "I'll tell you later.")

Set up an email account (you can get a free one with Yahoo or Hotmail) just for dating purposes. When corresponding with others, turn off your email signature file. Don't include your last name, email address, phone number, home

address, workplace, or other identifying information in your correspondence or in the profile on the dating site.

One study found it striking that Internet personals placed by college students were much longer than comparable newspaper personals, "yet people are revealing less personal information about themselves over the Internet" (Milewski et al. 1999). For example, 9% of Internet ad placers did not even state their gender, 33% did not reveal their sexual orientation, 25% did not mention their age, and 60% did not mention their year in school. In newspaper personals, by contrast, people would volunteer most such information.

- **Start slowly, exercise caution, and let others earn your trust:** Go at your own pace. You don't need to go beyond the computer or the phone until you feel at ease with the other person. You should take as much time as you need to assess

If a couple liked each other, the dating might evolve into "going steady"—the two would agree not to date others and to see only each other. Going steady might or might not lead to sexual intimacy or engagement and marriage, but at the very least it let other dating prospects know that the partners were "not available." Incidentally, going steady may ultimately be better than doing heavy dating. Research shows that lots of dating as a teenager may develop social skills, but it doesn't teach deeper skills such as how to communicate well and solve conflicts (Madsen and Collins 2005). Young people who dated moderately (an average of seven partners per year at age 16) have been found to fare the best in long-term relationships later in life (Musick et al. 2005).

The culmination of formal dating was and is the proposal of marriage, traditionally with the man asking the woman "for her hand" (after, perhaps, seeking the permission of her parents) and presenting her with an engagement

whether the other person is trustworthy.

"Watch out for someone who seems too good to be true," advises Trish McDermott (2002) on the *Match.com* website. "Look for odd behavior or inconsistencies. The person at the other end may not be who or what he or she says." Ask lots of questions, and watch for inconsistencies. Stay away from people who won't respect your space, who try to pressure you, or who won't take no for an answer.

The point is to let others gradually reveal whether their actions consist mostly of honorable, honest behavior. If someone makes you uncomfortable, don't continue.

In particular, watch for inconsistencies in answers about marital status, employment, interests, and so on or failure to respond to direct questions. Also watch for disrespectful comments, displays of anger, or attempts to control you.

- **Ask for a photo:** People who advertise in periodicals usually don't post photos. Those who post profiles about themselves on online relationship sites often do.

A photo will give you some idea of a person's appearance, suggests McDermott. "In fact," she says, "it's best to view several images of someone in various settings: casual, formal, indoor, and outdoors." Most important, if someone gives you excuses for not providing a photo, he or she might have something to hide.

- **Talk on the phone:** Talking on the phone will also help you determine the other person's communication and social skills. Don't reveal your own phone number. Use a pay phone or a cell phone or blocking techniques that will prevent your phone number from showing up on Caller ID.

- **If necessary, use verification services:** Some companies now offer background checks and client certification options to smoke out people who lie about everything from hair color to last name to criminal records. Examples are *Checkmates.com, LookBetterOnline .com, CertifiedDates.com, True.com, Verified Person.com,* and *Privacy RightsClearinghouse.com* (della Cava 2004).

If You Finally Meet

You never have to go beyond communicating by phone, letter, or online, regardless of the level of intimacy you've reached. But if you decide to meet, here are some tips:

- **Listen to your instincts:** Even if you have made plans to meet, do not go ahead with it if something doesn't feel right. You have to trust your instincts.

- **Meet somewhere safe:** Don't let your date pick you up; provide your own transportation to and from the meeting place. Meet in a public place, such as a coffee shop, with lots of people around. ALWAYS make sure a friend or family member knows your plans and how to find you.

If you meet out of town, don't allow the other person to make arrangements for you. Line up your own car and hotel, and arrange to meet at another location, such as a restaurant. If you can, carry a cell phone in case you feel uneasy about your environment and want to change plans. If necessary, don't be afraid to call the police.

ring. **Engagement is a period of time that begins with the marriage proposal and a formal announcement that the couple plans to be married.** Engagements average 12 to 16 months in duration; they serve two purposes:

■ **Sign of Commitment:** When you become engaged, you and your partner are making a public statement that your relationship has changed and you are now leaving the singles world. You are now expected to plan the date and nature of the marriage ceremony, where you will live, and other serious matters.

■ **Preparing to Expand Family Ties:** Engagement means that you and your partner are signaling your intentions to expand your kinship circle. That is, it is assumed that you will introduce each other to your respective family members and will enlarge your family system.

The traditional system of dating still exists—and for all age groups. Indeed, what's interesting is that despite the trend toward gender equality, studies find that young adults' first dates tend to adhere to strongly stereotyped gender behavior—woman as subordinate, sexual object, and as facilitator of men's plans and man as dominant, as planner, as economic provider, and as sexual initiator (Laner and Ventrone 1998, 2000). Even so, traditional dating practices have been replaced by other ways of getting together, as follows.

2. On Campus Today: Hanging Out, Hooking Up, & Joined at the Hip

Among college-age men and women, the idea of going steady, becoming engaged, and getting married seems to be virtually archaic, says sociologist Andrew Cherlin. Indeed, he says, "There is no true courtship today" (quoted in Peterson 2000b). More than this, as another writer puts it, "The date is all but dead" (Mulhauser 2001; see also Lavinthal and Rozler 2005).

Instead, what seems to be taking place on American campuses—and even in high schools—is what one study calls "hanging out, hooking up, or joined at the hip, with little in between" (Glenn and Marquardt 2001; see also Denizet-Lewis 2004). Sponsored by the Independent Women's Forum and conducted by the Institute for American Values, the study examined the heterosexual dating culture of 1,000 college women at 11 four-year U.S. colleges.

■ **Hanging Out:** Men and women don't date in the traditional sense. Indeed, only about half of senior women said that they had been asked on six or more man-pays-the-way dates since they started college. Instead, as one alternative, they might simply "hang out," or spend time in unstructured groups together. This is also called *pack dating*—students socializing in unpartnered groups (Gabriel 1997).

■ **Hooking Up:** *Hooking up* **is defined as a physical encounter that allows possible sexual interaction—ranging from kissing to having sex—without commitment.** The hookup might occur just once or more than once between the same two people over a period of weeks or months. About 40% of the women respondents reported having had at least one hookup, and 10% had had more than six (Sessions 2007).

■ **Joined at the Hip:** The opposite of hanging out or hooking up are what the study calls "joined-at-the-hip" relationships, also known as "the college marriage," in which two people do everything with each other—eat, study, do laundry, and perhaps sleep together.

These practices, the survey found, are encouraged by the freedoms that earlier generations of women fought for, such as sexual freedom. They are also exacerbated by the existence of co-ed dormitories. Interestingly, however, 39% of the respondents said that they were virgins. The study also found that most women students expected to meet their future husbands on campus and that they expected those marriages to last but that the women "were struggling to articulate rules and expectations that would help them to make sense of the prevailing confusion."

3. Dating in the Workplace

Americans now work an average of 47 hours a week, often in work teams and on joint projects, which provides more opportunity for office dating. Indeed, almost 40% of adults have dated a co-worker, according to one survey (Roper Starch, reported in Jackson 1999). As many as 8 million Americans enter into a romance with a fellow employee each year (Lardner 1998). One survey of 390 managers and executives found that 30% said they had dated a co-worker, and two-thirds said they approved of employees' dating in the workplace (American Management Association 2003). Another survey found 40% of employees being involved in an office romance (Parks 2006). Another found that 54% of single men and 40% of women said they would be open to dating a co-worker (Opinion Research Corp. 2005, cited in Jayson 2006b).

Yet another study found that 47% of women and 36% of men felt that openly dating a co-worker would jeopardize their job security or advancement opportunities (Harris Interactive/Spherion 2007). Are they right to be concerned? Only 12% of 391 companies surveyed by the American Management Association (cited in Shellenbarger 2005) had written guidelines on office dating. Some firms take the position that office romances are none of their business unless they occur between supervisors and their employees, where sexual harassment issues may arise.

4. Second-Time-Around Dating

For the single parent, the divorced, the widowed, and singles over age 65, dating has special challenges, especially if the person has children. We discuss these in detail in Chapter 14, "Uncoupling."

COURTIN'? Unlike the more structured dating and engagement patterns of past generations, the relationships of college students today range from the casually intimate (hooking up) to unstructured hanging out to the seriously attached (joined at the hip). Do you fall anywhere on this spectrum? ▲

5.3 Cohabitation: Living Together as an Unmarried Couple

MAJOR QUESTION Why might I live together with someone, and what would it be like?

PREVIEW We discuss the reasons people live together, their characteristics, and why living together has increased. We then discuss the experience of living together and how it may differ from marriage.

Cohabitation, **or living together, is defined as a couple living in an emotional and sexual relationship without being married.** A once somewhat uncommon arrangement, cohabitation began to be a trend in the late 1950s among less educated couples and since then has increased steadily. *(See* ■ *Panel 5.6.)* Indeed, today the majority of couples who marry have lived together first (Peterson 2002).

The U.S. Bureau of the Census includes couples in this kind of relationship under the term *POSSLQs*, **which stands for "People of the Opposite Sex Sharing Living Quarters."** Technically, POSSLQs include unmarried couples who are not related to each other and are of the opposite sex, perhaps with children under age 15. Thus, this could include not only cohabitants but also roommates of the opposite sex, a landlord and roomer, and a disabled or ill person and live-in caregiver. It also includes men and women who live together for economic reasons, such as an older couple who are widowed or divorced from previous spouses and who want to keep the financial benefits that might be lost if they married each other. (Social Security or pension benefits of a deceased spouse may be taken away on remarriage.) What we're concerned with, however, are unmarried heterosexual lovers who live together. (We discuss gay partners in Chapter 8, "Variations.")

People Who Live Together: Why & Who

Currently, about 5 million Americans live with partners of the opposite sex. This arrangement comprises about 8% of U.S. households with couples (Jayson 2005b.) Excluding the kind of POSSLQ households mentioned earlier, what are their reasons?

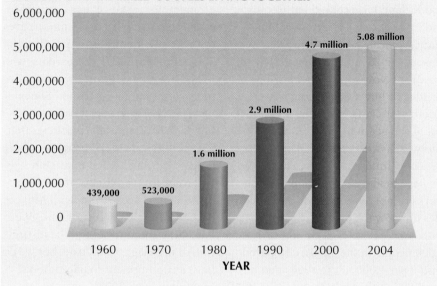

■ **PANEL 5.6   Cohabitation: Unmarried Couples Living Together, 1960–2004.** During this time, the number of unmarried couples living together increased tenfold. Most unmarried partners living together are 25 to 34 years old.

NUMBER OF UNMARRIED COUPLES LIVING TOGETHER

Four Reasons for Cohabiting

Among the causes that have been identified for lovers moving in together are the following (Ridley et al. 1978):

■ **The Linus Blanket:** The title comes from the *Peanuts* cartoon character Linus, with his security blanket. In this kind of cohabitation, one partner is highly insecure or dependent and prefers, in the study authors' words, "a relationship with *someone*, with little apparent regard for whom, or under what conditions. . . . To have someone to be with, even though he or she may treat you badly, is better than not having anyone at all" (p. 130). This type of cohabitation probably won't last because the more independent partner will tire of the dependent partner's demands.

■ **Emancipation:** One or both partners enter into the relationship to express independence from their parents' values about sexuality. The goal of cohabitation, then, is really to make a statement to the parents, and the unmarried partner is mainly a means for doing so. Developing intimacy is less important, so this relationship too probably won't survive.

■ **Convenience:** Two partners get their needs fulfilled without benefit of a traditional marriage. The woman, for instance, gets financial help, a roof over her head, and a sexual partner. The man gets "regularized sexual contact and the luxuries of domestic living" (p. 131). The woman, however, usually has less security. In fact, it is generally the man who resists getting married.

■ **Testing:** A couple lives together in a kind of trial marriage, to find out whether getting married would probably work for them. This could include people who are engaged. It could also include people who can't get married

EXAMPLE OF
Who's Living Together
Cohabitation among Europeans

Ms. Dorian Solot and Mr. Marshall Miller, who are in their thirties, are the founders of the Alternatives to Marriage Project as well as authors of *Unmarried to Each Other: The Essential Guide to Living Together* (2002). The two have been unmarried partners for over a decade, ever since they were undergraduates at Brown University. They decided to write the book because they were frustrated by assumptions in the United States such as those of the prospective landlord who wanted to know when they were getting married and the car-rental company that charged extra for one of them to be listed as a second driver (Mead 2002).

Although many couples in the United States are bypassing marriage in favor of cohabitation, it's an even bigger trend in Europe. For decades, couples in Sweden, Norway, Denmark, and Iceland have shared bathrooms and closet space without benefit of marriage license. Marianne Kristensen, age 28, and Tommy Pettersen, age 27, of Norway, for instance, decided to buy a house and move in together after she became pregnant—but not to get married. "We don't know each other quite well yet," said Pettersen (quoted in Knox 2004). "So we have to live together and see if it works or not." Indeed, unmarried couples are now the norm in Scandinavia, with marriage rates declining to 4 per 1,000 people in the 1990s, compared with 9 per 1,000 in the 1950s and 8.3 per 1,000 in the United States for 1998 (Williams 2000: A6).

The trend toward children being born to unmarried parents is far more prevalent in Scandinavian countries, as well as in France in Britain, than in the United States and less so in southern countries such as Switzerland and Italy. Whereas in the United States in 2003 only 34.6% of unmarried women had children, in Scandinavia they ranged from 44.9% in Denmark to 56% in Sweden (Knox 2004).

Such attitudes are substantially different from those in the United States, where the government announced in 2002 that it was actively committed to promoting marriage. The British government, for instance, has acknowledged that there are many alternatives to the classic family structure (Lyall 2002). In addition, single parents, who in general are better off economically in Europe than in the United States, have become a powerful political force, promoting welfare policies that give children financial benefits, inheritance rights, and equal treatment regardless of the parents' marital status. Says one sociologist, Karl Moxnes of the University of Trondheim, "We have little commitment to the institution of marriage, that's true, but we do have a commitment to parenthood" (quoted in Lyall 2002).

WHAT DO YOU THINK? Through its tax and benefit policies and the secularization of its culture, Swedish society has deinstutionalized marriage. If, asks David Popenoe (2005: 9), co-director of the National Marriage Project at Rutgers University, the institution of marriage in the United States is replaced by another form of human pair-bonding—nonmarital cohabitation (or "marriage lite")—do you see anything wrong with this?

right away because, for example, one is waiting to be divorced from a previous spouse.

There are some other variations on these patterns. For instance, those who reject traditional marriage might do so because they feel that their bond is emotional and that the legal contract of a marriage license detracts from the integrity of their emotional commitment. Some people want to keep their finances separate. Some with bad experiences in a previous marriage say, "I don't want to tie myself up again"—perhaps they want the option of just being able to walk away without legal complications. A final variation might be the lovers who maintain a long-term relationship but *don't* live together; they commute between separate residences or even separate cities yet in all other respects share the same characteristics as cohabiting partners. (This may evolve into a live-together arrangement.)

SENIORS WHO SHARE.
People live together without benefit of marriage for all kinds of reasons. Seniors, for instance, may share a household as roommates to make their incomes go farther. Do you know people like these? ◄

Cohabitation Nation: Who Are the Live-Togethers?

In the United States, people who live together before marriage tend to have the following characteristics compared to those who don't live together before marriage (Axinn and Thornton 1993; Thornton et al. 1995; Michael et al. 1994; Smock 2000):

▪ **Independence:** They are more independent.

▪ **Sex:** They have more sexual experience and have sex more often.

▪ **Attitudes:** They are more liberal, including in their views of gender roles.

▪ **Religion:** They are slightly less religious.

▪ **Income:** They have a slightly lower income.

▪ **Education:** They tend to be lower in education.

About 80% of cohabiting couples are under age 45 (and 19% are under age 25). Compared to married couples, cohabiting couples are more likely to be interracial (Glick and Spanier 1980). About 40% of cohabiting households have children under the age of 18 (Peterson 2002b).

Why Living Together Has Increased

At one time—and in some states still—cohabitation was against the law (a misdemeanor), although this was not often enforced. Now living together is more widespread and accepted, probably for the following reasons:

COMMITMENT? Compared to married couples, live-togethers don't have as deep a commitment toward each other during their time together. They are aware that the relationship can be ended at any time. Do you know any cohabiting couples who have been together for 10 years or more? ▶

■ **Social Tolerance:** Years ago, what made sex morally acceptable was marriage. Now social mores have changed, and many people regard sex between two people who are thought to be in love, whether married or not, as permissible behavior. The availability of reliable birth control has increased the prevalence and acceptability of premarital sex as well as cohabitation (Casper and Bianchi 2002).

■ **Female Equality:** More women are now in the workplace. Thus, women are more economically self-sufficient and no longer have to depend on marriage and a husband for their financial survival.

■ **Impermanence of Marriage:** High divorce rates make marriage seem a less permanent arrangement. Many people are afraid of rushing into marriage and want a trial period of living together.

Still, cohabitation doesn't have the same social acceptance as marriage, not just because it involves a sexual relationship outside of wedlock but also because it doesn't seem to represent a lifelong commitment. Your parents, for instance, might be less approving if you announce that you're living with someone than if you say that you're getting married. Therefore, most of the social support that cohabitants get probably comes from other couples who are living together.

The Experience of Living Together

Sarah Abbott and Daniel Price of San Francisco had lived together for about 18 months—somewhat unusual because by that point most cohabiting couples have either broken up or become married. And Sarah said that she would probably marry Daniel and definitely would do so if she were to have a child. When interviewed, however, she said that she was surprised by how well their cohabiting relationship was working. For the moment, she said, "I wouldn't want to do it any other way" (Peterson 2000a).

Is this something you've ever considered? Let's see how it might work.

Three Stages of Living Together

People in long-term cohabiting relationships (not just heterosexuals but gays and lesbians as well, as we discuss in Chapter 9, "Variations") may go through three stages (Kurdek and Schmitt 1986):

▪ **Year 1—Blending:** In this stage, the partners are infatuated with each other. They are at the height of passion—head over heels in love—and have a very active sex life.

▪ **Years 2 and 3—Nesting:** As passion subsides, the partners deemphasize sex and emphasize other grounds for compatibility, such as dealing with the household. Some ambivalence may creep in about their relationship.

▪ **Years 4 and 5—Maintaining:** If the relationship lasts this long, the partners will now begin to establish certain patterns of stability and establishing traditions, such as ways of dealing with conflict, frequency of sex, and handling of work and money matters.

In contrast to married couples, however, for unmarried cohabitants the commitment during their time together is not as deep. As long as they feel love for each other, they stay together. But they are aware that the escape hatch is always open, that the relationship can be ended at any time (Teachman and Polonko 1990; Lindsay 2000; Popenoe and Whitehead 2002). Indeed, the probability of a split within 5 years for people in a live-in relationship is 49% versus only 20% for those in a marriage, according to the National Center for Health Statistics (cited in Peterson 2002b).

Some Differences between Marriage & Living Together

Certain areas tend to be handled differently in cohabitant relationships than in married ones.

▪ **Work:** In traditional marriages, it has been considered the husband's role to provide financial support for the family, and whether the wife works is often determined by both. In cohabiting relationships, the two partners are individually expected to support themselves (Blumstein and Schwartz 1983). This is the case even if one member is still in school.

▪ **Finances:** As a sign of their commitment to each other, married partners generally consolidate their finances. Cohabiting partners generally maintain their financial independence—unless, perhaps, they expect to be together a long time or to become married (Blumstein and Schwartz 1983). Indeed, cohabitants may resist talking about money because it seems to reduce their love to numbers (Scherreik 1993).

▪ **Housework:** In traditional marriages, it has generally been the wife's role to be homemaker. In live-in relationships, the woman does not spend as much time on housework (Shelton and John 1993). Sometimes, cohabiting women are expected to be the traditional cook, cleaner, and bottle-washer, which some may resent.

The Advantages of Living Together

Cohabitants list several advantages to living together:

■ **Relationship Test:** Lovers can realistically see how workable their future marriage might be and learn about their partner's habits, values, and expectations.

■ **Companionship with Independence:** Cohabitation provides a sexual partner and companionship yet allows both people to maintain their independence in many ways.

■ **Easier Termination:** With fewer legal entanglements, it's easier to dissolve a cohabiting relationship than to end a marriage.

The Disadvantages of Living Together

There are clearly some disadvantages, however:

■ **Lack of Commitment:** Without binding marital commitment, couples are less inclined to stay faithful and to work through problems (Nock 1995; Waite 2000).

■ **Exploitation:** A woman might be asked to pay half of expenses even though her income may be less (Khoo 1987). She might also do more housekeeping tasks.

■ **Fewer Legal Rights:** Unless agreements are made legal by contract—such as property and paternity rights—ending a relationship can be full of hassles.

It needs to be pointed out that people in cohabiting relationships might have lower levels of happiness and higher rates of depression and alcohol problems than married couples have (Kurdek 1991; Horwitz and White 1998; Stack and Eshleman 1998). They might also see more incidents of fighting and domestic violence (Brown and Booth 1996; Magdol et al. 1998). These drawbacks diminish or disappear in live-together relationships in which the partners have declared that they intend to marry.

How likely are live-in partners to marry? In the 1970s, two-thirds of cohabiting couples married within 3 years. Today, only half as many women marry their live-in mates (Manning and Smock 2002). Still, one study found that unmarried lovers in a cohabiting relationship were more than three times as likely to declare their intent to marry their partner compared to lovers in non-cohabiting, steady dating relationships (Mcginnis 2003).

How likely are married people who formerly cohabited to stay together? About 40% of those who end up marrying later divorce (Nagourney 2000; Smock 2000). According to researcher Scott Stanley (cited in Peterson 2002a: 1D), men who cohabit with the women they eventually marry are less com-

PRACTICAL ACTION

Before Moving in Together: Setting Ground Rules for Understanding

Living together "is a big step, not to be taken lightly," says Stacey Whitman, coauthor of a book on the subject (Whitman and Whitman 2003). But, she says, "People tend to romanticize what it will be like" (quoted in Peterson 2002).

This view is echoed by Dorian Solot, cofounder of the Alternatives to Marriage Project and coauthor with her live-in boyfriend of *Unmarried to Each Other* (Solot and Miller 2002). "A lot of people jump into living together without thinking about it very long or thinking about it at all," says Solot (quoted in Peterson 2002b). "That can get you in trouble. It is important to have detailed information on what to talk about."

Issues Big & Small

The list of issues that live-in couples don't talk about beforehand is long. They frequently don't discuss why they want to live together; one person, for example, might see it as a step toward marriage, and the other might not. They don't talk about money issues, including how to divide up income and expenses or how to handle bank accounts, credit cards, taxes, or property ownership.

What the Experts Say

You and your partner don't have to agree on everything, but experts believe that you should resolve major issues before moving in together. Indeed, to give each person legal protection, they recommend that you even have a "cohabitation agreement" drawn up by a lawyer. This applies whether you're 25 or, as is happening more and more, whether you're 65 (Zaslow 2004).

Some questions to resolve are the following (Rowland 1994; Wu 1995; Peterson 2002; Solot and Miller 2002; Whitman and Whitman 2003; Williams 2004):

- **Do you know each other well enough?** Have you known each other long enough to commit to a live-together relationship? Are there any financial, alcohol, drug, or gambling problems to be discussed? STDs? Former sex partners? Are there religious differences? Career differences? How will you deal with each other's family and friends?

- **Why are you moving in together?** What's the purpose of your live-in relationship? Will it be short term

or long term? Is it a step toward marriage?

- **How will you handle money matters?** Will you keep your money separate? (Experts think you should.) How will you split income, expenses, taxes? Will you own property together, such as a car? Will you both sign an apartment lease?

- **How about lifestyle matters?** Where will you live? Will you be together every night? How will you divide up household chores? Will you have pets?

- **What about children?** Do you plan to have children? Will you both continue working? If one already has children, what should be the other partner's parenting role?

- **What about wills and health-care decisions?** To allow each other to inherit your property if one dies, should you make out two wills? Should you have a health-care proxy so that one partner can make medical decisions for the other? (We consider these legal matters in more detail in a Practical Action box in Chapter 9, "Variations.")

mitted to the marriage than are men who never lived with the women ahead of time. The reason, he speculates, is that men who want to "try out" marriage first are less committed to the institution in general and to their partners in particular compared with men who move directly to marriage without cohabiting.

5.4 Breaking Up Is Hard to Do

MAJOR QUESTION How do people react to a deteriorating relationship, and how can I handle a breakup?

PREVIEW We describe four ways of reacting to a deteriorating relationship. We also give some considerations to keep in mind if your partner breaks up with you or you break up with your partner.

Which gender more readily falls in love? Answer: males. Which more readily falls out of love? Females (Bradsher 1990). One reason, it's speculated, is that women are more sensitive than men about a relationship's emotional nuances, such as rapport. Because they have higher standards about what love should be, then, women are quicker to break up a relationship.

The reasons why couples break up can range from boredom to betrayal, from geographic separation to parental pressure, from meeting someone new to returning to an old lover. With college students, the main reason for a breakup, one study found, was "too many differences/different values" (43% of those surveyed) followed by "got tired of each other (27%), "cheating" (18%), and "dishonesty" (18%) (Knox et al. 1997).

Four Ways of Reacting to a Deteriorating Relationship

One scholar, **Caryl Rusbult** (1987), suggests that people typically try to deal with deteriorating relationships in four ways, which she has labeled the *exit-voice-loyalty-neglect model*. We will describe them in order of neglect, exit, loyalty, and voice responses.

1. The Neglect Response: "Just Let the Relationship Go Ahead & Fall Apart"

The *neglect response* is a destructive reaction that tends to occur when a person is not much invested in the relationship, doesn't want to deal with any problems in it, and is willing to let the partnership simply wither away.

This kind of reaction tends to be more typical with men than with women. It may be expressed in such ways as chronic complaints, frequent criticism, refusal to discuss difficulties, and spending less time with the partner—until the relationship finally dies. Sometimes a partner may start up an extramarital affair or an extrarelationship involvement.

2. The Exit Response: "We Have to End Our Relationship"

The *exit* kind of resolution—withdrawing or threatening to withdraw from a relationship—tends to happen with young people who have been involved with one another for only a short period of time. It is often the choice of people who are dissatisfied with or are only minimally invested in a relationship and who believe that alternative possible partners are available.

People who make the exit response might formally separate, move out of a joint residence, divorce, just stop seeing each other, or might decide to "just be friends."

3. The Loyalty Response: "Let's Just Stick It Out Despite Any Difficulties"

A passive but constructive response, the **loyalty kind of resolution consists of choosing to stay with one's partner despite any problems but making no attempt to try to resolve them, hoping that they will smooth out over time.** Sometimes the passive person will support the other person in the face of criticism, still continuing to have faith in the relationship and the partner.

People who favor the loyalty response might feel invested in, even satisfied with, the relationship and perceive the problems as being relatively minor. Loyalty is often the response favored by older people who have been together a long time, and it is also often more the choice of females than of males.

4. The Voice Response: "We Need to Talk about Improving Our Relationship"

The *voice response* is the choice of people who value the relationship and who are invested in it but who feel that it has problems that need to be discussed. The response seems to indicate a willingness to change things about the relationship—one's own behavior, the partner's behavior, or both.

This option, which is more apt to be pursued by females than males, is an active, constructive response. It can lead to talking, seeking compromises, going for counseling, and trying to change oneself or the partner.

The neglect response would seem to be the most immature and the voice response the most mature approach to dealing with relationship problems. Clearly, however, there are times when a partnership simply isn't working and ending it is the sensible outcome.

Ending a Relationship

The source of great joy can also be the source of great pain, but the process of falling out of love is equally as natural as that of falling in love (though not inevitable, of course). Most people have been involved in a relationship that came to an end. One study of college students found that 88% of women and 89% of men had experienced the breakup of at least one relationship (Laner 1995). According to another study of college students, most ended their last love relationship face to face (women 68%, men 75%) or by telephone (women 19%, men 9%), although some said that it just "faded away" (women 10%, men 16%) (Knox et al. 1998). In the digital age, when mementos of a relationship often exist in the form of emails and digital photos on one's computer, ending it may be as perfunctory as hitting the "delete" key (Bahney 2004). On the other hand, the amount of digital interaction also makes uncoupling more complicated, as ex-lovers scramble to clear cell-phone memories of phone numbers and old text messages, block names on instant-messaging buddy lists, and update profiles on social networking sites (Sharma 2006; Kornblum 2007).

For some people, the painful breakup of a love relationship can lead to what has been called "love addiction," when a person obsessively seeks to regain the pleasurable state that existed within a former love relationship (Timmreck 1990). The distrust, feelings of rejection, loss of self-worth, and feelings of failure, loss, and anger in the emotionally hurt person are all feelings that must be dealt with (Behrendt and Ruotola-Behrendt 2005).

What follows are some considerations to bear in mind whether you're the one receiving news of the breakup or the one initiating it.

If Your Partner Breaks Up with You

If you are the one being let down, don't spend a lot of time speculating about *why*. The other person might not even know why he or she is not in love, and it doesn't help to torture yourself trying to figure it out. The best thing is to simply put some distance between yourself and the other. Consider the following questions:

■ **Can You Accept That the Pain of Rejection Is Natural?** Is there anything worse than pain stemming from rejection by a loved one? It's important to realize that these feelings, however intense, will dwindle over time. Indeed, time is one of the two most helpful contributors to getting over a relationship, the other being getting involved with a new partner (Knox et al. 2000).

■ **What Steps Can You Take to Stop Thoughts about the Other Person?** In *How to Fall Out of Love*, Deborah Phillips (1980) suggests using methods borrowed from behavioral therapy to stop thinking about your former partner. For instance, you can make a list of positive scenes and pleasures that do not involve the former beloved. When a thought about the person enters your mind, say "Stop"; then think about one of the best scenes on your list.

■ **What Can You Do to Raise Your Self-Esteem?** Just as a love relationship builds self-esteem, being rejected lowers it. To raise your self-esteem, Phillips suggests that you use index cards on which you write two good things about

REJECTION. Is there anything worse than the pain that stems from being rejected by someone you love? How do you get over it? ◄

you every day, positive things that you have done recently or in the past. When negative thoughts creep in, say "Stop," and think one of these good things about you.

If You Break Up with Your Partner

You might think that it would be easier to be the one who initiates the termination of a relationship, but it's almost as difficult as being on the receiving end. Remember how it feels to be rejected, and try to be honest but gentle: "I no longer feel the way I once did about you." Don't promise to try to "work things out." Some questions to consider:

■ **Are You Really Sure You Want to Break Up—That the Relationship Can't Be Improved?** Sometimes people have unrealistic expectations about what a relationship should be, and after they end it, they realize that the other person was actually a fine partner. Or you might think that you want to end a relationship because it has so many conflicts—conflicts the two of you might be able to resolve through discussion and compromise. On the other hand, you shouldn't keep a damaged relationship going if it seems beyond repair.

■ **Can You Be Honest and Accept That Your Partner Will Be Hurt?** Usually, there's no painless way to end a relationship; inevitably, the other person will be hurt. But you're probably not being honest with yourself (or with your partner) if you try to be kind and put off the breakup to avoid hurting the other's feelings.

■ **Can You Put Off "Just Being Friends" and Terminate the Relationship Completely?** It is tempting to be ambivalent and to suggest that you remain "just good friends" with your former partner—partly to spare him or her pain but, less straightforwardly, to keep the relationship going on your terms. It's better, however, to put off friendship until a considerable amount of time has gone by or until your partner has become involved with someone else.

Self-Assessment: How Compatible Are You & Your Prospective Partner?

Both you and your partner should take the following quiz and then compare your answers. This quiz is not meant to be a valid scientific measure of your compatibility; it was put together to get you thinking about situations that can be difficult and cause stress in a relationship. It's perfectly OK to have some disagreement—provided that you're able to compromise or at least agree to disagree. Suggestions for each of the issues mentioned follow the quiz.

1. How many of the 10 items on this list do you have in common with your prospective mate: religion, career, same hometown or neighborhood, friends, education level, income level, cultural pastimes, sports/recreation activities, travel, physical attraction?

2. Would you prefer a relationship that is
   a. male-dominated?
   b. female-dominated?
   c. a partnership?

3. What banking arrangement sounds best after marriage?
   a. separate accounts
   b. joint account
   c. joint account but some cash for each of you to spend as you please with no accounting

4. If you share an account, whose responsibility is it to balance the checkbook and pay bills?
   a. the man in the family
   b. the woman in the family
   c. whoever is better at math and details

5. If you inherited $10,000, would you prefer it to be
   a. saved toward a major purchase?
   b. spent on something you could enjoy together, such as a vacation?
   c. spent on luxury items you could enjoy individually, such as a fur coat or golf clubs?

6. Where do you think you should spend major holidays?
   a. with his family
   b. with her family
   c. alternating between his family and her family

7. How frequently do you want to see your in-laws if they live in the same town?
   a. only on special occasions and holidays
   b. twice a month
   c. at least once a week

8. How frequently do you enjoy talking with your parents?
   a. every day
   b. once a week
   c. once a month or less

9. If you both have careers, what will be your priority?
   a. marriage before career
   b. marriage equally important as career
   c. career before marriage; my spouse is going to have to be understanding

10. If you are offered a career promotion with a hefty raise, making your income much more than your spouse's but involving a move out of state, would you
    a. expect your mate to be agreeable to relocation?
    b. try a commuter marriage, seeing each other only on weekends or occasionally?
    c. say no rather than move; money isn't everything?

11. If your new spouse sets aside one evening a week to go out with a friend or friends of his or her same sex, would you feel
    a. jealous of the time away from you?
    b. happy that he or she has friends?
    c. that this should not go on; let your feelings be known?

12. If you've had a bad day at the office and come home feeling moody, would you prefer that your mate
    a. back off, get out of the way?
    b. act sympathetic, be a good listener?
    c. discuss the events that led to your mood, perhaps offering some alternative suggestions for dealing with the people or problems that made you unhappy?

13. If your mate does something that makes you extremely angry, are you most likely to
    a. forgive and forget it?
    b. hurl insults?
    c. mention that you are angry at an appropriate time, preferably when the anger is first felt, and explain why without making derogatory accusations?

14. If you can't stand your partner's friends and he or she can't stand yours, how will you deal with this after marriage? (You may choose more than one.)

    a. Cultivate new friends you both can enjoy.

    b. See your friends by yourself; let your spouse do the same.

    c. Phase out the friends you knew before marriage; expect your spouse to do the same.

15. If you and your spouse-to-be practice different religions, would you expect to

    a. convert before marriage?

    b. have him or her convert before marriage?

    c. take turns attending each other's place of worship?

    d. observe religious days separately?

    e. not worry about it; religion is not an issue in your relationship?

16. When do you want to start a family?

    a. as soon as possible

    b. after you have spent a few years enjoying your relationship as a couple

    c. as soon as careers are firmly established

    d. never

17. What is your attitude about housework? (You may check more than one.)

    a. It is unmasculine for a man to do it. A woman should do all of it even if she chooses to have a career.

    b. It is fine for a man to help, but only with certain tasks, such as mowing the lawn or taking out the trash.

    c. If a woman works outside the home, cleaning should be shared.

    d. Even if a woman does not work outside the home, cleaning should be shared.

18. Before marriage, you go out as a couple several times a week. A few months after marriage, you realize that you are going out a lot less. You would consider this

    a. OK. The pace was exhausting.

    b. Dull. You worry that you are being taken for granted.

    c. Not OK. You and your mate should make plans for some evenings out or evenings at home with friends.

19. You need to buy a new suit. Your spouse wants to come along. Would you see this as a sign of

    a. interest in spending time with you?

    b. crowding your relationship?

    c. watchdogging your taste or pocketbook?

20. How would you prefer to spend your annual vacation? (Choose as many as apply.)

    a. on a trip by yourself

    b. on a trip with your mate

    c. on a trip with your mate and another couple

    d. visiting your relatives or in-laws at their homes

    e. at a beach relaxing

    f. engaged in an active sport such as skiing, tennis camp, or hiking/camping

    g. traveling to another city for sightseeing/s hopping

    h. at home catching up on repairs, appointments, books, visits with friends

    i. I would rather take a vacation less frequently than once a year and spend this money on rent or mortgage, enabling us to live in a more convenient or prestigious neighborhood.

21. If you were hunting for a place to live, would you prefer being in

    a. the country?

    b. the suburbs?

    c. the city?

22. If your spouse-to-be had many loves before he or she met you, would you prefer that he or she

    a. keep the details to himself or herself?

    b. tell you everything?

    c. answer truthfully but only the questions you ask, such as what broke up each relationship?

23. If your new spouse is in a romantic mood and you are not, how would you be most likely to respond?

    a. communicate your mood; suggest another time

    b. pretend that you are feeling romantic

    c. invent an excuse rather than communicate your mood

Once you and your prospective partner have completed the questionnaire, compare your answers with the following commentary in mind.

1. The more you have in common, the more of your life you can share and enjoy together.

2. Research and the experiences of many couples have shown that the equal relationship is the most successful.

3 and 4. There is not one right answer. Decide what works best for you and creates the least tension in your relationship.

5. You need to understand your priorities and be able to communicate them to your partner. Without this, you can find yourself in great financial conflict and tension.

6. Be able to compromise on this one.

7 and 8. Let your spouse know that he or she comes first before parents and in-laws, regardless of how often relatives will be seen.

9. Talk about career and marriage priorities. Can you accept your spouse's choice if he or she considers time spent on work more important right now than time spent with you?

10. There is not one right answer. Decide what works best for you and creates the least tension in your relationship.

11. It's healthy to have friends. You can't realistically expect your mate to spend 24 hours a day with you. If you or your mate goes off for a time with friends, it wouldn't be too mushy to kiss, hug, or otherwise reassure your mate by words or actions that he or she is still first in your life.

12. There are times when each answer would be best. Be sensitive to your mate's mood. If you are the one in the bad mood, don't expect your mate to read your mind as to whether you need space, sympathy, or discussion. Clue him or her in.

13. Answer c is best. You must learn how to express anger constructively.

14. Be careful here. If you make his or her old friends feel left out or unimportant, they could work on your prospective mate to break up your relationship.

15. If you have major differences on this one, you might want to consider terminating the relationship instead of committing to marriage.

16. It's impossible to have half a child. Compromise won't work on this one, so it is best to speak your mind before marriage.

17. The most successful marriages are the ones in which men and women do not limit themselves in the traditional masculine-feminine roles. The shar-ing of responsibility heightens a sense of trust, caring, and cooperation.

18. Sometimes the pace during dating is frantic. It is nice to calm down but not nice to settle down to the point that each of you is taking the other for granted. Marriage requires continual work if you are going to keep adventure and interest in the relationship.

19. Whether you see it as interest, crowding, or distrust, communicate your feelings to your mate. If you would rather shop alone, let that be known too.

20. Agree on your needs in advance of the annual vacation, or what should be a time of relaxation away from the daily grind will turn into a source of tension and arguments. There is nothing wrong with separate vacations if one of you wants to fish on the lake and the other enjoys sightseeing.

21. If you are set on a particular style of living and are not willing to change it after marriage, speak up before you say, "I do."

22. In general, it is not a good idea to go into great detail about past relationships because they are not totally relevant to your current one. However, trust and honesty are very important. If your partner asks a question, answer honestly but think very carefully. If you are the one doing the questioning, ask yourself, "Do I really want to hear this?"

23. There are times in your relationship when you might not want to go along with your spouse's romantic feelings, but it is generally best to communicate in a nice way without making him or her feel rejected or unloved because you simply are not in the mood. Do suggest another time.

Source: Hendrick, S. S. 1988. A generic measure of relationship satisfaction. *Journal of Marriage and the Family* 50:93–98. Copyright © 1988 by the National Council on Family Relations, 3989 Central Ave., N.E., Ste. 550, Minneapolis, MN 55421. Reprinted by permission of Wiley-Blackwell, publisher.

Key Terms Used in This Chapter

blind date, p. 158
blind marriage, p. 150
bride price, p. 150
closed fields, p. 158
cohabitation, p. 168
courtship, p. 149
dating, p. 152
dowry, p. 150
elope, p. 150
endogamy, p. 153
engagement, p. 166

exit response, p. 177
exogamy, p. 153
forced marriage, p. 150
green-card marriage, p. 150
homogamy, p. 153
hooking up, p. 166
loyalty response, p. 177
mail-order brides, p. 163
marriage bureaus, p. 163
marriage squeeze, p. 155
mating gradient, p. 155

neglect response, p. 176
open courtship system, p. 150
open fields, p. 157
POSSLQs, p. 168
propinquity, p. 153
relationship market, p. 151
socialization, p. 152
status, p. 153
video dating service, p. 163
voice response, p. 177

Summary

5.1 The Dating Game

- Courtship, the process by which a commitment to marriage is developed, was the major way in which people went about establishing a relationship before the eras of serial dating and cohabitation. The courtship process still exists today and can vary from a closed courtship system involving arranged marriages to an open system in which individuals generally make their own decisions about a suitable mate.

- Closed courtship, or arranged marriage, is evident in blind marriages, in which neither partner sees the other until the day of their wedding. It is also evident in marriages that involve a bride price, in which a man pay moneys or property to the bride's family for the right to marry her, or a dowry is given, in which case a bride is required to bring money, property, or goods to the marriage.

- Today's courtship system is an open system and is a relationship or marriage market in which prospective partners compare the personal, social, and financial resources of eligible mates and bargain for the best they can get. Everyone has a so-called market value that they use to try to obtain a mate. Today, individuals may be seeking a traditional partnership or one that is more egalitarian in nature.

- Dating is the process of meeting people socially for the purpose of possibly forming an exclusive long-term relationship. The main functions of dating include recreation, companionship, intimacy and sex, mate selection, socialization, and status achievement.

- Some scholars believe that in an attempt to find a suitable mate, people find one another more desirable on the basis of homogamy, or similarity in education, ethnicity, race, religion, age, and social class. Propinquity, or the nearness of a person in place and time, also plays a key role in the selection of people to date. People feel pressure to filter possible mates on the basis of endogamy, the cultural expectation that a person marries within his or her own social group, and exogamy, outside his or her family group.

5.2 Pairing Up: Finding & Choosing a Partner

- Finding and choosing a partner can be influenced by the type of setting in which one interacts. Open fields are settings in which people do not normally interact, such as large-crowd settings, and so potential partners are not likely to meet. Closed fields are settings in which people are likely to interact, such as the workplace, and so potential partners are more apt to meet.

- Today, people are exercising more control in how they meet others. Although many people meet through personal introductions, others are making use of classifieds ads, meeting online, and introduction services such as video dating services, marriage bureaus, and mail-order bride arrangements.

- Traditional courtship evolves from dating to going steady to engagement to marriage. Engagement, which extends from marriage proposal to formal wedding announcement, serves as a sign of commitment and indicates that the couple is planning to expand its family ties or kinship circle.

- Dating arrangements in college vary from just hanging out to hooking up (physical encounters that allow possible sexual interaction without commitment) to couples spending time all their time together.

- With an average work week of 47 hours, Americans have great opportunities to interact with and possibly date fellow employees.

- For many people, dating is a second-time-around experience in which they find themselves as a single parent or after a divorce or death of a spouse.

5.3 Cohabitation: Living Together as an Unmarried Couple

- Cohabitation, or living together, is defined as a couple in an emotional and sexual relationship sharing living quarters without being married. The U.S. Census Bureau identifies these relationships with the term POSSLQs, which stands for "People of the Opposite Sex Sharing Living Quarters."

- The primary reasons for cohabiting include security, emancipation from parents, convenience, and as a testing mechanism to determine whether marriage might be workable.

- Cohabitants tend to have similarities in independence, sex, attitudes, religion, income, and education.

- Cohabitation has increased in the United States as a result of increased social tolerance, increased female equality, and views of many people as to the impermanence of marriage.

- Cohabitants are expected to support themselves, frequently maintain financial independence, and might not follow traditional gender roles in performing housework.

- Cohabitation offers partners a time to test the relationship, companionship with independence, and greater ease in ending the relationship. However, it can involve a greater lack of commitment than a marriage, allow for individuals to be exploited, and provide partners with fewer legal rights.
- Couples who are considering living together should consider how well they know each other, why they are moving in together, how they will manage money, the similarities of their preferred lifestyles, their feelings on children and parenting, and legal issues such as wills and health-care proxies.

5.4 Breaking Up Is Hard to Do

- When relationships start to deteriorate, people may have several responses. The neglect response is char-acterized by avoidance and neglect. The exit response involves ending the relationship. The loyalty response involves partners staying together without working on the relationship, hoping that things will improve. The voice response is characterized by identifying the problems and working to save the relationship.
- In a breakup, it's important to consider whether you can accept that the pain of rejection is natural, identify what steps you can take to stop thinking about the other person, and focus on what you can do to raise your self-esteem. On the other hand, you should examine whether the relationship can't be improved, whether you can accept that your partner will be hurt, and whether you can terminate the relationship completely.

Take It to the Net

- **The Alternatives to Marriage Project.** A national nonprofit organization that advocates equality and fairness for unmarried people, including people who choose not to marry, cannot marry, or decide to live together before marriage.
www.unmarried.org

- **Life Innovations.** Offers a "premarital inventory" designed by University of Minnesota researchers, led by David H. Olson. Check the website for counselors who administer the PREP/ENRICH test.
www.lifeinnovations.com

CHAPTER 6

COMMUNICATION

Realizing Effective Intimacy

POPULAR CULTURE & THE MEDIA

Communication & Conflict

Jay Weil, 34, a San Francisco day trader, was building a close friendship with a woman whom he had met on a work-related Internet message board. That's over now, because email is different from conversation.

One day, Jay had said that he was going to practice his bass guitar instead of goofing off. When his friend emailed to ask how he was doing in that regard, Jay emailed back, "I don't need another mother."

It "was totally meant as an innocent joke," Weil said later. "She more or less blew up."

Although he knew his friend had misunderstood, the relationship was destroyed, and they never communicated again. The probable reason: "While email may be just fine for some communications," writes Janet Kornblum (2002), "it can't be a substitute for face-to-face conversation—or even a phone call. It's when people try to push email beyond its limitations that relationships suffer."

Communication and conflict— these are the underpinnings of so much storytelling. There are literally thousands of movies, TV shows, and novels in which the basic plot device (that is, the basic conflict

and its resolution) is built around miscommunication of one sort or another. For instance, various kinds of marital and family conflict involving faulty communication have been staples in television sitcom series ranging from the old-time *The Honeymooners* and *I Love Lucy* to *King of Queens* and *Everybody Loves Raymond.*

An interesting variation in recent times are plot lines involving misunderstandings that involve today's telecommunications and computer technology. Following are two examples:

■ *Cell phones:* In *One Fine Day* (1996), Michelle Pfeiffer plays a career-minded architect and supermom, taking on the demands of single parenting. George Clooney plays a hard-driving newspaper columnist and every-other-weekend dad. They meet by chance while taking care of their young children, and the only thing they have in common are identical cellular phones, which they keep getting

⦿ WHAT'S AHEAD IN THIS CHAPTER

We discuss how power works in intimate relationships and some explanations. We then consider conflict, both positive and negative, and how couples can learn to fight fair. Finally, we describe types of intimate communication, barriers to it, and ways in which partners can communicate more effectively.

mixed up, leading to involvement with each other's lives, jobs, and kids.

■ *Email:* In *You've Got Mail* (1998), Meg Ryan plays the owner of a neighborhood bookshop, and Tom Hanks plays the owner of superstore book chain that's poised to put her out of business. As it happens, they are already email pals, without knowing each other's identity. The Hanks character figures out who his online companion is and uses manipulation to meet her as a way to advance his business takeover. Ultimately, of course, they fall in love, but the situational meetings that occur as a result of their online discourse are quite distorted from reality.

What *is* the reality in trying to communicate using high technology? College students are completely comfortable with cell phones, text and instant messaging, mobile group-messaging services (Twitter, Dodgeball), and social networking websites (MySpace, Facebook). But they've also become more wary. Like Jay Weil, many have discovered email's "inherent ambiguity," as Ryder University psychology professor John Suler (2002) calls it. They've learned that, compared to face-to-face or phone communication, email has characteristics that can lead to escalation of conflicts. As researchers Raymond Friedman and Steven Currall (2002: 27) point out, email "reduces feedback and social cues, allows for excess attention to be focused on statements made, introduces new tactics (such as argument bundling) that can lead to the use of heavy tactics, makes the other's party's tactics seem more heavy, . . . enhances biased percep-

tions of the other party, and makes it harder to resolve disputes."

Students have also found that text messaging is an easy way to avoid humiliation—to ask for dates and escape hearing a "no" on the phone or in person or to cancel a night out to avoid having to call and explain (Pressner 2006). They've learned that one can sign up for a large number of contacts on a social network site but that "a good Facebook profile could make even the most boring person somewhat interesting," as Rollins College sophomore Steve Miller put it (quoted in Irvine 2006). Perhaps they've also had to deal with online bullies, since the anonymity of the Internet seems to allow people to say whatever they want in cyberspace (Noveck 2007). And finally, students may have had to confront privacy issues, as they've found that personal updates on their MySpace pages were being forwarded to contacts they did not necessarily want to have that information—or, worse, prospective employers were going online to look at their MySpace page, personal blog, or Flickr stream (Irvine 2006; Dubow 2007; Guynn 2007).

All these issues involve what Daniel Goleman (2006), author of *Social Intelligence: The New Science of Human Relationships,* calls "inexorable technocreep," in which "constant digital connection" can deaden us to the people around us. But, as we will discuss, our human brains are actually "wired to connect," and empathizing face to face or on the phone with a friend can activate the very same circuits in our own brains as in our friend's.

What should I be aware of about how power works in relationships?

What are principal areas of relationship conflict, how do people handle it, and how can I fight fairly?

How can I be better at communicating with my partner?

🌐 **ON THE WEB** Communication

www.gottman.com

The University of Washington Gottman Institute, dubbed the "Love Lab," was founded by marital communications experts Drs. John and Julie Schwartz Gottman. The website enables you to take a quiz about communication in your present relationship. Click on Marriage & Couples. Click on Relationship Quiz. Click on How Well Do You Know Your Partner? Take the quiz.

6.1 Power & Intimacy

MAJOR QUESTION What should I be aware of about how power works in a relationship?

PREVIEW We describe what power is and what unequal power does to relationships. We also discuss three explanations of how power works: Raven and colleagues' six types of power in a relationship, Blood and Wolfe's resource theory, and Waller's principle of least interest.

What's the best advice for preserving an intimate relationship or marriage?

■ **Continue to Say Sweet Nothings:** How partners talk to each other, more than what they actually say, is the best predictor of marriage success. Partners who express fondness and admiration for their partners after six months of marriage are less apt to divorce (Gottman et al. 1998).

■ **Lower Your Expectations:** Marriage doesn't offer sustained happiness, but you can be happy anyway, says Iris Krasnow (2002). "You've got to work [marriage] to the bone," she says (quoted in Kelly 2001). "Work on loving that person even if you think you're not in love."

Could both be right? In our fantasies, intimacy is a romantic adventure. In reality, it's a struggle as well. Much of how it turns out depends on how we share power, how we handle conflict, and how we communicate. We start by considering power.

Power & the Effects of Unequal Power

We would like to think that our most intimate relationship is one of equals, but is it? Must one person be the one who, in that unfortunate phrase, "wears the pants in the family"?

Traditionally, of course, the pants were worn by the husband, and in many countries, husbands still dominate over wives. This dominance derives from

- **How often do couples fight about money?** Money was the major focus of conflict in about a quarter of marriages according to one study and in about 38% according to another.[a, b] Even for couples in marriages lasting 50 years or more, money has been found to be the most common source of disagreement in 29% of them.[c]

- **When does affection cause resentment?** Women resent partners who are affectionate only when they are interested in sex or, worse, who force them to have sex against their will, as 9% of wives reported in one study.[d, e]

- **How often does cheating figure in divorce?** In one-third of divorces, one or both partners had been sexually involved with someone outside the marriage.[f]

- **How important is body language in communication?** An estimated 65 to 95% of face-to-face communication is interpreted through nonverbal means—that is, body language.[g]

- **What's a characteristic of lasting marriages?** Partners in lasting marriages show five times more positive feeling and interaction between them than negative.[h]

[a]Blood and Wolfe 1960. [b]Scanzoni 1970. [c] Alford-Cooper 1998. [d]Oggins et al. 1993. [e]Schrof and Wagner 1994. [f]South and Lloyd 1995. [g]Warfield 2000. [h]Gottman 1994: 41.

NUMBERS THAT MATTER

Communication & Power

the male's *authority*, a status that is usually rooted in the law. In the 20th century in the United States, however, the husband's dominance by virtue of legal authority steadily declined, and today a standard of equality prevails in most families, especially those in which the wife works outside the home (Sennett 1980). Instead of authority, then, power in a marriage often derives from *personality*. That is, whichever partner, male or female, has the more forceful personality and temperament might be the more dominant one in the relationship (Bernard 1982).

What Is Power & Why Is It Important?

As the preceding discussion suggests, ***power* is the ability or potential to impose one's will on other people—to get them to think, feel, or do something they would not ordinarily have done spontaneously** (Frieze et al. 1978). Power, an integral factor in human relationships, doesn't necessarily require the threat of physically overpowering someone, although it can.

Nor is power necessarily bad. A professor, for instance, might get you to take a positive action (such as studying how intimate relationships work—which might help you with your own) that you would not have considered doing by yourself. A spouse might get you to take up cooking or golf, which you then find brings you great enjoyment.

Having a sense of power is important, a concept that is best understood by recalling an instance when you haven't had power. How do you feel in an encounter with the police, for example, or the IRS or a bill-collection agency? People who feel powerless or helpless all the time, such as prison inmates or the very poor, are apt to become depressed and susceptible to physical and emotional disorders (McLeod 1986).

What Unequal Power Does to Relationships

In intimate relationships, power inequality is important for the following reasons:

■ **It Affects Self-Esteem:** Having power is important to one's self-image as a person who can control events. People in a relationship in which decision making is divided up so that each partner feels some power are more apt to feel self-esteem and equal to the task of handling most crises (Lauer and Lauer 1988; Beach and Tesser 1993).

■ **It Inhibits Satisfaction, Love, and Sharing of Feelings:** Inequality of power diminishes the less powerful partner's satisfaction with the marriage and love for his or her partner (Sampson 1966; Whisman and Jacobson 1990). It also discourages the expression of true feelings, so that the more vulnerable partner covers up or falsifies his or her feelings (Glazer-Malbin 1975).

■ **It Encourages Manipulation:** Unequal power encourages struggles to get or keep power. The partner who feels less powerful might, for example, develop physical or emotional illnesses as a way of consciously or unconsciously manipulating the more powerful spouse to do things that defer to the less powerful partner's handicap (Bagarozzi 1990).

Once an unequal power relationship is established, it might not be easy to change. Change can happen—through talking, counseling, and other means that we will discuss. Yet, as with change in general, the move entails some risk of failure. The question is whether there is enough of a fundamental basis for the relationship that the risk is worth taking.

How Power Works: Some Possible Explanations

Scholars have proposed various explanations for how power works. Here we consider three hypotheses or theories.

Raven & Colleagues' Six Types of Power in a Relationship

Bertram Raven and others (French and Raven 1959; Raven et al. 1975) suggested that there are six different kinds of power that people may exert in a marriage: *coercive, reward, expert, legitimate, referent,* and *informational.*

■ Coercive Power—"I'm worried you'll punish me": ***Coercive power* is based on your fear that your partner will inflict punishment.** The punishment can be emotional, such as sarcasm or contempt, or it can be physical, such as beatings. Partners in unsatisfying marriages are more apt than those in satisfying marriages to attribute coercive power to their spouses (Raven et al. 1975).
   Example: A wife gives in to a husband's demands for sex to avoid his hitting her.

■ Reward Power—"I'm going along with you in hopes that you'll reward me": ***Reward power* is based on your belief that your agreement with**

your partner will elicit rewards from that partner. Often, the rewards are verbal, such as praise, or at least the absence of criticism.

Example: A husband stops littering crumbs on the kitchen counter in expectation that his wife will praise him for keeping things neat.

■ **Expert Power—"You're the boss in this area":** *Expert power* **is based on your opinion that your partner has specialized knowledge.** The special knowledge can be mundane, such as knowing how often to service the car, or it can be sophisticated, such as knowing all about the family's investments. It used to be that women most frequently ascribed expert power to their husbands (Raven et al. 1975).

Example: A wife defers to her husband on financial matters (although, ironically, she might do the actual bill paying).

■ **Legitimate Power—"I agreed earlier to comply when you ask":** *Legitimate power* **is based on your partner's having the right to ask you and your having the duty to comply.** Gender roles have traditionally conferred legitimacy and still do in many traditional cultures, in which husbands may dictate and wives must obey.

Example: A husband agrees to care for the dog when asked because both partners agreed to have a pet.

■ **Referent Power—"I admire the things you do, so I want to please you":** *Referent power* **is based on your identifying with and admiring your spouse and receiving satisfaction by pleasing him or her.** Men most frequently ascribe referent power to their wives (Raven et al. 1975).

Example: A wife gets involved in the politics her husband supports to learn more about them.

■ **Informational Power—"You've convinced me of your viewpoint, so I'll do as you want":** *Informational power* **is persuasive power; you are persuaded by your partner that what he or she wants is in your best interest.**

Example: A husband agrees to attend church because he is persuaded by his wife that it will give a good moral example to the children.

Blood & Wolfe's Resource Theory: "Whoever Has the Most Resources Has the Most Power"

Formulated by sociologists **Robert Blood and Donald Wolfe** (1960), *resource theory* **suggests that the balance of power in a marriage reflects the relative resources of each spouse.** Resources might be money, education, or occupational status, but they might also be sex, emotional support, parenting skills, homemaking ability, or money management skills. The spouse who has more resources is able to make more decisions (decide how the money is spent, for example) that affect the marriage partner and so has more power.

Consider the following two examples of resources at work:

■ **Money:** The bigger income earner (traditionally the husband) usually has a bigger say in how the income is spent. One study (Blumstein and Schwartz 1983) found that in a third of marriages in which the husband made $8,000 more than the wife, the husband was the more powerful partner, having more authority to decide how the family income was spent.

EXAMPLE OF
Competing Power
Stepfamilies

A TYPICAL STEPFAMILY? Kathe and Frank Fanelli of northern Nevada, with children Hunter Marie, bottom, 10; Kristine, top left, 14; John, 15; and Katie, 12. When they married, Frank was single, and Kathe was divorced with five children; they later had a child of their own. Why are power relationships in blended families more complex than those in other families? ▲

As parents divorce and remarry, the number of stepfamilies increases. "Each person will bring into the new family his or her own history, lifestyle, finances, values, attitudes, and beliefs," says one writer (Hunter 2003: 1E). "That can be complicated."

It can also create complicated power relationships. Consider the stepfamily of Frank and Kathe Fanelli of Reno, Nevada. Frank was single when he met Kathe, who had recently divorced and had five children. After they married, Frank was a willing stepfather, but he had a different style of parenting and disciplining style from Kathe's. It was also different from that of the children's biological father, who lived nearby and was still very involved in their discipline and their lives. In addition, during the first year of marriage, Kathe became pregnant.

Complicated? Most certainly. "Blended families can be tough," says Kathe. "I know we struggle, and we're doing the best we can."

Among the areas of contention that stepfamilies must deal with:

■ **Loyalties and attention:** In many stepfamilies, loyalties are complicated because children and parents feel that they must make choices about whom to be loyal to. Children may feel abandoned as their custodial parent turns his or her attention to a new spouse and worry about how much love and attention they will receive. Parents may feel caught between whether to spend time with their children or

with their spouses. Children are also conflicted about their attachment to the noncustodial parent.

■ **Stresses:** Younger children worry about which parent's house they will live in and about being transported to the other biological parent's house; if it's the stepparent's house, this involves a whole new set of household rules. There may also be rivalries with stepsiblings, which cause more stresses than households that don't have stepsiblings (Lutz 1983).

■ **Discipline:** Discipline is one of the most common sources of conflict in stepfamilies (Ihinger-Tallman and Pasley 1987). Children who have grown up in a family where no one was spanked, for instance, may suddenly find themselves in a household with a stepparent who is inclined to use strong discipline.

■ **Finances:** Adults in stepfamilies tend to have lived alone for a while before coming together. Thus, they have their own financial systems. Because the financial arrangements of blended families can be complicated—involving questions of child support, alimony, tuition, and so on—a stepfamily household might have multiple checking accounts ("For Richer or Poorer Again" 2002).

WHAT DO YOU THINK? Are you part of a stepfamily or very familiar with one? How would you describe the different power arrangements in that family?

■ **Sex:** Sex can certainly be a balance-of-power resource (Blumstein and Schwartz 1983). Indeed, it seems to be an old story, for how often have we read about men with economic power yielding to women with sexual power? (Former Playmate of the Year Anna Nicole Smith's marriage to an oil-rich multimillionaire in his nineties comes to mind.)

GOT THE POWER. In many families, one spouse has more power than the other—that is, other family members follow at his or her will. Sometimes this power comes from just sheer force of personality, as would seem to be the case with the wife and mother here. What is the balance of power in your (or your parents') family? Why? ◀

As an explanation for power relationships, resource theory has some basis in fact, but there is also counterevidence. For example, men often continue to enjoy more power in the relationship even when their wives make more money or the husbands are stay-at-homes who make no money (Thompson and Walker 1989; Lips 1991; Cohen and Durst 2000).

Waller's Principle of Least Interest: "Whoever Has the Least Interest in the Relationship Has the Most Power"

A term coined by sociologist **Willard Waller** (Waller and Hill 1951), **the *principle of least interest* states that the partner who is least interested in the relationship has the most power.** Thus, if you are more committed to the relationship than your partner is, you might hold many of your wishes in check—do things you don't want to do, not express resentments, always strive to please your partner—for fear that he or she might walk out on you.

The principle of least interest may be considered an offshoot of the *relative love and need theory,* which proposes that the extent to which one spouse loves and needs the other is the most crucial variable in explaining power in relationships. In other words, the person who gains the most from a relationship is the most dependent and hence the least powerful (Safilios-Rothschild 1970).

6.2 Conflict & Growth

MAJOR QUESTION What are principal areas of relationship conflict, how do people handle it, and how can I fight fairly?

PREVIEW Conflict in a relationship is inevitable. Although it can be negative, it can also be positive—in fact, desirable. We discuss nine common areas of conflict in relationships. We also describe six ways in which people handle such conflict. We conclude with five rules for fighting fairly.

If you're rejected, could that make you stupid?

Surprisingly, maybe it could. In a two-year study, social psychologist Roy F. Baumeister and colleagues (2002) gave subjects various intelligence tests, then made them feel rejected. Some were given a false personality evaluation that made them think they were destined to live alone. Others mingled with strangers and were later told that the strangers wished to have nothing to do with them. After these ego-bruising experiences, the subjects were tested again for intelligence. It was found that their IQ scores had dropped about 25% and their analytical reasoning scores by 30%.

"Connecting with others is one of the deepest and most powerful human drives, and thwarting it has a big impact," says Baumeister (quoted in Briggs 2002) about these dramatic results. "After being rejected, people cannot think straight for a while."

Fortunately, the effects of a single rejection seem short-lived. But how might being in a relationship of constant conflict and frequent rejections affect you?

Out of Intimacy, Conflict

In any intimate relationship, we crave two contradictory things (Scarf 1995):

■ **Closeness:** We want to be close and cooperative—to have *agreement* with the other person.

■ **Independence:** We want personal autonomy—which means that we might have *disagreement* with that person.

The result is *conflict*, **the process of interaction that results when the behavior of one person interferes with the behavior of another,** according to one definition (Knox and Schacht 2002: 217). Conflict, according to one analysis (Canary et al. 1995), is about both (1) discrete, isolated problems (a dispute over which TV program to watch, for example) and (2) ongoing, chronic relational problems (such as always arguing about money). But, of course, conflict can also be caused by all kinds of things—different expectations, different gender norms, or inability to compromise, for example.

We often think in terms of opposites: love/hate, peace/war, cooperation/conflict. Thus, in our society, there exists a *conflict taboo*, **which considers conflict and anger wrong,** the opposite of cooperation and love. The conflict taboo particularly applies to relationships and families, which most people view as—ideally—havens of harmony and security against threats from the outside world (Crosby 1991). Indeed, conflict clearly challenges the notion of the *folk concept of the family*, **which emphasizes support, understanding, happiness, and warm holiday rituals** (Edwards 1991).

However, any couple in an intimate relationship that is engaged in a struggle about power is, by definition, in conflict. Indeed, all couples and families, no matter how caring and supportive of one another, experience conflict (Roberts and Krokoff 1990). Conflict, then, is *natural* to relationships. More than that, conflict is *desirable,* as we will explain.

Conflict is of two types: negative and positive.

Negative Conflict: Bad for Relationships

When people say that they dislike conflict (as most people say they do), they are thinking of negative conflict. *Negative conflict* is destructive behavior that is usually bad for relationships and families and even bad for health, delaying the healing of wounds, for example, and producing clogged arteries (Kiecolt-Glaser et al. 2003; Smith et al. 2005).

Some negative types of conflict are as follows:

■ Repressed Anger: *Repressed anger* **is the unconscious suppression of feelings of anger so that they are expressed in other ways.** One way is *gunnysacking*—**saving up, or putting in an imaginary sack, grievances until they spill over.** Another way is in overeating, apathy, or depression. The opposite way is shouting and violence.

Sometimes, in *displacement,* anger is directed toward things or people that are important to the other partner, such as his or her hobby or friends.

■ Passive-Aggression: *Passive-aggression* **is the expression of anger indirectly rather than directly.** In families and intimate relationships, this anger is masked by sarcasm, nagging, nitpicking, and procrastination—putting off completing a task you promised your partner you would do (Ferrari and Emmons 1994).

In another variation, **the *silent treatment*, you either ignore your partner or verbally say that things are all right while sending nonverbal signals that they are not.**

■ Scapegoating: *Scapegoating* **is the blaming of one particular family member for nearly everything that goes wrong in that family** (Vogel and Bell 1960). As you might guess, being the family scapegoat is not likely to build anyone's self-esteem, as we saw from the results of the Baumeister study on rejection resulting in temporarily lowering IQ.

CONFLICT BETWEEN EQUALS. When two people use conflict to define and maintain power as equals, they grow in self-assurance and power. Have you been in a relationship in which conflict actually improved the relationship? ▲

■ Gaslighting: In the 1944 movie *Gaslight* (starring Ingrid Bergman and Charles Boyer), a man tries to drive his wife crazy so that she'll be put in an insane asylum. He does this by gradually dimming the gaslight while denying that anything is wrong when she complains that the house is getting darker. ***Gaslighting* is when one partner, perhaps using sarcasm, constantly criticizes or denies the other's definition of reality, diminishing the other's self-esteem** (Bach and Wyden 1970).

Positive Conflict: Good for Relationships

A happy marriage and a conflict-free marriage—are they the same? Sociologist Judith Wallerstein interviewed 50 couples (mostly white and middle class, married for 10 to 40 years) who described their marriages as happy. She found that not only was conflict universal but that also "these couples considered learning to disagree and to stand one's ground one of the gifts of a good marriage" (Wallerstein and Blakeslee 1995: 144).

Positive conflict is the kind of airing of differences that bring partners closer together, that builds up each other's self-esteem rather than diminishing it. As we mentioned, conflict—when properly handled—is in fact *desirable*, providing the following benefits:

■ **Conflict Helps to Clarify Differences:** Without conscious conflict, differences stay underground. When issues are put out on the table, they can be clarified in ways that invite solution.

■ **Conflict Keeps Small Issues from Becoming Big Ones:** If small conflicts aren't dealt with on an ongoing basis, they can fester and breed resentments—until they culminate in a big blow-up.

■ **Conflict Can Improve Relationships:** For partners *with equal power*—an important matter—conflict helps to bolster each other's self-confidence and strengthens their relationship (Coser 1956; Gottman and Krokoff 1989; Noller et al. 1994).

With present-day levels of divorce, it would seem obvious that conflict can be the expression of important power struggles and a major threat to a marriage. But it is not just by coasting along that we prevail over the problems of life. By learning to manage conflict, we grow in self-assurance and power. And when two people use conflict to define and maintain power as equals, both of them grow.

What Do Couples Have Disagreements About?

How often do you think most couples fight? Every couple of days? Once a week? Once a month? One study (McGonagle et al. 1993) found that the majority averaged one to two "unpleasant disagreements" a month. Are they resolved? Actually, research shows that most disagreements that arise in a marriage are *never* resolved (Gottman and Silver 1999; Crawford et al. 2002; Smith and Huston 2004). Most couples, happy and unhappy, tend to argue, particularly in the early stages of marriage, and they tend to argue about the same things (Markman et al. 2001; Gottman 2002).

The matters over which most couples disagree, various studies suggest, are housework, money, sex, jobs, in-laws, alcohol, leisure, moodiness, anger, and children. Areas of disagreement change over time so that, for instance, conflicts about sex are infrequent during the first year of marriage but become significant by the fifth year. However, housework has been found to be the primary area of disagreement at six months, one year, and five years of marriage (Bader 1981).

Let us consider the following nine common areas of conflict: (1) household tasks, (2) money, (3) sex, (4) loyalty, (5) power, (6) nurturance, (7) privacy, (8) children, and (9) differences in style (Goldberg 1987; Betcher and Macauley 1990).

1. Household Tasks: Conflicts about "the Second Shift"

Conflict over division of household labor is especially pronounced among women (Kluwer et al. 1996). The term *the second shift* was coined by sociologist **Arlie Hochschild** (1989) and was the title of her celebrated study about the division of housework among 50 two-earner couples. **The *second shift* is defined as the housework and child care that employed women do after returning home from their jobs**—their jobs, of course, constituting "the first shift."

Men and women often have disagreements over household tasks. Traditionally, men have been the income earners and have not done much housework. Even with the rise in two-paycheck marriages, many wives have continued to bear the brunt of housework, producing serious resentments (Lye and Biblarz 1993; Davis et al. 2007; Stevenson and Wolfers 2007). As Hochschild put it, tensions were the result of "faster-changing women and slower-changing men" (1989: 11).

Conflicts aren't just about an imbalance in hours devoted to housework but also about management, schedules, and standards.

■ **Management:** Who organizes or supervises household tasks, from doing the dishes to mowing the lawn? If the windows need washing, who initiates the process and who might have to ask the other for help, risking procrastination or rejection?

■ **Schedules:** If something needs doing, who determines its priority? Whose nonhousework time is more valuable? Who takes off work to wait for the cable TV installer to come? Who takes the car to the mechanic and waits all day for its repair?

■ **Standards:** Who determines the standards of quality? Who gets to decide how clean the bathrooms and kitchen

THE SECOND SHIFT. Mother's home from her income-earning "first shift" job and, having picked up the kids, now has to start her "second shift"—dinner, housework, children's bedtime. One of the nine common areas of conflict, household tasks and the division of household and child-care labor, is a particularly irksome issue with married working women. Is this an issue in any household you're familiar with? ▼

have to be or how long the car can go without washing or the lawn without mowing?

We return to the discussion of housework in Chapter 12, "Work."

2. Money: The Power of the Purse

Money was the major focus of conflict in about a quarter of marriages, according to one study (Blood and Wolfe 1960), and in about 38%, according to another (Scanzoni 1970). Even for couples in long-term marriages, those lasting 50 years or more, money is the most common source of disagreement in 29% of them (Alford-Cooper 1998).

Some reasons why money matters generate conflict are as follows:

■ **Money Represents Secrecy:** Do you know what your parents' income is? Or what your partner's is, if you are in a relationship? In the United States, it's considered extremely rude to ask people how much money they make. (It would be like asking "How often do you and your partner have sex?")

As a result, we might come to a marriage or committed relationship without much experience in discussing money matters. And in the beginning, at least, we might be hesitant to raise uncomfortable questions ("Why do you spend so much money on clothes?") for fear of disturbing the spirit of harmony and cooperation.

■ **Money Represents Power:** If you are now in a dating or even a live-in relationship, you need to be aware that how the two of you handle money—one pays, you split the costs, or you take turns—is no guide to how it will be when you're married. Now you have separate incomes and hence separate sources of power. Most married couples, however, pool their incomes, which affects power relationships.

If only one spouse is working outside the home, for instance, that makes the other financially dependent, which can be a source of resentment. If both work outside the home, but one spouse has little say in money decisions, this can also generate resentment (Blair 1993).

■ **Money Represents Value Systems:** Suppose you come from a family background in which a dollar was hard to come by. Your partner was raised in a more affluent environment in which he or she rarely wanted for anything. So what do you do if there is suddenly an unusual infusion of money into your household (because one of you gets a bonus at work, say)? Do you blow it on a trip to the Caribbean or put it in the bank as a hedge against hard times?

Money decisions and priorities reflect our value systems, attitudes, and temperaments. If she is Ms. Frugality and he is Mr. Big Spender, how well do you think they're going to get along?

3. Sex: What Is the Conflict Really About?

Conflicts about sex can happen because the conflict really is just about that— sex. Or the conflict might actually be about sex but is expressed as disagreement about another matter altogether. Or the supposed argument about sex might really be about something else. Let's consider these possibilities.

■ **Conflicts about Sex:** He wants to have sex, but she does not because she's nervous about a big meeting at work the next day. Or she's feeling amorous, but he's bushed. So they have a fight. Women are particularly resentful of partners who are affectionate only when they are interested in sex (Oggins et al. 1993) or, worse, who force them to have sex against their will, as 9% of wives reported in one study (Schrof and Wagner 1994).

Sometimes a couple will have a fight about a different sexual matter than what is really the source of resentment. He, for instance, will criticize her for "always wanting to have sex late at night when he's tired" when the real problem is that he is an aging male who no longer gets erections quickly.

■ **Conflicts about Sex Disguised as Differences about Other Matters:** After sex, a woman might want to be held for a time, but he simply turns away and goes to sleep. The next day, she might start an argument about his always being late getting home from work. Or she might criticize him for never getting around to painting the deck as she had asked him to and as he had said he would do. The real message here is "You're not giving me enough attention and intimacy."

■ **Conflicts about Other Matters Disguised as Differences about Sex:** He criticizes her for not being sexually adventurous with him, for never wanting to try oral sex. But perhaps the real reason for the conflict is that he's angry because she never wants to go on any outings with him to ballgames or blues concerts. Or she might complain that he never wants to take the time to bring her to orgasm. But maybe what's really at issue is that she thinks he isn't a great income earner and is always looking for a better job instead of trying to do better at his present one.

4. Loyalty: Trust & Fidelity

Psychiatrist Martin Goldberg (1987) says that *trust* and *fidelity*, which we would sum up as loyalty, are two important areas affecting the level of conflict in a marriage.

■ **Trust:** Do you feel comfortable when your partner or spouse is off somewhere alone or at a party with other people? *Trust*—believing that your part-

FIGHTING ABOUT SEX. Conflict may be over differences about sex (when, what kind), over other matters disguised as sex, or over sex disguised as other matters. Do you see anything in this picture that relates to your own experience? ◀

ner is supportive and honest—allows the two of you to be away from each other without anxiety over something contrary to your relationship happening. However, if a wife immediately becomes worried when her husband returns from a business trip with a present for her ("Did he visit strip-tease clubs and is now feeling guilty?"), that means trust has broken down.

■ **Fidelity:** Fidelity is sexual faithfulness, certainly, but it is also faithfulness to the marriage vows that both partners swore to. Having sex with people outside the relationship is a clear violation of fidelity, but lesser breaches also count, such as spending too much time with other people (friends or relatives), revealing marital confidences through gossip, or lying in one form or another (Jones and Burdette 1994).

The gravest of offenses, extramarital sex, is a strong predictor of divorce. Indeed, one study found that in one-third of divorces, one or both partners had been sexually involved with someone outside the marriage (South and Lloyd 1995).

5. Power: The Issue of Control

Goldberg (1987) also says that *power and control* is an important area, because this is about which person gets to decide what to do. Indeed, men who don't share power with their spouses are a great source of conflict—so much so, suggests one study, that only newly married men who accept influence from their wives are ending up in happy marriages (Gottman et al. 1998). Arenas for power conflicts include not only the ones we have mentioned (housework, money, and sex) but also others such as disputes over how to discipline the children, alcohol and drug consumption, and involvement with relatives and in-laws.

6. Nurturance: Conflict over Who Takes Care of Whom

Another issue that Goldberg (1987) finds important is *nurturance,* defining who takes care of whom and in what ways. If one partner feels that his or her emotional needs are not being taken care of, there is apt to be conflict. For instance, one husband had a highly stressful job as a publishing executive and felt that he needed a lot of support from his wife. But when her sister and brother became seriously ill, one after the other, requiring her attention and care, he began to feel neglected and embarked on a series of affairs.

Incidentally, one study found that an indicator of this nurturance is how well partners respond to each other's triumphs, which are important for the health of a relationship (Gable et al. 2006). As one writer put it (Carey 2006), "The way a person responds to a partner's good fortune—with excitement or passive approval, shared pride or indifference—is the most crucial factor in tightening a couple's bond, or undermining it."

7. Privacy: Conflict over Aloneness versus Interaction

Are you thinking, "My partner is smothering me and doesn't give me enough space"? You're experiencing conflict over privacy versus intimacy, or aloneness versus interaction (Goldberg 1987). This can come about, for example, when a man retires from his job, and his stay-at-home wife, who was used to a certain amount of solitude and autonomy while he was away at work, now finds him around the house all the time. Or one partner might have grown up in a home where there was not a lot of touching and hugging, and people left one another alone, but is now married to someone who grew up in a physically affectionate family. In any event, most of us usually need some time alone, which is why, after dinner, a spouse might disappear into the garage workshop or to another room to read and watch TV.

8. Children: Coping with Offspring

Marital satisfaction declines slightly while parents are raising children, as we'll describe in Chapter 8, "Marriage." In part, this might be because, although children can be a source of great joy, they also require a lot of energy and attention. Thus, mothers and fathers, particularly if both are working, might find themselves in conflict over such issues as who should pick up a child after school or take him or her to a doctor. Or they might have different child-raising philosophies based on their own backgrounds, the husband being more of a disciplinarian and the wife being more sympathetic, for example.

We return to this subject again in Chapter 11, "Parenting."

9. Differences in Style: Variations in Preferences, Temperaments, & Tastes

She's from California, he's from New Jersey. She's laid-back, he's hardcharging. She's slow to burn, he's quick-tempered. Her home office is messy, his is highly organized. She likes spontaneity, he likes to plan ahead. She's emotional, he's rational. She dawdles in addressing problems, he meets them head-on. She likes to go out dancing, he prefers watching TV.

Can two people like this get along? Actually, people with different preferences, temperaments, and tastes such as these stay married for years—but they might have constant disagreements because of these differences in style. What both need to learn to recognize, however, is whether their conflict is over matters of style or over something else.

"HE'S MY KID, TOO!" Because children require a lot of investment of parental time and energy, they also create demands that may be very trying for parents. In addition, parents may disagree about how to impose discipline. Was this a problem in your household when you were growing up? ▲

How People Handle Conflict

Scholars have observed that people have different styles of conflicts (Wilmot and Wilmot 1978; Greeff and De Bruyne 2000). We describe five kinds: (1) competing, (2) parallel, (3) accommodating, (4) compromising, and (5) collaborating.

1. Competing: "Conflict Is War, and Only One Can Win!"

In the *competing style of conflict*, you are assertive and uncooperative, viewing conflict as a war in which you force your way in order to win. You have high concern for yourself and low concern for the other. If both partners are competitive, the battle can be drawn out and brutal.

"NO, MAN . . . !" Conflict is part of every intimate relationship, whether straight or gay. Does this exchange seem to represent the competing type of relationship—"conflict is war, and only one can win"? Which of the five types of conflict styles represents your approach to disputes? ▲

2. Parallel: "If We Ignore the Problem, Maybe It Will Go Away"

In the *parallel style of conflict*, you are unassertive and uncooperative. You and your partner completely deny and retreat from any discussion of a problem, hoping it will just disappear. After a while, you both will probably take up separate activities and stop being involved with each other.

3. Accommodating: "Let's Try to Find a Harmonious Solution"

In the *accommodating style of conflict*, you are unassertive but cooperative; you take a passive stance. Thus, you don't advance your own views but try to understand the other person's position, soothe the other's feelings, and be accommodating—work toward a harmonious solution to the problem.

4. Compromising: "Let's Seek a Solution We Can Both Live With"

In the *compromising style of conflict*, you are only somewhat assertive, but you are cooperative. You seek a solution that will be moderately but not optimally beneficial to you both. That is, you seek an outcome that you won't be overjoyed with but that you can both live with.

5. Collaborating: "Let's Really Work to Benefit Us Both"

In the *collaborating style of conflict*, you have a great deal of concern about advancing your interests but also those of your partner. You are *assertive and cooperative*. You will continue the conflict until you find the *optimum* mutually beneficial solution, not just a compromise. In your case, one or two styles might be dominant in most conflicts (Sternberg and Dobson 1987), and, in some instances, one style is more appropriate than another. However, if, on reflection, you think you are using styles that are not helping you get your way and/or are alienating your partner, you can change them. In the rest of the chapter, we discuss techniques for "good fighting" and couple communication.

Resolving Conflict: Five Rules for Fighting Fair & Preserving Your Relationship

Conflict is inevitable. Staying silent will only aggravate the relationship, producing tension and resentments. Ignoring problems, hoping that they will turn out all right, is usually ineffective. And shouting and insults never solve anything. The best way to deal with conflict is for both partners to learn how to fight, using the following rules.

1. Attack Problems, Not Your Partner, & Avoid Negativity

Both partners need to realize that the way to approach conflict is to attack problems but *not* attack each other (Gottman 1994; Markman et al. 1994). If you belittle, accuse, or threaten your partner or call names or give ultimatums, he or she will become defensive and angry. Some negative emotions that are used in arguments "are more toxic than others," says John Gottman. "Criticism, contempt, defensiveness, and stonewalling (withdrawing from a discussion, most frequently seen among men) are all particularly corrosive" (Gottman and Carrere 2000: 42).

The happiest couples try to reduce the negative emotion and express affection while ironing out differences (Carstensen et al. 1995). It helps to use humor, poking fun at yourself as a fallible human being—but don't laugh at your partner (Kurdek 1995).

2. Focus on Specific Issues, Use "I Feel" Language, & Avoid Mixed Messages

Even though you might be quite angry, try to concentrate on the *specific matter* that is causing the conflict. Stay in the present; don't dredge up past problems.

Use "I feel" language rather than "You always" or "You never" statements or "Why" questions. (Example: "I was worried about you being late" rather than "You're always late" or "Why are you so late?")

Avoid sending mixed messages, as in agreeing verbally ("Okay, I can go along with that") but not agreeing nonverbally (looking away and grimacing).

3. Be Sensitive about Timing & Place

An immediate problem need not demand immediate discussion. Sometimes, a conflict can go badly because one person is tired or extremely angry or tense because of overwork.

Place is important, too. Having a fight right before going in to a party or in the bedroom before going to sleep is best avoided. Suggest postponing the discussion until later. But when you do have it, strive to resolve it as quickly as possible so that resentments won't fester.

4. Say What You Mean, Don't Lie or Manipulate, & Ask for What You Want

When you don't feel like going out, should you lie to your partner by telling him or her that "something important came up"? Two-thirds of people, according to an Associated Press-IPsos poll (Noveck 2006), said it is okay to lie in certain situations, like protecting someone's feelings. For the most part, however, you should say what you really feel and what you really want, stating your wishes as clearly as you can and not beating around the bush, such as, "I really would rather stay home tonight than go to the movies."

Don't lie, sugarcoat, apologize, be seductive, or otherwise try to manipulate. For example, don't say, "I'm sorry about this, but . . ." or "You know, I went along with you last month when *you* wanted to see a movie."

When Partners Can't Handle Their Conflicts: Family Therapy & Counseling

"All too often," says health writer Jane Brody (2000), "the very characteristics that initially attracted partners to one another or the disturbing behavior that at first were ignored or considered unimportant eventually become marital sore points and the cause of repeated arguments and chronic unhappiness." Perhaps that is the time—before beginning the agonizing process of separation and divorce—to try couples counseling, which is designed to help couples and families learn more effective communication and support techniques.

How to Start

Be aware that all kinds of people call themselves marriage or couples counselors (Kantrowitz and Wingert 1999). You can start by getting a referral from a physician or college counselor. Most credentialed therapists are members of the American Association for Marital and Family Therapy (*www.aamft.org*). This means they hold

graduate degrees, have had special training in marriage and/or family therapy, and hold valid licenses issued by the state in which they practice. *(See ■ Panel 6.1.)* The National Registry of Marriage Friendly Therapists (*www.marriagefriendlytherapists.com*), launched in 2005 by William Doherty, a marriage and family therapist at the University of Minnesota, lists therapists who are sufficiently trained in couples counseling and who represent the view that they should actively try to save marriages/relationships rather than remain neutral and counsel couples as two individuals for whom divorce may very well be the best solution (Jayson 2005).

Counseling Approaches

A couple may be counseled one person at a time, both partners together, or with all family members present (family systems therapy). There are also two large nationwide marriage education programs, Practical Appli-

cation of Intimate Relationship Skills (PAIRS) and the Prevention and Relationship Enhancement Program (PREP), which offer workshops that teach couples how to get along without their having to air their problems.

Integrative couples therapy, also called acceptance therapy, refers to a number of approaches aimed at helping couples understand the problems in their relationship and learn to accept their differences. Three types of couples therapy are said to improve people's satisfaction with their marriage for at least a year after treatment is concluded (Gilbert 2005):

- **Behavioral marital therapy:** The oldest approach, this focuses on getting partners to learn to be nicer to each other, communicate better, and improve their skills at resolving conflicts.

- **Insight-oriented therapy:** This combines behavioral therapy with techniques for understanding the

5. Let Your Partner Know That You're Listening—Really Listening—& Work toward Resolution

Men who are accused by women of never listening to them now actually have an excuse—women's voices are more difficult for men to listen to than the voices of other men, because differences in the size and shape of vocal cords and larynx make women's voices more complex (Sokhi et al. 2005). Regardless, by not interrupting, not pretending to listen while actually preparing your counterargument, and not disrespecting your partner by carrying on other activities (watching TV, washing dishes) during your discussion, you show your partner that *you really are listening*. You thereby not only discover what your partner thinks and feels, you also set an example for your partner to follow in listening to your feelings (Broderick 1979).

■ PANEL 6.1   Different Types of Counselors.   Some therapists adjust their fees depending on clients' incomes.

TYPE OF COUNSELOR	DEGREE	EDUCATION	RATE
Psychiatrist	M.D. (medical doctor)	Physician with ten-plus years of postcollege medical and psychiatric training. The only type of therapist who is able to prescribe medications.	Most expensive hourly rate
Clinical psychologist	Ph.D. (doctor of philosophy)	Five-plus years of postcollege training and passing of state board.	Generally next highest hourly rate
Clinical social worker	L.C.S.W. (licensed clinical social work)	Degree with further training and passing of state board.	Usually affordable hourly rate
Marriage and family counselor or marital therapist	Master's degree	Degree plus 1,000 or more hours of supervised training with clients and passing of state board.	Usually affordable hourly rate
Advanced practice registered nurse	Master's degree in psychiatric/mental health nursing	Degree in psychiatric/mental health nursing and state license.	Affordable hourly rate
Pastoral counselor	Master's degree	Degree in psychology, counseling, social work, or marriage and family therapy plus theological training.	Affordable hourly rate

defense mechanisms, power struggles, and other negative behaviors that cause conflict in a relationship.

■ **Emotionally focused therapy:** This relatively new approach is designed to enable couples to identify and break free of the destructive emotional cycles they have fallen into by revealing their feelings during these cycles and building trust to strengthen their connection. Some research (Bradley and Johnson 2004; Johnson 2005) has found that after 8 to 12 sessions a majority of the couples had rebuilt their trust.

After the first visit, advises psychotherapist Paul Quinnett (1989), "consider carefully how comfortable you felt. Will you and the therapist be able to work together week after week?" If not, try someone else.

We discuss marriage education in more detail in Chapter 8, "Marriage."

Keep negotiating until the conflict is defused or resolved so as to keep the matter from festering, breeding misunderstandings and resentments. Work toward a specific, realistic solution that will satisfy both of you—a win-win solution.

6.3 The Nature of Communication

MAJOR QUESTION How can I be better at communicating with my partner?

PREVIEW We distinguish between verbal and nonverbal communication and describe types and uses of nonverbal communication. We then consider possible gender differences in communication. Next we consider barriers to communications: Satir's four styles, Gottman's five destructive interactions, and lack of self-disclosure. Finally, we offer four rules for effective communication.

"The brain is social," says Daniel Goleman (quoted in Matousek 2007: 36). "One person's inner state affects and drives the other person. . . . We actually catch each other's emotions like a cold."

The author of *Emotional Intelligence* (1995) and *Social Intelligence* (2006), Goleman is talking about how social interactions actually work on the neuronal level, thanks to new revelations revealed by brain imaging and other advanced technologies. Thus, for example, brain-scan studies have shown that being rejected by someone important, such as a spouse or a boss, actually registers in one of the key areas of the brain that responds to physical pain (Eisenberger et al. 2003; Eisenberger and Lieberman 2004). On the other hand, the verbal support of a loved one boosts the immune system and decreases stress hormones (Johnstone et al. 2006).

All such research suggests, as we stated at the beginning of this chapter, that communication in person or on the phone is far more important than being linked through texting and email, which may actually threaten meaningful social connection. Let us begin to consider how we can improve human communication, which is of two types: verbal and nonverbal. We consider nonverbal communication first.

Nonverbal Communication

You're listening to your partner discuss, say, what courses the two of you ought to take next semester. What do you find yourself responding to? The words? Or the twitching fingers, lack of eye contact, and flat tone of voice?

***Nonverbal communication* consists of messages sent outside the written or spoken word.** There are estimates that 65–95% of face-to-face communication is interpreted through body language (Warfield 2000).

Some Types of Nonverbal Communication: Five Kinds

Voice inflections can certainly be a kind of nonverbal communication. When your partner makes a suggestion, the way in which you emphasize the words in your response can indicates your approval or disapproval. (*"Allll*-right" signals resistance; "All-*right!"* indicates enthusiasm.) But there are other kinds of nonverbal cues that are equally indicative of your state of mind (Kinicki and Williams 2008):

■ **Interpersonal Space:** What is considered acceptable interpersonal space or proximity—how close or how far away one should be when talking with another person—varies among cultures. North Americans and northern Europeans tend to conduct conversations at a range of 3 to 4 feet. People in Latin American and Asian cultures are comfortable in a range of about 1 foot. For Arabs, it is even closer (Axtell 1991). Clearly, if an American moves back to get comfortable in a conversation with a non-European, the American could be inadvertently communicating rejection.

Even within American culture, however, one can send signals of acceptance or rejection by means of proximity. When you unconsciously begin to back away from someone during a conversation at a party (thinking to refill your glass perhaps), you could cause offense by signaling lack of interest.

■ **Eye Contact:** The social rules for eye contact vary by culture, but at least in North American culture it can serve three purposes in communication (Beier and Sternberg 1977):

1. It can signal the start and end of a conversation. Most of us tend to look away from others when we're beginning to speak to them and to look at them when we've finished speaking.

INTERPERSONAL SPACE. In Middle Eastern cultures, people are accustomed to conducting conversations at a range of a foot or less, compared to 3 to 4 feet for North Americans and Europeans. What is your comfort zone for talking to others? If people move toward or away from you, do you tend to move an equal distance to maintain your usual space? ◄

2. It can express emotion. For instance, most of us tend to avoid eye contact when we're conveying bad news or are in conflict. Rolling your eyes communicates skepticism or disgust.
3. Gazing signifies interest and attention, as when two people are attracted to each other.

■ **Facial Expressions:** Eye behavior is difficult to control, which is why salespeople are trained to hold eye contact with potential customers. Facial expressions aren't as difficult to control as eye contact is, but they are still difficult.

In North America, we are accustomed to thinking that smiling represents warmth, happiness, or friendship, whereas frowning represents dissatisfaction or anger. In other cultures, however, these facial expressions don't apply.

■ **Body Movements and Gestures:** Examples of *body movements* are leaning backward or forward. Examples of *gestures* are pointing or beckoning. Open body positions, such as leaning backward, can express openness, warmth, closeness, and availability for communication. Closed body positions, such as folding one's arms or crossing one's legs, can represent defensiveness.

Some body movements and gestures are associated more with one gender than the other. For instance, women nod their heads and move their hands more than men do. Men exhibit large body shifts and foot and leg movements more than women do (Hall 1985).

■ **Touch:** Touch is perhaps the most intimate type of nonverbal communication. Touching varies by culture, with French people in outdoor cafés, for instance, touching each other more often, at 142 touches per hour, than Londoners, at no touches per hour (Pease and Pease 2006). People also tend to touch those they like, and women tend to do more touching than men do (Hall 1985). People who touch seem to disclose more about themselves and to get others to be more open about themselves (Heslin and Alper 1983; Norton 1983). Between partners in an intimate relationship, a decline in touching suggests a decline in affection. Touching shows the importance of the neural connection we mentioned at the beginning of this section: Brain scans show that a husband's touch can bring immediate relief to his wife under extreme stress, more so than the touch of a stranger (Coan et al. 2006).

You can see that once you decide to be alert to nonverbal cues, these signs can give you lots of information.

The Uses of Nonverbal Communication: Six Functions

In their book *Nonverbal Communication*, **Loretta Malandro and Larry Barker** (1983) state that nonverbal communication has six functions in relation to our spoken words:

■ **It Can Complement Our Words—"I mean what I'm saying":** Nonverbal messages can *complement* the words we utter, reinforcing that we really mean what our words say.
Example: When your partner says "I love you" and simultaneously touches your arm, you are more apt to feel assured that he or she means it.

■ **It Can Contradict Our Words—"I don't really mean what I'm saying":** Our nonverbal messages can *contradict* what we say, leaving the other person puzzled or doubtful.

Example: When your partner says "I love you" but looks away, you might wonder just how sincere he or she is in professing love.

■ **It Can Accent Our Words—"This nonverbal sign means I'm emphasizing what I'm saying":** We frequently use nonverbal signs, such as a touch or a pause, to *accent* or give emphasis to what we say.

Example: When your partner touches you while saying "I love you," it conveys extra emphasis.

■ **It Can Repeat Our Words—"I meant what I said, and this nonverbal sign tells you so again":** Our nonverbal cues can *repeat* our verbal message in a nonverbal way.

Example: When your partner says "I love you" (first message), then follows up a half minute later by squeezing your hand (second message), the second message repeats the first.

■ **It Can Substitute for Our Words—"This sign means the same as if I'd spoken":** We often use nonverbal cues to *substitute* for words—to express wordlessly what we could say in words.

Example: Instead of saying "I love you," your partner might use his or her fingers to "blow you a kiss" to express the same thing.

■ **It Can Help Regulate Our Communication—"This sign means I agree, disagree, or need to interrupt":** We use nonverbal messages all the time to regulate the flow of conversation.

Example: Nodding the head means "Yes," shaking the head means "No," a shrug means "I don't know," and raising a hand slightly means "Allow me to speak here."

Gender Differences

Are there communication differences between men and women? John Gray (1990), author of the bestselling *Men Are from Mars, Women Are from Venus,* certainly thinks so. So does psychologist **Deborah Tannen** (1990), author of books about gender communication, such as *You Just Don't Understand.* Although some scholars (Crawford 1995) think that the Mars/Venus division is too simplistic and stereotypical, let's consider what the differences might be.

Do Women Mainly Communicate Emotionally?

If any generalizations can be made about women, it is that when there are relationship problems, women approach them *emotionally* (Derlega et al. 1993).

■ **For Women, Life Is Intimacy—Seeking Closeness:** For women, according to Tannen (1990), the goal is to avoid isolation and maintain intimacy. Thus, they seek intimacy, connection, closeness, and equality with friends. Accordingly, when they confer with their partner about future plans, they enjoy the feeling of being intertwined with someone else.

■ **Women Engage in "Rapport Talk"—Talk Is an End in Itself:** Women engage in what Tannen calls **rapport talk, aimed primarily at gaining rapport or intimacy.** Women respond to another's problem by listening and offering sympathy, support, and understanding. Because men are less apt to act this way, women often think that men are insensitive to women's problems (Tannen 1990).

■ **What Women Talk About—Leisure and Men:** After work and money, the next most popular subject for women was divided equally between (1) leisure activities and (2) members of the opposite sex—that is, men (Bischoping 1993). Women enjoy talking about life's small details because these represent caring and intimacy (Tannen 1990).

■ **Women's Speech Is Personal, Concrete, and Tentative:** Women often talk in terms of details, anecdotes, and personal disclosures—concrete language to clarify feelings. They also talk tentatively, using disclaimers and verbal hedges ("I could be wrong, but . . ."), especially when talking to men.

Do Men Mainly Communicate Cognitively?

Likewise, if any generalizations can be made about men, it is that where there are relationship problems, men approach them *cognitively* (Derlega et al. 1993).

■ **For Men, Life Is a Contest—Seeking Status:** For men, says Tannen (1990), the goal of life is to preserve independence and avoid failure. Thus, they seek to establish power and status. Accordingly, when they confer with their partner about plans, they feel that they are losing their independence; hence, they are more apt than women to act unilaterally in making decisions.

■ **Men Engage in "Report Talk"—Talk Is Used to Accomplish Specific Purposes:** Men engage in what Tannen calls *report talk*, **aimed primarily at conveying information.** Men respond to another's problem by trying to solve it—by offering information, directions, opinions, and advice. Indeed, men might feel that women complain without taking action to solve whatever the problem is (Tannen 1990).

■ **What Men Talk About—Leisure:** After work and money, the next most popular subject for men was leisure activities, including sports. Men were four times less likely to talk about women than women were to talk about men (Bischoping 1993). Men might be bored or irritated with talk about life's small details (Tannen 1990).

■ **Men's Speech Is Abstract, Authoritative, and Dominant:** Men often talk in abstract, assertive, forceful, and direct terms. They also seek to dominate conversations by speaking longer and more frequently and by interrupting other speakers. (Women are more apt to wait their turn instead of interrupting.)

The "Female-Demand/Male-Withdraw" Pattern

A consequence of the differing gender styles of communication in troubled marriages is the *female-demand/male-withdraw pattern*, **an ongoing cycle in which the wife frequently gives negative verbal expression and the husband withdraws** (Kurdek 1995). The unhealthy pattern is not necessarily initiated by the woman. She, in fact, might be trying to bring problems out into the light for discussion, since discussion of relationship problems is more frequently initiated by women than by men (Mackey and O'Brien 1999).

But her attitude might be considered demanding by her husband, who might first try to resolve the disagreement, then withdraw as the wife presses on because she feels that he is not recognizing her needs.

How Satisfied Are Couples with Their Communication?

In general, according to one study of 218 married couples, both husbands and wives were satisfied with the communication in their marriages (Houk and Daniel 1994). However, the wives tended to report less communication or to rate the quality of the partners' communication lower than their husbands did. For instance, 62% of the wives stated that they expressed their feelings more openly and freely than their husbands did. About 24% of the wives stated that they communicated more easily with their female friends than with their husbands. About 18% said that they felt neglected because their husbands spent so much time watching sports, and more than 37% stated that they sometimes thought their husbands liked watching TV better than talking to them. More than a third of the women stated that their husbands would withdraw if the two had a disagreement. Does this picture sound like any married couple you know?

Barriers to Communication

Although partners in a relationship might really want to have a meaningful interaction with each other and resolve problems, often they don't know what they are doing that throws up barriers. Let's consider some of them.

Satir's Four Styles of Miscommunication

Virginia Satir, author of two classic books on marital communication, *Peoplemaking* (1972) and *The New Peoplemaking* (1988), says that people use four styles of miscommunication: *placating, blaming, computing,* and *distracting.*

■ Placating—"Whatever makes you happy, dear": *Placaters* **are passive people who are always agreeable but act helpless.** Their greatest wish is to avoid having a scene—hence the wish to placate others. Consequently, whatever their real feelings—which they might not know themselves—they will give in to nearly any request by their partner.

■ Blaming—"It's not my fault!": *Blamers* **always try to put the responsibility for any problem on someone else.** Blamers are tense, often angry people who feel inadequate but can't admit it to themselves or anyone else. Because nothing is ever their fault, they rarely engage in constructive discussion about problems.

■ Computing—"One could be angry if one allowed it": *Computers* **always pretend to be reasonable and not reveal their feelings, because they find emotions threatening.** Thus, they might describe their feelings in the most expressionless, unemotional way, as in "If one were to observe the pounding vein in my temple, one would conclude I could be upset."

■ Distracting—"Oh my, there's something else I must deal with": *Distractors* **avoid disclosing relevant feelings, so they never discuss a problem but**

MISCOMMUNICATION. She's poking him in the chest (aggression). He's got his arms folded (resistance). An argument over who forgot to buy milk? Regardless, which of Virginia Satir's four styles of miscommunication—placating, blaming, computing, or distracting—seems to be represented by the man here? Which of these four styles do you tend to employ during an argument? ▲

instead change the subject. They always appear scattered and distracted, and because they don't feel that they belong anywhere, they constantly flit about from place to place.

Do these styles seem like cartoons? Or do they fit people you know—or yourself?

Gottman's Horsemen of the Apocalypse: Five Types of Destructive Interactions

If one partner (particularly the wife) rolls his or her eyes while the spouse is talking, is that a predictor of divorce? In fact, it is, says social psychologist **John Gottman** (Gottman and Krokoff 1989), a leading authority on marital communication, who has used videocameras to record couples' facial gestures. Gottman and his associates suggest that there are four kinds of couple interactions—to which he later added a fifth—that in 90% of cases are predictors of divorce (Gottman 1994; Gottman et al. 1998). Called by Gottman The Four Horsemen of the Apocalypse, they are *contempt, criticism, defensiveness,* and *stonewalling;* the fifth interaction is *belligerence.*

■ Contempt: *Contempt* (such as eye rolling) **expresses that your partner is inferior or undesirable.**
Example: "Well, the Master Leader is late for dinner again!"

■ Criticism: *Criticism* **is making disapproving judgments or evaluations about your partner.**
Example: "Hey, you know barbequing is not your talent. Why bother?"

■ Defensiveness: *Defensiveness* **is not listening but rather defending yourself against a presumed attack.**
Example: "Look, I know what you're going to say, and I resent it!"

■ Stonewalling: *Stonewalling* **is refusing to listen to your partner, particularly his or her complaints.**
Example: "We've been over this before, and there's no point discussing it again!"

■ Belligerence: *Belligerence* **is being provocative and challenging your partner's power and authority.**
Example: "Just a minute, who elected you God?"

The first four interactions, Gottman suggested, are apt to occur sequentially, each one being succeeded by another as marital communication deteriorates.

Hostility & Detachment as Destructive Behaviors

Two important behaviors contributing to marital distress, according to one study (Roberts 2000), are hostility and withdrawal.

■ Hostility: The primary predictor of marital dissatisfaction for wives was the husband's hostile responsiveness. This runs contrary to the traditional gender stereotype of the "uninvolved, withdrawn husband."

■ **Withdrawal:** The primary predictor of unhappiness for husbands was their wives' withdrawal, as expressed in three ways: (1) avoidance of intimacy, (2) avoidance of conflict, or (3) angry withdrawal. This, too, runs contrary to the gender stereotype of the "nagging, hostile wife."

Interestingly, another study concluded that the combination of hostility and detachment within the marital relationship "is the most destructive form of marital conflict and is associated with maladjustment throughout many levels of the family system" (Katz and Woodin 2002: 647). Children who are raised in families in which husbands and wives engaged in *both* attacking and withdrawing behavior in their communication with one another tended to show negative emotions and difficulties interacting with other children.

Lack of Self-Disclosure: The Need for Honesty & Leveling

So much of what we do consists of playing roles—jobholder, spouse, offspring, the strong man or the understanding woman. But these roles are surface ones; they do not represent our true selves, which are expressed only through self-disclosure. *Self-disclosure* **means telling another person deep personal information and feelings about yourself.** Women are more likely than men to practice self-disclosure, and they expect their partners to do the same (Gallmeier et al. 1997). Self-disclosure creates the conditions for mutual understanding, and the more spouses feel comfortable disclosing to each other, the deeper their intimacy and the more committed the relationship (Waring 1988; Derlega et al. 1993; Patford 2000).

Achieving self-disclosure requires *honesty* and *leveling*.

■ **Honesty:** Are you honest with yourself? Or do you deny or otherwise pretend not to recognize unpleasant realities about yourself (such as attitudes toward sex or money)? If you are not straightforward with yourself, you're not apt to be so with others (Lerner 1993).

Of course, people lie—by commission (stating outright untruths) or omission (withholding information)—all the time. Although a happy relationship might rest on withholding criticism of your partner (Finkenauer and Hazam 2000), serious deception will undermine intimacy.

■ **Leveling:** *Leveling* **consists of being specific, authentic, and transparent about how you feel, especially about matters in your relationship that create conflict or hurt.** Even when the years go by and spouses think they have achieved understanding, many conflicts are not resolved because the partners are unable to air grievances in a candid way.

A basic ingredient in leveling is kindness and gentleness. You want to be direct, avoiding contradictory messages, but you should always try to avoid being hurtful.

Guide to Effective Communication

Are there couples who thrive on confrontation and combat? Indeed, there are, says psychologist John Gottman, the marital communication expert. "This type of couple," he says, "is quite passionate and emotionally expressive. They fight a lot, but they also laugh a lot. They have a wide range of emotional expression" (Gottman 1994: 136–137).

But the confrontational approach is not for most people. The crucial thing about couples in lasting marriages, Gottman has found, is that they experience

five times more positive feelings and interaction than they do negative ones (Gottman 1994: 41). Other investigators (Boyd and Roach 1977) have found that satisfied couples tend to openly express respect and esteem for each other, to say what they really think, and to have good listening skills.

This and other research suggests the following four rules for effective communication, which overlap a bit with the tips we gave earlier about fighting fairly.

1. Create an Environment That Gives Communication High Priority & Values Others' Viewpoints

You and your partner—and other family members—need to create an environment of mutual affection and respect that gives a high priority to communicating everyone's wishes and needs. This will not occur naturally; it will require dedication and work.

An important part of this environment is learning to be able to see things from the other person's perspective.

2. Share Power & Hopes

Not sharing power is a great source of conflict—and ultimately of divorce (Kurdek 1995; Gottman et al. 1998). To build a satisfying relationship, partners need to consider themselves an alliance of best friends in which the goal is to share their power—over finances, over sex, over child rearing, and so on.

You also need to learn to share each other's hopes for the future, both near-term, such as weekend plans, and long-term, such as education, career, family, and retirement.

3. Be Specific, Honest, & Kind

Focus on specifics ("How about keeping your side of the bathroom sink neat?"), not generalities ("Why are you always so messy?").

Talk honestly—that is, directly, truthfully, and sincerely. Avoid such tactics of manipulation as sulking, martyrdom, bullying, indignant outrage, or other controlling emotional games.

By all means, avoid "brutal honesty" or "tough love" as an excuse to blame, criticize, or dominate the other person. Instead, use kindness, and say positive things about your partner. Express appreciation, and give compliments—often.

4. Tell Your Partner What You Want in Positive Terms, Ask for Information, & Listen Well

Learn to tell your partner what you want in positive rather than negative terms. (Positive: "Could you please turn off the porch light before going to bed?" Negative: "Don't always leave the porch light on.")

If your partner has a problem with something you're doing, ask for more information; don't be defensive.

When listening, give summations or feedback so that both you and your partner will know that you understand.

A final word from the famous Love Lab doctor, John Gottman, and his colleague Sybil Carrere, who say they have learned much from the couples they have studied that they try to bring to their own marriages—two things in particular. "One is the importance of building and maintaining a friendship in your marriage so that you give your partner the benefit of the doubt when times are tough. This takes constant work. The second thing is that you have a choice every time you say something to your partner. You can say something that will either nurture the relationship or tear it down. You may win a particular fight with your spouse, but you could lose the marriage in the long run" (Gottman and Carrere 2000: 42).

Self-Assessment: Accepting Your Partner

Assess how much acceptance you have for your partner. Report in the second column how many days in the past week your partner engaged in the activity in the first column. In the third column, rate how acceptable you find each behavior at its current frequency, using a scale of 0 to 9, with 0 totally unacceptable and 9 totally acceptable.

For ___ days in the past week, my partner	Number of days	Acceptability of behavior
1. Was physically affectionate (held my hand, kissed me, responded when I initiated affection)	____	____
2. Was verbally affectionate (complimented me, told me he/she loves me, said nice things to me)	____	____
3. Did housework (no matter who suggested it; cooked, took out trash, did dishes, laundry, shopping)	____	____
4. Did child care (took care of children, helped with homework, disciplined them, played with them)		
5. Confided in me (shared feelings, success, failures)	____	____
6. Engaged in sex with me (including intercourse or any other sexual activity initiated by you or partner)	____	____
7. Was supportive (listened to my problems, sympathized, helped with my difficulties)	____	____
8. Did social or recreational activities with me (movies, dinner, hiking, etc., no matter who initiated them)	____	____
9. Socialized with my family or friends and me	____	____
10. Discussed problems in our relationship with me	____	____
11. Showed consideration for me (tried to be quiet while I slept, offered me something from the kitchen)	____	____
12. Participated in financial responsibilities (helped make financial decisions, paid bills, consulted me on a purchase)	____	____
Total the numbers in the third column:		____

Scoring

If you're the female partner

Green light: 81 or above
Yellow light: 75–81
Red light: 74 or lower

If you're the male partner

Green light: 89 or above
Green light: 82–88
Red light: 81 or lower

GREEN LIGHT: Satisfied range. You are probably doing fine as a couple.

YELLOW LIGHT: Between happy and unhappy. There is possibly a cause for concern.

RED LIGHT: Dissatisfied range. Attention to the problems in your relationship is needed.

Source: Adapted from "Accepting Your Spouse." Karen S. Peterson. 2000. Breaking bickering barriers. *USA Today.* February 23, p. 7D. USA TODAY. Copyright February 23, 2000. Reprinted with permission. Based on Andrew Christensen and Neil S. Jacobson. 2000. *Reconcilable differences.* New York: The Guilford Press.

Key Terms Used in This Chapter

Summary

6.1 Power & Intimacy

- Many of the day-to-day interactions that couples experience are significantly influenced by how power is shared, how conflict is handled, and how the partners communicate. Power is the ability or the potential to impose one's will on other people, to get them to think, feel, or do something they would not ordinarily have done spontaneously. Unequal power in an intimate relationship affects self-esteem; inhibits satisfaction, love, and the sharing of feelings; and encourages manipulation.

- Six different types of power in relationships are as follows: (1) Coercive power is based on your fear that your partner will inflict punishment. The punishment can be emotional, such as sarcasm or contempt, or it can be physical, such as beatings. (2) Reward power is based on your belief that your agreement with your partner will elicit rewards from that partner. Often, the rewards are verbal, such as praise or at least the absence of criticism. (3) Expert power is based on your opinion that your partner has specialized knowledge. (4) Legitimate power is based on your partner's having the right to ask you and your having the duty to comply. (5) Referent power is based on your identifying with and admiring your spouse and receiving satisfaction by pleasing him or her. (6) Informational power is persuasive power; you are persuaded by your partner that what he or she wants is in your best interest.

- The resource theory developed by Blood and Wolfe suggests that the balance of power in a marriage reflects the relative resources of each spouse. Resources may be money, education, or occupational status, but they may also be sex, emotional support, parenting skills, homemaking ability, or money management skills.

- Waller's principle of least interest states that whoever has the least interest in the relationship has the most power.

- Stepfamilies represent the blending of families and consequently result in complicated power relationships. These relationships present challenges surrounding such issues as discipline and communication, divided loyalties, living arrangements and time, and money.

6.2 Conflict & Growth

- Conflict in a relationship is inevitable. Although it can be negative, it can also be positive—in fact, desirable. Because of the need for closeness and independence in relationships and the difficulty in trying to achieve both, conflict may result. Conflict is the process of interaction that results when the behavior of one person interferes with the behavior of another.

- Conflict in relationships can be negative conflict and can be bad for relationships, or it can be positive conflict and be good for relationships. Some negative types of conflict are the following: (1) Repressed anger is the unconscious suppression of feelings of anger so that they are expressed in other ways. One way is gunnysacking—saving up, or putting in an imaginary sack, grievances until they spill over. (2) Passive-aggression is the expression of anger indirectly rather than directly. In another variation, the silent treatment, you either ignore your partner or verbally say that things are all right while sending nonverbal signals that they are not. (3) Scapegoating is the blaming of one particular family member for nearly everything that goes wrong in that family. (4) Gaslighting is when one partner, perhaps using sarcasm, constantly criticizes or denies the other's definition of reality, diminishing the other's self-esteem.

- Conflict can also be positive for relationships by helping to clarify differences and keeping small issues from becoming big ones. It can also improve relationships through increasing each other's self-confidence and strengthening the relationship.

- Research indicates nine common areas of disagreement among couples involving such issues as household tasks, money, sex, loyalty, power, nurturance, privacy, children, and differences in style.

- A major area of conflict between couples is the division of household labor. Hochschild coined the term *the second shift*, defined as the housework and child care that employed women do after returning home from their jobs.

- Couples handle conflict in a variety of ways. Researchers have identified a number of methods of conflict and conflict resolution. Five major types include (1) competing, (2) parallel, (3) accommodating, (4) compromising, and (5) collaborating.

- Conflict is inevitable. The best way to deal with conflict is for both partners to learn about constructive conflict resolution. Five guidelines for handling conflict are as follows: (1) Attack problems, not your partner, and avoid negativity. (2) Focus on specific issues, use "I feel" language, and avoid mixed messages. (3) Be sensitive about timing and place. (4) Say what you mean, don't lie or manipulate, and ask for what you want. (5) Let your partner know that you're listening—really listening—and work toward resolution.

6.3 The Nature of Communication

- Communication can be verbal and nonverbal. Nonverbal communication, which consists of messages sent outside the written or spoken word, can be influ-

enced through such factors as interpersonal space, eye contact, facial expressions, body movements and gestures, and touch. Malandro and Barker state that nonverbal communication has six functions in relation to our spoken words: (1) It can complement the words we utter, reinforcing that we really mean what our words say. (2) It can contradict what we say, leaving the other person puzzled or doubtful. (3) It can accent or give emphasis to what we say. (4) It can repeat our verbal message in a nonverbal way. (5) It can substitute for words, expressing wordlessly what we could say in words. (6) It can regulate the flow of conversation.

- Research indicates that there are gender differences in communication. Tannen suggests that women communicate emotionally, while men tend to communicate cognitively. A consequence of the differing gender styles of communication in troubled marriages is the female-demand/male-withdraw pattern, an ongoing cycle in which the wife frequently gives negative verbal expression and the husband withdraws.

- Satir identifies four barriers to communication: (1) Placaters are passive people who are always agreeable but act helpless. (2) Blamers always try to put the responsibility for any problem on someone else. (3) Computers always pretend to be reasonable and not reveal their feelings, because they find emotions threatening. (4) Distractors avoid disclosing relevant feelings, so they never discuss a problem but instead change the subject.

- Gottman and associates suggest that there are four kinds of couple interactions—to which he later added a fifth—that in 90% of cases are predictors of divorce. Called by Gottman The Four Horsemen of the Apocalypse, they are contempt, criticism, defensiveness, and stonewalling; the fifth interaction is belligerence. (1) *Contempt* (such as eye rolling) expresses that your partner is inferior or undesirable. (2) *Criticism* is making disapproving judgments or evaluations about your partner. (3) *Defensiveness* is not listening but rather defending yourself against a presumed attack. (4) *Stonewalling* is refusing to listen to your partner, particularly his or her complaints. (5) *Belligerence* is being provocative and challenging your partner's power and authority.

- Self-disclosure means telling another person deep personal information and feelings about yourself. Achieving self-disclosure requires honesty and leveling. Leveling consists of being specific, authentic, and transparent about how you feel, especially about matters in your relationship that create conflict or hurt.

- Research suggests that to communicate effectively, you need to create an environment that gives communication high priority and values others' viewpoints; share power and hopes, be specific, honest, and kind; and tell your partner what you want in positive terms, ask for information, and listen well.

Take It to the Net

Among the Internet resources on communication are the following:

- **The American Association for Marital & Family Therapy.** Gives resources for finding a family therapist near you.
  www.aamft.org/index_nm.asp
- **Email Escalation: Dispute Exacerbating Elements of Electronic Communication.** Paper (40 pages long) by Raymond A. Friedman and Steven C. Currall analyzes email limitations.
  http://mba.vanderbilt.edu/ray.friedman/pdf/emailescalation.pdf
- **Lovegevity.** Offers various ideas for improving marriage.
  www.lovegevity.com/marriage/expertadvice/index.html

CHAPTER 7

SEXUALITY

Interpersonal Sexuality, Sexual Values, & Behavior

How Do We Learn about Sex?

"Television is the most powerful medium on the planet—that can't be said enough," says TV critic Tim Goodman (2003: D7). "Even people who say they don't watch, watch. Television is the shared experience of our country, a free (or mostly free) technology that bonds us together, the blue light flickering in our living rooms and bedrooms from coast to coast."

Television, other mass media, and the popular culture have a tremendous impact on what we think and feel about sex (McMahon 1990; Wolf and Kielwasser 1991). When asked by an adult what's new in the sexual realm since she was young, Chu Hui, 19, replied: "I

don't recall having sexuality pushed in my face when I was 10 or 11. But I have a younger half-sister who is 11 years old, and she's a very big fan of Britney Spears and the Spice Girls, and she tries to emulate them in the way she dresses and the way she acts. . . . I see her wanting to wear clothes that I would never have considered wearing. I don't remember going through that at her age" ("The naked truth" 2000: 59).

Watching television accounts for more than half of all media use. Adults spent an estimated 1,555 hours (equal to 65 days) in front of the TV in 2007 (*Statistical Abstract of the United States 2007* 2006: Table 1110), and one survey (Stodgill 1998) found that 29% of adult Americans said television was their most important source of information about sex. The average teenager watches TV more than three hours a day, and 83% of programs

popular with adolescents have been found to have sexual content; 20% contained explicit or implicit intercourse (Kunkel et al. 2005).

The average American youth spends one-third of each day with various forms of mass media, mostly without parental oversight (Escobar-Chaves et al. 2005). Thus, if we consider mass media and popular culture in general—everything from music to magazines to movies to ads to novels—the influence on sexuality is profound. One-third of respondents in one survey said contemporary pop culture was their most important source of ideas about sex (Moffatt 1989). Another study found that children ages 12 to 14 who had a high "sexual media diet" were more than two times more likely to have sex at ages 14 to 16 compared to teens exposed to lighter sexual media fare (Brown et al. 2006).

Yet teens themselves seem to be ambivalent about the usefulness of such information. In a Kaiser Foundation/U.S. News poll (reported in Mul-

🔍 WHAT'S AHEAD IN THIS CHAPTER

We discuss sexual values, learning, and scripts. Then we describe the varieties of sexual experience and include a short discussion about some sexual dysfunctions. The final section describes HIV/AIDS.

rine 2002: 47), 503 adolescents were asked about how helpful sexual scenes on TV would be applied to real life, 60% thought they would not help them "say no to an uncomfortable sexual situation," but 57% said they would be an aid in talking "to a boyfriend/girlfriend about safer sex."

It wouldn't be so bad if ideas about sex from MTV, *Playboy*, beer ads, and romance novels were factual. Unfortunately, quite often they're not. Consider:

■ *Television:* One study of adolescents' top ten TV programs found that more than a quarter had interactions of a sexual nature. Most of the messages showed men seeing women as sex objects, sex as a defining characteristic of masculinity, and sex as competition—in other words, the content is traditional and sex-role stereotyped (Ward 1995). Interestingly, women, but not men, are less apt to recall the content of TV commercials that appear in programs with a lot of sexual content (Parker and Furnham 2007).

Until recently there has almost never been any discussion of safer sex and contraception (Greenberg and Busselle 1996). That may be changing, however, since a recent survey (Kunkel et al. 2003) found that among shows with sexual content, references to such safe-sex issues as contraception had risen to 15% from 9% in 1999.

■ *Song lyrics and music videos:* Teens who listen to the raunchy, sexual lyrics of music are twice as likely to start having sex sooner than those who listen to other songs, according to one study (Martino et al. 2006). In addi-

tion, adolescent girls who watch a lot of music videos are more likely to say that dating is a game, that females are sex objects, and that males are sex driven (Strouse and Buerkel-Rothfuss 1987; Ward 2000).

■ *Advertising:* Young people view more than 40,000 ads a year on television alone (Shifrin et al. 2006). Many such commercials, of course, emphasize not only that sex is fun but that it is pervasive—that everyone engages in it (Strasburger 1997). A report by the American Psychological Association, which analyzed about 300 studies, found that ads in a variety of media showed body-baring doll clothes for preschoolers, children posing in suggestive ways, and young celebrities engaging in sexual antics, all images that may make girls think of their bodies as sexual objects (Zurbriggen et al. 2007). The American Academy of Pediatrics has called for limits on ads aimed at children, and recommended that commercials for erectile dysfunction drugs be shown only after 10 p.m. (Shifrin et al. 2006).

■ *Movies and the Internet:* Despite parental-guidance rating systems, most young people seem to have no problem seeing R- and even X-rated movies. Today, formerly hard-to-obtain adult-rated and pornographic materials are easily accessible. One study of college students found that more than 77% had visited a sexually explicit website (Knox et al. 2001). Other research reported that 42% of Internet users between the ages of 10 and 17 had viewed online porn (Wolak et al. 2007).

How did I learn to think what I think about sex?

What are all the forms of sexual expression?

How could having sex risk my health and my life?

⬤ **ON THE WEB** About Sex

www.siecus.org

No doubt you have at least one question about sex that the media has never answered satisfactorily. To begin to find out the truth, go to the website for the Sexuality Information and Education Council of the United States (SIECUS). A nonprofit organization formed in 1964, SIECUS collects and disseminates information about sex and making responsible sexual choices.

7.1 Sexual Values, Learning, & Scripts

MAJOR QUESTION How did I learn to think what I think about sex?

PREVIEW We first discuss sexual values, including four standards of pre-marital and nonmarital sex and age of first intercourse. We then describe how we learn about sex. Finally, we discuss sexual scripts, or expected ways of behaving.

"The more sex, the happier the person," write David Branchflower of Dartmouth College and Andrew Osmond of Warwick University (2004: 10). Indeed, the two economists say that regular sex brings people as much happiness as a $50,000-a-year raise.

Of course, the kind of sex that seems pleasurable for one person may not be for another. And pleasure also seems to have a lot to do with culture: Sex is more satisfying in countries in which women and men are considered equal, according to a study of 27,500 people in 29 nations (Laumann et al. 2006). *(See ■ Panel 7.1.)* As the lead researcher, University of Chicago sociologist Edward Laumann, suggests, "When mama's not happy, nobody's happy" (Laumann, quoted in Associated Press 2006).

When Sex Doesn't Work

The idea that great sex brings great joy is constantly reinforced. The very pinnacle of happiness, so we are often led to believe, is sex with a partner who wants to do everything you want to do, who wants to do it when you do, and who experiences the fireworks of ecstasy that good sex is supposed to be all about.

But what happens—as, in fact, often *does* happen in real life—when you and your partner don't want to engage in the same kinds of sexual activity or at the same time? For example, it has been found that about half of men like to receive oral sex and 37% like to give it. This compares with about one-third of women who like to receive oral sex and 19% who like to give it (Laumann

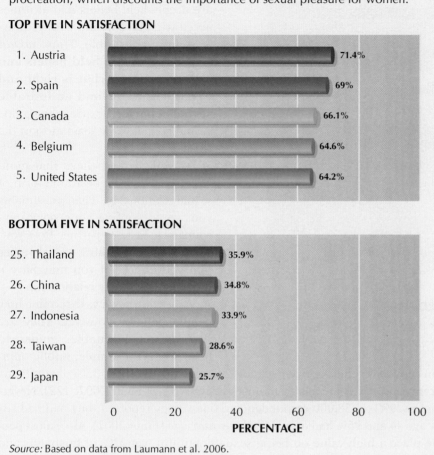

■ PANEL 7.1 "When Mama's Not Happy, Nobody's Happy": Nations Ranking Highest and Lowest in Sexual Satisfaction. The percentage of people in 10 of 29 countries who said they were satisfied with their sex lives. Rates are higher in countries in which women and men are considered equal. In male-centered countries, researchers suggest, sex is oriented more toward procreation, which discounts the importance of sexual pleasure for women.

TOP FIVE IN SATISFACTION

1. Austria — 71.4%
2. Spain — 69%
3. Canada — 66.1%
4. Belgium — 64.6%
5. United States — 64.2%

BOTTOM FIVE IN SATISFACTION

25. Thailand — 35.9%
26. China — 34.8%
27. Indonesia — 33.9%
28. Taiwan — 28.6%
29. Japan — 25.7%

PERCENTAGE

Source: Based on data from Laumann et al. 2006.

et al. 1994). Clearly, even if men and women were always agreeable to having sex at the same time, there would always be some differences in sexual preferences on the matter of oral sex alone.

Nearly everyone at some point has to deal with the possibility of engaging in sex that they don't want. A 2006 study of 279 teenage girls reported that 41% felt pressured into sex and that 1 in 10 felt forced to submit—especially when either member of a couple, but particularly the boy, had been using alcohol or marijuana (Blythe et al. 2006). A 1988 study of college students (507 men and 486 women) found that 97.5% of the women and 93.5% of the men had experienced unwanted sexual activity, including kissing, petting, and sexual intercourse (Muehlenhard and Cook 1988). Among them, 46.3% of the women and 62.7% of the men had had unwanted intercourse.

Why do people go against their own wishes and just give in? The reasons are shown in the accompanying chart. *(See ■ Panel 7.2, next page.)* *Enticement,* for instance, consists of seductive acts by the other person, such as touching. *Altruism* is satisfying the other person simply because he or she wants it. *Inexperience* is thinking that one needs to have the experience of the sexual activity. *Reluctance* is feeling obligated or not knowing what else to do.

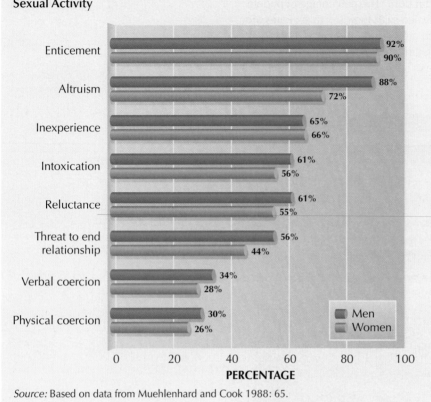

Enticement 92% / 90%
Altruism 88% / 72%
Inexperience 65% / 66%
Intoxication 61% / 56%
Reluctance 61% / 55%
Threat to end relationship 56% / 44%
Verbal coercion 34% / 28%
Physical coercion 30% / 26%

Men
Women

0 20 40 60 80 100
PERCENTAGE

Source: Based on data from Muehlenhard and Cook 1988: 65.

Sexual Values

Our preferences and beliefs about sex often reflect our sexual values. *Values,* as we said in Chapter 1, "Seeking," are deeply held beliefs and attitudes about what is right and wrong, desirable and undesirable. Thus, **sexual values are deeply held beliefs and attitudes about what is right and wrong, desirable and undesirable sexual behavior.** Sexual values guide sexual behavior—at least most of the time.

Do you firmly believe that monogamy is the most desirable form of sexual relationship? Then presumably you would confine your sexual encounters to just one partner. Does your partner have the same sexual values that you do? Then you may have a warm and workable relationship.

Values don't always determine how people behave, however. They are *general,* not inevitable, guides to behavior. For example, public opinions polls over the last two decades have shown that about 35% of adults say premarital sex is always or almost always wrong (Finer 2007: 122). Nevertheless, 99% of 38,000 respondents to one survey reported they had had sex by age 44 and 95% had done so before marriage (Finer 2007). Also, most people place a high value on being sexually faithful, yet 23% of husbands and 12% of wives are not, according to another study (Wiederman 1997).

Four Standards of Premarital & Nonmarital Sex

Sociologist **Ira Reiss** (1976) identified four values or societal standards about premarital sex—standards that also apply to nonmarital sex among the never-married, don't-intend-to-marry, formerly married, and married but separated.

■ The Double Standard: **The *double standard* is the standard according to which premarital or nonmarital sex is more acceptable for men than it is for women.**

In recent times, this standard has been modified so that unmarried women are sometimes permitted to have sex, provided that they are in love. Although the double standard seems to be declining in some parts of society, it still prevails in many quarters.

■ Permissiveness with Affection: The standard ***permissiveness with affection*** allows premarital or nonmarital sex for both women and men, provided that they have an affectionate and committed relationship.**

This standard seems to be widespread today, with many people feeling that having a few sexual partners enables one to have the experience to choose a sexually compatible mate (Whitman 1997).

- **How many experience unwanted sex?** One study of college students found that 97.5% of the women and 93.5% of the men had experienced unwanted sexual activity, including kissing, petting, and sexual intercourse.[a]

- **What percentage of people have had sex before marriage?** In one survey, 9970 of 38,000 respondents had had sex by age 44, and 95% had done so before marriage.[b]

- **Who's unfaithful?** Results from one study should that 23% of husbands and 12% of wives had been unfaithful.[b]

- **What's the age of first intercourse?** About 70% of American adolescent females and 65% of adolescent males have had sex (inter-course) by age 19.[d] Between 1994 and 2003, the median age at which people had their first sexual experience was 17.6.[e]

- **How often do people have sex?** Married and unmarried adults on average reported 57.4 instances of sexual intercourse the preceding year, or about once a week. Twenty-two percent of people, including 9% of married people, said that they had had no sex partners at all the previous year.[f]

- **Who suffers from STDs?** About two-thirds of sexually transmitted diseases occur among people under age 25.[g]

- **Who gets HIV/AIDS?** The rate of heterosexual HIV transmission is rising at three times the rate of homosexual transmission. More-over, heterosexual women are more than twice as likely as men to get HIV/AIDS, and they are apt to get it from heterosexual men.[h]

NUMBERS THAT MATTER
Sexuality

[a] Muehlenhard and Cook 1988. [b] Finer 2007. [c] Wiederman 1997. [d] Abma 2003. [e] Finer 2007. [f] National Opinion Research Center 1990. [g] Conforth 2004. [h] Centers for Disease Control and Prevention 2003.

■ **Permissiveness without Affection:** The standard ***permissiveness without affection*, also called recreational sex, allows premarital or nonmarital sex for women and men regardless of the amount of affection or stability in their relationship.**

This standard takes the point of view that casual sex is fine as a means of achieving sexual pleasure.

■ **Abstinence:** ***Abstinence* is defined as the voluntary avoidance of sexual intercourse.** Often endorsed by conservative religious groups, abstinence-only sex-education policies have become a way of life in many school districts (in fact, this is the only sex-education method taught in 55% of school districts in the South). There is as yet no evidence, however, that the "refrain until marriage" message prevents a significant amount of teen sex, pregnancy, or disease (Delgado 2002).

Sexual Values of College Students

Sociologist **David Knox** and his colleagues (2001) studied 620 never-married college undergraduates and identified three sexual values that guided their behavior in sexual decision making: *absolutism, hedonism,* and *relativism*:

■ **Absolutism:** People following this value adhere to strict codes, usually based on religion, that dictate what is right and wrong. The Knox study found that women were more likely than men to be absolutist. In addition, younger (ages 17 to 19) individuals, those who were involved in a relationship, and those who said that they would neither live together nor divorce were more likely to be absolutist.

IF IT FEELS GOOD. . . . College students tend to be influenced by one of three sexual values: absolutism (one should follow a strict sexual code), hedonism (sex is okay if it doesn't hurt others), and relativism (whether sex is right depends on the relationship). Which way do you tend to follow? ▶

■ **Hedonism:** Students subscribing to this value—"If it feels good, do it, but don't hurt anybody in the process"—were more apt to be men. Indeed, men were six times more likely to endorse hedonism than women were.

■ **Relativism:** People following this value would agree that "what you do sexually depends on the person you are with, how you feel about each other, and the nature of the relationship." Knox and associates found that university students are predominantly relativistic in their sexual beliefs—more so than either absolutist or hedonistic.

Age of First Sexual Experience

Virginity—**the state of not having experienced sexual intercourse**—and the consequences of no longer having it, particularly for females, has throughout human history been invested with a great deal of significance but attended by a great deal of ignorance. As scholar Hanne Blank (2007) writes in *Virgin: The Untouched History,* "The simple fact is that short of catching someone in the act of sex, virginity can be neither proven nor disproven" (Blank quoted in Blaisdell 2007). A partly or completely ruptured hymen—the skin covering the vaginal opening—is no more proof of loss of virginity than are measuring a woman's skull or the shape of her breasts or any other silly theories. Yet there are cultures today, such as that of the Zulus in South Africa, that make a great show of inspecting girls' hymens and passing judgment on their virgin status (LaFraniere 2005).

In the United States, because of the hypersexualization of our culture, adolescent girls often experience pressure not to retain but to lose their virginity. The same is true of boys. Nick, age 17, for instance, says: "I did feel pressure—from everything around me. Friends, media, everything. It was almost like afterwards it was almost a relief" ("The naked truth" 2000: 59). About 70% of American adolescent females and 65% of adolescent males have had sex (intercourse) by age 19, and few in this age group have married (Abma 2003). By age 20, 77% of respondents in one survey reported that they had had sex, and 75% had had premarital sex (Finer 2007). The age at which people have had their first sexual experience has dropped during the past 50 years, from a median of 20.4 years in 1954–1963 to 17.6 in 1994–2003. *(See ■ Panel 7.3)*

Throughout the world, according to one global study of 59 nations (Wellings et al. 2006), nearly everywhere men and women have their first sexual expe-

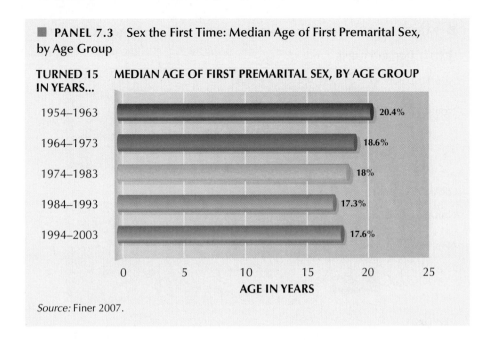

■ **PANEL 7.3**   Sex the First Time: Median Age of First Premarital Sex, by Age Group

TURNED 15 IN YEARS...	MEDIAN AGE OF FIRST PREMARITAL SEX, BY AGE GROUP
1954–1963	20.4%
1964–1973	18.6%
1974–1983	18%
1984–1993	17.3%
1994–2003	17.6%

AGE IN YEARS

Source: Finer 2007.

riences while in their late teens—from 15 to 19 years old—with generally younger ages for women than for men. Still, there are considerable variations, w ith men and women in Britain, for example, having their first sexual experience at ages 16½ and 17½, respectively, compared with men and women in Indonesia at 24½ and 18½, respectively.

In the United States, there seems to be a decline in the proportion of very young teenagers—those under age 15—who have had sex. The same is true with adolescents ages 15 to 19, with only 13% of never-married females and 15% of never-married males reporting in 2002 they had had sex before the age of 15, down from 19% and 21%, respectively, in 1995 (Terry-Humen et al. 2006). But here's an interesting wrinkle: Some adolescents who have not engaged in sexual intercourse have nevertheless engaged in oral sex. *(See* ■ *Panel 7.4, next page.)* Part of the reason for this is that adolescents may not see oral sex as a form of sex (Remez 2000). As junior college sophomore Natalie Fuller (quoted in Jayson 2005) put it, "For most teens, the only form of sex is penetration, and anything else doesn't count. You can have oral sex and be a virgin." (This is known as "technical virginity.")

How We Learn about Sex

We have already mentioned the mass media, popular culture, and the Internet as sources of our values and beliefs about sex. We also learn from parents, religion, friends and siblings, sex education, and our partners.

The Influence of Parents

A New Jersey girl, age 15 and a virgin, seeks out a housekeeper to talk about sex because "I asked both of my parents, and they wouldn't answer my questions" (reported in Mulrine 2002: 44). A California teen, age 16, who is close to her mother, one day confides that she and her boyfriend are ready to have sex for the first time. Although not thrilled, the mother is realistic, so she instructs her daughter in the use of condoms and spermicide and tells her she should bring her boyfriend home (Silver 2002: 46).

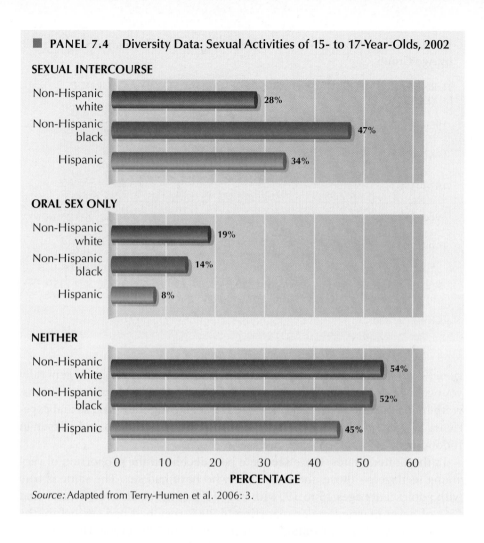

■ **PANEL 7.4** Diversity Data: Sexual Activities of 15- to 17-Year-Olds, 2002

SEXUAL INTERCOURSE

Non-Hispanic white — 28%
Non-Hispanic black — 47%
Hispanic — 34%

ORAL SEX ONLY

Non-Hispanic white — 19%
Non-Hispanic black — 14%
Hispanic — 8%

NEITHER

Non-Hispanic white — 54%
Non-Hispanic black — 52%
Hispanic — 45%

PERCENTAGE

Source: Adapted from Terry-Humen et al. 2006: 3.

The second story is the more unusual: Mother and daughter are actually talking with each other about sex. Research shows that mothers with good relationships with their teenage daughters have been able to influence their sexual activity (Taris et al. 1998). However, it's unclear how much influence parents actually have. Some research finds that 47% percent of teens say parents most influence their decisions about sex, although only 34% of parents of teens believe parents are most influential (Albert 2007). A Kaiser Family Foundation/*U.S. News* poll (cited in Silver 2002: 46) reports that 52% of teens say their parents "rarely" or "never" discuss sex with them. In another survey, only 7% of adults said their parents had been their most important source of information about sex (Stodgill 1998). But if parental communication may have little influence on a teen's first sexual involvement, research shows that it can be important in preventing teenage pregnancy (Hanson et al. 1987).

■ **How Parents Feel:** Most parents hold back because they are afraid they will embarrass their teenagers, will be asked a question they can't answer, or will impel their teens into becoming sexually active if they give them too much information. Some parents hold off having The Big Talk until a supposedly "appropriate time" or will discuss the subject only once, then be relieved that they've done their duty. (More frequent discussion is more effective.) Although the media tend to portray the "birds and bees" talk as being given by the father, in white families this is usually the case only between fathers and adolescent sons, and it is mothers who discuss sexual topics with daughters. In black and Hispanic families, by contrast, it is mothers more than fathers who perform this function, regardless of the adolescent's sex (Miller et al. 1998).

▪ **How Teenagers Feel:** Most teenagers are reluctant to discuss sex with their parents because of embarrassment, belief that their parents are "old-fashioned," fear that they will be asked personal questions, or a wish not to shock or upset their parents (Fullilove et al. 1994). How aware are parents about their children's sexual activities? Half of all mothers of sexually active teenagers mistakenly believe that their children are still virgins, according to some research (cited in Schemo 2002). Interestingly, according to another survey (cited in Meckler 2002), 56% of 664 teens surveyed in 2000 said they first had sex at their family's home or at the home of their partner's family.

In other countries, parents seem to be more tolerant of adolescent sexuality. For instance, a researcher who interviewed 14 American and 17 Dutch parents of teenagers in 1991–1992 found that the "American parents assume that teenagers cannot guard against unwanted consequences of sexual involvement—for instance, by using contraceptives. They suggest that teenagers are unable to regulate their sexual impulses, making any sexual involvement tantamount to irresponsibility" (Schalet 2000). The Dutch parents, in contrast, described teen sexuality as something that doesn't and shouldn't present many problems, believing that sex should be talked about and dealt with in a normal way.

The Influence of Religion

Religion can have direct and direct influences on sexual behavior.

▪ **Direct Influence:** According to some research, the strength of religious beliefs and frequency of church attendance are related to the delay of first intercourse (Heaton and Jacobson 1994; Udry et al. 1995). This seems to be particularly true for adolescent girls (Meier 2003).

▪ **Indirect Influence:** The more religious a person is, the less drinking he or she is apt to do, and lower alcohol consumption is related to lower frequency of risky sexual behavior (Poulson et al. 1998).

The Influence of Friends & Siblings

Only 18% of teens—compared to 41% of parents of teens—say friends most influence adolescents' decisions about sex (Albert 2007). Nevertheless, friends—not parents—are the most important source of information about sex. They also have the greatest influence on teenagers' sexual values and on a teen's decision to become sexually active (Thomsen & Chang 2000). Generally, adolescents report greater sexual activity when they believe that their friends are also sexually active, whether or not they actually are (Brooks-Gunn and Furstenburg 1989). Moreover, siblings rather than parents are twice as apt to be the source of information about reproductive anatomy and far more apt to influence a teenager's timing of first intercourse (East et al. 1993; Ansuini et al. 1996; Widmer 1997). About 45% of adults said that their friends were the most important source of information about sex (Stodgill 1998).

LARGER THAN LIFE. Many adolescents learn ideas about sex from their friends—who, like most people, are influenced in some way by the media and the commercial culture, such as the huge swimsuit photo in this Abercrombie & Fitch, San Francisco, store window. What did you learn from your friends that turned out to be helpful/erroneous? ▶

Friends and siblings can be positive influences, as in discussing maturational issues (such as the growth of body hair or breasts) and encouraging seeking of information about contraception (Gecas and Seff 1991). However, peers may have little accurate reproductive and contraceptive information (Buysse 1996).

The Influence of Sex Education

Sex-education programs in high schools generally seem to have a positive influence on teenagers' knowledge about sex (Finkel and Finkel 1985; Melchert and Burnett 1990; Song et al. 2000). However, they have not been found to influence teens' sexual attitudes or behaviors (Maslach and Kerr 1983; Finkel and Finkel 1985). Perhaps this is in part because teachers often feel that they lack support for their work and so restrict their discussion of controversial topics, limiting their lessons to "safe" topics such as anatomy and abstinence (Donovan 1998).

Some Europeans receive sex education in kindergarten, points out Gilbert Herdt (in Leff 2005), director of the National Sexuality Resource Center, but for Americans the subject is still controversial even in the higher grades. In middle schools and high schools across the United States, sex-education classes that discuss birth control and contraception as means of preventing pregnancy and disease are giving way to programs designed mainly to promote abstinence (Bernstein 2006; Freedman 2006). The warring views of what sex education should be, points out sociologist and law professor Kristen Luker (2006), represent the split between "sexual conservatives," for whom sex is *sacred* and demands formal structures—namely, marriage—to protect it, and "sexual liberals," for whom sex is *natural* and for whom marriage is just one among many acceptable options.

Social conservatives strongly favor abstinence-only education and deferring sex until marriage. Liberal groups advocate training in the use of contraceptives and urging young people to behave safely. According to a *Time*/MTV survey (reported in Morse 2002: 65) of 1,061 people ages 13 to 18, 15% of the teenagers have taken abstinence-only courses, yet 69% were opposed to federal funding for programs that teach abstinence only. Some researchers disagree with the usefulness of abstinence-only programs because they have not been found to reduce rates of pregnancy among students involved in them (Haffner 1997). Moreover, it has been found that ***virginity pledges*, in which young people make signed, public promises to abstain from sex until marriage,** have little staying power among those who take them, with more than half the adolescents who make them giving up on them within a year (Rosenbaum 2006).

Probably the most effective sex-education approaches involve teaching students to understand the pressure from media and peers to have sex and how to resist it and to understand the risks of unprotected sex and how to avoid them (Kirby et al. 1994).

The Influence of Sexual Partners

The preceding influences on our sexual learning are mostly abstract. Once we become involved with sexual partners, however, they become the most important factor in helping us to modify our sexual expectations—what are known as *sexual scripts*, as we discuss next.

Sexual Scripts

A *sexual script* is a set of expectations as to how one should behave in sexual situations, whether male or female, heterosexual or homosexual. (We discuss homosexuality and bisexuality in Chapter 9, "Variations.") Sexual scripts represent the interpretations and behaviors we have learned from society and others that are expected of us in sexual situations. For instance, males are expected to focus more on sex than on feelings and females to focus more on feelings than on sex. Sexual scripts are most influential and powerful during adolescence and young adulthood, when we are influenced by the media, friends, and parents; later, we are influenced more by our partners.

Many scripts are about taboos: Sex with children is frowned on, as are sex with animals and sex in public. Homosexuality has traditionally also been taboo—and still is in many places. Other traditional sexual scripts dictate how men and women are supposed to behave on the basis of their gender roles (Barbach 1982; Zilbergeld 1992; Brooks 1995).

■ **Men's Sexual Scripts:** Men are supposed to be in charge, confident, and aggressive, not tender and compassionate. The purpose of sex is orgasm rather than intimacy. Men know what women want, are always ready for sex, and any physical contact, even touching, is expected to lead to sex. Men objectify women, talking about physical aspects, size, and shapes of body parts.

■ **Women's Sexual Scripts:** Traditionally, women are expected to be beautiful, loving, nurturing, and accommodating. Unlike men, they are not supposed to talk about sex or to be overly interested in sex, especially casual sex (in which case they will be labeled "sluts," "nymphos," or "trash"). The exceptions are the slinky, come-hither females of men's fantasies.

Do any of these scripts sound familiar?

A Script for Women

Slim, Blond, & Youthful

Women seem to be obsessed with their appearance—or why would so many of them want to be slim, blond, and youthful?

Perhaps because they realize there are often cultural and material advantages. For instance, writer Amy Spindler (2001) followed blond model Sara Ziff, 19, around New York to see what her looks did for her. "Her beauty gets her tables in hot restaurants without a reservation," says Spindler (p. 136). "It gets off-duty cabs to stop for her. It gets her past the long lines at nightclubs and into V.I.P. rooms. It gets her discounts on clothes. More important, it got her a modeling agent and a Hollywood agent."

Researcher Emily Wilson (2002) cites a survey by *Glamour* magazine (Wooley and Wooley 1984) in which, when women were asked what they could accomplish if they could achieve any possible goal, "an overwhelming majority indicated that they would lose weight." She also cites a study (Patton et al. 1997) that shows that almost half of girls ages 12 to 17 have dieted. In addition, eating disorders

(anorexia, bulimia), stemming from negative images about being overweight, affect perhaps 5 million to 10 million American adolescent girls and women (Poirot 2002). (They also affect about 1 million American boys and men.)

As for being blond, a 1991 study (cited in Loftus 2000) reportedly found that 80% of American boys prefer blond females to brunets or redheads, although only 16% of American girls are actually born blond. Is this why among the half of all American women who color their hair, 40% of them choose the lightest hues? Is this why, according to one study (Hesse-Biber et al. 2004), African American girls have been found to be concerned about being unable to match white standards of hair (as well as skin color)?

Finally, the quest for youthfulness is seen in the continuing popularity of cosmetic plastic surgery. Probably reflecting public reaction to the entertainment industry's spotlighting of plastic surgery (as in ABC's *Extreme Makeover* and FX network's *Nip/Tuck*), cosmetic surgery procedures jumped from 8.7 million in 2003 to 11 million in 2006, according to the American Society of Plastic Surgeons (2007). The top five such procedures were breast augmentation, nose reshaping, liposuction, eyelid surgery, and tummy tuck. (Reconstructive plastic surgery, which improves function and appearance to abnormal structures, actually decreased in 2006.)

Even beautiful celebrities are often deemed not beautiful enough, points out Wilson, and their photographs are

altered to "improve" them. "A popular magazine airbrushed Cindy Crawford's thighs to make them appear smaller. . . . [and] photographs of Demi Moore were airbrushed to remove inches from her waist and hips. Photographers use lighting and angles, makeup artists and hairstylists are used, and then the images are airbrushed, removing any scars, lines, too-bigness, too-smallness, anything less than perfection" (Wilson 2002: 2). Jean Kilbourne, Ed.D., has spent many years researching and compiling examples of media images and their effects on young people, especially women. Her books include *Can't Buy My Love: How Advertising Changes the Way We Think and Feel* and *Deadly Persuasion: Why Women and Girls Must Fight the Addictive Power of Advertising.* Her videos, such as the three *Killing Us Softly* documentaries, analyze how so-called sexually attractive female bodies are depicted in advertising images and the devastating effects those images have on women's health. "Advertising is cumulative, and it's almost unconscious," Kilbourne told an interviewer (Simon 2000–2001). The result is that even when readers and viewers don't buy a product, she says, they buy into the consumer mind-set.

WHAT DO YOU THINK? No doubt you have heard that obesity is a great problem in the United States because of the nature of the American diet and the trend toward super-large portions. Yet media images stress thinness. How do these conflicting forces affect you?

7.2 The Varieties of Sexual Experience

MAJOR QUESTION What are all the forms of sexual expression?

PREVIEW This section first describes the different possible sexual experiences, ranging from sexual fantasies to atypical behavior. We then discuss two kinds of sexual difficulties.

Sexual intercourse occurs more than 100 times *every day* around the world, the World Health Organization (1992) once estimated. For all its frequency, however, sex has remained basically a private matter in North American culture—at least until recently.

Back in 1992, one sex therapist noted that "we don't observe others having sex, don't hear anyone discussing sexual experiences seriously, and don't have access to reliable information about what other people feel and do" (Klein 1992). The result, he said, was that many Americans had *normality anxiety:* They wondered whether what they were thinking, feeling, or doing about sex was normal. Today, however, we live in what journalist and author Pamela Paul (2005) calls a "pornified age," with pornography widely available on the Internet, on cable TV channels, and on hotel-room television sets, not to mention porn-style images everywhere, from billboards to reality shows. Are they offering examples of the "new normality"? (The stages of the human sexual response are described in Appendix A.)

The Different Kinds of Sexual Behavior

Basically, what is "normal" is what any adult finds pleasurable as long as the experience is engaged in willingly, under noncoercive, nonmanipulated circumstances, and places neither oneself nor one's partner (if a partner is involved) at risk for negative physical, emotional, or social consequences. Many college students, for instance, have widely varying ideas as to what constitutes "having sex," according to a Kinsey Institute survey. *(See ■ Panel 7.5.)*

Let's consider the different kinds of sexual behavior.

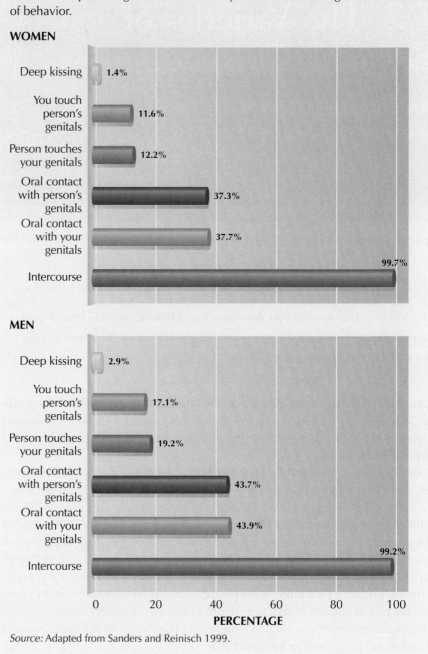

■ **PANEL 7.5   What Students Say "Having Sex" Means to Them.** A Kinsey Institute study of 599 college students from 29 states asked "Would you say you had sex with someone if the most intimate behavior you engaged in was . . . ." Here are the percentages who answered "yes" for the following intimate kinds of behavior.

Source: Adapted from Sanders and Reinisch 1999.

Sexual Fantasies & Dreams

Many questions about normality of sexual behavior have to do with fantasies. Sex is not just genitals and glands; a great part of it is the mind. For instance, a 24-year-old woman who had never had intercourse, interviewed by Nancy Friday (1991: 191), stated: "I am an extremely sexual person. I think about sex a lot and can become very horny if just the right word, sound, or suggestion is made."

A *sexual fantasy* is any mental representation of any kind of sexual activity (Zilbergeld 1992). It may be a single act, such as oral sex, or it may be like a movie, telling a story from beginning to end (for example, starting with a kiss and ending with orgasm). The fantasy may be stimulated by experience, by imagination, through words or pictures, whether an underwear ad or an erotic video. A *sexual dream* occurs during sleep, without a person's conscious control, and may produce a **nocturnal orgasm, an involuntary orgasm during sleep.** In males, this is also called a "wet dream," because ejaculation occurs while one is asleep.

Perhaps the principal purpose of sexual fantasies, when they occur during masturbation or sexual intercourse, is to help sexual arousal. Both men and women report fantasizing about one person—a former or imaginary lover—while making love to another (Sue 1979). Sexual fantasies also help to overcome anxiety or boredom, rehearse new sexual experiences, and express forbidden wishes, such as forced sex or same-sex encounters (Crooks and Baur 2002). And sexual fantasies often act as a safe outlet for people without partners.

How "normal" is sexual fantasizing? Research by Alfred Kinsey and his associates found that nearly all the males and two-thirds of the females who were studied reported having sexual fantasies (Kinsey et al. 1948, 1953). People who feel more guilt about sex are less apt to be aroused by sexual fantasies than are people who feel less guilt about sex (Follinstad and Kimbrell 1986).

Masturbation

Masturbation **is self-stimulation of the genitals for sexual pleasure,** as with one's hand or with a vibrator, resulting in orgasm.

Research shows that 61% of men and 42% of women masturbate, and that three times as many men as women report masturbating once a week or more (Laumann et al. 1994). Among college undergraduates, one study found that on average men masturbate 12 times a month and women 4.7 times a month (Pinkerton et al. 2002). The practice is not considered abnormal unless it somehow interferes with one's life or with enjoyable sexual sharing in a relationship (McAnulty and Burnette 2004: 399). As might be expected, single and divorced people masturbate more often than do people who are married or living together (Huey et al. 1981).

Kissing, Touching, & Genital Play

Kissing and touching ("petting") need not, of course, be preliminary steps toward sexual arousal or intercourse. When they are, however, they are considered part of *foreplay*, **or sex play.** Foreplay is stimulating activity that might or might not culminate in sexual intercourse. Touching or kissing *erogenous*, **or sexually sensitive,** areas—genitals, breasts, the anal area in some people—can lead to sexual excitement and even lead to orgasm. (Note that erogenous zones may, for many people, include nongenital areas such as ear, neck, stomach, and back.) *Outercourse* **is the name given to sexual acts that do not involve the exposure of a partner to semen, vaginal secretions, or blood.**

Setting and cleanliness are important for many lovers. Interestingly, big doses of cologne and perfume may actually work against sexual arousal—despite the ads.

FOREPLAY. Part of the enjoyment of sex is in the preamble to sexual intercourse itself—sexual play, as in the touching or kissing of sexually sensitive areas. Some people even attain sexual excitement from being touched in certain nongenital areas, such as the ear or neck. Does this apply to you? ▶

Oral-Genital Stimulation

Oral-genital stimulation **consists of mouth-to-genital contact** to stimulate sexual pleasure. One survey reported that 79% of men and 73% of women reported having received oral sex at least once (Michael et al. 1994). The most frequent practitioners of oral sex are married and cohabiting couples (92% to 93%) and white, college-educated men (80%), compared with, for example, African Americans (79%) and Hispanics (74%) (Laumann et al. 1994; Mosher et al. 2005).

Three basic forms of oral-genital stimulation are practiced by both heterosexual and homosexual couples.

■ Fellatio: *Fellatio* **is oral stimulation of the penis by a partner.** In one study, 28% of men reported that their last sexual event consisted of receiving fellatio (Michael et al. 1994).

■ Cunnilingus: *Cunnilingus* **is oral stimulation of the clitoris, labia, and vaginal opening.** Twenty percent of women reported that their last sexual event consisted of receiving cunnilingus (Michael et al. 1994).

■ Mutual Oral-Genital Stimulation: Couples sometimes practice **simultaneous oral-genital stimulation by facing each other while lying in opposite directions.** This arrangement is known as the "69 position."

Fellatio risks the exchange of bodily fluids and hence the passage of sexually transmitted diseases, including HIV (discussed shortly). This can occur through small openings in the skin of the mouth or genitals. Thus, couples who are not in a long-term mutually monogamous relationship should either avoid fellatio or always use a condom. Couples who are not in mutually monogamous relationships should also avoid practicing cunnilingus.

Anal Stimulation

Some people don't care to do anything sexual with the anus, but others find touching it to be highly erotic sex play. ***Anal intercourse* consists of inserting the penis into the anus** and is a sexual behavior engaged in by people regardless of sexual orientation. Though this is not a popular activity, 5% of men and 1% of women stated that anal sex was "very appealing" (Michael et al. 1994). Anal stimulation may include using the finger or the tongue.

Anal sex is one of the riskiest activities for transmission of sexual diseases, including HIV. Using a condom would seem to be mandatory for all but the most monogamous of sex partners, whether homosexual or heterosexual. However, one should be aware that condoms have a higher breakage rate for anal sex (1 in 105) than for vaginal sex (1 in 165) (Consumers Union 1989).

Sexual Intercourse

The term ***sexual intercourse* is generally thought to mean coitus, which involves penetration of the vagina by the penis.** This is the only sexual act that can achieve ***procreation*, or reproduction.** It may or may not produce orgasm in one or both partners.

What is the normal frequency of sexual intercourse? The answer is, there is no normal frequency. One study found that couples in their 20s and 30s *average* sex 2 to 3 times a week (Westoff 1974). However, the frequency for any couple tends to decrease over the years. The demands of work and child rearing may leave partners fatigued, and interest may decline owing to a familiar sexual routine (Trussell and Westoff 1980; Greenblatt 1983; Deveny 2003). Still, a recent survey (Lindau et al. 2007) found that older adults continue to remain sexually active: 73% of those ages 57 to 64, 53% of those ages 65 to 74, and 26% of those ages 75 to 85 reported having sex within the preceding 12 months, with 54% of the oldest respondents reporting they had sex at least twice a month. In a 1990 study, married and unmarried adults on average reported 57.4 instances of sexual intercourse in the preceding year—about once a week (National Opinion Research Center 1990). Married and cohabiting couples have much higher rates of sex than singles do, with the majority reporting intercourse "2 or 3 times a week" or "a few times a month" (Laumann et al. 1994). In sum, a wide range of frequency of intercourse is considered normal. And, not surprisingly, couples who have the most frequent sex are the most sexually satisfied (Laumann et al. 1994; Christopher and Sprecher 2000).

Celibacy

***Celibacy* may be either complete—a person has no sex at all—or partial. In partial celibacy, a person masturbates but has no sexual relations with others.** Being celibate is not done just for religious reasons or for lack of sexual partners. Some people choose to "renew their virginity" because of concern about sexually transmitted diseases. Others are celibate while they recover from a broken relationship or because of a health problem, including chemical dependency. How common is celibacy? A 1990 survey found that 22% of people—including 9% of married people—said they had no sex partners at all during the previous year (National Opinion Research Center 1990).

Pornography & Prostitution

Pornography and prostitution are two aspects of "commercial sex," which includes everything from phone sex ("dial-a-porn") to child prostitution. Paying for sex—or for sexual fantasies—seems to be as old as history. In our era, however, sex has also been exploited commercially and used to sell products. In other words, sex has shifted from the private world to the public world—it has become popularized (Marin 1983).

Here, we consider just two aspects of commercialized sex: pornography and prostitution.

■ **Pornography:** The word *pornography* comes from the ancient Greek word *pornographos*, which means "writing about prostitutes." It was not introduced into the English language until the 19th century, when it was used to describe erotic wall murals that were discovered in the ancient city of Pompeii in Italy. Today the word has taken on a different meaning.

Although defining pornography is difficult and involves a degree of subjectivity, *pornography* **can be defined as a depiction through words or pictures of sexual conduct involving opposite-sex or same-sex partners designed to cause sexual excitement.** Most buyers of pornography use it as a stimulus for masturbation. By identifying with the people in pornographic fantasies, some people may deny their fears about sexual inadequacy, sexual fatigue, or failing sexual interest (Byer and Shainberg 1991).

Some pornography is simply explicit portrayal of sexual acts such as we have described so far; some people call this material *erotica*. Couples sometimes use it as a stimulus for lovemaking. Some pornography, however, is violent, involving acts of rape, humiliation, degradation, and pain, often with female victims. Although particularly loathsome, child pornography is apparently widespread; a 2007 investigation by Austrian authorities, for instance, identified 2,361 Internet addresses in at least 77 countries, including the United States, where customers paid about $90 to view the abuse of infants and other children (Johnson 2007).

The Internet, of course, has created an opportunity for more viewers to access pornography. As you might expect, most people with access to porn are men, but a surprisingly high percentage are women. *(See* ■ *Panel 7.6.)* In addition, perhaps 40% of the nation's hotels make pornographic movies available to adult guests, generating perhaps 60 to 80% of their total in-room entertainment revenue (Crary 2006). As a *60 Minutes* documentary put it, "In the space of a generation, a product that once was available in the back alleys of big cities has gone corporate, delivered now directly into homes and hotel rooms by some of the biggest companies in the United States" ("Porn in the U.S.A." 2004).

■ **Prostitution:** *Prostitution* **is the exchange of sexual services for money** or sometimes drugs. The reality of prostitution is not like the glamorous depictions in some movies (such as Julia Roberts's *Pretty Woman*). The reality, as one writer puts it, is "about drugs and bad mistakes, and it's sometimes about violence" (Martin 1991). Often, men sentimentally believe that sex workers (prostitutes) enjoy their work. This might be true in some instances. However, even in countries such as Holland, Norway, and Sweden, where prostitution is often legal, most prostitutes express a wish to quit (Goldberg 1991).

Many people are split over legalization of prostitution. Some feminists, for instance, believe that the practice degrades not just the participants but all women. Others say that outlawing prostitution may reduce but never stop it, and if it has to exist, it is better done safely and hygienically ("Sex for sale" 1992). In Europe, there seems to be an expanding drive to legalize prostitution while at the same time to fight the crime and violence associated with it—including the explosion in human trafficking in recent years (Bilefsky 2005).

Atypical Sexuality

Many people would argue that the foregoing varieties of sexual expression may be considered to be fairly common. There are, however, a host of sexual behaviors that many people consider to be atypical, although we might recognize glimpses of them within ourselves.

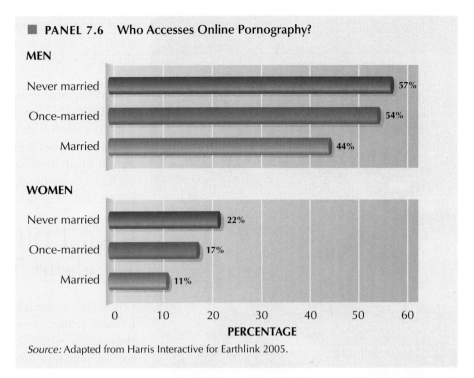

■ **PANEL 7.6**　**Who Accesses Online Pornography?**

Source: Adapted from Harris Interactive for Earthlink 2005.

Most of these behaviors are practiced principally by males rather than females. Some of the behaviors are harmful to others. However, we are *not* concerned here with the very damaging sexual aberrations having to do with issues of power and violence—sexual harassment, rape, incest, and child molestation (some of which are discussed in Chapter 13, "Crises").

Forms of atypical sexual expression include, but are not limited to, the following, ranging from passive behavior (not involving contact with others) to more aggressive behavior:

■ Voyeurism: *Voyeurism* **is behavior in which one becomes sexually aroused by looking at people, often strangers, undressing or having sex** without their being aware that they are being watched. Most, but not all, voyeurs are content just to look.

■ Fetishism: *Fetishism* **is behavior in which a person receives sexual arousal or pleasure from focusing on a nonsexual object or part of the body,** such as a shoe or the foot.

■ Exhibitionism: *Exhibitionism* **consists of exposing ("flashing") one's genitals in public to an involuntary observer,** usually female. The exhibitionistic male (who is often shy and unassertive) usually masturbates afterward, sexually excited by the victim's shocked reactions.

■ Sadomasochism: Also called *BDSM (bondage/discipline-dominance/submission-sadism-masochism),* **sadomasochism involves deriving sexual pleasure from the infliction or receiving of pain.** In sexual games, this implies mutual consent.

■ Obscene Phone Calls: Men who make obscene phone calls experience sexual arousal in much the same way as the exhibitionist does, and many masturbate during or immediately after the call. Often, victims are called at random from the phone book. The best way to deal with such a call is not to show emotional upset (the kind of stimulation the caller is seeking) but to just calmly hang up.

In describing these (and not some of the more bizarre and illegal sexual behaviors, such as necrophilia—sexual contact with the dead—and pedophilia—sexual contact with children), we do not mean to endorse them. If you express your sexual needs by engaging in any of these sexual behaviors exclusively or by engaging in illegal sexual activities, you might need professional assistance and support.

Sexual Difficulties & What to Do about Them

Our society raises all kinds of sexual expectations—about performance, about size, about having multiple orgasms. A lot of these ideas, which we get from our friends or from the mass media, promote an unrealistic view of sex. Even so, when real-life problems occur, we might perceive them as personal failures instead of talking about or seeking help for them.

Some sexual dysfunction is reasonably commonplace. Two common sexual dysfunctions for men are, as the TV commercials for Viagra and Cialis remind us, erection difficulties (erectile dysfunction) and premature ejaculation. For women, the chief sexual dysfunctions are inability to have an orgasm, painful intercourse, and spasms of the vaginal muscles. These are discussed in Appendix B. Here let us consider two others: inhibited sexual desire and sex addiction.

GLAMOROUS? The media often portray prostitution as cool and exciting, but the reality is quite different, involving drug addiction, violence, and degradation. What are your views about paying for sex? ▲

Inhibited Sexual Desire

Perhaps the most frequent sexual complaint of couples is that one or both individuals experience inhibited sexual desire. ***Inhibited sexual desire (ISD) is a lack of interest in sex or an inability to feel sexual*** or get sexually aroused.

Inhibited sexual desire can occur for various reasons. Perhaps the relationship has become too close for comfort; for a partner who is feeling suffocated, ISD can be a way of getting some space. Or one person might feel pushed around by a domineering partner, and ISD is a means of retaining some power in the relationship. Also, if a person has been sexually abused in the past, he or she might become sexually inhibited. There might be a lack of trust, fear of intimacy or rejection, or unresolved issues, anger, or resentment. Or ISD might result from frustration over lack of sexual arousal and organism. Stress outside the relationship, such as jobs, children, or the consumption of drugs, including alcohol, can turn a couple into roommates more than lovers. Indeed, some couples in long-term relationships have asexual partnerships, not having had sex in years (Josselson 1992).

A variation on ISD is dissatisfaction with the frequency or kind of sexual activity. One partner might want more (or less) sex than the other or different varieties of sex.

How do you maintain a vital sexual relationship within a committed partnership, or how do you rekindle the flame? Assuming that there is no physical problem, therapists suggest various techniques to break the cycle of routine sex. These include having sex in a different place (for example, the living room instead of the bedroom) and setting aside time when you're not stressed. Try different sexual positions, increase daily physical contact with each other (more touching and hugging), and have getaway weekends. Other ideas: buy sexy lingerie, watch erotic videos, and voice the desires you have been afraid to bring up (Bechtel 1991). If problems persist, see a marriage counselor or sex therapist to help you sort out the problem and develop strategies to solve it.

Sex Addiction: Compulsive Sexual Behavior

An obsessive-compulsive person might wash his or her hands 100 times a day. The sexual compulsive might take sex to a similar extreme, such as compulsive masturbation or insatiable sexual demands within a relationship. Other signs are feverish interest in pornography or phone sex, frenzied anonymous sex, or multiple affairs. **Sexual addiction**, or **compulsive sexual behavior**, **is an intense preoccupation with sex. It makes having a satisfying sexual relationship with just one lover difficult.**

Often, sexual compulsives were emotionally or physically abused as children and learned that sex was not a nurturing, natural experience. Thus, they alternate between profound anxiety and self-loathing. Like alcoholics, they are mainly intent on diverting their pain but use sex (Carnes 1983). Psychologists and other health professionals are uncertain what the condition is and how to treat it, but psychotherapy seems the best course. In addition, those who are sexually compulsive may find support by joining such organizations as Sexaholics Anonymous or Sexual Addicts Anonymous.

SEX ADDICT? The intense preoccupation with sex makes having a satisfying sexual relationship with just one lover difficult. Do you know of anyone who seems to be sexually compulsive? ◄

7.3 AIDS & Other Sexual Diseases

MAJOR QUESTION How could having sex risk my health and my life?

PREVIEW Here we consider one of the possible negative outcomes of sex—sexually transmitted diseases—beginning with a discussion of HIV/AIDS.

Love and passion are among the most powerful human forces. Love, or the belief in love, often leads people to take chances. Even if her boyfriend was also seeing other women, a San Francisco 17-year-old reports, "Nothing would happen because he says he'll never do anything that would mess me up, and I believe him." They don't need a condom, she states, "because he says he loves me" (quoted in Adler 1991).

Sexual passion sometimes leads people to take dangerous chances or make decisions they might not otherwise make. A survey of Stanford University students found that nearly three-quarters of those who engaged in heterosexual intercourse did not always use a condom. Two-thirds of homosexuals did not use a condom during anal sex. Students who did not use a condom often reported that had gotten carried away, had felt "out of control," or had not planned ahead when they became sexually involved (Workman 1991).

Love or sexual passion has often steamrolled over rationality, as people have risked their marriages, jobs, social standing, or concerns about morality or ethics to have sex with someone they really liked. That, however, was before the Age of AIDS. Has the knowledge that sex can be associated with a potentially fatal disease changed human behavior? For some people, yes, but not for all.

Sexually Transmitted Diseases

Formerly called venereal diseases, **sexually transmitted diseases (STDs) are infectious diseases that are transmitted as a result (usually) of sexual contact.** Although AIDS is the best-known STD, there are many others,

SEXUALLY TRANSMITTED DISEASES	2003	2004	2005
Gonorrhea	335,104	330,132	339,593
Syphilis	34,289	33,419	33,278
Chlamydia	877,478	929,462	976,445

Source: Centers for Disease Control and Prevention 2005: Table 1.

including hepatitis B, herpes, human papilloma virus, chlamydia, gonorrhea, syphilis, and parasite infections. These are growing rapidly, bringing suffering and even death. The number of reported cases of selected STDs is shown in the accompanying table. *(See ■ Panel 7.7.)*

About two-thirds of STDS occur among people under age 25 (Conforth 2004). *Many STDs cause no symptoms,* particularly in women, but can be passed on to sexual partners anyway. This poses a real dilemma, for even if one is currently in a monogamous relationship, it is not unusual for one or both partners to have a sexual encounter outside the relationship. And as public health officials like to point out, every time you have sex with someone, you are in effect having sex with every one of your partner's previous sexual partners during the past 10 years.

HIV & AIDS:
The Modern Scourge

We will focus on HIV and AIDS because they are relatively recent threats and because they have produced all kinds of misunderstandings.

■ **AIDS:** *AIDS stands for acquired immune deficiency syndrome, a sexually transmitted disease that is caused by a virus known as HIV. AIDS is characterized by irreversible damage to the body's immune system.* As a result, the body is unable to fight infections. Not everyone who is infected with HIV develops a full-scale case of AIDS; one study found about 30% of infected people still alive after 11 years (Gorman 1996: 65).

■ **HIV:** *HIV, or human immunodeficiency virus, the virus causing AIDS, brings about a variety of ills, including the breakdown of the immune system. This breakdown allows the development of certain infections and cancers,* most commonly *Pneumocystis carinii* pneumonia and the skin cancer called Kaposi's sarcoma. AIDS symptoms usually start to appear 7 to 10 years after initial infection with HIV.

Since 1981, when a gay man walked into San Francisco General Hospital with a mysterious immune disorder, approximately 988,376 cases of AIDS have been reported in the United States through the end of 2005, and about 550,394 have

■ PANEL 7.8 AIDS Cases by Age: Number of Cumulative AIDS Cases Reported through 2005 in the United States. This includes persons with a diagnosis of AIDS from the beginning of the epidemic. Patients' ages at time of diagnosis were distributed as follows. Note the highest number of cases occurred between the ages of 25 and 49, because of the time it takes for HIV to develop into full-blown AIDS.

AGE	NUMBER OF AIDS CASES
Under 13	9,089
13–14	1,015
15–19	5,309
20–24	34,987
25–29	114,519
30–34	194,529
35–39	209,210
40–44	165,497
45–49	103,326
50–54	57,336
55–59	30,631
60–64	16,611
65 or older	14,606

Source: Centers for Disease Control and Prevention 2006.

died (Centers for Disease Control and Prevention 2007). The highest incidence of AIDS is among people in their thirties. *(See* ■ *Panel 7.8.)* The epidemic is growing most rapidly among minority populations and is the leading killer of African American women ages 25–44 in the United States. For AIDS cases in 2005, about 44% were among non-Hispanic blacks, 36% among non-Hispanic whites, 19% among Hispanics, 1% among Asians/Pacific Islanders, and less than 1% among American Indians/Alaska Natives (AIDS Action 2007).

A growing proportion of people living with AIDS are women. Since 1985, the proportion of all AIDS cases reported among adult and adolescent women has more than tripled, from 7% in 1985 to 23% in 2005. The epidemic has increased most dramatically among women of color: Blacks represent only 13% of the U.S. population, but African American women accounted for 67% of new U.S. AIDS diagnoses in 2004 (Russell 2006).

How Do People Get Infected?

In the United States, the people who are most at risk for contracting HIV/AIDS are men who have sex with men, men and women who inject drugs, and men and women having heterosexual contact. *(See* ■ *Panel 7.9.)* (In Panel 7.9, the "Other" source of the disease might include transmission from mothers to infants and accidental contacts. At one point, it might have included infected blood from transfusions, but donated blood is now rigorously screened.)

Heterosexuals with HIV/AIDS

About 55% of people in the United States in 2002 infected with AIDS were gay and bisexual men. However, an estimated 20% of gay men marry at least once, perhaps to disguise their homosexuality (Buxton 1991; Schmitt 1993). The rate of heterosexual HIV transmission is rising at three times the rate for homosexual transmission. Moreover, heterosexual women are more than twice as likely as men to get HIV/AIDS, and they are apt to get it from heterosexual men. In 2002, about 42% of women received HIV/AIDS from men who were neither bisexual nor intravenous drug users (Centers for Disease Control and Prevention 2003: Table 16).

Why do heterosexual women seem to be more vulnerable than heterosexual men to HIV infection? Among the reasons are the following (Nicolosi et al. 1994):

■ **Exposure to Virus:** Men are exposed to the virus only during sexual intercourse. With women, infected semen lingers in the body after sex.

■ **Genital Surface Area:** Compared to men, women have a great deal more genital surface area that is exposed to the virus.

■ **Concentration of Virus:** The sperm of infected men is much more potent than are the vaginal secretions of infected women in packing high concentrations of HIV.

The heterosexuals who are at greatest risk for HIV are teenagers, adults with several sex partners, people living in areas where AIDS is more prevalent (such as southern and northeastern United States), and those who are afflicted with other STDs. The highest HIV rates, for example, are found in many sub-Saharan African populations because up to 40% of adolescent and adult males and females in those groups routinely have multiple and concurrent sex partners (Chin 2007).

The Future of HIV/AIDS: Could Things Get Better?

Some of the news about the AIDS epidemic is actually good. For instance, not everyone who gets infected gets sick; no one knows why, but perhaps further study will yield some useful clues (Zuger 2006). In addition, it turns out that circumcision may reduce a man's risk of contracting AIDS from heterosexual sex by as much as 65%, according to studies done in Africa (Wakabi 2007). Another piece of good news is that the spread of HIV in some of the hardest-hit African nations is actually slowing (Unaids 2006). Finally, American AIDS victims can now expect to live for an average of 24 years, the result mainly of effective (but very expensive—$25,200 a year) drug therapies (Schackman et al. 2006).

We discuss HIV/AIDS and other sexually transmitted diseases in detail in Appendices C and D.

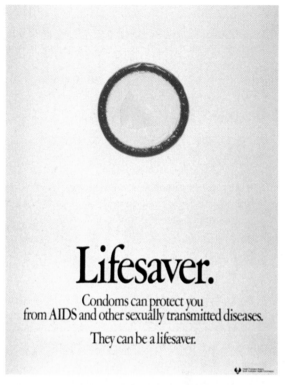

Lifesaver.
Condoms can protect you from AIDS and other sexually transmitted diseases. They can be a lifesaver.

STOPPING STDS. Sexual passion can lead people to take risks or make decisions they might not otherwise make. In one study, nearly three-quarters of the college students surveyed who engaged in heterosexual intercourse did not always use a condom. Have you ever taken this kind of chance? ▲

■ **PANEL 7.9 Estimated Cases of AIDS by Transmission Category, Reported to CDC through December 2005.** Following is the distribution of the estimated diagnosis of AIDS among adults and adolescents by transmission category in the United States, with breakdown by sex where appropriate.

TRANSMISSION CATEGORY	ADULT AND ADOLESCENT MALE	ADULT AND ADOLESCENT FEMALE	TOTAL
Male-to-male sexual contact	454,106	—	454,106
Injecting drug use	168,695	73,311	242,006
Male-to-male sexual contact and injection drug use	66,081	—	66,081
High-risk heterosexual contact*	61,914	102,936	164,850
Other**	13,967	6,575	20,542

*Heterosexual contact with a person known to have, or to be at high risk for, HIV infection.

**Includes hemophilia, blood transfusion, perinatal, and risk not reported or identified.

Source: Centers for Disease Control 2007.

The accompanying table shows how the topic of sexuality is viewed from three principal theoretical perspectives—structural-functional, conflict, and symbolic interaction. *(See ■ Panel 7.10.)*

■ **PANEL 7.10   Views on Sexuality: Three Sociological Theoretical Perspectives Compared**

STRUCTURAL-FUNCTIONAL (MACRO ORIENTATION)	CONFLICT (MACRO ORIENTATION)	SYMBOLIC INTERACTION (MICRO ORIENTATION)
■ Purpose of sexuality is viewed for reproduction/procreation and for maintaining a stable population and workforce. ■ There is consensus and agreement over the clearly defined sex roles. ■ Norms are developed to regulate sexual relations, such as sex being acceptable only within legal framework of marriage recognized by the government. ■ A manifest function is the control and regulation of human sexuality. ■ A latent function may include sexually transmitted diseases.	■ One's sexuality is related to the society's definition of gender. ■ Women are exploited (prostitution) to meet the sexual needs of men. ■ Double standard exists where men who engage in frequent sexual activities are seen in a positive way, whereas sexually active women are viewed as promiscuous. ■ Sexual exploitation of women and children keeps powerless groups from becoming powerful.	■ There is no one definition of sexuality; it is created through day-to-day interactions. ■ Cultural and subcultural differences result in a variety of sexual practices and beliefs. ■ People develop their own definitions of masculinity and femininity, and these social constructions affect one's perceptions. ■ Definitions of sexuality are socially created and can change over time as individuals create new definitions through interaction.

Self-Assessment: Test Your Knowledge of Sexuality

Part I. Your Sexual Knowledge

When 2,000 Americans were asked a series of questions about sexuality by the Kinsey Institute, only 45% of the respondents answered more than half the questions correctly. See how you do on this sample of true (**T**) or false (**F**) questions.

1. The average American first has sexual intercourse at about 16 or 17 years of age.   **T**   **F**
2. About 6 to 8 out of every 10 American women have masturbated.   **T**   **F**
3. Most women have orgasms from penile thrusting alone.   **T**   **F**
4. All men like large female breasts.   **T**   **F**
5. People usually lose interest in sexual activities after age 60.   **T**   **F**
6. Masturbation is physically harmful.   **T**   **F**
7. The average length of a man's erect penis is 5 to 7 inches.   **T**   **F**
8. Impotence usually cannot be treated successfully.   **T**   **F**
9. Petroleum jelly, Vaseline Intensive Care, and baby oil are not good lubricants to use with a diaphragm or condom.   **T**   **F**
10. Most women prefer a sexual partner who has a large penis.   **T**   **F**
11. A woman cannot get pregnant if she has sex during her menstrual period.   **T**   **F**
12. A woman cannot get pregnant if the man withdraws his penis before ejaculating.   **T**   **F**

Answers

1. T; 2. T; 3. F; 4. F; 5. F; 6. F; 7. T; 8. F; 9. T; 10. F; 11. F; 12. F

Sources: **Part I quiz:** Adapted from Reinisch, J. M., and R. Beasley. 1990. *The Kinsey Institute New Report on Sex*. New York: St. Martin's Press. Copyright © 1950 St. Martin's Press, Inc. **Part II quiz:** *Wellness Worksheet #34*, "Test Your Sexual Knowledge and Attitudes," from pp. 83–84 of *Wellness Worksheets, 2004 Update* by Paul M. Insel and Walton T. Roth, *Core concepts in health*, 9th ed. 2004 Update, The McGraw-Hill Companies, Inc. Wellness Sheets, p. 83. Reproduced with permission of The McGraw-Companies.

Part II. Your Sexual Attitudes

For each statement, circle the response that most closely reflects your position.

1 = Agree   **2 = Not sure**   **3 = Disagree**

1. Sex education encourages young people to have sex.   **1 2 3**
2. Homosexuality is a healthy, normal expression of sexuality.   **1 2 3**
3. Members of the other sex will think more highly of you if you remain mysterious.   **1 2 3**
4. It's better to wait until marriage to have sex.   **1 2 3**
5. Abortion should be a personal, private choice for a woman.   **1 2 3**
6. It's natural for men to have more sexual freedom than women.   **1 2 3**
7. Condoms should not be made available to teenagers.   **1 2 3**
8. Access to pornography should not be restricted for adults.   **1 2 3**
9. A woman who is raped usually does something to provoke it.   **1 2 3**
10. Contraception is the woman's responsibility.   **1 2 3**
11. Feminism has had a positive influence on society.   **1 2 3**
12. Masturbation is a healthy expression of sexuality.   **1 2 3**
13. I have many friends of the other sex.   **1 2 3**
14. Prostitution should be legalized.   **1 2 3**
15. Women use sex for love, men use love for sex.   **1 2 3**
16. Our society is too sexually permissive.   **1 2 3**
17. The man should be the undisputed head of the household.   **1 2 3**
18. Having sex just for pleasure is OK.   **1 2 3**

Scoring

Add up the numbers you circled to obtain your overall score. Find your score and rating below.

1–18   Traditional attitude about sexuality

19–36   Ambivalent or mixed attitude about sexuality

37–54   Open, progressive attitude about sexuality

Key Terms Used in This Chapter

abstinence, p. 225
AIDS, p. 243
anal intercourse, p. 237
celibacy, p. 237
cunnilingus, p. 236
double standard, p. 224
erogenous, p. 235
exhibitionism, p. 239
fellatio, p. 236
fetishism, p. 239
foreplay, p. 235
HIV, p. 243

inhibited sexual desire (ISD), p. 240
masturbation, p. 235
nocturnal orgasm, p. 235
oral-genital stimulation, p. 236
outercourse, p. 235
permissiveness with affection, p. 224
permissiveness without affection, p. 225
pornography, p. 238
procreation, p. 237
prostitution, p. 238

sadomasochism, p. 239
sexual addiction (compulsive sexual behavior), p. 241
sexual fantasy, p. 235
sexual intercourse, p. 237
sexual script, p. 231
sexual values, p. 224
sexually transmitted diseases (STDs), p. 242
virginity, p. 226
virginity pledges, p. 231
voyeurism, p. 239

Summary

7.1 Sexual Values, Learning, & Scripts

- Sexual values are deeply held beliefs and attitudes about what is right and wrong, desirable and undesirable sexual behavior.

- Many of the sexual values people acquire come from various forms of the media, including television, music videos, advertising, movies, and the Internet. Unfortunately, these sources of sexual values lack factuality and are distortions of the nature of sex, sexual roles, and treat women as sex objects.

- In today's society, premarital sex and nonmarital sex are more accepted than they were 50 years ago. Ira Reiss identified four values or societal standards concerning premarital and nonmarital sex: (1) The double standard is the standard in which premarital or nonmarital sex is more acceptable for men than for women. (2) Permissiveness with affection allows premarital or nonmarital sex for women and men equally. (3) Permissiveness without affection allows premarital or nonmarital sex for women and men regardless of the amount of affection. (4) Abstinence is the voluntary avoidance of sexual intercourse.

- Besides the effect of the media, sources of values and beliefs about sex include the following: (1) The relationship with parents can affect the initial sexual involvement and can also help to prevent teenage pregnancy. (2) Religion can have a direct influence on delaying first intercourse and an indirect influence on the risky sexual behavior through less use of alcohol. (3) Siblings and peers can have a significant impact on adolescent sexual behavior, especially when they believe that their friends are also sexually active. (4) Sex education has varying degrees of influence over one's sexual behavior, depending on the program, which can range from abstinence-only programs to

programs that help students understand the pressure from media and peers to have sex. (5) Sex partners with whom one becomes involved become the most important factor in helping people modify their sexual scripts, or set of expectations, as to how to behave sexually. The scripts represent the interpretations and behaviors we have learned from society and others that are expected of us in sexual situations.

7.2 The Varieties of Sexual Experience

- Sexual expression runs along a continuum of behaviors and involves both thoughts and actions. A sexual fantasy is any mental representation of any kind of sexual activity. Sexual fantasies can act as a safe outlet for people without partners.

- Masturbation, which is practiced both by people in relationships and by people who are not, is self-stimulation of the genitals for sexual pleasure. The practice is not considered abnormal unless it interferes with one's life or with enjoyable sexual sharing in a relationship.

- Foreplay or sex play may or may not lead to sexual arousal and intercourse. Kissing, touching, and genital play are examples of foreplay and may involve the touching or kissing of erogenous or sexually sensitive areas. Sexual acts that do not involve the exposure to semen, vaginal secretions, or blood are referred to as outercourse.

- Oral-genital stimulation consists of mouth-togenital contact to stimulate sexual pleasure. The three basic forms of oral-genital stimulation are (1) fellatio, oral stimulation of the penis by a partner; (2) cunnilingus, oral stimulation of the clitoris, labia, and vaginal opening by a partner; and (3) mutual oral-genital stimulation. Some partners also practice anal stimulation, which may include anal intercourse.

- Sexual intercourse, also referred to as coitus, involves the penetration of the vagina by the penis and is the only sexual act that can achieve procreation.
- Individuals may also practice celibacy—either complete celibacy, with no sex at all, or partial celibacy, involving masturbation but no sexual relations with others.
- Pornography and prostitution are referred to as commercialized sex. Pornography can be defined as a depiction through words or pictures of sexual conduct involving opposite-sex or same-sex partners designed to cause sexual excitement. Prostitution is the exchange of sexual services for money and in some cases money.
- Deviance is relative, varies from place to place, and changes over time. Nevertheless, a number of sexual behaviors are considered by many people to be atypical. They range from passive behavior that does not involve contact with others to more aggressive types of behavior. Five specific types of atypical sexual behavior are as follows: (1) Voyeurism is behavior in which one becomes sexually aroused by looking at people, often strangers, undressing or having sex without their being aware that they are being watched. (2) Fetishism is behavior in which a person experiences arousal or pleasure from focusing on a nonsexual object or part of the body, such as a shoe or the foot. (3) Exhibitionism consists of exposing one's genitals in public to an involuntary observer. (4) Sadomasochism involves deriving sexual pleasure from the infliction and/or receiving of pain. (5) Obscene phone calls made for the purpose of sexual arousal are similar to exhibitionism.

- Though the media are guilty of promoting and depicting unrealistic views of sex, real-life sexual difficulties occur and include the following: (1) Inhibited sexual desire is a lack of interest in sex, or an inability to feel sexual or get sexually aroused. (2) Sexual addiction or compulsive sexual behavior is an intense preoccupation with sex. It makes having a satisfying sexual relationship with just one lover difficult.

7.3 AIDS & Other Sexual Diseases

- Love and passion may lead people to take chances and possibly engage in risky sexual behavior, possibly resulting in a person's contracting an infectious disease or even a life-threatening virus. Sexually transmitted diseases are infections that are usually transmitted as a result of sexual contact.
- The most serious types of illness that can be transmitted through sexual contact are the human immunodeficiency disease (HIV) and acquired immune deficiency syndrome (AIDS). AIDS is a sexually transmitted disease that is caused by the HIV virus and is characterized by irreversible damage to the body's immune system. HIV is the virus that causes AIDS and can result in a variety of ills, including the breakdown of the body's immune system, resulting in certain infections and cancers. HIV and AIDS can be transmitted through homosexual or heterosexual contact with someone who has AIDS/HIV, intravenous drug use involving sharing of syringes with someone who has AIDS/HIV, exposure to the blood or other bodily fluids of an infected person, and blood transfusion with contaminated blood.

Take It to the Net

Among the Internet resources on sexuality and sexually transmitted diseases are the following.

- **American Social Health Association.** Offers information and statistics about STDs.
  www.ashastd.org
- **Guttmacher Institute.** Offers research, policy analysis, and public education on sexual and reproductive health.
  www.guttmacherinstitute.org
- **HIV/AIDS Treatment Information Service.** Offers federally approved treatment guidelines on HIV/AIDS and information on clinical trials of experimental drugs and other therapies.
  http://actis.org
- **HomeAccess Health Corporation.** Offers home HIV testing. Mail in a sample of blood, and call 7

days later for anonymous test results. Phone: 1-800-HIV-TEST.
  www.homeaccess.com
- **Sex, Etc.** Part of the National Teen-to-Teen Sexuality Education Project developed by the nonprofit Rutgers University–based Network for Family Life Education, which offers resources in support of balanced, comprehensive sexuality education.
  www.sxetc.org
- **Sexual Health InfoCenter.** A popular source of information for adults about sexuality and its nuances started by two students at McGill University in Montreal, Canada.
  www.sexhealth.org

CHAPTER 8

MARRIAGE

The Ultimate Commitment?

What Kind of Marriage & Family Is Really Real?

"The way the whole issue of family life in America is framed politically and culturally is dependent on utopian images of the family that come out of '50s television," says Robert Thompson (quoted in Jayson 2006), professor of media and popular culture at Syracuse University.

Even if you never watched reruns of Father Knows Best, Leave It to Beaver, *or* The Adventures of

Ozzie and Harriet—*all 1950s-era shows featuring nuclear families that were "unnaturally wholesome," as* USA Today *called them ("Dysfunction rules, man!" 2003)—your beliefs about families may have been influenced by these outmoded images, Thompson believes. Traditional TV families of the 1950s and 1960s (and even those that came later, such as* The Brady Bunch, The Waltons, The Cosby Show's Huxtables, *and* The Simpsons*) did not actually reflect the American family, says Thompson; rather, they established the notion of what a perfect American family is supposed to be.*

Since the 1990s, the dynamics, values, and humor of the television-family show have become increasingly edgy, if not downright dysfunctional. Ozzie and Harriet, for instance, yielded to a newer generation's Ozzy and Sharon of the MTV comedy *The Osbournes* (2002–2005), the real-life adventures of Beverly Hills oddballs—"an eccentric but loving family coping with dog poo on the rug, misplaced cats, and sibling rivalry," in one description. "Oh, and son Jack's pot use, daughter Kelly's vagina monologue, dad's Viagra habit, and mom's egg-throwing retaliation against noisy neighbors" (Gunderson 2002: 2E). Fox's animated series *Family Guy* (created in 1999)—described as "a traditional domestic sitcom soaked in battery acid" (Gordon 2005: 50)—has exhibited surprising longevity. Yet, says cultural observer Michael Medved (2002), even though we realize that the images of pop culture are "just TV" or "just a movie," they still inform what we think about marriage and families.

🔮 WHAT'S AHEAD IN THIS CHAPTER

We first discuss good and bad reasons for getting married, the expectations people have for marriage, and different marriage contracts. We then describe four phases in a family life cycle: beginning, child rearing, middle age, and aging. In the third section, we discuss three classifications for marriage relationships. Finally, we cover what makes for successful marriages.

■ **Television:** Besides the shows just mentioned, television has also brought us the unorthodox family values of New Jersey gangster Tony Soprano in *The Sopranos* (1998–2007). Although he murders people, "he is a surprisingly good father," says one account (Teachout 2002), "at once sternly moralistic and unambivalently loving." (Some might disagree this constitutes a "good father," though he might be a great godfather.)

One critic, Robert Bianco (2006: 2E), observes that, outside of CW's *Everybody Hates Chris* (created in 2005), loosely based on the experiences of comedian Chris Rock, "children have almost vanished from the sitcom sphere. And when they do appear, they're on comedies aimed at a much older audience, such as *Christine* and *Two and a Half Men*." Or they are pushed into the background, as in *Everybody Loves Raymond* (1996–2005) or turned into "a target of prepubescent jokes, as on [*Two and a Half*] *Men* or *The War at Home*." Bianco also points out that life on TV is, with rare exceptions, usually one of ceaseless prosperity. "How many people," he asks, "do you know who hold jobs that leave them struggling to pay current bills and worrying about their futures? How many of those do you see on TV?" Except for *Everybody Hates Chris*—and perhaps *My Name Is Earl, Friday Night Lights,* and *The Wire*—few shows examine the economic insecurities of working-class families.

So-called reality television has also given us *Who Wants to Marry a Multi-Millionaire,* in which we could watch two strangers tie the knot and then follow their breakup days later, as well as *Joe Millionaire, The Bachelor,* and *The Bachelorette*—all of which portray marriage not as sacred institutions but "exploitable, instantly disposable commodities," says one critic (Laurence 2003).

■ **Films:** The dysfunctional family has long been the subject of Hollywood films, ranging from *The Godfather* trilogy, through *Long Day's Journey into Night,* to *American Beauty.* Against these are more lighthearted family comedies such as the Ben Stiller films *Flirting with Disaster* (with Patricia Arquette) and *Meet the Parents* (with Robert De Niro) or the surprise 2002 hit, *My Big Fat Greek Wedding.*

■ **Books:** Can people cure their dysfunctionality by reading self-help advice books? If so, there is a never-ending supply, beginning with *The Complete Idiot's Guide to Being a Groom* and *Making Marriage Work for Dummies.* Seekers of a "happy marriage" may choose from *Seven Secrets of a Happy Marriage, 1008 Secrets of a Happy Marriage,* and *And They Lived Happily Ever After.*

Getting married and staying married: Clearly, this is a complex subject. Let us begin to explore it.

🌐 ON THE WEB The Marriage Surprise

www.google.com

One way to get into the subject of marriage is to use an Internet search engine to search for interesting topics:

1. Go to Google.
2. Click on *News.*
3. At the top of the screen, type in the keyword *Marriage.*
4. Click on *Search news.*
5. Scroll down until you see an interesting topic. Click on it and read. What startling things did you learn?

What are good and bad reasons for getting married, and what expectations do people have?

What four phases might a marriage go through, and how do they relate to marital satisfaction?

What are two ways in which I might classify marriage relationships?

What are the characteristics of successful marriages, and how could I achieve success in my own marriage?

8.1 Why Do People Marry?

MAJOR QUESTION What are good and bad reasons for getting married, and what expectations do people have?

PREVIEW Good reasons for marrying are emotional security, companionship, and the desire to be parents. Bad reasons are for physical attractiveness or economic security; pressure from others or pregnancy; and escape, rebellion, rebound, or rescue. In getting married, people expect to undergo a rite of passage, to have sexual exclusivity and permanence, and to make an important legal commitment to another person.

"Despite today's high divorce rates, more births to the unmarried, the rise in one-parent families, and other trends," writes sociologist Arlene Skolnick (2002: 149), "the United States today has the highest marriage rate among the advanced industrial countries. The Census Bureau estimates that about 90% of Americans will eventually marry." This is down from 95% in the 1950s and 1960s, but not greatly different from the marriage rate at the beginning of the 20th century, according to family studies scholar Stephanie Coontz (2006a). Even so, married-couple households are a minority in the United States, outnumbered by single-person households and cohabiting couples (Coontz 2004b).

How realistic are people's expectations for marriage? Studies show that adolescents and adults alike seem to have high expectations for the wedded state and are unprepared for the realities of marriage and family life (Martin et al. 2001; Bonds-Raacke et al. 2001). "There's an idealized state that people get into before they get married," says Reno, Nevada, psychologist Dean Hinitz (quoted in Steffens 2002). People often marry because of that euphoric, idealized feeling known as "being in love." But is that the only reason?

Why Individuals Get Married

Marriage has traditionally been defined as a socially approved mating relationship. We would go beyond that and say that, in North America, **marriage is a legal union between a man and a woman.** (This definition helps to distinguish marriage from cohabitation, which has been gaining more social

- **What would you miss if you never married?** In a study of the never married, 80% of the men and 75% of the women said what they would miss most if they never got married was companionship.[a]

- **How much does a wedding cost?** The median cost of a wedding in the United States in 2006 was about $15,000.[b]

- **Do married women usually keep their last names?** About 17% of college-educated married women kept their last name in 2000.[c]

- **Is sex still enjoyable during marriage?** In one study, 88% of married couples said that they experienced extreme physical pleasure with their partners, as opposed to 54% of single people not married or living with someone.[d]

- **Do men do as much housework as women?** In 1995, women—both full-time homemakers and employed wives—averaged 16 hours a week on housework, and men averaged 9, according to one study.[e] Another study found that in two-income families, women spent 34 hours a week on housework compared to their husbands' 18.[f]

[a]Edwards 2000. [b]Bialik 2007. [c]Goldin and Shim 2004. [d]Michael et al. 1994. [e]Robinson and Godbey 1997. [f]Presser 1993.

NUMBERS THAT MATTER
Holy Matrimony

acceptance in some areas, and civil unions, which are contractual relationships between gay or lesbian partners, which we discuss in Chapter 9, "Variations.")

People offer all kinds of justifications for why they got married, although one study (Patterson and Kim 1991) found that the principal reason was "because we're in love," followed by companionship, desire for children, and happiness. *(See ■ Panel 8.1).* In addition to these oft-stated answers, there are a host of others. Let's consider some of them.

■ **PANEL 8.1   Why People Say They Marry**

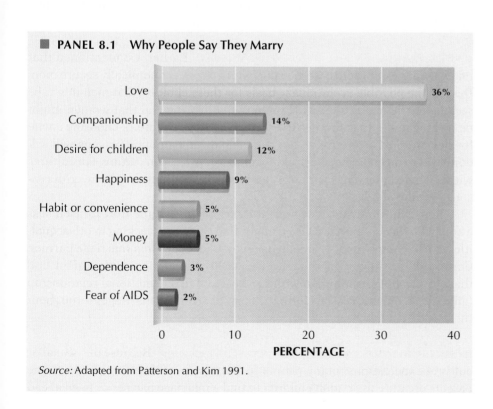

Source: Adapted from Patterson and Kim 1991.

Marriage for the Right Reasons

David Knox (1975) suggests three positive reasons for marrying:

■ **Emotional Security—"I want to fill an emptiness within myself":** In the United States, most people say they marry for love; indeed, only 4% of the respondents in one study reported that they would marry someone with whom they were not in love (Levine et al. 1995). By getting married, a person hopes to establish emotional security—an enduring, close emotional relationship (Knox 1975).

■ **Companionship—"I want to love and be loved by someone else":** Companionship—loving and being loved by another person—is actually the most important benefit that people in the United States expect to gain by getting married (Coontz 2000). One study of never-married adults found that four-fifths of the men and three-quarters of the women said what they would miss most if they never got married was companionship (Edwards 2000).

Seeking companionship is another way of saying "I want to avoid being alone." Some young people whose peers are already cohabiting or married might begin to be acutely sensitive to their own aloneness and singlehood (a topic we discuss in Chapter 9, "Variations").

■ **Desire to Be a Parent—"I want to have and raise children":** You don't have to be married to have children, of course. However, many Americans prefer to have them within the framework of marriage—probably because society's rules and expectations simply make life easier on parents and children when the father and mother are legally wed.

Marriage for the Wrong Reasons

There is a whole other list of reasons why people wed that are probably less likely to produce enduring marriages. Among them are the following:

■ **Physical Attractiveness or Economic Security:** Earlier, we mentioned that many men seek attractive women and women seek economically secure men. Despite the possible evolutionary basis for these choices (that men might be seeking fertile mates to provide them with offspring and that women might be seeking mates to guarantee the security of their children), choosing a wife for her physical attractiveness or a husband for economic reasons will seldom lead to an enduring marriage—at least in American culture. (In cultures with arranged marriages, finances and fertility may indeed be powerful reasons for marrying.)

A man who marries a woman for her beauty might find himself less attracted to her as she ages. Or he might find that she is lacking in other qualities, such as sensitivity or intelligence, that he values in a marriage partner. Conversely, a woman who marries for strictly economic reasons might find that she has little in common with her husband in an emotional relationship (although economic reasons form the basis of arranged marriages throughout the world).

■ **Pressure from Parents, Peers, Partners—Or Pregnancy:** Because of societal or cultural expectations, many people feel uncomfortable being single. Some parents pressure their adult children to find a marriage partner or to go ahead

THE RIGHT REASONS? Do you know of someone who got married more for reasons of parental pressure than for reasons of love? ◄

with an already announced engagement and have a wedding. Parents might also press their children to marry for religious reasons. Peers might encourage continuation of a long-term relationship so that it becomes more and more uncomfortable to back out. Partners—whether dating, cohabiting, or engaged—might, of course, bring pressure to continue.

Many women, especially teenagers, make the change from singlehood to being married because of premarital pregnancy. In fact, as many as 13% of females are pregnant at the time they marry (Abma et al. 1998). About one-quarter of teenagers' first births conceived out of marriage are made legitimate by marriage. Unfortunately, teenage females who marry to avoid being single usually get divorced, becoming single again after all (Teti and Lamb 1989).

■ **Escape, Rebellion, Rebound, or Rescue:** People may marry for reasons that even by the standards of passion might seem irrational.

Some young people might see marriage as an opportunity to escape abusive parents or even just parental authority. Some young people express their defiance of parental attempts at interference in a relationship by rebelling and marrying the object of their affections—mainly to show up the parents (Katz and Liu 1988). Some people, young or old, marry on the rebound from a broken relationship, their low self-esteem (as the result of being broken up with) a driving factor.

Sometimes people feel sorry for their partner—perhaps because he or she has a disability, a drinking problem, a history of sorrow, or the like—and decide to try to "rescue" or help that person. The rescuer might believe he or she can change the person, although change is usually not so easy.

In all such cases, the person who is targeted for marriage is less important than someone else, such as parents, a previous lover, or even one's own status as a "white knight" (rescuer). What kind of chance would you expect, therefore, for the longevity of the marriage?

Happiness, Marriage, & Race: The Interracial Experience

As we mentioned in Chapter 1, "Seeking," there is a strong cultural notion in the United States that "if we love each other enough, we can overcome all problems." Film director Michael Apted, intrigued that marriage is still idealized even though the divorce rate remains high, began a series of documentaries—*Made in America* (2002) and *Made in America 2* (2006)—in which he interviews several couples of varying race, religion, ethnicity, geography, and incomes over a 10-year period to see how well they do (Keveney 2002). For instance, Neal is Jewish, and Cheryl is a Catholic Filipina. Chris is a New York–born police officer, while Vanessa is a Colombian immigrant who works for an investment firm. Scott, from suburban Alabama, and Amber, who grew up in the Cayman Islands, have different ideas about where they would like to settle down.

However, even as such interracial—and interethnic and interfaith—partners profess their love for each other, they also express concern about the difficulties marriage could bring for them. Are they right to do so?

Interracial Marriage: The Background

In the United States, black–white marriages were banned in the late 1600s, when Virginia tobacco planters felt that they needed to shore up their new institution of slavery. Earlier, when servitude provided the basis for the labor force, sexual intimacy between races, even interracial marriage, was allowed. But as slavery became the basis of agricultural labor in the South, interracial sex and offspring threatened to blur the distinctions between white and black—and thus the basis between free and slave.

During the 18th century, all southern states and many northern ones outlawed all black–white marriages. Even after the Civil War, bans on *miscegenation,* **marriage or cohabitation between a white person and a person of another race,** continued. "In the West, 13 states passed new laws against interracial marriage, many of them targeting white-Asian unions along with white-black ones," says one account (Greenberg 1999).

The civil rights movement slowly began to change people's consciousness. In 1958, a black bricklayer named Richard Loving married the light of his life, a white woman named Mildred Jeter, in violation of Virginia's antimiscegenation law, an act that was punishable by 1 to 5 years in prison. In 1967,

INTERRACIAL MARRIAGE. Encouraging news is that since the early 1990s more Americans have expressed tolerance for interracial marriage. Biracial unions have also increased, now making up 1 in 15 marriages in the United States. How do you feel about interracial marriage? Do your views differ from those of your parents or grandparents? ◄

the U.S. Supreme Court, in the aptly named case of *Loving* v. *Virginia,* ruled the anti-miscegenation law in Virginia (and 15 other states) unconstitutional. Even so, laws banning interracial marriages remained on the books (though legally unenforceable) into the 1970s (Hartill 2001). The last state to strike its law, Alabama, did so in 2000.

As late as 1991, 66% of American whites said they would oppose a close relative marrying a black man, according to the National Opinion Research Center (cited in Hartill 2001). Ten years later, another survey—by *The Washington Post,* Henry J. Kaiser Family Foundation, and Harvard University—found that 53% of whites said it would make no difference if one married someone of their own or a different race, and acceptance was even higher among nonwhites (Fears and Deane 2001).

Between 1990 and 2000, biracial unions increased 65%, and interracial couples now comprise 1 in 15 marriages in the United States—up from 1 in 23 in 1990 (Frey 2003). But while the rate of marriages between black and whites rose significantly during that time, the share of Hispanics and Asians married to whites declined. Probably this is because the arrival of more than

11 million immigrants in the 1990s (more than half of adult Hispanics and about three-quarters of adult Asians are immigrants) created a larger marriage pool, allowing more Hispanics and Asians to marry among themselves (Qian and Lichter 2007).

Tolerance & Acceptance: Improved, but Could Be Better

Although biracial couples in the *Post*-Kaiser-Harvard surveys reported more tolerance and even acceptance, that doesn't mean the voyage is easy for everyone. Nearly half of black–white couples—significantly more than Latino–white or Asian–white couples—thought that marrying someone of a different race made marriage more difficult. More black–white couples also reported that a parent had a problem with the relationship. Some report being ignored by rude waiters in restaurants and receiving ugly stares from people in shopping malls. Cindy Terry, age 33, who is white, married an African American in Bremerton, Washington. When they went to New Orleans, however, she felt uncomfortable. "I felt like we were aliens, just the stares, and you knew they were saying something under their breath," she said (quoted in Fears and Deane 2001).

Acceptance of mixed-race couples is more likely to be found in black families. About three-quarters of Latino families would accept black people. Among Asian Americans, 77% would welcome a new white member, and 71% would accept a Latino. Black people are somewhat less likely to be accepted, at 66%.

Acceptance seems to increase from decade to decade, especially among younger people. Even so, an interracial or interethnic marriage can be difficult. White man Walter Simon, age 60, of Vacaville, California, said that his long-time marriage to his Mexican Cuban wife "hasn't been easy." The main difficulty involves culture rather than skin color. "My wife doesn't like to speak English," he said. "Certain places where we lived people were very racist. . . . They had reservations about meeting her" (quoted in Fears and Deane 2001).

One key to an interracial couple's married happiness is the extent to which—before their union—they are aware of how their union is perceived by others with regard to racial issues and how much social support they receive for their relationship from relatives and friends (Kenney 2002).

The Expectations People Have for Marriage

In getting married, people have several expectations: (1) that they will undergo certain rituals or a rite of passage—engagement, wedding ceremony, and honeymoon; (2) that they will have sexual exclusivity and permanence in their relationship; and (3) that they are making an important legal commitment.

1. Marriage as Rite of Passage

As we mentioned in Chapter 5, "Involvement," the culmination of the traditional courtship process is the engagement, which is followed (generally 12 to 16 months later) by the wedding, which is followed immediately by the honeymoon. All of these marriage-related rituals make up a critical ***rite of*** *passage*—**an event signaling a major change from one social status to another.** Let's consider these:

■ **Engagement:** *Engagement* is a couple's way of signaling to the world that they intend to marry. This is usually represented by the purchase of an *engagement ring,* which the future husband gives to his intended wife.

Today, because many couples live together before getting married (as we discussed in Chapter 5, "Involvement"), engagements often are not quite as formal as in times past. There might not be the ritual popping of the question over a romantic dinner, and the man might no longer ask the woman's parents "for her hand." Although we are made aware of splashy public proposals by such reality TV shows as *Perfect Proposal* or reports of Tom Cruise broaching the question atop the Eiffel Tower, in practice most people (91%) say that a private, intimate proposal is better (Zaslow 2005; "Private proposals go over better" 2007). In addition, nowadays many people buy their engagement rings at the same time they buy their wedding rings.

Beyond the ring, however, there are a couple of other rituals associated with engagement: the bridal shower and the bachelor party. The *bridal shower* is a party arranged by the bride-to-be's female friends, to which traditionally only women are invited, in which the prospective bride is "showered" with presents, such as household gifts. The *bachelor party* is a men-only party that the groom-to-be's friends organize, often involving a lot of drinking, where they "roast" the groom about his supposed loss of freedom. Sometimes these can go quite far afield: Some bachelor parties for British grooms-to-be take place in Eastern Europe, where hotel and bar prices are cheap (Bryan-Low 2007). In some areas, women get together and throw a *bachelorette party* for the prospective bride. These engagement rituals are also changing, however, with both men and women sometimes attending a single bridal/bachelor engagement party. (If a couple has been living together, sometimes friends will throw a "couple shower," getting together for a party and gift giving.) Finally, many couples now use websites ("Wed sites") and blogs to keep family and friends up on these events, with "confessional stories, courtship videos, and blow-by-blow accounts of the preparations," according to one report (Dodes 2007: A13).

The engagement period provides the new couple with a time to know each other better without the pressure of traditional dating. It is also an opportunity for couples to get premarital counseling (either religious or secular), discuss medical histories, and explore whether they want to have children (and whether genetic counseling might be called for). This may also be a time in which to create a *personal marriage agreement,* as we discuss at the end of this chapter.

■ **Wedding:** For the bride-to-be, the initial excitement of the engagement can be overwhelmed by the task of planning the wedding. Even a modest event can involve a lot of work: telling friends and family, putting an announcement in the paper, picking a date, choosing a location, settling on a theme, interviewing caterers and photographers, deciding on music and flowers, and trying on dresses.

Usually, the location, style, guest list, and other factors are determined by the couple's (or, traditionally, the bride's parents') spending budget. Wedding planners therefore suggest that the couple prioritize which elements are most important—whether, say, location and entertainment are more important than photographer or videographer. The engaged partners also, of course, need to decide who will be part of the wedding party and what their tasks will be: groomsmen, flower girls, ring bearers, ushers, parents, and grandparents. There is a whole wedding industry that offers clothing, gifts, and personal luxuries (hairdos, manicures, massages) for members of the wedding party.

Cost is a significant factor. The *mean* cost of a wedding in the United States in 2006 was a hefty $27,852, almost double the $15,208 spent in 1990, according to a study by the Condé Nast Bridal Group (cited in Parnes 2006). About 36% of couples spend more than they had planned, and only 30% of brides' parents pay for the whole event, down 8% since 1999. However, there is a difference between the *mean* cost and the *median* cost, which is the middle cost when you line up a set of numbers by order of size. Whereas the mean cost might be $27,852 (which might include a million-dollar wedding along with several $10,000 weddings), the median wedding cost is only about $15,000 (Bialik 2007).

Because weddings are at minimum a civil event, involving the power of the state, partners are required to obtain a marriage license (perhaps after having had a blood test to certify that neither has a sexually transmitted disease). Two-thirds of the states require a waiting period after the license is issued before the wedding can take place. Twenty percent of couples (mostly those being remarried) are married in a civil ceremony, by a judge or magistrate; 80% are married by a member of the clergy.

■ **Honeymoon:** Immediately following the wedding and wedding reception (and throwing of the bride's bouquet), the newlywed couple traditionally changes clothes and then rushes toward a car (in a shower of rice) to start their honeymoon. Whether the honeymoon takes place at an inexpensive inn or on a world cruise, its purpose is to allow the couple to recover from the stresses of the wedding and to begin to establish their new identity as legally wed husband and wife. The honeymoon is also the socially sanctioned period in which it is understood that the couple may freely have sexual relations with each other without fear of social disapproval.

2. Marriage in Expectation of Sexual Exclusivity & of Permanence

In making a pledge of monogamous marriage, most partners assume that their relationship will be built around two promises to each other: *sexual exclusivity* and *permanence*.

■ **Sexual Exclusivity—"Forsaking all others":** ***Sexual exclusivity* means that each partner promises to have sexual relations only with the other.** Although there are exceptions to this rule—called "open marriages"—the majority of marriages start out with the assumption that the spouses will be faithful to each other. Although a sizable number of married people stray from these marriage vows of exclusivity, one study found that 70% of Americans believe that sexual relations outside of marriage are always harmful to a marriage (Adler 1996).

■ **Permanence—"So long as we both shall live":** ***Permanence* means that the partners promise to stay together lifelong.** Historically, the reason that permanence was one of the marital vows is that society wanted to ensure an arrangement of economic stability for the safe rearing of children; later, emotional security and affection came to be the bonding agent. (Thus, some couples reword the vows to say, "So long as we both shall love.") Although we now live in an era of "serial marriages" or even "starter marriages" (as we'll discuss in Chapter 14, "Uncoupling"), people still enter each union hoping that they will find the lifelong emotional security and intimacy they seek.

Sexual exclusivity and permanence are truly major issues for many couples. In anticipation of the serious commitment that marriage requires, a growing number of engaged and cohabiting couples now seek couples therapy to help them work through their relationship problems (Wolff 2005).

3. Marriage as a Legal Commitment

In getting married, you make a commitment to your partner and, historically at least, to his or her family members. (Certainly very much in times past and even to a great extent today, couples who married realized that they also took on certain responsibilities toward each other's parents, such as sharing holiday visits and caring for them in periods of ill health or old age.) But you also make a *legal, contractual commitment* with the state in which you live. This means that the state has an interest in how you terminate the marriage and in how you divide property and share children if you divorce. When you marry someone, for instance, you might find yourself responsible for debts either or both of you take on after the marriage.

If you are a woman and don't want to take your husband's name, or want to take a hyphenated version of it (joining his last name with your last name, such as "Joan Cohen-Sanchez"), this needs to be made clear, especially if you are contemplating having children. (Will they take the hyphenated last name too?) Hyphenated names, although never common, are now increasingly rare. One study of college-educated women, who are more likely to keep their own names, found that only 17% kept them in 2000, down from 23% in 1990 (Goldin and Shim 2004). Another study, which analyzed 2000 *New York Times* wedding announcements from 1966 to 1996, found that 83% of women took their husband's name, 12.2% kept their own, and 1.5% took hyphenated names (Scheuble et al. 2000). Some women keep their own names for work and use their husband's name for everything else. On rare occasions, a man will take his wife's last name or combine his own last name with his wife's (as happened with Antonio Villar and Corina Raigosa, when they combined names as Villaraigosa; he's now the mayor of Los Angeles). However, most states make the couple pay extra fees and go through the red tape of a court petition (Kasindorf 2007; Friess 2007).

Because divorce looms so large as a possible outcome of so many marriages, three further contractual marital agreements have been developed: the *covenant marriage,* the *prenuptial agreement,* and the *postnuptial agreement.*

■ **The Covenant Marriage Contract—"We want to demonstrate a stronger commitment to our marriage":** In 1997, Louisiana passed the nation's first covenant marriage law, followed by Arizona in 1998 and Arkansas in 2001. (Covenant marriage bills have been introduced in several other states since then. Often, a license for a covenant marriage is cheaper to obtain than a traditional marriage license, although this financial incentive might make people less informed as to the legal commitment they are actually making.)

A *covenant marriage* **is an antidivorce contract in which couples demonstrate their strong commitment to marriage by (a) getting premarital counseling, (b) getting marital counseling in times of marital**

difficulties, and (c) agreeing not to divorce until after a separation of two years or after proving adultery or domestic abuse.

Supporters—who are often conservative Christians—argue that conventional marriage contracts are not binding enough in the face of today's "no-fault" divorce laws, which allow either partner to divorce on short notice. It's not clear that covenant marriage contracts by themselves would really reduce divorce, since it's possible they would be signed by people who tend to resist divorce anyway. Moreover, having to prove adultery or domestic abuse in court could be expensive—just as it was in the days before no-fault" divorce (which we discuss in Chapter 14, "Uncoupling").

■ **The Prenuptial Agreement—"Before marriage, we want to determine how property will be divided in the event of divorce":** Sort of the opposite of the covenant marriage, the *prenuptial agreement,* **or premarital agreement, is a contract signed by the couple before the wedding that specifies in advance how property will be divided and children cared for in the event of divorce or one partner's death.** Favored by people who remarry—particularly when one partner is wealthy—in essence, the prenuptial agreement describes how the assets the partners bring to the marriage are to be handled if the couple splits up. *(See ■ Panel 8.2.)* Prenups are particularly recommended for anyone who has children from a prior marriage; has $100,000 or more in assets (including retirement accounts); owns a business, is partner in a company, or is on a well-paying career fast track; or is supporting a spouse in getting an advanced degree (such as M.D.) in a profitable field (Hannon 2006: 55). Another legal device often used, especially by wealthy families looking to shield property from future divorce claims, are trusts, which are frequently used for tax planning and asset-protection purposes (Silverman 2005).

Nearly two-thirds of U.S. matrimonial lawyers surveyed said that prenups were eliciting high interest among remarrying Baby Boomers ("Surge in 'prenups'" 2007). Still, "Being asked to sign a prenup is a sensitive request," observes one writer (Hannon 2006: 53). "It conjures up feelings of distrust and heartlessness. It's as if your fiancé is planning the exit strategy even before the honeymoon." Perhaps this is why Paul McCartney didn't insist on one when he married Heather Mills, but the divorce may have cost him a quarter of his estimated $1 billion fortune. Because 60% of divorces occur during the first eight years of marriage, a prenuptial agreement can protect people "against the long-term consequences of a short-term marriage," says lawyer Arlene Dubin (quoted in Dugas 2002: 3B), who has written a prenuptial divorce book (Dubin 2001a). The expiration clause can be a compromise between a spouse who wants a prenuptial agreement and one who doesn't.

■ **PANEL 8.2   Possible Items in a Prenuptial Agreement**

A list of each person's assets, debts, and income.

What happens to assets if there is divorce or death.

Who are beneficiaries of pensions and retirement accounts.

Whether there will be a property settlement or alimony or spousal support.

Source: Adapted from Dubin 2001a.

PRACTICAL ACTION

Make It *Your* Wedding: Ideas for Today's Nuptials

About 2.2 million nuptials, or wedding ceremonies, are performed every year in the United States, making it a $70 billion business involving magazines, bridal gowns, tuxedo rentals, wedding ceremonies, flowers, music, photography, and catering, not to mention honeymoons. But this traditional industry is undergoing sometimes dramatic changes. One, for instance, is that more men are getting involved in wedding planning—as much as 80%, according to market researcher NPD Research (cited in Caplan 2005).

The Changing Wedding: Multicultural & Other Celebrations

The $10,000 white wedding dress with sheer sleeves and silver leaf embroidery will probably never go out of style, but now some brides are crossing over to other colors—startling reds, for instance.

"Brides have so many choices now, and many are moving into pale blues and greens," says Deborah Starks (quoted in Rubin 2002: 39), owner of an Oakland, California, bridal boutique. "There is less emphasis on the Judeo-Christian religious ceremonies, and women are not so heavily influenced by that."

Indeed, multicultural weddings are in. Her marriage "to Barukh, a Sephardic Jew, was a blend of Jewish, Chinese, Christian, and even Hawaiian

traditions," says Ami Chen Mills (2002: 18, 20). "Call it the melting pot of weddings. . . . But ours was just one in a tidal wave of colorful, wonderful multicultural and interfaith weddings."

Today, weddings are also complicated by the makeup of the postmodern family: "The typical 21st century wedding can now feature a supporting cast of stepparents, half-siblings, Dad's new girlfriend and her kids, the bride's first stepfather and his new wife, and sometimes even the bride and groom's ex-spouses," says one writer (Dickinson 2002). "The old rules of wedding etiquette don't stretch far enough to cover the shape of these families."

Some couples avoid these problems—and the considerable expense of fancy floral arrangements and hors d'oeuvres—by becoming "weddingmooners," folding their wedding and honeymoon into one far-flung trip, such as to Hawaii, Italy, Tahiti,

Anguilla, or Fiji (Klein 2003), which are the top five honeymoon destinations, according to travel agents (Sottili 2006). Some remarrying couples even bring along their children from their previous marriages—a "familymoon" (Greenberg and Kuchment 2006).

If you and your beloved met at a baseball game, you can celebrate your union by renting home plate for anywhere from $1,000 at Coors Field to $5,000 at Dodger Stadium (Frey 2002). You can even find services from Las Vegas to Zurich, Switzerland, that will broadcast your nuptials in real time via webcam so that family and friends far away can be included (Barker 2006).

Deal with Postwedding Letdown

This is a major life event. You're letting go of being single. Be prepared for postwedding withdrawal after being deluged with all the attention.

"WE'RE MARRIED!" The traditional wedding with formal dress will probably never go out of style, but more couples are now "customizing" their nuptials. What instances have you seen of this? ▶

Are These Prospective Marriage Partners Off Limits?

Is there someone of the opposite sex outside your immediate family that you've been told you should never marry? How about your first cousin?

Oh, right. Marrying your cousin, you've probably heard, violates some kind of stigma against inbreeding because it supposedly raises the risk that your children will have birth defects, such as mental retardation or cystic fibrosis.

Indeed, 24 states ban first-cousin marriages, and 5 others allow it only if the couple is unable to bear children. (You can get more information about the law in your state by going to *www.cousincouples.com*.)

But this prohibition has also frequently been ignored. Famed naturalist Charles Darwin married his first cousin, and they had 10 children, 4 of whom became brilliant scientists. Albert Einstein's second wife was his first cousin. In parts of Saudi Arabia, 39% of all marriages are between first cousins, and in Turkey and Morocco, it's 22% (Begley 2002; Corliss 2002). Some cultures encourage cousin marriages to keep dowries and other resources in the family.

But what about that biological taboo? A scientific task force reviewed studies stretching back to 1965 and concluded that the risk of having children with mental retardation is only about 1.7 to 2.8% higher for first-cousin couples than for unrelated partners.

Although this represents a near doubling of the risk, the result is not considered large enough to discourage cousins from having children, says study leader Arno Motulsky (Bennett et al. 2002; Grady 2002).

■ **The Postnuptial Agreement—"Because of new circumstances in our marriage, we now want to determine how property will be divided in the event of divorce"**: A relatively recent legal wrinkle is the postnuptial agreement. **A** *postnuptial agreement* **is the same as a prenuptial agreement except that it is worked out by partners who are already married to each other.** Most often, a postnuptial agreement is developed when one spouse comes into an inheritance or starts a business or when there are children from a previous marriage who need to be provided for (Lewin 2001).

Although Dubin (2001b) claims that such midmarriage agreements "provide a catalyst for communication and compromise" and "reduce probate problems and lessen the intensity of divorce," others disagree. Lawyer Thomas Oldham (quoted in Lewin 2001: A8) says, "If you look at the agreements, they're almost always to increase the rights of the wealthier partner and decrease the rights of the less wealthy one."

In addition to making use of these kinds of legal agreements, couples may benefit by having a personal marriage agreement, discussed at the end of this chapter.

8.2 Changes in the Family Life Cycle: Scenes from a Marriage

Major Question What four phases might a marriage go through, and how do they relate to marital satisfaction?

PREVIEW Family life has four phases: (1) beginning, with perhaps greatest marital satisfaction; (2) child rearing, often with less marital satisfaction; (3) middle age, with more marital satisfaction; and (4) aging.

Psychoanalyst Erik Erikson (1963) suggested that as individuals, we experience identity changes throughout our lives according to a human life cycle of eight stages but that these stages of identity are highly dependent on our relationships with others. Other scholars have suggested that marriages and families also have stages of development—a *family life cycle,* in the term coined by **Paul Glick** (Duvall and Miller 1985; Glick 1989). **In a *family life cycle,* members' roles and relationships change, largely depending on how they have to adapt themselves to the absence or presence of child-rearing responsibilities.** For ease of discussion, we divide the marital/family life cycle into four phases, as follows. (In general, these phases apply to the intact nuclear family. Alternative scenarios, such as cohabitation, single parenthood, childless marriages, and remarriage, may have their own variations. We discuss some of these in Chapter 9, "Variations.")

1. Beginning Phase: Greatest Marital Satisfaction?

Married life is different from single life. Suddenly, you're no longer responsible for just yourself but are sharing ties, responsibility, and even your identity with another person (Sarnoff and Sarnoff 1989). Indeed, it can be a shock to discover that the person you married is not the person you dated. Still, most partners say that they experience their greatest satisfaction with each other during this stage (Glenn 1991; Vaillant and Vaillant 1993; Benin, reported in Elias 1997). *(See ■ Panel 8.3.)* In one 17-year study, researchers at the University of Zurich (Stutzer and Frey 2006) asked several thousand couples to rate their happiness at various times and found that, on a scale of 1 to 10,

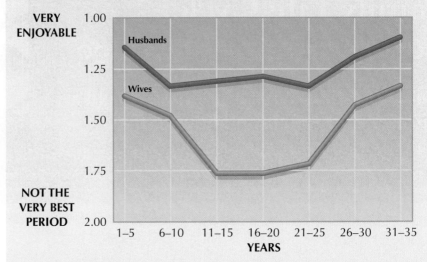

■ **PANEL 8.3 The U-Curve: How Marital Satisfaction Varies with Stages of Family Life Cycle—Up, Down, and Up.** The intact marriages of 52 couples (white, college-educated) were divided into seven consecutive 5-year periods. The periods are compared with how the couples retrospectively assessed their marital satisfaction during 35 years together.

Source: Caroline O. Vaillant and George Vaillant. 1993. Is the U-curve of marital satisfaction an illusion? A 40-year-study of marriage. *Journal of Marriage and the Family* 55: 237, Fig. 6. Copyright 1993 by the National Council on Family Relations, 3989 Central Avenue NE, Suite 550, Minneapolis, MN 55421. Reprinted by permission of Wiley-Blackwell, publisher.

singles rated themselves at 7.6, which rose to 7.8 after they married but dropped to 7.4 after a decade of marriage, in part because of the stress of raising children but also because of the woman's declining interest in sex.

Some changes during the beginning phase—which might last 2 to 3 years before children come along—are discussed next.

"Identity Bargaining"

The start of a marriage involves *identity bargaining*—**the realities of the marriage oblige spouses to adjust their idealized expectations of each other** (Blumstein 1976). If you thought your partner had been such a good sport when you were dating for not complaining about your staying out late, you might now find that role was one of the many small deceptions of courtship.

Loss of Independence

If you thrived on being independent during your single years, being married might take some getting used to. Indeed, some free spirits find themselves sorely frustrated by the responsibilities and confinements of marriage. On the other hand, even when their marriage isn't entirely equal, new spouses often talk a "language of equality" (Knudson-Martin and Mahoney 1998).

New Friends & Relatives

Getting married means getting to know your partner's family members and friends. The burden may fall on new wives in particular, who are often expected to manage social occasions and get-togethers with in-laws. You might also have less time for your own single friends because of the new demands on you as a spouse, and you might spend more time with other married couples.

Career & Domestic Roles

The first year is when you work out your respective career and domestic responsibilities, allocation of living expenses, and division of household tasks. Now that so many women work outside the home, the traditional bargain of the wife performing domestic services in exchange for the husband's financial support is no longer valid (Furstenberg 1996). Still, this situation can often create conflicts as newlyweds sort out their expectations of each other's role. However, finances are often not a problem because both partners are working; although their incomes might be low, so are their expenses.

2. Child-Rearing Phase: Less Marital Satisfaction?

Studies show that marital satisfaction changes during the family life cycle (Finkel and Hansen 1992; Glenn 1989, 1991; Vaillant and Vaillant 1993). Indeed, researchers speak of a U-shaped curve, as shown in Panel 8.3, in which satisfaction declines for the first 10 or 15 years, levels out, and then begins to rise during the later years of marriage. The period of less marital satisfaction corresponds to—though is not necessarily caused by—the most intense period of childbearing and child rearing. Sociologist Mary Benin also found in a study of 6,785 couples that marital happiness was highest before and after children were present. *(See ■ Panel 8.4.)* A survey of 90 studies of 31,000 married people found that marital satisfaction after the first baby's birth is 42% lower among the latest generation of parents (Twenge et al. 2003). A Pew Research Center (2007) survey found that children had fallen to eighth out of nine on a list of factors people associate with successful marriages.

As we will discuss in Chapter 11, "Parenting," children can bring great joy, but they also require a great deal of effort, time, and responsibility on the part of the parents. Children cost money that might otherwise have gone for enter-

■ **PANEL 8.4   Marital Contentment.** Time in the family life cycle when married couples are very happy (7 is highest) or least happy (1 is lowest).

Before children	6.24
WIth preschool children	5.95
WIth school-age children	5.89
With teenagers	5.79
WIth adult children	5.99
WIth adult children out of home	6.16
Never had children	6.26

Source: Adapted from M. Benin, reported in Elias 1997.

tainment or investment, detract from the parents' time with each other, and have needs that put a lot of stress on the couple. It is suggested that marital satisfaction is lowest about the time the oldest child enters school (or adolescence) but rises again after the children leave home.

We must point out, however, that there are probably contributors to marital dissatisfaction other than just the presence of children. We discuss some of these in Section 8.4, "What Makes for a Successful Marriage?"

Stages of Child Rearing

One approach divides childbearing and child rearing into five stages (Duvall and Miller 1985):

■ **Childbearing Family—Lasts about 2½ Years:** On average, American women have their first child at age 27. If there are other children, they tend to be born about 30 months apart.

■ **Family with Preschoolers—Lasts about 3½ Years:** In this stage, the couple's oldest child is 2½ to 6 years old. The parents (especially the mother) are quite preoccupied with child rearing.

■ **Family with School Children—Lasts about 7 Years:** By this stage, the oldest child is 6 to 13 years old. Often, the mother has returned to the job market, if only part time.

■ **Family with Adolescents—Lasts about 7 Years:** By this stage, the oldest child is 13 to 20 years old. This can be a particularly trying time for parents (Larson and Richards 1994). It's likely that both parents are working outside the home.

■ **Family as Launching Center—Lasts about 8 Years:** By this stage, the oldest child is an adult and has been "launched" into independence. At this point, marital satisfaction starts to rise.

It's apparent from this that a couple will devote their energies and finances to childbearing and child rearing for around 20 to 28 years—longer, perhaps, if they have more than one child.

Changes During the Child-Rearing Years

Some changes that occur during this phase are discussed next. (We elaborate on this subject in Chapter 11, "Parenting.")

■ **Work and Other Responsibilities:** Many two-paycheck families can't afford to have a stay-at-home parent, so both partners work outside the home, leaving the child or children in the care of someone else.

Working-class parents may be stressed by the demands of commuting, job insecurity, low pay, and child-care demands. Middle-class families may be strained by home, school, and after-school (children's sports, music lessons, and so on) responsibilities as well as career.

■ **Domestic Responsibilities:** Even before they become parents, partners in a marriage have to negotiate sharing of domestic work—cooking, shopping, cleaning, laundry, and home maintenance. Despite gains in egalitarianism between the sexes, however, women still do most household and child-care work—what has been called the "second shift"—even after performing at regular for-pay jobs all day. This perhaps occurs because of a tendency to follow their male partner's expectation that they will revert to traditional gender roles (Hochschild 1989; Nock 1995).

■ **Sexual Changes:** Even before the first child is born, a married couple will probably begin to experience change in their sex life. Indeed, even if you and your partner had sex while dating each other or lived together before marriage, you might find that the frequency with which you have sex declines.

Even so, most married partners report that sex with their partners is still satisfying. In one study, 88% of married partners said they experienced extreme physical pleasure with their partners, as opposed to 54% of single people who were not married or living with someone. And 85% of married partners said they experienced extreme emotional satisfaction with their partners, compared to only 30% of singles (Michael et al. 1994).

CHALLENGES WITH CHILDREN. During the child-rearing years of the family life cycle, there is an increase in domestic responsibilities. However, despite more equal sharing among husbands and wives, it is still women who do most household and child-care work. If you plan to have (or do have) children, how would you want to structure the next 20 to 28 years with your partner in terms of dividing child-care work and domestic responsibilities? ▲

3. Middle-Age Phase: More Marital Satisfaction?

In terms of the family cycle of a traditional nuclear family, middle age is considered to start at about the time the last child has left home and to continue until retirement. In this phase, some parents, particularly mothers, experience what's called **the *empty-nest syndrome*, a feeling of depression after the children have moved out or "fled the nest."**

On the other hand, there is also the reverse possibility—the "not-so-empty-nest" or "boomerang" effect. This occurs when adult children, after being away for a few years, return (like a boomerang) to live with their parents because of high housing costs, low income, or divorce (Mitchell and Gee 1996).

Among the changes that can happen during midlife are improved marital satisfaction and lack of marital satisfaction.

Improved Marital Satisfaction

In middle age, once the children leave home, the relationship between the marriage partners improves (Glenn 1991; Vaillant and Vaillant 1993). Without children in the house, the parents can begin to begin to enjoy each other more.

Satisfaction may vary by culture and gender, however. For example, Mexican American wives may react strongly to the empty-nest syndrome and not experience more marital satisfaction at midlife, although Mexican American husbands may (Markides et al. 1999).

Lack of Marital Satisfaction

Certain occurrences can actually reduce marital satisfaction at midlife: if an adult childhood returns home three times or more; if the child is returning to a household in which the parents are remarried rather than first-married; if the parents are in poor health (Willis and Reid 1999).

THE WAY WE WERE? Older couples hope that retirement will not only bring freedom from child-raising responsibilities but also enough income and leisure so that they can do the kinds of things they were unable to do when young, such as foreign travel, and to enjoy each other more. Of course, not everyone is so fortunate. Divorce, illness, job changes, financial reversals, and the need to care for older family members may erase such plans. What is the single most important thing you could do to try to make your later years fulfilling? ▶

In addition, if the families are taking care of elderly relatives, the extra responsibilities can contribute to diminished marital satisfaction.

4. Aging Phase

After 30 or 40 years of marriage, most income earners will be nearing retirement. This may require some adjustment, as, for example, if a wife who is accustomed to having her husband away at work now finds him around the house every day. Still, assuming that they are free of caregiving responsibilities (for grandchildren, older family members, or each other), this is a phase in which both partners can relax and enjoy each other more, although, of course, not all couples are so blessed. Eventually, one of the two, most often the woman, will outlive the other and will then live alone, with grown children, or in a retirement community.

All through their married years, however, the interaction of a couple often continues to change. For example, one study of 238 couples married 30 years or more found that women became less deferential to their husbands and more apt to challenge their authority and that men gradually became less patriarchal and more collaborative with their wives (Huyck and Gutmann 1992).

8.3 Different Kinds of Marriage Relationships

MAJOR QUESTION What are three ways in which I might classify marriage relationships?

PREVIEW We consider two different kinds of marriage relationships: (1) five types of enduring marriages and (2) four types of "good marriages" and their built-in "antimarriages."

Many social scientists have attempted to classify the different marriage relationships, although none of their studies has been based on representative samples of married couples. We will consider the following: (1) enduring marriages, studied by Cuber and Harroff, and (2) so-called "good marriages," studied by Wallerstein and Blakeslee.

1. Five Types of Enduring Marriages: Cuber & Harroff's Research

In their book *Sex and the Significant Americans,* **John Cuber and Peggy Harroff** (1965) proposed, on the basis of their interviews with 400 upper-middle-class couples in the 35 to 55 age range (not representative of most families, of course), that enduring marital relationships could be classified as five types divided between *utilitarian marriages* and *intrinsic marriages*. Although not all marriages were happy, all were enduring.

Utilitarian Marriages: Three Types of Unions Based on Convenience

A *utilitarian marriage* is one that is based on convenience. About 75 to 80% of the marriages in Cuber and Harroff's sample were in this category. There are three types of such marriages: *conflict-habituated, devitalized,* and *passive-congenial*.

■ Conflict-Habituated Marriages—"We thrive on conflict": **A *conflict-habituated marriage* is characterized by ongoing tension and unresolved**

conflict, "although it is largely controlled," say Cuber and Harroff (p. 44). Partners in this sort of relationship found fighting, whether verbal or physical, an acceptable way of dealing with each other.

Both spouses in these marriages privately acknowledged that incompatibility was pervasive and conflict was always a potential. As one physician married 25 years told the researchers (p. 45), "Of course we don't settle any of the issues. It's sort of a matter of principle *not* to. Because somebody would have to give in then and lose face for the next encounter."

■ **Devitalized Marriages—"Our marriage is a lost cause, but we're resigned to it": A *devitalized marriage* is one in which the partners have lost the strong emotional connection they once had but stay together out of duty.** These couples described themselves, say Cuper and Harroff, "as having been being 'deeply in love' during the early years, as having spent a great deal of time together, having enjoyed sex, and most importantly of all, having had a close identification with one another" (pp. 46–47). At the time of being interviewed, however, they spent little time together and enjoyed sex less.

Such time as they did spend together represented "duty time"—completing familial and community obligations together. Although one or both partners might feel dissatisfied or unfulfilled, they enjoy the comforts of the "habit cage," see no "engaging alternatives," and do not consider divorce.

■ **Passive-Congenial Marriages—"Our marriage is based on practicality, not emotion": In a *passive-congenial marriage*, the couple focuses on activities rather than emotional intimacy, but unlike those in devitalized marriages, these couples seem always to have done so.** These partners married with few emotional expectations of each other—and that continued to be the case. There was little conflict, but each person had separate interests and derived satisfaction from relationships with people other than each other, such as their children and friends.

These marriages were less likely to end in divorce than were marriages founded on higher expectations of emotional intensity.

Intrinsic Marriages: Two Types of Inherently Rewarding Unions

Intrinsic marriages **are marriages that are fundamentally rewarding.** Unlike utilitarian marriages, intrinsic marriages have little conflict and tension. Such marriages are of two types: *vital* and *total*.

■ **Vital Marriages—"We really enjoy being together and sharing most of our lives":** An uncommon form of enduring marriage, found in only 15% of Cuber and Harroff's sample, **a *vital marriage* is one in which the partners are intensely bound together psychologically and participate in each other's lives in many areas.** Couples in vital marriages find each other's company and sharing important. When these couples have conflicts, which are apt to be about real issues, they resolve them speedily. They are quick to compromise and often make sacrifices for each other. Sexuality is such a vital and pleasurable activity that it seems to pervade the relationship. "It's not only important, it's fun," says one. "You can't draw a line between being in bed together and just being alive together," says another (quoted in Cuber and Harroff 1965: 135–136).

■ **Total Marriages—"We intensely enjoy being together and sharing every area of our lives":** Even more uncommon than vital marriages and found in only 5% of the researchers' sample, a *total marriage* is one in which the partners are also intensely bound together psychologically but participate in each other's lives in all, not just some, areas and have very few areas of tension or conflict.

Such couples not only share their home life, friends, and recreational activities but may also even work together. Indeed, they may organize their time so that they are nearly always together. Although the mutual dependency of total-marriage couples can provide intense fulfillment, if the marriage ends with a death or divorce, it can be exceptionally difficult for the surviving partner.

2. Four Types of "Good Marriages" & Their Built-In "Antimarriages": Wallerstein & Blakeslee's Research

In their book *The Good Marriage: How and Why Love Lasts,* **Judith Wallerstein and Sandra Blakeslee** (1995) reported on their interviews with 50 northern California couples—white, well-educated, middle-class (again, you'll note, these couples are not representative of the population at large)—who had been married 10 to 40 years. Wallerstein and Blakeslee proposed four types of "good marriages": *romantic, rescue, companionate,* and *traditional.* Within each type, they suggested, are elements of an "antimarriage" that might endanger the relationship.

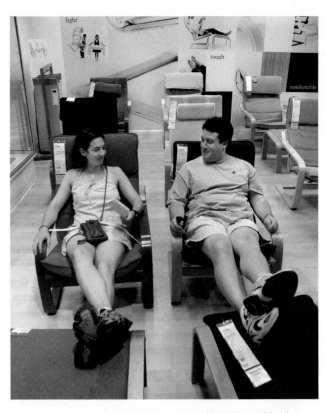

COMPANIONATE MARRIAGE. Unlike the romantic or other types of marriages, spouses in a companionate marriage base their relationship on equality and friendship. If you're presently in a relationship, is your partner also your good friend? ▲

The Romantic Marriage: "Our Passion Will Last Forever"

A *romantic marriage* **is filled with passion and sex. Romanic ideas of "destiny" and "ever after" pervade and keep the couple in a blissful state.**

The antimarriage: The built-in possible seeds of destruction are that the partners are so preoccupied with each other that they neglect their children and the rest of the world.

The Rescue Marriage: "We're Making Up for Our Past Unhappiness"

Partners in a *rescue marriage* base their relationship on the idea of healing. The point of the marriage is to provide each other with comfort for past suffering and unhappiness of early days or earlier relationships.

The antimarriage: Because husband and wife were wounded in the past, the relationship always allows the possibility for renewed strife based on earlier abuses.

EXAMPLE OF

An Intrinsic Marriage?

Bernard-Henry Lévy & Arielle Dombasle

Philosopher Bernard-Henry Lévy and actress Arielle Dombasle are the most famous couple in France. There is almost no equivalent in the United States, although married political advisors James Carville (he's a Democrat) and Mary Matalin (she's a Republican) may be closest.

Lévy, says writer Joan Juliet Buck, "is a unique figure, an action-driven intellectual who moves fast, writes fast, and is listened to with respect. Lévy's access to power and speed of action are virtually without precedent. Philosopher, publisher, novelist, journalist, filmmaker, defender of causes,

libertine, and provocateur, he is somewhere between gadfly and tribal sage, Superman and prophet" (Buck 2003: 88). Handsome and wealthy, Lévy, age 60, is able to alternate between a pleasant intellectual life in Paris and Morocco and adventurous travel to dangerous places such as war-torn Afghanistan.

Born in Connecticut in 1955, Arielle Dombasle has appeared in some 40 films but is best known for playing the sexy Marion in Eric Rohmer's 1983 *Pauline at the Beach*. Her "fragile little body with the astonishing figure, her constant good mood and crystalline singing voice are not the whole picture," writes Buck (p. 120). She also read philosophy at age 16, speaks four languages, and has lived in several countries. Buck (p. 120) quotes a friend as saying that Dombasle is a blessing for Lévy. "He needs to be loved, all the time. She's very intelligent and knows how to handle him." The only fight they have ever had, Lévy says, was over religion—he is an atheist and she is Catholic.

When they met, both were married to other people, and for seven years they conducted an affair in secret before leaving their respective spouses and marrying in 1993. "I felt this was exactly the woman I had been waiting for, who was right for me," Lévy says (in Buck, p. 121). "I understood that if I attached myself to her I would never leave her, that she would make all the others redundant, fill all the available space for passion and feelings."

WHAT DO YOU THINK? "Bernard and Arielle are where fact and fiction meet," a friend said about them. Does this kind of intrinsic relationship indeed seem like fiction—and unattainable to you? Are wealth, good looks, glamour, and experience with other lovers essential prerequisites? Or are intelligence and sensitivity all that's needed? What do you think of the fact that Lévy and Dombasle carried on a relationship for several years while married to other people? Do you think sexual fidelity—in our culture or any other—is a critical part of marital happiness and satisfaction?

The Companionate Marriage: "We Have a Friendly, Egalitarian Relationship"

In a *companionate marriage*, **the spouses base their relationship on equality and friendship.** They make time not only for each other but also equally for children and careers.

The antimarriage: If both spouses are too much involved in their respective careers, they might begin to spend less time with each other, and their relationship might become more like that of brother and sister.

The Traditional Marriage: "He's the Breadwinner, She's the Homemaker"

In a *traditional marriage*, **the husband is the income earner, and the wife takes care of the home and children.** This arrangement is, of course, the time-honored if stereotypical his-and-her partnership.

The antimarriage: In this classic relationship, the possibility is that the spouses will become so involved in their traditional roles and responsibilities that all they have in common is their interest in the children.

NONTRADITIONAL. Screen stars Ashton Kutcher, then age 26, who appeared in *Just Married*, and Demi Moore, then age 41, who acted in *Striptease* (back row center and right, respectively), before they married in September 2005. They are shown here with Moore's three daughters, whom she had with actor Bruce Willis during her second marriage. Asked by an interviewer whether he viewed Moore's children as "your little sisters or your kids," Kutcher said that he tried to help them with problems but that "to really define what I am to them would be very difficult." How would you feel about being in a relationship with an age gap of 15 years? Are you capable of being in a "random-type family"? ◀

What Can We Conclude?

If you consider the foregoing discussion carefully, you will probably be drawn to the following conclusions:

1. **Nonrepresentative samples:** None of the three classifications of marital/family relationships can be considered to reflect the North American population at large. The samples are too small or too nonrepresentative.
2. **Diverse marital relationships:** Whatever the marriage or family models you've observed in your own experience, these studies do not point to one kind being necessarily better than another. There are many ways in which a husband and a wife can relate to each other, and different people function better in one arrangement than in another.
3. **No pointers for happy marriage:** None of the relationships described seems to suggest a recipe for a stable and happy marriage. Are there pointers that can direct us to success? We consider this question next.

8.4 What Makes for a Successful Marriage?

MAJOR QUESTION What are the characteristics of successful marriages, and how could I achieve success in my own marriage?

PREVIEW Successful marriages are characterized by similar (homogamous) backgrounds, common characteristics and interests, economic security, and equity and equality in domestic work and child care. Marriage quality rests on commitment, acceptance and caring, and flexibility.

How do you define "success" in a marriage? By stability? There are many partnerships of mutual misery that last a lifetime. By happiness? No one is happy all the time. By flexibility? A couple need not agree on everything to be relatively comfortable with each other and able to solve problems together.

Perhaps the answer is all three qualities. That is, we suggest, ***marital success*, also called marital quality, is measured in terms of stability, happiness, and flexibility.**

Let us see what's required to increase the chances of a successful marriage. We look at what research shows about good marriages and specific suggestions for achieving your personal marital success.

Good Marriages: What the Research Shows

In 2007, a survey of 2,020 adults by the Pew Research Center (2007) found that the five top factors that people consider "very important" to a successful marriage are (1) faithfulness, (2) happy sexual relationship, (3) sharing household chores, (4) adequate income, and (5) good housing. (*See ■ Panel 8.5.*) Children ranked fairly low on the list—eighth, down from third in 1990.

These are people's opinions, of course. But are these really the characteristics of successful marriages? Many studies have looked into this matter (for example, Ortega et al. 1988; Billingsley et al. 1995; Wallerstein and Blakeslee 1995). Let us try to summarize some of their results.

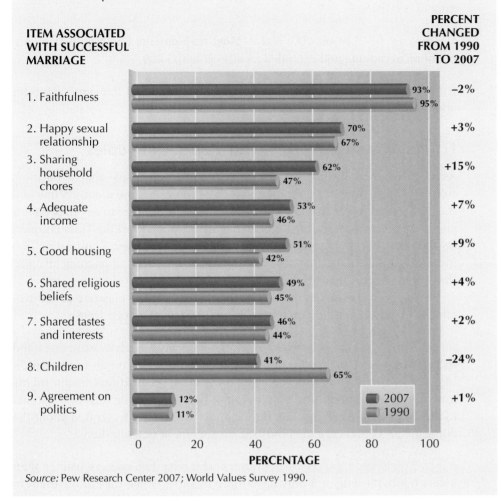

■ **PANEL 8.5 What Makes a Marriage Work?** Percent saying each is very important for a successful marriage: 2007 answers compared with 1990 answers. Children have fallen to eighth place in 2007 from third place in 1990. Sharing chores has assumed much more importance in 2007.

ITEM ASSOCIATED WITH SUCCESSFUL MARRIAGE	2007	1990	PERCENT CHANGED FROM 1990 TO 2007
1. Faithfulness	93%	95%	−2%
2. Happy sexual relationship	70%	67%	+3%
3. Sharing household chores	62%	47%	+15%
4. Adequate income	53%	46%	+7%
5. Good housing	51%	42%	+9%
6. Shared religious beliefs	49%	45%	+4%
7. Shared tastes and interests	46%	44%	+2%
8. Children	41%	65%	−24%
9. Agreement on politics	12%	11%	+1%

Source: Pew Research Center 2007; World Values Survey 1990.

Similar Backgrounds: Homogamy

*Homogamous marriages—that is, marriages between partners of similar education, ethnicity, race, religion, age, and social class—*are more apt to be successful than are heterogamous marriages (Ortega et al. 1988). *Heterogamous marriages are those in which the partners are of different education, ethnicity, race, religion, age, and/or social class.* The reason homogamous marriages seem to work better is, obviously, that people who share similar backgrounds and characteristics can adjust more readily to each other.

Commonalities: Similar Characteristics & Interests

Still, common background isn't everything. One study (Whyte 1990) of 459 successfully married women found that having similar social background was less important in marital quality than common characteristics, such as the following:

■ **Similar Temperaments:** The women reported that spouses had similarities in such characteristics as orderliness, temper, or being socially outgoing.

■ **Shared Interests:** Most also said the spouses had similar interests and recreational activities.

■ **Strong Family Ties on Both Sides:** Most respondents had supportive connections to parents and extended family on both sides.

■ **Similar Views on Children:** The couples generally had the same attitudes about child raising.

Economic Status, Work, & Two-Paycheck Couples

As we mentioned in Chapter 5, "Involvement," most people choose partners from within their socioeconomic class. The more income a couple has and the higher their occupational status, the more apt they are to say they have a good marriage (whether or not both partners work). Working-class couples, on the other hand, may find that juggling their work lives, commuting, job insecurity, inadequate finances, and child-care demands an ongoing struggle that severely taxes their marriage.

Having both spouses in the workforce can have either negative or positive effects, mostly depending on socioeconomic status (Kilborn 1994):

■ **Both Working—The Negatives:** Working-class wives such as waitresses and secretaries, whose paychecks are needed but whose jobs might not be fulfilling, are apt to come home bearing their work frustrations, resentments toward their husbands, and guilt over not being able to be full-time parents to their children. Working-class fathers may be similarly frustrated about the domestic and child-care demands the arrangement puts on them.

■ **Both Working—The Positives:** Couples who have two careers (rather than just two jobs) usually not only have more income, which may allow them to pay for child-care and domestic help. Both partners may also find their work sufficiently satisfying that it has a positive effect on their mental health and on their marriage.

Domestic Work & Child Care: The Importance of Equity & Equality

Two important factors in marital quality, according to one scholar (Schwartz 1994), are *equity* and *equality*.

■ **Equity:** Equity means that partners give in proportion to what they receive.

■ **Equality:** Equality means that the partners have equal status and are equally responsible for domestic, financial, and emotional tasks.

With these concepts in mind, how much time do you think married women spend on housework and child care? According to one study, in 1995, women—both full-time homemakers and employed wives—averaged 16 hours a week on housework, and men averaged 9 (Robinson and Godbey 1997). Another study found that in two-income families, women spent 34 hours a week on housework compared to their husbands' 18 (Presser 1993).

Clearly, the division of housework can create tension within a marriage. In her famous book *The Second Shift,* sociologist Arlie Hochschild (1989) argued that wives having to come from their jobs and work a "second shift" of housework and child care, without much help from their husbands, created great resentments that affected divorce rates.

Still, some men recognize the importance of equity and equality. Generally, the more educational achievement men have, they more they are apt to share the responsibility for traditional housework. Men whose wives have careers that are equally prestigious or more prestigious than their own also tend to participate more than do other husbands in housework.

Obviously, husbands and wives have to negotiate three matters here:

■ **Assignment of Responsibilities:** Who should do what? Who shops, who cooks? Who does laundry, who mows the lawn?

■ **Agreement on Schedule:** When will domestic chores be done? Will shopping be done twice a week? Will the house exterior be painted in the summer?

■ **Setting of Standards:** How perfectionistic should the execution be—that is, how clean, how neat, how orderly—and who determines that?

How well these matters are resolved reflects each spouse's commitment to the marriage. We return to this discussion in Chapter 12, "Work."

Your Personal Journey to Marriage Success

How can you achieve "marriage quality"—stability, happiness, and adjustment—in your own marriage, assuming that being married is what you want?

The first thing to realize is that marriage is a journey, not a destination, and that the journey should be its own reward. You might hope that this relationship will be fueled throughout by passionate, romantic love. The record shows, however, that unions of couples who marry amid passionate, whirlwind courtships are not apt to survive, mostly because the expectations and fantasies cannot be sustained (Pittman 1999). More to be hoped for is the transformation of that ecstasy and intensity into mature love—love that rests on commitment, acceptance and caring, and flexibility.

Commitment

Couples in happy marriages see their union as a long-term commitment. Divorce is not considered an option. This belief gives them the determination that will carry them through both good times and bad (Reiss 1980). It enables them to resist the signals of availability from others that might lead to extramarital affairs (Billingsley et al. 1995). It allows each partner to trust the other and be secure in the knowledge that the other will not leave.

Acceptance & Caring

Spouses in unhappy marriages often try to change each other to fulfill their own emotional needs, producing frustration and anger when they are unable to do so (Quinn and Odell 1998). By contrast, partners in happy marriages are accepting of each other for what they are—as individuals and as "good friends." More than that, they genuinely like each other and respect, cherish, and care about each other. They value each other's lives as ends in themselves. Finally, they are emotionally supportive of each other. During stressful times, they are able to provide mutual comfort and understanding.

Flexibility

It's important to recognize that marriages can be either static or flexible (O'Neill and O'Neill 1972; Scarf 1995; Lamanna and Riedmann 2000).

■ **Static:** *Static marriages* **don't change over time, don't allow for changes in the spouses, and rely on the fact of the legal marriage bond to enforce sexual exclusivity and permanence.**

■ **Flexible:** *Flexible marriages* **allow the partners to change over time and to grow as individuals and in the relationship.**

In flexible marriages, says one book, "partners are freer to reveal their changing selves and the parts of themselves that no longer fit into their established pattern. They can continue to be in touch at a deep emotional level while they alter the outer framework of their lives" (Lamanna and Riedmann 2000: 251).

Thus, a flexible marriage is one in which the spouses are able to make adjustments in the relationship while being in agreement on the issues that matter and are able to solve most of the problems that arise over time.

Vow Renewals & Personal Marriage Agreements

David P. Smalley has been married seven times in seven years—to the same woman. Smalley, age 59, and his wife, Marian, have participated in an annual "Say I Do Again" renewal-of-wedding-vows ceremony sponsored by their town, Cooper City, Florida. Smalley, who has been married for 21 years in all, says:

"We can't wait till next year to come so we can do it again. It just gets better and better" (quoted in Silverman 2003: D1).

Besides the formal and legal agreements we mentioned earlier—wedding vows, prenuptial agreements, and post-nuptial agreements—there are informal, nonlegal rites that many couples find satisfying. We consider *vow renewals* and *personal marriage agreements*.

■ **Vow Renewals:** **A** *vow renewal* **is a ceremony in which partners repeat their commitment to each other.** Vow-renewal ceremonies used to be held on special anniversaries, such as the 25th wedding anniversary. Today, however, many married couples—aided by an industry of resorts and cruises offering vow-renewal packages (including bouquet, renewal certificate, and photograph, as well as champagne, cake, and music)—are making it a regular event. An "officiant," who could be anyone, might state: "Having witnessed the vows you have just made to each other, I now pronounce you, once again, husband and wife" (Silverman 2003).

■ **Personal Marriage Agreements:** **A** *personal marriage agreement* **is a written agreement negotiated between**

CONTENTMENT. Over the long haul, do you think you could be happy in a static marriage? Or do you think flexibility is necessary to allow the two of you to be free "to reveal your changing selves"? ▼

STRUCTURAL-FUNCTIONAL (MACRO ORIENTATION)	CONFLICT (MACRO ORIENTATION)	SYMBOLIC INTERACTION (MICRO ORIENTATION)
■ Marriage helps maintain stability in society through manifest functions of sexual regulation and legitimacy of having children.	■ Traditional marriage and rigid sex/gender roles hinder potential for both males and females, exploit females, and result in stress for women (second shift) and men.	■ Through social interaction, people create the definition of marriage, ranging from traditional male-female unions to same-sex unions.
■ Marriage is viewed as means of providing economic and emotional support for spouses, as well as for offspring.	■ Changing nature of marriage (divorce, same-sex marriage, and contract marriage) reflects the adaptation of marriage to social pressures (economics, technology, social movements) and the need to legitimize other types of marriage.	■ They expect marriage to be a lifetime commitment or at least a form of socially acceptable serial monogamy.
■ Families of divorce and single-parent families are viewed as instances of family deterioration.	■ Traditional marriage is a source of social inequality and results in conflict over scarce resources and power.	■ People's personal experiences from their families of origin affect their views on the type of marriage they desire, even if they don't choose to wed.
■ Clearly defined sex/gender roles (instrumental and expressive) lend stability to marriage.		

married couples in which partners specify how they will behave in aspects of the relationship—their preferences, obligations, and sharing of labor and tasks. Although such an agreement might seem unromantic and legalistic, it can be very helpful not only in defining roles and role expectations in the relationship but also in encouraging communication and intimacy. Among the matters that couples may specify are (1) division of labor, both work and household; (2) how money will be handled and who will make what kinds of decisions; (3) privacy needs; (4) sexual relations, preferences and frequency; (5) relations with relatives and friends; (6) religious practices; (7) birth control and children; (8) vacations, whether together or separate; (9) renewal or renegotiation of marital agreements.

In Chapter 9, "Variations," we discuss the concept of relationship agreements and contracts between unmarried couples.

The accompanying table shows how the topic of marriage is viewed from three principal theoretical perspectives: structural-functional, conflict, and symbolic interaction. *(See ■ Panel 8.6.)*

Self-Assessment: Sternberg's Triangular Love Scale

We introduced Robert Sternberg's triangle of love in Chapter 4, "Love." This Self-Assessment applies some of those ideas to how you feel about your present spouse or, if you're in an unmarried relationship, your present lover.

Read each of the following statements, filling in the blank spaces with the name of one person you love or care for deeply. Rate your agreement with each statement according to the following scale, and enter the appropriate number between 1 and 9.

```
 1   2   3   4   5   6   7   8   9
Not at all    Moderately    Extremely
```

_____ 1. I am actively supportive of _____'s well-being.

_____ 2. I have a warm relationship with _____.

_____ 3. I am able to count on _____ in times of need.

_____ 4. _____ is able to count on me in times of need.

_____ 5. I am willing to share myself and my possessions with _____.

_____ 6. I receive considerable emotional support from _____.

_____ 7. I give considerable emotional support to _____.

_____ 8. I communicate well with _____.

_____ 9. I value _____ greatly in my life.

_____ 10. I feel close to _____.

_____ 11. I have a comfortable relationship with _____.

_____ 12. I feel that I really understand _____.

_____ 13. I feel that _____ really understands me.

_____ 14. I feel that I can really trust _____.

_____ 15. I share deeply personal information about myself with _____.

_____ 16. Just seeing _____ excites me.

_____ 17. I find myself thinking about _____ frequently during the day.

_____ 18. My relationship with _____ is very romantic.

_____ 19. I find _____ to be very personally attractive.

_____ 20. I idealize _____.

_____ 21. I cannot imagine another person making me as happy as _____ does.

_____ 22. I would rather be with _____ than with anyone else.

_____ 23. There is nothing more important to me than my relationship with _____.

_____ 24. I especially like physical contact with _____.

_____ 25. There is something almost "magical" about my relationship with _____.

_____ 26. I adore _____.

_____ 27. I cannot imagine life without _____.

_____ 28. My relationship with _____ is passionate.

_____ 29. When I see romantic movies and read romantic books, I think of _____.

_____ 30. I fantasize about _____.

_____ 31. I know that I care about _____.

_____ 32. I am committed to maintaining my relationship with _____.

_____ 33. Because of my commitment to _____, I would not let other people come between us.

_____ 34. I have confidence in the stability of my relationship with _____.

_____ 35. I could not let anything get in the way of my commitment to _____.

_____ 36. I expect my love for _____ to last for the rest of my life.

_____ 37. I will always feel a strong responsibility for _____.

_____ 38. I view my commitment to _____ as a solid one.

_____ 39. I cannot imagine ending my relationship with _____.

_____ 40. I am certain of my love for _____.

_____ 41. I view my relationship with _____ as permanent.

_____ 42. I view my relationship with _____ as a good decision.

_____ 43. I feel a sense of responsibility toward _____.

_____ 44. I plan to continue my relationship with _____.

_____ 45. Even when _____ is hard to deal with, I remain committed to our relationship.

Scoring

Psychologist Robert Sternberg sees love as being composed of three components: intimacy, passion, and commitment. The first 15 items in the scale reflect intimacy, the second 15 measure passion, and the final 15 reflect commitment. Add up your scores for each group of 15 items. Find the scores closest to your three totals in the appropriate column below to determine the degree to which you experience each of these three components of love.

According to Sternberg, high scores in all three components would indicate consummate love. However, uneven or low scores do not necessarily mean that a relationship is not strong: all relationships have ups and downs, and the nature of a relationship may change over time.

Source: Sternberg, R. 1988. The triangular love scale, from *The triangle of love: Intimacy, passion, commitment.* New York: Basic Books. Copyright © 1988 by Robert Sternberg. Reprinted by permission of the author.

Intimacy (Items 1–15)	Passion (Items 16–30)	Commitment (Items 31–45)	
93	73	85	Significantly below average
102	85	96	Somewhat below average
111	98	108	Average
120	110	120	Somewhat above average
129	123	131	Significantly above average

Key Terms Used in This Chapter

companionate marriage, p. 274
conflict-habituated marriage, p. 271
covenant marriage, p. 261
devitalized marriage, p. 272
empty-nest syndrome, p. 269
family life cycle, p. 265
flexible marriages, p. 280
heterogamous marriages, p. 277
homogamous marriages, p. 277
identity bargaining, p. 266

intrinsic marriages, p. 272
marital success, p. 276
marriage, p. 252
miscegenation, p. 256
passive-congenial marriage, p. 272
permanence, p. 260
personal marriage agreement, p. 280
postnuptial agreement, p. 264
prenuptial agreement, p. 262
rescue marriage, p. 273

rite of passage, p. 258
romantic marriage, p. 273
sexual exclusivity, p. 260
static marriages, p. 280
total marriage, p. 273
traditional marriage, p. 274
utilitarian marriage, p. 271
vital marriage, p. 272
vow renewal, p. 280

Summary

8.1 Why Do People Marry?

- Marriage can be defined as a legal union between a man and a woman.
- Positive reasons for marrying include emotional security, companionship, and the desire to be parents.
- Negative reasons for marrying include physical attractiveness or emotional security; pressure from parents, peers, partners, or pregnancy; and escape, rebellion, rebound, or rescue.

- In getting married, people have several expectations: (1) that they will undergo certain rituals or a rite of passage—engagement, wedding ceremony, and honeymoon; (2) that they will have sexual exclusivity and permanence in their relationship; and (3) that they are making an important legal commitment.
- A rite of passage can be viewed as an event that signals a major change from one social status to another. Other rites of passage include the engagement, the wedding, and the honeymoon.

- In making a pledge of monogamous marriage, most partners assume that their relationship will be built around the promises of sexual exclusivity and permanence. Sexual exclusivity means that each partner promises to have sexual relations only with the other. Permanence means that the partners promise to stay together for life.

- In addition to the commitments made to your partner regarding exclusivity and permanence, you also make a legal or contractual agreement with the state in which you live. This means that the state has an interest in how you terminate the marriage and in how you divide property and share children if you divorce.

- Because of the possibility of divorce in so many marriages, three additional contractual agreements—besides the legal contract a couple has with the state—have been developed: the covenant marriage, the prenuptial agreement, and the postnuptial agreement.

- A covenant marriage is an antidivorce contract in which couples demonstrate their strong commitment to marriage by (1) getting premarital counseling, (2) getting marital counseling in times of marital difficulties, and (3) agreeing not to divorce until after a separation of two years or after proving adultery or domestic abuse.

- The prenuptial agreement is a contract signed by the couple before the wedding that specifies in advance how property will be divided and children cared for in the event of divorce or one partner's death.

- A postnuptial agreement is the same as a prenuptial agreement except that it is worked out by partners who are already married to each other.

8.2 Changes in the Family Life Cycle: Scenes from a Marriage

- Family life has four phases: (1) beginning, with perhaps greatest marital satisfaction; (2) child rearing, often with less marital satisfaction; (3) middle age, with more marital satisfaction; and (4) aging.

- The beginning phase last about two to three years. During this stage, couples may experience the loss of independence, new friends and relatives, possible changes in career and domestic roles, and identity bargaining. Identity bargaining may occur when the realities of the marriage oblige spouses to adjust their idealized expectations of each other.

- The child-rearing stage can be characterized as a period of less marital satisfaction that corresponds to, though is not necessarily caused by, the most intense period of childbearing and child rearing.

- Child rearing can be viewed a encompassing a number of stages, beginning with the childbearing family that lasts about 2½ years, family with preschoolers that lasts about 3½ years, family with school children that lasts about 7 years, family with adolescents that lasts about 7 years, and finally family as launching center that lasts about 8 years. It is in this stage when children leave the family to establish their independence.

- During the child-rearing stage, couples may experience changes, including a decrease in the frequency of sexual relations, a shifting in domestic responsibilities, dependency on child-care services, and increased stress as a result of the additional responsibilities placed on them.

- The middle-age phase is normally a time when the last child has left the home and continues to retirement. In this phase, some parents, particularly mothers, experience what's called the empty-nest syndrome—a feeling of depression after the children have moved out—or the reverse possibility, which is referred to as the "not-so-empty-nest" or "boomerang" effect. This occurs when adult children, after being away for a few years, return to live with their parents because of high housing costs, low income, or divorce.

- The aging phase of marriage parallels the time when most income earners will be approaching retirement. Many people find this to be a time of adjustment to the new lifestyle and interaction with their spouse.

8.3 Different Kinds of Marriage Relationships

- Utilitarian marriages are marriages based on convenience. There are three types of such marriages. (1) A conflict-habituated marriage is characterized by ongoing tension and unresolved conflict. (2) A devitalized marriage is one in which the partners have lost the strong emotional connection they once had but stay together out of duty. (3) A passive-congenial marriage is one in which the couple focuses on activities rather than emotional intimacy, but unlike those in devitalized marriages, these couples seem always to have done so. Intrinsic marriages are marriages that are inherently rewarding. Such marriages are of two types: vital and total. A vital marriage is one in which the partners are intensely bound together psychologically and participate in each other's lives in many areas. A total marriage is one in which the partners are also intensely bound together psychologically but participate in each other's lives in all, not just some, areas and have very few areas of tension or conflict.

- Wallerstein and Blakeslee proposed four types of "good marriages": romantic, rescue, companionate, and traditional. Within each type, they suggested, are elements of an "antimarriage" that might put the relationship in jeopardy. (1) A romantic marriage is a passionate and lasting sexual relationship. The antimarriage: the built-in possible seeds of destruction are that the partners are so preoccupied with each other that they neglect their children and the rest of the world. (2) Partners in a rescue marriage base their relationship on the idea of healing. The point of the marriage is to provide each other with comfort for past suffering and unhappiness. The antimarriage: because husband and wife have wounded each other in the past, the relationship always allows the possibility for renewed strife based on earlier abuses. (3) In a companionate marriage, the spouses base their relationship on equality and friendship. The antimarriage: if both spouses are too much involved in their respective careers, they may begin to spend less time with each other, and their relationship can become more like that of brother and sister. (4) In a traditional marriage, the husband is the income earner, and the wife takes care of the home and children. This arrangement is, of course, the time-honored if stereotypical his-and-her partnership. The antimarriage: in this classic relationship, the possibility is that the spouses will become so involved in their traditional roles and responsibilities that all they have in common is their interest in the children.

8.4 What Makes for a Successful Marriage?

- Marital success, also called marital quality, is measured in terms of stability, happiness, and flexibility.

Take It to the Net

Among the Internet resources on marriage and families are the following:

- **Marriage Builders**
  www.marriagebuilders.com
- **The Nest.** Online community for newlyweds.
  www.thenest.com
- **Suite101 Interfaith Relationships.** Advice on interfaith relationships and weddings.
  www.suite101.com/article.cfm/interfaith_relationships

- Homogamous marriages are between partners of similar education, ethnicity, race, religion, age, and social class. Heterogamous marriages are those in which the partners are of different education, ethnicity, race, religion, age, and/or social class.
- Whyte's study found that similar characteristics and interests—such as similar temperaments, shared interests, strong family ties on both sides, and similar views on children—were important in marital quality.
- The more income a couple has and the higher their occupational status, the more apt they are to say they have a good marriage (whether or not both partners work). Working-class couples, however, may find that juggling their work lives, commuting, job insecurity, inadequate finances, and child-care demands an ongoing struggle that severely taxes their marriage.
- According to Schwartz (1994), two important factors in marital quality are equity and equality. Equity means that partners give in proportion to what they receive. Equality means that the partners have equal status and are equally responsible for domestic, financial, and emotional tasks.
- The first thing to realize is that marriage is a journey, not a destination, and that the journey should be its own reward. Mature love is based on commitment, acceptance and caring, and flexibility.
- Static marriages don't change over time, don't allow for changes in the spouses, and rely on the fact of the legal marriage bond to enforce sexual exclusivity and permanence. Flexible marriages allow the partners to change over time and to grow as individuals and in the relationship. Many couples repeat or define their commitment to each other through vow renewals, relationship agreements, or personal marriage agreements.

- **CousinCouples.com.** An interactive website for those who are romantically involved with their cousin. Provides support and factual information. *www.cousincouples.com*
- **Prenuptial Agreement.** Go to this website for Nolo ("Law for All"), and type in "prenuptial agreement" in the "Search the Site" space. (You can also use this site for information about postnuptial agreements.) *www.nolo.com/lawcenter/ency*

VARIATIONS
Nonmarital Families & Households

What about Alternatives?

Following is a letter to New York Times Magazine *advice columnist Randy Cohen (2003), otherwise known as* The Ethicist, *who answers readers' questions about their ethical dilemmas:*

"Senior citizens often pair off, not for marriage but for intimacy and someone to count on in an emergency. My companion of six years developed a debilitating, incurable condition three years ago and is no longer an active and engaging companion. He has family in other parts of the country and is well-off financially but expects me to stay with him. Were our situations reversed, he would surely leave me. May I leave him and seek other companionship?"
—Anonymous

How would you deal with this question? Are the obligations of friendship, even intimate friendship, the same as those in a marriage? Is the letter writer duty bound to act like this man's wife and become his full-time caretaker? Or, even though she is his friend, may she feel ethically free to abandon him in his hour of need, since he is financially comfortable and has family elsewhere?

The answers, says ethicist Cohen, are *no, no,* and *no.* The right thing to do, instead of dropping him, is to help him arrange for his continuing care, something that will be made easier by his having money and grown children. After that, the form the friendship takes is up to them both. "You are free to seek what companions you like—for folk dancing, card playing, or sex," Cohen says. "He can accept or reject such a relationship. However, if by 'stay with him' your friend means monogamously, then you have a gen-

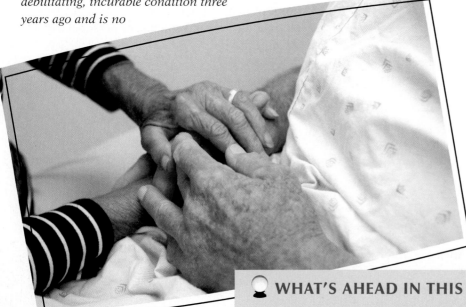

💡 WHAT'S AHEAD IN THIS CHAPTER

We give some examples of newer forms of living arrangements. We then discuss the world of singles and single parents. Next we discuss gay and lesbian relationships and conclude with a discussion of communal relationships.

uine conflict, one the two of you must resolve" (Cohen 2003: 29).

This, then, is the main lesson: As often happens in nonmarital relationships, the pair has drifted into an ambiguous association in which neither is sure what to expect from the other. "What you need," says Cohen, "is clarity, and that comes from conversation."

Older heterosexual couples living together as roommates don't get much play in the mass media and popular culture. But in the post–*Ozzie and Harriet* world, other nonmarital relationships are no longer rare:

■ *Singles:* Many TV dramas are based around the (often comic) problems of singles, from bachelors Jerry Seinfeld, Drew Carey, and Charlie Sheen (in *Two and a Half Men*) to the career-minded single women of *Grey's Anatomy* and *Boston Legal*. *Sex and the City* presented four glamorous New York females who, in one description, "discard men quicker than last season's bag and shoes" (Edwards 2000: 47). How true to life are they? In one poll (reported in Poniewozik 2000) asking 186 never-married women whether they had as much sex as those in *Sex and the City,* 21% said yes, 73% said no.

Television is often ahead of the curve in portraying unconventional households, especially those of single parents. In 1975, on *One Day at a Time,* divorcee Ann Romano raised two headstrong teens alone. On the 1987 show *Full House,* a widower is helped by his rock 'n' roller brother-in-law to raise his three girls. In 1992, Vice President Dan Quayle famously

caused a stir for criticizing reporter *Murphy Brown* for getting pregnant by her ex-husband and then declining marriage. In 1999, on *Once and Again,* a sexy, divorced father of two dated a newly divorced and also sexy mother of two. Is real life like this? Sometimes, perhaps—but not as easy.

■ *Gays:* Homosexuals have increasingly found acceptance in the mass media, with gay characters appearing in a variety of roles on prime-time TV—*ER, Will & Grace, Dawson's Creek, Brothers and Sisters,* and others. Interestly, the treatment of gays has become bolder over the years: The cable-TV show *Queer as Folk* (aired 2000–2005), which was billed as an "unapologetic celebration of gay life in all its forms" and featured lots of sex between young gays, was a far cry from the near-blackout of homosexuals in earlier TV—or even from the milder shows like *Will & Grace.* Focusing on a group of gay men and women living in Pittsburgh, *Queer as Folk* tracked this circle of friends through their "freewheeling nightlife and emotional ups and downs, AIDS, drug abuse, and harrowing gay-bashing," as one article put it ("Showtime revives 'Queer as Folk'" 2002). In its first year, *QAF* got overwhelmingly positive audience mail, an audience fairly evenly divided between gay men and straight women, with 100,000 messages of support versus only 100 of criticism. Ironically, the loudest denunciations came from homosexuals who resented the show's depiction of gay promiscuity.

ON THE WEB Alternatives to Marriage Project

www.unmarried.org

The Alternatives to Marriage Project was established to provide information and support to unmarried people, both heterosexual and homosexual. Visit its website to get a warm-up to the subject of this chapter.

MAJOR QUESTIONS
you should be able to answer

What kind of alternative household structure might I consider good for me?

What kind of single am I or could I be?

What is my understanding of homosexuality, and how does it relate to the research?

Would I ever consider communal living, group marriage, or open marriage?

9.1 Different Family & Household Relationships

MAJOR QUESTION What kind of alternative household structure might I consider good for me?

PREVIEW Family structures and households are changing. Four examples are platonic "roommate marriages"; commuter, living-apart-together, and transnational marriages; grandparents raising children alone; and "adultolescents" living with parents. We discuss families, nonfamily households, and lifestyles and consider principal shifts for household arrangements and their reasons.

"At least one had two wives," wrote Associated Press reporter David Crary (2002), "some were married but had children out of wedlock, while many others were divorced and remarried. Others, straight and gay, lived with long-term partners now in legal limbo."

Legal limbo indeed. Some of the kinship systems of the roughly 3,000 victims of the September 11, 2001, terrorist attack on New York's World Trade Center created considerable headaches for lawyers and survivors dealing with claims for compensation and inheritances. For instance, Marmily Carbrera, the female survivor of Pedro Checo, a man with whom she had lived for more than a decade and who had fathered her two young sons, feared being excluded from compensation because New York does not recognize common-law marriages. "She's not being recognized as Pedro's wife," said her lawyer, Helen MacFarlane (quoted in Crary 2002). "Our compassion should not be limited by some of the more narrow views [of relationships] that we have held historically."

Said one lawyer involved with the World Trade Center survivors: "I am struck, in meeting with families, by the concept of the extended nuclear family—children by multiple spouses, aunts and uncles who were pivotal to the victims' lives" (Kenneth Feinberg, quoted in Crary 2002). Other victims were single parents, whose surviving children had to be taken in by their grandparents.

Different Ways of Living: Four Examples

The family structures and households of the New York 9/11 victims reflect the remarkable diversity of relationships in U.S. society today, and there are

- **Is the percentage of married couples declining?** Married-couple families declined from 70.5% of all families in 1970 to 49.7% in 2005. The percentage of people living alone went from 17.1% to 25.5%.[a]

- **What is the increase in young people moving back in with their parents?** The number of young adults moving back home increased 50% between 1970 and 1990.[b]

- **What proportion of American adults are single divorced?** About 10.2% of the adult population in the United States in 2005 consists of single divorced men and women—up from 6.2% in 1980. [c]

- **Are single-parent households increasing?** U.S. families headed by single mothers increased from 5.4 million in 1980 to 9.9 million in 2005. Most single mothers are never-married or divorced, and the fastest-growing category is white women. Single-father households increased from 616,000 in 1980 to 2 million in 2005.[d]

- **How many grandparents are raising their grandchildren?** About 2.4 million grandparents were primary caregivers to a grandchild, according to the 2000 census, with most grandparents being white, ages 50 to 64, and living in nonurban areas.[e]

- **What percentage of the population is homosexual?** In one survey, 2.8% men and 1.4% women called themselves homosexual or bisexual. However, 9% of men and 4% of women said they had had a same-sex sexual experience.[f]

[a] Roberts 2006; American Association for Single People 2001. [b] Schoeni and Ross 2005. [c] U.S. Census Bureau 2006c: Table 54. [d] U.S. Census Bureau 2006c. [e]Clemetson 2000; Armas 2002b. [f] Laumann et al. 1994.

NUMBERS THAT MATTER
Different Folks

---

many others. By way of examples, consider the following four common variations: (1) platonic "roommate marriages"; (2) commuter, living-apart-together, and transnational marriages; (3) grandparents raising children alone; and (4) "adultolescents" living with parents.

1. Platonic "Roommate Marriages"

You've seen this kind of arrangement celebrated on such television programs as *Sister, Sister; Three's Company;* and *Two and a Half Men*—people living under the same roof as roommates for years and years. There is no sexual bond, but the roommates develop a deep emotional attachment to one another. As one article describes it, "These roommate couples build lives and connect in a way that was previously reserved only for those who are married" (Ahn 2001: B8).

Platonic "roommate marriages" are especially apt to develop in urban areas with high housing costs, such as San Francisco and New York City. According to the 2000 census, in 1998, among 25- to 34-year-olds, almost 2 million people lived in shared households; 34.7% of them were not married.

Living with a long-term roommate "can be a training ground for intimacy," says Leonard Donk (quoted in Ahn 2001: B8), a psychologist who specializes in personal relationships. "You're building a household with someone and learning to compromise."

2. Living Apart: Commuter, Living-Apart-Together, & Transnational Marriages

There have always been circumstances—war, imprisonment, economic necessity, a spouse's job-related travel—in which both partners in a marriage must live apart for some time. In 2003–2004, for instance, members of the U.S. military serving in Iraq were separated from their families for many months—and, in a switch from previous wars, many more of those who were divided by thousands of miles from their spouses and children were women (Alvarez 2007).

A so-called commuter marriage is somewhat different. **A *commuter marriage* is a dual-career marriage in which each partner lives in a different geographical area, yet the pair still maintain their commitment to their family.** A 2003 census report (cited in Lara 2005) found that 3 million married couples live in separate residences. These were people who did not declare themselves "separated," which could be a sign of a troubled marriage, and many were no doubt in the military. According to anecdotal evidence, however, long-distance marriages seem to be spreading beyond the armed services. One spouse, for instance, might be a college professor, the other a medical researcher. The distance between them might be a day's drive, or it might be a cross-country flight. They might unite with each other every weekend, once a month, or a few times a year. The important feature here is that both people are working at a demanding career that requires that they be separated (Kiefer 2000).

Commuter couples don't particularly want to be separated, but they also don't want to give up their respective careers—or each other. The marriage requires a great deal of effort, but couples don't see their decision to commute as a matter of choice (Gerstel and Gross 1987a, 1987b). Such marriages clearly are more successful when there are no children.

Other married couples willingly choose to not live together. Known as ***living-apart-together (LAT) couples* or dual dwelling duos (DDDs), these are happily married couples who are committed to each other but who live in separate quarters** (Hess and Catell 2001; Cagen 2004). For instance, San Francisco musician and comic Joshua Brody and his wife, financial consultant Juliana Grenzebeck, have been married for seven years, but all during that time they have lived across the street from each other (Lara 2005). LATs say that disregarding Hollywood expectations of what marriage is supposed to be like and living in separate residences helps keep their relationship alive and fresh.

***Transnational marriages* are those in which one partner is in the United States and the other—and perhaps the children—are in another country** (Chavez 1992). This kind of arrangement, which may involve separations of months or years, is characteristic of many immigrant families, both among the approximately 1 million immigrants who win permanent resident status every year as among the 500,000 people who enter the United States illegally. Because of tougher immigration rules, such as the 1996 Illegal Immigration Reform and Immigrant Responsibility Act, it is harder for illegal immigrant parents to return home to see their families and children (Suárez-Orozco et al. 2005; Hendricks 2005).

3. Skipped-Generation Households: Grandparents Raising Grandchildren

Harriet Jackson-Lyons raised six children alone in a tough Boston neighborhood and put them through college. But in her seventies, she again became a full-time parent, raising her 9-year-old grand-child after her daughter died of a massive coronary. Jackson-Lyons is one of more than 2.4 million grandparents found by the 2000 census to be primary caregivers to a grand-child, usually because of death, drugs, divorce, abandonment, incarceration, or mental ill-ness. In the majority of such "skipped-genera-tion households," the grandparents are white, between the ages of 50 and 64, and live in nonurban areas (Clemetson 2000; Armas 2002b). Nationally, 4.5 million children are living in grandparent-headed households, according to the 2000 census, a 30% increase from 1990 to 2000. In 1999, 19% of the grand-parents serving as primary caregivers were liv-ing in poverty (Haskell 2003).

MAMA GRANDMA. Grandparent-headed households have increased significantly in recent years, and many grandparents are pri-mary caregivers to a grandchild. Do you know of any "skipped-generation" older per-son currently raising children? Why did this come about? ▲

The biggest hardship is financial, although the sudden responsibility late in life also results in stress, resentment toward the grand-children's parents, and legal conflicts. A few states have programs that provide guardianship subsidies for grandparents, but sometimes getting legal custody requires suing the grandparent's own child. Without custody, however, grand-parents have few rights, so it can be difficult to get medical care or even enroll the grandchild in school. A housing experiment in New York City called GrandParentFamily Apartments offers 51 apartments built exclusively for grandparents raising grandchildren (Williams 2005).

4. "Adultolescents" Living with Parents: Failure to Launch?

What are your plans after graduation? Get a job, get a place of your own, get married, have children? Or go home and live with your parents?

Just as certain bird species continue to support (feed) their offspring after they are supposed to leave the nest (Radford and Ridley 2006), so many young, single college graduates also enter a period known as "postmodern postadolescence" (Kay Hymowitz, cited in Furstenberg et al. 2004) by return-ing to the homes of their parents. Otherwise known as boomerangs, Peter Pans, bungee-kids, twixters, kidults, and thresholders, such **adultolescents are adult children, usually in their twenties, who have moved back in with their parents.** The phenomenon has been the subject of the movie *Failure to Launch* (with Matthew McConaughey playing a 35-year-old who lives with his parents); syndicated television series such as *Seinfield* and *Friends* (featuring young Americans living more like teenagers than adults); and several recent books, including *The Myth of Maturity* (Apter 2001), *Mom, Can I Move Back in with You?* (Gordon and Shaffer 2004), and *Boomerang Nation* (Furman 2005). According to a University of Michigan study of 6,000 young adults, the proportion of people in their twenties living with their par-ents increased 50% between 1970 and 1990 (Schoeni and Ross 2005). Forty-eight percent of students graduating in 2006 said they would move back into their parents' home after graduation, and 44% of 2005 graduates were still living with their parents the following year (Kantrowitz and Tyre 2006: 56).

People from certain ethnic groups (Asian, African American, and Hispanic) and cultures (such as Mexico and Italy) often have particularly close family

ADULTOLESCENT? Many single, college-age children report that they plan to move back in with their parents after graduation. Is this something you might consider? ▲

ties, and adult children stay home longer (Jayson 2006a). But others are latecomers to this trend, driven by today's economic realities—student loans, credit card debt, high housing costs, stalled paychecks, the need for graduate training, and the like—forcing them to rely more on help from their parents (Kamenetz 2006, Draut 2007). Although some critics say that the willingness of parents to subsidize their adult children prolongs their adolescence, others argue that the material support helps them make a smoother transition than those struggling on their own. Most young adults find a way to make the transition to independent singlehood before the age of 34 (Arnett 2006).

New Family Arrangements

The variations just discussed are only four examples of today's kinds of living arrangements. We are also seeing many more instances in which the wife is the family's better-paid or even sole breadwinner—a so-called "Alpha Earner"—while the husband stays home to look after the children and the household. According to a *Newsweek* poll, 54% of Americans know a couple in which the woman is clearly the major wage earner and the man's career is secondary (Tyre and McGinn 2003). There is also an increase in the number of extended families whose members, instead of scattering throughout the country, are moving in with one another. In fact, according to the 2000 census (cited in Fletcher 2002), the number of households with three generations under one roof has doubled since 1980, and the number of young adults moving back home is up 6%.

Are all these examples of alternative families? And what do the trends mean?

Traditional Families, Nonfamily Households, & Alternative Arrangements

To bring some clarity to this discussion, let us distinguish among the following:

■ **Family:** As we stated in Chapter 1, "Seeking," **a traditional *family* is a unit made up of two or more people who are related by blood, marriage, or adoption and who live together.** This definition therefore excludes foster families, couples who cohabit, homosexual couples, and communal arrangements in which a child is reared by several people besides the parents.

■ **Nonfamily Household:** A category used by the Census Bureau, **a *nonfamily household* consists of (1) a person who lives alone or (2) people who live with unrelated individuals within a housing unit,** such as a room, apartment, or house. Clearly, all families form households, but not all households contain families. They could contain singles, college students, seniors, live-together couples (straight or gay), and so on (Ahlburg and De Vita 1992).

■ **Alternative Arrangements or Lifestyles:** **A *lifestyle* is the pattern by which a person organizes his or her living arrangements in relation to others,** whether a single parent, cohabiting heterosexual, one-half of a gay couple, or whatever. The word *variations* in our chapter title suggests that we are discussing living arrangements that are alternatives to traditional heterosexual marriage, although we certainly don't suggest that these alternatives are either better or worse than the traditional institution.

The word *lifestyle* also seems to imply choice, but many people's lifestyles—and the ability to escape or reshape them—are constrained by such matters as education, finances, and perhaps even biology.

Principal Shifts in Household Arrangements

Several patterns have emerged in recent years that signify a move away from traditional families, reflecting social forces such as increased cost of living, need for more education, new forms of birth control, and more liberated views about women's roles.

■ **Decline in the Percentage of Married-Couple Households:** Between 1970 and 2005, according to census figures, the percentage of U.S. households with married couples dropped from 70.5% to 49.7%. More than one in four households—27%—now consist of people living alone (Roberts 2006). *(See* ■ *Panel 9.1.)* Does this mean that marriage is doomed? Actually, as sociologist Stephanie Coontz (2006) points out, 90% of Americans will eventually marry (down from 95% in the 1950s and 1960s). Indeed, census data show that the majority (71%) of men and women in 2006 had been married by the time they were 30 to 34 years old, and among men and women age 65 and older, 96% had been married (U.S. Census Bureau 2007).

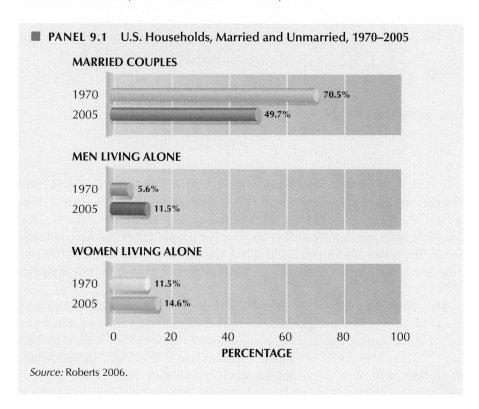

■ **PANEL 9.1   U.S. Households, Married and Unmarried, 1970–2005**

MARRIED COUPLES

1970   70.5%
2005   49.7%

MEN LIVING ALONE

1970   5.6%
2005   11.5%

WOMEN LIVING ALONE

1970   11.5%
2005   14.6%

0   20   40   60   80   100
PERCENTAGE

Source: Roberts 2006.

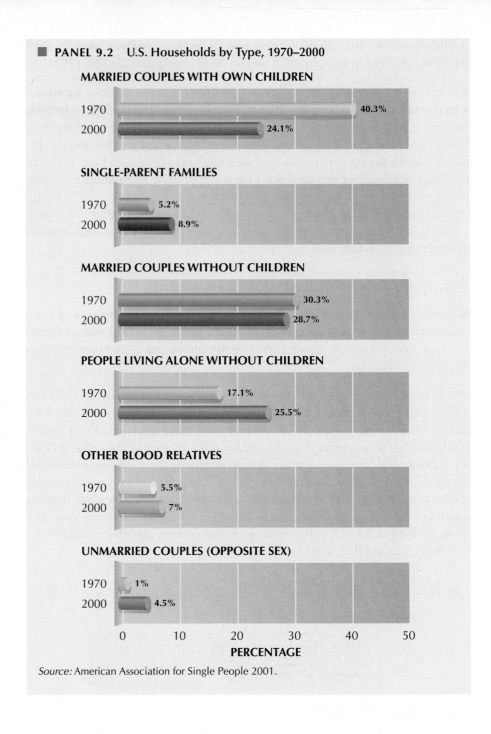

■ PANEL 9.2   U.S. Households by Type, 1970–2000

MARRIED COUPLES WITH OWN CHILDREN

1970   40.3%
2000   24.1%

SINGLE-PARENT FAMILIES

1970   5.2%
2000   8.9%

MARRIED COUPLES WITHOUT CHILDREN

1970   30.3%
2000   28.7%

PEOPLE LIVING ALONE WITHOUT CHILDREN

1970   17.1%
2000   25.5%

OTHER BLOOD RELATIVES

1970   5.5%
2000   7%

UNMARRIED COUPLES (OPPOSITE SEX)

1970   1%
2000   4.5%

0   10   20   30   40   50
PERCENTAGE

Source: American Association for Single People 2001.

■ **Decline in Percentage of Households with Children:** Between 1970 and 2000, the percentage of households with children dropped from 45% to 36%. *(See* ■ *Panel 9.2.)* Among the factors contributing to this decline: lower birth rates, fewer children per family, delays by younger people in getting married, and longer life spans (DeVita 1996). In 2004, the birth rate was 14 per 1,000 persons, down from 16.7 per 1,000 in 1990 (National Center for Health Statistics 2006).

Minorities are much more likely than whites are to live in households with children, primarily, it's suggested, because a higher proportion of minorities are of child-bearing age and because minorities tend to have higher fertility rates. Whereas only 32% of white households had at least one child under age 18 in 1995, 40% of minority households did (De Vita 1996).

The days of the suburbs being dominated by families consisting of Mom, Dad, and the kids are gone. Today, the married-with-children suburban household is, like housing in the cities, yielding to nonfamily households—homes headed by young, single professionals, single parents, and elderly widows, for instance. The 2000 census showed that in suburbs in the nation's 102 largest metropolitan areas, nonfamilies made up 29% of households, up from 27% ten years earlier. Married-with-children homes had declined from 28% to 27%.

Among the reasons for the changes: increase in divorce, causing a rise in single-parent homes; the death of a spouse, leaving more widows and widowers; departure of children of the Baby Boom generation, leaving aged, "empty-nester" parents; and the influx of young professionals from the cities, escaping high urban rents or moving closer to jobs in suburban office parks (Brookings Institution, cited in Armas 2002a).

The Reasons for Changes in Families & Households

The reasons for the changes in households and families are as follows (Bruce et al. 1995):

■ **Women's Age at Marriage and Childbearing:** More adults are remaining single longer. The median age at first marriage has been rising since the 1950s: In 1970, it was 23.2 years for men and 20.8 years for women; in 2005, it was 27.1 for men and 25.8 for women (U.S. Census Bureau 2006a: Table MS-2). Also, women are having their first child at a later age: The mean age for American women between ages 15 and 44 at the birth of their first baby rose from 21.4 years in 1970 to 26.5 in 2005 (Hamilton et al. 2007: Table 7).

■ **Smaller Households:** Families and households have gotten smaller. In 1970, the average household in the United States was 3.14 people. In 2007, it was 2.57 (U.S. Census Bureau 2006b). The changes in household size have much to do with the kinds of households being formed—married couple, single parent, nonfamily (Bryson and Casper 1998).

■ **More Burden on Working Parents:** The burden on parents who are still of working age has increased because of having to support not just younger dependents but also older ones: their own parents and other elderly relatives.

■ **More Female Households:** The proportion of households headed by females has increased enormously. The number of families headed by single mothers increased from 3 million in 1970 to 10.4 million in 2006 (U.S. Census Bureau 2007).

■ **More Women Workers:** The percentage of women working has increased as the percentage of men has declined. Families in which both parents are working doubled from 1976 to 1998—from 31% to 62%. In 2002, over 71% of mothers with children under the age of 18 were in the workforce.

In the next three sections, we discuss single, gay and lesbian, and communal households.

9.2 The Single Way of Life

MAJOR QUESTION What kind of single am I or could I be?

PREVIEW We describe the three types of heterosexual singles: never married, widowed, and divorced. We also discuss myths and realities about singles and explain some different categories of singles. Finally, we briefly discuss single parents.

"WHO NEEDS A HUSBAND?" shouted the *Time* magazine cover blurb over a photo of the stars of the television drama *Sex and the City*. "More women are saying no to marriage and embracing the single life. Are they happy?"

The inside article described a 32-year-old project manager for Chase Bank of Texas in Houston, who had dated several men but decided that marriage was something she wanted only if she found the right companion. "I've finally matured enough to acknowledge that there's more to life than being married," said Jodie Hannaman (quoted in Edwards 2000: 47). "I'd like to get married and have kids, but something in the last few years has changed. I'm happier being single."

The World of Heterosexual Singles

Single is defined as, among heterosexuals, the never-married, widowed, or divorced. During the first half of the 20th century, most people tended to marry, and to marry at younger ages. Since then, the trend has been reversed, and many youths and young adults seem to be committed to themselves first and marriage later, if and when it happens at all. As a result, single adults without children went from 17.1% in 1970 to 25.5% in 2000 (American Association for Single People 2001). More and more people are putting off wedded bliss: In 2003, according to Census Bureau figures (cited in Armas 2004), one-third of men and nearly one-quarter of women ages 30 to 34 have never been married, nearly four times the rates in 1970.

When Hannaman says she's happier being single, is she just putting up a brave front? Or can unmarried, childless women—and men—really find happiness? Would having a child—but without a spouse or partner—make their lives more fulfilling? Let's consider these and other questions. We begin by considering the three types of singles: (1) never-marrieds, (2) widowed, and (3) divorced.

1. The Never-Married

Never-married singles consist principally of those who, like Jodie Hannaman, would like to get married. Indeed, by age 65, only 4.8% of men and 4.1% of women in the United States have never been married (U.S. Census Bureau 2006c: Table 55). In 2005, 29.6% of adults had never been married in the United States—up from 20.3% in 1980 (U.S Census Bureau 2006c: Table 54).

Some social trends that encourage youths or young adults to not marry or to delay marriage are discussed next.

■ **Lack of Potential Marriage Partners: The *sex ratio* is the ratio of men to women within a particular social group,** usually expressed as the number of males for every 100 females. In 1948, the sex ratio was about even; by 1996, there were 95 men for every 100 women (U.S. Census Bureau 1998: Table 15). Today, most of the shortage of men is in older age groups, with more men than women among those in their twenties and early thirties (Weeks 1996).

However, African American, Chinese American, and Japanese American women, for instance, perceive that there are fewer suitable marriage partners (Ferguson 2000). Singlehood is increasing among Latinos and African Americans, both men and women.

■ **Economic Changes:** Economic changes may make marriage at earlier ages seem less attractive (Lloyd and South 1996). For instance, more employment options are currently open to women than existed previously, and more women are enrolled in college. Thus, women need not marry for economic support.

On the other hand, during economic downturns, men tend to postpone marriage (Rodgers and Thornton 1985). Among African Americans, both men and women are more apt not to marry when fewer jobs are available (Lichter et al. 1991; Fossett and Kiecolt 1993).

■ **More Liberal and Individualistic Sexual and Social Standards:** Especially with widespread contraceptive techniques available, men and women need not be forced into marriage because of unexpected pregnancy (Cherlin 1981). In addition, as we discussed in Chapter 5, "Involvement," because of society's relatively greater tolerance of cohabitation, more people may be postponing or rejecting marriage, electing for a more individualistic rather than familial lifestyle (Montgomery and Sorell 1997). And as sociologist Peter Stein (1981) has suggested, more people are moving away from marriage and family norms as these norms conflict with the possibility for individual development.

Are unmarried singles happy? It seems that most are. One 12-year study that compared never-marrieds with first-marrieds and remarrieds after divorce (controlled for age, race, income, and education) found that most never-married reported that they were "a great deal" happy or "quite a bit" happy (Jacques 1998). We explore this subject a bit further later in the chapter.

2. The Widowed

About 6.4% of the adult population in the United States consists of widows and widowers, down from 8% in 1980 (U.S. Census Bureau 2006c: Table 54). The decline in death rates during the past century has reduced the probability that young and middle-aged adults will become widowed. However, as they grow older, women are more apt to become widowed than men are—perhaps because men treat their bodies with more indifference owing to a "macho" world view (Williams 2003). Widowed females are less apt to find new spouses because of the *marriage gradient* and the *marriage squeeze*, as we discussed in Chapter 5, "Involvement." In terms of happiness, the widowed are less happy than married people, but are happier than divorced people (Glenn and Weaver 1988).

3. The Divorced

About 10.2% of the adult population in the United States consists of single divorced men and women—up from 6.2% in 1980 (U.S. Census Bureau 2006c: Table 54). As has been mentioned, divorced people are considerably less happy than married people and also less happy than the widowed. We discuss separation and divorce in detail in Chapter 14, "Uncoupling."

Myths & Realities about Singles

Never-married heterosexuals approaching age 50 have to cope with all kinds of stereotypes. He is said to be a "confirmed bachelor," she is a "lifelong spinster." He is "commitment-phobic" or "has too-high standards." She is "flighty" or "unable to catch a husband." Even younger singles have to deal with exaggerations good and bad. Let's consider what some of these are.

What's Not True about Singles

Two scholars, **Leonard Cargan and Matthew Melko** (1982), found that a number of popular myths exist about being single. Although their research was done some time ago, you might still hear erroneous statements such as the following:

■ *"Singles Are Self-Centered":* The reality: Singles actually are more involved with friends than married people are. They also tend to be more active in community service projects, probably because they make more time for them.

■ *"Singles Are Financially Better Off":* The reality: Although there are, of course, affluent professionals who are single, more singles than marrieds live below the poverty level. In general, married couples are better off, often because both spouses are employed.

■ *"Singles Are Happier":* The reality: Singles tend to believe they are happier than married people, perhaps because they spend more time at leisure activities (movies, clubs, restaurants) than marrieds do. However, they are also more likely to be lonely, depressed, anxious, and stressed.

■ *"Singles Are Confirmed in Their Singlehood":* The reality: Most singles expect to be single for only a short period of time and to be married within five years.

Some feel, however, that the benefits of being married do not outweigh the benefits of being unattached.

What Is True about Singles

Cargan and Melko also found the following characterizations of singles to be fairly accurate:

■ **Singles Have More Free Time:** Compared to married people, singles have more time and more opportunities for leisure and volunteer activities. As a result, they are more apt to go out two or three evenings a week.

■ **Singles Have More Fun:** Being happy and having fun are different things. Singles might be less happy than married people, but they go out more, engage in more physical activity, and have more sex partners—in short, have more fun.

■ **Singles Tend to Be More Comfortable with Other Singles:** Because married people tend to think in terms of couples, they don't realize that singles don't fit well in married socializing—and so they often invite opposite-sex singles as "company" for their single friends.

■ **Singles Are Lonely:** As has been noted, singles are apt to feel more lonely than married people do. In particular, divorced singles experience loneliness more than never-married singles do.

Different Kinds of Singles

Being single is not always a matter of choice, though it can be. Moreover, how single people structure their relationships with others can also vary. Let's explore these two questions (some of which may be applicable to gays as well as heterosexuals).

Is Singlehood Voluntary or Involuntary, Temporary or Stable?

Peter Stein (1981) suggests that singles can be classified according to a typology of whether (1) they are voluntarily or involuntarily single and (2) their singlehood is temporary or stable.

■ **Voluntary Temporary Singles:** *Voluntary temporary singles* **are those who are open to marriage but find seeking a mate a lower priority than other activities,** such as gaining an education, starting a career, or self-development. People in this group tend to be younger never-marrieds and the divorced, including people in cohabiting relationships.

■ **Voluntary Stable Singles:** *Voluntary stable singles* **are those who are satisfied not to be married.** This group includes the never-married, divorced not seeking remarriage, single parents not wanting marriage, cohabitants not intending to marry, and people such as priests and nuns whose lifestyles don't permit marriage.

"SINGLES HAVE MORE FUN." Younger singles in particular have more free time, engage in more physical activity, and go out more—in other words, have more fun. This does not mean, however, that they are happier compared to married people. Indeed, singles are apt to feel more lonely than do people who are married. If you're currently single, does this description seem to fit? ▶

■ Involuntary Temporary Singles: *Involuntary temporary singles* **are those who would like to marry and are actively seeking mates.** People in this group may be never-married singles, widows and widowers, divorced people, single parents desiring marriage, and older people who have postponed marriage.

■ Involuntary Stable Singles: *Involuntary stable singles* **are those who would like to marry, have not found a mate, and have come to accept their single status.** People in this group are older never-married, widowed, and divorced people, as well as those with physical or psychological impairments that make them less attractive as mates.

Throughout life, people may move from one status from another—for example, from being a voluntary temporary single seeking an education and career to ultimately being an involuntary stable single three decades later.

Is Singlehood Freely Chosen?

Robert Staples (1981) suggests that singles can be classified according to five types based on whether or not their status is freely chosen. The classification describes the single person's relationship to possible partners.

■ The Free-Floating Single: **The** *free-floating single* **is an unattached single who dates randomly.** This could be someone of almost any age, including older singles.

■ The Open-Couple Single: **The** *open-couple single* **has a steady partner, but the relationship is open enough that he or she can have romantic or sexual relationships with others.**

■ The Closed-Couple Single: **The** *closed-couple single* **is expected to be faithful to his or her partner and not go outside the relationship for romance or sex.**

■ The Committed Single: **The** *committed single* **lives in the same household with his or her partner and perhaps is engaged to be married or has agreed to maintain fidelity to the relationship.**

■ **The Accommodationist Single:** The *accommodationist single* has accommodated himself or herself to an unattached life, getting together with friends but refusing romantic or sexual contacts.

Singlehood: Lifestyle Choice or Life Stage?

Clearly, being single can be a *lifestyle choice,* and a beneficial one at that. People stay single because having no partner is better than having the wrong partner—that is, one who is abusive, dependent, and so on (Ross 1995). Singlehood means that you're responsible only for yourself, free to do what you want to do—spontaneously, when you want to do it, spending what you want to spend on it—without having to feel influenced by the wishes of a spouse or partner.

Yet singlehood can also be a *life stage,* an interval between other arrangements in which you trade freedom and spontaneity for intimacy, closeness, and companionship with a partner.

Being a Single Parent

"Today's single mothers may be divorced or never-wed, rich or poor, living with men or on their own. But with traditional households in decline, they're the new faces of America's family."

So begins the lead-in (to which might be added lesbian single mothers, too) to a *Newsweek* cover story headlined "The New Single Mom" (Kantrowitz and Wingert 2001: 46). Not just in the United States but throughout the world, the number of single-parent homes is on the rise, from England to Australia, from Belgium to Japan. In the United States, according to the 2000 census, 9% of households (up from 8% in 1990) were headed by a man or a woman raising a child alone or without a spouse living at home (U.S. Census, cited in Armas 2001). By contrast, 24% of U.S. households in 2000 were the traditional "Ozzie and Harriet" home with married parents and children—down from 26% reported in the 1990 census. And we're only at the beginning: In the future, according to some (Demo 2000), more than half of the children who were born in the United States in the 1990s will spend some time in a single-parent household.

We discuss child rearing in detail in Chapter 11, "Parenting." However, because so many never-married singles have said they would consider raising a child on their own—61% of women and 55% of men, according to one survey (Edwards 2000)—and because so many babies, about a third of all births, are born to unmarried women, up from 3.8% in 1940 (Curtin and Martin 2000), we need to briefly consider the subject of single parenting here.

Single mothers and fathers present different pictures.

Single Mothers Raising Children

When Carolyn Feuer, age 30, of New York became pregnant, she chose to go ahead and have her baby without marrying her boyfriend. "It wouldn't have been a good marriage," she said. "It's better for both of us this way, especially my son." Her salary as a nurse gave her choices. "I had an apartment," she said. "I had a car. I felt there was no reason why I shouldn't have the baby. I felt I could give it whatever it needed as far as love and support, and I haven't

SINGLE PARENTS. From 1990 to 2000, single-mother households increased 25%, and single-father households increased 62%. What do you think accounts for this? Could you—or do you—handle raising children while simultaneously pursuing a career? ▲

regretted it for even a minute since" (Feuer, quoted in Kantrowitz and Wingert 2001: 49).

The number of families in the United States headed by single mothers increased from 5.4 million in 1980 to 9.9 million in 2005 (U.S. Census Bureau 2006c). Low education increases the likelihood of planned and unplanned childbearing outside of marriage for all racial and ethnic groups (Musick 2002). Even so, most such single mothers don't fit the stereotype of unwed teenagers on welfare: The median age is the late 20s, and the fastest-growing category is white women, although, unlike Carolyn Feuer, single mothers are still apt to be financially insecure. Although one myth is that single mothers are predominantly women who have never been married to the father of their child, they are more apt to be divorced, separated, or widowed. In 2000, for example, 55% of single mothers were divorced or separated, and another 4% were widowed (Sugarman 2003).

Single Fathers Raising Children

Charles Claudius, age 30, of Concord, California, a Home Depot supervisor, gained custody of his three children, ages 3 to 7, after separating from his wife. The pair had married young and produced children two years apart, but after nine years, the wife decided that she was in a rut and wanted to go to medical school. Eventually, they settled on a 70–30% custody arrangement, with the children spending the majority of the time with him. "Mothers want it shared a little more," he said, "so they can have time [for a] professional life" (quoted in Ginsburg 2001: A12).

Single-father households increased from 616,000 in 1980 to over 2 million in 2005 (U.S. Census Bureau 2006c). Indeed, during the decade of 1990–2000, single-father households increased 10 times faster than did traditional homes and 2½ times faster than did single-mother households. That is, in about 1 in 45 households, fathers raise their children without a mother. This is still a small percentage of the overall picture, however, with single-father homes making up only 3% of the households in the United States.

The Challenges to Single Parenting

Raising children can be difficult enough with a married couple, but at least the work is usually somewhat divided between two people. It's possible that many single parents have help that doesn't show up in census statistics—a partner such as a live-in boyfriend or girlfriend or another parental figure. Still, being a single parent can involve many challenges, among them the following:

■ **Money Matters:** Some single mothers—those known as single mothers by choice—may be financially stable (Bock 2000). However, consider that the median income for an unmarried female head of household in 2005 was $30,650, compared with $66,067 for married-couple households (DeNavas-Walt et al. 2006; Table 1). Divorced single mothers earn less than widowed single mothers (Biblarz and Gottainer 2000). Unmarried men who fathered children are more apt to be poor than are those who didn't father children before marriage (Nock 1998).

One problem for single mothers who are seeking help from absentee fathers is that some "deadbeat dads," fathers who refuse to provide court-ordered child support, turn out, once caught, to be "dead-broke dads," too poor to pay. Although most of the estimated 11 million fathers in the United States who are not living with their children have stable jobs and can afford support, about 2.5 million poor noncustodial fathers are unable to do so. Nearly 30% are in prison, among the rest half are unemployed, and those who do have jobs earn an average of $5,600 a year, which is below the poverty line (Harden 2002).

■ **Children's Stability:** Among sixth- to twelfth-graders, according to a study of 75,000 students, the percentage of students who said they used drugs was as follows: those living with both parents, 20.4%; those living with mothers only, 28.3%; those living with fathers only, 38.4% (Parents' Resource Institute for Drug Education 2001). Another study (Weitoft et al. 2003) of about 1 million children in Sweden found that children with single parents were twice as likely as others to develop a psychiatric illness such as severe depression or schizophrenia, to commit or attempt suicide, or to develop an alcohol-related disease. Girls living with one parent were three times more likely to become drug addicts, and boys were four times more likely, compared to children in two-parent households.

An earlier study of children of single parents found that they were twice as likely to quit high school, have alcohol problems, or become pregnant before marriage (McLanahan and Booth 1989; McLanahan 1991). Financial hardship of single parents may play a role, but it is suggested that once financial stability has been achieved, the quality of parenting is not an issue among single parents (Pong and Dong 2000).

Of course, there are plenty of single parents and plenty of single-parent children who don't have these kinds of serious problems, and despite the stresses, many unmarried parents wouldn't trade the experience of love and intimacy for anything. We return to a discussion of single parenting in Chapter 11, "Parenting."

9.3 The Gay & Lesbian Way of Life

MAJOR QUESTION What is my understanding of homosexuality, and how does it relate to the research?

PREVIEW We distinguish among heterosexuality, homosexuality, and bisexuality. We also discuss the problem of trying to define the percentage of people who are homosexual. Next, we describe the acquiring of a gay identity, discrimination and violence against gays, various kinds of gay couples and same-sex commitments, gays as parents, and the effect of gay parents on children.

Before 1973, the American Psychiatric Association defined homosexuality as a mental disorder, with treatments ranging from lobotomies to castration. Today, the medical system takes a far more enlightened view. But how tolerant is the rest of society about gayness?

Sexual Orientation: Heterosexuality, Homosexuality, & Bisexuality

Sexuality, which we introduced in Chapter 7, is a topic of endless fascination. At heart, it would seem to be principally about the biological process of *procreation,* **the bringing forth of children.** But though procreation may indeed be nature's ultimate purpose, *sexuality,* **the state of being sexual, encompasses not only the biological aspects of sex but psychological, social, and cultural aspects as well.** Indeed, your sexuality involves your emotions, thoughts, beliefs, values, identity, relationships, behaviors, and lifestyles and, finally, your sexual orientation.

The Kinds of Sexual Orientation

Sexual orientation **refers to sexual inclinations—feelings and sexual interactions—whether for the opposite sex, the same sex, or both.** These inclinations are expressed as heterosexuality, homosexuality, and bisexuality.

■ **Heterosexuality:** *Heterosexuality* **is the sexual inclination toward members of the opposite sex.** Among some groups, being heterosexual is referred to as being *straight*. The actual percentage of the population that is exclusively heterosexual is not known. This statement will make more sense as we discuss homosexuality and bisexuality.

■ **Homosexuality:** *Homosexuality* **is the sexual inclination toward members of the same sex.** Whether man or woman, a person who is homosexual is also said to be *gay*. In this book, however, we principally use *gay* in the term *gay male* **to refer to male homosexuals.** We use *lesbian* **to refer to female homosexuals.**

■ **Bisexuality:** *Bisexuality* **is the sexual inclination toward both sexes.** This doesn't necessarily mean an *equal* preference. A study of 100 members of a bisexual organization found that some were inclined toward the same sex and some toward the opposite, but most had primary heterosexual relationships and secondary homosexual relationships (Weinberg et al. 1994).

In recent years, the latter two groups have grouped themselves under the initials *LGBT*—short for "lesbian, gay, bisexual, and transgender (or transgendered) people." *Transgender*, you'll recall from Chapter 3, "Gender," is the adjective applied to a person with the biological sex of one gender who has the identity of the other gender. There is debate as to whether transgender belongs in the same group as homosexuals and bisexuals.

Is One Out of Ten People Gay?

Perhaps you have heard it said that "one out of ten people is gay" or "4–10% of adults are exclusively or mostly homosexual." Where do these figures come from, and are they true?

Pioneering sex researcher Alfred Kinsey and his associates (1948, 1953), who showed that homosexuality was much more common than anyone had previously suspected, found that among American males 10% were predominantly gay for at least three years, and 4% were exclusively gay throughout their entire lives. However, they also found that a much higher figure— 20–37% of males, including adolescents—had had orgasms with other men. As for American females, only 1–3% identified themselves as lesbian, but around 13% said that they had had orgasms with other women (Kinsey et al. 1948; Fay et al. 1989). (It should be noted that because of the populations chosen for the surveys, Kinsey's samplings might have been somewhat biased toward homosexual respondents.)

Other studies have come up with different kinds of numbers, as the accompanying chart shows. (See ■ *Panel 9.3, next page.*)

The Problem of Trying to Determine the Percentage of Gays

What should we think about the different outcomes of the studies just described? Why can't we be more specific in determining who is gay and who's not? Here are some possible reasons (Michael et al. 1994; Black et al. 2000; Diamond 2000).

■ **Different Study Approaches:** Variations in study results can be attributed to different definitions of homosexuality, different sampling techniques, different ways of interviewing, and different methodologies and technical analyses.

■ PANEL 9.3   What Percentage of People Are Gay? Different studies produce different numbers.

- **4.5% of adult men—1991 study:**   One review of 20 years of male same-sex studies from 1970 on determined that 5–7% of adult males had had same-sex sexual contact. From this, it's suggested, about 4.5% of adult men are exclusively gay (Rogers and Turner 1991).

- **6% of adult heterosexual men—1992 study:**   From a study of 52 men who called themselves heterosexual, 6% reported they had had sex with men in the past two years, and 23% said they had had sex with both men and women (Doll et al. 1992).

- **2% of adult men—1992 study:**   From a study of 6,982 men who had reported having sex with both men and women, 2% considered themselves gay, 29% bisexual, and 69% heterosexual (Lever et al. 1992).

- **1% of adult men—1993 study:**   A study of 3,300 males ages 20–39 found that 2% had had same-sex contact and 1% considered themselves gay (Billy et al. 1993).

- **2.8% men and 1.4% women gay or bisexual—1994 study:**   In this survey, 2.8% men and 1.4% women called themselves homosexual or bisexual. However, 9% of men and 4% of women said they had had a same-sex sexual experience (Laumann et al. 1994).

- **6% men and 14% women in late teens and 20s had same-sex encounter—2005 survey:**   About 6% of men and 14% of women in their late teens and 20s said they'd had at least one same-sex encounter (Mosher et al. 2005).

- **6.5% of men and 11% of women aged 25–44 had same-sex experience—2005 survey:**   About 6.5% of men 25–44 years of age have had oral or anal sex with another man; 11% of women 25–44 years of age reported having had a sexual experience with another woman (Mosher et al. 2005).

- **2.3% of men said they are homosexual and 1.8% said they are bisexual—2005 survey:**   About 2.3% of men 18–44 years of age said they think of themselves as homosexual and 1.8% said they think of themselves as bisexual (Mosher et al. 2005).

- **1.3% of women said they are homosexual and 2.8% said they are bisexual—2005 survey:**   About 1.8% of women 18–44 years of age said they think of themselves as homosexual and 2.8% said they think of themselves as bisexual (Mosher et al. 2005).

■ **Reluctance to Reveal Orientation:** Despite a more accepting climate for homosexuality in many locations, many people are reluctant, for fear of persecution, to reveal (as on census reports) a homosexual orientation.

■ **Changing Sexual Behavior:** People do not stay the same throughout their lives, even in something as basic as sexual orientation. Because people change their sexual behavior over time, it's difficult to say that particular behaviors indicate that a person is gay or not gay.

■ **Sexual Orientation Is Not Expressed Just through Behavior:** Behavior alone is not a definitive indicator of sexual orientation. Desires and attraction are also

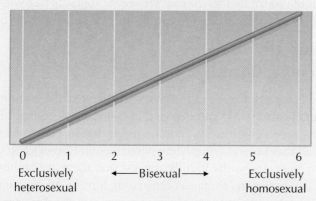

■ PANEL 9.4   The Heterosexual-Homosexual Rating Scale

| 0 | 1 | 2 | 3 | 4 | 5 | 6 |

Exclusively
heterosexual   ◄——Bisexual——►   Exclusively
homosexual

Source: The Hetero-Homosexual Rating Scale. Kinsey, A. C., W. B. Pomeroy, C. H. Martin, and P. H. Gebhard. 1953. *Sexual behavior in the human female.* Philadelphia: W. B. Saunders. Reproduced by permission of the Kinsey Institute for Research in Sex, Gender, and Reproduction, Inc.

important. One can be a virgin or abstain from sex and still be heterosexual, homosexual, or bisexual. Also, studies have shown that people may identify themselves as bisexual but physical attraction patterns (as measured by physical arousal) may differ from their professed desires (Chivers et al. 2004; Rieger et al. 2005).

■ Sexual Orientation May Lie along a Continuum: Finally, it might be that sexual orientation is not either/or. Rather, as Kinsey and associates (1953) suggested, it may be expressed as a continuum, with few people being either entirely straight or entirely gay. *(See ■ Panel 9.4.)* This continuum was later refined by Fritz Klein's so-called Klein Grid, which added sexual attraction, fantasies, emotional and social attraction, lifestyle, and self-identification to Kinsey's scale. Klein (1993) argued that an individual's sexual attraction cannot fit in a simple category.

Whatever the actual percentage of gays in the population, research suggests that from 1988 to 1998, there was an increasing likelihood that American men and women had had a same-gender sexual partner during the previous year. The increase cannot be accounted for by changes in age structure, increasing urbanization, increasing educational attainment, or the changing racial and ethnic mix in the United States during that period. An alternative explanation is declining social, legal, and economic sanctions against same-sex sexual behavior in recent years. In addition, suggests one writer, "more positive images of gay men and lesbians in the media may have made it easier for people to recognize their same-gender sexual interest and to act on it" (Butler 2000: 341).

Acquiring a Gay Identity

Do you think that gays *have a sexual orientation*? Or, rather, do they *express their sexual preferences*? Although many people use the terms *sexual orientation* and *sexual preference* interchangeably, they do not have the same meaning. *Sexual orientation* suggests determinism—that people's sexual identities are the result of inborn factors. *Sexual preference* suggests free will—that people choose their sexual identities (Weinrich and Williams 1991). Which is true?

Sexual Identity: Chance or Choice?

The Rev. Ted Haggard, forced to resign as president of the National Association of Evangelicals after being exposed in a three-year sexual affair with a man who was a gay prostitute, later announced that he had come out of therapy convinced that he was completely heterosexual (Banerjee 2007). Ex-gay backers such as Focus on the Family suggest that there are highly motivated people who can overcome same-sex attraction, but the American Psychiatric Association, the American Medical Association, and the American Academy of Pediatrics oppose the kind of reparative therapy that it and other conservative Christian organizations support (cited in Buchanan 2005; see also Jenkins and Johnston 2004). Research by one gay organization (Cianciotto and Cahill 2006) argues that such efforts can even be harmful.

Although homosexuality is no longer considered a mental disorder—a classification the Pentagon only recently dropped, years after mental health experts did (Baldor 2006a, 2006b)—can we determine whether our sexual identities are the result of biology or the result of environment? According to one poll, 75% of gay men and lesbians (compared to only 33% in the overall population) thought that homosexuality was something they were born with—that is, a matter of chance—not the result of upbringing or environmental influence (Leland and Miller 1998). The same poll found that only 11% of gay men and lesbians (compared with 56% in the overall population) felt that homosexuals could change their sexual orientation through therapy, willpower, or religious conviction—that is, a matter of choice.

■ **The Evidence for Chance—Biological Factors:** The biological explanation means that your sexual identity results from genetics or hormones. One review of genetic research on straight versus gay sexual orientations concluded that (1) at least half of the reasons for sexual orientation variances could be traced to genetics and (2) sexual orientation tended to run in families (Pillard and Bailey 1998). Other research finds that a boy's chances of growing up gay increase with the number of brothers he has and that the sexual orientation seems to be established before birth (Bogaert 2006). In addition, it's been found that lesbians seem to have different brain circuitry than heterosexual women do, processing the aromoa of sex hormones in ways similar to those of straight men, and that gay and straight men respond differently to two odors that may be involved in sexual arousal, perhaps providing a biological basis for sexual orientation (Berglund et al. 2006). One scientific team has even been looking at physiological differences between gay and straight sheep (Roselli et al. 2004a, 2004b).

■ **The Evidence for Choice—Environmental Factors:** If you had a frightening experience with a member of the opposite sex (or a highly pleasurable experience with a member of the same sex), would that later affect your gender preference in sexual partners? Not according to one study of the effect of sexually traumatic experiences on straight and lesbian women (Brannock and Chapman 1990). Yet people do change their sexual orientations, as was revealed by one study of 80 lesbian, bisexual, and so-called unlabeled women over several years (Diamond 2000).

Four Stages in Acquiring a Gay or Lesbian Identity

Whatever its causes, it's thought that one's sexual inclination is usually established by age 4 or 5 (Marmor 1980a, 1980b). Even at this tender age, there can be *erotic feelings*—**feelings of sensuality or sexuality.** When **erotic attraction is directed toward a member of the same gender, it is known as** *homoeroticism*.

According to a model by **Richard R. Troiden** (1988), the process of identifying oneself as gay begins in late childhood or early adolescence and occurs in four stages.

■ **Stage 1—Sensitization: "Am I different?":** This stage occurs before puberty. Most children and adolescents assume that they are heterosexual, but future gays suspect that they may be different. These children's attraction toward members of the same gender may be characterized by confusion and denial—and fear that their family will discover their true sexual interests.

■ **Stage 2—Identity Confusion: "I'll prove I'm not gay":** This stage occurs during adolescence. Here, people become aware of homosexual feelings, fantasies, or behaviors, but because these inclinations go against their self-image, they might try to prove the opposite. A gay man, for instance, might date a lot of women or take a public anti-gay stance.

■ **Stage 3—Identity Assumption: "I know I'm gay, but which people should I tell?":** This stage occurs on average for males at ages 19 to 21 and for females at ages 21 to 23. Here, people accept that they are gay, but they then struggle with determining whether they should "stay in the closet" (hide their sexual identity) or *"come out"*—**publicly reveal their gayness**—and to whom.

■ **Stage 4—Commitment: "I'm gay, but that's not all I am":** In the end, of course, one's sexual identity is not *everything* that a person is. In the fourth stage, gay people reveal their sexual orientation to others, both homosexuals and (some) heterosexuals. There is increased self-satisfaction and happiness. Homosexuality becomes a relatively less important part of one's overall identity.

Prejudice, Discrimination, & Violence against Gays

Two things gays have to deal with are prejudice and discrimination. Although many people tend to think these are the same thing, they're not: One is an attitude, the other is an act.

■ *Prejudice* **is an attitude or prejudging, usually negative, of an individual or group.**

- **Discrimination** **is an act of unfair treatment directed against an individual or a group.**

The majority of cultures, including those in North America, are "heterosexist," most people believing that heterosexuality is superior to homosexuality. "Heterosexuality is equated with 'normal' masculinity and 'normal' femininity," says one account, "whereas homosexuality is equated with violating norms of gender. . . . This dynamic contains the ingredients for the violence experienced by more and more lesbians and gay men" (Appleby and Anastas 1998: 18). This view results in *homophobia*—**also called** *anti-gay prejudice*—**which is defined as negative attitudes toward homosexuality and homosexuals.** (A variation on homophobia is biphobia—negative attitudes toward bisexuality. Bisexuals may experience victimization not only from heterosexuals, but also from homosexuals.)

Anti-Gay Prejudice Can Escalate

It's possible for people to be prejudiced without being discriminatory. For instance, one survey (Schmalz 1993) found that a majority of respondents, 55%, believed that behavior between homosexuals was wrong—an example of prej-

PRACTICAL ACTION
The Other Side of Gay Liberation: The Effect on Straight Family Members

In 1984, after 25 years and two children, Amity Pierce Buxton (2004) addressed an Oakland, California, crowd of 50 in her new role as the soon-to-be ex-wife of a man who had recently come out of the closet. The audience was visibly moved as Buxton and three other women talked of their love for their gay husbands, their efforts to understand their husbands' dilemma, and their own sadness and sense of loss.

"It takes persistence to make people wake up to the fact that there's another side of gay liberation," said Buxton (quoted in Marech 2003: A1). "There are casualties along the way."

Since that night, Buxton, who has a Ph.D. and is remarried, has become perhaps the leading expert

on the issues faced by straight spouses. She founded a support organization, the Straight Spouse Network, and is author of a book on "mixed-orientation" marriages, *The Other Side of the Closet: The Coming-Out Crisis for Straight Spouses and Families.*

Some Issues in "Mixed-Orientation" Marriages

An estimated 3.9% of American men who have ever been married have had sex with men in the previous five years, according to one study (Laumann et al. 1994), and 2 to 4% of ever-married American women (1.7 million to 3.4 million) knowingly or unknowingly have been in what are labeled "mixed-orientation marriages," also

now called "Brokeback marriages" after the movie *Brokeback Mountain,* about two gay, married cowboys (Butler 2006). Most homosexual or bisexual men go into heterosexual marriages believing that their same-sex attractions are controllable; then, as the feelings gain in intensity, they hide the feelings before coming out to their spouses.

Once the truth is out, straight spouses have to deal with a number of issues, with which support groups may be of help. Among those Buxton (2004) mentions are deception, hurt, anger, powerlessness, and recriminations; sexual rejection; sexually transmitted diseases; effects on children and other family members; and their own crisis of identity.

udice. Yet a majority, 78%, also believed that homosexuals should not be barred from having equal job opportunities—they were against discrimination.

But prejudice can also escalate. Famed psychologist Gordon Allport (1958) suggested that prejudice can be acted out in three stages.

■ **Stage 1—Offensive Language:** Gay men and women are often called offensive names—"queer," "faggot," "dyke," "lesbo"—though some younger gays use "queer" as a point of pride (Heredia 2001).

Straight male students in one school said the worst putdown they could experience was to be called a "fag" (Thompson 1995). At one university, 68% of first-year students said they had heard fellow students make disparaging remarks about a person's sexual orientation (Mather 2000). Nearly two-thirds of gay and lesbian students in schools nationwide experienced verbal harassment in 2005 because of their sexual orientation, according to a survey conducted by a gay student rights group (Kosciw and Diaz 2006).

■ **Stage 2—Discrimination:** Homosexuals are denied equal employment opportunities, parental rights, adoption, and the like.

One study (Berg and Lien 2002) found that gay men earn about 22% less than similarly qualified straight men. On the other hand, gay women earn

It's a mistake, however, to conclude that all such marriages are doomed. "Once the truth comes out, you're closer," Buxton says (quoted in Marech 2003: A11). "For those married a long time, there's the history. It's too hard to pull apart and open the threads."

Should You Tell Your Parents That You're Gay?

Some parents—26% in one study (Robinson et al. 1989)—suspect that their children are gay even before they're told. Whether or not this is so, disclosing one's homosexual orientation to parents is often quite difficult. Some parents are happier not knowing, some may punish their offspring (withdraw financial support), and others may be in a closer relationship with their children for knowing the truth.

Not everyone should come out to their parents or family members. But if you're thinking of doing so, here are some things to consider (Sauerman 1995; Stewart 2002; "Coming out" 2004; "Coming out to your parents" 2004):

■ **Be clear in your own mind:** Are you sure about your sexuality? Don't raise the issue unless you are comfortable with being gay.

■ **Prepare for their reactions:** Think how your parents have reacted to gay people in the media and whether they have been supportive or critical with you about other issues in your life. Choose a time when they're relaxed, not in an emotional, financial, or health crisis. Think about the statement you will make (for example, "There's something about me that I want to share with you because I love you very much and I want you to know me fully"). Plan to reassure them that your being gay isn't a mark of parental failure.

Consider telling one parent first (but also consider whether the other will have hurt feelings if he or she feels ignored). Generally, young people are more apt to come out to their mothers than to their fathers (Cohen and Savin-Williams 1996). It might be useful to test the waters by telling a sibling first.

In the event that your parents' reactions turn out to be devastating to you, have someone else to whom you can turn for support.

■ **Be ready for six stages of understanding:** General stages that families may move through—some take months, some take years—are (1) shock, (2) denial, (3) guilty, (4) expressing feelings, (5) making decisions, and (6) true acceptance ("Coming out to your parents" 2004). For an explanation of these stages, go to *www.4therapy.com/ consumer/life_topics/item.php?uniq ueid=5532&categoryid=442.*

ANTI-GAY PREJUDICE. Prejudice against gays may be rooted in people's personal insecurities, fundamentalist religious orientation, or simple ignorance about homosexuality. Can you recall someone making anti-gay statements? What do you think were the causes? ▶

30% more than similarly qualified straight women—possibly because gay women might be more career-minded than married women with children (who may suffer another kind of workplace discrimination).

■ **Stage 3—Violence:** Gays are threatened, verbally abused, attacked, beaten up ("gay bashing"), raped, and even killed. About 17% of gay and lesbian students said they were physically harassed in 2005 (Kosciw and Diaz 2006).

In 1998, Matthew Shepard, age 22, an openly gay college student, died after being robbed, burned, pistol-whipped, and tied to a fence of a ranch near Laramie, Wyoming, where he was left for 18 hours in near freezing temperatures. Two homophobic young men were convicted of the crime (Brooke 1998a, 1998b).

The Roots of Anti-Gay Feelings

In the United States, prejudice against gays has several possible roots (Marmor 1980b):

■ **Personal Insecurity:** People who hate gays might have deep insecurities about their own gender identity and sexuality. This may derive from rigid ideas about gender roles.

■ **Fundamentalist Religion:** Many people who are anti-gay have a strong fundamentalist religious orientation. The Roman Catholic Church has rejected homosexuality, as did the 1998 Southern Baptist Convention.

■ **Ignorance about Homosexuality:** Many homophobic people simply know little about gay and lesbian life. They may think that gays are promiscuous, are possible child molesters, and are conduits for transmission of HIV/AIDS.

Gay Couples

Like heterosexual couples, gays and lesbians want to be in close, stable relationships with someone they love. Also, like straight couples, gay couples have similar experiences in their relationships, including working through power and communication issues (Blumstein and Schwartz 1983; Meyer 1990; Peplau et al. 1996). The incidence of violence or battering tends to be the same—25 to 33%—as it is for heterosexual couples (Brand and Kidd 1986; Lundy 1993). Finally, same-sex couples are like straight couples in seeking steady relationships, in using their relationships as the main source of affection and companionship, and in having similar relationship quality (Risman and Schwartz 1988).

Yet despite the similarities, gay and lesbian couples show some differences.

Five Types of Gays: From "Happily Married" to Lonely

One classic study of gays and lesbians was conducted by Alan Bell and Martin Weinberg (1978), who studied 979 male and female, black and white homosexuals. On the basis of interviews and questionnaires, the researchers determined that there were five categories of gays:

■ **Closed Couples—The "Happily Married"**: Members of *closed couples* described themselves as being "happily married" and "closely bound together." They derive personal satisfaction and sexual gratification from each other rather than from people outside the relationship.

■ **Open Couples—The "Unhappily Married"**: Although they were living with a single sexual partner, members of the category labeled *open couples* stated that they were "not happy with their circumstances." They tended to try to seek sexual and interpersonal satisfaction with people outside the relationship.

■ **The Functionals—The Highly Sexual**: So-called *functional* homosexuals, both single males and single females, engaged in a variety of sexual activity and constructed their lives around their sexual experiences.

■ **The Dysfunctionals—The Tormented**: The *dysfunctional* gay men and lesbian women reported suffering many problems, even torments, stemming from their sexual orientation.

■ **The Asexuals—The Lonely**: These single males and females reported having few friends and feeling lonely. *Asexuals* were less explicit than gays in the other categories about expressing their homosexual orientation.

How Gay Couples Differ from Straight Couples

Of course, many heterosexuals are also highly sexually active, or are lonely, or are happily or unhappily married. But gay couples differ from straight couples in the following ways:

■ **Egalitarian, Dual-Worker Relationships**: Despite the stereotypes, homosexual relationships are not divided into "butch and femme" or "husband and wife" roles. Rather, they are apt to be egalitarian, dual-worker relationships, with income or household responsibilities based on factors other than traditional masculine/feminine, breadwinner/homemaker roles (Kurdek 1993; Allen and Demo 1995; Peplau et al. 1996). Equality in decision making and sharing of household tasks is apt to be more equal than it is among heterosexual couples (Harry 1982; Kurdek 1993).

■ **Less Family Support and Openness:** Same-sex couples often receive less social and emotional support from family members, and they feel less open about expressing their sexual preferences and relationships or public affection toward their partners (Blumstein and Schwartz 1983). African American gay men and women in particular find little acceptance in the black community (Bell and Weinberg 1978; Staples 1982; Morales 1990). Compared to straight couples, gay couples get more support from friends than from their extended families (Kurdek and Schmitt 1987).

Gay Relationships

More than their sexual orientation, gender socialization often seems to have a great influence on the intimate relationships of lesbians and gays. That is, gay men resemble heterosexual men, and lesbians are similar to heterosexual women (Risman and Schwartz 1988). Even so, there are some differences.

■ **Gay Men:** Gay men seem to have more casual sex than either heterosexual men or lesbians do, and their sexuality seems to be more body centered than personality centered (Ruefli et al. 1992). About 50% of gay men are estimated to be in stable long-term relationships at any one time (Bell and Weinberg 1978; Riedmann 1995). Gay male couples are twice as likely as heterosexual couples to report the highest levels of closeness in their relationships (Green et al. 1996). When gay men have sex outside their relationship, it is usually infrequent (Green et al. 1996). However, violence seems to happen more often in gay male relationships than in either heterosexual cohabiting relationships or lesbian relationships, with 16% of same-sex gay cohabiting males saying they had been raped or physically assaulted by their partners (Tjaden et al. 1999).

■ **Gay Women:** Gay women seem to emphasize committed relationships more than gay men do. Lesbians also have less casual sex than gay men do, and their sexuality is more personality centered than body centered (Ruefli et al. 1992). Lesbians report greater sexual satisfaction than do heterosexual women, including more orgasms (Konner 1990). More gay women—about 75%—than gay men are in domestic relationships at any one time (Bell and Weinberg 1978; Riedmann 1995). Moreover, compared with married couples and gay male couples, lesbian couples have been found to be the closest, the most satisfied, and the most flexible in roles in their relationships (Green et al. 1996). Violence by their partners was reported by only 11% of lesbians, compared with 16% for gay males (Tjaden et al. 1999).

Same-Sex Commitments

Are gays sexually promiscuous? That is indeed one stereotype. Although a great many homosexuals define faithfulness to a partner as *emotional* rather than *sexual* fidelity (McWhirter and Mattison 1984), it's estimated that 50% of gay men and 75% of gay women are in monogamous relationships at any one time (Riedmann 1995). More and more gays also are in families with children. Let us consider same-sex commitments.

Six Stages in a Gay Relationship

Researchers David McWhirter and Andrew Mattison (1984) determined that there were six stages through which a gay couple's relationship moves over time. It's apparent that growth of intimacy, bonding, and commitment is very similar to that of heterosexual couples.

■ **Year 1—Blending:** Stage 1 is characterized by intense feelings, frequent sexual activity, bonding, and attempts to make the relationship an egalitarian one.

■ **Years 2–3—Nesting:** In stage 2, sexual passion may decline (as it does in heterosexual couples), and one or both partners may begin to feel ambivalence, but they also explore their areas of compatibility and establish themselves in homemaking.

■ **Years 4–5—Maintaining:** In stage 3, the partners begin to establish family traditions, regain their sense of independence as individuals within the framework of the relationship, and find ways to resolve, avoid, or neutralize conflicts.

■ **Years 6–10—Building:** In stage 4, the partners further establish their individuality, become more productive in their work, and learn to become more dependent on each other.

■ **Years 11–20—Releasing:** Stage 5 is characterized by the combining of each other's possessions and money, of deepening trust in each other, and possibly taking each other for granted.

■ **Years 20 on—Renewing:** During the final stage, the partners have learned to feel secure with each other and have developed a shared history of experiences.

Domestic Partners & Civil Unions

On Valentine's Day, February 14, 2003, the Rev. Troy D. Perry, founder of the predominantly gay Metropolitan Community Churches, and his partner of 18 years applied for a marriage license at a Los Angeles courthouse. They and four other gay couples were politely turned down, along with many other same-sex partners seeking marriage licenses at 120 other cities and towns around the country that day. "For me it's not a religious issue, it's a legal issue," said Perry. "It's a matter of equality and simple justice" (quoted in Whitaker 2003). Other gays who seek to be married in a church associate the event with "overcoming the outsider status they had long assumed to be an inalterable fact of homosexuality" (Lewin 2002: 100).

The American Law Institute, an influential group of lawyers and judges, has recommended sweeping changes in family law that would not only increase alimony and property rights for divorced women but also extend such rights to cohabiting domestic partners, including gays (Ellman et al. 2002). Conservatives, such as Brigham Young University law professor Lynn Wardle (quoted in Pear 2002: A1), say that such proposals to make "domestic partnerships" more like marriage "could undermine the institution of marriage and reflect an ideological bias against family relations based on marriage. On the other hand, an analysis of 150 studies published over the last 30

GAY WEDDING. Although civil unions of same-sex couples are lawful in several foreign countries and Canadian provinces, in the United States in 2007 only a handful of states allow them. Allowing them were Connecticut, New Hampshire, New Jersey, and Vermont. In Massachusetts, same-sex marriage is legal. Do you think gay couples should be allowed to marry and have marriage rights just as heterosexual couples do? Why or why not? ▶

years (Herdt and Kertzner 2006) found that heterosexual married couples generally have better mental health, more emotional support, less psychological distress, and lower rates of psychiatric disorders than unmarried heterosexuals. The researchers concluded that the denial of marriage causes some homosexuals—and their families—to devalue their relationships and to establish ambiguous commitments, thereby negatively affecting their mental health.

Two stepping-stones toward the legalization of gay partnerships are as follows:

■ **Domestic Partnerships:** ***Domestic partners* are two people, gay or straight, who have chosen to cohabit or share each other's lives in an intimate and committed relationship without being married.**

However, there are efforts to legalize this status. That is, **the *domestic partnership movement* is an attempt to give some kind of official recognition to providing domestic partners with the legal and economic benefits of marriage.** These include recognition of health benefits from corporations; partners' right to claim alimony, custody, or visitation rights after a partnership ends; and inheritance rights.

■ Civil Unions: A key institution of the domestic partnership movement is the ***civil union*, a civil status similar to marriage, typically created for the purposes of allowing gay couples access to the benefits enjoyed by married heterosexuals.**

Civil unions are of three types:

1. Some are simple registries of domestic partners, including statement of joint residence and finances.
2. Some have many but not all of the rights accorded married couples.
3. Some are marriages in every way except name.

Various nationwide surveys of Americans age 18 and older suggest that the public seems to be split on the question of civil unions, or granting of spousal benefits to gay and lesbian partners. For instance, one poll found that 45% would support a law allowing same-sex couples to form civil unions but 52% would oppose it. In general, those polled were mostly against the idea of gay marriage (by 63% to 34%) but opposed (by 54% to 43%) a constitutional amendment to ban gay marriage (Quinnipiac University Poll 2006).

Where Are Same-Sex Civil Unions & Marriages Allowed?

Most legislation recognizing some form of civil union and same-sex marriage has taken place outside the United States:

■ **Trends Outside the U.S.:** Countries that recognize same-sex civil unions and marriages are shown in the accompanying chart. *(See ■ Panel 9.5.)* Denmark first recognized nationwide civil unions in 1989. In 2001, the Netherlands became the first country to allow gay couples to marry with all the rights afforded straight couples (but they can't adopt non-Dutch children—a move aimed at preventing confrontations with other nations), and Belgium followed suit in 2003.

■ **Trends Inside the U.S.:** Massachusetts is the only state where gay marriage is legal statewide. Four states allow same-sex civil unions: Connecticut, New Hampshire, New Jersey, and Vermont. California, Hawaii, Maine, Oregon, Washington, and the District of Columbia recognize same-sex civil union in some parts. All together, then, 10 states give all or some spousal rights to same-sex couples—California, Connecticut, Hawaii, Maine, Massachusetts, New Hampshire, New Jersey, Oregon, Vermont, and Washington—along with the District of Columbia.

In 2000, Vermont became the first state to recognize civil unions nearly identical to marriage, granting partners next-of-kin rights and the right to divorce. The result was a "modest boomlet in gay tourism," according to one description (Drummond 2001), with 80% of the gay-union licenses being issued to out-of-state residents. But Vermont civil unions aren't recognized by other states; therefore, couples cannot be legally divorced except in Vermont (Ferdinand 2002). The Defense of Marriage Act also prohibits the federal government from acknowledging state-recognized gay marriage (Eskridge 2002).

■ **PANEL 9.5** Countries and States Recognizing Civil Unions and Same-Sex Marriages

Throughout the world, same-sex civil unions are recognized in . . .
Denmark (1989)
Norway (1993)
Israel (1994)
Sweden (1995)
Greenland (1996)
Hungary (1996)
Iceland (1996)
France (1999)
Germany (2001)
Portugal (2001)
Finland (2002)
Croatia (2003)
Austria (2003)
Luxembourg (2004)
New Zealand (2005)
United Kingdom (2005)
Andorra (2005)
Czech Republic (2006)
Slovenia (2006)
Switzerland (2007)
Colombia (2007)

In the United States, same-sex civil unions are recognized in all or some parts of . . .
California
Connecticut
Hawaii
Maine
New Hampshire
New Jersey
Oregon
Vermont
Washington
District of Colombia

Throughout the world, same-sex marriage is legal in . . .
Netherlands (2001)
Belgium (2003)
Spain (2005)
Canada (2005)
South Africa (2006)

In the United States, same-sex marriage is legal in . . .
Massachusetts (2004)

Gays as Parents: The "Gayby Boom"

Many gays have children who were born when their fathers or mothers were part of a heterosexual marriage, before "coming out." But today, the United States seems to be in the midst of a "gayby boom," with thousands of gays and lesbians making the decision to become parents. "Planned lesbian and gay families," says one account, "most fully realize the early Planned Parenthood goal, 'every child a wanted child'" (Stacey 2003: 163). Some of this impulse is demonstrated in the 2002 documentary *Daddy & Papa*, which explores the lives of some gay males who made the decision to raise children themselves. Director/producer Johnny Symons and his partner, for example, are a San Francisco Bay Area interracial gay couple who adopted an African American baby, a story that was complicated by a devoutly religious foster mother who was reluctant to let go of the child she had raised from birth—especially when her friends told her that these men would want to "do things to him" and that they would undoubtedly "make him gay."

Gay couples become parents (1) by *adoption* or (2) by *biological* means.

1. Having Children by Adoption

Adoption **is the legal process by which adult couples or singles voluntarily take a child born of other parents and raise him or her as their own child.** The ability of gays to adopt a child varies significantly, being affected by a welter of conflicting state laws, local rules, and court rulings. Adoptions by gays are banned by law or court ruling in Colorado, Florida, Michigan, Mississippi, Nebraska, Ohio, Utah, and Wisconsin. Adoptions statewide by gays are permitted in Washington, DC, and 11 states: California, Connecticut, Illinois, Indiana, Maryland, Massachusetts, Nevada, New Jersey, New York, Pennsylvania, and Vermont. (In Canada, adoption by same-sex couples is illegal in New Brunswick, Prince Edward Island, and Nunavut and is ambiguous in Yukon but is legal in other provinces and territories.) In a CNN.com (2007) poll of 515 Americans, 57% said gay and lesbian couples should have the legal right to adopt children; 40% said they should not.

Adoptions may be of two types:

■ **Second-Parent Adoptions:** *Second-parent adoptions,* **also known as co-parent adoptions, are situations in which the gay or lesbian partner of a biological or adoptive parent is given full legal status as the child's second parent.**

In 2002, in an unprecedented show of mainstream support for gay parents, the 65,000-member American Academy of Pediatrics endorsed the idea that adoptions by the same-sex partner of a legally recognized parent should be made legal because it was better for children to have two fully sanctioned and legally defined parents (Goode 2002; Perrin et al. 2002). Without second-parent adoptions, the pediatricians noted, children can suffer severe hurts in battles over child support and in medical coverage and custody, particularly after the breakup of the same-sex relationship or the death of the legally recognized parent (Hall 2002).

■ **Foster-Parent Adoptions:** **A** *foster parent* **is an adult who raises a child who is not his or her own for a short period of time but does not formally**

GAY PARENTS. Gays become parents either through adoptions or through biological means, such as use of surrogate mothers or sperm donors. Do you think gays and lesbians could actually be better parents than heterosexuals? ▲

adopt that child. Children who are removed by state and county child-welfare agencies from abusive or neglectful parents are often placed with foster parents. If qualified, foster parents may become adoptive parents. Gays and their supporters say that there are large numbers of children in foster care in America who are in need of mature, responsible, loving adoptive parents—no matter what their sexual orientation (Alpert 2002). In 2003, there were 119,000 children awaiting adoption from the child-welfare system, according to the U.S. Children's Bureau (cited in Howard 2006).

Daddy & Papa tells the story of Kelly Wallace, age 38, a San Francisco single white gay man who adopts two brothers, ages 2 and 3, from foster care. The children are typical of those who languish in the foster system: They are boys and they are non-white. The film shows the challenges of single parenting, the difficulties of raising hard-to-place children, and the isolation of being a family in a virtually childless neighborhood.

2. Having Children by Biological Means

Gays and lesbians may also decide they want a child that is biologically half their own. The ways of doing this are as follows:

■ **Gay Men Having Children—Using Surrogate Mothers:** A gay man or two gay men might decide to adopt a baby through arrangements with a birth mother known as a *surrogate*. **A *surrogate mother* may be artificially inseminated by a gay man. *Artificial insemination* is a process in which sperm are**

introduced artificially into the woman's vagina or uterus at about the time of ovulation. (With heterosexual couples, a surrogate mother may also be a woman who is implanted with the female partner's egg after it has been fertilized by her mate. We discuss this type in Chapter 10, "Reproduction.")

In *Daddy & Papa*, two gay men arranged with a friend, a surrogate mother, to bear their child. A decade later, they have split up, and each has a new partner. Their 11-year-old daughter's biggest problem now is not that her fathers are gay but that they are divorced.

■ **Lesbians Having Children—Using Sperm Donors:** A lesbian women might decide to become pregnant from a *sperm donor*—**a male who makes his sperm available for artificial insemination.** The type of donor determines what rights the biological father may have later in relation to the child. There are three types:

1. **Known sperm donor:** This could be a close friend or other person known to the mother. In some jurisdictions, he could be considered a legal parent and could exercise custody rights despite the mother's wishes. (To prevent this, she could try executing a donor-recipient agreement.)

2. **Knowable sperm donor:** This is someone whose identity is held in confidence by a third party. That identity could be revealed later at the mother's request.

3. **Unknown sperm donor:** This is someone who has contributed to a *sperm bank*—**a depository for storing sperm**—and whose identity is kept secret.

ROSIE. Former talk-show host Rosie O'Donnell, a publicly declared lesbian, is mother to three adopted children. Do you think that the children of gay parents are apt to grow up gay themselves? ▲

How Are Children Affected by Having Gay Parents?

When talk-show host Rosie O'Donnell described herself in 2002 as a lesbian who was also the responsible mother of three adopted children, she restarted an emotional debate between gays and opponents in which both sides declared that they were protecting the welfare of children (Alpert 2002; Oldenburg 2002). Opponents worry that gays will push children into a gay lifestyle—or, worse, that they will actually engage in child molestation. Gays say that such concerns are misplaced—that the research shows that children of lesbian mothers, for instance, are as just as likely to be well adjusted as the children of non-gay mothers (Patterson 1996; Tasker and Golombok 1997).

A year earlier, however, two University of Southern California sociologists published a

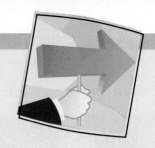

PRACTICAL ACTION

Legal & Financial Considerations for Unmarried Couples, Straight or Gay

Legal marriage is considered a binding contract, even if the ceremony took place in a tacky Las Vegas drive-through wedding chapel. Unmarried couples, by contrast, don't have such rights as inheritance and entitlement to property, as well as custody of any children, if the partners split up or one of them dies. This was made apparent in the film *The Break-Up*, an "anti-romantic comedy," in which Vince Vaughn and Jennifer Aniston play a cohabiting couple who have bought a condo together without a living-together contract dividing assets, then when their relationship implodes, neither wants to move out (Jayson 2006b).

A living-together agreement should show that you're a couple, not just roommates or friends. Thus, it should spell out how you'll share your income and property, so that if the relationship fails, it will be easier to divide up property. "Putting the details of your shared lives in writing," says writer Sandra Block (1999), "will help convince family, employers, and even courts that you're in a committed relationship."

The Cost of Procrastination

But will you actually make such an agreement—even though perhaps you know you should? People often hate to deal with financial issues. "We'd rather avoid doing things now that make us feel uncomfortable, even though we stand to gain in the long run," says Sonja Lyubomirsky (quoted in Dunleavey 2006), a psychology professor who studies decision-making behavior and its impact on people's happiness. Indeed, economists even

call this phenomenon "hyperbolic discounting"—the tendency to value what you have now and discount what you might gain later. Clearly, though, procrastination has a cost.

Factors that both straight and gay unmarried couples should consider are living-together agreements, domestic partner registries, wills, health-care proxies, durable power of attorney for financial management, insurance, joint tenancy, and retirement savings (Chu 2006).

Common-Law Marriage

One factor that unmarried heterosexual couples should be aware of is *common-law marriage*, a cohabiting relationship that is based on the mutual consent of the partners, is not solemnized by a ceremony, and is recognized as valid by the state. The Alternatives to Marriage Project (ATMP) website (2007) points out that there is a common misperception that if partners live together for seven years, they are considered common-law married. In fact, as the website explains, at least in the United States, there is no time component—seven years or otherwise—and common-law marriage is recognized in only 15 states and the District of Columbia. *(See ▪ Panel 9.6.)* If you live in one of these states and "intend to be married" by acting as if and telling the community that you are married, calling each other husband and wife, using the same last name, filing joint income tax returns, and the like, you might be able to establish that you are in a common-law marriage. This is considered legally identical to a regular civil marriage. (And if

you end the relationship, you'll need to go through a formal divorce.)

Living-Together Agreements

A living-together agreement is a contract that specifies what each partner owns and how property is to be divided if the relationship ends. "Since divorce laws don't apply when unmarried couples break up," points out the ATMP website, "it can be an important form of protection and provide guidance if the couple winds up in court." If, for instance, you are the wealthier member of an unmarried heterosexual couple and your relationship breaks up, your partner might sue you for *palimony*, claiming that you promised to support him or her for life and that all property acquired during the relationship would belong to both of you (Laskin 2003). Having a cohabitation agreement can help to avoid such problems. An example of a cohabitation agreement, or "romantic-love contract," appears at www.neo-tech.com/love-contract.

Domestic Partner Registries

Domestic partners are defined differently in different U.S. towns, cities, and states. Most include both straight and gay couples, but some include same-sex couples only. About 100 localities offer domestic partner registries, where you and your significant other can, if you meet certain criteria, pay a small fee and be registered as domestic partners. (A list of such localities may be found at *www.hrc.org/Template.cfm?Section=Domestic_partners1&Template=/CustomSource/Agency/AgencySearch1.cfm.*)

(continues)

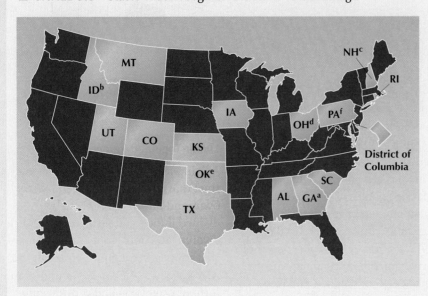

Notes about the following states:

[a]**Georgia** (if relationship created before January 1997)

[b]**Idaho** (if relationship created before January 1996)

[c]**New Hampshire** (for inheritance purposes only)

[d]**Ohio** (if relationship created before October 10, 1991)

[e]**Oklahoma** (possibly if created before November 1, 1998)

[f]**Pennsylvania** (if relationship created before September 2003)

Source: Alternatives for Marriage Project 2007.

The ATMP website (2007) points out that these registries usually offer no immediate benefits but that employers or insurance companies can, if they wish, rely on the registry's information to decide who is eligible for domestic partner health benefits, different insurance rates, and the like. It also points out that registries aren't the same thing as domestic partner benefits, which some organizations offer employees with unmarried partners so that they will have the same benefits for partners as married people do for spouses (health benefits, different insurance rates, and the like).

Wills

An advantage of the marriage contract is that a spouse is a legal heir, even when no will exists. If you're in a non-marital relationship, your partner won't inherit property from you unless you make formal provisions—in other words, have a will or a living trust. (For a description of the advantages and disadvantages of wills versus living trusts, go to *www.palimony.com/4 .html*.) If you die without a will, a pro-bate court will determine how your estate—your money and property—is to be divided and will probably distribute it to your closest blood relative, such as your parents, rather than to your partner.

Sometimes a handwritten will is sufficient. However, because such wills aren't recognized in all states and might have to be executed precisely (with no scratch-outs or insertions), it's best to consult a lawyer. Standard wills are relatively inexpensive, perhaps a couple of hundred dollars. Living trusts are more expensive, though

study that worried and pleased both sides of the argument. Judith Stacey and Timothy Biblarz reevaluated 21 psychological studies conducted between 1981 and 1998 that suggested children raised by same-sex parents were no different from those raised by straight parents. They concluded, however, that children with lesbian and gay parents are, in fact, different: They show more empathy for social diversity, and they are less confined by gender stereotypes. Finally, they are probably more likely to explore homosexual activity themselves (Stacey and Biblarz 2001).

"We say that there are some differences and that [scholars sympathetic to gays] have shied away from acknowledging them for fear that this would inflame homophobia," Stacey told a newspaper interviewer (Crary

easier on the survivor, and much harder for relatives to challenge in court.

Health-Care Proxy (Durable Power of Attorney for Health Care)

A *health-care proxy*, also known as a *durable power of attorney for health care*, gives your partner (or other designated person) the authority to make health-care decisions in case you're not able to do so. The form varies for each state. (You can download the form for your state by going to the Partnership for Caring website at *www.partnershipforcaring.com*.)

Durable Power of Attorney for Financial Management

A *durable power of attorney for financial management* gives your partner (or other designed person) the authority to manage your property and finances if you unable to do so. (More about legal and financial matters for unmarried partners is available at *www.unmarried.org/res.html#legal*.)

Insurance: Health, Car, Life

Unmarried couples should familiarize themselves with the following kinds of insurance (Block 1999):

- **Health insurance:** People in unmarried partnerships are much less likely than married couples to have health insurance, with 20% of same-sex couples and 35% of unmarried heterosexual couples uninsured compared with only 10% of married people and 15% of the overall population (Ash and Badgett 2006). Among people ages 18 to 34, incidentally, more than one-quarter lack health insurance (Lee 2006).

  Most company-funded health insurance plans allow employees to include spouses, but not unmarried partners, as dependents. Therefore, each partner needs to get his or her own medical insurance because, otherwise, each could be wiped out by medical bills.

- **Car insurance:** With married people, one's car insurance policy probably covers the spouse. Unmarried couples are usually obliged to get separate coverage. Beware, incidentally, of driving each other's cars unless you have listed each other as an occasional driver on your policy. (Incidentally, if you rent a car for a long trip, you might have to pay extra to the car-rental company for both you and your partner to drive—something that spouses don't have to worry about. Different companies have different exceptions to the rule, but you have to ask.)

- **Life insurance:** If you and your unmarried partner own a house, you should get a life insurance policy that names each other as beneficiaries. Otherwise, if one partner dies, the other might be unable to afford the mortgage payments.

Home Ownership: Joint Tenancy with Right of Survivorship

If you and your unmarried partner buy a house, you'll need to take steps to ensure that if one of you dies the surviving partner doesn't wind up on the street. (This is not a problem for married couples.) The mechanism for doing this is to include the phrase *joint tenancy with right of survivorship* in the title to the house. The joint tenancy agreement will also help to avoid probate.

Retirement Savings

Unlike married couples, a survivor in an unmarried couple has no right to the partner's Social Security benefits. In addition, some company pension plans exclude unmarried partners from being beneficiaries. It's important, therefore, if you and your unmarried partner plan on growing old together, that you contribute more to your respective retirement plans.

2001). Yet, she said, nothing in their research justified discrimination against gay families or altered her conviction that gays could be excellent parents raising well-adjusted children. Although some supporters worried that the Stacey/Biblarz research might reinforce attitudes against gay parenting, some leaders of national gay groups welcomed the article. "The stereotype is that gay parents make their children gay and want them to be gay," said the executive director of Children of Lesbians And Gays Everywhere, Felicia Park-Rogers (in Crary 2001). "The reality is that gay parents allow being gay to be an option. They know there are still difficulties about it."

9.4 Communal Living, Group Marriages, & Open Marriages

MAJOR QUESTION Would I ever consider communal living, group marriage, or open marriage?

PREVIEW Three types of communal arrangements or variations are described: communes, or people living and sharing together; group marriages, such as polygamy; and open marriages.

"Many people believe that the essence of [today's] marriage revolution is the multiplication of diverse family forms," Stephanie Coontz (2005) writes. This is not the case, however. "Through most of history," she continues, "family diversity was the norm, and some of the variations in marriage that were acceptable in the past make our own supposedly 'anything goes' society look downright conservative."

Consider a 1,400-year-old tradition that seems to be making a comeback in parts of Iraq—*mutaa,* also known as "pleasure marriage" and "temporary marriage." **A *mutaa* marriage is a secret betrothal in which a Shiite Muslim unmarried woman is allowed to enter into a pleasure marriage with a man (married or not) for periods as brief as a few minutes or as long as a lifetime** (Moore 2006). Although people who participate in *mutaa*—especially women—risk their reputations and prospects for permanent marriage, it has been used by divorced women whose former husbands have left them without financial support.

Or consider a new kind of housing development concept being used by seniors known as co-housing, an idea that has been on the rise in the United States since the first one opened in 1991. ***Co-housing* is communal housing that residents help design and share ownership in and that encourages interaction through common facilities and shared land** (Kornblum 2005; Brown 2006). Co-housing is not new. It began in Denmark in the 1960s among groups of families who were dissatisfied with existing housing and communities.

Communes

We are accustomed to thinking of relationships in either-or ways: A person is either alone or one-half of a couple. But for hundreds of years people have also lived in groups known as communes. **A *commune* is a group of adults, perhaps including children, who live together, sharing different aspects of their lives.**

Types of Communal Living

Communes have been in existence for at least a couple of thousand years, and in the widest sense of the term, communal living is not at all unusual today. Examples include:

■ **College Living Arrangements:** Many student readers of this book probably live in rented housing or fraternities or sororities and share a number of social and economic activities.

■ **Elder Living Arrangements:** Some senior citizens derive economic and emotional support from sharing living arrangements and living costs. Co-housing is one example.

■ **Co-Housing Communities:** As mentioned, a co-housing community consists of residents who vote on household decisions, share expenses and chores, and develop close emotional ties.

■ **Israeli Farming Cooperatives:** Kibbutzes are long-established farming cooperatives that have had great success in Israel.

The Shakers

One of the longest-lasting of communal living arrangements has been that of the Shakers, a religious group of self-governing communities established in 1774 that is still in existence. The Shakers have insisted on strict celibacy, believing that sexual activity leads to self-indulgence and other ills; therefore, the communities grow by converting outsiders to their faith rather than through procreation. As a result, however, the sect is on the verge of dying out.

Group Marriage

In *group marriage*, each member of the group is married to all other group members of the opposite sex. One famous example, the 1840s Oneida Community of New York State, practiced what its founder, John Humphrey Noyes, called "complex marriage," with every adult married to every other opposite-sex member. No exclusive personal relationships were permitted. Children were removed from their mothers as infants and raised communally, a matter that gave some mothers great difficulty (Dalsimer 1981).

Perhaps the modern kind of group marriage that has received the most attention recently—both because of the HBO TV drama *Big Love* about a Utah businessman with three wives and because of the long hunt, trial, and conviction of real-life polygamous leader Warren Jeffs for performing illegal marriages and abetting rape involving young girls—is the form of polygamy known as *polygyny*, the marriage of a man to two or more wives. Polygyny is still practiced in other countries of the world, such as Kenya, Guinea, Mali, and Tajikistan (Lacey 2003; Greenberg 2006; Bernstein 2007). In the United States, although illegal in all states, polygyny has been practiced by small groups of former Mormons who say they are following their religious beliefs

POLYGAMIST. Tom Green, 52, of Partoun, Utah, in a 2001 pose with his five wives. From left: Hannah, 24; LeeAnn, 28; Shirley, 31; Linda, 28 (the "head wife"); and Cari, 25. Green went to prison for bigamy, child support violations, and child rape. If no criminal behavior is involved, do you think the government should make monogamy public policy and criminalize other marital arrangements among consenting adults? ▶

(Altman and Ginat 1996). There are perhaps 30,000 to 50,000 members of polygamist families in the American West today who practice a form of Mormonism, although the Mormon church—the Church of Jesus Christ of Latter-day Saints—disavowed polygamy in 1890 (Soukup 2006).

Some public officials and former "plural wives" have been pushing for the prosecution of polygamy and the secret crimes that sometimes accompany it, such as incest, wife and child abuse, forced and underage marriages, and welfare and tax fraud (Madigan 2005). In late 2007, Warren Jeffs, a leader of one of Utah's largest sects, was convicted of arranging marriages with underage girls. Earlier, Tom Green, who had five wives and 31 children, went to prison for bigamy and child-support violations as well as for child rape for marrying a 13-year-old girl and conceiving a child with her.

But organizations advocating the decriminalization of polygamous marriage, such as the Centennial Park Action Committee, TruthBearer, and Principle Voices, argue that polygamy rights is the next civil rights battle (Soukup 2006). One journalist who has covered polygamy in rural Africa found that plural wives thought that "it was better to share one prosperous husband than to marry someone else without land, cows, or a job" (Tierney 2006). Although poor men may end up with no wives, women benefit because polygamy increases their marriage prospects, the only way in traditional societies that women can improve their lives. A former Utah wife (cited in Tierney 2006) who was married to a polygamist said she appreciated such benefits as round-the-clock day care and an opportunity when tired and stressed to let other wives take over chores.

Open Marriages

Yuri Shiller, age 48, and Lana Trumm, age 35, both born in Russia, have been married for 10 years and now live in San Francisco, where they practice conceptual art. They also practice something else: For two years, they have been regular visitors to Lush, one of 22 couples-only Bay Area sex clubs listed with NASCA International, formerly known as the North American Swing Club Association. At Lush, couples pay $80 per visit, and singles are not admitted.

A dress code is enforced: Patrons may not wear jeans or athletic clothing. If one is asked to "play"—have sex—a "no" answer is to be accepted as unequivocally as a "yes" (Guthrie 2002).

Swinging **is an arrangement in which committed couples exchange partners to engage in purely recreational sex.** Ted McIlvenna, president of the Institute for Advanced Study of Human Sexuality in San Francisco, who has studied sex clubs and swingers for many years, says that it's generally the man who wants to try swinging, but it's the woman who wants to go back to the club, because "she likes the sense of community" (quoted in Guthrie 2002: A4).

Swinging can be (but need not be) a component of an open marriage. In an ***open marriage,*** **or** *sexually open marriage,* **a married couple agrees that each may have emotional and sexual relations with others—they go out separately as well as together—while still keeping the marriage the primary relationship.** The movement toward swinging seems to have received some impetus with the publication of the 1972 book *Open Marriage* (O'Neill and O'Neill 1972).

"We are living our fantasy," Yuri Shiller says. "I'm glad when Lana finds something good at Lush." Says Trumm: "Lush has made our life much more interesting. We are closer than ever before. It's very sexy" (quoted in Guthrie 2002: A4). But while supporters of swinging and open marriage tout its benefits—variety, honesty—others mention problems with jealousy, guilt, fear of discovery by family and friends, and other unexpected problems (Macklin 1987; Masters et al. 1994).

Self-Assessment: Homophobia Scale

In 1996, as part of his study on homophobia, Dr. Henry Adams and his colleagues at the University of Georgia developed a 25-item homophobia scale "designed to measure your thoughts, feelings and behaviors with regards to homosexuality." What came to be known as the Wright, Adams, and Bernat Homophobia Scale appears on the website for PBS Online and WGBH Frontline. The instructions stress that this scale "is not a perfect measure of anti-gay feelings or ideas, and is not a predictor of potential for anti-gay violence." Nevertheless, the website says, "the scale can be used as a rough but worthwhile measure of heterosexual attitudes toward homosexuals."

To do this self-assessment, go to *www.pbs.org/wgbh/ pages/frontline/shows/assault/etc/quiz.html*.

Source: Wright, Adams, and Bernat Homophobia Scale. © 2000 PBS Online and WGBH Frontline. Based on Adams, Henry E., Lester W. Wright, Jr., and Bethany A. Lohr. 1996. Is homophobia associated with homosexual arousal? *Journal of Abnormal Psychology* 105(2):440–45; Wright, Lester W., Henry E. Adams, and Jeffrey Bernat. 1999. Development and validation of the homophobia scale. *Journal of Psychopathology and Behavioral Assessment* 21(4):337–47.

Key Terms Used in This Chapter

accommodationist single, p. 301
adoption, p. 318
adultolescents, p. 291
anti-gay prejudice, p. 310
artificial insemination, p. 319
bisexuality, p. 305
civil union, p. 316
closed-couple single, p. 300
co-housing, p. 324
"come out," p. 309
committed single, p. 300
commune, p. 325
commuter marriage, p. 290
discrimination, p. 310
domestic partners, p. 316
domestic partnership movement, p. 316
erotic feelings, p. 309
family, p. 292

foster parent, p. 318
free-floating single, p. 300
gay male, p. 305
group marriage, p. 325
heterosexuality, p. 305
homoeroticism, p. 309
homophobia, p. 310
homosexuality, p. 305
involuntary stable singles, p. 300
involuntary temporary singles, p. 300
lesbian, p. 305
LGBT, p. 305
lifestyle, p. 293
living-a part-together (LAT) couples, p. 290
mutaa, p. 324
nonfamily household, p. 292
open-couple single, p. 300

open marriage, p. 327
prejudice, p. 309
procreation, p. 304
second-parent adoptions, p. 318
sex ratio, p. 297
sexual orientation, p. 304
sexuality, p. 304
sexually open marriage, p. 327
single, p. 296
sperm bank, p. 320
sperm donor, p. 320
surrogate mother, p. 319
swinging, p. 327
transnational marriages, p. 290
voluntary stable singles, p. 299
voluntary temporary singles, p. 299

Summary

9.1 Different Family & Household Relationships

- Besides the more common nuclear and extended family structures, a number of new family structures have emerged. Four new variations are (1) platonic "roommate marriages"; (2) commuter, living-apart-together and transnational marriages; (3) grandparents raising children alone; and (4) adultolescents.

- In platonic or "roommate marriages," there is no sexual bond, but the roommates develop a deep emotional attachment for each other. A commuter marriage is a dual-career marriage in which each partner lives in a different location yet both of them still maintain their commitment to their family. Living-apart-together couples live in separate quarters. Transnational marriages are those in which one partner is in the United States and the other (and perhaps the children) is in another country.

- Skipped-generation households are family structures in which grandparents raise grandchildren. According to the 2000 census, more than 2.4 million grandparents are primary caregivers to a grandchild, usually because of death, drugs, divorce, abandonment, incarceration, or mental illness. Adultolescents are adult children who have moved back in with their parents.

- U.S. society is also seeing other variations in family structure and living arrangements, such as instances in which the wife is the family's primary or even sole breadwinner.

9.2 The Single Way of Life

- The single way of life includes the never-married, widowed, and divorced.
- Social trends today that encourage youths and young adults not to marry or to delay marriage include lack of potential marriage partners reflected through the sex ratio or the ratio of men to women within a particular social group, economic changes, and more liberal and individualistic sexual and social standards.
- The widowed represent approximately 6.4% of the adult population in the United States. Women are more apt to become widowed than men.
- The divorced represent approximately 10.2% of the adult population in the United States. Studies have shown that divorced people are considerably less happy than married people and are also less happy than the widowed.
- Compared to the first half of the 20th century, many youths and adults seemed to be committed to themselves first and marriage later. Among the stereotypes of singles and single life are that singles are self-centered, financially better off, happier, and confirmed in their singlehood.
- Research has found that singles have more time, have more fun, tend to be more comfortable with other singles, and are more apt to feel lonely than marrieds.
- Singles can be classified according to a typology of whether (1) they are voluntarily or involuntarily single and (2) their singlehood is temporary or stable. Voluntary temporary singles are those who are open to marriage but find seeking a mate a lower priority than other activities, such as gaining an education, starting a career, or self-development. Voluntary stable singles are those who are satisfied not to be married. Involuntary temporary singles are those who would like to marry and are actively seeking mates. Involuntary stable singles are those who would like to marry, have not found a mate, and have come to accept their single status.
- Singles can be classified according to five types based on whether or not their status is freely chosen:

free-floating, open-couple, closed-couple, committed, and accommodationist.

- Singlehood can be viewed as a lifestyle choice and life stage.
- An increasing number of singles are also parents, with women outnumbering men, although the number of men who are single parents is increasing at a faster rate.
- Single parents face many challenges. The median income for single mothers is significantly lower than is the median income for two-parent households. Children of single parents tend to have higher incidences of drug use and psychiatric illness.

9.3 The Gay & Lesbian Way of Life

- Procreation is the biological purpose of sex, or the bringing forth of children. Sexuality is the state of sexual being that encompasses not only the biological aspects of sex but psychological, social, and cultural aspects as well. Sexual orientation refers to sexual inclinations, such as one's feelings and sexual interactions, whether for the opposite gender, same gender, or both.
- Heterosexuality is the sexual inclination toward members of the opposite gender. Among some groups, being heterosexual is referred to as being straight. Homosexuality is the sexual inclination toward members of the same gender. Whether man or woman, if one is homosexual, one is also said to be gay. Bisexuality is the sexual inclination toward both genders.
- Accurate statistics regarding the percentage of gay men in the United States are difficult to obtain. Some of the difficulty in acquiring accurate results comes from different definitions or methodological approaches, reluctance to reveal one's sexual orientation, people's changing sexual behavior over their lifetime, the fact that sexual orientation is not just expressed through behavior, and the idea that sexual orientation may lie along a continuum.
- Research on the acquisition of a gay identity looks at biological and environmental factors, with evidence supporting both views.
- Erotic feelings are feelings of sensuality or sexuality. Homoeroticism is erotic attraction to a member of the same gender.
- Gays in society confront and deal with prejudice and discrimination. Prejudice is an attitude, usually negative, toward an individual or group. Discrimination is an act of unfair treatment directed against an individual or a group. Homophobia, or anti-gay prejudice, is defined as negative attitudes toward

homosexuality and homosexuals. Prejudice can be acted out in three ways: stage 1, offensive language; stage 2, discrimination; and stage 3, violence. Anti-gay feelings in the United States may result from personal insecurity, fundamentalist religious views, and ignorance about homosexuality.

■ Gay couples differ from straight couples in the following ways: egalitarian, dual-worker relationships with income or household responsibilities based on factors other than traditional masculine/feminine, breadwinner/homemaker roles and less family support and openness.

■ Gay men seem to have more casual sex than do either heterosexual men or lesbians, and their sexuality seems to be more body centered than personality centered, whereas gay women seem to emphasize committed relationships more than gay men do. Lesbians also have less casual sex than gay men do, and their sexuality is more personality centered than body centered.

■ Collective behavior and social movements have helped to bring greater public awareness of issues involving gay rights in the United States. Two types of relationships that might serve as stepping-stones in the move toward legalization of gay marriages are domestic partnerships and civil unions. Domestic partners are two people, gay or straight, who have chosen to cohabit or share one another's lives in an intimate and committed relationship without being married. The domestic partnership movement is an attempt to give some kind of official recognition to providing domestic partners with the legal and economic benefits of marriage. A civil union is a civil status similar to marriage, typically created for the purposes of allowing gay couples access to the benefits enjoyed by married heterosexuals. Most legislation recognizing some form of civil union has taken place outside the United States.

■ Many gays have children who were born when their fathers or mothers were part of a heterosexual marriage, before "coming out." Today, thousands of gays and lesbians in the United States are making the decision to become parents. Gay couples become parents by adoption or by biological means. Adoption is the legal process by which adult couples or singles voluntarily take a child born of other parents and raise him or her as their own child. Adoptions may be of two types: Second-parent adoptions, also known as co-parent adoptions, are situations in which the gay or lesbian partner of a biological or adoptive parent is given full legal status as the child's second parent; in a foster-parent adoption, an adult who raises a child not his or her own for a short period of time but does not formally adopt that child. Having children by biological means includes gay men having children with surrogate mothers. A surrogate mother may be artificially inseminated by a gay man. Artificial insemination is a process in which sperm are introduced artificially into the woman's vagina or uterus at about the time of ovulation. Lesbians may have children through using sperm donors. A lesbian might decide to become pregnant from a sperm donor, a male who makes his sperm available for artificial insemination.

9.4 Communal Living, Group Marriages, & Open Marriages

■ A commune is a group of adults, perhaps including children, who live together, sharing different aspects of their lives. Examples of communal living include college living arrangements, elder living arrangements, co-housing communities, and Israeli farming cooperatives, called kibbutzes.

■ Group marriages are marriages in which each member of the group is married to all other group members of the opposite sex. An example is polygamy.

■ In an open marriage, also referred to as a sexually open marriage, the married partners agree that each may have emotional and sexual relations with others. They go out separately as well as together while still keeping the marriage the primary relationship. Open marriages may also involve swinging, in which couples exchange partners to engage in purely recreational sex.

Take It to the Net

Among the Internet resources are the following:

■ **Alternatives to Marriage Project.** Offers financial and legal advice for people in unmarried relationships. *www.unmarried.org/faq.html*

■ **Children of Lesbians & Gays Everywhere (COLAGE).** Offers resources for homosexuals considering adoption. *www.colage.org*

- **Coalition for Marriage, Family, and Couples Education.** An independent, nonpartisan, nondenominational clearinghouse to help people find the information they need to strengthen marriages and families—their own or those in their community. *www.smartmarriages.com*
- **Domestic Partnership Benefits.** Lots of information about domestic partnership benefits for gay couples. *www.buddybuddy.com/d-p-1.html*
- **Family Pride Coalition.** National group supporting gay, lesbian, bisexual, and transgendered parents and their families. *familypride.org*
- **GayChristian, Net.** Provides resources to gay, lesbian, and bisexual christians. *www.gaychristian.net*
- **GayData.org.** Website grounded in scientific knowledge for those looking for information about lesbians, gays, and bisexuals. *www.gaydata.org*
- **Gay & Lesbian Alliance Against Defamation (GLAAD).** An organization dedicated to promoting and ensuring fair, accurate, and inclusive representation of people and events in the media as a means of eliminating homophobia and discrimination based on gender identity and sexual orientation. Has a list of newspapers that allow same-sex celebration announcements. *www.glaad.org*
- **Gay Financial Network.** Offers financial advice for gay consumers. *www.gfn.com*
- **Generations United.** National organization focusing on promoting intergenerational strategies for families in which youth and elderly people live together. *www.gu.org*
- **Human Rights Campaign.** An organization that works for lesbian, gay, bisexual, and transgender equal rights. *www.hrc.org*
- **NASCA International.** Known as the North American Swing Club Association before it went international. *http://nasca.com/states/nasca_faq.html*
- **National Shared Housing Resource Center.** A network of more than 300 programs under the auspices of nonprofit agencies, which offer a matching process for finding roommates of all ages to share housing. *www.nationalsharedhousing.org*
- **Soulforce.** Provides information about gay adoptions and foster care. *www.soulforce.org/main/adopt.shtml*
- **Straight Spouse Network.** Offers services for heterosexuals whose partners have disclosed that they are gay, lesbian, bisexual, or transgender. *www.ssnetwk.org*

CHAPTER 10

REPRODUCTION

Decisions about Having or Not Having Children

Reproduction by High-Tech Means

Jeffrey Harrison, 50 years old, was the son of an Ivy League–educated financial executive, but he opted for a more unconventional life-path and today lives with four dogs in a recreational vehicle near the Venice section of Los Angeles, where he survives by doing odd jobs, such as taking care of dogs. "I make a meager living," he reports. Back in the late 1980s, however, he earned $400

a month as donor number 150, giving his sperm twice weekly to a sperm bank, where he was one of the most-requested donors, profiled as 6 feet tall, blue-eyed, and with interests in philosophy, music, and drama (Harmon 2007; Kolata 2007).

Years later Harrison read in a newspaper that two teenagers whose mothers had used his sperm to conceive were looking for their father—donor number 150. The sperm bank, which had promised anonymity to its customers and donors, refused to offer assistance. Harrison then logged on to the Donor Sibling Registry, a website devoted to facilitating connections between donor-conceived offspring, where he discovered six teenagers for whom he was the biological father.

He worried that they might be disappointed in his humble circumstances, but when 17-year-old Danielle P. first spoke to him by phone, she was upbeat. "He's sort of a free spirit," she says, "and I don't care what career he has. I got to talk to his dogs." Since then, other offspring around the country who have contacted him marvel over the shared love of animals and the distinctive forehead evident in photos he has emailed them.

As we mentioned in Chapter 1, "Seeking," the theme of this book is finding happiness in intimacy in a complex world. One of the things that makes the world complex, of course, is ongoing changes in technology—and nowhere is this more apparent than in

💡 WHAT'S AHEAD IN THIS CHAPTER

We discuss possible reactions to having children, the choices prospective parents have, what influences people to have children, and the costs of raising children. We then discuss five general methods of birth control. Next, we focus on abortion and safe haven laws. Finally, we describe causes of infertility, six types of assisted reproduction technology, and the subject of adoption.

what is known as "assisted reproductive technology," the various treatments and procedures by which human eggs and sperm may be manipulated to produce a pregnancy.

Perhaps for you, having a child, if you want one, will be easy (or has been easy), and maybe your main concern now is to *not* have one by mistake. (We discuss the latest information on contraception and abortion in this chapter.) But there are many millions of people who have difficulty conceiving, and more than 1 million babies worldwide—1 to 2% of births in the United States and Canada—are due to laboratory-induced fertility (Marchione 2007).

The mass media report all kinds of medical wonders. Some example headlines:

■ *Fortune:* "So You Want a Girl?"— about letting parents order up the sex of their child (Wadman 2001).

■ *Time:* "Eggs on Ice: A Woman's Fertility Often Peaks Before She's Ready to Have Babies. Does Banking Her Eggs Make Sense?" (Hamilton 2002).

■ *USA Today:* "Donor Eggs Can Let Women Over 50 Produce Viable Babies" (Rubin 2002).

■ *Reno Gazette-Journal:* "Mother, 66, Well After Historic Birth" (2005).

■ *San Francisco Chronicle:* "Manufacture of Human Eggs on Horizon" (Ross 2001).

Sometimes the news stories verge on the fantastic:

■ *San Francisco Chronicle:* "55-Year-Old Mom: Surrogate Gives Birth to Triplets—Her Own Grandkids"—about an older woman, acting as a surrogate for her daughter, giving birth to triplets (Associated Press 2004).

■ *USA Today:* "Blueprint for Life . . . 'Designer Baby' Technology Could Be the Next Big Thing"—about labs screening test-tube embryos for genetic diseases and to create healthy babies (Friend 2003).

■ *The Week:* "Her Daughter Would Be Her Sister" (2007)—about a Canadian mother who had frozen her eggs for her infertile daughter, meaning the daughter might one day give birth to her own sister.

■ *Reno Gazette-Journal:* "U.S. Couple to Try Cloning . . ." (2002)—about a Kentucky reproductive physiologist who had found couples willing to try a cloning procedure at an undisclosed foreign clinic.

■ *San Francisco Chronicle:* And finally the most bizarre: "Cloned Baby Girl Is on the Way, Scientist Promises: Group Linked to Belief in Extraterrestrials"—about a report saying supposedly a baby was about to be born that was cloned from a woman's cell fused with one of her eggs, an event that never happened (Ritter 2002).

Technology offers more possible choices. Even so, advancing age decreases your ability to produce offspring. You and your partner therefore need to decide the best time to have children. The twenties and early thirties are the most fertile time—regardless of the technology miracles reported in the media.

ON THE WEB Safe Haven Laws

www.religioustolerance.org/saf_have.htm

There are many ways in which one might begin the study of reproduction. To take an unusual approach, consider what you might do if you had an unwanted child. Do you know what safe haven laws are? To find out, go to the website listed above.

MAJOR QUESTIONS
you should be able to answer

What are my feelings about having children, and what influences these feelings?

Which kind of birth-control method would probably be best for me and my partner?

What have I learned about abortion and safe haven laws that I didn't know?

If I wanted children but had difficulty conceiving them, what would my options be?

10.1 Having or Not Having Children: Choice or Fate?

MAJOR QUESTION What are my feelings about having children, and what influences these feelings?

PREVIEW In this section, we describe possible reactions to having children. We then discuss four choices prospective parents have: to be child-free, to postpone having children, to have one child, or to have many children. Then we consider what influences people to have children: general fertility trends; race, ethnicity, and religion; and education and income. Finally, we describe the costs of raising children.

How important are children to your happiness? Could you actually be happy without children? These are crucial questions, for the answers could make a vast difference in your life.

Perhaps you already have children. Or perhaps you would like to be a parent some day—most people think they would. Only a minority of Americans—about 4%—say that they never want children or are glad they don't have kids (Exter 1991). According to Halle (2000: Table 1), 65% of American males and 74% of American females have had biological children. Most young people express a desire to have children, according to a study of 505 undergraduate students, even those who say they are "unsure," although women are more sensitive than men to the effect of parenthood on their employment and career prospects (O'Laughlin and Anderson 2001). Do these findings mean that most people consider children to be an important part of happiness?

How Would You React If You Suddenly Learned That You'll Be a Parent?

Suppose you suddenly learn that you or your partner is expecting a baby. How would you react? In their book *When Partners Become Parents*, University of California, Berkeley, psychologists **Carolyn and Philip Cowan** (2000) identify four kinds of reactions.

Planner Partners: "A Baby! Hallelujah!"

Couples who have planned to have children, who have discussed the issue in detail and have come to a joint decision to do so, will express jubilation on learning that a baby could be on the way. The partners look forward to having a committed, intimate relationship with their children as they grow up.

Acceptance-of-Fate Partners: "What a Pleasant Surprise!"

Often, couples will not actively discuss or plan to have children, but they might unconsciously be in favor of the idea, perhaps not being rigorous about practicing contraception. For them, the announcement of pregnancy might come as a pleasant surprise.

Ambivalent Partners: "We Really Didn't Want a Baby, but We'll Go Ahead with It"

Couples of this sort usually didn't plan to have a baby and are shocked when they receive the news of pregnancy. Although they might have mixed feelings, they will proceed with the pregnancy anyway, perhaps because one partner wants the baby and the other concedes or because neither believes in abortion, or because an abortion might be wanted but be unobtainable.

Yes–No Partners: "I Want a Baby, My Partner Doesn't, but I'll Have It Anyway"

In this case, one partner (usually the man) doesn't want to have the baby, but the other partner (usually the woman) decides to have it anyway. Often, the result is that the pregnancy or the birth leads to separation or divorce.

At this point in your life, which one of these reactions would you be most likely to express? How about 5 years from now? Ten years? Can you think of other reactions a person might have?

NEW LIFE. Some pregnancies are planned, some unplanned but accepted, and some unwanted. How would you react if you learned that you or your partner were expecting a baby? ▲

The Choices: Child-Free, Postponing Children, One Child, or Many Children?

Oprah Winfrey decided never to have children. Actor Tony Randall was 77 years old when he and his 27-year-old wife had a child. David Letterman and his wife have one child. George W. and Laura Bush have two children. Former President George H. W. and Barbara Bush have five children, including George W. (a sixth died in childhood). Clearly, many kinds of approaches are possible when it comes to being a parent or not being a parent. Consider the choices available: no children, having children later, having one child, or having several children.

NUMBERS THAT MATTER
Having or Not Having Children

■ **How many people don't want kids?** Only about 4% of Americans say that they never want children or are glad they don't have kids. Among American adults, 65% of males and 74% of females have had a biological child.[a]

■ **Are fewer children being born?** Children as a percentage of the U.S. population are decreasing. Among women ages 15–44, 8.9% have said that they don't expect to have children.[b] Among women ages 18 to 34, 9.3% of whites and African Americans and 5.7% of Latinas said that they plan to remain child-free.[c]

■ **Which women have the highest fertility rates?** Among women ages 15 to 29, fertility rates are highest among low-income women (under $10,000 annually) and lowest among high-income women (making $75,000 or more). But among women ages 30–44, high-income women have the highest fertility rates, and lower-income women ($10,000–$29,999) have the lowest.[d]

■ **How much does it cost to raise a child?** For middle-income parents, raising a child (in a two-child family) to age 18 will cost an average of $197,700.[e]

■ **How long does it usually take to conceive a child?** One researcher found that the average (median) time for a sexually active couple using no contraception to conceive was 2½ months. The majority conceived within 6 months, but some couples took 2 years or more.[f]

■ **Which foster children are hardest to find adoptions for?** Most in demand are children age 5 or younger; hardest to place are 16- to 18-year-olds.[g]

[a]Halle 2002; Exeter 1991. [b]Abma et al. 1997. [c]U.S. Census Bureau 1997, Table 107. [d]Legislative Commission on the Economic Status of Women 1999. [e]Lino 2007. [f]Guttmacher 1983. [g]Adoption and Foster Care Analysis and Reporting System 2006.

Child-Free: Voluntarily Having No Children

Alicia and Doug Strauss of Menlo Park, California, decided that they would have a *child-free marriage*—**a marriage that is voluntarily without children.** ("Child-free" is to be distinguished from "*childless*," **which is involuntary.**) Doug feels the world is too heavily populated. Alicia, while in the Peace Corps in Africa, saw the effects of overpopulation in badly malnourished babies. The couple belongs to a loose-knit social organization of child-free couples called "No Kidding!" "It's a nice way to meet people," Alicia says (Dremann 2002).

Children as a percentage of the population are decreasing. *(See ■ Panel 10.1.)* Among American women ages 15 to 44, 8.9% have said that they don't expect to have children (Abma et al. 1997). Among women ages 18 to 34, 9.3% of whites and African Americans and 5.7% of Latinas said that they plan to remain child-free (U.S. Census Bureau 1997: Table 107). The reasons for opting out of child raising range from religion to ideology to simple lifestyle preference ("Childless by choice" 2001).

Most women who opt to be child-free have college or graduate/professional degrees and are career oriented (Ambry 1992). In general, married couples with kids have less discretionary income than their married-without-children counterparts. In 2003, families in which husbands worked full time and their wives also worked earned a median yearly income of $81,255, but those who had no related children made over $4,000 more (U.S. Census Bureau 2006: Table 681).

However, many people who opt to be without children as a deliberate choice have to deal with our society's *pronatalist bias* **(the word "natal"**

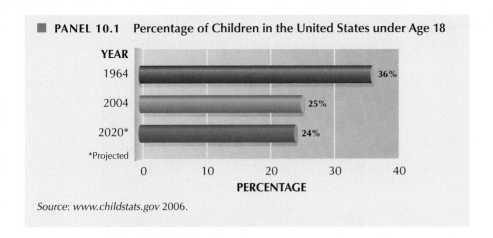

PANEL 10.1 Percentage of Children in the United States under Age 18

YEAR

1964   36%

2004   25%

2020*   24%

*Projected

0   10   20   30   40

PERCENTAGE

Source: www.childstats.gov 2006.

relates to birth), the cultural attitude that takes having children for granted (May 1997). One study, for example, found that college students considered employed women with two children to be the norm—they perceived voluntarily child-free women as an aberrant (Mueller and Yoder 1997). Pronatalist pressure may especially be felt by couples with middle-aged parents who would like to become grandparents.

Yet despite feeling negatively stereotyped by society, child-free couples have been found to be more satisfied with their relationships than are couples who are parents (Somers 1993).

Indeed, as we saw in our look at the family life cycle (Chapter 8, "Marriage"), most couples say that they experience their greatest satisfaction with each other before children come along and after grown children have left home (Glenn 1991; Vaillant and Vaillant 1993). Other studies also find higher levels of marital happiness in child-free marriages compared to unions with children (Somers 1993; Twenge et al. 2003; Whitehead and Popenoe 2006). On the other hand, it must be pointed out that unhappy married couples who are parents might be more apt to stay together ("for the sake of the children"), whereas unhappy couples who are child-free are more apt to divorce (White et al. 1986).

Postponing Children: Having Babies Later

Women are waiting longer to have their first child. *(See* ■ *Panel 10.2.)* In the 1970s, only 4% of American women had first babies at age 30 or over. By 1998, the figure was 23%, and the trend seems to be continuing, especially among women who are better educated and economically better off (Edmondson et al. 1993; Bachu 1999; Ventura et al. 2000). Key factors in postponing children, of course, have been the availability of effective birth control and legal abortion, as well as reproductive technologies, as we will describe. The result is that the United States has become a much more adult-focused rather than child-focused society because longer life expectancy, delayed marriage and childbearing, and increased childlessness add up to a longer life without kids (Whitehead and Popenoe 2006).

There are advantages and disadvantages to deferring parenthood:

■ **Advantages:** Delaying having children allows couples to finish their educations, get established in their careers, have more time to develop their rela-

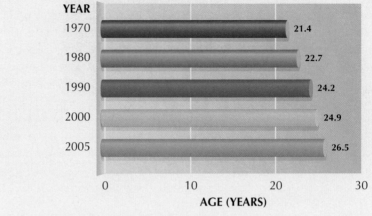

■ **PANEL 10.2   Women Waiting Longer.** The average age of American mothers, 15 to 44 years old, giving birth to first child is rising.

Source: Centers for Disease Control & Prevention 2003; Hamilton et al. 2006.

tionship with each other, and build the economic resources to provide for children (who, as we will see, are one of the greatest expenses one can take on).

■ **Disadvantages:** Couples who wait until after age 30 to have children might find themselves with heavy career demands just at the time they are expected to care for young children, and they might also be anxious to return to the happier child-free time when they could enjoy their own privacy and absence of responsibility. Of course, fertility tends to diminish with age, so that the later one waits to have children, the greater is the possibility that it will be too late (although use of reproductive technologies can help, as we'll describe). Women in their forties also have a higher risk for bearing children with ***Down*** **(or *Down's*) *syndrome*, a genetic condition that leads to various degrees of mental retardation and physical disability.**

One Child: Are "Only Children" Different?

According to recent figures from the U.S. Census Bureau, the proportion of only children has nearly doubled in the past 25 years or so—from about 9.6% of all families in the 1970s to more than 17% in 1998 and to more than 20% in 2005 (U.S. Census Bureau 2006; Table 66).

Many people stereotype only children as being spoiled, lonely, and selfish, but the research shows there are no major differences in these traits in only children compared with other children (Falbo 1976; Pines 1981). Indeed, only children tend to have more self-confidence and self-reliance and higher IQs and verbal skills, and they get good to excellent grades (Hawke and Knox 1978).

More Than One Child

Eighteen percent of American families in 2005 had two children under 18 years old (down from 19% 15 years earlier). Ten percent of families had three children or more (U.S. Census Bureau 2006: Table 66).

Parents who have a second child tend to do so for the following reasons: They believe that the first child should have a sibling companion. They want "a little insurance" in case something happens to the first child. They hope that the second child will be of a different sex from the first so that the family will have both a boy and a girl. They are apt to have a third child if they already have two children of the same sex—particularly if those children are girls—in hopes of getting a child of the opposite sex (Knox and Wilson 1978; Jones et al. 1995). Economists argue that the costs, in time and money, involved in raising children are a key consideration in determining the number of children and the expenditure on each (Duncan and Magnuson 2002).

Every child who is added to a family changes the dynamics within that family. For instance, older children often slip in reading achievement and in grades as the parents' attention turns to the newborn (Baydar et al. 1997; Barber 1998). As other children come along, the older children receive even less attention (Menaghan and Parcel 1995). Conversely, recent research on birth order also suggests that the very existence of an older sibling increases the chances that a younger sibling will get involved in risky behaviors—smoke, use marijuana, or have sex (Argys et al. 2006). On the other hand, members of large families tend to emphasize cooperation over independence, stressing sharing rather than personal development, compared to people in smaller families.

What Influences People to Have Children?

There are many individual reasons why you might want to have or not have children—and many reasons for deciding how many to have, when, and the preferred gender (if one is preferred). Teenagers and women in their twenties might have children to be accepted by their friends, who might also be having babies. Some young women do it to avoid having to settle on a career—or because they don't have the opportunity to develop feelings of competence and achievement outside the family (White and Kim 1987). Others might want to fulfill their own parents' wish for a grandchild. Some do it for religious reasons (Gerson 1986). Some have children to please their spouses—a significant influence, in fact (Thompson 1997). Some do it to leave a legacy, to extend the family line (Berelson 1979). Finally, many do it in the belief that it will add to their happiness, fulfill their uniqueness as human beings, and give them a sense of accomplishment (Gallup and Newport 1990; Groat et al. 1997).

In addition, there are larger social and economic factors that influence people's having children: (1) general trends in family size; (2) race and ethnicity; and (3) education, income, and workforce status.

1. General Trends in Family Size

Fertility refers to both the ability to reproduce biologically and a person's actual reproductive performance. **Fertility rates** refer to the number of births per year per thousand women of child-bearing age (ages 15 to 44).

In general, families have been getting smaller. In the 18th and early 19th centuries, for example, families with five children or more were not uncommon. Children were an asset as workers in a predominantly agricultural society that had a high infant mortality rate. But as the Industrial Revolution brought more

EXAMPLE OF
Being Childless in a Child-Oriented Society

A Woman's View, a Man's View

How do people who have never had children feel about their status? Here are two views, taken from the *Child-Free Zone: Why More People Are Choosing NOT to Be Parents*, at *www.childfree.net*:

One Woman's View

"I never made a conscious decision not to have children. I just never decided to have them. I remember when I was about 12, my aunt and uncle came to visit with my cousin and her new baby. They put the baby on my lap and I remember carefully sliding it slowly to the floor while they were talking. When they saw what I had done my aunt said: 'Don't you want one some day?' My response was 'I'd rather have a llama.' I wanted to be a zookeeper when I was 12.

"My husband told me that he never thought one way or the other about having kids, he just thought that whoever he married would probably want them. Several of our male friends say the same thing. He's actually very good with children and would have made a great father but he says he's glad that we don't have them. So I would say that we are equal in our decision. I'm glad that I didn't fall for someone who desperately wanted kids. I think that when I was younger, I may have changed my mind just to please them and it would have been a disaster. Now that I'm older, I know for a fact that I would be miserable if I had a child. . . .

"A friend of mine who has recently started a family told me that your relationship is never the same after the kids come along. . . . At the moment, I prefer spending time with people whose kids have grown up or who are child-free. I don't like feeling guilty because I don't get a warm fuzzy feeling when I see a small child or baby and I'm sick of pretending I do."

One Man's View

"I never made a decision not to have children as such. Children were just never a high personal priority for me. My wife is more against having children. There was some peer pressure earlier in our marriage. But generally this decision did not cause any significant strain in our relationship. We were too busy in career building (we started a business) in the early years of our marriage. Both my wife and I worked in the business, and we used to travel a lot for a period of four to five years. . . . I also think that current social and environmental conditions are not conducive to having children. Do we really want to bring more children into a world where thousands of other kids die each day, an overpopulated world with an increasing crime rate and global warming?

"The main benefit is that I retain my personal identity. I am John the person rather than being so-and-so's father. I am also able to concentrate more on personal development and maintain a younger outlook in life.

---

women into the workplace and as improved public health and medical technology reduced the rates of infant mortality, families became smaller, with most parents opting to have two children (Thornton and Freedman 1983).

2. Race, Ethnicity, & Religion

Fertility rates vary for different ethnic and racial groups, with Hispanics/Latinos having the highest rates and whites having the lowest. For example, the average number of children per woman in 2005 was as follows: Hispanics—2.9; non-Hispanic blacks—2.0; Asian and Pacific Islanders—1.9; non-Hispanic whites—1.8; and American Indians and Alaska Natives—1.7 (Kent 2007).

Possible reasons for the high rates are that Hispanics/Latinos who are immigrants tend to be Catholic, to be from rural areas favoring large families, and to rely on children for additional family income and support of parents

However, at times I feel like [my wife and I are] social outcast[s]. As most of our friends have children and they all want to do children's things, we are on the bottom of their priority list. We had some pressure from family and friends when we first got married. Fortunately our respective parents are quite liberal in their thinking and after a while, everyone got used to the idea.

"As far as I am concerned, a child is a poor legacy to leave as my mark on this world. I would like to be remembered for such things like achievements [or], if not, at least to leave behind some fond memories by my friends and people I touched that I was a good and kind and sincere person."

Some people are childless by choice; others remain childless because they cannot afford reproduction-assisted technology or adoption or because of ill health or other life problems. Does society view childless people as worthless?

In one episode on the former TV sitcom *Ally McBeal*, Calista Flockhart played an unmarried, highly paid lawyer who saw dancing babies in the middle of dates with men. Columnist Julianne Malveaux (2002) points out the cultural ambivalence this reveals about our society: "You could make six figures, live in a nice place, and have a full life, but the dancing baby told you that you were unfulfilled."

Of course, most women don't work in professional or managerial jobs or make $100,000 or more a year (in fact, only 1.1% do, compared with 5.4% of men). In reality, for many working mothers, whether married or single, juggling job and children is a continuing struggle.

According to 2004 Census Bureau data, the proportion of the American female population ages 15 to 44 that was childless was 44.6%, up from 35% in 1976, representing the fastest-growing demographic group to emerge in decades. The trend may reflect social forces such as the changing nature of the economy or the increased economic independence of women. Regardless, these women, says Madelyn Cain in *The Childless Revolution* (2002), are reshaping the definition of womanhood in a fundamental way, yet they are largely misunderstood. Whether childless by choice or by chance, they are alternately pitied and scorned and are rarely asked directly about their childlessness; like the "crazy aunt in the attic," childlessness is a taboo subject. However, many people who have made the choice to be child-free are happy with their decisions, as the statements above show.

The case can certainly be made that being childless need not mean a short-changed life. Many childless women, points out Malveaux, lead fulfilling lives by helping friends with their offspring. "We are the women who scoop the kids up on a Saturday to give a mother a much-needed break," she writes. "We're the impartial shoulder that some youngsters lean on—and our lives are enhanced because we have young people in them."

WHAT DO YOU THINK? Having a child is one of the most important decisions one can make. How would you feel if you were never to have children?

Source: Adapted from stories on the website *www.childfree.com.au* for *Child-Free Zone: Why More People Are Choosing Not to Be Parents* by Susan J. and David L. Moore, available at *www.authors@childfree.com* and *www.cafepress.com/cfz.*

in their old age. In general, families whose religions are Catholic or Mormon tend to have higher fertility rates.

3. Education & Income Status

In general, though not invariably, the more education and income a woman has, the lower is the fertility rate. *(See ■ Panel 10.3, next page.)* Women with high school degrees have the highest birth rates, followed by college-educated women and those with less than a high school education.

Among women ages 15 to 29, fertility rates are highest among low-income women (under $10,000 annually) and lowest among high-income women (making $75,000 or more). But among women ages 30 to 44, this trend is almost reversed: High-income women have the highest fertility rates, and lower-income women ($10,000 to $29,999) have the lowest (Dye 2005).

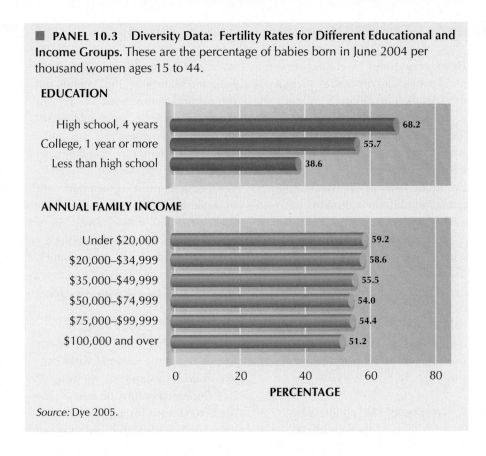

■ **PANEL 10.3 Diversity Data: Fertility Rates for Different Educational and Income Groups.** These are the percentage of babies born in June 2004 per thousand women ages 15 to 44.

EDUCATION

High school, 4 years — 68.2
College, 1 year or more — 55.7
Less than high school — 38.6

ANNUAL FAMILY INCOME

Under $20,000 — 59.2
$20,000–$34,999 — 58.6
$35,000–$49,999 — 55.5
$50,000–$74,999 — 54.0
$75,000–$99,999 — 54.4
$100,000 and over — 51.2

PERCENTAGE

Source: Dye 2005.

The Costs of Raising Children

How much does it cost to raise a child? A middle-income family (earning $44,500 to $74,900 a year) with two children might well spend 40 to 45% or more of their after-tax income on their offspring. For a child born in 2006 of a middle-income family with two children, the cost before age 18 could be $197,700 (in 2006 dollar values). And college expenses are yet to come!

College expenses and what economists call ***opportunity costs—the loss of wages and investments that parents sacrifice by devoting their time and energy to other pursuits (namely, child rearing)***—drive the cost even higher. For example, based on a survey of more than 40,000 mothers, Salary.com (2007) determined that the time mothers spend performing 10 typical job functions would equate to an annual salary of $138,095 for a stay-at-home mom—a salary that, of course, she does not collect, which represents an opportunity cost. (A working mother's "at-home" salary would be equivalent to $85,939 in 2007; this would be in addition to the salary she earned in the workplace.)

The cost of parenting varies, of course, depending on whether a family is low, middle, or high income and also whether it is a two-parent or single-parent family (single parents spend less). It also varies depending on the region of the country, with the West being most expensive, followed by the Northeast, South, and Midwest. *(See ■ Panel 10.4.)* These estimated costs may seem fearsome enough, but *The Wall Street Journal* looked at what parents are currently spending on children through age 17 in the way of "extras"—including every-

■ PANEL 10.4   The Costs of Raising a Child. Estimated average expenditures of raising a child to age 18 by a husband-and-wife family in urban regions of the United States in 2006. The West is most expensive; the Midwest is the least. Rural areas are cheaper than urban areas. College and other costs beyond age 18 are additional.

GEOGRAPHICAL AREA (URBAN)	FAMILY INCOME RANGE		COST OF RAISING A CHILD TO AGE 18*
West	Low	Less than $44,900	$161,250
	Middle	$44,900–$75,600	$215,520
	High	More than $75,600	$304,740
Northeast	Low	Less than $45,200	$155,220
	Middle	$45,200–$76,100	$208,680
	High	More than $76,100	$297,210
South	Low	Less than $44,200	$145,050
	Middle	$44,200–$74,400	$200,040
	High	More than $74,400	$289,350
Urban	Low	Less than $44,000	$130,230
	Middle	$44,000–$74,000	$183,510
	High	More than $74,000	$270,630

*Costs include housing, food, transportation, clothing, healthcare, child care and education, and miscellaneous expenses such as personal-care items, entertainment, and reading materials.

Source: Lino 2007: Appendix 2, Tables 2–5.

thing from orthodontia to clothing to cars to college saving plans—and projected that some well-off parents might spend between $776,000 and $1.6 million per child (Daspin and Gamerman 2007).

Another cost in raising children, as we will see in Chapter 11, "Parenting," is the anxiety, stress, and fatigue that children can bring, particularly during the infant years, when it's difficult for parents to find time for themselves.

Thus, although children can clearly bring great benefits, pleasure, and joy, parents also pay a price for making the decision to raise them. Consequently, the best thing people can do—both for themselves and for prospective children—is to make sure having children is a *choice,* not an accident. The basis for this is our next topic: contraception.

10.2 Contraception: Practical Methods of Birth Control

MAJOR QUESTION Which kind of birth-control method would probably be best for me and my partner?

PREVIEW This section describes five general methods of birth control: (1) natural family planning methods, (2) barrier methods, (3) hormonal methods, (4) sterilization, and (5) emergency contraception. In general, we consider them in order from least effective to most effective.

A major theme of this book, as we have stated, is happiness and how to realize it in intimate relations. How happy do you think you would be if you suddenly found out that you were going to be responsible for a child you had not planned on? How would it affect your future?

There are many different contraceptive methods, and no one can tell others which method is best for them. Today, however, concerns about preventing pregnancy often have to be linked with concerns about protection from sexually transmitted diseases (STDs). In general, for anyone who is sexually active and not in a long-term, mutually monogamous relationship, there is a single method of contraception and protection. That method is *condoms*, especially combined with *nonoxynol-9*, an antiviral, antibacterial spermicidal agent. Heterosexual couples who need not worry about STDs, however, have a great many choices in contraception.

The Abstinence Controversy: Bad Science at Work?

In recent years, teenage pregnancies have declined 36% between 1991 and 2002, according to figures from the U.S. government and the Alan Guttmacher Institute (cited in Koch 2006). In part it might be because sexually active teens are more apt to use birth control, spurred by fear of AIDS and by expanded options in contraception. It could also be the result of a governmental focus on abstinence-only programs and virginity pledges, as claimed by, for example, conclusions to studies by the conservative Heritage Foundation (Rector and Johnson 2005a, 2005b). The federal government spends about $176 million annually on abstinence-until-marriage education, a cornerstone of Bush administration social policy (Stepp 2007).

But does abstinence-only education work? Not according to a taxpayer-funded study ordered by Congress and conducted by Mathematica Policy Research Inc. (Trenholm et al. 2007). Mathematica looked at 2,057 students in grades 3 through 8 in rural and urban communities who had been randomly assigned to one of four abstinence-only programs, as well as a control group of students who did not participate in such programs. The result: By age 16½, abstinence-only students were just as likely to have had sex as those in the control group. Those who became sexually active—about half of each group—started at the same age, 14.9 years on average, and had the same number of sexual partners. As for the drop in teenage pregnancies, other researchers (Santelli et al. 2007) attribute 86% of the decline to greater and more effective use of contraceptives and only 14% to teens deciding to wait longer before having sex.

What about all the research that shows that abstinence-only education works? Douglas Kirby (2001), of the National Campaign to Prevent Teen Pregnancy, has analyzed a great many sex-education programs. Recently, when he started to update his research, according to journalist Sharon Begley (2007), "he had 111 studies that were scientifically sound, using rigorous methods to evaluate whether a program met its goals. . . . He also had a pile of studies that were too poorly designed to include. It measured three feet high." Some abstinence studies, for example, follow their subjects for only a few months, not several years. Or they evaluate only those who stay in a just-say-no program, not those who were expelled for having sex. Or they don't count teens who, when they begin having sex, pretend to forget they ever made a virginity pledge. Is this junk science? "No one is alleging that scientists stack the deck on purpose," says Begley. "Let's just say that depending on how you design a study you can practically preordain the outcome."

Contraceptive Choices

There are many criteria for choosing a method of contraception. These criteria range from availability to effectiveness to cost to considerations of personal comfort, health, and religious beliefs. Many people also recognize the benefits of combining methods, which increases effectiveness.

"Contraceptive" Methods That Usually Don't Work

People have highly mistaken ideas about what they can do to prevent conception. These include the following:

■ **No Method at All:** Using no method of contraception at all has the highest failure rate for birth control. In one study, 85% of fertile women were estimated to have become pregnant using this "method" within one year (Kost et al. 1991). This was at least four times as high as the rate among those using *any* method of birth control.

■ **Breast Feeding:** Nursing delays fertility in many women after childbirth. However, it is an unreliable form of birth control, since no one can predict in whom ovulation is suppressed and for how long. About 80% of women ovulate before their menstrual periods return after childbirth. Nursing mothers should therefore use other methods of contraception.

■ Douching: *Douching* **is the practice of rinsing out the vagina with a chemical solution right after sexual intercourse.** From the standpoint of birth control it is almost worthless. Although douching is an attempt to "wash out" the ejaculate, it actually often brings the sperm into contact with the cervix. Moreover, some sperm are able to enter the uterus within seconds of ejaculation, before a woman has a chance to begin douching.

Five Categories of Contraception

The five principal categories of birth control are (1) natural planning methods, (2) emergency contraception, (3) barrier methods, (4) hormonal methods, and (5) sterilization. We describe these methods here, in general proceeding from contraceptive methods that are *least effective* to those that are *most effective. (See* ■ *Panel 10.5.)* The specific forms of birth control are discussed in Appendix E, "Contraceptive Choices."

1. Natural Family Planning Methods

Natural family planning methods **of birth control mainly include various ways of gauging times for periodic abstinence—the calendar method, the BBT method, the cervical mucus method.** It can also include withdrawal.

2. Emergency Contraception

Emergency contraception, **also known as** *postcoital birth control,* **refers to various methods of protecting a woman from getting pregnant after having unprotected vaginal intercourse.** It is *not* supposed to be a regular method of birth control (National Women's Health Information Center 2005). It should be used when a contraceptive method fails, such as a condom breaking, or when a woman may have forgotten to take her birth control pills. It is also used in cases of unwanted sex or rape. The main type of emergency contraception consists of *morning-after pills*.

3. Barrier Methods

Most of the birth-control methods available without a doctor's prescription are so-called *barrier methods of contraception,* **with devices that put physical barriers between egg and sperm: diaphragms, cervical caps, condoms, and the contraceptive sponge.** Another, the vaginal sponge, was off the market for several years and is not discussed in much of the recent literature.

4. Hormonal Methods

Hormonal methods **are female forms of birth control that use chemicals to prevent cervical shield, ovulation or implantation of the fertilized egg in the uterus, using pill, vaginal ring, vaginal insertion, skin patch, injection, or implant.** All require a doctor's prescription. However, they are usually more convenient and less messy than barrier methods, as well as being more reliable at preventing pregnancy. A recent addition to this category are birth-control pills (Seasonale, Seasonique, Lybrel) that eliminate monthly menstruation entirely (Saul 2007).

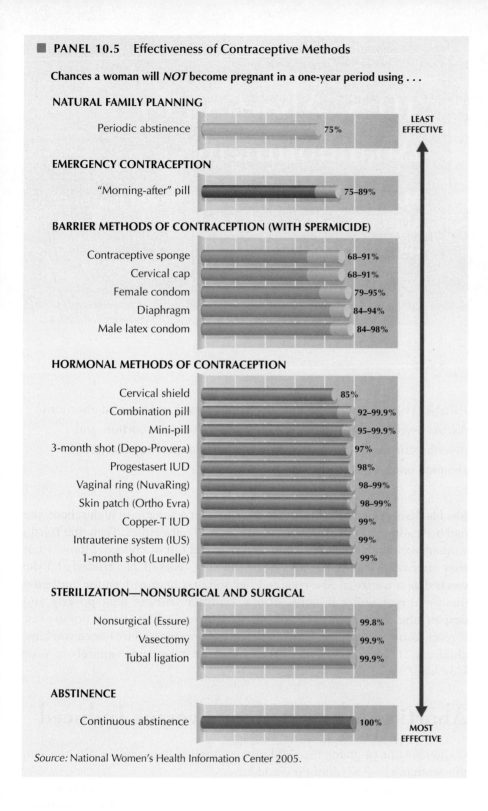

PANEL 10.5   Effectiveness of Contraceptive Methods

Chances a woman will *NOT* become pregnant in a one-year period using . . .

NATURAL FAMILY PLANNING

Periodic abstinence — 75%

LEAST EFFECTIVE

EMERGENCY CONTRACEPTION

"Morning-after" pill — 75–89%

BARRIER METHODS OF CONTRACEPTION (WITH SPERMICIDE)

Contraceptive sponge — 68–91%
Cervical cap — 68–91%
Female condom — 79–95%
Diaphragm — 84–94%
Male latex condom — 84–98%

HORMONAL METHODS OF CONTRACEPTION

Cervical shield — 85%
Combination pill — 92–99.9%
Mini-pill — 95–99.9%
3-month shot (Depo-Provera) — 97%
Progestasert IUD — 98%
Vaginal ring (NuvaRing) — 98–99%
Skin patch (Ortho Evra) — 98–99%
Copper-T IUD — 99%
Intrauterine system (IUS) — 99%
1-month shot (Lunelle) — 99%

STERILIZATION—NONSURGICAL AND SURGICAL

Nonsurgical (Essure) — 99.8%
Vasectomy — 99.9%
Tubal ligation — 99.9%

ABSTINENCE

Continuous abstinence — 100%

MOST EFFECTIVE

Source: National Women's Health Information Center 2005.

5. Sterilization—Nonsurgical & Surgical

***Sterilization* is the nonsurgical or surgical interruption of a person's reproductive capacity—generally for people who want a permanent method of birth control.** Sterilization prevents the normal passage of sperm or ova. Sterilization may be done surgically for both men and women, but women may also avail themselves of nonsurgical sterilization (Essure).

10.3 Abortion & Abandonment

MAJOR QUESTION What have I learned about abortion and safe haven laws that I didn't know?

PREVIEW We distinguish between spontaneous and induced abortions, discuss psychological and moral issues associated with abortion, and describe safe haven laws that most states have for parents who want to abandon unwanted infants.

She had had a promising future ahead of her. An A student in high school, she had been admitted to both Cornell and Stanford universities. Then, the Toledo woman accidentally got pregnant and dropped out of college. Life was not easy after that. The father, whom she married, worked as a roofer, and she worked as a waitress. She resented her son and blamed him for her being unable to realize her dreams. At age 32, after years of near poverty and despair, she wrote columnist Abigail Van Buren (2003): "Youth doesn't last forever. You will no longer have a chance to be young and free once you have children. The pain left in the wake of your mistake lands squarely in your kids' laps."

Abortions: Spontaneous versus Induced

Could abortion or giving the child up for adoption have made a difference in this woman's life? No doubt it could have.

Abortion* is the removal or expulsion of an embryo (the fertilized egg in its second through eighth week) or fetus (the successor to the embryo) from the uterus before it can survive on its own.** Not all abortions are induced. **An abortion can happen spontaneously, owing to medical, hormonal, genetic, or other problems; this is called a *spontaneous abortion* or *miscarriage. A spontaneous abortion is a miscarriage that occurs within the first 20 weeks of pregnancy. About 20% of all known pregnancies end in a spontaneous abortion, usually during the first 3 months (trimester) of pregnancy. A miscarriage often represents a significant loss to the woman and her partner that must be grieved for.

In contrast with spontaneous abortions, **in an *induced abortion,* or *elective abortion,* a decision has been made to purposefully terminate a pregnancy.** Every year, about 1.29 million women in the United States terminate their pregnancies by means of abortion (Alan Guttmacher Institute 2006). Another important statistic: Almost half of the pregnancies that occur in the United States every year are not planned; of these, 4 in 10 are terminated by induced abortion (Alan Guttmacher Institute 2006).

We mentioned some types of emergency contraception, including the "abortion pill," RU-486. The most common forms of induced abortions, however, are surgical. These are described in Appendix F.

Abortion, Psychological Health, & Moral Issues

There are, of course, alternatives to abortion. Assuming the absence of a serious threat to a woman's life or health, the pregnancy can be carried to term. The child can then be kept, put up for adoption, or placed in a foster home.

Psychological Health

Some women and couples who have planned or wanted pregnancies but lose their babies through spontaneous abortion (miscarriage) may become quite distraught and might have to grieve for their loss, although some feel little effect (Lasker and Borg 1990).

In some ways, the reactions are predictable: The more a pregnancy is wanted and personally meaningful to the woman, and often her partner, the more difficult emotionally abortion may be for her or them. But if a pregnancy is unintended, women seem not to experience negative psychological responses, under two conditions: (1) the idea of abortion does not violate their deeply held beliefs and (2) it does not have a perceived social stigma. In fact, emotional distress is usually greater *before* an abortion than it is afterward, when women frequently report relief and other positive emotions (Adler et al. 1990; Lunneborg 1992).

Equally important, at least one study (Dagg 1991) reports that women who are denied abortions only rarely give up their unwanted babies for adoption. Many harbor resentment and anger toward their children for years, as we saw with the "Dear Abby" letter writer.

Also, the study found, children who are born to women whose abortion requests were denied are more likely to have problems than wanted offspring are. Unwanted children are more likely to be troubled and depressed, to have drug and alcohol problems, to drop out of school, and to commit crimes. More of them suffer from serious illnesses and express dissatisfaction with life.

Moral Issues

Abortion is an issue about which many Americans profoundly disagree. For instance, one Ipsos poll (reported in Benac 2006) found that 19% of Americans thought that abortion should be legal in all cases, 32% that it should be legal in most cases, 16% that it should be illegal in all cases, 27% that it should be illegal in most cases, and 6% not sure. This is why laws about it vary from state to state. *(See ■ Panel 10.6.)*

■ **PANEL 10.6** **Abortion Laws across the Nation.** Restrictions on abortion laws vary from state to state. Here are some of the most common ones. "Enjoined" means the state court has prohibited the law from being in effect because they say the restrictions violate their state constitution.

STATE	ABORTION PROHIBITED EXCEPT IN CASES OF LIFE OR HEALTH ENDANGERMENT IF AT:	PARENTAL NOTICE REQUIRED IF CHILD UNDER 18	PARENTAL CONSENT REQUIRED IF CHILD UNDER 18	MANDATED COUNSELING	WAITING PERIOD (IN HOURS) AFTER COUNSELING BEFORE ABORTION
Alabama	Viability		✓	✓	24
Alaska		Enjoined	Enjoined	✓	
Arizona	Viability		✓		
Arkansas	Viability		✓	✓	Day before
California	Viability	Enjoined	Enjoined		
Colorado		✓			
Connecticut	Viability				
Delaware	Enjoined	✓*		✓	Enjoined
District of Columbia					
Florida	24 weeks	✓			24
Georgia	3rd trimester	✓		✓	
Hawaii					
Idaho	Viability		✓		24
Illinois	Viability	Enjoined	Enjoined	✓	
Indiana	Viability		✓	✓	18
Iowa	3rd trimester	✓			
Kansas	Viability	✓		✓	24
Kentucky	Viability		✓	✓	24
Louisiana	Viability		✓	✓	24
Maine	Viability				
Maryland	Viability	✓*			
Massachusetts	24 weeks		✓		Enjoined
Michigan	Viability		✓	✓	24
Minnesota	Enjoined	✓**		✓	24
Mississippi			✓**	✓	24
Missouri	Viability		✓		24
Montana	Viability	Enjoined	Enjoined		Enjoined
Nebraska	Viability	✓		✓	24
Nevada	24 weeks	Enjoined		✓	
New Hampshire		Enjoined	Enjoined		
New Jersey		Enjoined	Enjoined		
New Mexico		Enjoined	Enjoined		
New York	24 weeks				
North Carolina	20 weeks		✓		
North Dakota	Viability		✓	✓	24
Ohio	Enjoined		✓	✓	24
Oklahoma	Viability	✓	✓	✓	24
Oregon					
Pennsylvania	24 weeks		✓	✓	24
Rhode Island	24 weeks		✓	✓	
South Carolina	3rd trimester		✓	✓	1
South Dakota	24 weeks	✓		✓	24
Tennessee	Viability		✓	✓	Enjoined
Texas	3rd trimester		✓	✓	24
Utah	Enjoined	✓	✓	✓	24+
Vermont					
Virginia	3rd trimester		✓	✓	24
Washington	Viability				
West Virginia		✓*		✓	24
Wisconsin	Viability		✓*	✓	24
Wyoming	Viability		✓		

*Specified health professionals may waive parental involvement in certain circumstances.

**Both parents must consent to abortion.

+The waiting period is waived if the pregnancy is the result of rape or incest, the fetus has grave defects, or the patient is younger than age 15.

Source: Adapted from Alan Guttmacher Institute, 2007. *State policies in brief: Overview of abortion law,* July 1. *http://www.guttmacher.org/ statecenter/spibs/spib_OAL.pdf* (accessed July 10, 2007).

Strictly from a public health standpoint, however, when abortions are illegal, maternal deaths increase because of botched illegal abortions by unqualified practitioners. In 1972, there were probably thousands of deaths from illegal abortions in the United States. The next year, the U.S. Supreme Court upheld the decision of *Roe* v. *Wade*. That decision stated that an abortion in the first 3 months of pregnancy is a matter to be determined by a woman and her physician. (It said that abortions in later months can be performed on the basis of health risks and the danger to the mother's health.) By 1985, there were only six deaths from abortion, making it safer than pregnancy or childbirth.

People of different religious beliefs have different attitudes toward abortion. However, as one writer (Rosenblatt 1992) points out, in all of human history, no culture has been able to satisfactorily answer three questions: (1) When is a fetus a person? (2) What circumstances justify abortion? (3) Who decides?

And in our time, abortion continues to polarize the political dialogue.

Safe Havens for Placing Abandoned Babies

There are alternatives to abortion, of course, but Jamie Marie Smith, age 19, didn't seem to be much aware of them. Smith was unmarried and—except for her 2-year-old son—alone when she gave birth to a baby on the floor of her trailer home in South Bend, Indiana. The next night, she abandoned her sleeping newborn son in a cardboard box in the hallway of an apartment complex. The infant was found and adopted. Smith, however, was prosecuted for criminal neglect. "I wasn't doing a whole lot of thinking," Smith said later. "I just knew I wanted him to be taken care of and I couldn't do it" (quoted in Bernstein 2001: A1).

Smith was unaware of a law existing in Indiana and in 46 other states called a safe haven law. **Safe haven laws, or *abandoned baby laws*, allow a person—anonymously and without fear of prosecution—to leave an unwanted newborn at a hospital emergency room, fire station, or other designated place.** The laws stem from a centuries-long tradition in Europe, in which desperately poor mothers could slip their newborns into a dark slot within a wooden turntable in a convent wall, hoping their child would have a better life. Originally known as "the wheel" and recently revived in Europe, the system currently has names like "babbyklappe" (baby slot) in Austria and Germany; "babyfenster" (baby window) in Switzerland; "babybox" in the Czech Republic; and "culle per vite" (cradles for life) in Italy. Many are sophisticated incubator-like containers that warm up when a baby is placed inside and sound an alarm a few minutes after the mother leaves (D'emilio 2005).

The chief purpose of safe haven laws is to reduce *neonaticide*, **the murdering of infants within 24 hours of their birth.** In the United States, the first such law was enacted in Texas in 1999 in response to the discovery of 13 abandoned babies in 10 months, and other states followed suit. (As of 2007, Alaska, Hawaii, and Nebraska still had not passed such legislation.) States vary in the grace period allowed before a parent can be prosecuted for abandonment, with some states insisting the infant must be newborn and others allowing 30 or 45 days as a grace period.

Arguments for Safe Haven Laws

The laws have been embraced by people on both sides of the political spectrum. "Conservatives like the fact that the laws promised to save babies without spending money; liberals like the idea that they were not punitive," says one account. "Anti-abortion groups promoted them in their fight against abortion, and some Planned Parenthood affiliates latched on to promote contraception" (Bernstein 2001: A1, A14). Dawn Geras, president of the Save Abandoned Babies Foundation of Illinois, argues that the number of babies illegally abandoned and found dead has been decreasing since 1999 (Geras, cited in Buckley 2007).

Arguments against Safe Haven Laws

Critic Adam Pertman (2000), author of *Adoption Nation* and director of a nonprofit adoption organization, says that safe haven laws have unintended consequences. A report issued by his organization (Evan B. Donaldson Institute 2003) argues that such laws induce abandonment by women who otherwise would not have done so because it is perceived as easier than receiving counseling. Such laws also deprive biological fathers of their legal rights to care for their offspring and ensure that the children who are abandoned can never learn their medical or genealogical histories. Although parents abandoning newborns may be asked to fill out a brief family history, they may refuse (Bell 2001).

The chief problem seems to be that many people do not know about safe haven laws, and the effectiveness of such laws has been very difficult to judge. Few states have implemented tracking systems to see how well the laws work or of the numbers of babies abandoned, dead or alive (Buckley 2007).

10.4 Infertility, Reproductive Technology, & Adoption

MAJOR QUESTION If I wanted children but had difficulty conceiving them, what would my options be?

PREVIEW We discuss causes of infertility in couples, males, and females. We then describe six types of assisted reproductive technology to help conception: (1) artificial insemination, (2) fertility-enhancing drugs, (3) in vitro fertilization, (4) intrafallopian transfer, (5) embryo transfer, and (6) surrogate mothers. We conclude with a discussion of adoption.

Baby-making would seem to just happen naturally. One researcher (Guttmacher 1983) found that the average (median) time for a sexually active couple using no contraception to conceive was 2½ months. (The majority conceived within 6 months, but some couples took 2 years or more.)

For about a third of all couples in the United States, however, having a child is difficult—either because they cannot conceive or because the woman is physiologically unable to carry the child to term. About 10 to 15% of couples of reproductive age cannot ever have children (McCary and McCary 1984; Rosenthal 1997).

The Causes of Infertility

Although definitions vary, we use the term *infertility* **to mean the failure to conceive after 1 year of regular sexual intercourse without contraception or the inability to carry a pregnancy to live birth.** Infertility is differentiated from *sterility,* **the total inability to conceive** (Marchbanks et al. 1989; Crooks and Baur 1990).

Infertility is a couple's problem that requires an evaluation of both partners.

The Causes of Infertility in Couples

Twenty percent of infertility problems may be attributed to both partners. A couple's inability to conceive can have any number of causes:

- **Not Enough Sex:** The couple might not be having enough intercourse—once or less per week.
- **Too Much Sex:** The couple might be having too much intercourse—several times a day or over the course of several days, which keeps sperm from collecting in the testicles.
- **Sex at Wrong Times of the Month:** Intercourse that occurs during times of the month when the woman is less apt to conceive might not lead to conception.
- **Use of Vaginal Lubricants:** The use of some vaginal lubricants, such as Vaseline, can prevent sperm from entering the cervix.
- **Health Problems:** Either partner suffers from anemia, fatigue, emotional stress, being either underweight or overweight, or the effects of sexually transmitted diseases (such as chlamydia, gonorrhea, and syphilis). Smoking can stretch out the time to conceive by a year or more. Diets high in trans fats may affect fertility. Exercising four or more hours per week can make women less likely to conceive.

The Causes of Infertility in Males

Forty percent of infertility problems can be attributed to males. Principal causes are the following:

- **Low-Quality Sperm:** There might be a reduced number of sperm or more defective sperm, owing to untreated sexually transmitted diseases and environmental toxins.
- **Blockage:** There might be blockage somewhere between the testicle and the end of the penis, so that the sperm cannot pass through.
- **Erection or Ejaculation Problems:** The man might be unable to sustain an erection or be unable to ejaculate.

The Causes of Infertility in Females

Forty percent of infertility problems can be attributed to females. Some of the main causes of infertility in women are as follows:

- **Age:** The woman's age might be a problem, since fertility decreases slightly as women become older.
- **Failure to Ovulate:** The woman might fail to ovulate, owing to such factors as hormonal deficiencies, defective ovaries, metabolic imbalances, genetic factors, various medical conditions, or cigarettes or other drugs.
- **Blockage:** There might be a blockage of the fallopian tubes, preventing fertilization from taking place and keeping the eggs from passing from the ovaries to the uterus.
- **Abnormalities of the Uterus:** There might be abnormalities of the uterus, such as *endometriosis*, **in which some cells of the inner lining of the uterus grow in the pelvic and abdominal cavities.**
- **Inhospitable Environment for Sperm:** There might be an immune response or acidic chemical climate in the vagina, which can immobilize sperm.

If none of these problems occur and the sperm and egg are united, there is still no guarantee of full-term pregnancy. About 20% of pregnancies end in miscarriages, or spontaneous abortions (Bates and Boone 1991).

Recently, a new at-home screening test, called Fertell, allows couples to find out if they have fertility problems without going to a doctor's office. The kit has a component for men that measures the concentration of motile sperm, and a test for women that measures a hormone considered a marker of egg quality (Rabin 2007a).

Treating Infertility: Assisted Reproductive Technology

After a couple has tried to conceive for a year or more, they might seek alternative methods of conceptions. ***Assisted reproductive technology (ART) is the collective name for all treatments and procedures by which human eggs and sperm may be manipulated to produce a pregnancy.*** They include (1) artificial insemination, (2) fertility-enhancing drugs, (3) in vitro fertilization, (4) intrafallopian transfer, (5) embryo transfer, and (6) surrogate mothers. These methods of treating infertility can be very expensive; thus, a couple's economic status can influence their ability to do something about their infertility.

1. Artificial Insemination: AIH & AID

Sometimes sperm don't have the strength, mobility, necessary enzymes, or ability to bypass hostile vaginal secretions and pierce the outer shell of the egg (ovum). Or a man might be unable to produce viable sperm at all.

In ***artificial insemination,* sperm are collected from the male partner— or an anonymous male donor—by masturbation. With the help of a powerful microscope, the sperm cells are injected by syringe directly into the woman's vagina or uterus.**

Artificial insemination is of two types: AIH and AID:

■ **AIH:** In *artificial insemination by husband (AIH),* used when a husband's sperm count is low, the husband's sperm may be collected over several ejaculations and preserved by refrigeration until a greater quantity of sperm is available for injection into the vagina.

■ **AID:** In cases in which AIH fails or no male partner is present, the woman might seek *artificial insemination by donor (AID).* Lesbians, either single or in couples, have increasingly used AID as a way to have children. AID has led to the establishment of *sperm banks* to meet demand, some of which exclusively serve lesbians.

2. Fertility-Enhancing Drugs: Ovulating-Stimulating Hormones

Some women have difficulty ovulating naturally. Others produce eggs that cannot be fertilized. One solution is to give large doses of ***fertility-enhancing drugs,* drugs that stimulate hormones to produce eggs.** When large doses of ovulation-stimulating hormones (Clomid, Pergonal, and HCG—human chorionic gonadotropin—a hormone derived from human placenta) are administered, dozens of eggs may be produced.

One common result of this treatment is multiple births—twins, triplets, even quadruplets. Unfortunately, in many multiple births, the babies are premature mature and have low birth weights, which put them at risk for many problems (Luke et al. 1991; Luke and Keith 1992). *(See ■ Panel 10.7.)*

■ **PANEL 10.7** **The Risks of Being a Twin or a Triplet.** Babies born in multiple births have higher risks of low birth weight and infant mortality.

RATE PER 1,000 LIVE BIRTHS	SINGLETON	TWINS	TRIPLETS
Very low birth weight (3.3 lbs or less)	10.3	98.7	336.6
Low birth weight (5.5 lbs or less)	59.2	502.0	911.8
Mortality	8.6	56.6	166.7

Source: Adapted from Luke and Keith 1992.

3. In Vitro Fertilization: "Test-Tube Babies"

The term *in vitro* means "in glass" and is the origin of the term "test-tube babies." During an ***in vitro fertilization (IVF) procedure, the egg and the sperm are taken from the parents and kept in a laboratory setting until the mother's uterus is hormonally ready; then the fertilized egg is implanted in the wall of the uterus.*** This procedure is useful when the woman's fallopian tubes are blocked or otherwise unable to transport an egg. Beware an in vitro technique called *pre-implantation genetic diagnosis*, touted to help older women achieve fertility, since it actually *reduces* births by one-third (Mastenbroek et al. 2007).

4. Intrafallopian Transfer: GIFT & ZIFT

Two processes related to in vitro fertilization are GIFT and ZIFT:

■ **GIFT: In *GIFT*, which stands for *gamete intrafallopian transfer*,** the woman's egg and the man's sperm are collected and then united inside the woman's fallopian tubes. (A gamete is a mature sexual reproductive cell, a sperm or an egg, that unites with another cell to form a new organism.) The

MULTIPLE BIRTHS. A frequent consequence of assisted reproductive technology, particularly in the use of fertility-enhancing drugs, is that parents who were looking forward to having one child experience an embarrassment of riches—twins, triplets, even quadruplets. What would you think if you were in your forties or fifties and found yourself having to consider funding college educations for three children—at a time when you were hoping for a blissful retirement? ▶

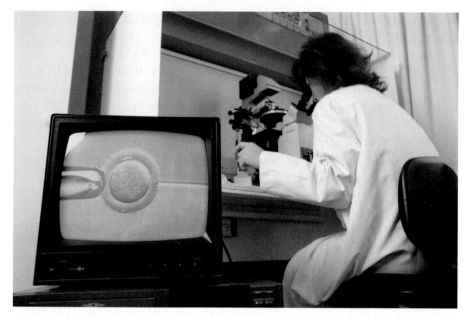

LAB WORK. As the television monitor shows, this laboratory worker looking into a microscope is holding an egg steady with a pipette (left) while injecting a single sperm into it through a tiny needle (right). After fertilization takes place, the zygote can be placed in a woman's fallopian tubes. Such a procedure may cost $10,000 or more. Would you consider this option if it were the only one? ◀

GIFT procedure, which has a 50 to 60% success rate, is often tried when the cause of fertility is unclear.

■ **ZIFT: In *ZIFT*, which stands for *zygote intrafallopian transfer*, the mother's egg and the father's sperm are collected and placed in a laboratory dish. Then, one day after fertilization takes place, the zygote is placed in the woman's fallopian tubes.** (A *zygote* is the cell formed by the union of two gametes before it splits and then continues to subdivide.)

5. Embryo Transfer

In *embryo transfer*, **the sperm of a male partner of an infertile woman is placed in another woman's uterus during ovulation. Five days later, the embryo is transferred to the uterus of the infertile woman,** who carries the embryo and delivers the baby.

6. Surrogate Mothers

A *surrogate mother* **is a consenting woman who is artificially inseminated with the sperm of the male partner of a woman who is infertile. Usually for a fee, the surrogate mother carries the child through pregnancy and gives the newborn to the couple with whom she contracted.**

Personal & Ethical Problems with Assisted Reproductive Technology

Lesbian couple Jennifer Lee Shultz-Jacob and Jodilynn Jacob lived together in Pennsylvania, after being united in a Vermont civil union, and Jacob bore two children after artificial insemination with the sperm of her friend Carl L. Frampton Jr. Later, when the couple separated, a court ordered Shultz-Jacob to pay child support to Jacob—and over his objections the sperm donor, Frampton, was required to pay as well (Sheffield 2007). Was this fair? And what kind of social risks are children being introduced to when sociology and biology combine to give them *three* adults all with legal claims on them (Marquardt 2007)?

This story, and others mentioned at the outset of this chapter, show some of the personal and ethical complexities arising from ART. For example, there have been a few cases in which surrogate mothers changed their minds about giving the babies away, resulting in legal disputes with the sponsoring parents (Hanafin 1996); most surrogates, however, report being quite satisfied with their experience (Kleinpeter and Hohman 2000). As was suggested in the Jeffrey Harrison incident at the beginning of this chapter, there are also questions of privacy: What kind of privacy rights do biological fathers (the sperm donors) have, and how much contact should their offspring be allowed to have with them?

When a couple divorces, what happens to their frozen embryos? Should an ex-wife have the right to continue a pregnancy over her former spouse's objections even if the embryo hasn't been implanted yet (Daar 1999)? Should the ex-husband have the right to implant the embryo in some other woman? Can surplus embryos be put up for adoption, to be used by others?

In addition, how much should an infertile couple be expected to pay for an egg donor, and does this favor the rich? Samantha Carolan was 23 years old and fresh out of graduate school when she decided to donate eggs to help pay off her student loans. She received $7,000 the first time and $8,000 the second time (Rabin 2007b). One survey found that the national average compensation for donors was $4,217 (Covington and Gibbons 2007). Ads trying to recruit students from elite universities to donate promise tens of thousands of dollars. A problem, however, is that the risks of donation have not been thoroughly studied, and questions have been raised whether extraction of eggs may jeopardize the donor's fertility. What is known is that the procedure is time consuming, involves taking drugs for several weeks, and is not comfortable—indeed, may even be painful (Rabin 2007b).

Finally, there are ethical issues about how much ART (especially matters related to genetic engineering) can vary the nature of the family—indeed, even vary the concept of perfection (Sandel 2007).

When Fertility Treatment Fails

What happens when involuntarily childless couples find that there is no solution? What is it like to face the difficult task of reconstructing their identities as infertile? "They have to re-envision their 'self' and their life based on the reality that they will never know what it is like to birth a child, to see the things they love most about their partners reflected in their offspring," says one researcher, "and to experience the sense of genetic continuity that for many is an important part of procreation" (Daniluk 2001: 49). They must acknowledge the losses associated with this state and be able to "reject the socially constructed link between fertility and self-worth." Not surprisingly, working through this "identity shock" is most difficult for those who are unable to see the value in their own selves and in their lives apart from their ability to produce a child.

Adoption

Adults who cannot become biological parents may still become parents by *adoption*—**voluntarily the child of other parents as one's own child.** In

2000 and 2001, about 127,000 children were adopted annually in the United States (U.S. Department of Health and Human Services 2004). There are 1.5 million adopted children in the United States, over 2% of all U.S. children (Fields 2001). In 2002, about 300,000 women ages 18 to 44 were currently seeking to adopt and had taken specific steps toward adoption; about 1% of women ages 18 to 44 (or about 600,000 women) in that year were found to have ever adopted a child (Chandra et al. 2005: 40).

Some adoptions are of stepchildren by stepparents: For example, in 1992, 42% of all adoptions were stepparent adoptions. Overall, about two-fifths of adoptions are private agency, tribal, or kinship (including stepparent) adoptions; another two-fifths are through publicly funded child welfare agencies; and the remaining 15% are intercountry (international) adoptions (U.S. Department of Health and Human Services 2004). A fairly recent phenomenon is adoption via the Internet (Mansnerus 2001; Elias 2002).

Public versus Private Adoptions

As a single, 36-year-old man trying to adopt an inner-city child, Brian Saber (2003) of New York was spurned by public agencies. "I was told that I would be put in a 'don't call us, we'll call you' category because I was single, male, and white and therefore didn't fit the 'ideal' scenario," he said. "Instead, I went halfway around the world to adopt a beautiful baby boy from Vietnam."

Saber's account would seem to illustrate some of the differences between the two types of adoption: public or private.

■ **Public:** *Public adoptions* **are those that are arranged through licensed agencies that place children in adoptive families.** Often such children have been in foster care.

Although licensed agencies might better explain legal rights and offer counseling to both parties to the adoption—birth parents and adoptive parents—they also can take a long time, up to 7 years, to arrange adoptions—although recently some agencies are saying they desperately need couples to adopt babies in the United States (Hwang 2004). They may also, as in Saber's case, screen for their own views of acceptability in marital status, age, income, and other standards in prospective adoptive parents.

■ **Private:** *Private adoptions,* **also called** *independent adoptions,* **are those that are arranged directly between birth mother and adoptive parent or parents.** Usually, this type of adoption is handled by a lawyer or an adoption facilitator; no licensed agency is involved.

Private adoptions can offer both birth and adoptive parents more control and a quicker transaction then public adoptions can. But they can also be thousands of dollars more expensive. And they can be exploitative, as when desperate, pregnant young Mexicans are smuggled into the United States to give their babies up for adoption (Brooks and Sanders 2002).

Closed, Semi-Open, or Open Adoptions

An adoption, whether public or private, can involve three kinds of communication—or lack of communication—between the biological parent(s) and the adoptive parent(s): closed, semi-open, or open.

- **Closed:** *Closed adoptions* **are those in which birth parents and adoptive parents do not know one another's identities and do not communicate.** This has been the traditional arrangement.

- **Semi-Open:** A step up from closed, *semi-open adoptions* **are those in which the biological and adoptive parents exchange information such as photographs or letters but don't otherwise communicate.**

- **Open:** *Open adoptions* **are those in which both birth parents and adoptive parents have more active contact, as in a meeting before the birth or even lifelong communication.**

One study that examined the experience of contact between adoptive and birth families found that not one parent felt less comfortable with such open adoption 7 years after they adopted their infants. Adoptive parents' remarks ranged from "I feel very comfortable being in each others' homes now" to "My initial fears and anxieties are gone" to "Things have worked . . . better than I thought" (Siegel 2003).

Who Adopts?

Celebrities such as Madonna, Angelina Jolie, and Rosie O'Donnell have gained widespread publicity for their adoptions, but traditionally people who adopt have been couples who are infertile, are highly educated, have high incomes, have wives not working full time, or all of these. However, in recent years single parents and gays and lesbians have also adopted children. *(See ■ Panel 10.8.)* In addition, some biological parents have broadened their families by adopting disabled and older children. Nearly 50% of employers offer adoption benefits, such as adoption-related legal services and paid time off, according to a survey by benefits consultants Watson Wyatt Worldwide (reported in Armour 2007).

Who Puts a Child Up for Adoption?

People often think the kind of woman who surrenders her baby for adoption is a teenager, an unmarried high school dropout. Actually, she is more apt to be in her 20s, likely a high school (or even college) graduate, living on her own, often raising other children, perhaps even married. And, rather than simply giving up her infant and never looking back, the birth mother typically wants periodic contact and regular updates, and she is likely to suffer chronic grief if she fails to achieve it (Smith 2007).

Foster Children

One principal source of closed adoptions are foster children. There were 513,000 children in the U.S. foster-care system in 2005, averaging 10 years old, 52% male and 48% female. Most children are placed in foster care because of parent abuse or neglect, and the average amount of time they spend in the system is 28.6 months. As a percentage, there are more children of color in the foster-care system than in the general

ADOPTED. Adoptions can produce multiracial or multiethnic families. If you were to adopt, would it be important to you that the child be of a certain race, ethnicity, gender, or age? ▼

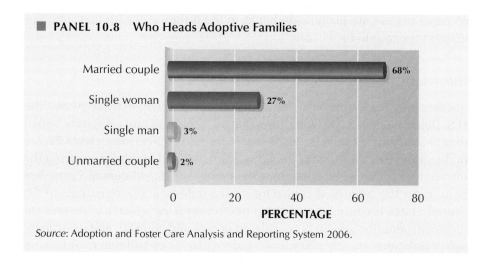

PANEL 10.8 Who Heads Adoptive Families

Married couple — 68%
Single woman — 27%
Single man — 3%
Unmarried couple — 2%

PERCENTAGE

Source: Adoption and Foster Care Analysis and Reporting System 2006.

U.S. population. *(See ■ Panel 10.9.)* Fifty-four percent of children exiting foster care are reunited with parents or primary caretakers (Adoption and Foster Care Analysis and Reporting System 2006).

As you might expect, the easiest foster children to place for adoption are age 5 and younger (53% of adoptions), followed by children ages 6 to 10 (28%), then adolescents from 11 to 15 years old (16%), and finally those who are ages 16 to 18 (3%) (Adoption and Foster Care Analysis and Reporting System 2006). However, an enormous number of teens—24,407 in 2005—leave the system at age 18 without a family to help them (Freundlich et al. 2007). Accordingly, the U.S. government launched a media campaign urging Americans to adopt teenagers, who fare particularly poorly when they turn 18 years old and "age out" of the foster system (Crary 2007a). Many children who spent some time between ages 14 to 18 in foster care have been found at ages 20 to 33 to suffer from problems such as post-traumatic stress disorder, major depression, and social phobia (Pecora et al. 2003). Indeed, one study (Doyle 2007) of 15,000 children found that minors whose families are investigated for

PANEL 10.9 Diversity Data: Race and Ethnicity of Children Ages 1 to 19 in U.S. Foster-Care System

RACE/ETHNICITY	IN OUT-OF-HOME CARE	IN GENERAL U.S. POPULATION
Black (non-Hispanic)	32%	15%
White (non-Hispanic)	41%	61%
Hispanic	18%	17%
American Indian/Alaska Native (non-Hispanic)	2%	1%
Asian/Pacific Islander (non-Hispanic)	1%	3%
2 or more races (non-Hispanic)	3%	4%
Unknown	2%	–

Sources: Adoption and Foster Care Analysis and Reporting System 2006; U.S. Census Bureau 2004: Table 1.

abuse or neglect are likely to do better in life if they stay with their families than if they go into foster care.

International Adoptions

Another primary source of closed adoptions are international adoptions. The U.S. Department of State (2007) says that 20,679 immigrant visas were issued to orphans coming to the United States in fiscal year 2006, down from 22,928 in the prior year, with China, Guatemala, Russia, and South Korea being the top sources for adopted children. *(See ■ Panel 10.10.)* Mainland China has been by far the country of choice for most would-be adoptive parents in the United States because, according to one report (Crary 2007b), "its government-run adoption system is considered honest and efficient, and its orphan-age population—mostly abandoned baby girls—is considered healthier on average than those in many other countries." Guatemala, by contrast, has come in for U.S. government scrutiny for suspected widespread fraud in its adoption practices, and Russia began curtailing its adoptions to the United States in the wake of reports of abuse by adoptive American parents. In the past five years, these three countries accounted for 70% of the orphans who came to the United States—about 10% of all U.S. adoptions (Friess 2007; Koch 2007).

■ **PANEL 10.10** **Top Countries of Origin for International Adoptions.** Immigrant visas issued to orphans coming to the United States, fiscal year 2006.

RANK	COUNTRY	NUMBER OF VISAS
1	China (Mainland)	6,493
2	Guatemala	4,135
3	Russia	3,706
4	South Korea	1,376
5	Ethiopia	732
6	Kazakhstan	587
7	Ukraine	460
8	Liberia	353
9	Colombia	344
10	India	320
11	Haiti	309
12	Philippines	245
13	China (Taiwan born)	137
14	Vietnam	163
15	Mexico	70

Source: U.S. Department of State 2007.

One concern of prospective adoptive parents is that children adopted from overseas will have physical and emotional problems that can't be forecast from photos or brief visits to orphanages. This has brought about the rise of *adoption medicine*, a specialty recognized by the American Academy of Pediatrics, in which doctors try to assess for prospective parents the risks of children they are considering adopting, which can range from attention deficit disorder to fetal alcohol syndrome (Gross 2006).

However, an analysis by Dutch researchers found that children adopted from overseas are better adjusted than had been expected—with fewer problems than children adopted within their own countries—and only slightly more than nonadopted children. Femmie Juffer and Marinus van Ijzendoorn (2005) pooled results from 137 studies on adoptions by parents living in the United States, Canada, Europe, Australia, New Zealand, and Israel and found that international adoptees had only a 20% higher chance of being disruptive owing to behavioral problems such as aggressiveness and anxiety than nonadopted children, compared with a 50% chance for domestically adopted children.

The Post-Adoption Blues

You may be aware that many birth mothers, perhaps 25 to 50%, experience *post-partum blues,* a period of sadness and anxiety following the birth of their child (as we discuss in Chapter 11, "Parenting"). Is it possible this kind of depression could afflict new adoptive parents as well? Although there is no research on the syndrome, adoption professionals recognize that some adoptive parents can experience the **post-adoption blues, or post-adoption depression, a condition ranging from a low mood to a full-fledged plunge into despair** (Foli and Thompson 2004).

According to a 1999 survey by Harriet White McCarthy (2005) of subscribers to an online site for parents in the Eastern European Adoption Coalition, 77% of those reporting post-adoption depression said their symptoms lasted from two months to more than a year. As Karen Foli, author of *The Post-Adoption Blues,* says, people want to become adoptive parents for so long, "and they're dumbfounded and feel tremendous guilt and shame admitting they have anything less than positive feelings" (Foli, quoted in Tarkan 2006: D5). To weather the storm, McCarthy suggests would-be parents alert and educate families, spouses, and mental health care providers in advance that they may need extra emotional support in the same way that new birth families do.

Self-Assessment: How Would You Deal with an Unexpected Pregnancy?

Suppose it develops that you or your partner has a positive pregnancy test and the pregnancy is unexpected. The questions in this self-assessment—about parenthood, marriage, adoption, and abortion—address the kinds of considerations that would have to be weighed, questions geared toward helping you sort out your rational and emotional feelings about the options that are available. Every option has emotional, social, spiritual, and physical considerations. Unlike previous self-assessments in this book, this one has no ready-made scoring system at the end. When a pregnancy is unplanned, there is no such thing as an easy way out. Each choice represents gains and losses. Each woman must weigh her perceived gains and losses in her particular situation to make her own best decision, as must her partner. To take this Self-Assessment, go to *www .heritageclinic.com/decision/decision_making_process .htm.*

Source: Courtesy of Kathryn Barker MSW and the Heritage Clinic for Women. 2004. *Decision making process.* Heritage Clinic for Women, 320 East Fulton, Grand Rapids, MI 49503. Tel.: 616-458-3694. *www.heritageclinic.com/decision/decision_making_process .htm.*

Key Terms Used in This Chapter

abandoned-baby laws, p. 351
abortion, p. 348
adoption, p. 348
artificial insemination, p. 355
assisted reproductive technology (ART), p. 355
barrier methods of contraception, p. 346
childless, p. 336
child-free marriage, p. 336
closed adoptions, p. 360
douching, p. 346
Down (Down's) syndrome, p. 338
elective abortion, p. 349
embryo transfer, p. 357
emergency contraception, p. 346

endometriosis, p. 354
fertility, p. 339
fertility-enhancing drugs, p. 355
fertility rates, p. 339
gamete intrafallopian transfer, p. 356
GIFT, p. 356
hormonal methods, p. 346
in vitro fertilization (IVF), p. 356
independent adoptions, p. 359
induced abortion, p. 349
infertility, p. 353
miscarriage, p. 348
natural family planning methods, p. 346
neonaticide, p. 351

open adoptions, p. 360
opportunity costs, p. 342
post-adoption blues, p. 363
postcoital birth control, p. 346
private adoptions, p. 359
pronatalist bias, p. 336
public adoptions, p. 359
safe haven laws, p. 351
semi-open adoptions, p. 360
spontaneous abortion, p. 348
sterility, p. 353
sterilization, p. 347
surrogate mother, p. 357
ZIFT, p. 357
zygote intrafallopian transfer, p. 357

Summary

10.1 Having or Not Having Children: Choice or Fate?

- Carolyn and Phillip Cowan identify four kinds of reactions partners have to pregnancy: (1) planner partners, (2) acceptance-of-fate partners, (3) ambivalent partners, and (4) yes-no partners.
- Couples have a number of choices about being a parent or not being a parent: no children, having children later, having one child, or having several children.
- Child-free marriages involve a choice on the couple's part not to have children.

- Many people who opt not to have children must deal with society's pronatalist bias, the cultural attitude that takes having children for granted.
- Couples might postpone having children to finish their educations and get established in their careers, to have more time to develop their relationship with each other, and to build the economic resources to provide for children. However, couples who wait until after age 30 to have children might find themselves with heavy career demands just at the time they are expected to care for young children, and they might also be anxious to return to the happier child-free time when they could enjoy their own pri-

vacy and absence of responsibility. Also, fertility tends to diminish with age, so that the later one waits to have children, the greater is the possibility that it will be too late. Postponing having children until a woman is in her forties incurs an increased risk of having a baby with Down (Down's) syndrome, a condition that leads to various degrees of mental retardation and physical disability.

- Social and economic factors influence people's decision to have children: (1) general trends in family size; (2) race, ethnicity, and religion; and (3) education, income, and workforce status.
- Fertility refers to both the ability to reproduce biologically and a person's actual reproductive performance.
- Fertility rates refer to the number of births per year per thousand women of child-bearing age (ages 15 to 44).
- Raising children can be expensive. In addition to the basics of food, clothing, and shelter, there are opportunity costs, or the loss of wages and investments that parents sacrifice by devoting their time and energy to child rearing.

10.2 Contraception: Practical Methods of Birth Control

- A couple's choice in deciding whether or not to have children has been greatly affected by the development of effective methods of birth control including (1) natural family planning methods, (2) emergency contraception, (3) barrier methods, (4) hormonal methods, and (5) sterilization.
- Pregnancy "protection" approaches that usually don't work include (1) no method at all, (2) breastfeeding, and (3) douching.
- Natural family planning methods of birth control include (a) various ways of gauging times for periodic abstinence—the calendar method, the BBT method, the cervical mucus method—and (b) withdrawal.
- Barrier methods of contraception involve the use of devices that put physical barriers between egg and sperm. They include diaphragms, cervical caps, and condoms.
- Hormonal methods are female forms of birth control that use chemicals to prevent ovulation or implantation of the fertilized egg in the uterus, using pills, vaginal rings, insertion devices, skin patches, injections, or implants.
- Sterilization is the surgical or nonsurgical interruption of a person's reproductive capacity, generally for

people who want a permanent method of birth control.

- Emergency contraception, also known as postcoital birth control, refers to various methods of protecting a woman from getting pregnant after having unprotected vaginal intercourse. It is not supposed to be a regular method of birth control and is intended to be used when a contraceptive method fails, such as a condom breaking, or when a woman might have forgotten to take her birthcontrol pills. It is also used in cases of unwanted sex or rape. The main types of emergency contraception are morning-after pills and RU-486 pills.

10.3 Abortion & Abandonment

- Abortion is the removal or expulsion of an embryo (the fertilized egg in its second through eighth week) or a fetus (the successor to the embryo) from the uterus before it can survive on its own.
- An abortion can happen spontaneously, owing to medical, hormonal, genetic, or other problems; this is called a spontaneous abortion, or miscarriage.
- Induced, or elective, abortion involves a decision to purposefully terminate a pregnancy.
- Alternatives to abortion include deciding to keep the child, adoption, and foster care.
- The more a pregnancy is wanted and personally meaningful to the woman, and often to her partner, the more difficult emotionally abortion may be for her or them. But if a pregnancy is unintended, women seem not to experience negative psychological responses (1) if the idea of abortion does not violate their deeply held beliefs and (2) if it does not have a perceived social stigma.
- Safe haven laws, or abandoned-baby laws, allow a person, anonymously and without fear of prosecution, to leave an unwanted newborn at a hospital emergency room, fire station, or other designated place. The chief purpose of such laws is to avoid neonaticide, murder of infants.

10.4 Infertility, Reproductive Technology, & Adoption

- Infertility is the failure to conceive after 1 year of regular sexual intercourse without contraception or the inability to carry a pregnancy to live birth. Infertility is differentiated from sterility, the total inability to conceive.
- A couple's inability to conceive can have any number of causes, including not enough sex, too much sex, sex at wrong times of the month, use of vaginal

lubricants, and health problems such as anemia, fatigue, emotional stress, poor nutrition, and effects of sexually transmitted diseases.

- Male infertility may be caused by low sperm count, blockage so that sperm can not pass from the testicle to the end of the penis, or erection or ejaculation problems.

- Infertility in females may be caused by age (fertility decreases slightly as women age), failure to ovulate, blockage of the fallopian tubes, abnormalities of the uterus, or an inhospitable environment for sperm.

- Assisted reproductive technology (ART) is the collective name for all treatments and procedures by which human eggs and sperm may be manipulated to produce a pregnancy. They include (1) artificial insemination, (2) fertility-enhancing drugs, (3) in vitro fertilization, (4) intrafallopian transfer, (5) embryo transfer, and (6) surrogate mothers.

- In artificial insemination, sperm are collected from the male partner or an anonymous male donor by masturbation.

- Fertility-enhancing drugs stimulate hormones to produce eggs.

- Through the in vitro fertilization (IVF) procedure, the egg and sperm are taken from the parents and kept in a laboratory setting until the mother's uterus is hormonally ready; then the fertilized egg is implanted in the wall of the uterus.

- In GIFT, which stands for gamete intrafallopian transfer, the woman's egg and the man's sperm—each a gamete, or mature reproductive cell—are collected and united inside the woman's fallopian tubes. When two gametes unite, a zygote is formed.

- In ZIFT, which stands for zygote intrafallopian transfer, the mother's egg and the father's sperm are collected and placed in a laboratory dish. Then, one day after fertilization takes place, the zygote is placed in the woman's fallopian tubes.

- In embryo transfer, the sperm of a male partner of an infertile woman is placed in another woman's uterus during ovulation. Five days later, the embryo is transferred to the uterus of the infertile woman, who carries the embryo and delivers the baby.

- A surrogate mother is a consenting woman who is artificially inseminated with the sperm of the male partner of a woman who is infertile. Usually for a fee, the surrogate mother carries the child through pregnancy and gives the newborn to the couple with whom she contracted.

- Adults who cannot become biological parents can still become parents by adoption, whereby one voluntarily takes the child of other parents as one's own child.

- Public adoptions are arranged through licensed agencies that place children in adoptive families.

- Private adoptions, also called independent adoptions, are arranged directly between the birth mother and the adoptive parent or parents.

- Closed adoptions are those in which birth parents and adoptive parents do not know one another's identities and don't communicate.

- Semi-open adoptions are those in which the biological parents and the adoptive parents exchange some information such as photographs or letters but don't otherwise communicate.

- Open adoptions are those in which birth parents and adoptive parents have more active contact, as in a meeting before the birth or even lifelong communication.

- Traditionally, people wanting to adopt have been couples who are infertile, are highly educated, have high incomes, or have wives not working full-time, or all of these. However, single parents and gay and lesbian people now also adopt children. In addition, some parents who have their own biological children have widened their families by adopting disabled and older children. Most in demand are healthy infants; hardest to place are older children.

Take It to the Net

Among the Internet resources are the following:

- **Adoption Online.** Online adoption services. *www.adoptiononline.com/index.cfm*

- **AdoptUSKids.org.** A national photo listing service for children who are awaiting adoption across the United States. You may learn about the children without registering to become a site member and access in-depth information about a child. *www.adoptuskids.org*

- **The Alan Guttmacher Institute.** The mission of this nonprofit organization is to protect the reproductive choices of all women and men and to support their ability to obtain the information and services needed. *www.agi-usa.org/index.html*

- **American College of Obstetricians and Gynecologists (ACOG) Resource Center.** Resource for finding women's health physicians and other information. *www.acog.org/*
- **Birdsandbees.org.** Information on sex. *www.birdsandbees.org*
- **Center for Reproductive Rights.** This website gives the current status of laws on reproductive rights and abortion. *www.reproductiverights.org/st_laws.html*
- **Child-free support groups** *www.nokidding.net* *www.overpopulation.org* *www.populationconnection.org*
- **Planned Parenthood Federation of America.** Provides comprehensive reproductive and complementary health-care services in settings that preserve and protect the essential privacy and rights of each individual. *www.plannedparenthood.org/*
- **Population Council.** Research group aimed at addressing problems of reproductive health and population growth. *www.popcouncil.org/*
- **Safe Place for Newborns.** This website has a map of the United States that allows you to click on your state and find out details about its safe haven law, if it has one. *www.safeplacefornewborns.com/statemap.html*

CHAPTER 11

PARENTING
Children, Families, & Generations

"Will My Kids Turn Out All Right?"

*"**Meet the parents:** role models, confidants, weekend buddies.*

"Not a bad list of labels, especially since it came from the kids.

"Almost 75% of high school students say they get along very well or even extremely well with their

parents or guardians, a [2003] survey finds. Most of the rest call the relationship 'just OK,' and only 3% say they and their parents don't get along well.

"Overall, teenagers have a lot more admiration than animosity for their families, despite popular notions to the contrary" (Feller 2003).

The foregoing conclusions, from the annual State of Our Nation's Youth survey (Horatio Alger Association 2003; 2005), would delight any parent. Parents would also be pleased to hear that among children in grades 7 through 12, according to research by Ellen Galinsky (1999), 61% would give their parents an "A" for "encouraging me to want to learn," and 72% would give them an "A" for "raising me with good values."

Along with raising children who are self-reliant, honest, caring, and happy, isn't this the kind of praise you would hope to hear as a parent? Considering all the effort involved in raising children—and make no mistake, raising children entails a great many obligations—what kinds of ideas would keep you going when times get rough?

☼ WHAT'S AHEAD IN THIS CHAPTER

We first describe the status and rights of children and different kinds of people who make up the category *parents*; we then consider the role of a dysfunctional family background in parenting and show that other factors influence child development besides parents. Next, we consider both the mother's and the father's adjustment to pregnancy and childbirth and the transition to parenting. We then describe three parenting approaches and five parenting styles and consider ways to be an effective parent. Finally, we consider the aging family and grandparenting.

Consider the following images, as expressed in the mass media and popular culture (LeMasters and DeFrain 1989):

■ *"Raising children will be fun":* "A child is the ultimate pet," says one print ad (for jeans). "What's important is right in front of you," says another ad (for shoes) showing a little girl running into the arms of a woman who is presumably her mother (cited in Kilbourne 1999: 78, 80). Of course, people do have fun with their children—and children with their parents. But in the words of Northwestern University psychologist David Guttman (1987), parenting can also be a "chronic emergency." As he explains, "After children come, dedicated parents can never completely relax into self-absorption or self-indulgence. From then on, even rest becomes a nurse's sleep, the parent waiting for the child's cry or the alarm in the night."

■ *"I want to do things for my kids because I know they'll show appreciation":* "I want my kids to have the things that I didn't have as a kid" is a common expression. But will parental self-sacrifice—perhaps giving up hours of family time to earn the money to give the children "the finer things of life"—really result in your children thanking you? Gratitude is one of life's underutilized emotions, a cynic once said. Indeed, children might simply assume that it's a parent's role to give them everything—and show no appreciation at all.

■ *"Parenting is simply doing what comes naturally":* Because so many people *have* a child by "just doing what comes naturally," it's assumed that almost anyone can *raise* a child the same way—that child rearing is an instinctual process for which no particular training is necessary. Few people would say that the ability to read and write doesn't improve with training, yet they are unwilling to take the same view about training for parenting.

■ *"Just give kids enough love, and they'll turn out all right":* This belief is sort of a corollary to the one just described—namely, parents don't need to know much about child raising, all they need to do is give their children enough love. But giving children love won't guarantee that they'll turn into responsible, empathic, moral, successful adults—any more than giving frequent spankings or stern lectures on morality guarantees the same outcome.

■ *"Good parents raise good children":* Abusive parents often produce children who feel that they are worthless, unlovable, and inadequate, but this is not an *inevitable* outcome. Similarly, parents who invest a lot of emotional and material resources often produce stable, responsible children, but here, too, there are no guarantees. Later in life, kind and well-intentioned parents might blame themselves because their kids got into drugs or flunked out of school. But it needs to be pointed out that parents are only *one* of several influences on a child's development.

🌐 **ON THE WEB** "Leave No Child Behind"

www.childrensdefensefund.org

The mission of the Children's Defense Fund is to leave no child behind (it was their motto before George W. Bush adopted the slogan "No child left behind") and to ensure that every child successfully makes the passage to adulthood with the help of caring families and communities. Go to its website and read about the needs of poor and minority children and those with disabilities.

MAJOR QUESTIONS
you should be able to answer

Who are different people I might meet who could call themselves parents?

What sorts of transitions might I have to make to adjust to parenthood?

What kind of parent would I probably be, and how might I be a better parent?

What should I be prepared for when I and my parents get older?

369

11.1 Parenthood: The Varieties of Experience

MAJOR QUESTION Who are different people I might meet who could call themselves parents?

PREVIEW We first describe the status and rights of children, then the varieties of parents: teenage parents, single parents, older parents, minority parents, nontraditional parents—single fathers, relatives, and gays and lesbians—and working parents. We then consider the role of a dysfunctional family background in parenting. Finally, we show that other factors influence child development besides parents.

Will children bring you happiness? Many people say that becoming a parent gives them self-esteem, feelings of accomplishment, and the sense of exploring new frontiers within themselves. For most healthy parents, the presence of a child is not a *substitute* for happiness they might feel is missing from their lives. Rather, they feel that a child brings them *additional* happiness.

But a lot of your happiness as a parent may depend on how *you* were brought up. If the family in which you were raised was a healthy, *functional* family, then you were raised (generally) with love and respect—and this positive picture of parenthood is probably one you would bring to your own parenting.

One of the purposes of a family, sociologically speaking, is to nurture and protect the young. Here, then, is an important consideration: *If people are not ready to protect and nurture children, should they become parents?* All children should be wanted children, and parenting is one of the most important responsibilities anyone can ever have. Are you willing to devote 18-plus years of your life to being responsible for a child? How would having a child affect your career, your interests, your intimate relationship with your partner? Do you *like* children—and will you like them even if and when they turn out to have ideas different from yours?

The Status & the Rights of Children

For some children and adolescents, things have been improving over the years. For instance, between 2000 and 2004, the number of minors engaged

■ **PANEL 11.1**   **Child Well-Being in 21 Wealthy Countries.**   Lowest figures
indicate the best result. Countries were ranked on the individual categories of
material well-being, health and safety, education, peer and family relationships,
behaviors and risks, and young people's own subjective sense of well-being,
then averaged into a single number. The United States and Britain scored low
because of such factors as economic inequality, poor levels of public support
for families, and high incidences of single-parent families.

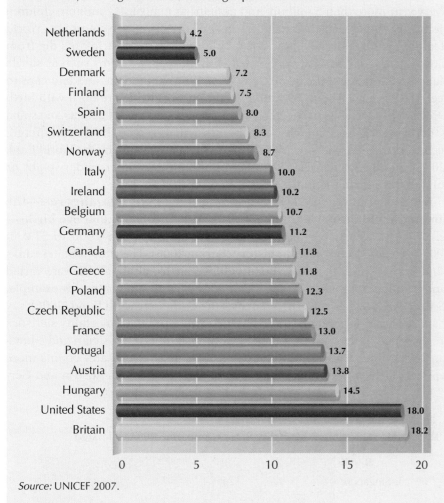

Netherlands 4.2
Sweden 5.0
Denmark 7.2
Finland 7.5
Spain 8.0
Switzerland 8.3
Norway 8.7
Italy 10.0
Ireland 10.2
Belgium 10.7
Germany 11.2
Canada 11.8
Greece 11.8
Poland 12.3
Czech Republic 12.5
France 13.0
Portugal 13.7
Austria 13.8
Hungary 14.5
United States 18.0
Britain 18.2

Source: UNICEF 2007.

in child labor fell by 11% throughout the world, and more than 30 nations
have set a deadline of 2016 to abolish the worst forms of this practice (International Labour Office 2006). In the United States, more children are performing at grade level in school and are taking lessons after class and on
weekends, compared with a decade ago (Dye and Johnson 2006). Since 1993,
they have also been taking fewer drugs, committing fewer crimes, and having
fewer babies (Land 2007). In other respects, however, children are not doing
well in the United States, let alone the world. Indeed, the United States and
Britain ranked at the bottom of a United Nations survey of child welfare in 21
wealthy countries. *(See* ■ *Panel 11.1.)*

The study assessed everything from infant mortality to whether children ate
dinner with their parents and whether they were bullied in school (UNICEF
2007). Also indicative of the investment in children's well-being, economic
historian John Komlos and other researchers (reported in Crenson 2007) have

found that the average height of non-Hispanic white and black Americans has risen at a slower pace compared to people in other industrialized nations over the last several generations; thus, for instance, the typical Dutch male now measures 6 feet—2 inches more than his average American counterpart.

High Mortality Rate for Babies

Every year more than 5 million, and perhaps as many as 11 million, children die before they reach the age of 5, most of them in poor countries (World Health Organization 2006; Save the Children 2007). Most infants die from causes that could be easily prevented with inexpensive items such as sterile blades to cut the umbilical cord, antibiotics for pneumonia, and knit caps to keep them warm. About 7.9 million children worldwide are born with birth defects caused at least partly by a genetic flaw, such as heart defects and spina bifida, about 70% of which could be prevented, repaired, or ameliorated, according to researchers (Christianson et al. 2006). A study by the World Bank (2006) found that nearly 100 million children are either underweight or stunted from malnutrition.

Yet there is also good news: The worldwide *infant mortality rate*—**the number of children who die before 1 year of age per 1,000 live births**—fell 7% in the last five years, from 61.5 deaths in 1995–2000 to 57.0 in 2000–2005, the lowest level in history (Sorkin 2006). The United States ranks 42nd in the world, with 6.37 per 1,000 live births, although the rate varied among different groups—it was 13.8 among African Americans, for example. *(See ■ Panel 11.2.)* Some critics, such as the Commonwealth Fund (2006), say that America's rather high (for a developed nation) infant mortality statistics are evidence of the country's failed health system. But physician and educator Bernardine Healy (2006) points out that the United States counts more types of births as live than many other countries (such as Austria and Ger-

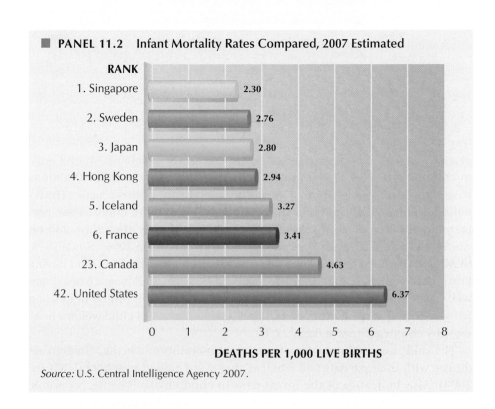

■ **PANEL 11.2** Infant Mortality Rates Compared, 2007 Estimated

DEATHS PER 1,000 LIVE BIRTHS

Source: U.S. Central Intelligence Agency 2007.

many) do, which have less restrictive standards, thus presenting a more favorable picture of their infant mortality rates.

Premature Births & Low Birth Weights

In the United States, 12.5% of babies born in 2004, or about half a million infants, were born prematurely, up from 9.4% in 1981 (Mathews and Mac-Dorman 2007). Traditionally, doctors have estimated women's due dates as 40 weeks, but now the most common gestational age for single live births is 39 weeks and the percentage of babies born between 34 and 36 weeks has increased (Davidoff et al. 2006). **Premature birth, which is defined as a birth that occurs during less than 37 weeks of pregnancy**, is the chief risk factor in about one-third of all infant deaths (Callaghan et al. 2006). Every socioeconomic class and race/ethnicity is affected, although rates are highest among non-Hispanic black women, which is twice that of white women (Mac-Dorman et al. 2007).

What accounts for the increase in premature births? Although the answer remains largely a public health mystery, there is speculation that it may be because of the rising rates of labor inductions and scheduled C-sections. Most at risk are women who had a previous preterm baby, who are carrying twins, who became pregnant through certain infertility treatments (because they're more likely to have multiple births), who are poor, and who are under age 16 or over age 35 (Waitzman et al. 2006).

Infants born with low birth weights—under 5.5 pounds, a condition that foreshadows many problems—made up 8.2% of births in the United States in 2005 (Child Trends DataBank 2007a). Infants weighing less than 3 pounds 4 ounces at birth have a 25% chance of dying before age 1.

The percentage of African American babies born with low birth weight is more than double that of white babies; the discrepancy is smaller among Native American, Asian American, and white babies, which can be partly attributed to educational attainment. Mothers with 12 or more years of education are considerably less likely to have low-birth-weight babies than are those who haven't finished high school.

Childhood Poverty

The official U.S. child poverty rate (which is based on a 1965 definition that many social scientists think is outdated) was reduced in the 1990s, probably mostly as a result of the economic boom, although it was still well above the historic lows of the late 1960s and 1970s (Madrick 2002). According to the U.S. government, 17% of children live in families with incomes below the poverty line. The groups most likely to be living in poor families, however, are black children, with 34%, and Hispanic children at 28% (Child Trends DataBank 2007b). Children are also much more likely to be poor if they live in single-mother families (43%) than in married-couple families (9%). One-half of black and Hispanic children in single-mother families were poor in 2005.

Government policies, such as tax policy and transfers of wealth, have the potential to greatly reduce child poverty rates, and indeed this has been the case with many other industrialized countries. *(See ■ Panel 11.3.)* The policies of the United States, however, have been relatively ineffective in supplementing poverty-level incomes to keep children out of poverty (Burman and Wheaton 2005; Allegretto 2006). The consequences of child poverty are severe:

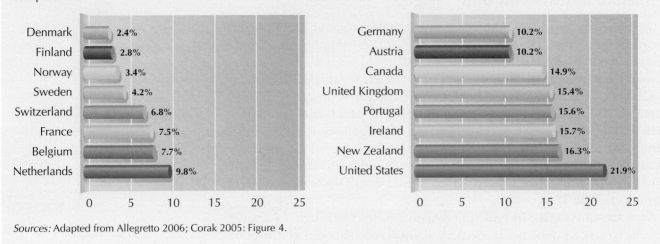

■ **PANEL 11.3 Percentage of Child Poverty in 16 Developed Countries, 2000.** The United States still led in child poverty even after taking into account anti-poverty tax policy and wealth transfers. *Poverty* is defined as families with incomes below one-half the median income for that country, which is a traditional measure of poverty for international comparisons.

Sources: Adapted from Allegretto 2006; Corak 2005: Figure 4.

Children who grow up poor cost the economy $500 billion a year because they are less productive, earn less money, commit more crimes, and have more health-related expenses (Holzer et al. 2007).

Why Are So Many American Children Suffering?

The biggest reason for the deplorable state of America's children is economics. Eighteen percent of American women have minimal or no prenatal care, higher than the rate in any other rich nation, according to Guy Stevens, a senior economist at the Federal Reserve (cited in Madrick 2002). An increasingly selective health-care system in the United States has left a rising percentage of children—11.2% in 2005—with no health insurance. In addition, the childcare system in the United States is "a fragmentary patchwork, both at the level of the individual child and at the level of the overall system," according to research (Clawson and Gerstel 2002: 34). Only 60% of 3- and 4-year-olds go to daycare, well below the European rate, and many of those that do go attend child-care centers that are inadequate.

Economic factors have also meant that two-parent families have become more dependent than ever on the mother's income to meet the family's financial needs. As a result, adults in households with children had fewer hours available each week to provide children with things such as home-cooked meals and help with homework. In addition, the growing incidence of divorce and single motherhood has led to an increase in the number of children living in single-parent families and a consequent decline in the money available to spend on children.

Elsewhere in the world, the status of children is even more tragic. Millions are starved, undernourished, sick, uneducated, homeless, or enslaved; are brutally exploited sexually and for their labor; are both victims and killers in war; and are even hunted down and murdered by sadistic police or death squads. As a result, in 1989, the Convention of the Rights of the Child (a bill of rights for children) was adopted by the United Nations General Assembly after a decade of discussion. It has been ratified by 192 countries; only 2 have not ratified it: the United States and Somalia. *(See* ■ *Panel 11.4.)*

- ***How does the U.S. child poverty rate compare?*** The United States has a child poverty rate of 21.9%, the highest among 16 rich nations. Our poorest children, those in the bottom 10%, have a lower standard of living than those in the bottom 10% of any other nations measured.[a]

- ***How many teenage girls become pregnant every year?*** Although the teen pregnancy rate seems to be declining, about 75 of 1,000 girls ages 15 to 19 become pregnant each year.[b]

- ***What usually happens to children of divorced parents?*** Among parents who divorce, the mother winds up with custody of the children 90% of the time.[c] Another study found that in the previous year, only 17% of children in divorced

families had at least weekly visits with the noncustodial parent, usually the father, and over half had no direct contact.[d]

- ***How often do women over age 30 have babies?*** In the 1970s, only 4% of American women age 30 or over had first babies. By 1998, the figure was 23%. The trend is particularly the case among women who are well educated and economically well off.[e]

- ***What percentage of family income is spent on child care?*** The average family pays about 10% of its family income for child care. Among low-income parents, however, the costs are 23%, about the same proportion as for housing.[f]

- ***What percentage of parents discipline their children with physical force?*** One study found that physi-

NUMBERS THAT MATTER
Parenting

cal force, such as spanking, was inflicted by 94% of parents of children ages 3 and 4, declining to 13% of parents of 17-year-olds.[g]

[a]Allegretto 2006; Corak 2005. [b]Guttmacher Institute 2006. [c]Kreider and Fields 2005. [d]Furstenberg et al. 1983. [e]Ventura et al. 2000. [f]Shellenbarger 1992a. [g]Straus and Stewart 1999.

Young Parents: Teen Pregnancies

The teen (ages 15 to 19) pregnancy rate has declined 36% between 1990 and 2002, owing to increased use of condoms, adoption of effective injectable and implant contraceptives, and reduced sexual activity (Guttmacher Institute 2006: 3). Even so, about 75 of 1,000 girls ages 15 to 19 become pregnant each year.

The problems with children having children are twofold: difficulties for the parent(s) and difficulties for the child(ren).

Difficulties for the Parent

Research shows that teenage girls who have babies end up poorer and less educated than other women. Perhaps, for many young women who are already in poverty, having babies might follow from their sense that they have nothing better to look forward to. Yet having babies makes it even more difficult to break out of poverty. Managing schoolwork and child care is difficult when social support systems such as counseling and daycare are absent. On top of that, many teenagers are single parents: Over half the children of teenage mothers never live with their biological fathers (McGrew and Shore 1991).

Women who bear only one child during adolescence seem to have a better chance of educational and economic achievement. Teenage women who bear a second child are less able to achieve an education and financial security (Furstenberg et al. 1987). In general, the higher the mother's educational and

■ **PANEL 11.4 Children's Rights.** The United Nations Convention of the Rights of the Child states that every human being below the age of 18 should have these rights. For more information, see *www.unicef.org/crc/convention.htm.*

■ The right to affection, love, and understanding.

■ The right to adequate nutrition and medical care.

■ The right to free education.

■ The right to full opportunity for play and recreation.

■ The right to a name and a nationality.

■ The right to be among the first to receive relief in times of disaster.

■ The right to learn to be a useful member of society and to develop individual abilities.

■ The right to be brought up in a spirit of universal peace and brother/ sisterhood.

■ The right to enjoy these rights, regardless of race, color, sex, religion, or national or social origin.

occupational aspirations, the older she is apt to be at the birth of her first child (Stewart 2003).

Difficulties for the Child

Some good news: Only about a third of the daughters of poor teenage mothers become teenage mothers themselves, according to one study, indicating that a cycle of adolescent parents repeating from generation to generation is not inevitable (Furstenberg et al. 1990). The bad news: The study found that the offspring who *do* become teenage mothers might have less chance of breaking out of poverty than their mothers did.

Children of adolescent parents are more apt to fail a grade in school, the study suggests, with up to half repeating at least one grade. Incidents of substance abuse, fighting, and problems with the law are also higher among the offspring of teenage parents.

Compared with older mothers, teenage mothers have a higher possibility of going on welfare and tend to spend more years on welfare over their lifetimes. Accordingly, the Personal Responsibility and Work Opportunity Reconciliation Act of 1996, the welfare reform act that was passed during the Clinton administration, offers several programs to help teenage parents on welfare be better parents (Kisker et al. 1998). (A starting point for exploring these programs can be found at *www.aspe.dhhs.gov/hsp/isp/tpd/synthes/lessons.htm.*)

Single Parents: Unmarried & Divorced

Single-parent families are definitely on the upswing. One-parent families jumped from 9% in 1960 to about 31% in 2001. Births to unmarried women went from 11% in 1970 to 36.8% in 2005. More and more children are also being raised by single-parent fathers.

Who are today's single parents? Probably the two largest groups are the *unmarried* and the *divorced*. (Other single parents include the widowed, grandparents and other guardians, and gay families, as we will describe.)

Unmarried Parents

Think Angelina Jolie and Brad Pitt, or Goldie Hawn and Kurt Russell, or Susan Sarandon and Tim Robbins—all celebrities with longtime live-together relationships who have raised children (Jayson 2007). They are emblematic of the startling rise in out-of-wedlock births in the United States, in which 38.6%, or nearly 4 in 10, babies are born to unmarried parents (Hamilton et al. 2006; Pew Research Center 2007). Most of the increase, however, is among women in their twenties and thirties, not among teenage mothers, whose rates have actually dropped (National Institute of Child Health and Human Development 2007a). The increase occurred among all racial and ethnic groups but was steepest among Hispanics.

This does not mean that children of unwed mothers are necessarily born into single-parent families. About one-quarter of the children born to unmarried parents are born into two-parent families because the parents live together (Pear 1991). Often, a child lives in a single-parent situation for only a year or two, until the parent marries.

Although cohabitation and childbearing outside marriage are increasingly common family arrangements in the United States, research shows that they are unlikely anytime soon to achieve the same standing as marriage and childbearing within marriage in terms of social and kinship acceptability (Seltzer 2000).

DISORDER. Before one has children, it's hard to anticipate the great disruptions that they impose on adult life. Could you handle two decades or so of this kind of responsibility? ▲

Divorced Parents

Married adults now divorce two-and-a-half times as often as adults did 20 years ago and four times as often as they did 50 years ago. If all marriages are considered, about 2 to 3% end in divorce in any particular year. However, between 40 and 60% of *new* marriages will eventually end in divorce. The probability of a first marriage ending in separation or divorce within the first five years is 20%, and the probability of its ending within the first 10 years is 33% (National Center for Health Statistics 2002). More than 90% of the time, the mother winds up having custody of the children. In 2001, 15% of children (10.6 million) lived in blended families; about half (5.1 million) lived with at least one stepparent (Kreider and Fields 2005:3).

The experiences of divorced mothers and fathers differ:

■ **Divorced Mothers:** Divorced women with children often don't do as well as their ex-husbands financially. Many experience a marked decline in their standard of living (Weitzman 1985). The primary reason is that ex-husbands contribute far less to child care than they did before the divorce. Beginning in

1994, however, employers must deduct all child-support payments for workers from their paychecks, whether the absent parent is delinquent or not. A lack of child support is a major cause of poverty among American children (Shellenbarger 1992b).

■ **Divorced Fathers:** Divorced fathers tend to become less and less involved with their children's lives (Furstenberg and Nord 1985). One survey of children from divorced families found that only 17% had had at least weekly visits with the noncustodial parent in the previous year, and over half had had no direct contact (Furstenberg et al. 1983).

Older Parents

At one time, physicians routinely advised women not to wait until they were older to have children. However, as we have seen (Chapter 10, "Reproduction"), more effective birth control and the increased opportunities for women for education and careers have allowed many women to delay childbearing until their later years, bringing about a profound shift in childbearing patterns. In the 1970s, only 4% of American women had first babies at age 30 or over; by 1998, it was 23%. Between 2004 and 2005, the rise in the birth rate for women ages 30 to 34 was the highest since 1965, for women ages 40 to 44, it was the highest since 1968, and for women ages 45 to 49, it was the highest since 1970 (Hamilton et al. 2006). More than 8,000 men age 50 or older became fathers in 2002 (Tyre 2004).

Although women who postpone childbirth until their thirties might have more pregnancy complications, older parents often speak enthusiastically about having children and say that they are more prepared emotionally to be parents than they were when they were younger (Berkowitz et al. 1990; Hardie 1991). Children of older fathers find that their dads are more involved in their lives, perhaps because these fathers are more mature and more ready to focus on parenting (Tyre 2004: 71).

Minority Parents

In some cases, race and ethnicity don't seem to matter. For instance, did you often disagree with your parents when you were a teenager? One study found that parents and adolescents still argued daily about clothes, school, chores, and the like, regardless of color—whether white, black, or Latino (Barber 1994). Other research suggests that within a certain socioeconomic class, parents' expectations and aspirations for their children are similar to those of other parents—whether black, Hispanic, or Asian American (Julian et al. 1994).

However, whether a family is of recent immigrant status can make a difference. For example, parents born in Mexico might insist that children adhere to family discipline and rules at the same time they are encouraged to be self-reliant, whereas parents of Mexican descent who were born in the United States might expect proper behavior but also give their children emotional support (Becerra 1988; Buriel 1993). Parents who were born in Asia seem to expect discipline and obedience and use physical punishment, whereas those of Asian descent who were born in the United States generally allow their children more independence (Tran 1988; Wong 1988).

African American Parents

No doubt one of the greatest factors affecting parenting among African Americans is the matter of race itself: Even financial security is not enough to protect parents or their children from unexpected incidents of racism. A recent newspaper story, for instance, described the difficulties of blacks with upper-middle-class incomes trying to employ nannies for their children, with even nannies of African American or Caribbean descent themselves refusing to work for them (because of fears about low pay, extra work, and notions that the neighborhoods would be unsafe) (Kantor 2006). Many African American parents, fed up with the public school system, are moving toward home-schooling their children (Fulbright 2006).

Still, the evidence seems to show that economic class differences do affect parenting approaches (Blackwell 1991; Sugrue 1999).

■ **The Working Poor and Underclass:** Being involved in a constant financial struggle often leaves poor parents—especially if they see no way of improving their status—unable to direct their children or influence their behavior. Parents who are functionally illiterate or have only grade school educations might try to influence their children's obedience by pointing to themselves as models of what not to aspire to.

■ **The Working Class and Middle Class:** Among the working class, when some parental direction is possible, parents tend to emphasize conformity, obedience, good behavior, respect for authority, and staying out of trouble with the police. Middle-class families also frequently stress these values and promote respect for property, achievement, and high educational and occupational goals.

Hispanic Parents

Now the largest minority group, Hispanics tend to stress the authority of the father, to demand that children (even grown children) respect their parents, and to insist that older children set a positive example for their younger siblings (Becerra 1988).

Asian American Parents

Asian American parents tend to emphasize the authority of the family, encourage respect for and obedience to the parents, and discourage expressions of individuality and aggression (Tran 1988; Wong 1988; Cooper and Cooper 1992). They are also often strong believers in educational success (Fejgin 1995).

Native American Parents

Native American parents tend to try to instill in their children a sense of family and tribal unity and to discipline them with persuasion and nonverbal behavior (such as disapproving looks) rather than physical punishment. Children are expected to show respect for their parents and others, to suppress aggression, and to be independent (John 1988).

Nontraditional Parents: Single Fathers, Relatives, & Gays & Lesbians

Today, parents don't consist of just traditional biological mom and dad. Following are some variations:

Single Fathers

We considered single parents, including single fathers, in Chapter 9, "Variations." Among American households with working parents and children, those headed by single fathers are increasing fastest. The 2000 U.S. Census data show that there were 2.2 million households across the country in which single men were raising children, a 62% increase since 1990. In 2001, among the 18.5 million children living with only one unmarried parent, 2.2 million lived with their fathers (Kreider and Fields 2005: 2).

EXAMPLES OF

Two New Kinds of Parent–Child Arrangements

A Pair of Fathers, a Son Never Officially Adopted

One hallmark of families in our time seems to be that parent-child relationships are more fluid than people might once have thought. Children are raised not only by parents but also by grandparents, relatives, and family friends. There are other variations as well. Two examples follow:

Two Gay Fathers, with One Happy to Stay Home

Jamie McConnell used to be a corporate litigator for a prestigious Minneapolis law firm. Now he stays home full time to raise Ben, age 3, whom he and his partner of 8 years adopted. His partner, Bill Atmore, an anesthesiologist, works full time.

The pair are representative of same-sex couples analyzed by the U.S. Census Bureau (reported in Bellafante 2004: A1). Twenty-six percent of male couples include a stay-at-home parent—quite a bit more than the number of men in married heterosexual couples who stay home, in part perhaps because gay men find it difficult to locate surrogate mothers and in part because they don't want to adopt only to turn the child over to a daycare provider. Many same-sex couples are electing for one partner to stay home even though their median household income is only $35,000, compared to $45,000 for a heterosexual married couple with a stay-at-home parent.

Even though many gay fathers believe that having one partner stay home to raise their child is the right thing to do, the idea of putting a professional career on hold can be even more anxiety provoking than it is for nonworking mothers, given that, as one reporter puts it, "male identity is largely defined by achievements outside the confines of nurseries, mud rooms and kitchens" (Bellafante 2004: A17). Tom Howard, who holds a Ph.D. in microbiology and gave up a research and medical school position at the University of Southern California to be a stay-at-home dad of three adopted children, says, "I can truly empathize with the women's movement now. I know that I've committed career suicide." Yet it seemed more practical for his partner of 17 years, Ken Yood, to continue to pursue a partnership at his Los Angeles law firm. "We realized pretty quickly that Ken's pay scale was going to support the family," said Howard. Often gay household fathers also feel the loss of

Grandparents & Other Relatives

Grandparents and other relatives increasingly end up raising children because the biological parents are incapable of doing so themselves (perhaps because of chemical dependency) or a court determines that the biological parent is not the best nurturer for a child. Indeed, the number of children living with grandparents as their primary caregivers increased 31% between 1990 and 1997, according to the 2000 U.S. Census (cited in Briggs 2007: 34).

Gays & Lesbians

We discussed gays as parents in Chapter 8, "Variations." Children become part of gay and lesbian families through custody in the dissolution of hetero-sexual marriages in which one parent is homosexual or bisexual, through adoption, and through alternative means of conception, such as artificial insemination or surrogate birth mothers (both avenues by which single gays

financial independence and experi-ence guilt feelings about the loss of their credit rating or making even an inexpensive impulse buy.

A Nonbiological Son & the Concept of "Equitable Adoption"

In 1955, after being abandoned by his mother, Terrold Bean, age 21 months, was placed in foster care with Pat and Kathleen Ford. He stayed with them for 19 years, and they became the only family he ever knew.

"They bought him a new bike every Christmas, helped him get his first car, and embraced him as their own," says a newspaper story. "In turn, he cared for the San Francisco couple he called Mom and Dad, overseeing their affairs as they grew older and tending to them when they became ill" (Chiang 2004: A1).

When Pat Ford died in 2000, he left no will and an estate worth about $640,000. Kathleen had died in 1973 and their only biological child, a daugh-ter, passed away in 1999. However, Bean was not Pat's heir because the Fords had never formally adopted him.

Pat Ford's nearest blood relatives, a nephew and a niece who had not seen him in 15 years and didn't bother to attend his funeral, tried to claim the estate. But Bean, age 50, filed a suit in which he argued that he was "equi-tably adopted" because the Fords had raised him as their son.

The lawyer for the nephew and niece argued that the courts had made it clear that a child is equitably adopted "only if there is clear and con-vincing evidence that the parents intended to adopt the child." In the Fords' case, he said, "they never men-tioned adoption, they never promised to leave him anything" (Chiang 2004: A1). Bean argued that the Fords, who took in other foster children who were later adopted out, never allowed him to be interviewed by prospective par-ents, referred to him as their son, encouraged a sibling relationship between him and their biological daughter, and changed his religion to the Ford family's Catholicism. A fam-ily friend said that the couple wanted to adopt Bean but were worried that his natural mother might try to block

the adoption, though she gave up her legal rights to him when he was 3 years old.

Unfortunately for Bean, the Califor-nia Supreme Court ruled that even though he had stayed in close touch with Pat Ford for 45 years and had helped to care for him and arrange for his funeral, Bean had no claim to the estate. The court said that the line between caregiving by a foster parent and adoption should remain clear. Making it too easy for a foster child to claim the status of an adopted child "would leave open to competing claims the estate of any foster parent or stepparent who treats a foster child or stepchild lovingly" and might dis-courage foster parenting (California Supreme Court, reported in Egelko 2004).

WHAT DO YOU THINK? These two exam-ples express unusual variations on the parent-child bond. What kinds of con-cerns do they illustrate that might apply to heterosexual marriages with biological children?

SINGLE DAD. Among U.S. households with working parents and children, the number of those headed by single fathers jumped to 2.2 million in 2000—a 62% increase since 1998. Do you know any single fathers (or are you one yourself)? ▶

or lesbians can have children). The 2000 U.S. Census (cited in Bellafante 2004: A17) found that there were about 60,000 male couple households with children and close to 96,000 female couple households with children.

Working Parents

Mom's role has undergone a serious change in the last couple of decades—and this has affected Dad's role. Mom has gotten a job, either because she wants to or because she has to help meet the family budget. Families in which both parents are working outside the home more than doubled from 1976 to 2002—from 31 to 68%. Between 1970 and 2002, the percentage of married women with children under age 6 who were in the labor force went from 30 to 63%. In 2002, over 71% of mothers with children under age 18 were in the workforce.

The fact of both parents working outside the home has amounted to a social revolution. Among the consequences are the following.

Career-Parenting Conflict

Mothers (and fathers) who don't work outside the home—who choose to stay at home, particularly when the children are old enough to go to school—might find their role devalued by their own family members, other parents, and society in general (Spring 1991). Alternatively, parents who want to pursue a career might worry about the effect of their absence on their child's upbringing. Despite the surge of women into the workforce, however, mothers today are spending at least as much time with their children as they did 40 years ago. What's different is that the amount of child care and housework performed by fathers has sharply increased, although women still do twice as much as men (Bianchi et al. 2006).

Family-Oriented Workplace Policies

The United States lags far behind almost all wealthy countries on family-oriented workplace policies, such as parental and maternal leave, as well as for paid sick days and support for breast feeding at work, according to a study by Harvard and McGill University researchers (Heymann et al. 2007). For instance, at least 145 countries require paid sick days and at least 107 countries protect working women's right to breast-feed, but the United States does not. As a result, the proportion of U.S. working mothers with very young children peaked at 58% in 1998, but has since fallen to 53% and is continuing to drop (Cohany and Sok 2007).

Only recently has the United States required employers to allow workers to take unpaid leaves of absence from their jobs for pregnancy, postchildbirth maternity or paternity leave, care of sick children, or family emergencies. Family leave has been a reality for some time in countries such as Germany and Japan, with government and/or employers supporting a certain number of paid weeks. Only in 1993 did Congress finally pass legislation allowing unpaid family leave.

At present, some parents who take time off either for pregnancy or for childbirth experience employer discrimination and often suffer career setbacks (Hughes 1991; Bernstein 1992). Men seem reluctant to use unpaid leave, even in the states that require large employers to provide them. According to one survey, only about 1% of eligible men actually use the leave, perhaps in part because of a social and cultural stigma associated with men taking care of children (Brott 1992).

Child-Care Services

Single working parents find worries about child care and flexible scheduling one of their major concerns. Indeed, the youngest children of working women are now more likely to be cared for by a nonrelative (51%) than by a family member (49%).

Child care is also a preoccupation of married working parents, particularly those who are poor. Although the average family pays about 10% of its family income for child care, the costs are 23% for low-income parents, about the same proportion as for housing (Shellenbarger 1992a). Average child-care prices in the United States range from $3,016 for a 4-year-old child in Alabama to $13,480 for infant child care in Massachusetts (NACCRRA 2005: 2).

Child care is such a major dilemma for many two-paycheck couples with children that they try to avoid child care and its costs by asking their employers for split shifts. Others borrow money to pay for high-quality care. Because child care is expensive, some parents are forced to leave their children alone at home; indeed, nearly one in four children is **a *latchkey child*—a school-age child who regularly spends part of the day unsupervised at home while his or her parents are at work** (Hofferth et al. 2000). Preteens and teenagers left unsupervised after school may be far more prone than other kids to get involved with alcohol and illegal drugs (Richardson 1989; Miller 1990).

Although some daycare centers offer children excellent age-appropriate care and educational opportunities, some have been known to resort to "child packing"—rows of children in cribs and high chairs with an adult sitting nearby reading a magazine (Miller 1990). Indeed, recent research suggests that the quality of care for young children is "poor or fair" in well over half of child-care settings (Clawson and Gerstel 2002). Whether or not child-care facilities have a negative or positive impact on the children depends, of course, on the level of care, which depends in turn on such matters as pay and training of staffers. Overall, some studies have found that children in full-time daycare whose mothers worked outside the home when their children were under 1 year old did less well on tests predicting school performance than those whose mothers stayed at home (Desai et al. 1989). A major federally financed study that tracked 1,364 children from birth through elementary school found that the more time preschoolers spent in daycare centers—not with nannies or family daycare homes—the more aggressive and disobedient they were in sixth grade (National Institute of Child Health and Human Development 2007b). Still, the difference was not statistically significant unless preschoolers were in group care for four years.

Even working parents who have satisfactory child-care arrangements come to dread the phone call from the sitter or child-care center saying, "I'm sorry to bother you at work, but your child is running a high temperature and needs to go home." Work and sick children are one of the top conflicts in a working parent's life. Despite all the talk about changing gender roles, it is mothers rather than fathers who bear most of the burden of child care. Among parents with preschoolers, more women than men missed work in an average week, usually owing to sick children or problems in child-care scheduling arrangements (Schellhardt 1990).

We return to the subject of child care in Chapter 12, "Work."

Making Time for Children

Jobs, school, and financial responsibilities can be terribly demanding of adults. Sooner or later, many find that they've reached a decision point: Should they continue a single-minded devotion to career at the expense of attention to their family? Or should they scale back their career ambitions to devote more time to their families? Certainly, the stress of overwork does not make for good parenting or a good relationship with one's partner. Yet the transition from a socially and intellectually involving job to a renewed emphasis on family is not always easy. Some people who cut back on work to focus on family initially feel a sense of loss. Still, on balance, the news is encouraging: A Canadian study found that professional women who take time out to marry and to have children are far more content than are those who put their career above all (Recer 1992). Unfortunately, we know little about the effect of men scaling back on or taking a break from their careers for the sake of their children. However, one study of more than 80 part-time professionals, both men and women, found that going part time in order to take care of children won't dead-end a career: Most received at least one promotion and pay increases comparable to those of workers who returned to work full time after taking family leave (Lee and Kossek 2005).

Your Own Background: Functional or Dysfunctional Parents?

Unfortunately, many people are raised in dysfunctional families, such as those in which a parent is impaired by alcohol or other drugs or is somehow emotionally handicapped, bringing many woes to his or her children.

A *dysfunctional family* **is one in which the parents demon-strate negative or destructive behavior toward each other and/or toward their children.** Children may be physically or sexually abused, emotionally or verbally abused, neglected, isolated, overcontrolled, overburdened, or otherwise mistreated. As a result, they usually have a low sense of self-esteem, feeling unworthy, unvalued, and unloved. Unfortunately, the children of abusive or neglectful parents may themselves becomes abusive or neglectful with their own children, perpetuating a cycle that might well extend over several generations.

Being raised in a dysfunctional family should not negate the possibility of becoming a parent. Rather, it may serve as an invitation to prospective parents to participate actively in their own recovery from the effect of their dysfunctional families. In addition, as we'll discuss, parenting programs can be helpful in developing the knowledge, skills, and perspectives a person needs to be a nurturing, effective parent.

ABUSE. Adults who were physically or emotionally abused, neglected, or otherwise mistreated as children often feel unworthy and unloved—and are abusive or neglectful of their own children. Did you suffer such parental misbehavior when you were a child? ▲

A Sense of Perspective: Parents Aren't the Only Influences on Their Children

Parents tend to wonder later in life what they could have done better in raising their children. Asked "What do you regret most?" after their children have left home, parents told one interviewer (Shellenbarger 2003) that it was mainly "the small stuff." Most parents thought they did well enough teaching values and keeping their children safe but regretted doing too much for their kids, such as managing their money and preventing them from learning self-reliance.

Of course, there are other influences, which are discussed next.

Biology & Heredity

Every parent must wonder sometimes where a child got "that drawing ability" or why the child seems to have a temper no one else in the family has. Clearly, genetics and physiology are important influences on behavior, thinking, and personality (Reiss 1995).

The Social Environment

Children who are born into a large, impoverished family living in a rural area will, of course, have an entirely different upbringing from that of an only child born into an upscale family living in an urban area. Among the environmental influences are socioeconomic class, race and ethnicity, religion, geography, and family size. For instance, how rapidly California immigrant children attain English proficiency in "English learner" classes depends a lot on the education and income levels of their parents, with fast-learning Mandarin and

Toxic Parents & Transcenders: How Do Some People Survive Abusive Parents?

Even if you're not engaged in raising children yourself, you might be interested in how you were affected by the way you were raised. You might also wonder about how your own abilities as a parent might be affected by how you were parented.

"Toxic Parents": There Is a Difference between Discipline & Abuse

Even the best of parents are only human. They lose their tempers with their children, aren't always emotionally available, and are occasionally domineering or controlling. And in the United States at least, physical force, ranging from slaps to batterings, is a common form of punishment (Straus 1994a; Straus and Stewart 1999). Indeed, one survey in Ohio found that more than two-thirds of family physicians and pediatricians supported the use of spanking—even though the U.S. Surgeon General in 1985 said that corporal punishment should be discour-

aged (McCormick 1992). In Sweden, incidentally, people think that such corporal punishment of children is harmful. There, spanking is outlawed (Greven 1991).

If your parents lost their tempers or were domineering or emotionally distant from time to time, does this mean that they were abusive? Probably not. Parents are subject to many stresses and strains, and we might argue that they may be excused if *occasionally* they have such lapses, especially if the rest of the time they treat their children with warmth, affection, and respect. However, there are some parents (including stepparents and guardians) who *consistently* act in negative ways toward their children, inflicting ongoing trauma, abuse, and denigration. Sometimes, the trauma is not ongoing but happens only once, as in the case of sexual abuse. Quite often, the mistreatment takes the form of *emotional abuse*, such as excessive

criticism or withholding of affection. Susan Forward (1989) has dubbed such harmful parents "toxic parents." The emotional damage inflicted by such parents, she says, spreads through a child's being like a chemical toxin, and as the child grows, so does the pain.

If you were left alone a lot, overprotected, made to feel guilty, repeatedly humiliated, beaten, or sexually abused, you probably suffer what most abused children do: feelings that you are worthless, unlovable, and inadequate. These feelings come about, Forward points out, because children of "toxic parents" largely blame themselves for their parents' abuse. As she writes, "It is easier for a defenseless, dependent child to feel guilty for having done something 'bad' to deserve Daddy's rage than it is for that child to accept the frightening fact that Daddy, the protector, can't be trusted."

Cantonese students being found principally in suburban schools with greater resources (Jepsen and de Alth 2005).

Siblings & Relatives

Brothers and sisters, aunts and uncles, cousins and grandparents can sometimes have influences that are equal to those of some parents. In lieu of an absentee father, for example, another older male figure might become a model for children's behavior.

Teachers & Friends

Many successful adults from unpromising backgrounds point to the influence of a teacher or a friend in steering them on a course that helped them to overcome family disadvantages.

We discuss child abuse in more detail in Chapter 13, "Crises."

Transcenders: Even Abused Children Can Turn Out All Right

Many children never rise above their abusive backgrounds. Some develop health problems that require more than usual medical care as adults (Bachman et al. 1988). Some who experience harsh punishment at home become accustomed to expressing violence against other children, teachers, and society (Martin 1975). Some become the homicidal teenagers who make headlines for killing their parents (Heide 1992). Others continue to have problems accepting and valuing themselves and forming intimate relationships with others.

However, some people who had abusive childhoods have managed to overcome problems or disabilities that would seem to sink most others. Called "transcenders," they offer lessons for those who have trouble rising above the circumstances of their lives. Transcenders, writes psychologist Donna LaMar, author of *Transcending Turmoil: Survivors of Dysfunctional Families*, "are individuals who grow up in difficult, painful, destructive families and emerge with a meaningful, productive way of life" (LaMar 1992: 3).

Several famous people were abused as children. Television talk-show hostess Oprah Winfrey was sexually molested by male relatives and family friends when she was 9 years old. British actor Michael Caine was physically abused by his foster mother and kept on a starvation diet until he was rescued by his natural mother. Former U.S. Senator Paula Hawkins was molested at age 5 by an elderly man. Poet Rod McKuen was battered by his stepfather, to the extent of having both arms broken, and was raped by a male family member at age 7.

Other transcenders are "ordinary heroes." A young West Virginian named Elizabeth was abandoned by her mother, subjected to bone-breaking beatings by her aunt, and sexually molested by her uncle from the age of 8. The turning point came in fourth grade, when her aunt shaved off Elizabeth's long, blonde curls, her secret pride. "After that," reports Karen Northcraft (quoted in Rogers 1991: B1), a psychiatric social worker who wrote her doctoral dissertation on transcenders, Elizabeth "was able to reject what her aunt was saying and start making her life better."

What is it that transcenders have that others don't? Why do they not succumb to the pressures of the psychological and social problems of their surroundings? "They have self-confidence, and early on, they think for themselves," says Northcraft. "They emotionally distance themselves from their parents, and they choose their actions rather than do what would be expected in their environment." When things are at their worst, they are able to imagine themselves somewhere else, envisioning that they can do great things despite their present circumstances.

Source: From *Healthy for Life: Wellness & the Art of Living* 1/e by Williams/Knight © 1994. Reprinted with permission of Brooks/Cole, a division of Thomson Learning. www.thomsonrights.com; fax 800-730-2215.

The Mass Media

As we have noted all along in this book, television, movies, music videos, magazines, and now the Internet can have a tremendous effect on children's values and behavior. Indeed, a survey of 1,000 parents by Common Sense Media (reported in Nevius 2003) found that an overwhelming majority believed that unsuitable TV, movies, video games, and contemporary music lead to violent, antisocial behavior, and sex at younger ages. Common Sense Media (*www.commonsensemedia.org*) evaluates the kinds of films, TV shows, and music a child is likely to encounter, makes recommendations, and describes content but does not call for banning offensive material. The purpose is to let parents know what their kids are getting into.

The American Academy of Pediatrics (2007) recommends that babies under 2 years old not watch any screen (television and video) media and that children age 2 and older watch no more than 1 to 2 hours a day. However, one recent study (Zimmerman et al. 2007) found that the average amount of viewing time for all children up to age 2 was a little more than 40 minutes a day.

ELECTRONIC BABYSITTER. Although parents, teachers, and friends all influence a child's upbringing, the mass media—and most especially television—are important contributors. Can you pinpoint any ideas that you as a child got from TV that were significant influences? ▶

Another study found that on a typical day 61% of babies 1 year old or younger watch TV or videos, with average viewing of more than an hour. A third of children under age 6 have a TV in their bedroom (Rideout and Hamel 2006). "There has been this sense that it is kids clamoring for media and parents trying to hold back the wave," said study co-author Vicky Rideout (quoted in Clemetson 2006). "But what came out is that parents themselves are very enthusiastic about using media in their children's lives." Despite concerns about the potentially harmful effects of TV on young children—exposure to messages about violence, sex, alcohol, faulty nutrition, and so on—it seems that a great many parents feel the need to use it as an electronic babysitter or subscribe to the belief that programs such as those on the BabyFirst TV channel will provide beneficial experiences. Although BabyFirst TV—a TV channel exclusively for babies—bills itself as offering content "tailored to meet the needs of infants and children" through age 3, the consensus of pediatricians is pretty clear: You should turn it off (DeFao 2006).

11.2 Becoming a Parent

MAJOR QUESTION What sorts of transitions might I have to make to adjust to parenthood?

PREVIEW In this section, we consider both the mother's and the father's adjustment to pregnancy and childbirth. We then examine the transition to parenting by both parents, the transition to motherhood, and the transition to fatherhood.

At what time of year are obstetricians least likely to take their vacations? Late summer, especially September, says one report (Waldrop 1991). That's when the largest group of babies is born—at least in the United States. Although most people would prefer to have their babies in the spring, it can take 3 to 4 months or more to conceive, which is why most birth dates can't be preplanned.

In other parts of the world, peak months for births vary according to the latitude and the climate in which conception occurred, according to one study (Rosenberg and Aschoff 1990). Air conditioning and heating in industrialized nations have changed this somewhat.

Adjusting to Pregnancy & Childbirth

How parents-to-be react to the news of the woman's pregnancy depends in great part on whether the pregnancy was planned or not, whether the mother is in love with the father, whether financial hard times mean that the baby is merely another mouth to feed, and all kinds of other factors. Women having second or subsequent pregnancies view them more negatively than first ones, perhaps because of their awareness of the costs and responsibilities (Westbrook 1978). Pregnancy seems more desirable if the man is employed (Meyerowitz 1970). In addition, the woman's reactions can vary depending on the extent of the father's support (Leifer 1980).

Pregnancy: The Mother's Story

In the early months (the first trimester), the woman experiences signs of pregnancy such as enlarged and tender breasts and recurring **morning sickness, nausea and vomiting that happen frequently in the early morning but also during other times of the day.**

During the second 3 months (second trimester), the mother begins to notice her waistline expanding and perhaps experiences craving for new foods—not just the classic pickles and peppermint ice cream but also foods she might not even have liked before. By the fourth or fifth month, she experiences "quickening"—the fetus moving and kicking inside her.

During months 7 through 9 (the third trimester), she will likely experience increasing discomfort as the growing fetus puts pressure on her bladder, lungs, and other organs. She might also have difficulty sleeping and have backaches and swollen legs, and her moods might swing from anxiety to apprehension to excitement and anticipation of the impending arrival. Then one day—or, often, one night—the time that she thought would never come finally does. The baby signals that it is ready to be born.

Pregnancy: The Father's Story

The father's story is mainly an emotional one. Even the most involved father, however, is less apt to get attention than is the prospective mother.

Some fathers are excited participants, identifying with all the stages of pregnancy (Antle 1978). Indeed, there are men who so completely identify with the woman's pregnancy that they even experience some of the same physical symptoms (a condition called *couvade*) (Conner and Denson 1990). Some fathers-to-be become preoccupied with themselves, overexercising or overeating (Jackson 1984). Others become so resentful that they actually harm their partners; in fact, the incidence of wife-beating increases during pregnancy (Gelles 1975). Many partners, however, find that the event brings them closer together than they have ever been (Kitzinger 1983).

One study found that whether or not men felt ready to be receptive to a pregnancy depended on the stability of the relationship, their sense of financial security, whether they intended to be parents at some point, and the sense of the childless part of their life coming to an end (May 1982). Their readiness, then, depends on the goals they had set earlier in their lives.

After the Baby Is Born: Postpartum Adjustment

The *postpartum period* **is a 3-month period following the birth, during which critical family and emotional adjustments are made.** Of the many matters with which new parents must deal, we single out the following for special attention:

■ Bonding: Sometimes separation between mother and child immediately after birth cannot be avoided; however, if the separation is prolonged, it can have important negative effects. In general, the more time the family can spend together after the baby's arrival, the better the **bonding, or close emotional attachment among them** (Klaus and Kennel 1982). Indeed, frequent contact between both parents and the baby is important in developing future attachments (Harlow and Suomi 1970).

■ **Postpartum Blues:** After 9 months of pregnancy, hours of fatiguing and stressful labor, hormonal changes after delivery, and the incredible emotional high of seeing the baby born, many women (perhaps 25 to 50%) experience **a period of sadness and anxiety, the** *postpartum blues*. A woman might cry easily, be alternately ecstatic and lethargic, and feel helpless and out of control, even "crazy" (Hopkins et al. 1984). Because these fluctuating moods can persist for weeks or even months, it helps to know that they are normal, universal, and temporary.

■ **Postpartum Depression:** However, we need to distinguish *postpartum blues* from *postpartum depression*, **severe persistent symptoms of a major depression that warrant the assistance of a health-care professional.** The consequences of postpartum depression for mothers who have limited or no emotional support or who have a history of depression can be serious (Beck et al. 1992). Even some fathers—up to 7%, according to one study (Ramchandani et al. 2005)—report low moods and feelings of sadness, irritability, and hopelessness.

Of course the emotions of both parents are strained by the sudden responsibilities of caring for a new infant and the continuing fatigue because the baby likely does not sleep through the night and often fusses during the day. As one expert, C. G. Coll (quoted in Kutner 1991), put it, "One of the frustrating things is the lack of control, especially during the first 3 months. The baby is constantly demanding things of you, but is giving very little back." In addition, there are all the other responsibilities that must be attended to—taking care of other children, doing housework, going off to a job. One way to reduce this stress is for the mother to mobilize her social support network, including her partner, close relatives, or friends, to help her.

Adjusting to Parenting

We mentioned in Chapter 8, "Marriage," that a couple will devote their energies and finances to childbearing and rearing for around 20 to 28 years, or longer if they have more than one child. This effort, it has been suggested, occurs in five stages. *(See* ■ *Panel 11.5.)*

Adjustments are made, of course, throughout this time. Let us consider some of the highlights.

Transition to Parenthood

Is making the transition to parenthood just like the transition to any other adult role, such as getting married or embarking on a new job? Actually, it is more difficult, suggested sociologist **Alice Rossi** (1968), for several reasons:

■ **You Can't Undo Parenthood:** Adults, especially married couples, feel pressured by the culture to have children even when they don't want to. But once a child is born, most adults feel that they have to be committed to parenthood.

■ **Parenting Is an Immediate 24/7 Job:** Parenting is an experience in which one abruptly has to be responsible for a **continuous coverage system, in which parents must become fully responsible for a fragile infant—immediately, 24 hours every day—**which can create conflict between partners about who's on duty and who has free time (LaRossa and LaRossa 1981).

■ **Childbearing family—lasts about 2½ years:** On average, American women have their first child at age 27. If there are other children, they tend to appear about 30 months apart.

■ **Family with preschoolers—lasts about 3½ years:** In this stage, the couple's oldest child is 2 to 6 years old. The parents (especially the mother) are quite preoccupied with child rearing.

■ **Family with schoolchildren—lasts about 7 years:** By this stage, the oldest child is 6 to 13 years old. Often, the mother has returned to the job market, if only part time.

■ **Family with adolescents—lasts about 7 years:** By this stage, the oldest child is 13 to 20 years old. This can be a particularly trying time for parents. It's likely that both parents are working outside the home.

■ **Family as launching center—lasts about 8 years:**   By this stage, the oldest child is an adult and has been "launched" into independence.

Source: Based on data from Duvall and Miller 1985.

■ **Unrealistic Expectations Can Lead to Disillusionment:** Very few parents have any training or previous experience with child raising, so they might romanticize it. Thus, the hard work of actual parenthood might lead to disillusionment, anger, and guilt.

■ **There Is No Instruction Manual for Parenting:** True, there is *Dr. Spock's Baby and Child Care* book, supposedly the bible of child raising, but there are also many other experts. Most parents are uncertain about what is the correct way to proceed in bringing their children up to be healthy adults.

■ **Parenting Changes the Couple's Relationship:** If you're a man who is used to receiving your partner's attention, how will you adjust to having less of it? If you're a working woman in an egalitarian relationship with your partner, how will you deal with having to stay home as a homemaker? Most couples are unprepared for their changing roles with each other. Marital satisfaction after the first baby's birth has been found to be 42% lower among the latest generation of parents, according to a survey of 90 studies of 31,000 married people (Twenge et al. 2003). However, some research (Shapiro et al. 2000) has found that couples that appeared to have a strong marital friendship were the most resilient to decline in marital satisfaction when they became parents.

These are not the only transitions. California psychologists **Carolyn and Phillip Cowan** (1992, 2000) have identified some changes that new parents might expect:

■ ***"I No Longer Think about Myself the Same Way":*** Once children come along, people think about themselves differently. Often, they feel that they are now full-fledged adults, charged with one of the most important of life's responsibilities. Matters that once seemed abstract and unimportant—life insurance, school systems, child care—suddenly become very personal.

■ ***"My Partner and I Are Really Having to Adjust":*** The new family member forces Mom and Dad to consider how they will divide their tasks. Who is the

income earner? Who stays home? Deciding who does what about child care is a big issue, and there can be many resentments. The fatigue and additional work occasioned by the newcomer will also force changes in the quality of the couple's relationship.

■ **"My Parents and I Are Having to Adjust Our Relationship":** Becoming a new parent usually alters your relationship with your own parents. Perhaps you will now respect them more for what they went through and feel closer to them. Yet you might also resent them if they try to express their views about parenting, especially if these views are different from yours.

■ **"My Employer and My Friends and I Are Having to Adjust":** Other relationships change as well. New parental responsibilities will probably affect your role at work, at least to the extent that you or your partner might have to take some parental leave and later might experience conflict between sick-child demands and work demands. And you probably won't be able to be as flexible about seeing your friends as in the past.

Not surprisingly, the Cowans point out, when couples report high outside-the-family life stress during pregnancy, they are "more likely to be unhappy in their marriages and stressed in their parenting roles during the early years of parenthood" (Cowan and Cowan 2003: 209).

Transition to Motherhood

For some women, motherhood is their ultimate destiny, a condition that they choose deliberately and joyfully and that they find a profoundly happy time

(Demo and Acock 1996). For others, it is a condition that just happens to them and to which they willingly adapt, seeing it as the confirmation of their identity as adults. A third group, however, feels ambivalence, and a fourth finds motherhood the ultimate frustration, a condition involving menial tasks—laundry, cooking, housekeeping—that are not valued by society (Koch 1987). Nearly all women, as you might expect, find motherhood a truly life-changing event (Lerner 1997).

Transition to Fatherhood

Whereas traditionally the mother's role was expressive, giving emotional support to spouse and children, the father's role was instrumental—as the income provider and family protector. Even today, some fathers view themselves principally in economic terms—so-called *breadwinner fathers*—and others, so-called *autonomous fathers*, distance themselves from family commitments (Gerson 1997). But a third category, *involved fathers*, are deeply involved with their children—being present at birth, providing or participating in child care, helping with household tasks, and the like (Pleck 1990).

Even so, many of today's fathers are confused, uncertain about what is expected of them as parents, in large part because (unlike women, who learned parenting skills by modeling their mothers) their own fathers did not provide sufficient models (Daly 1993). Still, the research shows that becoming a father represents a "moral transformation" in that it shifts men's priorities and sense of responsibility, so the responsibility for children found its provide sufficient models (Daly 1993). Indeed, unlike TV fathers, who appear to be more supportive and accepting, students are apt to rate their own real-life fathers as being too consumed with work demands to be very good at parenting (Kelly 2007). Still, the research shows that becoming a father represents a "moral transformation" in that it shifts men's priorities and sense of responsibility toward a focus on working to provide for their children (Townsend 2003). And fathers have been found to be important in children's language development, independent of mothers' behavior (Pancsofar and Vernon-Feagans 2006; Shannon et al. 2006).

11.3 Parenting Approaches

MAJOR QUESTION What kind of parent would I probably be, and how might I be a better parent?

PREVIEW We describe three parenting approaches: authoritarian, permissive, and authoritative. We then consider five parenting styles: martyr, pal, police officer, teacher-counselor, and athletic coach. Finally, we look at ways to be an effective parent: positive reinforcement, instilling values and a sense of responsibility, practicing good communication, and avoiding physical punishment.

Most new parents tend to copy the child-rearing methods of their own parents—if they liked their parents. If they did not like their parents, they tend to practice the opposite methods (Simons et al. 1993). In any event, your techniques as a parent will probably be influenced by how you were raised.

Three Parenting Approaches

Psychologist **Diana Baumrind** (1968, 1989) has identified three general approaches to child rearing: *authoritarian, permissive,* and *authoritative.*

Authoritarian Child Rearing: "Do What's Expected Because I Said So!"

In *authoritarian child rearing*, parents are repressive, controlling, and often unreasonably strict. Working-class parents tend to be more authoritarian than are middle-class parents. Such parents tend to be cold and unsupportive, to discourage verbal give-and-take, and to use physical force to control behavior. Children in such families tend to be more moody, less cheerful, more passively hostile, and more vulnerable to stress.

Example of authoritarian parenting: "The reason you can't stay out late is because I said so!" Authoritarian mothers, incidentally, are five times more likely to raise overweight first-graders than mothers who treated their children with flexibility and respect while also setting clear rules (Rhee et al. 2006).

Permissive Child Rearing: "Do What's Expected Because You Want to Do It"

In *permissive child rearing*, parents are warm and reasonable. Found more in middle-class than in working-class families, the permissive approach is characterized by an absence of rules and regulations, and parents tend not to be demanding about performing chores. But permissive parents might also practice manipulation, persuading children to follow internal codes of behavior because they supposedly "willingly" elect to follow such constraints.

Example of permissive parenting: "The reason you can't stay out late is because you know what your duty is."

Authoritative Child Rearing: "You Know What's Expected; It's Up to You"

In *authoritative child rearing*, parents are, on the one hand, strict and controlling yet, on the other hand, also warm and supportive. Such parents tend to use positive reinforcement rather than punishment. They show awareness of the child's feelings and encourage open communication, independence, and self-reliance. Instead of being bound by many rules and restrictions, the child is expected to be disciplined, but everything is up for discussion according to specific situations. Such children show self-reliance, curiosity, and creativity in dealing with new situations.

Example of authoritative parenting: "You remember we have a 1:00 o'clock curfew, but if your homework is done for tomorrow, it's up to you how late you want to stay out up until 1:00."

Baumrind's categories don't cover all kinds of parenting. For example, there are neglectful parents who don't attend to their children much at all.

Five Parenting Styles

Somewhat similar to Baumrind's approaches are five parenting styles proposed by **E. E. LeMasters** and **John DeFrain** (1989): *martyr, pal, police officer, teacher-counselor,* and *athletic coach.*

Martyr: "There's Nothing I Wouldn't Do for My Kids"

In the *martyr parenting style*, parents make great sacrifices for their children and exercise little or no authority over them. Such parents spoil their children with material things, let the children make most decisions, and allow them to dictate what they want, when they want it. These children often never learn to be self-sufficient.

Pal: "My Kids & I Are Buddies Because I Want Them to Like Me"

In the *pal parenting style* —also known as *laissez-faire parenting* —parents let children set their own goals, rules, and limits, Although parents might adopt this style because they want their children to like them, they risk losing their authority when conflicts arise.

Police Officer: "If My Kids Don't Obey Me, They Get Punished"

The opposite of the pal parenting style, **the *police officer parenting style* is an authoritarian and repressive style in which parents insist that their children follow rules and punish them when they don't.** The risk of this style is that in adolescence, children might revolt, insisting on more independence and avoiding the family in favor of friends from less authoritarian families.

Teacher-Counselor: "I Want to Positively Shape Every Part of My Children's Lives"

In the *teacher-counselor parenting style*, parents are intensely focused on guiding their children's behavior, always helping them with homework, being available to answer every question, and in general putting the needs of the child before those of the parents. Although this approach can have some positive results, it can make children feel as if they are the be-all and end-all of everyone else's life.

Athletic Coach: "I Want to Encourage My Children to Do Well within a Framework of Family Rules"

In the *athletic coach parenting style*, parents set rules ("team rules") for the house, helped by input from the family, teach the children the rules, and apply appropriate penalties for infractions. Children are encouraged to work at developing their individual talents but also to put the needs of the family ahead of their own when necessary. LeMasters and DeFrain believe that the athletic coach style, which resembles the Baumrind authoritative approach, is the most effective form of parenting.

How to Be an Effective Parent

If you were to try to get children of, say, between ages 6 and 10 to do something that they might not be inclined to do (clean up their rooms, do their homework, turn off the TV and go to bed, or whatever), what do you think you would do? Request politely? Explain reasonably? Beg pleadingly? Threaten darkly? Command forcefully? Yell loudly? Promise to spank the living daylights out of them *if they don't start moving their feet RIGHT NOW?*

Any of these might be appropriate in certain circumstances (though we'll discuss spanking in a minute), but probably none will work consistently. What follows are some principles of child rearing drawn from diverse sources that have been found to be effective. We discuss (1) positive reinforcement (predictability, praise, and love); (2) instilling values and a sense of responsibility; (3) practicing good communication; and (4) avoiding physical punishment.

1. Positive Reinforcement: Predictability, Praise, & Love

The point of parenting, of course, is (or should be) to give children the sense of self-reliance they will need to be successful outside the family. The key to doing this is to provide a reliable environment with predictable routines so that children feel that they have a secure place from which to venture out into

DADDY'S GIRL. How do you feel about bringing children to work? Would you try to do this if you became a parent, or have you already done this? What kind of hindrances would you have to overcome? ▶

the world and to which they may return. In other words, what children need is a secure relationship with adults who adore them (Knudsen et al. 2006). And the kind of mother-baby interaction they have suggest ultimately how secure they themselves will be in their relationships with future lovers (Simpson et al. 2007).

Giving praise and love helps encourage not only positive social behavior but also a positive self-image and a feeling of comfort about engaging in love relationships as an adult.

2. Instilling Values & a Sense of Responsibility

As a parent, you will no doubt want your children to have personal integrity, show respect for others, and be responsible about keeping commitments. This can be done by giving children sufficient freedom to enable them to feel increased independence while being firm about adherence to certain standards.

3. Practicing Good Communication

As we discussed in Chapter 6, "Communication," partners need to communicate well not only with each other but also with other family members. Certainly, many of the practices we discussed there about resolving conflict and

PANEL 11.6 Rules for Resolving Conflict and Communicating Well

■ **Attack problems and avoid negativity:** Attack problems, not each other. Don't belittle, accuse, or threaten others, call names, or give ultimatums, which will only make others defensive and angry.

■ **Focus on specific issues, use "I feel" language, and avoid mixed messages:** Concentrate on the specific problem you are trying to resolve, use "I feel" language, and avoid sending mixed messages (as in agreeing verbally but not agreeing nonverbally).

■ **Be sensitive about timing:** An immediate problem need not require immediate discussion. Sometimes, a conflict can go badly because one person is tired, angry, or tense from overwork.

■ **Say what you mean, don't manipulate, and ask for what you want:** State what you really feel, and don't beat around the bush. Don't lie, sugarcoat, apologize, be seductive, or otherwise try to manipulate. Ask for what you want, stating your wishes as clearly as you can.

■ **Let others know you're really listening and work toward resolution:** Don't interrupt, don't pretend to listen while actually preparing your counterargument, and don't disrespect the other(s) by carrying on other activities such as watching TV. That is, show that *you really are listening.* Keep talking until any conflict is resolved or the problem is solved. Work toward a specific, realistic solution that will satisfy everyone.

communicating well apply here as well. (*See* ■ *Panel 11.6.*) Avoid nagging, lecturing, questioning, demanding, and threatening.

One way of doing this is to have weekly family get-togethers to hear complaints, make plans, and solve problems, with decisions being reached by common consensus rather than parental dictates (Nelsen 1987).

4. Avoiding Physical Punishment

According to a 2000 study of 991 parents from different socioeconomic groups, 90% of parents use verbal and psychological aggression to control children ages 2 to 17 (Straus and Field 2003).

In addition, many parents seem to favor *corporal punishment*, **the use of physical force to cause a child to experience pain but not injury, with the intent of correcting or controlling the child's behavior.** Examples of physical punishment range from pinching to slapping to shaking to hitting with a belt or paddle. Another variant, *spanking*, **consists of hitting a child, usually on the buttocks, with an open hand without causing physical injury.** One study found that such forms of punishment were inflicted by 94% of parents of children ages 3 and 4, declining to 13% of parents of 17-year-olds (Straus and Stewart 1999).

Is spanking ever appropriate? Researchers disagree. One expert on domestic violence, sociologist Murray Straus, finds all kinds of adverse effects linked to spanking: that children who were spanked (even infrequently) are later more apt to lie, cheat, or be mean to others; to be disobedient in school; to experience depression, drug abuse, or suicide in adolescence; and to be linked to dating violence and child-to-parent violence (Straus 1994b, 1996; Straus and Kantor 1994; Straus and Yodanis 1996; Straus et al. 1997; Straus and Mouradian 1998; Straus 2001). Interestingly, Straus's research finds that, par-

LEARNING RESPONSIBILITY. Being a coach or counselor during adolescence can help instill positive values and a sense of responsibility. Did you do anything of this nature during your high school years? ▶

adoxically, professionals advising parents, including professionals who are opposed to spanking, generally fail to tell parents not to spank, thinking that they are avoiding a "negative approach" (Straus 2001). Other social scientists think that spanking may be acceptable under certain conditions and within certain cultures (Baumrind 1996).

11.4 The Aging Family: When Parents & Children Get Older

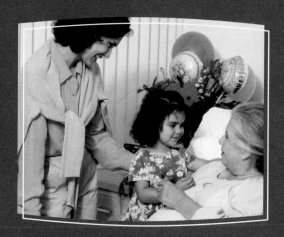

MAJOR QUESTION What should I be prepared for when I and my parents get older?

PREVIEW We describe what happens when children become adults and have to be concerned about the welfare of their own parents, a kind of role reversal, and different ways of interrelating. We also discuss grandparenthood and different types of grandparenting and ways of interacting with grandchildren.

Barry Orenstein, an independent market researcher in Lexington, Massachusetts, has had to drop everything and rush home a dozen times in recent years. He arranges his business calendar with alternate plans in mind and occasionally postpones work until late in the day when he's free to catch up. "You're always thinking, 'What if?'" he says. "You have to remain as flexible as you can" (Orenstein, quoted in Jackson 2003).

It is he a conscientious father who is concerned about his children? No, Orenstein, age 61, is being a responsible son, sharing the care of his mother, Phyllis, age 88, with his brother, Steve. "More men are stepping in to care for elderly mothers, fathers, and other relatives and are conducting a difficult balancing act between work and home life," says one report. "Men are shopping, cleaning, and doling out medicines while reworking schedules to accommodate the needs of older relatives" (Jackson 2003).

It's not just men who do this, of course. Women have long assumed, or been cast in, the role of main caregivers to the elderly. Regardless of gender, there is a significant cost for working adults taking care of their parents. One study found that two-thirds of men and women who provide such care said that their careers had suffered as a result (MetLife Mature Market Institute 2003).

Parental Transitions

Research on families in the middle and later years blossomed in the 1990s (Allen et al. 2000). For instance, it is evident that as parents enter middle age, they might find themselves members of the *sandwich generation*—**that is,**

sandwiched between taking care of their children and taking care of their own aging parents (Harris and Bichler 1997). Research shows that 37% of Americans ages 53 to 61 have at least one child and at least one living parent, and 27% have a grandchild as well (Kolata 1993).

Role Reversal: Taking Care of Mom & Dad

During the difficult economic times of the early 2000s, many middle-aged people, after seeing their children leave home and accelerating their own savings for retirement, found an unexpected cost that they never planned for: supporting their own parents. For instance, Rae Mauro, age 66, a research analyst from Valencia, California, decided not to retire because, without a salary, she could not afford a home help aide for her 87-year-old mother, who suffers from Alzheimer's disease (Higgins 2003: D1).

■ **Helping One's Parents While Helping Oneself:** "Instead of getting financial help from their parents," says one account, "children are having to give them regular handouts. Some are shelling out tens of thousands of dollars to cover basic costs, from medical and credit-card bills to vacation and retirement-home expenses" (Higgins 2003: D1). Accordingly, financial planners are suggesting ways to help older children supporting their even older parents: They can buy their parents' homes or rental property and rent it back to them, buy valuables from the parents that they might inherit some day (it keeps family mementos in the family), and take tax deductions for supporting parents or paying heavy medical expenses for them. If the younger generation has enough foresight, they should also urge their parents to buy insurance to pay for possible nursing home care.

■ **Being Realistic about Social Security:** Another tactic is to urge retirees not to take Social Security starting at age 62, as so many people do. *(See ■ Panel 11.7.)* "In recent years," says one analysis, "almost 70% of retirees took Social Security before age 65, thus accepting a permanent reduction in their monthly benefits. But this doesn't make any sense at all, especially with folks living longer and longer" (Clements 2003). These days, retirement might last 20 to 25 years, but taking Social Security at age 62 instead of 65 means that people receive 20% less in benefits—a sizable amount if you think you will live to be at least age 84. (People who are age 65 today on average will live until their early eighties. Social Security payments average about $1,000 a month, with a slight cost-of-living adjustment every year.)

Relationships of Adult Children to Their Parents

As the concerns just discussed would suggest, money matters can lead to a lot of stresses. Even when finances are not a factor, however, the relationship between adult children and their aging parents becomes ambivalent (Luescher and Pillemer 1998). Both children and parents tend to want to let the elders live independently, but as the older generation becomes more frail or disabled, they might be reluctant to ask for help. In fact, they might become more controlling, making it difficult for their children to know when to intervene (Cicerelli 1990; Hansson et al. 1990).

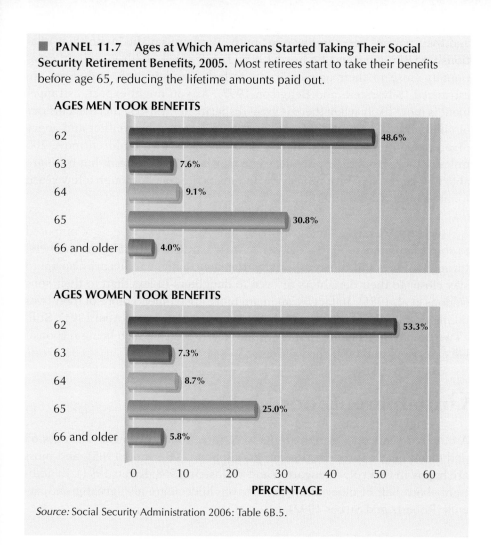

■ **PANEL 11.7   Ages at Which Americans Started Taking Their Social Security Retirement Benefits, 2005.** Most retirees start to take their benefits before age 65, reducing the lifetime amounts paid out.

AGES MEN TOOK BENEFITS

62 — 48.6%
63 — 7.6%
64 — 9.1%
65 — 30.8%
66 and older — 4.0%

AGES WOMEN TOOK BENEFITS

62 — 53.3%
63 — 7.3%
64 — 8.7%
65 — 25.0%
66 and older — 5.8%

0   10   20   30   40   50   60
PERCENTAGE

Source: Social Security Administration 2006: Table 6B.5.

Let's consider some other characteristics of the relationship between adult children and their parents:

■ **Most Elderly People Are Not Supported by the Government:** Most elderly needy people are supported not by the government but by family and friends. Indeed, 70% of those who are not in health-care institutions rely exclusively on this kind of personal support (Schenck-Yglesias 1995). Although the notion has grown that because most elderly people live alone, they must therefore be neglected, in actuality 50 to 60% have at least one child living within 10 minutes of their home (Lin and Rogerson 1995).

■ **Both Generations Generally Assume That Children Will Assist Parents if Needed:** In general, adult children continue to get substantial support from their parents, such as financial help, child care, or advice, especially when the adult children are in crisis, such as going through divorce. In return, both older parents and their adult children expect that the children will help the older generation if the need arises (Hogan and Farkas 1995).

■ **Emotional Closeness of Adult Children to Their Parents Varies:** According to one study of 2,095 Americans over age 80, as many as 85% saw or spoke to their children two to seven times a week (Kolata 1993). Most adult children and their parents seem to like one another and are satisfied with their relationship (Blieszner and Bedford 1995). But if some children remain emotionally close to their aging parents, others are detached, and some are estranged (Silverstein and Bengtson 1997). As you might expect, estrangement is more likely when there is great disparity in lifestyles, there is a history of child abuse by the parents, or the family was torn by conflict and angry divorce (Kaufman and Uhlenberg 1998). When grown children move 200 miles or more from their parents, some may become estranged, but most are able to take the separation in stride and to stay in touch, though a few yearn to move back (Climo 1992).

■ **Daughters Are Generally Closer Than Sons Are to Their Parents:** Compared to sons, daughters tend to be closer to their parents, especially the mothers, throughout life, and this is especially true later in life. Parents are also apt to stay closer to their daughters or even to daughters-in-law than to their sons (Aldous et al. 1985). In fact, women are more apt to spend more of their lives taking care of an elderly person than of their own children (Abel 1991). Still, as we saw in the opening to this section, many men are also being responsible caregivers to their elderly parents.

Grandparenthood

A hundred years ago, grandparents were rare. Today, of Americans ages 65 and older, nearly three-fourths are grandparents (Barranti 1985), and most are happy in that role (Neugarten and Weinstein 1968; Kivett 1991). In addition, about half of older adults who have children are also great-grandparents (Roberts and Stroes 1992).

Why Grandparents Like Being Grandparents— & the Benefits They Offer

If you talk to older adults whose friends of the same age all seem to be crowing about their grandchildren (or about the fact that they have become grandparents), you might wonder why having grandchildren seems to be so important. According to one researcher (Barranti 1985), the presence of a grandchild reassures the grandparent that something of him or her will continue after death—a kind of immortality. Grandparents also benefit by keeping up with cultural and social events through their grandchildren and by being assisted in the performance of chores, such as shopping or running errands.

In addition, many grandparents gain self-esteem from playing what others (Kornhaber and Woodward 1981) list as the five roles of historian, mentor, role model, wizard, and nurturer/great parent:

■ **Historian:** As the family historian, a grandparent can provide a cultural and family sense of history and thus a sense of continuity and belonging.

■ **Mentor:** The mentor provides guidance in ways of living, as in helping mothers care for their infants during the first weeks and months of life.

■ **Role Model:** The grandparent as role model holds up an ideal of appropriate behavior for both children and grandchildren.

- **Wizard:** The wizard tells fascinating stories of times past and excites the child's imagination.

- **Nurturer/Great Parent:** As a nurturer/great parent, the grandparent provides the child with an expanded family support system and can act as a surrogate parent in times of need.

These roles also, of course, benefit the grandchildren. In addition, grandparents can provide practical assistance, such as child care or financial help—including, among those who can afford it, help with college tuition or purchase of a house (King and Elder 1995). Some research shows that when grandchildren enter college, the mentoring role of grandparents and the grandparent-grandchild relationship are enhanced (Crosnoe and Elder 2002).

How Grandparents Interact with Their Grandchildren: Neugarten & Weinstein's Five Types

Researchers **Bernice Neugarten** and **Karol Weinstein** (1964, 1968) studied 70 pairs of middle-class grandparents. They classified their interactions with their grandchildren into five types of behavior, from distant and formal (usually older grandparents) to highly interactive and informal (usually younger):

- **The Distant Figure—"I don't see my grandchildren much":** The *distant figure* kind of grandparent is rarely in contact with the grandchild, generally limiting interaction to holidays and special occasions. Although such grandparents might behave kindly toward the grandchildren, their contact is brief and infrequent, perhaps because of geographical distance, perhaps simply because of personal choice.

- **The Formal Grandparent—"I'm a grandparent, not a parent":** *Formal* grandparents follow what they perceive to be a role of grandparenting that is clearly different from a parent's role. For example, they leave child-care tasks in the hands of the parents, and they don't dispense parental advice, although they express a lot of interest in the child and will play with the child and even do some babysitting.

- **The Reservoir of Family Wisdom—"I know what's good for these kids":** The *reservoir of family wisdom*, a rather rare kind of grandparent, acts as a source of special skills or resources, such as the family matriarch who supposedly knows all about child raising. Both parents and grandchildren defer to the wisdom and judgment of this authority figure.

- **The Fun Seeker—"These little tykes are my pals":** *Fun-seeker* grandparents interact informally and playfully with their grandchildren. In fact, they play with their grandchildren almost as if they were playmates, playing dollhouse or cops and robbers as though they were friends the same age.

- **The Surrogate Parent—"I'm having to raise my kid's kids":** The *surrogate parent* type is a grandparent who has assumed the child-care responsibilities for the grandchild. As we mentioned, many grandparents have assumed sole responsibility for raising their children's children. According to the 2000 U.S. Census, 2.3 million grandparents were raising their own grandchildren (Grandsplace 2004). About 1.4 million were grandmothers, and 889,000 were grandfathers.

In many cases, having grandchildren reassures an older person that something of her or him will continue after death. ▶

How Grandparents Interact with Their Grandchildren: Cherlin & Furstenberg's Three Styles

A more recent analysis of grandparenting, based on interviews with 510 grandparents, was done by **Andrew Cherlin** and **Frank Furstenberg** (1986). They identified three styles of grandparenting, which correspond roughly to Neugarten and Weinstein's types.

■ Remote—"I see my grandchildren only every 2 to 3 months or so": Like distant grandparents, *remote grandparents,* who constituted 30% of those surveyed, did not interact often with their grandchildren, less often than once every 2 or 3 months. Usually, this was because they lived far away. Thus, their relationship was mainly symbolic or ritualistic, as in seeing the children mostly on holidays.

■ Companionate—"I see my grandchildren about once a week or more": *Companionate grandparents,* who made up about 55% of the sample, saw their grandchildren one or more times a week but less often than every day. They tended to be informal and easygoing in their interactions with their grandchildren but exercised little formal authority over the children. Companionate grandparents were often involved in their own work and leisure lives.

■ **Involved—"I see my grandchildren every day":** *Involved grandparents,* about 15% of those surveyed, saw their grandchildren every day and were active participants in raising them, imposing sometimes demanding expectations and having substantial authority. Some lived with their grandchildren.

What's important about Cherlin and Furstenberg's analysis is that it is more flexible than Neugarten and Weinstein's. That is, a grandparent's style of inter-action might change over time as a child grows older. A grandparent might also interact differently with one grandchild than with another, being distant (remote) with one and close (companionate) with another. Such differences come about not only because of the number and the ages of grandchildren, sex, birth order, and personality differences but also because of the age and the economic need of the grandparents, how close they are geographically to the grandchildren, and their relationships with their own adult children.

In general, it seems clear that the role of grandparent is affected by the relationship with the adult child. If grandparents don't get along with their grown children, they are apt to have less contact with their grandchildren (Whitbeck et al. 1993). In addition, research shows that children seem to feel closer to their maternal grandparents, especially to their maternal grand-mothers (Matthews and Sprey 1985). This might because the rise in divorce rates has led to more households in which the mother, rather than the father, has custody of the children, and the grandchild might lose touch with his or her father's parents.

Race, Ethnicity, & Grandparenting

Although the majority of adults become grandparents in their forties and fifties, blacks differ from whites in that they are apt to become grandparents—and even great-grandparents—at younger ages (Perry 1999). Grandmothers in low-income African American families are able to offer important assistance to unmarried daughters with children and can have a stabilizing effect on families (Apfel and Seitz 1991; Hunter 1997). In addition, in black families, being a grandfather offers a more important role for these men than it does for grandfathers in white families (Kivitt 1991).

Asian Americans, Hispanics, and Native Americans, as well as African Americans, are also more apt to be involved in the lives of their grandchil-dren compared with other groups, perhaps because of greater extended kin-ship networks (National Indian Council on Aging 1981; Cavanaugh 1993).

The Childless or Child-Free Older Adult

In Chapter 10, "Reproduction," we discussed the option of being child-free or childless and pointed out its benefits. The possible downside, of course, is that older adults without children might have less chance of having a family support system. As a result, such older adults are apt to have fewer social con-tacts and have a greater chance of being institutionalized (Bachrach 1980; Cantor and Little 1985).

This means that older adults who are not married or in a couple relation-ship at some point need to deliberately work on setting up a support network. Some make connections to blood relatives, such as nephews, nieces, and sib-lings. Others link up with friends or younger adults to create bonds that can become important means of support in later life (Chappell 1991).

Self-Assessment: Assessing Your Readiness to Become a Parent

Many factors have to be taken into account when you are considering parenthood. The following are some questions you should ask yourself and some issues you should consider when making this decision. Some issues are relevant to both men and women; others apply only to women. There are no "right" answers—you must decide for yourself what your answers reveal about your aptitude for parenthood. Circle "Yes" or "No," whichever applies.

Physical Health

1. Are you in reasonably good health? **Yes   No**

2. Do you have any behaviors or conditions that could be of special concern? **Yes   No**

   _____ Obesity   _____ Anemia

   _____ Smoking   _____ Diabetes

   _____ Hypertension   _____ Epilepsy

   _____ Alcohol and drug use

   _____ Sexually transmitted diseases

   _____ Previous problems with pregnancy or delivery

   _____ Prenatal exposure to diethylstilbestrol (DES)

   _____ Asthma

3. Are you under 20 or over 35 years of age? **Yes   No**

4. Do you or your partner have a family history of a genetic problem that a baby might inherit? **Yes   No**

   _____ Hemophilia

   _____ Phenylketonuria (PKU)

   _____ Sickle-cell disease

   _____ Cystic fibrosis

   _____ Down syndrome

   _____ Thalassemia

   _____ Tay-Sachs disease

   _____ Other _____

Financial Circumstances

1. Will your health insurance cover the costs of pregnancy, prenatal tests, delivery, and medical attention for the mother and baby before and after the birth? **Yes   No**

2. Can you afford supplies for the baby: diapers, bedding, crib, stroller, car seat, clothing, food, and medical supplies? **Yes   No**

3. Will one parent leave his or her job to care for the baby? **Yes   No**

4. If so, can the decrease in family income be worked into the family budget? **Yes   No**

5. If both parents will continue to work, has affordable child care been set up? **Yes   No**

6. The annual cost of raising a child is about $9,000; can you save and/or provide the necessary money? **Yes   No**

Education, Career, & Child-Care Plans

1. Have you completed as much of your education as you want? **Yes   No**

2. Have you sufficiently established yourself in a career, if that is important to you? **Yes   No**

3. Have you investigated parental leave and company-sponsored child care? **Yes   No**

4. Do both parents agree on child-care arrangements? **Yes   No**

Lifestyle & Social Support

1. Would you be willing to give up the freedom to do what you want to do when you want to do it? **Yes   No**

2. Would you be willing to restrict your social life, to lose leisure time and privacy? **Yes   No**

3. Would you and your partner be prepared to spend more time at home? Would you have enough time to spend with a child? **Yes   No**

4. Are you prepared to be a single parent if your partner leaves or dies? **Yes   No**

5. Do you have a network of family and friends who will help you with the baby? Are there community resources you can call on for additional assistance? **Yes   No**

Readiness

1. Are you prepared to have a helpless being completely dependent on you 24 hours a day? **Yes   No**

2. Do you like children? Have you enough experiences with babies, toddlers, and teenagers? **Yes   No**

3. Do you think time spent with children is time well spent? **Yes No**

4. Do you communicate easily with others? **Yes No**

5. Do you have enough love to give a child? Can you express affection easily? Yes No

6. Do you feel good enough about yourself to respect and nurture others? **Yes No**

7. Do you have safe ways of handling anger, frustration, and impatience? **Yes No**

8. Would you be willing to devote a great part of your life, at least 18 years, to being responsible for a child? **Yes No**

Relationship with Partner

1. Does your partner want to have a child? Is he or she willing to ask these same questions of himself or herself? **Yes No**

2. Have you adequately discussed your reasons for wanting a child? **Yes No**

3. Does either of you have philosophical objections to adding to the world's population? **Yes No**

4. Have you and your partner discussed each other's feelings about religion, work, family, and child raising? Are your feelings compatible and conducive to good parenting? **Yes No**

5. Would both you and your partner contribute in raising the child? **Yes No**

6. Is your relationship stable? Could you provide a child with a really good home environment? **Yes No**

7. After having a child, would your partner and you be able to separate if you should have unsolvable problems? Or would you feel obligated to remain together for the sake of the child? **Yes No**

Source: Paul M. Insel and Walton T. Roth. 2004. *Wellness worksheets: 2004 update,* #41. Assessing your readiness to become a parent. San Francisco: McGraw-Hill, pp. 97–98. © 2004 The McGraw-Hill Companies, Inc.

Key Terms Used in This Chapter

athletic coach parenting style, p. 397

authoritarian child rearing, p. 395

authoritative child rearing, p. 396

bonding, p. 390

continuous coverage system, p. 391

corporal punishment, p. 399

dysfunctional family, p. 385

infant mortality rate, p. 372

latchkey child, p. 383

martyr parenting style, p. 396

morning sickness, p. 390

pal parenting (laissez-faire parenting) style, p. 396

permissive child rearing, p. 396

police officer (or drill sergeant) parenting style, p. 397

postpartum blues, p. 391

postpartum depression, p. 391

postpartum period, p. 390

premature birth, p. 373

sandwich generation, p. 401

spanking, p. 399

teacher-counselor parenting style, p. 397

Summary

11.1 Parenthood: The Varieties of Experience

■ If your family raised you with love and respect, you will probably bring this positive picture of parenthood to your own parenting. Unfortunately, many children are not so fortunate. Many live in poverty, which can lead to high infant mortality rates, low birth rates, unstable home environments, higher divorce rates, poor nutrition, and substandard medical and dental care.

■ There are a variety of types of parents. Teen parents often face a number of problems, with teenage mothers often ending up as single parents and poorer and less educated than other mothers; their children are more apt to fail in school, be involved in substance abuse, and have problems with the law. Single parents include the unmarried and the divorced as well as widows and widowers, grandparents and other guardians, and gay families. Divorced women with children often don't do as well as their ex-husbands financially and might suffer a marked decline in living standards; divorced fathers tend to become less and less involved in their children's lives. Many women delay childbearing, significantly increasing the number of older parents. Among American households with working parents and children, those headed by single fathers are increasing fastest. Minority parents may differ depending on whether or not they are recent immigrants, who might insist more on their children's discipline and obedience. Nontraditional parents, such as single fathers, grandparents and other relatives, and gays and lesbians face their own particular types of problems.

- Changes in the U.S. economy often require that both parents work outside the home, which can lead to conflicts over staying home with one's children or pursuing a career outside the family, dealing with society's view and support of parental and maternal leave, dependency on child-care services, and career demands and expectations.

- Families can be viewed along a continuum of dysfunctional to functional. A dysfunctional family is one in which the parents demonstrate negative or destructive behavior toward each other or toward their children. Consequences of this abuse include a low sense of self-esteem and feeling unworthy, unvalued, and unloved. The children of abusive or neglectful parents might become abusive or neglectful with their own children, perpetuating a cycle.

- Although parents are a primary influence on the development and socialization of children, there are other significant influences: biology and heredity, the social environment, siblings and relatives, teachers and friends, and the mass media.

11.2 Becoming a Parent

- Pregnancy and childbirth involves both physical and psychological adjustments. Women experience signs of pregnancy such as enlarged and tender breasts and morning sickness, nausea and vomiting that occur early in the morning or at other times of the day. Expectant mothers may also experience mood swings from anxiety to apprehension to excitement and anticipation of the impending arrival. Men's experience of pregnancy and childbirth is primarily on the emotional level.

- After the baby is born, parents often undergo postpartum adjustment, a 3-month period of critical family and emotional adjustments, including bonding of mother and child, postpartum blues, and postpartum depression. Postpartum blues come about as a result of the whole childbirth process, which may can involve hours of fatiguing and stressful labor, hormonal changes after delivery, and the incredible emotional high of seeing the baby. Approximately 25 to 50% of women experience sadness and anxiety. A woman might cry easily, be alternately ecstatic and lethargic, and feel helpless and out of control. Post-

partum depression involves severe symptoms of a major depression that warrant the assistance of a health-care professional. Consequences of postpartum depression for those who have limited or no emotional support or who have a history of depression can be serious.

- It has been suggested that the parenting or child rearing goes through five stages: childbearing family (lasting about 2½ years), family with preschoolers (about 3½ years), family with schoolchildren (about 7 years), family with adolescents (about 7 years), and family as launching center (about 8 years).

- The transition to parenthood can be more difficult than the transition required for other adult roles such as getting married or starting a new job. Parenting is an immediate 24/7 job in which parents must become fully responsible for a fragile infant immediately and in which a couple's own relationship changes. Some changes that new parents might expect include not thinking about themselves the same way and having to make adjustments with each other, their parents, and their employers and friends.

- Transition to motherhood and fatherhood can be helped or hindered by one's family upbringing and socialization. For women, the experience can be a time of complete happiness, something that happens that can be accepted and helps to confirm their identity as an adult, an event about which they are ambivalent, or a time of extreme frustration. Fathers frequently view themselves primarily as breadwinners performing instrumental roles. Some try to adjust to the home and career expectations by becoming autonomous fathers who distance themselves from family commitments. Other fathers are viewed as involved fathers who are deeply involved in their children's lives. Some new fathers face the experience uncertain about what is expected of them as parents. Unlike women, who learned their parenting skills by modeling their mothers, many new fathers had fathers who did not provide a sufficient role model.

11.3 Parenting Approaches

- New parents' parenting style is heavily influenced by the type of parenting they received themselves.

- Baumrind has identified three general approaches to child rearing. In authoritarian child rearing, parents are demanding, controlling, and punitive and require absolute obedience. In permissive child rearing, parents are warm, responsive, and nondemanding and rely on reasoning and explanations. In authoritative child rearing, parents are, on the one hand, demanding and controlling yet, on the other hand, also responsive and supportive.

- LeMasters and DeFrain identified five parenting approaches. In the martyr parenting style, parents sacrifice everything for their children and let the children do whatever they want. In the pal parenting style, parents let children set their own goals, rules, and limits. The police officer parenting style is an authoritarian and punitive style in which parents insist that their children follow rules and punish them when they don't. In the teachercounselor parenting style, parents are intensely focused on guiding their children's behavior. In the athletic coach parenting style, parents set rules ("team rules") for the house, helped by input from the family, teach the children the rules, and apply appropriate penalties for infractions.

- Some child-rearing principles that have been found to help in effective parenting include (1) positive reinforcement (predictability, praise, and love); (2) instilling values and a sense of responsibility; (3) practicing good communication; and (4) avoiding physical punishment.

11.4 The Aging Family: When Parents & Children Get Older

- As parents enter middle age, they might find themselves members of the sandwich generation, taking care of both their children and their own aging parents. Taking care of elderly parents can involve helping them sort out their finances.

- Since most elderly needy parents are not supported by the government, they are largely supported by family and friends. In general, both generations generally assume that children will assist their parents if needed. However, the emotional closeness of adult children to their children varies a lot depending on physical distance, lifestyle, and temperament. Daughters are generally closer than sons to their parents.

- Most grandparents like being grandparents. Many gain self-esteem from playing such roles as historian, mentor, role model, wizard (storyteller), and nurturer/great parent.

- Five ways in which grandparents interact with their grandchildren have been described as the distant figure, the formal grandparent, the reservoir of family wisdom, the fun seeker, and the surrogate parent. Three styles of grandparenting are remote (seeing grandchildren only every 2 to 3 months or so), companionate (seeing them about once a week or more), and involved (seeing them every day). In general, the role of the grandparent is affected by the relationship with the adult child.

- Most people become grandparents in their forties and fifties, but blacks differ from whites in that they are apt to become grandparents at younger ages. In low-income African American families, grandparents can be a stabilizing influence. African Americans, Asian Americans, Hispanics, and Native Americans are more apt to be involved in the lives of their grandchildren compared with other groups, perhaps because of extended kinship networks. Older adults without children have less chance of having a family support system.

Take It to the Net

Among the Internet resources on parenting and families are the following:

- **Child Care Aware.** A nonprofit initiative committed to helping parents find the best information on locating high-quality child care and child-care resources in their community.
www.childcareaware.org
- **Common Sense Media Guide.** A nonpartisan, nonprofit organization whose purpose is to give parents, educators, and children a choice and a voice about the media they consume. By creating a grassroots movement of concerned citizens, the organization hopes to make media producers present programming that serves the interests of our kids.
www.commonsensemedia.org/mediaguide

- **iVillage.** Child-rearing advice and connections to parent discussion groups.
http://parenting.ivillage.com
- **National Child Care Information Center.** Offers links to other child-care resources.
www.nccic.org
- **National Fatherhood Initiative.** Tips on effective parenting for fathers.
www.fatherhood.org
- **Parenthood.** Tips on general parenting.
www.parenthoodweb.com
- **Teenage Parent Demonstration.** Demonstration programs associated with welfare reform to help teenage parents be better parents.
www.aspe.dhhs.gov/hsp/isp/tpd/synthes/lessons.htm

CHAPTER 12

WORK

Economics, Jobs, & Balancing Family Demands

Is Money the Measure of Love?

"Somehow people need to believe *that love is too important an experience to be contaminated with considerations of money," write clinical psychologists Herb Goldberg and Robert Lewis (1979: 20–21).*

"Since money is supposedly ruled by the head and love is ruled by the heart, money views are usually hidden, and individuals get married pretending *money does not exist. But money feelings are all too real, and if conflicting feelings about money are present, as they often are, they will soon become evident. Too often, the course of the relationship goes from (a) denial of the importance of money during courtship, to (b) arguments over money dur-* ing marriage, to (c) an attempt to destroy each other financially during divorce."

It is foolish to pretend that money is irrelevant to love, says sociologist Marcia Millman (1991). "In a market economy, money is not only power but also the ultimate measure of value; for this reason, it insinuates itself into even the most intimate settings" (p. 4). Thus, money is used, often unconsciously, as a symbolic manifestation of and measure of family members' feelings: to curry favor with a partner, to gauge our parents' true love for us, to discriminate among our children, and so on.

Money may be the means by which goods and services are allocated within a society. But it also has many psychological meanings that affect marriage, families, and intimate relationships. Four of the most important psychological motives for acquiring and using money are *security, power, love,* and *freedom* (Goldberg and Lewis 1979: 67–79):

■ *Security:* In the movie *Trading Places,* Eddie Murphy plays a street-

🔮 WHAT'S AHEAD IN THIS CHAPTER

We first discuss the history of work and its effect on family, as well as unequal distribution of income and economic factors affecting families today. We next consider various arrangements of work and family life. Finally, we consider different strategies for dealing with work-life balance.

wise hustler who is made to exchange places with a rich commodity broker played by Dan Aykroyd, who gets tossed onto the mean city streets, where he has to learn firsthand that lack of money means lack of security. Most of today's movies don't ask us to confront how insecure it is to be without money (films such as *Grapes of Wrath* and *Harlan County* have done so). Security, however, seems to be the preeminent reason for wanting money. In an intimate relationship, the need for security can mean that one partner, for instance, might be so averse to spending money that the other feels that he or she has almost no enjoyment.

■ *Power:* Money is a primary source of power in relationships, points out Millman. "Having money allows us to control other people or be free of them, even rid of them, as it allows the other to be free of us" (p. 5). When Jacqueline Kennedy, widow of President John Kennedy, married shipping magnate Aristotle Onassis, she had a formal marriage agreement that gave her considerable power. According to reports (Goldberg and Lewis 1979: 22), she was to receive $25,000 a month for expenses and spending money while married and would receive $10 million for each year of marriage if he should leave her and $18 million if she should leave him. Among two-income couples, partners generally are more equal in decision-making power than are those in one-income marriages (Rosenbluth et al. 1998).

■ *Love:* The lavish wedding in *The Godfather*—is this the truest expression of love by a father for his offspring? Many people think money is symbolic of love. Emotionally inhibited parents, for example, might offer presents or cash in lieu of affection, and the child then learns "Money equals love." Does a husband's not earning big bucks show that he's not loving? If you don't overtip, are you concerned a waitperson won't "like you"? Even ordinary people might feel that the more expensive a gift (the restaurant dinner, the engagement ring), the more it is presumed to be the fullest expression of love.

■ *Freedom:* In the movie *The Talented Mr. Ripley*, the undistinguished Tom Ripley, played by Matt Damon, craves the freedom that wealth provides to play amid the idyllic landscape of sun-drenched Italy, so he takes on the identity of a rich playboy—because it's better to be a rich fake somebody than a poor real nobody. People who are motivated by a desire for freedom (as opposed to security) are less interested in money per se than in money as the means to personal gratification.

"To the extent that you understand how money is used and what it means to you psychologically," say Goldberg and Lewis (p. 79), "you can better assess whether your handling of it is rational or not." Such assessment is the subject of this chapter.

What economic factors affect my family situation?

Which arrangement describes my family/work situation, and how would I like it to be?

Which work-life strategy would best work for me?

🌐 ON THE WEB Money Matters

www.moneyworkbook.com/finpers.htm

Dr. Jon Rich, author of *The Couple's Guide to Love and Money*, offers an informal survey to determine what type of money handler you are. The test consists of 36 items, each rated on a five-point scale, from "Strongly Disagree" to "Strongly Agree." The test has been validated on a sample of hundreds of Internet visitors. When you click "submit" at the end of the test, you will receive a detailed report describing your financial personality. Your results will also be sent to a database so that Rich can use the data for further research efforts and further refine the test. Go to the website, read the directions, and try the test.

12.1 Work, Wealth, & Well-Being

MAJOR QUESTION What economic factors affect my family situation?

PREVIEW This section discusses how work and its effect on families have changed over time. We also describe the unequal distribution of income and wealth and various economic classes. Finally, we examine economic factors that affect families today.

"Everyone wants a clear reason to get up in the morning," says journalist Dick Leider (1988: 52). "As humans we hunger for meaning and purpose in our lives. At the very core of who we are, we need to feel our lives matter . . . that we do make a difference."

Do you think your life has meaning and purpose? What are they?

"Life never lacks purpose," says Leider. "Purpose is innate—but it is up to each of us individually to discover or rediscover it. And, it must be discovered by oneself, by one's own conscience."

As we saw in Chapter 1, "Seeking," purpose is synonymous with happiness, at least in the sense of knowing and using your strengths in work, love, parenting, and the like or, more important, in using your strengths to serve a higher purpose (Seligman 2002). What is the purpose of your life? For most people, said Sigmund Freud, founder of psychoanalysis, the two biggest things that provide meaning and purpose are *love* and *work*. Or, as he put it, "Love and work . . . work and love, that's all there is."

Unfortunately, many people do not feel that work does give them a sense of purpose. According to one Gallup poll, only 41% of the respondents consciously chose the job or career they were in. Of the rest, 18% got started in their present job through chance circumstances, and 12% took the only job that was available ("Working at the wrong job" 1990). The remaining 29% said they were influenced by relatives or friends. Perhaps the most important finding was this: Nearly *two-thirds* of the respondents said that, given a chance to start over, they would have tried to learn more about career options.

It is not the point of this chapter to look at career options, although for the sake of your future happiness, we would certainly urge you to get as much information as you can about them. But because, as one observer (Crawford

NUMBERS THAT MATTER
Working Families

■ **How much of employee compensation consists of benefits?** In many countries, health, retirement, and similar benefits are government programs, but in the United States, they are usually offered by employers. Indeed, whereas in 1929 only 1.4% of U.S. employee compensation consisted of benefits rather than cash, by 2002 they accounted for 16.3%.[a]

■ **How do U.S. household incomes compare?** In 2001, the top fifth income-earning households (averaging $145,970 per household a year) took in 50.2% of the total U.S. aggregate income, up from 43.3% in 1976. The middle fifth ($42,629) saw their share of aggregate income decline from 17.1% to 14.6%. And the share for the poorest fifth of households slipped from 4.4% to 3.5%.[b]

■ **How does family income compare between blacks and whites?** In 2004, the median net worth of black families was only 58% of that for non-Hispanic white families.[c] Among workers with advanced degrees, blacks earned $2.5 million over the course of their careers and Hispanic workers earned $2.6 million, compared with $3.1 million for white and Asian American workers.[d]

■ **In what percentage of families does the husband not work?** Just 5.6% of married couples have a husband who doesn't work and a wife who does.[e]

■ **What percentage of married women with children work?** Between 1970 and 2002, the percentage of married women with children under age 6 who were in the labor force went from 30% to 63%. In 2002, over 71% of mothers with children under age 18 were in the workforce.[f]

■ **How many men and women work part time?** A quarter of working women work part time, compared with only 10% of working men, which enables them to take care of children or elderly parents while still maintaining job skills. Women who work part time earn a median of $1.15 for every dollar their male counterparts make—the reverse of the 76 cents on the dollar that women earn for full-time work compared to men.[g]

■ **How does gender affect employment?** Although women have been recently achieving more high-status managerial and professional jobs, traditionally they have been and still are concentrated in relatively low-paying occupations. According to one study, the average working women's family would earn $4,205 more per year if women were paid as much as men.[h]

[a]Bureau of Economic Analysis, cited in Wiener 2003. [b]U.S. Census Bureau 2002c. [c]Ferguson 2005. [d]Day and Newburger 2002. [e]Tyre and McGinn 2003. [f]"Single-earner households shrink" 2002. [g]"Women's pay tops men's as part timers" 2002. [h]Lewin 1999.

2000) points out, the workplace affects the family more than the family affects the workplace, we do want to describe how the important matters of work and money bear on intimacy and family relationships.

How Work Has Changed

At one time, in preindustrial society, "work and family were practically the same thing," points out Rutgers University historian John Gillis (quoted in Curry 2003: 50). That is, for centuries the household was the unit of production, with whole families engaged in the enterprise, whether farming, milling, wagon making, or whatever.

From Work & Family to Families in the Workforce

The Industrial Revolution in England in the late 1700s changed all that, with factories and mills requiring a substantial workforce and constant attention. Thus, work and families were divided, and instead of selling what they produced, men, women, and children sold their time—they became part of a *labor force,* **wage earners who hired out their labor to someone else.** The jobs that skilled craftsmen used to do were broken down into measurable component tasks that, as in Henry Ford's automobile assembly line, could easily be taught to almost anyone, which made workers easily replaceable.

In addition, to get the most out of their production lines, businesses began insisting that workers put in longer hours. This led to the glorification of the work ethic, as embodied in the tales of Horatio Alger. As a counterforce to this exploitation, labor unions were formed to push for higher wages and fewer hours. The result of their efforts was that between 1830 and 1930, work hours were reduced nearly in half.

More Working Hours, Less Leisure

As jobs disappeared during the Great Depression of the 1930s, President Franklin Delano Roosevelt suggested that to increase employment, more people should become consumers. "The aim . . . is to restore our rich domestic market by raising its vast consuming capacity," Roosevelt said (quoted in Curry 2003: 54). Since then, the dominant view of both business and government is that the purpose of industry is to create more and more things, which requires heavy advertising to induce people to buy them, making people want more and therefore have to work more to afford these things.

Lost in this process is the idea that people should work fewer hours and enjoy more *leisure*—**time not taken up by work in which to engage in freely chosen satisfying activities.** In addition, the labor unions, which reached the peak of their influence in the 1950s, failed to extend their organizing efforts to the increasing number of white-collar jobs, and, since then, workers' hours have steadily increased. *(See ■ Panel 12.1.)* As a result, U.S. workers have the fewest vacation days in the industrialized world—averaging 14 paid days off a year—but 35% of employed U.S. adults usually do not take all their vacation days, on average leaving 3 vacation days per year "on the table," according to a Harris Interactive survey for Expedia.com (2007). Other figures show that Americans take only 10.2 vacation days a year, compared with 25 to 30 days for citizens in many European countries. *(See ■ Panel 12.2.)* The largest increase in working time has occurred among dual-earner couples; husbands and

■ **PANEL 12.1** Annual Hours Worked per Employed Person in Industrialized Countries, 2004

Country	Annual Average Hours
Netherlands	1,357
Norway	1,363
France	1,441
Germany	1,443
Denmark	1,454
Austria	1,550
Italy	1,585
Sweden	1,585
Ireland	1,642
United Kingdom	1,669
Portugal	1,694
Canada	1,751
Japan	1,789
Spain	1,799
Australia	1,816
United States	1,824
New Zealand	1,826
Mexico	1,848
Korea	2,380

ANNUAL AVERAGE HOURS

Source: Adapted from Organization for Economic Cooperation and Development, cited in U.S. Department of Labor 2007: Chart 2.8.

wives in these marriages jointly devoted 81.3 hours per week to paid employment—up more than 3 hours from the 78 hours per week reported in 1970 (Jacobs and Gerson 2001).

However, a great many people—48%, according to one survey (Haralson and Mullins 2000)—would prefer more vacation time to more pay. This is what has happened in Europe, where, it is suggested (Alesina et al. 2005), powerful labor unions have pushed for more vacation time instead of wage increases. As a result, because Americans spend more hours at work than Europeans do, they spend fewer hours on household and child-care tasks, which they then often pay other people to do (Surowiecki 2005). However, both Americans and many Europeans find that money and work are daily major causes of stress in their lives (AP-Ipsos poll, reported in Lester 2006). In the United States, finances were cited most frequently (by 34%) as the top source of stress and jobs (at 28%) as the second top source.

"While there are surely exceptions," says one analysis, "most [U.S.] workers are not working long hours in order to escape their homes and families. Rather, in the competition among work, family, and self, the self appears to be losing" (Gerson and Jacobs 2003: 351–352). In the 1990s, information technology made further inroads into leisure time, as fax machines, home computers, email, pagers, and cell phones became ways to extend work processes into supposedly off-work time, making home an outpost of the office. The logical extension of this is *telecommuting,* **working at home while in telecommunication contact—by Internet, phone, and fax—with the office.** Historian Gillis (quoted in Curry 2003: 56) sees telecommuting as coming full circle: "We may be seeing the return of households where work is the central element again."

Noncash Benefits: Alternative Community Welfare

In many industrialized countries, such as those in Europe, health, disability, retirement, sick leave, unemployment benefits, and other forms of community *welfare—***aid to those in need—**are largely programs of the state. In the United States, by contrast, much of the welfare state (apart from Social Security and Medicaid) is run largely through fringe benefits offered by employers. Indeed, whereas in 1929, only 1.4% of employee compensation consisted of benefits rather than cash, by 2002, they accounted for 16.3%—and even more in some companies (Bureau of Economic Analysis, cited in Wiener

■ **PANEL 12.2** Annual Vacation Days for Industrialized Countries

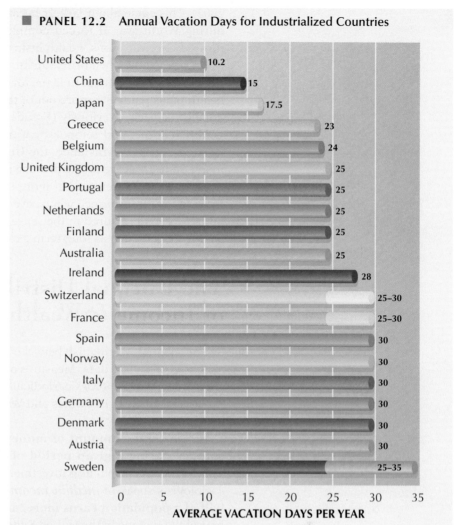

Source: Adapted from data in Valenti 2003.

2003). This came about largely because government-imposed wage controls during World War II forced companies to offer inducements in noncash forms: better vacations, health insurance, retirement benefits.

Unfortunately, when firms run into hard times, benefits are among the first things that are trimmed. In 2003, for instance, people in employer-sponsored health plans paid 48% more out of their own pockets for care than they had done three years previously (Freudenheim 2003). Other employees—lower-paid, part-time, and temporary workers—receive few such benefits at all (Wiener 2003). For instance, the United States spends more than twice as much on health care as the average of other developed nations, all of which boast universal coverage. Yet more than 46 million Americans (nearly 16%) have no health insurance whatsoever (U.S. Census Bureau 2007a), and most others are underinsured in the sense that they lack adequate coverage for all contingencies, such as long-term care and prescription drug costs.

The Unequal Distribution of Income & Wealth

Social scientists distinguish between income and wealth. Measures of income are based on census data. Measures of wealth are harder to come by, although magazines such as *Forbes* periodically make "guesstimates" of the wealthiest Americans (such as Bill Gates and Warren Buffett) based on all kinds of publicly available data.

***Income* is the amount of money a household receives from various sources during a given period of time.** The sources may be wages and salaries, of course, but also investment income, dividends, and the like. When sociologists speak of ***median income*, they mean the income midpoint— half of a population earns more, and half earns less.** In 2005, the median household income in the United States was $42,326, with Asian and non-Hispanic white households above the median and Hispanic and black households below the median. *(See ■ Panel 12.3.)* Incomes are distributed extremely unequally, with the top 0.1%—one out of 1,000 taxpayers—bringing in 11% of the nation's total income, three times the share that they did just a generation ago. In other words, the rich have grown richer, but rank-and-file Americans' incomes have grown not much faster than the inflation rate (Leonhardt 2007: C1). Indeed, research shows that American men in their thirties now actually

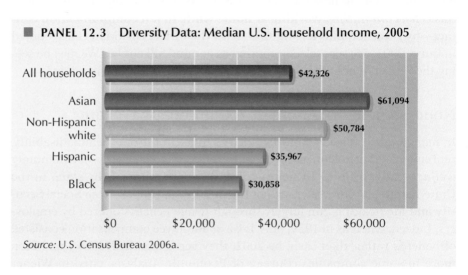

■ **PANEL 12.3** Diversity Data: Median U.S. Household Income, 2005

Source: U.S. Census Bureau 2006a.

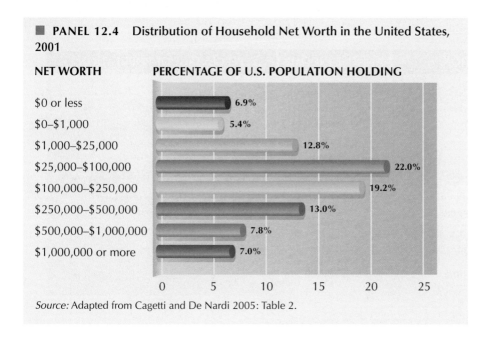

PANEL 12.4 Distribution of Household Net Worth in the United States, 2001

NET WORTH	PERCENTAGE OF U.S. POPULATION HOLDING
$0 or less	6.9%
$0–$1,000	5.4%
$1,000–$25,000	12.8%
$25,000–$100,000	22.0%
$100,000–$250,000	19.2%
$250,000–$500,000	13.0%
$500,000–$1,000,000	7.8%
$1,000,000 or more	7.0%

Source: Adapted from Cagetti and De Nardi 2005: Table 2.

make *less* than their fathers did—a 12.5% drop from $40,000 median annual income in 1974 to $35,000 in 2004 when adjusted for inflation (Sawhill and Morton 2007).

Wealth, also called *net worth*, is the monetary value of everything one actually owns—such as property, stocks, and insurance—minus debts. Wealth is also distributed extremely unequally, with the richest 2% of adults owning more than half of the world's household wealth in 2001 (Atkinson 2006). "So much of the world's wealth is concentrated in few hands," says one journalist, "that if all the world's wealth was distributed evenly, each person would have $20,500 of assets to use" (Giles 2006). In the United States, the top 1% owns 32% of the nation's wealth, and the richest 10% owns nearly 70% of the country's wealth. *(See ■ Panel 12.4.)* Viewed another way, the household net worth for the top 7% is $1 million or more and for the bottom 7% is zero or less (Cagetti and De Nardi 2005: Table 2). Unlike income, wealth tends to increase through investment and can be passed along to heirs, which gives those who inherit wealth a big advantage in accumulating even more wealth.

Which Economic Class Are You a Member Of?

About 45% of Americans identify themselves as being "middle class," according to one survey ("A middle-class nation" 1999). This figure is actually pretty close to the percentage of middle-class people in a six-class model formulated by Dennis Gilbert and Joseph Kahl (1993; Gilbert 1997). *(See ■ Panel 12.5.)*

■ **The Capitalist Class, 1%—Incomes of $1,000,000-Plus:** The super-rich members of the capitalist class are worth more than the entire bottom 90%. Consisting of investors and heirs plus a few top corporate executives, these are the people whose power can affect the jobs of millions, who are on the *Forbes* list of the 400 wealthiest individuals, whose ownership of the media and access to politicians wield tremendous influence. Some members are heirs to old money (for example, the Rockefellers, the Kennedys, and the Fords), some have new money (for example, Microsoft's Bill Gates, GE's Jack Welch). They are usually graduates of prestigious universities—Harvard, Princeton, Stanford, Yale, and the like.

SOCIAL CLASS	OCCUPATION	ANNUAL INCOME	PERCENTAGE OF POPULATION
Capitalist	Investors, heirs, top executives	$1,000,000+	1%
Upper middle	Professionals, upper managers	$125,000+	15%
Lower middle	Semiprofessionals, lower managers, craftspeople	About $60,000	34%
Working class	Factory and clerical workers, retail sales, craftspeople	About $35,000	30%
Working poor	Laborers, service workers, low-paid salespeople	About $17,000	16%
Underclass	Unemployed, part-time, or on welfare	Under $10,000	4%

Source: Adapted from Henslin 2007: 269.

■ **The Upper Middle Class, 15%—Incomes of $125,000-Plus:** These are professionals and upper managers, those who manage the corporations owned by the super-rich or who run their own businesses. They owe much of their success to education, since most of them have college degrees and often postgraduate degrees in business, law, or medicine.

■ **The Lower Middle Class, 34%—Incomes of about $60,000:** These are people in technical and lower-level management positions who work for those in the upper middle class as lower managers, craftspeople, and the like. They enjoy a reasonably comfortable standard of living, although it is constantly threatened by taxes and inflation. Generally, they have a high school education and perhaps some college or apprenticeship education.

■ **The Working Class, 30%—Incomes of about $35,000:** Compared to those in the lower middle class, members of the working class have jobs that are lower paying, more routine, and less secure. With occupations such as factory workers, clerical workers, low-paid salespeople, and the like, they frequently fear that they will be laid off during economic hard times. Generally, they have only a high school diploma.

■ **The Working Poor, 16%—Incomes of about $17,000:** The working poor are those who hold unskilled, low-paying jobs such as house cleaners, day laborers, and migrant workers. Although they work full time, they depend on help such as food stamps to supplement their incomes. Quite often, the working poor are high school dropouts, and many are functionally illiterate. Their major fear is that they might become homeless.

■ **The Underclass, 4%—Incomes of under $10,000:** These are the unskilled people who in an earlier time—before industrialized farming and disappearing factory jobs—might have found work but now endure poverty and despair sometimes for years and even for generations. When they are able to find work, it is in menial, low-paying, temporary jobs such as washing dishes or unloading trucks. They draw their main support from government aid, food stamps, and nonprofit food kitchens.

It needs to be pointed out, however, that in some localities—such as the San Francisco Bay area and New York City—a family might have a high income, such as $125,000 a year, and still have trouble making ends meet because of family size, high housing and commuting costs, and other expenses. Indeed, one in five workers who earn $100,000 or more report they often or always live paycheck to paycheck, according to a survey by Harris Interactive (reported in Armour 2007).

The Rich Get Richer, the Poor Get Poorer, the Middle Class Loses Ground

During the late 20th century, the share of aggregate U.S. income acquired by the top fifth income-earning households increased significantly—from 43.3% in 1976 to 50.2% in 2001. These are households with a mean (not median) yearly income of $145,970 in 2001. Meanwhile, the other four-fifths of U.S. households lost ground. For instance, those in the middle fifth of households (median income $42,629) went from earning 17.1% of aggregate U.S. income to 14.6%. And the poorest fifth households slipped from a 4.4% share in 1976 to 3.5% in 2001 (U.S. Census Bureau 2002c). Stated another way, today the top 20% of the population receives more than half the nation's income, and the bottom 60% receives only about 27%. (See ■ Panel 12.6.)

Also during the 1990s and early 2000s, despite the biggest economic boom in 30 years, African Americans closed little, if any, of the gap between themselves and whites on important measures of economic success (Crockett and Coy 2003: 100). In 2004, the median net worth of black families was only 58% of that for non-Hispanic white families (Ferguson 2005). A U.S. Census Bureau study (Day and Newburger 2002) found that among workers with advanced degrees, blacks earned $2.5 million over the course of their careers and Hispanic workers $2.6 million, compared with $3.1 million for white and Asian American workers.

OUTFLOW. Unless you have a personal money manager to handle your financial affairs, you probably pay your own bills and write your own checks. How are you at doing this? Do you pay bills the same time every month? Or do you procrastinate and delay sending them because it's too unpleasant for you? ▲

■ **PANEL 12.6   Unequal Distribution of Income.** Proportion of income received by each fifth of the U.S. population, 2001.

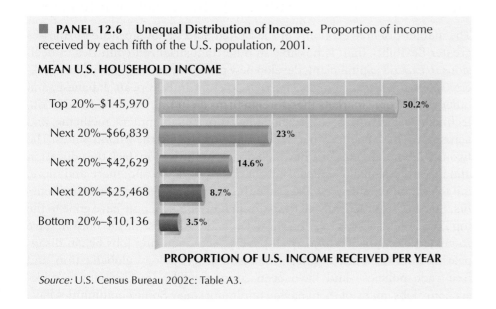

MEAN U.S. HOUSEHOLD INCOME

Top 20%–$145,970	50.2%
Next 20%–$66,839	23%
Next 20%–$42,629	14.6%
Next 20%–$25,468	8.7%
Bottom 20%–$10,136	3.5%

PROPORTION OF U.S. INCOME RECEIVED PER YEAR

Source: U.S. Census Bureau 2002c: Table A3.

Economic Changes Affecting the Family Today

Jill Naves, a Kansas widow living on Social Security who supports four children on $17,820 a year, wasn't surprised when the U.S. Census Bureau reported in 2002 that the number of impoverished people had increased the previous year. "It seems like the cost of living is going up, but no one's income is going up," she said. "Most of my friends, even if they are married, still depend on family or some other kind of help" (quoted in Murphy 2002).

Why hasn't the economic expansion in the United States of the last 25 years benefited everyone? Let's consider some of the reasons.

Long-Term Inflation & the Decline in Purchasing Power

The average hourly earnings in 2007 were four times higher than they were in 1970—that is, $17.30 versus $3.23 three and a half decades ago (Bureau of Labor Statistics 2007: Table B-3). But adjusted for inflation, the dollars don't have the same amount of buying power, so that $17 today won't buy you as much as $3 did earlier. The median price of a house in the San Francisco Bay area in 1970 was $23,000. In 2007, the median house price throughout the United States was $212,300, but in the San Francisco Bay area it was $748,100.

The minimum wage has also not kept up with long-term inflation. The *minimum wage* was first set in 1938 by Congress in the Fair Labor Standards Act (FLSA) in an attempt to bring all families' income above the poverty line. The minimum hourly wage started at 25 cents in 1938 and rose to $5.15 in 2007 (and is expected to go to $7.25 by 2009). However, minimum wages have never been sufficient to raise a family out of poverty, if only one member of the family works. The minimum wage has varied from a maximum of 90% of the poverty level in 1968 and has been between 53 and 62% since 1985. This is the lowest percentage since the poverty level was established in 1959. Today, $5.15 is the equivalent of only $3.95 in 1995 (Economic Policy Institute 2007).

The Two-Tier Labor Market: The Bottom Half Slips Behind

The market-oriented economy of the United States allows private businesses greater flexibility than is possible in other industrialized countries in decisions to expand capital plant, develop new products, and lay off surplus workers. Yet businesses face higher barriers to entry in European, Japanese, and other rivals' home markets than foreign firms do in U.S. markets. In addition, technological advances—especially innovations in computers, medicine, and aerospace—have resulted in a two-tier labor market in the United States. The two-tier labor market is one in which people at the bottom lack the education and the professional/technical skills of those at the top and, more and more, fail to get comparable pay raises, health insurance coverage, and other benefits. Since 1975, practically all the gains in household income have gone to the top 20% of households (NationMaster.com 2003). Those at the bottom have stagnated or slipped behind. Well-paying manufacturing jobs began disappearing from the United States—the result of technology, globalization, and free-trade policies—and have been supplanted by lower-paying service-economy jobs, many of them paying minimum wage. Some communities have tried to counteract this trend by instituting *living wage laws,* **in which wages and benefits take into account the area's cost of living** and which are higher than the federal minimum wage.

Poverty

The *poverty line* is officially defined as the minimum level of income the U.S. government considers necessary for individual and family subsistence. The poverty line, which changes every year (it is pegged to changes in the government's Consumer Price Index), is income measured before income taxes and payroll taxes and does not include cash and noncash benefits such as food stamps, housing support, and medical subsidies.

The official definition of poverty, which was created in 1959, is widely considered to be inadequate, since it ignores the needs of single mothers requiring child care and transportation assistance, and subsistence needs vary by geographical areas (Bergmann 1994; Burtless and Smeeding 2001).

■ **Who's Below the Poverty Line?** In 2005, the poverty line was $19,971 a year for a four-person family. At that time, nearly 37 million people lived at or below the poverty level, 12.6% of the total U.S. population, according to the Census Bureau (2006a). Roughly 17.6% of American children, or 12.9 million, lived in poverty in 2005—up from 16.4% in 2001.

■ **Poverty and Race/Ethnicity:** Poverty rates vary by race and ethnicity, being significantly greater among most nonwhites. *(See ■ Panel 12.7.)* Most of those who fall below the poverty limit are there temporarily rather than permanently. Indeed, nearly a quarter of the U.S. population needs government aid (welfare) at some point during their lives, owing to divorce, disability, or unemployment. But most regain self-sufficiency within a year or two (Rank and Cheng 1995).

Poverty also varies by sex. In 2005, 14.1% of the female population in the United States and 11.1% of the male population lived below the poverty level. Poverty rates were highest for children: 17.6%, or one in six children. And of the families living in poverty, 28.7% were maintained by women with no husband present; only 13% were maintained by men with no wife present (DeNavas-Walt et al. 2006).

Long-term poverty, however, is rare among whites, with fewer than 1% remaining poor for 10 years or more, but common among African American children, with 29% poor for 10 years or more. Moreover, by ages 25 to 27, only 1 in 14 whites were still poor, whereas 1 in 3 African Americans were (Corcoran 2001).

■ **The Feminization of Poverty:** A term coined by researcher **Diana Pearce** (1978), **the *feminization of poverty* denotes the likelihood that female heads of households will be poor, owing to job and**

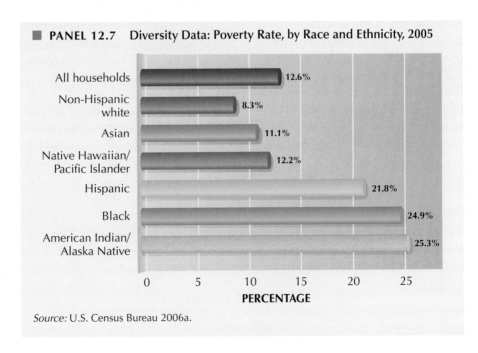

■ **PANEL 12.7 Diversity Data: Poverty Rate, by Race and Ethnicity, 2005**

	Percentage
All households	12.6%
Non-Hispanic white	8.3%
Asian	11.1%
Native Hawaiian/Pacific Islander	12.2%
Hispanic	21.8%
Black	24.9%
American Indian/Alaska Native	25.3%

PERCENTAGE

Source: U.S. Census Bureau 2006a.

EXAMPLE OF

The Effects of Unemployment

Coping with the Spiral of Stress

When Robert Todaro of Middleboro, Massachusetts, lost his job as a technical writer at General Dynamics, it was nothing personal; he was just one of many employees let go when the company downsized in 2001. But the effect was nonetheless "utterly devastating," he said. "You feel as though you've done something wrong. You worry about money. You worry about what's going to happen in the future. And it depresses you—emotionally, physically, all sorts of ways" (Todaro, quoted in Duenwald 2002).

Mary, the wife of a 44-year-old executive who had had a great 20-year career with a big company and was promoted eight times, then laid off, said that "for the past few months he has grown more and more depressed, and now he isn't even looking anymore" (Fisher 2003).

As we discuss in Chapter 13, "Crises," being unemployed—or even *under*employed—is one of the most severe problems one can encounter, and it can have an enormous effect on family relations. Says Sherry Cadoratte (quoted in Fisher 2003), president of an outplacement firm, "When

someone is out of work, it does become a family issue. As the spouse's anxiety builds, it can create even more pressure on the unemployed person and contribute to a downward spiral."

Richard H. Price, a University of Michigan psychologist who studied the effects of unemployment on 756 people for two years, says that people tend to think the greatest shock is at the moment of job loss. But, he says, "it's the cascade of events that is triggered by it that causes greater and more lasting harm" (Price, quoted in Duenwald 2002). The layoff leads to financial insecurity, which then causes depression, which leads to people feeling that they have little control over events, which is followed by hopelessness and then sleeplessness, headaches, and chronically upset stomachs and fatigue (Price et al. 2002).

Some people who lose their jobs are able to use the stressful transition to explore career alternatives or connect better with their children. When Mark Gozonsky lost his job as a manager for America Online, he enlisted his twin 7-year-old daughters to help him find a new career. "You should work in an art museum telling people stories about art, because you love art and telling stories," said one. "You should design theme-park rides so we can help you test them," said the other. "Finding out about the jobs my kids dreamed up for me was a great place to start looking for my dream job," Gozonsky said. And when he found a job as an elementary school teacher, his daughters were almost as excited as he was. Inviting his children into his job search also helped him become more involved with them in a way that he had never imagined (Zaslow 2002).

Gozonsky's story is one of the more upbeat ones among the unemployed. But there are solutions for those who are suffering from unemployment-related depression. One exercise for the discouraged: Write down five anecdotes describing things you did well in the past and enjoyed doing, whether work related or not. This helps you realize that you have succeeded at things you liked—the first step in believing it could happen again (Fisher 2003). Another activity is to simply become more adept at looking for work, as in improving interviewing skills, presentation, and focus. Finding a job seekers' club, such as WIND (Wednesday Is Networking Day) in New England, gives the unemployed a place to meet and hear advice from career counselors and other specialists. Having a session or two with a career coach can also help.

What if you are Mary, the wife of the unemployed executive, and he refuses to see a career coach or join a group? In that case, says Alan Kramer, a consultant for an outplacement firm, she should enlist a third party to help persuade him. "In every family or circle of friends," he says, "there is someone whose opinion counts and who is close to the situation—but one crucial step more removed from it, emotionally, than you are. Who holds sway with your husband? Ideally, it should be a friend or relative who has been through a tough spell of unemployment too" (Kramer, quoted in Fisher 2003).

WHAT DO YOU THINK? No doubt you have known people who were unemployed for a long time, or perhaps you have been so yourself. What effects did you observe? What kind of advice would you give?

wage discrimination, high divorce rates, and births to unmarried women. Poverty rates were higher for single-female households, 28.7%, than for married-couple households, only 5.1%, in 2005 (U.S. Census Bureau 2006a).

■ **The Consequences of Being Poor:** Studies document that poor people have greater exposure to environmental toxins, from lead paint to proximity to chemical plants and waste incinerators that are consistently built in poorer neighborhoods. The high-fat, high-salt, and low-vegetable/fruit diets found in disadvantaged populations are often less the result of bad choices than of the unfortunate consequence of the shrinking number of good, affordable supermarkets in inner-city neighborhoods, the explosion of fast-food restaurants in urban areas, and food traditions originating in deprivation. Higher rates of smoking and alcohol use related to higher levels of chronic disease in African American communities are more a response to the stresses of poverty and lack of employment opportunities than "lifestyle choices."

Particularly destructive aspects of poverty in the African American community are the chronically higher levels of unemployment embedded in it. Each 1% rise in the unemployment rate is accompanied by a 2% increase in the mortality rate, a 5 to 6% increase in homicides, a 5% increase in imprisonment, a 3 to 4% increase in first admissions to mental hospitals, and a nearly 5% increase in infant mortality rates. Loss of insurance is at least partially to blame for this frightening list of social ills—a loss that affects minorities at significantly high rates. A great many Americans, almost 47 million, or 15.9%, according to the Census Bureau (2006a), are without health insurance, but the percentages are even higher for most minorities. (*See ■ Panel 12.8.*) These include millions of full-time workers in low-wage jobs that don't offer insurance benefits and those who lost Medicaid benefits through the 1996 welfare reforms. In a market-driven health care system that links insurance coverage to high-paying jobs, it can be argued that poor health outcomes for minorities and other disadvantaged groups is almost a given.

A Kaiser Family Foundation report also states that 40% of uninsured people, compared to 8% of those with insurance, postponed necessary care owing to costs, and 30% of uninsured Americans, compared to 11% of the insured, didn't fill their prescriptions. Without access to early treatment and regular care, the uninsured are at least twice as likely to be hospitalized for avoidable complications of manageable conditions such as diabetes and hypertension. More than 40% are more likely to be diagnosed with late-stage breast and prostate cancer, and uninsured women with breast cancer are 40 to 50% more likely to die from the disease (Harvard Public Health Review 2002).

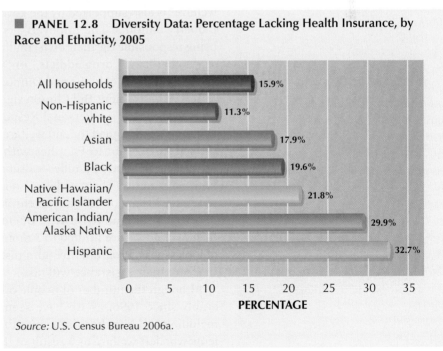

■ **PANEL 12.8** Diversity Data: Percentage Lacking Health Insurance, by Race and Ethnicity, 2005

Source: U.S. Census Bureau 2006a.

POVERTY. This rural, poor family in Louisiana includes a mother and her three small children who live in a dilapidated trailer. Roughly 17.6% of American children lived in poverty in 2005. Do you know of any children who are this poor? What should be done for them? What could you do for them?

▶

What about the "Social Safety Net"?

What help is available for poor families? Not a great deal, it can be argued. The social programs that originated with the War on Poverty in the 1960s are no longer popular, and in recent times there has been considerable antagonism toward the idea of government aid to those who can't support themselves, such as the unemployed, the disabled, and the poor. Of course, the government provides many programs of support to those who are not poor—student loans, farm subsidies, and home-mortgage deductions. "Corporate welfare" is also supported by the government in the form of tax subsidies and industry bailouts. The impoverished, however, have come to be viewed as being responsible for their own conditions because of character flaws; they are said to be "lazy," "drug addicts," or "welfare cheats" and undeserving of government support (Aldous and Dumon 1991).

In 1996, President Bill Clinton signed what came to be known as the "Welfare Reform Act," or Personal Responsibility and Work Opportunity Reconciliation Act, designed to "end welfare as we know it." This legislation replaced the old AFDC (Aid to Families with Dependent Children) with Temporary Assistance to Needy Families—a set amount of dollars with a 5-year lifetime limit on benefits. The new law also requires welfare recipients to work after receiving 2 years of benefits, to enroll in vocational or on-the-job training, or to perform community service. Unemployed people ages 18 to 50 who are not raising children are limited to 3 months of food stamps for any 3-year period of joblessness. Programs are administered by the various states, which decide the form their assistance will take.

Although the number of people on the welfare rolls has decreased considerably since 1996, as we have seen, the number of impoverished people, including children, has risen since then. Moreover, about a third of the recipients who left welfare as a result of the 1996 legislation returned to receiving benefits the next year (Loprest 1999).

12.2 Changing Family Work Patterns

MAJOR QUESTION Which arrangement describes my family/work situation, and how would I like it to be?

PREVIEW In this section, we discuss various alternative types of work and family life. We consider the traditional family arrangement of good-provider husband and homemaker wife, along with the exception of men as house-husbands. We then consider co-provider families, in which husbands and wives act as economic partners.

"Maybe it is time for a new kind of prenuptial agreement," says *Wall Street Journal* work and family columnist Sue Shellenbarger (2003), "an 'economic prenup.' It wouldn't be legally binding; it could simply be an unwritten understanding or an informal written checklist. It would lay ground rules for keeping a marriage together, rather than splitting assets in a divorce, as conventional prenuptial agreements do."

The idea is for a couple to discuss in advance of marriage such matters as whose job comes first and who stays home with children. Sample questions: Will we both avoid jobs that demand workaholic hours? If we have kids, will the lower-earning spouse switch to part time? If the primary breadwinner is laid off, will the other spouse try to make more money? Should the family accept a company transfer while the kids are still in school? Indeed, should the couple agree that they hope to derive meaning in life primarily through family rather than careers, as many law and business students told interviewers in one study (Orrange 2003)? Despite all the economic changes, it seems that individuals are no less psychologically invested in their families than people were in the past (Kiecolt 2003).

Too often, couples have different expectations of each other in the event of a job layoff. They also find that they need to be flexible about prioritizing one partner's career over the other's, since today's economy "may decide the other gets the bigger paycheck and better job security," Shellenbarger says. Another matter: "You never know how you are going to feel about returning to work until you hold your newborn in your arms," points out Shellenbarger. "Therefore, decisions about career priorities need to be flexible, to make room for new parents' desires."

How do you feel about how work and family life should be organized? In this section, we consider the various alternatives.

Traditional Families: Good-Provider Husband, Homemaker Wife

Earlier we considered the traditional roles that have typified most families in the past. This is the family form known as the ***two-person single career,*** **in which the husband works outside the home and the wife—even if she is also employed—helps the husband's career by being responsible for domestic tasks and child rearing** (Papanek 1979; Demo and Acock 1993). This means that one spouse, usually the husband, takes on the so-called *good-provider role* and the other spouse, usually the wife, takes on the *homemaker role.*

The Good-Provider Role: Traditional "Man's Work"

Accepted since the 1830s in the United States, **the *good-provider role* emphasizes that the man is the principal or sole economic provider for the family** (Bernard 1986). This stereotypical role held sway until the 1980s, when the U.S. Census Bureau no longer made the automatic assumption that the head of a household was male. The good-provider role still endures, of course, and for many women, marital satisfaction rests on their perception of how well their husbands are fulfilling the role of provider (Blair 1993).

If men are expected to be good at "bringing home the bacon"—at providing income to support the family—they are also traditionally expected to contribute to household work in stereotypical ways, such as mowing the lawn, repairing roofs and plumbing, doing painting, and the like. Other tasks, such as child care, vacuuming, and washing dishes, are perceived as done simply to help out the spouse, not as areas of equal responsibility (Hochschild 1989).

The Homemaker Role: Traditional "Woman's Work"

The *homemaker role* emphasizes that the woman should be principally responsible for housework, child raising, and maintaining family ties to parents and in-laws (Thompson 1991; Brayfield 1992). Although the homemaker role traditionally takes priority over other demands, it is usually viewed as not constituting "real work"—as when a woman is asked whether she works and answers, "No, I'm just a housewife" (Oakley 1974). This overlooks such economic benefits to society as the unpaid nursing care that older homemakers provide to ailing family members.

Among the characteristics of housework is that it tends to be isolating, and homemakers may complain of loneliness—or, if they are raising children, of a longing for adult company (Oakley 1985; Bird and Ross 1993). Because homemaking is unpaid, a housewife is economically dependent on her husband. Homemaking is also monotonous, repetitive, and unending—it goes on 24 hours a day, 7 days a week. However, it is also unstructured and autonomous—there is no "employer" looking over one's shoulder—and many wives find satisfaction in child rearing, entertaining, and networking with friends and relatives.

THE "GOOD PROVIDER." In the 1950s and 1960s, men's and women's roles in the nuclear family were such that the husband went out and worked, playing the good provider role of being sole economic provider for his family, and the woman played the homemaker role, being responsible for housework and child raising. What do you think of the changes in work arrangements since then—dual-income earners, "Mr. Mom" househusbands, working mothers, single working parents? Do these changes give men and women more freedom? ◄

The number of full-time stay-at-home mothers went from 4.5 million in 1994 to nearly 5.6 million in 2005, up about 20% in a decade (U.S. Census Bureau 2006b). Three possible reasons for the increase are (1) the economic boom of the late 1990s and early 21st century, which enabled more families to survive on one income; (2) the cultural influence of the growing Hispanic population in the United States, which tends to favor traditional family models; and (3) the entry into parenthood of a generation of Americans who were raised as "latchkey" children and want to offer their own children closer parenting (Armas 2003).

"Mr. Mom" as the Exception:
Men as Full-Time Homemakers

The reverse of wife as homemaker is **the *househusband*, also known as *stay-at-home dad*, a man who is a full-time homemaker.** Just 5.6% of married couples have a husband who doesn't work and a wife who does, according to the Bureau of Labor Statistics (cited in Tyre and McGinn 2003: 46). The U.S. Census Bureau (2006b) estimates that there are 142,000 stay-at-home dads, married fathers with children younger than age 15 who have chosen to care for the family while their wives work outside the home.

Some men voluntarily choose the househusband role. Dan and Lynn Murray were both Chicago lawyers when Lynn became pregnant with triplets. After the babies were born, the couple decided that Lynn was happier in the office. Today, Dan cares for their five children, and Lynn hopes that he will never return to work (Tyre and McGinn 2003: 48).

Many men, however, become "Mr. Moms" inadvertently, the result of downsizing at work. When Alex Wright of Redwood City, California, was laid off from his job as marketing director at a graphics design firm in late 2002, his wife, Cherlene, a juvenile probation officer, became the breadwinner, and Alex became the one who helped their 10-year-old twin boys with their homework and took on the bulk of the housework. "My wife jokes that the house has never been cleaner," he observed. "She likes having a househusband." Even so, the loss of his salary meant that they had to learn to live on less, and Alex devoted most mornings to searching for a new job (Lynem 2003).

Indeed, the number of men who act as full-time fathers seems to fluctuate with economic conditions. For instance, in 1991, a time of downsizing, about 20% of fathers were taking care of young children at home. However, in 1993, it decreased to 16% as economic conditions improved (Adler 1996).

Co-Provider Families: Husbands & Wives as Economic Partners

During the prosperous 1950s and 1960s, the one-paycheck, good-provider/homemaker model was an efficient family form, although many women chafed at being homebound, and many men felt trapped in their breadwinner roles. In the 1970s, however, changes in the economy put extreme pressure on families' purchasing power. The rate of inflation soared, and well-paying manufacturing jobs began to disappear from the United States—the result of technology, globalization, and free-trade policies—and were supplanted by lower-paying service-economy jobs.

The result was a significant rise in *co-provider marriages*, **also known as** *dual-earner marriages*, **in which both married partners are employed outside the home.** By 2000, only 21% of households followed the traditional single-earner married-couple model, down from 63% a half century earlier, and dual-earner married couples went from 20% in 1950 to 37% in 2000 ("Single-earner households shrink" 2002). As we mentioned in Chapter 11, "Parenting," between 1970 and 2002, the percentage of married women with children under age 6 who were in the labor force went from 30% to 63%. In 2002, over 71% of mothers with children under age 18 were in the workforce.

Working Women

During some national emergencies, such as the two world wars, more women than usual have gone into the workplace. Even without these, women's workplace participation has steadily increased: Except for a short time after World War II, the percentage of women in the workforce grew every decade throughout the 20th century—from being 20% of all women in 1900 to 59% in 2005 (U.S. Census Bureau 2007). (Of course, one must remember that almost all postslavery African American women had to work outside the home just to enable their families to survive, and that reality lasted a long time.)

A quarter of employed women work part time, compared with only 10% of working men, which enables them to take care of children or elderly parents while still maintaining job skills. Many more working mothers—60%, in fact—said they would prefer to work only part time, up from 48% a decade earlier (Pew Research Center 2007a). Indeed, working part time is a better financial deal for women, since they earn $1.15 for every dollar their male counterparts make—the reverse of the 76 cents on the dollar that women earn for full-time work compared to men ("Women's pay tops men's as part timers" 2002). The desire to work part time also seems to be a reflection of the difficulties of combining responsibilities at work and home. Researchers have found that women still do twice as much housework and child care as men do in two-parent families, although total hours of work by mothers and fathers are roughly equal (about 65 hours a week), when both paid and unpaid work is tallied up (Bianchi et al. 2006). No wonder couples find sharing of household chores more important than raising children to realizing a successful marriage (Pew Research Center 2007b).

The obstacles to women's employment progress are known as the glass ceiling and the mommy track.

■ **The Glass Ceiling:** **The *glass ceiling* is a metaphor for an invisible barrier preventing women and minorities from being promoted to top executive jobs.** Generally, negative stereotypes are a main factor holding women back. These stereotypes are contradicted by several studies showing that female managers, for example, outshine their male counterparts on almost every measure (Sharpe 2000).

■ **The Mommy Track:** The *mommy track* offers women flexibility but compels them to surrender ambition (Hochschild 1997). The "mommy track" refers to the idea that the career path for women in an organization should be split into two tracks, one for career-primary women and the other for career-and-family women (Purola 2001). Generally, the career-primary woman is promoted more frequently and receives higher pay than does the career-and-family woman. This is based on the fact that many corporations still retain outdated traditional gender role stereotypes of women taking care of the child and the working man receiving more promotions and pay based on work put into the corporation. They don't assume that a businessman who becomes a father for the first time will automatically become less interested in his career.

Working Mothers

In her book *Women's Two Roles: A Contemporary Dilemma*, Cornell University sociologist **Phyllis Moen** (1992) suggested that there are four types of working mothers, most of whom do not have complete choice about how to handle their work/family roles:

■ **The Captives—"I'd rather be a homemaker, but I have to work":** Captive women are single, unmarried, or married mothers who would like to take care of their children full time. However, their economic status—working poor, working class, or lower middle class—requires them to work.

■ **The Conflicted—"If the job conflicts with my family, I'll quit":** Conflicted women believe that their job hinders their parenting, so they are likely to quit work whenever they can afford to, as when their spouse obtains a better-paying job.

■ **The Copers—"I'll work if the job lets me cope with my family demands":** Copers take jobs that are generally flexible, part time, and/or low paying so that they can concentrate principally on parenting. As we mentioned earlier, women who try to balance a career with family demands are often unfairly restricted to the mommy track in favor of the "more-job-dedicated" male, even though many men would like more job flexibility in order to help take care of family matters.

■ **The Committed—"I'm committed to both my career and my family":** The committed, who are probably the smallest group, have the most freedom. They are generally women with career ambitions who have enough income to hire good child care; however, these women are frequently held back by the glass ceiling, also mentioned earlier, and thus—as the result of negative stereotypes—end up earning less than, and having less power than, men in their organization.

Some women are able to be both copers and committed. Christina Stoever, for example, is an account executive for KPS3, an advertising and public relations firm in Reno, Nevada, who works two and a half days at the office and spends the rest of her workweek at home. This enables her to take care of her son Jason, age 2, while still maintaining a career (McAndrew 2003).

Single Working Parents

We discussed single parents in Chapter 9, "Variations." As we mentioned there, 9% of households in the United States are headed by a man or a woman raising a child alone or without a spouse or partner living at home. From the standpoint of work and money, the greatest challenge for single parents is that they are usually unable to divide both income-earning work and family-household work between two people, although some may be helped by friends or relatives in child-care arrangements.

Indeed, both single working parents and dual-wage-earner families frequently have a difficult time finding high-quality day care for their children.

12.3 Balancing Work & Family Demands: Some Practical Strategies

MAJOR QUESTION Which work-life strategy would best work for me?

PREVIEW Here we consider the major role disruptions—overload, conflict, and ambiguity—that can occur in work-family arrangements. We then discuss six strategies for balancing work and family demands.

Connie Faircloth, age 34, of suburban Atlanta says she would never do what her own mother did: work full time while raising her children. "A lot of times my mom had to work late. I was a latchkey child," says Faircloth. "I came home to a house alone. I cannot even imagine doing that with my children" (quoted in Peterson 2003: 1D).

Faircloth is a member of so-called Generation X, born from 1965 to 1982, people who are now in their mid-twenties to early forties. The Baby Boom generation—born from 1946 to 1964—helped to give the Gen Xers options that are now often taken for granted. According to Neil Howe (cited in Peterson 2003: 2D), coauthor of *13th-Gen,* a book on the generation, Gen X women who can afford to are putting families ahead of career—and are willing to make financial sacrifices to do so. Whereas her own mother felt that she had to work for financial reasons and Connie Faircloth herself misses getting a paycheck, she is satisfied with her choice of being more available to her children. "I want to be home for them when they are in their high school years," she says. "That is when they need a mom the most."

When Major Role Disruptions Occur: Overload, Conflict, & Ambiguity

Faircloth is lucky. Not everyone is able to choose to put parenting before working. Indeed, while there are many who would like to spend less time at work, there are also many who would like to increase their working hours—mainly people with children who want to be able to support their families (Reynolds 2003). In any event, those who are obliged to hold a job find that

Choosing Good Daycare: Help for Working Parents

If you have decided to enroll your child in a child-care center or family daycare home, you want the very best situation for your child. When choosing child care, you should visit more than one program. If possible, take your child with you on the visits.

There are three types of regulated child-care options. (1) *Child-care centers* include daycare centers, preschools, nursery schools, drop-in centers, and Head Start Programs. State laws require them to be licensed. (Go to *www.daycare.com* to find the licensing requirements for the state you live in.) (2) A *family daycare home* is a private home in which an adult provides care for a specific number of children. The law requires such providers to be licensed. (3) A *group daycare home* is a private home in which two or more adults provide care for a specific number of children. The law also requires this kind of home to be licensed.

The following guidelines will help you make good choices (Watson 1984; Carroll 2001; daycare.com 2004; Michigan 4C Association 2004):

Visit the Daycare Center—Preferably Unannounced and More than Once

Visit the facilities more than once and stay as long as you can to get a feel for the place. Try to visit unannounced. If the staff does not allow this, it may mean they have something to hide. Visit again after your child is enrolled.

Observe the Children's and Staff Members' Demeanor

Are children busy in their play, interacting with other children, reading books, doing art projects? What sounds do you hear? If the place is too quiet, it might mean a lack of activities; if too noisy, a lack of control. Listen to the staff members' voices. Are they patient, cheerful, and responsive to the children? These are essential qualities for children's development.

Observe Whether the Environment Is Adequate and the Curriculum Stimulating

Is the facility cleaned daily, especially the bathrooms and kitchen? Is there sufficient indoor space (at least 35 square feet per child) and outdoor space (75 square feet)? Are toys and play equipment in good repair? Is the curriculum stimulating, with a mix of physical activity, individual activities, quiet time, group programs, snacks, and free time?

Ask What the Staff-to-Child Ratio Is

The best ratios are 1 adult per 3 or 4 infants, 1 adult per 2 to 6 2-year-olds, 1 adult per 10 5- and 6-year-olds, and 1 adult per 10 to 12 children over age 6. When visiting a daycare center, count the number of children in a playgroup and then count the number of adults supervising them.

Ask What the Rate of Staff Turnover Is

Frequent turnover is disturbing to children. If half the staff leaves every year, it probably means they are not paid well or they don't like the way the daycare program is run.

Ask about Staff Training

Daycare work is not a remunerative line of work. Nevertheless, you should ask if the staff members have advanced training, preferably at least two years of college and preferably in fields such as child psychology or child development. Ask about the center director's background as well. Ask if the center has been accredited by the National Association for the Education of Young Children or the National Association of Family Child Care.

Ask about References

By all means get the names and telephone numbers of other parents whose children are enrolled. Call them and ask about both good and bad aspects of the center. Don't go with a daycare center that does not give references.

Source: Adapted from checklist developed by Michigan 4C Association, 2875 Northwind Drive, Suite 200, East Lansing, MI 48823, (517) 351-4171; The Children's Resource Network, *www.crn.nu/checklist.html*; and "Tips for Evaluating Quality Daycare," posted on *www.daycare.com/news/tips.html*.

events at work—deadlines, overtime, difficult clients and bosses—affect the emotional life at home and even household scheduling and financial arrangements. But the reverse is true as well: Family demands can affect one's ability to concentrate or perform well at work—or even to be available (as when a parent must stay home to care for a sick child). If one is also married, there can be further problems with juggling not only working and parenting but also being a spouse (Voydanoff and Donnelly 1989). These can lead to several role disruptions.

Role Conflict: "Different People Want Me to Do Different Things!"

Have you ever felt that you were being torn apart by the conflicting demands of those around you? If so, you were the victim of *role conflict,* in which an individual experiences others' conflicting or inconsistent expectations. As we mentioned in Chapter 3, "Gender," **role conflict occurs when the expectations of two or more roles are incompatible.** Managers often experience conflicting demands between work and family (Wharton and Erickson 1993; Shellenbarger 1996a). Women who hold full-time jobs find that they can't also be good mothers—look after sick children, go to school events, and the like. Men who assume housework or child-care duties might feel inadequate for not doing these things as well as their spouses might.

Role conflicts can produce stress-related problems, including anxiety attacks, insomnia, headaches, various tensions, and poor mental health (Weber et al. 1997). And, interestingly, it might be that family interfering with work is more detrimental to mental health than work interfering with family (Grzywacz and Bass 2003).

Role Overload: "I Can't Do What They Expect of Me!"

Role overload **occurs when others' expectations exceed one's ability to meet them.** Students who attempt to handle a full course load and maintain a decent social life while working 30 or more hours a week know full well the consequences of role overload. Similarly, being a parent, worker, and spouse can make us feel we unable to do all the things we are asked to handle.

As one tries to do more and more in less and less time, stress mounts, and personal effectiveness slips.

Role Ambiguity: "I Don't Know What People Want Me to Do!"

In *role ambiguity,* **others' expectations are unknown. When you don't know what others expect of you—either because they don't have the necessary information or because they deliberately withhold it from you—you are experiencing role ambiguity.** New employees in an organization, for instance, often complain about unclear job descriptions and vague promotion criteria. Similarly, husband and wife might have unclear understanding as to who will do what when both have to work late—who will pick up the kids from daycare, who will get dinner on the table, and so on. Prolonged role ambiguity can foster dissatisfaction, hamper performance, and erode self-confidence.

How Some People Reduce Role Disruptions

As you might expect, unmarried women without children experience less difficulty about defining their roles, and they are more likely to be employed full time and to be farther along in their careers than married women are (Houseknecht et al. 1987). Working women who are married or in a live-in relationship, with or without children, are apt to try to reduce role disruptions by trying to work part time or on different shifts from their partners (Warren and Johnson 1995; Love 2000). Men seem able to reduce role disruptions either by (1) putting their family roles ahead of their work roles by spending less time at work or taking more flexible or less demanding jobs or by (2) being equally committed to work and family roles (O'Neil and Greenberger 1994). However, a recent survey by the AFL-CIO (American Federation of Labor–Congress of Industrial Organizations) indicated that working men share the concerns of working women on issues that are critical to families. For the first time since this survey had been conducted, working men demonstrated strong support for child care, paid family leave, strengthening working women's rights, and fighting gender discrimination and unequal pay (AFL-CIO 2002).

Both men and women might try some practical strategies for juggling work and family demands, as we discuss next.

ROLE CONFLICT? Do you think this mother experiences role conflict—feeling she can't be a good mother because the job demands too much of her? How about the father— does being in charge of child care make him feel inadequate because he is not acting like the traditional breadwinner? Have you asked parents performing these kinds of (until recently) unconventional roles how they feel? What do they tell you? ▲

Strategy #1: Mentally Separate Work & Home Roles

Some parents, whether single or in a partnership, are able to mentally separate their work roles from their spouse/parent/home roles. That is, while at work, they give no thought to home, and while at home, they give no thought to work. Social scientists call this *role compartmentalization*—**separating one's various roles within the mind so that the worries associated with one role (such as work) don't disturb one's feelings and performance in the other role (such as home).**

Such a strategy would seem to be achievable if you view it as an attempt to achieve the goal of "work-life balance," a notion that has gained currency in some organizations (Friedman et al. 1998). Still, it obviously takes a certain amount of mental discipline to avoid the effect of work spillover—all the worries about job and career that remain in our thoughts while at home (Small and Riley 1990). Perhaps married couples without children and without demanding, high-pressure careers are more easily able to achieve this kind of mental compartmentalization.

Strategy #2: Use Positive Self-Talk to Replace Negative Thoughts

This strategy too attempts to use the mind to alter the *perception* of the situation rather than to change any objective realities. ***Positive self-talk* consists**

of giving yourself positive messages so that you can view a situation in beneficial terms. Thus, if you are one-half of a dual-career couple, you can say that the extra hours you put into your career enable you to afford a better life than you would otherwise have. Or that the work gives you a wider view of the world and makes you a better intellectual and conversational companion for your partner. Or that your home life gives you a better appreciation for the kinds of problems faced by co-workers and makes you a better manager of the people you supervise.

Strategy #3: Develop Good Time-Management & Task-Delegation Skills

Some working spouses are as effective at employing management skills for their households as they are for their jobs. They set goals. They keep a master calendar, showing recurring events, such as music lessons or orthodontist appointments. To this they add unusual events, such as birthdays, parent-teacher meetings, doctor's appointments, and the like. Along with the master calendar—whether it is a wall calendar next to the kitchen phone, a pocket week-at-a-glance diary, or a PDA (personal digital assistant)—these individuals maintain a daily to-do list. "Back-to-school nights, mother-daughter things, and other family commitments are on the calendar just like client meetings," says DeAnne Aguirre, a partner at consulting firm Booz Allen Hamilton, "so that I can do them from home and minimize my commuting time" (quoted in Nusbaum 2002: 14).

In a two-earner family, partners agree on who will do which tasks, such as picking up a child at daycare or dropping off the car for servicing. Sometimes, children are assigned to do chores such as yard work, dishwashing, or dog walking. Some dual-income couples hire extra help, such as gardeners or house-cleaning services. Finally, some households in which both partners are working outside the home simply take a more tolerant attitude toward the standards of domesticity; they are less fastidious about the amount of dusting and vacuuming required or the absence of weeds from flowerbeds and lawns.

Strategy #4: Employ Customized Work Arrangements

Depending on the level of one's education and income, support from the spouse, sympathetic employers, and similar variables, different kinds of work/family arrangements might be tried.

Parents Work Alternate Shifts

Flight attendant Kim Murphy, married and the mother of a 9-year-old son, had enough seniority that she was able to work a schedule in which she flew from Virginia to Europe every weekend. This allowed her to be home with her son much of the week while her husband worked (Swoboda 2000).

Murphy is like many millions of partners in two-income families who face the need to work different hours in an effort to balance the pressures of work and child care. Indeed, a survey of 765 women age 18 and older by the Work-

PERSONAL ASSISTANT. While this father reads a message from work on his personal digital assistant (PDA), he is also acting as the personal daddy assistant to his infant. How do you think he and others who balance home and work reduce their role disruptions? ▲

ing Women's Department of the AFL-CIO (cited in Swoboda 2000) showed that 46% of all women who are married or living with someone work a different schedule than their partners do. In addition, 51% of married women with young children work different hours from their husbands. Finally, the survey showed that one of four working women work at least part of their hours in the evening or on the weekend. This is especially true of women in low-wage jobs, with annual incomes of less than $25,000.

As you might expect, working alternate shifts, such as Mom working during the day while Dad works at night, not only can lead to fatigue and sleep deprivation but also can have a negative effect on a spousal relationship.

One Parent Is Self-Employed

Some college graduates, encountering dismal job prospects, start their own businesses instead, becoming entrepreneurs or hiring themselves out as contract workers. Other people become self-employed because they are hoping for a better work-life balance (Armour 2002).

For example, Ernie Ting, a single father in Oakland, California, was able to take a morning off from his telecommunications consulting business to attend his daughter's end-of-school picnic (where he was assigned to give manicures to the girls). Ting had voluntarily resigned from a full-time government job to become a self-employed consultant, partly to have more time during the day for his children (DeBare 1998a).

One woman resigned from an unsatisfying executive position to start her own real-estate management business. She found herself working hard but felt in control of her life again, happier than she had ever been. She also noticed an unexpected benefit: Her daughter, age 5, used to be very unhappy at school but now was going to school "skipping and singing." The probable reason? Because the child's mother feels better about her work and her life, she is better able to hear and observe her child (Shellenbarger 1996b). Indeed, one study has found fewer behavioral problems in children whose parents have control over how, where, and when their work gets done (Friedman and Greenhaus 2000).

One or Both Partners Use a Flexible Workplace Program

Employers have begun to recognize the idea of a so-called *flexible workplace* as a way of recruiting, retaining, and motivating employees. Among the alternative types of work schedules available are the following:

■ **Part-Time Work—Less than 40 Hours:** Part-time workers work less than the standard 40-hour workweek. Some temporary workers and contingency workers would like to work 40 hours or more but can't find full-time jobs. Others, however, work part time by choice to have more time with their families. And there are some professional women, such as some lawyers, who take part-time work to escape the fatigue and isolation of intensive parenting and to maintain power in their marital relationship. "Part-time work," says a study of these individuals, "allows them to keep some control over their financial resources, social networks, and professional identities" (Epstein et al. 2003: 348).

■ **Flextime—Flexible Working Hours:** *Flextime,* or *flexible time,* **consists of flexible working hours or any schedule that gives one some choices in working hours.** For example, if an organization's normal working hours are 9:00 A.M. to 5:00 P.M., a flextime worker might be allowed to start and finish an hour earlier or an hour later—that is, to work from 8:00 A.M. to 4:00 P.M. The main requirement is that the employee be at work during certain core hours so as to be available for meetings, consultations, and so on.

■ **Compressed Workweek—40 Hours in Four Days:** **In a *compressed workweek,* employees perform a full-time job in less than five days of standard 8- (or 9-) hour shifts, such as four days of 10 hours each.** In this arrangement, employees get three instead of two consecutive days off.

■ **Job Sharing—Two Co-Workers Split the Same Job:** **In *job sharing,* two co-workers divide one full-time job.** Usually, each person works half a day, although there can be other arrangements (working alternate days or alternate weeks, for example). The disadvantage of job sharing from the employer's point of view is that it can result in communication problems with co-workers or customers. Job sharers can divide duties by clients, by functions, or in some other way, but it's important that their work styles mesh. It's also important for them to keep a running notebook that logs events throughout the day.

■ **Telecommuting and Other Work-at-Home Schedules:** As we mentioned earlier, *telecommuting* is working at home while in telecommunication contact—by Internet, phone, and fax—with the office. Analee Edwards, a quality consultant for Hewlett-Packard in Palo Alto, California, advises against mix-

TELECOMMUTER. The presence of information technology—computer, the Internet, phone, and fax machine—allows all kinds of people to work at home and telecommute with the office. Some people like working from home, but others miss the social interaction of the office. Which kind of worker do you think you would be? ◀

ing work life with personal life. On the two days that she telecommutes each week, she doesn't do laundry or chat with friends. The company encourages its telecommuters to write down project plans and completion dates, which keeps telecommuters on track and reassures managers that real work is being done (Flynn 1997: J2).

If you want a new work-life arrangement—especially in a tough job market—you should try to sell the organization on the business purpose, not the personal reasons, suggests Lisa Williams, human resources director for Fireman's Fund Insurance Company in San Francisco (Flynn 1997: J1). For example, you could present a convincing case that telecommuting from home two days a week will help you get more done or that working 10-hour days on a compressed schedule will expand customer-service hours.

Some employers evidently use work-life programs as incentives for the best employees—that is, they believe that such benefits shouldn't be handed out unless they are earned. Others think that this is the wrong approach, pointing out that some employees might be low performers precisely because they lack balance between their work and personal lives (Kleiman 2000).

Strategy #5: Take Other Forms of Time Off

The foregoing kinds of flexible work revolve around set schedules, which employers like because they are predictable. However, some employers are more flexible—or employees simply take time off any way they can to help their children. Indeed, flexibility policies are less popular and less frequently used than family care policies used on an as-needed basis (Blair-Loy and Wharton 2002).

Some examples of taking time off are as follows.

Take Unpaid Time Off

Some forms of time off are permitted by law, although they are unpaid. **The *Family and Medical Leave Act (FMLA)* requires U.S. companies that employ 50 or more workers to provide up to 12 weeks of unpaid leave a year to employees with a newborn or newly adopted child, serious personal illness, or a seriously ill family member.**

For example, Amy Calhoun, a California mortgage company supervisor, used an FMLA leave to fly to Utah when her father suffered a brain aneurysm. Another Californian, Scott Jones, a Federal Express account executive, took 12 weeks off to care for his baby daughter—right after his wife finished her leave, so that the baby wouldn't have to be in daycare until she was 6 months old (DeBare 1998b).

Take Personal Time Off

Many single parents find that they simply have to take personal time for family responsibilities. "At some companies, you'll get raised eyebrows when you leave early for a parent-teacher meeting," said Jim Lindsay, a computer programmer at Extensity, a company in Emeryville, California. "But this place is real good. There are no eyebrows raised. The attitude is, 'OK, as long as you get your work done'" (quoted in DeBare 1998a).

Use Sick Days for Family Reasons

More workers are now taking sick days for family and personal reasons rather than illness, according to a survey by business information publisher CCH Inc. (cited in Geller 2002). That is, more workers are calling in absent because of family issues, stress, and personal needs. Only a third of unscheduled days off are taken because of illness.

Take Children to Work

Taking children to work might seem a real act of desperation, but parents do it all the time. James Morando, a commercial litigator in a San Francisco law firm, is also a divorced father whose two young daughters live with him half the time. His computer calendar contains client meetings, filing deadlines, and settlement conferences—and his children's schedules. Sometimes, he brings his daughters to work. In fact, he has taken them to court with him when they have been mildly sick (DeBare 1998a).

Strategy #6: Scale Down Your Career— At Least for a While

Obviously, there are a great many parents, whether single or partnered, who can't afford *not* to work. But some people—those in higher-income families— do have the choice. Kristin Mascha of Pasadena, California, for instance, planned for both children and a high-powered career but was laid off when the 2000s dot.com bubble burst. When she then gave birth to a child, she and her husband, a lawyer, decided that they could afford to live on one salary. Mascha rejects the working mother/stay-at-home mother division. "I anticipate wearing many labels," she says. "In a few years, I may be a working mom." Any particular day "is just a snapshot of where I am" (quoted in Peterson 2003). However, one study of 100 similar people in high-powered, two-career couples who were engaged in scaling back found that it was wives, not husbands, who disproportionately did the scaling back (Becker and Moen 1999).

For many couples, when one partner stops working, the first concern is usually reducing expenses—slashing 30% from their budget, or clipping coupons, canceling cable TV, or joining a wholesale club. But some also worry that by working less, they will sidetrack their careers. However, one two-year study of 87 corporate professionals and managers found that scaled-back work weeks slowed down employees' careers but didn't stop them (MacDermid et al. 2001). In fact, about 35% were actually promoted after they started working less. Critical to success is that the professionals who were studied had supervisors who fully supported them.

One person in the study was Sue Halliday, director of finance for a vendor of medication delivery products, who shared her job with another woman, which enabled Halliday to work three days one week and four the next, giving her time to raise her children. Halliday says that she was supported by the company CEO, who was "very open about not losing out on talent in the marketplace" (Halliday, quoted in Kleiman 1999).

A Final Word: The Effects on Children of Mothers Working Are Not Purely Negative

Many people assume that children are affected only negatively when both their parents—especially their mothers—work outside the home. In fact, children get some benefits from having working mothers. Often, of course, the family has more money to obtain the goods, services, and entertainment/recreation that everyone wants. In addition, the children learn a greater degree of independence. Finally, daughters have good female role models, especially since—unless the economy changes dramatically—they will probably also have to work outside the home when they have families.

Susan Chira, author of *A Mother's Place: Taking the Debate about Working Mothers beyond Guilt and Blame,* maintains that it's not whether a mother works in the home or in the labor force but the kind of mother she is that matters. The main issue, she writes, "is whether or not she is sensitive to her child." Chira discusses ways in which society and the government can enhance support systems for families, including subsidized child care, welfare reform, and more flexible employment arrangements. She encourages us to focus on "true hallmarks of motherly love": an unwavering commitment to the children, a sense of responsibility (that often includes breadwinning), and emotional sensitivity. Her final hope is that "no mother should curb her dreams—whether to be at home or at work—out of baseless fear or guilt" (Chira 1998).

A study in the journal *Developmental Psychology* concludes that the negative effects on children aren't very great. Elizabeth Harvey, a psychology professor at the University of Massachusetts at Amherst, analyzed data from the long-running National Longitudinal Survey of Youth (NLSY), conducted by the U.S. Department of Labor, to determine how parental employment affects children's academic achievement, behavior, and emotional development. She found that having parents who work has both positive and negative effects on children that counteract each other. The effects overall, however, are small (Jacobson 1999).

Harvey's research shows that working more hours may have greater benefits for children in low-income families than for those in families with higher incomes. She concludes that the income that working parents bring home has positive effects on children's behavior and academic achievement. Although her study did not take into account the quality of the child-care settings in which children spend time while their mothers are at work, that question has been the subject of ongoing research sponsored by the National Institute of Child Health and Human Development (2007). The federally funded study has shown that the quality of child care matters much more than whether or not a mother is working outside the home (Jacobson 1999).

Self-Assessment: How Well Do You Balance Work & Life?

People face many conflicts among self, work, family, and community demands. This self-assessment enables you to quickly determine how well you are balancing work and private life, including family, and to figure out how you might make changes. Now and then it's helpful to take a step back and analyze what we're doing and why.

To do this self-assessment, go to "How Well Are You Balancing Work and Family?" at *www.fhahelps.com/ employresources/tools_balancing.html.*

Source: Frank Horton Associates, workplace consulting and counseling services and Employee Assistance Program (EPA) services.

Key Terms Used in This Chapter

Summary

12.1 Work, Wealth, & Well-Being

- Money is relevant to marriage and intimate relationships through its power to increase security, power, love, and freedom (or its power to decrease them through its lack).

- Before the industrialization of society, the family household was the major economic unit; work and family were almost the same thing.

- The Industrial Revolution in England in the late 1700s dramatically changed the nature of the family. Instead of working out of the home and selling what one produced, many family members became part of the labor force as wage earners who hired out their labor to someone else.

- As a result of the industrialization, workers were expected to work long hours to meet the demands of production. These expectations lead to abuse of the workforce, and labor unions emerged to fight for better working conditions. As a result of these early union efforts, the number of hours employees worked was significantly reduced.

- As a consequence of the Great Depression of the 1930s, a more rigid work ethic evolved. Lost in this

process was the idea that people should work fewer hours and enjoy more leisure, time not taken up by work in which to engage in freely chosen satisfying activities.

- In the 1990s, information technology also significantly affected the nature of work. Things like fax machines, home computers, email, pagers, and cell phones have make further inroads into leisure time. Today, many people are engaged in telecommuting, or working at home while in contact with the office via Internet, phone, and fax.

- In many parts of the industrialized world, states offer noncash benefits to workers; however, in the United States, most noncash benefits are offered by employers. When the economy slows, these benefits are often cut, leaving many people without health insurance, for example.

- In the study of social class and stratification, social scientists distinguish between income and wealth. Income is the amount of money a household receives from various sources during a given period of time. Median income refers to the income midpoint of a population: half earn more, half earn less. Wealth, also called net worth, is the monetary value of everything one owns, such as property, stocks, and insurance minus debts. In the United States, 10% of the wealthiest people control 86% of U.S. wealth. Unlike income, wealth can be passed along to heirs, who can use that wealth to accumulate even more.

- Sociologists view society as comprising social classes based on income and wealth. Gilbert and Kahl developed a six-class model: (1) the capitalist class (1%—incomes of $1,000,000-plus and great wealth), (2) the upper middle class (15%—incomes of $125,000-plus), (3) the lower middle class (34%—incomes of about $60,000), (4) the working class (30%—incomes of about $35,000), (5) the working poor, 16%—incomes of about $17,000, and (6) the underclass, 4%—incomes of under $10,000.

- The more affluent social classes benefited greatly from the economic expansion of the last quarter of the 20th century. Yet this economic expansion has not helped everyone. Inflation, the decline in purchasing power, and a two-tier labor market have resulted in the lower half of society falling behind financially, and the gap between the net worth of white families and minority families has widened.

- The poverty line, established in 1959, is officially defined as the minimum level of income the U.S. government considers necessary for individual and family subsistence. The poverty line is income measured before income and payroll taxes and does not include cash and noncash benefits such as food stamps, housing support, and medical subsidies. Poverty rates vary by race and ethnicity, being significantly greater among nonwhites and among women and children.

- The feminization of poverty denotes the likelihood that female heads of households will be poor, owing to job and wage discrimination, high divorce rates, and births to unmarried women. Also, women in the workforce must contend with the glass ceiling and the mommy track, obstacles that mend do not face.

- Some of the consequences of being poor include greater exposure to environmental toxins; poor diets; higher rates of chronic disease, higher mortality rates; higher homicide, imprisonment, and mental-hospital admission rates; and the loss or lack of insurance.

- Welfare or government aid for those who can't support themselves, such as the unemployed, the disabled, and the poor, is no longer popular. Recently, there has been considerable antagonism toward the idea of this type of public assistance, and new laws have reduced the benefits that are provided.

12.2 Changing Family Work Patterns

- Economic and social forces have influenced the nature and composition of the family. These influences shape the roles expected and performed by men and women in intimate relationships. Today, it is best for a couple to discuss in advance of marriage or live-in arrangements such matters as whose job comes first and who stays home with the children.

- In the past, most families adhered to stereotypic sex roles. This is the family form known as the two-person single career, in which the husband works outside the home and the wife, even if she is also employed, helps the husband's career by being responsible for domestic tasks and child rearing. This traditional view of the family views men as the good provider and emphasizes that the man is the principal or sole economic provider for the family. The traditional view of women sees them as homemakers. This homemaker role emphasizes that the woman should be principally responsible for housework, child raising, and maintaining family ties to parents and in-laws.

- A newer family form has emerged that reverses the role of the wife as homemaker. Instead, the man is a househusband, also known as a stay-at-home dad, and is a full-time homemaker.

- Changes in the economy have put extreme pressure on the purchasing power of families; thus, the one-paycheck family model often no longer works. The result is a significant rise in co-provider marriages, also known as dual-earner marriages, in which both married partners are employed outside the home.

- Some working mothers are "captives"—they'd rather be homemakers but work because they have to. Others are "conflicted"—they want to work but they quit if the job conflicts with family needs. Still others are "copers"—they work jobs that are flexible enough to allow them to deal with family demands. However, copers often are disadvantaged by the "mommy track." The last group of working mothers is the "committed"—they are committed to both career and family. These women are often held back on the job, however, by the "glass ceiling."

12.3 Balancing Work & Family Demands: Some Practical Strategies

- Family and career both involve the performance of various roles. At times, role expectations can be very stressful and can result in role conflict, role overload, and role ambiguity.

- Role conflict occurs when the expectations of two or more roles are incompatible.

- Role overload occurs when others' expectations exceeds one's ability to meet them.
- Role ambiguity involves unclear or unknown expectations of other people. When you don't know what others expect of you, either because they don't have the necessary information or because they deliberately withhold it from you, you are experiencing role ambiguity.
- People handle role disruptions in a variety of ways as they attempt to juggle work and family demands.
- Role compartmentalization involves separating one's various roles within the mind so that the worries associated with one role (such as work) don't disturb one's feelings and performance in another role (such as home).
- Like role compartmentalization, positive self-talk attempts to use the mind to alter the perception of the situation rather than to change any objective realities; positive self-talk consists of giving yourself positive messages so that you can view a situation in beneficial terms.
- Time-management and task-delegation skills are also beneficial in handling the various expectations and responsibilities of maintaining a household and a career.
- Many families are able to employ customized work arrangements including parents working alternate shifts; one parent being self-employed and thereby having more control over schedules and time; and one or both parents using a flexible workplace program such as part-time work, flextime, a compressed workweek, job sharing, and/or telecommuting.
- Many individuals have the option of taking time off to handle various family responsibilities. Some examples are taking unpaid time off, taking personal time off, using sick days for family reasons, and, where it is allowed, taking children to work.
- Scaling down one's career—perhaps temporarily—may also be another option for working couples who can afford to take a reduction in income.
- Although many people assume that it is bad for children to have two working parents—especially a working mother—studies show that advantages do exist. The family has more money for the goods, services, and entertainment/recreation that everyone in the family wants; the children can learn a greater degree of independence; and daughters have good role models for the time when they also may have to work outside the home to help support a family. Some studies show that higher income has a positive effect on children's behavior and academic achievement. In any case, the quality of any child-care arrangements made by working parents is critical to their children's well-being.

Take It to the Net

Among the Internet resources on work, money, and family matters are the following:

- **The Couple's Guide to Love & Money.** Offers a guide to your "money personality."
  www.moneyworkbook.com/
- **Daycare.com** A resource for parents and daycare providers.
  www.daycare.com
- **Family & Home Network.** Formerly Mothers at Home, this website also offers support to women who favor parenting over working.
  www.familyandhome.org
- **Mothers & More.** Offers support to mothers making all kinds of life choices.
  www.mothersandmore.org
- **myGoals.com.** A personalized service that translates your goal into a personal plan: career goals, time management, health and fitness, and so on.
  www.mygoals.com
- **The Relate Institute.** Helps couples to assess their values.
  http://relate.byu.edu

CHAPTER 13

CRISES

Managing Stress, Disaster, Violence, & Abuse

Crises: A Way of Life?

*"**I could hardly breathe.** Gulping for air, I started crying and yelling at him, 'What do you mean? What are you saying? Why did you lie to me?'*

"I was furious and getting more so by the second. He just stood there saying over and over again, 'I'm sorry. I'm so sorry.' . . . I couldn't believe he would do anything to endanger our marriage and our family. I was dumbfounded, heartbroken, and outraged that I'd believed him at all. . . .

"He had betrayed the trust in our marriage, and we both knew it might be an irreparable breach. And he had to tell [our daughter] that he had lied to her too. These were terrible moments for all of us. I didn't know whether our marriage could—or should—survive such a stinging betrayal, but I knew I had to work through my feelings carefully, on my own timetable. . . . This was the most devastating, shocking, and hurtful experience of my life. I could not figure out what to do, but I knew I had to find a calm place in my heart and mind to sort out my feelings."

Thus Hillary Rodham Clinton (2003: 34, 36) describes her reactions when her husband, President Bill Clinton, in July 1998, admitted to her his affair with White House intern Monica Lewinsky. The crisis, Hillary Clinton wrote later, nearly ended their marriage. For days afterward, she said, "I wasn't ready to be in the same room with him, let alone forgive him. I would have to go deep inside myself and my faith to discover any remaining belief in our marriage, to find some path to understanding" (p. 37). Eventually, Clinton was able to forgive her husband, but, she said, "it

WHAT'S AHEAD IN THIS CHAPTER

We first distinguish among stresses, hassles, and crises. We then consider some predictable crises of family life and then some unpredictable crises. Next we describe various aspects of intimate and family violence and abuse. Finally, we discuss steps you can take to alleviate the stresses in your life.

took a long time" to let go of her anger and disappointment. Marital counseling helped her decide that she wanted to preserve her marriage (Peterson 2003).

■ *Family crises in the media:* Although they are not always this disturbing, crises and stresses are ongoing features of family life—indeed, of life in general. Movies, drama, and novels, as we pointed out in Chapter 6, "Communication," depend on conflict and crises to create a plot—a tension between two opposing forces—and then to move the story action forward toward a resolution. But the crises that are portrayed in mass media fiction are usually resolved unambiguously.

In the 1987 movie *Fatal Attraction,* for instance, a happily married man (played by Michael Douglas) has a brief affair with a sexy woman (Glenn Close) who turns out to be psychotic and makes his and his family's life a living hell. However, the movie concludes with "a finale more appropriate to *Rambo,*" as one reviewer describes it (Maltin 1999: 436). He points out that the original ending was more subtle and intriguing but was dumped after an unsuccessful preview.

Even when a movie is adapted from a nonfiction account, nuances go by the board. The 1992 Nick Nolte/Susan Sarandon film *Lorenzo's Oil* is based on a true story about a couple who learned that their son had an incurable degenerative disease (adrenoleukodystrophy), then began their own intensive research efforts for a cure that ultimately prolonged their son's life. The film received favorable reviews in the lay press, but reviews in medical journals focused on factual inaccuracies (Jones 2000).

Some works of fiction, however, give us deeper understanding of family crises. Eugene O'Neill's 1940 masterpiece *Long Day's Journey Into Night* (made into a movie in 1962, revived as a Broadway play in 2003) portrays a sickly adult son, another alcoholic son, a drug-addicted mother, and a pompous father as they interact with one another.

■ *Do people imitate the movies?* Whether or not the mass media portray family problems and violence accurately, they do sometimes seem to inspire people to take action. The night NBC aired its 1984 TV movie *The Burning Bed,* a story about a battered wife who sets her husband on fire one night after living with his beatings and humiliations for years, battered-spouse centers were overwhelmed with calls from women wanting to extricate themselves from abusive mates. On the negative side, one man set his wife on fire, and another beat his wife senseless; both claimed to have been inspired by *The Burning Bed* (Vivian 2001: 373–374).

What factors affect stress?

What are some major crisis events I might have to face?

What kinds of abuse are couples and families capable of?

What factors affect stress, and how can I handle it?

◉ ON THE WEB Dealing with the Ultimate Crisis

www.jedfoundation.org

One of the greatest crises an individual or family can face is the prospect of suicide, whether contemplated by oneself or by a friend or family member. The Jed Foundation is a nonprofit public charity that is committed to reducing the young adult suicide rate and improving mental health support provided to college students nationwide. To begin to explore this subject, go to the foundation's website.

13.1 Stresses, Hassles, & Crises: Seeking Hardiness

MAJOR QUESTION What factors affect stress?

PREVIEW We discuss stress and types of stressors—hassles versus crises. We also describe what influences psychological stress reactions: (1) the number, kind, and magnitude of stressors; (2) your emotional predisposition and self-esteem; and (3) your resilience. Finally, we consider hardiness.

Two years after Kay Bartlett (1990) suffered a neck injury from a fall in her kitchen, she wrote that pain had become her constant companion. Pain, she stated, "regulates nearly every moment of my waking life, holding me captive to its savage dictates." Indeed, she said, "Pain has changed my life, narrowing it as old age will eventually do. But, at 49, I'm not old enough to be this old. I feel like the last two years I have aged 30."

How well do you think you would cope with such a terrible event? For Bartlett, chronic pain clearly generated significant stress that dramatically changed her life.

Stress & Stressors

Stress **is the reaction of our minds and bodies to an unusual or substantial demand made on it.** Stress has both physical and emotional components. Physical reactions to stress may be tense muscles, high blood pressure, perspiration, tension headaches, intestinal distress, and the like. Emotional reactions to stress are nervousness and anxiety, emotional and mental exhaustion, and even violence.

Types of Stressors: Hassles versus Crises

Stresses are triggered by *stressors*, **precipitating events that cause the stress.** Stressors range from hassles to crises.

■ Hassles: *Hassles* **are simply frustrating irritants,** but their cumulative effect can be significant and even hazardous to health. For instance, college

- **Do spouses often cheat on each other?** One study of a national sample of U.S. adults found that 23% of husbands and 12% of wives said that they had had sex with someone else sometime during their marriage.[a]

- **How prevalent is alcohol and drug addiction?** According to one study, 1 in 12 full-time U.S. workers has illicit drug or alcohol abuse problems serious enough to require treatment.[b]

- **Do people who attempt suicide ultimately succeed at it?** About one-third of people who survive a suicide attempt eventually do kill themselves.[c]

- **How often does abuse happen in a dating relationship?** One study of daters age 30 and under found that nearly a third had either inflicted or suffered physical vio- lence in their relationships within the preceding year.[d]

- **Is violence the same among gay partners as straights?** Violence occurs in 11% to over 45% of gay and lesbian relationships, and the dynamics are similar to those in abusive straight relationships, with alcohol, drugs, and jealousy often major factors.[e]

- **How prevalent is sexual abuse?** One national study found that 27% of the women and 16% of the men surveyed had been sexually abused as children.[f] Another found that 12% of adult women reported that as children they had had physical sexual contact with an adult.[g]

[a]Wiederman 1997. [b]Larson et al. 2007. [c]Blumenthal and Kupfer 1986. [d]Lloyd 1995. [e]Renzetti 1995; Kurdek 1994, 1998. [f]Finkelhor et al. 1990. [g]Browning and Laumann 1998.

students are most hassled by anxiety over wasting time, pressure to meet high standards, and feeling lonely, says psychologist Richard Lazarus (1981).

Lazarus also says that nearly everyone, regardless of age, complains about three kinds of hassles: misplacing or losing things, physical appearance, and having too many things to do.

- **Crises:** **A *crisis* is an especially strong source of stress, a crucial change in the course of events that requires changes in people's normal patterns of behavior.** For instance, it could be a seemingly normal life event, such as pregnancy, childbirth, job change, or retirement. Or it could be an untoward event such as an auto accident, a physical illness, unemployment, an act of infidelity, a death in the family, or drug abuse. Kay Bartlett, described on the previous page, clearly was affected by a crisis. Severe and chronic emotional stress can age people biologically (Epel et al. 2004).

Psychological Stress Reactions

How you respond psychologically to stress is an individual matter and is influenced by, among other things, (1) the number, kind, and magnitude of stressors in your life; (2) your emotional predisposition and self-esteem; and (3) your resilience. It also depends on your coping resources, as we describe later in this chapter.

1. Number, Kind, & Magnitude of Stressors in Your Life

We have said that too many negative stresses can make a person ill. Working from this proposition, in the early 1960s, physicians Thomas Holmes and Richard Rahe (1967) devised a "future illness" scale and tried it out on several medical students. The scale, known as the Holmes-Rahe Life Events Scale or the Social Readjustment Rating Scale, identifies certain stressors (life events), both positive and negative examples that range from (at the most stressful end) death of a spouse, divorce, a jail term, marriage, and sex difficulties to (at the least stressful end) a change in sleeping habits, vacation, Christmas, and minor violations of the law. By adding up the values assigned to the stressful events they have encountered in the past year, people can see how much adapting they had had to do and what the implications are for their health. (A variation on the scale, "Major Life Events & Stress," is presented as a Self-Assessment at the end of this chapter.)

2. Your Emotional Predisposition & Self-Esteem

Emotional predisposition—your intensity of feeling—can influence how you perceive stressors and react to stress. Often, because the source of the stress is other people, your reactions can depend in part on *how you feel about yourself in relation to other people*—that is, your level of self-esteem.

Emotional predisposition and level of self-esteem are, at least in part, learned behavior. If, in the past, you learned from parents or others that expressing anger is "impolite" or "bad" or you are unable to direct anger toward its source for fear of being criticized, you might turn your anger inward. Lacking the self-esteem to direct the anger appropriately, you might express it in unhealthy ways: (1) by attempting to ease the stress with alcohol, drugs, binge eating, or similar escapist activities or (2) by overreacting to the stress with expressions of fly-off-the-handle rage and even violence.

3. Your Resilience

How did life stresses affect you as a child? That depends on the *vulnerabilities* to which you were exposed and your *resilience*. **Vulnerability refers to psychological or environmental difficulties that make children more at risk for developing later personality, behavioral, or social problems.** A study that followed 600 children growing up in rural Hawaii from birth to almost age 20 (Werner 1989) found that such life stressors as lower-class social environment and parents' mental and financial difficulties left a third of the children with behavioral or learning problems.

However, the other two-thirds of the children showed resilience, or stress resistance, and became competent, independent adults. **Resilience is defined as various personal, family, or environmental factors that compensate for increased life stresses so that expected problems do not develop** (Plotnik 1999: 394). Among the factors that contribute to resilience are these:

■ **Positive Temperament:** Resilient children seem to be born with a genetic inclination toward being socially responsive to their caregivers, so they receive more attention.

■ **Substitute Caregiver:** Resilient children have a loving caregiver or mentor whose social skills they can imitate and who can substitute for an indifferent parent.

MAJOR CRISIS. Leslie Gil of Tennessee grieves over a memorial representing her son Pedro Espaipilat Jr., age 20, who died in Iraq. The memorial in New York City, which coincided with the 2004 Republican Convention, included a pair of boots for every U.S. soldier killed in Iraq. The death of a family member or close friend is considered to be among the most stressful of the life stressors that can happen to people. What other life events would you find to be the most stressful? ◀

■ **Social Support:** Resilient children received support and trust from caregivers and other children and learned positive social skills.

Toward Becoming a Hardy Person

Resilience is found in some children; hardiness is found in some adults. According to psychologist Suzanne Kobasa, *hardiness* **is a combination of three personality traits—commitment, control, and challenge—that protect us from the potentially harmful effects of stressful situations and reduce our chances of developing illness** (Kobasa 1979; Kobasa et al. 1982):

■ **Commitment:** People who are *committed* have high self-esteem, enthusiasm, and a sense of purpose in their lives.

■ **Control:** People who have the belief that they can control or influence events in their lives accept responsibility for their actions and make changes in harmful behaviors.

■ **Challenge:** Hardy people perceive changes in life as *challenges,* or as stimulating opportunities for personal growth, rather than as threats. Hardy people, in other words, are optimists, not pessimists, and optimistic people are less likely to die of heart disease and other causes, some research shows (Giltay et al. 2004).

As an example of challenge, a hardy person will see the breakup of a relationship less as a sad event than as the end of a chapter in which he or she has learned lessons that will be applicable to the next relationship. Could this be your point of view as well?

13.2 Crises & Disasters

MAJOR QUESTION What are some major crisis events I might have to face?

PREVIEW Stressors may be internal or external. The four phases of the family life cycle produce somewhat predictable stressors. Some unpredictable stressors are unemployment, infidelity, alcohol and drug abuse, mental disorders, physical disability and illness, and death.

Malik Miah, age 51, and his wife borrowed $50,000 to remodel their house in South San Francisco. A few months later, under a new cost-cutting contract with his employer, Miah's pay fell 13%; he now had to pay his own medical premiums, which were $120 a month, and he worried that his job as an airline mechanic might be outsourced to a private company. A diabetic whose left foot had been amputated, Miah would have difficulty finding another job that would pay as well. His wife, a nurse who has had breast cancer, could find herself in a similar bind (Arndt 2003).

Are these the kind of stresses that are just normal bumps in the road of life? Or are these extraordinary events of the kind that ask us to draw on extra resources to survive?

Types of Stressor Events: Internal versus External

With all the stressors that can afflict us, how can we make sense of them? Sociologist Pauline Boss (1988: 40) has distinguished between *internal* and *external* stressor events:

■ **Internal Stressors:** *Internal stressors* **are those events that begin inside the family.** Examples are those that are expected over the normal family life cycle, events that are sought out, such as a new job, and situations of long duration such as diabetes or chemical addiction.

■ **External Stressors:** *External stressors* **are those that begin with someone or something outside the family.** Examples are earthquakes, terrorism, the inflation rate, cultural attitudes toward women or minorities, unexpected events such as divorce or a lottery win, and severe but short-term events such as the sudden loss of a job. The stress of combat clearly applies here, and it should be no surprise that the percentage of marriages of active-duty Army officers that ended in 2004 were almost four times the number in 2000, the result of the stresses of the Iraq and Afghanistan wars (Zoroya 2005).

For Kay Bartlett, the type of stressor would seem to be an external stressor—an isolated event. By contrast, as we mentioned, many internal stressors occur within the family life cycle, as we discuss next.

Some Predictable Stressors of the Family Life Cycle

As you'll recall from Chapter 8, "Marriage," in a *family life cycle*, members' roles and relationships change, largely depending on how family members have to adapt themselves to the absence or presence of child-rearing responsibilities. Family life, we said, has four phases: (1) beginning, with perhaps greatest marital satisfaction (though a stressful period of adjustment); (2) child rearing, often with less marital satisfaction; (3) middle age, with more marital satisfaction; and (4) aging. Some stressors that are somewhat predictable but that vary with these stages are discussed below (Olson and McCubbin 1983).

1. The Beginning Phase: The Stresses of Newly Marrieds

Some stressors during the beginning phase of a marriage—which might last 2 to 3 years before children come along—are, as we mentioned in Chapter 8, identity bargaining, loss of independence, new friends and relatives, and conflicts over career and domestic roles (Knudson-Martin and Mahoney 1998).

Work and family stresses may be particularly acute as recently wed young couples work out the stresses between their work problems and marital roles (Bolger et al. 1989; Hamilton et al. 1996).

2. The Child-Rearing Phase: Stresses with Children

As we have seen in earlier Chapter 9, the birth of the first child is certainly a stressor even if it is planned, and even more so if it is not planned. Either way, the parents have now embarked on years of child rearing, which can at times severely tax them financially, because of all the expenses that are required to sustain a child, from clothing to college, and psychologically because of disputes over chores and homework, sibling quarrels, and unexpected child illnesses.

Some couples may also find themselves in the *sandwich generation—* **sandwiched between taking care of their children and of their own aging parents** (Harris and Bichler 1997).

3. The Middle-Age Phase: The Empty Nest—Or Not

Recall that we said that, in middle age, some parents feel the *empty-nest syndrome*—some depression and a sense of less well-being after the children have

GOING OFF TO COLLEGE. Parents might feel that a child leaving home, whether to attend college, to marry, or for another reason, is a moderately stressful experience—almost as stressful as being demoted at work. What kind of stressor is this—internal or external? ▲

left home. Conversely, they may experience the *boomerang effect*—their grown children returning to live with them because of high housing costs, low income, or divorce.

Either way, the couple might find themselves stressed by financial problems, sexual difficulties, lower job satisfaction, taking care of elderly parents, and dealing with the deaths of aging friends and relatives. Or they may finally find this a welcome time when they have the house to themselves.

4. The Aging Phase: Stresses of Health & Financial Worries

After 30 or 40 years of marriage, most income earners will be nearing retirement. Some retired couples find themselves well situated financially. Others find themselves worrying about financial matters, since income typically declines by 30 to 50% on retirement (Soldo and Agree 1988). Health is also a concern, since health-care costs are continually going up and health insurance programs generally don't cover the entire amounts. Finally, the aged may have to deal with physical decline, perhaps requiring admission to a nursing home, and the death of a spouse. (We discuss death later in this section.)

Some Unpredictable Stressors

The strains of ordinary living that we just described can seem daunting enough. Perhaps the real tests of life, however, are in meeting the challenges of unexpected crises. Among the more important are (1) unemployment, (2) infidelity, (3) drug and alcohol abuse, (4) mental disorders, (5) physical illness, and (6) death.

1. Unemployment & Underemployment

Perhaps you have been unemployed once or twice. But only if you've been looking for work for six months or more can you really know the unemployed person's feelings of helplessness, self-doubt, and desperation as the bills pile up—and the stress affecting the families (Voydanoff 1991). Even concern about possible loss of a job can create a lot of anxiety, depression, and stress (Larson et al. 1994; Uchitelle 2004).

Who Are the Unemployed?

The U.S. labor force consists of the employed and the unemployed, and the Bureau of Labor Statistics divides the number of unemployed by the number in the labor force to determine the unemployment rate—4.5%, or 6.8 million, nonfarm payroll employees in May 2007 (Bureau of Labor Statistics 2007). In reality, probably more than 70 million adult Americans are not working, but some people are not officially counted among the unemployed (Uchitelle 2004; Walker 2006).

UNEMPLOYMENT. A long line of unemployed people wait outside an office of the State of California Employment Development Department. Families affected by or threatened with unemployment experience deteriorating personal relationships as stress increases. Depression, alcoholism, and family violence also rise under such circumstances. What have you observed regarding the effects of unemployment on family relationships? ◀

■ **Unemployed Workers:** *Unemployed workers* **are those seeking work who are new to the labor force or have been laid off (temporarily dismissed), downsized (permanently dismissed), or fired (dismissed for cause, such as absenteeism).** They may be recent high school graduates, parents who gave up their jobs to have children and who are returning to the workforce, and all those coal miners, dot.com-ers, and the like who lost jobs when their industries or economic conditions changed.

■ **Discouraged Workers:** *Discouraged workers* **are those who have given up looking for work and have simply dropped out of the labor force.** Therefore, they are not "officially" unemployed because they are not actively seeking work. The reasons are many: too old, too young, low skills, or discrimination because of race and ethnicity. What is a recession for whites can be a depression for blacks, whose unemployment rate is more than twice that for whites (U.S. Department of Labor 2007).

■ **Underemployed Workers:** *Underemployed workers* **are those who hold jobs below their level of qualification or are working part time but want to work full time.** They also are not counted as "unemployed." Especially during recessionary times, many college graduates, for instance, may work as sales clerks, receptionists, cab drivers, and the like—dead-end, low-wage positions that certainly don't require a bachelor's degree.

The Stress of Being Unemployed or Underemployed

Being jobless or in financially reduced straits has a number of effects on families:

■ **More Conflict and Problems:** Families that are threatened by unemployment experience deteriorating relationships among spouses and children as arguments increase and communication suffers (Larson et al. 1994; Wilson and Larson 1994; Uchitelle 2004). As family battles heat up, children's psychological and physical health are particularly affected (Voydanoff 1991).

Increases in depression, alcoholism, separation, divorce, infant mortality, suicide, violence against spouses, and homicide are all associated with unemployment, especially if the unemployment lasts beyond a year (Voydanoff 1991; Teachman et al. 1994; Macmillan and Gartner 2000).

■ **Change in Family Roles and Routine:** In some cases, a shared family emergency, such as bankruptcy, brings a couple closer together, and family communication improves (Burr and Klein et al. 1994). In other cases, a job loss affects family roles: Men, whose self-identities are more bound up in their work, might feel that they have lost a part of themselves. Women might need to seek employment and feel that their husbands aren't contributing to household tasks even though they're always around (Rubin 1994; Teachman et al. 1994).

2. Infidelity: Sexual & Emotional Unfaithfulness

Infidelity, **also called extramarital sex, adultery, having an affair, or "cheating," is marital unfaithfulness—usually considered sexual contact outside the marriage or primary relationship.** Unlike extramarital sex in an open marriage (discussed in Chapter 9, "Variations"), the unfaithfulness occurs without the permission or, ordinarily, the knowledge of the partner. According to one study (Wiederman 1997) involving a national sample of U.S. adults, 23% of husbands and 12% of wives admitted having had sex with someone else sometime during their marriage. This, of course, amounts to tens of millions of people.

Infidelity in women may have some evolutionary connection to ovulation, the most fertile part of the menstrual cycle (Haselton and Gangestad 2006). From a psychological and sociological standpoint, however, affairs seem to be principally related to two variables: premarital sexual permissiveness and unhappiness in the marriage (Reiss 1980). People—both men and women—who have a strong need for sex and who have permissive sexual values plus some dissatisfaction with their present relationship (but not enough to seek divorce) are more inclined to seek extramarital relationships (Wiederman and Allgeier 1996; Treas and Giesen 2000).

Extramarital adventures can range from one-night stands to full-fledged affairs that last weeks, months, or even years.

Short-Term Extramarital Involvements

Many short-term affairs begin as a sexual encounter at an office party or an out-of-town meeting, a brief reacquaintance with an old flame, or a tentative fling before an anticipated divorce. For men, the short-term extramarital involvement is often sex without love—sex with a prostitute or a one-night stand. For women, the affair frequently involves love as well as sex (Glass 1998). Men are apt to have an affair for the feeling of conquest and sexual excitement, women because they are angry with their husbands and seek revenge (Grosskopf 1983; Masters et al. 1994).

Long-Term Extramarital Involvements

Famous human sexuality researchers **William Masters and Virginia Johnson,** with their colleague Robert Kolodny (1994), categorized long-term affairs into the following types (among others): *marriage maintenance, intimacy reduction, reactive,* and *hedonistic.*

■ **Marriage Maintenance—"To supply what's missing from my marriage":** ***Marriage maintenance affairs*** **are those that provide something missing from the marriage,** such as unusual sex. Such affairs can sometimes actually help to sustain the marriage.

■ **Intimacy Reduction—"To buffer against too much closeness in my marriage":** ***Intimacy reduction affairs*** **are involvements by a spouse who feels uncomfortable with too much closeness in his or her marriage.**

■ **Reactive—"To reassure me of my sexuality":** ***Reactive affairs*** **are engaged in by partners, such as spouses in middle age, who are seeking reassurance about their youthfulness and sexuality.**

■ **Hedonistic—"Just for the fun and sensuality of it":** ***Hedonistic affairs*** **are acts of playfulness** by partners who are often sexually fulfilled and happy in their own marriages (Cano and O'Leary 1997).

Affairs without Sex

Although most of us think of affairs as involving sex, they can be emotional without being sexual (Thompson 1984). An example is the ***cybersex affair,*** **in which a person has a secret online relationship with someone in an Internet chat room** that drains off emotional energy that would otherwise be devoted to the spouse. Says psychologist and therapist Shirley Glass, two people who meet online in a chat room might "begin to share more about themselves and their fantasies," and "soon they're switching screens when their spouse walks in on them" (Glass, quoted in Wingert 2003). Some Internet or e-mail affairs progress to actual extramarital sex, especially those involving contact with a former lover (Kalish 1997).

Consequences of Extramarital Sex: The End of Trust?

Although a marriage might be held together by an affair (as in marriage maintenance and intimacy reduction), once the affair is revealed to the spouse who has been in the dark, the resulting shock and outrage usually produce a major crisis. An affair, of course, is a spear in the heart of what's central to a marriage: trust and intimacy. Once you have broken your partner's trust, how will you ever be able to prove that you can be trusted again? The offended spouse might forgive, but can complete trust ever be regained? Alternatively, scorned spouses may try to seek revenge by, for instance, trying to damage their mates' careers by contacting their employers (Lublin and Hymowitz 2005).

If you are the victimized spouse, you will probably not only suffer the great pain of the broken commitment but also wonder whether your spouse strayed because you were inadequate, uninteresting, or unattractive (Scarf 1987). You might also worry about whether you are at risk for sexually transmitted diseases and be enraged that some of your joint finances might have been frittered away on romantic dinners, gifts, and trips with somebody else. The damage to the family is even deeper if the children learn of it, particularly if the ultimate result is divorce.

A Loving Marriage Won't Prevent Infidelity

The Lessons of Shirley Glass

His mother, says her son, Ira Glass (2003), was a psychologist, scholar, and therapist known as "the godmother of infidelity research." Shirley P. Glass, Ph.D., wrote a book, *NOT "JUST FRIENDS": Protect Your Relationship from Infidelity and Heal the Trauma of Betrayal* (Glass and Staeheli 2003), and she was quoted regularly in national media and appeared on all sorts of TV interview shows.

"Mom explained her interest in the subject this way," says her son. "Back in the 70's, she and my dad ran into a guy they'd known for years at a restaurant on a Saturday night. He was obviously on a date, cheating on his wife. It just didn't make sense to my mom. She'd always believed the conventional wisdom . . . that only people in unhappy marriages have affairs. This couple's marriage seemed exceptionally good, enviable even. Yet here he was" (I. Glass 2003: 48). It developed that the man had been having sexual flings for decades without his wife's ever knowing.

After this revelation—that is, learning that infidelity could happen in even a loving marriage—Shirley Glass began to do research into the subject of extramarital affairs. What she discovered in her surveys confirmed what she also learned from the hundreds of couples she counseled: when a person is unfaithful, it *does not* necessarily mean that there's a problem in the marriage. In fact, as she reported in her book, over half of the men and a third of the women she surveyed who'd had affairs said that they were happy with their spouses.

Among some of Glass's other findings (Glass and Staeheli 2003):

■ **The workplace is the new meeting place:** The workplace has become "the new danger zone of romantic attraction and opportunity." Many affairs begin at work, starting as peer relationships. From 1991 to 2000, the number of work affairs among unfaithful wives in Glass's clinical practice increased from 38% to 50%. Among men, 62% of unfaithful men met their affair partners at work.

■ **Being a loving partner won't prevent infidelity:** Glass calls this the "Prevention Myth." A happy marriage, according to her research and clinical practice, is not insurance against affairs. Affairs are "less about love and more about sliding across boundaries," she says.

■ **In the "new infidelity," affairs don't have to involve sexual contact.** Some extramarital affairs, such as Internet affairs, are primarily emotional. Indeed, it is a myth, she says, that affairs occur mostly because of sexual attraction. "The lure of an affair is how the unfaithful partner is mirrored back through the adoring eyes of the new love," she says. "Another appeal is that individuals experience new roles and opportunities for growth in new relationships."

■ **A cheating spouse doesn't always leave clues that the faithful spouse could detect:** The conventional wisdom is that clues are there for the naïve spouse to read—if he or she would only choose to notice (Houston 2003). Most affairs are never detected, says Glass, because people are good liars or are able to compartmentalize their lives (as in business travel) so that their spouses never find out. For instance, it's assumed that a person in an affair shows less interest in sex at home, but actually the excitement of an affair can increase passion at home and make sex even more interesting.

■ **If an affair is discovered, talking about it will not necessarily create more upset:** People think that talking about an affair afterward will only create more upset, but Glass says that not discussing the betrayal is "like waxing a dirty floor" and that exploring vulnerabilities can help lead to a more intimate relationship.

■ **Divorcing the old spouse and marrying the conspirator in the affair does not lead to eternal bliss:** Seventy-five percent of all people who marry their affair partners end up divorced, says Glass.

WHAT DO YOU THINK? Do you agree with Glass's findings? What would you do if you found out your partner was having an affair?

3. Drug & Alcohol Abuse

Drugs **are chemical substances other than those required for the maintenance of normal health, such as food.** The kind of drugs that can bring severe stress to a family are legal prescription drugs, legal mind-altering drugs such as alcohol, and illegal mind-altering drugs such as marijuana. Drugs are everywhere, of course. One analysis of 10 million online messages written by teenagers found that they regularly chat about drinking alcohol, smoking marijuana, partying, and hooking up (Simon and Majewski 2007). A study by the Substance Abuse and Mental Health Services Administration (Larson et al. 2007) found that nearly 1 in 12 full-time U.S. workers has illicit drug or alcohol abuse problems serious enough to require treatment. That amounts to 9.4 million illicit drug users and 10.1 million heavy drinkers who hold full-time jobs.

Drug Abuse & Dependency

Drug abuse, **or** *substance abuse,* **is defined as the use of a drug in violation of legal restrictions or for other nonmedical reasons.** *Substance dependence* **differs from substance abuse in that the user becomes biologically dependent on the substance.**

Mind-altering (psychoactive) drugs—both legal and illegal—are classified according to the primary effects they produce.

■ Stimulants: Examples are caffeine and nicotine (mild stimulants), amphetamines and cocaine (major stimulants). Stimulants speed up brain activity, increasing arousal.

■ Depressants: Examples are alcohol, solvents and inhalants, sedativehypnotics, and tranquilizers. Depressants slow down or sedate brain activity.

■ Cannabis: This category includes marijuana and hashish, which produce mild sedation at low doses and hallucinations at high doses.

■ Hallucinogens: These include LSD, mescaline, psilocybin, and phencyclidine (PCP), which produce hallucinations, scrambling of senses, and depersonalization.

■ Opiates: These are narcotics and include opium, morphine, codeine, and heroin. They are sleep-inducing painkillers that produce euphoria.

Other categories are inhalants, such as glue, and designer drugs, such as MDA and Ecstasy. Another type of drug, steroids, which are synthetic hormones used by weight lifters and other athletes to enhance performance, can be responsible for mood changes as well.

Colleges are rife with drug use, with 49% (3.8 million) full-time college students binge drinking or misusing prescription drugs (such as Ritalin, Adderall, Vicodin, or OxyContin) or illegal drugs, according to the National Center on Addiction and Substance Abuse (CASA) at Columbia University (2007). But alcohol and drug use is also widespread in American households, with, for example, seven states in the South and Midwest showing an increase in people who drink alcohol even as drug use is down, according to the Substance Abuse and Mental Health Services Administration (2007). Illegal drug use by teenagers is on the decline, according to a survey by the National Institute of Drug Abuse (Johnston et al. 2006), but teen prescription drug use is soaring, according to CASA. A *USA Today*/HBO nationwide poll (reported in Rubin 2006) found that one in five adults said they had an immediate relative who at some point had been addicted to alcohol or drugs. On a worldwide basis, abuse of prescription drugs—painkillers, stimulants, tranquilizers—will soon exceed the use of illicit street narcotics, according to the International Narcotics Control Board (2007). One final interesting discovery is that, despite the conventional wisdom, substance abuse *does not* decline as people age; research by the Substance Abuse and Mental Health Services Administration (2007) estimates that aging Baby Boomers will actually double the amount of drug abuse by 2020.

Alcohol Abuse

***Alcoholism*, a form of substance dependence, is defined as a chronic, progressive, and potentially fatal disease characterized by a growing compulsion to drink.** Although many people think of alcohol as being separate from drugs, alcohol *is* a drug. In fact, it constitutes North America's (and perhaps the world's) largest drug problem. More than 30% of American adults have abused alcohol or suffered from alcoholism at some point in their lives, and those who get treatment first receive it, on average, at about age 30—eight years after they developed their dependency on drinking (Hasin et al. 2007). Only 24% of alcoholics, however, receive any treatment at all.

In a family, the effects of alcoholism as a stressor can range from almost no effect, especially if it is the wife rather than the husband who is alcoholic (Noel et al. 1991), to abuse and family violence (Coleman and Straus 1983). Even when the abuser is not drinking, the household is apt to be a place of frequent conflict and dissatisfaction (O'Farrell and Birchler 1987; Weinberg and Vogler 1990). Children of both practicing and recovering alcoholics show more insecurity, fear, and anxiety than do other children (Whipple and Noble 1991). When these children get married, they are more apt to experience dissatisfaction and conflict within their marriages (Domenico and Windle 1993).

4. Mental Disorders

Many people aren't very sympathetic to problems of psychological or mental illness because they don't believe that mental difficulties can happen to them. They have, as novelist William Styron (1990: 15) put it, "a smug belief in the impregnability of my psychic health." Styron himself was well along in life when he experienced clinical depression, a disorder that affects 1 out of 20 Americans at some time in their lives, according to practicing psychologists (Robins et al. 1984), although debated by some sociologists.

Depression is one of a great number of ***mental disorders*, defined as psychiatric illness or diseases manifested by breakdowns in the adaptational process and expressed primarily as abnormalities of thought, feeling, and behavior, producing either distress or impairment of function** (Medical Dictionary Search Engine 2007). Mental illness has been linked to shortened lives, probably because of obesity and use of antipsychotic drugs, with mentally ill adults in public systems dying about 25 years earlier than Americans overall, according to one report (by Linda Rosenberg and Joseph Parks, reported in Bender 2007).

Among the many mental disorders, three are the most commonly experienced by Americans: anxiety disorders; alcohol and drug abuse; and mood disorders, such as depression. Having already considered alcohol and drug abuse, let us consider anxiety disorders and mood disorders. We'll also consider eating disorders.

Anxiety Disorders

Anxiety disorders **include four common mental disorders: generalized anxiety disorders, panic attacks, phobias, and obsessive-compulsive disorder.** *Generalized anxiety disorder* consists of excessive or unrealistic worries extending 6 months or more. *Panic attacks* are episodes that are experienced as intense fear or terror. *Phobias* are specific fears associated with particular places, things, or people. *Obsessive-compulsive disorder* is marked by repetitive thought patterns and actions.

Mood Disorders: Depression & Suicide

Mood disorders **are mental disorders usually characterized by periods of depression, sometimes alternating with periods of elevated mood.** The essential feature of these mental disorders, also referred to as *affective disorders,* is persistent or episodic exaggeration of mood state. The term *mood* may include depression, mania, euphoria, elation, anger, irritability, happiness, sadness, and many others (*DSM-IV-TR* 2001). Deep depression, says author Styron (1990: 56), "is a howling tempest in the brain," a daily horror that rolls in "like some poisonous fogbank." Clinical depression generally lasts more than 2 weeks, impairs one's everyday ability to function, and is associated with such symptoms as feelings of worthlessness, loss of energy and motivation, unrelenting fatigue, difficulty concentrating, and thoughts of death and suicide.

About 9.6% of Americans suffer from depression or bipolar disorder, which is the highest rate among 14 nations surveyed, according to one long-term study (Merikangas et al. 2007), perhaps because in some of the other nations (Lebanon, Mexico, Nigeria) with which the United States was compared the life struggle is so severe that people don't have time to "indulge in existential despair" (Stephens 2007). Women are twice as likely as men to experience depression, and, if untreated, mothers with depression are more apt to find that their children are depressed as well (Weissman et al. 2006). Nevertheless, it is often difficult for family members to see the "illness" of such a mental illness, says one observer. "Empathy gets lost with exhaustion from the unending crises associated with the illness" (Hyde 2001: 111).

Eating Disorders: Anorexia & Bulimia

Eating disorders **consist of anorexia, or self-starvation, and bulimia, or binge eating.**

■ **Anorexia Nervosa:** *Anorexia nervosa* **is self-starvation, resulting from a distorted body self-image that leads to the conviction that one is grossly overweight.** The disorder is in response to the cultural emphasis on thinness—indeed, it may be manifested particularly right before spring break, when college students want to become "bikini ready" (Williams 2006). Anorexia typically develops during the teen years or twenties, mostly among

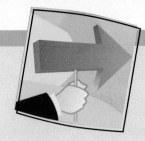

How Do You Know If Someone Is Likely to Attempt Suicide?

There are no dependable patterns that will enable you to predict that someone will try to commit suicide, but here are some considerations:

- **Look for changes in mood and habit:** Be alert to the signs of depression—sadness, hopelessness, helplessness, apathy. In addition, studies of adolescents suggest looking for school problems, antisocial behavior, social isolation, running away, and preoccupation with death (Low and Andrews 1990). Another sign is when a person gives away valued personal possessions. An additional signal might be the occurrence of a suddenly positive outlook on life after a period of severe depression.

- **Look for changes in life events:** People who are experiencing very stressful life events, such as a major loss associated with a death or relationship loss, are at a higher risk for suicide (Low and Andrews 1990).

- **Beware of previous attempts:** A previous suicide attempt is always significant. About one-third of people who survive a suicide attempt eventually do kill themselves (Blumenthal and Kupfer 1986).

- **Talkers may be doers:** If a person talks about suicide, always take it seriously. Don't believe the myth that the people who talk about suicide are not the ones who commit it. Such talk might be about life not being worth living, about the suicide of someone else, or about how others will or will not miss them when they are gone.

- **Warnings versus no warnings:** Usually, people who are contemplating suicide send out warning signals in advance. However, one study (Peterson et al. 1985) found that more than half the people who attempt suicide do so on the spur of the moment; that is, they make a decision less than 24 hours before making the attempt.

women, who make up 94 to 95% of those who are afflicted (Storrow 1984: 407). It is also common among white middle-class and upper-class individuals. A controversial underground movement of "pro-ana," or pro-anorexia, devotees maintain message boards on MySpace, Xanga, and LiveJournal.com that promote the "anorexic lifestyle."

Anorexics are often rigid and perfectionistic (Szabo and Blanche 1997). They might exercise compulsively and force vomiting or use laxatives (drugs that stimulate evacuation of the bowels) or diuretics (drugs that increase the flow of urine). Because anorexics frequently deny their symptoms, there is often powerful resistance to treatment. With therapy, about 70% of patients are improved. Unfortunately, the disease can cause irreversible physiological changes and even be fatal for those who are not able to seek treatment or don't respond to treatment (Hsu 1980, 1988).

■ Bulimia: **Bulimia consists of episodes of binge eating alternating with purging**—that is, repeated attempts to lose weight by self-induced vomiting or use of laxatives or diuretics. Bulimia seems to be more in evidence than anorexia. Estimates run at 2 to 19% among college women—the group at greatest risk—and as high as 5% for men (Halmi et al. 1981; Lustic 1985). Bulimia is found mostly among women in their teens and twenties, although it is also encountered among females in middle age and later.

Like anorexics, bulimics may come from traditional families with "old-fashioned" parents—mothers who don't work outside the home and fathers

"OH, NO!" Physical disability or illness, whether acute or chronic, can put a major strain on a family. If the illness is a long-term disorder, such as Alzheimer's, most families suffer disruption and decline in marital satisfaction. Have you been part of a family that has been affected by the presence of severe illness or disability? How did it affect interaction among family members? ◄

who do and are emotionally distant. Bulimics are inclined to be people-pleasers who do not deal easily with their feelings (Arbetter 1989). Bulimics wait an average of 5½ years before seeking help, and some never seek help, which can be fatal (Johnson 1982).

Clearly, these and other kinds of mental disorders can have a tremendously stressful impact on a family.

5. Physical Disability & Illness

"Everyone who is born holds dual citizenship, in the kingdom of the well and in the kingdom of the sick," states philosopher and critic Susan Sontag (1978: 3). When we are well, it is difficult to understand what it is like to be unwell. When we are sick, it is difficult to avoid self-pity and not to feel that we are stigmatized by the culture.

Physical disorders may be **_acute_, which are of short duration, or _chronic_, which are of long duration or are recurring.** An illness or disability of a few days or weeks can be stressful enough for a family. A long-term disorder, especially one with no cure, such as diabetes, Lou Gehrig's disease (amyotrophic lateral sclerosis, or ALS), or Alzheimer's, can put a tremendous strain on a family. Indeed, one study ranked "Family member becomes physically disabled or chronically ill" as fifth in a list of Family Life Events and Changes or severe family stressors (McCubbin and Patterson 1983: 285–86). Most families suffer disruption and decline in marital satisfaction when a person is chronically ill, although that is not always the case (Hafstrom and Schram 1984). Older people whose sick spouses go to the hospital for dementia, hip fracture, psychiatric disease, and other disorders have a greater risk of dying than do the spouses of healthy people (Christakis and Allison 2006). One study found severe psychological stress in 67% of the caregivers of cancer patients and 64% of those caring for Alzheimer's patients (Kim et al. 2005).

If either you or your partner becomes severely ill, it's suggested (Rolland 1994a, 1994b), there are three areas you need to discuss. The support of a counselor (especially a certified rehabilitation counselor) may also be well advised.

Keep the Illness from Completely Dominating Your Lives

It's difficult not to let a serious illness become the "third partner" in a marriage, dominating all discussion. To keep it from becoming the main focus of their emotions, couples should declare it off-limits for conversation in certain areas, such as the bedroom and living room, so that romance may continue as well as visits and socializing with others.

View the Adversity as a Challenge to Be Faced Together

Chronic illness can threaten intimacy by making partners want to withdraw from or cling to each other. Viewing the disability not with dread but as a challenge to be faced together can put the situation in a more positive light—a more beneficial coping mechanism. One person (quoted in Peyrot et al. 1988) said that the experience "pulled us closer together, made our marriage stronger. It's pointed out the more important things."

Review the Balance between Closeness & Autonomy

In intimacy, we've said, we crave two contradictory things: to be close and to be autonomous (Scarf 1995). When a serious illness occurs, this balance needs to be discussed. The ill partner's fears might trigger a need for more closeness, but the other partner might desire detachment as a step toward the final separation of death. In reviewing this balance, both partners need to recognize that the caretaker needs time with others away from the caretaker role.

6. Death

It is possible that you will be blessed with a sudden, virtually painless end. But before that day, you might well be caught up in the dying and deaths of family members or friends—involved in events that you can't control and that are tremendously saddening and stressful but that call on you to give comfort as well.

In the Family Inventory of Life Events and Changes, the most severe family stressor was found to be "death of a child," followed by "death of a spouse/parent" (McCubbin and Patterson 1983). We consider these in reverse order.

Death of a Parent

"It happens without you even consciously thinking about it," said Ernestina Higuera, age 44. "Maybe you'll be driving to work . . . , and suddenly you start crying in the car." Higuera (quoted in Larson 1990) was talking about experiencing the death of her parents, both in their eighties, 3 years earlier.

At least 25% of adults still cry or become upset when they think of the deceased parent—even 1 to 5 years after the parent's death, according to researcher Andrew Scharlach (cited in Larson 1990). More than 20% continue to be preoccupied with thoughts of the parent. Especially profound responses among adult children include an overwhelming sense of feeling orphaned and the sense that one no longer fits the role of a child. As Scharlach says, "As long as a parent is alive, there is somebody between us and what we fear."

The death of a parent, particularly the second parent, can also profoundly change adult siblings' relationships with one another as they reevaluate the meaning of family and their roles within it (Kutner 1990, 1992). Some marriages suffer when the parent of one spouse dies (Umberson 1995). The grieving spouse might feel that he or she is not getting enough understanding and emotional support. The other spouse might feel that he or she is being imposed on by the continuing distress of the survivor.

Death of a Spouse

Despite today's high divorce rates, most marriages end with death, making the survivor a **widow, a wife who outlives her husband,** or **widower, a husband who outlives his wife.** In unmarried partnerships, whether straight or gay, the living member is generally called simply "the survivor" or "surviving partner." Most of the time, at almost every age, women outlive men, because, on average, women live about 7 years longer than men. Indeed, three out of four wives will become widowed.

Losing a spouse or a partner means not only the loss of intimacy and companionship, the struggle with grief, loneliness, depression, and sometimes (especially for low-income traditional women) financial hardship (Smith and Zick 1986). It also means the shattering of an identity—that of *wife* or *husband*, a role that might have been played for many years. Men are more depressed than women after their mate's death (Siegel and Kuykendall 1990). Recovery is often long and difficult, and widowed men and women are more apt to experience health problems in the year following a spouse's death than are those of a similar age who still have their spouses (Hooyman and Kiyak 1991).

Eventually, most survivors regain their emotional and physical health. Most widowers and many widows also begin to date again, primarily for friendship and companionship and to avoid isolation and loneliness.

Death of a Child

This is the most severe kind of stressor that most people can face, according to some researchers (McCubbin and Patterson 1983; Brotherson 2000). It's the second most severe—after the death of a spouse—according to others (Hobson et al. 1998). Indeed, one study finds that the death of a child not only alters a family forever but also sharply increases the risk that parents will later be hospitalized for mental illness (Li et al. 2005).

■ **Miscarriage or Stillbirth:** **A *miscarriage,* or *spontaneous abortion,* is the natural expulsion of a fetus from the uterus before birth,** an event that occurs in about 15% of pregnancies (Nielsen and Hahlin 1995). Most miscarriages occur during the sixth to eighth weeks of pregnancy. **A *stillbirth* means that the fetus is born dead.**

Although some parents grieve very little, the loss can be shattering because most women become attached to the child even before birth. Most parents recover, but some mourn the loss as much as 40 years later (Stinson et al. 1992).

■ **Infant Death:** A sad but common event in times past, infant mortality is still frequent in the United States, with 6.37 infant deaths per 1,000 live births, making the United States 42nd in the world in this category. This is rather far behind such countries as first-place Singapore (2.30), fifth-place Iceland (3.27), and tenth-place Czech Republic (3.86), which provide health care for all pregnant women and children. Canada is 23rd, with 4.63; Mexico is 110th, with 19.63 (U.S. Central Intelligence Agency 2007).

Many babies in the United States die because of problems associated with poverty; others die from disease, accidents, or health problems appearing at birth. If a baby dies from *sudden infant death syndrome (SIDS)*, **or "crib death," an event in which an apparently healthy infant under 1 year of age dies suddenly—and inexplicably—while sleeping,** the parents may be wracked with guilt as well as sadness. This is because society often perceives the parents as being somehow at fault for the death, and the parents always wonder whether they could have done anything to prevent the death. According to government statistics, about 0.55 SIDS deaths occurred per 1,000 live births in 2004, down from about 1.53 in 1980; most of these deaths occur between 2 and 4 months of age (National SIDS/Infant Death Resource Center 2007). In the United States, more SIDS cases are reported in the fall and winter than in spring or summer. SIDS occurs more often in infant boys than in girls (approximately a 6-to-4 male-to-female ratio). African American and American Indian infants are two to three times more likely to die from SIDS than are other infants (National SIDS/Infant Death Resource Center 2007). Several government agencies are intensifying efforts to reach these populations with the latest information about SIDS (such as putting infants to sleep on their stomachs instead of their backs).

A team of researchers funded by the National Institute of Child Health and Human Development (NICHD) has discovered that infants who die of SIDS might have abnormalities in several parts of the brain stem. This finding builds on the results of an earlier study that identified abnormalities in the region of the brain known as the arcuate nucleus in babies who died of SIDS. This region of the brain is thought to play a crucial role in regulating breathing, heartbeat, body temperature, and arousal.

■ **Loss of Older Child:** If a child who died was old enough to have a distinct personality and if his or her death was violent and sudden (as such deaths often are between ages 1 and 24—car accidents being the greatest cause), the loss is particularly powerful. There may be strong feelings not only of sorrow but also of guilt and anger, which might cause parents (and siblings) to inflict pain on each other just at a time when they most need each other's support (Sobieski 1994).

Even when the child who dies is fully grown, the loss never really heals for many parents and siblings. One father (quoted in Greene 1990) who lost his 17-year-old daughter in a freak auto accident says that even 2 years later, he cannot handle her death. When he is lunching with friends and the conversation turns to their college-age children, he has to leave the table. The feelings can be even more intense if the young person committed suicide (Chance 1992).

13.3 Violence & Abuse: The Dark Side of Intimate Relationships

MAJOR QUESTION What kinds of abuse are couples and families capable of?

PREVIEW We describe the kinds of violence, physical and emotional, against adults and children. We then discuss violence applied to dating and live-together relationships, marriage, children, and elders.

At the age of 14, Martha Tschetter of Fallon, Nevada, met an 18-year-old boy and began a romantic relationship. "We argued over simple things," she said later, "and he'd always say the reason he was so jealous was because he didn't want to lose me." When she was 15, halfway through her first pregnancy, during a heated argument about his drug use, he punched her in the stomach and spit his tobacco chew on her—the first of several acts of physical violence. "But I loved him and wanted to believe he could change," she said. Later, he began to isolate her from family and friends and to come home drunk, which led to even worse outbursts. Eventually, he decided to move out of state. At that point, Martha realized that she would never be able to please him and filed for divorce (Hiller 2002).

Tschetter is one of the lucky ones in that she did not suffer even greater harm. Still, her story presents a classic picture of domestic violence, a situation that victimizes not only women but also men. It also is important to note that family violence happens in all socioeconomic, ethnic, and racial groups. Who would have guessed, for instance, that the self-assured TV personality Meredith Viera, co-host of NBC's *Today* show, as a young newswoman working in local TV had such low self-esteem that she couldn't bring herself to leave a boyfriend who beat her (Johnson 2006)?

Violence & Abuse among Intimates: Some Definitions

Violence is a special kind of stressor—ugly, brutal, often sudden, and terrifying. Whether experienced or witnessed, *violence—**the threat of or infliction of physical or emotional harm on another***—within an intimate relationship

FAMILY VIOLENCE. Three-quarters of marital abuse consists of verbal assaults (threatening, cursing), according to some research, but 12% of heterosexual couples suffer some sort of physical abuse from their partners. Children may be even more at risk, suffering emotional and developmental problems as well as physical injuries. Did you grow up in a household in which adults were abusive toward each other? How did it affect you? ▶

or family produces both physical consequences and often lifelong psychological effects. There are various categories of violence, but there is much disagreement as to the exact numbers and percentages because this is behavior that is often hidden and is certainly underreported.

In the Family Inventory of Life Events and Changes, the category "Physical or sexual abuse or violence between family members" ranks as fourth in severity in the list of stressors—behind death of a child, death of a spouse/parent, and separation or divorce of a spouse/parent (McCubbin and Patterson 1983). The research literature on partner violence is handicapped by a failure to attend to distinctions—for example, lumping face slapping and shoving matches in with homicides (Johnson and Ferraro 2000). Even so, we may begin by at least distinguishing between physical violence and emotional abuse.

Physical Violence

***Physical violence*, also called *battering*, is the infliction or threat of physical harm.** This ranges from pushing and shoving to hitting and kicking to biting and choking to stabbing and shooting. Women are more apt to slap men; men are more apt to grab or push women (Lloyd and Emery 2000).

A specific kind of physical violence is ***sexual assault*, a legal term for rape.** Rape may be stranger rape, acquaintance rape (including date rape), and marital rape, as we'll explain shortly. A report by Amnesty International (2007) found that American Indian women are more than twice as likely to be raped as other U.S. women, that 86% of such sexual assaults were by non-Indian men, and that the suspects often go free because of confusing police jurisdictions and lack of nurses with rape-evidence kits. Violence against women, however, is a global problem; according to the World Health Organization (2005), rates vary between as low as 15% of women having been victims of domestic violence in their lifetimes in Japan to as high as 71% in Ethiopia. (It is about 20% in the United States.)

Emotional Violence

Emotional violence, or emotional abuse, is verbal and psychological abuse that inflicts or threatens to inflict emotional distress. This can take the form of criticism ("Can't you have dinner ready when I get home?"); sarcasm, ridicule, and insults ("You really need to take off about 200 pounds," "You're pathetic"); refusing to talk to or touch the partner; restricting the partner in the use of money, the use of a car, or visits with friends; and threats of all kinds—to leave, to beat up, to institutionalize, even to kill the partner.

Violence in Dating & Live-Together Relationships

You might think that when two people are dating, they would be on their best behavior. Unhappily, violence does happen, and it happens often. In fact, estimates are that it occurs in 9% to as much as 82% of dating relationships (Riggs and Caulfield 1997; Simons et al. 1998; Shook et al. 2000; Eaton et al. 2006: Table 10).

One study of high school students who were dating found that 96% had experienced emotional abuse, 59% reported physical violence at least once, and 15% reported unwanted sexual activity (Jezl et al. 1996). The longer and more involved the dating relationship, the higher is the potential for violence and the more likely the violence is to be mutual, according to one study of adolescents (Gray and Foshee 1997). The availability of cell phones and the Internet make it easier for teenagers to be intimidated or emotionally abused by boyfriends or girlfriends without their parents' knowledge (Jayson 2007). As for young adults, one study of daters age 30 and under found that nearly a third had either inflicted or suffered physical violence in their relationships within the preceding year (Lloyd 1995).

Causes of Dating Violence

Daters become violent because of jealousy issues, when one person refuses to have sex, and/or because of excessive drinking or quarreling about drinking behavior (Makepeace 1981, 1986; Riggs 1993). Indeed, alcohol and drugs play a particularly important role in dating violence (O'Keefe 1997; Simons et al. 1998).

Unwanted Sex, Including Date Rape

The usual definition of **rape is unwanted sexual penetration, perpetrated by force, threat of harm, or when the victim is intoxicated or unconscious** (Koss and Cook 1993). Although the picture that emerges from the news media is one of rapists as strangers who attack unsuspecting women on lonely streets or break into their homes, this is not generally accurate. The most common form of rape is **acquaintance rape—nonconsensual sex between adults who know each other.** Acquaintances could be friends, neighbors, or co-workers. A particular kind of acquaintance rape, **date rape, is nonconsensual sex between dating partners.** Up to 20% of college women report that they have been raped on a date (Patterson and Kim 1991).

The term *date rape*, however, may be misleading in indicating the frequency of sexual violence. It's more useful to think of the notion of *unwanted sex*, in which people are forced into unwanted sexual activity, from kissing to sexual intercourse, without their permission. By this definition, 11.2% of high school females and 5.9% of high school males said they were physically forced to have sex (Eaton et al. 2006: Table 11). One-half to three-quarters of college women reported they had experienced sexual aggression while dating, according to a 1992 study (Cate and Lloyd 1992). Indeed, during a time (1973 to 2004) when rapes and attempted rapes declined more than 80%, the sexual violence rates (including nonconsensual sex) among young women of high school and college age remained as serious as ever (U.S. Department of Justice 2006).

Often alcohol or drugs (such as GHB, Rohypnol, and Ketamine—the so-called date rape drugs, which reduce inhibitions, especially when used with alcohol) are a factor. In one study, 79% of women who were date-raped said that they had been drinking and/or taking drugs beforehand, and 71% said that their date had, too (Copenhaver and Grauerholz 1991). The accompanying box gives some tips on how to avoid date rape. *(See ■ Panel 13.1.)*

Different Experiences of Men & Women

Although both sexes engage in physical and emotional aggression, there are differences in experience and background:

■ **Men:** Men are more likely to say that they have beat up the woman they were dating or threatened her with a gun (Makepeace 1981; Riggs 1993). Men who were raised by physically abusive fathers might be apt to be verbally and/or physically abusive in dating relationships (Alexander et al. 1991; Simons et al. 1998).

Date rapists also tend to hold traditional views about women and sex, to show hostility toward women, to have been sexually promiscuous as adolescents, to report a great number of sexual experiences, to have a propensity

---

■ **PANEL 13.1   How You Can Reduce the Risk of Date Rape**

■ **Know your own mind, and don't give mixed messages.** Examine your feelings, and decide whether you want to have sex—in advance, not in the heat of the moment. Be aware of the signals you send with your posture, tone of voice, clothing, gestures, and eye contact. Say yes when you mean yes and no when you mean no. Don't expect your partner to read your mind. Be forceful and firm. Don't worry about being impolite.

■ **Think about where you're meeting, and watch alcohol and drug use.** Especially on a first date, avoid secluded places where you might be vulnerable. Go where there are other people. Be aware that drug and alcohol use (yours or the other party's) is associated with date rape. Have your own transportation arrangements so that you can get home by yourself. Pay your own way so you that won't feel obligated to your date.

■ **For women—be independent, and trust your gut feelings.** Women are socialized to be polite, but don't yield to rape just to avoid a scene. If you are worried about hurting his feelings, remember that he is ignoring yours. If things start to get out of hand, be loud in protesting, leave, go for help. Do not wait for someone else to rescue you or for things to get better.

for jealousy, and to have difficulty expressing their feelings (Lloyd and Emery 2000; Senn et al. 2000).

■ **Women:** Women are more likely to say that they have pushed or slapped a man they were dating (Makepeace 1981; Riggs 1993). There is no evidence that women who were raised by physically abusive fathers themselves become verbally or physically abusive in dating relationships (Alexander et al. 1991).

Women are more apt than men to be the victims of physical and emotional violence and sexual assaults (Stets and Henderson 1991). College women who have been date-raped reported higher levels of sexual dysfunction, anger, depression, and anxiety than did comparable women who had not been date-raped (Shapiro and Schwarz 1997). Sadly, fewer than half of women injured by rape or sexual assault each year report the crime to police (Rennison 2002: 1).

Violence in Cohabiting Relationships

Couples in live-together relationships are more apt to be physically violent— mostly grabbing, pushing, and slapping—than are couples in dating relationships (Magdol et al. 1998). Often, the abuse occurs in couples in which partners, particularly women, are insecure about the level of emotional commitment (Hanley and O'Neill 1997; O'Hearn and Davis 1997).

Violence in Gay & Lesbian Relationships

Although sparse, the research on relationship violence between gay partners and between lesbian partners suggests that they are much the same as in straight relationships. That is, violence occurs in 11% to over 45% of relationships, and the dynamics are similar to those in abusive straight relationships, with alcohol, drugs, and jealousy often major factors (Kurdek 1994, 1998; Renzetti 1995).

There are, however, certain differences in comparison with heterosexual abusive relationships. For one thing, an additional abusive threat is that of "outing," or exposing the partner's homosexual status to parents or employer. Lesbian victims, as well as gay male victims, are more apt to fight back than is the case with straight women (Island and Letellier 1991). Gay men are less abusive than heterosexual men are toward their partners, but lesbians are more abusive than heterosexual women are toward their partners (Bowman and Morgan 1998). Finally, lesbians who batter are more apt to seek treatment than are gays who batter, although in either case, there is not a great variety of resources or sources of support (Obejas 1995; Renzetti 1995).

Stalking: The Abuse after Abusive Relationships End

***Stalking* is the repeated and malicious following or harassment of another person.** We read in the press about unstable individuals (as portrayed in the 1981 Lauren Bacall movie *The Fan*) stalking celebrities such as entertainers Madonna, Michael J. Fox, and David Letterman or supermodel Claudia Schiffer. But stalking can also happen after one partner tries to end a physically and/or emotionally abusive relationship, when the possessive, jealous, rejected partner attempts either to win the other one back or to take revenge. In one study of 144 college women, those who had been in abusive relationships were more apt to be stalked than were those who had not (Coleman 1997).

Violence between Husband & Wife

Older terms such as *wife beating* and *spouse abuse* have yielded to a more general term: ***intimate partner violence*, which is defined as physical and/or emotional abuse of one partner by another—male or female, married or unmarried, straight or gay, current or former.** *Marital violence* is husbands attacking wives and wives attacking husbands.

What Is the Incidence of Marital Violence?

Much of intimate violence is never reported to the police or admitted to inquiring researchers, but here are a few indicators:

■ **Some Violent Incident—One of Six:** A study of almost 9 million married couples found that some violent episode occurred in one out of six marriages every year (Gelles and Straus 1988; Newman 1999).

■ **Verbal Assaults—Three-Fourths:** In a national study, three-fourths of both males and females admitted to verbally assaulting (threatening, cursing) their partners the preceding year (Straus and Sweet 1992).

■ **Physical Abuse—12%:** A study of heterosexual couples found that 12% of adult intimates suffered some sort of physical abuse from their partners (Renzetti and Curran 1999).

■ **Severe Wife Beating—30%:** In a study of 6,002 representative households, 30% of wives reported having suffered severe beatings (Gelles and Straus 1988).

■ **Victims of Intimate Violence—92% Are Women:** Among victims of nonfatal intimate violence, 92% are women (U.S. Department of Justice 1994, 1998).

Clearly, women suffer more violence than men do. Indeed, 1 of 50 women ages 16 to 24 are victims of intimate violence, and 10 times as many women as men are seriously hurt by current or former partners (Gelles and Cornell 1990; Campbell 1995).

Two Kinds of Marital Violence: Patriarchal & Common Couple Violence

Pennsylvania State University sociologist **Michael Johnson,** who has done a great deal of work in abusive relationships, has identified two kinds of violence (Johnson 1995):

■ **Patriarchal Terrorism—From the Need to Control Generally:** The more extreme and less common of the two forms of violence, ***patriarchal terrorism* is violence by men who feel that they must control "their" women by any means necessary.** This is one-way violence, directed by a man against a woman. The woman is viewed as "my property" who must be beaten to "keep her in her place."

■ **Common Couple Violence—From the Need to Control a Specific Situation:** Usually less severe in the kinds of injuries inflicted, *common couple violence* **consists of violence between partners arising from everyday disagreements that have gone too far.** Such violence, which may be female against male as well as male against female, is motivated by the need to control the specific situation under dispute.

The Cycle of Violence: Three Phases

In a pattern that especially applies to patriarchal terrorism, **Lenore Walker** (1984) has proposed a three-phase *cycle of violence* **of (1) rising tension, (2) escalation and explosion, and (3) calmness, contrition, and kindness following the violent episode**—before the cycle begins again:

■ **Phase 1—Rising Tension:** Tension builds as a result of minor conflicts. There may be minor acts of physical abuse by the husband toward the wife. The wife tries to be conciliatory or stay out of the way to avoid aggravating her husband, but her—and his—anger keeps rising. The tension continues to increase, and the husband becomes more aggressive.

■ **Phase 2—Escalation and Explosion:** The situation escalates until the husband explodes in rage (sometimes, in the case of a long-time abuser, triggered by the wife to "get it over with") and beats his spouse. Alcohol problems often play a big part in the cycle—perhaps anywhere in the range of 35 to 93% of assaults on wives by their husbands (Gelles 1993).

■ **Phase 3—Calmness, Contrition, and Kindness:** With tension released, calmness returns. This phase is often described as the honeymoon phase, because of the element of intense emotion—relief and renewed love. The husband expresses contrition and kindness—giving flowers and gifts—and promises never to repeat his sins. The wife chooses to think that "This time, he really means it" and forgives him. The calm exists until Phase 1 starts again. This is why it's important that police officers taking the initial report of beatings photograph the victim's wounds (not Polaroids, but higher-quality digital photos), because oftentimes she or he recants the story later (Buckley 2007).

Marital Rape

Traditionally, the notion of *marital rape*—**forcible rape by one's spouse**— by a husband of a wife was considered nonsensical, since she was regarded as his property. The women's movement has changed that outlook, and now marital rape is against the law in every state (but in some states is illegal only if the couple is separated). Still it continues. According to one study, about 10 to 14% of wives have been forced by their husbands to have sex involuntarily, which may have included sex acts other than intercourse, such as oral or anal sex, that the wife did not want to do (Yllo 1995).

After the rape, some wives blame themselves, feel guilty for not being better spouses, and regard their lack of interest in sex as stemming from their own failures, not from the experience of violence. Others are enraged at their husbands, feeling intense humiliation and betrayal (Finkelhor and Yllo 1985). Unfortunately, very few wives report marital rape to the police (Michael et al.

1994). Moreover, many people, both police and victimized wives, regard marital rape as just part of normal "husband-and-wife stuff"—not serious like stranger or acquaintance rape (Yllo 1995).

Characteristics of Violent Families

Family violence occurs among people of all social classes, races, and ages. Even middle- or upper-class families may experience violence, although it is less likely to attract the attention of police because they have more privacy (they don't live in crowded conditions), their physicians are less apt to report injuries, and they have more access to friends and counselors compared with people in lower-class families (Buzawa and Buzawa 1990; Fineman and Mykitiuk 1994).

Even so, some risk factors are more associated with family violence than others, as the box shows. (See ■ Panel 13.2.) In general, domestic violence is found more frequently among young, low-income, blue-collar couples in which alcohol or drugs are abused and in which the man tends to believe in traditional gender roles, is jealous, and believes that violence is acceptable. As Johnson (1995: 287) says, "The central motivating factor behind the violence is a man's desire to exercise general control over 'his' woman."

An important contributor to domestic violence is *spillover*, **the effect of participation in one of life's domains (such as work) on other domains (such as family).** As you might expect, men who are experiencing feelings of job strain and men who are working at the lower rungs of the occupational ladder, with the consequent lack of financial resources, are more apt to be violent toward their partners (Fox et al. 2002). Men in physically violent and dangerous workplaces, such as the military and the police, are likewise more likely to engage in violence; interestingly, so are men in female-dominated workplaces, such as nursing and clerical work (Melzer 2002). In contrast to workers in service jobs, managers and professionals report more negative spillover from work to family (Almeida et al. 2002).

■ PANEL 13.2   Household Risk Factors Portending Violence

■ Man is 18 to 24 years old.

■ Family is at poverty level and has financial worries.

■ Man is unemployed or employed part time; woman is employed.

■ Man is a high school dropout.

■ One or both abuse alcohol or other drugs.

■ Man abuses wife verbally as well as physically.

■ Family is socially isolated from neighbors and relatives.

■ Man believes in traditional family and gender stereotypes.

■ Man is jealous and has frequent conflicts with wife.

Sources: Gelles and Cornell 1990; Hotaling and Sugarman 1990; Leonard and Senchak 1993; Straus 1993; Bachman 1994; Gelles 1995; Sorenson et al. 1996; Straus and Yodanis 1996; Brookoff et al. 1997; Hutchison 1999; Macmillan and Gartner 2000.

Why Do People Stay in Violent Relationships?

There are many reasons why victims—particularly women living with violent men—stay with their abusive partners:

■ **Fear of Partner, Isolation, or Poverty:** Some victims are afraid they will suffer dreadful violence if they leave—perhaps even be killed. Indeed, in about three-quarters of cases in which women were murdered by their male partners, the women were trying to leave (de Santis 1990). Victims might also fear being alone, particularly if the abuser has effectively cut off all the abused partner's outside relationships (Nielsen et al. 1992; Forte et al. 1996). Finally, particularly for low-income women who are dependent on their husbands, there is fear of economic hardship. Indeed, the victim might feel that she has nowhere else to go.

■ **Love, Pity, Duty, Guilt, Hope:** The victim may, in fact, love and be committed to the abuser. Indeed, she or he might pity the partner, especially when, after a violent episode, the abuser makes abject apologies and promises to change. Wives might feel that it is their duty to serve their marriage vows and to keep the family together, particularly if children are involved. They might feel guilty that they are at fault for their marriage not working well—in fact, think that they deserve the violence. Finally, they might have hopes that the abuser will reform—that he or she can be forgiven one more time and at last will change.

■ **Low Self-Esteem, Childhood Experience, Learned Helplessness:** Would a self-respecting victim stay in such a relationship? Lack of self-respect can indeed be a major problem. Because many abusers convince their victims that they are worthless, the victims might believe this to be the case (Goode 1994). One theory is that battered women stay in such relationships because of *learned helplessness—because of their battering experience, people perceive that they have no control over the major events affecting them* (Walker 1984, 1993). The seeds for this negativity and low self-esteem may already have been sown during childhood, in which beatings (of spouses and children) might have been a part of life (Torr and Swisher 1999).

Escaping Family Violence

There is some good news: When women in abusive relationships believe that they are able to stop the violence and become determined to do so, many are able to make this happen. According to one study by Karen Rosen and Sandra Stith (1997) of 22 women ages 16 to 32 who had been in abusive relationships ranging from 10 months to 9 years, the process of escape develops in five stages, as follows:

■ **Experiencing Doubts:** The woman begins to experience seeds of doubts about the wisdom of remaining in the relationship.

■ **Turning Point:** There follows a turning point that affects the woman's motivations, such as a particularly severe beating.

■ **Detachment and Reevaluation:** Next occurs a period of objective reflection—taking a detached look at the situation—followed by reappraisal—reevaluating its meaning and what might be done.

■ **Shift in Thinking:** Perhaps prompted by some last-straw abusive event, the woman begins to shift her thinking from staying in the relationship to getting out of it.

■ **Breaking Free:** The last stage is particularly difficult. The woman might need to have the man arrested, obtain a legal restraining order against him, go to a shelter or safe house, or leave town.

A sixth stage might be the rebuilding of family life, as in obtaining job skills and a new job, putting the children in new schools, and so on. Rebuilding can be very difficult, and sometimes a woman will return to an abusive relationship if her attempt to rebuild is unsuccessful.

Dealing with Family Violence

There are three important issues in addressing family violence, as follows:

■ **Intervention:** Victims of violence can begin to turn things around when they seek help from friends, the police, or public agencies or even when they adopt passive means of defense, such as covering themselves with their hands (Bowker 1983; Gondolf 1987, 1988). One study found that women who sought a *protection order*—**a court order that prohibits a person from threatening, harassing, or hurting a victim**—experienced significantly lower levels of threats of abuse, stalking, work harassment, and the like from the offending partner (McFarlane et al. 2004). Without intervention, it has been estimated that 32% of victimized women will very shortly become victimized again, and the violence will increase as time goes on (Langan and Innes 1986).

In the past, the police generally avoided making arrests in cases of husband-wife violence, but changes in the law in recent years have made arrests and prosecution for battery easier. Mandatory arrest policies for abuse do deter repeated assaults and even beginning assaults, according to some studies, although the effectiveness of mandatory arrests is still questionable (Sherman and Berk 1984; Berk 1993; Buzawa and Buzawa 1993; Schmidt and Sherman 1993; Berk and Newton 1995). Some localities also have "no drop" prosecution policies, in which the state, not the victim, presses charges. The rationale for this is that some victims of violence are too fearful of retribution by their abusive mates or former mates to press charges, so the state takes the responsibility of doing so.

■ **Shelters and Safe Houses:** In many cities, women and children can escape abusive partners by going to a *women's shelter*, or *victim shelter*, **which provides not only food and accommodation but also other help such as money, food stamps, counseling, and legal, medical, and employment assistance.** Equally important, the shelters enable battered women to realize that they are not alone in their problems.

Operating in conjunction with many shelters, *women's safe houses*, **whose existence is known only to residents and shelter workers, are private homes that provide temporary housing for abused women.**

Most victims of abuse are women, but there are also some victimized men. They are not allowed to stay at women's shelters and safe houses, but they may receive help in the form of motel rooms and other support services.

■ **Treatment Programs for Abusers:** Treatment programs aimed at changing the behavior of abusive men consist of group and individual therapy concerned with reducing stress, improving communication techniques, and similar matters. The influence of the victimized women who insist that their partners get this kind of help can be very important (Gondolf 1987, 1988).

Although such programs may have some success, effectiveness is difficult to determine (Gelles and Conte 1991; Davis and Taylor 1999). Among those who went through voluntary programs, according to some research, between two-thirds and three-quarters were found to have relinquished their violent behavior (Gondolf 1987, 1988).

Child Abuse & Neglect

How likely is it that you as a college student would have been subject to abuse as a child? In one study of 1,770 undergraduates, 6.3% said that they had been abused by a parent. Their parents, they said, were apt to be either too strict or too permissive, depressed and angry, abusing alcohol or drugs, and generally always in conflict and unsupportive (Wright 1985). Does this kind of family background sound familiar? We sincerely hope not.

Child abuse and neglect are very serious problems. ***Child abuse* refers to acts of aggression by an adult against a child,** generally under the age of 18, whether physical or verbal. Sexual abuse is also a form of child abuse. ***Sexual abuse* involves manipulated or coerced sexual behavior of a minor by an adult.** It may vary from exposure and unwanted kissing to fondling and rape to *incest*—**sexual relations between persons who are related to each other.**

***Child neglect* is *physical neglect*, as in not providing enough food, clothing, health care, or security, or *emotional neglect*, as in not providing sufficient care, attention, and guidance.** Physical neglect nearly always results in emotional neglect as well, although the reverse is not necessarily true—emotional abuse need not entail physical abuse.

In 1997, the U.S. Department of Health and Human Services released a survey, the congressionally mandated Third National Incidence Study of Child Abuse and Neglect (NIS-3), which estimated that child abuse and neglect nearly doubled in the United States, from 1.4 million in 1986 to more than 2.8 million in 1993. During the same period, the number of children who were seriously injured quadrupled from about 143,000 to nearly 570,000. The report also estimated that in 1993 only 28% of the children who were identified by the study as harmed by abuse and neglect had been investigated by state child protective services, a significant decrease from the 44% investigated in 1986. Schools identified the largest number of children at risk, yet states investigated only 16% of these children. A Fourth National Incidence Study (NIS-4) is to be completed at the end of 2008.

Other findings from the NIS-3 survey include the following:

■ **Children of Single Parents:** Children of single parents had a 77% greater risk of being harmed by physical abuse, an 87% greater risk of being harmed by physical neglect, and an 80% greater risk of suffering serious injury or harm from abuse and neglect.

■ **Children in Large Families:** Children in the largest families were physically neglected at nearly three times the rate of those who came from single-child families.

■ **Children in Low-Income Families:** Children from families with annual incomes below $15,000 were more than 22 times more likely to experience maltreatment than were children from families whose incomes exceeded $30,000. Poorer children were also 18 times more likely to be sexually abused, almost 56 times more likely to be educationally neglected, and more than 22 times more likely to be seriously injured.

■ **Girls:** Girls are sexually abused three times more often than boys; however, boys are at greater risk of emotional neglect and serious injury than girls are. Yet all children are consistently more vulnerable to sexual abuse from age 3. Although childhood physical abuse is more prevalent among males, the long-term health consequences are more significant for females (Thompson et al. 2004).

■ **Race and Ethnicity:** There were no significant race/ethnicity differences in the incidence of maltreatment.

The U.S. Department of Health and Human Services reported that in 2005, about 12.1 of every 1,000 children were victims of abuse or neglect (U.S. Department of Health and Human Services 2007). A sense of the details is provided by the Children's Defense Fund (2007), which says that every day in America, the following occur:

4 children are killed by abuse or neglect
5 children or teens commit suicide
8 children or teens are killed by firearms
192 children are arrested for violent crimes
383 children are arrested for drug abuse
2,383 children are confirmed as abused or neglected

Risk Factors for Child Abuse

Abused children are found in families of all income levels, races, ethnicities, and religions, although more abuse is reported in poor and nonwhite families than in middle-class and upper-class white families. Other risk factors are as follows:

■ **History of Physical Punishment:** Abusive parents were often physically punished by their own parents, and they tend to believe (as many people do) in corporal punishment (spankings) as a means of maintaining discipline. (However, most parents who were abused as children do not themselves become abusers.) In some families that stress physical punishment, there may also be abuse between husband and wife.

■ **Unrealistic Expectations for the Child:** Parents often have unrealistic views about their child's development, as in expecting a child to be toilet-trained by age 1. Parents might think their child "unsatisfactory" simply for being born outside marriage, of the "wrong" sex, born with congenital defects (developmental disabilities, mental retardation), or fussy and hyperactive (Steele 1980).

■ **Other Factors:** Often the abusive adult is a boyfriend or a stepfather, who is less likely to be invested in the child than blood relatives are (Daly and Wilson 1994). Frequently, alcohol or drug abuse is present (Fleming et al. 1996). Many abused children are raised in socially isolated, crowded, economically stressed households located in low-income, unsafe neighborhoods.

Effects of Child Abuse

Adults who have experienced abuse as children are apt to show a number of adverse effects (Felitti et al. 1998; Garnefski and Arends 1998; Mullen et al. 1996; Windom 1999; Muller and Lemieux 2000; Bernstein 2006).

■ **Physical and Mental Problems:** Many abused children suffer physical injuries that result in scars and physical disabilities and even posttraumatic stress disorder and attempts at suicide.

■ **Emotional and Developmental Problems:** Often, abused children show low self-esteem, higher levels of aggression, depression, anxiety, behavior problems at home and in school, lower intellectual development, alcohol and drug problems, and generalized unhappiness. Females who were sexually abused may tend to become promiscuous.

■ **Intimacy Problems:** Abused children are likely to have problems that interfere with fostering intimate relationships—feelings of isolation, communication problems, and difficulty trusting others. About a third will grow up to be abusers themselves.

Child Sexual Abuse

Data on child sexual abuse vary. The U.S. Department of Health and Human Services (2007:17) found that 9.3% of mistreated children suffered sexual abuse. An earlier national study found that 27% of the women and 16% of the men surveyed had been sexually abused as children (Finkelhor et al. 1990). Another found that 12% of adult women reported that as children, they had had physical sexual contact with an adult (Browning and Laumann 1998). **Sexual child abuse may be by nonrelated individuals—*extrafamilial abuse*. Or it may be by related individuals, including steprelatives—*intrafamilial abuse*.** One study of nearly 4,000 intrafamilial cases found that 85% of the sexually abused children were female, and 15% were male (Solomon 1992).

Sexual abuse can take many forms: exposure of private parts, unwanted hugging and kissing, attempted sexual contact, fondling of genitals, intercourse, oral sex, and incest. (It does not include mutually desired sex between siblings.) Probably the most common form of incest is that between a girl and her father, stepfather, or older brother (Canavan et al. 1992). Father–daughter incest is apt to occur when the girl is between ages 6 and 11 and to last about 2 years (Stark 1984).

Many of the effects of child sexual abuse are the same as those for general child abuse. In addition, people who were sexually abused may develop sexual problems. Women report having more sexual partners, more difficulty with sexual activity, and inhibited sexual desire (Mullen et al. 1996). Men report having difficulty with ejaculation (Elliott and Briere 1992).

Elder Abuse & Neglect

There are other forms of family violence—for instance, teenagers against parents or sibling against sibling. A study by David Finkelhor and colleagues (2005) found that 35% of children reported they had been attacked by a sibling in the previous year. One form of such violence that has come to the attention of the public in recent years is elder abuse and elder neglect—child (or grandchild or caretaker) violence against older people (Wolf 1995; Henningson 1997; Carp 2000). **Elder abuse consists of acts of aggression against the elderly—physical assaults, emotional humiliation, verbal abuse, financial exploitation, isolation from friends. Elder neglect consists of acts of omission in the care and treatment of the elderly.** Perhaps 4 to 6% of the elderly are abused, according to the National Committee for the Prevention of Elder Abuse (NCPEA) (2007).

The NCPEA (cited in France 2006) also identifies three types of abuse:

■ **Person in New Relationship Turns Out to Be Abusive:** Although one may have had the good fortune to have been happy with a previous spouse or spouses, it's possible to arrive at the end of life with a partner who turns out to be abusive.

■ **Late-Onset Domestic Violence:** This abuse occurs when a long, ordinary marriage unexpectedly leads to an environment of brutality and fear, perhaps triggered by an event such as a spouse's failing health (brain impairments, strokes, incontinence, and other old-age disorders).

■ **Domestic Violence Grown Old:** Perhaps the most common sort, this type of abuse involves violence that begins in early marriage and continues for decades. A variant has been identified in Japan, where older wives have reported suffering from "retired husband syndrome (RHS)," stress-related symptoms caused by the sudden daily presence of a fault-finding, backbiting husband recently retired from his job (Faiola 2005).

Other reasons for abuse are impairment (as with Alzheimer's) of the victim, which taxes the patience of the caregiver; having to pay for the elder's medical costs; and dependence of the elder on the caregiver or vice-versa (Harris 1990; Kilburn 1996; Gelles 1997). Some adult children or grandchildren, tired of the responsibility, may resort to *granny dumping*—**abandoning an elderly person at a hospital entrance with no identification.**

The most likely to be victimized are very elderly women (often suffering from mental disabilities such as Alzheimer's), probably because they live longer than men; most perpetrators of abuse and neglect, 53%, are men (Tatara 1998). Some characteristics of perpetrators of elder abuse are shown in the accompanying chart. *(See ■ Panel 13.3.)*

■ **PANEL 13.3**   Perpetrators and Victims of Elder Abuse

PERPETRATORS OF ELDER ABUSE

Adult child—53%

Spouse—19%

Grandchild—9%

Other relative—9%

Friend/neighbor—6%

In-home service provider—3%

Out-of-home service provider—1%

Men—53%

Ages 41–59—38%

Ages 4 and under—27%

VICTIMS OF ELDER ABUSE (AGE 60 AND OVER)

Likeliest victims in later life: middle- and lower-middle-class white women ages 75–85 with physical or mental impairment

Physical abuse—62%

Abandonment—56%

Emotional/psychological abuse—54%

Financial/material abuse—45%

Neglect—41%

White—84%

Black—8%

Latino—5%

Asian—2%

Sources: Based on data from Gabarino 1989; Tatara et al. 1998.

13.4 Coping Strategies: Successful Ways of Handling Stresses & Crises

MAJOR QUESTION What factors affect stress, and how can I handle it?

PREVIEW We discuss good and bad types of stressors and eight types of defense mechanisms people use to deal with them. We also describe five strategies for living to reduce the stressors.

As we have seen, a stressor can be bad, such as being rejected in love, being fired, or being beaten up. The depressing catalog of crises and violence that we discussed in the first three sections of this chapter clearly represents a long list of bad stressors. But a stressor can also be good.

Good versus Bad Stressors

Famed Canadian stress researcher **Hans Selye** points out that it "is immaterial whether the agent or situation we face is pleasant or unpleasant; all that counts is the intensity of the demand for adjustment and adaptation" (Selye 1974: 28–29).

When the source of stress is a positive event, it is called a *eustressor*, and its effect is called *eustress* (pronounced "*you*-stress"). Eustress can stimulate a person to better coping and adaptation, to do one's best.

When the source of stress is a negative event, it is called a *distressor*, and its effect is called *distress*. Although distress can be helpful when one is facing a physical threat, too much of this kind of stress can result in illness. When distressors follow one after the other, they can produce ***stressor overload*—that is, the unrelated but unrelenting small stressors can produce a breakdown in a person or family's morale,** perhaps leading to physical illness, mental illness, or family violence (Boss 1988; Hamilton et al. 1996). We can't always prevent distressors, but we can learn to recognize them and develop ways of managing both stressors and stress.

Defense Mechanisms[*]

Distressors cause anxiety and frustration, often leading us to employ a number of **defense mechanisms**, **or unconscious methods for denying, excusing, disguising, or changing the behaviors that cause anxiety and frustration.** Although defense mechanisms are often normal and even healthy ways of dealing with difficulty, they can become problems if they prevent someone from dealing with reality or communicating about problems.

Eight important defense mechanisms are as follows:

■ Repression: *Repression* **is "motivated forgetting," the unconscious blocking of whatever is causing one stress.**
Example: Victims of sexual abuse or incest in childhood might push the events that happened to them deep into their memories.

■ Denial: *Denial* **is the refusal to believe information that provokes anxiety.**
Example: A man who is married to an alcoholic might deny that she has a severe drinking problem, choosing to think rather that "she can party with the best of them."

■ Rationalization: *Rationalization* **is the assertion that the reasons for illogical behavior are "rational" and "good."**
Example: Someone who hates the work of college might rationalize dropping out by saying, "No one's hiring college graduates now."

■ Displacement: *Displacement* **is redirecting one's feelings from the true target to a less threatening substitute.**
Example: A student who fails an exam and is angry about it might take her anger out on her boyfriend that evening.

■ Projection: *Projection* **is the attributing of unacceptable impulses or characteristics to other people.** This is the basis for *scapegoating*—blaming one group for the mistakes of another.
Example: People who say "Everyone cheats" (on tests, their spouses, their taxes) might well be doing some cheating themselves.

■ Reaction Formation: *Reaction formation* **occurs when people present themselves as feeling the opposite of what they really feel.**
Example: To "prove" to the world that he can't possibly wish for his father dead, an indifferent son might insist that physicians do everything possible to save his dying parent.

■ Regression: *Regression* **is a relapse into a more childlike or juvenile form of behavior** to "avoid" the threat of the moment.
Example: A child might begin to wet the bed again or suck her thumb after her parents go through a divorce or a new brother or sister is born.

---

[*]This section adapted from *Healthy for Life: Wellness & the Art of Living*, 1st edition, by Williams/Knight, 1994. Used with permission of Brooks/Cole, a division of Thomson Learning. www.thomsonrights.com; fax 800-730-2215.

■ **Sublimation:** ***Sublimation* is socially constructive behavior that is formed to disguise unacceptable behavior.**

Example: Hostile impulses might be sublimated into seeking work as a police officer, or sexual impulses into becoming a sculptor of nudes.

Adaptation versus Coping Strategies

Although a survey of about 2,000 U.S. adults found that 47% were concerned about the levels of stress in their lives, only about half of them were making an effort to manage it, according to a survey by the American Psychological Association (2006). Others tried to cope by overeating, smoking, and other bad habits. Many people, men more than women, are apt to adapt to stress by using denial, suppressing and not sharing their feelings, blaming others, and abusing alcohol (Burr and Klein et al. 1994; Bouchard et al. 1998). ***Adaptation* is not changing the stressor or the stress.**

By contrast, other people, women more so than men, are apt to use positive coping strategies, among them expressing emotions and sharing their concerns. ***Coping* is changing the stressor or changing your reaction to it.** Whereas defense mechanisms are unconscious, coping strategies are conscious (Cramer 1998, 2000). ***Coping strategies* are generally realistic and helpful ways of dealing with stress, pain, fear, and other problems caused by stressors.** It's important to realize that there are positive, proactive things that you can do in response to crises, violence, and abuse.

We describe five kinds of coping strategies—strategies for living—that fight stress: (1) reduce the stressors, (2) manage your emotional response, (3) develop a support system, (4) take care of your body, and (5) develop relaxation techniques (Williams and Knight 1994).

Strategy for Living #1: Reduce the Stressors

"Reducing the stressors" seems like obvious advice, but it's surprising how long we can let something go on being a source of stress—usually because dealing with it is so uncomfortable. Examples are falling behind in your work and having to explain your problem to your instructor or your boss, running up debts on a credit card, or owing back taxes to the IRS.

It might not be easy, but all these problems are matters you can do something about, although getting the advice of a counselor might help. Avoidance and procrastination only make things worse.

Strategy for Living #2: Manage Your Emotional Response

Learning how to manage your emotional response is crucial. Quite often you can't do anything about a stressor, but you can do something about your *reaction* to it. Some techniques for managing your emotional response are the following.

STRATEGY FOR LIVING. All of us need to find realistic ways to deal with stress and fear. Humor, optimism, hope—and just plain relaxation—are all ways to improve mental well-being. What works for you? ◄

Be Realistic & Keep Control of Any Destructive Impulses

It might be tempting to become enraged, to blame others, to play the victim game, to fall into helplessness, to disengage emotionally from your partner or family, or to retreat into alcohol or drugs. However, all such activities will only aggravate a crisis situation and your ability to communicate with your partner. A better approach, found in one study of 50 successful marriages, is to try to take a realistic view of the situation and to address it early (Wallerstein and Blakeslee 1995).

Use Reframing to Feel & Act Positively

Can you actually *will* yourself to feel and act positively and affirmatively? Perhaps so. Some studies have found that putting a smile on your face produces the feelings that the expression represents. Indeed, facial action can lead to changes in mood (Zajonc 1985; Adelmann and Zajonc 1989).

You can also use your "inner voice" as a force for success. Positive self-talk, says clinical psychologist Harriet Braiker (1989), consists of giving yourself positive messages—such as "You can do it. You've done it well before"—that correct distortions in your thinking. This is known as **reframing—you redefine the meaning of a situation as a way of changing your perspective on it** (Easley and Epstein 1991).

Have Fun, Keep Your Sense of Humor, & Have Hope

Successful couples dealing with crisis manage to try to have fun—eat out, rent movies, take trips—to avoid letting tragedy take over their lives and send them into depression (Wallerstein and Blakeslee 1995).

There has also been a growing body of literature that seems to show that humor, optimism, and hope can help people conquer disease, reduce stress, and improve psychic well-being (Siegel 1986; Frankenfield 1996; Kamei et al. 1997). Although there is some disagreement as to how much effect laughter and hope have on healing, so many accounts have been written of the positive results of these two qualities that they cannot be ignored.

Strategy for Living #3: Develop a Support System

It can be tough to do things by yourself, so it's important to grasp a lesson that many people never learn: *You are not alone. No matter what troubles you, emotional support is available—but you have to reach out for it.*

Social Support Systems

Social support systems, or their absence, can make a vast difference in how well you deal with stress (Vaux 1988). Some examples:

■ **Being Single:** Single men between the ages of 25 and 64 have a higher rate of deaths from heart disease than married men in the same age range do. Indeed, the single, the divorced, and the widowed have higher death rates in general than married people do.

■ **Social Isolation:** People who are uninvolved with other people or organizations are more vulnerable to chronic disease. Those who are more geographically mobile—and hence presumably less socially connected—tend to have higher rates of depression, heart disease, and lung cancer.

■ **Altruistic Egoism:** **Altruistic egoism is the process of cooperation in which you help others satisfy their needs and they in turn help you satisfy yours** (Selye 1974). In one study, students who scored high on a test for adaptive potential, which included altruism, had fewer physical problems than those who didn't (Colby 1987).

Your Coping Resources

How strong your ties are to others can have an important bearing on how well you handle stress. Belonging to a group of kindred spirits can go a long way toward helping one deal with the stressors and stresses of life. Some forms of support are as follows:

■ **Find Support in Your Family Members:** Family members are one of the most important resources of love and emotional support for handling crises and reducing stress (Harper et al. 2000). In some families, religious beliefs are of considerable help (Weigel and Weigel 1987). Research shows that a simple snuggle can actually lower blood pressure and reduce stress (Grewen et al. 2005) and that women facing a stressful event experience less anxiety when they hold their husbands' hands (Coan et al. 2006).

■ **Talk to and Do Things with Friends:** True friends are not just people you know. They are people you can trust, talk to honestly, and draw emotional sustenance from. Studies show, for instance, that the more students participate in activities with other students, the less they suffer from depression (Reifman and Dunkel-Schetter 1990).

■ **Join a Support Group or Talk to a Counselor:** The areas of concern covered by self-help groups (Alcoholics Anonymous is the most famous) range from drug addiction to spouse abuse to compulsive shopping to stroke victims to various forms of bereavement. You can also get emotional support from counselors, paid or unpaid, including telephone hot lines.

Strategy for Living #4: Take Care of Your Body

The interaction between mind and body becomes particularly evident when you're stressed. If you're not eating and exercising well, are short on sleep, or are using drugs, these mistreatments of the body will only make the mind feel worse. Some related stress-buster techniques are as follows:

■ **Eat Right:** Sugar is seductive. When you're feeling run down, a candy bar or a couple of beers (alcohol contains sugar) seem to provide a pick-me-up. However, a sugar lift wears off very quickly. Fat, such as that found in hamburgers, French fries, and ice cream, can make you feel sluggish (and too much can make you at high risk for heart attack and stroke). The best advice: Most health experts today recommend that you reduce fats of animal origin; eat whole grains, vegetables, and fruit; and drink water and juice rather than sweetened soft drinks or alcohol.

■ **Exercise Right:** Exercise is a terrific stress reducer, energy enhancer, mental relaxant, sleep inducer, confidence builder, and (when done right) form of *fun* (Williams and Lord 1997). Forty minutes of exercise can reduce stress for up to 3 hours afterward, whereas an equal period of rest and relaxation lowers stress for only 20 minutes, according to John Ragland (cited in Busey 1990: 78) of the University of Wisconsin's sports psychology laboratory.

■ **Sleep Right:** We might envy the people we read about who supposedly need only 4 hours sleep a night, but if you sleep 6 to 9 hours, you're within the normal range. Most people are sleep deprived, but sleep is important because it's restorative: It helps you recover from the previous day's stresses and gives you energy to meet the stresses of the next day. The quality of sleep is also important. Sleeping pills or alcohol can actually disrupt sleep so that you wake up feeling tired rather than energetic.

■ **Avoid Drugs:** The temptation of many drugs, whether legal or illegal, is that they *do* alleviate stress—in the short run. But in the long run, they not only come to have a powerful grip on your life but also damage the body. For instance, alcohol has extremely harmful effects on the liver, brain, and nervous system—and thus greatly adds to the stress in one's life.

Strategy for Living #5: Develop Relaxation Techniques

There is an entire body of activities that many people in North America have never tried at all that nonetheless have been found to be extremely effective stress reducers (Snyder 1988). They include deep breathing, progressive muscular relaxation (reducing stress by tightening and relaxing major muscle groups throughout your body), guided imagery (in which you essentially daydream an image or desired change, anticipating that your body will respond as if the image were real), and meditation. *(See ■ Panel 13.4.)* All are worth your investigation.

■ **PANEL 13.4 Meditation.** Meditation includes the repetition of a word, sound, phrase, or prayer for 10 to 20 minutes, practiced once or twice daily.

■ Pick a focus word or short phrase that is firmly rooted in your personal belief system. For example, a Christian person might choose the opening words of Psalm 23, "The Lord is my shepherd"; a Jewish person might choose "Shalom"; a nonreligious individual might choose a neutral word such as "One" or "Peace."

■ Sit quietly in a comfortable position.

■ Relax your muscles.

■ Breathe slowly and naturally, and as you do, repeat your focus word or phrase as you exhale.

■ Assume a passive attitude. Don't worry about how well you're doing. When other thoughts come to mind, simply say to yourself, "Oh, well," and gently return to the repetition.

Source: Adapted from Benson 1989.

Self-Assessment: Major Life Events & Stress

To get a feel for the possible health impact of the various recent events or changes in your life, think back over the past year, and circle the points listed for each of the events that you experienced during that time.

Health

An injury or illness which:

kept you in bed a week or more or sent you to the hospital	74
was less serious than that	44
Major dental work	26
Major change in eating habits	27
Major change in sleeping habits	26
Major change in your usual type or amount of recreation	28

Work

Change to a new type of work	51
Change in your work hours or conditions	35

Change in your responsibilities at work:

more responsibilities	29
fewer responsibilities	21
promotion	31
demotion	42
transfer	32

Troubles at work:

with your boss	29
with co-workers	35
with persons under your supervision	35
other work troubles	28
Major business adjustment	60
Retirement	52

Loss of job:

laid off from work	68
fired from work	79
Correspondence course to help you in your work	18

Home & Family

Major change in living conditions	42

Change in residence:

move within the same town or city	25
move to a different town, city, or state	47
Change in family get-togethers	25

Major change in health or behavior of family

member	55
Marriage	50
Pregnancy	67
Miscarriage or abortion	65

Gain of a new family member:

birth of a child	66
adoption of a child	65
a relative moving in with you	59
Spouse beginning or ending work	46

Child leaving home:

to attend college	41
owing to marriage	41
for other reasons	45
Change in arguments with spouse	50
In-law problems	38

Change in marital status of your parents:

divorce	59
remarriage	50

Separation from spouse:

because of work	53
because of marital problems	76
Divorce	96
Birth of grandchild	43
Death of spouse	119

Death of other family member:

child	123
brother or sister	102
parent	100

Personal & Social

Change in personal habits	26
Beginning or ending school or college	38
Change of school or college	35
Change of political beliefs	24
Change in religious beliefs	29
Change in social activities	27
vacation trip	24
new, close, personal relationship	37
engagement to marry	45
girlfriend or boyfriend problems	39
sexual difficulties	44
"falling out" of a close personal relationship	47

An accident	48	Major purchase	37
Minor violation of the law	20	Foreclosure on a mortgage or loan	58
Being held in jail	75		
Death of a close friend	70		
Major decision about your immediate future	51	**Total score:** _____
Major personal achievement	36		

Financial

Major change in finances:	
increased income	38
decreased income	60
investment or credit difficulties	56
Loss or damage of personal property	43
Moderate purchase	20

Scoring

Add up your points. A total score of anywhere from about 250 to 500 or so would be considered a moderate amount of stress. If you score higher than that, you may face an increased risk of illness; if you score lower than that, consider yourself fortunate.

Source: Reprinted from Miller, M. A., and R. H. Rahe. 1997. Life changes scaling for the 1990s, *Journal of Psychosomatic Research* 43(3): 279–292. Copyright 1997, with permission from Elsevier.

Key Terms Used in This Chapter

acquaintance rape, p. 469

acute, p. 463

adaptation, p. 484

alcoholism, p. 460

altruistic egoism, p. 486

anorexia nervosa, p. 461

anxiety disorders, p. 461

battering, p. 468

bulimia, p. 462

child abuse, p. 477

child neglect, p. 477

chronic, p. 463

common couple violence, p. 473

coping, p. 484

coping strategies, p. 484

crisis, p. 449

cybersex affair, p. 457

cycle of violence, p. 473

date rape, p. 469

defense mechanism, p. 483

denial, p. 483

discouraged workers, p. 455

displacement, p. 483

distress, p. 482

distressor, p. 482

drug abuse, p. 459

drugs, p. 459

eating disorders, p. 461

elder abuse, p. 480

elder neglect, p. 480

emotional abuse, p. 469

emotional neglect, p. 477

emotional violence, p. 469

eustress, p. 482

eustressor, p. 482

external stressors, p. 453

extrafamilial abuse, p. 480

granny dumping, p. 481

hardiness, p. 451

hassles, p. 448

hedonistic affairs, p. 457

incest, p. 477

infidelity, p. 456

internal stressors, p. 452

intimacy reduction affairs, p. 457

intimate partner violence, p. 472

intrafamilial abuse, p. 480

learned helplessness, p. 475

marital rape, p. 473

marriage maintenance affairs, p. 457

mental disorders, p. 460

miscarriage, p. 465

mood disorders, p. 461

patriarchal terrorism, p. 472

physical neglect, p. 477

physical violence, p. 468

projection, p. 483

protection order, p. 476

rape, p. 469

rationalization, p. 483

reaction formation, p. 483

reactive affairs, p. 457

reframing, p. 485

regression, p. 483

repression, p. 483

resilience, p. 450

sandwich generation, p. 453

sexual abuse, p. 477

sexual assault, p. 468

spillover, p. 474

spontaneous abortion, p. 465

stalking, p. 471

stillbirth, p. 465

stress, p. 448

stressor overload, p. 482

stressors, p. 448

sublimation, p. 483

substance abuse, p. 459

substance dependence, p. 459

sudden infant death syndrome (SIDS), p. 466

underemployed workers, p. 455

unemployed workers, p. 455

victim shelter, p. 476

violence, p. 467

vulnerability, p. 450

widow, p. 465

widower, p. 465

women's safe house, p. 476

women's shelter, p. 476

Summary

13.1 Stresses, Hassles, & Crises: Seeking Hardiness

- Stress is the reaction of our bodies to an unusual or substantial demand made on it. Stress has both physical and emotional components. Physical reactions to stress may be tense muscles, high blood pressure, perspiration, tension headaches, intestinal distress, and the like. Emotional reactions to stress are nervousness and anxiety, emotional and mental exhaustion, and even violence.

- Stresses are triggered by stressors, precipitating events that cause the stress.

- Stressors range from hassles to crises. Hassles are simply frustrating irritants such as anxiety over wasting time and pressure to meet high standards at work or college. A crisis is an especially strong source of stress, a crucial change in the course of events that requires changes in people's normal patterns of behavior. Crises can range from normal life events such as pregnancy, childbirth, and job change to more serious events like an auto accident, a physical illness, or an act of infidelity.

- One's psychological response to stress is influenced by the number, kind, and magnitude of stressors, as well as one's emotional predisposition and self-esteem, resilience, coping resources, and hardiness.

13.2 Crises & Disasters

- Stressors can be both external and internal. Internal stressors are those events that begin inside the family. External stressors are those that begin with someone or something outside the family.

- Stressors can be predictable and unpredictable. Each of the four phases of the family life cycle has predictable stressors ranging from those of the newly married to those relating to child rearing and health and financial worries, children leaving home, and aging.

- Unpredictable stressors include such crises as unemployment and underemployment, infidelity, alcohol and drug abuse, mental disorders, physical illness, and death.

13.3 Violence & Abuse: The Dark Side of Intimate Relationships

- Violence is the threat of or infliction of physical or emotional harm on another. It is an especially ugly form of stressor that, whether witnessed or experi-

enced, can have lifelong physical and psychological consequences.

- Physical violence, also called battering, is the infliction or threat of physical harm. This ranges from pushing and shoving to hitting and kicking to biting and choking to stabbing and shooting. A specific kind of physical violence is sexual assault, a legal term for rape.

- Emotional violence, or emotional abuse, is verbal and psychological abuse that inflicts or threatens to inflict emotional distress. This can take the form of criticism, sarcasm, ridicule, and insults, refusing to talk to or touch the partner; restricting the partner in the use of money, the use of a car, or visits with friends; and threats of all kinds, such as to leave, to beat up, to institutionalize, even to kill the partner.

- Violence can occur in dating, cohabitating, and marriage relationships.

- Dating violence can result from jealousy and sexual disagreements and/or be a consequence of the use of alcohol and drugs.

- Unwanted sex may range from people being forced to engage in sexual activities from kissing to sexual intercourse. Rape is unwanted sexual penetration, perpetrated by force, threat of harm, or when the victim is intoxicated or unconscious. The most common type of rape is acquaintance rape, which is nonconsensual sex between adults who know each other. Date rape is nonconsensual sex between dating partners.

- Stalking is the repeated and malicious following or harassment of another person that may occur after that person tries to end a physically or emotionally abusive relationship.

- Intimate partner violence, which is defined as physical and/or emotional abuse of one partner by another male or female, married or unmarried, straight or gay, current or former.

- Marital violence is husbands attacking wives and wives attacking husbands.

- Marital violence can be patriarchal terrorism or common couple violence. Patriarchal terrorism is violence by men who feel that they must control "their" women by any means necessary. Common couple violence consists of violence between partners arising from everyday disagreements that have gone too far.

- Lenore Walker suggested a three-phase cycle of violence of (1) rising tension, (2) escalation and explosion, and (3) calmness, contrition, and kindness following the violent episode before the cycle begins again.

- Rape that happens within a marriage is referred to as marital rape and involves the use of force against one's spouse; it is illegal in every state.

- Individuals stay in abusive relationships because of fear of one's partner, of isolation, or of poverty or out of love, pity, duty, guilt, and hope that the relationship will improve. Individuals may also stay in abusive relationships as a consequence of low self-esteem or childhood experiences. Some people stay in abusive relationships because of learned helplessness—the abuse they have endured has convinced them they have no control over the major events affecting them.

- Family violence may be addressed through intervention, shelters, and safe houses. Women's shelters and victim shelters provide not only food and accommodation but also help with money, food stamps, and counseling and offer legal, medical, and employment assistance.

- Women's safe houses, whose existence is known only to residents and shelter workers, are private homes that provide temporary housing for abused women.

- Treatment programs for abusers aim at changing the behavior of abusive men; they consist of group and individual therapy concerned with reducing stress, improving communication techniques, and similar matters.

- Violence in intimate relationships is not confined to just adults; it extends to children as well. Child abuse refers to acts of aggression by an adult against a child, generally under the age of 18, whether physical or verbal. Sexual abuse is also a form of child abuse. Sexual abuse involves manipulated or coerced sexual behavior of a minor by an adult. It may vary from exposure of private parts and unwanted kissing to fondling and rape to incest—sexual relations between persons who are related to each other. Child neglect is physical neglect, as in not providing enough food, clothing, health care, or security, or emotional neglect, as in not providing sufficient care, attention, and guidance. Physical neglect nearly always results in emotional neglect as well, although the reverse is not necessarily true—emotional abuse need not entail physical abuse.

- Risk factors for child abuse include a family history of physical punishment; unrealistic expectations for the child; alcohol or drug abuse; being raised in socially isolated, overcrowded homes; and economically stressed households located in low-income, unsafe neighborhoods.

- The effects of child abuse can last long into adulthood and may include physical and mental problems, emotional and developmental problems, and intimacy problems.

- Elder abuse consists of acts of aggression against the elderly, including physical assaults, emotional humiliation, verbal abuse, financial exploitation, isolation from friends, and granny dumping.

- Elder neglect consists of acts of omission in the care and treatment of the elderly.

13.4 Coping Strategies: Successful Ways of Handling Stresses & Crises

- Stress in one's life can result from good and bad events. When the source of stress is a positive event, it is called a eustressor, and its effect is called eustress. When the source of stress is a negative event, it is called a distressor, and its effect is called distress.

- As a result of distress, individuals may employ the use of defense mechanisms. Defense mechanisms are unconscious methods for denying, excusing, disguising, or changing the behaviors that cause anxiety and frustration. Although defense mechanisms are often normal and even healthy ways of dealing with difficulty, they can become problems if they prevent you from dealing with reality or communicating about problems.

- Eight common defense mechanisms are repression, denial, rationalization, displacement, projection, reaction formation, regression, and sublimation.

- In handling stress, individuals adapt or cope with the stressors. Adaptation is not changing the stressor or the stress. Coping is changing the stressor or changing your reaction to it.

- To effectively cope with stress, you can reduce the stressors, manage your emotional response, develop a support system, take care of your body, and develop relaxation techniques.

Take It to the Net

Among the Internet resources on stresses, crises, and family violence are the following:

- **American Anorexia Bulimia Association, Inc.** Provides information and services related to eating disorders.
  www.aabainc.org
- **American Association of Suicidology.** Referrals to local self-help groups for survivors.
  www.suicidology.org
- **Childabuse.com** Comprehensive resource bringing awareness and education in preventing child abuse and related issues.
  www.childabuse.com
- **Child Welfare Information Gateway.** Concerned with protecting children and strengthening families.
  www.childwelfare.gov
- **Jed Foundation.** This website of a nonprofit public charity is committed to reducing the young adult suicide rate and improving mental health support pro-

vided to college students nationwide.
www.jedfoundation.org

- **Male Survivor.** Concerned with overcoming sexual victimization of boys and men.
  www.malesurvivor.org
- **National Coalition against Domestic Violence.** Describes counseling, legal aid, and women's shelters.
  www.ncadv.org
- **National Committee for the Prevention of Elder Abuse.** Describes types of abuse and provides referral services.
  www.preventelderabuse.org
- **Rape, Abuse, & Incest National Network (RAINN).** Operates national toll-free hotline for victims of sexual assault.
  www.rainn.org
- **Stop It Now.** Campaign to prevent child sexual abuse.
  www.stopitnow.com

UNCOUPLING
Separation & Divorce

Marriage & Divorce, Love & Heartbreak

*"**You can't leave the dishes** for later, wash the dishes badly, not use soap, drink straight from the container, make crumbs without wiping them up (now, not later), or load the dishwasher according to the method that seems most sensible to you. . . .*

"You can't not make the bed. You can't not express appreciation when the other person makes the bed even if you don't care. You can't sleep apart, you can't go to bed at different times, you can't fall asleep on the couch without getting woken up to go to bed. You can't eat in bed. You can't get out of bed right away after sex. You can't have insomnia without being grilled about what's really bothering you."

These are among hundreds of answers to what Laura Kipnis, in *Against Love: A Polemic* (2003: 85–86), says is the simple question "What can't you do because you're in a couple?" In this "droll, overstated" book, as one reviewer called it, Kipnis says that "the domestic captivity that is marriage is complete and relent-

less, with surveillance, repression, and prohibition built into its very structure" (Mead 2003: 79).

Indeed, Kipnis (pp. 99, 100), a Northwestern University media studies professor, points out that for every film that insists love is "the path to future happiness and fulfillment—fading quickly to black once our lovers, having overcome some temporary series of obstacles, are finally united—the anti-love story is not quite so optimistic. . . . Anti-love films begin where the fade-to-black leaves off," as in the bickering and fighting in Ingmar Bergman's *Scenes from a Marriage* and Mike Nichols's cinematic adaptation of Edward Albee's *Who's Afraid of Virginia Woolf*? Or the couples in the more recent films *American Beauty* and *The Story of Us*.

Do the people who do the acting in celluloid fantasies know more about marital unhappiness than the rest of

🔍 WHAT'S AHEAD IN THIS CHAPTER

The first section discusses different marital endings and trends in divorce. We next discuss the risk factors associated with divorce. We then describe the various processes of divorce, such as the emotional and the financial. Finally, we look at the effects of divorce on the ex-spouses and on the children.

us? Or are they just less patient? Consider these short celebrity marriages (Giantis 2003):

■ **20 months—Lisa Marie Presley & Michael Jackson:** Her next marriage, to Nicolas Cage, ended after 3½ months.

■ **9 months—Jennifer Lopez & Cris Judd:** Choreographer Judd was Lopez's second husband; her first marriage had lasted a year.

■ **5 months—Drew Barrymore & Tom Green, Shannen Doherty & Ashley Hamilton, Charlie Sheen & Donna Peele:** Barrymore's previous marriage lasted 19 days. Doherty's former marriage lasted 8 months. Hamilton's marriage to Angie Everhart lasted 3 months.

■ **A matter of days—Ernest Borgnine & Ethel Merman (32), Cher & Gregg Allman (8), Dennis Hopper & Michelle Phillips (8):** Phillips: They were "the happiest eight days of my life." Hopper: "Seven of those days were pretty good. The eighth day was the bad one."

And then there was the 1919 marriage of "The Great Lover" Rudolph Valentino to actress Jean Acker. They split after 6 hours. (This was even briefer than Britney Spears's 55-hour quickie marriage to Jason Allan Alexander in 2003.)

Perhaps the personal lives of celebrities are merely leading indicators of social trends, the kind that the trend spotters who work for Hallmark greeting cards look for. Hallmark was too early when it introduced divorce cards in 1973 because people didn't want to talk about the subject. "But, oh," says a card company spokesperson, "it's the right time now. We have a nice array" (quoted in Wilson 2001: 2D).

Why do so many loves end in heartbreak, so many marriages in divorce? Is it all just about suddenly getting fed up with the daily irritants of living with another human being—as so well documented by Laura Kipnis? "You can't leave the bathroom door open, it's offensive," she continues (2003: 85, 92). "You can't leave the bathroom door closed, they need to get in. . . . You can't drive too fast, or faster than the mate defines as fast. You can't tailgate, you can't honk. You may not criticize the other person's driving, signaling, or lane-changing habits." And so on.

One divorced woman (quoted in Blakely 1995: 37) said that it took her and her husband only 10 minutes to pronounce the "I dos" at their wedding, "but we would spend the next 10 years trying to figure out who, exactly, was supposed to do what: who was responsible for providing child care, finding babysitters and tutors, driving car pools, for which periods and where?"

In our yearnings for happiness, is marriage just a setup for disappointment?

⊙ ON THE WEB Learning about the Aftermath of Divorce

www.makinglemonade.com/spwanna.htm

If you're an unhappy parent in a marriage and are fantasizing about divorce, this is the place to take a preview into what single parenting is really like, says this website, called Making Lemonade: The Single-Parent Network. If you are married and have children (or even if you aren't), visit the website.

MAJOR QUESTIONS
you should be able to answer

What are the chances that a marriage will end, and how might it happen?

What factors raise the risk that I might divorce, assuming that I were married?

What are the paths people take when they go through divorce?

If I were anticipating a divorce, what are some of the negative consequences I could envision?

14.1 Separation, Divorce, & Trends

MAJOR QUESTION What are the chances that a marriage will end, and how might it happen?

PREVIEW We consider the continuing search for happiness, and its possible connection to separation and divorce, or "uncoupling." We also examine the differences between desertion, separation, annulment, and divorce. Then we discuss various ways to measure divorce and trends in divorce.

James Mooring, age 24, of Dyersburg, Tennessee, was brought up in a close-knit family in which everyone did everything together. "I want a family so bad I can't stand it," says Mooring (quoted in Rimer 2002). When he discovered that his girlfriend of a short time was pregnant, Mooring married her. "I loved her, I just wasn't totally in love," he says. "But I said, I'm just going to make the best of it. As long as she's happy, I'll be happy." They divorced, however, when it turned out that they were "arguing and partying" and neither was happy.

It's not just younger people who seek fulfillment in marriage. Kit Levedahl's husband divorced her after 48 years of marriage and three children. She was 72; her husband, age 74, had met a younger woman. Average life expectancy today being 76 years, older people "see many healthy years ahead of them," says Kate Vetrano, chair of the American Bar Association's elder-law committee. "They decide, 'I'm going to make those years happy'" (quoted in Springen 2000: 56).

The Continuing Search for Happiness: Are Our Expectations for Intimacy Too High?

University of Chicago sociologist Linda Waite says that marriage remains "the gold standard" of American life, because of the emotional, health, and financial benefits marriage can provide (quoted in Melendez 2002: A14). Indeed, as University of Nebraska–Lincoln sociologist Lynn White points out, "for a substantial portion of Americans, it works" (cited in Melendez 2002: A1).

- **Can being fired lead to divorce?**
Married men who are fired have an 18% greater chance of being divorced within the next 3 years, and married women have a 13% higher chance, according to one study.[a]

- **Do some races have higher divorce rates?** Skin color doesn't cause divorce, but race and ethnicity are often associated with other factors, such as education and income level, that may be predictors of divorce. Blacks generally have higher divorce rates than whites because they are disproportionately poor.[b] However, as income levels rise, divorce rates for blacks decrease, resembling those for whites.[c]

- **What are the leading causes of divorce?** One study found that in 47% of divorces, the leading cause of the breakup was incompatibility, or basic personality differences, and another cause was alcohol or substance abuse problems (for 24% of women and 6% of men).[d]

- **How long does it take to cope emotionally with divorce?** Most people take 2 to 4 years to work through the negative emotions of a divorce.[e] However, one study found that about 20% of fathers and 25% of mothers were still coping emotionally with their divorces 10 years after the event.[f]

- **How does divorce change one's standard of living?** One study found that 40% of divorcing wives lost half their family income, compared to 17% of men.[g] Among Latinos, married and divorced men had essentially equal incomes, but divorced women's incomes dropped about 24%.[h] African American divorced women are especially at risk economically because of differences in male and female incomes.[i]

- **What percentage of divorced fathers don't support their children?** About 50% of men don't support their children at all after divorce—or even see them.[j] Two-thirds of noncustodial fathers were found to have spent more on their car payments than on child support.[k]

[a]Charles and Stephens 2001. [b]Blackwell 1991. [c]Raschke 1987. [d]Colasanto and Shriver 1989. [e]Lauer and Lauer 1988. [f]Wallerstein and Blakeslee 1989. [g]Arendell 1995. [h]Stroup and Pollack 1999. [i]Stroup and Pollack 1999; Smock 1993. [j]Sorenson and Zibman 2000. [k]Kitson and Holmes 1992.

However, the high, maybe extravagant hopes that people have for intimacy in marriage might be a primary reason the U.S. divorce rate has continued to be so high for two decades, with half of new marriages ending in dissolution (Glenn 1996). "The right to divorce," suggests one commentator, "is deeply ingrained in American culture precisely because so is the ideal of a mutually fulfilling marriage" (Talbot 2000: 10).

High Hopes

Recall all the expectations we mentioned in Chapter 1, "Seeking":

- Somewhere there is a soul mate for each of us.
- If we love each other enough, we can overcome all problems.
- A marriage partner should be everything—best friend, terrific sex partner, sympathetic confidante, good provider.
- A "normal" family is a close-knit unit consisting of father, mother, and children plus close relatives.

- Perfect families are "always there for us," providing love and solidarity, nurturing and support.

Since the 1950s, people have increasingly emphasized individualistic values, stressing personal growth and self-fulfillment (Guttman 1993). When these values conflict with everyday marital demands ("You can't leave the dishes for later"), divorce can seem to be an obvious way out. Couples with more down-to-earth expectations, however, seem to find more satisfaction in their marriages than do those who expect a lot more emotionally expressive and intense relationships (Troll et al. 1979).

Uncoupling: The Ending of Relationships

Sociologist Diane Vaughan (1986) coined the term ***uncoupling to describe the series of stages by which couples—whether married or cohabiting, heterosexual or homosexual—move toward ending their relationship.*** Uncoupling proceeds something like this:

- **Dissatisfaction:** The initiator of the process—whom we'll call "she" here, although it could be "he"—gradually becomes dissatisfied and begins to think about what she wants out of life.
- **Attempts at change:** She might try to make changes in the relationship but not be successful, perhaps because she doesn't really know what's wrong.
- **Turning elsewhere:** She will then begin to turn away to try to find satisfaction and personal self-validation elsewhere, without at first intending to leave the relationship.
- **Further distancing:** She will voice more complaints, which will have the effect of making the other partner be less desirable, and will begin to weigh the benefits of staying and leaving.
- **Resolution:** Eventually, she will decide that continuing the relationship is no longer possible.
- **Informing the other partner:** She might then simply tell her partner that the relationship is over. Or she might consciously or unconsciously break a basic rule, such as having an affair, and then let her partner find out about it.
- **Acknowledging the ending:** The process of uncoupling ends when both partners acknowledge that the relationship can't be saved and can put it behind them.

What about "Divorce" among Gay & Nonmarried Couples?

Necessarily, this chapter is mostly about divorce within the framework of marital law—the dissolution of marriages between heterosexual men and women. But, of course, unmarried couples who live together—whether heterosexual or homosexual—must deal with the same kinds of issues, such as property distribution, financial support, child custody, and child support. Some examples are as follows:

■ **Gay Couples:** In February 2002, Texas residents John Anthony and Russell Smith went to Vermont to enter into a *civil union*, which, in the United States was then the closest gay and lesbian couples could legally get to marriage. By the end of that year, the two had split up. However, they have not been able to dissolve their civil union, because only partners who live in Vermont for at least a year can have their civil union legally dissolved in that state, and other states don't recognize the civil union at all—putting the Texas ex-couple into a legal limbo (Bernstein 2003).

In another case, Shari Bandes became pregnant by artificial insemination, but then her relationship with her lesbian partner, Mindy Storch, cooled. Seven months after the child was born, the couple separated—and suddenly faced questions about custody and responsibility, issues that were complicated by the fact that they had been unable to be legally married in the first place (Graves 2002).

■ **Unmarried Straight Couples:** Similar kinds of problems apply to nonmarried straight partners who live together and acquire property and children along the way. In one unique case, a southern California man who had raised his ex-girlfriend's son for 7 years, since the child's birth, was awarded legal custody of the boy, despite not being his biological father and despite the mother's objections (Chiang 2002).

In addition, married partners who are growing older find themselves facing custody issues when there is the equivalent of a state-mandated divorce, as when a court appoints a protective service agency to take care of a spouse who has been disabled by Alzheimer's disease or dementia (Hendrix 2002).

A 10-year study by the American Law Institute (Ellman et al. 2002), a prestigious organization of judges and lawyers, recommended sweeping changes in family law that would not only increase property and spousal support protections for divorced women but also extend such rights for the first time to many live-together partners, both straight and gay. The report said that a parent's sexual orientation should not influence decisions about child custody; judges, it said, should not be swayed by stereotypes or "prejudicial attitudes" (quoted in Pear 2002: A1). Although not encouraging cohabitation, the report's coauthors dealt with the subject because they said that divorce court judges advising the project said that 20% of their caseloads involved nonmarried couples (Peterson 2002a).

Conservative critics, such as law professor Lynn Wardle (quoted in Pear 2002: A1), said that the proposals "could undermine the institution of marriage and reflect an ideological bias against family relations based on marriage."

People end dating and live-together relationships all the time, sometimes cordially, often with great bitterness and acrimony. However, these kinds of uncouplings differ from marriage in one important respect: The state is not usually involved. The marriage contract, in contrast, makes the government a third party to a couple's relationship. Let us consider this subject further.

Marital Endings: Desertion, Separation, Annulment, & Divorce

Marriage vows stress perpetuity and longevity: "until death do us part . . . ," "so long as you both shall live . . . ," "let no one put asunder. . . ." Besides death, however, there are four ways in which a marriage can end: *desertion, separation, annulment, divorce.*

Desertion: Abandonment & No Further Contact

When reading the history of the American West, one might begin to notice the great numbers of cases in which families were simply deserted. ***Desertion***

means that one spouse simply abandons the marriage and family and has no subsequent contact.

Today, most desertions occur among the poor and are done by men, who frequently leave because they find the financial demands unbearable. Women might leave because of spousal abuse, because they are overwhelmed by family and child-care responsibilities, or because they visualize a life of greater possibilities than being trapped as a housewife and mother.

When desertion results, as it usually does, in no further financial support by the former income-earning spouse, it can be considered a crime. If children are involved, the deserter (particularly if a woman) might feel extreme anguish.

Separation: No Longer Living Together but Still Married

Separation **is the state in which married partners decide to no longer live together.** Separation might or might not lead to divorce. In fact, many more people have separated than are divorced.

There are three kinds of separation—informal, formal, and controlled.

■ **Informal Separation:** With an *informal separation,* **spouses settle financial, child-custody, child-support, and visitation arrangements informally between themselves; no legal papers are drawn up.** (We explain the meanings of *custody* and *visitation* later in this section.)

The couple remains officially married, they are still legally responsible for each other's debts, and they are not allowed to remarry. According to Constance Ahrons (cited in Dickinson 1999), director of the Marriage and Family Therapy Training Program at the University of Southern California, separations work best if the couple can establish some basic ground rules first, such as agreeing on the length of the separation—3 to 6 months is average—staying away from lawyers (who have a way of moving the process toward divorce), and working on their own individual problems, with or without a counselor.

■ **Formal Separation:** With a *formal separation,* **a couple uses a lawyer to draw up a legal agreement enabling them to live separately but specifying financial, child-custody, child-support, and visitation arrangements between them.** Formal separation is less common than informal separation.

The agreement permits them to have emotional (and sexual) relationships with other people, but neither is allowed to remarry. A formal separation may last for life, or it may be the preliminary step toward divorce.

■ **Controlled Separation:** States no longer require formal or informal separation as part of the divorce process, but many couples try separation either as a last-ditch effort to save their relationship or to do some soul-searching about themselves. Unfortunately, separation often becomes essentially a prelude to divorce. Wisconsin marriage and family therapist Lee Raffel (1998), author of *Should I Stay or Go?,* developed the idea of controlled separation after observing that couples who separated usually had a terrible time. "They didn't know if they wanted to stay or go," she says (quoted in Stout 2005). "They only knew they were unhappy. They didn't know how to solve their problems and they did a lot of nasty things to each other." She developed controlled separation as a way of addressing the failures of formal and informal separations and to halt the move toward divorce.

Controlled separation, usually negotiated in a therapist's office, never a lawyer's, has the ultimate goal of saving a marriage by having a contract or written commitment specifying the time limits (usually no more than 6 months), living arrangements, finances, and contact between the two. For example, a contract might specify a separation of 5 weeks, with one person moving in with a friend and the other staying in the residence; purchases over $500 requiring mutual consultation; contact of no more than three phone calls, unlimited emails, and a date with each other on Saturday night, with sex being optional.

Separations need to be distinguished from a **marriage sabbatical, defined as a personal timeout from daily routines for creative, professional, or spiritual growth, for study, reflection, or renewal** (Jarvis 2001). For example, Cheryl Jarvis, author of *The Marriage Sabbatical*, suggests that the time can be spent on "anything from writing the first draft of a manuscript to painting to walking the Appalachian Trail" (quoted in Stout 2001). This taking leave from family and work obligations (with the agreement of the spouse, as well as the employer) to foster personal growth can range from weeks to months, but the duration should be set in advance. Of course, not everyone can afford to go off to Italy and paint for 6 months (Peterson 2001).

THE BEGINNING OF SEPARATION. Does separation always begin with anger and tears? Many more couples go through separation, but it doesn't always lead to divorce. If you've been through the ending of a serious relationship or marriage, what led you to the point of separation? ▲

Annulment: Marriage Is Declared to Have Never Been Valid

Annulment is a pronouncement that declares that a couple never had a valid marriage, returning both partners to single status and allowing them to marry others. Annulments may be religious or civil.

■ **Religious Annulment:** The Catholic Church does not recognize divorce, but it does recognize annulment, which in essence declares that a marriage never existed. Besides a church annulment, Catholics must also get a civil annulment for the action to be recognized legally by the state.

Most Catholics simply get divorced and remarried, avoiding annulment entirely. However, this means that they are prohibited from full participation in the religious rites of their faith.

■ **Civil Annulment:** A civil annulment, which is granted by a state civil court, declares that the marriage was not valid, returns property to the respective partners, and allows both to remarry. These state-sanctioned annulments occur even with marriages in which children are involved.

> ■ **PANEL 14.1** Some Reasons for Granting a Civil Annulment
>
> ■ **Under age:** Being under the state's legal age, if parents do not approve of the pair's union.
>
> ■ **Unable to have intercourse:** Impotent, disabled, or unwilling to have sex with partner.
>
> ■ **Insane or unable to understand marriage agreement:** Being mentally disabled or intellectually deficient.
>
> ■ **Fraud or bigamy:** A partner misrepresents himself or herself before marriage or is already married.

Civil annulments are granted for any number of reasons, although most of them are for fraud. *(See ■ Panel 14.1.)* (Basketball bad boy Dennis Rodman claimed fraud and an unsound mind when he filed for an annulment against *Baywatch* actress Carmen Electra in 1998. Britney Spears also had her 2003 marriage to Jason Allan Alexander immediately annulled.)

Divorce: Legal Ending to a Valid Marriage

***Divorce* is defined as the legal dissolution of a valid marriage.** Divorce, which has become common in all age, socioeconomic, religious, and racial/ethnic groups, has changed quite a bit during the last few decades.

■ **Divorce before the 1970s—The Fault System:** Before the 1970s, divorce was treated like other cases in the law's adversarial system. The two parties hired lawyers and faced off against each other in court, with one (the plaintiff) suing the other (the defendant). The party who brought suit had to prove that the other was at fault on grounds such as desertion, adultery, impotence, cruelty, insanity, or criminality. The court judged one spouse to be the loser, which influenced the awarding of child custody and property settlement and alimony (Fine and Fine 1994).

In the 1930s and 1940s, Reno, Nevada, became the "divorce capital of the world" because a 1931 law allowed a person to obtain a divorce after residing in the state for 6 weeks, whereas most other states required long waiting periods and often proof or admission of adultery. In New York, for instance, a couple that agreed amicably to divorce might be forced, with the help of a photographer, to stage a charade in which one spouse pretended to be trapped in an act of adultery (with a hired accomplice).

Although, as we discuss next, most states have been making it easier to get divorced by removing "fault" requirements like adultery, seven states have held on to statutes that allow people to sue others and recover damages for sexual indiscretions. *(See ■ Panel 14.2.)* **Alienation of affection laws allow a spouse to bring a suit for damages against a third party with whom his or her spouse has had an extramarital affair and who is alleged to be responsible for the failure of the marriage.** Although rarely used in most states, claims may be filed as leverage in divorce and custody proceedings (Scelfo 2006).

■ Divorce after the 1970s—No-Fault Divorce: Since 1970, beginning in California, all states have adopted *no-fault divorce,* **in which neither partner is found guilty or at fault; the marriage is declared unworkable and is legally dissolved for irreconcilable differences.** No-fault divorce takes the case out of the realm of the legal adversarial process, and financial and child-custody considerations are no longer supposed to be decided on the basis of "morality." In some states, *community property*—**property acquired by the couple during their marriage**—is supposed to be divided equally, reflecting the idea of gender equality and of equal contributions to the marriage.

Thus, the man is no longer automatically considered to be the head of the household, and the mother is no longer automatically considered to be the best parent for the child. *Child custody*—**the court-mandated decision as to which parent will be primarily responsible for the upbringing and welfare of the child**—is supposed to be determined according to "the best interests of the child." Among the decisions to be made are *visitation schedules,* **the days and times on which the noncustodial parent is allowed to visit the children.**

About 90% of divorces are settled out of court through negotiations rather than being contested.

<table>
<tr><td colspan="2">**■ PANEL 14.2   States with Alienation of Affection Statutes, 2007**</td></tr>
<tr><td>■ Hawaii</td></tr>
<tr><td>■ Illinois</td></tr>
<tr><td>■ Mississippi</td></tr>
<tr><td>■ New Mexico</td></tr>
<tr><td>■ North Carolina</td></tr>
<tr><td>■ South Dakota</td></tr>
<tr><td>■ Utah</td></tr>
</table>

Trends in Divorce

If the average (median) wedding cost is $15,000 and if half of all those marrying end up divorced within seven years, does this represent, in that cynical phrase, "the triumph of hope over experience"? What *are* the trends in divorce, and why are the rates so high?

RENO'S AMERICAN DIVORCE COURT, 1935. Reno, Nevada, became known as a place to go in the 1930s and 1940s for "quicky divorces," since only 6 weeks of residence were required in that state, whereas other states had long waiting periods and difficult divorce laws. A whole industry of "divorce ranches" sprang up, dude ranches where wives would go to fulfill their state residency requirements before obtaining their divorce. What would you guess the socioeconomic class would be of such women? ◄

Before we can answer these questions, we need to consider how divorce rates are reported.

What Is the Most Useful Measure of Divorce?

Divorce rates are reported in several ways, some more valuable than others.

■ **Raw Numbers—Not Useful: The *raw numbers* are the actual numbers of people who marry and divorce.** In 2004, the raw numbers show that slightly under 2.3 million people married and about 950,000 divorced (Munson and Sutton 2005). This suggests that about 41% of marriages ended in divorce. However, the raw numbers are not useful for generalizing about marriage and divorce because the numbers are all within *the same year.* The people who were married in 2004 were not necessarily the same people who were divorced in that year.

■ **Crude Divorce Rate—Also Not Very Useful: The *crude divorce rate* is the number of divorces in a given year per 1,000 population.** In 2004, the number was 3.7 per thousand people in the United States. The rate has come steadily downward in recent years, from 5.0 in 1985 to 4.4 in 1995 to 3.8 in 2003. The difficulty with this measure is that within the 1,000 population there are all kinds of unmarried people—singles, divorced, children, widowed, and so on—who are not at risk for divorce.

■ **Refined Divorce Rate—Most Useful: The *refined divorce rate* reflects the number of divorces in a given year for every 1,000 married women over age 15.** *(See* ■ *Panel 14.3.)* In 1997, the refined rate was 19.8 divorces for every 1,000 marriages for married women over age 15, which means that about 2% of marriages in a year end in divorce—a much more reassuring figure than the

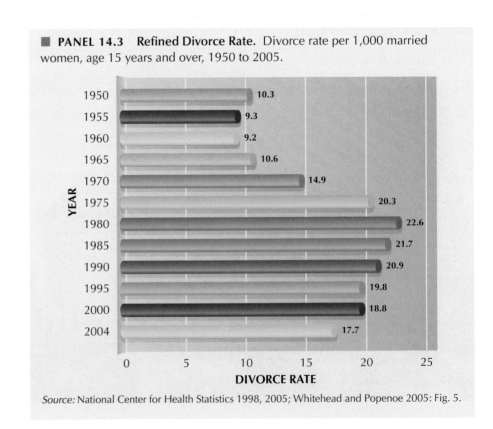

■ **PANEL 14.3   Refined Divorce Rate.** Divorce rate per 1,000 married women, age 15 years and over, 1950 to 2005.

Source: National Center for Health Statistics 1998, 2005; Whitehead and Popenoe 2005: Fig. 5.

"1 out of 2," or 50%, rate that we hear so much about. The refined divorce rate, considered the most useful way to measure divorce, has gone from 9.2 in 1960 to a high of 22.8 in 1979, but since then has declined steadily to 17.4 in 2005, which means that it is now at its lowest level since 1970.

Today's Divorce Rates

If all marriages are considered, about 2 to 3% end in divorce in any particular year. However, anywhere from 40 to 60% of *new* marriages will eventually end in divorce—or about the 1 out of 2 figure we are accustomed to hearing. The probability of a first marriage ending in separation or divorce within the first five years is 20%, and the probability of its ending within the first 10 years is 33% (National Center for Health Statistics 2002). The U.S. divorce rate is the highest of those among industrialized nations, according to the U.S. Census Bureau (2007). *(See ■ Panel 14.4.)*

Also, in a given year, in about half of all couples marrying, one or both partners will have been previously married. The median length of time for a marriage until divorce is about 11 years.

■ **PANEL 14.4   Divorce Rates Worldwide.** Divorce rate per 1,000 population ages 15 to 64 years, 2003.

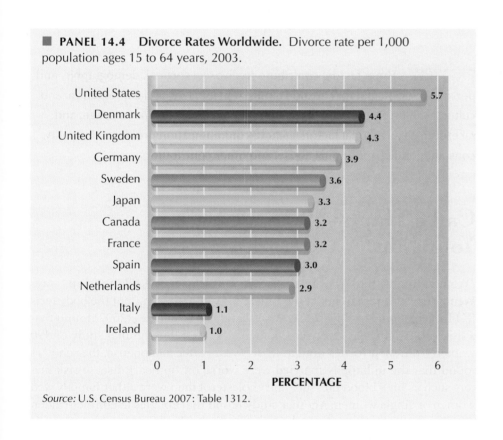

Source: U.S. Census Bureau 2007: Table 1312.

14.2 Why People Divorce

MAJOR QUESTION What factors raise the risk that I might divorce, assuming that I were married?

PREVIEW Three factors contribute to divorce: societal, demographic, and personal. Societal factors include family, religion, law, social integration, and cultural values. Demographic factors include education, income, age, and race/ethnicity. Personal factors include communication problems, infidelity, constant conflict, emotional abuse, and other contributors.

Can a Happy Marriage Save Your Life?

"Women might think they're shrugging off a miserable relationship," says Wendy Troxel, a researcher at the University of Pittsburgh, "but the body feels it" (Troxel, quoted in Elias 2001). Troxel and her colleagues (2002) found that a miserable marriage can make women sick. In a longitudinal study of 490 women from their forties until at least 5 years after menopause, the scholars found that the unhappily married were worse off on heart disease risk factors such as high blood pressure and cholesterol than were either happily wed women or single women. Another study found that couples in conflict-ridden marriages take longer than the happily married to heal from various wounds, from minor scrapes to major surgery (Kiecolt-Glaser et al. 2005). Although in the year after a separation most people report being less happy, according to one British study (Gardner and Oswald 2006), one year after divorce they are happier for their decision.

Of course, many women (and men) stay in unhappy marriages despite the effects on their physical or emotional health. Let us therefore consider the causes of divorce—first the societal and demographic factors, then the personal ones. *(See ■ Panel 14.5.)*

SOCIETAL & DEMOGRAPHIC FACTORS	PERSONAL FACTORS
Family	Communication problems
Religion	Infidelity
Law	Constant conflict
Social integration	Emotional abuse
Individual cultural values	Falling out of love
Education	Unsatisfactory sex
Income	Insufficient income
Age at marriage	Physical abuse
Living together	Falling in love with someone else
Pregnancy before marriage	Boredom
Existence of children	
Race/ethnicity	
Divorced parents	
Remarriage and redivorce	

Societal & Demographic Factors Associated with Divorce

It is hard to consider the big picture when you're involved in the personal pain of divorce. As marital sociologist Joseph Guttman (1993) says, social and structural factors connected with divorce "are largely invisible to people who must cope with the personal consequences of those factors on a daily basis." Nevertheless, let us consider what some of these factors are.

Family, Religious, & Legal Institutions: Have Changes Encouraged More Divorce?

At one time, family, religious, and legal institutions made divorce a difficult process, but as the United States changed from an agricultural to an industrial society, these institutions changed as well.

■ **Family:** Many of the family's traditional functions of child care, protection, and recreation have been taken over by outside institutions: hospitals, schools, police, and the mass media, for example. In the past, large, extended families meant that more people were available to meet one's emotional needs. Today, the stresses of life are often concentrated within a small nuclear family.

■ **Religion:** Many religious leaders now view divorce as being more acceptable, although some still subscribe to *divorcism*, **the belief that divorce is harmful.** People who are church members and regularly attend religious

MOBILITY. One possible explanation for the high divorce rates in the United States is that Americans move around a lot, and the consequent lack of social integration—not being close to family members and familiar friends—weakens social bonds and makes married couples unduly dependent on each other. How many times have you moved in your life? Has this cost you close association with friends and extended family? ▶

services are less likely to divorce than are people who are not members. In fact, the more frequently they attend services, the less apt they are to divorce (Glenn and Supancic 1984). Spouses who have the same religion are also more likely to have stable marriages (Lehrer and Chiswick 1993).

■ **Law:** It is unclear whether the prevalence of no-fault divorce laws contributed to the rise in divorce rates or whether these laws merely reflect a liberalization of attitudes about divorce that was already occurring (Glenn 1997). Certainly, however, legal assistance is easier to obtain, ranging from do-it-yourself books and websites that show you how to fill out forms to legal clinics and storefront law firms.

Less Social Integration: Is Mobility Linked to Divorce?

Social integration **is the degree of cohesion and strength of social bonds that people have with each other and their community.** Social scientists who favor the social integration approach suggest that spouses who are members of extended families, are active churchgoers, live in ethnic neighborhoods, and don't move often are less apt to divorce (Glenn and Supancic 1984; Glenn and Shelton 1985; Shelton 1987). It has been found, for instance, that husbands' and wives' closeness to their in-laws predict higher levels of marital happiness in the first year of a marriage (Timmer and Veroff 2000). The high mobility of people in the United States, plus the diversity of neighborhoods, religions, and languages, might be associated with the high divorce rates.

Individualistic Cultural Values: Is Individual Happiness Valued over Family Connections?

Since the 1950s, Americans have increasingly learned to put personal happiness and growth ahead of family connections and responsibilities (Guttman

1993; Popenoe 1996; Whitehead 1997). As we have noted throughout this book, people expect love and marriage to bring them happiness. In addition, gender roles have become much more egalitarian. With increased economic independence, many women are now less inclined to stay in unsatisfying relationships. Indeed, with 70% of women now employed outside the home, women are more likely to have egalitarian views of gender roles and to distance themselves from their mates (Guilbert et al. 2000). Moreover, employed women are more apt to divorce than are nonemployed women (Heckert et al. 1998). This is not to say that women's employment necessarily leads to divorce; the research seems to show that the employment does not lead to divorce in happy marriages but does increase the risk of marital disruption in unhappy marriages (Schoen et al. 2002).

Education & Income: Do More Schooling & More Money Encourage Marital Stability?

In general, the lower a couple's educational level and income, the higher is the likelihood of divorce (Kurdek 1993).

■ **Education:** One study found that men and women with only a high school education were more apt to become divorced than were those with a college degree (Glick 1984), perhaps because the extra time spent in school gives them more time to mature as well as presents better economic opportunities. The U.S. Census Bureau reported that about 36% of women ages 35 to 39 with less than 12 years of school divorced, compared to about 28% of women with 17 or more years of education (U.S. Census Bureau 2002). *(See* ■ *Panel 14.6.)* Because of the steep decline in the rate of divorce among college graduates, a "divorce divide" may have opened up between people with and without college degrees (Martin 2004).

Sociologist Stephanie Coontz points out that the link between education and divorce is different for women and men. In general, the more years of education a man has, the less he is apt to divorce. Women who don't complete high school have higher divorce rates than women who do, and female high school graduates have higher divorce rates than women who go on to college, writes Coontz. However, "with further higher education, divorce rates to up again" (Coontz 1997: 82). But there is an important qualifier: "People

■ **PANEL 14.6** Percentage of Women Divorced after First Marriage, by Years of School Completed

YEARS OF SCHOOL COMPLETED	AGE AT SURVEY DATE				
	35–39	40–44	45–49	50–54	55–59
Less than 12 years	36.1%	32.7%	36.3%	31.0%	25.8%
12 years	35.0	37.9	34.7	25.8	24.0
13–15 years	38.8	37.8	41.0	35.7	31.2
16 years	25.2	31.5	26.5	24.5	18.1
17 or more years	27.9	32.5	33.0	38.4	25.8

Source: U.S. Census Bureau 2002.

who have started toward *but failed to complete* a particular degree or diploma, whatever its level, are more likely to divorce than those who secure a precise diploma or degree."

■ **Income:** The higher a family's income, the less apt spouses in first marriages are to divorce (Bramlett and Mosher 2002). Couples below the poverty line are twice as likely to divorce within 2 years as are those above the line (Hernandez 1993). Divorce is also more likely if a husband has a low income and the wife doesn't work outside the home or is employed but earns a low income (Ono 1998). However, the higher a woman's income, the greater is the possibility of divorce—again, perhaps because the income gives her more options.

One study (Charles and Stephens 2001) found that being fired from a job significantly raised the probability of getting divorced. Married men who are fired have an 18% greater chance of being divorced within the next 3 years, and married women have a 13% higher chance. (This did not apply to people who lost their jobs because of a plant closing or because of disability.)

Age at Time of Marriage: Is Being Older Better?

People who marry as teenagers are more likely to divorce than are people who marry when in their twenties or older (Martin and Bumpass 1989; Kurdek 1993; Bramlett and Mosher 2002). In general, people who marry young are not well prepared for their spousal roles, owing to lack of emotional maturity, lack of financial stability, inability to handle jealousy and conflict, and so on (Booth and Edwards 1985). Early marriage also makes it more difficult to achieve a higher education, with consequent lower income (South 1995).

After age 23 for women and age 26 for men, however, the age at which a person marries seems to make little difference as a predictor of divorce (Glenn and Supancic 1984).

Living Together: Are Former Cohabitors More Likely to Divorce?

Compared to married couples who did not cohabit, spouses who lived together before marriage have higher rates of marital separation and divorce (Bennett et al. 1988; Bramlett and Mosher 2002). One reason might be that couples with single and multiple cohabitation experiences display poorer communication and marital problem-solving skills. In addition, it's suggested that "the uncertain future of many cohabiting relationships may also engender a sense of . . . being perpetually in the market for a more attractive partner," which perhaps contributes to relationship instability (Cohan and Kleinbaum 2002: 192).

Pregnancy & Children: Does Having Children Before or After Marriage Affect Risk of Divorce?

The way in which children contribute to marital stability or instability depends in part on whether the children existed before or after marriage.

■ **Pregnancy Before Marriage:** Women who are pregnant or have a child before getting married are at higher risk for divorce than are women who conceive or bear children after getting married—at least for first marriages (Norton and Miller 1992). The risk is particularly high for women who are teens, high school dropouts, or of low income (Martin and Bumpass 1989).

■ **Existence of Children during Marriage:** The presence of young children seems to keep spouses together or at least to postpone divorce. However, the presence of teenagers between ages 13 and 17 makes separation and divorce more likely, perhaps because the strains of adolescence aggravate already existing spousal tensions (Heaton 1990).

Race & Ethnicity: Do National Origins & Culture Matter?

African American couples are twice as likely to end their marriages as white and Hispanic couples are (Bramlett and Mosher 2002; Raley et al. 2004; Sweeney and Phillips 2004). The color of one's skin does not cause one to divorce, of course. However, race and ethnicity are often associated with other factors, such as education and income level, that may be predictors of divorce. Thus, African Americans in general have higher divorce rates than do whites because they are disproportionately poor (Blackwell 1991). Black women in particular have extremely high divorce rates—about half their marriages end in 15 years, compared with 17% of marriages for white women—because they are more likely to run the risk of teen pregnancy, premarital pregnancy, or poverty (Garfinkel et al. 1994). However, as income levels rise, divorce rates for blacks decrease, resembling those for whites (Raschke 1987). Latinos have relatively low divorce rates, in part because Catholicism, the religion of many, frowns on divorce.

Divorced Parents: Does Being from a Split Family Encourage Divorce in Children's Marriages?

About a quarter of all first-year American college students have parents who were divorced (American Council on Education and University of California 2000). Are you among them? Unfortunately, if your parents split while you were a child, this increases the likelihood that your marriage will end in divorce as well (Raschke 1987; McLanahan and Bumpass 1988; Teachman 2002). In fact, parents' divorce may increase their children's probability of divorce within 5 years of marriage by 70% (Amato 1996).

In part, this predictor may once again be linked to education and income: children whose parents were divorced are less apt to afford college and more apt to marry early, particularly if they are women (Keith and Findlay 1988; Amato 1996).

Incidentally, there is strong evidence that children who were born out of wedlock are as likely as, if not more likely than, children of divorce to see their own marriages dissolve (Teachman 2002).

Remarriage & Redivorce: Is Dissolution More Likely the Next Time Around?

First marriages that end in divorce last close to 8 years on average, with about 1 year between separation and divorce (Kreider and Fields 2002: 9). However, a new trend has emerged—***redivorce, divorces during second or subsequent marriages, with the median length of time for length of marriage declining.*** *(See* ■ *Panel 14.7.)* The median duration of second marriages that

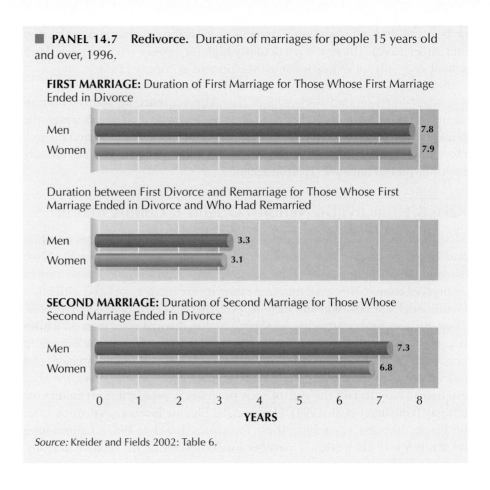

■ **PANEL 14.7** **Redivorce.** Duration of marriages for people 15 years old and over, 1996.

FIRST MARRIAGE: Duration of First Marriage for Those Whose First Marriage Ended in Divorce

Men 7.8
Women 7.9

Duration between First Divorce and Remarriage for Those Whose First Marriage Ended in Divorce and Who Had Remarried

Men 3.3
Women 3.1

SECOND MARRIAGE: Duration of Second Marriage for Those Whose Second Marriage Ended in Divorce

Men 7.3
Women 6.8

0   1   2   3   4   5   6   7   8
YEARS

Source: Kreider and Fields 2002: Table 6.

ended in divorce was about 7 years. In 1995, 15% of remarriages dissolved after 3 years and almost a quarter after 5 years (Bramlett and Mosher 2002: Table 41).

Why is there an increased risk during later marriages? It might be that the existence of stepchildren adds to marital tensions (White and Booth 1985). It might also be that the same factors that were associated with first divorces, such as low education level and low income, are still present in later marriages (Martin and Bumpass 1989).

Personal Factors Associated with Divorce

As we have said, when you're in the midst of the pain of divorce, the big picture is not what you think about. Instead, everything boils down to the personal factors. For instance, one study found that in 47% of divorces, the leading cause of the breakup was incompatibility, or basic personality differences, and another cause was alcohol or substance abuse problems (for 24% of women and 6% of men) (Colasanto and Shriver 1989).

In general, as we indicated in Panel 14.5, the 10 biggest personal issues, in order of frequency, are the following, according to one national study (Patterson and Kim 1991). These reasons overlap because respondents were allowed to give as many as they wished. We will flesh out this list with findings from more recent research (Amato and Rogers 1997; Fu 2000; Amato 2001).

INFIDELITY. One of the main reasons people give for divorce is an extramarital affair. Yet not all infidelities necessarily lead to divorce—indeed, some couples stay together for years despite the ongoing "cheating" of one or both partners. Do you think you could handle this obvious betrayal of trust in your own relationship? ◄

1. Communication Problems: "She/He Doesn't Know Me"

Communication problems were listed as the most frequent reason why Americans said they got divorced. A husband might complain that his wife "doesn't know me." A wife might say that her husband "doesn't understand who I am." If a couple has faulty communication skills, issues go unresolved and build up over time.

2. Infidelity: "He/She Has Broken My Trust"

It is not clear whether infidelity contributes to the decline in a relationship or develops as a result of dissatisfaction with the marriage. Nevertheless, a review of nine studies analyzing reasons people gave for divorce found that extramarital relationships were mentioned in eight of them (Kitson et al. 1985). Compared to the problems of nagging, anger, and financial problems associated with a spouse, a lover seems to offer only positive benefits: exciting sex, romantic dinners, close attention.

Although infidelity ranked high in the Patterson and Kim (1991) study, another study found that extramarital affairs ranked seventh as the most common reason for divorce (Kitson and Sussman 1982).

3. Constant Conflict: "We Never Get Along"

"You never pick your dirty clothes off the floor." "You come home late without calling." Every marriage experiences conflict, but some relationships involve continual conflict, over issues ranging from domestic chores to extramarital affairs to disagreements about how to discipline children (Stewart et al. 1997). Or sometimes the conflict may come about because some event has raised the tension level in the household, as in a home-renovation project (Breslau 2006). Couples who can't reduce their disputes, according to Gottman and colleagues (1998), are at high risk for divorce.

As we have seen (in Chapter 6, "Communication," and Chapter 13, "Crises"), some couples simply don't have good conflict-resolution skills. According to one study, about half of couples who divorced had frequent, intense conflict (Kelly 1988).

4. Emotional Abuse: "She/He Doesn't Treat Me Well"

Emotional problems and negativity can cause a relationship to deteriorate (Caughlin et al. 2000). For example, husbands might resent their wives' being critical, being quick to anger, moodiness, having easily hurt feelings, and not talking (Amato and Rogers 1997). Wives might be upset that their husbands are moody, don't talk, are quick to anger, are not home enough, and have irritating habits (Amato and Rogers 1997).

5. Falling Out of Love: "My Perspective Changed"

On her fortieth wedding anniversary, Terry Martin Hekker (2006) was stunned and devastated when her husband presented her with a divorce. ("He got to take his girlfriend to Cancun," she wrote, "while I got to sell my engagement ring to pay the roofer.") People might begin a marriage with a similar outlook, but their perspectives change during their lifetimes, as they do for most people. The love that two people felt for each other at the start changes because the partners themselves change. Even if there is little conflict in the marriage, the partners find that they no longer enjoy being with each other or doing the same kinds of things, or one or both don't like the way their partner has changed (Kelly 1988). Having little in common weakens marital bonds.

6. Unsatisfactory Sex: "The Thrill Is Gone"

Newspapers, magazines, and other mass media frequently run advertisements for services (such as clinics) or products (such as Viagra) that are intended to "rejuvenate your sex life." Indeed, boredom with sex is the reason why some couples enter into extramarital affairs.

7. Insufficient Income: "There's Never Any Money"

Limited education and limited income, as we have seen, increase the stresses in a relationship. This, of course, is one reason why people of lower socio-economic status are at higher risk for divorce (Hernandez 1993; Ono 1998; Lawson and Thompson 1999). Amato and Rogers (1997) found that husbands who divorced reported anger over their wives spending money and wives resented their husbands spending money foolishly or having an insufficient income.

8. Physical Abuse: "He/She Beats Me Up!"

Physical abuse—often associated with alcohol and/or substance abuse—is the ultimate expression of disrespect for one's spouse. Under such circumstances, clearly there comes a point when the benefits of the relationship no longer outweigh the drawbacks.

9. Falling in Love with Someone Else: "This Is the Person I Should Have Married!"

This reason, of course, overlaps with others—falling out of love with one's spouse or having an extramarital affair—and even with the reason to follow, boredom.

10. Boredom: "It Was Just the Same Old Same Old"

Although 64% of the respondents listed personal reason #1, "communication problems," as the reason for divorce, the last reason—boredom—nevertheless was mentioned by 22%. Another name for boredom is *satiation*, **the term for what occurs when a stimulus no longer stimulates because of repeated exposure** (the "cry wolf" phenomenon). Routine, of course, is endemic to all relationships, and part of the challenge for long-term couples is to keep a measure of enjoyment in their union by finding pleasurable experiences, taking trips, going out to dinner, and so on.

14.3 The Process of Divorce

MAJOR QUESTION What are the paths people take when they go through divorce?

PREVIEW One scholar has proposed six "stations" or processes of divorce: (1) emotional, or loss of affection and trust; (2) legal, the court-ordered termination of a marriage; (3) economic, or the settlement of property; (4) co-parental, or decisions about child custody, support, and visitation; (5) community, or the giving up of relatives and mutual friends; and (6) psychic, or the complete emotional separation from the former spouse. We discuss two variations on traditional divorce: divorce mediation and collaborative divorce.

You can find a relationship, fill out a bridal registry, and plan a honeymoon—all online (Sharp 2002). Now you can also use the Web to put it all asunder. For fees ranging from $50 to $300, a great deal less than what most divorce lawyers charge even for uncontested divorces, you can go online and obtain the appropriate forms and various degrees of help in completing them.

"I filled out the forms in the course of a night—it took three hours—and saved $2,000," says John Chang of South Pasadena, California, who paid a firm called LegalZoom $300 to help him obtain an uncontested divorce. "When you don't have children or a lot of assets, it's the way to go" (Chang, quoted in Crary 2003: 6A).

In California, a reported 80% of people who file for divorce handle their own paperwork, probably because of rising lawyers' fees, decreasing legal services for poor people, and a "Home Depot philosophy of people feeling they can do things on their own," suggests Richard Zorza (quoted in Associated Press 2007), who coordinates a national network of organizations working on self-representation. A concern to court officials and legal experts, however, is that many people, perhaps a third, are so stumped by complex paperwork and court procedures that they don't finalize their divorce petitions—which means they really aren't divorced.

Uncoupling can be a long, complicated process. Let us consider how it develops.

The Long Good-Bye: Bohannan's Six Stations of Divorce

Anthropologist **Paul Bohannan** (1970) proposed a psychological model consisting of *six stations, or processes, of divorce:* **emotional, legal, economic, co-parental, community, and psychic.** (The co-parental process doesn't occur in every case.) As people divorce, they go through these six processes, though not in any particular order or simultaneously and with varying degrees of intensity of feeling. Whereas in marriage, Bohannan says, you feel good partly because you have been selected from among a host of others to be someone's intimate partner, in divorce you feel awful partly because of the opposite—you have been "de-selected." The six stations are discussed next.

1. The Emotional Divorce: "I Don't Care for Him/Her Anymore; I'm No Longer Involved"

The *emotional divorce* involves loss of affection, trust, and respect for each other and replaces positive emotions with indifference or destructive emotions. In the emotional divorce, which begins before any legal actions are taken, the partners might engage in sarcasm, blame, quarreling, and acts that are intended to wound each other. Or they might be simply aloof and indifferent. They might mentally already be distancing themselves from each other, even though they might remain together "for the sake of my . . . (wedding vows/children/religion/whatever)."

The emotional divorce has three phases:

■ **Beginning Phase:** Here, you and your partner begin to feel disappointment with each other. However, you might still hope the relationship will improve.

■ **Middle Phase:** Anger and hurt feelings increase as the marriage difficulties remain unresolved. Whichever of you is the unhappier will begin weighing whether or not to leave.

■ **End Phase:** You and your partner completely stop caring about each other. You become apathetic and indifferent to the other's feelings, although you might seek counseling to put off the final breakup. You might have a period of trial separation. Later, you and your partner might seek legal advice.

2. The Legal Divorce: "I Wanted Out, but I Miss What We Once Had—& Why Is the Legal System So Difficult?"

The *legal divorce* is the court-ordered termination of a marriage. The purpose of this station, the only one that actually benefits the two parties, is to end the marriage contract so that the two former partners can have economically separate lives and, if they wish, be free to remarry. The partners come to agreement on the important issues of property division, child custody, and perhaps spousal support (alimony), as we'll discuss.

The legal divorce can be particularly painful because of two factors:

■ **Ambivalence and Grieving:** Divorcing partners might wonder whether they are really doing the right thing in divorcing. They might also grieve for the loss of a relationship that at one point provided splendid benefits—love, familiarity, comfort, and intimacy. However, few divorce attorneys—most of whom are more concerned with protecting or advancing their client's economic position—have much time to spare for hand-holding and grief counseling.

■ **Adversarial Aggravation:** Although a few lawyers specialize in divorce mediation (as we'll discuss), the U.S. legal system is largely an adversarial arena in which lawyers are supposed to fight for the rights of their clients. Consequently, even parties in a supposedly amicable divorce may find themselves highly aggravated by the zeal with which the opposing attorneys aggressively strive to achieve the best deal for the individuals rather than for both parties.

Some jurisdictions have family courts that try to ameliorate marital failure or at least ensure a fair legal divorce. One lawyer-free court in Kane County, Illinois, allows ex-couples to represent themselves in divorce and related custody matters (Wilgoren 2002).

3. The Economic Divorce: "I'm Afraid I Won't Have Enough to Live on, & I Dread Losing Things I've Become Attached To"

The *economic divorce* **involves settlement of the property.** In most states, property that is acquired during the marriage—not just cars and houses, but everything—is considered joint property (unless it is declared off-limits by a premarital agreement). As you might imagine (or have experienced), this area can involve considerable conflict.

The economic divorce is often quite painful, for the following reasons:

■ **Threat of Declining Living Standards:** Usually, there is not enough money and property (savings, houses, furniture, pensions) to allow the former partners to maintain the same living standards separately that they had jointly.

■ **Disputes over Who Gets What:** Who gets the dog? The car? The silverware? The great rug you acquired on your overseas trip? People's attachments to things can generate a lot of conflict.

■ **Loss of Favorite Things:** The prospect of living without certain items that you learned to cherish—ranging from the cat to the vacation home—can produce a lot of sadness.

We expand on the consequences of economic divorce later in the chapter.

4. The Co-Parental Divorce: "He/She Can't Take Away My Children!"

Applying only to couples who have children (about two-thirds of all couples), **the *co-parental divorce* involves decisions about child custody, child support, visitation rights, and the ongoing responsibilities of each parent.**

This is one of the most difficult, and even tragic, areas of divorce. Divorcing partners might be so enraged at each other that the children become unwilling, frightened pawns in their dispute—and continue to be long afterward. Some people might have been indifferent parents during the marriage but will pull out all stops in the battle for custody. Or in using the children to try to extract large child-support payments and minimal visitation rights.

We discuss the effect of divorce on children—and the recommended course of action for divorcing parents—later in the chapter.

5. The Community Divorce: "So Long, In-Laws; Good-Bye, Common Friends"

The *community divorce* means that each partner reduces or leaves membership in a common community of relatives and friends. This community might be replaced with new communities—or even no communities, as when a newly single parent finds herself or himself too exhausted from work and child raising to make new friends.

When people marry, they usually acquire a community of relatives and perhaps mutual friends. After divorce, these relationships might become strained or might disappear entirely. The wife's old high school friends that a married couple used to have over for dinner might revert to being just her friends. The husband's kid brother whom they took in when he was between jobs might never meet up with his former sister-in-law again.

The station of community divorce can have considerable impact in two areas:

■ **Relations with Relatives from the Marriage:** Extended families can be profoundly affected by divorce, as when grandparents find the custodial parent taking their only grandchild and moving out of state. Although the relationships between former relatives often decline or disappear, quite often ties are still maintained to former in-laws (Ambert 1988).

Indeed, the term *relatives of divorce* **has been coined to describe kinship ties that were established during marriage but continue after divorce** (Johnson 1988). For example, an ex-daughter-in-law and ex-mother-in-law might continue to see each other even though one (or both) has remarried.

Postdivorce in-law relationships seem to thrive best when the family members haven't taken sides in the divorce and have made their primary commitment to the children (Wallerstein and Blakeslee 1989). Women are more apt to stay in close touch with their in-laws after divorce, especially if they did so before and especially if children are involved (Serovich et al. 1991).

■ **Relations with Friends from the Marriage:** When people are single, they might have a lot of single friends. When they marry, they might then find more couples as friends. And when they divorce, they might find themselves losing friends—in one study, three-fourths of women said that they lost friends during or after divorce (Arendell 1986).

Divorced new singles and their married friends might find themselves suddenly no longer comfortable with each other. Married couples might feel that they should take sides in the divorce, suffer grief over the loss of another couple with whom they used to share many experiences, and feel their own marriage threatened by the presence of a single. Divorced singles, on the other hand, might feel awkward about no longer being a member of a couple and might be eager to find support and new relationships among other single and divorced people.

Moving from one community of relationships to another can be difficult, and divorced people often feel isolated and lonely during this time.

6. The Psychic Divorce: "Now, Finally, I Don't Care about Him/Her Anymore; I'm My Own Person"

Bohannon regards this last station as the most important of the six. **The *psychic divorce*, which follows a period of mourning, means that you**

Alternatives to the Courtroom: Rent-a-Judge, Divorce Mediation, & Collaborative Divorce

"Divorce is just an absolutely awful process," says Birmingham, Alabama, lawyer and divorce mediator Lee Borden *(www.divorceinfo.com)*. "Whether you're the leaver or the left, whether you have children or not, divorce stinks."

There is probably no way to avoid the pain that characterizes most couples' separation and divorce. However, rent-a-judges, divorce mediation, and collaborative divorce might help to reduce the acrimony and expense and to advance the healing process.

Rent-a-Judge: Quicker, Cheaper Third-Party Help

Clogged courts and changing statutes in states such as California, Colorado, Florida, Ohio, and Texas have cleared the way for private judges, who can save a divorcing couple perhaps 30 to 50% in time and fees. "The practice is gaining a foothold in part because, unlike binding arbitration, the decisions can be appealed," says one report (Daily 2006). "It also helps that the jurists, many of them retired from the bench or attorneys who changed careers, may be surer and swifter

than the government judge who happens to get your case." The fee can be $350 to $475 an hour, but that rate is split with the divorcing spouse. Most cases are settled in days instead of weeks.

Divorce Mediation: Other Third-Party Help

Mediators try to help about-to-be-divorced people to develop communication skills to negotiate with each other and arrive at mutually agreed-on solutions. The mediator acts as a neutral advisor who presents options for the couple to consider.

Mediators may be attorneys or mental health experts—from social work, family therapy, or marriage counseling backgrounds—but others, such as accountants, are also seeking training in mediation (DeWitt 1994). Sometimes, two people—a lawyer and a mental health professional—will act as mediators together. There are also online divorce mediation sites (Maltais 2001; Flynn 2002).

The main beneficiaries of mediation are not just the spouses but also any children who are involved

(Marlow and Sauber 1990; Kelly 2000). Among the benefits are the following:

■ **Better communication, reduced conflict, increased cooperation:** Mediation increases communication between the partners, decreasing the level of anger.

When divorced parents are able to discuss differences (about visitation schedules, say) without sarcasm, bitterness, or shouting matches, the chances of reaching workable outcomes are much improved. Moreover, the outcome of the mediation is apt to generate more satisfaction than a solution imposed by a judge. The two partners must agree to enter into the mediation in a spirit of fairness and to not withhold information about assets, income, and debts.

■ **Savings in money and time:** Mediation offers considerable monetary savings. *(See ■ Panel 14.8.)* Also, whereas divorce litigation can take 2 to 3 years, mediation might take only 2 to 3 months—once again a special benefit to children,

separate from your former partner emotionally and are free from his or her influence.

The mourning period consists of at least three stages (Brodie 1999):

■ **Denial:** Usually occurring early, even before the legal divorce, denial is the inability to accept that uncoupling is necessary—until frustrations build up and lead to the emotional divorce that forces both partners to this realization.

■ **Anger and Depression:** Is it possible to be both angry with your former partner and also depressed that he or she is no longer in your life? Divorced

520   CHAPTER 14 UNCOUPLING: SEPARATION & DIVORCE

who won't have to wait a long time for custody arrangements and visitation schedules to be finalized.

- **More privacy:** Because mediation occurs in private, participants avoid having their finances and personal lives aired in open court. Also, mediators are not allowed to divulge information without the spouses' permission.

Collaborative Divorce: No Third Party

There is a considerable overlap between divorce mediation and collaborative divorce, but the collaborative process differs in that there is no third party. Each spouse has his or her own lawyer present. As one account describes it, "The main distinction is the couple and their lawyers try to resolve all issues themselves, then present their agreement to a judge for approval" (Gullapalli 2002: D3).

Sometimes other professionals are called on to assist in collaborative negotiations, such as accountants, mental-health practitioners, parenting coaches, and even clergy. (Divorce mediators also may draw on such professionals.)

Like mediation, collaborative divorce is a good process for people who value their privacy. It is also a faster process than a typical divorce, with resolution occurring in about 3

■ **PANEL 14.8   Mediation versus Divorce: How Much?**

■ **Mediation—$2,000–$5,000:** At $75–$250 an hour, it's not cheap—but it's cheaper than most methods of divorce.

■ **Internet divorce—$20–$250 per spouse:** Takes only a few hours. Note: You need to be sure the service properly transfers the legal paperwork and that it is processed at court.

■ **No-fault divorce—$1,000–$1,200 per spouse:** Wal-Mart will sell you the book *Divorce Yourself: The National No-Fault Divorce Kit* for $22 (Sitarz 1998). Involving lawyers costs more but can offer couples better protection. Couples must agree neither is at fault and not to litigate.

■ **Collaborative divorce—$1,000–$3,000 per spouse:** Faster than litigation. when property and child custody issues are simple.

■ **Litigated divorce—$20,000–$75,000 per spouse:** Takes up to 3 years. Traditional litigation should be reserved for cases involving complex finances, property, and custody issues.

Sources: Adapted from Gullapalli 2002; www.divorce.com 2002; National Conflict Resolution Center 2007.

---

months, as opposed to an average of 20 months for a courtroom divorce. Finally, it is less expensive, with lawyers receiving an average of $3,000 per spouse, compared with $10,000 to $25,000 per spouse in standard divorces.

There are some risks, however. The process should not be used in cases involving domestic abuse or drug or alcohol addiction, since batterers might try to use verbal and nonverbal cues to inspire fear in the other spouse—and the lawyers might not pick up on them.

In addition, if the collaborative process breaks down, it can end up being even more expensive, because the couple can end up hiring new attorneys (and paying more fees) and starting over again. Therefore, couples have to be willing to n egotiate, compromise, and act cooperatively.

People seeking lawyers for a collaborative divorce can contact family lawyers in their community or a local collaborative law institute, who can refer them to local collaborative practitioners.

---

people often experience a seesaw of emotions, one alternating with the other.

■ **Acceptance and Forgiveness:** This final stage represents the culmination of the psychic divorce: You accept responsibility for your part in ending the relationship, forgive yourself and your partner, and realize that you're your own person, able to cope with the world on your own.

Some divorced people never achieve psychic divorce. To the extent that you are still preoccupied with and angry toward your former partner, you are still connected to the relationship. The lingering resentments, bitterness, and

UNCOUPLING. The process of divorce takes many forms—emotional, legal, economic, and so on. An overriding characteristic is that of loss—of things, of pets, of favorite places, of friends and in-laws, perhaps of children. If you have not been through divorce, how do you think you would handle it? ▶

hatred keep you from distancing yourself and prevent you from feeling whole. We consider this further in a few pages.

Divorce Mediation & Collaborative Divorce

The six stations of divorce represent a process that can be painful, acrimonious, and difficult. Are there ways to ameliorate this?

The courts are supposed to act in the best interests of both parties, and legal observers might tend to think that a good settlement is one in which neither ex-spouse leaves the courtroom satisfied. A quicker, less expensive alternative to litigation is *divorce mediation*, **a process in which divorcing spouses make agreements with a third party about property division, spousal support, child custody, and child support.**

Another recent innovation is the so-called *collaborative divorce*, **in which a couple and their lawyers sign a contract agreeing to dissolve the marriage without litigation—and if they fail, the lawyers pledge to drop out of the case before it goes to court** (Gullapalli 2002).

We discuss these processes in the Practical Action box beginning on page 520.

14.4 The Effects of Divorce

MAJOR QUESTION If I were anticipating a divorce, what are some of the negative consequences I could envision?

PREVIEW The consequences of divorce can be emotional, psychological, and physical, producing depression, anger, stress, and health problems. The consequences are also financial, depending on the arrangements for property settlement, spousal support, and child support. There are important effects in how child custody is awarded—sole, joint, split, or third party. Finally, there are both short-term and long-term effects on the children of divorce.

Rachel Harris (2003) was a divorced, 55-year-old woman whose parents were dead, who was estranged from her brother, and whose only child was away at college. Harris had no other close relatives when, in 2002, she was hit with some dismaying news: Three of her neck vertebrae had deteriorated badly, owing to a long-ago injury, and she faced immediate surgery or life-long disability. From her doctor's office, she says, she "drove home to an empty house where there was no husband, life partner, or lover to call or comfort me. I was alone and scared."

She had never imagined that her life could be like this. "I'd always assumed that there would be a man in my life, that we would share a future together, weathering whatever problems arose. I was wrong. I divorced in my late forties fully expecting to remarry. But I was a devoted mother who didn't want to take my energy away from my teenage daughter to concentrate on dating. No one I met inspired me to change my mind. I didn't understand the social reality of being a postmenopausal woman. . . . I had to adjust to a level of independence I'd never chosen."

Divorce often has unintended consequences. Fortunately for Harris, however, she was able to call on a network of friends who were willing to interrupt their own lives and help her through surgery and the reconstruction of her spine. The lesson, says Harris, for the growing number of women living on their own: "We will, all of us, need help from our friends at one time or another."

Emotional, Psychological, & Physical Effects

Divorce doesn't always result in loneliness. But it is usually an agonizing process emotionally for everyone involved, regardless of sex, race and ethnicity, and socioeconomic status. One study of 80 people whose divorces had become final 6 to 12 months earlier found that 87% had "felt angry toward my former spouse," 86% said they had "felt insecure," and 86% had "been depressed" (Buehler and Langenbrunner 1987).

Most people take 2 to 4 years to work through the negative emotions of a divorce, but some feel the effects for decades (Lauer and Lauer 1988). One study found that about 20% of the fathers and 25% of the mothers were still coping emotionally with their divorces 10 years after the event (Wallerstein and Blakeslee 1989). For many, the anger, hostility, and hurt don't go away even after 25 years (Wallerstein et al. 2000). Those who are unable to complete their "psychic divorce" (described previously) suffer from what has been called *divorce hangover*—**they are unable to let go of the fact of their divorce, reorient themselves as single parents, or develop new friendships** (Walther 1991).

The following are among the emotional, psychological, and physical effects of divorce.

Separation Distress: Depression, Anger, & Anxiety

The term *separation distress* **has been given to the psychological state following separation, which may feature feelings of depression, loss, and anxiety, as well as intense loneliness.** The loss of emotional and sexual intimacy and of one's identity as part of a couple can be devastating—especially for the spouse whose partner initiated the divorce. However, the initiating spouse also experiences depression, anger, and guilt, although usually earlier in the divorce process (Buehler 1987). When compared to married people and other singles, divorced people have been found to be the most depressed and even suicidal (Kurdek 1991; Waite and Gallagher 2000). Particularly in the beginning, the former partners are often highly angry and bitter, fighting over property and children and blaming each other for everything.

Loneliness & Feelings of Being Stigmatized

Moving out or watching your partner move out, sleeping alone, eating by yourself, and seeking out friends and strangers for companionship all heighten your feelings of loneliness. Being separated or divorced can also make you feel stigmatized by your own parents and siblings, as well as by your ex-partner's family and even by friends and co-workers (Gerstel 1987; Gasser and Taylor 1990; Kitson and Morgan 1991). You might feel, for example, that you have somehow disgraced yourself and them by not succeeding in your marriage.

Stress

Needless to say, all such negative feelings are exceedingly stressful, although the amount of stress will probably vary depending on the amount of stress in the marriage before the divorce (Wheaton 1990). Even so, divorce is said to

be the greatest stress-producing event that one can experience in life, next to the death of a spouse or a child (Holmes and Rahe 1967).

Health Problems

Divorced people are at higher risk for health problems in part because the ongoing stress can tax their immune systems (Gottman 1994). Divorced people have higher likelihood of heart or lung disease, cancer, high blood pressure, diabetes, stroke, and difficulties with mobility (Hughes et al. 2004). They also show higher rates of alcoholism, mental problems, accidents, and suicide (Hemstrom 1996; Richards et al. 1997). After 10 years, divorced women in one study reported 37% more physical illness than those who stayed married, from simple respiratory infections to heart disease and cancer (Wickrama et al. 2006). A study of 127,545 adults showed that divorced people reported more smoking, physical inactivity, and heavy drinking than married individuals (Schoenborn 2004).

Positive Effects

Perhaps surprisingly, however, many people say that being divorced yields positive effects, especially in the long run. The same study we cited earlier (Buehler and Langenbrunner 1987) of 80 people whose divorces had become final 6 to 12 months before found that the majority expressed such positive feelings as "felt worthwhile as a person" (96%), "experienced personal growth and maturity" (94%), "felt relieved" (92%), "felt closer to my children" (89%), and "felt competent" (89%). Divorce is apt to be positive for young, highly educated females in short-lived marriages (Veevers 1991) and for those with good social support systems (Garvin et al. 1993). Even so, only a minority of divorced couples in Judith Wallerstein's long-term research were able to recreate fuller, happier lives after the divorce (Wallerstein and Blakeslee 1989; Wallerstein et al. 2000).

Interaction with Ex-Spouse

Interaction with former spouses varies a great deal. As might be expected, when children are in the picture, there is more contact after a divorce between ex-spouses, although the relationship might involve more conflict than will postdivorce relationships among the childless (Masheter 1991). One researcher, Constance Ahrons (reported in Stark 1986; Ahrons and Rodgers 1987), found four kinds of relationships among 98 pairs of former spouses, ranging from cooperative colleagues to fiery foes to angry associates to perfect pals. *(See ■ Panel 14.9.)*

Financial Effects

No-fault laws were intended to make economic and child-custody matters more equitable. Do they? Let's consider the answer to this question in relation to three financial areas: (1) *property settlements,* (2) *spousal support* (alimony), and (3) *child support.*

Property Settlements: Are "Equal" & "Equitable" the Same?

No-fault law operates on the assumption that, except for inheritances or gifts from parents, both partners contributed to the marriage equally, and therefore the money and property (and debts) accumulated during the marriage should be divided fairly. What does *fairly* mean? Depending on which of the 50 states you live in, it can be either equal or equitable.

Consider the famous 1997 Connecticut case of Lorna Wendt, who for 31 years was married to a man who became GE Credit Corporation's chief executive. In their divorce, Lorna was initially awarded a settlement worth $20 million from a family fortune worth about $100 million. Was this fair?

Family divorce mediator Anju Jessani (2003) makes the following important distinction:

■ **Property Divided Equally, Not Equitably:** A few states, influenced by their French or Spanish heritage, have the continental system of community property (50–50). In such *equal-distribution states*, **property that was acquired by either spouse during their marriage (except gifts from third parties) belong equally to the husband or wife.** These states include Arizona, California, Idaho, Louisiana, Nevada, New Mexico, Texas, and Washington.

LORNA WENDT. The wife of General Electric executive Gary Wendt is surrounded by members of the media in Stamford, Connecticut, outside the courthouse in which her divorce case was being heard. She was initially awarded $20 million of the couple's $100 million fortune, not half as is mandated in other states. What do you think of this decision? ◄

Had the Wendts filed for divorce in these states, points out Jessani, Lorna Wendt should have received approximately half the assets, or $50 million.

■ **Property Divided Equitably, not Equally:** However, the majority of states—including Connecticut, New Jersey, New York, and Pennsylvania—base their domestic-relations law on British common law. In such *equitable-distribution states,* **the court determines a fair and reasonable distribution that may be more than or less than 50% of any asset to either of the divorcing parties.** Consequently, divorce settlements are often intended to provide nonworking spouses with sufficient financial resources to live in their accustomed manner.

For Lorna Wendt, $20 million was considered equitable on the basis of her lifestyle and set of circumstances. Had the family fortune been $5 million rather than $100 million, she might have gotten 50% rather than 20% of the assets (Jessani 2003). Fortunately for Lorna Wendt, after two years of court wrangling she actually did end up with closer to half of the assets, although she won't disclose the exact amount (Benjamin 2005).

New Jersey law is indicative of equitable distribution states in that it directs the court to consider 16 factors in determining what is an equitable, fair, and just division of property. *(See ■ Panel 14.10.)*

Property, also called *assets,* does not consist of just houses and bank accounts. Except for very wealthy people like the Wendts, truly valuable property today lies in "human capital"—the earning power residing in work experience, a skilled trade, a professional degree, or a business position (Glendon 1981). Thus, the gender-neutral emphasis of no-fault divorce law can actually work against women. A divorced wife who stayed home for many years raising children, even if she gets half the property and savings, is apt not to have the earning power of her ex-husband. Indeed, most divorced women experience dramatic declines in their economic status (Morgan 1991; Beller et al. 1996). So-called *displaced homemakers—***full-time housewives who lose**

■ PANEL 14.10 Guidelines for Equitable Distribution of Assets.

Sixteen factors a New Jersey court should consider in determining an equitable division of assets.

1. **Duration:** The duration of the marriage

2. **Health:** The age and physical and emotional health of the parties

3. **Income:** The income or property brought to the marriage by each party

4. **Living standards:** The standard of living established during the marriage

5. **Property agreement:** Any written agreement made by the parties before or during the marriage concerning an arrangement of property distribution

6. **Economic circumstances:** The economic circumstances of each party at the time the division of property becomes effective

7. **Earning capacity:** The income and earning capacity of each party, including education background, training, etc.

8. **Contribution to earning power:** The contribution by each party to the education, training, or earning power of the other

9. **Value of marital property:** The contribution of each party to the acquisition, dissipation, preservation, depreciation, or appreciation in the amount or value of the marital property, as well as the contribution of a party as a homemaker

10. **Taxes:** The tax consequences of the proposed distribution to each party

11. **Present value:** The present value of the property

12. **Child custody:** The need of a parent who has physical custody of a child to own or occupy the marital residence and to use or own the household effects

13. **Debts:** The debts and liabilities of the parties

14. **Trust fund:** The need for creation, now or in the future, of a trust fund to secure reasonably foreseeable medical or educational costs for a spouse or children

15. **Deferred career:** The extent to which a party deferred achieving their career goals

16. **Other:** Any other factors that the court might deem relevant

Source: Adapted from A. D. Jessani 2003. What does equitable distribution mean? *www.divorce source.com/NJ/ARTICLES/jessani9.html.*

their economic support owing to divorce or widowhood—are particularly vulnerable.

This discussion logically brings us to the subject of spousal support.

Spousal Support & the "Alimony Myth": Are Better Arrangements Possible?

***Spousal support*, or *spousal maintenance*, the terms that are now usually preferred to *alimony*, consists of court-ordered financial support by a spouse or a former spouse to the other following separation or divorce.** Let us consider some of the facts of spousal support.

According to sociologist Lenore Weitzman (1985), in her landmark book *The Divorce Revolution,* most people subscribe to what she calls the ***"alimony myth"*—namely, that most women profit from divorce by receiving high alimony payments.** There are many refutations of this point of view.

One study (Peterson 1996) reports that ex-husbands experienced a 10% improvement in their standard of living but ex-wives experienced a *27% decline.* Another study finds that 40% of divorcing wives lost half their family income, compared to 17% of men (Arendell 1995). Yet another study (Hetherington 1993) found that 18% of divorced mothers had been on public assistance at some time (compared with 10% of remarried mothers and 2% of nondivorced mothers in a comparison group). Among Latinos, married and divorced men had essentially equal incomes, but divorced women's incomes dropped about 24% (Stroup and Pollack 1999). African American divorced women are especially at risk economically (Stroup and Pollack 1999). The main reason for the difference is the inequality in men's versus women's incomes (Smock 1993).

Why does the alimony myth endure? Among the possible reasons are the following (Weitzman 1985):

■ **Ignorance about Actual Alimony Awards:** Most people don't know that only a few divorcing women receive alimony—in 1989, about 16% of divorcing white women, 11% of black women, and 11% of Latina women (U.S. Census Bureau 1994). Moreover, in most cases, the amount that is awarded is low. The amount of spousal support depends on the recipient's need and the payer's ability to pay. Factors might include the former standard of living of the parties, the duration of the marriage, the extent to which child-care responsibilities or other home responsibilities affected one spouse's earning capacity, each person's tax liabilities, the age and health of each party, and so on. However, a spouse or partner has a duty to provide for himself or herself. His or her spouse is entitled to spousal support only if he or she is unable to be self-supporting. This means that any ex-spouse or partner who can work and earn income is expected to do so. Spousal support is ordered only if the person cannot earn enough money to live on or cannot work for one reason or another. One goal of spousal support is to make the supported party self-sufficient in a number of years.

■ **Confusion of "Spousal" with "Child" Support:** Many people think of spousal support and child support as being essentially the same—money that divorced men have to pay their ex-wives.

■ **Media Reports about Wealthy Divorces:** Sensational alimony awards made by celebrities or wealthy people to their spouses receive huge media attention. For example, Frances Lear, a former self-described Hollywood wife, was awarded $112 million in a 1986 divorce settlement from legendary television producer Norman Lear (*All in the Family, Maude*). Real estate mogul (and star of TV's *The Apprentice*) Donald Trump was obliged to pay ex-wife Ivana $25 million in 1990.

In some cases, ex-wives have received court-ordered ***rehabilitative alimony*, or short-term financial payments to help a wife go to school and "rehabilitate" her vocational skills** to enable her to work independently. However, a few classes in learning office skills will certainly not put her on an equal footing with a husband who has spent years working his way up through a company's management levels. Perhaps a better idea than alimony, therefore, is ***spousal entitlement*, in which a nonworking spouse receives a kind of severance pay for her or his "investment" in the marriage—for helping to advance the income earner's career during the marriage,** as by entertaining colleagues and clients.

Child Support: How Well Does the System Work?

***Child support* is the ongoing financial assistance for child-care expenses that the separated or divorced parent with custody of the child receives from the noncustodial parent.** Because mothers gain custody in 85% of cases, most court-ordered child support is required of fathers. Unfortunately, the facts about child support are not happy ones.

■ **Not Every Custodial Parent Gets Child Support:** Only about 59% of custodial parents were awarded child support in 2002, and the average amount was $5,044 a year (Grall 2003).

■ **Payments Vary by Race/Ethnicity and Education:** Support payments tended to be higher for white women. *(See ■ Panel 14.11.)* As might be expected, they also tended to be higher for women with more education. *(See ■ Panel 14.12.)*

■ **Many Men Don't Provide Support:** About 50% of men don't support their children at all after divorce—or even see them (Sorenson and Zibman 2000). The amounts that are paid vary more according to the father's circumstances than the mother and child's needs (Teachman 1991). Two-thirds of noncustodial fathers were found to have spent more on their car payments than on child support (Kitson and Holmes 1992).

■ **Noncustodial Parents Are More Apt to Pay When They Are Involved with Their Children:** Even men with the financial resources to support their children and former wives resist doing so if they disagree with the child-custody arrangements and visitation rights (Finkel and Roberts 1994). Eighty-five percent of custodial parents who share custody and visitation with the other spouse are more apt to receive at least some support payments, compared with only 36% of those who do not (Grall 2000).

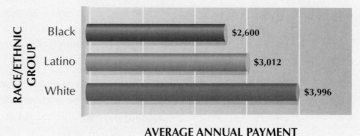

■ **PANEL 14.11   Diversity Data: Custody Payments by Race/Ethnicity.** Average yearly child support payments received by custodial mothers by race/ethnicity, 1997.

Source: Grall 2000, Table B.

So-called *deadbeat dads*—**fathers who don't meet their court-ordered child-support responsibilities**—aren't all angry and vengeful, although some are. One scholar (Nuta 1986) suggests that there are at least four categories of nonpaying fathers. *(See* ■ *Panel 14.13.)* However, evading payment was made more difficult with the passage of the 1984 ***Child Support Enforcement Amendments,*** **which require states to deduct from fathers' paychecks and tax returns delinquent child-support payments.** This legislation was reinforced by the 1988 ***Family Support Act,*** **which authorizes judges to use their discretion when support agreements cannot be met and requires periodic reviews of award levels to keep up with the rate of inflation.** In 1994, all states implemented automatic wage withholding on the paychecks of noncustodial parents who are required to pay child support.

Although such legislation and enforcement have stepped up the percentages of support payments, states vary in the effectiveness of their enforcement (Williams 1994; Meyer and Bartfeld 1996, Meyer et al. 1996, Koch 2006). The greatest guarantee of reliable support payments and parental involvement with their children seems to be whether there are good relationships between the divorced parents (Garfinkel et al. 1994).

Other countries solve the problem of child support by other means. One system, practiced by nearly all industrialized countries except the United States, is a ***children's allowance,*** **whereby the government provides a grant of child support to all families based on the number of children they have**—and irrespective of the parents' marital status or income level. Another system, practiced in France and Sweden, is ***guaranteed child support,*** **whereby the government sends to the custodial parent the amount of child-support payment that was awarded** and then it's the government's task to collect this amount from the noncustodial parent.

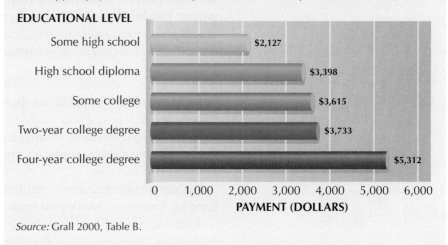

■ **PANEL 14.12   Custody Payments by Educational Level.** Average yearly child support payments received by custodial mothers by educational level, 1997.

Source: Grall 2000, Table B.

Effects of Child Custody Arrangements

Child custody, as we said, is the court-mandated decision as to which parent will be primarily responsible for the upbringing and welfare of the child or children.

Four Types of Child Custody

There are three major types of custody for children living with parents: *sole, joint,* and *split.* In some cases, children live with adults who are not their parents, referred to as *third-party custody.*

■ **Sole Custody—Children with One Parent:** In **sole custody, children live with one parent, who is solely responsible for raising them, and the other parent has legally specified visitation rights.** Sole custody occurs in 81% of cases, and most children live with their mothers. In 13% of cases, mothers are noncustodial parents (Christensen et al. 1990).

■ **Joint Custody—Children with Both Parents:** Occurring in about 16% of cases, in **joint custody, the children divide their time between both parents.** There are two types of joint custody.

In **joint legal custody, children live with one parent, but both share decisions about their children's upbringing,** such as education, health care, and religious training.

In **joint physical custody, children live with both parents, dividing their time on a more or less equal basis between the separate households.**

A new variant of joint custody, occurring in about 1% of cases, is called *birdnesting* or *nesting.* **In birdnesting, the children stay in the family home and the parents alternate staying with them.** Sometimes used temporarily during early stages of separation, this arrangement "is akin to birds who leave their babies in the nest to gather food," says one report. "The aim is to give the kids more stability and save them from the wrenching experience of boomeranging between each parent's home" (Silverman and Higgins 2003: D1). However, it might not work in the long term because it doesn't allow the parents to live their own lives, and most divorced parents can't handle the cooperation needed to make it work. Moreover, it requires enough income to afford three residences: his, hers, and the children's.

■ **Split Custody—Some of the Children with One Parent, Some with the Other:** Occurring in about 2% of cases, in ***split custody*, the children are divided between the two parents.** Perhaps the mother gets custody of the daughters and the father gets custody of the sons, or perhaps the children are allowed to choose the parent they want to live with. Split custody can have adverse effects on sibling attachments to one another (Kaplan et al. 1993).

■ **Third-Party Custody—Children Live with Someone Other Than a Parent:** **In *third-party custody*, which occurs very occasionally, in perhaps 1% of cases, child custody is awarded to a grandparent, other relative, or some other adult instead of the parents.** This might occur, for instance, if both the children's parents have been deemed unfit owing to drug abuse, criminality, or other negative factors.

What happens if one parent moves out of state? The Internet offers the opportunity for ***virtual visitation*, the use of such online tools as videoconferencing, webcams, and other wired or wireless technologies with which a noncustodial divorced parent can visit his or her child** (Thomas 2001; Clemetson 2006; Sanner 2006). Email can also be used by ex-spouses to "talk" to each other in a civil way, keeping their emotions in check (Zaslow 2005).

Issues about Child Custody: Hurt & Rage in Noncustodial Parents, Particularly Fathers

Some of the varieties of child custody arrangements are described in the accompanying box. *(See* ■ *Panel 14.14.)* It's clear that the way custody is structured depends on a great number of factors, including available income, whether the parents live near one another, the number of children and their ages, and whether the parents are on reasonably good terms with each other after the divorce.

The rise of the ***fathers' rights movement*, which urges that divorced male parents have equal treatment with divorced female parents in matters of child custody, visitation, and support**, has called attention to several custody-related issues:

■ **Father's Separation—The Loss to Both Parent and Children:** During a one-year period, according to one national survey, over 60% of noncustodial fathers did not have contact with their children (Bianchi 1990). Another study (Dudley 1991) of 84 fathers who were divorced an average of 6 years said that they saw their children infrequently. Of these, 40% said that the main reason was that the ex-wife did not allow access to the children or talked negatively about the father to the children.

Even when there is no obstruction by the former spouse, many fathers experience role confusion and suffer greatly after divorce, feeling guilty, anxious, and depressed (Arditti 1990). Fathers who are considering staying involved with their children might feel that they have to weigh the benefits of connectedness against the costs of emotional pain (Braver et al. 1993a, 1993b). Often, fathers become frustrated about their loss of influence over their children, and visiting declines over time (Seltzer 1991; Wallerstein 1998). Divorced fathers who live with their minor children have a relationship quality similar to that found with continuously married fathers who live with their children. Noncustodial fathers are likely to experience depression and other negative effects on their psychological well-being compared to men in intact marriages. This state might not be solely due to the event of divorce; rather, it might be caused at least partly by the separation of fathers from their children (Shapiro 1999).

What happens to the bonds between divorced fathers and their children? Research suggests that closeness between them does suffer (Cooney 1994). One study of young adult children of divorce, ages 18 to 22, found that two-thirds had poor relationships with their fathers and one-third had poor relationships with their mothers, which was about double the percentage in similar children from nondivorced families (Zill et al. 1993).

■ **Parent Alienation Syndrome—When Children Hate Their Parents:** ***Parent alienation syndrome (PAS) is defined as a disturbance in which children are preoccupied with viewing one parent as all good and the other parent as all bad. The "bad" parent is hated and verbally marginalized, whereas the "good" parent is idealized and loved*** (Vestal 1999).

Richard Gardner (1998), who originated the term, says that the disorder arises primarily in the context of child-custody disputes. Its primary manifestation, he says, "is the child's campaign of denigration against a parent, a campaign that has no justification. It results from the combination of a programming (brainwashing) parent's indoctrinations and the child's own contributions to the vilification of the target parent." The PAS is not applicable when true parental abuse or neglect has occurred, which would fuel a legitimate reason for the child's dislike of the parent.

Parent alienation syndrome can stem from the father, but it is more often caused by the mother (Gardner 1998). This has led to what has been called ***divorce-related malicious mother syndrome, in which a mother unjustifiably punishes her divorcing or divorced husband by attempting to alienate their mutual children from him, involving others (including lawyers) in malicious actions against him, and denying him visitation, telephone access, and participation in their school and after-school activities***

(Turkat 1995). (The male counterpart might be the deadbeat dad syndrome—especially the vengeful parent form.)

Parent alienation syndrome is now said to be the leading defense for parents accused of abuse in custody cases, who use PAS to claim that their children have been corrupted or coached to lie by the other parent (Chandress 2006). One small survey in which 39 women in custody cases involving spousal abuse were interviewed (Silverman et al. 2004) found that 54% were decided in favor of the alleged abusers. But do abusive fathers use PAS to force access to their children where none should be granted? Some critics, including the writers of a report put out by the National Council of Juvenile and Family Court Judges (Dalton et al. 2006), claim that the theory is junk science and has no place in custody cases.

■ **Child Stealing—Kidnapping Children from the Other Parent:** Child custody disputes, both during and after divorce, can become quite heated and even nasty, in some cases resulting in so-called child stealing. Usually the result of a noncustodial parent's frustration over custody and visitation arrangements, *child stealing,* **also known as** *child abduction,* **is the act in which one parent kidnaps his or her children from the other parent.**

Most children are returned within 2 to 7 days, and the custodial parent is usually aware of the child's whereabouts (Hotaling and Finkelhor 1990). However, one study (Finkelhor et al. 1991) suggested that there could be as many as about 163,000 kidnappings each year by noncustodial parents who have the intention of keeping the children or of taking them out of state. The recourse for the custodial parent is to press his or her state to find and extradite the child-stealing parent (Fass 1998).

■ **Supervised Visitation—Presence of a Third Party during Visits:** One way to alleviate the tensions surrounding custody and visitation is *supervised visitation,* **in which a noncustodial parent is allowed to visit his or her child only with a third party present, such as a court employee or social worker.** This person may be called a *parenting coordinator,* **a qualified neutral person appointed by the court or agreed to by the parties to assist the parties in resolving issues relating to parenting** (Navarro 2005). This approach is particularly recommended for noncustodial parents who have a history of abusiveness or domestic violence (Perkins and Ansay 1998). Unfortunately, a growing problem is that many poor parents cannot afford to pay for supervised visits, which may routinely cost $100 an hour (Kaufman 2007).

The Effect of Divorce on Children

Which child is more vulnerable to emotional stress and loss of self-esteem: the one who stays in an intact family that is constantly roiled by tension and conflict or the one who loses financial advantages and the attention of one parent (usually the father) because of divorce?

The choices are not always so grim, but they can be. Let's consider the short- and long-range consequences of divorce for children—realizing as we do so that there are contradictory findings.

The Short-Term Consequences

If you are in a high-conflict marriage, will your children do better if you divorce? One study (Jekielek 1998) found that such children reported heightened emotional well-being and feelings of relief that they were removed from the scene of continuing parental warfare. Other studies also support this view (Kline et al. 1991; L'Heureax-Dube 1998). A 17-year study of two generations found that children who are raised in angry and miserable but intact marriages are more likely to be unhappily married themselves (Amato and Booth 2001). The more discord there was in the parents' marriage, the more unhappily married their grown children were.

Much of the time, the short-term effects of divorce are negative, according to some research:

■ **Unwanted Split:** Most children don't want their parents to split up. In one study of 28 children whose parents had separated, all wanted their parents back together (Holroyd and Sheppard 1997). They especially resent it when parents "fight through the children" or when one parent induces the children to spy on his or her former spouse and report back.

■ **Guilt, Anger, Depression, Anxiety, Withdrawal:** Generally, children feel guilty, depressed, anxious, intensely angry, and withdrawn in the short term (Hetherington 1973, 1993; Wallerstein and Kelly 1980; Dawson 1991). One study of teenagers and young adults in 34 countries even found a link between divorce rates and suicide rates (Johnson et al. 2000).

■ **Less Social and School Competence:** Children of divorced parents are less sociable and feel less confident in their social skills (Baker et al. 1993; Peretti and di Vitorrio 1993). They also have more behavioral problems at school, including more absences and lower grades (Dawson 1991; Downey 1994).

■ **Health Problems:** Children from divorced families have lower physical health ratings, and they are more likely to experience eating problems and disorders (Guidubaldi and Cleminshaw 1985; Wynn and Bowering 1990).

The Long-Term Consequences

Is there hope for the long term? Do children survive the initial awful period and become happy and well adjusted? Two scholars, Judith S. Wallerstein and E. Mavis Hetherington, represent opposite sides of the debate—the dark view and the rosy view:

■ **Wallerstein's Pessimistic View:** Since 1971, Wallerstein, a clinical psychologist, has followed the postdivorce lives of the same 60 families from Marin County, California. In a 1989 book (Wallerstein and Blakelee 1989), she reported that 10 and 15 years after their parents split up, children were entering adulthood as "worried, underachieving, self-deprecating and sometimes angry young men and women." In a later book, *The Unexpected Legacy of Divorce: A 25-Year Landmark Study* (Wallerstein et al. 2000), Wallerstein reported that only 40% of the grown-up children (ranging in age from late twenties to early forties) had ever married—compared with 81% of men and 87% of women of those ages in the general population. Because such children did not grow up in loving, contented families, they did not know what one ought to be like.

Overcoming the effects of divorce, Wallerstein suggests, often means that the children must go through a painful struggle. Because of the lack of healthy role models and difficult stepfamily arrangements, she says, these children have less social competence than do children from intact families, are at greater risk for drug and alcohol abuse, and are less apt to attend college, and the girls are more likely to have early sexual experiences. Wallerstein finds that children are usually happier if their parents stay together—even if the marriage is an unhappy and loveless one.

■ **Hetherington's More Optimistic View:** Two years after Wallerstein and associates' best-selling *The Unexpected Legacy of Divorce* appeared, Hetherington, a developmental psychologist, published *For Better or for Worse: Divorce Reconsidered* (Hetherington and Kelly 2002), which was also based on three decades of research. Although some findings about children of divorce are disturbing, Hetherington believes that the harm of divorce has been exaggerated and the positive effects have been ignored.

Whereas Wallerstein saw burdens and worries, Hetherington saw increased resilience, with 75 to 80% of children whose parents divorced adapting to the change. Although the other 20 to 25% were found to be at risk for lifelong emotional or behavioral problems (compared with only 10% of children from intact families), the greater percentage "are functioning in the normal range," says Hetherington (quoted in Duenwald 2002), "and some are functioning remarkably well." Indeed, within 6 years after the divorce, she and her researchers found, these children were as well adjusted and happy as were children whose parents stayed married.

■ **Why Do Wallerstein and Hetherington's Findings Differ?** Both psychologists spent three decades studying white middle-class families, most of whom split up during the 1970s. So what are we to make of these different outcomes? A lot has to do with their research methods (Corliss 2002; Duenwald 2002; Peterson 2003).

Developmental psychologist Hetherington, assisted by a crew of researchers, interviewed the children and parents of more than 1,400 families, about half divorced and half not, and observed families interacting in their homes. The subjects kept journals recording their actions and feelings and were given standardized personality tests. Reports were also gathered from peers as well as parents and children. For many, data were collected seven different times during the course of 24 years.

Clinical psychologist Wallerstein, on the other hand, intimately interviewed the children and parents of 60 families five times over 25 years. The grown children of divorced parents were compared with 44 adults who had grown up in intact families.

The difference between the two research approaches, as one commentator put it, is that "one tactic is broad but shallow, the other deep but narrow" (Corliss 2002). Thus, Hetherington's sample is considered more representative (at least of white middle-class families), and her standards of data collection are thought to be more scientifically rigorous. Wallerstein has been faulted for

CHILDREN OF DIVORCE. Which of the two adults would you guess is the custodial parent in this picture? Generally, the noncustodial parent gets "visitation rights," which allows him or her access to the children a few days a month. Most children don't want their parents to split up and want them to stay together. In addition, children in divorced families feel guilty, anxious, and withdrawn in the short term and may even suffer school and health problems. What kinds of consequences would you expect children of divorce to suffer in the long run? ▲

EXAMPLE OF

The Pain of Children

How Can Parents Help Them Adjust to Divorce?

"My parents are devvorst," a child wrote to children's book author Beverly Cleary. "My dad is the kind of person who never wants to be around kids." "I wish I could sue my parents for malpractice," another girl confides, "but I know I can't so I just try to forget what they do."

These are two examples quoted by Barbara Dafoe Whitehead, author of *The Divorce Culture* (1996), of plain-

tive messages written by children to their favorite authors, seeking information, advice, and solace. "Few scholars have paid close attention to the emergence of a children's literature devoted to divorce," says Whitehead (1997). "Yet this literature provides a remarkable account of children's experience of divorce, a story radically at odds with the story told in scores of books on divorce for adults."

Divorce books for children, which began issuing forth from publishers in the 1970s, are written for all ages: picture books with divorcing dinosaurs, workbooks and coloring books to help children express feelings, divorce dictionaries and advice manuals, and divorce novels, such as Judy Blume's *It's Not the End of the World*. These books have been joined by others on the subjects of isolation and abandonment, difficulty with stepparents and stepsiblings, and even sexual abuse. Whitehead points out that although liberation is often a theme of adult literature on divorce, loss is the com-

mon theme for much of this kind of children's fiction—especially the pain of loss caused by the absence or separation from the father, as in *Will Dad Ever Move Back Home?* When mothers are described, they are often distracted and sad. Even the absence of grandparents and the loss of pets become subjects for such books.

"Parents are children's greatest resource," say two medical professors at New York University. "When parents are hurting, parenting suffers. Unfortunately, it is precisely at this time of depletion that children need their parents most" (Koplewicz and Gurian 2001:1). Scholars note that redefining relationships and roles after divorce is difficult for ex-spouses because there are no institutional models for doing so (Walzer and Oles 2003).

There are several pieces of advice that can help children at this troubled time (Koplewicz and Gurian 2001; Garber 2003; Divorce Recovery.net 2004):

having examined too few families and claiming that they are representative of all divorces. Moreover, her clinical sample was composed of people who had asked for help dealing with problems associated with divorce, so this group would naturally have a higher level of difficulty than a random population. Still, her methodology has been praised for having dug more deeply than Hetherington did. "She got at something I think the standardized instruments wouldn't necessarily pick up on," says University of Texas sociologist Norval Glenn (quoted in Duenwald 2002).

A Third View: Children of Divorce Suffer Even When Parents' Conflict Is Minimal

It has been pointed out (Peterson 2002b) that some of Hetherington's findings might initially seem positive but that some of the comments about the children themselves are less so—for instance, that children of divorce show a reluctance to commit and an uncertainty in relationships. This point of view is reinforced by **Elizabeth Marquardt's** (2005) study of 1,500 adults ages 18 to 35 that shows that even in a "quiet" divorce—one in which parents amicably minimize their conflict—children undergo hardships not experienced by children from intact families.

Such children "feel strongly and intensely that their parents are polar opposites, even if they don't fight," says Marquardt (quoted in Tyre 2005). "They feel

- **Tell the children about the divorce:** Children who are old enough to acknowledge their parents need to be told something about their parents splitting up, with the message tailored according to the child's level of understanding. If possible, both parents should inform the child together; otherwise, the news should be broken by the parent to whom the child is closest. Parents should not assess blame, which identifies one parent as bad and induces children to choose sides. Children should be told that the divorce is between the parents, to allay the children's fear that the parents will divorce them too. Emphasize that they did not cause the divorce. Allow plenty of time for questions, which might go on for several months.

- **Understand that children feel guilty about the separation and hope for a reunion:** Children should be told that they did not cause the divorce, since most blame themselves rather than a parent for the painful experience. They should be told that they cannot bring the parents back together, even though fantasies about reunion will remain strong for some time.

- **Recognize the child's strong emotions:** Most children will express sadness and will show some signs of depression, such as sleeplessness, restlessness, and difficulty concentrating. They will also feel rejected by one or both parents and worry about being abandoned or left alone. They will likely express anger against one or both parents as well as themselves. The parents should let the children know that they are loved and wanted.

- **Don't put the child in the middle, and be clear about family boundaries:** Parents should not put children in the middle of adult conflicts or ask them to be spies or messengers. The co-parents should work to create as much consistency, continuity, and security in the children's lives as possible, including giving them advance knowledge about where they will be at any given time. Agreements should be reached between the former parents about the boundaries between the two households—whether belongings will go back and forth, whether holidays will be celebrated together, how separate and distinct each family will be.

- **Parents should attend to their own anger and guilt:** Parents should seek support from other adults. They should not voice their own strong feelings to their children or seek to make the children emotional caretakers.

they must take care of their parents rather than be taken care of. They feel loss and anger." Elsewhere she adds, "Even a good divorce restructures children's childhoods and leaves them traveling between two distinct worlds. It becomes their job, not their parents', to make sense of those two worlds" (Marquardt, quoted in Lewin 2005). In other words, children of divorce said they felt like a different person with each parent, that they felt like outsiders in their own home. Although Marquardt is a scholar with the Institute for American Values, a pro-marriage organization, her findings are supported by other research. Child psychologist Robert Emery (2004) found that about half of children from divorced families felt they had had a harder childhood than most people, compared with 14% of children from intact married families.

The Good Divorce

How does one calm roiling emotions, especially when dealing with an ex-spouse? Mab Nulty of Edina, Minnesota, who was an in-home child-care provider at the time of her divorce and now is a psychologist, said she took the following advice of a friend: "Until your own emotions settle down, you [have to] get very good at acting 'as if' . . . *as if* you are like the other person, and *as if* you can talk easily with that person" (Nulty, quoted in Cummins 2002).

Increasingly, it seems, ex-spouses are willing to make the effort to try to employ strategies that will reduce the damage to their children: communicating on Web message boards instead of arguing, joining in the collaborative law movement to avoid going to court, and hiring "parenting coordinators" to make decisions for them (Navarro 2005). To foster a more loving parent-child bond, they have also discovered the benefits of mediation over litigation in custody disputes. As Robert Emery found in a 12-year study (Emery et al. 2001), in families that have gone through mediation, the noncustodial parent is several times more likely to have weekly phone contact with his or her children. Reflecting the changing role of fathers, such couples are also shifting to more equitable custody arrangements; one study finds, in fact, that over a span of 70 years mothers and fathers have been favored roughly equally by the courts in child-custody disputes (Mason and Quirk 1997). In sum: *how* parents divorce is even more important than the divorce itself.

The accompanying table shows how the topic of divorce is viewed from three principal theoretical perspectives: structural-functional, conflict, and symbolic interaction. *(See ■ Panel 14.15.)*

PANEL 14.15   Views on Divorce: Three Sociological Theoretical Perspectives Compared

STRUCTURAL-FUNCTIONAL (MACRO ORIENTATION)	CONFLICT (MACRO ORIENTATION)	SYMBOLIC INTERACTION (MICRO ORIENTATION)
Manifest functions: Divorce brings new stability to the family and provides a healthier, less stressful environment for children.	The search for happiness results in conflict, and divorce produces competition for scarce resources (the couple's accumulated money and assets).	People's immediate environments (family, religious views) affect their feelings about marriage and divorce.
Latent functions: Leaving a bad relationship can increase self-esteem, benefit certain parts of society (such as the legal system), and affect other aspects of the social structure (such as law enforcement and health care).	A divorced couple's lack of consensus can lead to health-care issues for both males and females (divorce hangover).	Many children of divorce are negatively affected in their views on marriage.
Changes in one part of society (increased or decreased divorce rates) bring about changes in other parts (such as health care, law enforcement, and education).	Lack of agreement leads to a breakup in the family relationship, producing instability and displacement of the children.	The mass media can affect people's views on divorce and marriage and their ideas as to what constitutes happiness.
The parts of the social structure work to deal positively with the impact of divorce and bring more stability to society.		

Self-Assessment: How's Your Marital Adjustment?

There's no way to predict with certainty whether a specific couple is "affair-proof." Responding to the statements below will help identify relationship vulnerabilities that make marriages susceptible.

Directions

Circle the appropriate number to the right of each statement:

1 = No, disagree completely

2 = Yes, agree somewhat

3 = Yes, agree completely

NA = Not applicable

1. We had problems trusting each other before we got married.   1 2 3 NA

2. Our marriage revolves around our children. Or (for childless couples) We disagree on whether or not to have children.   1 2 3 NA

3. My partner spends too much time away from home.   1 2 3 NA

4. My partner rarely takes my side in anything.   1 2 3 NA

5. We've grown apart.   1 2 3 NA

6. I have felt alone and unsupported at times of loss or crises.   1 2 3 NA

7. We don't have equal input for important decisions.   1 2 3 NA

8. We argue about the frequency of sex.   1 2 3 NA

9. Our interactions feel more like a parent-child relationship than one between equals.   1 2 3 NA

10. We are uncomfortable about exposing our inner selves to each other.   1 2 3 NA

11. We sweep things under the rug so we hardly ever fight.   1 2 3 NA

12. There's a disparity in how invested we are in the relationship.   1 2 3 NA

13. I feel I can't influence my partner to do what I request.   1 2 3 NA

14. I don't know if I really love my partner.   1 2 3 NA

15. We don't know how to repair after a conflict.   1 2 3 NA

16. We don't have much in common.   1 2 3 NA

Total score _____

Scoring Key

Add up your total number of points to interpret your relationship vulnerability score.

16–20 = A safe harbor

21–29 = Choppy waters

30–39 = Rough seas

40–48 = Watch out! You're headed for the rocks.

Take another look at those statements that you rated 2 or 3. You and your partner can work on these issues to build a better marriage. Sharing your responses will give you another way to discuss your marital lifeline and relationship patterns.

Remember that your relationship vulnerability score is *not a predictor of infidelity*. It is an assessment of your marital adjustment. Remember that affairs can and do happen in good relationships. Even a score that indicates high vulnerability does not mean that infidelity is inevitable. Just as there are happily married people who are unfaithful, there are also many dissatisfied individuals who remain faithful because of individual or cultural factors.

Source: Reprinted from Quiz: The Relationship Vulnerability Map. Shirley P. Glass with Jean Coppock Staeheli. 2003. *NOT "JUST FRIENDS": Protect your relationship from infidelity and heal the trauma of betrayal.* New York: Free Press. See *www.shirleyglass .com/quizrelationship.php*. Reprinted with the permission of The Free Press, a Division of Simon & Schuster Adult Publishing Group, from *NOT "JUST FRIENDS": Protect Your Relationship from Infidelity and Heal the Trauma of Betrayal* by Shirley P. Glass, Ph.D., with Jean Coppock Staeheli. Copyright © 2003 by Shirley P. Glass, Ph.D. All rights reserved.

Key Terms Used in This Chapter

Summary

14.1 Separation, Divorce, & Trends

- The American belief in the right to divorce seems connected to the search for happiness in intimacy and marriage. The term *uncoupling* describes the series of steps by which couples move toward ending their relationship. These steps involve dissatisfaction, attempts at change, turning elsewhere, further distancing, resolution, informing the other partner, and acknowledging the ending of the relationship.

- Besides death, there are four other ways in which a marriage can end: desertion, separation, annulment, and divorce. Desertion means that one spouse simply abandons the marriage and family and has no subsequent contact. Separation, in which a married couple decides to no longer live together, can be of three kinds: With informal separation, spouses settle financial, child-custody, child-support, and visitation arrangements informally between themselves, with no legal papers drawn up; with a formal separation, a lawyer draws up a legal agreement enabling a cou-

ple to live separately but specifying financial, child-custody, child support, and visitation arrangements between them; in controlled separations, which have the goal of saving the marriage, a contract specifies time limits, living arrangements, finances, and contact. Annulments, declaring a couple's marriage invalid, may be religious (pronounced by the church) or civil (a judicial pronouncement). Divorce is defined as the legal dissolution of a valid marriage.

- Before the 1970s, divorce was treated as an adversarial matter, with spouses attempting to prove each other legally at fault. Since then, divorce has evolved into a no-fault system, in which neither partner has to prove fault, and the marriage is simply declared legally dissolved.

- Community property—property acquired by a couple during their marriage—is supposed to be divided equally, reflecting the idea of equal contributions to the marriage. Child custody, the court-mandated decision as to which parent will be primarily responsible for raising the couple's children, is supposed to be determined according to the best interests of the children.

- In studying divorce, it is important to understand how it is measured. The ratio measure of divorce is the ratio within a given year of the number of marriages to the number of divorces. The crude divorce rate is the number of divorces in a given year per 1,000 population. The refined divorce rate reflects the number of divorces in a given year for every 1,000 married women over age 15.

14.2 Why People Divorce

- Divorce is more acceptable today than it used to be, in part because cultural values now mainly stress individual happiness over family togetherness. Because of mobility and focus on careers, many people also don't have an extended family to provide assistance when there are stresses on a marriage. Greater social acceptance of divorce also is leading to more remarriages and more redivorces.
- Lack of education is correlated with higher divorce rates. For men, the more education they have, the less likely they are to divorce. However, for women, additional education can increase financial independence from men so that the women are less likely to stay in a bad marriage. Women from the lower socioeconomic class who have not completed high school are at greater risk of divorce. The younger the age at which a couple marries, the greater is the chance that they will divorce, owing to lack of maturity and inability to handle marriage responsibilities. The presence of young children can strengthen the family bonds and commitment to family responsibilities and consequently serve to prevent or delay divorce; however, the presence of teenagers makes separation and divorce more likely.
- Personal factors that are associated with divorce include communication problems, infidelity, constant conflict, emotional abuse, falling out of love, unsatisfactory sex, insufficient income, physical abuse, falling in love with someone else, and boredom.

14.3 The Process of Divorce

- Anthropologist Paul Bohannan developed a psychological model of divorce consisting of six "stations" or processes: (1) Emotional divorce involves loss of affection, trust, and respect for each other and replaces positive emotions with indifference or destructive emotions. (2) Legal divorce is the court-ordered termination of a marriage. (3) Economic divorce involves settlement of the property. (4) Co-

parental divorce involves decisions about child custody, child support, visitation rights, and the ongoing responsibilities of each parent. (5) Community divorce means that each partner reduces or leaves membership in a common community of relatives and friends. (6) Psychic divorce, which follows a period of mourning, means emotional separation from the former partner.

- The postdivorce mourning period consists of at least three stages, including denial, anger and depression, and acceptance and forgiveness.
- To help reduce the negative impact of divorce, two techniques have been developed. In divorce mediation, divorcing spouses make agreements with a third party about property division, spousal support, child custody, and child support. In collaborative divorce, a couple and their lawyers agree to dissolve the marriage without litigation and, if they fail, for the lawyers to drop out of the case before it goes to court.

14.4 The Effects of Divorce

- Divorce can have long-term consequences for an individual's emotional, psychological, and physical state. Many people who are unable to complete their psychic divorce suffer "divorce hangover," unable to let go of the fact of their divorce, reorient themselves as single parents, or develop new friendships. Separation distress, a psychological state following separation, may feature feelings of depression, loss, and anxiety as well as intense loneliness. People who are going through separation and divorce are at greater risk of experiencing health problems.
- Some people experience positive effects of divorce— for example, increased self-esteem and feelings of competency, relief, and better relationships with children.
- Divorcing couples are affected financially by property settlements, spousal support, and child support. Settlements can be equal distribution or equitable distribution. In equal-distribution settlements, property acquired by either spouse during their marriage, except gifts from third parties, belong equally to the husband or wife. In equitable-distribution settlements, the court determines a fair and reasonable distribution that might be more than or less than 50% of any asset to either of the divorcing parties.
- Divorce settlements are often intended to provide nonworking spouses, especially displaced homemakers, with sufficient financial resources to live in their accustomed manner. Alimony, or spousal support, consists of court-ordered financial support by a

spouse or a former spouse to the other following separation or divorce. Courts have also used rehabilitative alimony, or short-term financial payments, to help displaced homemakers go to school and learn new vocational skills. Spousal entitlement occurs when a nonworking spouse receives a kind of severance pay for helping the income earner's career during the marriage.

- Child support is the ongoing financial assistance for child-care expenses that the noncustodial parent gives the separated or divorced parent who has physical custody of the child. Various compliance laws have been enacted to identify deadbeat dads, or fathers who don't meet their court-ordered child-support payments. The Child Support Enforcement Amendments (1984) require states to deduct from fathers' paychecks and tax returns delinquent child-support payments; the Family Support Act (1988) authorizes judges to use their discretion when support agreements cannot be met and requires periodic reviews of award levels to keep up with the rate of inflation. In 1994, all states began implementing automatic wage withholding from the paychecks of noncustodial parents who are required to pay child support.

- Two other systems of child support that are used outside the United States are a children's allowance, whereby the government provides a grant of child support to all families based on the number of children they have and irrespective of the parents' marital status or income level, and guaranteed child support, whereby the government sends to the custodial parent the amount of child-support payment that was awarded—then it's the government's task to collect this amount from the noncustodial parent.

- Child custody is the court-mandated decision as to which parent will be primarily responsible for the upbringing and welfare of the child or children. Child custody may be sole custody, joint custody, split custody, or third-party custody. In sole custody, children live with one parent, who is solely responsible for raising them, and the other parent has legally specified visitation rights. In joint custody, children divide their time between the two parents. Joint custody may be joint legal custody, whereby children live with one parent but both share decisions about their children's upbringing, such as education, health care, and religious training, or joint physical custody, whereby children live with both

parents, dividing their time on a more or less equal basis between the separate households. A new and relatively unused form of joint custody is birdnesting, which involves the children living in the family home and the parents alternating staying with them. In split custody, which is uncommon, some of the children live with one parent, some with the other. In third-party custody, children live with someone other than a parent. Historically, custody settlements favored women, which led the fathers' rights movement, which urges that divorced male parents be treated equally with divorced female parents in matters of child custody, visitation, and support.

- Divorce can have serious emotional effect on everyone involved, particularly children, and can result in parent alienation syndrome, divorce-related malicious mother syndrome, and child stealing. Parent alienation syndrome (PAS) is defined as a disturbance in which children are preoccupied with viewing one parent as all good and the other parent as all bad. The "bad" parent is hated and verbally marginalized, whereas the "good" parent is idealized and loved. In divorce-related malicious mother syndrome, a mother unjustifiably punishes her divorcing or divorced husband by attempting to alienate their mutual children from him, involving others in malicious actions against him, and denying him visitation and other access. Child stealing is the act in which one parent kidnaps his or her children from the other parent. One way to relieve tensions that are part of custody and visitation is supervised visitation, in which a noncustodial parent is allowed to visit his or her child only with a third party present, such as a court employee or social worker.

- Short-term effects of divorce on children include guilt, anger, depression, anxiety, withdrawal, less social and school competence, and health problems such as eating disorders.

- Studies by Wallerstein and colleagues found that many children of divorce entered adulthood as worried, underachieving, self-deprecating, and sometimes angry women and men. Growing up in a family experience marked by divorce might provide no positive role model of a loving, caring, and functional family. Studies by Heatherington and colleagues suggest that the harm of divorce has been exaggerated and the positive effects have been ignored and that children show increased resilience and are as well adjusted and happy as children from intact families.

Take It to the Net

Among the Internet resources on divorce are the following:

- **Bill Ferguson's Divorce As Friends.** This site suggests ground rules for peaceful divorce, including ways to keep divorce attorneys at bay.
  www.DivorceAsFriends.com
- **The Coalition for Collaborative Divorce.** This nonprofit organization is dedicated to addressing divorce needs in a positive and cooperative manner so as to resolve conflict, avoid litigation, and help people restructure their lives to benefit all family members during and after the divorce.
  www.nocourtdivorce.com
- **Divorce Central.** Features four topic-specific areas important to people who are dealing with divorce: a legal center (about state laws), the DC Lifeline (for emotional support), a parenting center, and a financial center.
  www.divorcecentral.com
- **DivorceDirectory.com.** Although divorce is never easy, this site can make it less complicated. It offers 100 divorce-related online resources.
  www.divorcedirectory.com
- **Divorce Magazine.** This website features links to other divorce-related sites.
  www.divorcemag.com
- **Divorce Recovery.net.** This website offers education and support for people who are ending a relationship. It also has good information for children of divorce.
  www.divorcerecovery.net
- **Divorce Source.** This website offers an effective way to locate information and communicate with professionals and individuals sharing similar thoughts and experiences.
  www.divorcesource.com
- **Divorce-Without-War.** This website offers information on mediation services.
  www.DivorceWithoutWar.com
- **The Gottman Institute.** A top marriage researcher offers marriage tips, as well as quizzes for assessing your relationship skills.
  www.gottman.com
- **The National Marriage Project.** This promarriage nonprofit offers links to many helpful organizations and resources.
  http://marriage.rutgers.edu
- **Shared Parenting Information Group.** This website promotes responsible shared parenting after separation and divorce. It is a good website for information about parent alienation syndrome (PAS).
  www.spig.clara.net/issues/pas.htm
- **therapistlocator.net.** This website offers a list of 15,000 licensed marriage therapists by ZIP code.
  www.therapistlocator.net

CHAPTER 15

REMARRIAGE

Reinvented, Renewed, & Blended Families

Makeovers: Remarriages & Stepfamilies

"Your wart-covered , foul-smelling, evil stepmother asks you, 'Please clean your room.' "

That's how Meg Schlefer, of Brooklyn, New York, says she tries to get her stepdaughters to help with chores. In the tricky territory of step-relationships, she finds, humor can go a long way (Herbert 1999a: 64).

There is the happy "Brady Bunch" ideal of stepparents and stepchildren. But there are

also 900 stories written about evil or wicked stepmothers, according to one account (Recker 2001), and few of them are humorous. Not only does the malevolent stepmother appear in fairy tales such as *Cinderella* and *Snow White*, but the stereotypes appeared even earlier, in Greek and Roman myths, perhaps embodying an anti-female tradition that flourished in those ancient civilizations (Watson 1995).

In classical literature, apart from Quasimodo's cruel stepfather in *The Hunchback of Notre Dame*, stepfathers seem to come off rather more easily than stepmothers do. However, movies such as *Home Fries* (with Chris Ellis), *Domestic Disturbance* (Vince

Vaughn), and *Night of the Hunter* (Robert Mitchum) more than make up for that imbalance, showing stepfathers as cheats, murderers, and psychopaths.

■ *Are movie depictions of stepparents based on fact?* Do these stereotypes have any effect? Real flesh-and-blood stepfathers tend to view themselves as less effective parents, compared to the way biological fathers view themselves. But stepmothers have the most negative image (being perceived as less affectionate, less fair, and more cruel) and consequent self-image of any member of a stepfamily. In addition, stepfamilies are thought to be somehow not as good as first-marriage families.

With these kinds of reports, it seems extraordinary that any divorced or widowed parent would ever bring his or her children into another marriage. Or that any single man or woman would willingly join what's

⬤ WHAT'S AHEAD IN THIS CHAPTER

The first section discusses the trend toward remarriage. The next focuses on the characteristics and stages of development of blended families. We then describe the new family as viewed by the stepmother, the stepfather, and the stepchildren. Finally, we discuss some benefits of being in a stepfamily and ways to try to ensure its success.

sometimes known as a "reconstituted" family. Yet about 40% of all unions are now remarriages, 65% of remarriages involve children, and one out of every four children in the United States today is a stepchild. Capitalizing on this cultural change, hotels and resorts now offer *familymoons* in lieu of honeymoons, catering to new couples who want to bring the whole clan along on their after-wedding getaway (Silverman 2003).

■ *Mismatched expectations:* At the other extreme are stepfamilies in name only, in which a divorced, successful older man who has already raised children proposes marriage to a younger woman (pejoratively called "the trophy wife"), but there is a catch: He doesn't want any more children. (The reverse can be true, too: A divorced mother contemplating remarriage might not want any more children.) Some remarried spouses might willingly agree—and even sign prenuptial agreements to that effect—but then feel great resentment later, which can adversely affect the marriage (Brooke 2002).

Today, says Andrew Hacker, author of *Mismatch: The Growing Gulf between Men and Women* (2003), "brides and grooms are less embarking on a *journey* together than on a trip with two separate destinations" (Hacker, quoted in Johnson 2003: 35). What's going on here? What do people hope for in marriages (and other kinds of committed relationships) the second time around?

■ *The makeover culture:* Perhaps we can draw some insights from the "makeover" shows that have attained popularity on TV, such as *What Not to Wear, Extreme Makeover,* and *Trading Spaces.* What accounts for their success? Two social observers, Robert Thompson and Virginia Blum (both quoted in "Finding Happiness between Commercials" 2003), offer some thoughts: It's about reinvention and transformation.

Thompson, a Syracuse University professor of media and popular culture, suggests that "if you had to describe the American mythos in one single word, 'reinvention' would not be a bad choice." From the time of the Pilgrims' arrival at Plymouth Rock through the westward movement, he says, America has been about reinvention, leaving the Old World for the New. "In a very real sort of way," says Thompson, "the history of the United States is one big fat makeover show."

Blum, an English professor at the University of Kentucky and author of a book about cosmetic surgery, says that "we're a transformational culture. We have an ongoing before-and-after story. . . . We are also an immigrant culture. You get a makeover story that we tell again and again throughout the 20th century because of these waves of immigration."

Perhaps remarriage is another expression of the hope for makeover. Does it happen? As we'll see, there can be many surprises.

MAJOR QUESTIONS
you should be able to answer

If I were a newly single adult, what should I be alert for in the dating scene?

How does a blended family differ from a nuclear family in characteristics and stages of development?

What are three perspectives of the stepmother, the stepfather, and the stepchild on the blended family?

What are the benefits of being in a stepfamily, and what are ways to help ensure success?

ON THE WEB About Stepfamilies

www.bonusfamilies.com

The founders of this nonprofit organization couldn't get along at first. The reason: One was the ex-wife of the other's husband. After years of butting heads, they formed Bonus Families to offer support for people combining families after divorce. Visit the website.

15.1 Moving toward Remarriage

MAJOR QUESTION If I were a newly single adult, what should I be alert for in the dating scene?

PREVIEW Returning to dating after divorce or widowhood can be both exciting and frightening, especially for older adults. The newly dating need to realize that they may still be in emotional recovery and might be in too much of a hurry to remarry, and that children can complicate the dating process. Middle-aged singles have different needs than young singles.

Screen star Elizabeth Taylor, who was married eight times, including twice to actor Richard Burton, told CNN's "Larry King Live" in 2001 that she would never marry again (although she added, "I'd live with someone if he were cute, intelligent, compassionate, adorable, had a good sense of humor"). Taylor has clearly been a serious practitioner of *serial marriage,* or *serial monogamy,* **defined as participation in a sequence of marital partnerships, one at a time.** Although eight trips to the altar is uncommon, serial marriage is no longer unusual: At least 3.6% of the currently married population, or more than 2.1 million people, have been married three times or more (Kreider 2005: 1). No doubt you know at least one person who has been thrice-married.

Imagine the complexities in stepfamilies—remarriages involving children from previous marriages or relationships—springing out of a couple with a history of multiple marriages and children, with all their family networks. But as we'll explain in this chapter, it can be complicated enough even when only one partner in a newly married couple brings his or her own children to the union.

After the First Marriage: Returning to the Single Life & Dating Again

When a separated or divorced person begins dating, it not only sends a signal to the community and the former spouse that one is once again, as they say, "available," it also enables the person to experiment with roles, friendships, and self-esteem–enhancing adventures that could only be fantasized about before (Spanier and Thompson 1987). Yet whether one is under 30 and just

- **What percentage of people have been married three times or more?** At least 3.6% of the ever-married U.S. population, or more than 2.1 million people, have been married three times or more.[a]

- **Do people spend less time on courtship before second marriages?** Respondents in one study said that before their first marriages, they spent an average (median time) of 17 months in courtship (dating plus engagement). Before their second marriages, they spent only about 9 months in courtship.[b]

- **What proportion of unmarried women date men younger than themselves?** A survey of 1,407 single men and 2,094 single women ages 40–69 found that more than a third of unmarried American women who date were going out with younger men. About two thirds of the men said that they were dating younger women.[c]

- **Are remarriages more likely to end in divorce?** Remarriages are 20% more likely to end in divorce than are first marriages.[d]

- **What percentage of children live in blended families?** About 17% of all children live in stepfamilies.[e]

- **Is a remarried adult required by law to support his or her stepchildren?** Only 20 states require stepparents to support their stepchildren, whereas all states require biological parents to support their children.[f]

[a]Kreider 2005. [b]O'Flaherty and Eels 1988. [c]Montenegro et al. 2003. [d]Martin and Bumpass 1989. [e]U.S. Census Bureau 2001. [f]Morgan 2002.

NUMBERS THAT MATTER
Remarried Couples & Blended Families

out of (or leaving) a first marriage or well over 30 and divorced after many years of spousal, parenting, and work responsibilities, the return to the singles world can be both exciting and frightening.

Exciting: It can be exciting, particularly for young adults, because one might remember the thrills and energy of being in a white-hot romance, with all the hopes for intimacy and renewed hopes of finding a truly satisfying soul mate and life partner.

Frightening: It can be frightening, particularly for people who were long married, because one has little idea of today's dating norms and feels as awkward and insecure as a newly dating adolescent.

With people emerging from first marriages, dating can differ quite a bit from what it was like when they were in their teens or twenties. Following are some facts to be aware of.

Divorced People Who Date May Still Be in Emotional Recovery

It takes some people longer than others to recover emotionally from the separation and divorce. In going about creating their new selves, people tend to go through two phases: transition and recovery (Weiss 1975).

Transition Phase—1 Year: During the transition phase, which starts with separation and lasts about a year, one experiences the anxiety, loneliness, and depression of separation distress. But one has also begun making important decisions—about residence, custody, career, finances, dating, and so on—that help to shape one's new identity.

■ **Recovery Phase—1 to 3 Years:** During the recovery phase, which lasts 1 to 3 years, the divorced person's life and emotions have become more stable, with fewer pangs of loneliness, periods of depression, and moments of rage against the former spouse. Even so, insecurities about a romantic partner, squabbles with children, or a bad day at work can trigger self-doubts.

You can see from this why psychotherapists recommend holding off for 3 years or so before remarriage (Sager et al. 1980, 1983).: However, most people don't wait this long.

Divorced People May Be in a Hurry to Remarry

Before their first marriages, according to one study of 248 remarried subjects (O'Flaherty and Eels 1988), respondents said that they spent a median time of 17 months in courtship (12 months dating, 5 months engaged), whereas before their second marriages they spent just about half that time in courtship: only about 9 months (7 months dating, 2 months engaged).

The accelerated courtship might be propelled by loneliness, desperation for financial or child-care help, concerns that "life is passing me by," or other reasons that we'll describe. In any case, many divorced people seek to rush into remarriage—which in turn might be a reason that the divorce rate is higher for later marriages than for first marriages.

Children Can Complicate the Dating Process

Any custodial parent with young children will tell you that it's difficult to be spontaneous about dating ("Hey, want to go for coffee?") when one has to put child-care arrangements in place first. Children also affect dating in other ways—for example, some custodial parents feel guilty that their dating causes them to not be quite so available to their children (Montgomery et al. 1992). Even so, it seems that divorced parents often don't discuss dating with their offspring (Sumner 1997). Some parents might delay dating for fear it will upset their children's lives.

Children can also affect one's finances and hence the amount of money a divorced parent has to put toward dating and entertainment. If you're a father, your income is probably affected by child-support or spousal-support obligations. If you're a mother, you might not be receiving such support, or you might be obliged to work outside the home in addition to meet expenses. Or nowadays the reverse may be true: You might be a custodial father who isn't receiving child support from the mother.

Sex Can Be a Whole New World

For the newly single, most of whom had been sexually faithful in marriage, having sexual relations with other people can be a challenge to self-esteem, a dramatic confidence booster, or both, depending on the partners. In general, divorced men tend to enjoy sex after separation and are bolstered by it. Women, however, do not find it quite as enjoyable, and their sense of well-being is not as linked to sexual activity (Spanier and Thompson 1987). We expand on this a bit next.

Middle-Aged Singles: Dating, Sex, & Lifestyles

Was divorced actress Demi Moore, age 40, boldly departing from social norms about dating younger men when in 2003 she took up with Ashton Kutcher, 15 years her junior? (They wed in September 2005.)

Not according to a sweeping survey (Montenegro et al. 2003) conducted by Knowledge Networks for *AARP The Magazine*. (AARP, an advocacy group for people over age 50, was formerly called the American Association of Retired People.) The survey's sample of 1,407 single men and 2,094 single women ages 40 to 69 yielded the surprise that more than a third of unmarried American women who date were going out with younger men.

"There seems to be no stigma now for dating men a few years younger," said the magazine's editor, Steve Slon (quoted in Crary 2003). "Today they [women] have the jobs, they have the money, they can call the shots." (About 66% of the men said they were dating younger women.)

Although we might tend to think of singles as being in their twenties or thirties, the AARP survey clearly shows there are a great many singles in their forties, fifties, and sixties. Not all singles in the survey were divorced (indeed, a number had never been married—a startling 42% of the men and 24% of the women). However, 56% of all the singles were separated or divorced; 70% of the formerly married singles in their fifties had been single for 5 years or more. The study's authors attached particular importance to the increased prevalence of divorce, linking it to many of the trends they found in dating habits, sex lives, and lifestyles among middle-aged singles, who are no longer dominated by the widowed and the never-married. (The survey drew on a randomly recruited and nationally representative sample of the U.S. population.)

Dating

The AARP survey turned up a number of interesting results regarding dating:

■ **Reasons for Dating:** The principal reason for dating (49%) among both men and women was to have someone to talk to or do things with, followed by (at 18%) "to simply have fun." Only 11% of men and 2% of women cited sex as the primary reason. And only 10% of men and 7% of women said that the goal of dating was marriage (Montenegro et al. 2003: 7).

■ **Types of Dating:** About 9% of singles ages 40 to 69 are not interested in dating at all. Others are not dating but would be interested in finding a date or would date if the right person came along (27%). Of the rest, 31% were in exclusive dating relationships, and 32% were in nonexclusive dating relationships. Seven percent of men and 3% of women reported same-sex dating partners (Montenegro et al. 2003: 2).

■ **Finding Dates:** About 29% said that they had difficulty finding dates. The best sources for dates were friends and relatives or the workplace, but several were trying singles organizations, match-making services, and online services, as well as church. The hindrances to dating might be recognized by many pre-teens and teens: being shy, feeling self-conscious, not knowing where to meet people, and meeting too few people.

Sex

There is a "vast chasm," the study authors observe, "between men and women in their dating attitudes and sexual desire" (p. 3). Among the differences are the following:

■ **Desire:** Fifty-nine percent of men believed that they didn't have sex often enough. Only 35% of women believed that.

■ **Number of Partners:** More than twice as many men as women—46% versus 21%—said that they had sex with more than one person during the same time period.

■ **Sex on First Date:** Twenty-one percent of men in their forties and fifties thought that sex on the first date is acceptable, but only 2% of women believed this, and the gap grows wider for men and women in their sixties.

Why Remarry?

Like most people, midlife singles want the best of both worlds of independence and intimacy—the eternal conflict we've mentioned elsewhere. On the one hand, they like having the personal freedom that singlehood gives them and not having to answer to someone else. *(See ■ Panel 15.1.)* On the other hand, they hate not having someone to do things with, and they worry about being alone in the future. *(See ■ Panel 15.2.)*

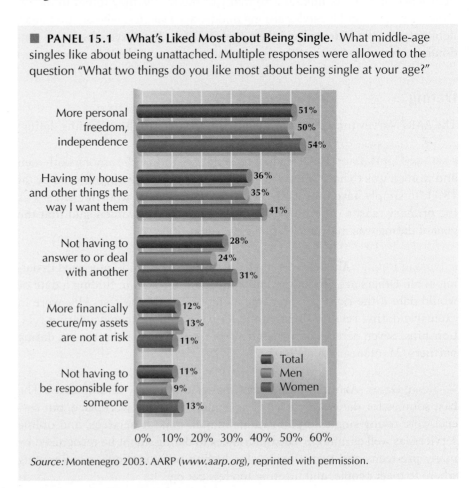

■ **PANEL 15.1 What's Liked Most about Being Single.** What middle-age singles like about being unattached. Multiple responses were allowed to the question "What two things do you like most about being single at your age?"

Source: Montenegro 2003. AARP (*www.aarp.org*), reprinted with permission.

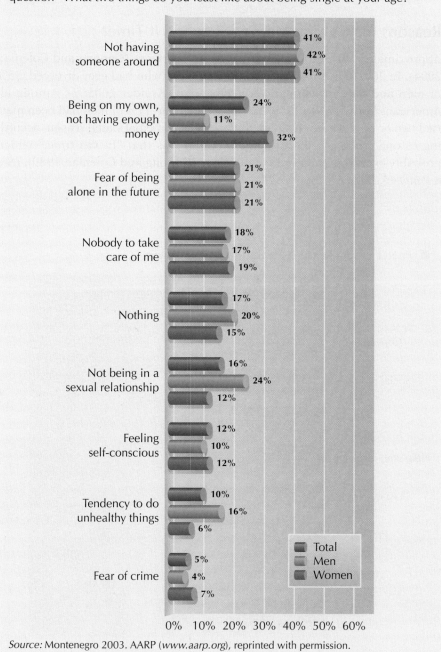

■ **PANEL 15.2   What's Liked Least about Being Single.** What middle-age singles hate about being unattached. Multiple responses were allowed to the question "What two things do you least like about being single at your age?"

Not having someone around — Total 41%, Men 42%, Women 41%

Being on my own, not having enough money — Total 24%, Men 11%, Women 32%

Fear of being alone in the future — Total 21%, Men 21%, Women 21%

Nobody to take care of me — Total 18%, Men 17%, Women 19%

Nothing — Total 17%, Men 20%, Women 15%

Not being in a sexual relationship — Total 16%, Men 24%, Women 12%

Feeling self-conscious — Total 12%, Men 10%, Women 12%

Tendency to do unhealthy things — Total 10%, Men 16%, Women 6%

Fear of crime — Total 5%, Men 4%, Women 7%

Legend: Total, Men, Women

0% 10% 20% 30% 40% 50% 60%

Source: Montenegro 2003. AARP (*www.aarp.org*), reprinted with permission.

Moving beyond Dating: Cohabitation or Remarriage?

About a third of men (32%) and women (34%) in the AARP survey said that they weren't sure whether they would marry if and when they found themselves in a committed exclusive relationship (Montenegro et al. 2003: 10). Another third of men said that they would enter into a cohabitation relationship, compared to about a fifth of the women. Almost a third of women, versus one in four men, said that they would get married. Another study of U.S. women 15 to 44 years of age (Bramlett and Mosher 2002) found that the probability of remarriage among divorced women was 54% in 5 years (58% for white women, 44% for Hispanic women, and 32% for black women).

Reasons for Getting Married Again: Is it Time?

Approximately 40% of all marriages are remarriages (Ganong and Coleman 2004). In 2001, for Americans age 25 and older who had ever divorced, 55% of men and 44% of women were remarried (Kreider 2005: 7). Among all Americans born 1955 to 1959, 22% of women and 17% of men had been married two or more times (Kreider 2005: 4). The principal stated reason, according to one study of 205 men and women, was that "It was time," which probably expresses the need for intimacy (Ganong and Coleman 1989). *(See* ■ *Panel 15.3.)*

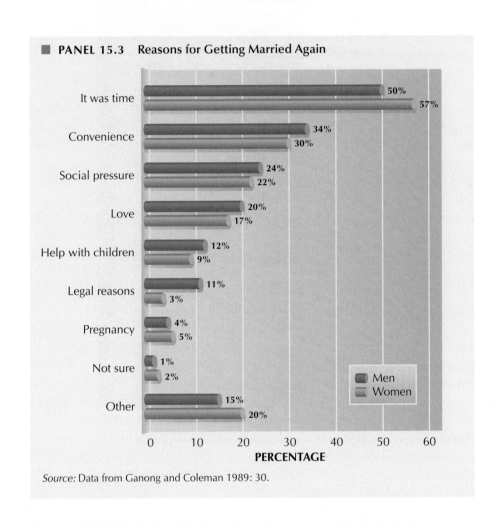

■ **PANEL 15.3   Reasons for Getting Married Again**

Source: Data from Ganong and Coleman 1989: 30.

15.2 Remarried & Blended Families

MAJOR QUESTION How does a blended family differ from a nuclear family in characteristics and stages of development?

PREVIEW People who remarry are either equally happy or less happy compared to people in first marriages, but subsequent marriages don't usually last as long. There are three common forms of blended families, but kinship (quasi-kin) arrangements can be quite elaborate. At least five major characteristics differentiate the stepfamily from the nuclear family. Stepfamilies often go through a series of predictable stages over several years of integration.

Will the second marriage be the same as the first? As we saw in the introduction about mass media depiction of stepparents, a fair amount of "stepism" exists. Like racism and sexism, **stepism is an attitude of prejudice and discrimination; it assumes that stepfamilies are inferior to biological families.**

One observer, social work professor Irene Levin (1997), suggests that many people measure themselves against a **nuclear-family model monopoly, in which the first-marriage family is seen as the legitimate model for how families should be and all other forms are seen as deficient alternatives.** "The privileged status of the biological nuclear family in American society," says another scholar, "contributes to the stigmatization of all nonnuclear family, but especially that of stepfamilies" (Jones 2003: 1).

Is this true? How *do* later remarriages and stepfamilies resemble or differ from first marriages and families?

Remarriage: "This Time It Will Be Different"

Notions of love and happiness exert as much pull the second time around as the first. Divorced people who are contemplating remarriage think that "this time it will be different," that they married the wrong person the first time, that the troubles in that marriage were the fault of the ex-spouse, and that they now have better prospects. Finally, having been through one divorce, they are less afraid of another one (Furstenberg 1980; Marano 2000). It has been found, in fact, that failure in a first marriage does not necessarily affect the quality of a second marriage (Johnson and Booth 1998).

How much better are second and subsequent marriages than first marriages? To answer this question, we need to distinguish between happiness (quality in the marriage) and stability (duration of the marriage).

Happiness: Better the Second Time Around?

"Love is lovelier the second time around," according to a popular song. Is it? Actually, the evidence seems to be that, compared with first marriages, second marriages either show no difference in satisfaction or even show less satisfaction.

■ **Evidence for Equal Satisfaction:** A number of studies have concluded that there are few differences in marital satisfaction between couples in first marriages and those in second or later marriages (White and Booth 1985; Vemer et al. 1989; Coleman and Ganong 1990, 1991; Demo and Acock 1996; Ihinger-Tallman and Pasley 1997). This seemed to be the case despite the complexities of stepchildren and other factors that are specific to remarriages (MacDonald and DeMaris 1995).

One study (Kurdeck 1989) found that it was not whether the marriage was the first or second that affected satisfaction but whether the partners tended to be highly expressive and whether the spouses received social support from their families. Other research (Ono 2005) finds that previously married people are twice as likely to marry those with similar marital histories—for example, when ex-spouses of alcoholics find each other—which can have advantages over "mixed-history" unions.

■ **Evidence for Less Satisfaction:** Yet there is some evidence that remarriages can be less satisfying. One study (Booth and Edwards 1992) found that, compared to subjects in first marriages, subjects in second marriages were more likely to report a decline in marital quality during the first 8 years of marriage. In part, this could be because spouses might have less interaction with parents, in-laws, and others who can lend social support. In addition, compared with couples in first marriages, they might not handle conflicts as well, resorting to anger and shouting (Larson and Allgood 1987).

Stability: How Long Lasting Are Later Marriages?

Stability is another matter. As a general rule, second and third marriages don't last as long as first marriages. Indeed, remarriages are 20% more likely to end in divorce than are first marriages (Martin and Bumpass 1989). And as we saw in Chapter 14, "Uncoupling," subsequent marriages are apt not to last as long as first marriages.

What are the reasons for the higher divorce rates of remarriages? Among the possibilities are the following:

■ **People Who Remarry Are More Accepting of Divorce:** The formerly divorced evidently have a different point of view about marriage than do people in first marriages. They are more likely to go through divorce again than to stick it out in another unhappy marriage (White and Booth 1985; Booth and Edwards 1992).

■ **Remarried Partners Receive Less Social Support:** Remarried couples tend to have less social support from their families of origin as well as their parents and in-laws (Booth and Edwards 1992; Goldenberg and Goldenberg 1994).

■ **Stepchildren Create More Stresses:** The presence of stepchildren who compete for parental attention can distract from the remarried spouses' interactions with each other. Remarriages involving stepchildren have higher divorce rates than remarriages without stepchildren (Ihinger-Tallman and Pasley 1987a; Ganong and Coleman 1994).

■ **Lack of a Cultural Script Adds More Uncertainty:** Even though divorce, remarriage, and stepfamilies seem to have been around forever, remarriage, in the opinion of sociologist Andrew Cherlin (1978, 1981), is an "incomplete institution." That is, society has not yet created a ***cultural script*, or set of social norms for guiding the various participants in their relations with one another.** How are first and second spouses supposed to deal with each other? If you're the child/stepchild, are you supposed to call both male parental figures "Dad" or both female parental figures "Mom"? (Some children find ways never to call their stepparents by name at all.)

However, not all remarried people are more at risk for divorce. According to one nationwide study (Clarke and Wilson 1994), although remarriages are likely to end in divorce during the early years of the union, those who remarried at ages 25 to 44 had lower divorce rates than those who married in their teens. Indeed, after 15 years of marriage, those in remarriage are not more likely to divorce than are those in first marriages. Possible reasons are that older people choose their second partners more judiciously; have more patience, finances, and other resources to make the marriage successful; and are not as willing to divorce again.

In addition, people in ***single remarriages*—marriages in which only one of the partners was previously married—**are no more apt to divorce than are people in first marriages. On the other hand, people in ***double remarriages*—marriages in which both partners were previously married—**are twice as apt to divorce as are people in first marriages. The presence of stepchildren is said to make the risk rise even further—by 50% (White et al. 1986; White 1990, 1991). Interestingly, though, other research concludes that marital conflict occurs less frequently in double remarriages than in first marriages—perhaps because the partners are apt to be more realistic in their expectations than are those in first marriages (MacDonald and DeMaris 1995).

Blended Families & Kinship Networks

The postdivorce (or postmodern) family, as we discussed in Chapter 1, "Seeking," is represented by single parents, binuclear families, and blended families. We already considered single parenting in Chapter 9, "Variations," and Chapter 11, "Parenting."

A ***binuclear family* is a family in which former spouses and children live in two different households.** A single-parent family is one form of a binuclear family—so is a ***blended family*, or *stepfamily*, which is created**

HIS KIDS, HER KIDS. Children of single, divorced, or widowed parents often enjoy close relationships with their biological parents. How do you think this affects them if one parent (or both) remarries? ▲

when two people marry and one or both brings into the household a child or children from a previous marriage. In 1996 (the latest year for which statistics are available), 17% of all children lived in blended families (U.S. Census Bureau 2001).

Common Forms of Blended Families

Looking beyond single parents, there are three basic forms of blended families:

■ Biological Father + Stepmother: In the *biological father–stepmother family*, **all children are biological children of the father and are stepchildren of the stepmother.** (The children's biological mother lives elsewhere or is deceased.) This was a more common form of blended family in earlier times when more mothers died in childbirth and a father remarried principally to have someone to take care of his children.

■ Biological Mother + Stepfather: In the reverse of the preceding form, the *biological mother–stepfather family*, **all children in the family unit are biological children of the mother and are stepchildren of the stepfather.** (The children's biological father is elsewhere or deceased.) This is a more common form of blended family nowadays because of the high number of instances of unmarried mothers or of divorced mothers with children who then marry a man who becomes the children's stepfather.

■ Joint Biological + Stepfamily: In the *joint biological–stepfamily*, **(1) at least one child is the biological child of both parents and (2) at least one child is the biological child of one parent and the stepchild of the other parent.**

Of course, blended families can become far more complicated than this, featuring adopted children, children from more than one former marriage, and siblings and half-siblings, some of whom live within the household part or all of the time and some of whom live somewhere else (Trost 1997). There may also, of course, be wildly varying ages among the children, ranging from babies to adults. And nowadays it is not unheard of for adult children of divorce to find that their father has remarried a woman who is younger than they are.

New Kin, or "Quasi-Kin"

If your parents divorced and then remarried, you might feel (and might still feel) a sense of loss, as so many children of divorce do. Ironically, however, you now have *more* relatives and kin rather than fewer: not just stepparents and stepsiblings, perhaps, but also possibly stepgrandparents, step in-laws (perhaps your stepsister's husband, for instance), and other step-relatives, not to mention the grandparents, aunts, uncles, and cousins of your half-siblings. Indeed, because of the steep rise in divorce starting in the 1970s, now nearly half of American families with children have at least one set of grandparents who have been divorced, compared with just one-fifth in the mid-1980s, according to professor of gerontology Merrill Silverstein (cited in Harmon 2005). Grandparents' decisions to divorce, incidentally, can generate family problems two generations later, predicting less education, more marital discord, and weaker ties with parents (Amato and Cheadle 2005).

Then there's your biological father's new wife and your biological mother's new husband—how do you refer to your parents' new spouses by remarriage? Anthropologist Paul Bohannan (1970) suggests the term **quasi-kin to describe the person a former spouse remarries or, more broadly, to describe any in-laws, both former ones from the previous marriage and added ones from remarriage.**

Discovering Kin Relationships with a Genogram

A blended family can make for an interesting **genogram, a diagram that shows clearly all the people who genetically, emotionally, and legally constitute a particular family.** An example of one such blended family is shown here. *(See ■ Panel 15.4.)* With extra information and symbols, points out Peter Gerlach (2003) of the Stepfamily Association of America, "genograms can show family alliances, conflicts, relationship cut-offs, and other important factors that help describe the family's structure and dynamics." They can be especially helpful, he adds, for new stepfamily members who wonder "Who are we all, now?" (Mental health experts often use a genogram to identify positive and negative influences surrounding an individual.)

Characteristics of Stepfamilies: From Sad Beginnings

People who have not been in stepfamilies might tend to view them as being essentially no different from nuclear families. That is, everyone thinks of the second family as "more or less the same as the first" (Levin 1997: 124). After all, don't both consist of a married adult couple with one or more children all living under the same roof?

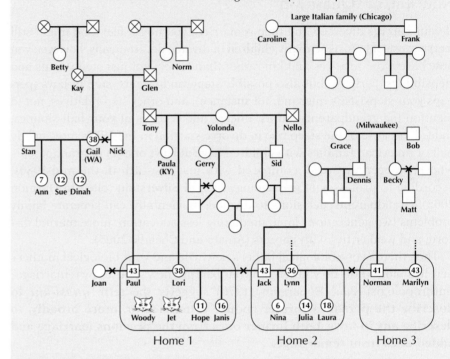

■ **PANEL 15.4 Genogram of a Blended Family.** This real stepfamily has six active co-parents living in three homes with five dependent children. There are nine emotionally important co-grandparents (both living and dead), and many biologically related and legal relatives. Only four of the six biological families are shown. The full three-generational stepfamily has 78 adults and children, with the potential for [(78 × 77)/2] = 3,003 relationships! A male is drawn as a square, a female is drawn as a circle, and a triangle is used when the sex is not known. An "X" or a slash is drawn through the shape if the person is deceased.

Source: Copyright © 1997–2003, by Peter K. Gerlach, MSW, Stepfamily inFormation, *http://sfhelp.org.*

Within the blended-family household, however, is a family with real differences (Peek et al. 1988; Visher and Visher 1979, 1991, 1996).

1. Most Stepfamily Members Have Suffered Some Sort of Loss

A blended family begins with sadness: Most of its members in some way grieve for the loss of an important love relationship with a parent or a former mate, even if the former marriages weren't happy. (The exception would be an unmarried, unwidowed childless person who marries someone with children.) The great majority of children are not living with their biological father, and many divorced fathers simply cut off contact with their offspring, or at the least paternal nurturance and involvement is lessened (Amato and Gilbreth 1999; Schwartz and Finley 2005). (Therefore, many children fantasize that the father will suddenly magically show up and bring the family together again "just like it used to be in happier times.") Indeed, some children might not even see their siblings, who might be distributed among different households.

Many children have been uprooted and have had to move away from a previous residence, giving them less contact with former neighborhoods, schools, and friends. Nuclear families can experience this kind of loss, too, but step-families all start with histories of separation, disconnection, and isolation, which can produce feelings of depression, anxiety, anger, and resentment.

2. Blended Families Have a More Complex Structure

A blended family has a more complex structure than does a first-marriage family. For one thing, stepchildren are biologically related to only one parent, whereas in a nuclear family, children are related to both parents. This means that in a stepfamily, one biological parent lives outside the current household, although in some cases, the children take turns living with different biological parents.

With the new stepfamily household, children find themselves occupying new roles—stepchild, half-sibling, stepsibling—and having new "quasi-kin": stepgrandparents and other steprelatives, with whom they might or might not have contact. Although most stepgrandparents accept their new stepgrand-children rather quickly (Spanier and Furstenberg 1982), whether the ties are close or distant depends mostly on the effort the stepgrandparents make (Cherlin and Furstenberg 1994).

3. Family Boundaries Are Uncertain

Family boundary **refers to rules about who is and is not considered a member of the family and the extent to which each member is allowed to participate.** In a stepfamily, the family boundaries are apt to be vague and uncertain, with members having differing ideas (compared to those in a nuclear family) about which people are and are not "part of our family."

For example, a father's second wife might not want to have nonresidential children from his first marriage visit whenever they want ("because it's our house, not theirs"), whereas the father might want them to be able to come and go as they please ("because I'm their father and they're part of the family").

Children in a stepfamily may also have different outlooks. Sociologist Penny Gross (1986) studied 60 teenagers whose parents had divorced and found that they had four different views of who was and was not considered to be a legitimate member of the family. *(See ■ Panel 15.5.)*

4. Roles Are Ill-Defined, So There Might Be More Tension

Anyone who has stepped into the role of stepparent probably thinks that he or she has to improvise as things go along. No instructions come with the job. Legally, in fact, you are a nonparent, with no prescribed rights or duties (Mason 1998). You are never sure what you are supposed to do. ("Should I rebuke Johnny for breaking the vase? Or let his father do it when he gets home?") You might try on one role after another (the pal, the older advisor, the distant relation, whatever) until you find one that seems to work.

Children also, of course, find that they have to shift roles. Many move between different households, or different stepsiblings and half-siblings appear in their households. The different, perhaps exclusive bonds they had with their biological parents must now be shared. Stepparents and stepsib-lings might compete for their custodial parent's attention. Each household and each arrangement might have different rules and different expectations about allowable behavior. ("Why can't I watch TV like I do at Dad's house?") There may be struggles about turf rights and property rights.

All this might be aggravated by money problems that began with the previous divorce (Mason 1998). For example, the ex-spouse, usually the husband, might fail to make, or be irregular with, child-support payments. Yet the resentful custodial spouse, usually the mother, might still be obliged to turn over the children on weekends for scheduled visitation (Whitsett and Land 1992). These and many other reasons are why stepfamily environments can be sources of tension and conflict. And unlike first-marriage families, stepfamilies aren't usually allowed to adjust gradually.

5. With Different Loyalties, Family Integration Comes Slowly

What if you, a boy, feel closer to your father and his new wife, who live elsewhere, than you do to your mother and her new husband, whose house you live in? Imagine the resentment you would feel toward your custodial parent. Or what if you, a young adult woman, put yourself through college without financial help from your biological, noncustodial father, then observe him giving help to his stepdaughter (your younger stepsister) for the same thing? Incidentally, although all states require biological parents to support their children, only 20 states require stepparents to support their stepchildren (Morgan 2002). Clearly, problems about family loyalty can be much more accentuated in blended families.

With all the shifting power balances, continual transitions, resentments, and lack of shared family history, integration comes slowly. According to one study, stepfamily members did not begin to think and act like a family until the end of the second or third year of the remarriage (Bray and Kelly 1998). The entire process of integration of stepfamilies, as we shall see, usually takes 7 to 10 years, although some families do it in as little as 4 years and some never do it at all.

Stages in Becoming a Blended Family

Just as there are developmental stages in becoming married or becoming divorced, there are stages in building a blended family. Researchers such as Patricia Papernow (1988, 1993) and James Bray and John Kelly (1998) have divided this developmental process into phases, a "stepfamily life cycle," each subdivided into stages, as shown here.

1. The Turbulent Early Phase: Fantasy, Immersion, & Awareness

The early phase, which might last 2 years and includes the courtship and early part of remarriage, is characterized by fantasy, confusion and chaos, and learning to know one another.

■ **Stage 1: Fantasy—"I'll love the children, and they'll love me":** The remarriage and stepfamily development begins with each person having his or her fantasy of what the new family will be like ("We'll be a normal family again"). Many hope that they will step into another nuclear family (not realizing that stepfamilies are different), only perhaps better than any first-marriage family, in which everyone will love and be loved.

Children, however, might have different fantasies, in which they feel the loss of their original families and hope that their original parents will get back together again. They might be afraid that if they come to like the new stepparent, they will somehow harm one or both of their biological parents. Or they might fear that their new family will also fail, bringing about renewed upheavals.

■ **Stage 2: Immersion—"I didn't realize there would be so much confusion":** Now fantasy is replaced by reality, as unanticipated problems and struggles emerge. The stepparents might feel excluded from the parent-child union, prompting feelings of resentment and inadequacy. The biological parents might feel that they have to please everyone, or perhaps they will try to deny that problems exist.

Children might feel that they are caught in a web of new rules, conflicts of loyalties, and confusion. They might feel that showing affection to the stepparent is betraying loyalties to the absent biological parent.

■ **Stage 3: Awareness—"I think we're beginning to figure one another out now":** In the awareness stage, family members become familiar with one another and aware of one another's peculiarities and needs. That is, they "map the territory" of each family member. Stepparents learn about their stepchildren's histories, preferences, friends, and so on and try to discover their own need for distance with the stepchildren. Biological parents might become aware of their own feelings of resentment toward their children and their new spouses—or the reverse, of overprotecting them—and begin to take leave of feelings about having a perfect family.

Children might feel that the stepparent has replaced them in their biological father or mother's affections ("Mom never cuddles me in bed in the morning anymore") and be resentful of the stepparent. As long as they are not told "how wonderful" they are supposed to feel about the new family and are

HIS, HERS, THEIRS. Blended families can become quite complicated, perhaps combining older children from previous marriages with newborns or young children from the present marriage. What kind of interaction would you expect in such families? ▶

encouraged to look at the positive things the stepparent has to offer, perhaps they will begin to appreciate the benefits of the new person who will play with them and take them to restaurants, movies, horseback riding, and on other outings.

2. The Middle Phase: Mobilization & Action

In the middle phase, the family begins to restructure. Many of the fantasies have been given up, and the members have learned more about one another's needs; however, the children remain attached to the biological parent. In this phase, the family might fall apart unless it learns how to make changes in the emotional structure as a whole. Phase 2, then, is the stage of hard work.

■ **Stage 4: Mobilization—"No more Mr. Nice Guy with this family; I'm taking a stand for myself":** The catalyst is usually the stepparent, who suddenly realizes that he or she can't be the ideal stepparent and can't be the insider and is tired of not having his or her needs met. The stepparent's sudden demands (that children pick up their own clothes or do their own chores) might be frightening to the biological parent, who, feeling caught in the middle, might either try to support and empathize with both the children and the stepspouse or simply stop trying to be a buffer and let the other parties work out their own relationships.

Tired of divided loyalties and of bickering parents, the children might begin to express their own needs, bringing their resentments more into the open.

■ **Stage 5: Action—"We've begun to make some joint decisions and to accept that we're each different":** In this stage, the family begins to take some actions that will reorganize its structure, routines, and rituals so that it can function effectively as a stepfamily. The family members might institute family meetings to handle issues, compromise on standards of household cleanliness and order, and make new arrangements about which households the children will spend holidays at. They develop realistic expectations about one another.

The stepparent becomes more active in decision-making and disciplinary matters, the biological parent no longer feels that he or she has to be every-

REMARRIAGE, NO CHILDREN. Jeff Gundersen, age 50, a successful Wall Street executive headhunter and divorced father of three, was dating younger women, most of them in their thirties and most of whom wanted to have children. He, however, felt that he had paid his dues with diapers, weekend soccer games, and late nights with kids' homework and was happy to have his life back. Lorraine White, a decade younger, was able to see it differently: "What's more important? A great relationship or a child?" Before marrying in 2000, she agreed not to start a second family. Could you see yourself making this kind of bargain? ◄

thing to everybody, and the stepparents begin taking time for themselves in a way that doesn't involve the children. The result, if all goes well, is that the bonds between everyone are strengthened.

3. Later Stages: Contact & Resolution

In the later phase, the family achieves its own identity and begins to solidify itself as a family.

■ **Stage 6: Contact—"Our relationships with one another have become more easy and honest":** In this stage, family members make emotional contact with one another, communicating more easily, intimately, and authentically. The stepparent becomes an "intimate outsider" with whom the stepchildren (or some of them at least) can talk about matters that are too sensitive to discuss with their biological parents (drugs, relationships, sex, religion, and divorce, for example).

■ **Stage 7: Resolution—"We're all comfortable with one another now":** Relationships will always vary depending on the personality of each individual, and some will be closer than others. Nevertheless, by the end stage, which can take 7 to 10 years or even more, there will be a sense of acceptance by everyone in the family. Assuming that the major issues have been worked through, many of the stepchildren will have come to accept the stepparent as someone who offers certain benefits, even a mentoring relationship. And the married partners will have found comfort and support in their own relationship.

15.3 Inside the Blended Family

MAJOR QUESTION What are three perspectives of the stepmother, the stepfather, and the stepchild on the blended family?

PREVIEW The experience of being in a blended family depends on whether you're the stepmother, stepfather, or stepchild. Stepmothers bear the greatest burden, being expected to be unduly nice while having to deal with the "evil stepmother" stereotype. A stepfather's role may vary depending on whether he has children and is marrying a childless woman, has no children and is marrying a woman with children, or has children and is marrying a woman with children. Stepchildren must cope with feelings of abandonment, uncertainty about discipline, and adjusting to stepsiblings. All need to be aware of sexual boundaries.

Most participants in a stepfamily—stepmother, stepfather, stepchildren—come to the new arrangement with a *hidden agenda,* **expectations about how everyone should behave, but often these expectations are not communicated to everyone.**

For instance, the mother who comes to the marriage with her own biological children might assume that the stepfather will willingly contribute to their well-being (including paying college costs, say) as if they were his own children. The stepfather might assume that he will be allowed to step in and have his own way as disciplinarian. The stepchildren might assume that whatever allocation of chores had been worked out with their mother will continue to prevail.

Then there are the resentments that are unique to stepfamilies compared to nuclear families—the wife's irritation about her new husband's paying all that money in spousal support to his ex-wife, the husband's indignation about his new wife's not allowing his own biological children to visit at any time, the stepchildren's bitterness over the first divorce and the presence of an "interloper" stepparent, and so on.

As we have indicated throughout the chapter, stepfamilies really are different from nuclear families. Let us consider some of the specifics.

STEPMOTHERS AND STEPDAUGHTERS. Discipline is a tricky area for stepmothers. If the stepmother is the principal stay-at-home parent, she may be expected to be the disciplinarian, but this situation will probably not result in her developing a good relationship with her stepchildren. However, a stepdaughter might find it easier to talk to her stepmother rather than her biological mother about uncomfortable subjects. What have been your observations about the interaction between stepmothers and stepdaughters? ▲

Being a Stepmother

Sociologist Phyllis Raphael (1978) calls it the "stepmother trap," in which a stepmother is caught between two conflicting societal views: one sentimental, one harsh. **In the *stepmother trap*, a stepmother is, on the one hand, expected to be unnaturally loving toward her stepchildren, yet, on the other hand, she is viewed as being mean, abusive, and vain,** like Cinderella's and other stepmothers in the old folktales.

As we have seen, stepmothers join their new families with high hopes of loving the stepchildren just as they do their own biological children, making up for the pain of the divorce, keeping everyone happy, and creating a close-knit family. In return, they hope to prove that they are not wicked stepmothers and to receive immediate affection from their stepchildren (Visher and Visher 1979, 1991). Unfortunately, most stepmothers are frustrated in their expectations (Church 1994). Some of the problems are as follows.

Expectations of Love & Acceptance by Stepchildren

Although society might expect stepparents and stepchildren to love one another in the same way as biologically related parents and children, this doesn't usually happen (Smith 1990). Nor, say therapists, should stepfamilies expect to feel that way (Pasley et al. 1996). Stepmothering is particularly difficult for women who are married to noncustodial fathers who see their children on a regularly scheduled but part-time basis, in which the stepmother might feel excluded from the father-child relationship (Coleman and Ganong 1997). In addition, stepmother-stepdaughter relationships are particularly difficult (Clingempeel et al. 1984).

Furthermore, stepmothers might be accused by their stepchildren of giving special treatment to their own biological children (Coleman and Ganong 1997). And the stepchildren might be right: It's possible that stepparents have a "genetic propensity," say MacDonald and DeMaris (1996), to express greater solicitude toward their biological children than toward their stepchildren.

Being a Disciplinarian

Another dilemma for many stepmothers is the matter of discipline. If the stepmother is at home most of the time, the role of disciplinarian most likely falls to her, as a result of which she is less likely to have good relationships with the children (Kurdek and Fine 1993). Therefore, it is advisable for stepparents to wait a while before becoming disciplinarians (Visher and Visher 1996).

Problems with the Former Wife

A remarried wife can't help but feel great resentment when her husband pays spousal and/or child support to his ex-wife in an amount that represents perhaps a third of his income—maybe equivalent to the remarried wife's own income. In addition, her husband might spend a fair amount of time communicating with his ex about school, child care, summer activities, and other matters concerning their joint children.

Being a Stepfather

Stepfathers don't have a centuries-old stereotype of "cruel stepfather" to deal with (except for Quasimodo's evil stepfather), and they tend to spend less time with children or stepchildren than do stepmothers and biological mothers (Kyungok 1994). Compared with biological fathers, as we mentioned, stepfathers are also apt to view themselves as being less effective with their stepchildren (Beer 1992). Still, many stepfathers—55%, according to one survey (Sweet et al. 1988)—find having stepchildren just as satisfying as having their own biological children. Indeed, the more a stepfather is involved with his stepchildren, including their discipline, the greater is his satisfaction in parenting (Fine et al. 1997).

A stepfather will confront his own challenges, depending on which of the following scenarios occurs.

Childless Man Marries Woman with Children

About 86% of children in blended families live with their biological mother and stepfather (Rutter 1994). A woman who already has her own children might have had years to establish strong emotional bonds. Consequently, the new stepfather must not only accept their attachment to one another but also deal with their resentments that he is interfering with their special relationship (Wallerstein and Kelly 1980a, 1980b). He must also cope with their established ways of doing things, such as how household chores are handled. The

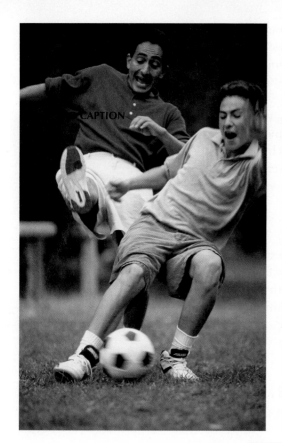

STEPFATHERS AND STEPSONS. Discipline can be a difficult matter for stepfathers, especially if there is some sort of competition for influence with the stepson's biological father. In general, stepfathers are inclined to view themselves as being less effective with their stepchildren compared with biological fathers. Even so, some find having stepchildren just as satisfying as having their own biological children, especially when they can become engaged in shared activities. What have you observed about the interaction between stepfathers and stepsons? ▲

bottom line is that the man is the outsider and must work his way into the closed circle of mother and children (Cherlin and Furstenberg 1994).

Man with Children Marries Childless Woman

About 14% of children in blended families live with their biological father and stepmother (Rutter 1994). A man with children who marries a woman without children may face several issues. If his children don't live with him and he sees them part time, he might feel guilty about not being a full-time father and want to play "Disneyland Dad," devoting lots of time to the children and spoiling them with treats at a time when money might be tight, sparking resentments in the new spouse. In fact, stepmothers whose stepchildren visit have greater difficulty than do those whose stepchildren live in the home (Ambert 1986).

In addition, whether the children are with him part time or full time, the father might expect his new wife to actively engage in raising the children and to establish an emotional connection with them. Since, as we have seen, this kind of bonding can take 2 to 7 years or more, attempts to accelerate it might only incur resentments from the new wife ("They're not *my* kids!") and the children ("She's not *my* mother!"). Stepmothers who are married to men whose children live with them full time rather than part time seem to have an especially rocky road. Perhaps this is because the children are there owing to an angry custody dispute or were removed by court order from their biological mother's home and therefore are especially apt to resent their stepmother for "trying to take over as my mother" (Furstenberg and Nord 1985).

Man with Children Marries Woman with Children

If both partners in a remarried couple have biological children from previous marriages—especially if all live together full time in one household—this situation can significantly lower satisfaction in comparison to the situation in which only one partner brings children into the remarriage (Clingempeel 1981). Yet the first situation can also be a beneficial arrangement. The father/stepfather is impelled to take a more active role with regard to all the children and to deal with both sets in a fair-minded manner (Palisi et al. 1991).

Of course, in this as in any other stepfamily, the two stepparents might not agree about discipline and other matters regarding their children's behavior. In addition, there might be competition with the influence of the stepchildren's biological father, especially if he is regularly involved in his children's lives.

Being a Stepchild

As we mentioned, in 1996, about 17% of all U.S. children were found to be living in stepfamilies. In Canada, 4.3% of children ages 11 or younger live with a biological parent and a stepparent (National Longitudinal Study of Children and Youth 1997). Children, especially young children, might be willing to accept a stepparent as a new mother or father, but many will have an instant dislike or fear of the stepparent. Adolescents and young adults might regard the newcomer as "Dad's wife" or "Mom's husband" rather than as a stepparent.

Are children who grow up in blended families greatly different from those who grow up in nuclear families? Are they weakened or made stronger by the experience? Educators have assumed that children in families reconstituted after divorce do better academically than do children in divorced single-parent families, but this notion is not supported by research; indeed, sometimes children in the former situation are worse off (Jeynes 1999). Research also shows that grown children of stepfamilies reported less cohesion, less closeness, less adaptability, and more stress in their family life compared with children raised in intact families (Kennedy 1985; Pink and Wampler 1985; Peek et al. 1988). This does not mean, however, that grown children of stepfamilies were damaged by their experience; the good news is that 80% of children in blended families are doing well, turning out much like those raised in nuclear families (Pasley 2000). Indeed, they have no more negative attitudes toward themselves and others than do children in nuclear families (Ganong and Coleman 1993).

Still, stepchildren often have to deal with some unique challenges.

Feelings of Abandonment

Some problems that stepchildren suffer are a consequence of their parents' divorce. As we described in Chapter 14, "Uncoupling," in the short term, such children feel guilty, depressed, anxious, intensely angry, and withdrawn. In addition, when the parents split up, children feel abandoned. But then, when they find that they are part of a stepfamily, they often feel abandoned a second time, as their custodial parent turns his or her attention to the new spouse. The task for the parent, then, is to spend sufficient time with his or her children as well as the new partner and to impress on the children that the divorce was not their fault and that they are loved equally by both biological parents.

Conflicts

The greatest source of problems for children in blended families is conflict between parents left over from the first marriage (Rutter 1994). Of course, every family, first family or stepfamily, has conflicts. And a family that has gone through divorce might have seen even more conflict. Once a family has split up, however, conflicts take on a different nature. Most are over such matters as divided loyalties, discipline, and stepsibling rivalry.

Divided Loyalties

In Chapter 14, "Uncoupling," we mentioned the problems of *parent alienation syndrome,* in which children are preoccupied with viewing one parent as all good and the other parent as all bad, and of *divorce-related malicious mother syndrome*, in which a mother unjustifiably punishes her divorced husband by attempting to alienate their mutual children from him (Turkat 1995). Fathers may also have similar motivations, especially the vengeful type of "deadbeat dad." These are battles for the children's loyalty, forcing them to take sides or at least to pretend to agree.

One study (Lutz 1983) of adolescents found that half said one divorced parent talked negatively of the other, which most of the children found stressful. Sometimes, however, the quarrel is over loyalty to a stepparent for whom a child has developed a liking but who is disliked by the "rival" biological parent, such as a biological father for a stepfather.

Discipline

Suppose you have spent half your childhood growing up in a family where no one ever spanked you, then you suddenly find yourself in a new household with a stepparent who believes in stern discipline. Clearly, discipline—on top of the shock of all the new living arrangements—can be a major issue for stepchildren, and it is one of the most common sources of conflict in blended families (Ihinger-Tallman and Pasley 1987b).

For children, discipline seems to be more difficult to adjust to with a stepmother than with a stepfather, probably because the stepmother is apt to be the more actively involved parent (Fine and Kurdek 1992). The problem of discipline is often aggravated by interference from the biological parent, which can undermine the stepparent's authority (Mills 1984).

Stepsibling Rivalry

Even in nuclear families, of course, the parents might favor one child over another ("She's so smart, but he can never get his homework done," or "He's always so sunny, but she's so grumpy"). In stepfamilies, however, a stepchild might perceive that a stepsibling is receiving more favorable treatment simply on the basis of a biological relationship ("Dad's wife always gives her own kid more leeway when it comes to making mistakes"). Indeed, it has been found that biological children in blended families with stepsiblings suffer more stress than do those in families without stepsiblings, perhaps because of disputes among the adults when both sets of children are present (Lutz 1983).

The Special Problem of Sexual Boundaries

You are Soon-Yi Previn, age 23, and your stepfather is filmmaker Woody Allen, age 58. Or you're a 14-year-old boy when your mom remarries a man with a daughter near your age, to whom—after 2 years of fighting——you find

SEXUAL BOUNDARIES. Stepfamilies may have to take special pains to make sure members don't cross sexual boundaries, as with sexual abuse of young women (or men) perpetrated by stepfathers, uncles, stepbrothers, or male friends of the parents. Are you aware of any instances of sexual abuse in stepfamilies? ◀

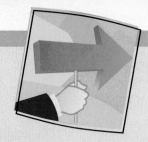

PRACTICAL ACTION
Sexual Abuse & Sexual Boundaries in Stepfamilies

Sexual abuse, we pointed out in Chapter 13, "Crises," can take many forms: exposure, unwanted hugging and kissing, attempted sexual contact, fondling of genitals, intercourse, oral sex, and incest. Most children are between 8 and 12 years old when they suffer the abuse.

Although the abuse might be by nonrelatives, here we are more concerned with relatives, including steprelatives (intrafamilial abuse). Perhaps 85% of abused children in intrafamilial cases are female, and 15% are male (Solomon 1992). The most common form of incest (defined as sexual abuse between people who are too closely related to marry) is that between a girl and her father, stepfather, or older brother (Canavan et al. 1992).

Mother-son sexual relations are apparently rare.

Intrafamilial Sexual Abuse: Three Types

There are three categories of intrafamilial sexual abuse, as follows:

- **Uncle and niece:** Although uncles are technically not members of a family, whether nuclear or blended, they are apparently the most common perpetrators of intrafamilial sexual abuse, and victims suffer considerable long-term emotional distress (Kinsey et al. 1953; Russell 1986).

- **Stepfather and stepdaughter:** Sexual abusers of daughters can be biological fathers, but they are more often stepfathers (Jensen and

Doxey 1996). At one time, stepfather sexual abuse was not considered incest, since the perpetrator and the victim aren't biologically related. Regardless, this type of sexual abuse is considered the most traumatic, and not surprisingly, women who were abused as children tend as adults to be less secure and trusting in relationships (Lang 1997).

- **Stepbrother and his stepsister:** Incest can also occur between biological brothers and sisters. Russell (1986) found that at the time of incest, the age of the brother averaged 17.9 and that of the sister averaged 10.7—representing a power differential that belies any pretensions about consent.

yourself powerfully attracted. Or you're a 15-year-old girl, and your new stepdad's male friends, who are twice your age, clearly have eyes for you.

Sexual boundaries are an area of special sensitivity in blended families. (After their sexual relationship became highly publicized, Allen and Previn, the adopted daughter of Allen's 10-year companion, Mia Farrow, were married in 1997.) Although research seems to show that incest is more common in stepfamilies and that stepdaughters are the ones more apt to be sexually abused, the abuse is less apt to be committed by stepfathers; rather, the abusers are more likely to be their stepfather's friends (Finkelhor 1987; Ganong and Coleman 1994; Giles-Sims 1997). We discuss more about sexual abuse and sexual boundaries in stepfamilies in the Practical Action box on these pages.

Conditions under Which Sexual Abuse Takes Place

David Finkelhor (1984) suggests that sexual abuse may take place when four preconditions exist:

- **Precondition 1—motivation:** For the perpetrator, (a) relating to the child fulfills an important emotional need, (b) he (the abuser is almost always male) is sexually aroused by the child, and (c) alternative means of sexual gratification are not available or are less satisfying.

- **Precondition 2—inhibitions overcome:** Alcohol, drugs, senility, social approval of child sex, or other factors overcome internal prohibitions.

- **Precondition 3—obstacles overcome:** The usual external obstacles that protect the child are overcome, as when the mother is absent, ill, or incapacitated.

- **Precondition 4—child's resistance overcome:** A child's ability to resist is overcome by force, persuasion, attention, bribes, and the like.

Reducing Chances for Abuse in Blended Families

Emily and John Visher (1982: 162–166) offer some suggestions for reducing the chance for sexual abuse in stepfamilies:

- **Arrange the living space appropriately:** If stepsiblings are of an age at which sexual relations could develop, arrange the living situation to head off temptations—for example, avoid adjoining bedrooms.

- **Avoid being sexually provocative:** Even with young children present but especially with teenagers, adults shouldn't walk around the house in their underwear. Scantily clad adolescents should be told to go to their rooms and put on appropriate clothing.

- **Curtail roughhousing and some intimate behavior with children over age 10 or 11:** Roughhousing or having the child sit on one's lap and kissing might become physical turn-ons.

- **Be affectionate but not passionate when you're with your spouse in public:** Because of their own awakening sexuality, teenagers in particular are highly sensitive to displays of passion, including stolen kisses and embraces.

- **Don't turn to stepchildren for emotional support when you and your partner aren't getting along:** Asking for emotional support from a stepchild might lead to the encouragement of feelings of intimacy that should not be allowed.

We considered other aspects of sexual abuse in Chapter 13, "Crises."

15.4 Strengthening Stepfamilies

MAJOR QUESTION What are the benefits of being in a stepfamily, and what are ways to help ensure success?

PREVIEW Despite the difficulties, living in a stepfamily provides five potential benefits, especially for the children, that are not found in nuclear families. Experts provide several pieces of advice about how a blended family can be successful.

Are all the problems we've described inevitable? Or is there a pool of wisdom available that can make life easier for stepfamilies? Let's consider, first, the kind of strengths and benefits stepfamilies have and, second, how stepfamilies can be strengthened even further.

Five Potential Benefits of Stepfamilies

If you grew up in a stepfamily, you might not have had the family closeness, security, and stability that someone growing up in an intact family would have had. However, the first family you started out with, before your parents' divorce, might have been no picnic. Perhaps it was roiled by conflict, drug abuse, violence, and even sexual abuse. This begins to suggest some of the possible benefits of blended families (Coleman et al. 1985).

Potential Benefit #1: Families Are Happier

Although stepfamilies might not have as much emotional closeness as first families, they might be calmer, with fewer crises (Ihinger-Tallman and Pasley 1987a). Wives in particular seem happier than husbands in blended families (Kurdek and Fine 1991). Research shows that a mother will less often yell at, spank, or hit children if she is living with a new husband or partner (Thomson 2001). A formerly single parent is apt to have fewer childraising stresses and feel fewer financial burdens after remarrying, and the child's financial situation might improve as a result. From the child's point of view, when his or her mother remarries, the new intact partnership can improve the mother-child relationship (Thomson 2001).

STEPFAMILY INTERACTION. One of the overlooked benefits of stepfamilies is interaction among the extended kinship network of stepsiblings, stepgrandparents, and other relatives. What successful large stepfamilies are you familiar with? ▲

Potential Benefit #2: Children Gain Role Models

Stepfamily parents might provide happier, and therefore more positive, marital role models for their children than those in a conflict-ridden nuclear family (Rutter 1994). Moreover, a child might now have as many as four parental role models: mother, father, stepmother, and stepfather.

Potential Benefit #3: Parents Might Be More Objective

Because they have had to make several adjustments regarding divorce and remarriage and have become more mature themselves, stepparents might be able to handle problems with each other and with their children more objectively. Is an adolescent or college-age daughter, for example, having relationship problems or worrying about getting HIV/AIDS? She might find it easier to talk about it with her stepmother, who might be less emotionally involved and less uncomfortable with the subject than her biological mother.

Potential Benefit #4: Children Gain More Siblings & Kin

An only child in a first family might in the second family gain the older brother or younger sister that he or she never had but fantasized about having. Of course, not all stepchildren get along with their stepsiblings or half-siblings, but some find their lives enriched by the experience.

In addition, a child who moves into a stepfamily also may gain an extended kinship network of assorted grandparents and other relatives, who might be able to provide love and security as well.

Potential Benefit #5: Children Become More Flexible

In experiencing the merger of two families, children might be forced to learn negotiation skills and to become more flexible and accommodating in working out differences. They might be exposed to new ideas, alternative political views, different values, and even different interests—such as an interest in sports or music that did not exist in the first family. Thus, children might become more adaptable in their adult relationships.

Steps toward Becoming a Successful Stepfamily

You would expect that the same factors that make a first marriage work would be applicable to remarriage, such as having good communication. But are there other matters that apply specifically to remarriage and stepfamilies? The following suggestions to the parents in a blended family draw on a variety of sources (U.S. Department of Health, Education, and Welfare 1978; Turnbull and Turnbull 1983; Van Pelt 1985; Visher and Visher 1993; Lauer and Lauer 1999).

1. Harmonize Your Finances: "We Want to Be Fair to Everyone with the Limited Resources We Have"

"Reviewing each partner's finances in detail [preferably before marriage] may not be your idea of some enchanted evening," says a *Consumer Reports* article ("For Richer or Poorer Again" 2002: 60), "but doing so may prevent a great deal of heartache later on." Indeed, says the article, the primary reason a second marriage may fall apart is disagreement over money. In fact, remarrying couples are advised to develop a prenuptial agreement (or postnuptial, if they are already married) if either one has more than $100,000 in assets and children or other heirs to whom they want to leave money. A prenuptial agreement will also shield a large inheritance one partner might want kept separate from marital property in any future divorce.

Among the things to be done, advises *Consumer Reports*: (1) Disclose your financial information to each other. (2) Set up a family budget and decide how you'll pay joint expenses. (3) Decide how to title your joint assets. (4) Develop an estate plan, including new wills, living wills, durable powers of attorney, health-care proxies, and trusts. (5) Update all your papers.

2. Develop Realistic Expectations: "I Know We're Not Going to Become an Instant Happy Family"

Successful blended families replace fantasy expectations, such as the hope for immediate love or an improved version of the nuclear family, with realistic ones. A new stepparent should realize that love and friendship with stepchildren can't be hurried and that he or she can't replace a lost parent.

It's important also that, rather than wishing the children were different, the stepparent try to accept them as they are—and let them know of that acceptance through praise and affectionate gestures.

3. Let Everyone Mourn Their Losses: "We All Lost Someone or Something Important, & I Know It Still Hurts"

Family members need to help each other cope with the feelings of loss of a former spouse or biological parent arising out of the disruption of previous families (Marano 2000). Children especially need time to mourn—to express their sadness, fear, and anger—and the adults should not take the reactions as personal rejection. Evidently, African American families are better at giving this kind of support than white families are (Crosbie-Burnett and Lewis 1993).

4. Maintain the Primacy of the Relationship with Your New Partner: "We Need to Focus on Each Other as Well as on the Children"

In successful stepfamilies, the remarried partners take care to build a strong relationship with each other, spending time alone and having fun with each other. This is important because too many stepparents concentrate principally on the children and fail to nurture each other. When the adults have a strong relationship, it also gives the children a pair of strong role models to follow in terms of problem solving and stability and reduces the children's anxiety about another breakup occurring (Kheshgi-Genovese and Genovese 1997).

5. Treat Children the Same Way & Give Them Their Own Space: "The Stepchildren Should Be Made to Feel at Home—Because That's Where They Are"

Fairness is often a big issue with stepchildren, who might be forced into new kinds of sharing (such as a bedroom) that they don't like. Therefore, it is important that everyone plays by the same rules and that all the children understand that they have responsibilities and receive rewards just as everyone else does.

Stepchildren have a strong sense of ownership, but the children who have been already occupying the residence or the room that the stepchildren now are in have a certain territorial power. If a stepfamily can't afford to move to neutral territory, such as a new house, it's advisable to give all children their own space, to let them put their own pictures up on the wall, and to encourage them to make their own friends and to invite them over. If children can't be given their own rooms, each should have his or her own bed and space in the dresser and bookshelves so that each child "owns" part of the bedroom.

6. Don't Rush Being a Stepparent: "It Can Take a Few Years to Build a Good Relationship"

Stepparents need to realize that developing a relationship with the stepchildren has to happen gradually. Acknowledge that you might be compared with the absent parent. Don't play some preconceived role, which children will probably spot as phony anyway. It can take 3 years before everyone begins to feel comfortable with one another (Bray and Kelly 1998), and building a sup-

EXAMPLE OF

Blended Bonds

Establishing Great Relationships within Stepfamilies

Sarah Albright, age 15, of Alexandria, Virginia, thinks her stepmother is "cool" and gives her spontaneous hugs. "You have to be mindful and respectful of your stepparent," says Sarah (quoted in Peterson 2002b: 2D). After all, "she is married to one of your biological parents."

The stepmother, Kristin Lee Mead, age 34, has been married for 4 years to her husband, Luis Albright, age 47, and lives with him and Sarah. Another daughter, age 14, lives nearby with her single mother. Luis's 20-year-old son, who lived with them earlier for 2 years, now has his own household. Mead says that she and Sarah are totally "on the same wavelength."

About 48% of adult children whose mothers had remarried were happy

with the new union, and half thought of their stepfathers as parents, according to Constance Ahrons (1987, 1994). However, only about 29% of those whose fathers remarried like the idea of a stepmother, and only about a third regard their stepmothers as parents. According to E. Mavis Hetherington, only about 20% of adult stepchildren feel close to their stepmothers (Hetherington and Kelly 2002)

What explains these differences between closeness to stepmothers and stepfathers? Ahrons says that stepmothers tend to become too involved in their stepchildren's affairs (even when the children don't live with them), whereas stepfathers tend to stand back. Stepmothers, suggests Ahrons (quoted in Peterson 2002: 2D), need to approach the stepchildren "very, very slowly. The women want so badly to be part of the family, and they tend to come on too strong too soon."

What do stepmothers like Mead do right to ensure bonding with the stepchildren? Jennifer Green and Susan Wisdom, authors of *Step-coupling: Creating and Sustaining a Strong Marriage in Today's Blended Family* (2001), have extended clans that include four biological children and four stepchildren, two stepgrand-children, two ex-husbands, two hus-

bands' ex-wives, one ex-wife's new partner, and two ex-husbands' new spouses. One of their most important suggestions they offer is that the new couple have a strong relationship with each other.

- **Develop a committed, bonded relationship with the new spouse:** A healthy relationship in which the parents connect at least once a day—sharing, laughing, being physically intimate—will help to stabilize the new family. It sends a message to the children of a strong relationship that makes them feel secure.

- **Listen, stay detached, don't parent:** Her role in the family, says Mead, "is to listen. . . . Let the biological parent parent. If you want to be a mother, then have your own baby." Let the biological parents get involved in the discipline and problem solving.

- **Join a stepparent group:** More and more stepparents attend workshops and conferences and get help from people like them in Internet chat rooms and on message boards. Some join (or start) local chapters of the Stepfamily Association of America.

portive stepfamily takes longer than that—perhaps 4 to 10 years, as we mentioned earlier (Beer 1988; Papernow 1993; Gamache 1997).

Although it's important to integrate a stepparent into children's lives, it's also important that that he or she not rush to assume authority or intimacy, especially during the first year. The stepparent will need the support of his or her spouse in child rearing, and it's important that the two see eye to eye. In matters of discipline, some parents and stepparents will agree that they are allowed to discipline their own biological children but not the stepchildren. (This might mean that when the biological parent is absent, the children will test the stepparent by being unruly.) In any event, both adults should try to treat their own children and stepchildren with equal fairness and to deal with problems openly and honestly.

7. Cooperate with the Absent Parent & Other Kin: "I Don't Have to Like Them, but They Belong in the Children's Lives"

Maybe neither you nor your spouse likes your ex-spouse. Regardless of your anger and resentments, however, the children must be able to maintain a relationship with both biological parents. The same is true for both sets of grandparents, who can be a stabilizing influence. Therefore, it's important to develop a working relationship with ex-partners so that school activities, summer vacations, graduations, and other important events can proceed smoothly for the children.

8. Develop Your Own Family Rituals: "Let's Try Out New Ways of Doing Things"

A family ritual can be anything from doing the laundry on a certain day to decorating the house for a holiday to visiting relatives to taking a vacation to the same place every year. The purpose of a ritual in stepfamilies, as in nuclear families, is to foster bonding among their members. In a blended family, the rituals can be combined out of previous ways of doing things, although it might be best if they don't resemble past patterns. For instance, if the dinner hour was once the sacred get-together time in previous households, it might be best to vary this, letting children fix their own meals sometimes, eating out, or having the job of cook rotate.

9. Thinking of the Stepparent on Mother's Day or Father's Day

Stepchildren, especially teenagers busy grappling with the stresses of young adulthood, might not convey much gratitude for what their stepparent has done for them. But as one stepmother (McClenon 2002) of adolescents writes, "You have a scant few years together, and someday they will regard you differently. . . . And someday you just may not be able to believe how close you've become."

When that day of realization comes, some stepchildren make their appreciation known by sending Mother's Day or Father's Day cards to their stepparents.

Self-Assessment: Rate Your Family's Strengths

This Family Strengths Inventory was developed by researchers who studied the strengths of more than 3,000 families. To assess your family (the family you grew up in, the family you're in now, or the family you're planning on joining), circle the number that best reflects how your family rates on each strength. A number 1 represents the lowest rating, and a number 5 represents the highest.

	Low	High
1. Spending time together and doing things with one another	1 2 3 4 5	
2. Commitment to one another	1 2 3 4 5	
3. Good communication (talking with one another often, listening well, sharing feelings with one another)	1 2 3 4 5	
4. Dealing with crises in a positive manner	1 2 3 4 5	
5. Expressing appreciation to one another	1 2 3 4 5	
6. Spiritual wellness	1 2 3 4 5	
7. Closeness of relationship between spouses	1 2 3 4 5	
8. Closeness of relationship between parents and children	1 2 3 4 5	
9. Happiness of relationship between spouses	1 2 3 4 5	

10. Happiness of relationship between parents and children   1 2 3 4 5

11. Extent to which each spouse makes the other feel good about himself/herself (self-confident, worthy, competent, happy)   1 2 3 4 5

12. Extent to which parents help children feel good about themselves   1 2 3 4 5

Total score_____

Scoring & Interpretation

- Add the numbers you have circled.
- A score below 39 indicates below-average family strengths.
- Scores between 39 and 52 are in the average range.
- Scores above 53 indicate a strong family.
- Low scores on individual items identify areas that families can profitably spend time on.
- High scores are worthy of celebration but shouldn't lead to complacency. Like gardens, families need loving care to remain strong.

What do you think is your family's or potential family's major strength? What do you like best about your family or potential family?

Source: Adapted from SECRETS OF STRONG FAMILIES by Nick Stinnett and John De Frain. Little, Brown and Company. Copyright © 1985 by Nick Stinnett and John DeFrain. By permission of Little, Brown and Co., Inc.

Key Terms Used in This Chapter

binuclear family, p. 557
biological father–stepmother family, p. 558
biological mother–stepfather family, p. 558
blended family, p. 557
cultural script, p. 557

double remarriages, p. 557
family boundary, p. 561
genogram, p. 559
hidden agenda, p. 567
joint biological–stepfamily, p. 558
nuclear-family model monopoly, p. 555

quasi-kin, p. 559
serial marriage, p. 548
serial monogamy, p. 548
single remarriages, p. 557
stepfamily, p. 557
stepism, p. 555
stepmother trap, p. 568

Summary

15.1 Moving toward Remarriage

- During the last 50 years in the United States, young adults have waited longer to get married for the first

time. One reason for this delay might be the need for individuals to get more education to find gainful employment and spend more time establishing a career. Many people also have reservations about entering into marriage because of their experiences as a child or an adolescent with the divorce of their parents.

- It takes some people longer than others to recover emotionally from separation and divorce. The transition phase lasts about 1 year; during this phase, one commonly experiences anxiety, loneliness, and depression. The recovery phase lasts about 1 to 3 years; during this phase, one's life and emotions become more stable, although loneliness and depression can still occur.

- Some divorced people are in a hurry to remarry; reasons might be loneliness, need for financial or child-care help, and/or feeling that life is passing by.

- Many individuals who start dating after the end of a relationship find that the situation is complicated by being the custodial parent of young children. Adults frequently feel a sense of guilt over possibly neglecting their children and might put the development of new relationships on hold until their children are older.

- Sex can also complicate new relationships after divorce or separation. Divorced men tend to enjoy sex more; their self-esteem is increased. Women do not find it quite as enjoyable; their sense of well-being is not linked to sexual activity.

Remarried & Blended Families

- Although many divorced people think that the second marriage will be more successful than the first because of lessons learned from past experience, the second marriage is not necessarily affected by the first. Some experts believe that it is not whether the marriage is the first or second that affects satisfaction but whether the partners are highly expressive and receive social support from their families.

- In general, when both partners have been previously married, second and third marriages don't last as long as first marriages. Reasons for this might include the following: People who remarry are more accepting of divorce; remarried partners receive less social support; stepchildren create more stresses; lack of a cultural script adds uncertainty.

- Single remarriages—marriages in which only one of the partners was previously married—are no more apt to end in divorce than are first marriages.

- The postdivorce family is represented by single parents, binuclear families, and blended families. A binuclear family is a family in which former spouses and children live in two different households. A single-parent family may be one form of a binuclear family. A blended family (stepfamily) is created when

two people marry and one or both brings into the household a child or children from a previous marriage.

- Blended families may be one of three basic types: (1) the biological father–stepmother family, in which all the children are biological children of the father and stepchildren of the mother; (2) the biological mother–stepfather family, in which all the children are biological children of the mother and stepchildren of the stepfather; and (3) the joint biological–stepfamily, in which at least one child is the biological child of both parents and at least one child is the biological child of one parent and the stepchild of the other parent.

- *Quasi-kin* is the term used to describe the person a former spouse married, as well as any previous in-laws and new in-laws from remarriage.

- Blended families may have interesting genograms. A genogram is a diagram that shows clearly all the people who genetically, emotionally, and legally constitute a particular family.

- Stepfamilies have significant adjustments to make in the blending of the two families. This time of adjustment is further complicated by the stepism existing in society. Stepism is an attitude of prejudice and discrimination; it assumes that stepfamilies are inferior to biological families.

- Beyond the three basic forms of blended families there exist other more complicated structures featuring adopted children, children from more than one former marriage, and siblings and half-siblings, some of whom live within the household and some of whom live somewhere else.

- Research has identified a number of characteristics of stepfamilies, including the following: (1) Most stepfamily members have suffered some sort of loss; (2) blended families have a more complex structure; (3) family boundaries or rules about who is a member of the family and the extent to which each member is allowed to participate are uncertain; (4) roles are ill-defined, thereby possibly creating more tension; and (5) with different loyalties, family integration comes slowly.

- Paralleling the stages one goes through in getting married or divorced, researchers have identified seven stages that are involved in the building of a blended family: (1) fantasy—"I'll love the children, and they'll love me"; (2) immersion—"I didn't realize there would be so much confusion"; (3) awareness—"I think we're beginning to figure one another out now"; (4) mobilization—"No more Mr. Nice Guy with this family; I'm taking a stand for myself"; (5) action—"We've begun to make some joint decisions and to accept that we're each different"; (6) contact—"Our relationships with one another have become more easy and honest"; and (7) resolution—"We're all comfortable with one other now."

Inside the Blended Family

- One's experience of being in a blended family can vary according to who one is and the role one is expected to play. Stepmothers, stepfathers, and stepchildren all experience being a part of a blended family differently. Each participant comes to the new arrangement with a hidden agenda that consists of expectations about how everyone should behave; however, these expectations are often not clearly stated to one another.

- According to sociologist Phyllis Raphael, stepmothers can find themselves in the stepmother trap, in which they are expected to be unnaturally loving toward their stepchildren yet are simultaneously seen as being mean, abusive, and vain. Stepmothers may also find themselves in role conflicts involving the expectations that they be loving and accepting while also being disciplinarians. Husbands paying spousal and or child support to ex-wives may also become problematic for stepmothers.

- Stepfathers are also apt to view themselves as less effective with their stepchildren. Their challenges are somewhat defined by what type of relationship they are in: childless and married to a woman with children, having children and married to a childless woman, or having children and married to a woman with children.

- Being a stepchild can also present a number of challenges and issues that can make the adjustment to the new family relationship difficult. Stepchildren frequently have feelings of abandonment and being involved in conflicts between parents from the first marriage. The conflicts can involve such issues as divided loyalties, changes in the type of parenting and discipline styles, and stepsibling rivalry.

- As a result of the composition of blended families, sexual boundaries are an area of special sensitivity. Consequently, sexual abuse is an area of concern. The three major types of intrafamilial sexual abuse involve uncle and niece, stepfather and daughter, and stepbrother and stepsister.

- David Finkelhor suggests that sexual abuse may occur when four preconditions exist: (1) motivation, (2) inhibitions overcome, (3) obstacles overcome, (4) child's resistance overcome.

- Emily and John Visher provide some suggestions for preventing abuse in stepfamilies: arrange the living space appropriately, avoid being sexually provocative, curtail roughhousing and some intimate behavior with children over age 10 or 11, be affectionate but not passionate with your spouse in public, and don't turn to stepchildren for emotional support when you and you partner aren't getting along.

Strengthening Stepfamilies

- Even though stepfamilies may deal with a number of significant adjustments and challenges, research indicates that stepfamilies have a number of potential benefits: families can be happier and calmer, with fewer crises and stresses, and might have fewer financial burdens; children can gain role models; stepparents might be more objective; children can gain more siblings and kin; and children can become more flexible.

- In addition to factors that help to make first marriages successful, researchers have identified a number of influences specific to stepfamilies that help to ensure success: harmonize finances, develop realistic expectations, let everyone mourn their losses, maintain the primacy of the relationship with one's new partner, treat children equally and give them their own space, don't rush being a stepparent, cooperate with the absent parent and other kin, develop one's own family rituals, and think of and recognize the stepparent on Mother's or Father's Day.

Take It to the Net

Among the Internet resources on remarriage and stepfamilies are the following:

- **Bonus Families.** This nonprofit organization promotes a positive image for stepfamilies and prefers the word "bonus" rather than the word "step." *www.bonusfamilies.com*

- **Creating genograms.** How to Make a Multi-generation Map (Genogram) to See Who You All Are by Peter K. Gerlach, Stepfamily Association of America. *http://sfhelp.org/03/geno1.htm*

- **The Rape, Abuse & Incest National Network (RAINN).** The nation's largest anti–sexual-assault organization carries out programs to prevent sexual assault, help rape and incest victims, and offer counseling resources. *www.rainn.org*

- **Shared Parenting Information Group.** This organization promotes responsible shared parenting after separation and divorce. This is a good website for information about parent alienation syndrome (PAS). *www.spig.clara.net/issues/pas.htm*
- **Step-Carefully for Stepparents.** From divorce recovery to stepchild woes to working with ex-spouses—that's what Step-Carefully is all about. *www.stepcarefully.com*
- **Stepfamily Association of America.** This national, nonprofit membership organization is dedicated to successful stepfamily living. Its website provides educational information and resources for anyone interested in stepfamilies and their issues. *www.saafamilies.org*
- **The Stepfamily Foundation.** Advice and information for stepfamily members and professionals. *www.stepfamily.org*
- **The StepParent's Web.** It is not easy for a stepfamily to become a real family. This website is for stepparents or people who are soon to become stepparents. *www.cyberparent.com/step*
- **Step Together.** This organization has been providing "virtual" support to stepparents since 1998. *www.steptogether.org*

Appendices

Appendix A
The Human Sexual Response

Humans have been having sex for hundreds of thousands of years, of course. But the study of sex was considered off limits until the 1940s and 1950s, when groundbreaking research was done by Alfred Kinsey and colleagues (1948, 1953). Also among the pioneers, **William Masters and Virginia Johnson** (1966) developed a four-phase **model of *sexual response* of how both men and women respond to sex physiologically: (1) excitement, (2) plateau, (3) orgasm, and (4) resolution.**

1. Excitement

The *excitement phase* consists of a physical reaction to erotic stimulation, whether thought, touch, taste, sight, and/or sound. Both men and women experience increased respiration and heart rates, erect nipples, and increased congestion of blood in the genital area.

■ **Men:** The penis becomes erect, although the erection may subside and return several times. The testes lift and increase in size. A man's initial physical response to sexual arousal is erection.

■ **Women:** The clitoris swells, the vaginal walls begin to lubricate, and the uterus enlarges. A woman's initial physical response to sexual arousal is believed to be vaginal lubrication.

Some practitioners working with the Masters and Johnson model felt that something was missing from stage 1. Helen Singer Kaplan (1979) added a "desire" stage before "excitement" and changed the name of that stage to "arousal." This preliminary stage of desire involves a person's readiness for and interest in sexual activity. Without sexual desire, arousal is less likely to occur. Thus, this expanded model has five stages: desire, arousal, plateau, orgasm, and resolution.

Source: Appendices A–F adapted from *Healthy for Life: Wellness & the Art of Living* 1/e by Williams/Knight © 1994. Reprinted with permission of Brooks/Cole, a division of Thomson Learning. *www.thomsonrights.com;* fax 800-730-2215.

2. Plateau

During the ***plateau phase*, sexual excitement and muscle tension continue to build.** Blood pressure and heart rate continue to rise, and breathing becomes faster.

■ **Men:** The penis becomes fully erect, and the testes continue to swell and elevate.

■ **Women:** The clitoris retracts under its hood. The inner two-thirds of the vagina enlarges, and the muscles in the outer third of the vagina tighten.

3. Orgasm

The third stage observed by Masters and Johnson, the ***orgasmic phase*, is the most ecstatic** for those who experience it. Here, rhythmic contractions cause the release of neuromuscular tension and feelings of intense pleasure. This experience is an orgasm (also known as a "climax" or "coming"). Blood pressure, heart rate, and breathing reach their highest levels, and there are involuntary muscle spasms throughout the body. All this lasts only a few seconds. The intensity of the orgasm seems to vary with experience, setting, partner, expectations, and level of anxiety.

■ **Men:** Males ejaculate in two stages. First, semen is released into the urethra, and it is during this time that a man may feel a sense of orgasmic inevitability. A few seconds later, the semen is ejaculated out of the urethra and penis, accompanied by contractions of the urethra and anus. The first two or three contractions are most intense.

■ **Women:** Contractions occur in the uterus, the vaginal opening, and anal areas. Masters and Johnson identified three patterns: (1) one or more orgasms without dropping below the plateau level, (2) extended plateau with no orgasms, and (3) a rapid rise to orgasm with no plateau. Masters and Johnson found that there is no physiological difference between a *vaginal orgasm,* achieved by stimulation of the vagina, and *clitoral orgasm,* achieved by stimulation of the clitoris.

4. Resolution

The *resolution phase* is the return of the body to its unaroused state. Heart rate, blood pressure, breathing, muscle tension, and nipple erection all subside.

■ **Men:** The penis returns to its nonerect state, and the testes return to normal. Most men are unable to resume erection and ejaculation for a period that may range from seconds to hours. With age, the recovery period is considerably longer, up to several hours.

■ **Women:** The clitoris, uterus, vagina, and vaginal lips return to their normal unaroused positions.

The Varieties of Orgasms

We owe much to Masters and Johnson in gaining insight into many of the physiological mysteries of sex. For example, they found that most men are not *multiorgasmic*—**able to have multiple orgasms within a single period of sexual arousal.** However, 10 to 30% of adult females are routinely able to have multiple orgasms. In contrast, Masters and Johnson found, some 10% of females are *anorgasmic*, **unable to have an orgasm.** Or they can experience orgasms during masturbation but not during conventional sexual intercourse.

Appendix B
Sexual Dysfunctions

Sexual Dysfunctions in Men

Common sexual problems in men include *erection difficulties* and *premature ejaculation.*

■ **Erection Difficulties:** Sexual adequacy is important to men, so they can be devastated by erection (erectile) dysfunction. ***Erectile dysfunction, or impotence, is failure to achieve or maintain an erection.*** The problem affects almost every man at some time; only when an erection cannot be maintained in one out of four sexual encounters is the problem considered serious. Problems may come from "performance anxiety" (self-consciousness about having an erection), tension, or too much to eat or drink. Other factors are marital strife, prescription or "street" drugs, fatigue, lack of privacy, or a new partner. Sometimes there are physical causes, such as diabetes or blood-vessel disorders, when the body cannot deliver enough blood to engorge the penis, or prostate gland surgery. Impotence can also be a side effect of medication.

A man cannot simply *will* an erection to happen. Therefore, therapists recommend that couples try nondemanding techniques, such as massage or simply lying together for 10 to 20 minutes. These can reduce anxiety and allow sexual arousal to occur naturally.

Some men resolve their erection difficulties with Viagra (silenafil citrate), a medicine that became available in 1998. Studies show that Viagra works for many men, regardless of what caused erectile dysfunction. Viagra works by increasing blood flow to the penis. It is not a hormone or an aphrodisiac (an agent, such as a food or drug, that arouses sexual desire). However, men are advised to get a medical exam before using Viagra. Newer competitors to Viagra are Levitra and Cialis.

■ **Premature Ejaculation:** After a period of abstinence, almost any man will ejaculate rapidly. However, ***premature ejaculation* is a man's inability to reasonably control his ejaculatory reflex on a regular basis.** That is, he reaches orgasm so quickly that his partner may consistently have trouble achieving orgasm. This is usually a psychological problem rather than a physical one.

Sometimes a condom can dull sensation and boost staying power. Sometimes masturbating before sex will make the second ejaculation occur less rapidly. There is also a squeeze-and-release technique suggested by Masters and Johnson: When the man is about to ejaculate, he withdraws his penis. The partner squeezes the neck of the penis between thumb and first and second fingers for 4 seconds. After 15 to 30 seconds, stimulation of the penis is resumed.

In addition, condoms are available that contain a mild anesthetic, Benzocaine, that is supposed to be able to postpone climax for up to 5 minutes.

Sometimes men are unable to ejaculate. This temporary condition is usually caused by fatigue, stress, alcohol, illness, or lack of emotional involvement with the partner.

Sexual Dysfunctions in Women

Sexual enjoyment is now expected of women, although once it was not. So women, too, have sexual expectations that they sometimes can't meet, such as pressure to achieve multiple or simultaneous orgasms. Chief among the female dysfunctions are *inability to have an orgasm, painful intercourse,* and *spasms of the vaginal muscles.*

■ **Inability to Have an Orgasm:** ***Inhibited female orgasm* is a term that is now used instead of frigidity**

to describe an inability to reach orgasm. Perhaps 7% of women have never experienced orgasm (Levin and Levin 1975). Others have orgasms infrequently. One reason might be that orgasm is difficult to accomplish through sexual intercourse, that additional, direct stimulation of the clitoris is required.

Therapists can help a woman give herself permission to express her sexual feelings and eliminate inhibitions. Learning how to explore her body, masturbate, and tell her partner how to touch and stimulate her in a pleasurable way might help.

■ Painful Intercourse: **Painful or difficult sexual intercourse is called** *dyspareunia*. Occasionally, women experience a burning or sharp pain when the penis is inserted into the vagina. Causes include inadequate lubrication, infection of the vagina, a tight hymen, irritation by contraceptive creams, and the penis touching the cervix. If dyspareunia persists, the woman should see a health care professional.

■ Involuntary Spasms of Vaginal Muscles: **Known as** *vaginismus*, **involuntary spasms of the muscles surrounding the lower third of the vagina** prevent the penis from entering. Sometimes it is a normal response when a woman is expecting pain (as on first intercourse). Or she might not want sex, perhaps as a reaction to sexual trauma such as rape. When the problem is chronic, the woman needs to seek assistance from a health-care provider. After exploring the underlying problem, some therapists teach a woman to explore her genital area and learn to relax her vaginal muscles.

Appendix C
Sexually Transmitted Diseases

HIV/AIDS

If you have shared needles or syringes to inject drugs or steroids or if you have had sex with someone whose sexual history you don't know or with numerous sex partners, you should consider being tested. Most tests don't test for HIV itself but rather to see whether the body has developed antibodies in response to HIV infection (suggesting, of course, that HIV is present). Unfortunately, people usually don't develop antibodies until 3 months after exposure. Discussion about the four tests follows.

■ ELISA Test: The enzyme-linked immunosorbent assay (ELISA) test is an inexpensive, basic screening test that evaluates a blood sample taken from one's arm for the presence of antibodies to HIV in the bloodstream. Although it can assess antibodies for a person who was exposed to HIV as little as 2 weeks earlier, the test becomes more accurate as time goes on because it takes time for antibodies to build in the body.

■ Western Blot Test: After one has been tested twice with ELISA, one should take the Western blot test, a more expensive but also more definitive kind of screening. If the result is negative, it is probable that the person being tested does not have HIV; if positive, it is probable that the person does have HIV; if neither negative nor positive, the person should repeat the test a month later when the antibodies, if any, have developed further.

■ OraQuick Test: Approved for use in late 2002, the OraQuick is a "while you wait" test with a 99.6% accuracy rate, making it the first one that is highly reliable. Results can be available in as little as 20 minutes, compared to 2 days to 2 weeks with other tests. The test may help reduce mother-to-infant transmissions of HIV by enabling doctors to test pregnant women while they are in labor (Stolberg 2002).

■ VAL-I.D. PCR Test: An alternative to a second Western blot test, the VAL-I.D. PCR (polymerase chain reaction) screens for the presence of HIV itself, not just the buildup of antibodies. The test is supposed to be accurate as early as 6 weeks after HIV exposure.

Dealing with HIV/AIDS

At present, no vaccine is available to prevent or cure HIV or subsequent AIDS symptoms. Drugs (such as AZT, 3TC, Indnavir, Ritonavir, and Saquinavir) that were developed in the 1990s promised to help AIDS sufferers live longer and be more comfortable. However, although some slow the progress of AIDS and increase the survival rate, they seem to have negative side effects than was predicted. In addition, HIV has mutated into some drug-resistant strains (Kalb 1998).

Other STDs

The sexually transmitted diseases caused by viruses—HIV, hepatitis B, herpes, and genital warts—cannot be cured, although in many cases, they can be controlled. STDs caused by *bacteria*—chlamydia, gonorrhea, and syphilis—can be cured. Unfortunately, however, they are often difficult to detect because many have no obvious symptoms and thus can lead to grave difficulties later. Both these kinds of STDs are discussed next.

Hepatitis B: A Disease of the Liver

Hepatitis covers five virus-caused inflammatory diseases of the liver (A, B, C, D, and E), which have similar symptoms but otherwise are different. Hepatitis B is transmitted through infected blood, saliva, mucus, or semen by sexual contact or sharing of drug needles.

Among those who are at risk are the million of heterosexuals who have multiple partners or whose partners have had multiple partners.

■ Symptoms: Symptoms include fever, chills, headache, nausea, diarrhea, loss of appetite, skin rashes, and sometimes jaundice (yellowing of skin and eyes).

■ Outcome: The disease lasts 2 to 6 months. People usually recover on their own, although in 1 to 3% of cases, there are fatalities from liver failure.

■ Treatment: No treatment is available. Patients are advised to rest and consume fluids until the illness runs its course. In terms of prevention, a vaccine is available that has been found to be 80 to 95% effective.

Herpes: The Secret Virus

Herpes is a viral infection that evades the body's immune defenses by hiding in the nervous system until reactivation of the virus occurs. Tens of millions of people have been infected with herpes, and perhaps as many as a million more join their ranks every year. The most common strains are the *herpes simplex virus, types 1 and 2,* which are sexually transmitted.

■ Symptoms: Both types of herpes viruses produce cold sore–like blisters in the areas of the genitals and mouth. One may experience numbness, itching, or tingling in the area where there has been contact with the virus, followed by an often painful eruption of water-filled blisters. Within 10 days of an initial exposure to the virus, people may feel flulike symptoms: fever, chills, nausea, headaches, fatigue, and muscle aches. The eruption crusts and scabs over, and in about 2 weeks the skin appears normal.

After the first episode, the virus seems to disappear. Thereafter, it emerges from time to time—sometimes as frequently as four or more times a year. Sometimes, it will produce no symptoms. At other times, it will produce outbreaks of blistering sores. As time goes on, many people find that the duration of symptoms becomes shorter and less severe.

■ Outcome: Among adults, the principal effects of herpes seem to be feelings of desperation and social inhibition. A great many herpes victims feel isolated and depressed and fear rejection in social situations. Stress, depression, and other psychological upsets seem to trigger recurrences among infected people.

■ Treatment: There is also no cure for herpes, although a prescription drug called acyclovir, if taken during the initial herpes outbreak, can ease the symptoms. People with herpes who have learned relaxation and other coping techniques seem to suffer fewer outbreaks.

HPV: More Serious Than Just Genital Warts

HPV (human papilloma virus), which causes genital warts, is widespread in the United States, in particular infecting a great many college women who have been sexually active with several sex partners. HPV is very contagious, being readily transmitted by sexual contact.

■ Symptoms: HPV causes *genital warts*—unpleasant fleshy growths in the areas of the genitals and mouth. Unfortunately, in the vast majority of cases (99%), HPV is painless and shows no symptoms, in both females and males. On average, the incubation period is 2 to 3 months after contact. One test for HPV infection is the Southern blot technique.

■ Outcome: HPV should not be taken lightly. Some types of HPV have been found to be associated with cancer of the anus, penis, vulva, or cervix.

■ Treatment: Genital warts are treated by freezing, heat, cauterization, laser therapy, chemicals such as podophyllin, or surgical removal. The virus still remains in the body after the warts have been removed.

Chlamydia: The Most Common STD

Chlamydia is perhaps the most common STD in the United States, with perhaps as many as 4 million new cases appearing every year. *Chlamydia*—or, more accurately, *chlamydia infections*—consists of a family of sexually transmitted diseases caused by a bacterium (*Chlamydia trachomatis*).

■ Symptoms: Diagnosis must be made by a health care professional. A major problem associated with this STD is that the organism often does not cause any symptoms. About 50 to 70% of infected females and 30% of infected males show no signs of early symptoms. Those who do show signs may experience itching and burning during urination 2 to 7 days after infection.

■ Outcome: If untreated, chlamydia can cause lifelong damage, such as pelvic inflammatory disease in women, urinary infections in men, and sterility, infertility, and blindness in both sexes.

■ **Treatment:** Standard treatment is with antibiotics (doxycycline, tetracycline, erythromycin).

Gonorrhea: An Old Enemy Comes Back

Once upon a time, when the phrase *venereal disease* was in use, when people thought of STDs they thought principally of gonorrhea and syphilis. For a time, in the 1970s and early 1980s, the incidence of these two diseases declined. Recently, unfortunately, both the old enemies, gonorrhea and syphilis, have had a resurgence.

Gonorrhea is caused by the sexual transmission of a bacterium *Neisseria gonorrhoeae*. It is an organism that is easily transmitted. A man who has had sexual intercourse once with an infected woman has a 20 to 25% risk of getting the disease; a woman who has had intercourse once with an infected man has a 50% chance of getting it.

Because the gonorrhea bacterium needs warmth and humidity to thrive, it is harbored principally in warm, moist areas of the human body. Thus, one may contract gonorrhea from an infected person through genital, anal, and oral contact. Toilet seats are not a means of transmission.

■ **Symptoms:** Symptoms appear 2 to 8 days after one has been infected.

Some men, perhaps 10 to 20%, show no signs of infection at all. Otherwise, the main manifestation is burning pain during urination and later discharge (pus) from the urinary tract. The burning sensation may subside in 2 to 3 weeks, but the disease may remain.

In women, early symptoms may be so slight that they might be overlooked. Indeed, up to 80% of women show no symptoms at all. When symptoms appear, they may take the form of irritation of the vagina and painful and frequent urination.

■ **Outcome:** If the disease, which is diagnosed primarily through laboratory tests, is untreated, it spreads throughout the urinary and reproductive systems, causing scarring, sterility, and infertility.

■ **Treatment:** Treatment is use of antibiotics, such as penicillin or tetracycline.

Syphilis: The "Great Imitator" Returns

Syphilis, another old enemy, like gonorrhea, is known as the "great imitator" because its sores and other symptoms mimic those of other disorders and diseases, such as cancers, abscesses, hemorrhoids, and hernias. Once thought to be under control in the United States, syphilis has returned with a vengeance; syphilis rates rose between 2000 and 2001—a 15% jump among men, especially among men who have sex with men (Kalb 2003). *Syphilis* is a sexually transmitted disease caused by a bacterium (a long, slender, spiral bacterium, or spirochete, called *Treponema pallidum*). Syphilis is serious because it can become a systemic infection, possibly leading to brain damage, heart failure, and death.

■ **Symptoms and Outcome:** Diagnosed by means of blood tests, syphilis appears in four stages:

Primary stage: Within 10 to 90 days of infection, one or more pink or red dime-sized or smaller sores called *chancres* appear on the sex organs, mouth, or other parts of the body. Because the sores do not cause pain, they might not be noticed. The chancres disappear by themselves in 3 to 6 weeks, but this does not mean that the disease has disappeared.

Secondary stage: About 6 to 8 weeks later, symptoms appear that can be mistaken for the flu: swollen lymph nodes, sore throat, headache, and fever. There may also be loss of hair. In addition, the disease produces a rash, which may appear on the hands or feet or all over the body and does not itch. Finally, large, moist sores may appear around the mouth or genitals. The sores disappear in 2 to 6 weeks, but this means only that the disease has entered the next stage.

Latent stage: In this stage, the disease goes underground. Although 50 to 70% of people with untreated syphilis remain in this latent stage for the rest of their lives and experience no further problems, the rest develop late-stage syphilis.

Tertiary stage: Years after the initial exposure, the effects of untreated syphilis can result in damage to the heart and major blood vessels, the central nervous system, or other organs. This can cause blindness, paralysis, neurological disorders, insanity, and death.

■ **Treatment:** Penicillin or other antibiotics are the most common treatment.

Pelvic Inflammatory Disease

Pelvic inflammatory disease (PID), often caused by untreated chlamydia or gonorrhea, is an infection in females of the lower abdomen, cervix, and uterus.

■ **Symptoms:** Symptoms may include lower abdominal pain, painful intercourse, irregular menstrual bleeding, abnormal vaginal discharge, painful urination, fever, nausea and vomiting, and elevated white blood cell count. Sometimes, there are no symptoms at all.

- **Outcome:** If untreated, PID can sometimes spread to the liver and the appendix. It can cause scarring of the fallopian tubes and infertility and can lead to ectopic pregnancy, in which a fertilized egg implants itself outside the lining of the uterus.

- **Treatment:** Treatment is by antibiotics such as penicillin and by surgery.

Appendix D
Reducing Risks of Acquiring STDs

Truth is the first casualty in war, it is said. Some think that it is also the first casualty in sexual behavior. Clearly, the bottom line is that simply *asking* a prospective sex partner about HIV does not by itself guarantee safer sex.

The Principles of Prevention

So how *should* one pursue sexual relationships? There are two principal pieces of advice:

- **Use Precautions Universally:** If you choose to have sex, then *consistently* use safer-sex measures (such as condom and spermicide) with *all* partners. This means *all* sex partners, not just those you don't know well or those you think might be higher risk. This means learning to overcome any embarrassment you might feel associated with condom use.

- **Keep Your Head Clear:** Be careful about using alcohol and other drugs with a prospective sex partner. Drugs cloud your judgment, placing you in a position of increased vulnerability. A decrease in alcohol consumption rates on a state level has been associated with a decrease in STDs such as gonorrhea and syphilis (Chesson et al. 2003).

No doubt you have heard the phrase *safe sex*. However, only abstinence is considered truly safe. In general, there are three levels of risk in sexual behavior: "saved sex," "safer sex," and high-risk sex.

Lower Risk: "Saved" Sex, Including Abstinence

The safest kind of sex avoids the exchange of semen, vaginal secretions, saliva, or blood. The principal kind of "saved sex" is *abstinence*, which, as we said, is the voluntary avoidance of sexual intercourse. Saved sex includes massage, hugging, rubbing of bodies, dry kissing (not exchanging saliva), masturbation, and mutual manual stimulation of the genitals. (In all cases, contact with body fluids is avoided.)

Thus, abstinence can mean anything from avoiding all sexual activity to avoiding only those, such as intercourse or oral sex, in which fluids are exchanged. The trick with saved sexual activity is not to get swept away and end up practicing unsafe sex.

Somewhat Risky: "Safer" Sex, Including Use of Condoms

The next best step to ensuring safe sex—actually, only *safer* sex—is to use *latex:* condoms and dental dams. "Safer" sex is still somewhat risky, but at least it minimizes the exchange of body fluids (semen, vaginal secretions, saliva, or blood). Examples of safer-sex behavior include deep (French) kissing and vaginal intercourse using latex condoms with the spermicide nonoxynol-9 (which kills STD organisms). Other examples are fellatio with the male wearing a condom and cunnilingus with a menstruating female using a latex dental dam.

Let us consider the two principal means of protection: condoms and dental dams.

- **Condoms: A** *condom* **(also known as a "prophylactic" or "rubber") is a thin sheath made of latex rubber or lamb intestine.** (Though called "natural skin," lamb intestine is not as safe as latex.) Packaged in rolled-up form, the condom is unrolled over a male's erect penis, leaving a little room at the top to catch the semen. Some condoms are made with a "reservoir" at the end for this purpose.

  A latex condom provides protection for both partners during vaginal, oral, or anal intercourse. It keeps semen from being transmitted to a man's sex partner and shields against contact with any infection on his penis. It also protects the male's penis from contact with his partner's secretions, blood, and saliva.

- **Dental Dams:** Every major sexually transmitted disease can be acquired during oral sex, although not as easily as during intercourse. Males receiving oral sex should wear a condom. If a female is the recipient, she should use a dental dam. Sold in pharmacies and medical supply stores, **a** *dental dam* **(designed for use in dental surgery) is a flat 5-inch-square piece of latex. It may be placed over the vaginal opening and surrounding area.**

  Before you use the dam, you should rinse it in warm water, dry it with a towel, then hold it up to the light to ensure that it is free of holes. Only one side of the dam should come into contact with the genitals, and the dam should be used only once.

Unfortunately, *condoms are not perfect protection.* They only *reduce* the risk of acquiring HIV infection and other STDs. Note that *reducing the risk is not the same as eliminating the risk.* If the condom is flawed or it slips off or breaks during intercourse, there is suddenly 100% exposure—possibly to a disease that is 100% fatal.

Condoms break most frequently when couples use oil-based lubricants or engage in prolonged sex. A condom can also be weakened if couples attempt their own "quality testing" (such as blowing up condoms to test for leaks). There are several precautions that people can take to ensure that condoms are used properly. *(See ■ Panel D.1.)*

Whether made by U.S. or overseas manufacturers, condoms are tested for leakage by the Food and Drug Administration. Unfortunately, the Joint United Nations Programme on HIV/AIDS has found that even when people use condoms consistently, the failure rate for protection against HIV is an estimated 10% (Chaya et al. 2002). This does not mean that every tenth condom is defective but only that something has gone wrong in about 10% of their use, as when condoms slip off, break, or are not put on early enough. (The report also stated that the failure rate to protect against HIV was probably the same as the failure rate in preventing pregnancy.)

Very Risky: Unprotected Sex & Other Behavior

Behavior that involves high risk for the transmission of STDs includes unprotected sex or any behavior that involves sharing intravenous needles. This includes vaginal or anal intercourse without a condom, fellatio without a condom, cunnilingus without a dental dam, and anal-oral sex without a condom or dental dam. It includes all forms of sex in which body fluids may be exchanged: semen in the mouth or contact with a partner's blood (including menstrual blood). Any sexual behavior that leads to bleeding or tissue damage also risks fluid exchange.

Finally, high risks include people or behavior having to do with intravenous (IV) injection of drugs, a prime means of transmitting some STDs. Don't share IV needles yourself, and avoid sexual contact with an injectable-drug user or someone whose previous partner was such a person. Avoid having sexual contact with people who sell or buy sex, who are often injectable-drug users.

Mutual Monogamy

Having multiple sex partners is one of the leading risk factors for the transmission of STDs. Clearly, mutual monogamy is one way to avoid infection. However, even apparent monogamy may have its risks.

■ **"Fooling Around":** If one partner secretly has a sexual adventure outside the supposedly monogamous relationship, especially without using condoms, it does not just breach a trust. It can endanger the other partner's life, whether the outside relationship is heterosexual, bisexual, or homosexual. Having extramarital affairs or otherwise "fooling around" or "cheating" outside the relationship means, of course, that the commitment is not truly monogamous.

■ **The AIDS Time Bomb:** A person can be infected with HIV for perhaps 10 years before AIDS itself beings to appear. *And there may be no outward signs or symptoms at all during that time.* This poses a dilemma, for you could be in a monogamous relationship but have no idea if your partner was infected previously. You can wait several months while remaining faithful to each other and then take a test to see if HIV antibodies are present. This gives some indication (though not absolutely) that the partner is currently free of infection.

Despite AIDS and the rise of other STDs, many of our cultural images remain the same. Movies and magazines still celebrate the glories of passion, of losing oneself in sexual ecstasy, of having relationships with exciting strangers. But clearly the world itself has changed.

Appendix E
Contraceptive Choices

Natural Family Planning Methods: Periodic Abstinence & Withdrawal

***Natural family planning methods* of birth control include (1) various ways of gauging times for periodic abstinence—the calendar method, the BBT method, the cervical mucus method—and (2) withdrawal.**

1. Periodic Abstinence

As we have mentioned (Chapter 7, "Sexuality"), *abstinence* is the voluntary avoidance of sexual intercourse. ***Periodic abstinence*—which goes by the names of fertility awareness, natural family planning, and the rhythm method—is avoidance of sexual intercourse during perceived fertile periods of the woman's menstrual cycle.**

How to Buy

Materials: Buy latex, not natural membrane or lambskin. Latex is less apt to leak and better able to protect against HIV transmission. Inexpensive foreign brands are suspect.

Sizes: The Food and Drug Administration (FDA) says condoms must be between 6 and 8 inches in length when unrolled. (The average erect penis is $6^{1}/_{2}$ inches.) Condoms labeled *Regular* are $7^{1}/_{2}$ inches. Instead of "Small" for condoms under $7^{1}/_{2}$ inches, manufacturers use labels such as *Snug Fit.* Instead of "Large" for condoms over $7^{1}/_{2}$ inches, manufacturers used labels such as *Max* or *Magnum.*

Shapes: Most condoms are *straight-walled.* Some are labeled *contoured,* which means they are anatomically shaped to fit the penis and thus are more comfortable.

Tips: Some condoms have a *reservoir* at the end to catch semen upon ejaculation. Others do not have a reservoir, in which case they should be twisted at the tip while being put on.

Plain or lubricated: Condoms can be purchased *plain* (unlubricated) or *lubricated,* which means they feel more slippery to the touch. There are four options:

■ Buy a plain condom and don't use a lubricant.
■ Buy a plain condom and use your own lubricant, preferably water-based (such as K-Y Jelly or Astroglide). (Do not use a petroleum-based lubricant such as Vaseline; these products can weaken latex.)
■ Buy a lubricated condom pregreased with silicone-, jelly-, or water-based lubricants.
■ Buy a *spermicidally lubricated* condom, which contains *nonoxynol-9,* a chemical that kills sperm and HIV. This is probably the best option.

Strength: A standard condom will do for vaginal and oral sex. Some people an *"extra-strength"* condom is less apt to break during anal sex, although this is debatable.

Gimmicks: In addition, condoms come with all kinds of other features:

■ *"Climax control":* Some condoms (Trojan Extended Pleasure, Durex Performax) contain a mild anesthetic, Benzocaine, that is supposed to desensitize the penis and delay climax for as long as 5 minutes.
■ *Colors:* Red, blue, green, and yellow are safe. Avoid black and "glow in the dark," says the FDA, since dyes may rub off.
■ *Smell and taste:* Latex smells and tastes rubbery, but some fragranced condoms mask this odor.
■ *Adhesive:* Condoms are available with adhesive to hold them in place so they won't slip off during withdrawal.

■ *Marketing gimmicks:* Condoms are sold with ribs, nubs, bumps, and so on, but unless the additions are at the tip and can reach the clitoris they do no good whatsoever.

How to Use

Storage: Condoms should be stored in a cool, dry place. Keeping them in a hot glove compartment or wallet in the back pocket for weeks can cause the latex to fail.

Opening package: Look to see that the foil or plastic packaging is not broken; if it is, don't use the condom. Open the package carefully. Fingernails can easily damage a condom.

Inspection: Make sure a condom is soft and pliable. Don't use it if it's brittle, sticky, or discolored. Don't try to test it for leaks by unrolling, stretching, or blowing it up, which will only weaken it.

Putting it on: Put the condom on before any genital contract to prevent exposure to fluids. Hold the tip of the condom and unroll it directly onto the erect penis. (If the man is not circumcised, pull back the foreskin before rolling on the condom.) Gently pinch the tip to remove air bubbles, which can cause the condom to break. Condoms without a reservoir tip need a half-inch free at the tip.

Lubricants: *Important!* If you're using a lubricant of your own, *don't use an oil/petroleum-based lubricant.* Oil-based lubricants—examples are hand lotion, baby oil, mineral oil, and Vaseline—can reduce a latex condom's strength by 90% in as little as 60 seconds. Saliva is not recommended either.

Use a water-based or silicone-based product designed for such use, such as K-Y Jelly or spermicidal compounds containing nonoxynol-9.

Add lubricant to the outside of the condom before entry. If not enough lubricant is used, the condom can tear or pull off.

Slippage and breakage: If the condom begins to slip, hold your fingers around the base to make it stay on. If a condom breaks, it should be replaced immediately. *If ejaculation occurs after a condom breaks, apply a foam spermicide to the vagina at once.*

After ejaculation: After sex, hold the base of the condom to prevent it from slipping off and to avoid spillage during withdrawal. Withdraw while the penis is still erect. Throw the used condom away. (Never reuse condoms.) Wash the genitals.

Source: From *Healthy for Life: Wellness & the Art of Living* 1/e by Williams/Knight © 1994. Reprinted with permission of Brooks/Cole, a division of Thomson Learning. *www .thomsonrights.com;* fax 800-730-2215.

Periodic abstinence cannot be used by women who have irregular menstrual cycles or who are at risk for STD exposure. Using this method to prevent pregnancy requires a motivated, knowledgeable couple who has undergone training. They must be able to abstain or use another contraceptive method during those times when the woman is likely to be fertile.

Four methods of periodic abstinence are presented in the box on the next page. (See ■ Panel E.1.)

2. Withdrawal

The birth-control technique known as **withdrawal, or coitus interruptus, consists of removing the penis from the vagina before ejaculation.** The theory, which dates back to biblical times, is that withdrawal prevents sperm from being deposited in or around the vagina.

This method is flawed: 14.7% of women using the technique are estimated to become pregnant. Probably one reason is that withdrawal requires unusual willpower. In any case, all it takes is the little bit of fluid that is released from the penis *before* ejaculation to send sperm into the vagina.

Barrier Methods: Diaphragms, Cervical Caps, & Condoms Used with Spermicide

Most of the birth-control methods that are available without a doctor's prescription are so-called **barrier methods of contraception, with devices that put physical barriers between egg and sperm: diaphragms, cervical caps, and condoms.** (Another, the vaginal sponge, was off the market for several years and is not discussed in much of the recent literature.)

Diaphragm

A **diaphragm is a soft latex rubber dome stretched over a metal spring or ring. The size varies from 2 to 4 inches depending on the length of the vagina. When in place, the diaphragm covers the ceiling of the vagina, including the cervix.** (See ■ Panel E.2.)

A diaphragm should always be used with a vaginal **spermicide, which contains a sperm-killing chemical.** The spermicide should be placed in the vagina no more than an hour before intercourse and should be left in place at least 6 to 8 hours afterward. Spermicides are available in drug stores in several forms: foam, gel, cream, film, suppository, or tablet. Creams or gels are used with a diaphragm; gels, films, and suppositories are intended to be used alone or with a condom. Some spermicides also contain nonoxynol-9, which can protect women from the STDs gonorrhea and chlamydia, although not from HIV/AIDS. Used by themselves, sper-

micides are about 74% effective at preventing pregnancy (National Women's Health Information Center 2002).

Cervical Cap

A **cervical cap operates in much the same way as the diaphragm. It is a much smaller, thimble-shaped rubber or plastic cap that fits directly onto the cervix.** (See ■ Panel E.3.) Insertion of the cervical cap can present more of a challenge to first-time users than does the diaphragm. The cervical cap cannot be used during menstruation. However, it can be left in place for up to 48 hours. Like the diaphragm, the cervical cap requires a visit to a health-care provider for proper fitting.

Female Condom

We have already discussed the male condom. A more recent variant is the **female condom, a lubricated, polyurethane pouch about 7 inches long that is inserted into the vagina and extends outside it to cover the outer lips.** (See ■ Panel E.4.) The condom has flexible rings at both ends. When inserted into the vagina, the inner ring fits behind the pubic bone. The outer ring remains outside the body.

The female condom is marketed under the brand names Reality and Femidom. Advantages are that the condom is available without a prescription, may be placed in the body up to 8 hours before use, and, unlike many other contraceptives, helps to protect against STDs, including HIV. However, the female condom is not reusable, and some women may have difficulty inserting it on their first attempts.

Hormonal Methods: Pill, Vaginal Ring, Insertion, Patch, Injection, & Implant

Hormonal methods **are female forms of birth control that use chemicals to prevent ovulation or implantation of the fertilized egg in the uterus, using pills, vaginal rings, vaginal insertion, skin patches, injections, or implants.** All require a doctor's prescription. However, they are usually more convenient and less messy than barrier methods, as well as being more reliable at preventing pregnancy.

Oral Contraceptives

The most commonly used method of all nonsurgical forms of birth control, **oral contraceptives, known simply as *The Pill*, consist of synthetic female hormones that are administered in pill form and that prevent ovulation or implantation.** The two basic types of pills are the combination pill and the mini-pill.

■ **PANEL E.1 Four Methods of Periodic Abstinence.** The time in a woman's cycle when she is at increased risk of ovulation can be assessed in four ways.

1. **The calendar method: The *calendar method* of periodic abstinence involves counting days.** Each month for 6 to 12 months the beginning and the end of the menstrual cycle are charted on a calendar. At the end of this time, the shortest and longest cycles are determined. *(See illustration at right.)*

    Most women's cycles are not a consistent 28 days but can vary as much as 8 to 9 days (for a cycle of 21 to 35 days). A cycle ranges from day 1 of one menstrual period to day 1 of the next menstrual period. A formula is then used to estimate the days of the month when the woman is most likely to be fertile. Because women can ovulate at unpredictable times, this method is not particularly reliable.

2. ***Basal-body-temperature method:* In the *basal-body-temperature (BBT) method,* a woman uses a special thermometer to record her body temperature daily.** She takes her temperature *immediately* on waking (before going to the bathroom or any physical activity). Records are kept for 6 to 12 months.

    The pattern that many women experience includes a slight drop in *basal body temperature* 1 to 3 days before ovulation. A sharp rise occurs at the beginning of ovulation. *(See illustration at right.)* Note the periods of low risk for conception. Ovulation is confirmed if the rise is sustained at least 3 days. It is unsafe to have intercourse from the day the temperature drops until 3 days after it rises.

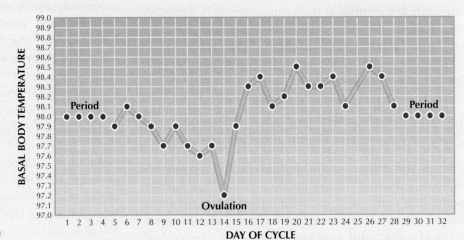

26 days = shortest cycle
First fertile day =
26 – 20 = day 6

29 days = longest cycle
Last fertile day =
29 – 10 = day 19

SEPTEMBER

First fertile day is day 6 of cycle
Last fertile day is day 19 of cycle
First day of bleeding
Fertile period

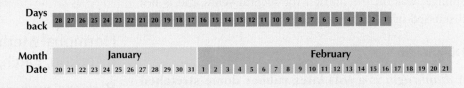

3. **Cervical mucus method:** The *cervical mucus method* of periodic abstinence—also called the *Billings method* or the *fertility awareness method*—requires that a woman evaluate the appearance, amount, and consistency of the daily mucus discharge from her cervix. Unsafe days for intercourse are indicated by a discharge that is clear, thin, and elastic rather than cloudy and thick.

    The woman generally must abstain from intercourse about 9 days in each 28-day cycle. This method must be learned from a family-planning professional or physician.

4. **Symptom-thermal method:** The symptom-thermal method of periodic abstinence combines all three previous methods: calendar, BBT, and cervical mucus. It provides the most reliable means of determining high- and low-risk times for sexual intercourse.

Note: One of the problems with these natural planning methods is that ovulation is difficult to predict accurately and consistently. The only relatively accurate way to determine ovulation is by hindsight: On day 1 of the menstrual period, one can look *back* and say that 2 weeks *ago*, ovulation probably occurred. The problem, however, is in trying to predict ovulation *ahead* of time.

Spermicide is applied.

Diaphragm is folded for
easier insertion.

Diaphragm is inserted
into vagina.

Placement of diaphragm
is checked.

■ Combination Pill: The *combination pill* **contains two hormones: estrogen and progestin. These hormones, independently or together, prevent pregnancy in three ways:** (1) They primarily prevent ovulation. (2) They change cervical mucus, making it difficult for the sperm to enter the cervix. (3) They change the lining of the uterus (endometrium), preventing implantation of the fertilized egg. This type of pill is taken for 21 days, with 7 days off to permit menstrual healing. A new combination pill, designed to be taken 365 days a year, is Lybrel, whose advantage is that women who take it never get their periods (Houppert 2007).

■ Mini-Pill: **The *mini-pill* contains only one hormone: progestin.** Thus, it is a good option for women who are breastfeeding, because it won't affect their milk supply; for women who can't take estrogen; or for women who have a risk of blood clots. This kind of pill is associated with higher rates of menstrual bleeding. Although oral contraceptives have several advantages, there are certain risks, such as adding to risk of heart disease, including high blood pressure, blood clots, and blockage of the arteries. Women who are over age 35 and smoke are often advised not to use this form of birth control.

Vaginal Ring

Approved by the Food and Drug Administration in 2001, **the *vaginal ring*—brand name NuvaRing—is a hormonal ring that is placed inside the vagina to go around the cervix; it releases the hormones progestin and estrogen.** The ring is worn for 3 weeks, then taken out the week a woman has her period, then replaced with a new ring. This hormonal contraceptive requires a doctor's prescription, and users will need to visit their health-care provider to make sure they are not having problems.

Insertion

The *intrauterine device (IUD)* is a small, often T-shaped plastic device that is inserted by a health-care professional inside the uterus. It is designed to interfere with fertilization or, if fertilization does take place, with implantation of the fertilized embryo, because the IUD changes the lining of the uterus. (*See* ■ *Panel E.5.*) IUDs require the user to visit a health-care provider to have the device inserted and to make sure they're not having any problems. Once the IUD has been inserted, the wearer must locate its string after every menstrual period to be sure the device remains in place.

Depending on the type, an IUD may remain in the uterus for 1 to 10 years. The principal types of IUD are Progestasert, Copper-T, and intrauterine system (IUS).

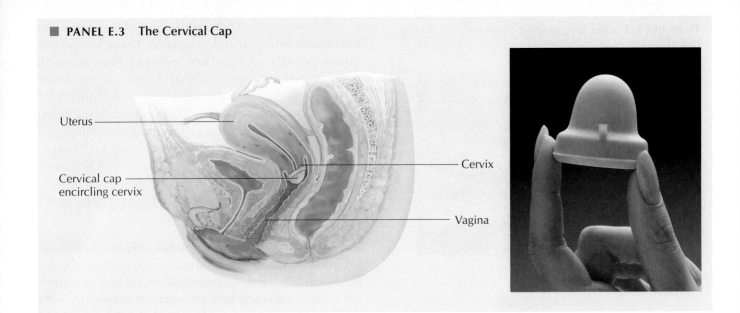

Uterus

Cervical cap encircling cervix

Cervix

Vagina

■ **Progestasert IUD—Good for 1 Year:** The *Progestasert IUD* is a small, plastic T-shaped device that contains the hormone progesterone—the same hormone that a woman's ovaries produce during the monthly menstrual cycle. This type of IUD can stay in the uterus for one year.

■ **Copper-T IUD—Good for Up to 10 Years: The *Copper-T IUD* contains copper, which interferes with fertilization and implantation.** This kind of IUD can stay in the uterus for up to 10 years.

■ **Intrauterine System (IUS)—Good for Up to 5 years: The *intrauterine system (IUS)* is a small T-shaped device that releases a small amount of hormone each day to prevent pregnancy.** The IUS (brand name: Mirena) is good for up to 5 years.

Hormone Injections

Contraception is available as hormone injections requiring visits to a health-care provider either every 3 months or once a month.

■ **Depo-Provera—Every 3 Months: *Depo-Provera* is a synthetic compound similar to progesterone that is injected into a woman's arm or buttock.** It offers birth-control protection for 3 months.

■ **Lunelle—Once a Month:** Approved by the FDA in 2000, *Lunelle* **is administered as monthly hormone shots given in the arm, buttocks, or thigh.**

Implant

The contraceptive *Norplant* **consists of small, removable silicone-rubber, sticklike rods that are implanted surgically by a physician, using a local anesthetic, under the woman's skin, in the arm or leg. The rods release a low, steady level of a steroid that prevents pregnancy.**

Norplant was taken off the market in July 2002 (Schwartz and Gabelnick 2002). Some users had reported such side effects such as migraine headaches, shortness of breath, and weight gain.

Sterilization: Surgical & Nonsurgical Methods

Sterilization **is the surgical or nonsurgical interruption of a person's reproductive capacity, generally for people who want a permanent method of birth control.** Sterilization prevents the normal passage of sperm or ova.

Sterilization may be done surgically for both men and women, but women may also avail themselves of nonsurgical sterilization.

Male Surgical Sterilization: Vasectomy

Male sterilization is accomplished by *vasectomy*, **a surgical procedure that involves making a pair of incisions in the scrotum and cutting and tying two sperm-carrying tubes** called the *ductili efferentes testis* (singular: *vas deferens* or *ductus deferens*). (See ■ *Panel E.6.*) After the operation—a 20-minute procedure that is

PANEL E.4 The Female Condom

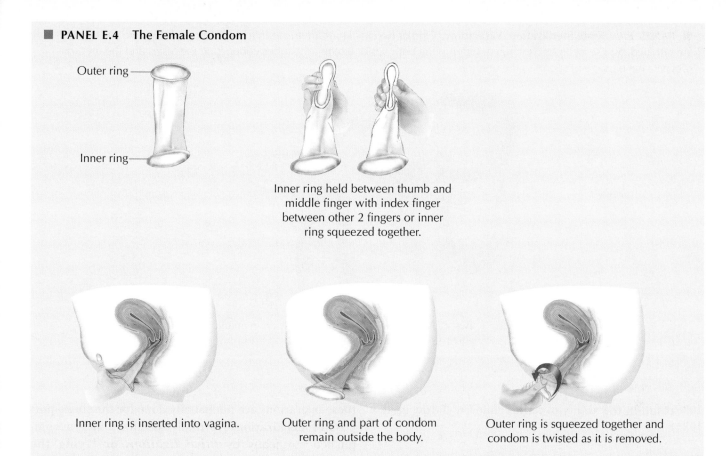

Outer ring

Inner ring

Inner ring held between thumb and middle finger with index finger between other 2 fingers or inner ring squeezed together.

Inner ring is inserted into vagina.

Outer ring and part of condom remain outside the body.

Outer ring is squeezed together and condom is twisted as it is removed.

performed in a physician's office using a local anesthetic—sperm still continue to form but are absorbed by the body. The man continues to be able to have erections, enjoy orgasms, and produce semen, but the ejaculate contains no sperm cells.

A man who is contemplating a vasectomy should proceed as though the procedure were irreversible—that he will never be able to sire children again (a subject that might come up in a later marriage). Although 90% of the operations to reopen the tubes are successful, only 40 to

PANEL E.5 Four Types of Intrauterine Devices

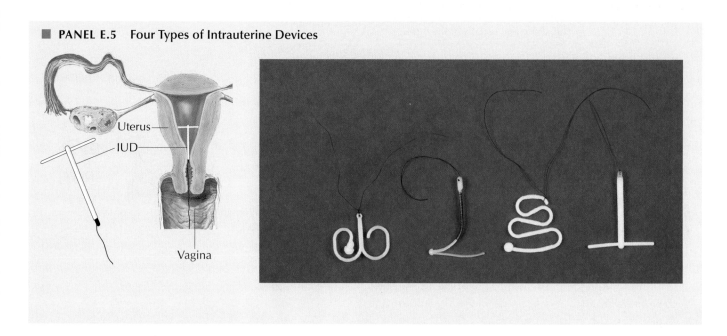

Uterus

IUD

Vagina

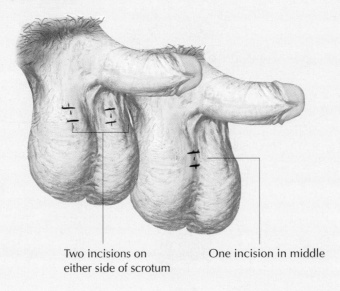

Two incisions on
either side of scrotum

One incision in middle

70% result in the ability to father children (Jarow et al. 1985).

Female Surgical Sterilization: Tubal Ligation

Female sterilization may be accomplished by removal of the ovaries (oophorectomy) or uterus (hysterectomy), but these operations are not usually done for the single purpose of sterilization. Normally, sterilization is accomplished surgically by ***tubal ligation*, or "tying the tubes," which involves the blocking or cutting of the fallopian tubes to prevent passage of the eggs down to the uterus, where they might be fertilized.** *(See ■ Panel E.7.)*

■ **PANEL E.7** **Female Sterilization: Tubal Ligation.** The fallopian tubes are interrupted surgically—cut and tied or blocked. This prevents passage of the eggs to the uterus.

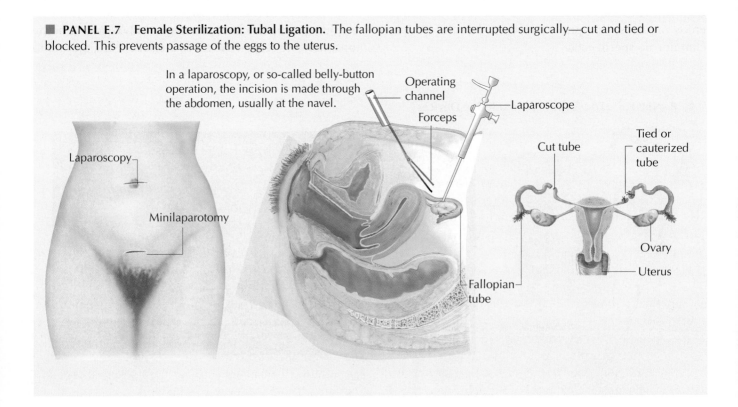

In a laparoscopy, or so-called belly-button operation, the incision is made through the abdomen, usually at the navel.

Laparoscopy

Minilaparotomy

Operating channel

Forceps

Laparoscope

Cut tube

Tied or cauterized tube

Fallopian tube

Ovary

Uterus

There are three procedures for accomplishing tubal sterilization, the choice having to do with the place and extent of the incision and the anticipated anesthesia and length of hospitalization needed.

■ **Laparotomy: In a *laparotomy*, a surgeon makes a 2-inch-long incision in the woman's abdomen and cuts the fallopian tubes.** The procedure is performed with anesthesia in a hospital and might require a few days of recovery in the hospital and at home. A laparotomy leaves a 2-inch scar.

A variant, a ***minilaparotomy***, attempts to leave a less-visible scar by making a 1-inch-long incision just above the pubic hairline. It uses a local anesthestic, takes only 30 minutes, and allows the patient to go home the same day.

■ Laparoscopy: **In a *laparoscopy*, a tubelike instrument called a laparoscope is inserted through a half-inch incision in the area of the navel. This is the most common means of female sterilization.** The fallopian tubes are closed by using instruments inserted through the laparoscope. The operation may be performed in 30 minutes, and the patient is usually discharged in a few hours.

■ Colpotomy: **In a *colpotomy*, an incision is made through the back of the vagina.** Although the operation leaves no outside scar, it is somewhat more difficult and hazardous than the other procedures are.

Female Nonsurgical Sterilization: Essure

Approved by the Food and Drug Administration in November 2002, the Essure Permanent Birth Control System involves no incisions and can be put it place in a doctor's office in 30 minutes with a local anesthetic, after which most women can resume normal activities within a day. **The *Essure procedure* consists of a physician's inserting a tiny metal implant into the fallopian tube using a thin tube that passes through the vagina and the uterus. Once the tube (catheter) is removed, the implant expands, and scar tissue grows around it, completely blocking the tube** (National Women's Health Information Center 2002; Davis 2003).

Essure does have some drawbacks. Unlike tubal ligation, which can be reversed in some cases, Essure cannot be undone. Moreover, contraception doesn't begin right away; women need to continue using other forms of birth control for the first 3 months. After that, a special X-ray must be taken to confirm that the inserts are properly placed. Finally, the procedure is so new that many obstetrician/gynecologists may not have much experience in

the technique; in fact, one study (cited in Davis 2003) found that doctors failed on their first attempt in 14% of the patients.

Emergency Contraception

***Emergency contraception*, also known as *postcoital birth control*, refers to various methods of protecting a woman from getting pregnant after having unprotected vaginal intercourse.** It is *not* supposed to be a regular method of birth control (National Women's Health Information Center 2002). It should be used when a contraceptive method fails, such as a condom breaking, or when a woman might have forgotten to take her birth-control pills. It is also used in cases of unwanted sex or rape. There are two types of emergency contraception: *morning-after pills* and *RU-486 pills*.

Morning-After Pill

The so-called *morning-after pill* (brand names: Preven, Plan B) are combined estrogen-progesterone oral contraceptives (hormone pills), a number of which are taken within 72 hours of unprotected intercourse. The pills prevent the fertilized egg from entering the uterus or being implanted in the uterus. A urine test should be given first to be sure that the woman is not already pregnant; then one pill is taken within 72 hours of intercourse followed by another dose 12 hours later. Another pregnancy test should be given 3 weeks later. Plan B is available without a prescription.

If the combined estrogen-progesterone pills are taken within 12 hours of unprotected intercourse, the pregnancy rate is 1.2%; if they are taken within 48 hours, it is 2.3%; if they are taken within 72 hours, it is 4.9% (Rosenfeld 1997). Minor side effects are possible nausea, tender breasts, headaches, and perhaps abdominal pain. According to another source, the pills are 75 to 89% effective in preventing pregnancy (National Women's Health Information Center 2002).

RU-486 (Mifepristone)

Approved for use by the FDA in September 2000, ***RU-486*, or *mifepristone* (brand name: Mifeprex), is a synthetic steroid often referred to as the abortion pill. If taken within 7 weeks of pregnancy, it acts to prevent the cells of the uterine lining from getting the progesterone they need to support implantation of a fertilized egg.** The body is tricked into thinking that it's the end of the menstrual cycle, and so it sheds the uterine lining in what appears to be a heavy menstrual period. The pregnancy rate is 1.6%.

Appendix F
Abortion

Five principal methods of induced abortion that we will describe (there are others as well) are *vacuum aspiration, D and C, D and E, saline induction/use of prostaglandins,* and *hysterotomy.*

Each method is appropriate for a different stage or stages of pregnancy. From a medical standpoint, abortions are least risky during the first 3 months of pregnancy. During the second 3 months, the woman is more apt to suffer complications. Abortions are generally not performed after the 24th week of pregnancy.

Vacuum Aspiration: Performed in First 12 Weeks

The most common method of abortion—used for about 96% of all abortions—is vacuum aspiration, usually performed during weeks 6 to 12. The procedure itself usually takes about 10 to 15 minutes. **In *vacuum aspiration*, after the cervix is numbed with a local anesthetic, the cervix is dilated—that is, gradually expanded. A small plastic tube is then inserted through the woman's cervix into the uterus. The tube is attached to a suction pump, and the contents of the uterus are then drawn out into the vacuum system.**

When performed during the first trimester, this kind of abortion usually takes place in a clinic or physician's office. Vacuum aspiration is one of safest surgical procedures when performed by a trained, experienced health-care professional; in fact the complication and death rates are lower than those for childbirth (Physicians for Reproductive Choice and Health and The Alan Guttmacher Institute 2006). However, risks do exist: perforation of the uterus, bleeding, uterine cramping, or incomplete evacuation of the uterine contents.

D & C, Dilation & Curettage: Performed in Weeks 9 to 14

A benefit of vacuum aspiration is that it reduces the risk of the physician accidentally perforating the uterus. From the ninth to fourteenth weeks, however, a physician may use the ***D and C* technique, which stands for *dilation and curettage*. After general anesthesia is administered, the cervical canal is dilated. The physician then uses a small, spoon-shaped curette to scrape the uterine wall of fetal tissue.** Because of the risk of perforation of the uterus and bleeding and infection, hospitalization is often required.

D & E, Dilation & Evacuation: Performed in Weeks 13 to 20

Similar to the D and C method, ***D and E* stands for *dilation and evacuation*. Performed with general anesthesia in a hospital because of the risk of perforation, the D and E starts with dilation of the cervix. The physician then uses a combination of vacuum aspiration and forceps (an instrument for grasping) to extract fetal tissue.**

Saline Induction/Use of Prostaglandins: Performed in Weeks 16 to 20

There are two methods that are used during weeks 16 to 20:

- *Saline induction method:* **In the *saline induction method*, a physician instills a saline (salt) solution by needle through the abdominal wall and into the amniotic sac surrounding the fetus. This induces the uterus to contract and thus simulate labor,** which results in the expulsion of the fetus within 24 hours.
- *Use of prostaglandins:* Instead of using salt solutions, physicians may use ***prostaglandins*, naturally occurring hormonelike substances.** These produce labor contractions faster but can also cause vomiting and diarrhea.

Hysterotomy: Performed in Weeks 16 to 24

A hysterotomy is a surgical procedure that is performed late in a woman's pregnancy, in weeks 16 to 24. A hysterotomy is used mainly when the woman's life is in danger and other abortion methods are considered too risky. Called a "small cesarean section," this procedure requires hospitalization. **In a *hysterotomy*, the physician makes a surgical incision in the abdomen and uterus and removes the fetus.** A hysterotomy should not be confused with a hysterectomy (removal of the uterus).

After the 24th Week

After week 24, abortion by any method is not considered advisable or at least will not be performed by very many doctors. This creates hardship for prospective parents who learn late in the pregnancy that the fetus is severely deformed or brain-damaged and would like to consider having an abortion (Kolata 1992).

Glossary

abandoned baby laws See *safe-haven laws.*

abortion Removal or expulsion from the uterus of an embryo (the fertilized egg in its second through eighth week) or fetus (successor to the embryo) before it can survive on its own; can be induced or spontaneous.

abstinence Voluntary avoidance of sexual intercourse.

accommodating style of conflict A means of handling conflict whereby one is cooperative, taking a passive stance.

accommodationist single A person who has accommodated himself or herself to an unattached life, getting together with friends but refusing romantic or sexual contacts.

acquaintance rape Nonconsensual sex between adults who know each other.

acute Of short duration.

ad hominem See *irrelevant attack on opponent.*

adaptation Adjusting to the situation, not changing the stressor or the stress.

adolescence Separate social and psychological stage of development coinciding with puberty and characterized by rebellion and crises; the term was coined in 1903.

adoption Legal process by which adult couples or singles voluntarily take a child born of other parents and raise him or her as their own child.

adultolescents Also known as *Peter Pans, bungee kids, twixters, kidults,* and *thresholders;* adult children, usually in their twenties, who have moved back in with their parents.

affiliated kin Unrelated individuals who are treated as if they are related.

agape ("ah-*gah*-pay") According to sociologist John Alan Lee's theory of the origin of love, one of six basic styles of loving: altruistic love—unselfish, self-giving, self-sacrificing love.

AIDS (acquired immune deficiency syndrome) Sexually transmitted disease that is caused by a virus, HIV (human immunodeficiency virus). It is characterized by irreversible damage to the body's immune system.

alcoholism Form of substance abuse; a chronic, progressive, and potentially fatal disease characterized by a growing compulsion to consume alcohol.

alienation of affection laws Laws allowing a spouse to bring a suit for damages against a third party with whom his or her spouse has had an extramarital affair and who is alleged to be responsible for the failure of the marriage.

alimony myth According to Lenore Weitzman, the fallacious belief that most women profit from divorce by receiving high alimony payments.

altruistic egoism The process of cooperation in which one helps others to satisfy their needs, and they in turn help one to satisfy one's own needs.

anal intercourse Insertion of the penis into the anus.

androgyny ("an-*droj*-en-ee") The quality of having in one person the characteristics, as culturally defined, of both males and females.

annulment ("an-*null*-ment") Pronouncement that declares that a couple never had a valid marriage, returning both partners to single status and allowing them to marry others; can be religious or civil.

anorexia nervosa ("an-or-*reks*-see-uh ner-*voh*-suh") Self-starvation, resulting from a distorted body self-image that leads to the conviction that one is grossly overweight.

anorgasmic ("an-or-*gaz*-mik") Unable to have an orgasm.

antifeminists The conservative branch of the men's movement, antifeminists believe that male dominance is natural and therefore women's attempts to attain gender equality must be resisted.

anti-gay prejudice Also called *homophobia;* negative attitudes toward homosexuality and homosexuals.

anxiety disorders Four common psychological disorders: generalized anxiety disorders, panic attacks, phobias, and obsessive-compulsive disorder.

appeal to authority Also known as *argumentum ad verecundiam;* argumentation fallacy that uses an authority in one area to pretend to validate claims in another area in which the person is not an expert.

appeal to pity Argumentation fallacy that appeals to emotion rather than arguing the merits of the case itself.

arguments One or more premises, or reasons, that logically support a result or outcome called a *conclusion.*

arranged marriage A marriage in which the partners are determined by their families; the partners do not choose each other.

artificial insemination Procedure whereby sperm are collected from the male partner—or an anonymous male donor—by masturbation. With the help of a powerful microscope, the sperm cells are injected by syringe directly into the woman's vagina or uterus.

assisted reproductive technology (ART) The collective name for all treatments and procedures by which human eggs and sperm may be manipulated to produce a pregnancy.

athletic coach parenting style Parenting style in which parents set rules ("team rules") for the house, helped by input from the family, teach the children the rules, and apply appropriate penalties for infractions.

attachment theory A theory of the origin of love; it suggests our primary motivation in life "is to be connected with other people—because it is the only security we ever have."

authoritarian child rearing Parenting approach in which parents are repressive, controlling, and often unreasonable strict.

authoritative child rearing Parenting approach in which parents are, on the one hand, demanding and controlling yet, on the other hand, also warm and supportive.

avoidant adults Adults who are somewhat uncomfortable being close to, trusting, and being dependant on others. See *avoiding style of conflict.*

avoiding style of conflict A means of handling conflict whereby one is unassertive and uncooperative and is mainly avoiding confrontation.

barrier methods of contraception Birth control devices using devices that put physical barriers between the egg and the sperm: diaphragms, cervical caps, and condoms.

basal-body-temperature method In the basal-body-temperature (BBT) method, a woman uses a special thermometer to record her body temperature daily.

battering See *physical violence.*

beliefs Definitions and explanations people have about what is true; convictions of the truth of a statement or the reality of some being or phenomenon.

belligerence ("bel-*lij*-er-ence") The behavior of being provocative and challenging one's partner's power and authority.

binuclear family Family in which members live in two different households.

biochemical theory A theory about the origin of love; it suggests that love results from our biological, chemical, and hormonal origins.

biological father–stepmother family Family in which all children are biological children of the father and are stepchildren of the stepmother.

biological mother–stepfather family Family in which all children in the family unit are biological children of the mother and are stepchildren of the stepfather.

birdnesting A variation of joint custody whereby the children stay in the family home and the parents alternate staying with them.

bisexuality Sexual inclination toward both genders.

blamers People who always try to put the responsibility for any problem on someone else.

blended family Stepfamily; family created when two people marry and one or both bring into the household a child or children from a previous marriage or relationship.

blind date Also known as the *setup;* a classic form of personal introduction in which a common friend or relative introduces two singles who are unknown to each other.

blind marriage A marriage in which neither partner saw the other until the day of their wedding.

bonding The development of close emotional attachment among family members and a new baby.

bride price A courtship custom in which a man must pay money or property to the future bride's family for the right to marry her.

bulimia ("boo-*lee*-me-uh") Eating disorder in which binge eating is alternated with purging.

calendar method of periodic abstinence Natural family-planning method that involves counting days from the last menstrual period in order to determine the woman's fertile period.

case study method Used in clinical research studies; clinical practitioners work one on one with individuals or families using interviews, direct observation, and analysis of records.

celibacy ("*sell*-uh-bah-see") Abstention for sexual intercourse; may be either complete—a person has no sex at all—or partial. In partial celibacy, a person masturbates but has no sexual relations with others.

cervical ("*ser*-vik-al") cap Barrier method of birth control that uses a thimble-shaped rubber or plastic cap that fits directly onto the cervix.

cervical mucus method The cervical mucus method of periodic abstinence—also called the Billings method or the fertility awareness method—requires that a woman evaluate the appearance, amount, and consistency of the daily mucus discharge from her cervix.

child abduction See *child stealing.*

child abuse Acts of aggression by an adult against a child.

child custody The charge and control of a child mandated by the court; the decision as to which parent will be primarily responsible for the upbringing and welfare of the child.

child neglect Physical neglect of a child, as in not providing enough food, clothing, health care, or security.

child stealing Also known as *child abduction* or *child snatching;* the act in which one parent kidnaps his or her children from the other parent.

child support The ongoing financial assistance for child-care expenses that the separated or divorced parent with custody of the child receives from the noncustodial parent.

Child Support Enforcement Amendments U.S. act passed in 1984 that requires states to deduct from fathers' paychecks and tax returns delinquent child-support payments.

child-free marriage A marriage that is voluntarily without children.

childless marriage A marriage that is involuntarily without children.

children's allowance Practice in industrialized countries other than the United Sates whereby the government provides a grant of child support to all families based on the number of children they have.

chronic Of long duration, or recurring.

circular reasoning Argumentation fallacy that rephrases the statement to be proven true. It then uses the new, similar statement as supposed proof that the original statement is in fact true.

civil union Civil status similar to marriage, typically created for the purposes of allowing gay couples access to the benefits enjoyed by married heterosexuals.

clinical research Research that entails in-depth study of individuals or small groups who have sought counseling for psychological, relationship, or marital/family problems from mental health professionals.

closed adoptions Adoptions in which birth parents and adoptive parents do not know each other's identities and don't communicate.

closed fields Settings in which people are likely to interact and thus make it relatively easy to meet a potential partner. Compare *open fields.*

closed-couple single Single people who are expected to be faithful to their partner and not go outside the relationship for romance or sex.

closed-type family Marriage/family system that values the family over the individual and emphasizes tradition, stability, belonging, and caring for one another; one of three types of marriage/family systems proposed by David Kantor and William Lehr (1975).

coercive ("koh-*er*-siv") power Type of power based on a person's fear that his or her partner will inflict punishment if the person does not do what the partner wants. Compare *expert power, informational power, legitimate power, referent power, reward power.*

cognitive development theory Theory that attributes gender differences to the fact that how children think, understand, and reason changes as they grow older, the result of biological maturation and increasing social experience. Social learning theory suggests that children and adults learn in the same way. By contrast, cognitive development theory suggests that the way we learn depends on our age. This perspective is based on the findings of Swiss psychologist Jean Piaget (1950, 1954) and was later reinforced by Lawrence Kohlberg (1966, 1969).

cohabitation Living together as if a married couple.

co-housing Communal housing that residents help to design and that they share ownership in and that encourages interaction through common facilities and shared land.

coitus ("*coit*-us") Penetration of the vagina by the penis.

coitus interruptus Also called *withdrawal;* birth control method that involves removing the penis from the vagina before ejaculation.

collaborating style of conflict A means of handling conflict whereby one has a great deal of concern in advancing one's interests but also those of the partner.

collaborative divorce Divorce in which a couple and their lawyers sign a contract agreeing to dissolve the marriage without litigation—and if they fail, the lawyers pledge to drop out of the case before it goes to court.

colpotomy ("kohl-*poh*-toh-me") Female sterilization procedure done via an incision made through the back of the vagina.

combination pill Hormonal form of birth control for females that contains two hormones, estrogen and progestin.

come out To publicly reveal one's gayness (one's homosexuality).

committed single Person who lives in the same household with his or her partner and is engaged to be married or has agreed to be faithful to the partner.

common couple violence Mutual violence between partners arising from everyday disagreements that have gone too far.

common-law marriage Type of living arrangement in which a man and a woman living together present themselves as being married and are legally recognized as such; marriage existing by mutual agreement or by the fact of cohabitation, without a civil or religious ceremony.

commune A group of adults, perhaps including children, who live together, sharing different aspects of their lives.

community divorce Paul Bohannon's fifth of six stations of divorce: each partner reduces or leaves membership in a common community of relatives and friends.

community property Property acquired by a couple during their marriage.

commuter marriage Dual-career marriage in which each partner lives in a different location yet the pair still maintain their commitment to their family.

companionate family According to Steven Mintz and Susan Kellogg (1988), a relatively recently evolved (early 1900s) form of family whereby marriage is supposed to provide "romance, emotional growth, and sexual fulfillment"; wives are no longer supposed to exercise sexual restraint; spouses share decisions and tasks equally; and adolescent children are allowed greater freedom from parental supervision.

companionate love Love that emphasizes intimacy with, affection for, and commitment to another person. Compare *romantic love.*

companionate marriage Marriage in which the spouses base their relationship on equality and friendship; one of four types of "good marriage" described by Judith Wallerstein and Sandra Blakeslee (1995).

competing style of conflict A means of handling conflict whereby one is assertive and uncooperative, viewing conflict as a war in which one forces one's way in order to win.

compressed workweek Work period in which employees perform a full-time job in less than five days of standard eight- (or nine-) hour shifts, such as in four days of ten hours each.

compromising style of conflict A means of handling conflict whereby one is assertive, but one is cooperative.

compulsive sexual behavior (CSB) See *sexual addiction.*

computers People who always pretend to be reasonable and not reveal their feelings, because they find emotions threatening.

conclusion Result or outcome.

condom Also called a *prophylactic* or a *rubber*; a thin sheath made of latex rubber or lamb intestine that is pulled over the erect penis to prevent semen from entering the vagina.

conflict Process of interaction that results when the behavior of one person interferes with the behavior of another.

conflict perspective The sociological approach that views individuals and groups as being basically in conflict with each other for power and scarce resources.

conflict taboo A societal attitude that considers conflict and anger wrong.

conflict-habituated marriage Marriage characterized by ongoing tension and unresolved conflict.

consummate ("*con*-soo-met") **love** When you and your partner's intimacy, passion, and decision/commitment are of the same intensity.

contempt The expression of one's feeling that one's partner is inferior or undesirable.

content analysis Systematic examination of cultural artifacts or various forms of communication to extract thematic data and draw conclusions about social life.

continuous coverage system Situation in which parents become fully responsible for a fragile infant 24 hours every day.

control group In an experiment, subjects who are not introduced to the independent variable by the researcher. Compare *experimental group.*

controlled separation A separation between husband and wife usually negotiated in a therapist's office (never a lawyer's), which has the ultimate goal of saving a marriage; it institutes a contract or written commitment specifying the time limits (usually no more than six months), living arrangements, finances, and contact between the two.

co-parental divorce Paul Bohannon's fourth of six stations of divorce: involves decisions about child custody, child support, visitation rights, and the ongoing responsibilities of each parent.

coping Changing the stressor or changing one's reaction to it.

coping strategies Realistic and helpful ways of dealing with stress, pain, fear, and other problems caused by stressors.

Copper-T IUD Intrauterine device that contains copper, which interferes with fertilization and implantation. This kind of IUD can stay in the uterus for up to 10 years.

co-provider marriages Also known as *dual-earner marriages*; both married partners are employed outside the home.

corporal punishment The use of physical force to cause a child to experience pain but not injury, with the intent of correcting or controlling the child's behavior.

courtship The process by which a commitment to marriage is developed.

covenant marriage An antidivorce contract in which couples demonstrate their strong commitment to marriage by (1) getting premarital counseling, (2) getting marital counseling in times of marital difficulties, and (3) agreeing not to divorce until after a separation of two years or after proving adultery or domestic abuse.

crisis An especially strong source of stress, a crucial change in the course of events that requires changes in people's normal patterns of behavior.

critical thinking Clear thinking, skeptical thinking, active thinking—actively seeking to understand, analyze, and evaluate information in order to solve specific problems.

criticism The expression of disapproving judgments or evaluations about one's partner.

cross-dressers People of one gender who dress up in clothes, wigs, and so on to appear to be members of the other gender.

cross-cultural studies Type of research whereby social scientists compare data on family life among different kinds of societies.

crude divorce rate The number of divorces in a given year per 1,000 population.

cultural script Set of social norms for guiding the various participants in a remarriage in their relations with one another.

cunnilingus ("cun-nih-*ling*-us") Oral stimulation of the clitoris, labia, and vaginal opening.

cybersex affair Type of sexual affair in which a person has a secret online relationship with someone in an Internet chat room.

cycle of violence Lenore Walker's three-phases of violence: (1) rising tension, (2) escalation and explosion, and (3) calmness, contrition, and kindness following the violent episode.

D and E (dilation and evacuation) Method of abortion usually performed in weeks 13 through 20 of pregnancy; performed with general anesthesia in a hospital because of the risk of perforation, the D and E starts with dilation of the cervix. The physician then uses a combination of vacuum aspiration and forceps (instrument for grasping) to extract fetal tissue.

D and C (dilation and curettage) ("dye-*lay*-shen" and "ker-reh-*tahj*") Method of abortion usually performed in weeks 9 to 14 of pregnancy; after general anesthesia is administered, the cervical canal is dilated. The physician then uses a small, spoon-shaped curette to scrape the uterine wall of fetal tissue. Because of the risk of perforation of the uterus and bleeding and infection, hospitalization is often required.

date rape Nonconsensual sex between dating partners.

dating The process of meeting people socially for the purpose of possibly forming an exclusive long-term relationship.

deadbeat dads Fathers who don't meet their court-ordered child-support responsibilities.

deductive argument Type of valid argument whereby if the premises are true, then the conclusions are true also.

defense mechanisms Unconscious methods for denying, excusing, disguising, or changing the behaviors that cause anxiety and frustration.

defensiveness The behavior of not listening but rather defending oneself against a presumed attack.

demographics Population characteristics such as family size, marriage and divorce rates, and ethnicity and race.

demography The study of population and population characteristics.

denial The refusal to believe information that provokes anxiety.

dental dam Originally designed for use in dental surgery, a flat 5-inch-square piece of latex that can be used to cover the vaginal opening during oral sex.

dependent variables In an experiment, factors or behaviors that are affected by changes in the independent variables. Compare *independent variables*.

Depo-Provera Female contraceptive; synthetic compound similar to progesterone that is injected into a woman's arm or buttock.

desertion The abandonment of marriage and family by one spouse.

developmental tasks According to the family development perspective, the task—specific role expectations and responsibilities—that family members must fulfill as they move through the life cycle.

devitalized marriage Marriage in which the partners have lost the strong emotional connection they once had but stay together out of duty or resignation.

diaphragm ("*dy*-uh-fram") Barrier method of birth control made of a soft latex rubber dome stretched over a metal spring or ring. The size varies from 2 to 4 inches depending on the length of the vagina. When in place, the diaphragm covers the ceiling of the vagina, including the cervix.

discouraged workers People who have given up looking for work and have simply dropped out of the labor force.

discrimination An act of unfair treatment directed against an individual or a group.

displaced homemakers Full-time housewives who lose their economic support owing to divorce or widowhood.

displacement The redirection of one's feelings from the true target to a less-threatening substitute.

distractors People who avoid disclosing relevant feelings, so they never discuss a problem but instead change the subject.

distress The effect of a *distressor*.

distressor A negative event that is a source of stress.

divorce The legal dissolution of a valid marriage.

divorce hangover Situation in which ex-partners are unable to let go of the fact of their divorce, reorient themselves as single parents, or develop new friendships.

divorce mediation Process in which divorcing spouses make agreements with a third party about property division, spousal support, child custody, and child support.

divorce-related malicious mother syndome Situation in which a mother unjustifiably punishes her divorcing or divorced husband by attempting to alienate their mutual children from him, involving others (including lawyers) in malicious actions against him, and denying him visitation, telephone access, and participation in their school and after-school activities.

divorcism Belief that divorce is harmful.

domestic partners Two people, gay or straight, who have chosen to cohabit or share each other's lives in an intimate and committed relationship, without being married.

domestic partnership movement Movement that attempts to obtain some kind of official recognition of domestic partners in order to provide them with the legal and economic benefits of marriage.

double remarriages Marriages in which both partners were previously married.

double standard The standard according to which premarital or nonmarital sex is more acceptable for men than it is for women.

douching The practice of rinsing out the vagina with a chemical solution right after sexual intercourse.

Down (or Down's) syndrome Genetic condition that leads to various degrees of mental retardation and physical disability.

dowry The money, property, or goods a woman brings to a marriage.

drug abuse Use of a drug in violation of legal restrictions or for nonmedical reasons.

drugs Chemical substances other than those required for the maintenance of normal health.

dual-earner marriages See *co-provider marriages*.

dysfunctional family Family in which the parents demonstrate negative or destructive behavior toward each other and/or toward their children.

dyspareunia ("dis-pair-*yune*-yuh") Painful sexual intercourse, experienced by the woman when the penis is inserted into the vagina.

eating disorders Anorexia (self-starvation) and bulimia (binge-eating/ purging). See *anorexia* and *bulimia*.

ecological perspective A sociological/psychological approach that examines how a family is influenced by and influences its environment.

economic divorce The third of Paul Bohannon's six stations of divorce: involves settlement of the property.

elder abuse Acts of aggression against the elderly—physical assaults, emotional humiliation, verbal abuse, financial exploitation, isolation from friends.

elder neglect Consists of acts of omission in the care and treatment of the elderly.

elective abortion See *induced abortion*.

elope To run away and be married somewhere away from the partners' families.

embryo The developing human being from the time of implantation in the uterus to the end of the 8th week after conception.

embryo transfer Fertilization procedure whereby the sperm of a male partner of an infertile woman is placed in another woman's uterus during ovulation. Five days later, the embryo is transferred to the uterus of the infertile woman, who carries the embryo and delivers the baby.

emergency contraception Also known as *postcoital birth control, morning-after pill,* and *RU-486;* refers to various methods of protecting a woman from getting pregnant after having unprotected vaginal intercourse.

emotional abuse See *emotional violence*.

emotional divorce The first of Paul Bohannon's six stations of divorce; involves loss of affection, trust, and respect for each other and replaces positive emotions with indifference or destructive emotions.

emotional neglect Absence of sufficient care, attention, and guidance.

emotional security Quality of an enduring, close emotional relationship.

emotional violence Also called *emotional abuse*; verbal and psychological abuse that inflicts or threatens to inflict emotional distress.

empty-nest syndrome Parents' feelings of depression and lessened well-being after the children have left home.

endogamy A factor in the dating process; the cultural expectation, which acts as a filter, that a person marries within his or her own social group in terms of race, religion, and social class.

endometriosis (*"en-doh-mee-tree-oh-sis"*) Abnormality of the uterus in which some cells of the inner lining grow in the pelvic and abdominal cavities.

engagement Period of time beginning with the marriage proposal and a formal announcement that the couple plans to be married and ending with the marriage (or the termination of the engagement).

equal-distribution states Eight U.S. states in which the property acquired by either spouse during the marriage (except gifts from third parties) belongs equally to the husband or wife.

equality Situation in which partners have equal status and are equally responsible for domestic, financial, and emotional tasks.

equitable-distribution states U.S. states in which the court determines a fair and reasonable distribution that may be more than or less than 50% of any asset to either of the divorcing parties.

equity Means that partners give in proportion to what they receive.

erectile dysfunction (ED) Also called *impotence*; failure to achieve or maintain an erection.

erogenous (*"er-roh-jen-us"*) Sexually sensitive.

eros (*"air-ros"*) According to sociologist John Alan Lee's theory of the origin of love, one of six basic styles of loving: the love of beauty, characterized by intense emotional attachment and powerful sexual feelings.

erotic (*"e-rah-tik"*) **feelings** Feelings of sensuality or sexuality.

Essure procedure Female nonsurgical sterilization procedure that involves a physician inserting a tiny metal implant into the fallopian tube using a thin tube that passes through the vagina and the uterus. Once the tube (catheter) is removed, the implant expands, and scar tissue grows around it, completely blocking the tube.

ethnicity The cultural characteristics that distinguish one group from another. Compare *race*.

ethnocentrism One kind of mind-set; the belief that one's native country, culture, language, abilities, and/or behavior are superior to those of another culture.

eustress (*"you-stress"*) The effect of an *eustressor*.

eustressor A positive event that is a source of stress.

excitement phase The first phase of the four-phase description, developed in 1966 by William Masters and Virginia Johnson, of how men and women respond to sex physiologically: (1) excitement, (2) plateau, (3) orgasm, and (4) resolution; (1) consists of a physical reaction to erotic stimulation.

exhibitionism (*"egs-ih-bish-in-niz-em"*) Behavior that consists of exposing ("flashing") one's genitals in public to an involuntary observer.

exit response As a response to a deteriorating relationship, withdrawing or threatening to withdraw from the relationship.

exogamy (*"ex-og-am-ee"*) A factor in the dating process; the cultural expectation that one marry outside one's family group and not practice sex with a sibling.

experiment A test or trial in which factors or behaviors are measured or monitored under closely controlled circumstances.

experimental group In an experiment, the subjects who are exposed to an independent variable introduced by the researcher. Compare *control group*.

experimental research Process in which researchers try to isolate a single factor or behavior under controlled conditions to determine its effect.

expert power Type of power based on a person's opinion that his or her partner has specialized knowledge. Compare *coercive power, informational power, legitimate power, referent power, reward power*.

expressive role According to the structural-functional perspective, the female role of being the homemaker and being nurturing and supportive. Compare *instrumental role*.

extended family Family that includes not only the nuclear family but others as well—uncles and aunts, nieces and nephews, cousins, grandparents, great-grandparents.

external stressors Stressful events that begin with someone or something outside the family.

extrafamilial abuse Sexual child abuse by nonrelated individuals.

fallacies Patterns of incorrect reasoning.

false cause (irrelevant reason) Fallacy whereby the conclusion does not follow logically from the supposed reasons stated earlier. See *non sequitor*.

familism (*"fam-il-izm"*) The decision-making philosophy of the traditional family as an economic unit before the Industrial Revolution: when decisions were made, family collective concerns took priority over individual concerns. Compare *individualism*.

family Traditionally, a unit of two or more people who are related by blood, marriage, or adoption and who live together.

Family and Medical Leave (FMLA) Act Requires U.S. companies employing 50 or more workers to provide up to 12 weeks of unpaid leave a year to employees with a newborn or a newly adopted child, serious personal illness, or a seriously ill family member.

family boundaries Rules about who is a member of the family and the extent to which each member is allowed to participate.

family development perspective Sociological approach that proposes that family members accomplish developmental tasks as they move through stages in the family life cycle.

family life cycle According to the family development perspective, family members' roles and relationships change, largely depending on how they have to adapt themselves to the absence or presence of child-rearing responsibilities.

family of origin Also called *family of orientation*; family into which a person was born or grew up.

family of procreation Also called *family of cohabitation*; family one begins if and when one gets married and has children.

Family Support Act U.S. legislation passed in 1988 that authorizes judges to use their discretion when support agreements cannot be met and requires periodic reviews of award levels to keep up with the rate of inflation.

family systems perspective The sociological approach that suggests that family members make up a system of interconnected parts of a whole and that changes in one part change the other parts.

fathers' rights movement Movement that urges that divorced male parents have equal treatment with divorced female parents in matters of child custody, visitation, and support.

fellatio (*"fel-lay-sho"*) Oral stimulation of the penis by a partner.

female condom Barrier method of birth control that uses a lubricated, polyurethane pouch about 7 inches long that is inserted into the vagina and that extends outside it to cover the outer lips.

female-demand/male-withdraw pattern Ongoing cycle in which the wife frequently expresses herself negatively, and the husband withdraws.

feminism The view that women should have the same economic, social, and political rights as men have.

feminist perspective The sociological approach that holds that inequality in women's roles is the result of male dominance in the family and in society.

feminization of poverty Refers to the likelihood that female heads of households will be poor, owing to job and wage discrimination, high divorce rates, and single parenthood.

fertility (1) The ability to reproduce biologically; (2) a person's actual reproductive performance.

fertility rates The number of births per year per thousand women of child-bearing age, 15 to 44.

fertility-enhancing drugs Drugs that stimulate hormones to produce eggs.

fetishism (*"fet-is-shizm"*) Behavior in which a person experiences sexual arousal or pleasure from focusing on a nonsexual object or part of the body.

flexible marriages Marriages in which the partners change over time and grow as individuals and in the relationship. Compare *static marriages.*

flextime Flexible time; flexible working hours or any schedule that gives one some choices in working hours.

folk concept of the family Societal attitude that emphasizes support, understanding, happiness, and warm holiday rituals.

forced marriage An extreme form of arranged marriage in which the bride, groom, or both are coerced to marry against their will and under duress that includes both physical and emotional pressure.

foreplay Sex play; preliminary steps toward sexual arousal or intercourse.

formal separation Type of separation in which married partners use a lawyer to draw up a legal agreement enabling them to live separately but specifying financial, child-custody, child support, and visitation arrangements.

foster parent Adult who raises a child not his or her own for a short period of time but does not formally adopt that child.

free-floating single An unattached single who dates randomly.

friendship An attachment between people; the basis for a strong love relationship.

gamete A mature sexual reproductive cell (sperm or egg).

gaslighting When one partner, perhaps using sarcasm, constantly criticizes the other's definition of reality, diminishing the other's self-esteem.

gay Homosexual; usually refers to a male.

gay male See *homosexuality.*

gender The socially learned attitudes and behaviors associated with being male or female.

gender identity A person's psychological sense of whether he or she is male or female.

gender role The behavior expected of a female or a male in a particular culture.

gender schema theory Field of study of gender differences that suggests that as children people develop a framework of knowledge—a gender schema—about what they think males and females typically do and then use that framework to interpret new information about gender.

gender stereotype The belief that men and women each display traditional gender-role characteristics.

gender variance An intense psychological discomfort with one's sex. Also called *gender identity disorder (G.I.D.),* it is the American Psychiatric Association's diagnosis for people who repeatedly show, or feel, a strong desire to be the other sex.

generalized A term that refers to survey results: the results of the survey sample can be said to apply to the population, the larger group.

genogram (*"jen*-uh-gram") Diagram that shows clearly all the people who genetically, emotionally, and legally constitute a particular family.

GIFT (gamete intrafallopian transfer) Fertilization procedure whereby the woman's egg and the man's sperm are collected and united inside the woman's fallopian tubes.

globalization Trend of the world economy toward becoming a more interdependent system.

good-provider role Traditional role whereby the man is the principal or sole economic provider for the family.

granny dumping Abandoning an elderly person at a hospital entrance with no identification.

green-card marriage A sham marriage in which an American marries, or pretends to marry, usually in exchange for money, an immigrant for the purpose of giving him or her a green card that grants permanent U.S. residency.

group marriage Type of marriage in which each member of the group is married to all other group members of the opposite sex.

guaranteed child support System in France and Sweden whereby the government sends to the custodial parent the amount of child-support awarded.

gunnysacking Saving up, or putting in an imaginary sack, grievances until they spill over.

hardiness The combination of three personality traits—commitment, control, and challenge—that protect us from the potentially harmful effects of stressful situations and reduce our chances of developing illness.

hassles Frustrating irritants.

Hawthorne effect Factor that applies to participant observer research, when subjects of research change their typical behavior because they realize they are under observation.

hedonistic (*"hed-doh-nist*-ik") **affairs** Extramarital affairs that are acts of playfulness.

hermaphrodite Also called *intersexual;* a person who has both male and female sexual organs, or organs that are not distinct, as when a female's sex organ (the clitoris) resembles a male's (the penis).

heterogamous marriages Marriages in which the partners are of different education, ethnicity, race, religion, age, and social class. Compare *homogamous marriages.*

heterosexism One kind of mind-set; the belief that the standard family is heterosexual, with homosexual families—lesbians and gays—not being viewed as true families.

heterosexuality Sexual inclination toward members of the opposite gender.

hidden agenda In a blended family, expectations about how everyone should behave that often are not communicated.

historical studies Type of research whereby researchers compare census, social agency, or demographic data to ascertain changing patterns of family life.

HIV (human immunodeficiency virus) The virus that causes AIDS by bringing about a variety of ills and the breakdown of the immune system, which allows the development of certain infections and cancers.

homemaker role Traditional role whereby the woman is principally responsible for housework, child raising, and maintaining family ties to parents and in-laws.

homoeroticism (*"ho-mo-ee-rah*-tih-siz-im") Erotic attraction toward a member of the same gender.

homogamous marriages Marriages between partners of similar education, ethnicity, race, religion, age, and social class. Compare *heterogamous marriages.*

homogamy Marriage between partners of similar education, ethnicity, race, religion, age, and social class.

homophobia ("ho-mo-*fobe*-be-uh") Also called *anti-gay prejudice*; negative attitudes toward homosexuality and homosexuals.

homosexuality Sexual inclination toward members of the same gender.

hookup A physical encounter that allows possible sexual interaction—ranging from kissing to having sex—without commitment.

hormonal methods Female forms of contraception that use chemicals to prevent ovulation or implantation of the fertilized egg in the uterus, via pill, vaginal ring, vaginal insertion, skin patch, injection, or implant.

hormones Chemical substances secreted into the bloodstream by the endocrine glands. Men usually have more testosterone (produced by the testes), and women usually have more estrogen and progesterone (produced by the ovaries). These hormones and the different sex chromosomes underlying them are certainly what produce different physical characteristics—for example, facial hair on men and breasts on women.

househusband Also known as *stay-at-home dad*; a man who is a full-time homemaker.

hysterotomy ("his-ter-*ah*-toh-me") Surgical abortion performed late in a woman's pregnancy, in weeks 16 to 24; used mainly when the woman's life is in danger and other abortion methods are considered too risky. Also called a "small cesarean section," this procedure requires hospitalization; the physician makes a surgical incision in the abdomen and uterus and removes the fetus.

identity bargaining Process whereby the realities of the marriage oblige spouses to adjust their idealized expectations of each other.

immature love Passionate or romantic love. Compare *mature love*.

impotence See *erectile dysfunction*.

in vitro fertilization (IVF) Procedure in which the egg and the sperm are taken from the parents and kept in a laboratory setting until the mother's uterus is hormonally ready; then the fertilized egg is implanted in the wall of the uterus.

incest Sexual relations between persons who are related.

income The amount of money a household receives from various sources during a given period of time.

independent variables In an experiment, factors or behaviors that can be controlled or manipulated by the experimenter. Compare *dependent variables*.

individualism Post-industrialization family economic philosophy: when decisions are made, individual concerns take priority over family collective concerns. Compare *familism*.

induced abortion Also called *elective abortion*; purposeful termination of a pregnancy.

inductive argument Type of valid argument whereby if the premises are true, the conclusions are probably true, but the truth is not guaranteed.

infant mortality rate The number of children who die before 1 year of age per 1,000 live births.

infertility The failure to conceive after 1 year of regular sexual intercourse without contraception, or the inability to carry a pregnancy to live birth.

infidelity Also called *extramarital sex, adultery, having an affair,* or *cheating*; marital unfaithfulness—usually considered sexual contact outside the marriage or the primary relationship.

informal separation Type of separation in which the spouses settle financial, child-custody, child-support, and visitation arrangements informally; no legal papers are drawn up.

informational power Type of power that is persuasive, whereby a person is persuaded by his or her partner that what the partner wants is in the person's best interest. Compare *coercive power, expert power, legitimate power, referent power, reward power.*

inhibited female orgasm Previously called *frigidity*; inability to reach orgasm.

inhibited sexual desire (ISD) Lack of interest in sex, or an inability to feel sexual.

instrumental role According to the structural-functional perspective, the male role of being the breadwinner and being hard-working, tough, and competitive. Compare *expressive role*.

intercourse See *sexual intercourse*.

internal stressors Stressful events that begin inside the family.

interviewer bias A drawback of interviews: interviewers allow their own preconceptions to influence how they ask questions.

intimacy The intense affection for, commitment to, and sharing of intellectual, physical, and emotional connections with another person.

intimacy reduction affairs Extramarital affairs that entail involvements by a spouse who feels uncomfortable with too much closeness in his or her marriage.

intimate partner violence Physical and/or emotional abuse of one partner by another—male or female, married or unmarried, straight or gay, current or former.

intrafallopian transfer See *GIFT* and *ZIFT*.

intrafamilial abuse Sexual child abuse by related individuals, including steprelatives.

intrauterine ("in-tra-*yu*-ter-in") **device (IUD) (Progestasert and Copper-T)** Birth control device for females; small, often T-shaped plastic device that is inserted by a physician inside the uterus. It is designed to interfere with fertilization or, if it does take place, with implantation, because it changes the lining of the uterus.

intrauterine system (IUS) (Mirena) Small T-shaped birth-control device (similar to the IUD) that is placed inside the uterus by a physician. It releases a small amount of hormone each day to prevent pregnancy.

intrinsic marriages Marriages that are inherently rewarding.

involuntary stable singles People who would like to marry, have not found a mate, and have come to accept their single status. Compare *involuntary temporary singles, voluntary stable singles, voluntary temporary singles.*

involuntary temporary singles People who would like to marry and are actively seeking mates. Compare *involuntary stable singles, voluntary stable singles, voluntary temporary singles.*

irrelevant attack on an opponent Also called *ad hominem* argument; argumentation fallacy that attacks a person's reputation or beliefs rather than his or her argument.

irrelevant reason See *false cause*.

IUD See *intrauterine device*.

jealousy A usually intolerant or even hostile response to a real or imagined threat to a love relationship.

job sharing The sharing of one full-time job by two co-workers.

joint biological–stepfamily Family in which at least one child is the biological child of both parents, and at least one child is the biological child of one parent and the stepchild of the other parent.

joint custody Situation in which the children divide their time between both parents.

joint legal custody Joint custody arrangement whereby the children live with one parent, but both parents share decisions about their children's upbringing.

joint physical custody Joint custody arrangement whereby the children live with both parents, dividing their time on a more or less equal basis between the separate households.

jumping to conclusions Also known as *hasty generalization*; fallacy whereby a conclusion has been reached when not all the facts are available.

kin A person's relatives by blood, marriage, remarriage, or adoption, varying from grandparents to nieces to brothers-in-law.

labor force Wage earners who hire out their labor to someone else.

laissez-faire ("lay-say fair") parenting See *pal parenting style.*

laparoscopy ("lah-pah-*roh*-skoh-pe") Female sterilization procedure whereby a tubelike instrument called a *laparoscope* is inserted through a half-inch incision in the area of the navel. This is the most common means of female sterilization.

laparotomy ("lah-pah-*roh*-toh-me") Female sterilization procedure whereby a surgeon makes a 2-inch-long incision in the woman's abdomen and cuts the fallopian tubes.

latchkey child A school-age child who regularly spends part of the day unsupervised at home while his or her parents are at work.

latent ("*lay*-tent") functions According to the structural-functional perspective, functions that are unconscious or unintended; they have hidden purposes. Compare *manifest functions.*

learned helplessness A response to being battered: people perceive that they have no control over the major events affecting them.

Lee's six styles of love Sociologist John Alan Lee's theory of the origin of love, which suggests there are six basic styles of loving: (1) love of beauty and the physical, or *eros;* (2) obsessive love, or*mania;* (3) playful love, or *ludus;* (4) companionate love, or *storge;* (5) altruistic love, or *agape;* and (6) practical love, or *pragma.*

legal divorce The second of Paul Bohannon's six stations of marriage: the court-ordered termination of a marriage.

legitimate power Type of power based on a person's partner having the right to ask you to do something and you having the duty to comply. Compare *coercive power, expert power, referent power, reward power, informational power.*

leisure Time not taken up by work in which to engage in freely chosen satisfying activities.

lesbian Female homosexual.

leveling Being specific, authentic, and transparent about how one feels, especially about matters in one's relationship that create conflict or hurt.

LGBT Short for "lesbian, gay, bisexual, and transgender (or transgendered) people."

liberal feminism Also called *equal rights feminism;* movement principally concerned with achieving equal opportunities for women through legal and social reforms.

lifestyle A pattern by which a person organizes his or her living arrangements in relation to others.

living apart together (LAT) couples Also known as *dual dwelling duos (DDDs);* these are happily married couples who are committed to each other but who live in separate quarters.

longitudinal studies Type of research whereby researchers use questionnaires or interviews over a number of years to follow up on earlier investigations.

living wage laws Laws mandating that wages and benefits take into account the area's cost of living; they are higher than the federal minimum wage.

love Intimacy with, caring for, and commitment to another person.

loyalty response A passive, constructive response to a deteriorating relationship; choosing to stay with one's partner despite any problems but making no attempt to try to resolve them, hoping they will smooth out over time.

ludus ("*lewd*-us") According to sociologist John Alan Lee's theory of the origin of love, one of six basic styles of loving: playful love, love as pleasure and fun and games. This love style focuses on sex as recreation, the enjoyment of many sexual partners rather than concentrating on one serious relationship.

Lunelle Contraceptive for females; is administered as monthly hormone shots given in the arm, buttocks, or thigh.

macro-level orientation Theory focusing on large-scale patterns of society; examples are the structural-functional perspective and the conflict perspective.

magical thinking Interpreting of two closely occurring events as though one caused the other, without any concern for causal link.

mail-order brides Agencies specializing in so-called mail-order brides publish profiles and photos of women mainly for the benefit of American men seeking wives.

mania ("*may*-nee-uh") According to sociologist John Alan Lee's theory of the origin of love, one of six basic styles of loving: obsessive love, which consists of strong sexual attraction and emotional intensity, extreme jealousy, and mood swings alternating between ecstasy and despair.

manifest functions According to the structural-functional perspective, functions that are open, stated, and conscious. Compare *latent functions.*

marital quality Marriage success measured in terms of stability, happiness, and flexibility.

marital rape Sexual assault by one's spouse.

marital success Also called *marital quality,* characteristic of marriage measured in terms of stability, happiness, and flexibility.

marriage A socially approved mating relationship; a legal union between a woman and a man.

marriage bureaus Services that arrange introductions for a fee.

marriage gradient See*mating gradient.*

marriage maintenance affairs Extramarital affairs that provide something missing from the marriage.

marriage sabbatical ("suh-*bat*-ih-kel") A personal timeout from daily routines for creative, professional, or spiritual growth, for study, reflection, or renewal.

marriage squeeze A factor that influences dating: one sex has a more limited pool of eligible marriage candidates than the other sex has.

martyr parenting style Parenting style in which parents sacrifice everything for their children and exercise little or no authority over them.

masculinists People who believe that the patriarchal system causes oppression and isolation but who are in favor of males' trying to achieve self-realization and self-expression.

masturbation Self-stimulation of the genitals for sexual pleasure.

mating (marriage) gradient An aspect of social class and dating behavior; it refers to the tendency of men to marry downward in class and women to marry upward with respect to age, education, and occupational success.

matriarchal ("may-tree-*ark*-kel") Female-dominated, female-identified, and female-centered.

matriarchal family Family in which the mother holds the power.

matrilineal ("ma-trih-*lin*-ee-al") Family/kinship system whereby children trace their descent, and perhaps rights and property, through the mother's line.

matrilocal residence Situation in which newly married partners reside with the wife's family.

mature love Companionate love. Compare *immature love.*

mental disorders Psychiatric illnesses or diseases manifested by breakdowns in the adaptational process and expressed primarily as abnormalities of thought, feeling, and behavior, producing either distress or impairment of function.

median income The income midpoint—half of a population earns more and half earns less.

micro-level orientation Theory focusing on small-scale patterns of society, concentrating on individual interactions in specific settings; an example is the symbolic interaction perspective.

mindfulness Term coined by Ellen J. Langer; state of mind characterized by three features: (1) creation of new categories,

(2) openness to new information, and (3) awareness of more than one perspective.

mindlessness Term coined by Ellen J. Langer; state of mind characterized by three features: (1) entrapment in old categories, (2) automatic behavior, and (3) acting from a single perspective.

minilaparotomy ("min-ee lah-pah-*roh*-toh-me") Type of laparotomy that leaves a smaller scar.

mini-pill Hormonal form of birth control for females that contains only one hormone, progestin.

miscarriage See *spontaneous abortion.*

miscegenation Marriage or cohabitation between a white person and a person of another race.

Mirena See *intrauterine system.*

modeling Learning through imitation of other people.

modern family See *nuclear family.*

monogamy ("muh-*nog*-uh-mee") A marital or sexual relationship in which a person is committed exclusively to one partner.

mood disorders Prolonged or severe depression or mania (elation) or swings between these extremes.

morning sickness Early pregnancy (first trimester) problem of nausea and vomiting that happen frequently in the early morning or during other times of the day.

morning-after pill (Preven, Plan B) Combined estrogen-progesterone oral emergency contraceptives (hormone pills).

multiorgasmic Being able to have multiple orgasms within a single period of sexual arousal.

mutaa (or *Muta'a*) **marriage** Also known as an *enjoyment marriage* or *pleasure marriage;* secret betrothal in Iraq in which a Shiite Muslim unmarried woman is allowed to enter into a pleasure marriage with a man (married or not) for periods as brief as a few minutes or as long as a lifetime.

mutual dependency The sharing of pleasures, ideas, jokes, and sexual desires.

mutual oral-genital simulation Simultaneous oral-genital stimulation while partners are facing each other while lying in opposite directions. This arrangement is known as the "69 position."

natural family planning methods Birth control methods that include various ways of gauging times for periodic abstinence—the calendar method, the BBT method, the cervical mucus method—and withdrawal.

neglect response A destructive reaction that tends to occur when a person is not much invested in the relationship, doesn't want to deal with any problems in it, and is willing to let the partnership simply wither away.

neolocal residence Situation in which newly married partners set up their own household, not connected with the parents of the bride or the groom.

neonaticide The murdering of infants within 24 hours of their birth.

nocturnal orgasm Involuntary orgasm during sleep.

no-fault divorce The legal dissolution of a valid marriage in which neither partner is found guilty or at fault; the marriage is declared unworkable and is legally dissolved for irreconcilable differences.

non sequitur Latin for "it does not follow"; also called *false cause* or *irrelevant reason;* the conclusion does not follow logically from the supposed reasons stated earlier.

nonfamily household Household that consists of (1) a person who lives alone or (2) people who live with unrelated individuals within a housing unit.

nonlove Situation in which all elements are missing from a relationship between two people.

nonoxynol-9 ("non-*ox*-ee-noll-9") Antiviral, antibacterial spermicidal agent.

nonparticipant observation Observational research method whereby researchers observe their subjects without interacting with them. Compare *participant observation.*

nonrepresentative sample Not scientifically valid, a sample in which researchers pick people for convenience or availability.

nonverbal communication Messages sent by means other than the written or the spoken word.

Norplant Contraceptive for females; small, removable silicone-rubber, sticklike rods implanted surgically, using a local anesthetic, by a physician under the woman's skin, in the arm or leg. The rods release a low, steady level of a steroid that prevents pregnancy.

nuclear family Also once thought of as the modern family; family consisting of father, mother, and children living in one household (the idealized version of "family"); this term was coined by Robert Murdock in 1949.

nuclear-family model monopoly Model in which the first-marriage family is seen as the legitimate model for how families should be, and all other forms are seen as deficient alternatives.

NuvaRing See *vaginal ring.*

observational research Research method whereby researchers collect data by observing people in their usual surroundings.

open adoptions Adoptions in which both birth parents and adoptive parents have more active contact, as in a meeting before the birth or even lifelong communication.

open courtship system Society in which people make their own decisions about marriage.

open fields Settings in which people do not normally interact and thus make it difficult to meet a potential partner. Compare *closed fields.*

open marriage Also called *sexually open marriage;* marriage in which a married couple agrees that each may have emotional and sexual relations with others—they go out separately as well as together—while still keeping the marriage the primary relationship.

open-couple single A single person with a steady partner, but the relationship is open enough that he or she can have romantic or sexual relationships with others.

open-type family Marriage/family system that is sensitive to both individual and family needs and tries to achieve consensus in ideas and feelings; one of three types of marriage/family systems proposed by David Kantor and William Lehr in 1975.

opportunity costs The loss of wages and investments that parents sacrifice by devoting their time and energy to other.

oral contraceptives Synthetic female hormones administered in pill form that prevent ovulation or implantation; The Pill.

oral-genital stimulation Mouth-to-genital contact.

orgasmic phase The third phase of the four-phase description, developed in 1966 by William Masters and Virginia Johnson, of how men and women respond to sex physiologically: (1) excitement, (2) plateau, (3) orgasm, and (4) resolution; (3) is the most ecstatic stage, as rhythmic contractions cause the release of neuromuscular tension. Blood pressure, heart rate, and breathing reach their highest levels, and there are involuntary muscle spasms throughout the body.

outercourse Sexual acts not involving the exposure of a partner to semen, vaginal secretions, or blood.

pal parenting style Also known as *laissez-faire parenting;* parents let children set their own goals, rules, and limits.

parallel style of conflict A means of handling conflict whereby one is unassertive and uncooperative; the arguers completely deny and retreat from any discussion of a problem, hoping it will just disappear.

parent alienation syndrome (PAS) Disturbance in which children are preoccupied with viewing one parent as all good and the other parent as all bad. The "bad" parent is hated and verbally marginalized, whereas the "good" parent is idealized and loved.

parenting coordinator A qualified neutral person appointed by the court or agreed to by the parties in a divorce to assist the divorced mothers and fathers in resolving issues relating to parenting.

participant observation Type of observational research whereby researchers interact naturally with the subjects they are observing but do not reveal that they are researchers. Compare *nonparticipant observation*.

passive-aggression The expression of anger indirectly rather than directly.

passive-congenial marriage Marriage in which the couple focuses on activities rather than intimacy, but unlike people in devitalized marriages, they have always done so.

patriarchal ("pay-tree-*ark*-el") Male-dominated, male-identified, and male-centered.

patriarchal family A family in which the father holds the power.

patriarchal terrorism Violence committed by men who feel they must control "their" women by any means necessary.

patriarchy ("pay-tree-*ark*-ee") The social arrangement in which positions of power and authority are mostly held by men.

patrilineal ("pa-trih-*lin*-ee-al") Family/kinship system whereby descent and ownership of property is traced through the father's lines.

patrilocal residence Situation in which newly married partners live with the husband's family.

peers People of equal status in age, class, and the like.

periodic abstinence Also called *fertility awareness, natural family planning*, and *rhythm method*; avoidance of sexual intercourse during perceived fertile periods of the woman's menstrual cycle.

permanence Situation in which the partners promise to stay together lifelong.

permissive child rearing Parenting approach in which parents are warm and reasonable.

permissiveness with affection The standard that allows premarital or nonmarital sex for women and men equally, provided they have an affectionate and reasonably stable relationship.

permissiveness without affection Also called *recreational sex*; the standard that allows premarital or nonmarital sex for both women and men regardless of the amount of affection or stability in their relationship.

personal marriage agreement Written agreement negotiated between married partners that specifies how they will behave in aspects of the relationship—preferences, obligations, and sharing of labor and tasks.

physical neglect See *child neglect*.

physical violence Also called *battering*; the infliction or threat of physical harm.

The Pill Hormonal birth-control method for females administered in pill form to prevent ovulation or implantation.

placaters Passive people who are always agreeable but act helpless.

plateau phase The second phase of the four-phase description, developed in 1966 by William Masters and Virginia Johnson, of how men and women respond to sex physiologically: (1) excitement, (2) plateau, (3) orgasm, and (4) resolution; (2) consists of sexual excitement as muscle tension continues to build.

police officer parenting style Authoritarian and punitive parenting style in which parents insist that their children follow rules and punish them when they don't.

polyandry ("pol-lee-*an*-dree") Form of marriage in which one wife has more than one husband.

polygamy ("poh-*lig*-am-mee") Form of marriage in which one person has several spouses.

polygyny ("poh-*lij*-in-nee") Form of marriage in which one husband has more than one wife.

population Social scientists' term that describes any well-known group of people they want to study.

pornography Material—such as books and films—designed to cause sexual excitement.

positive self-talk Giving oneself positive messages so that one can view a situation in beneficial terms.

POSSLQs ("*poss*-el-kews") People of the Opposite Sex Sharing Living Quarters.

postadoption blues Also known as *postadoption depression;* a condition experienced by some adoptive parents ranging from a low mood to a full-fledged plunge into despair.

postcoital birth control See *emergency contraception*.

postmodern family Relatively new term that describes the great variability in family forms beyond traditional families; includes *binuclear families* and *blended families*.

postnuptial agreement Similar to a prenuptial agreement, a contract signed by the couple that specifies in advance how property will be divided and children cared for in the event of divorce or one partner's death; however, in this case the agreement is worked out and signed after the partners have married each other.

postpartum blues The period of sadness and anxiety experienced by some women after giving birth.

postpartum depression Severe persistent symptoms of a major depression that warrant the assistance of a health-care professional; experienced by some women after giving birth.

postpartum period Three-month period following birth during which critical family and emotional adjustments are made.

poverty line The minimum level of income the U.S. government considers necessary for individual and family subsistence.

power The ability or the potential to impose one's will on other people—to get them to think, feel, or do something they would not ordinarily have done spontaneously.

pragma ("*prag*-ma") According to sociologist John Alan Lee's theory of the origin of love, one of six basic styles of loving: practical love, the type of love that makes a rational assessment of a potential partner's positives and negatives.

prejudice Prejudgment; the biased attitude, usually negative, pertaining to an individual or to a group.

premature birth A birth that occurs during less than 37 weeks of pregnancy.

premature ejaculation ("ee-jak-yu-*lay*-shen") Inability of a man to reasonably control his ejaculatory reflex on a regular basis.

premises Reasons that logically support a result or an outcome.

prenuptial agreement Contract signed by the couple before the wedding that specifies in advance how property will be divided and children cared for in the event of divorce or one partner's death.

principle of least interest Proposed rule of Willard Waller (1951) that the partner who is least interested in the relationship has the most power.

private adoptions Also called *independent adoptions*; adoptions arranged directly between birth mother and adoptive parent or parents.

procreation Reproduction, or the bringing forth of children.

profeminists The liberal branch of the men's movement, profeminists agree with feminist women that a system of patriarchy benefits white heterosexual males but forces all men, including minorities and gays, into restrictive gender roles.

Progestasert IUD Small, plastic T-shaped intrauterine device that contains the hormone progesterone—the same hormone produced by a woman's ovaries during the monthly menstrual cycle. This type of IUD can stay in the uterus for one year.

projection The attribution of unacceptable impulses or characteristics to other people.

pronatalist ("pro-*nay*-tal-ist") **bias** The cultural attitude that takes having children for granted.

propinquity A factor in the dating process; the nearness to a person of a potential date in place and time acts as a filter—it's easier to meet people locally at school, work, or church or through social networks.

prostaglandin ("pros-tah-*glan*-din") **induction** Method of induced abortion used in weeks 16 to 20 of pregnancy whereby physicians use prostaglandins, which are naturally occurring hormonelike substances, to produce labor contractions.

prostitution The exchange of sexual services for money.

protection order A court order that prohibits a person from threatening, harassing, or hurting a victim.

psychic divorce The sixth of Paul Bohannon's six stations of divorce: after a period of mourning one separates from one's former partner emotionally and is free from his or her influence.

psychological disorders Behaviors associated with distress (pain), disability (impaired functioning), and risk of pain, death, or loss of freedom.

puberty ("*pew*-ber-tee") Period during which one develops secondary sex characteristics (such as breasts or facial hair).

public adoptions Adoptions arranged through licensed agencies that place children in adoptive families.

quasi-kin ("*kway*-zee kin") The person a former spouse marries or any in-laws, both former ones from the previous marriage and added ones from remarriage.

race Inherited physical characteristics that distinguish one group from another. Compare *ethnicity*.

random sample See *representative sample*.

random-type family Marriage/family system that focuses on the needs of individuals and tends to value freedom, intensity, and spontaneity; one of three types of marriage/family systems proposed by David Kantor and William Lehr in 1975.

rape Unwanted sexual penetration, perpetrated by force, by threat of harm, or when the victim is intoxicated or unconscious.

rapport ("rap-*pore*") **talk** Style of communication, often engaged in by women, that is aimed primarily at gaining rapport or intimacy. Contrast *report talk*.

ratio measure of divorce The ratio within a given year of the number of marriages to the number of divorces.

rationalization The assertion that the reasons for illogical behavior are "rational" and "good."

raw numbers In divorce statistics, the actual numbers of people who marry and divorce; raw numbers are not useful for generalizing about marriage and divorce because the numbers are all within the same year.

reaction formation Behavior whereby people present themselves as the opposite of what they really feel.

reactive affairs Extramarital affairs engaged in by partners, such as spouses in middle age, seeking reassurance about their youthfulness and sexuality.

reactive jealousy The type of jealousy that occurs when evidence is revealed of a partner's past, present, or anticipated relationship with another person. Compare *suspicious jealousy*.

reasoning Giving reasons in favor of this assertion or that; justifying or supporting a premise with reasons.

redivorce Divorce during second or subsequent marriages, with the median length of time for length of marriage declining in each instance.

referent power Type of power based on a person's identifying with and admiring his or her spouse and receiving satisfaction by pleasing him or her. Compare *coercive power, expert power, informational power, legitimate power, reward power*.

refined divorce rate The rate that reflects the number of divorces in a given year for every 1,000 married women over age 15.

reframing Redefining the meaning of a situation as a way of changing one's perspective on it.

regression Relapse into a more childlike or juvenile form of behavior.

rehabilitative alimony Short-term financial payments to help an ex-wife to go to school and "rehabilitate" her vocational skills.

relationship market Also called a *marriage market*; situation in which prospective partners compare the personal, social, and financial resources of eligible mates and then bargain for the best they can get.

relatives of divorce Kinship ties that were established during marriage but continue after divorce.

reliability The degree to which a measurement method produces the same results when repeated by the same or other researchers.

report talk Style of communication, often engaged in by men, used to accomplish specific purposes. Contrast *rapport talk*.

representative sample Also called *random sample*; sample in which everyone in the targeted population has the same chance of being included.

repressed anger The unconscious suppression of feelings of anger, so that they are expressed in other ways.

repression "Motivated forgetting"; the unconscious blocking of whatever is causing one stress.

rescue marriage Marriage based on a relationship centered on the idea of healing; one of four types of "good marriage" described by Judith Wallerstein and Sandra Blakeslee in 1995.

resilience The ability to recover after stress; various personal, family, and/or environmental factors compensate for increased life stresses so that expected problems do not develop.

resolution phase The fourth phase of the four-phase description, developed in 1966 by William Masters and Virginia Johnson, of how men and women respond to sex physiologically: (1) excitement, (2) plateau, (3) orgasm, and (4) resolution; in (4) the body returns to its unaroused state.

resource theory Theory of Robert Blood and Donald Wolfe (1960) that suggests that the balance of power in a marriage reflects the relative resources of each spouse.

reward power Type of power based on a person's belief that an agreement with his or her partner will elicit rewards from that partner. Compare *coercive power, expert power, legitimate power, referent power, informational power*.

rite of passage An event signaling a major change from one social status to another.

role Pattern of behaviors expected of a person occupying a certain social position within a certain group or culture; the behavior expected of someone who holds a particular status.

role ambiguity Situation in which role expectations are unknown.

role compartmentalization The separation of one's various roles within the mind so that the worries associated with one role (such as work) don't disturb one's feelings and performance in another role (such as home).

role conflict Situation that occurs when the expectations of two or more roles are incompatible.

role overload Situation in which others' expectations exceeds one's ability to meet them.

romantic love An intense, passionate love in which a person believes that there is love at first sight, that there is only one true love, and that love conquers all. Compare *companionate love*.

romantic marriage Marriage based on a passionate and lasting sexual relationship; one of four types of "good marriage" described by Judith Wallerstein and Sandra Blakeslee in 1995.

RU-486 (mifepristone, Mifeprex) Emergency contraception; synthetic steroid referred to as the abortion pill. If taken within 7 weeks of pregnancy, it acts to prevent the cells of the uterine lining from getting the progesterone they need to support implantation of a fertilized egg.

sadomasochism Also called *BDSM (bondage/discipline-dominance/submission-sadism/masochism)*; behavior that involves deriving sexual pleasure from inflicting or receiving pain.

safe haven laws Also called *abandoned baby laws*; laws in 42 states that allow a person—anonymously and without fear of prosecution—to leave an unwanted newborn at a hospital emergency room, fire station, or other designated place.

saline induction method Induced abortion method used during weeks 16 to 20 of pregnancy whereby a physician instills a saline (salt) solution by needle through the abdominal wall and into the amniotic sac surrounding the fetus. This induces the uterus to contract and thus simulate labor, which results in the expulsion of the fetus within 24 hours.

sample The small group of the population to be studied.

sandwich generation Middle-aged parents who are "sandwiched" between taking care of their children and also of their own aging parents.

satiation ("say-she-ay-shen") Situation in which a stimulus no longer stimulates because of repeated exposure.

scapegoating The blaming of one particular family member for nearly everything that goes wrong in that family.

second shift The housework and child care that employed women do after returning home from their jobs.

secondary analysis The analysis of data collected by other researchers.

second-parent adoption Also known as *co-parent adoption*; situation in which the gay or lesbian partner of a biological or adoptive parent is given full legal status as the child's second parent.

self-disclosure Telling another person deep personal information and feelings about oneself.

semi-open adoptions Adoptions in which the biological and the adoptive parents exchange information such as photographs or letters but don't otherwise communicate.

separation Cessation of cohabitation; the state in which married partners no longer live together.

separation distress Term given to the psychological state following separation, which may feature feelings of depression, loss, and anxiety, as well as intense loneliness.

serial marriage Also called *serial monogamy*, participation in a sequence of marital partnerships, one at a time.

serial monogamy See *serial marriage*.

sex The biological characteristics with which one is born that determine whether one is male or female.

sex ratio Ratio of men to women within a particular social group.

sex role The behavior defined by biological constraints.

sexism Unjust discrimination based on a person's sex or the belief that one sex is innately superior to the other.

sexual abuse Manipulated or coerced sexual behavior of a minor by an adult.

sexual addiction Also called *compulsive sexual behavior (CSB)*; an intense preoccupation with sex. It makes having a satisfying sexual relationship with just one lover difficult.

sexual assault Legal term for rape.

sexual exclusivity Situation in which each partner promises to have sexual relations only with the other partner.

sexual fantasy Any mental representation of any kind of sexual activity.

sexual harassment The abuse of one's position of authority to force unwanted sexual attention on another person.

sexual intercourse Generally means coitus, penetration of the vagina by the penis.

sexual orientation Sexual inclinations—feelings and sexual interactions—whether for the opposite gender, same gender, or both.

sexual response A four-phase description, developed in 1966 by William Masters and Virginia Johnson, of how men and women respond to sex physiologically: (1) excitement, (2) plateau, (3) orgasm, and (4) resolution.

sexual script The set of expectations of how one is to behave sexually.

sexual values Deeply held beliefs and attitudes about what is right and wrong, desirable and undesirable sexual behavior.

sexuality The state of being sexual; encompasses not only the biological aspects of sex but psychological, social, and cultural aspects as well.

sexually transmitted diseases (STDs) Infectious diseases that are transmitted as a result (usually) of sexual contact. They include hepatitis B, herpes, human papilloma virus, chlamydia, gonorrhea, syphilis, and parasitic infections.

silent treatment A version of passive-aggression in which one either ignores one's partner or says things are all right while sending nonverbal signals that they are not.

single Among heterosexuals, the never-married, the widowed, or the divorced.

single remarriages Marriages in which only one of the partners was previously married.

six stations (processes) of divorce According to Paul Bohannon's psychological model: emotional, legal, economic, co-parental, community, and psychic divorce.

slippery slope Argumentation fallacy whereby one fails to see that the first step in a possible series of steps does not lead inevitably to subsequent ones.

social exchange perspective Sociological approach that proposes that people's interactions represent the efforts of each person to maximize his or her benefits and minimize costs.

social integration The degree of cohesion and strength of social bonds that people have with one another and with their community.

social learning theory The field of study of gender differences that suggests that we learn attitudes and behaviors through our interaction with the environment.

social networking websites Online communities of Internet users who share a common bond; examples are MySpace and Facebook.

socialist feminism Movement that advocates government support for parental leave and child care to enable women to achieve a better quality of life.

socialization Process by which people learn the characteristics of their group—the attitudes, values, and actions thought appropriate for them, to their society and culture; also the process by which people learn the skills needed to survive as individuals and as members of society.

sociobiology The field of study of gender differences that suggests that our social behavior—and gender behavior—results from biological differences.

sole custody Situation in which the children live with one parent, who is solely responsible for raising them, and the other parent has legally specified visitation rights.

soul mate A person who is temperamentally suited to another—one's best friend, confidant, and romantic partner.

spanking Hitting a child, usually on the buttocks, with an open hand without causing physical injury.

sperm bank A depository for storing sperm.

sperm donor A male who makes his sperm available for artificial insemination.

spermicide ("sperm-uh-side") Sperm-killing chemical, often used with a diaphragm.

spillover The effect of participation in one of life's domains (such as work) on other domains (such as family).

split custody Custody arrangement whereby the children are divided between the two parents.

spontaneous abortion Also called *miscarriage*; spontaneous loss or the embryo/fetus that occurs within the first 20 weeks of pregnancy.

spousal entitlement An alternative to alimony in which a non-working spouse receives a kind of severance pay for her or his "investment" in the marriage—for helping the income earner's career during the marriage.

spousal support Also called *spousal maintenance* (now usually preferred to alimony); court-ordered financial support payments by a spouse or a former spouse to the other person following separation or divorce.

stalking Maliciously following, pursuing, and/or harassing another person.

static marriages Marriages that don't change over time, don't allow for changes in the spouses, and rely on the fact of the legal marriage bond to enforce sexual exclusivity and permanence. Compare *flexible marriages*.

status The social ranking or the prestige attached to a particular position in society.

stay-at-home dad See *househusband*.

stepfamily See *blended family*.

stepism The attitude of prejudice and discrimination that assumes that stepfamilies are inferior to biological families.

stepmother trap Two conflicting societal views that can "trap" a stepmother; a stepmother is, on the one hand, expected to be unnaturally loving toward her stepchildren and yet she is, on the other hand, viewed as being mean, abusive, and vain.

sterility The total inability to conceive.

sterilization The surgical or nonsurgical interruption of a person's reproductive capacity—generally for people who want a permanent method of birth control.

stillbirth Birth of a dead fetus.

stonewalling The behavior of refusing to listen to one's partner, particularly his or her complaints.

storge ("*stor*-gay") According to sociologist John Alan Lee's theory of the origin of love, one of six basic styles of loving: an affectionate, peaceful, companionate style of loving, also referred to as companionate love.

stratified random sample Sample of specific subgroups of the targeted population in which everyone in the subgroups has an equal chance of being included in the study.

straw man argument Argumentation fallacy whereby one misrepresents one's opponent's position to make it easier to attack or attacks a weaker position while ignoring a stronger one.

stress The reaction of one's body to an unusual or substantial demand made on it.

stressor overload The situation in which unrelated but unrelenting small stressors produce a breakdown in a person or family's morale.

stressors Precipitating events that cause stress.

structural-functional perspective Sociological approach that views the family as a social institution that performs essential functions for society in order to ensure its stability.

study method Consists of clinical practitioners working one on one with individuals or families using interviews, direct observation, and analysis of records.

sublimation ("sub-lih-*may*-shen") Socially constructive behavior that is formed in order to disguise unacceptable behavior.

substance abuse See *drug abuse*.

sudden infant death syndrome (SIDS) Also called *crib death*; event in which an apparently healthy infant dies suddenly—and inexplicably—while sleeping.

supervised visitation A way to alleviate tensions surrounding custody and visitation; the noncustodial parent is allowed to visit his or her child only with a third party present, such as a court employee or a social worker.

surrogate ("*sir*-eh-get") **mother** A consenting woman who is legally contracted to be artificially inseminated with the sperm of the male partner of an infertile woman. For a fee (usually), the surrogate mother carries the child through pregnancy and gives the newborn to the couple with whom she contracted.

survey research Research that uses questionnaires or interviews to collect data from small representative groups (samples), which are then used to generalize conclusions valid for larger groups (populations).

suspicious jealousy The type of jealousy that occurs when there is no evidence, or only ambiguous evidence, for suspecting a partner is involved with someone else. Compare *reactive jealousy*.

swinging Arrangement in which committed couples exchange partners in order to engage in purely recreational sex.

symbolic interaction perspective Sociological approach that focuses on internal family interactions, the ongoing action and the response of family members to one another. In this perspective, a family is not considered to be a standard structure (as it is in structural functionalism) but rather the creation of its members.

symptom-thermal method (of periodic abstinence) Combines all three methods of natural family-planning method—calendar, BBT, and cervical mucus.

teacher-counselor parenting style Parenting style in which parents are intensely focused on guiding their children's behavior.

telecommuting Working at home while in telecommunication contact—by Internet, phone, and fax—with the office.

theory A perspective or a set of statements that explains why processes and events occur.

third-party custody Custody arrangement whereby the children live with someone other than a parent.

Thomas theorem Statement by William I. Thomas, a sociologist who represented the symbolic interaction perspective: "If people define situations as real, they are real in their consequences."

total marriage Marriage in which the partners are intensely bound together psychologically and participate in each other's lives in all, not just some, areas and have very few areas of tension or conflict.

traditional family Family in which the man's role is primarily husband, father, and income earner, and the woman's role is wife, mother, and homemaker.

traditional marriage Marriage in which the husband is the income earner, and the wife takes care of the home and the children; one of four types of "good marriage" described by Judith Wallerstein and Sandra Blakeslee in 1995.

transgenderist A person with the biological sex of one gender who has the identity of the other gender and lives the full-time life of that gender but does not undergo medical procedures to change to that gender.

transnational marriages Marriages in which one partner is in the United States and the other—and perhaps the children—are in another country.

transsexual A person with the biological sex of one gender who has the identity or self-concept of the other gender and undergoes medical procedures to change to that gender.

transvestite A cross-dresser, usually a male, who dresses provocatively in order to appeal to men.

triangular theory A theory of the origin of love that emphasizes three important elements of love, which interact with one another: intimacy, passion, and decision/commitment.

tubal ligation Also called *tying the tubes*; sterilization procedure that blocks or cuts the fallopian tubes to prevent passage of the eggs down to the uterus where they might be fertilized.

tubal sterilization Sterilization procedure whereby the fallopian tubes are interrupted surgically—cut and tied or blocked. This prevents passage of the eggs to the uterus.

two-person single career Traditional family form in which the husband works outside the home and the wife—even if she is also employed—helps the husband's career by being responsible for domestic tasks and child rearing.

U-curve Graphic representation of variations in marital satisfaction according to stages of family life cycle.

uncoupling Going through the series of stages by which partners—whether married or cohabiting, heterosexual or homosexual—move toward ending their relationship.

underemployed workers People holding jobs below their level of qualification or are working part-time but wanting to work full-time.

unemployed workers People seeking work who are new to the labor force or have been laid off (temporarily dismissed), downsized (permanently dismissed), or fired (dismissed for cause, such as absenteeism).

unrequited love Love that is not returned, not reciprocated.

utilitarian marriage A marriage based on convenience.

vacuum aspiration The most common form of induced abortion; performed in the first 12 weeks of pregnancy; after the cervix is numbed with a local anesthetic, the cervix is dilated—that is, gradually expanded. A small, plastic tube is then inserted through the woman's cervix into the uterus. The tube is attached to a suction pump, and the contents of the uterus are then drawn out into the vacuum system.

vaginal ring (NuvaRing) Hormonal form of birth control for females in the shape of a ring that is placed inside the vagina and that releases progestin and estrogen.

vaginismus ("vaj-in-*is*-mus") Involuntary spasms of the muscles surrounding the lower third of the vagina.

validity The degree to which a measurement method actually measures what it claims to measure and is free of bias.

values Deeply held beliefs and attitudes about what is right and wrong, desirable and undesirable; principles and qualities thought to be of high worth, to be extremely valuable.

variable Factor that can be varied or manipulated in an experiment.

vasectomy ("vah-*sek*-toh-me") Sterilization procedure for males; surgical procedure that involves making a pair of incisions in the scrotum and cutting and tying the two sperm-carrying vas deferens tubes.

video dating service Dating service that allows one to watch videotapes of others talking and in various activities in return for allowing others to watch one's own tape.

violence The threat of or infliction of physical or emotional harm on a person.

virtual visitation The use of such online tools as videoconferencing, webcams, and other wired technologies with which a noncustodial divorced parent can visit his or her child.

visitation schedules The days and times on which the noncustodial parent is allowed to visit the children.

vital marriage Marriage in which the partners are intensely bound together psychologically and participate in many areas of each other's lives.

voice response Valuing the relationship and being invested in it but feeling that it has problems that need to be discussed.

voluntary stable singles People who are satisfied not to be married. Compare *involuntary temporary singles, involuntary stable singles, voluntary temporary singles.*

voluntary temporary singles People who are open to marriage but for whom seeking a mate is a lower priority than are other activities, such as gaining an education, starting a career, or self-development. Compare *involuntary temporary singles, involuntary stable singles, voluntary stable singles.*

vow renewals Ceremonies in which partners repeat their commitment to each other.

voyeurism ("*voy*-yur-izm") Behavior in which one becomes sexually aroused by looking at people, often strangers, undressing or having sex.

vulnerability Psychological or environmental difficulties that make children more at risk for developing later personality, behavioral, or social problems.

wealth Also called *net worth;* the monetary value of everything one owns—such as property, stocks, and insurance—minus debts.

Web 2.0 Name for new part of World Wide Web that includes communication tools, social networking websites, and wikis—websites that allow visitors to edit content.

welfare Government aid to those who can't support themselves.

wheel theory A theory of the origin of love; it suggests that love develops and is maintained through four stages: (1) rapport, (2) self-revelation, (3) mutual dependency, and (4) intimacy need fulfillment.

widow Wife who outlives her husband.

widower Husband who outlives his wife.

withdrawal Also called *coitus interruptus;* birth control method that involves removing the penis from the vagina before ejaculation.

women's safe house A place whose location is known only to residents and shelter workers; a private home that provides temporary housing for abused women.

women's shelter Also called *victim shelter;* provides not only food and accommodation but also other help such as money, food stamps, counseling, and legal, medical, and employment assistance.

ZIFT (zygote intrafallopian transfer) Fertilization procedure whereby the mother's egg and the father's sperm are collected and placed in a laboratory dish. Then, 1 day after fertilization takes place, the zygote is placed in the woman's fallopian tubes.

zygote Cell formed by the union of two gametes before it splits and then continues to subdivide.

References

CHAPTER 1

Allen, K., J. Blascovich, and W.B. Mendes. 2002. Cardiovascular reactivity and the presence of pets, friends, and spouses: The truth about cats and dogs. *Psychosomatic Medicine* 64:727–39.

Baker, D., and C. Stauth. 2002. *What happy people know: How the new science of happiness can change your life for the better.* Emmaus, PA: Rodale Press.

Barnes, J.S., and C.E. Bennett. 2002. The Asian population: 2000. *Census 2000 Brief.* C2KBR/01-16. U.S. Census Bureau, February. Washington, DC: U.S. Government Printing Office, www.census.gov/prod/2002pubs/c2kbr01-16.pdf (accessed May 13, 2007).

Barringer, F. 1991. Immigration brings new diversity Asian population in the U.S. *New York Times,* June 12, A1, D25.

Biddle, B.J. 1979. *Role theory: Expectations, identities, and behaviors.* Chicago: Dryden Press.

Brickman, P., and D.T. Campbell. 1971. Hedonic relativism and planning the good society. In *Adaptation-level theory: A symposium.* Edited by M.H. Apley. New York: Academic Press, 287–302.

Brittingham, A., and G.P. de la Cruz. 2004. Ancestry: 2000. *Census 2000 Brief.* C2KBR-35. U.S. Census Bureau, June. Washington, DC: U.S. Government Printing Office, www.census.gov/prod/2004pubs/c2kbr-35.pdf (accessed May 13, 2007).

Brown, P. 1995. *The death of intimacy.* New York: Haworth Press.

Christensen, K., A.M. Herskind, and J.W. Vaupel. 2006. Why Danes are smug: Comparative study of life satisfaction in the European Union. *British Medical Journal* 333:1289–91.

Clark, J. 2003. Animal lovers are 'ruffing it' at upscale lodgings. *USA Today,* February 27, 6D.

Clements, J. 2006. Money and happiness: Here's why you won't laugh all the way to the bank. *The Wall Street Journal,* August 16, D1.

Cole, D. 2007. Divorceproof your marriage. *U.S. News & World Report,* January 1, 72.

Corliss, R. 2003. Is there a formula for joy? *Time,* January 20, 72–74.

Cowley, G. 2002. The science of happiness. *Newsweek,* September 16, 46–48.

Crook, J.H., and S.J. Crook. 1988. Tibetan polyandry: Problems of adaptation and fitness. In *Human reproductive behavior: A Darwinian perspective.* Edited by L. Betzig, M.B. Bulder, and P. Turke. Cambridge: Cambridge University Press, 97–114.

Csikszentmihalyi, M. 1990. *Flow: The psychology of optimal experience.* New York: Harper & Row.

Davidson, R.J., and A. Harrington, eds. 2002. *Visions of compassion: Western scientists and Tibetan Buddhists examine human nature.* New York: Oxford University Press.

Davidson, R.J., H.H. Goldsmith, and K. Scherer, eds. 2003. *Handbook of affective science.* New York: Oxford University Press.

Day, J.C. 2001. National population projections, U.S. Census Bureau, Population Division and Housing and Household Economics Statistics Division, last revised January 18, 2001, www.census.gov/population/www/pop-profile/natproj.html (accessed May 11, 2007).

DeNavas-Walt, C., B.D. Proctor, and C.H. Lee. 2006. *Income, poverty, and insurance coverage in the United States: 2005.* U.S. Census Bureau, Current Population Reports, P60-231. Washington, DC: U.S. Government Printing Office.

Diener, E., and S. Oishi. 2000. Money and happiness: Income and subjective well-being across nations. In *Culture and subjective well-being.* Edited by E. Diener and E.M. Suh. Cambridge, MA: MIT Press, 185–218.

The Donald Richard Gavagan Fund and Project Kids Worldwide. 2003. www.mpfoundation.org.

Drucker, P. 1993. *Post-capitalist society.* New York: Harper-Collins.

Edwards, J.N. 1991. New conceptions: Biosocial innovations and the family. *Journal of Marriage and the Family* 53:349–60.

Elias, M. 2002a. What makes people happy: Psychologists now know. *USA Today,* December 9, 1A–2A.

Elias, M. 2002b. Families provide antidote to unhappiness. *USA Today,* December 9, 11D.

Elias, M. 2002c. Ask 'Dr. Happiness.' *USA Today,* December 9, 11D.

Fields, J. 2004. *America's families and living arrangements: 2003.* U.S. Census Bureau, Current Population Reports, P20-553. Washington, DC: U.S. Government Printing Office, www.census.gov/prod/2004pubs/p20-553.pdf (accessed May 13, 2007).

Finn, J. 2004. Man's best friend becoming travelers' favorite perk: More hotels, shelters offer "loaner" dogs. *San Francisco Chronicle,* October 17, D9.

Gerstel, N., and N. Sarkisian. 2007. Marriage reduces social ties. Discussion paper for Council on Contemporary Families, January 2, www.contemporaryfamilies.org/subtemplate.php?t=briefingPapers&ext=socialties (accessed May 17, 2007).

Giddens, A. 2003. The global revolution in family and personal life. In *Family in transition.* Edited by A.S. Skolnick and J.H. Skolnick. Boston: Allyn & Bacon, 17–23.

Gilbert, D. 2006. *Stumbling on happiness.* New York: Alfred A. Knopf.

Gilbert, D.T., and J.E.J. Ebert. 2002. Decisions and revisions: The affective forecasting of changeable outcomes. *Journal of Personality and Social Psychology* 82:503–14.

Goode, W., ed. 1982. *The family.* 2nd ed. Englewood Cliffs, NJ: Prentice-Hall.

Gottman, J., J.S. Gottman, and J. DeClaire. 2006. *Ten lessons to transform your marriage: America's Love Lab experts share their strategies for strengthening your relationship.* New York: Crown.

Hamilton, B.E., J.A. Martin, and S.J. Ventura. 2006. *Births: Preliminary data for 2005.* Health E-Stats. Released November 21. Hyattsville, MD: National Center for Health Statistics, www.cdc.gov/nchs/products/pubs/pubd/hestats/prelimbirths05/prelimbirths05.htm (accessed May 13, 2007).

Harper, J. 2001. Road worriers: Tourists concerns while traveling. *Insight on the News,* October 1, www.findarticles.com/p/articles/mi_m1571/is_37_17/ai_79051724 (accessed May 11, 2007).

Hawkley, L.C., C.M. Masi, J.D. Berry, and J.T. Cacioppo. 2006. Loneliness is a unique predictor of age-related differences in systolic blood pressure. *Psychology and Aging* 21(1):152–64.

Hewlett, S.A. 1992. *When the bough breaks: The cost of neglecting our children.* New York: HarperCollins.

Inglehart, R., M. Basáñez, J. Díez-Medrano, L. Halmann, and R. Luijkx, eds. 2004. *Human beliefs and values. A cross-cultural sourcebook based on the 1999–2002 values surveys.* Coyoacan (Mexico City): Siglo veintiuno editores.

Ishii-Kuntz, M. 1997. Japanese American families. In *Families in cultural context.* Edited by M.K. DeGenova. Mountain View, CA: Mayfield.

Kahneman, D., A.B. Krueger, D. Schkade, N. Schwartz, and A.A. Stone. 2006. Would you be happier if you were richer? A focusing illusion. *Science* 312:1908–10.

Kahneman, D., A.B. Krueger, D.A. Schkade, N. Schwartz, and A.A. Stone. 2004. A survey method for characterizing daily life experience: The Day Reconstruction Method. *Science* 306:1776–80.

Kahneman, D., and A.B. Krueger. 2006. Developments in the measurement of subjective well-being. *Journal of Economic Perspectives* 20(1):3–24.

Kieffer, C. 1977. New depths in intimacy. In

Marriages and alternatives: Exploring intimate relationships. Edited by R. Libby and R. Whitehurst. Glenview, IL: Scott, Foresman, 267–93.

Kitano, K., and H. Kitano. 1998. The Japanese-American family. In *Ethnic families in America: Patterns and variations,* 4th ed. Edited by C. Mindel, R. Habenstein, and R. Wright, Jr. Upper Saddle River, NJ: Prentice-Hall, 311–30.

Kleiman, C. 1995. Global knowledge helps in making career decisions. *San Jose Mercury News,* September 24, 1PC.

Kochakian, M.J. 1992. Study finds many marriages unhappy. *San Francisco Chronicle,* October 27, D3; reprinted from *Hartford Courant.*

Kotchemidova, C. 2005. From good cheer to "drive-by smiling": A social history of cheerfulness. *Journal of Social History* 39(1):5–38.

Kreider, R.M., and J. Fields. 2005. *Living arrangements of children: 2001.* U.S. Census Bureau, Current Population Reports, P70-104. Washington, DC: U.S. Government Printing Office, www.census.gov/prod/2005pubs/p70-104.pdf (accessed May 13, 2007).

Ladbrook, D. 2000. *Relationship quality and the future of death.* Talk given at the Building Family Strengths International Symposium. University of Nebraska, Lincoln, May 10–12.

Lavee, Y., and D.H. Olson. 1992. Seven types of marriage: An empirical typology based on ENRICH. *Journal of Family Psychology* 6(1):10–21.

Levine, R., S. Sato, T. Hashimoto, and J. Verma. 1995. Love and marriage in eleven cultures. *Journal of Cross-Cultural Psychology* 26:554–71.

Lieberson, S., and M. Waters. 1988. *From many strands: Ethnic and racial groups in contemporary America.* New York: Russell Sage Foundation.

Lin, C.C., and V.R. Fu. 1990. A comparison of child-rearing practices among Chinese, immigrant Chinese, and Caucasian-American parents. *Child Development* 61:429–33.

Lucas, R.E., A.E. Clark, Y. Georgellis, and E. Diener. 2004. Unemployment alters the set point for life satisfaction. *Psychological Science,* 15(1):8–13.

Lyubomirsky, S., K.M. Sheldon, and D. Schkade. 2005. Pursuing happiness: The architecture of sustainable change. *Review of General Psychology* 9(2):111–32.

Malone, M.S. 1995. The tiniest transformer. *San Jose Mercury News,* September 10, 1D, 2D.

Marin, G., and B.V. Marin. 1991. *Research with Hispanic populations.* Thousand Oaks, CA: Sage.

Marriage today. 2007. Fact Monster, January 11. © 2000–2006 Pearson Education, publishing as Fact Monster, www.factmonster.com/ipka/A0767670.html (accessed May 11, 2007).

Max, D.T. 2007. Happiness 101. *New York Times Magazine,* January 7, 46–51.

McLuhan, M. 1951. *The mechanical bride: Folklore of industrial man.* New York: Vanguard Press.

McLuhan, M. 1960. *Explorations in communication: An anthology.* Boston: Beacon Press.

McLuhan, M. 1964. *Understanding media: The extensions of man.* New York: McGraw-Hill.

McLuhan, M., and Q. Fiore. 1967. *The medium is the message.* New York: Bantam Books/Random House.

Murdock, G. 1949. *Social structure.* New York: Macmillan.

Myers, D.G. 1992. *The pursuit of happiness: Who is happy—and why.* New York: William Morrow.

National Center for Health Statistics. 2005. *Child health USA 2005.* Centers for Disease Control, http://mchb.hrsa.gov/mchirc/chusa_05/pages/pdf/c05pc.pdf (accessed May 13, 2007).

Nettle, D. 2005. *Happiness: The science behind your smile.* New York: Oxford University Press.

Olson, D.H. 2000. *Empowering couples: Building on your strengths.* Life Innovations. www.lifeinnovations.com.

Peterson, C., and M.E.P. Seligman. 2004. *Character strengths and virtues: A handbook and classification.* New York: Oxford University Press.

Pew Research Center. 2006a. *Are we happy yet?* February 13, http://pewresearch.org/assets/social/pdf/AreWeHappyYet.pdf (accessed May 10, 2007).

Pew Research Center. 2006b. *Gauging family intimacy,* March 7, http://pewresearch.org/social/pack.php?PackID=3 (accessed May 11, 2007).

Platoni, K. 2006. Joy to the world. *Stanford Magazine,* September/October, 33–35.

Pryor, F.L. 2002. *The future of U.S. capitalism.* Cambridge: Cambridge University Press.

Rabin, R. 2007. Screen all pregnancies for Down syndrome, doctors say. *The New York Times,* January 9, D5.

Revkin, A.C. 2005. A new measure of well-being from a happy little kingdom. *The New York Times,* October 4, D1, D6.

Rivenburg, R. 2003. Boredom: Can it be (yawn) destructive? *Reno Gazette-Journal,* March 1, 1D, 4D; reprinted from *Los Angeles Times.*

Ryan, J. 2003. Child prostitute—criminal or victim? *San Francisco Chronicle,* March 2, D4.

Sapolsky, R.M. 2003. 'Pseudokinship' and real war. *San Francisco Chronicle,* March 2, D3.

Savage, H., and P. Fronczek. 1993. *Who can afford to buy a house in 1991?* U.S. Census Bureau, Housing and Household Economic Statistics Division. Washington, DC: U.S. Government Printing Office.

Schkade, D.A., and D. Kahneman. 1998. Does living in California make people happy? A focusing illusion in judgments of life satisfaction. *Psychological Science* 9:340–46.

Seligman, M. 2002a. *Authentic happiness: Using the new positive psychology to realize your potential for lasting fulfillment.* New York: Free Press.

Seligman, M. 2002b. How to see the glass half full. *Newsweek,* September 16, 48–49.

Solnick, J., and D. Hemenway. 1998. Is more always better? A survey on positional concerns. *Journal of Economic Behavior and Organization* 37(3):373–83.

Spencer, J. 2003. How much is your time worth? *The Wall Street Journal,* February 26, D1, D2.

Stacey, J. 1996. *In the name of the family: Rethinking family values in the postmodern age.* Boston: Beacon Press.

Stallones, L., M.B. Marx, T.F. Garrity, and T.P. Johnson. 1990. Pet ownership and attachment in relation to the health of U.S. adults, 21 to 64 years of age. *Anthozoos* 4(2):100–12.

Stossel, S. 2006. The joy of delusion. *The New York Times Book Review,* May 7, 16.

U.S. Census Bureau. 2000. *Statistical abstract of the United States.* Washington, DC: U.S. Government Printing Office, www.census.gov/prod/www/statistical-abstract-1995_2000.html (accessed May 13, 2007).

U.S. Census Bureau. 2001. *America's families and living arrangements 2000.* Washington, DC: U.S. Government Printing Office.

U.S. Census Bureau. 2006a. *Current Population Survey, March and Annual Social and Economic Supplements, 2005 and earlier.* Washington, DC: U.S. Government Printing Office, www.census.gov/population/socdemo/hh-fam/ms2.pdf (accessed May 13, 2007).

U.S. Census Bureau. 2006b. *Statistical abstract of the United States.* Washington, DC: U.S. Government Printing Office, www.census.gov/prod/2006pubs/07statab/pop.pdf (accessed May 13, 2007).

U.S. Department of Labor. 2005a. Tomorrow's jobs. *Occupational outlook handbook.* Washington, DC: Bureau of Labor Statistics, www.bls.gov/oco/oco2003.htm, last updated December 20, 2005 (accessed May 11, 2007).

U.S. Department of Labor. 2005b. *Women in the labor force: A databook.* Report 985, May 2005. Washington, DC: Bureau of Labor Statistics, www.bls.gov/cps/wlf-databook-2005.pdf (accessed May 16, 2007).

Veenhoven, R. 2007. *Average happiness in 95 nations 1995–2005,* World Database of Happiness, RankReport 2006, http://worlddatabaseofhappiness.eur.nl/hap_nat/nat_fp.htm (accessed May 11, 2007).

Wagner, C.G. 2006. The well-being of nations. *The Futurist,* November/December, 12.

Waite, L.J. 2005. Marriage and family. In *Handbook of Population.* Edited by D. Poston and M. Micklin. New York: Kluwer Academic/Plenum, 87–108.

Waite, L.J., and M. Gallagher. 2000. *The case for marriage: Why married people are happier, healthier, and better off financially.* New York: Doubleday, Chapter 12.

Ward, G.C., R. Burns, and K. Burns. 1990. *The Civil War: An illustrated history.* New York: Knopf.

White, A.G. 2007. *A global projection of subjective well-being: A challenge to positive psychology?* University of Leicester, School of Psychology, www.le.ac.uk/pc/aw57/world/sample.html (accessed May 11, 2007).

Wilson, A. 2007. What is social networking? *Social Networking,* http://socialnetworking.knowhow-now.com/blog/ (accessed May 11, 2007).

Wilson, C. 2004. How much would make you smile? *USA Today*, December 27, 1D, 2D.

Wilson, T.D., J. Meyers, and D.T. Gilbert. 2001. Lessons from the past: Do people learn from experience that emotional reactions are short lived? *Personality and Social Psychology Bulletin* 27:1648–61.

Wu, L.L. 1996. Effects of family instability, income, and income instability on the risk of a premarital birth. *American Sociological Review* 61:386–406.

Zaretsky, E. 1996. *Capitalism, the family, and personal life*. New York: Harper & Row.

Zuckoff, M. 2002. *Choosing Naia: A family's journey*. Boston: Beacon Press.

CHAPTER 2

Alcock, J. 1995. The belief engine. *Skeptical Inquirer*, May/June, www.csicop.org/si/9505/belif.html (accessed May 17, 2007).

Alvarez, L. 2006. A growing stream of illegal immigrants choose to remain despite the risks. *The New York Times*, December 20, A20.

American Academy of Pediatrics. 2006. Policy statement: Children, adolescents, and advertising. *Pediatrics* 118(6):2563–69.

Baca Zinn, M., and B. Wells. 1999. Diversity within Latino families: New lessons for family social science. In *The handbook of family diversity*. Edited by D.H. Demo, K.R. Allan, and M.A. Fine. New York: Oxford University Press, 389–414.

Ball, D. 2007. As vodka sales skyrocket, many newcomers pour in. *The Wall Street Journal*, January 26, A1, A8.

Begley, S. 2006. Critical thinking: Part skill, part mindset and totally up to you. *The Wall Street Journal*, October 20, B1.

Bengtson, V.L., T.J. Biblarz, and R.E.L. Roberts. 2002. *How families still matter: A longitudinal study of youth in two generations*. Cambridge: Cambridge University Press.

Blair, S.L., and Z. Qian. 1998. Family and Asian students' educational performance. *Journal of Family Issues* 19:355–74.

Blassingame, J.W. 1979. *The slave community: Plantation life in the antebellum South*, rev. ed. New York: Oxford University Press.

Blau, P.M. 1964. *Exchange and power in social life*. New York: Wiley.

Blumer, H.G. 1969. The methodological position of symbolic interaction. In *Symbolic interactionism: Perspective and method*. Englewood Cliffs, NJ: Prentice-Hall.

Brofenbrenner, U. 1979. *The ecology of human development: Experiment by nature and design*. Cambridge, MA: Harvard University Press.

Bubolz, M.M., and M.S. Sontag. 1993. Human ecology theory. In *Sourcebook of family theories and methods: A contextual approach*. Edited by P.G. Boss, W.J. Dohert, R. LaRossa, W.R. Schumm, and S.K. Steinmetz. New York: Plenum, 419–48.

Camarillo, A. 1979. *Chicanos in a changing society: From Mexican pueblos to American barrios in Santa Barbara and Southern California, 1848–1930*. Cambridge, MA: Harvard University Press.

Carey, B. 2007. Do you believe in magic? *The New York Times*, January 23, D1, D6.

Christakis, D.A., F.J. Zimmerman, D.L. DiGiuseppe, and C.A. McCarty. 2004. Early television exposure and subsequent attentional problems in children. *Pediatrics* 113:708–13.

Collins, L.V. 1997. Facts for Asian and Pacific Islander American Heritage Month. *Census Bureau Fact Sheet*. Washington, DC: U.S. Bureau of the Census.

Cooley, C.H. 1909. *Social organization*. New York: Scribner's.

Coontz, S. 1992. *The way we never were: American families and the nostalgia trap*. New York: Basic Books.

Coontz, S. 1997. *The way we really are: Coming to terms with America's changing families*. New York: Basic Books.

Coontz, S. 2005. *Marriage, a history: From obedience to intimacy, or How love conquered marriage*. New York: Viking.

Curiel, J. 2001. Love and marriage. *San Francisco Chronicle*, June 10, C7, C8.

Day, R.D. 1995. Family-systems theory. In *Research and theory in family science*. Edited by R.E. Day, K.R. Gilbert, B.H. Settles, and W.R. Burr. Pacific Grove, CA: Brooks/Cole, 91–101.

De Vaus, D. 2002. Marriage and mental health: Does marriage improve the mental health of men at the expense of women? *Family Matters*, no. 62 (Winter):26–32.

Demos, J. 1970. *A little commonwealth: Family life in Plymouth colony*. New York: Oxford University Press.

Duvall, E. 1957. *Family development*. Philadelphia, PA: Lippincott.

Duvall, E.M., and B.C. Miller. 1985. *Marriage and family development*. 6th ed. Boston: Allyn & Bacon.

Escobar, G. 2006. The complex tapestry of the undocumented. Pew Hispanic Center, March 28, http://pewresearch.org/pubs/14/the-complex-tapestry-of-the-undocumented (accessed May 17, 2007).

Filene, P. 1986. *Him/Her/Self sex roles in modern America*, 2nd ed. Baltimore: Johns Hopkins University Press.

Frey, W.H. 2003. Married with children. *American Demographics*, March 1, 17–19.

Gamboa, S. 2006. Illegal immigrants estimated at 11 million. *San Francisco Chronicle*, August 19, A5.

Ganong, L., M. Coleman, and M. Fine. 1995. Remarriage and stepfamilies. In *Research and theory in family science*. Edited by R.D. Day, K.R. Gilbert, B.H. Settles, and W.R. Burr. Pacific Grove, CA: Brooks/Cole, 287–303.

Genovese, E.D. 1981. Husbands and fathers, wives and mothers, during slavery. In *Family life in America: 1620–2000*. Edited by M. Albin and D. Cavallo. St. James, NY: Revisionary Press, 237–51.

Goode, E. 2003. Babies pick up emotional clues from TV, experts find. *New York Times*, January 21, D5.

Goode, W.J., ed. 1982. *The family*. 2nd ed. Englewood Cliffs, NJ: Prentice-Hall.

Gordon, L. 1988. *Heroes of their own lives: The politics and history of family violence*. New York: Viking.

Griswold del Castillo, R. 1984. *La familia*. Notre Dame, IN: University of Notre Dame Press.

Gutman, H. 1976. *The black family in slavery and freedom, 1750–1925*. New York: Pantheon.

Gutman, H. 1983. Persistent myths about the AfroAmerican family. In *The American family in social-historical perspective*, 3rd ed. Edited by M. Gordon. New York: St. Martin's, 459–81.

Hamilton, B. 1996. Ethnicity and the family life cycle: The Chinese-American family. *Family Therapy* 23:199–212.

Harari, S.E., and M.A. Vinovskis. 1993. Adolescent sexuality, pregnancy, and childbearing in the past. In *The politics of pregnancy: Adolescent sexuality and public policy*. Edited by A. Lawson and D. I. Rhode. New Haven, CT: Yale University Press, 23–45.

Hilts, P.J. 1997. A scholar of the absent mind. *New York Times*, September 23, B9, B13.

Hogan, D.P. and N.M. Astone. 1986. The transition to adulthood. *Annual Review of Sociology* 12:109–30.

Homans, G. 1958. *Social behavior: Its elementary forms*. New York: Harcourt Brace.

International Communications Research. 2003. 'Honey' easiest pet name for couples to swallow. *USA Today*, March 10, 1D.

John, R. 1988. The Native American family. In *Ethnic families in America: Patterns and variations*, 3rd ed. Edited by C.H. Mindcl, R.W. Habenstein, and R. Wright, Jr. New York: Elsevier, 325–66.

Jones, J. 1985. *Labor of love, labor of sorrow: Black women, work and the family from slavery to the present*. New York: Basic Books.

Kahane, H. 1988. *Logic and contemporary rhetoric: The use of reason in everyday life*. 5th ed. Belmont, CA: Wadsworth.

Kao, E.M., D.K. Nagata, and C. Peterson. 1997. Explanatory style, family expressiveness, and self-esteem among Asian American and European American college students. *Journal of Social Psychology* 137:435–44.

Kilbourne, J. 1999. *Can't buy my love: How advertising changes the way we think and feel*. New York: Touchstone.

Klein, D.M., and J.M. White. 1996. *Family theories: An introduction*. Thousand Oaks, CA: Sage.

Krakauer, J. 2003. *Under the banner of heaven: A story of violent faith*. New York: Doubleday.

Laird, J. 1993. Lesbian and gay families. In *Normal family processes*, 2nd ed. Edited by F. Walsh. New York: Guilford, 282–330.

Langer, E.J. 1989. *Mindfulness*. Reading, MA: Addison-Wesley.

Langer, E.J. 1997. *The power of mindful learning*. Reading, MA: Addison-Wesley.

Lorber, J. 1998. *Gender inequality: Feminist theories and politics*. Los Angeles: Roxbury.

Mann, S.A., M.D. Grimes, A.A. Kemp, and P.J. Jenkins. 1997. Paradigm shifts in family sociology? Evidence from three decades of family textbooks. *Journal of Family Issues* 18:315–49.

Matthaei, J.A. 1982. *An economic history of women in America*. New York: Schoken.

Maynard, M. 1994. Methods, practice and epistemology: The debate about feminism and research. In *Research in women's lives from a feminist perspective*. Edited by

M. Maynard and J. Purvis. London: Taylor & Francis, 10–26.

McGoldrick, M., M. Heiman, and B. Carter. 1993. The changing family life cycle: A perspective on normalcy. In *Normal family processes*, 2nd ed. Edited by F. Walsh. New York: Guilford, 405–43.

Mead, G.H. 1934. *Mind, self, and society*. Chicago: University of Chicago Press.

Melito, R. 1985. Adaptation in family systems: A developmental perspective. *Family Processes* 24:89–100.

Miller, W.L., and B.F. Crabtree. 1994. Clinical research. In *Handbook of qualitative research*. Edited by N.K. Denzin and Y.S. Lincoln. Thousand Oaks, CA: Sage, 340–52.

Mintz, S., and S. Kellogg. 1988. *Domestic revolutions: A social history of American family life*. New York: Free Press.

Morgan, E.S. 1966. *The Puritan family: Religion and domestic relations in seventeenth-century New England*. New York: Harper Torchbooks.

Mullings, L. 1997. *On our own terms: Race, class, and gender in the lives of African American women*. New York: Routledge.

Mumme, D.L, and A. Fernald. 2003. The infant as onlooker: Learning from emotional reactions observed in a television scenario. *Child Development* 74:221–37.

Navarro, M. 2006. Traditional round trip for workers is becoming a one-way migration north. *The New York Times*, December 21, A20.

Newman, K. 1988. *Falling from grace*. New York: Free Press.

Nye, F.I. 1988. Fifty years of family research. *Journal of Marriage and the Family* 50(2):305–16.

Parsons, T., and R.F. Bales. 1955. *Family socialization and interaction process*. New York: Free Press.

Peterson, K.S. 2000. Research reveals quick lessons for a long marriage. *USA Today*, July 3, 6D.

Peterson, K.S. 2003. There's a gut feeling about this whole intuition thing. *USA Today*, February 27, 8D.

Pettys, G.L., and P.R. Balgopal. 1998. Multigenerational conflicts and new immigrants: An Indo-American experience. *Journal of Contemporary Human Services* 79(4):410–24.

Popenoe, D. 1993. American family decline, 1960–1990: A review and appraisal. *Journal of Marriage and the Family* 55:527–55.

Ramirez, O., and C.H. Arce. 1981. The contemporary Chicano family: An empirically based review. In *Explorations in Chicano psychology*. Edited by A. Baron, Jr. New York: Praeger, 3–28.

Randi, J. 1992. Help stamp out absurd beliefs. *Time*, April 13, 80.

Rasool, J., C. Banks, and M.J. McCarthy. 1993. *Critical thinking: Reading and writing in a diverse world*. Belmont, CA: Wadsworth.

Rodgers, R.H. and J.M. White. 1993. Family development theory. In *Sourcebook of family theories and methods: A contextual approach*. Edited by P.G. Boss, W.J. Doherty, R. LaRossa, W.R. Schumm, and S.K. Steinmetz. New York: Plenum, 225–54.

Ruchlis, H., and S. Oddo. 1990. *Clear thinking: A practical introduction*. Buffalo, NY: Prometheus.

Sahlman, S. 2002. Executive summary insert: 2002. Demographic characteristics of immigrants. Population Resource Center, August. www.prcdc.org/summaries/immigrationinsert02/immigrationinsert02.html

Schvaneveldt, J. 1981. The interactional framework in the study of the family. In *Emerging conceptual frameworks in family analysis*, 2nd ed. Edited by F.I. Nye and F. Berardo. New York: Praeger.

Silsby, G. 2003. Talkin' about my gen-er-a-tion: External factors have mild effects on teens. *College Magazine*, Winter; www.usc.edu/schools/college/college_magazine/winter_2003/generation.html (accessed April 2, 2007).

Slater, S. 1995. *The lesbian family life cycle*. New York: Free Press.

Staples, R., and A. Mirande. 1980. Racial and cultural variations among American families: A decennial review of the literature on minority families. *Journal of Marriage and the Family* 42:887–903.

Therrien, M., and R.R. Ramirez. 2001. The Hispanic population in the United States: Population characteristics, March 2000. *Current Population Reports*. P20-535. Washington, DC: U.S. Census Bureau. www.census.gov/population/socdemo/hispanic/p20-535/p20-535.pdf (accessed October 8, 2004).

Thomas, W.I., and D.S. Thomas. 1928. *The child in America: Behavior problems and programs*. New York: Knopf.

U.S. Census Bureau. 2007. *Statistical abstract of the United States: 2007*. Washington, DC: U.S. Government Printing Office, www.census.gov/prod/www/statistical-abstract.html (accessed May 17, 2007).

Waters, M.C., and K. Eschbach. 1995. Immigration and ethnic and racial inequality in the United States. *Annual of Review of Sociology* 21:419–46.

Weiner-Davis, M. 1993. *Divorce busting: A revolutionary and rapid program for staying together*. New York: Simon & Schuster.

Williams, N. 1990. *The Mexican American family: Tradition and change*. Dix Hills, NY: General Hall.

Winton, C. 1995. *Frameworks for studying families*. Guilford, CT: Dushkin.

Zaslow, J. 2003. Divorce makes a comeback. *The Wall Street Journal*, January 14, D1, D10.

CHAPTER 3

Abelson, R. 2001. Men, increasingly are the ones claiming sex harassment by men. *The New York Times*, June 10, sec. 1, 1, 29.

Al-Jadda, S. 2005. Move over, Barbie. *USA Today*, December 14, 23A.

August, M., H. Barovick, E.L. Bland, S. Gregory, D. Robinson, and H.W. Tesoriero. 2002. Numbers. *Time*, July 15, 19.

Basow, S.A. 1992. *Gender: Stereotypes and roles*, 3rd ed. Pacific Grove, CA: Brooks/Cole.

Baxter, J., and E.W. Kane. 1995. Dependence and independence: A cross-national analysis of gender inequality and gender attitudes. *Gender and Society* 9:193–215.

Bem, S.L. 1975. Androgyny vs. the tight little lives of fluffy women and chesty men. *Psychology Today* 9:58–62.

Bem, S.L. 1981. Gender schema theory: A cognitive account of sex typing. *Psychological Review* 88:354–64.

Berglund, D.M., and T. Inman. 2000. Gender role stereotypes and family roles in comic strips. 62nd Annual Meeting of National Council on Family Relations, Minneapolis, November 12.

Blair, S.L. 1992. The sex-typing of children's household labor: Parental influence on daughters' and sons' housework. *Youth and Society* 24:178–203.

Bly, R. 1990. *Iron John: A book about men*. Reading, MA: Addison-Wesley.

Brizendine, L. 2006. *The female brain*. New York: Morgan Road Books.

Brown, P.L. 2006. Supporting boys or girls when the line isn't clear. *The New York Times*, December 2, A1, A11.

Buchanan, W. 2007. More U.S. employers cover transsexual surgery. *San Francisco Chronicle*, January 31, B4.

Burns, A., and R. Homel. 1989. Gender division of tasks by parents and their children. *Psychology of Women Quarterly* 13:113–25.

Buss, D.M. 1989. Sex differences in human mate preferences: Evolutionary hypotheses tested in 37 cultures. *Behavioral and Brain Sciences* 12:1–13.

Caldera, Y.M., A.C. Huston, and M. O'Brien. 1989. Social interactions and play patterns of parents and toddlers with feminine, masculine, and neutral toys. *Child Development* 60:70–76.

Callimachi, R. 2007. Women, not men, chose mate on this African isle. *Reno Gazette-Journal*, February 3, 4B.

Cargan, L., ed. 1991. *Marriage and families: Coping with change*. 3rd ed. Upper Saddle River, NJ: Prentice-Hall.

Carter, B. 1991. Children's TV, where boys are king. *The New York Times*, May 1, A1, C18.

Carter, D.B., ed. 1987. *Current conceptions of sex roles and sex typing*. New York: Praeger.

Chafetz, J.S., and A.G. Dworkin. 1986. *Female revolt: Women's movements in world and historical perspective*. Totowa, NJ: Rowman and Allanheld.

Cherry, R. 1998. Rational choice and the price of marriage. *Feminist Economics* 4:27–49.

Children Now. 2002. *Fall colors: Prime time diversity report 2001–02*. Oakland, CA: Children Now.

Chodorow, N. 1978. *The reproduction of mothering: Psychoanalysis and the sociology of gender*. Berkeley: University of California Press.

Culp, R.E., A.S. Cook, and P.C. Housley. 1983. A comparison of observed and reported adult-infant interactions: Effects of perceived sex. *Sex Roles* 9:475–79.

Demarest, M., and J. Garner. 1992. The representation of women's roles in women's magazines over the past 30 years. *Journal of Psychology* 126(4):357–69.

Derlega, V.J.S., S. Meits, S. Petronio, and S.T.

Margulis. 1993. *Self-disclosure.* Newbury Park, CA: Sage.

Devitt, J. 1999. *Framing gender on the campaign trail: Women's executive leadership and the press.* Washington, DC: The Women's Leadership Fund.

Eder, D., with C.C. Evans and S. Parker. 1995. *School talk: Gender and adolescent culture.* New Brunswick, NJ: Rutgers University Press.

Ellis, B.J., and D. Symons. 1990. Sex differences in sexual fantasy: An evolutionary psychological approach. *Journal of Sex Research* 27:527–56.

Fagot, B., and M. Leinbach. 1987. Socialization of sex roles within the family. In *Current conceptions of sex roles and sex typing.* Edited by D.B. Carter. New York: Praeger.

Falvey, J. 1986. *After college: The business of getting jobs.* Charlotte, VT: Williamson.

Franklin, C.W. 1988. *Men and society.* Chicago: Nelson-Hall.

Friedan, B. 1963. *The feminine mystique.* New York: Dell.

Fuentes, A. 2007. Out-of-style thinking. *USA Today,* February 13, 11A.

Furham, A., and L. Gasson. 1998. Sex differences in parental estimates of their children's intelligence. *Sex Roles* 38:151–62.

Gallup Organization. 1990. Working at the wrong job. *San Francisco Chronicle,* January 12, C1.

Gaylin, W. 1992. *The male ego.* New York: Viking.

Garofoli, J. 2002. On college campuses, it's a woman's world. *San Francisco Chronicle,* August 26, B1, B3.

Gecas, V., and M. Seff. 1991. Families and adolescents. In *Contemporary families: Looking forward, looking back.* Edited by A. Booth. Minneapolis: National Council on Family Relations.

Gerson, K. 1985. *Hard choices: How women decide about work, career, and motherhood.* Berkeley: University of California Press.

Gerson, K. 1993. *No man's land: Men's changing commitments to family and work.* New York: Basic Books.

Gerson, K. 2001. Children of the gender revolution: Some theoretical questions and findings from the field. In *Reconstructing work and the life course.* Edited by V.W. Marshall, W.R. Heinz, H. Krueger, and A. Verma. Toronto: University of Toronto Press, 103–14.

Goodwin, R. 1990. Sex differences among partner preferences: Are the sexes really very similar? *Sex Roles* 23:501–14.

Greenwald, J. 1996. Barbie boots up. *Time,* November 11, 48–50.

Harris, M. 1994. *Down from the pedestal: Moving beyond idealized images of womanhood.* New York: Doubleday.

Henig, R. M. 2006. How women think [review]. *The New York Times Book Revew,* September 10, 12.

Hibbard, D.R., and D. Buhrmester. 1998. The role of peers in the socialization of gender-related social interaction styles. *Sex Roles* 39:185–203.

Internal Revenue Service. 2002. *Statistics of Income Bulletin.* Winter 2001–2002. Reported in Johnson, D.C. 2002. As salary grows, so does a gender gap. *The New York Times,* May 12, sec. 3; 8.

Jackson, R.M. 1998. *Destined for equality: The inevitable rise of women's status.* Cambridge, MA: Harvard University Press.

Jones, D.C., N. Bloys, and M. Wood. 1990. Sex roles and friendship patterns. *Sex Roles* 23: 133–45.

Johnson, A.G. 1997. *The gender knot: Unraveling our patriarchal legacy.* Philadelphia, PA: Temple University Press.

Jorgensen, C. 1967. *Christine Jorgensen: A personal autobiography.* New York: Paul S. Erickson.

Kalof, L. 1993. Dilemmas of femininity: Gender and the social construction of sexual imagery. *The Sociological Quarterly* 34(4):639–52.

Kimmel, M.S. 1995a. Misogynists, masculinist mentors, and male supporters: Men's responses to feminism. In *Women: A feminist perspective,* 5th ed. Edited by J. Freeman. Mountain View, CA: Mayfield, 561–72.

Kimmel, M.S. 1995b. *Manhood in America: A cultural history.* Berkeley: University of California Press.

Kindlon, D., and M. Thompson. 1998. *Raising Cain: Protecting the emotional life of boys.* London: Michael Joseph Publishers.

Kluger, B. 2006. Dolls lose their innocence. *USA Today,* December 12, 23A.

Kohlberg, L. 1966. A cognitive-developmental analysis of children's sex-role concepts and attitudes. In *The development of sex differences.* Edited by E.E. Maccoby. Stanford, CA: Stanford University Press.

Koivula, N. 1999. Gender stereotyping in televised media sport coverage. *Sex Roles* 41:589–604.

Kohlberg, L. 1969. Stage and sequence: The cognitive-developmental approach to socialization. In *Handbook of socialization theory and research.* Edited by D.A. Goslin. Chicago: Rand McNally, 347–480.

LaRossa, R., C. Jaret, M. Gadgil, and G.R. Wynn. 2000. The changing culture of fatherhood in comic strip families: A six-decade analysis. *Journal of Marriage and the Family* 62:375–87.

Lavelle, M. 1998. The new rules of sexual harassment. *U.S. News & World Report,* June 6, 30–31.

Leaper, C. 2002. Parenting girls and boys. In *Handbook of parenting.* 2nd ed., Vol. 1. Edited by M.H. Bornstein. Mahwah, NJ: Erlbaum, 198–215.

Lehrman, S. 1997. Billy Tipton: Self-made man. *Stanford Today,* May/June.

Leonhardt, D. 2006. Gender paygap, once narrowing, is still in place. *The New York Times,* December 24, A1, A18.

Leve, L.D., and B.I. Fagot. 1997. Gender-role socialization and discipline processes in one and two parent families. *Sex Roles* 36:1–21.

Lewin, T. 2006. At colleges, women are leaving men in the dust. *The New York Times,* July 9, sec. 1, 1, 18–19.

Liebowitz, E. 2002. Macho in miniature. *Smithsonian,* August, 26–28.

Lindsey, L.L. 1997. *Gender roles: A sociological perspective,* 3rd ed. Upper Saddle River, NJ: Prentice-Hall.

Lips, H.M. 1995. Gender-role socialization: Lessons in femininity. In *Women: A feminist perspective,* 5th ed. Edited by J. Freeman. Mountain View, CA: Mayfield, 128–48.

Lips, H. 1997. *Sex and gender.* 3rd ed. Mountain View, CA: Mayfield.

Macionis, J.J. 2001. *Sociology.* 8th ed. Upper Saddle River, NJ: Prentice-Hall.

Majors, R.G., and J.M. Billson. 1992. *Cool pose: The dilemmas of black manhood in America.* Lexington, MA: Heath.

McNeely, C.A. 1998. Lagging behind the times: Parenthood, custody, and gender bias in family court. *Florida State University Law Review* 25:891.

Mead, M. 1935. *Sex and temperament in three primitive societies.* New York: William Morrow.

Middlebrook, D.W. 1997. *Suits me: The double life of Billy Tipton.* Boston: Houghton Mifflin.

Morse, S. 1995. Why girls don't like computer games. *AAUW Outlook* 88:14–17.

National Women's Health Information Center. 2002. *Frequently asked questions about eating disorders,* www.4woman.gov/faq/Eatingdi.pdf (accessed February 7, 2004).

Noveck, J. 2006. The speaker has nice clothes: Is it sexist to discuss Pelosi's wardrobe? *Reno Gazette-Journal,* November 22, 6C.

Mulrine, A. 2001. Are boys the weaker sex? *U.S. News & World Report,* July 30, 40–47.

Oakley, A., ed. 1985. *Sex, gender, and society,* rev. ed. New York: Harper & Row.

Overholser, G. 1996. Front page story: Women. *Washington Post,* April 21, C6.

Parsons, T., and R.F. Bales. 1955. *Family, socialization, and interaction process.* Glencoe, IL: Free Press.

Phillips, L. 1998. *The girls report: What we know and need to know about growing up female.* New York: National Council for Research on Women.

Piaget, J. 1950. *The psychology of intelligence.* London: Routledge & Kegan Paul.

Piaget, J. 1954. *The construction of reality in the child.* New York: Basic Books.

Pollack, W. 1998. *Real boys: Rescuing our sons from the myths of boyhood.* New York: Random House.

Rapping, E. 1994. *Mediations: Forays into the culture and gender wars.* Boston: South End Press.

Reisberg, L. 1999. To help Latino students, a college looks to parents. *The Chronicle of Higher Education,* January 15, A43–A44.

Rettig, K.D., and M.M. Bubolz. 1983. Interpersonal resource exchanges as indicators of quality of marriage. *Journal of Marriage and the Family* 45:497–510.

Renzetti, C.M., and D.J. Curran. 1995. *Women, men, and society,* 3rd ed. Boston: Allyn & Bacon.

Risman, B.J., and D. Johnson-Sumerford. 1998. Doing it fairly: A study of postgender marriages. *Journal of Marriage and the Family* 60: 23–40.

Rodgers, A. 2007. Faiths seeing wider spectrum of female clergy. *Post-gazette.com,*

January 2, www.post-gazette.com/pg/pp/o7002/750584.stm (accessed May 17, 2007).

Roper Starch Worldwide, Inc. 1994. *Teens talk about sex: Adolescent sexuality in the 90s.* New York: Sexuality Information and Education Council of the United States.

Ross, C.E., and M. Van Willigen. 1997. Education and the subjective quality of life. *Journal of Health and Social Behavior* 38:275–97.

Roy, R., J.F. Benenson, and F. Lilly. 2000. Beyond intimacy: Conceptualizing sex differences in same-sex friendships. *Journal of Psychology* 134:93–101.

Sadker, M., and D. Sadker 1995. *Failing at fairness: How American schools cheat girls.* New York: Touchstone.

Shapiro, L. 1990. Guns and dolls. *Newsweek,* May 26, 56–65.

Shellenbarger, S. 2006. Boys mow lawns, girls do dishes: Are parents perpetuating the chore wars? *The Wall Street Journal,* December 7, D1.

Smith, K.M. 1995. *First-year student survey.* Report 9596-I. East Carolina University, Research, Assessment, and Testing. Greenville, NC.

Smith, S. L. 2006a. Where the girls aren't: Gender disparity saturates G-rated films. Research brief commissioned by the See Jane Program at Dads & Daughters, February. www.DadsandDaughters.org (accessed May 17, 2007).

Smith, S. L. 2006b. G movies give boys a D: Portraying males as dominant, disconnected, and dangerous. Research brief commissioned by the See Jane Program at Dads & Daughters, May. www.DadsandDaughters.org (accessed May 17, 2007).

Spence, J., and L.L. Sawin. 1985. Images of masculinity and femininity. In *Sex, gender, and social psychology.* Edited by V. O'Leary, R. Unger, and B. Wallston. Hillsdale, NJ: Erlbaum.

Starrels, M.E., S. Bould, and L.J. Nicholas. 1994. The feminization of poverty in the United States. *Journal of Family Issues* 15:590–607.

Statistical Abstract of the United States. 2007. Washington, DC: U.S. Bureau of the Census.

Symons, D. 1987. An evolutionary approach: Can Darwin's view of life shed light on human sexuality? In *Theories of human sexuality.* Edited by J.H. Greer and W.T. O'Donohue. New York: Plenum.

Symons, D., and B. Ellis. 1989. Human male-female differences in sexual desire. In *Sociobiology of sexual and reproductive strategies.* Edited by A. E. Rasa, C. Vogel, and E. Voland. London: Chapman and Hall, 131–46.

Taylor, R.L., ed. 1994. *Minority families in the United States: A multicultural perspective.* Englewood Cliffs, NJ: Prentice-Hall.

Thelen, M.H., W. Vander-Wal, J.S.A. Muir-Thomas, and R. Harmon. 2000. Fear of intimacy among dating couples. *Behavior Modification* 24:223–40.

Thorne, B. 1993. *Gender play: Girls and boys in school.* New Brunswick, NJ: Rutgers University Press.

Torassa, U. 2002. Boy or girl? Advocate for intersex children influences attitudes. *San Francisco Chronicle,* August 4, E10, E11.

U.S. Census Bureau. 2006. Nearly half of our lives spent with TV, radio, Internet, newspapers, according to Census Bureau publication (press release) *U.S. Census Bureau News.* December 15. www.census.gov/Press-Release/www/releases/archives/miscellaneous/007871.html (accessed May 17, 2007).

U.S. Department of Labor, Bureau of Labor Statistics. 2002. *Employment and Earnings* 47(1): 178–83.

U.S. Department of Labor Women's Bureau. 2005. 20 leading occupations of employed women: Full-time wage and salary workers, 2005 annual averages. www.dol.gov/wb/factsheets/20lead2005.htm (accessed May 17, 2007).

Vande Berg, L.R., and D. Streckfuss. 1992. Prime-time television's portrayal of women and the world of work: A demographic profile. *Journal of Broadcasting and Electronic Media* (March):195–207.

Vonk, R., and R.D. Ashmore. 1993. The multifaceted self: Androgyny reassessed by open-ended self-descriptions. *Social Psychology Quarterly* 56(4):278–88.

Weber, L., T. Hancick, and, E. Higginbotham.1997. Women, power, and mental health. In *Women's health: Complexities and differences.* Edited by S.B. Ruzek, V.L. Olesen, and A.E. Clarke. Columbus: Ohio State University Press, 380–96.

White House Project. 2005. Who's talking now: A followup analysis of guest appearances by women on the Sunday morning talk shows, October. New York: The White House Project, www.thewhitehouseproject.org/v2/researchandreports/whostalking/whos_talking_2005.pdf (accessed May 17, 2007).

Whittier, N. 1995. *Feminist generations: The persistence of the radical women's movement.* Philadelphia, PA: Temple University Press.

Willets-Bloom, M.C., and S.L. Nock. 1994. The influence of maternal employment on gender role attitudes of men and women. *Sex Roles* 30:371–89.

Wright, D.W., and R. Young. 1998. The effects of family structure and maternal employment on the development of gender-related attitudes among men and women. *Journal of Family Issues* 19:300–14.

Zinn, M.B. 1994. Adaptation and continuity in Mexican-origin families. In *Minority families in the United States: A multicultural perspective.* Edited by R.L. Taylor. Englewood Cliffs, NJ: Prentice-Hall.

CHAPTER 4

Ainsworth, M.D.S., M.C. Blehar, E. Waters, and S. Wall. 1978. *Patterns of attachment: A psychological study of the strange situation.* Hillsdale, NJ: Erlbaum.

Aron, A., E.N. Aron, and J. Allen. 1998. Motivations for unrequited love. *Personality and Social Psychology Bulletin* 24(8):787–97.

Aron, A., T. McLaughlin-Volpe, D. Mashek, G. Lewandowski, S. C. Wright, and E. Aron. 2005. Including others in the self. In *European review of social psychology,* Vol. 14. Edited by W. Stoebe and M. Hewstone. Hove, UK: Psychology Press, 102–32.

Associated Press. 2003. Soldier punished for marriage to Iraqi, will be discharged. *Reno Gazette-Journal,* December 2, 2A.

Babwin, D. 2006. Study finds women like kid-friendly male faces. *Reno Gazette-Journal,* May 10, 1C, 4C.

Bartels, A., and S. Zeki. 2000. The neural basis of romantic love. *NeuroReport* 11 (17):3829–34.

Baumeister, R.F., and S.R. Wotman. 1992. *Breaking hearts: The two sides of unrequited love.* New York: Guilford.

Baumeister, R.F., S.R. Wotman, and A.M. Stillwell. 1993. Unrequited love: On heartbreak, anger, guilt, scriptlessness, and humiliation. *Journal of Personality and Social Psychology* 64(3):377–94.

Bornstein, R.F., and M.A. Languirand. 2003. *Healthy dependency: Leaning on others without losing yourself—The four keys to achieving balance in love, family, parenting, friendship, and work.* New York: Newmarket Press.

Brehm, S.S. 1992. *Intimate relationships.* 2nd ed. New York: McGraw-Hill.

Brennan, K.A., and P.R. Shaver. 1995. Dimensions of adult attachment, affect regulation, and romantic relationship functioning. *Personality and Social Psychology Bulletin* 21(3):267–84.

Bringle, R., and B. Buunk. 1991. Extradyadic relationships and sexual jealousy. In *Sexuality in close relationships.* Edited by K. McKinney and S. Sprecher. Hillsdale, NJ: Erlbaum.

Burcky, W., N. Reuterman, and S. Kopsky. 1988. Dating violence among high school students. *School Counselor* 35(5):353–58.

Buss, D.M., R.J. Larsen, D. Westen, and J. Semmeiroth. 1992. Sex differences in jealousy: Evolution, physiology and psychology. *Psychological Science* 3(4):251–55.

Buunk, B. 1991. Jealousy in close relationships: An exchange theoretical perspective. In *Psychology of jealousy and envy.* Edited by P. Salovey. New York: Guilford, 148–77.

Buunk, B.P., A. Angleitner, V. Oubaid, and D.M. Buss. 1996. Sex differences in jealousy in evolutionary and cultural perspective: Tests from the Netherlands, Germany and the United States. *Psychological Science* 7:359–63.

Cano, A., and D. O'Leary. 1997. Romantic jealousy and affairs: Research and implications for couple therapy. *Journal of Sex and Marital Therapy* 23(4):249–75.

Carey, B. 2007. Insufferable clinginess, or healthy dependence? *The New York Times,* March 6, D1, D8.

Clarke, J.W. 1990. *On being mad or merely angry: John W Hinckley, Jr., and other dangerous people.* Princeton, NJ: Princeton University Press.

Cohen, J. 2001. On the Internet, love really is blind. *New York Times,* January 18, D1, D9.

Corbett, S. 2001. When Debbie met Christina, who then became Chris. *New York Times Magazine,* October 14, 84–87.

Davis, K., and M. Todd. 1985. Assessing friendship: Prototypes, paradigm cases and relationship description. In *Understanding personal relationships: An interdisciplinary approach.* Edited by S. Duck and D. Perlman. London: Sage, 17–38.

Edlund, L., and N.-P. Lagerlöf. 2002. Implication of marriage institutions for redistribution and growth. www.columbia.edu/∼le93/love.pdf (accessed August 9, 2007).

Fisher, H. 1992. *Anatomy of love: The natural history of monogamy, adultery, and divorce.* New York: Norton.

Fisher, H.E. 2004. *Why we love: The nature and chemistry of romantic love.* New York: Henry Holt.

Flora, C. 2004. Chemistry lessons. *Psychology Today,* September/October, 38–50.

Ganahl, J. 2002a. The book on love. *San Francisco Chronicle,* January 13, E3.

Ganahl, J. 2002b. Putting love to the test. *San Francisco Chronicle,* January 13, E3.

Goode, W., ed. 1982. *The Family.* 2nd ed. Englewood Cliffs, NJ: Prentice-Hall.

Gupta, S. 2002. The chemistry of love. *Time,* February 18, 78.

Hansen, G.L. 1985. Perceived threats and marital jealousy? *Social Psychology Quarterly* 48:262–68.

Harris, C.R., and N. Christenfeld. 1996. Gender, jealousy, and reason. *Psychological Science* 7:364–66.

Hassebrauck, M., and T. Buhl. 1996. Three-dimensional love. *Journal of Social Psychology* 136(1):121–22.

Hatfield, E., and S. Sprecher. 1986. Measuring passionate love in intimate relationships. *Journal of Adolescence* 9:383–410.

Hazan, C., and P.R. Shaver. 1987. Conceptualizing romantic love as an attachment process. *Journal of Personality and Social Psychology* 52:511–24.

Heslin, R. 2005. With the Internet, the blind date is vanishing. *USA Today,* August 22, 4D.

Hitsch, G.J., A. Hortaçsu, and D. Ariely. 2005. What makes you click: An empirical analysis of online dating. January, www.aeaweb.org/annual_mtg_papers/2006/0106_0800_0502.pdf (accessed May 17, 2007).

Hook, M.K., L.H. Gerstein, L. Detterich, and B. Gridley. 2003. How close are we? Measuring intimacy and examining gender differences. *Journal of Counseling and Development* 81(4):462–73.

Hupka, R.B., B. Buunk, G. Falus, A. Fulgosi, E. Orgeta, R. Swain, and N.V. Tarabrina. 1985. Romantic jealousy and romantic envy: A seven-nation study. *Journal of Cross-Cultural Psychology* 16:423–46.

Hyde, J.S. 1986. *Understanding human sexuality.* 3rd ed. New York: McGraw-Hill.

Jacob, S., M.K. McClintock, B. Zelano and C. Ober. 2002. Paternally inherited HLA alleles are associated with women's choice of male odor. *Nature Genetics* 30(2):175–79.

Jankowiak, W.R., and E.F. Fischer. 1992. A cross-cultural perspective on romantic love. *Ethnology* 31:149–55.

Jayson, S. 2006. Couples can be too close for comfort. *USA Today,* February 6, 6D.

Johnson, S., and H.E. Marano. 1994. Love: The immutable longing for contact. *Psychology Today* (March/April), 32 passim.

Jones, D. 2006. One of USA's exports: Love, American style. *USA Today,* February 14, 1B, 2B.

King-Casas, B., D. Tomlin, C. Anen, C.F. Camerer, S.R. Quartz, and P.R. Montague. 2005. Getting to know you: Reputation and trust in a two-person economic exchange. *Science* 308:78–83.

Kipnis, L. 2003. *Against love: A polemic.* New York: Pantheon.

Knox, D., C. Schacht, and M.E. Zusman. 1999a. Love relationships among college students. *College Student Journal* 33 (1):149–52.

Knox, D., M.E. Zusman, L. Mabon, and L. Shriver. 1999b. Jealousy in college student relationships. *College Student Journal* 33(3): 328.

Laner, M.R. 1990. Violence or its precipitators: Which is more likely to be identified as a dating problem? *Deviant Behavior* 11(4): 319–29.

Lee, J.A. 1973. *The colors of love: An exploration of the ways of loving.* Don Mills, Ontario: New Press.

Lee, J.A. 1988. Love-styles. In *The psychology of love.* Edited by R. Sternberg and M. Barnes. New Haven, CT: Yale University Press, 38–67.

Lindholm, C. 2002. What is this thing we call love? *Los Angeles Times,* February 10, M6.

Loewenstein, S.F. 1985. On the diversity of love object orientations among women. In *Feminist perspectives on social work and human sexuality.* Edited by M. Valentich and J. Gripton. New York: Haworth Press, 7–24.

Madden, M., and A. Lenhart. 2006. *Online dating.* Washington, DC: Pew Internet & American Life Project, March 5, www.pewinternet.org/pdfs/PIP_Online_Dating.pdf (accessed May 17, 2007).

Mashek, D., and A. Aron, eds. 2004. *Handbook of closeness and intimacy.* Mahwah, NJ: Lawrence Erlbaum Associates.

Mintz, S., and S. Kellogg. 1988. *Domestic revolutions: A social history of American family life.* New York: Free Press.

Murstein, B.I. 1971. A theory of marital choice. In *Theories of attraction and love.* Edited by B.I. Murstein. New York: Springer, 100–51.

Murstein, B.I. 1986. *Paths to marriage: Family studies,* Vol. 5. Beverly Hills, CA: Sage.

Newman, D.M. 1995. *Sociology: Exploring the architecture of everyday life.* Thousand Oaks, CA: Pine Forge Press.

Parker-Pope, T. 2006. Where is the love? Antidepressants may inadvertently blunt feelings of romance. *The Wall Street Journal,* February 14, D1.

Peele, S., and A. Brodsky. 1976. *Love and addiction.* New York: New American Library.

Peterson, K.S. 2002. Read my lips: Give me a big kiss. *USA Today,* November 1, 1D, 2D.

Pines, A.M. 1992. *Romantic jealousy: Understanding and conquering the shadow of love.* New York: St. Martin's.

Radecki Bush, C.R., J.P. Bush, and J. Jennings. 1988. Effects of jealousy threats on relationship perceptions and emotions. *Journal of Social and Personal Relationships* 5:285–303.

Regan, P.C., and E. Berscheid. 1999. *Lust: What we know about human sexual desire.* Thousand Oaks, CA: Sage.

Reiss, I. 1960. Toward a sociology of the heterosexual love relationship. *Marriage and Family Living* 22:139–45.

Reiss, I. 1980. A multivariate model of the determinants of extramarital sexual permissiveness. *Journal of Marriage and the Family* 42(2):395–411.

Reiss, I.L., and G.R. Lee. 1988. *Family systems in America.* 4th ed. New York: Holt, Rinehart & Winston.

Riggs, D.S. 1993. Relationship problems and dating aggression: A potential treatment target. *Journal of Interpersonal Violence* 8(1):18–35.

Romance.com. 2006. *Consumer Reports,* December, 43–45.

Roney, J.R., K.N. Hanson, K.M. Durante, and D. Maestripieri. 2006. Reading men's faces: Women's mate attractiveness judgments track men's testosterone and interest in infants. *Proceedings of the Royal Society B: Biological Sciences* 273(1598):2169–75.

Rossi, H.L. 2006. With Beliefnet.com. *Newsweek,* October 2, 9.

Salovey, B. 1985. The heart of jealousy. *Psychology Today* 19:22–25, 28–29.

Salovey, P., and J. Rodin. 1985. The heart of jealousy. *Psychology Today,* September 19, 22–29.

Schneider, M. 2007. NASA fires astronaut charged with attempted kidnapping; Nowak will return to Navy. *Houston Chronicle,* March 8, www.chron.com/disp/story.mpl/ap/tx/4612533.html (accessed May 17, 2007).

Shaver, P., and C. Hazan. 1988. A biased overview of the study of love. *Journal of Social and Personal Relationships* 5(4):473–501.

Shulman, P. 2004. Great expectations. *Psychology Today,* March/April, 33–42.

Snowden, L. 1995. How to kiss a woman. *Esquire* (Fall):41–42.

Sternberg, R.J. 1986. A triangular theory of love. *Psychological Review* 93(2):119–35.

Sternberg, R.J. 1988. *The triangle of love.* New York: Basic Books.

Stone, B. 2007. Hot but virtuous is an unlikely match for an online dating service. *The New York Times,* March 19, C1, C2.

Tjaden, P., and N. Thoennes. 1998. *Stalking in America: Findings from the National Violence Against Women Survey.* Washington, DC: National Institute of Justice and National Center for Injury Prevention and Control.

Tucker, P., and A. Aron. 1993. Passionate love and marital satisfaction at key transition points in the family life cycle. *Journal of Social and Clinical Psychology* 12:135–47.

Tuller, D. 1994. Men, women respond differently to jealousy. *San Francisco Chronicle,* June 24, A17.

Twenge, J.M. 2006. *Generation me: Why today's young Americans are more confident, assertive, entitled—and more miserable than ever before.* New York: Free Press.

Vanderkam, L. 2006. Love (or not) in an iPod world. *USA Today,* February 14, 13A.

Vitzthum, V. 2007. *I love you, let's meet: Adventures in online dating.* Boston: Little, Brown.

Walsh, Anthony. 1991. *The science of love: Understanding love and its effects on mind and body.* Buffalo, NY: Prometheus.

Watters, E. 2001. In my tribe. *The New York Times Magazine,* October 14, 25–26.

White, G. 1981. Jealousy and partner's perceived motives for attraction to a rival. *Social Psychology Quarterly* (44):24–30.

White, G.L., and P.E. Mullen. 1989. *Jealousy: Theory, research, and clinical strategies.* New York: Guilford.

Wilson, C. 2005. What did we learn in "Kissing School"? *USA Today,* February 10, 6D.

Winch, R.R., T. Ktsanes, and V. Ktsanes. 1954. The theory of complementary needs in mate selection: An analytic and descriptive study. *American Sociological Review* 19:241–49.

CHAPTER 5

Adler, J. 1997. A matter of faith. *Newsweek,* December 15, 49–54.

Ahuvia, A.C., and M.B. Adelman. 1992. Formal intermediaries in the marriage market: A typology and review. *Journal of Marriage and the Family* 54:452–63.

American Management Association. 2003. *Survey on workplace dating,* www.amanet.org/research/pdfs/dating_workplace03.pdf (accessed September 4, 2007).

Armour, S. 2003. Cupid finds work as office romance no longer taboo. *USA Today,* February 11, 1B.

Axinn, W.G. and A. Thornton. 1993. Mothers, children, and cohabitation: The intergenerational effects of attitudes and behavior. *American Sociological Review* 58(2):233–45.

Bahney, A. 2004. Zapping old flames into digital ash. *The New York Times,* April 4, sec. 9, 1–2.

Bailey, B.L. 1989. *From front porch to back seat: Courtship in twentieth-century America.* Baltimore: Johns Hopkins University Press.

Barker, O. 2002. 8 minutes to a love connection. *USA Today,* December 12, 1D, 2D.

Barker, O. 2003. No time for dating? You're not alone. *USA Today,* November 12, 1A, 2A.

Barker, O. 2005. Blind dating gets back in the game. *USA Today,* December 12, 1D, 2D.

Behrendt, G., and A. Ruotola-Behrendt. 2005. *It's called a breakup because it's broken: The smart girl's breakup buddy.* New York: Broadway Books.

Berger, C.R. 1987. Planning and scheming: Strategies for initiating relationships. In *Accounting for relationships: Explanations, representation and knowledge.* Edited by R. Burnett, P. McChee, and D. Clarke. New York: Methuen.

Berscheid, E., K. Dion, E. Walster, and G.W. Walster. 1982. Physical attractiveness and dating choice: A test of the matching hypothesis. *Journal of Experimental Social Psychology* 1:173–89.

Blackwell, D.I., and D.T. Lichter. 2000. Mate selection among married and cohabiting couples. *Journal of Family Issues* 21:275–302.

Blumstein, P., and P. Schwartz. 1983. *American couples.* New York: McGraw-Hill.

Booth, R., and M. Jung. 1998. *Romancing the Net: A "tell-all" guide to love online.* Rocklin, CA: Prima.

Bounds, G. 2004a. Get me rewrite! Personal ads are big; big on clichés, too. *The Wall Street Journal,* August 16, A1, A7.

Bounds, G. 2004b. In search of single men—must have pulse. *The Wall Street Journal,* March 9, B1, B4.

Bradsher, K. 1990. For the man under 30, where is the woman? *The New York Times,* January 17.

Brooks, M. 2007. Nielsen//NetRatings February U.S. Rankings, *Online Personals Watch,* March 16, http://onlinepersonalswatch.typepad.com/news/nielsen_netratings/index.html (accessed May 17, 2007).

Brown, S., and A. Booth. 1996. Cohabitation versus marriage: A comparison of relationship quality. *Journal of Marriage and the Family* 58:668–78.

Bulcroft, R.A., K.A. Bulcroft, K. Bradley, and C. Simpson. 2000. The management and production of risk in romantic relationships: A postmodern paradox. *Journal of Family History* 25:63–92.

Casper, L.M., and S.H. Bianchi. 2002. *Continuity and change in the American family.* Thousand Oaks, CA: Sage.

Chang, A. 2002. Love by mail. ABCNews.com. May 23.

Cherlin, A.J., and A. Chamratrithirong. 1993. Variations in marriage patterns in Central Thailand. In *Next of kin: An international reader on changing families.* Edited by L. Tepperman and S.J. Wilson. Englewood Cliffs, NJ: Prentice-Hall, 84–89.

Cicerello, A., and E.P. Sheehan. 1995. Personal advertisements: A content analysis. *Journal of Social Behavior and Personality* 10:751–56.

Coltrane, S. 1998. *Gender and families.* Thousand Oaks, CA: Pine Forge Press.

Crary, D. 2002. In search of emotionally engaged mates. *San Francisco Chronicle,* September 9, A2.

Cullen, L.T. 2004. Cupid academy. *Time,* February 16, 67–68.

Davis, S. 1990. Men as success objects and women as sex objects: A study of personal advertisements. *Sex Roles* 23(1/2):43–50.

Dell'Orto, G. 2006. Authorities crack down on green-card weddings. *Reno Gazette-Journal,* October 21, 4C.

della Cava, M.R. 2004. Truth in advertising hits Internet dating. *USA Today,* April 20, 1D, 2D.

Denizet-Lewis, B. 2004. Friends, friends with benefits, and the benefits of the local mall. *The New York Times Magazine,* May 30, 30–35, 54–58.

Dunbar, R. 1995. Are you lonesome tonight? *New Scientist* 145:26–31.

Egan, J. 2003. Love in the time of no time. *The New York Times Magazine,* November 23, 66.

Erard, M. 2003. Decoding the new cues in online society. *The New York Times,* November 27, G1.

Fine, D. 2005. *The fine art of small talk: How to start a conversation, keep it going, build networking skills—and leave a positive impression!* New York: Hyperion.

Fowlkes, M.R. 1994. Single worlds and homosexual lifestyles: Patterns of sexuality and intimacy. In *Sexuality across the life course.* Edited by A.S. Rossi. Chicago: University of Chicago Press, 347–60.

Gabriel, T. 1997. Pack dating: For a good time, call a crowd. *The New York Times,* January 5, 22.

Garwood, P. 2006. Nations combat forced marriage. *Reno Gazette-Journal,* August 30, 6C.

Gaulin, S.J.C., and J.S. Boster. 1990. Dowry as female competition. *American Anthropologist* 92:994–1005.

Geiger, E. 2005. Muslim girls in Austria fighting forced marriages. *San Francisco Chronicle,* December 14, A15, A18.

Glenn, N., and E. Marquardt. 2001. *Hooking up, hanging out, and hoping for Mr. Right: College women on mating and dating today.* New York: Institute for American Values.

Glick, P.C., and G. Spanier. 1980. Married and unmarried cohabitation in the United States. *Journal of Marriage and the Family* 48(4):737–47.

Gwinnell, E. 1998. *Online seductions: Falling in love with strangers on the Internet.* New York: Kodansha.

Hafner, K. 2002. Searching for a safety zone. *New York Times,* October 31, E1, E5.

Harley, W.F. Jr. 2003. Letter #1: How to resolve conflicts before marriage. Marriage Builders. March 12. www.marriagebuilders.com/graphic/mbi5068a_qa.html.

Harris Interactive/Spherion. 2007. Be my valentine? Nearly 40% of workers have had a workplace romance, according to latest Spherion survey. Spherion Workplace Snapshot, January 29, www.spherion.com/press/releases/2007/workplace-romance.jsp (accessed May 17, 2007).

Hatfield, E., and R.L. Rapson. 1996. *Love and sex: Cross-cultural perspectives.* Boston: Allyn & Bacon.

Headley, M.D. 2007. *The year of yes: The story of a girl, a few hundred dates, and fate.* New York: Hyperion.

Horwitz, A., and H. White. 1998. The relationship of cohabitation and mental health: A study of a young adult cohort. *Journal of Marriage and the Family* 60:505–14.

Hymowitz, C., and J.S. Lublin. 2005. Many companies look the other way at employee affairs. *The Wall Street Journal,* March 8, B1, B6.

Internet now third most popular way to get a date. 2005. *Netimperative,* March 8, www.netimperative.com/2005/08/03/Internet_dating_popular (accessed May 17, 2007).

Jackson, M. 1999. Office is fertile ground for romance. *San Francisco Chronicle,* February 13, D1, D2.

Jana, R. 2000. Arranged marriages, minus the parents. *The New York Times,* August 17, D1, D10.

Jayson, S. 2005a. Meet a real-life "Hitch." *USA Today,* February 17, 9D.

Jayson, S. 2005b. Cohabitation is replacing dating. *USA Today,* July 18, 6D.

Jayson, S. 2006a. A new generation doesn't

blink an eye at interracial relationships. *USA Today*, February 8, 1A, 2A.

Jayson, S. 2006b. Workplace romance no longer gets the kiss-off. *USA Today*, February 9, 9D.

Kerchoff, A.C., and K.E. Davis. 1962. Value consensus and need complementarity in mate selection. *American Sociological Review* 27: 295–303.

Kesmodel, D. 2006. "Adult" dating sites flourish as people seek sex over love. *The Wall Street Journal*, March 1, http://online.wsj.com/public/article/SB114113606338 885286kKdCK_sy2Ly87GC5blGHG GrYq1s_20070301.html?mod=tff_main_ tff_top (accessed May 17, 2007).

Khoo, S.-E. 1987. Living together as married: A profile of de facto couples in Australia. *Journal of Marriage and the Family* 49:185–91.

Klaff, L.G. 2001. Companies want intra-office couples to sign "love contracts." *Reno Gazette-Journal*, June 15, 3A.

Knox, D., L. Gibson, M.E. Zusman, and C. Gallmeier. 1997. Why college student relationships end. *College Student Journal* 32:449–52.

Knox, D., M. E. Zusman, and W. Nieves. 1998. How college students end love relationships. *College Student Journal* 32:482–84.

Knox, D., M.E. Zusman, M. Kaluzny, and C. Cooper. 2000. College student recovery from a broken heart. *College Student Journal* 34: 322–24.

Knox, N. 2004. Nordic family ties don't mean tying the knot. *USA Today*, December 16, 15A, 16A.

Kornblum, J. 2004. Web singles seek dater encryption. *USA Today*, August 24, 14B.

Kornblum, J. 2007. Getting "singled" out is tough on the Web. *USA Today*, March 8, 4D.

Kuczynski, A. 2002. She's got to be a macho girl. *The New York Times*, November 3, sec. 9, 1, 12.

Kugiya, H. 2007. Brimming with dating advice, the Professional Dater looks for love herself. *USA Today*, February 7, www.usatoday.com/life/lifestyle/2007-02-10-dater_x.htm?csp=34 (accessed May 17, 2007).

Kurdek, L.A. 1991. The relations between reported well-being and divorce history, availability of a proximate adult, and gender. *Journal of Marriage and the Family* 253:956–57.

Kurdek, L.A., and J.P. Schmitt. 1986. Early development of relationship quality in heterosexual married, heterosexual cohabiting, gay, and lesbian couples. *Developmental Psychology* 22:305–9.

Kurlantzick, J. 2001. Hello, goodbye, hey maybe I love you? *U.S. News & World Report*, June 4, 43.

LaFraniere, S. 2005. Forced to marry before puberty, African girls pay lasting price. *The New York Times*, November 27, sec. 1, pp. 1, 14.

Lancaster, J. 2005. Young woman challenges India's child-marriage tradition. *Reno Gazette-Journal*, September 10, 7C; reprinted from *The Washington Post*.

Lance, L.M. 1998. Gender differences in heterosexual dating: A content analysis of personal ads. *The Journal of Men's Studies* 6(3): 297–396.

Laner, M.R. 1995. *Dating: Delights, discontents and dilemmas*. 2nd ed. Salem, MA: Sheffield.

Laner, M.R., and N.A. Ventrone. 1998. Egalitarian daters/traditionalist dates. *Journal of Family Issues* 19(4):468–78.

Laner, M.R., and N.A. Ventrone. 2000. Dating scripts revisited. *Journal of Family Issues* 21(4):488–500.

Lardner, J. 1998. Cupid's cubicles. *U.S. News & World Report*, December 14, 44–54.

Lavinthal, A., and J. Rozler. 2005. *The hookup handbook: A single girl's guide to living it up*. New York: Simon Spotlight Entertainment.

Lehrer, E.L., and C.U. Chiswick. 1993. Religion as a determinant of marital stability. *Demography* 30(3):385–404.

Lieberman, D. 2005. Dating On Demand puts those looking for love on TV. *USA Today*, February 10, 1B.

Lindsay, J.M. 2000. An ambiguous commitment: Moving into a cohabiting relationship. *Journal of Family Studies* 6:120–34.

Lloyd, S.A., R.M. Cate, and J.M. Henton. 1984. Predicting premarital relationship stability: A methodological refinement. *Journal of Marriage and the Family* 46:71–76.

Lyall, S. 2002. For Europeans, love, yes; marriage, maybe. *The New York Times*, March 24, sec. 1; 1, 8.

Madsen, S., and W.A. Collins. 2005. Longitudinal links and divergences in interactions in parent-child and romantic relationships, www.education.umn.edu/icd/Parent-Child/SRA%202004%20Handouts/SRA%202004%20Madsen-Collins.pdf (accessed May 17, 2007).

Magdol, L., T.E. Moffitt, A. Caspi, and P.A. Silva. 1998. Hitting without a license: Testing explanations for differences in partner abuse between young adult daters and cohabitors. *Journal of Marriage and the Family* 60(1): 41–55.

Maloney, L. 1986. Behind rise in mixed marriages. *U.S. News & World Report*, February 10, 68–69.

Manning, W., and P. Smock. 2002. First comes cohabitation and then comes marriage? *Journal of Family Issues*. November 23(8): 1065–88.

Manning, W.D., P.C. Giordano, and M.A. Longmore. 2006. Hooking up: The relationship contexts of "non-relationship" sex. *Journal of Adolescent Research* 21(5):459–83.

McDermott, T. 2002. 10 tips for online dating safety. Match.com. www.match.com/Matchscene, December 20.

McGinn, D. 2006. Dating: Positive thinking. *Newsweek*, January 16, http://msnbc.msn.com/id/10753452/site/newsweek (accessed May 17, 2007).

Mcginnis, S.L. 2003. Cohabiting, dating, and perceived costs of marriage: A model of marriage entry. *Journal of Marriage and the Family* 65(1):105–12.

Mead, R. 2002. Unmarital bliss. *The New Yorker*, December 9, 48, 50.

Michael, R.T., J.H. Gagnon, E.O. Laumann, and G. Kolata. 1994. *Sex in America: A definitive survey*. Boston: Little, Brown.

Milewski, K., M.N. Hatala, and D.W. Baack. 1999. Downloading love: A content analysis of Internet personal advertisements placed by college students. *College Student Journal* 33(1):124.

Mindel, C.H., R.W. Habenstein, and R. Wright Jr., eds. 1988. *Ethnic families in America: Patterns and variations*. 3rd ed. New York: Elsevier.

Mixed Media Watch. 2005. Most approve of interracial relationships . . . but don't count the Asians. *Racialicious*, June 6–25, www.mixedmediawatch.com/2005/10/10/most-approve-of-interracial-relationships-but-dont-count-the-asians (accessed May 17, 2007).

Mulhauser, D. 2001. Dating among college students is all but dead, survey finds. *The Chronicle of Higher Education*, August 10, A51.

Murstein, B.I. 1976. *Who will marry whom: Theories and research in marital choice*. New York: Springer.

Murstein, B.I. 1986. *Paths to marriage*. Newbury Park, CA: Sage.

Murstein, B.I. 1987. A clarification and extension of the SVR theory of dyadic pairing. *Journal of Marriage and the Family* 49:929–33.

Musick, K., A. Meier, and L. Bumpass. 2005. Influences of family structure, conflict, and change on transitions to adulthood. Annual meeting of the American Sociological Association, Montreal, Canada, August. Described in Shellenbarger, S. 2005. The case for going steady: Studies say teen dating habits affect marriage skills. *The Wall Street Journal*, September 8, D1.

Nagourney, E. 2000. Study finds families bypassing marriage. *The New York Times*, Feburary 15, D8.

Navarro, M. 2005. Love the job? What about your boss? *The New York Times*, July 24, sec. 9, 1, 9.

Nelson, S. 1992. It's not black and white. *Seventeen*, January, 80–83.

Nielsen/NetRatings. 2004. Top 10 matchmaking sites. *USA Today*, May 26, 9D.

Nock, S.L. 1995. A comparison of marriages and cohabiting relationships. *Journal of Family Issues* 16:53–76.

Nussbaum, E. 2004. Are we a match? *New York Times*, April 25, sec. 4A, 20–21.

O'Hear, S. 2007. Social network traffic up 11.5 percent; MySpace still dominates. *ZDNet*, March 15, http://blogs.zdnet.com/social/?p=114 (accessed May 17, 2007).

Olander, M., E.H. Kirby, and K. Schmitt. 2005. *Attitudes of young people toward diversity*. College Park, MD: Center for Information & Research on Civic Learning & Engagement, University of Maryland, School of Public Policy, February, http://www.civicyouth.org/PopUps/FactSheets/Attitudes%202.25.pdf (accessed May 17, 2007).

Oldenburg, A. 2005. Love is no longer color-coded on TV. *USA Today*, December 21, D1, D2.

Onishi, N. 2007. Betrothed at first sight: A

Korean-Vietnamese courtship. *The New York Times,* February 22, A1, A12.

Parks, M. 2006. *2006 workplace romance: Poll findings.* A study by the Society for Human Resource Management and CareerJournal.com, January. Alexandria, VA: Society for Human Resource Management, www.shrm.org/hrresources/surveys_published/2006%20Workplace%20Romance%20Poll%20Findings.pdf (accessed May 17, 2007).

Peterson, K.S. 2000a. Wedded to their relationship but not to marriage. *USA Today,* April 18, 7D.

Peterson, K.S. 2000b. Wooing the past: Courtship flirts with a comeback. *USA Today,* September 27, 9D.

Peterson, K.S. 2002. Shacking up: Lots to puzzle over. *USA Today,* November 27, 11D.

Peterson, K.S. 2003. Dating game has changed. *USA Today,* February 11, 2003, 9D.

Phillips, D. 1980. *How to fall out of love.* New York: Fawcett.

Popenoe, D. 2005. *The state of our unions: The social health of marriage in America. Marriage and family: What does the Scandinavian experience tell us?* Rutgers, the State University of New Jersey. Piscataway, NJ: The National Marriage Project, http://marriage.rutgers.edu/Publications/SOOU/TEXTSOOU2005.htm (accessed May 17, 2007).

Popenoe, D., and B.D. Whitehead. 2002. *Should we live together? What young adults need to know about cohabitation before marriage.* 2nd ed. Rutgers, the State University of New Jersey. Piscataway, NJ: The National Marriage Project, June, http://marriage.rutgers.edu/Publications/SOOU/TEXTSOOU2005.htm (accessed May 17, 2007).

Rainie, L., and M. Madden. 2006. *Not looking for love: The state of romance in America.* Washington, DC: Pew Internet & American Life Project, February 13, www.pewinternet.org/pdfs/PIP_Romance_in_America_feb06.pdf (accessed May 17, 2007).

Ramu, G.N. 1989. Patterns of mate selection. In *Family and marriage: Cross-cultural perspectives.* Edited by K. Ishwaran. Toronto: Wall and Thompson, 165–78.

Raybeck, D., S. Dorenbosch, M. Sarapata, and D. Herrman. 1996. SWF ISO LTR: The quest for love and meaning in the personals. Paper read at 98th Annual Meeting of the American Anthropological Association, at Chicago, IL.

Ricketts, C. 2004. What's race got to do with it? *Stanford Magazine,* May/June, 40–41.

Ridley, C.D., J. Peterman, and A.W. Avery. 1978. Cohabitation: Does it make for a better marriage? *Family Coordinator* 27:129–36.

Rogers, C.R. 1954. The case of Mrs. Oak: A research analysis. In *Psychotherapy and personality change: Coordinated research studies in the client-centered approach.* Edited by C.R. Rogers and R.F. Dymond. Chicago: University of Chicago Press.

Rogers, M., C.B. Taylor, D. Cunning, M. Jones, and K. Taylor. 2006. Parental restrictions on adolescent Internet use. *Pediatrics* 118(4):1804–05.

Romance.com. 2007. *Consumer Reports,* December, 43–45.

Roscoe, B., M.S. Diana, and R.H. Brooks II. 1987. Early, middle, and late adolescents' views on dating and factors influencing partner selection. *Adolescence* 22:59–68.

Rowland, M. 1994. Hurdles for unmarried partners. *The New York Times,* May 22, sec. 3, 15.

Rusbult, C.E. 1987. Responses to dissatisfaction in close relationships. In *Intimate relationships: Development, dynamics, and deterioration.* Edited by D. Penman and S. Duck. Beverly Hills, CA: Sage.

Ruvolo, A.P., and C.J. Brennan. 1997. What's love got to do with it? Close relationships and perceived growth. *Personality and Social Psychology Bulletin* 23(8): 814–23.

Scherreik, S. 1993. The practical part of living together. *The New York Times,* March 6, 142.

Schneider, P. 2005. The new Berlin Wall. *The New York Times Magazine,* December 14, 66–71.

Sessions, L.S. 2007. *Unhooked: How young women pursue sex, delay love, and lose at both.* New York: Riverhead/Putnam.

Sharma, A. 2006. Love, shift, delete: Saying bye-byte in a digital age. *The Wall Street Journal,* March 27, A1, A14.

Shellenbarger, S. 2005. Employers often ignore office affairs, leaving co-workers in difficult spot. *The Wall Street Journal,* March 10, D1.

Shelton, B.A., and D. John. 1993. Does marital status make a difference? Housework among married and cohabit-ing men and women. *Journal of Family Issues* 14 (3):401–20.

Shostak, A.B. 1987. Singlehood. In *Handbook of marriage and the family.* Edited by M. Sussman and S. Steinmetz. New York: Plenum Press.

Simenauer, J., and D. Carroll. 1982. *Singles: The new Americans.* New York: Simon & Schuster.

Smith, C. S. 2005. Abduction, often violent, a Kyrgyz wedding rite. *The New York Times,* April 30, A1, A7.

Smock, P.J. 2000. Cohabitation in the United States: An appraisal of research themes, findings, and implications. *Annual Review of Sociology* 26:1–20.

Solot, D., and M. Miller. 2002. *Unmarried to each other: The essential guide to living together as an unmarried couple.* New York: Marlowe & Company.

Soriano, C. S. 2006. Groups try to break bonds of forced marriage. *USA Today,* April 20, 7A.

Sprecher, S., and K. McKinney. 1993. *Sexuality.* Newbury Park, CA: Sage.

Sprecher, S., Q. Sullivan, and E. Hatfield. 1994. Mate selection preferences: Gender differences examined in a national sample. *Journal of Personality and Social Psychology* 66(6): 1074–81.

St. John, W. 2002. Young, single and dating at hyperspeed. *The New York Times,* April 21, sec. 9, 1, 2.

Stack, S., and J.R. Eshleman. 1998. Marital status and happiness: A 17-nation study. *Journal of Marriage and the Family* 60:527–36.

Strauss, N. 2005. *The game: Penetrating the secret society of pickup artists.* New York: HarperCollins.

Sullivan, K. 2007. Clicking on community: On-line newsgroups move coffee klatch to cyberspace. *San Francisco Chronicle,* January 6, F1, F4.

Surra, C.A., and D.K. Hughes. 1997. Commitment processes in accounts of the development of premarital relationships. *Journal of Marriage and the Family* 59:5–21.

Teachman, J.D., and K.A. Polonko. 1990. Cohabitation and marital stability in the United States. *Social Forces* 69(1):207–20.

Thornton, A., W.G. Axinn, and J.D. Teachman. 1995. The influence of school enrollment and accumulation on cohabitation and marriage in early adulthood. *American Sociological Review* 60:762–74.

Timmreck, T.C. 1990. Overcoming the loss of love: Preventing love addiction and promoting positive emotional health. *Psychological Reports* 66:515–28.

Waite, L.J. 2000. *The ties that bind: Perspectives on marriage and cohabitation.* New York: Aldine de Gruyter.

Wallack, T. 2005. Singles turn to the pros to boost their chances: Experts provide photos, profiles, background checks. *San Francisco Chronicle,* February 14, E1.

Walsh, D. 2006. Team rescues women from forced marriages. *San Francisco Chronicle,* January 1, A1, A2.

Whitman, S., and W. Whitman. 2003. *Shacking up: The smart girl's guide to living in sin without getting burned.* New York: Broadway Books.

Whyte, M.K. 1990. *Dating, mating, and marriage.* New York: Aldine de Gruyter.

Williams, C.J. 2000. When love is never having to say 'I do.' *Los Angeles Times,* March 31, A1, A6.

Williams, E. 2004. Plan even sans ring. *Newsweek,* April 19, 68.

With this ring . . . A national survey on marriage in America. 2005. Gaithersburg, MD: National Fatherhood Initiative, November 17, www.smartmarriages.com/nms.pdf (accessed May 17, 2007).

Wu, Z. 1995. The stability of cohabitation relationships: The role of children. *Journal of Marriage and the Family* 57(1):231–36.

Zaslow, J. 2004. Unmarried with grandchildren: Seniors shacking up face unexpected issues. *The Wall Street Journal,* March 4, D1.

CHAPTER 6

Abma, J. 2003. Sexual activity among teenagers in the United States. In *Long-term trends in the well-being of children and youth.* Edited by R.P. Weissberg, H.J. Walberg, M.U. O'Brien, and C.B. Kuster. Washington, DC: Child Welfare League of America Press.

Alford-Cooper, F. 1998. *For keeps: Marriages that last a lifetime.* Armonk, NY: M.E. Sharpe.

Axtell, R.E. 1991. *Gestures: The do's and taboos of body language around the world.* New York: John Wiley.

Bach, G.R., and P. Wyden. 1970. *The intimate*

enemy: How to fight fair in love and marriage. New York: Avon Books.

Bader, E. 1981. Do marriage preparation programs really help? Paper presented at the annual conference of the National Council on Family Relations, Milwaukee.

Bagarozzi, D.A. 1990. Marital power discrepancies and symptom development in spouses: An empirical investigation. *American Journal of Family Therapy* 18:51–64.

Baumeister, R.F., J.M. Twenge, and C. Nuss. 2002. Effects of social exclusion on cognitive processes: Anticipated aloneness reduces intelligent thought. *Journal of Personality and Social Psychology* 83:817–27.

Beach, S.R.H., and A. Tesser. 1993. Decision-making power and marital satisfaction: A self-evaluation maintenance perspective. *Journal of Social and Clinical Psychology* 12:471–94.

Beier, E.G., and D.P. Sternberg. 1977. Beier Sternberg discord questionnaire. In *Measure for clinical practice: A sourcebook*, 3rd ed. Edited by K. Corcoran and J. Fisher. 2000. New York: Free Press.

Bernard, J. 1982. *The future of marriage.* 2nd ed. New York: Columbia University Press.

Betcher, W., and R. Macauley. 1990. *The seven basic quarrels of marriage: Recognize, defuse, negotiate, and resolve your conflicts.* New York: Villard.

Bischoping, K. 1993. Gender differences in conversation topics, 1922–1990. *Sex Roles* 28: 1–18.

Blair, S.L. 1993. Employment, family, and perceptions of marital quality among husbands and wives. *Journal of Family Issues* 14:189–212.

Blood, R.O., Jr., and D.M. Wolfe. 1960. *Husbands and wives.* New York: Free Press.

Blumstein, P., and P. Schwartz. 1983. *American couples: Money, work, sex.* New York: William Morrow.

Boyd, L.A., and A.J. Roach. 1977. Interpersonal communication skills differentiating more satisfying from less satisfying marital relationships. *Journal of Counseling Psychology* 24:540–42.

Bradley, B., and S.M. Johnson. 2004. Emotionally focused couples therapy: An integrative contemporary approach. In *Handbook of couples therapy*, edited by M. Haraway. New York: John Wiley & Sons, 179–93.

Briggs, J. 2002. IQ bruised as ego battered. *Popular Science* (August):42.

Broderick, C.B. 1979. *Couples: How to confront problems and maintain loving relationships.* New York: Simon & Schuster.

Brody, J. 2000. A matter of compromise and acceptance. *The New York Times*, February 15, D8.

Canary, D.J., W.R. Cupach, and S.J. Messamn. 1995. *Relationship conflict: Conflict in parent child, friendship, and romantic relationships.* Thousand Oaks, CA: Sage.

Carey, B. 2006. For couples, reaction to good news matters more than reaction to bad. *The New York Times*, December 5, D5.

Carstensen, L.L., J.M. Gottman, and R.W. Levenson. 1995. Emotional behavior in long-term marriage. *Psychology and Aging* 10:140–49.

Coan, J.A., H.S. Schaefer, and R.J. Davidson. 2006. Lending a hand: Social regulation of the neural response to threat. *Psychological Science* 17(12):1032–39.

Cohen, T., and J.C. Durst. 2000. Leaving work and staying home: The impact on men of terminating the male economic provider role. In *Men and masculinity: A text-reader.* Edited by T. Cohen. Belmont, CA: Wadsworth.

Coser, L. 1956. *The functions of social conflict.* New York: Free Press.

Crawford, D.W., R.M. Houts, and T.L. Huston. 2002. Compatibility, leisure and satisfaction in marriage. *Journal of Marriage and the Family* 64(2):433–49.

Crawford, M. 1995. *Talking difference: On gender and language.* Thousand Oaks, CA: Sage.

Crosby, F.J. 1991. *Juggling: The unexpected advantages of balancing career and home for women and their families.* New York: Free Press.

Davis, S.N., T.N. Greenstein, and J.P.G. Marks. 2007. Effects of union type on division of household labor. *Journal of Family Issues* 28:1246–72.

Derlega, V.J., S. Metts, S. Petronio, and S.T. Margulis. 1993. *Self disclosure.* Newbury Park, CA: Sage.

Dubow, B. 2007. What 2 say when u know 2 much? *USA Today*, March 8, 4D.

Edwards, J.N. 1991. New conceptions: Biosocial innovations and the family. *Journal of Marriage and the Family* 53:349–60.

Eisenberger, N.I., and M.D. Lieberman. 2004. Why rejection hurts: A common neural alarm system for physical and social pain. *Trends in Cognitive Sciences* 8:294–300.

Eisenberger, N.I., M.D. Lieberman, and K.D. Williams. 2003. Does rejection hurt? An fMRI study of social exclusion. *Science* 302:290–92.

Ferrari, J.R., and R.A. Emmons. 1994. Procrastination as revenge: Do people report using delays as a strategy for vengeance? *Personality and Individual Differences* 17(4):539–42.

Finkenauer, C., and H. Hazam. 2000. Disclosure and secrecy in marriage: Do both contribute to marital *satisfaction? Journal of Social and Personal Relationships* 17:245–63.

For richer or poorer again. 2002. *Consumer Reports.* June, 60–61.

French, J.P., and B. Raven. 1959. The bases of social power. In *Studies in social power.* Edited by L. Cartwright. Ann Arbor: University of Michigan Press.

Friedman, R.A., and S.C. Currall. 2002. E-mail escalation: Dispute exacerbating elements of electronic communication, www2.owen.vanderbilt.edu/ray.friedman/pdf/emailescalation.pdf (accessed May 17, 2007).

Frieze, I.H., J.E. Parsons, P.B. Johnson, D.N. Ruble, and G.L. Zeliman. 1978. *Women and sex roles.* New York: W.W. Norton.

Gable, S., G. Gonzaga, and A. Strachman. 2006. Will you be there for me when things go right? Supportive responses to positive event disclosures. *Journal of Personality and Social Psychology* 91:904–17.

Gallmeier, C.P., M.E. Zusman, D. Knox, and L. Gibson. 1997. Can we talk? Gender differences in disclosure patterns and expectations. *Free Inquiry in Creative Sociology* 25:129–225.

Gilbert, S. 2005. Married with problems? Therapy may not help. *The New York Times*, April 19, D1, D6.

Glazer-Malbin, N., ed. 1975. *Old family/new family.* New York: Van Nostrand.

Goldberg, M. 1987. Patterns of disagreement in marriage. *Medical Aspects of Human Sexuality* 21:42–52.

Goleman, D. 1995. *Emotional intelligence: Why it can matter more than IQ.* New York: Bantam Books.

Goleman, D. 2006. *Social intelligence: The new science of human relationships.* New York: Bantam Books.

Gottman, J. 2002. *The relationship cure: A 5-step guide to strengthening your marriage, family, and friendships.* New York: Random House.

Gottman, J., and N. Silver. 1999. *The seven principles for making marriage work: A practical guide from the country's foremost relationship expert.* New York: Three Rivers/Random House.

Gottman, J., and S. Carrere. 2000. Welcome to the Love Lab. *Psychology Today* (September):42.

Gottman, J., J. Coan, S. Carrere, and C. Swanson. 1998. Predicting marital happiness and stability from newlywed interactions. *Journal of Marriage and the Family* 50:5–22.

Gottman, J.M. 1994. *What predicts divorce: The relationship between marital processes and marital outcomes.* Hillsdale, NJ: Lawrence Erlbaum Associates.

Gottman, J.M., and L.J. Krokoff. 1989. Marital interaction and satisfaction: A longitudinal view. *Journal of Consulting and Clinical Psychology* 57:47–52.

Gray, J. 1990. *Men are from Mars, women are from Venus: A practical guide for improving communications and getting what you want in your relationships.* New York: HarperCollins.

Greeff, A.P., and T. De Bruyne. 2000. Conflict management style and marital satisfaction. *Journal of Sex and Marital Satisfaction* 26:321–34.

Guynn, J. 2007. Tech's younger generation leans on Web 2.0 for love. *San Francisco Chronicle*, February 14, A10.

Hall, J.A. 1985. Male and female nonverbal behavior. In *Multichannel integrations of nonverbal behavior.* Edited by A.W. Siegman and S. Feldstein. Hillsdale, NJ: Lawrence Erlbaum, 195–226.

Heslin, R., and T. Alper 1983. Touch: A bonding gesture. In *Nonverbal interaction.* Edited by J.M. Wiemann and R.P. Harrison. Beverly Hills, CA: Sage, 47–75.

Hochschild, A. 1989. *The second shift: Working parents and the revolution at home.* New York: Viking.

Houk, J.W., and R.W. Daniel. 1994. Husbands' and wives' views of the communication in their marriages. *Journal of Humanistic Education and Development* 33(1):21–32.

Hunter, S. 2003. The blended bunch: Stepfamilies create new problems and new opportunities for growth. *Reno Gazette-Journal*, May 17, 1E, 3E.

Ihinger-Tallman, M., and K. Pasley. 1987. *Remarriage*. Newbury Park, CA: Sage.

Irvine, M. 2006. High technology losing its sheen for some users. *San Francisco Chronicle*, October 9, E3.

Jayson, S. 2005. Hearts divide over marital therapy. *USA Today*, June 22, 1D, 2D.

Johnson, S.M. 2005. The evolution of couples therapy: A new era. *The Psychologist: British Psychological Association* 18:538–39.

Johnstone, T., C.M. van Reekum, T.R. Oakes, and R.J. Davidson. 2006. The voice of emotion: An fMRI study of neural responses to angry and happy vocal expressions. *Social, Cognitive, and Affective Neuroscience* 1(3):242–49.

Jones, W.H., and M.P. Burdette, 1994. Betrayal in relationships. In *Perspectives on close relationships*. Edited by A.L. Weber and J.H. Harvey. Boston: Allyn & Bacon, 243–62.

Kantrowitz, B., and P. Wingert. 1999. The truth about tweens. *Newsweek*, October, 62–72.

Katz, L.F., and E.M. Woodin. 2002. Hostility, hostile detachment, and conflict engagement in marriages: Effects on child and family functioning. *Child Development* 73(2):636–52.

Kelly, K. 2001. Recipe for wedded bliss: Lower your expectations. *U.S. News & World Report*, May 28, 50.

Kiecolt-Glaser, J.K., C. Bane, R. Glaser, and W.B. Malarkey. 2003. Love, marriage, and divorce: Newlyweds stress hormones foreshadow relationship changes. *Journal of Consulting and Clinical Psychology* 71:176–88.

Kinicki, A., and B.K. Williams. 2008. *Management: A practical introduction*. 3rd ed. Burr Ridge, IL: McGraw-Hill/Irwin.

Kluwer, E.S., J.M. Heesink, and E. Van de Vliert. 1996. Marital conflict about the division of household labor and paid work. *Journal of Marriage and the Family* 58:968–69.

Knox, D., and Schacht, C. 2002. *Choices in relationships: An introduction to marriage and the family*. 7th ed. Belmont, CA: Wadsworth/Thomson Learning.

Kornblum, J. 2002. E-mail's limits create confusion, hurt feelings. *USA Today*, February 5, 6D.

Krasnow, I. 2002. *Surrendering to marriage: Husbands, wives, and other imperfections*. New York: Miramax Paperback.

Kurdek, L.A. 1995. Predicting change in marital satisfaction from husbands' and wives' conflict resolution styles. *Journal of Marriage and the Family* 57(1):153–64.

Lauer, R.H., and J.C. Lauer. 1988. *Watersheds: Mastering life's unpredictable crises*. Boston: Little, Brown.

Lerner, H.G. 1993.*The dance of deception: Pretending and truth-telling in women's lives*. New York: HarperCollins.

Lips, H.M. 1991. *Women, men, and power*. Mountain View, CA: Mayfield.

Lutz, P. 1983. The stepfamily: An adolescent perspective. *Family Relations* 32(3):367–75.

Lye, D.N., and T.J. Biblarz. 1993. The effects of attitudes toward family life and gender roles on marital satisfaction. *Journal of Family Issues* 14:157–88.

Mackey, R.A., and B.A. O'Brien. 1999. Adaptation in lasting marriages. *Families in Society: The Journal of Contemporary Human Services* 80:587–96.

Malandro, L.A., and L. Barker. 1983. *Nonverbal communication*. Reading, MA: Addison Wesley.

Markman, H., S. Stanley, and S.L. Blumberg. 1994. *Fighting for your marriage*. San Francisco: Jossey-Bass.

Markman, H., S. Stanley, and S.L. Blumberg. 2001. *Fighting for your marriage*, rev. ed. San Francisco: Jossey-Bass.

Matousek, M. 2007. We're wired to connect. *AARP*, January/February, 36–38.

McGonagle, K.A., R.C. Kessler, and I.H. Gotlib. 1993. The effects of marital disagreement style, frequency, and outcome on marital disruption. *Journal of Social and Personal Relationships*, 10:385–404.

McLeod, B. 1986. Rx for health: A dose of self-confidence. *Psychology Today* (October): 46–49.

Noller, P., J.A. Feeney, D. Bonnell, and V.J. Callan. 1994. A longitudinal study of conflict in early marriage. *Journal of Social and Personal Relationships* 11:233–52.

Norton, A.J. 1983. Family life cycle: 1980. *Journal of Marriage and the Family* 45:267–75.

Noveck, J. 2007. Internet offers forum to be nasty. *Reno Gazette-Journal*, March 21, 3C.

Oggins, J., J. Veroff, and D. Leber. 1993. Perceptions of marital interaction among black and white newlyweds. *Journal of Personality and Social Psychology* 65:94–511.

Patford, J.L. 2000. Partners and cross-sex friends: A preliminary study of the way marital and de facto partnerships affect verbal intimacy with cross-sex friends. *Journal of Family Studies* 6:106–19.

Pease, A., and B. Pease. 2006. *The definitive book of body language*. New York: Bantam Books.

Pressner, A. 2006. Can love blossom in a text message? *USA Today*, January 30, 7D.

Quinnett, P.G. 1989. The key to successful therapy. *Psychology Today* (April):46.

Raven, B.H., R. Centers, and A. Rodrigues. 1975. The bases of conjugal power. In *Power in families*. Edited by R. Cromwell and D. Olson. New York: Halstead Press.

Roberts, L., and L.J. Krokoff. 1990. A time-series analysis of withdrawal, hostility, and displeasure in satisfied and dissatisfied marriages. *Journal of Marriage and the Family* 52:95–105.

Roberts, L.J. 2000. Fire and ice in marital communication: Hostile and distancing behaviors as predictors of marital distress. *Journal of Marriage and the Family* 62(3):693–708.

Safilios-Rothschild, C. 1970. The study of the family power structure. *Journal of Marriage and the Family* 32(4):539–43.

Sampson, R. 1966. *The problem of power*. New York: Pantheon.

Satir, V. 1972. *Peoplemaking*. Palo Alto, CA: Science and Behavior Books.

Satir, V. 1988. *The new peoplemaking*. Mountain View, CA: Science and Behavior Books.

Scanzoni, J. 1970. *Opportunity and the family*. New York: Free Press.

Scarf, M. 1995. *Intimate worlds: Life inside the family*. New York: Random House.

Schrof, J.M., with B. Wagner. 1994. Sex in America. *U.S. News & World Report*, October 17, 75–81.

Sennett, R. 1980. *Authority*. New York: Knopf.

Smith, S.E., and T.L. Huston. 2004. How and why marriages change over time: Shifting patterns of companionship and partnership. In *Continuity and change: Family structure and family process*, edited by R. Conger, F.O. Lorenz, and K.A.S. Wicrama. Mahwah, NJ: Erlbaum Associates, 145–80.

Smith, T.W., C.A. Berg, B.N. Uchino, P. Florsheim, and G. Pearce. 2005. Association of spouse ratings of anxiety, anger, and depression with coronary artery calcification in healthy older adults. Paper presented at the annual meetings of the American Psychosomatic Society, Vancouver, March.

Sokhi, D.S., M.D. Hunter, I.D. Wilkinson, and P.W.R. Woodruff. 2005. Male and female voices activate distinct regions in the male brain. *NeuroImage* 27(3):572–78.

South, S., and K. Lloyd. 1995. A longitudinal study of marital problems and subsequent divorce. *American Sociological Review* 60: 21–35.

Sternberg, R.J., and D.M. Dobson. 1987. Resolving Interpersonal conflicts: An analysis of stylistic consistency. *Journal of Personality and Social Psychology* 52:794–812.

Stevenson, B., and J. Wolfers. 2007. The paradox of declining female happiness (draft). September 17, http://bpp.wharton.upenn .edu/jwolfers/Papers/WomensHappiness .pdf (accessed September 28, 2007).

Suler, J. 2002. The basic psychological features of cyberspace. In *The psychology of cyberspace*, www.rider.edu/suler/psycyber/ basicfeat.html (article orig. pub. 1996) (accessed May 17, 2007).

Tannen, D. 1990. *You just don't understand: Women and men in conversation*. New York: Morrow.

Thompson, L., and A.J. Walker 1989. Gender in families: Women and men in marriage, work, and parenthood. *Journal of Marriage and the Family* 51(4):845–72.

Vogel, E.F., and N.W. Bell. 1960. The emotionally disturbed child as family scapegoat. In *Modern introduction to the family*. Edited by N.W. Bell and E.F. Vogel. Glencoe, IL: Free Press, 382–97.

Waller, W., and R. Hill. 1951. *The family: A dynamic interpretation*. New York: Dryden Press.

Wallerstein, J.S., and S. Blakeslee. 1995. *The good marriage: How and why love lasts*. Boston: Houghton Mifflin.

Warfield, A. 2000. Do you speak body language? *Training and Development*, April, 60–61.

Waring, E.M. 1988. *Enhancing marital intimacy through facilitating cognitive self-disclosure*. New York: Brunner/Mazel.

Whisman, M.A., and N.S. Jacobson. 1990. Power, marital satisfaction, and response to marital therapy. *Journal of Family Psychology* 4:202–12.

Wilmot, J.H., and W.W. Wilmot. 1978. *Interpersonal conflict.* Dubuque, IA: Wm C. Brown.

CHAPTER 7

Abma, J.C., G.M. Martinez, W.D. Mosher, and B.S. Dawson. 2005. Teenagers in the United States: Sexual activity, contraceptive use, and childbearing, 2002. *Vital Health Statistics* 23(24):1–48.

Adler, J. 1991. Safer sex. *Newsweek,* December 9, 52–56.

AIDS Action. 2007. *HIV/AIDS in the United States.* Washington, DC: AIDS Action. www.aidsaction.org/communications/publications/statefactsheets/pdfs/2005/usa_2005L.pdf (accessed May 17, 2007).

Albert, B. 2007. *With one voice: America's adults and teens sound off about teen pregnancy.* Washington, DC: National Campaign to Prevent Teen Pregnancy, www.teenpregnancy.org/resources/data/pdf/WOV2007_fulltext.pdf (accessed May 17, 2007).

American Society of Plastic Surgeons. 2007. 11 million cosmetic plastic surgery procedures in 2006—up 7%. Press release, March 22, www.plasticsurgery.org/media/press_releases/2006-Stats-Overall-Release.cfm (accessed May 17, 2007).

Ansuini, C.G., J. Fiddler-Woite, and R.S. Woite. 1996. The source, accuracy, and impact of initial sexuality information on lifetime wellness. *Adolescence* 31(Summer):283–89.

Associated Press. 2006. Study shows equality improves sexual satisfaction. *San Francisco Chronicle,* April 20, A2.

Barbach, L. 1982. *For each other: Sharing sexual intimacy.* Garden City, NY: Doubleday.

Bechtel, S. 1991. Burning down the house. *Men's Health,* August, 78–80.

Bernstein, E. 2006. Sex-ed class becomes latest school battleground. *The Wall Street Journal,* March 30, D1, D6.

Bilefsky, D. 2005. Belgian experiment: Make prostitution legal to fight its ills. *The Wall Street Journal,* May 26, A1, A8.

Blaisdell, B. 2007. Behind men's obsession with virginity. *San Francisco Chronicle,* March 11, M1, M3.

Blank, H. 2007. *Virgin: The untouched history.* New York: Bloomsbury.

Blythe, M.J., J.D. Fortenberry, M. Temkit, W. Tu, and D.P. Orr. 2006. Incidence and correlates of unwanted sex in relationships of middle and late adolescent women. *Archives of Pediatric & Adolescent Medicine* 160:591–95.

Branchflower, D.G., and A.J. Oswald. 2004. Money, sex, and happiness: An empirical study. *Scandinavian Journal of Economics* 106(3):393–415, www2.warwick.ac.uk/fac/soc/economics/staff/faculty/oswald/finalsentscanjsex04.pdf (accessed May 17, 2007).

Brooks, G.R. 1995. *The centerfold syndrome: How men can overcome objectification and achieve intimacy with women.* San Francisco: Jossey-Bass.

Brooks-Gunn, J., and F. Furstenberg Jr. 1989. Adolescent sexual behavior. *American Psychologist* 44:249–57.

Brown, J.D., K.L. L'Engle, C.J. Pardun, G. Guo, K. Kenneavy, and C. Jackson. 2006. Sexy media matter: Exposure to sexual content in music, movies, television, and magazines predict black and white adolescents' sexual behavior. *Pediatrics* 117(4):1018–27.

Buxton, A.P. 1991. *The other side of the closet: The coming-out crisis for straight spouses.* Santa Monica, CA: IBS Press.

Buysse, A. 1996. Adolescents, young adults and AIDS: A study of actual knowledge vs. perceived need for additional information. *Journal of Youth and Adolescence* 25:259–71.

Byer, C.O., and L.W. Shainberg. 1991. *Dimensions of human sexuality.* 3rd ed. Dubuque, IA: Wm. C. Brown.

Carnes, P. 1983. *Out of the shadows: Understanding sexual addiction.* Minneapolis: CompCare.

Centers for Disease Control and Prevention. 2002. *HIV/AIDS surveillance report.* Atlanta: U.S. Department of Health and Human Services, Centers for Disease Control and Prevention, www.cdc.gov/hiv/stats/hasrlink.htm (accessed May 17, 2007).

Centers for Disease Control and Prevention. 2003. *Basic statistics: Cumulative cases by age.* Atlanta: U.S. Department of Health and Human Services, Centers for Disease Control and Prevision, www.cdc.gov/hiv/stats.htm#cumage (accessed May 17, 2007).

Centers for Disease Control and Prevention. 2005. *STD surveillance 2005 tables.* Atlanta: U.S. Department of Health and Human Services, Centers for Disease Control and Prevention, www.cdc.gov/std/stats/Tables/Table1.htm (accessed May 17, 2007).

Centers for Disease Control and Prevention. 2006. *HIV/AIDS surveillance report: HIV infection and AIDS in the United States and dependent areas, 2005.* Vol. 17. Atlanta: U.S. Department of Health and Human Services, Centers for Disease Control and Prevention, www.cdc.gov/hiv/topics/surveillance/basic.htm#aidsage (accessed May 17, 2007).

Centers for Disease Control and Prevention. 2007. *Basic statistics.* Atlanta: U.S. Department of Health and Human Services, Centers for Disease Control and Prevention, www.cdc.gov/hiv/topics/surveillance/basic.htm#exposure (accessed May 17, 2007).

Chin, J. 2007. Myths and misconceptions of the AIDS pandemic. *San Francisco Chronicle,* March 11, E5.

Christopher, F.S., and S. Sprecher. 2000. Sexuality in marriage, dating, and other relationships. *Journal of Marriage and the Family* 62(4):999–1018.

Conforth, T. 2004. STDs FAQs: Answers to frequently asked questions about sexually transmitted diseases. http://womenshealth.about.com/cs/stds/a/stdfaqs.htm (accessed April 29, 2007).

Consumers Union. 1989. Can you rely on condoms? *Consumer Reports,* March, 135–41.

Crary, D. 2006. Activists try to curtail hotel porn. *Reno Gazette-Journal,* August 23, 4C.

Crooks, R., and K. Baur. 2002. *Our sexuality.* 8th ed. Pacific Grove, CA: Wadsworth.

Delgado, R. 2002. Abstinence-only sex ed—does it work? *San Francisco Chronicle,* April 25, A1, A15.

Deveny, K. 2003. We're not in the mood. *Newsweek,* June 30, 40–46.

Donovan, P. 1998. School-based sexuality education: The issues and challenges. *Family Planning Perspectives* 30(4):188–94.

East, P., M. Felice, and M. Morgan. 1993. Sisters' and girlfriends' sexual and childbearing behavior: Effects on early adolescent girls' sexual outcomes. *Journal of Marriage and the Family* 55:953–63.

Escobar-Chaves, S.L., S.R. Tortolero, C.M. Markham, B.J. Low, P. Eitel, and P. Thickstun. 2005. Impact of the media on adolescent sexual attitudes and behavior. *Pediatrics* 116(1):303–26.

Finer, L.B. 2007. Trends in premarital sex in the United States, 1954–2003. *Public Health Reports* 122(1):73–78.

Finkel, M.L., and Finkel, S. 1985. Sex education in high school. *Society* 23:48–53.

Follingstad, D., and D. Kimbrell. 1986. Sexual fantasies revisited: An expansion and further clarification of variables affecting sex fantasy production. *Archives of Sexual Behavior* 15:475–86.

Freedman, S.G. 2006. Muzzling sex education on anything but abstinence. *The New York Times,* July 19, A21.

Friday, N. 1991. *Women on top: How real life has changed women's sexual fantasies.* New York: Simon & Schuster.

Fullilove, R.E., W. Barksdale, and M.T. Fullilove. 1994. Teens talk sex: Can we talk back? In *Sexual cultures and the construction of adolescent identities.* Edited by J. M. Irvine. Philadelphia, PA: Temple University Press, 31–32.

Gecas, V., and M.A. Seff. 1991. Families and adolescents: A review of the 1980s. In *Contemporary families: Looking forward, looking back.* Edited by A. Booth. Minneapolis: National Council on Family Relations, 208–25.

Goldberg, L. 1991. Walking away from the wild side. *San Francisco Chronicle,* November 10, C5.

Goodman, T. 2003. Death march with cocktails. *San Francisco Chronicle,* July 18, D1, D7.

Gorman, C. 1996. Battling the AIDS virus. *Time,* February 12, 62–65.

Greenberg, B.S., and R. Busselle. 1996. What's old, what's new: Sexuality on the soaps. *SIECUS Report* 24:14–16.

Greenblatt, C.S. 1983. The salience of sexuality in the early years of marriage. *Journal of Marriage and the Family* 45:289–99.

Haffner, D.W. 1997. What's wrong with abstinence-only sexuality education programs? *SIECUS Report* 25, April/May, 9–13.

Halpern-Felsher, B.L., J.L. Cornell, R.Y. Kropp, and J.M. Tschann. 2005. Oral versus vaginal sex among adolescents: Perceptions, attitudes, and behavior. *Pediatrics* 115(4):845–51.

Hanson, S.L., D. Myers, A.L. Ginsburg. 1987.

The role of responsibility and knowledge in reducing teenage out-of-wedlock childbearing. *Journal of Marriage and the Family* 49(2):241–56.

Harris Interactive for Earthlink. 2005. Who looks at online porn. *USA Today*, March 1, 1D.

Heaton, T.B., and C.K. Jacobson. 1994. Race differences in changing family demographics in the 1980s. *Journal of Marriage and the Family* 15:290–308.

Hesse-Biber, S.N., S.A. Howling, P. Leavy, and M. Lovejoy. 2004. Racial identity and the development of body image issues among African American adolescent girls. *The Qualitative Report* 9(1):49–79.

Huey, C., G. Kline-Graber, and B. Graber. 1981. Time factors and orgasmic response. *Archives of Sexual Behavior* 21:111–18.

Jayson, S. 2005.What is sex? "Technical virginity" becomes part of teens' equation. *USA Today*, October 19, 7D.

Johnson, K. 2007. Investigation of child porn site hits 77 nations. *USA Today*, February 8, 13A.

Josselson, R. 1992. *The space between us.* San Francisco: Jossey-Bass.

Kinsey, A., W. Pomeroy, and C. Martin. 1948. *Sexual behavior in the human male.* Philadelphia, PA: Saunders.

Kinsey, A., W. Pomeroy, and C. Martin. 1953. *Sexual behavior in the human female.* Philadelphia, PA: Saunders.

Kirby, D., L. Short, J. Collins, D. Rugg, L. Kolbe, M. Howard, B. Miller, F. Sonenstein, and L.S. Zabin. 1994. School-based programs to reduce sexual risk behaviors: A review of effectiveness. *Public Health Reports* 109(3): 339–60.

Klein, M. 1992. The answer guy. *Men's Health*, June, 84–85.

Knox, D., C. Cooper, and M.E. Zusman. 2001. Sexual values of college students. *College Student Journal* 35(1):24–27.

Kunkel, D., E. Biely, K. Eyal, K. Cope-Farrar, E. Donnerstein, and R. Fandrich. 2003. *Sex on TV 2003: A biennial report to the Kaiser Family Foundation.* Washington, DC: Henry J. Kaiser Family Foundation. www.kff.org/entmedia/loader.cfm?url=/commonspot/security/getfile.cfm&PageID=14209 (accessed September 17, 2007).

Kunkel, D., K. Eyal, K. Finnerty, E. Biely, and E. Donnerstein. 2005. *Sex on TV 4: A Kaiser Family Foundation report.* Menlo Park, CA: Henry J. Kaiser Family Foundation, www.kff.org/entmedia/upload/Sex-on-TV-4-Full-Report.pdf (accessed May 17, 2007).

LaFraniere, S. 2005. Women's rights and African custom clash. *The New York Times,* December 30, A1, A10.

Laumann, E.O., A. Paik, D.B. Glasser, J.-H. Kang, T. Wang, B. Levinson, E.D. Moreira Jr., A. Nicolosi, and C. Gingell. 2006. A cross-national study of subjective sexual well-being among older women and men: Findings from the Global Study of Sexual Attitudes and Behaviors. *Archives of Sexual Behavior* 35(2):145–61.

Laumann, E.O., J.H. Gagnon, R.T. Michael, and S. Michaels. 1994. *The social organization of sexuality: Sexual practices in the United States.* Chicago: University of Chicago Press.

Leff, L. 2005. Sex researchers convene to study "moral panics." *Reno Gazette-Journal,* June 20, 4B.

Lindau, S.T., L.P. Schumm, E.O. Laumann, W. Levinson, C.A. O'Muircheartaigh, and L.J. Waite. 2007. A study of sexuality and health among older adults in the United States. *New England Journal of Medicine* 357:762–74.

Loftus, M. 2000. The roots of being blond. *U.S. News & World Report,* March 13, 52.

Luker, K. 2006. *When sex goes to school: Warring views on sex—and sex education—since the sixties.* New York: W. W. Norton.

Marin, P. 1983. A revolution's broken promises. *Psychology Today* (July):50–57.

Martin, G. 1991. The body trade. *San Francisco Chronicle, This World.* August 11, 7–10.

Martino, S.C., R.L. Collins, M.N. Elliott, A. Strachman, D.E. Kanouse, and S.H. Berry. 2006. Exposure to degrading versus nondegrading music lyrics and sexual behavior among youth. *Pediatrics* 118(2):430–41.

Maslach, G., and G.B. Kerr. 1983. Tailoring sex-education programs to adolescents: A strategy for the primary prevention of unwanted adolescent pregnancies. *Adolescence* 18(70): 449–56.

McAnulty, R.D., and M.M. Burnette. 2004. *Exploring human sexuality: Making healthy decisions,* 2nd ed. Boston: Allyn & Bacon.

McMahon, K. 1990. The cosmopolitan ideology and the management of desire. *Journal of Sex Research* 27(3):381–96.

Meckler, L. 2002. Teen sex often begins right at home, study finds. *San Francisco Chronicle,* September 26, A2.

Meier, A.M. 2003. Adolescents' transition to first intercourse, religiosity, and attitudes about sex. *Social Forces* 81(3):103–25.

Melchert, T., and K.F. Burnett. 1990. Attitudes, knowledge, and sexual behavior of high-risk adolescents: Implications for counseling and sexuality education. *Journal of Counseling and Development* 68:293–98.

Michael, R.T., J.H. Gagnon, E.O. Laumann, and G. Kolata. 1994. *Sex in America.* Boston: Little, Brown.

Miller, K.S., B.A. Kotchick, S. Doresey, R. Forehand, and A.Y. Ham. 1998. Family communication about sex: What are parents saying and are their adolescents listening? *Family Planning Perspectives* 30(5):218–23.

Moffatt, M. 1989. *Coming of age in New Jersey: College and American culture.* New Brunswick, NJ: Rutgers University Press.

Morse, J. 2002. An Rx for teen sex. *Time,* October 7, 64–65.

Mosher, W.D., A. Chandra, and J. Jones. 2005. *Sexual behavior and selected health measures: Men and women 15–44 years of age, United States, 2002.* Advance data from vital and health statistics; no. 362. Hyattsville, MD: National Center for Health Statistics, www.cdc.gov.nchs/data/ad/ad362.pdf (accessed May 17, 2007).

Muehlenhard, C.L., and S.W. Cook. 1988. Men's self-reports of unwanted sexual activity. *The Journal of Sex Research* 24:58–72.

Mulrine, A. 2002. Risky business. *U.S. News & World Report,* May 27, 42–49.

National Opinion Research Center, University of Chicago. 1990. *Report on sexual behavior.* Presented to February 1990 American Association for the Advancement of Science Meeting, New Orleans.

Nicolosi, A., M.L. Correa Leite, M. Musicco, C. Arici, G. Gavazzeni, and A. Lazzarin. 1994. The efficiency of male to-female and female-to-male sexual transmission of the human immunodeficiency virus: A study of 730 stable couples. Italian Study Group on HIV Heterosexual Transmission. *Epidemiology* 5(6):570–75.

Parker, E., and A. Furnham. 2007. Does sex sell? The effect of sexual programme content on the recall of sexual and non-sexual advertisements, *Applied Cognitive Psychology,* January 26, www3.interscience.wiley.com/cgi-bin/abstract/114082375/ABSTRACT (accessed May 17, 2007).

Patton, G.C., J.B. Carlin, Q. Shao, M.E. Hibbert, M. Rosier, R. Selzer, and G. Bowes. 1997. Healthy weight control or borderline eating disorder? *Journal of Child Psychology and Psychiatry and Allied Disciplines* 38(3):299–306.

Paul, P. 2005. *Pornified: How pornography is transforming our lives, our relationships, and our families.* New York: Times Books/Henry Holt & Company.

Pinkerton, S., L. Bogart, H. Cecil, and P. Abramson. 2002. Factors associated with masturbation in a collegiate sample. *Journal of Psychology and Human Sexuality* 14(2/3):103–21.

Poirot, C. 2002. Eating disorders strike younger children. *Reno Gazette-Journal,* October 22, 4F.

Porn in the U.S.A. 2004. 60 Minutes. September 5. www.cbsnews.com/stories/2003/11/21/60minutes/main585049.shtml (accessed September 5, 2007).

Poulson, R.L., M.A. Eppler, T.N. Satterwhite, K.L. Wuench, and L.A. Bass. 1998. Alcohol consumption, strength of religious beliefs, and risky sexual behavior in college students. *Journal of American College Health* 46: 227–34.

Reiss, Ira L. 1976. *Family systems in America.* 2nd ed. Hinsdale, IL: Dryden.

Remez, L. 2000. Oral sex among adolescents: Is it sex or is it abstinence? *Family Planning Perspectives* 32(6):298–304.

Rosenbaum, J. 2006. Reborn a virgin: Adolescents' retracting of virginity pledges and sexual histories. *American Journal of Public Health* 96:1098–1103.

Russell, S. 2006. Black leaders call for more HIV testing. *San Francisco Chronicle,* August 15, A3.

Sanders, S.A., and J.M. Reinisch. 1999. Would you say you "had sex" if . . .? *Journal of the American Medical Association* 281:275–77.

Schackman, B.R., K.A. Gebo, R.P. Walensky, E. Losina, T. Muccio, P.E. Sax, M.C. Weinstein, G.R. Seage 3rd, R.D. Moore, and K.A. Freedberg. 2006. The lifetime cost of current human immunodeficiency virus care in the United States. *Medical Care* 44(11):990–97.

Schalet, A.T. 2000. Raging hormones, regulated loved: Adolescent sexuality in the United States and the Netherlands. *Body and Society* 6(1):75–105.

Schemo, D.J. 2002. Mothers of sex-active youths often think they're virgins. *The New York Times*, September 5, A14.

Schmitt, E. 1993. In fear, gay soldiers marry for camouflage. *New York Times*, July 12, A7.

Sex for sale (editorial). 1992. *The Times* (London), April 23, 13.

Shifrin, D. L., A. Brown, B.P. Dreyer, K.R. Ginsburg, R.M. Milteer, K.G. Nelson, and D.A. Mulligan. 2006. Children, adolescents, and advertising. *Pediatrics* 118(6):2563–69.

Simon, C. 2000–2001. Hooked. *Ms. Magazine*. December/January. www.msmagazine .com/jan01/hooked_jan01.html (accessed September 16, 2004).

Song, E.Y., B.E. Pruitt, J. McNamara, and B. Colwell. 2000. A meta-analysis examining effects of school sexuality education programs on adolescents' sexual knowledge, 1960–1977. *Journal of School Health* 70(10):413–16.

Spindler, A.M. 2001. Beheld: The alternate reality of the prettiest girl. *The New York Times Magazine*, September 9, 132–36.

Statistical Abstract of the United States: 2007. 2006. Washington, DC: U.S. Census Bureau, December 15, www.census.gov/prod/ 2006pubs/07statab/infocomm.pdf (accessed May 17, 2007).

Stodgill, R. 1998. Where'd you learn that? A Time/CNN poll. *Time*, 15 June, 52 passim.

Strasburger, V.C. 1997. Tuning in to teenagers. *Newsweek*, May 19, 18–19.

Strouse, J.S., and N.L. Buerkel-Rothfuss. 1987. Media exposure and the sexual attitudes and behaviors of col-lege students. *Journal of Sex Education and Therapy* 13:43–51.

Sue, D. 1979. Erotic fantasies of college students during coitus. *Journal of Sex Research* 15:299–305.

Taris, T.W., C.R. Semin, and I.A. Bok. 1998. The effect of quality of family interaction and intergenerational transmission of values on sexual permissiveness. *Journal of Genetic Psychology* 159:237–51.

Terry-Humen, E., J. Manlove, and S. Cottingham. 2006. *Trends and recent estimates: Sexual activity among U.S. teens*. Research brief, June. Washington, DC: Child Trends, www.childtrends.org/Files//Child_Trends 2006_06_01_RB_SexualActivity.pdf (accessed May 17, 2007).

"The naked truth." 2000. *Newsweek*, May 8, 58–59.

Thomsen, D., and I.J. Chang. 2000. Predictors of satisfaction with first intercourse: A new perspective for sexuality education. Poster presentation at 62nd Annual Conference of the National Council on Family Relations, Minneapolis, November.

Trussell, J., and C.F. Westoff. 1980. Contraceptive practice and trends in coital frequency. *Family Planning Perspectives* 12:246–49.

Udry, J.R., J. Kovenock, N.M. Morris, and B.J. van den Berg. 1995. Childhood precursors of age at first intercourse for females. *Archives of Sexual Behavior* 24:329–37.

UNAIDS. 2006. *2006 report on global AIDS epidemic*. Joint United Nations Programme on HIV/AIDS, May, www.unaids.org/en/ HIV_data/2006GlobalReport (accessed May 17, 2007).

Wakabi, W. 2007. Circumcision trials halted. *The Lancet* 7(2):86–87.

Ward, M. 1995. Talking about sex: Common themes about sexuality in the prime-time television programs children and adolescents view most. *Journal of Youth and Adolescence* 24:595–615.

Ward, M. 2000. Does television exposure affect adolescents' sexual attitudes and expectations? Correlational and experimental confirmation. Paper presented at annual meeting of the Society for Research on Adolescence, Chicago. March.

Wellings, K., M. Collumbien, E. Slaymaker, S. Singh, Z. Hodges, D. Patel, and N. Majos. 2006. Sexual behaviour in context: A global perspective. *The Lancet* 368(9548):1706–28.

Westoff, C. 1974. Coital frequency and contraception. *Family Planning Perspectives* 6:136–41.

Whitman, D. 1997. Was it good for us? *U.S. News & World Report*, May 19, 56–64.

Widmer, E.D. 1997. Influence of older siblings on initiation of sexual intercourse. *Journal of Marriage and the Family* 59:928–38.

Wiederman, M.W. 1997. Extramarital sex: Prevalence and correlates in a national survey. *Journal of Sex Research* 34:167–74.

Wilson, E. 2002. The media's portrayal of women. http://pages.towson.edu/itrow/ fact%20sheets/media_images_of_women .htm (accessed April 29, 2004).

Wolak, J.D., K. Mitchell, and D. Finkelhor. 2007. Unwanted and wanted exposure to online pornography in a national sample of youth Internet users. *Pediatrics* 119(2):247–57.

Wolf, M., and A. Kielwasser. 1991. Introduction: The body electric: Human sexuality and the mass media. *Journal of Homosexuality* 21(1/2):7–18.

Wong, M. 2006. Internet video sharing gets too graphic. *San Francisco Chronicle*, July 10, C1, C6.

Wooley, S.C., and O.W. Wooley. 1984. Feeling fat in a thin society. *Glamour*, February, 198–252.

Workman, B. 1991. Sex at Stanford not always safe, poll finds. *San Francisco Chronicle*, May 2, A20.

World Health Organization. 1992. *Reproductive health: A key to a brighter future*. Cited in Associated Press. 1992. U.N. agency on sex: Pitfalls and promise. *The New York Times*, June 25, A4.

Zilbergeld, B. 1992. *The new male sexuality: The truth about men, sex, and pleasure*. New York: Bantam.

Zuger, A. 2006. A long life? A death sentence? AIDS still offers no easy answers. *The New York Times*, June 6, D1, D6.

Zurbriggen, E.L., R.L. Collins, S. Lamb, T.-A. Roberts, D.L. Tolman, L.M. Ward, and J. Blake. 2007. *Report of the APA Task Force on the Sexualization of Girls*. Washington, DC: American Psychological Association.

CHAPTER 8

Abma, J., A. Driscoll, and K. Moore. 1998. Young women's degree of control over first intercourse: An exploratory analysis. *Family Planning Perspectives* 30:12–18.

Adler, J. 1996. Adultery: A new furor over an old sin. *Newsweek*, September 30, 54–60.

Barker, O. 2006. Wedding webcasts engage more interest. *USA Today*, July 18, 1D.

Begley, S. 2002. Kissing-cousin taboo: Can love conquer biological destiny? *The Wall Street Journal*, May 17, B1.

Bennett, R.L., A.G. Motulsky, A. Bittles, L. Hudgins, S. Uhrich, D.L. Doyle, K. Silvey, C.R. Scott, E. Cheng, B. McGillivray, R. Steiner, and D. Olson. 2002. Genetic counseling and screening consanguineous couples and their offspring: Recommendations of the National Society of Genetic Counselors. *Journal of Genetic Counseling* 11:97–119.

Bialik, C. 2007. Weddings are not the budget drains some surveys suggest. *The Wall Street Journal*, August 24, B1.

Bianco, R. 2006. What happened to the really big shows? *USA Today*, December 15, 1E, 2E.

Billingsley, S., M. Lim, and G. Jennings. 1995. Themes of long-term, satisfied marriages consummated between 1952–1967. *Family Perspective* 29:283–95.

Blumstein, P. 1976. Identity bargaining and self-conception. *Social Forces* 53(3):476–85.

Bonds-Raacke, J.M., E.S. Bearden, N.J. Carriere, E.M. Anderson, and S.D. Nicks. 2001. Engaging distortions: Are we idealizing marriage? *Journal of Psychology* 135 (2):179–85.

Bryan-Low, C. 2007. British bridegrooms bring stag revelry to Eastern Europe. *The Wall Street Journal*, April 10, A1, A10.

Buck, J.J. 2003. France's prophet provocateur. *Vanity Fair*, January, 86–92, 118–121.

Caplan, J. 2005. Metrosexual matrimony. *Time*, October 3, 67.

Coontz, S. 2000. Marriage: Then and now. *Phi Kappa Phi Journal* 80:16–20.

Coontz, S. 2006a. Marriage as a social contract. *Philadelphia Inquirer*, October 22, www.contemporaryfamilies.org/subtem plate.php?t=inTheNews&ext=marriageas contract (accessed July 6, 2007).

Coontz, S. 2006b. How to stay married. *The Times of London*, November 30, http:// stephaniecoontz.com/articles/article34 .htm (accessed July 6, 2007).

Corliss, R. 2002. Cousins: A new theory of relativity. *Time*, April 15, 60.

Cuber, J., and P. Harroff. 1965. *Sex and the significant Americans*. Baltimore: Penguin.

Dickinson, A. 2002. The rules for modern weddings. *Time*, May 20, 89.

Dodes, R. 2007. Webbed bliss: Brides and grooms tell all online. *The Wall Street Journal*, May 31, A1, A13.

Dubin, A. 2001a. *Prenups for lovers: A romantic guide to prenuptial agreement*. New York: Random House.

Dubin, A. 2001b. Ah, romance! Our love, my money [letter]. *The New York Times*, July 14, A28.

Dugas, C. 2002. Some prenups are set up to expire. *USA Today*, March 15, 3B.

Duvall, E., and B. Miller. 1985. *Marriage and family development*. 6th ed. New York: Harper & Row.

Dysfunction rules, man! 2003. *USA Today*, January 21, 11A.

Edwards, T.M. 2000. Flying solo. *Time*, August 28, 47–53.

Elias, M. 1997. Couples in pre-kid, no-kid marriages happiest. *USA Today*, August 12, D1.

Erikson, E. 1963. *Childhood and society*. New York: Norton.

Fears, D., and C. Deane. 2001. Biracial couples report tolerance. National survey by *The Washington Post*, the Henry J. Kaiser Family Foundation, and Harvard University. *Washington Post*, July 5, A1.

Finkel, J.A., and F. Hansen. 1992. Correlates of retrospective marital satisfaction in long-lived marriages: A social constructivist perspective. *Family Therapy* 19(1):1–16.

Frey, C. 2002. Eat, drink and be married at the ballpark: From coast to coast, couples are shirking tradition, choosing instead to tie the knot in stadiums. *Los Angeles Times*, April 21, E1.

Frey, W. 2003. Rainbow nation: Mixed race marriages among states. *Milkin Institute Review*, Third Quarter, 7–10, http://www.frey-demographer.org/reports/Rainbow nation.pdf (accessed July 6, 2007).

Friess, S. 2007. What's in a name? A radical change. *USA Today*, March 21, 6D.

Furstenberg, F.F. Jr. 1996. The future of marriage. *American Demographis* 18(6):34–40.

Glenn, N. 1989. Duration of marriage, family composition, and marital happiness. *National Journal of Sociology* 3:3–24.

Glenn, N. 1991. The recent trend in marital success in the United States. *Journal of Marriage and the Family* 53(2):261–70.

Glick, P. 1989. The family life cycle and social change. *Family Relations* 38(2):123–29.

Goldin, C., and M. Shim. 2004. Making a name: Women's surnames at marriage and beyond. *Journal of Economic Perspectives* 18:143–160.

Gordon, D. 2005. Family reunion. *Newsweek*, April 4, 50–51.

Grady, D. 2002. Few risks seen to the children of 1st cousins. *The New York Times*, April 4, A1, A16.

Greenberg, D. 1999. White weddings: The incredible staying power of the laws against interracial marriage. Slate. June 15. http://slate.msn.com/id/30352/ (accessed April 15, 2007).

Greenberg, S.H., and A. Kuchment. 2006. The "familymoon." *Newsweek*, January 9, 46–47.

Gunderson, E. 2002. Uncovering the real Osbournes. *USA Today*, November 22, 1E, 2E.

Hannon, K. 2006. Planning for love and money. *U.S. News & World Report*, July 24, 53–55.

Hartill, L. 2001. A brief history of interracial marriage. *Christian Science Monitor*, July 25. http://search.csmonitor.com/durable/2001/07/25/p15s1.htm (accessed May 1, 2007).

Hochschild, A. 1989. *The second shift: Working parents and the revolution at home*. New York: Avon Books.

Huyck, M.H., and U.L. Gutmann. 1992. Thirtysomething years of marriage: Understanding experiences of women and men in enduring family relationships. *Family Perspective* 26:249–65.

Jayson, S. 2006. Experts: TV doesn't always know best. *USA Today*, March 20, 6D.

Kasindorf, M. 2007. L.A. man sues to take wife's last name. *USA Today*, January 12, 3A.

Katz, S.J., and A.E. Liu. 1988. *False love and other romantic illusions: Why love goes wrong and how to make it right*. New York: Ticknor & Fields.

Kenney, K.R. 2002. Counseling interracial couples and multiracial individuals: Applying a multicultural counseling competency framework. *Counseling and Human Development* 35(14):1–13.

Keveney, B. 2002. "Married" films the state of the union. *USA Today*, June 17, 3D.

Kilborn, P.T. 1994. More women take low-wage jobs so their families can get by. *The New York Times*, March 13, A1.

Klein, D.A. 2003. The "weddingmooners." *Newsweek*, January 27, 70–71.

Knox, D.H. Jr. 1975. *Marriage: Who? When? Why?* Englewood Cliffs, NJ: Prentice-Hall.

Knudson-Martin, C., and A. Mahoney. 1998. Language and processes in the construction of marital equality in new marriages. *Family Relations* 47:81–91.

Lamanna, M.A., and R. Riedmann. 2000. *Marriages and families: Making choices in a diverse society*. 7th ed. Belmont, CA: Wadsworth/Thomson Learning.

Larson, R., and M.H. Richards. 1994. *Divergent realities: The emotional lives of mothers, fathers, and adolescents*. New York: Basic Books.

Laurence, R.P. 2003. Reality shows now taking bite out of marriage, family. *San Diego Union-Tribune*, March 18, D1.

Levine, R., S. Sato, T. Hashimoto, and J. Verma. 1995. Love and marriage in eleven cultures. *Journal of Cross-Cultural Psychology* 26: 554–71.

Lewin, T. 2001. Among nuptial agreements, post- has now joined pre-. *The New York Times*, July 7, A1, A8.

Markides, K.S., J. Roberts-Jolly, L.A. Ray, S.K. Hoppe, and L. Rudkin. 1999. Changes in marital satisfaction in three generations of Mexican Americans. *Research on Aging* 21:36–45.

Martin, P.D., M. Martin, and D. Martin. 2001. Adolescent premarital sexual activity, cohabitation, and attitudes toward marriage. *Adolescence* 36(143):601–10.

Medved, M. 2002. Pop culture embraces weird but realistic families. *USA Today*, September 24, 13A.

Michael, R.T., J.H. Gagnon, E.O. Laumann, and G. Kolata. 1994. *Sex in America*. Boston: Little, Brown.

Mills, A.C. 2002. Multi culti weddings. *San Francisco Chronicle Magazine*, June 23, 18, 20–23.

Mitchell, B.A., and E.M. Gee. 1996. "Boomerang kids" and midlife parental marital satisfaction. *Family Relations* 45: 442–48.

Nock, S.L. 1995. A comparison of marriages and cohabiting relationships. *Journal of Family Issues* 16:53–76.

O'Neill, N., and G. O'Neill. 1972. *Open marriage: A new life style for couples*. New York: M. Evans.

Ortega, S.T., H.P. Whitt, and J.A. Williams Jr. 1988. Religious homogamy and marital happiness. *Journal of Family Issues* 9:224–39.

Parnes, F. 2006. Avert a fractured fairy tale, a wedding planner. *The New York Times*, July 23, sec. 3, p. 6.

Patterson, J., and P. Kim. 1991. *The day America told the truth: What people really believe about everything that really matters*. Upper Saddle River, NJ: Prentice-Hall.

Pew Research Center. 2007. *As marriage and parenthood drift apart, public is concerned about social impact: Generation gap in values, behaviors*, July 1. New York: Pew Research Center, http://pewresearch.org/assets/social/pdf/Marriage.pdf (accessed July 7, 2007).

Pittman, F. 1999. *Grow up! How taking responsibility can make you a happy adult*. New York: Golden Books.

Presser, H.B. 1993. The housework gender gap. *Population Today* 21:5.

Private proposals go over better. 2007. Harris Interactive survey via QuickQuery of 2,288 adults for Blue Nile, November 14–16, 2006, reported in *USA Today*, April 9, 1D.

Qian, Z., and D.T. Lichter. 2007. Social boundaries and marital assimilation: Interpreting trends in racial and ethnic intermarriage. *American Sociological Review* 72:68–94.

Quinn, W., and M. Odell. 1998. Predictors of marital adjustment during the first two years. *Marriage and Family Review* 27(1/2):113–30.

Reiss, I. 1980. *Family systems in America*. 3rd ed. New York: Holt, Rinehart, & Winston.

Robinson, J.P., and G. Godbey. 1997. *Time for life: The surprising ways Americans use their time*. University Park: Pennsylvania State University Press.

Rubin, S. 2002. And the bride wore red? *San Francisco Chronicle Magazine*, June 23, 25, 39.

Sarnoff, I., and S. Sarnoff. 1989. The dialectic of marriage. *Psychology Today* (October):54–57.

Scarf, M. 1995. *Intimate worlds: Life inside the family*. New York: Random House.

Scheuble, L.K., K. Klingemann, and D.R. Johnson. 2000. Trends in women's marital name choice: A content analysis of marriage announcements in the *New York Times* from 1966–1996. *Names* 48:51–63.

Schwartz, P. 1994. *Peer marriage: Love between equals*. New York: Free Press.

Silverman, R. E. 2005. Beyond the prenup. *The Wall Street Journal*, September 22, D1, D2.

Silverman, R.E. 2003. 'I do, I do, I do, I do . . .' *The Wall Street Journal*, August 28, D1, D15.

Skolnick, A. 2002. Grounds for marriage: Reflections and research on an institution in transition. In *Inside the American couple: New thinking/new challenges*. Edited by M. Yalom and L.L. Carstensen. Berkeley: University of California Press, 149–63.

Steffens, S. 2002. Before the wedding, learn

marriage skills, counselors say. *Reno Gazette-Journal*, June 16, 2B.

Stutzer, A., and B.S. Frey. 2006. Does marriage make people happy, or do happy people get married? *Journal of Socio-Economics* 35(2):326–347.

Surge in "prenups." 2007. Survey by American Academy of Matrimonial Lawyers, reported in *The Futurist*, January/February, www.wfs.org/tibsjf07.htm (accessed July 6, 2007).

Teachout, T. 2002. Is Tony Soprano today's Ward Cleaver? *The New York Times*, September 15, sec. 4, 3.

Teti, D.M., and M. Lamb. 1989. Socioeconomic and marital outcomes of adolescent marriage, adolescent childbirth, and their co-occurrence. *Journal of Marriage and the Family* 51:103–12.

Twenge, J.M., W.K. Campbell, and C.A. Foster. 2003. Parenthood and marital satisfaction: A meta-analytic review. *Journal of Marriage and the Family* 65:574–83.

Vaillant, C.O., and G.E. Vaillant. 1993. Is the U-curve of marital satisfaction an illusion? A 40-year study of marriage. *Journal of Marriage and the Family* 55(1):230–40.

Wallerstein, J.S., and S. Blakeslee. 1995. *The good marriage: How and why love lasts.* Boston: Houghton Mifflin.

Whyte, M.K. 1990. *Dating, mating, and marriage.* New York: Aldine de Gruyter.

Willis, S.L., and J.D. Reid, eds. 1999. *Life in the middle: Psychological and social development in middle age.* San Diego, CA: Academic Press.

Wolff, Z. 2005. Going to the therapist en route to the altar. *The New York Times*, June 16, E1, E2.

World Values Survey. 1990. *World Values Survey*, www.worldvaluessurvey.org/ (accessed July 7, 2007).

Zaslow, J. 2005. Love and the Jumbotron: Why men turn marriage proposals into public events. *The Wall Street Journal*, August 4, D1.

CHAPTER 9

Ahlburg, D.A., and C.J. De Vita. 1992. New realities of the American family. *Population Bulletin* 47 (August): entire issue.

Ahn, K. 2001. Loyal live-ins. *San Francisco Chronicle*, August 12, B8, B9.

Allen, K., and D.H. Demo. 1995. The families of lesbians and gay men: A new frontier in family research. *Journal of Marriage and the Family* 57:111–27.

Allport, G. 1958. *The nature of prejudice.* Garden City, NY: Doubleday.

Alpert, B. 2002. Both sides in gay adoption debate say children's welfare is at stake. *San Francisco Chronicle*, April 5, H6.

Alternatives to Marriage Project. 2007. FAQ: Frequently asked questions. www.unmarried.org/ (accessed September 27, 2007).

Altman, I., and J. Ginat. 1996. *Polygamous families in contemporary societies.* Cambridge, MA: Cambridge University Press.

Alvarez, L. 2007. Long Iraq tours can make home a trying front. *The New York Times*, February 23, A1, A14.

American Association for Single People. 2001.

Households by type: 1980–2000. *2000 Census—ASSP Report.* www.unmarriedamerica.org/Census%202000/households-type-trends-family%20diversity.htm (accessed September 26, 2007).

Appleby, G.A., and J.W. Anastas. 1998. *Not just a passing phase: Social work with gay, lesbian, and bisexual people.* New York: Columbia University Press.

Apter, T. 2001. *The myth of maturity: What teenagers need from parents to become adults.* New York: W.W. Norton.

Armas, G.C. 2001. One-parent families on rise around the world. *Reno Gazette-Journal*, November 22, 16A.

Armas, G.C. 2002a. 'Burbs increasingly filled with single families. *Reno Gazette-Journal*, March 15, 3D.

Armas, G.C. 2002b. More kids in care of grandmas, grandpas. *San Francisco Chronicle*, July 8, A2.

Armas, G.C. 2004. Census shows more people putting off wedded bless. *Reno Gazette-Journal*, December 2, 7A.

Arnett, J.J. 2006. *Emerging adulthood: The winding road from the late teens through the twenties.* New York: Oxford University Press.

Ash, M.A., and M.V.L. Badgett. 2006. Separate and unequal: The effect of unequal access to employment-based health insurance on same-sex and unmarried different-sex couples. *Contemporary Economic Policy* 24(4):582–99.

Baldor, L.C. 2006a. Homosexuality listed as a mental disorder. *San Francisco Chronicle*, June 20, A2.

Baldor, L.C. 2006b. Pentagon redefines homosexuality. *San Francisco Chronicle*, November 17, A2.

Banerjee, N. 2007. Sex scandal pastor says after therapy he's heterosexual. *San Francisco Chronicle*, February 7, A9; reprinted from *The New York Times*.

Bell, A.P., and M.S. Weinberg. 1978. *Homosexualities: A study of human diversity.* New York: Simon & Schuster.

Berg, N., and D. Lien. 2002. Measuring the effect of sexual orientation on income: Evidence of discrimination? *Contemporary Economic Policy* 20(4):394–414.

Berglund, H., P. Lindström, and I. Savic. 2006. Brain response to putative pheromones in lesbian women. *Proceedings of the National Academy of Sciences* 103(21):8269–74.

Bernstein, N. 2007. Polygamy, practiced in secrecy, follows Africans to New York City. *The New York Times*, March 23, A1, A20.

Biblarz, T.J., and G. Gottainer. 2000. Family structure and children's success: A comparison of widowed and divorced single-mother families. *Journal of Marriage and the Family* 62:533–48.

Billy, J., K. Tanfer, W.R. Grady, and D.H. Kiepinger. 1993. The sexual behavior of men in the United States. *Family Planning Perspectives* 25(2):52–60.

Black, D., C. Gates, S. Sanders, and L. Taylor. 2000. Demographics of the gay and lesbian population in the United States: Evidence from available systematic data sources. *Demography* 37:139–54.

Block, S. 1999. Living together? Commit to contract. *USA Today*, October 15, 3B.

Blumstein, P., and P. Schwartz. 1983. *American couples: Money, work, sex.* New York: William Morrow.

Bock, J.D. 2000. Doing the right thing? Single mothers by choice and the struggle for legitimacy. *Gender and Society* 14:62–86.

Bogaert, A.F. 2006. Biological versus nonbiological older brothers and men's sexual attraction. *Proceedings of the National Academy of Sciences* 103(28):10771–74.

Brand, P.A., and A.H. Kidd. 1986. Frequency of physical aggression in heterosexual and female homosexual dyads. *Psychological Reports* 59: 1307–13.

Brannock, J.C., and B.E. Chapman. 1990. Negative sexual experiences with men among heterosexual women and lesbians. *Journal of Homosexuality* 19:105–10.

Brooke, J. 1998a. Gay man beaten and left for dead; 2 are charged. *The New York Times*, October 10, A9.

Brooke, J. 1998b. Gay man dies from attack, fanning outrage and debate. *New York Times*, October 13, A1.

Brown, P.L. 2006. Growing old together, in a new kind of commune. *The New York Times*, February 20, A1, A16.

Bruce, J., C.B. Lloyd, and A. Leonard. 1995. Introduction to *Families in focus: New perspectives on mothers, fathers, and children.* New York: The Population Council.

Bryson, K., and L. Casper. 1998. Household and family characteristics: March 1997. *Current Population Reports.* Washington, DC: U.S. Census Bureau.

Buchanan, W. 2005. Report: "Ex-gay" therapy claims deceptive. *San Francisco Chronicle*, March 3, A4.

Butler, A.C. 2000. Trends in same-gender sexual partnering, 1988–1998. *Journal of Sex Research* 37(4):333–43.

Butler, K. 2006. Many couples must negotiate terms of "Brokeback" marriages. *The New York Times*, March 7, D5, D7.

Buxton, A.P. 2004. Straight Spouse Network: What we do. www.ssnetwk.org/whatwe.shtml (accessed October 11, 2007).

Cagen, S. 2004. *Quirky alone: A manifesto for uncompromising romantics.* San Francisco: HarperSanFrancisco.

Cargan, L., and M. Melko. 1982. *Singles: Myths and realities.* Beverly Hills, CA: Sage.

Chavez, L.R. 1992. *Shadowed lives: Undocumented immigrants in American society.* Orlando, FL: Harcourt Brace.

Cherlin, A.J. 1981. *Marriage, divorce, remarriage.* Cambridge, MA: Harvard University Press.

Chivers, M.L., G. Rieger, E. Latty, and J.M. Bailey. 2004. A sex difference in the specificity of sexual arousal. *Psychological Science* 15(11):736–44.

Chu, K. 2006. Unwed pairs need legal protection. *USA Today*, May 12, 3B.

Cianciotto, J., and S. Cahill. 2006. *Youth in the crosshairs: The third wave of ex-gay activism*, March 2. New York and Washington, DC: National Gay and Lesbian Task Force Institute, www.thetaskforce.org/

downloads/reports/reports/YouthInThe Crosshairs.pdf (accessed April 20, 2007).

Clemetson, L. 2000. Grandma knows best. *Newsweek*, June 12, 60–61.

CNN.com. 2007. Poll majority: Gays' orientation can't change. CNN/Opinion Research Corporation poll, June 27, www.cnn.com/2007/US/06/27/poll.gay/index.html (accessed July 9, 2007).

Cohen, K.M., and R.C. Savin-Williams. 1996. Developmental perspectives on coming out to self and others. In *The lives of lesbians, gays, and bisexuals: Children to adults*. Edited by R.C. Savin-Williams and K.M. Cohen. Fort Worth, TX: Harcourt Brace, 113–51.

Cohen, R. 2003. Senior moment. *New York Times Magazine*, April 20, 29–30.

Coming out to your parents. 2004. www.4therapy.com/consumer/life_topics/item.php?uniqueid=5532&categoryid=442 (accessed May 7, 2007).

Coming out: The complete guide. 2004. University College London Union, Lesbian, Gay, and Bisexual Society. May 9. www.lgb.uclu.org/comingout.asp (accessed May 7, 2004).

Coontz, S. 2005. The evolution of matrimony: The changing social context of marriage. *Annals of the American Psychotherapy Association*, December 22, www.mywire.com/pubs/AnnalsoftheAmericanPsychotherapyAssociation/2005/12/22/1329538?page=2 (accessed April 18, 2007).

Coontz, S. 2006. Marriage as a social contract. *Philadelphia Inquirer*, October 22, www.contemporaryfamilies.org/subtemplate.php?t=inTheNews&ext=marriageascontract (accessed April 18, 2007).

Crary, D. 2001. New view of same-sex parents fires mixed reaction in gays. *San Francisco Chronicle*, June 17, A7.

Crary, D. 2002. Atypical families test relief effort. *San Francisco Chronicle*, February 17, A18.

Curtin, S.C., and J.A. Martin. 2000. Preliminary data for 1999. *National vital statistics reports* 48(14). Hyattsville, MD: National Center for Health Statistics.

Dalsimer, M. 1981. Bible communists: Female socialization and family life in the Oneida Community. In *Family life in America: 1620–2000*. Edited by M. Albin and D. Cavallo. New York: Revisionary Press, 30–46.

De Vita, C.J. 1996. The United States at mid-decade. *Population Bulletin* 50 (March): entire issue.

Demo, D.H. 2000. Children's experience of family diversity. *Phi Kappa Phi Journal* 80:16–20.

DeNavas-Walt, C., B.D. Proctor, and C.H. Lee. 2006. *Income, poverty, and health insurance coverage in the United States: 2005*. U.S. Census Bureau, Current Population Reports, P60-231. Washington, DC: U.S. Government Printing Office.

Diamond, L.M. 2000. Sexual identity, attractions, and behavior among young sexual-minority women over a 2-year period. *Developmental Psychology* 36:241–50.

Doll, L.S., L.R. Petersen, C.R. White, E.S. Johnson, J.W. Ward, and the Blood Donor Study Group. 1992. Homosexual and nonhomosexual identified men: A behavioral comparison. *Journal of Sex Research* 29:1–14.

Draut, T. 2007. *Strapped: Why America's 20- and 30-somethings can't get ahead*. New York: Anchor.

Drummond, T. 2001. The marrying kind. *Time*, May 14, 52.

Dunleavy, M.P. 2006. Procrastination can have its own cost. *The New York Times*, December 30, B6.

Edwards, T.M. 2000. Flying solo. *Time*, August 28, 47–55.

Ellman, I.M., K.T. Bartlett, and G.G. Blumberg. 2002. *Principles of the law of family dissolution: Analysis and recommendations*. Philadelphia, PA: American Law Institute.

Eskridge Jr., W.N. 2002. *Equality practice: Civil unions and the future of gay rights*. New York: Routledge.

Fay, R., C. Turner, A. Klassen, and J. Gagnon. 1989. Prevalence and patterns of same-gender sexual contact among men. *Science* 243:338–48.

Ferdinand, P. 2002. Dissolving Vermont's same-sex unions proving difficult. *San Francisco Chronicle*, November 30, A5; reprinted from *Washington Post*.

Ferguson, S.J. 2000. Challenging traditional marriage: Never married Chinese American and Japanese American women. *Gender and Society* 14:136–59.

Fletcher, J. 2002. Your new neighbor: Mom. *The Wall Street Journal*, December 20, W1, W4.

Fossett, M.A., and K.J Kiecolt. 1993. Mate availability and family structure among African Americans in U.S. metropolitan areas. *Journal of Marriage and the Family* 55:288–302.

Furman, E. 2005. *Boomerang nation: How to survive living with your parents . . . the second time around*. New York: Simon & Schuster.

Furstenberg Jr., F.F., S. Kennedy, V.C. McLoyd, R.G. Rumbaut, and R.A. Settersten Jr. 2004. Growing up is harder to do. *Contexts* 3(3):33–41, www.contextsmagazine.org/content_sample_v3-3.php (accessed April 18, 2007).

Gerstel, N., and H.E. Gross, eds. 1987a. Commuter marriage: A microcosm of career and family conflict. Edited by N. Gerstel and H.E. Gross. *Families and work*. Philadelphia, PA: Temple University Press, 222–33.

Gerstel, N., and H.E. Gross, eds. 1987b. *Families and work*. Philadelphia, PA: Temple University Press.

Ginsburg, M. 2001. More U.S. fathers raising families by themselves. *San Francisco Chronicle*, May 18, A1, A12.

Glenn, N.D., and C.N. Weaver. 1988. The changing relationship of marital status to reported happiness. *Journal of Marriage and the Family* 50:317–24.

Goode, E. 2002. Group backs gays who seek to adopt a partner's child. *The New York Times*, February 4, A1, A21.

Gordon, L.P., and S.M. Shaffer. 2004. *Mom, can I move back in with you? A survival guide for parents of twentysomethings*. New York: Tarcher/Penguin.

Green, R.J., J. Bettinger, and E. Sacks. 1996. Are lesbian couples fused and gay male couples disengaged? In *Lesbians and gays in couples and families*. Edited by J. Laird & R.J. Green. San Francisco: Jossey-Bass, 185–230.

Greenberg, I. 2006. After a century, public polygamy is re-emerging in Tajikistan. *The New York Times*, November 13, A10.

Guthrie, J. 2002. Swinging into the mainstream. *San Francisco Chronicle*, July 4, A1, A4.

Hall, C.T. 2002. Pediatricians endorse gay, lesbian adoption. *San Francisco Chronicle*, February 4, A1, A11.

Hamilton, B.E., J.A. Martin, and S.J. Ventura. 2007. *Births: Preliminary data for 2005*. Hyattsville, MD: Centers for Disease Control, National Center for Health Statistics, www.cdc.gov/nchs/products/pubs/pubd/hestats/prelimbirths05/prelimbirths05.htm (accessed April 19, 2007).

Harden, B. 2002. "Dead broke" dads' child-support struggle. *The New York Times*, January 29, A19.

Harry, J. 1982. Decision making and age differences among gay couples. *Journal of Homosexuality* 2:9–21.

Haskell, K. 2003. When grandparents step into the child care gap, money can be scarce. *The New York Times*, November 30, sec. 1; 29.

Hendricks, T. 2005. Immigrant families frequently separated. *San Francisco Chronicle*, July 6, B1, B5.

Herdt, G., and R.M. Kertzner. 2006. I do, but I can't: The impact of marriage denial on the mental health and sexual citizenship of lesbians and gay men in the United States. *Sexuality Research and Social Policy* 3(1):33–49.

Heredia, C. 2001. Older generation sneers at "queer." *San Francisco Chronicle*, June 24, A1, A24.

Hess, J., and P. Catell. 2001. Dual dwelling duos: An alternative for long-term relationships. *Journal of Couples Therapy* 10(3/4):25–31.

Howard, J. 2006. *Expanding resources for children: Is adoption by gays and lesbians part of the answer for boys and girls who need homes?* New York: Evan B. Donaldson Adoption Institute, www.adoptioninstitute.org/policy/2006_Expanding_Resources_for_Children.php (accessed April 27, 2007).

Jacoby, J. 2007. Are women giving up on marriage? *Boston Globe*, January 21, www.boston.com/news/globe/editorial_opinion/oped/articles/2007/01/21/are_women_giving_up_on_marriage/ (accessed April 18, 2007).

Jacques, J.M. 1998. Changing marital and family patterns: A test of the post-modern perspective. *Sociological Perspectives* 41:381–413.

Jayson, S. 2006a. Is "failure to launch" really a failure? *USA Today*, March 16, 1D, 2D.

Jayson, S. 2006b. Real break-ups? Not so funny. *USA Today*, June 6, 9D.

Jenkins, D., and L.B. Johnston. 2004. Unethical treatment of gay and lesbian people with conversion therapy. *Families in Society, The Journal of Contemporary Social Service* 85(4):557–61.

Kamenetz, A. 2006. *Generation debt: Why now is a terrible time to be young.* New York: Riverhead Books.

Kantrowitz, B., and P. Tyre. 2006. The fine art of letting go. *Newsweek,* May 26.

Kantrowitz, B., and P. Wingert. 2001. Unmarried with children. *Newsweek,* May 28, 46–54.

Kiefer, F. 2000. Commuter marriages test more Americans. *The Christian Science Monitor.* January 9. http://search.csmonitor.com/durable/2000/01/07/f-p1s4.shtml

Kinsey, A., W. Pomeroy, and C. Martin. 1948. *Sexual behavior in the human male.* Philadelphia: Saunders.

Kinsey, A., W. Pomeroy, and C. Martin. 1953. *Sexual behavior in the human female.* Philadelphia: Saunders.

Klein, F. 1993. *The bisexual option.* 2nd ed. New York: Haworth Press.

Konner, M. 1990. Women and sexuality. *The New York Times Magazine.* April 29, 24, 26.

Kornblum, J. 2006. Shared lives, shared space. *USA Today,* January 17, 4D.

Kosciw, J.G., and E.D. Diaz. 2006. *The 2005 national school climate survey: The experiences of lesbian, gay, bisexual and transgender youth in our schools.* New York: Gay, Lesbian & Straight Education Network.

Kurdek, L. 1993. The allocation of household labor in gay, lesbian, and heterosexual married couples. *Journal of Social Issues* 49(3):127–39.

Kurdek, L.A., and J.P. Schmitt. 1987. Perceived emotional support from family and friends in members of homosexual, married, and heterosexual cohabiting couples. *Journal of Homosexuality* 14:57–68.

Lacey, M. 2003. Is polygamy confusing, or just a matter of family values? *The New York Times,* December 16, A4.

Lara, A. 2005. One for the price of two. *San Francisco Chronicle,* June 29, www.sfgate.com/cgi-bin/article.cgi?f=/c/a/2005/06/29/HOG7HDEB7B1.DTL&hw=Lara+2003+Joshua+Brody&sn=001&sc=1000 (accessed September 30, 2007).

Laskin, J. 2003. Why you should have a cohabitation agreement. www.palimony.com/2.html (accessed May 7, 2007).

Laumann, E., R. Michael, S. Michaels, and J. Gagnon. 1994. Thermidor in the sexual revolution? *National Review,* November 7, 18.

Laumann, E.O., J.H. Gagnon, R.T. Michael, and S. Michaels. 1994. *The organization of sexuality: Sexual practices in the United States.* Chicago: University of Chicago.

Lee, J. 2006. For insurance, adult children ride piggyback. *The New York Times,* September 17, sec. 1, 1, 18.

Leland, J., and M. Miller. 1998. Can gays convert? *Newsweek,* August 17, 46–51.

Lever, J., D.E. Kanouse, W.H. Rogers, S. Carson, and R. Hertz. 1992. Behavior patterns and sexual identity of bisexual males. *Journal of Sex Research* 29(2):141–67.

Lewin, E. 2002. "You'll never walk alone": Lesbian and gay weddings and the authenticity of the same-sex couple. In *Inside the American couple: New thinking, new challenges.* Edited by M. Yalom and L.L.

Carstensen. Berkeley: University of California Press, 87–107.

Lichter, S.R., L.S. Lichter, and S. Rothman. 1991. *Watching America.* Upper Saddle River, NJ: Prentice-Hall.

Lloyd, K.M., and S.J. South. 1996. Contextual influences on young men's transition to first marriage. *Social Forces* 74:1097–119.

Lundy, S.E. 1993. Abuse that dare not speak its name: Assisting victims of lesbian and gay domestic violence in Massachusetts. *New England Law Review* 28 (Winter):272–311.

Macklin, E.D. 1987. Nontraditional family forms. In *Handbook of marriage and the family.* Edited by M.B. Sussman and S.K. Steinmetz. New York: Plenum, 317–53.

Madigan, N. 2005. After fleeing polygamist community, an opportunity for influence. *The New York Times,* June 29, A14.

Marech, R. 2003. Devastating side of gay liberation. *San Francisco Chronicle,* January 6, A1, A11.

Marmor, J. 1980a. Homosexuality and the issue of mental illness. In *Homosexual behavior.* Edited by J. Marmor. New York: Basic Books.

Marmor, J. 1980b. The multiple roots of homosexual behavior. In *Homosexual behavior.* Edited by J. Marmor. New York: Basic Books.

Masters, W.H., V.E. Johnson, and R.C. Kolodny. 1994. *Heterosexuality.* New York: HarperCollins.

McLanahan, S., and K. Booth. 1989. Mother-only families: Problems, prospects and politics. *Journal of Marriage and the Family* 51:557–80.

McLanahan, S.S. 1991. The long-term effects of family dissolution. In *When families fail: The social costs.* Edited by B.J. Christensen. New York: University Press of America for the Rockford Institute, 5–26.

McWhirter, D.P., and A.M. Mattison. 1984. *The male couple.* Englewood Cliffs, NJ: Prentice-Hall.

Meyer, J. 1990. Guess who's coming to dinner this time? A study of gay intimate relationships and the support for those relationships. In *Homosexuality and family relations.* Edited by F.W. Bozett and M.B. Sussman. New York: Harrington Park Press, 59–82.

Michael, R.T., J.H. Gagnon, E.O. Laumann, and G. Kolata. 1994. *Sex in America.* Boston: Little, Brown.

Montgomery, M.J., and G.T. Sorell. 1997. Differences in love attitudes across family life stages. *Family Relations* 46:55–61.

Moore, S. 2006. Temporary marriages regaining popularity. *Reno Gazette-Journal,* January 15, 2C; reprinted from *Los Angeles Times.*

Morales, E. 1990. Ethnic minority families and minority gays and lesbians. In *Homosexuality and family relations.* Edited by F.W. Bozett and M.B. Sussman. New York: Harrington Park Press, 217–39.

Mosher, W.D., A. Chandra, and J. Jones. 2005. Sexual behavior and selected health measures: Men and women 15–44 years of age, United States, 2002. *Advance Data from Vital and Health Statistics,* no. 362,

September 15. Hyattsville, MD: National Center for Health Statistics, www.gaydata.org/02_Data_Sources/ds005_NSFG/ds005_NSFG_Results_2002.pdf (accessed April 20, 2007).

Musick, K. 2002. Planned and unplanned childbearing among unmarried women. *Journal of Marriage and the Family* 64 (4):915–30.

National Center for Health Statistics. 2006. Births/natality. Hyattville, MD: National Centers for Health Statistics, www.cdc.gov/nchs/fastats/births.htm (accessed April 30, 2007).

Nock, S.L. 1998. The consequences of premarital fatherhood. *American Sociological Review* 63: 250–63.

O'Neil, G.C., and N. O'Neill. 1972. *Open marriage.* New York: M. Evans. [Paperback version 1984.]

Oldenberg, A. 2002. For Rosie, coming out is merely about what's right. *USA Today,* March 12, A1, A2.

Parents' Resource Institute for Drug Education. 2001. PRIDE Questionnaire Report: 2000–01 national summary grades 6 through 12. Atlanta, GA: Parents' Resource Institute for Drug Education.

Patterson, C.J. 1996. Lesbian and gay parents and their children. In *The lives of lesbians, gays, and bisexuals: From children to adults.* Edited by R.C. Savin-Williams and K.M. Cohen. Fort Worth, TX: Harcourt Brace, 274–304.

Pear, R. 2002. Legal group urges states to update their family law. *The New York Times,* November 30, A1, A12.

Peplau, L.A., R.C. Veniegas, and S.N. Campbell. 1996. Gay and lesbian relationships. In *The lives of lesbians, gays, and bisexuals: Children to adults.* Edited by R.C. Savin-Williams and K.M. Cohen. Fort Worth, TX: Harcourt Brace, 250–73.

Perrin, E.C., and the Committee on Psychosocial Aspects of Child and Family Health. 2002. Technical report: Coparent or second-parent adoption by same-sex parents. *Pediatrics* 109:341–44.

Pillard, R.C., and J.M. Bailey. 1998. Human sexuality has a heritable component. *Human Biology* 70:347–65.

Pong, S.L., and B. Dong. 2000. The effects of change in family structure and income on dropping out of middle and high school. *Journal of Family Issues* 21:147–69.

Poniewozik, J. 2000. Waiting for Prince Charming. *Time,* August 28, 50–51.

Quinnipiac University Poll. 2006. Polling Report.com, November 13–19, www.pollingreport.com/civil.htm (accessed April 24, 2007).

Radford, A.N., and A.R. Ridley. 2006. Recruitment calling: A novel form of extended parental care in an altricial species. *Current Biology* 16:1700–04.

Riedmann, A. 1995. Lesbian and gay male families. *Primis* 4:66–83.

Rieger, G., M.L. Chivers, and J.M. Bailey. 2005. Sexual arousal patterns of bisexual men. *Psychological Science* 16(8):579–84.

Risman, B.J., and P. Schwartz. 1988. Sociological research on male and female homosexuality. *Annual Review of Sociology* 14:125–47.

Roberts, S. 2006. Married couples now a minority. *The New York Times*, October 15, www.nytimes.com/2006/10/15/us/15census.html?ei=5090&en=e788ed47b459cd7f&ex=1318564800 (accessed April 17, 2007).

Robinson, B.E., L.H. Walters, and P. Skeen. 1989. Response of parents to learning that their child is homosexual and concern over AIDS: A national study. *Journal of Homosexuality* 18:59–80.

Rodgers, W.L., and A. Thornton. 1985. Changing patterns of first marriage in the United States. *Demography* 22:265–79.

Rogers, S.M., and C.F. Turner. 1991. Male-male sexual contact in the U.S.A.: Findings from five sample surveys, 1970–1990. *Journal of Sex Research* 28(4):491–519.

Roselli, C.E., K. Larkin, J.A. Resko, J.N. Stellflug, and F. Stormshak. 2004a. The sexually dimorphic nucleus of the preoptic area varies with sexual partner preference in sheep. *Endocrinology* 145:478–83.

Roselli, C.E., K. Larkin, J.M. Schrunk, and F. Stormshak 2004b. Sexual partner preference, hypothalamic morphology, and aromatase in rams. *Physiology and Behavior* 83:233–45.

Ross, C.E. 1995. Reconceptualizing marital status as a continuum of social attachment. *Journal of Marriage and the Family* 57:129–40.

Rozhon, T. 2007. To have, hold and cherish, until bedtime. *The New York Times*, March 11, sec. 1, 1, 16.

Ruefli, T., O. Yu, and J. Barton. 1992. Brief report: Sexual risk taking in smaller cities. *Journal of Sex Research* 29(1):95–108.

Sauerman, T. 1995. Read this before coming out to your parents. OutProud. www.outproud.org/brochure_coming_out.html (accessed May 7, 2004).

Schmalz, J. 1993. Homosexuals wake to see a referendum: It's on them. *The New York Times*, January 31, sec. 4, E1.

Schoeni, R.F., and K. Ross. 2005. Material assistance received from families during the transition to adulthood. In *On the frontier of adulthood: Theory, research, and public policy*. Edited by R.A. Settersten Jr., F.F. Furstenberg Jr., and R.G. Rumbaut. Chicago: University of Chicago Press.

Showtime revives "Queer as Folk." 2002. *Reno Gazette-Journal*, January 2, 3E.

Soukup, E. 2006. Polygamists, unite! *Newsweek*, March 20, 52.

Stacey, J. 2003. Gay and lesbian families: Queer like us. In *All our families: New policies for a new century—A report of the Berkeley Family Forum*, 2nd ed. Edited by M.A. Mason, A. Skolnick, and S.D. Sugarman. New York: Oxford University Press, 144–69.

Stacey, J., and T.J. Biblarz. 2001. (How) does the sexual orientation of parents matter? *American Sociological Review* 66:159–83.

Staples, R. 1981. Black singles in America. In *Single life: Unmarried adults in social context*. Edited by P.J. Stein. New York: St. Martin's, 40–51.

Staples, R. 1982. *Black masculinity: The black male role in American society*. San Francisco: The Black Scholar Press.

Stein, P.J., ed. 1981. *Single life: Unmarried adults in social context*. New York: St. Martin's.

Stewart, T. 2002. Telling parents you're gay . . . from a parent's perspective. *Gayline Wellington*. November 17. www.gayline.gen.nz (accessed May 7, 2007).

Suárez-Orozco, M., C. Suárez-Orozco, and D.B. Qin-Hillard, eds. 2005. *The new immigration: An interdisciplinary reader*. New York: Routledge.

Sugarman, S.D. 2003. Single-parent families. In *All our families: New policies for a new century—A report of the Berkeley Family Forum*, 2nd ed. Edited by M.A. Mason, A. Skolnick, and S.D. Sugarman. New York: Oxford University Press, 87–107.

Tasker, F.L., and S. Golombok. 1997. *Growing up in a lesbian family: Effects on child development*. New York: Guilford.

Thompson, C. 1995. A new vision of masculinity. In *Race, class, and gender in the United States*, 3rd ed. Edited by P.S. Rothenberg. New York: St. Martin's, 475–81.

Tierney, J. 2006. Who's afraid of polygamy? *The New York Times*, March 11, A27.

Tjaden, P., N. Thoennes, and C.J. Allison. 1999. Comparing violence over the life span in samples of same-sex and opposite-sex cohabitants. *Violence and Victims* 14:413–25.

Troiden, R.R. 1988. *Gay and lesbian identity: A sociological analysis*. New York: General Hall.

Tyre, P., and D. McGinn. 2003. She works, he doesn't. *Newsweek*, May 12, 44–52.

U.S. Census Bureau. 1998. *Statistical Abstract of the United States: 1998*. www.census.gov/prod/3/98pubs/98statab/sasec1.pdf

U.S. Census Bureau. 2006a. *Current Population Survey*, March, and Annual Social and Economic Supplements, 2005 and earlier. Washington, DC: U.S. Census Bureau, www.census.gov/population/socdemo/hhfam/ms2.pdf (accessed April 18, 2007).

U.S. Census Bureau. 2006b. *America's families and living arrangements*. Washington, DC: U.S. Census Bureau, www.census.gov/population/www/socdemo/hhfam/cps2005.html (accessed April 18, 2007).

U.S. Census Bureau. 2006c. *Statistical Abstract of the United States: 2006*, www.census.gov/prod/2006pubs/07statab/pop.pdf (accessed April 30, 2007).

U.S. Census Bureau. 2007. Single-parent households showed little variation since 1994, Census Bureau reports. *U.S. Census Bureau News*, March 27, www.census.gov/Press-Release/www/releases/archives/families_households/009842.html (accessed April 18, 2007).

Weeks, J.R. 1996. *Population*. 6th ed. Belmont, CA: Wadsworth.

Weinberg, M., C. Williams, and D. Pryor. 1994. *Dual attraction: Understanding bisexuality*. New York: Oxford University Press.

Weinrich, J.D., and W.L. Williams. 1991. Strange customs, familiar lives: Homosexualities in other cultures. In *Homosexuality: Research implications for public policy*. Edited by J.C. Gonsiorek and J.D. Weinrich. Newbury Park, CA: Sage.

Weitoft, G.R., A. Hjern, B. Haglund, and M. Rosen. 2003. Mortality, severe morbidity, and injury in children living with single parents in Sweden: A population-based study. *The Lancet* 361:289–95.

Whitaker, B. 2003. Gay couples pop big question, but the states' reply is the same. *The New York Times*, February 15, A13.

Williams, D.R. 2003. The health of men: Structured inequalities and opportunities. *American Journal of Public Health* 93(5):724–31.

Williams, T. 2005. A place for grandparents who are parents again. *The New York Times*, May 21, A12.

CHAPTER 10

Abma, J.C., A. Chandra, W. Mosher L. Peterson, and L. Piccinino. 1997. Fertility, family planning, and women's health: New data from the 1995 National Survey of Family Growth. Washington, DC: National Center for Health Statistics. *Vital and Health Statistics*, Series 23: No. 19 (May).

Adler, N.E., H.P. David, B.N. Major, S. Roth, N.F. Russo, and G. Wyatt. 1990. Psychological responses after abortion. *Science* 248:41–44.

Adoption and Foster Care Analysis and Reporting System (AFCARS). 2006. *The AFCARS report: Preliminary FY 2005 estimates as of September 2006*. Washington, DC: U.S. Department of Health and Human Services, Administration for Children and Families, www.acf.dhhs.gov/programs/cb/stats_research/afcars/tar/report13.htm (accessed July 10, 2007).

Alan Guttmacher Institute. 2006. *Facts on induced abortion in the United States*, May. New York: Alan Guttmacher Institute. www.guttmacher.org/pubs/fb_induced_abortion.html (accessed July 10, 2007).

Ambry, M.K. 1992. Childless chances. *American Demographics* 14(4):55.

Argys, L.M., D.I. Rees, S.L. Averett, and B. Witoonchart. 2006. Birth order and risky adolescent behavior. *Economic Inquiry* 44(2):215–33.

Armour, S. 2007. More companies add benefits for employees who adopt. *USA Today*, June 20, 1B.

Associated Press. 2004. 55-year-old mom. *San Francisco Chronicle*, December 29, A2.

Bachu A. 1999. *Fertility of American women: June 1994*. Current Population Reports P20-482. Washington, DC: U.S. Census Bureau.

Bachu, A. 1993. *Fertility of American women: June 1992*. Current Population Reports P20-470. Washington, DC: U.S. Census Bureau.

Bachu, A. 1999. Is childlessness among American women on the rise? *Population Division Working Paper*, No. 37, May. Washington, DC: U.S. Census Bureau.

Bachu, A. A current populations report. Series pp. 20-482. Washington, DC: U.S. Bureau of the Census.

Barber, N. 1998. The role of reproductive strategies in academic attainment. *Sex Roles* 38:313–27.

Bates, G.W., and W.R. Boone. 1991. The female reproductive cycle: New variations on an old theme. *Current Opinion in Obstetrics and Gynecology* 3:838–43.

Baydar, N., P. Hyle, and J. Brooks-Gunn. 1997. A longitudinal study of the effects of the birth of a sibling during preschool and early grade school years. *Journal of Marriage and the Family* 59:957–65.

Begley, S. 2007. Just say no—to bad science. *Newsweek*, May 7, 57.

Bell, E. 2001. New law is saving babies' lives, but is too little-known. *San Francisco Chronicle*, August 6, A15.

Benac, N. 2006. Poll discovers contradictory abortion views. *Reno Gazette-Journal*, March 13, 1C, 7C.

Berelson, B. 1979. The value of children: A taxonomical essay. In *Current issues in marriage and the family*, 2nd ed. Edited by J.G. Wells. New York: Macmillan.

Bernstein, N. 2001. Few choose legal havens to abandon babies. *The New York Times*, August 31, A1, A14.

Boyce, N. 2003. A law's fetal flaw. *U.S. News & World Report*, July 21, 48–51.

Brooks, K., and B.R. Sanders. 2002. Woman strives to get baby back. *Star-Telegram*, September 22. www.dfw.com/mld/dfw/news/state

Buckley, C. 2007. Despite alternatives, many newborns are abandoned. *The New York Times*, January 30, A14.

Cain, M. 2002. *The childless revolution*. Cambridge, MA: Perseus.

Centers for Disease Control and Prevention, Division of HIV/AIDS Prevention. 2003. *Basic statistics: Cumulative cases by age*. December 31. Atlanta, GA: Centers for Disease Control and Prevention. www.cdc.gov/hiv/stats.htm#cumage (accessed April 28, 2007).

Chandra, A., G.M. Martinez, W.D. Mosher, J.C. Abma, and J. Jones. 2005. Fertility, family planning, and reproductive health of U.S. women: Data from the 2002 National Survey of Family Growth. National Center for Health Statistics. *Vital Health Statistics* 23(25), www.cdc.gov/nchs/data/series/sr_23/sr23_025.pdf (accessed July 10, 2007).

Childless by choice. 2001. *American Demographics*, November 1, 44.

Covington, S., and W. Gibbons. 2007. What is happening to the price of eggs? *Fertility and Sterility* 87(5):A15–A26.

Cowan, C.P., and P.A. Cowan. 2000. *When partners become parents: The big life change for couples*. Mahwah, NJ: Lawrence Erlbaum Associates.

Crary, D. 2007a. Tough times often await youths aging out of foster system. *Reno Gazette-Journal*, January 14, 10C.

Crary, D. 2007b. Foreign adoptions decline after many years of growth. *San Francisco Chronicle*, January 7, A13.

Crooks, R., and K. Baur. 1990. *Our sexuality*. 4th ed. Redwood City, CA: Benjamin/Cummings.

D'emilio, F. 2005. Revived tradition credited with saving newborns. *San Francisco Chronicle*, October 30, A22.

Daar, H. 1999. Assisted reproductive technologies and the pregnancy process: Developing an equality model to protect reproductive liberties. *American Journal of Law & Medicine* 25:455–77.

Dagg, P.K. 1991. The psychological sequelae of therapeutic abortion—denied and completed. *American Journal of Psychiatry* 148(5):578–85.

Daniluk, J.C. 2001. Reconstructing their lives: A longitudinal, qualitative analysis of the transition to biological childlessness for infertile couples. *Journal of Counseling and Development* 19(4):439–50.

Daspin, E., and E. Gamerman. 2007. The million dollar kid. *The Wall Street Journal*, March 3–4, P1, P5.

Doyle Jr., J.J. 2007. Child protection and child outcomes: Measuring the effects of foster care. *American Economic Review*, March. www.mit/edu/~jjdoyle/doyle_fosterlt_march07_aer.pdf (accessed December 24, 2007).

Dremann, S. 2002. Child-free: By nature or design. *Palo Alto* (California) *Weekly Online Edition*, February 13. www.paweekly.com/weekly/morgue/2002/2002_02_13.child13.html

Duncan, G.J., and K.A. Magnuson. 2002. Economics and parenting. *Parenting: Science and Practice* 2(4):437–50.

Dye, J.L. 2005. *Fertility of American women: June 2004*. Current Population Reports, December. P20-555. Washington, DC: U.S. Census Bureau.

Edmondson, B., J. Waidrop, D. Crispell, and L. Jacobsen. 1993. The big picture. *American Demographics* 15(12):28–30.

Elias, M. 2002. Adopt U.S. kids online. *USA Today*, July 23, 8D.

Evan B. Donaldson Institute. 2003. *Unintended consequences: "Safe haven" laws are causing problems, not solving them*. New York: New York: Evan B. Donaldson Adoption Institute, www.adoptioninstitute.org/whowe/Last%20report.pdf (accessed May 9, 2007).

Exter, T. 1991. The costs of growing up. *American Demographics*, August, 59.

Falbo, T. 1976. Does the only child grow up miserable? *Psychology Today* 9:60–65.

Fields, J. 2001. Living arrangements of children, *Current Population Reports*, Series P70, No. 74, April. Washington, DC: U.S. Census Bureau.

Foli, K.J., and J.R. Thompson. 2004. *The post-adoption blues: Overcoming the unforeseen challenges of adoption*. Emmaus, PA: Rodale Books.

Freundlich, M., Excal Consulting, and staff from The Pew Charitable Trust. 2007. *Time for reform: Aging out and on their own*. Report by the Pew Charitable Trusts' Kids Are Waiting campaign and the Jim Casey Youth Opportunities Initiative, May 24, www.pewtrusts.org/pdf/Aging_Out_May2007.pdf (accessed July 13, 2007).

Friend, T. 2003. Blueprint for life: Never mind human cloning. 'Designer baby' technology could be the next big thing. *USA Today*, January 27, 1D, 2D.

Friess, S. 2007. U.S. government scrutinizes Guatemalan adoptions. *USA Today*, March 19, 6D.

Gallup, G. Jr., and F. Newport. 1990. Virtually all adults want children, but many of the reasons are intangible. *The Gallup Poll Monthly*, June, 8–14.

Gerson, M.-J. 1986. The prospect of parenthood for women and men. *Psychology of Women Quarterly* 10:49–62.

Glenn, N. 1991. The recent trend in marital success in the United States. *Journal of Marriage and the Family* 53(2):261–70.

Groat, H.T., P.C. Giordano, S.A. Cernkovich, and M.D. Pugh. 1997. Attitudes toward child rearing among young parents. *Journal of Marriage and the Family* 59:568–81.

Gross, J. 2006. Seeking doctors' advice in adoptions from afar. *The New York Times*, January 3, A1, A12.

Guttmacher, A.F. 1983. *Pregnancy, birth, and family planning*, rev. ed. New York: New American Library.

Halle, T. 2002. Charting parenthood: A statistical portrait of fathers and mothers in America. Washington, DC: Child Trends, http://fatherhood.hhs.gov/charting02/index.htm (accessed May 5, 2007).

Hamilton, A. 2002. Eggs on ice. *Time*, July 1, 54–55.

Hamilton, B.E., J.A. Martin, and S.J. Ventura. 2006. Births: Preliminary data for 2005. *Health E-Stats*. Released November 21. Hyattsville, MD: Centers for Disease Control and Prevention, National Center for Health Statistics, www.cdc.gov/nchs/products/pubs/pubd/hestats/prelimbirths05/prelimbirths05.htm (accessed May 3, 2007).

Hanafin, H. 1996. Overview of surrogacy parenting: An overview of the psychological evaluation and counseling in surrogacy parenting. Marietta, GA: American Surrogacy Center, www.surrogacy.com/psychres/article/eval.html (accessed July 10, 2007).

Harmon, A. 2007. Sperm donor father ends his anonymity. *The New York Times*, February 14, A15.

Hawke, S., and D. Knox. 1978. The one-child family: A new life-style. *Family Coordinator* 27:215–19.

Her Daughter Would Be Her Sister. 2007. *The Week*, July 20, 22.

Hwang, S. 2004. Adoptions get easier thanks to "open" agreements. *The Wall Street Journal*, September 28, http://online.wsj.com/public/us (accessed September 30, 2007).

Jones, C.L., L. Tepperman, and S.J. Wilson. 1995. *The future of the family*. Englewood Cliffs, NJ: Prentice-Hall.

Juffer, F., and M.H. van Ijzendoorn. 2005. Behavior problems and mental health referrals of international adoptees: A meta-analytic approach. *Journal of the American Medical Association* 293:2501–15.

Kent, M. 2007. U.S. birth rate: Still fueling population growth? Online discussion, March 22. Population Reference Bureau, http://discuss.prb.org/content/interview/detail/1172/ (accessed May 6, 2007).

Kirby, D. 2001. *Emerging answers: Research findings on programs to reduce teen pregnancy (summary)*. Washington, DC: National Campaign to Prevent Teen Pregnancy, www.teenpregnancy.org/resources/data/pdf/emeranswsum.pdf (accessed May 8, 2007).

Kleinpeter, C.H., and M.M. Hohman. 2000.

Surrogate motherhood: Personality traits and satisfaction with service providers. *Psychological Reports* 87:957–70.

Knox, D., and K. Wilson. 1978. The differences between having one and two children. *Family Coordinator* 27:23–25.

Koch, W. 2006. Strong messages get girls to wait on motherhood. *USA Today*, October 30, 2A.

Koch, W. 2007. Russia curtails American adoptions. *USA Today*, April 11, 1A.

Kolata, G. 2007. Psst! Ask for donor 1913. *The New York Times*, February 18, sec. 4, 5.

Kost, K., J.D. Forrest, and S. Harlap. 1991. Comparing the health risks and benefits of contraceptive choices. *Family Planning Perspectives* 19:133.

Lasker, J., and S. Borg. 1990. *When pregnancy fails: Families coping with miscarriage, ectopic pregnancy, stillbirth, and infant death.* 2nd ed. New York: Bantam.

Lino, M. 2007. *Expenditures on children by families, 2006.* Washington, DC: U.S. Department of Agriculture, Center for Nutrition Policy and Promotion. Miscellaneous Publication No. 1528-2006, www.cnpp .usda.gov/Publications/CRC/crc2006.pdf (accessed May 6, 2007).

Luke, B., and L.G. Keith. 1992. The contribution of singletons, twins and triplets to low birth weight, infant mortality and handicap in the United States. *Journal of Reproductive Medicine* 37:661–62.

Luke, B., F.R. Witter, H. Abbey, T. Feng, A.B. Namnoum, D.M. Paige, and T.R. Johnson. 1991. Gestational age-specific birthweights of twins versus singletons. *Acta Geneticae Medicae Et Gemellogiae* 40:69–76.

Lunneborg, P. 1992. *Abortion: A positive decision.* South Hadley, MA: Bergin & Garvey.

Malveaux, J. 2002. Childless doesn't mean worthless. *USA Today*, May 3, 15A.

Mansnerus, L. 2001. Couples looking to adopt find a shifting spotlight. *The New York Times*, September 26, 11.

Marchbanks, P.A., H.B. Peterson, G.L. Rubin, and P.A. Wingo. 1989. Research on infertility: Definition makes a difference. The Cancer and Steroid Hormone Study Group. *American Journal of Epidemiology* 130:259–67.

Marchione, M. 2007. Fertility treatment may raise defect rate. *San Francisco Chronicle*, February 9, A4.

Marquardt, E. 2007. When 3 really is a crowd. *The New York Times*, July 16, A17.

Mastenbroek, S., M. Twisk, J. van Echten-Arends, B. Sikkema-Raddatz, J.C. Korevaar, H.R. Verhoeve, N.E.A. Vogel, E.GJ.M. Arts, J.W.A. de Vries, P.M. Bossuyt, C.H.C.M. Buys, M.J. Heineman, S. Repping, and F. van der Veen. 2007. In vitro fertilization with preimplantation genetic screening. *New England Journal of Medicine* 357(1):9–17.

May, E.T. 1997. *Barren in the promised land: Childless Americans and the pursuit of happiness.* Cambridge, MA: Harvard University Press.

McCarthy, H.W. 2005. Post-adoption depression: The unacknowledged hazard. International adoptions articles directory,

Post-Adoption Learning Center, www .adoptionarticlesdirectory.com/Article/Post-Adoption-Depression-The-Unacknowledged-Hazard/53 (accessed May 10, 2007).

McCary, S.P., and J.L. McCary. 1984. *Human sexuality.* 3rd ed. Belmont, CA: Wadsworth.

Mother, 66, well after historic birth. 2005. *Reno Gazette-Journal*, January 18, 2A.

Mueller, K.A., and J.D. Yoder. 1997. Gendered norms for family size, employment, and occupation: Are there personal costs for violating them? *Sex Roles* 35(3-4):207–21.

National Women's Health Information Center. 2005. Birth control methods. November. 4woman.gov. U.S. Department of Health and Human Services, Office on Women's Health. www.4woman.gov/faq/birthcont.htm#7.

O'Laughlin, E.M., and V.N. Anderson. 2001. Perceptions of parenthood among young adults: Implications for career and family planning. *American Journal of Family Therapy* 29(2):95–109.

Pecora, P.J., J. Williams, R.C. Kessler, A.C. Downs, K. O'Brien, E. Hiripi, and S. Morello. 2003. *Assessing the effects of foster care: Early results from the Casey National Alumni Study.* New York: Casey Family Programs, www.casey.org/NR/rdonlyres/CEFBB1B6-7ED1-440D-925A-E5BAF602294D/302/casey_alumni_studies_report.pdf (accessed May 12, 2007).

Pertman, A. 2000. *Adoption nation: How the adoption revolution is transforming America.* New York: Basic Books.

Pines, M. 1981. Only isn't lonely (or spoiled or selfish). *Psychology Today* 15:15–19.

Rabin, R. C. 2007a. At-home fertility tests for men hitting stores. *The New York Times*, June 4, A4.

Rabin, R. C. 2007b. As demand for donor eggs soars, high prices stir ethical concerns. *The New York Times*, May 15, D6.

Rector, R., and K.A. Johnson. 2005a. Adolescent virginity pledges, condom use, and sexually transmitted diseases among young adults. *Conference Paper*, June 14. Heritage Foundation, www.heritage.org/Research/Abstinence/whitepaper06142005-1.cfm (accessed May 8, 2007).

Rector, R., and K.A. Johnson. 2005b. Adolescent virginity pledges and risky sexual behaviors. *Conference Paper*, June 14. Heritage Foundation, www.heritage.org/Research/Abstinence/whitepaper06142005-2.cfm (accessed May 8, 2007).

Ritter, M. 2002. Cloned baby girl is on the way, scientist promises. *San Francisco Chronicle*, December 20, A4.

Rosenblatt, B. 1992. *Life itself: Abortion in the American mind.* New York: Random House.

Rosenthal, M.B. 1997. Infertility. In *Women's health in primary care.* Edited by J. Rosenfeld. Baltimore: Williams & Wilkins, 351–62.

Ross, E. 2001. Manufacture of human eggs on horizon. *San Francisco Chronicle*, July 3, A3.

Rubin, R. 2002. Donor eggs can let women over 50 produce viable babies. *USA Today*, November 13, 9D.

Saber, B. 2003. Child welfare disgrace [letter]. *The New York Times*, July 15, A24.

Salary.com. 2007. What is your mom worth?

Salary.com, http://swz.salary.com/momsalarywizard/htmls/mswl_momcenter.html (accessed May 6, 2007).

Sandel, M. 2007. *The case against perfection: Ethics in the age of genetic engineering.* Cambridge, MA: Harvard University Press.

Santelli, J.S., L.D. Lindbergt, L.B. Finer, and S. Singh. 2007. Explaining recent declines in adolescent pregnancy in the United States: The contribution of abstinence and improved contraceptive use. *American Journal of Public Health* 97(1):150–56.

Saul, S. 2007. Pill that eliminates the period gets decidedly mixed reviews. *The New York Times*, April 20, A1, C4.

Sheffield, R. 2007. Sperm donor liable for child support. *San Francisco Chronicle*, May 11, A4.

Siegel, D.H. 2003. Open adoption of infants: Adoptive parents' feelings seven years later. *Social Work* 48(3):409–20.

Smith, S. 2007. *Safeguarding the rights and well-being of birthparents in the adoption process*, revised with foreword. New York: Evan B. Donaldson Adoption Institute, www.adoptioninstitute.org/publications/2007_01_Birthparent_Study_All.pdf (accessed May 10, 2007).

Somers, M.D. 1993. A comparison of voluntarily childfree adults and parents. *Journal of Marriage and the Family* 55(3):643–50.

Stepp, L. S. 2007. Study casts doubt on abstinence-only programs. *The Washington Post*, April 14, A2.

Tarkan, L. 2006. After the adoption, a new child and the blues. *The New York Times*, April 25, D5, D8.

Thompson, E. 1997. Couple childbearing desires, intentions, and births. *Demography* 34:343–45.

Thornton, A., and D. Freedman. 1983. The changing American family. *Population Bulletin* 38. Washington, DC: Population Reference Bureau.

Trenholm, C., B. Devaney, K. Forston, L. Quay, J. Wheeler, and M. Clark. 2007. *Impacts of four Title V, Section 510 abstinence education programs.* Washington, DC: Mathematica Policy Research Inc., www.mathematica-mpr.com (accessed May 8, 2007).

Twenge, J.M., W.K. Campbell, and C.A. Foster. 2003. Parenthood and marital satisfaction: A meta-analytic review. *Journal of Marriage and the Family* 65:574–83.

U.S. Census Bureau. 2004. *Characteristics of children under 18 years, by age, for the United States, regions, states, and Puerto Rico: 2000 (PHC-T-30).* Washington, DC: U.S. Government Printing Office, www.census .gov/population/cen2000/phc-t30/tab01.pdf (accessed May 10, 2007).

U.S. Census Bureau. 2006. *Statistical abstract of the United States: 2006.* Washington, DC: U.S. Government Printing Office, www .census.gov/prod/www/statistical-abstract .html (accessed May 10, 2007).

U.S. couple to try cloning, report says. 2002. *Reno Gazette-Journal*, August 7, A1.

U.S. Department of Health and Human Services. 2004. *How many children were adopted in 2000 and 2001?* Washington, DC: Child Welfare Information Gateway, www

.childwelfare.gov/pubs/s_adopted/s_adopted .cfm (accessed May 10, 2007).

U.S. Department of State. 2007. Immigrant visas issued to orphans coming to the U.S. http://travel.state.gov/family/adoption/stats/ stats_451.html (accessed May 10, 2007).

U.S. Census Bureau. 2000. *Statistical abstract of the United States.* Washington, DC: U.S. Government Printing Office.

Vaillant, C.O., and G.E. Vaillant. 1993. Is the U-curve of marital satisfaction an illusion? A 40-year study of marriage. *Journal of Marriage and the Family* 55:230–39.

Van Buren, A. 2003. Prom plan could haunt teen virgin. *Pioneer Press,* May 13. www .twincities.com/mld/twincities/living/ columnists/dear_abby/5844856.htm

Ventura, S.J., J.A. Martin, S.C. Curtin, T.J. Mathews, and M.M. Park. 2000. Births: Final data for 1998. *National Vital Statistical Reports* 48, March 28, Centers for Disease Control and Prevention.

Wadman, M. 2001. So you want a girl? *Fortune,* February 19, 174–82.

White, L.K., A. Booth, and J.N. Edwards. 1986. Children and marital happiness. *Journal of Family Issues* 7(2):131–47.

White, L.K., and H. Kim. 1987. The family-building process: Childbearing choices by parity. *Journal of Marriage and the Family* 49:271–79.

Whitehead, B.D., and D. Popenoe. 2006. Essay: Life without children. *The state of our unions: The social health of marriage in America, 2006.* National Marriage Project. Piscataway, NJ: Rutgers, the State University of New Jersey.

CHAPTER 11

Abel, E.K. 1991. *Who cares for the elderly? Public policy and the experiences of adult daughters.* Philadelphia, PA: Temple University Press.

Aldous, J., E. Klaus, and D. Klein. 1985. The understanding heart: Aging parents and their favorite children. *Child Development* 56:303–16.

Allegretto, S.A. 2006. U.S. government does relatively little to lessen child poverty rates. *Economic Snapshots,* July 19. Washington, DC: Economic Policy Institute, www.epi .org/content.cfm/webfeatures_snapshots_ 20060719 (accessed July 17, 2007).

Allen, K.R., R. Blieszner, and K.A. Roberto. 2000. Families in the middle and later years: A review and critique of research in the 1990s. *Journal of Marriage and the Family* 62(4):911–27.

American Academy of Pediatrics. 2007. Television and the family. Elk Grove Village, IL: American Academy of Pediatrics, www.aap .org/family/tv1.htm (accessed July 17, 2007).

Antle, K. 1978. Active involvement of expectant fathers in pregnancy: Some further considerations. *Journal of Obstetric, Gynecologic, and Neonatal Nursing* 7:7–12.

Apfel, N.H., and V. Seitz. 1991. Four models of adolescent mother–grandmother relationships in black inner-city families. *Family Relations* 40:421–29.

Bachmann, G.A., T.P. Moeller, and J. Benett.

1988. Childhood sexual abuse and the consequences in adult women. *Obstetrics & Gynecology* 71:631–42.

Bachrach, C.A. 1980. Childlessness and social isolation among the elderly. *Journal of Marriage and the Family* 42:627–37.

Barber, B.K. 1994. Cultural, family, and personal contexts of parent-adolescent conflict. *Journal of Marriage and the Family* 56:375–86.

Barranti, C.C.R. 1985. The grandparent/grandchild relationship: Family resource in an era of voluntary bonds. *Family Relations* 34: 343–52.

Baumrind, D. 1968. Authoritarian versus authoritative parental control. *Adolescence* 3:255–72.

Baumrind, D. 1989. Rearing competent children. In *Child development today and tomorrow.* Edited by W. Damon. San Francisco: Jossey-Bass, 349–78.

Baumrind, D. 1996. The discipline controversy revisited (child discipline). *Family Relations* 45(4):405–15.

Becerra, R. 1988. The Mexican American family. In *Ethnic families in America: Patterns and variations.* 3rd ed. Edited by C. H. Mindel, R.W. Habenstein, and R. Wright Jr. New York: Elsevier.

Beck, C.T., M.A. Reynolds, and P. Rutowski. 1992. Maternity blues and postpartum depression. *Journal of Obstetric, Gynecologic, and Neonatal Nursing* 21:287–93.

Bellafante, G. 2004. Two fathers, with one happy to stay at home. *The New York Times,* January 12, A1, A17.

Berkowitz, G.S., M.L. Skovron, R.H. Lapinski, and R.L. Berkowitz. 1990. Delayed childbearing and the outcome of pregnancy. *New England Journal of Medicine* 322:659–64.

Bernstein, A. 1992. The mommy backlash. *Business Week,* August 10, 42–43.

Bianchi, S.M., J.P. Robinson, and M.A. Milkie. 2006. *Changing rhythms of American family life.* New York: Russell Sage Foundation/American Sociological Association.

Blackwell, J.E. 1991. *The black community: Diversity and unity.* 3rd ed. New York: HarperCollins.

Blieszner, R., and V.H. Bedford, eds. 1995. *Handbook of aging and the family.* Westport, CT: Greenwood.

Briggs, J. 2007. To grandmother's house we go. *The Crisis,* January/February, 34–37.

Brott, A.A. 1992. Paternity leave given a wide berth. *San Francisco Examiner,* September 20, A6.

Buriel, R. 1993. Childrearing orientations in Mexican American families: The influence of generation and sociocultural factors. *Journal of Marriage and the Family* 55:987–1000.

Burman, L.E., and L. Wheaton. 2005. Who gets the child tax credit? *Tax Notes,* October 27. Washington, DC: Tax Policy Institute, www.urban.org/UploadedPDF/ 411232_child_tax_credit.pdf (accessed July 17, 2007).

Callaghan, W., M. MacDorman, S. Rasmussen, C. Qin, and E. Lackritz. 2006. The contribution of pre-term birth to infant

mortality rates in the United States. *Pediatrics* 118(4):1566–73.

Cantor, M.H., and V. Little. 1985. Aging and social care. In *Handbook of aging.* Edited by R.H. Binstock and E. Shanas. New York: Van Nostrand Reinhold, 745–81.

Cavanaugh, J. 1993. *Adult development and aging.* 2nd ed. Pacific Grove, CA: Brooks/ Cole.

Chappell, N. 1991. Living arrangements and sources of caring. *Journal of Gerontology* 46(1):51–58.

Cherlin, A., and F.F. Furstenberg Jr. 1986. Styles and strategies of grandparenting. In *Grandparenthood.* Edited by V.L. Bengston and J. Robertson. Beverly Hills, CA: Sage, 97–116.

Chiang, H. 2004. State law adapting to new kinds of families. *San Francisco Chronicle,* January 12, A1, A6.

Child Trends DataBank. 2007a. Low and very low birthweight infants. Washington, DC: Child Trends, www.childtrendsdatabank .org/indicators/57LowBirthweight.cfm (accessed July 17, 2007).

Child Trends DataBank. 2007b. Children in poverty. Washington, DC: Child Trends, www.childtrendsdatabank.org/indicators/ 4Poverty.cfm (accessed July 17, 2007).

Christianson, A., C.P. Howson, and B. Modell. 2006. *March of Dimes global report on birth defects: The hidden toll of dying and disabled children.* White Plains, NY: March of Dimes Birth Defects Foundation, http:// mod.hoffmanpr.com/MOD-Report.pdf (accessed July 17, 2007).

Cicerelli, V.G. 1990. Family support in relation to health problems of the elderly. In *Family relations in later life,* 2nd ed. Edited by T. H. Brubaker. Newbury Park, CA: Sage, 212–28.

Clawson, D., and N. Gerstel. 2002. Caring for our young: Child care in Europe and the United States. *Contexts* (Fall/Winter): 28–35.

Clements, J. 2003. Why it pays to delay: Too many retirees start collecting Social Security early. *The Wall Street Journal,* April 23, D1.

Clemetson, L. 2006. Parents making use of TV despite risks. *The New York Times,* May 25, A16.

Climo, J. 1992. *Distant parents.* New Brunswick, NJ: Rutgers University Press.

Cohany, S.R., and E. Sok. 2007. Trends in labor force participation of married mothers of infants. *Monthly Labor Review,* February. Washington, DC: Bureau of Labor Statistics, 9–16.

Commonwealth Fund Commission on a High Performance Health System. 2006. *Why not the best? Results from a national scorecard on U.S. health system performance,* September. New York: The Commonwealth Fund, www.commonwealthfund.org/usr_doc/ Commission_whynotthebest_951.pdf? section=4039 (accessed July 17, 2007).

Conner, G.K., and V. Denson. 1990. Expectant fathers' response to pregnancy: Review of literature and implications for research in high-risk pregnancy. *Journal of Perinatal and Neonatal Nursing* 4:33–42.

Cooper, C.R., and R.G. Cooper Jr. 1992. Links

between adolescents' relationships with their parents and peers: Models, evidence, and mechanisms. In *Family-peer relations: Modes of linkage.* Edited by R.D. Parke and G.W. Ladd. Hillsdale, NJ: Lawrence Erlbaum Associates, 135–58.

Corak, M. 2005. *Principles and practicalities in measuring child poverty for the rich countries.* Innocenti Working Paper 2005-01. Florence, Italy: UNICEF Innocenti Research Centre, www.unicef-icdc.org/publications/pdf/iwp_2005_01.pdf (accessed July 17, 2007).

Cowan, C.P, and P.A. Cowan. 2003. New families: Modern couples as new pioneers. In *All our families: New policies for a new century.* A report of the Berkeley Family Forum. Edited by M. A. Mason, A. Skolnick, and S.D. Sugarman, New York: Oxford University Press, 196–219.

Cowan, C.P., and P.A. Cowan. 1992. *When partners become parents: The big life change for couples.* New York: Basic Books.

Cowan, C.P., and P.A. Cowan. 2000. *When partners become parents: The big life change for couples.* Mahwah, NJ: Lawrence Erlbaum Associates.

Crenson, M. 2007. Industrialized nations outgrow U.S. *Reno Gazette-Journal,* July 16, 3B.

Crosnoe, R., and G.H. Elder Jr. 2002. Life course transitions, the generational stake, and grandparent-grandchild relationships. *Journal of Marriage and Family* 64:1089–96.

Daly, K. 1993. Reshaping fatherhood: Finding the models. *Journal of Family Issues* 14(4):510–30.

Davidoff, M.J., T. Dias, K. Damus, R. Russell, B.R. Bettegowda, S. Dolan, R.H. Schwarz, N.S. Green, and J. Petrini. 2006. Changes in the gestational age distribution among U.S. singleton births: Impact on rates of late preterm birth, 1992 to 2002. *Seminars in Perinatology* 30(1):8–15.

DeFao, J. 2006. TV channel for babies? Pediatricians say turn it off. *San Francisco Chronicle,* September 11, A1, A8.

Demo, D.H., and A.C. Acock. 1996. Singlehood, marriage, and remarriage: The effects of family structure and family relationships on mother's well-being. *Journal of Family Issues* 17:388–407.

Desai, S., P.L. Chase-Lansdale, and R.T. Michael. 1989. Mother or market? Effects of maternal employment on the intellectual ability of 4-year-old children. *Demography* 26:545–61.

Duvall, E., and B. Miller. 1985. *Marriage and family development.* 6th ed. New York: Harper & Row.

Dye, J.L., and T.D. Johnson. 2006. A child's day: 2003 (Selected indicators of child well-being). *Current Population Reports,* P70-109. Washington, DC: U.S. Census Bureau, www.census.gov/prod/2007pubs/p70-109.pdf (accessed July 17, 2007).

Egelko, B. 2004. State's top court strikes down foster child's claim to estate. *San Francisco Chronicle,* January 16, A21.

Fejgin, N. 1995. Factors contributing to the academic excellence of American Jewish and Asian students. *Sociology of Education* 68(1):18–30.

Feller, B. 2003. Teens like their parents, according to survey. *San Francisco Chronicle,* August 6, A2.

Forward, S. 1989. *Toxic parents: Overcoming their hurtful legacy and reclaiming your life.* New York: Bantam.

Fulbright, L. 2006. Blacks take education into their own hands. *San Francisco Chronicle,* September 23, A1, A8.

Furstenberg, F.F. Jr., and C.W. Nord. 1985. Parenting apart: Patterns of childbearing after marital disruption. *Journal of Marriage and the Family* 47:893–912.

Furstenberg, F.F. Jr., C.W. Nord, J.L. Peterson, and N. Zill. 1983. The life course of children of divorce: Marital disruption and parental contact. *American Sociology Review* 48:656.

Furstenberg, F.F. Jr., J.A. Levine, and J. Brooks-Gunn. 1990. The children of teenage mothers: Patterns of early childbearing in two generations. *Family Planning Perspectives* 22:54–61.

Furstenberg, F.F., J. Brooks-Gunn, and S. Morgan. 1987. Adolescent mothers and their children in later life. *Family Planning Perspectives* 19:142–51.

Galinsky, E. 1999. *Ask the children*: *What America's children really think about working parents*. New York: William Morrow.

Gelles, R.J. 1975. Violence and pregnancy: A note on the extent of the problem and needed services. *Family Coordinator* 24:81–86.

Gerson, K. 1997. The social construction of fatherhood. In *Contemporary parenting: Challenges and issues.* Edited by T. Arendeli. Thousand Oaks, CA: Sage, 119–53.

Grandsplace. 2004. U.S. Census 2000 figures on grandparents raising grandchildren. www.grandsplace.com (accessed January 14, 2007).

Greven, P. 1991. *Spare the child: The religious roots of punishment and the psychological impact of physical abuse.* New York: Knopf.

Guttmacher Institute. 2006. *U.S. teenage pregnancy statistics: National and state trends and trends by race and ethnicity,* September. New York: The Guttmacher Institute, www.guttmacher.org/pubs/2006/09/12/USTPstats.pdf (accessed July 17, 2007).

Guttman, D. 1987. *Reclaimed powers.* New York: Basic Books.

Hamilton, B.E., J.A. Martin, and S.J. Ventura. 2006. Births: Preliminary data for 2005. *National Vital Statistics Reports*; vol 55. Hyattsville, MD: National Center for Health Statistics, www.cdc.gov/nchs/products/pubs/pubd/hestats/prelimbirths05/prelimbirths05.htm (accessed July 15, 2007).

Hansson, R.O., R.E. Nelson, M.D. Carver, D.H. NeeSmith, E.M. Dowling, W.L. Fletcher, and P. Suhr. 1990. Adult children with frail elderly parents: When to intervene? *Family Relations* 39:153–58.

Hardie, A. 1991. Aging boomers having babies. *San Francisco Chronicle,* September 2, D1, D5.

Harlow, H.F., and S.J. Suomi. 1970. Nature of love—simplified. *American Psychologist* 25:161–68.

Harris, P.B., and J. Bichler. 1997. *Men giving care: Reflections of husbands and sons.* New York: Garland.

Healy, B. 2006. Behind the baby count. *U.S. News & World Report,* October 2, 76.

Heide, K.M. 1992. Why kids kill parents. *Psychology Today* (September/October):62–66, 76–77.

Heymann, J., A. Earle, and J. Hayes. 2007. *The work, family, & equity index: How does the United States measure up?* Boston/Montreal: Project on Global Working Families, www.mcgill.ca/files/ihsp/WFEIFinal2007.pdf (accessed July 17, 2007).

Higgins, M. 2003. How to protect yourself from your parents. *The Wall Street Journal,* April 23, D1, D2.

Hofferth, S.L, Z. Jankuniene, and P.D. Brandon. 2000. Self-care among school-age children. University of Michigan, Institute for Social Research. Paper presented at the biennial meeting of the Society for Research on Adolescence, Minneapolis.

Hogan, D.P., and J.I. Farkas. 1995. The demography of changing intergenerational relationships. In *Adult intergenerational relations: Effects of societal change.* Edited by V.L. Bengtson and K.W. Schaie. New York: Springer, 1–18.

Holzer, H.J., D.W. Schanzenbach, G.J. Duncan, and J. Ludwig. 2007. *The economic costs of poverty in the United States: Subsequent effects of children growing up poor,* April. IRP discussion paper no. 1327-07. Madison, WI: University of Wisconsin–Madison, Institute for Research on Poverty, www.irp.wisc.edu/publications/dps/pdfs/dp132707.pdf (accessed July 17, 2007).

Hopkins, J., M. Marcues, and S.B. Cambell. 1984. Postpartum depression: A critical review. *Psychological Bulletin* 95:498–515.

Horatio Alger Association. 2003. *The state of our nation's youth.* Alexandria, VA: Horatio Alger Association of Distinquished Americans.

Horatio Alger Association. 2005. *The state of our nation's youth: 2005–2006.* Alexandria, VA: Horatio Alger Association of Distinguished Americans, www.horatioalger.com/pdfs/state05.pdf (accessed July 17, 2007).

Hughes, K.A. 1991. Mothers-to-be sue, charging discrimination. *The Wall Street Journal,* February 6, B1, B6.

Hunter, A.G. 1997. Counting on grandmothers: Black mothers' and fathers' reliance on grandmothers for parenting support. *Journal of Family Issues* 18(3):251–69.

International Labour Office. 2006. *The end of child labour: Within reach.* Global report under the follow-up to the ILO Declaration on Fundamental Principles and Rights at Work, International Labour Conference, 95th session, report I (B). Geneva: International Labour Office, www.ilo.org/iloroot/docstore/ipec/prod/eng/2006_cl_global report_en.pdf (accessed July 17, 2007).

Jackson, B. 1984. *Fatherhood.* London: George Allen and Unwin.

Jackson, M. 2003. More sons are juggling jobs and care for parents. *The New York Times,* June 15, sec. 5; 9.

Jayson, S. 2007. Unwed births shift to older, cohabiting couples. *USA Today,* July 2, 7D.

Jepsen, C., and S. de Alth. 2005. *English learners in California schools*. San Francisco: Public Policy Institute of California.

John, R. 1988. The Native American family. In *Ethnic families in America: Patterns and variations*, 3rd ed. Edited by C.H. Mindel, R.W. Habenstein, and R. Wright Jr. New York: Elsevier.

Julian, T.W., P.C. McKenry, and M.W. McKelvey. 1994. Cultural variations in parenting. *Family Relations* 43:30–37.

Kantor, J. 2006. Nanny hunt can be a "slap in the face" for blacks. *The New York Times*, December 26, A1, A20.

Kaufman, G., and P. Uhlenberg. 1998. Effects of life course transitions on the quality of relationships between adult children and their parents. *Journal of Marriage and the Family* 60(4):924–38.

Kelly, J. 2007. Comparison between television and real fathers and children involvement. *The Journal of Men, Masculinity and Politics*. (in press)

Kilbourne, J. 1999. *Can't buy my love: How advertising changes the way we think and feel*. New York: Touchstone.

King, V., and G.H. Elder Jr. 1995. American children view their grandparents: Linked lives across three rural generations. *Journal of Marriage and the Family* 57(1):165–78.

Kisker, E.E., R.A. Maynard, A. Rangarajan, and K. Boller. 1998. Moving teenage parents into self sufficiency: Lessons from recent demonstrations. Final report. Washington, DC: U.S. Department of Health and Human Services. www.aspe.dhhs.gov/hsp/isp/tpd/synthes/lessons.htm (accessed January 16, 2007).

Kitzinger, S. 1983. *The complete book of pregnancy and childbirth*. New York: Knopf.

Kivett, B.R. 1991. The grandparent-grandchild connection. *Marriage and Family Review* 16:267–90.

Klaus, M., and J. Kennel. 1982. *Preparing for parenthood*. New York: Bantam.

Knudsen, E.I., J.J. Heckman, J.L. Cameron, and J.P. Shonkoff. 2006. Economic, neurobiological, and behavioral perspectives on building America's future workforce. *Proceedings of the National Academy of Sciences* 103(27):10155–62.

Koch, L. 1987. Mothering: An honorable profession. *The Doula* 2(2):4–6.

Kolata, G. 1993. Family aid to elderly is very strong, study shows. *The New York Times*, May 3, A16.

Kornhaber, A., and K.L. Woodward. 1981. *Grandparents/grandchildren: The vital connection*. Garden City, NY: Doubleday/Anchor.

Kreider, R.M., and J. Fields. 2005. *Living arrangements of children: 2001*. Current Population Reports, P70-104. Washington, DC: U.S. Census Bureau, www.census.gov/prod/2005pubs/p70-104.pdf (accessed July 17, 2007).

Kutner, L. 1991. First comes the baby, then anger and frustration when not all goes according to expectations. *The New York Times*, November 7, B4.

LaMar, D.G. 1992. *Transcending turmoil: Survivors of dysfunctional families*. New York: Plenum Press.

Land, K.C. 2007. *2007 report: The Foundation for Child Development and youth well-being index (CWI), 1975–2005, with projections for 2006*, April 17. New York: Foundation for Child Development, www.fcd-us.org/usr_doc/2007CWIReport-Embargoed.pdf (accessed July 17, 2007).

LaRossa, R., and M.M. LaRossa. 1981. *The transition to parenthood: How infants change families*. Beverly Hills, CA: Sage.

Lee, M.D., and E.E. Kossek. 2005. *Crafting lives that work: A six-year retrospective on reduced-load work in the careers & lives of professionals and managers*. Boston: Sloan Work and Family Research Network, Boston College, www.polisci.msu.edu/kossek/final.pdf (accessed July 17, 2007).

Leifer, M. 1980. *Psychological effects of motherhood: A study of first pregnancy*. New York: Praeger.

LeMasters, E.E., and J. DeFrain. 1989. *Parents in contemporary America: A sympathetic view*. 5th ed. Belmont, CA: Wadsworth.

Lerner, H. 1997. *The mother dance*. New York: HarperCollins.

Lin, G., and P.A. Rogerson. 1995. Elderly parents and the geographic availability of their adult children. *Research on Aging* 17 (3):303–31.

Luescher, K., and K. Pillemer. 1998. Intergenerational ambivalence: A new approach to the study of parent–child relations in later life. *Journal of Marriage and the Family* 60(2):413–25.

MacDorman, M.F., W.M. Callaghan, T.J. Mathews, D.L. Hoyert, and K.D. Kochanek. 2007. Trends in preterm-related infant mortality by race and ethnicity: United States, 1999–2004. *Health E-Stats*, May 21. Hyattsville, MD: National Center for Health Statistics, www.cdc.gov/nchs/products/pubs/pubd/hestats/infantmort99-04/infantmort99-04.htm (accessed July 17, 2007).

Madrick, J. 2002. There have been significant changes in the welfare system, yet a rise in child poverty rates is now a real risk in the U.S. *The New York Times*, June 13, C2.

Martin, B. 1975. Parent-child relations. In *Review of child development research*, Vol. IV. Edited by F.D. Horowitz. Chicago: University of Chicago Press.

Mathews, T.J., and M.F. MacDorman. 2007. Infant mortality statistics from the 2004 period linked birth/infant death data set. *National Vital Statistics Reports* 55(15). Hyattsville, MD: National Center for Health Statistics, www.cdc.gov/nchs/data/nvsr/nvsr55/nvsr55_14.pdf (accessed July 17, 2007).

Matthews, S.H., and J. Sprey. 1985. Adolescents' relationships with grandparents: An empirical contribution to conceptual clarification. *Journal of Gerontology: Social Sciences* 50B:S312–20.

May, K.A. 1982. Factors contributing to first-time father's readiness for fatherhood: An exploratory study. *Family Relations* 31:353–61.

McCormick, K.F. 1992. Attitudes of primary care physicians toward corporal punishment. *Journal of the American Medical Association* 267:3161–65.

McGrew, M.C., and W.B. Shore. 1991. The problem of teenage pregnancy. *Journal of Family Practice* 32:17–25.

MetLife Mature Market Institute. 2003. *The MetLife study of sons at work: Balancing employment and eldercare*. Findings from a national study by the National Alliance for Caregiving and The Center for Productive Aging at Towson University. June. www.metlife.com/WPSAssets/20358015231056137413V1FSonsAtWork.pdf (accessed January 10, 2007).

Meyerowitz, J.H. 1970. Satisfaction during pregnancy. *Journal of Marriage and the Family* 32:38–42.

Miller, A.B. 1990. *The daycare dilemma: Critical concerns for American families*. New York: Plenum.

NACCRRA. 2006. *Breaking the piggy bank: Parents and the high price of child care*. Arlington, VA: National Association of Child Care Resource and Referral Agencies, www.naccrra.org/docs/policy/breaking_the_piggy_bank.pdf (accessed July 17, 2007).

National Center for Health Statistics. 2002b. New report sheds light on trends and patterns in marriage, divorce, and cohabitation. www.cdc.gov/nchs/releases/02news/div_mar_cohab.htm (accessed January 12, 2007).

National Indian Council on Aging. 1981. 1981 White House Conference on Aging: The Indian issues. *National Indian Council on Aging Quarterly* 4:1.

National Institute of Child Health and Human Development. 2007a. *America's children: Key national indicators of well-being, 2007*. National Institutes of Health, Department of Health and Human Services. Washington, DC: U.S. Government Printing Office, www.nichd.nih.gov/publications/pubs/upload/report2007.pdf (accessed July 17, 2007).

National Institute of Child Health and Human Development. 2007b. *The NICHD study of early child care and youth development*. Bethesda, MD: National Institutes of Health, http://secc.rti.org/home.cfm (accessed July 18, 2007).

Nelsen, J. 1987. *Positive discipline*. New York: Ballantine.

Neugarten, B.L., and K.K. Weinstein. 1964. The changing American grandparent. *Journal of Marriage and the Family* 26:199–204.

Neugarten, B.L., and K.K. Weinstein. 1968. The changing American grandparent. In *Middle age and aging*. Edited by B.L. Neugarten. Chicago: University of Chicago Press.

Nevius, C.W. 2003. Parents fear perils of media, polls show. *San Francisco Chronicle*, May 22, A1, A17.

Pancsofar, N., and L. Vernon-Feagans. 2006. Mother and father language input to young children: Contributions to later language development. *Journal of Applied Developmental Psychology* 27(6):571–87.

Pear, B. 1991. Bigger number of new mothers are unmarried. *The New York Times*, December 4, A11.

Perry, C. 1999. Extended family support among older black females. In *The black family: Essays and studies*. 6th ed. Edited by R. Staples. Belmont, CA: Wadsworth, 70–76.

Pew Research Center. 2007. *As marriage and parenthood drift apart, public is concerned about social impact.* Pew Research Center, a Social & Demographic Trends Report, July 1, http://pewresearch.org/assets/social/pdf/Marriage.pdf (accessed July 17, 2007).

Pleck, J.H. 1990. American fathering in historical perspective. In *Perspectives on the family: History, class, and feminism.* Edited by C. Carlson. Belmont, CA: Wadsworth, 377–89.

Ramchandani, P., A. Stein, J. Evans, T.G. O'Connor, and the ALSPAC study team. 2005. Paternal postnatal depressive symptoms predict behavioral problems in children independent of maternal postnatal depression. *The Lancet* 365:2201–05.

Recer, P. 1992. Executive moms more content than careerists. *San Francisco Examiner,* November 22, A10.

Reiss, D. 1995. Genetic influence on family systems: Implications for development. *Journal of Marriage and the Family* 57:543–60.

Rhee, K.E., J.C. Lumeng, D.P. Appugliese, N. Kaciroti, and R.H. Bradley. 2006. Parenting styles and overweight status in first grade. *Pediatrics* 117(6):2047–54.

Richardson, J. 1989. Substance use among eighth grade students who take care of themselves after school. *Pediatrics* 84:556–66.

Rideout, V., and E. Hamel. 2006. *The media family: Electronic media in the lives of infants, toddlers, preschoolers, and their parents,* May. Menlo Park, CA: Henry J. Kaiser Family Foundation, www.kff.org/entmedia/upload/7500.pdf (accessed July 17, 2007).

Roberts, K.A., and J. Stroes. 1992. Grandchildren and grandparents: Roles, influences, and relationships. *Journal of Aging and Human Development* 34:227–39.

Rogers, T. 1991. Why some people transcend their traumatic childhoods. *San Francisco Chronicle,* January 2, B1, B4.

Rosenberg, T., and J. Aschoff. 1990. Annual rhythm of human reproduction: Environmental correlates. *Biological Rhythms* 5:217–39.

Rossi, A.S. 1968. Transition to parenthood. *Journal of Marriage and the Family* 30:26–39.

Save the Children. 2007. *State of the world's mothers 2007.* Westport, CT: Save the Children, www.savethechildren.org/publications/mothers/2007/SOWM-2007-final.pdf (accessed July 17, 2007).

Schellhardt, T.P. 1990. It still isn't dad at home with sick kids. *The Wall Street Journal,* September 19, B1.

Schenck-Yglesias, C.G. 1995. A frail mom is a full-time job. *American Demographics,* September, 14–15.

Seltzer, J.A. 2000. Families formed outside of marriage. *Journal of Marriage and the Family* 62(4):1247–69.

Shannon, J.D., C.S. Tamis-LeMonda, and N.J. Cabrera. 2006. Fathering in infancy: Mutuality and stability between 8 and 16 months. *Parenting* 6(2&3):167–88.

Shapiro, A.F., J.M. Gottman, and S. Carrère. 2000. The baby and the marriage: Identifying factors that buffer against decline in marital satisfaction. *Journal of Family Psychology* 14(1):59–70.

Shellenbarger, S. 1992a. Parents' heavy burden of child-care costs. *The Wall Street Journal,* January 7, B1.

Shellenbarger, S. 1992b. Child-support rules shake parents, firms. *The Wall Street Journal,* January 20, B1.

Shellenbarger, S. 2003. No turning back: Parents debate whether they messed up their kids. *The Wall Street Journal,* July 31, D1.

Silverstein, M., and V.L. Bengston. 1997. Intergenerational solidarity and the structure of adult child–parent relationships in American families. *American Journal of Sociology* 103(2):429–60.

Simons, R.L., J. Beaman, R.D. Conger, and W. Chao. 1993. Childhood experience, conceptions of parenting, and attitudes of spouse as determinants of parental behavior. *Journal of Marriage and the Family* 55:91–106.

Simpson, J.A., W.A. Collins, S. Tran, and K.C. Haydon. 2007. Attachment and the experience and expression of emotions in adult romantic relationships: A developmental perspective. *Journal of Personality and Social Psychology* 92:355–67.

Sorkin, L. 2006. Infant mortality rate falls again. In *Vital signs 2006–2007: The trends that are shaping our future.* New York: The Worldwatch Institute.

Spring, I. 1991. Only a mother. *American Health,* June, 83.

Stewart, J. 2003. The mommy track: The consequences of gender ideology and aspirations on age at first motherhood. *Journal of Sociology and Social Welfare* 30(2):3–30.

Straus, M.A. 1994a. *Beating the devil out of them: Corporal punishment in American families.* New York: Lexington Books/Macmillan.

Straus, M.A. 1994b. State-to-state differences in social inequality and social bonds in relation to assaults on wives in the United States. (Special Issue: Family Violence) *Journal of Comparative Family Studies* 25(1): 7–25.

Straus, M.A. 1996. Spanking and the making of a violent society. (The short- and long-term consequences of corporal punishment: Proceedings of a Conference, February 9 and 10, 1996 in Elk Grove Village, IL.) *Pediatrics* 98(4):837–43.

Straus, M.A. 2001. New evidence for the benefits of never spanking. *Society* 38(6):52–61.

Straus, M.A., and C.J. Field. 2003. Psychological aggression by American parents: National data on prevalence, chronicity, and severity. *Journal of Marriage and the Family* 65:795–808. http://pubpages.unh.edu/∼mas2/CTS27.pdf (accessed January 12, 2007).

Straus, M.A., and C.L. Yodanis. 1996. Corporal punishment in adolescence and physical assaults on spouses in later life: What accounts for the link? *Journal of Marriage and the Family* 58:825–41.

Straus, M.A., and G.K. Kantor. 1994. Corporal punishment of adolescents by parents: a risk factor in the epidemiology of depression, suicide, alcohol abuse, child abuse, and wife beating. *Adolescence* 29(115):543–62.

Straus, M.A., and J.H. Stewart. 1999. Corporal punishment by American parents: National data on prevalence, chronicity, severity, and duration, in relation to child and family characteristics. *Clinics of Child Family Psychology Review* 2:55–70.

Straus, M.A., and V.E. Mouradian. 1998. Impulsive corporal punishment by mothers and antisocial behavior and impulsiveness of children. *Behavioral Sciences and the Law* 16(3):353–74.

Straus, M.A., D.B. Sugarman, and J. Giles-Sims. 1997. Spanking by parents and subsequent antisocial behavior of children. *Archives of Pediatrics and Adolescent Medicine* 151(8):761–68.

Sugrue, T.J. 1999. Poor families in an era of urban transformation: The "underclass" family in myth and reality. In *American families: A multicultural reader.* Edited by S. Coontz. New York: Routledge, 243–57.

Townsend, N.W. 2003. The four facets of fatherhood. In *The package deal: Marriage, work, and fatherhood in men's lives.* Philadelphia, PA: Temple University Press, 50–80.

Tran, T.V. 1988. The Vietnamese American family. In *Ethnic families in America: Patterns and variations,* 3rd ed. Edited by C.H. Mindel, R.W. Habenstein, and R. Wright Jr. New York: Elsevier.

Twenge, J.M., W.K. Campbell, and C.A. Foster. 2003. Parenthood and marital satisfaction: A meta-analytic review. *Journal of Marriage and the Family* 65:574–83.

Tyre, P. 2004. A new generation gap. *Newsweek,* January 19, 68–71.

U.S. Central Intelligence Agency. 2007. Rank order—infant mortality rate. *The world factbook,* www.cia.gov/library/publications/the-world-factbook/rankorder/2091rank.html (accessed July 17, 2007).

UNICEF. 2007. *Child poverty in perspective: An overview of child well-being in rich countries.* Innocenti Report Card 7, February 14. Florence, Italy: UNICEF Innocenti Research Centre, www.unicef.org/media/files/ChildPovertyReport.pdf (accessed July 17, 2007).

Ventura, S.J., J.A. Martin, S.C. Curtin, T.J. Mathews, and M.M. Park. 2000. Births: Final data for 1998. *National Vital Statistic Reports* 48, March 28. Centers for Disease Control and Prevention.

Waitzman, N.J., J.D. Iams, R.E. Behrman, and J. Howse. 2006. *Preterm birth: Causes, consequences, and prevention,* July 13. Washington, DC: Institute of Medicine.

Waldrop, J. 1991. The birthday boost. *American Demographics,* September, 4.

Weitzman, L.J. 1985. *The divorce revolution: The unexpected social and economic consequences for women and children in America.* New York: Free Press.

Westbrook, M.T. 1978. The effects of the order of a birth on women's experience of childbearing. *Journal of Marriage and the Family* 40:165–72.

Whitbeck, L.B., D.R. Hoyt, and S.M. Huck. 1993. Family relationship history, contemporary parent–grandparent relationship quality, and the grandparent–

grandchild relationship. *Journal of Marriage and the Family* 55(4):1025–35.

Wong, M.G. 1988. The Chinese American family. In *Ethnic families in America: Patterns and variations*, 3rd ed. Edited by C.H. Mindel, R.W. Habenstein, and R. Wright Jr. New York: Elsevier.

World Bank. 2006. *Repositioning nutrition as central to development: A strategy for large-scale action.* Washington, DC: World Bank, http://siteresources.worldbank.org/NUTRITION/Resources/281846-1131636806329/NutritionStrategy.pdf (accessed July 17, 2007).

World Health Organization. 2006. *The world health report 2006: Working together for health.* Geneva: World Health Organization, www.who.int/whr/2006/06_overview_en.pdf (accessed July 17, 2007).

Zimmerman, F.J., D.A. Christakis, and A.N. Meltzoff. 2007. Television and DVD/video viewing in children younger than 2 years. *Archives of Pediatrics and Adolescent Medicine* 161:473–79.

CHAPTER 12

A middle-class nation. 1999. *Public Perspective* 10:13.

Adler, J. 1996. Building a better dad. *Newsweek*, June 17, 58–64.

AFL-CIO. 2002. Ask a working woman, May 7, www.aflcio.org/mediacenter/prsptm/pr05072002a.cfm (accessed January 4, 2007).

Aldous, J., and W. Dumon. 1991. Family policy in the 1980s: Controversy and consensus. In *Contemporary families: Looking forward, looking back.* Edited by A. Booth. Minneapolis: National Council on Family Relations.

Alesina, A., E. Glaeser, and B. Sacerdote. 2005. Work and leisure in the U.S. and Europe: Why so different? Discussion Paper No. 2068, April, Harvard Institute of Economic Research, http://post.economics.harvard.edu/hier/2005papers/HIER2068.pdf (accessed July 18, 2007).

Armas, G.C. 2003. More mothers choosing to stay at home with kids. *Reno GazetteJournal*, June 17, 1A, 5A.

Armour, S. 2002. With job market tight, students start own businesses. *USA Today*, March 5, 1B.

Armour. S. 2007. High earners can still struggle. *USA Today*, June 28, 3B.

Atkinson, A.B. 2006. *Concentration among the rich.* United Nations University, World Institute for Development Economics Research, research paper 2006/151, December. Helsinki: UNU-WIDER, www.wider.unu.edu/research/research.htm (accessed July 18, 2007).

Becker, P.E., and P. Moen. 1999. Scaling back: Dual-earner couples' work-family strategies. *Journal of Marriage and the Family* 61(4):995–1007.

Bergmann, B. 1994. The economic support of child-raising: Curing child poverty in the United States. *AEA Papers and Proceedings* 84:76–80.

Bernard, J. 1986. The good-provider role: Its rise and fall. In *Family in transition: Rethinking marriage, sexuality, child rearing, and family organization,* 5th ed. Edited by A.S. Skolnick and J.H. Skolnick. Boston: Little, Brown, 125–44.

Bianchi, S.M., J.P. Robinson, and A. Milkie. 2006. *Changing rhythms of American family life.* New York: Russell Sage Foundation.

Bird, C.E., and C.E. Ross. 1993. Houseworkers and paid workers: Qualities of the word and effects on personal control. *Journal of Marriage and the Family* 55:913–25.

Blair, S.L. 1993. Employment, family, and perceptions of marital quality among husbands and wives. *Journal of Family Issues* 14(2):189–212.

Blair-Loy, M., and A.S. Wharton. 2002. Employees' use of work-family policies and the workplace social context. *Social Forces* 80(2):813–46.

Brayfield, A.A. 1992. Employment resources and housework in Canada. *Journal of Marriage and the Family* 54(1):19–30.

Bureau of Labor Statistics. 2007. Average hourly and weekly earnings of production and nonsupervisory workers (1) on private nonfarm payrolls by industry sector and selected industry detail. *Bureau of Labor Statistics News*, June 1, www.bls.gov/news.release/empsit.t16.htm (accessed July 18, 2007).

Burtless, G., and T.M. Smeeding. 2001. The level, trend, and composition of poverty. In *Understanding poverty.* Edited by S.H. Danziger, and R.H. Haveman. New York: Russell Sage Foundation.

Cagetti, M., and M. De Nardi. 2005. *Wealth inequality: Data and models.* FRB Chicago Working Paper 2005-10, August 17. Chicago: Federal Reserve Bank, www.chicagofed.org/publications/workingpapers/wp2005_10.pdf (accessed July 18, 2007).

Carroll, C. 2001. Finding good daycare. *The Pacer.* April 24. www.angelina.cc.tx.us/OnlinePaper/childcare.htm (accessed October 6, 2007).

Chira, S. 1998. *A mother's place: Taking the debate about working mothers beyond guilt and blame.* New York: HarperCollins.

Corcoran, M. 2001. Mobility, persistence, and the consequences of poverty for children: Child and adult outcomes. In *Understanding poverty.* Edited by S.H. Danziger, and R.H. Haveman. New York: Russell Sage Foundation.

Crawford, D.W. 2000. Occupational characteristics and marital leisure involvement. *Family and Consumer Sciences Research Journal* 28:52–70.

Crockett, R.O., and P. Coy. 2003. Progress without parity. *Business Week*, July 14, 100–102.

Curry, A. 2003. The history of work in America over the past century. *U.S. News & World Report*, February 24/March 3, 50–56.

Day, J.C., and E.C. Newburger. 2002. *The big payoff: Educational attainment and synthetic estimates of work-life earnings.* Current Population Reports, P23-210, July. Washington, DC: U.S. Census Bureau, www.census.gov/prod/2002pubs/p23-210.pdf (accessed July 18, 2007).

Daycare.com. 2004. Tips for evaluating quality daycare. www.daycare.com/news/tips.html (accessed October 6, 2007).

DeBare, I. 1998a. Double-duty dads. *San Francisco Chronicle*, June 15, B1, B3.

DeBare, I. 1998b. A time for caring. *San Francisco Chronicle*, August 3, B1, B3.

Demo, D.H., and A.C. Acock. 1993. Family diversity and the division of domestic labor: How much have things really changed? *Family Relations* 42(3):323–31.

DeNavas-Walt, C., B.D. Proctor, and C.H. Lee. 2006. *Income, poverty, and health insurance coverage in the United States: 2005.* Current Population Reports, P60-231, August. Washington, DC: U.S. Census Bureau, www.census.gov/prod/2006pubs/p60-231.pdf (accessed July 18, 2007).

Duenwald, M. 2002. Coping with the spiral of stress that layoffs create. *The New York Times*, October 29, E3.

Economic Policy Institute. 2007. *Minimum wage issue guide: Facts at a glance,* April. Washington, DC: Economic Policy Institute, www.epi.org/issueguides/minwage/epi_minimum_wage_issue_guide.pdf (accessed July 18, 2007).

Epstein, C.F., Seron, C., B. Oglensky, and R. Sauté. 2003. The family and part-time work. In *Family in transition*, 12th ed. Edited by A.S. Skolnick and J.H. Skolnick. Boston: Allyn & Bacon, 335–49.

Expedia.com. 2007. International vacation deprivation survey results, online survey conducted by Harris Interactive for Expedia.com., http://media.expedia.com/media/content/expus/graphics/promos/vacations/Expedia_International_Vacation_Deprivation_Survey_Results_2007.pdf (accessed July 18, 2007).

Ferguson Jr., R.W. 2005. Remarks by vice chairman Roger W. Ferguson Jr., Federal Reserve Board, November 18, www.federalreserve.gov/BOARDDOCS/Speeches/2005/20051129/default.htm (accessed July 18, 2007).

Fisher, A.F. 2003. My husband lost his job, and then he lost his drive. *Fortune*, April 28, 144.

Flynn, G. 1997. Flex appeal. *San Francisco Examiner*, November 16, J1, J2.

Freudenheim, M. 2003. Employees paying ever-bigger share for health care. *New York Times*, September 10, A1, C2.

Friedman, S.D., and J.H. Greenhaus. 2000. *Work and family allies or enemies? What happens when business professionals confront life choices.* New York: Oxford University Press.

Friedman, S.D., P. Christensen, and J. DeGroot. 1998. Work and life: The end of the zero-sum game. *Harvard Business Review,* November–December, 119–29.

Geller, A. 2002. Sick days are less about being ill. *Reno Gazette-Journal*, October 17, 1D, 5D.

Gerson, K., and J.A. Jacobs. 2003. Changing the structure and culture of work: Work and family conflict, work flexibility, and gender equity in the modern workplace. In *Family in transition.* 12th ed. Edited by A.S. Skolnick and J.H. Skolnick. Boston: Allyn & Bacon, 349–63.

Gilbert, D., and J.A. Kahl. 1993. *The American*

class structure: A new synthesis. 4th ed. Homewood, IL: Dorsey.

Gilbert, D.L. 1997. The American class structure: In an age of growing inequality. Belmont, CA: Wadsworth.

Giles, C. 2006. Richest 2% hold half the world's assets. Financial Times, December 5, www.ft.com/cms/s/41470ec0-845b-11db-87e0-0000779e2340.html (accessed July 18, 2007).

Goldberg, H., and R.T. Lewis. 1979. Money madness: The psychology of saving, spending, loving, and hating money. New York: Signet Books.

Grzywacz, J.G., and B.L. Bass. 2003. Work, family, and mental health: Testing different models of work-family fit. Journal of Marriage and the Family 65(1):248–62.

Haralson, D., and M.K. Mullins. 2000. Less pay, more play. USA Today, November 6, B1.

Harvard Public Health Review. 2002. www.hsph.harvard.edu/review/review_winter_02/featurerace.html (accessed January 5, 2007).

Henslin, J.M. 2007. Sociology: A down-to-earth approach, 8th ed. Boston: Allyn & Bacon.

Hochschild, A. 1989. The second shift: Working parents and the revolution at home. New York: Viking.

Hochschild, A. 1997. Time bind: When work becomes home and home becomes work. New York: Henry Holt.

Houseknecht, S.K., S. Vaughan, and A. Statham. 1987. The impact of singlehood on the career patterns of professional women. Journal of Marriage and the Family 49(2):353–66.

Jacobs, J.A., and K. Gerson. 2001. Overworked individuals or overworked families? Work and Occupations 28(1):40–63.

Jacobson, L. 1999. Mothers' jobs have modest effect on children. Education Week on the Web, March 10, www.edweek.com/ew/vol18/26moms.h18 (accessed January 4, 2007).

Kiecolt, K.J. 2003. Satisfaction with work and family life: No evidence of a cultural reversal. Journal of Marriage and the Family 65(1):23–36.

Kleiman, C. 1999. Work less, get promoted? Study says it's possible. San Jose Mercury News, April 11, PC1.

Kleiman, C. 2000. Work-life rewards grow. San Francisco Chronicle, January 16, J2; reprinted from Chicago Tribune.

Leider, D. 1988. Purposeful work. Utne Reader, July/August, 52.

Leonhardt, D. 2007. Middle-class squeeze comes with nuances. The New York Times, April 25, C1, C12.

Lester, W. 2006. Stress is a common bond for those in developed nations. San Francisco Chronicle, December 21, A14. Report on Associated Press-Ipsos poll on stress.

Lewin, T. 1999. Union links women's pay to poverty among families, The New York Times, February 25, A17.

Loprest, P. 1999. Families who left welfare: Who are they and how are they doing? Washington, DC: Urban Institute. newfederalism.urban.org/pdf/discussion99-02.pdf (accessed January 8, 2007).

Love, A.A. 2000. A challenge for working couples: Poll finds many women are working

different shifts from spouses. South Coast Today, March 10. www.s-t.com/daily/03-00/03-10-00/a02wn013.htm (accessed January 8, 2007).

Lynem, J.N. 2003. Manning the house. San Francisco Chronicle, June 14, B1, B2.

MacDermid, S.M., M.D. Lee, M. Buck, and M.L. Williams. 2001. Alternative work arrangements among professionals and managers: Rethinking career development and success. The Journal of Management Development 20(4):305–317.

McAndrew, S. 2003. The importance of being flexible. Reno Gazette-Journal, March 17, 1D, 3D.

Millman, M. 1991. Warm hearts and cold cash: The intimate dynamics of families and money. New York: Free Press.

Moen, P. 1992. Women's two roles: A contemporary dilemma. Westport, CT: Auburn House.

Murphy, K. 2002. More people fall below poverty line in 2001 over previous year. Kansas City Star, September 25. www.kansascity.com/mld/kansascity/news/local

National Institute of Child Health and Human Development. 2007. The NICHD study of early child care and youth development. Bethesda, MD: National Institutes of Health, http://secc.rti.org/home.cfm (accessed July 18, 2007).

NationMaster.com. 2003. www.nationmaster.com/graph-T/eco_eco_ove/NAM (accessed January 5, 2007).

Nusbaum, M.A. 2002. Creative thinking by a working mom. The New York Times, October 27, sec. 3; 14.

O'Neil, R., and E. Greenberger. 1994. Patterns of commitment to work and parenting: Implications for role strain. Journal of Marriage and the Family 52(1):101–15.

Oakley, A. 1974. Sociology of housework New York: Pantheon.

Oakley, A., ed. 1985. Sex, gender, and society, rev. ed. New York: Harper & Row.

Orrange, R.M. 2003. The emerging mutable self: Gender dynamics and creative adaptations in defining work, family, and the future. Social Forces 82(1):1–34.

Papaneck, H. 1979. Family status production. Signs 4:775–81.

Pearce, D. 1978. The feminization of poverty: Women, work, and welfare. Urban and Social Change Review 11:28–36.

Peterson, K.S. 2003. Gen X moms have it their way. USA Today, May 7, 1D, 2D.

Pew Research Center. 2007a. Fewer mothers prefer full-time work: From 1997 to 2007. July 12. New York: Pew Research Center, http://pewresearch.org/assets/social/pdf/Women Working.pdf (accessed July 18, 2007).

Pew Research Center. 2007b. As marriage and parenthood drift apart, public is concerned about social impact: Generation gap in values, behaviors, July 1. New York: Pew Research Center, http://pewresearch.org/assets/social/pdf/Marriage.pdf (accessed July 18, 2007).

Price, R.H., J.N. Choi, and A.D. Vinokur. 2002. Links in the chain of adversity following job loss: How financial strain and loss of personal control lead to depression, impaired functioning, and poor health.

Journal of Occupational Health Psychology 5(1):32–47.

Purola, J. 2001. The "mommy track" role: Traditional gender roles manifest in the mommy track, www.ashtabulaart.com/jp/Papers/MommyTrack.htm (accessed January 6, 2007).

Rank, M.R., and L.-C. Cheng. 1995. Welfare use across generations: How important are the ties that bind? Journal of Marriage and the Family 57(3):673–84.

Reynolds, J. 2003. You can't always get the hours you want: Mismatches between actual and preferred work hours in the U.S. Social Forces 81(4):1171–200.

Rosenbluth, S.C., J.M. Steil, and J.H. Whitcomb. 1998. Marital equality: What does it mean? Journal of Family Issues 19:227–44.

Sawhill, I., and J. E. Morton. 2007. Economic mobility: Is the American dream alive and well? A report of the Economic Mobility Project, The Pew Charitable Trusts. Washington, DC: Pew Charitable Trusts, www.economicmobility.org/assets/pdfs/EMP%20American%20Dream%20Report.pdf%20 (accessed July 18, 2007).

Seligman, M.E.P. 2002. Authentic happiness. New York: Free Press.

Sharpe, R. 2000. As leaders, women rule. Business Week, November 20, 75–84.

Shellenbarger, S. 1996a. Feel like you need to be cloned? Even that wouldn't work. The Wall Street Journal, July 10, B1.

Shellenbarger, S. 1996b. It's the type of job you have that affects the kids, studies say. The Wall Street Journal, July 31, B1.

Shellenbarger, S. 2003. The new prenup: Planning whose job comes first, who stays home with kids. The Wall Street Journal, June 26, D1.

Single-earner households shrink. 2002. USA Today. April 22, 1B. Citing Employment Policy Foundation's Center for Work and Family Balance of Decennial Census and current population survey data.

Small, S., and D. Riley. 1990. Toward a multidimensional assessment of work spillover into family life. Journal of Marriage and the Family 52(1):51–61.

Surowiecki, J. 2005. No work and no play. The New Yorker, November 28, 68.

Swoboda, F. 2000. Stress in women's work schedule. San Francisco Chronicle, March 10, B3; reprinted from Washington Post.

Thompson, L. 1991. Family work: Women's sense of fairness. Journal of Family Issues 12(2):181–96.

Tyre, P., and D. McGinn. 2003. She works, he doesn't. Newsweek, May 12, 44–52.

U.S. Census Bureau. 2002. Money income in the United States: 2001. www.census.gov/prod/2002pubs/p60-218.pdf (accessed May 15, 2007).

U.S. Census Bureau. 2006a. Income climbs, poverty stabilizes, uninsured rate increases, August 29, www.census.gov/Press-Release/www/releases/archives/income_wealth/007419.html (accessed July 18, 2007).

U.S. Census Bureau. 2006b. Parents and children in stay-at-home family groups: 1994 to present, September 21, www.census.gov/

population/socdemo/hh-fam/shp1.pdf (accessed July 18, 2007).

U.S. Census Bureau. 2007. Women's history month: March 2007. *Facts for Features*, January 4, www.census.gov/Press-Release/www/releases/archives/cb07ff-03.pdf (accessed July 18, 2007).

U.S. Census Bureau. 2007a. U.S. Census Bureau revises 2004 and 2005 health insurance coverage estimates, March 23, www.census.gov/Press-Release/www/releases/archives/health_care_insurance/009789.html (accessed July 18, 2007).

U.S. Department of Labor. 2007b. *Report: A chartbook of international labor comparisons: The Americas, Asia, Europe—June 2006*, Chart 2.8. Washington, DC: U.S. Department of Labor, www.dol.gov/asp/media/reports/chartbook/index.htm (accessed July 18, 2007).

U.S. Office of Personnel Management. 1999. *The child care resources handbook*. www.opm.gov/wrkfam/html/cchb500.asp (accessed May 15, 2007).

United Nations International Labor Organization. 2002. Reported in G.T. Anderson. 2003. Should America be France? CNNMoney. October 9. http://money.cnn.com/2003/10/06/pf/work_less/ (accessed May 12, 2007).

Valenti, C. 2003. Vacation deprivation. *ABC News moneyscope*. June 23. http://abcnews.go.com/sections/business/USvacation_030625.html (accessed January 8, 2007).

Voydanoff, P., and B. Donnelly. 1989. Work and family roles and psychological distress. *Journal of Marriage and the Family* 51(4):933–41.

Warren, J.A., and P.J. Johnson. 1995. The impact of workplace support on work-family role strain. *Family Relations* 44(2):163–69.

Watson, R. 1984. What price day care? *Newsweek*, September 10, 14–21.

Weber, L., T. Hancick, and E. Higginbotham. 1997. Women, power, and mental health. In *Women's health: Complexities and differences*. Edited by S.B. Ruzek, V.L. Olesen, and A.E. Clarke. Columbus: Ohio State University Press, 380–96.

Wharton, A.S., and R.J. Erickson. 1993. Managing emotions on the job and at home: Understanding the consequences of multiple emotional roles. *Academy of Management Review*, July, 457–86.

Wiener, L. 2003. Paycheck plus. *U.S. News & World Report*, February 24/March 3, 48.

Women's pay tops men's as part timers. 2002. *Los Angeles Times*, April 17, C7.

Working at the wrong job. 1990. *San Francisco Chronicle*, January 12, C1. Gallup Organization October 1989 survey for National Occupational Information Coordinating Committee.

Zaslow, J. 2002. Who's the new guy at dinner? It's Dad; laid-off fathers face tough job at home. *The Wall Street Journal*, October 1, D1.

CHAPTER 13

Adelmann, P.K., and R.B. Zajonc. 1989. Facial efference and the experience of emotion. *Annual Review of Psychology* 40:249–80.

Alexander, P.C., S. Moore, and E.R. Alexander III. 1991. What is transmitted in the intergenerational transmission of violence? *Journal of Marriage and the Family* 53(3):657–68.

Almeida, D.M., D.A. McDonald, and J.G. Grzywacz. 2002. Work-family spillover and daily reports of work and family stress in the adult labor force. *Family Relations* 61(1):28–37.

American Psychological Association. 2006. Americans engage in unhealthy behaviors to manage stress. Press release, February 23, http://apahelpcenter.mediaroom.com/index.php?s=press_releases&item=23 (accessed June 27, 2007).

Amnesty International. 2007. Maze of injustice: The failure to protect indigenous women from sexual violence in the USA. Report by Amnesty International, April 24, http://web.amnesty.org/library/index/ENGAMR510352007 (accessed June 25, 2007).

Arbetter, S.R. 1989. Emotional food fights. *Current Health 2*, 15:4–10.

Arndt, M. 2003. People are basically defeated. *Business Week*, June 2, 57–58.

Bachman, R. 1994. *Violence against women: A national crime victimization survey report*. Washington, DC: U.S. Department of Justice, Office of Justice Programs, Bureau of Justice Statistics. Fall.

Bartlett, K. 1990. After a fall, pain is both her constant companion and her jailer. *Los Angeles Times*, March 25, A2.

Bender, E. 2007. Action sought to close gap in hospital, outpatient care. *Psychiatric News* 42(10):18.

Benson, H. 1989. Editorial: Hypnosis and the relaxation response. *Gastroenterology* 96:1610.

Berk, R.A. 1993. What the scientific evidence shows: On the average, we can do no better than arrest. In *Current controversies in family violence*. Edited by R. Gelles and D. Loseke. Newbury Park, CA: Sage.

Berk, R.A., and P.J. Newton. 1985. Does arrest really deter wife battery? An effort to replicate the findings of the Minneapolis Spouse Abuse Experiment. *American Sociological Review* 50:253–62.

Bernstein, N. 2006. A tough road for siblings who survived cases of abuse. *The New York Times*, January 15, sec. 1, 21.

Blumenthal, S.J., and D.J. Kupfer. 1986. Generalizable treatment strategies for suicidal behavior. *Annals of the New York Academy of Sciences* 487:327–40.

Bolger, N., A. DeLongis, R.C. Kessler, and E. Wethington. 1989. The contagion of stress across multiple roles. *Journal of Marriage and the Family* 5(1):175–83.

Boss, P. 1988. *Family stress management*. Newbury Park, CA: Sage.

Bouchard, G., J. Wright, Y. Lussier, and C. Richer. 1998. Predictive validity of coping strategies on marital satisfaction: Cross-sectional and longitudinal evidence. *Journal of Family Psychology* 12:112–31.

Bowker, L. 1983. *Beating wife beating*. Lexington, MA: Lexington Books.

Bowman, R.L., and H.M. Morgan. 1998. A comparison of rates of verbal and physical abuse on campus by gender and sexual orientation. *College Student Journal* 32:43–52.

Braiker, H.B. 1989. The power of self-talk. *Psychology Today* (December):24.

Brookoff, D., K. O'Brien, C.S. Cook, and T.D. Thompson. 1997. Characteristics of participants in domestic violence. *Journal of the American Medical Association* 277:1369–73.

Brotherson, S.E. 2000. When a child dies: Primary parenting concerns during the loss of a child. Poster presentation at the Annual Conference of the National Council on Family Relations, Minneapolis, November.

Browning, C.R., and E.O. Laumann. 1998. Sexual contact between children and adults: A life course perspective. *American Sociological Review* 62:540–60.

Buckley, C. 2007. In domestic violence cases, digital photos often say more than the victims. *The New York Times*, May 7, A22.

Bureau of Labor Statistics. 2007. *Employment situation summary*, June 1. Washington, DC: U.S. Department of Labor, www.bls.gov/news.release/empsit.nor0.htm (accessed June 12, 2007).

Burr, W.R., and S.R. Klein and Associates. 1994. *Reexamining family stress: New theory and research*. Thousand Oaks, CA: Sage.

Busey, M. 1990. Industrial-strength stress dissolvers. *Men's Health*, October, 78–80.

Butler, K. 2006. Beyond rivalry, a hidden world of sibling violence. *The New York Times*, February 28, D1, D6.

Buzawa, E.S., and C.G. Buzawa. 1990. *Domestic violence: The criminal justice response*. Newbury Park, CA: Sage.

Buzawa, E.S., and C.G. Buzawa. 1993. The scientific evidence is not conclusive: Arrest is no panacea. In *Current controversies in family violence*. Edited by R. Gelles and D. Loseke. Newbury Park, CA: Sage.

Campbell, J. 1995. Violence toward women: Homicide and battering. In *Vision 2010: Families and violence, abuse and neglect*. Edited by R.J. Gelles. Minneapolis: National Council on Family Relations.

Canavan, M.M., W.J. Meyer III, and D.C. Higgs. 1992. The female experience of sibling incest. *Journal of Marital and Family Therapy* 18(2):129–42.

Cano, A., and D. O'Leary. 1997. Romantic jealousy and affairs: Research and implications for couple therapy. *Journal of Sex and Marital Therapy* 23(4):249–75.

Carp, F.M. 2000. *Elder abuse in the family: An interdisciplinary model for research*. New York: Springer.

Cate, R.M., and S.A. Lloyd. 1992. *Courtship*. Newbury Park, CA: Sage.

Chance, S. 1992. *Stronger than death*. New York: W.W. Norton.

Children's Defense Fund. 2007. *Every day in America*, May, www.childrensdefense.org/site/PageServer?pagename=research_national_data_each_day (accessed June 11, 2007).

Christakis, N.A., and P.D. Allison. 2006. Mortality after the hospitalization of a spouse. *The New England Journal of Medicine* 354:719–30.

Clinton, H.R. 2003. Hilary unbound, *Time*,

June 16, 24–38. Book except from H.R. Clinton, *Living history*. New York: Simon & Schuster, 2003.

Coan, J.A., H.S. Schaefer, and R.J. Davidson. 2006. Lending a hand: Social regulation of the neural response to threat. *Psychological Science* 17(2):1032–39.

Colby, B.N. 1987. Well-being: A theoretical program. *American Anthropologist* 89:879–95.

Coleman, D.H., and M.A. Straus. 1983. Alcohol abuse and family violence. In *Alcohol, drug abuse, and aggression*. Edited by E. Gottheil, K.A. Druley, T.E. Skoloda, and H.M. Waxman. Springfield, IL: Charles C. Thomas.

Coleman, F.L. 1997. Stalking behavior and the cycle of domestic violence. *Journal of Interpersonal Violence* 12:420–32.

Copenhaver, S., and E. Grauerholz. 1991. Sexual victimization among sorority women: Exploring the link between sexual violence and institutional practices. *Sex Roles* 24(1/2):31–41.

Cramer, P. 1998. Coping and defense mechanisms: What's the difference? *Journal of Personality* 66:895–918.

Cramer, P. 2000. Defense mechanisms in psychology today. *American Psychologist*, June, 637–46.

Daly, M., and M.I. Wilson. 1994. Some differential attributes of lethal assaults on small children by stepfathers versus genetic fathers. *Ethology and Sociobiology* 15:207–17.

Davis, R.C., and B.G. Taylor. 1999. Does batterers' treatment reduce violence? A synthesis of the literature. In *Women and domestic violence: An interdisciplinary approach*. Edited by L. Fedeç. New York: Haworth Press, 69–93.

de Santis, M. 1990. Hate crimes bill excludes women. *Off our backs*. June.

Domenico, D., and M. Windle. 1993. Intrapersonal and interpersonal functioning among middle-aged female adult children of alcoholics. *Journal of Consulting and Clinical Psychology* 61:659–66.

DSM-IV-TR. 2001. *Diagnostic and statistical manual of mental disorders (text revision)*. Washington, DC: American Psychiatric Association.

Easley, M.J., and N. Epstein. 1991. Coping with stress in a family with an alcoholic parent. *Family Relations* 40:218–24.

Eaton, D.K., L. Kann, S. Kinchen, J. Ross, J. Hawkins, W.A. Harris, R. Lowry, T. McManus, D. Chyen, S. Shanklin, C. Lim, J.A. Grunbaum, and H. Wechsler. 2006. Youth risk behavior surveillance—United States, 2005. *MMWR Surveillance Summaries*, June 9. Washington, DC: Centers for Disease Control and Prevention.

Elliott, D.M., and J. Briere. 1992. The sexually abused boy: Problems in manhood. *Medical Aspects of Human Sexuality* 26:68–71.

Epel, E.S., E.H. Blackburn, J. Lin, F.S. Dhabhar, N.E. Adler, J.D. Morrow, and R.M. Cawthon. 2004. Accelerated telomere shortening in response to life stress. *Proceedings of the National Academy of Sciences* 101(49):17312–15.

Faiola, A. 2005. Retired husbands making wives in Japan sick, therapists report. *Reno Gazette-Journal*, October 18, 4C; reprinted from *The Washington Post*.

Felitti, V.J, R.F. Anda, D. Nordenberg, et al. 1998. Relationship of childhood abuse and household dysfunction to many of the leading causes of death in adults. The Adverse Childhood Experiences (ACE) Study. *American Journal of Preventive Medicine* 14(4):245–58.

Fineman, M.A., and R. Mykitiuk. 1994. *The public nature of private violence: The discovery of domestic abuse*. New York: Routledge.

Finkelhor, D., and K. Yllo. 1985. *License to rape: Sexual abuse of wives*. New York: Holt.

Finkelhor, D., G. Hotaling, I.A. Lewis, and C. Smith. 1990. *Missing, abducted, runaway, and throwaway children in America*. Washington, DC: U.S. Department of Justice.

Finkelhor, D., R. Ormrod, H. Turner, and S.L. Hamby. 2005. The victimization of children and youth: A comprehensive, national survey. *Child Maltreatment* 10(1):5–23.

Fleming, J., P. Mullen, and C. Bammer. 1996. A study of potential risk factors for sexual abuse in childhood. *Child Abuse and Neglect* 21(1):49–58.

Forte, J.A., D.D. Franks, J.A. Forte, and D. Rigsby. 1996. Asymmetrical role-taking: Comparing battered and nonbattered women. *Social Work* 41:59–73.

Fox, G.L., M.L. Benson, A.A. DeMaris, and J.V. Wyk. 2002. Economic distress and intimate violence: Testing family stress and resources theories. *Journal of Marriage and the Family* 64(3):793–808.

France, D. 2006. And then he hit me. *AARP Magazine*. January & February 2006, 73–77, 105–06.

Frankenfield, P.K. 1996. The power of humor and play as nursing interventions for a child with cancer. *Journal of Pediatric Oncology Nursing* 13:15–20.

Gabarino, J. 1989. The incidence and prevalence of child maltreatment. In *Family violence*. Edited by L. Ohlin and M. Tonry. Chicago: University of Chicago Press, 219–61.

Garnefski, N., and E. Arends. 1998. Sexual abuse and adolescent maladjustment. *Journal of Adolescence 2* 1:99–107.

Gelles, R., and C. Cornell. 1990. *Intimate violence in families*. 2nd ed. Newbury Park, CA: Sage.

Gelles, R.J. 1993. Alcohol and other drugs are associated with violence: They are not its cause. In *Current controversies in family violence*. Edited by R. Gelles and D. Leseke. Newbury Park, CA: Sage.

Gelles, R.J. 1995. *Contemporary families: A sociological view*. Thousand Oaks, CA: Sage.

Gelles, R.J. 1997. *Intimate violence in families*. 3rd ed. Thousand Oaks, CA: Sage.

Gelles, R.J., and J.R. Conte. 1991. Domestic violence and sexual abuse of children: A review of research in the eighties. In *Contemporary families: Looking forward, looking back*. Edited by A. Booth. Minneapolis: National Council on Family Relations.

Gelles, R.J., and M.A. Straus. 1988. *Intimate violence*. New York: Simon & Schuster.

Giltay, E.J., J.M. Geleijnse, F.G. Zitman, T. Koekstra, and E.G. Schouten. 2004. Dispositional optimism and all-cause and cardiovascular mortality in a prospective cohort of elderly Dutch men and women. *Archives of General Psychiatry* 61:1126–35.

Glass, I. 2003. The doctor of dalliance. *The New York Times Magazine*, December 28, 48–49.

Glass, S. 1998. Shattered vows. *Psychology Today* (July 1):34 passim.

Glass, S., and J.C. Staeheli. 2003. *NOT "just friends": Protect your relationship from infidelity and heal the trauma of betrayal*. New York: Free Press.

Gondolf, E.W. 1987. Evaluating progress for men who batter. *Journal of Family Violence* 2:95–108.

Gondolf, E.W. 1988. The effect of batterer counseling on shelter outcome. *Journal of Interpersonal Violence* 3(3):275–89.

Goode, E. 1994. Till death do them part? *U.S. News & World Report*, July 4, 24–28.

Gray, H.M., and V. Foshee. 1997. Adolescent dating violence: Differences between one-sided and mutually violent profiles. *Journal of Interpersonal Violence* 12:126–41.

Greene, B. 1990. Some wounds never really heal. *San Francisco Chronicle, This World*, February 25, 5–6.

Grosskopf, D. 1983. *Sex and the married woman*. New York: Simon & Schuster.

Hafstrom, J., and V. Schram. 1984. Chronic illness in couples: Selected characteristics, including wife's satisfaction with and perception of marital relationships. *Family Relations* 33:195–203.

Halmi, K.A., J.R. Flak, and E. Schwartz. 1981. Binge-eating and vomiting: A survey of a college population. *Psychology and Medicine* 11:697–706.

Hamilton, I., A.I. Thompson, and M.A. McCubbin. 1996. *Family assessment: Resiliency, coping and adaptation*. Madison, WI: University of Wisconsin Publishers.

Hanley, M.J., and P. O'Neill. 1997. Violence and commitment: A study of dating couples. *Journal of Interpersonal Violence* 12:685–703.

Harper, J.M., B.C. Schaalje, and J.C. Sandberg. 2000. Daily hassles, intimacy, and marital quality in later marriages. *American Journal of Family Therapy* 28:1–18.

Harris, D.K. 1990. *Sociology of aging*. 2nd ed. New York: Harper & Row.

Harris, P.B., and J. Bichler. 1997. *Men giving care: Reflections of husbands and sons*. New York: Garland.

Haselton, M.G., and S.W. Gangestad. 2006. Conditional expression of women's desires and men's mate guarding across the ovulatory cycle. *Hormones and Behavior* 49:509–18.

Hasin, D.S., F.S. Stinson, E. Ogburn, and B.F. Grant. 2007. Prevalence, correlates, disability, and comorbidity of *DSM-IV* alcohol abuse and dependence in the United States: Results from the National Epidemiologic Survey on Alcohol and Related Conditions. *Archives of General Psychiatry* 64:830–42.

Henningson, E. 1997. *Financial abuse of the elderly*. Wisconsin Department of Health and Family Services. http://maxpages.com/

savinggrace/Elder_Financial_Abuse (accessed May 15, 2004).

Hiller, L. 2002. At 20, she's a survivor with a promising future. *Reno Gazette-Journal*, October 14, 1B, 4B.

Hobson, C.J., J. Kamen, J. Szostek, C.M. Nethercut, J.W. Tiedmann, and S. Wojnarowiez. 1998. Stressful life events: A revision and update of the social readjustment rating scale. *International Journal of Stress Management* 5:1–23.

Hoffman, L. 2007. Baby Boomers becoming generation of aging addicts. *San Francisco Chronicle*, January 25, A6.

Holmes, T.H., and R.H. Rahe. 1967. The social readjustment rating scale. *Journal of Psychosomatic Research* 11:213–18.

Hooyman, N.K., and H.A. Kiyak. 1991. *Social gerontology: A multidisciplinary perspective.* 2nd ed. Boston: Allyn & Bacon.

Hotaling, G.T., and D.B. Sugarman. 1990. A risk marker analysis of assaulted wives. *Journal of Family Violence* 5:1–13.

Houston, R. 2003. *Is he cheating on you? 829 telltale signs.* Winter Park, FL: Lifestyle Publications.

Hsu, L.K.G. 1980. Outcome of anorexia nervosa: A review of the literature. *Archives of General Psychiatry* 37:1041–46.

Hsu, L.K.G. 1988. The outcome of anorexia nervosa: A reappraisal. *Psychology and Medicine* 18:807–12.

Hutchison, I.W. 1999. The effect of children's presence on alcohol use by spouse abusers and their victims. *Family Relations* 48:57–65.

Hyde, J.A. 2001. Bipolar illness and the family. *Psychiatric Quarterly* 72(2):109–18.

International Narcotics Control Board. 2007. *Report of the International Narcotics Control Board for 2006.* New York: United Nations, www.incb.org/pdf/e/ar/2006/annual-report-2006-en.pdf (accessed June 25, 2007).

Island, D., and P. Letellier. 1991. *Men who beat the men who love them: Battered gay men and domestic violence.* New York: Haworth.

Jayson, S. 2007. Abusive teen dating behavior goes high-tech. *USA Today*, February 8, 6D.

Jezl, D.R., C.E. Molidor, and T.L. Wright. 1996. Physical, sexual and psychological abuse in high school dating relationships: Prevalence rates and self-esteem issues. *Child and Adolescent Social Work Journal* 13(1):69–87.

Johnson, C. 1982. Bulimia: An analysis of moods and behavior. *Psychosomatic Medicine* 44:34–51.

Johnson, M. 2006. Meredith's view: Meredith Vieira on her career, family, and future. *More*, May, www.more.com/more/story.jsp;jsessionid=EAKBCQ00WVVGZQFIBQPSCAQ?catref=cat5360022&page=2&storyid=/templatedata/more/story/data/1145638684682.xml (accessed June 27, 2007).

Johnson, M.P. 1995. Patriarchal terrorism and common couple violence. *Journal of Marriage and the Family* 57:238–94.

Johnson, M.P., and K.J. Ferraro. 2000. Research on domestic violence in the 1990s: Making distinctions. *Journal of Marriage and the Family* 62(4):948–63.

Johnston, L.D., P.M. O'Malley, J.G. Bachman, and J.E. Schulenberg. 2006. *Monitoring the future national results on adolescent drug use: Overview of key findings.* Washington, DC: National Institute of Drug Abuse.

Jones, A.H. 2000. Medicine and the movies: *Lorenzo's Oil* at century's end. *Annals of Internal Medicine* 133:567–71.

Jordan, L.C. 2001. Elder abuse and domestic violence: Overlapping issues and legal remedies. *American Journal of Family Law* 15(2):147–56.

K.M. Grewen, S.S. Girdler, J. Amico, and K.C. Light. 2005. Effects of partner support on resting oxytocin, cortisol, norepinephrine, and blood pressure before and after warm partner contact. *Psychosomatic Medicine* 67:531–38.

Kalish, N. 1997. *Lost & found lovers: Facts and fantasies of rekindled romances.* New York: Morrow.

Kamei, T., H. Kumano, and S. Masumura. 1997. Changes of immunoregulatory cells associated with psychological stress and humor. *Perceptual and Motor Skills* 84:1296–98.

Kilburn, J.C. Jr. 1996. Network effects in caregiver to care-recipient violence: A study of caregivers to those diagnosed with Alzheimer's disease. *Journal of Elder Abuse and Neglect* 8(1):69–80.

Kim, Y., P.R. Duberstein, S. Sörensen, and M.R. Larson. 2005. Depression in spouses of people with lung cancer: Effects of personality, social support, and caregiving burden. *Psychosomatics* 46(2):123–30.

Knudson-Martin, C., and A. Mahoney. 1998. Language and processes in the construction of marital equality in new marriages. *Family Relations* 47:81–91.

Kobasa, S. 1979. Stressful life events, personality and health: An inquiry into hardiness. *Journal of Psychology and Social Psychology* 37:1–11.

Kobasa, S.C., S.R. Maddi, and S. Kahn. 1982. Hardiness and health: A prospective study. *Journal of Personality and Social Psychology* 42:168–77.

Koss, M.P., and S.L. Cook. 1993. Facing the facts: Date and acquaintance rape are significant problems for women. In *Current controversies in family violence.* Edited by R. Gelles and D. Loseke. Newbury Park, CA: Sage.

Kurdek, L.A. 1994. Areas of conflict for gay, lesbian, and heterosexual couples: What couples argue about Influences relationship satisfaction. *Journal of Marriage and the Family* 56(4):923–34.

Kurdek, L.A. 1998. Relationship outcomes and their predictors: Longitudinal evidence from heterosexual married, gay cohabiting, and lesbian cohabiting couples. *Journal of Marriage and the Family* 60(3):553–68.

Kutner, L. 1990. The death of a parent can profoundly alter the relationships of adult siblings. *The New York Times*, December 6, B7.

Kutner, L. 1992. A parent's impending death can lead family members to reassess relationships with the parent. *The New York Times*, January 9, B3.

Langan, P., and C. Innes. 1986. *Preventing domestic violence against women.* Bureau of Justice Statistics. Washington, DC: Department of Justice.

Larson, D. 1990. The "orphaned" adult. *San Francisco Chronicle*, February 2, B5; reprinted from *Los Angeles Times*.

Larson, J.H., S.M. Wilson, and R. Beley. 1994. The impact of job insecurity on marital and family relationships. *Family Relations* 43(2):138–43.

Larson, S.L., J. Eyerman, M.S. Foster, and J.C. Gfroerer. 2007. *Worker substance use and workplace policies and programs.* DHHS Publication No. SMA 07-4273, Analytic Series A-29. Rockville, MD: Substance Abuse and Mental Health Services, http://oas.samhsa.gov/work2k7/work.pdf (accessed July 19, 2007).

Lazarus, R.S. 1981. Little hassles can be hazardous to health. *Psychology Today* (July):61.

Leonard, K.E., and M. Senchak. 1993. Alcohol and premarital aggression among newlywed couples. *Journal of Studies on Alcohol*, Suppl. 11, 96–108.

Lester, W. 2006. Stress is common bond for those in developed countries. *San Francisco Chronicle*, December 21, A14.

Li, J., T.M. Laursen, D.H. Precht, J. Olsen, and P.B. Mortensen. 2005. Hospitalization for mental illness among parents after the death of a child. *The New England Journal of Medicine* 352:1190–96.

Lloyd, S.A. 1995. Physical and sexual violence during dating and courtship. In *Vision 2010: Families and violence, abuse and neglect.* Edited by R.J. Celles. Minneapolis: National Council on Family Relations.

Lloyd, S.A., and B.C. Emery. 2000. *The dark side of courtship: Physical and sexual aggression.* Thousand Oaks, CA: Sage.

Low, B.P., and S.F. Andrews. 1990. Adolescent suicide. *Medical Clinics of North America* 74:1251–64.

Lublin, J.S., and C. Hymowitz. 2005. Scorned spouses can wreak havoc with mates' careers. *The Wall Street Journal*, June 14, B1, B8.

Lustic, M.J. 1985. Bulimia in adolescents: A review. *Pediatrics* 76:685–90.

Macmillan, K., and R. Gartner. 2000. When she brings home the bacon: Labor-force participation and the risk of spousal violence against women. *Journal of Marriage and the Family* 61:947–58.

Magdol, L., T.E. Moffitt, A. Caspi, and P.A. Silva. 1998. Hitting without a license: Testing explanations for differences in partner abuse between young adult daters and cohabitors. *Journal of Marriage and the Family* 60(l): 41–55.

Makepeace, J.M. 1981. Courtship violence among college students. *Family Relations* 30: 97–102.

Makepeace, J.M. 1986. Gender differences in courtship violence victimization. *Family Relations* 35:383–88.

Maltin, L. 1999. *Leonard Maltin's movie and video guide, 2000 edition.* New York: Signet.

Masters, W.H., V.E. Johnson, and R.C. Kolodny. 1994. *Heterosexuality.* New York: HarperCollins.

McCubbin, H.I., and J.M. Patterson. 1983. Stress: The family inventory of life events and changes. In *Marriage and family assessment: A sourcebook for family therapy.* Edited by E.E. Filsinger. Beverly Hills, CA: Sage, 285–86.

McFarlane, J., A. Malecha, J. Gist, K. Watson, E. Batten, I. Hall, and S. Smith. 2004. Protection orders and intimate partner violence: An 18-month study of 150 black, Hispanic, and white women. *American Journal of Public Health* 94(4):613–19.

Medical Dictionary Search Engine. 2007. www.online-medical-dictionary.org/searchengine/search.php?page=1&currPath=&search=mental+disorders (accessed June 14, 2007).

Melzer, S.A. 2002. Gender, work, and intimate violence: Men's occupational violence spillover and compensatory violence. *Journal of Marriage and the Family* 64(4):820–33.

Merikangas, K.R., H.S. Akiskal, J. Angst, P.E. Greenberg, R.M.A. Hirschfeld, M. Petukhova, and R.C. Kessler. 2007. Lifetime and 12-month prevalence of bipolar spectrum disorder in the National Comorbidity Survey Replication. *Archives of General Psychiatry* 64:543–52.

Michael, R.T, J.H. Gagnon, E.O. Laumann, and G. Kolata. 1994. *Sex in America: A definitive study.* Boston: Little, Brown.

Mullen, P.E., J.L. Martin, J.C. Anderson, S.E. Romans, and C.P. Herbison. 1996. The long-term impact of the physical, emotional, and sexual abuse of children: A community study. *Child Abuse and Neglect* 20:7–21.

Muller, R.T., and K.E. Lemieux. 2000. Social support, attachment, and psychopathology in high risk formerly maltreated adults. *Child Abuse and Neglect* 24(7):883–900.

National Center on Addiction and Substance Abuse at Columbia University. 2007. *Wasting the best and the brightest: Substance abuse at America's colleges and universities,* March. New York: Columbia University.

National Committee for the Prevention of Elder Abuse. 2007. What is elder abuse? NCPEA website, www.preventelderabuse.org/elderabuse/elderabuse.html (accessed June 26, 2007).

National SIDS/Infant Death Resource Center. 2007. Statistics. www.sidscenter.org/Statistics.aspx?fromparent=parent&id=6&heading=Statistics (accessed June 11, 2007).

Newman, D. 1999. *Sociology of families.* Thousand Oaks, CA: Pine Forge.

Nielsen, J.M., R.K. Endo, and B.L. Ellington. 1992. Social isolation and wife abuse: A research report. In *Intimate violence.* Edited by E. Viano. Washington, DC: Hemisphere.

Nielsen, S., and M. Hahlin. 1995. Expectant management of first-trimester spontaneous abortion. *Lancet* 345:84–86.

Noel, N.E., B.S. McCrady, R.L. Stout, and H. Fisher-Nelson. 1991. Gender differences in marital functioning of male and female alcoholics. *Family Dynamics of Addiction Quarterly* 1:31–38.

O'Farrell, T.J., and G.R. Birchler. 1987. Marital relationships of alcoholic, conflicted, and non-conflicted couples. *Journal of Marital and Family Therapy* 13:259–74.

O'Hearn, R.E., and K.E. Davis. 1997. Women's experience of giving and receiving emotional abuse: An attachment perspective. *Journal of Interpersonal Violence* 12:375–91.

O'Keefe, M. 1997. Predictors of dating violence among high school students. *Journal of Interpersonal Violence* 12:546–68.

Obejas, A. 1995. Women who batter women. *Ms. Magazine,* September/October, 53.

Olson, D.H., and H.I. McCubbin. 1983. *Families: What makes them work?* Beverly Hills, CA: Sage.

Patterson, J., and P. Kim. 1991. *The day America told the truth.* New York: Prentice-Hall.

Peterson, K.S. 2003. She stayed with a president who strayed. *USA Today,* June 10, 8D.

Peterson, L.G., M. Peterson, G.J. O'Shanick, and M. Schwann. 1985. Self-inflicted gunshot wounds: Lethality of method versus intent. *Journal of Psychiatry* 142:228–31.

Peyrot, M., J. McMurry, and R. Hedges. 1988. Marital adjustment to adult diabetes: Interpersonal congruence and spouse satisfaction. *Journal of Marriage and the Family* 50(2):363–76.

Plotnik, R. 1999. *Introduction to psychology.* 5th ed. Belmont, CA: Wadsworth.

Reifman, A., and C. Dunkel-Schetter. 1990. Stress, structural social support, and well-being in university students. *Journal of American College Health* 38:271–77.

Reiss, I. 1980. A multivariate model of the determinants of extramarital sexual permissiveness. *Journal of Marriage and the Family* 42(2):395–411.

Rennison, C.M. 2002. Rape and sexual assault: Reporting to police and medical attention, 1992–2000, *Bureau of Justice Statistics, Selected Findings,* April. Washington, DC: U.S. Department of Justice, www.ojp.usdoj.gov/bjs/pub/pdf/rsarp00.pdf (accessed June 26, 2007).

Renzetti, C. 1995. Violence in gay and lesbian relationships. In *Vision 2010: Families and violence, abuse and neglect.* Edited by R.J. Gelles. Minneapolis: National Council on Family Relations.

Renzetti, C., and D. Curran. 1999. *Women, men, and society.* 4th ed. Boston: Allyn & Bacon.

Riggs, D.S. 1993. Relationship problems and dating aggression: A potential treatment target. *Journal of Interpersonal Violence* 8:18–35.

Riggs, D.S., and M.B. Caulfield. 1997. Expected consequences of male violence against their female dating partners. *Journal of Interpersonal Violence* 12:229–40.

Robins, L.N., J.E. Helzer, M.M. Weissman, H. Orvaschel, E. Gruenberg, J.D. Burke Jr. and D.A. Regier. 1984. Lifetime prevalence of specific psychiatric disorders in three sites. *Archives of General Psychiatry* 41:949–58.

Rolland, J.S. 1994a. *Families, illness, and disability.* New York: Basic Books.

Rolland, J.S. 1994b. In sickness and in health: The impact on illness of couples relationship. *Journal of Marital and Family Therapy* 20:327–47.

Rosen, K.H., and S.M. Stith. 1997. Surviving abusive dating relationships. In *Out of the darkness: Contemporary perspectives on family violence.* Edited by G.K. Kantor and J.L. Jasinski. Thousand Oaks, CA: Sage, 171–82.

Rubin, L. 1994. *Families on the faultline: America's working class speaks about the family, the economy, race, and ethnicity.* New York: HarperCollins.

Rubin, R. 2006. 1 in 5 adults have a close relative who is or was addicted to drugs or alcohol. *USA Today,* July 20, 1A, 2A.

Scarf, M. 1987. *Intimate partners: Patterns in love and marriage.* New York: Random House.

Scarf, M. 1995. *Intimate worlds: Life inside the family.* New York: Random House.

Schmidt, J.D., and L.W. Sherman. 1993. Does arrest deter domestic violence? *American Behavioral Scientist* 36:601–09.

Selye, H. 1974. *Stress without distress.* New York: Lippincott.

Senn, C., V.S. Desmarais, N. Verberg, and E. Wood. 2000. Predicting coercive sexual behavior across the lifespan in a random sample of Canadian men. *Journal of Social and Personal Relationships* 17:95–113.

Shapiro, B.L., and J.C. Schwarz. 1997. Date rape: The relationship to trauma symptoms and sexual self-esteem. *Journal of Interpersonal Violence* 12:407–19.

Sherman, L.W., and R.A. Berk. 1984. Deterrent effects of arrest for domestic assault. *American Sociological Review* 49:261–72.

Shook, N.J., D.A. Gerrity, J. Jurich, and A.E. Segrist. 2000. Courtship violence among college students: A comparison of verbally and physically abusive couples. *Journal of Family Violence* 15:1–22.

Siegel, B. 1986. *Love, medicine, and miracles.* New York: Harper & Row.

Siegel, J.M., and D.H. Kuykendall. 1990. Loss, widowhood, and psychological distress among the elderly. *Journal of Consulting and Clinical Psychology* 58(5):519–24.

Simon, E., and E. Majewski. 2007. *A qualitative study of online discussions about teen alcohol and drug use: A word-of-mouth audit,* April 20. Study by Nielsen BuzzMetrics for Caron Treatment Centers. Wernersville, PA: Caron Treatment Centers, www.caron.org/pdfs/Report%20on%20Teen%20Online%20Conversations.pdf (accessed July 19, 2007).

Simons, R.L., K.-H. Lin, and L.C. Gordon. 1998. Socialization in the family of origin and male dating violence: A prospective study. *Journal of Marriage and the Family* 60:467–78.

Smith, K., and C. Zick. 1986. The incidence of poverty among the recently widowed: Mediating factors in the life course. *Journal of Marriage and the Family* 48:619–30.

Snyder, M. 1988. Relaxation. In *Annual review of nursing research, 8.* Edited by J.J. Fitzpatrick, R.I. Taunton, and J.Q. Benoliel. New York: Springer, 111–28.

Sobieski, R. 1994. *Men and mourning: A father's journey through grief.* Mothers Against Drunk Driving (MADD), 511 E. John

Carpenter Freeway, Suite 700, Irving, TX 75062-8187.

Soldo, B.J., and E.M. Agree. 1988. *America's elderly. Population Bulletin* 43(3). Washington, DC: Population Reference Bureau.

Solomon, J.C. 1992. Child sexual abuse by family members: A radical feminist perspective. *Sex Roles* 27:473–85.

Sontag, S. 1978. *Illness as metaphor.* New York: Farrar, Straus & Giroux.

Sorenson, S.B., D.M. Upchurch, and H. Shen. 1996. Violence and injury in marital arguments. *American Journal of Public Health* 86:35–40.

Stark, E. 1984. The unspeakable family secret. *Psychology Today* (May):39–46.

Steele, B.E. 1980. Psychodynamic factors in child abuse. In *The battered child.* Edited by C.H. Kempe and R. Heifer. Chicago: University of Chicago Press.

Stephens, B. 2007. The great depression. *The Wall Street Journal,* March 9, www.opinionjournal.com/best/?id=110009785 (accessed July 19, 2007).

Stets, J.E., and D.A. Henderson. 1991. Contextual factors surrounding conflict resolution while dating: Results from a national study. *Family Relations* 40:29–40.

Stinson, K.M., J.N. Lasker, J. Lohmann, and L.J. Toedter. 1992. Parents' grief following pregnancy loss: A comparison of mothers and fathers. *Family Relations* 41:218–23.

Storrow, H.A. 1984. Eating disorders. In *Encyclopedia of psychology* (Vol. 1). Edited by R.J. Corsini. New York: Wiley.

Straus, M.A. 1993. Identifying offenders in criminal justice research on domestic assault. *American Behavioral Scientist* 36:587–600.

Straus, M.A., and C.L. Yodanis. 1996. Corporal punishment in adolescence and physical assaults on spouses in later life. *Journal of Marriage and the Family* 58:825–41.

Straus, M.A., and S. Sweet. 1992. Verbal aggression in couples: Incidence rates and relationships to personal characteristics. *Journal of Marriage and the Family* 54:346–57.

Styron, W. 1990. *Darkness visible: A memoir of madness.* New York: Random House.

Substance Abuse and Mental Health Services Administration. 2007. *Results from the 2005 national survey on drug use and health: National findings.* Washington, DC: Substance Abuse and Mental Health Services Administration, Department of Health and Human Services, http://oas.samhsa.gov/nsduh/2k5nsduh/2k5Results.pdf (accessed June 25, 2007).

Szabo, X.P., and M.J.T. Blanche. 1997. Perfectionism in anorexia nervosa. *American Journal of Psychiatry* 154:132.

Tatara, T., L. Kuzmeskus-Blumerman, and E. Duckhorn et al. 1998. *The national elder abuse incidence study: Final report.* The National Center on Elder Abuse at the American Public Human Services Association. www.aoa.gov/eldfam/Elder_Rights/Elder_Abuse/AbuseReport_full.pdf (accessed July 2002).

Teachman, J.D., R. Vaughn, A. Call, and K.P. Carver. 1994. Marital status and duration of joblessness among white men. *Journal of Marriage and the Family* 56(2):415–28.

Thompson, A. 1984. Emotional and sexual components of extramarital relations. *Journal of Marriage and the Family* 46(1):35–42.

Thompson, M.P., J.B. Kingree, and S. Desai. 2004. Gender differences in long-term health consequences of physical abuse of children: Data from a nationally representative survey. *American Journal of Public Health* 94(4):599–605.

Torr, J.D., and K. Swisher. 1999. *Violence against women.* San Diego, CA: Greenhaven.

Treas, J., and D. Giesen. 2000. Sexual infidelity among married and cohabiting Americans. *Journal of Marriage and the Family* 62:48–60.

U.S. Central Intelligence Agency. 2007. Rank order—infant mortality rate. *The world factbook,* www.cia.gov/library/publications/the-world-factbook/rankorder/2091rank.html (accessed June 11, 2007).

U.S. Department of Health and Human Services, Administration on Children, Youth, and Families. 2007. *Child maltreatment 2005.* Washington, DC: U.S. Government Printing Office, www.acf.dhhs.gov/programs/cb/pubs/cm05/cm05.pdf (accessed June 11, 2007).

U.S. Department of Justice. 1994. Violence between intimates. *Bureau of Justice Statistics Selected Findings: Domestic Violence.* Nov. No. NCJ–149259. Washington, DC: U.S. Department of Justice, Office of Justice Programs.

U.S. Department of Justice. 1998. Violence by intimates: Analysis of data on crimes by current or former spouses, boyfriends, and girlfriends. *Bureau of Justice Statistics Selected Findings: Domestic Violence.* March. No. NCJ–167237. Washington, DC. U.S. Government Printing Office. www.ojp.usdoj.gov.

U.S. Department of Justice. 2006. Statistical overviews and resources, *2006 National Crime Victims' Rights Week Resource Guide.* Washington, DC: Office for Victims of Crime, Department of Justice, www.ojp.usdoj.gov/ovc/ncvrw/2006/pdf/statistical_overviews.pdf (accessed June 26, 2007).

Uchitelle, L. 2004. *The disposable American: Layoffs and their consequences.* New York: Knopf.

Umberson, D. 1995. Marriage as support or strain? Marital quality following the death of a parent. *Journal of Marriage and the Family* 57:709–25.

Vaux, A. 1988. *Social support: Theory, research, and intervention.* New York: Praeger.

Vivian, J. 2001. *The media of mass communication: Updated online edition.* Boston: Allyn & Bacon.

Voydanoff, P. 1991. Economic distress and family relations: A review of the eighties. In *Contemporary families: Looking forward, looking back.* Edited by A. Booth. Minneapolis: National Council on Family Relations.

Walker, L. 1984. *The battered woman syndrome.* New York: Springer.

Walker, L. 1993. The battered woman syndrome is a psychological consequence of abuse. In *Current controversies in family violence.* Edited by R. Gelles and D. Loseke. Newbury Park, CA: Sage.

Walker, R. 2006. Help wanted—A broader measure of unemployment needed. *San Francisco Chronicle,* September 4, B7.

Wallerstein, J.S., and S. Blakeslee. 1995. *The good marriage.* Boston: Houghton Mifflin.

Weigel, R.R., and D.J. Weigel. 1987. Identifying stressors and coping Strategies in two generation farm families. *Family Relations* 36:379–84.

Weinberg, T.S., and C.C. Vogler. 1990. Wives of alcoholics: Stigma management and adjustments to husband-wife interaction. *Deviant Behavior* 11:331–43.

Weissman, M.M., D.J. Pilowsky, P.J. Wickramaratne, A. Talati, S.R. Wisniewski, M. Fava, C.W. Hughes, J. Garber, E. Molloy, C.A. King, G. Cerda, A.B. Sood, J.E. Alpert, M.H. Trivedi, and A.J. Rush. 2006. Remissions in maternal depression and child psychopathology: A STAR*D-child report. *Journal of the American Medical Association* 295:1389–98.

Werner, E.E. 1989. Children of the garden island. *Scientific American* 206:106–11.

Whipple, S.C., and E.P. Noble. 1991. Personality characteristics of alcoholic fathers and their sons. *Journal of Studies on Alcohol* 52:331–37.

Wiederman, M.W. 1997. Extramarital sex: Prevalence and correlates in a national survey. *Journal of Sex Research* 34:167–74.

Wiederman, M.W., and E.R. A1lgeier. 1996. Expectations and attributions regarding extramarital sex among young married individuals. *Journal of Psychology and Human Sexuality* 8:21–35.

Williams, A. 2006. Before spring break, the anorexic challenge. *The New York Times,* April 2, sec. 9, 1, 6.

Williams, B.K., and S.M. Knight. 1994. *Healthy for life: Wellness and the art of living.* Pacific Grove: Brooks/Cole.

Williams, P., and S.R. Lord. 1997. Effects of group exercise on cognitive functioning and mood in older women. *Australian and New Zealand Journal of Public Health* 21:45–52.

Windom, C.S. 1999. Posttraumatic stress disorder in abused and neglected children grown up. *American Journal of Psychiatry* 156:1223–29.

Wingert, P. 2003. Infidelity: Some friendly advice. *Newsweek,* March 3, 10.

Wolf, R.S. 1995. Abuse and neglect of the elderly. In *Vision 2010: Families and violence, abuse and neglect.* Edited by R.J. Gelles. Minneapolis: National Council on Family Relations.

World Health Organization. 2005. *WHO multicountry study on women's health and domestic violence against women: Summary report of initial results on prevalence, health outcomes and women's responses.* Geneva: World Health Organization.

Wright, L.S. 1985. Correlates of perceived child abuse among college undergraduates. *Family Perspective* 19:171–88.

Yllo, K. 1995. Marital rape. In *Vision 2010: Families and violence, abuse and neglect.*

Edited by R.J. Gelles. Minneapolis: National Council on Family Relations.

Zajonc, R.B. 1985. Emotion and facial efference: A theory reclaimed. *Science* 228:15–21.

Zoroya, G. 2005. Combat stress wearing away at marriages. *Reno Gazette-Journal*, June 8, 4C; reprinted from *USA Today*.

CHAPTER 14

Amato P.R., and S.J. Rogers. 1997. A longitudinal study of marital problems and subsequent divorce. *Journal of Marriage and the Family* 59:612–24.

Amato, P. 1996. Explaining the intergenerational transmission of divorce. *Journal of Marriage and the Family* 58:628–40.

Amato, P.R. 2001. The consequences of divorce for adults and children. In *Understanding families into the new millennium: A decade in review.* Edited by R.M. Milardo. Minneapolis: National Council on Family Relations, 488–506.

Amato, P.R., and A. Booth. 2001. The legacy of parents' marital discord: Consequences for children's marital quality. *Journal of Personality and Social Psychology* 81 (4):627–38.

Ambert, A.-M. 1988. Relationships with former in-laws after divorce: A research note. *Journal of Marriage and the Family* 50:679–86.

American Council on Education and University of California. 2000. *The American freshman: National norms for fall 2000.* Los Angeles: Los Angeles Higher Education Research Institute.

Arditti, J.A. 1990. Noncustodial fathers: An overview of policy and resources. *Family Relations* 39(4):460–65.

Arendell, T. 1986. *Mothers and divorce: Legal, economic, and social dilemmas.* Berkeley: University of California Press.

Arendell, T. 1995. *Fathers and divorce.* New York: Sage.

Associated Press. 2007. Do-it-yourself divorces daunting novices. *Reno Gazette-Journal,* January 2, 4C.

Baker, A.K., K.J. Barthelemy, and L.A. Kurdek. 1993. The relation between fifth and sixth graders' peer-rated classroom social status and their perceptions of family and neighborhood factors. *Journal of Applied Developmental Psychology* 14:547–56.

Beller, A.H., J.I. Lieberman, and J.W. Graham. 1996. *Small change: The economics of child support.* New Haven, CT: Yale University Press.

Benjamin, M. 2005. Update: Lorna Wendt. *U.S. News & World Report,* March 28, EE8.

Bennett, N.G., A.K. Blanc, and D.E. Bloom. 1988. Commitment and the modern union: Assessing the link between premarital cohabitation and subsequent marital stability. *American Sociological Review* 53:127–38.

Bernstein, F.A. 2003. Gay unions were only half the battle. *The New York Times,* April 6, sec. 9, 2.

Bianchi, S. 1990. America's Children. *Population Bulletin* 45:3–41.

Blackwell, J.E. 1991. *The black community: Diversity and unity.* 3rd ed. New York: HarperCollins.

Blakely, M.K. 1995. An outlaw mom tells all. *Ms. Magazine,* January/February, 34–45.

Bohannan, P. 1970. *Divorce and after.* New York: Doubleday.

Booth A., and J.N. Edwards. 1985. Age at marriage and marital instability. *Journal of Marriage and the Family* 47:67–75.

Bramlett, M.D., and W.D. Mosher. 2002. Cohabitation, marriage, divorce, and remarriage in the United States. *Vital Health Statistics* 23(2). Hyattsville, MD: National Center for Health Statistics, www.cdc.gov/nchs/data/series/sr_23/sr23_022.pdf (accessed July 1, 2007).

Braver, S.L., S.A. Wolchik, I.N. Sandler, and V.L. Sheets. 1993a. A social exchange model of nonresidential parent involvement. In *Nonresidential parenting: New vistas in family living.* Edited by C.E. Depner and J.H. Bray. Newbury Park, CA: Sage.

Braver, S.L., S.A. Wolchik, I.N. Sandler, V.L. Sheets, B. Fogas, and R.C. Bay. 1993b. A longitudinal study of noncustodial parents: Parents without children. *Journal of Family Psychology* 7:9–23.

Breslau, K. 2006. Till faucets do us part. *Newsweek,* January 30, 57.

Brodie, D. 1999. *Untying the knot: Ex-husbands, ex-wives, and other experts on the passage of divorce.* New York: St. Martin's Griffin.

Buehler, C. 1987. Initiator status and the divorce transition. *Family Relations* 36:82–86.

Buehler, C., and M. Langenbrunner. 1987. Divorce-related stressors: Occurrence, disruptiveness of life change. *Journal of Divorce* 11:25–50.

Caughlin, J.K, T.L. Huston, and K.M. Houts. 2000. How does personality matter in marriage? An examination of trait anxiety, interpersonal negativity, and marital satisfaction. *Journal of Personality and Social Psychology* 78:326–36.

Chandress, S. 2006. Fighting over the kids. *Newsweek,* September 26, 35.

Charles, K.K., and M. Stephens Jr. 2001. Job displacement, disability, and divorce. In *New Economics Papers,* nep-dcm-2001-11-05. *NEP Report on Discrete Choice Models.* Edited by P. Yu. Cambridge, MA: National Bureau of Economic Research, Inc.

Chiang, H. 2002. Father figure wins custody. *San Francisco Chronicle,* June 7, A1, A18.

Christensen, D.H., C.M. Dahl, and K.D. Rettig. 1990. Noncustodial mothers and child support: Examining the larger context. (Noncustodial parents) *Family Relations* 39(4):388–95.

Clemetson, L. 2006. Weekends with dad, courtesy of D.S.L. *The New York Times,* March 19, sec. 9, 1, 6.

Cohan, C.L., and S. Kleinbaum. 2002. Toward a greater understanding of the cohabitation effect: Premarital cohabitation and marital communication. *Journal of Marriage and the Family* 64(1):180–93.

Colasanto D., and J. Shriver. 1989. Middle-aged face marital crisis. *Gallup Report,* no. 284. May, 34–38.

Cooney, T.M. 1994. Young adults' relations with parents: The influence of recent parental divorce. *Journal of Marriage and the Family* 56:45–56.

Coontz, S. 1997. *The way we really are: Coming to terms with America's changing families.* New York: Basic Books.

Corliss, R. 2002. Does divorce hurt kids? *Time,* January 28, 40.

Crary, D. 2003. Online divorces gaining popularity. *Reno Gazette-Journal,* May 29, 1A, 6A.

Cummings, H.J. 2002. Is divorce good or bad? Well, it depends, new book says. *Minneapolis– St. Paul Star-Tribune,* January 28. www.startribune.com/stories/1017/1123990.html (accessed January 11, 2007).

Daily, L. 2006. Trial offer. *AARP,* May & June, 26.

Dalton, C., L.M. Drozd, and F.Q.F. Wong. 2006. *Navigating custody and visitation evaluations in cases with domestic violence: A judge's guide.* Reno, NV: National Council of Juvenile and Family Court Judges.

Dawson, D.A. 1991. Family structure and children's health and well-being: Data from the 1988 National Health Interview Survey on Child Health. *Journal of Marriage and the Family* 53:573–84.

DeWitt, P.M. 1994. Breaking up is hard to do. *American Demographics* (reprint package), October, 14–16.

Dickinson, A. 1999. Divided we stand. *Time,* October 25, 138.

Divorce Recovery.net. 2004. Children of divorce. www.divorcerecovery.net/children/children.htm (accessed January 17, 2007).

Downey, D.B. 1994. The school performance of children from single-mother and single-father families: Economic or interpersonal deprivation? *Journal of Family Issues* 15:129–47.

Dudley, J.R. 1991. Increasing our understanding of divorced fathers who have infrequent contact with their children. *Family Relations* 40:279–85.

Duenwald, M. 2002. 2 portraits of children of divorce: Rosy and dark. *The New York Times,* March 26, D6, D10.

Elias, M. 2001. Miserable marriages can make you sick. *USA Today,* March 12, 1D.

Ellman, I.M., G.G. Blumberg, and K.T. Bartlett. 2002. *Principles of the law of family dissolution: Analysis and recommendations—tentative draft no. 4.* May 8. Washington, DC: American Law Institute.

Emery, R.E. 2004. *The truth about children and divorce: Dealing with the emotions so you and your children can thrive.* New York: Viking/Penguin.

Emery, R.E., L. Laumann-Billings, M. Waldron, D.A. Sbarra, and P. Dillon. 2001. Child custody mediation and litigation: Custody, contact, and co-parenting 12 years after initial dispute resolution. *Journal of Consulting and Clinical Psychology* 69:323–32.

Fass, P.S. 1998. A sign of family disorder? Changing representations of parental kidnapping. In *All our families: New policies for a new century.* Edited by M.A. Mason, A. Skolnick, and S.D. Sugarman. New York: Oxford University Press, 144–68.

Fine, M.A., and D.R. Fine. 1994. An examination and evaluation of recent changes in divorce laws in five western countries: The critical role of values. *Journal of Marriage and the Family* 56(2):249–63.

Finkel, J., and P. Roberts. 1994. *The incomes of noncustodial fathers.* Washington, DC: Center for Law and Social Policy.

Finkelhor, D., G. Hotaling, and A. Sedlak. 1991. Abduction of children by family members. *Journal of Marriage and the Family* 53(3):805–17.

Flynn, L.J. 2002. Clicking on Splitsville with divorce web site. *The New York Times,* May 6, C4.

Fu, X. 2000. An interracial study of marital disruption in Hawaii: 1983 to 1996. *Journal of Divorce and Remarriage* 32:73–92.

Garber, B.D. 2003. Helping kids cope with parental conflict, separation, and divorce. http://healthyparent.com/Divorce.html (accessed January 17, 2007).

Gardner, J., and A.J. Osward. 2006. Do divorcing couples become happier by breaking up? *Journal of the Royal Statistical Society Series A* 127(2):319–36.

Gardner, R.A. 1998. *The parental alienation syndrome.* 2nd ed. Cresskill, NJ: Creative Therapeutics.

Garfinkel, I., S.S. McLanahan, and P.K. Robbins, eds. 1994. *Child support and child well-being.* Washington, DC: Urban Institute Press.

Garvin, V., N. Kalter, and J. Hansell. 1993. Divorced women: Factors contributing to resiliency and vulnerability. *Journal of Divorce and Remarriage* 21:21–39.

Gasser R.D., and C.M. Taylor. 1990. Role adjustment of single parent fathers with dependent children. *Family Relations* 40:397–400.

Gerstel, N. 1987. Divorce and stigma. *Social Problems* 34:172–86.

Giantis, K. 2003. When the vow breaks: We dissect the top 10 shortest celebrity marriages. MSN Entertainment. http://entertainment.msn.com/news/article.aspx?news=114177 (accessed May 10, 2007).

Glendon, M. 1981. *The new family and the new property.* Toronto: Butterworths.

Glenn N.D., and B.A. Shelton. 1985. Regional differences in divorce in the United States. *Journal of Marriage and the Family* 47:641–52.

Glenn, N.D. 1996. Values, attitudes, and the state of American marriage. In *Promises to keep: The decline and renewal of marriage in America.* Edited by D. Popenoe, J.B. Elshtain, and D. Blankenhorn. Lanham, MD: Rowman and Littlefield, 15–33.

Glenn, N.D. 1997. A reconsideration of the effect of no-fault divorce on divorce rates. *Journal of Marriage and the Family* 59:1023–30.

Glenn, N.D., and M. Supancic. 1984. The social and demographic correlates of divorce and separation in the United States: An update and reconsideration. *Journal of Marriage and the Family* 46:563–75.

Glick, P. 1984. Marriage, divorce, and living arrangements: Prospective changes. *Journal of Family Issues* 4(1):7–26.

Gottman, J., J. Coan, S. Carrere, and C. Swanson. 1998. Predicting marital happiness and stability from newlywed interactions. *Journal of Marriage and the Family* 60:5–22.

Gottman, J.M. 1994. *What predicts divorce?* Hillsdale, NJ: Lawrence Erlbaum Associates.

Grall, T. 2000. Child support for custodial mothers and fathers. *Current Population Reports,* P60-212. Washington, DC: U.S. Census Bureau. www.census.gov/prod/2000pubs/p60-212.pdf (accessed May 15, 2007).

Grall, T. 2003. Custodial mothers and fathers and their child support: 2001. *Current Population Reports,* P60-225. Washington, DC: U.S. Census Bureau. www.census.gov/prod/2003pubs/p60-225.pdf (accessed January 12, 2007).

Graves, B. 2002. Parting same-sex parents reinventing family law. *San Francisco Chronicle,* April 2, F10.

Guidubaldi, J., and H. Cleminshaw. 1985. Divorce, family health, and child adjustment. *Family Relations* 34:35–41.

Guilbert, D.E., N.A. Vacc, and K. Pasley. 2000. The relationship of gender role beliefs, negativity, distancing and marital instability. *The Family Journal* 8:124–32.

Gullapalli, D. 2002. A growing number of unhappy couples try "collaborative divorce." *The Wall Street Journal,* July 17, D1, D3.

Guttman, J. 1993. *Divorce in psychosocial perspective: Theory and research.* Hillsdale, NJ: Erlbaum.

Harris, R. 2003. I'm not married, but I'm far from alone. *Newsweek,* May 19, 13.

Heaton, T.B. 1990. Marital stability throughout the child-rearing years. *Demography* 27:55–63.

Heckert, D.A., T.C. Nowak, and K.A. Snyder. 1998. The impact of husbands' and wives' relative earnings on marital disruption.*Journal of Marriage and the Family* 60(3):690–703.

Hekker, T. M. 2006. Paradise lost (domestic division). *The New York Times,* January 1, sec. 1, 9.

Hemstrom, O. 1996. Is marriage dissolution linked to differences in mortality risks for men and women? *Journal of Marriage and the Family* 58:366–78.

Hendrix, A. 2002. Until the state do us part. *San Francisco Chronicle,* June 14, A21, A25.

Hernandez, D.J. 1993. When families break up. *Current Population Reports.* P20-478. Washington, DC: U.S. Census Bureau.

Hetherington, E.M. 1973. Girls without fathers. *Psychology Today* 6:47–52.

Hetherington, E.M. 1993. An overview of the Virginia Longitudinal Study of Divorce and Remarriage with a focus on early adolescence.*Journal of Family Psychology* 7:39–56.

Hetherington, E.M., and J. Kelly. 2002. *For better or for worse: Divorce reconsidered.* New York: Norton.

Holmes, T., and R. Rahe. 1967. The Social Readjustment Rating Scale. *Journal of Psychosomatic Medicine* 11:213–18.

Holroyd, R., and A. Sheppard. 1997. Parental separation: Effects on children; implications for services. *Child Care, Health and Development* 23:369–78.

Hotaling, G.T, and D. Finkelhor. 1990. Estimating the number of stranger-abduction homicides of children: A review of available evidence. *Journal of Criminal Justice* 18:5385–399.

Hughes, M., L.J. Waite, J.T. Cacioppo, and L. Hawkley. 2004. Marital biography and health at mid-life. Paper presented at the annual meeting of the American Sociological Association, Hilton San Francisco & Renaissance Parc 55 Hotel, San Francisco, August, www.allacademic.com/meta/p109970_index.html (accessed June 28, 2007).

Jarvis, C. 2001. *The marriage sabbatical: The journey that brings you home.* New York: Perseus.

Jekielek, S.M. 1998. Parental conflict, marital disruption and children's emotional well-being. *Social Forces* 76:905–36.

Jessani, A.D. 2003. What does equitable distribution mean? www.divorcesource.com/NJ/ARTICLES/jessani9.html (accessed May 15, 2007).

Johnson, C.J. 1988. *Ex-familia: Grandparents, parents, and children adjust to divorce.* New Brunswick, NJ: Rutgers University Press.

Johnson, G.R., E.G. Krug, and L.B. Potter. 2000. Suicide among adolescents and young adults. A cross-national comparison of 34 countries. *Suicide and Life Threatening Behavior* 30:74–82.

Kaplan, L., C.B. Hennon, and L. Ade-Ridder. 1993. Splitting custody of children between parents: Impact on the sibling system. *Families in Society: The Journal of Contemporary Human Services* 74(3):131–45.

Kaufman, L. 2007. In custody fights, a hurdle for the poor. *The New York Times,* April 8, sec. 1, 21.

Keith, V.M., and B. Findlay. 1988. The impact of parental divorce on children's educational attainment, marital timings, and likelihood of divorce. *Journal of Marriage and the Family* 50:797–809.

Kelly, J.B. 1988. Longer-term adjustment in children of divorce: Converging findings and implications for practice. *Journal of Family Psychology* 2:119–40.

Kelly, J.B. 2000. Children's adjustment in conflicted marriage and divorce: A decade review of research. *Journal of the American Academy of Child and Adolescent Psychiatry* 39:963–73.

Kiecolt-Glaser, J.K., T.J. Loving, J.R. Stowell, W.B. Malarkey, S. Lemeshow, S.L. Dickinson, and R. Glaser. 2005. Hostile marital interactions, proinflammatory cytokine production, and wound healing. *Archives of General Psychiatry* 62:1377–84.

Kipnis, L. 2003. *Against love: A polemic.* New York: Pantheon.

Kitson, G., and M. Sussman. 1982. Marital complaints, demographic characteristics, and symptoms of mental distress in divorce. *Journal of Marriage and the Family* 44(1):87–101.

Kitson, G.C., and L.A. Morgan. 1991. The multiple consequences of divorce. In *Contemporary families: Looking forward, looking back.* Edited by A. Booth. Minneapolis: National Council on Family Relations, 150–61.

Kitson, G.C., and W.M. Holmes. 1992. *Portrait*

of divorce: Adjustment to marital breakdown. New York: Guilford.

Kitson, G.C., K.B. Babri, and M.J. Roach. 1985. Who divorces and why: A review. *Journal of Family Issues* 6:255–93.

Kline, M., J.R. Johnston, and J.M. Tschann. 1991. The long shadow of marital conflict: A model of children's postdivorce adjustment. *Journal of Marriage and the Family* 53(2):297–309.

Koch, W. 2006. Creative efforts ensure parents pay: States find new ways to collect child support. *USA Today*, March 15, 1A.

Koplewicz, H.S., and A. Gurian. 2001. Divorce and children. *Child Study Center Letter* 6(1):1–5.

Kreider, R.M., and J.M. Fields. 2002. Number, timing, and duration of marriages and divorces: 1996. *Currrent Population Reports*, P70-80, February. Washington, DC: U.S. Census Bureau, www.census.gov/prod/2002pubs/p70-80.pdf (accessed July 1, 2007).

Kurdek, L.A. 1991. The relations between reported well-being and divorce history, availability of a proximate adult, and gender. *Journal of Marriage and the Family* 53:71–78.

Kurdek, L.A. 1993. Predicting marital dissolution: A 5-year prospective longitudinal study of newlywed couples. *Journal of Personality and Social Psychology* 64(2):221–42.

L'Heureax-Dube, C. 1998. A response to remarks by Dr. Judith Wallerstein on the long-term impact of divorce on children. *Family and Conciliation Courts Review* 36(3):384–86.

Lauer, R.H., and J.C. Lauer. 1988. *Watersheds: Mastering life's unpredictable crises.* Boston: Little, Brown.

Lawson, E.J., and A. Thompson. 1999. *Black men and divorce.* Thousand Oaks, CA: Sage.

Lehrer E.L., and C.U. Chiswick. 1993. Religion as a determinant of marital stability. *Demography* 30:385–404.

Lewin, T. 2005. Messy or not, divorce is hard on kids, survey finds. *San Francisco Chronicle*, November 5, A2; reprinted from *The New York Times*.

Maltais, M. 2001. Split screens. *Los Angeles Times*, June 14, T2.

Marlow, L., and S.R. Sauber. 1990. *The handbook of divorce mediation.* New York: Plenum.

Marquardt, E. 2005. *Between two worlds: The inner lives of children of divorce.* New York: Crown.

Martin, S.P. 2004. Growing evidence for a divorce divide? Education and marital dissolution rates in the United States since the 1970's. Russell Sage Foundation Working Papers: Series on Social Dimensions of Inequality. Reported in D. Hurley. 2005. Divorce rate: It's not as high as you think. *The New York Times*, April 19, D7.

Martin, T.C., and L.L. Bumpass. 1989. Recent trends in marital disruption. *Demography* 26: 37–51.

Masheter, C. 1991. Postdivorce relationships between ex-spouses: The roles of attachment and interpersonal conflict. *Journal of Marriage and the Family* 53:103–10.

Mason, M.A., and A. Quirk. 1997. Are mothers losing custody? Read my lips: Trends in judicial decision-making in custody disputes—1920, 1960, 1990, and 1995. *Family Law Quarterly* 31(1):215–36.

McLanahan, S., and L. Bumpass. 1988. Intergenerational consequences of family disruption. *American Journal of Sociology* 94:130–52.

Mead, R. 2003. Love's labors: Monogamy, marriage, and other menaces. *The New Yorker*, August 11, 79–82.

Melendez, M.M. 2002. Ninety percent of Americans will marry, Census Bureau says. Newhouse News Service. www.newhouse.com/archive/story1b0w08.2.html (accessed January 14, 2007).

Meyer, D.R., and J. Bartfeld. 1996. Compliance with child support orders in divorce cases. *Journal of Marriage and the Family* 58(1):201–12.

Meyer, D.R., J. Bartfeld, I. Garfinkel, and P. Brown. 1996. Child support reform: Lessons from Wisconsin. *Family Relations* 45:11–18.

Morgan, L.A. 1991. Women's life cycle and economic insecurity: Problems and proposals. *Contemporary Sociology* 20(1):129–31.

Munson, M.L., and P.D. Sutton. 2005. Births, marriages, divorces, and deaths: Provisional data for 2004. *National Vital Statistics Report* 53(21). Hyattsville, MD: National Center for Health Statistics.

National Center for Health Statistics. 1998. Centers for Disease Control and Prevention. Births, marriages, divorces, and deaths: Provisional data for June 1997. *Monthly Vital Statistics Report* 46(6). Hyattsville, MD: National Center for Health Statistics.

National Center for Health Statistics. 2002. New report sheds light on trends and patterns in marriage, divorce, and cohabitation. www.cdc.gov/nchs/releases/02news/div_mar_cohab.htm (accessed January 12, 2004).

National Center for Health Statistics. 2005. Births, marriages, divorces, and deaths: Provisional data for 2004. *National Vital Statistics Report* 53:21, June 26. Hyattsville, MD: National Center for Health Statistics. www.cdc.gov/hchs/data/nvsr/nvsr53/ncsr53_21.pdf (accessed December 14, 2007).

National Conflict Resolution Center. 2007. Divorce mediation FAQs, www.ncrconline.com/FAQs/DivorceFAQ.shtml (accessed July 2, 2007).

Navarro, M. 2005. More options to answer "what about the kids?" *The New York Times*, November 27, sec. 9, 1, 6.

Norton, A.J., and L.F. Miller. 1992. Marriage, divorce, and remarriage in the 1990s. *Current Population Reports*. P23–ISO. Washington, DC: U.S. Census Bureau.

Nuta, V.R. 1986. Emotional aspects of child support enforcement. *Family Relations* 35: 177–82.

Ono, H. 1998. Husbands' and wives' resources and marital dissolution. *Journal of Marriage and the Family* 60:674–89.

Patterson, J., and P. Kim. 1991. *The day America told the truth.* New York: Prentice-Hall.

Pear, R. 2002. Legal group urges states to update their family law. *The New York Times*, November 30, A1, A12.

Peretti, P.O., and A. di Vitorrio. 1993. Effect of loss of father through divorce on personality of the preschool child. *Social Behavior and Personality* 21:33–38.

Perkins, D.F., and S.J. Ansay. 1998. The effectiveness of a visitation program in fostering visits with noncustodial parents. *Family Relations* 47(3):253–58.

Peterson, K.S. 2001. Relationship respite: Women find "marriage sabbaticals" help them pursue dreams, find direction. *USA Today*, July 19, 1D, 2D.

Peterson, K.S. 2002a. Love and the law: A reality check. *USA Today*, December 4, 8D.

Peterson, K.S. 2002b. Kids, parents can make the best of divorce: Negatives overstated, in-depth study says. *USA Today*, January 14, 1A, 2A.

Peterson, K.S. 2003. Children of divorce straddle a divided world: Torn between homes, caught in conflicting research. *USA Today*, July 14, 6D.

Peterson, R.R. 1996. A re-evaluation of the economic consequences of divorce. *American Sociological Review* 61:528–36.

Popenoe, D. 1996. *Life without father: Compelling new evidence that fatherhood and marriage are indispensable for the good of children and society.* New York: Martin Kessler.

Raffel, L. 1998. *Should I stay or go? How controlled separation (CS) can save your marriage.* New York: McGraw-Hill.

Raley, R.K., T.E. Durden, and E. Wildsmith. 2004. Understanding Mexican-American marriage patterns using a life-course approach. *Social Science Quarterly* 85:872–90.

Raschke, H. 1987. Divorce. In *Handbook of marriage and the family.* Edited by M. Sussman and S. Steinmetz. New York: Plenum.

Richards, M., R. Hardy, and M. Wadsworth. 1997. The effects of divorce and separation on mental health in a national U.K. birth cohort. *Psychological Medicine* 27:1121–28.

Rimer, S. 2002. Sad song in Splitsville, Tenn.: "I said I do but now I don't." *The New York Times*, June 11, A12.

Sanner, A. 2006. Video visits help families stay in touch after divorce. *San Francisco Chronicle*, March 1, A2.

Scelfo, J. 2006. Heartbreak's revenge. *Newsweek*, December 4, 57.

Schoen, R., N.A. Astone, K. Rothert, N.J. Standish, and Y.J. Kim. 2002. Women's employment, marital happiness, and divorce. *Social Forces* 81(2):643–63.

Schoenborn, C.A. 2004. Marital status and health: United States, 1999–2002. *Advance Data from Vital and Health Statistics*, No. 351, December 15. Hyattsville, MD: National Center for Health Statistics, www.cdc.gov/nchs/data/ad/ad351.pdf (accessed June 28, 2007).

Seltzer, J.A. 1991. Relationships between fathers and children who live apart: The father's role after separation. *Journal of Marriage and the Family* 53(1):79–101.

Serovich, J.M., S.J. Price, and S.F. Chapman. 1991. Former in-laws as a source of support.

Journal of Divorce and Remarriage 17(1/2): 17–26.

Shapiro, A. 1999. Longitudinal effects of divorce on the quality of the father-child relationship and on fathers' psychological well-being. *Journal of Marriage and the Family* 61(2):397–409.

Sharp, D. 2002. Web site offers point-and-click splits: Unhappily married can now prepare their divorce online. *USA Today*, March 6, 3A.

Shelton, B.A. 1987. Variations in divorce rates by community size: A test of the social integration explanation. *Journal of Marriage and the Family* 49:827–32.

Silverman, J.G., C.M. Mesh, C.V. Cuthbert, K. Slote, and L. Bancroft. 2004. Child custody determinations in cases involving intimate partner violence: A human rights analysis. *American Journal of Public Health* 94 (6):951–57.

Silverman, R.E., and M. Higgins. 2003. When the kids get the house in a divorce. *The Wall Street Journal*, September 17, D1, D2.

Sitarz, D. 1998. *Divorce yourself: The national no-fault divorce kit*. Carbondale, IL: Nova.

Smock, P.J. 1993. The economic costs of marital disruption for young women over the past two decades. *Demography* 30(3):353–71.

Sorenson, E., and C. Zibman. 2000. *Child support offers some protection against poverty*. Washington, DC: Urban Institute.

South, S.J. 1995. Do you need to shop around? Age at marriage, spousal alternatives, and marital dissolution. *Journal of Family Issues* 16:432–49.

Springen, K. 2000. Feeling the 50-year itch. *Newsweek*. December 4, 56–57.

Stark, E. 1986. Friends through it all. *Psychology Today* (May):54–60.

Stewart, A.J., A.P. Copeland, N.L. Chester, J.E. Malley, and N.B. Barenbaum. 1997. *Separating together: How divorce transforms families*. New York: Guilford.

Stout, F. 2001. Take a break—From your marriage. *USA Weekend*. February 2–4, 9.

Stout, H. 2005. A time out for troubled marriages: Therapists push "controlled separation." *The Wall Street Journal*, July 7, D1.

Stroup, A.L., and G.E. Pollack. 1999. Economic consequences of marital dissolution for Hispanics. *Journal of Divorce and Remarriage* 30(1/2):149–66.

Sweeney, M.M., and J.A. Phillips. 2004. Understanding racial differences in marital disruption: Recent trends and explanations. *Journal of Marriage and Family* 66:239–50.

Talbot, M. 2000. The price of divorce. *The New York Times Book Review*, October 1, 10–11.

Teachman, J. 1991. Receipt of child support in the United States. *Journal of Marriage and the Family* 53(3):759–72.

Teachman, J.D. 2002. Childhood living arrangements and the intergenerational transmission of divorce. *Journal of Marriage and the Family* 64(3):717–30.

Thomas, K. 2001. "Virtual visitation" gains acceptance. *USA Today*, April 9, 3D.

Timmer, S.G., and J. Veroff. 2000. Family ties and the discontinuity of divorce in black and white newlywed couples. *Journal of Marriage and the Family* 62(2):349–62.

Troll, L.E., S.J. Miller, and R.C. Atchley. 1979. *Families in later life*. Belmont, CA: Wadsworth.

Troxel, W.M., K.M. Matthews, J.T. Bromberger, and K. Sutton-Tyrrell. 2002. Chronic stress burden, discrimination, and subclinical cardiovascular disease in African American and Caucasian women. *Health Psychology* 22(3):300–09.

Turkat, I.D. 1995. Divorce-related malicious mother syndrome. *Journal of Family Violence* 10 (3):253–64.

Tyre, P. 2005. The secret pain of divorce. *Newsweek*, October 24, www.msnbc.msn.com/id/9707663/site/newsweek/ (accessed July 2, 2007).

U.S. Census Bureau. 1994. *Statistical abstract of the United States*. Washington, DC: U.S. Government Printing Office.

U.S. Census Bureau. 2002. *Statistical abstract of the United States*. Washington, DC: U.S. Government Printing Office.

U.S. Census Bureau. 2007. *Statistical abstract of the United States 2007*. Washington, DC: U.S. Census Bureau, www.census.gov/compendia/statab/ (accessed June 29, 2007).

Vaughan, D. 1986. *Uncoupling: Turning points in intimate relationships*. New York: Oxford University Press.

Veevers, J.E. 1991. Traumas versus stress: A paradigm of positive versus negative divorce outcomes. *Journal of Divorce and Remarriage* 15:99–126.

Vestal, A. 1999. Mediation and Parental Alienation Syndrome: Considerations for an intervention model. *Family and Conciliation Courts Review* 37(4):487–503.

Waite, L., and M. Gallagher. 2000. *The case for marriage: Why married people are happier, healthier and better off financially*. New York: Doubleday.

Wallerstein, J.S. 1998. Children of divorce: A society in search of policy. In *All our families: New policies for a new century*. Edited by M.A. Mason, A. Skolnick, and S.D. Sugarman. New York: Oxford University Press, 66–94.

Wallerstein, J.S., and J. Kelly. 1980. *Surviving the break-up: How children actually cope with divorce*. New York: Basic Books.

Wallerstein, J.S., and S. Blakeslee. 1989. *Second chances: Men, women, and children a decade after divorce*. New York: Ticknor & Fields.

Wallerstein, J.S., J.M. Lewis, and S. Blakeslee. 2000. *The unexpected legacy of divorce: A 25-year landmark study*. New York: Hyperion.

Walther, A.N. 1991. *Divorce hangover*. New York: Pocket Books.

Walzer, S., and T.P. Oles. 2003. Managing conflict after marriages end: A qualitative study of narratives of ex-spouses. *Journal of Contemporary Human Services* 84(2):192–201.

Weitzman, L. 1985. *The divorce revolution*. New York: Free Press.

Wheaton, B. 1990. Life transitions, role histories, and mental health. *American Sociological Review* 55(2):209–23.

White, L., and A. Booth. 1985. The transition to parenthood and marital quality. *Journal of Family Issues* 6:435–49.

Whitehead, B.D. 1996. *The divorce culture*. New York: Knopf.

Whitebread, B.D., and D. Popenoe. 2005. *The state of our unions: The social health of marriage in America*. New Brunswick, NJ: The National Marriage Project, The State University of New Jersey, http://marriage.rutgers.edu/Publications/SOOU/TEXTSOOU2005.htm#Divorce (accessed December 14, 2007)

Whitehead, B.D. 1997. The children's story of divorce. *Books & Culture Magazine*, September/October, 3; www.christianitytoday.com/bc/7b5/7b5003.html (accessed January 11, 2007).

Wickrama, K.A.S., F.O. Lorenz, R.D. Conger, and G. Elder Jr. 2006. Married and recently divorced mothers' changes in family financial strain and physical health: An investigation of trajectories during the middle years. *Social Science and Medicine* 63:123–36.

Wilgoren, J. 2002. Divorce court proceeds in a lawyer-free zone. *The New York Times*, February 9, A10.

Williams, B.L. 1994. Reflections on family poverty. *Families in Society: The Journal of Contemporary Human Services* 75:47–50.

Wilson, C. 2001. Hallmark hits the mark. *USA Today*, June 14, 1D, 2D.

Wynn, R.L., and J. Bowenng. 1990. Homemaking practices and evening meals in married and separated families with young children. *Journal of Divorce and Remarriage* 14:107–23.

Zaslow, J. 2005. Emailing the ex: Technology can help ease dealings between divorced couples. *The Wall Street Journal*, November 3, D1.

Zill, N., D.R. Morrison, and M.J. Coiro. 1993. Long-term effects of parental divorce on parent-child relationships, adjustment, and achievement in young adulthood. *Journal of Family Psychology* 7(1):91–103.

CHAPTER 15

Ahrons, C.R. 1987. *Divorced families: A multidisciplinary developmental view*. New York: Norton.

Ahrons, C.R. 1994. *The good divorce: Keeping your family together when your marriage comes apart*. New York: HarperCollins.

Amato, P.R., and J. Cheadle. 2005. The long reach of divorce: Divorce and child well-being across three generations. *Journal of Marriage and Family* 67:191–206.

Amato, P.R., and J.G. Gilbreth. 1999. Divorced fathers and children's well-being: A meta-analysis. *Journal of Marriage and Family* 61:557–73.

Ambert, A.-M. 1986. Being a stepparent: Live-in and visiting stepchildren. *Journal of Marriage and the Family* 48:795–804.

Beer, W. 1992. *American stepfamilies*. New Brunswick, NJ: Transaction.

Beer, W.R., ed. 1988. *Relative strangers*. Lanham, MD: Rowan & Littlefield.

Bohannan, P. 1970. Divorce chains, households of remarriage, and multiple divorces.

In *Divorce and after*. Edited by P. Bohannan. New York: Doubleday, 113–23.

Booth, A., and J.N. Edwards. 1992. Starting over: Why remarriages are more unstable. *Journal of Family Issues* 13:179–94.

Bramlett, M.D., and W.D. Mosher. 2002. Cohabitation, marriage, divorce, and remarriage in the United States. *Vital Health Statistics* 23(2). Hyattsville, MD: National Center for Health Statistics, www.cdc.gov/nchs/data/series/sr_23/sr23_022.pdf (accessed July 3, 2007).

Bray, J.H., and J. Kelly. 1998. *Stepfamilies: Love, marriage and parenting in the first decade*. New York: Broadway Books.

Brooke, J. 2002. A promise to love, honor and bear no children. *The New York Times*, October 13, sec. 9, 1, 11.

Canavan, M.M., W.J. Meyer III, and D.C. Higgs. 1992. The female experience of sibling incest. *Journal of Marital and Family Therapy* 18(2):129–42.

Cherlin, A. 1981. *Marriage, divorce, remarriage*. Cambridge, MA: Harvard University Press.

Cherlin, A.J. 1978. Remarriage as incomplete institution. *American Journal of Sociology* 84:634–50.

Cherlin, A.J., and F.F. Furstenberg Jr. 1994. Stepfamilies in the United States: A reconsideration. *Annual Review of Sociology* 20:359–81.

Church, E. 1994. What is a good stepmother? In *Families and justice: From neighborhoods to nations. Proceedings*, Annual Conference of the National Council on Family Relations, no. 4, 60.

Clarke, S.C., and B.F. Wilson. 1994. The relative stability of remarriages: A cohort approach using vital statistics. *Family Relations* 43: 305–10.

Clingempeel, W.G. 1981. Quasi-kin relationships and marital quality in stepfather families. *Journal of Personality and Social Psychology* 41:890–901.

Clingempeel, W.G., E. Brand, and R. Ievoli. 1984. Stepparent-stepchild relationships in stepmother and stepfather families: A multimethod study. *Family Relations* 33:465–73.

Coleman, M., and L.H. Ganong. 1990. Remarriage and stepfamily research in the 1980s: Increased interest in an old family form. *Journal of Marriage and the Family* 52 925–40.

Coleman, M., and L.H. Ganong. 1991. Remarriage and stepfamily research in the 1980s. In *Contemporary families: Looking forward, looking back*. Edited by A. Booth. Minneapolis: National Council on Family Relations, 192–207.

Coleman, M., and L.H. Ganong. 1997. Stepfamilies from the stepfamily's perspective. In *Stepfamilies: History, research, and policy*. Edited by I. Levin and M.B. Sussman. New York: Haworth, 107–22.

Coleman, M., L.H. Ganong, and R. Gingrich. 1985. Stepfamily strengths: A review of popular literature. *Family Relations* 34:583–89.

Crary, D. 2003. Dating habits, sex lives of middle-age singles. *San Francisco Chronicle*, September 29, A2.

Crosbie-Burnett, M., and E.A. Lewis. 1993. Use of African-American family structures and functionmg to address the challenges of European-American postdivorce families. *Family Relations* 42:243–48.

Demo, D.H., and A.C. Acock. 1996. Singlehood, marriage, and remarriage: The effects of family structure and family relationships on mothers' well-being. *Journal of Family Issues* 17(3):388–407.

Finding happiness between commercials. 2003. *The Chronicle of Higher Education*, October 17, B4.

Fine, M.A., and L.A. Kurdek. 1992. The adjustment of adolescents in stepfather and stepmother families. *Journal of Marriage and the Family* 54:725–36.

Fine, M.A., L.H. Ganong, and M. Coleman. 1997. The relation between role constructions and adjustment among stepfathers. *Journal of Family Issues* 18:503–25.

Finkelhor, D. 1987. The sexual abuse of children: Current research reviewed. *Psychiatric Annals* 17:233–41

Finkelor, D. 1984. *Child sexual abuse: New theory and research*. New York: Free Press.

For richer or poorer again. 2002. *Consumer Reports*, June, 60–61.

Furstenberg, F.F. Jr. 1980. Reflections on remarriage. *Journal of Family Issues* 1(4):443–53.

Furstenberg, F.F. Jr., and C. Nord. 1985. Parenting apart: Patterns in childrearing after marital disruption. *Journal of Marriage and the Family* 47(4):893–904.

Gamache, S.J. 1997. Confronting nuclear family bias in stepfamily research. *Marriage and Family Review* 26(1-2):41–50.

Gangong, L.H., and M. Coleman. 1989. Preparing for remarriage: Anticipating the issues, seeking solutions. *Family Relations* 38:28–33.

Ganong, L., and M. Coleman. 1994. *Remarried family relationships*. Newbury Park, CA: Sage.

Ganong, L.H., and H. Coleman. 2004. *Stepfamily relationships: Development, dynamics, and interventions*. New York: Kluwer Academic/Plenum.

Ganong, L.H., and M. Coleman. 1993. A meta-analytic comparison of the self-esteem and behavior problems of stepchildren to children in other family structures. *Journal of Divorce and Remarriage* 19:143–63.

Gerlach, P.K. 2003. Who belongs to our (multi-home) stepfamily? How to make a multi-generation map ("genogram") to see who you all are. Stepfamily inFormation, Stepfamily Association of America. http://sfhelp.org/03/geno1.htm (accessed May 15, 2007).

Giles-Sims, J. 1997. Current knowledge about child abuse. In *Stepfamilies: History, research, and policy*. Edited by I. Levin and M. Sussman. New York: Haworth, 215–30.

Goldenberg, H., and I. Goldenberg. 1994. *Counseling today's families*. 2nd ed. Pacific Grove, CA: Brooks/Cole.

Green, J., and S. Wisdom. 2001. *Stepcoupling: Creating and sustaining a strong marriage in today's blended family*. New York: Crown/Three Rivers.

Gross, P. 1986. Defining post-divorce remar-

riage families: A typology based on the subjective perceptions of children. *Journal of Divorce* 10:205–17.

Hacker, A. 2003. *Mismatch: The growing gulf between men and women*. New York: Scribner's.

Harmon, A. 2005. Ask them (all 8 of them) about their grandson. *The New York Times*, March 20, sec. 1, 1, 18.

Herbert, W. 1999a. When strangers become family. *U.S. News & World Report*, November 29, 58–65.

Hetherington, E.M., and J. Kelly. 2002. *For better or for worse: Divorce reconsidered*. New York: Norton.

Ihinger-Tallman, M., and K. Pasley. 1987a. Divorce and remarriage in the American family: A historical review. In *Remarriage and stepparenting: Current research and theory*. Edited by K. Pasley and M. Ihinger-Tallmann. New York: Guilford.

Ihinger-Tallman, M., and K. Pasley. 1987b. *Remarriage*. Newbury Park, CA: Sage.

Ihinger-Tallman, M., and K. Pasley. 1997. Stepfamilies in 1984 and today—A scholarly perspective. In *Stepfamilies: History, research, and policy*. Edited by I. Levin and M.B. Sussman. New York: Haworth, 19–40.

Jensen, L., and C. Doxey. 1996. Family, type, and denomination in reported sexual abuse. Poster session presented at the 58th Annual Conference of the National Council on Family Relations, Kansas City, Missouri.

Jeynes, W.H. 1999. Effects of remarriage following divorce on the academic achievement of children. *Journal of Youth and Adolescence* 28(3):385–94.

Johnson, D. 2003. The war between men and women (cont'd). *The New York Review of Books*, October 23, 35–37.

Johnson, D.R., and A. Booth. 1998. Marital quality: A product of the dyadic environment or individual factors. *Social Force* 76:883–905.

Jones, A.C. 2003. Reconstructing the stepfamily: Old myths, new stories. *Social Work* 48(2):228–37.

Kennedy, G.E. 1985. Family relationships as perceived by college students from single-parent, blended, and intact families. *Family Perspective* 19:117–26.

Kheshgi-Genovese, Z., and T.A. Genovese 1997. Developing the spousal relationship within stepfamilies. *Families in Society: The Journal of Contemporary Human Services* 78:255–64.

Kinsey, A., W. Pomeroy, C. Martin, and P. Gebhard. 1953. *Sexual behavior in the human female*. Philadelphia, PA: Saunders.

Kreider, R.M. 2005. Number, timing, and duration of marriages and divorces: 2001. *Current Population Reports*, P70-97, February. Washington, DC: U.S. Census Bureau, www.census.gov/prod/2005pubs/p70-97.pdf (accessed July 3, 2007).

Kurdek, L.A. 1989. Relationship quality for newly married husbands and wives: Marital history, stepchildren, and individual difference predictors. *Journal of Marriage and the Family* 51(4):1053–64.

Kurdek, L.A., and M.A. Fine. 1991. Cognitive correlates of satisfaction for mothers and stepfathers in stepfather families. *Journal of Marriage and the Family* 53:565–72.

Kurdek, L.A., and M.A. Fine. 1993. The relation between family structure and young adolescents' appraisals of family climate and parenting behavior. *Journal of Family Issues* 14:279–90.

Kyungok, H. 1994. Father's child care time across family types. In *Families and justice: From neighborhoods to nations. Proceedings,* Annual Conference of the National Council on Family Relations, no. 4, 22.

Lang, S.S. 1997. Childhood sexual abuse affects relationships in adulthood. *Human Ecology Forum* 25:3–4.

Larson, J.H., and S.M. Allgood. 1987. A comparison of intimacy in first-married and remarried couples. *Journal of Family Issues* 8:319–31.

Lauer, J.C., and R.H. Lauer. 1999. *Becoming family: How to built a stepfamily that really works.* Minneapolis: Aubsburg.

Levin, I. 1997. Stepfamily as project. In *Stepfamilies: History, research, and policy.* Edited by I. Levin and M.B. Sussman. New York: Haworth, 123–33.

Lutz, P. 1983. The stepfamily: An adolescent perspective. *Family Relations* 32(3):367–75.

MacDonald, W., and A. DeMaris. 1996. Parenting stepchildren and biological children: The effects of stepparent's gender and new biological children. *Journal of Family Issues* 17:5–25.

MacDonald, W.L., and A. DeMaris. 1995. Remarriage, stepchildren, and marital conflict: Challenges to the incomplete institutionalization hypothesis. *Journal of Marriage and the Family* 57:387–98.

Marano, H.E. 2000. Divorced? Don't even think of remarrying until you read this. *Psychology Today* (March/April):56–64.

Martin, T.C., and L. Bumpass. 1989. Trends in marital disruption. *Demography* 26:37–52.

Mason, M. 1998. The modern American stepfamily: Problems and possibilities. In *All our families: New policies for a new century.* Edited by M.A. Mason, A. Skolnick, and S.D. Sugarman. New York: Oxford University Press, 95–116.

McClenon, J.B. 2002. Blended families: The Brady Bunch were a fraud. *San Francisco Chronicle,* April 14, E2.

Mills, D. 1984. A model for stepparent development. *Family Relations* 33:365–72.

Montenegro, X. P., T. Needham, S. Gross, M. Jacquet, A.D. Stewart, S. Taie, and L. Fisher. 2003. Lifestyles, dating and romance: A study of midlife singles. Executive summary for *AARP The Magazine.* Survey conducted by Knowledge Networks, Inc., September. Washington, DC: AARP. http://research.aarp.org/general/singles_1.pdf (accessed May 15, 2007).

Montgomery, M.J., E.R. Anderson, E.M. Hetherington, and W.G. Clingempeel. 1992. Patterns of courtship for remarriage: Implications for child adjustment and parent-child relationships. *Journal of Marriage and the Family* 54:686–98.

Morgan, L.W. 2002. The duty of stepparents to support their stepchildren. Supportguidelines.com www.childsupportguidelines.com/articles/art199908.html (accessed May 15, 2007).

National Longitudinal Study of Children and Youth. 1997. *Applied Research Bulletin* 3(2). Human Resources Development Canada. www.hrdc-drhc.gc.ca/ (accessed May 15, 2007).

O'Flaherty, K.M., and L.W. Eels. 1988. Courtship behavior of the remarried. *Journal of Marriage* and *the Family* 50:499–506.

Ono, H. 2005. Marital history homogamy between the divorced and the never married among non-Hispanic whites. *Social Science Research* 34(2):333–56.

Palisi, B.J., M. Orleans, D. Caddell, and B. Korn. 1991. Adjustment to stepfatherhood: The effects of marital history and relations with children. *Journal of Divorce and Remarriage* 14:89–106.

Papernow, P.L. 1988. Stepparent role development: From outsider to intimate. In *Relative strangers.* Edited by W.R. Beer. Lanham, MD: Rowman & Littlefield, 54–82.

Papernow, P.L. 1993. *Becoming a stepfamily: Patterns of development in remarried families.* San Francisco: Jossey-Bass.

Pasley, K. 2000. Stepfamilies doing well despite challenges. *National Council on Family Relations* Report 45:6–7.

Pasley, K., L. Rhoden, E.B. Visher, and J.S. Visher. 1996. Successful stepfamily therapy: Clients' perspectives. *Journal of Marital and Family Therapy* 22(3):343–57.

Peek, C.W., N.J. Bell, T. Waidren, and G.T. Sorrell. 1988. Patterns of functioning in families of remarried and first-married couples. *Journal of Marriage and the Family* 50:699–708.

Peterson, K.S. 2002. Stepmoms step up to the plate. *USA Today,* May 7, 1D, 2D.

Pink, J.E.T., and K.S. Wampler. 1985. Problem areas in stepfamilies: Cohesion, adaptability, and the stepfather-adolescent relationship. *Family Relations* 34:327–35.

Raphael, P. 1978. The stepmother trap. *McCall's,* February, 188–94.

Recker, N.K. 2001. The wicked stepmother myth. Fact sheet FLM-FS-4-01, Ohio State University Extension, Family Life Month Packet 2001. http://ohioline.osu.edu/flm01/FS04.html (accessed May 15, 2007).

Russell, D.E. 1986. *The secret trauma: Incest in the lives of girls and women.* New York: Basic Books.

Rutter, V. 1994. Lessons from stepfamilies. *Psychology Today.* (May/June):27, 30 passim.

Sager, C.J., H. Steer, H. Crohn, E. Rodstein, and E. Walker. 1980. Remarriage revisited. *Family and Child Mental Health Journal* 6:19–33.

Sager, C.J., H.S. Brown, H. Crohn, T. Engel, E. Rodstein, and L. Walker. 1983. *Treating the remarried family.* New York: Brunner/Mazel.

Schwartz, S.J., and G.E. Finley. 2005. Fathering in intact and divorced families: Ethnic differences in retrospective reports. *Journal of Marriage and Family* 67:207–15.

Silverman, R.E. 2003. Just married, with children: The familymoon. *The Wall Street Journal,* May 21, D1, D3.

Smith, D. 1990. *Stepmothering.* New York: St. Martin's.

Solomon, J.C. 1992. Child sexual abuse by family members: A radical feminist perspective. *Sex Roles* 27:473–85.

Spanier, G., and L. Thompson. 1987. *Parting: The aftermath of separation and divorce,* updated edition. Newbury Park, CA: Sage.

Spanier, G.B., and F. Furstenberg Jr. 1982. Remarriage after divorce: A longitudinal analysis of well-being. *Journal of Marriage and the Family* 44(3):709–20.

Sumner, W.C. 1997. The effects of parental dating on latency children living with one custodial parent. *Journal of Divorce and Remarriage* 27:137–57.

Sweet, J.A., L.L. Bumpass, and V.R.A. Call. 1988. *The design and content of the National Survey of Families and Households.* (Working Paper NSFH-1). Madison: University of Wisconsin, Center for Demography and Ecology.

Thomson, E. 2001. Remarriage, cohabitation, and changes in mothering behavior. *Journal of Marriage and the Family* 63(2):370–81.

Trost, J. 1997. Step-family variations. In *Stepfamilies: History, research, and policy.* Edited by I. Levin and M.B. Sussman. New York: Haworth, 71–84.

Turkat, I.D. 1995. Divorce-related malicious mother syndrome. *Journal of Family Violence* 10(3):253–64.

Turnbull, S.K., and J.M. Turnbull. 1983. To dream the impossible dream: An agenda for discussion with stepparents. *Family Relations* 32:227–30.

U.S. Census Bureau. 2001. *Population profile of the United States: 2000 (Internet release).* Washington, DC: U.S. Government Printing Office.

U.S. Department of Health, Education, and Welfare. 1978. *Yours, mine, and ours: Tips for stepparents.* Washington, DC: U.S. Government Printing Office.

Van Pelt, N.L. 1985. *How to turn minuses into pluses: Tips for working moms, single parents, and stepparents.* Washington, DC: Review and Herald, Better Living Series.

Vemer, E., M. Coleman, L.H. Ganong, and H. Cooper. 1989. Marital satisfaction in remarriage: A meta-analysis. *Journal of Marriage and the Family* 51:713–25.

Visher, E.B., and J. Visher. 1982. *How to win as a stepfamily.* New York: Taylor & Francis.

Visher, E.B., and J. Visher. 1993. Remarriage families and stepparenting. In *Normal family processes.* 2nd ed. Edited by F. Walsh. New York: Guilford, 235–53.

Visher, E.B., and J.S. Visher. 1979. *Stepfamilies: A guide to working with stepparents and stepchildren.* New York: Brunner/Mazel.

Visher, E.B., and J.S. Visher. 1991. *How to win as a stepfamily.* New York: Brunner/Mazel.

Visher, E.B., and J.S. Visher. 1996. *Therapy with stepfamilies.* New York: Brunner/Mazel.

Wallerstein, J., and J. Kelly. 1980a. Effects of divorce on the visiting father-child relationship. *American Journal of Psychiatry* 137(12):1534–39.

Wallerstein, J., and J. Kelly. 1980b. *Surviving the breakup: How children and parents cope with divorce.* New York: Basic Books.

Watson, P.A. 1995. *Ancient stepmothers: Myth, misogyny and reality.* Leiden: E.J. Brill.

Weiss, R. 1975. *Marital separation.* New York: Basic Books.

White, L.K. 1990. Determinants of divorce: A review of research in the eighties. *Journal of Marriage and the Family* 52:904–12.

White, L.K. 1991. Divorce over the life course: The role of marital happiness. *Journal of Family Issues* 12(1):5–21.

White, L.K., and A. Booth. 1985. Stepchildren in remarriages. *American Sociological Review* 50:689–98.

White, L.K., A. Booth, and J.N. Edwards. 1986. Children and marital happiness. *Journal of Family Issues* 7(2):131–47.

Whitsett, D., and H. Land 1992. The development of a role strain index for stepparents. *Families in Society: The Journal of Contemporary Human Services* 73:14–22.

APPENDICES

Amato, P.R., and J.G. Gilbreth. 1999. Divorced fathers and children's well-being: A meta-analysis. *Journal of Marriage and Family* 61:557–73.

Chaya, N., K.-A. Amen, and M. Fox. 2002. *Condoms count: Meeting the need in the era of HIV/AIDS.* Washington, DC: Population Action International.

Chesson, H.W., P. Harrison, and R. Stall. 2003. Changes in alcohol consumption and in sexually transmitted disease incidence rates in the United States: 1983–1998. *Journal of Studies on Alcohol* 16(5):623–31.

Davis, R.J. 2003. A new choice for birth control. *The Wall Street Journal,* July 8, D3.

Houppert, K. 2007. Final period. *The New York Times,* July 17, www.nytimes.com/2007/07/17/opinion/17houppert.html?_r=1&pagewanted=print&oref=slogin (accessed July 23, 2007).

Jarow, J., R.E. Budin, M. Dym, B.R. Zirkin, S. Noren, and F.F. Marshall. 1985. Quantitative pathologic changes in the human testis after vasectomy. *New England Journal of Medicine* 20:1252–56.

Kalb, C. 1998. Now, a scary strain of drug-resistant HIV. *Newsweek,* July 13, 63.

Kalb, C. 2003. An old enemy is back. *Newsweek,* February 10, 60.

Kaplan, H.S. 1979. *Disorders of sexual desire: And other new concepts and techniques in sex therapy.* New York: Brunner/Mazel.

Kinsey, A., W. Pomeroy, and C. Martin. 1948. *Sexual behavior in the human male.* Philadelphia, PA: Saunders.

Kinsey, A., W. Pomeroy, and C. Martin. 1953. *Sexual behavior in the human female.* Philadelphia, PA: Saunders.

Kolata, G. 1992. In late abortions, decisions are painful and options few. *The New York Times,* January 5, sec. 1, 1, 12.

Levin, R., and A. Levin. 1975. Sexual pleasure: The surprising preferences of 100,000 women. *Redbook,* September, 51–68.

Masters, W., and V. Johnson. 1966. *Human sexual response.* Boston: Little, Brown.

National Women's Health Information Center. 2002. Birth control methods. November. *4woman.gov.* U.S. Department of Health and Human Services, Office on Women's Health. www.4woman.gov/faq/birthcont.htm#7. (accessed July 23, 2007).

Physicians for Reproductive Choice and Health and The Alan Guttmacher Institute. 2006. *An overview of abortion in the United States,* May, www.guttmacher.org/presentations/ab_slides.html (accessed July 23, 2007).

Rosenfeld, J. 1997. Postcoital contraception and abortion. In *Women's health in primary care.* Edited by J. Rosenfeld. Baltimore: Williams & Wilkins, 315–29.

Schwartz, J.L., and H.I. Gabelnick. 2002. Current contraceptive research. *Perspectives on Sexual and Reproductive Health* 34(6), www.guttmacher.org/pubs/journals/3431002.html (accessed July 23, 2007).

Stolberg, S.G. 2002. Drug agency approves a quick test for HIV. *The New York Times,* November 8, A14.

Name Index

Rosenberg, Linda, 460
Rosenberg, T., 389
Rosenblatt, B., 351
Rosenbluth, S. C., 413
Rosenfeld, J., A15
Rosenthal, M. B., 353
Rosler, J., 166
Ross, C. E., 109, 428
Ross, E., 333
Ross, K., 289, 291
Rossi, A. S., 391
Rossi, H. L., 121
Roth, Walton T., 409
Rowland, M., 175
Roy, R., 107
Rubenstein, Alma, 148
Rubin, L., 456, 460
Rubin, R., 333
Rubin, S., 263
Ruchlis, H., 53–54
Ruefli, T., 314
Ruotola-Behrendt, A., 178
Rusbult, Caryl, 176
Russell, D. E., 574
Russell, Kurt, 377
Russell, S., 243
Rutter, V., 569, 570, 572, 577
Ruvolo, A. P., 156
Ryan, J., 9
Ryan, Meg, 187

S

Saber, Brian, 359
Sadker, D., 103, 105
Sadker, M., 103, 105
Safilios-Rothschild, C., 193
Sager, C. J., 550
Sahlman, S., 49
Salovey, P., 136–137
Sampson, R., 190
Sandel, M., 358
Sanders, B. R., 359
Sanders, S. A., 234
Sanner, A., 533
Santelli, J. S., 345
Sapolsky, Robert M., 18
Sarandon, Susan, 377, 447
Sarkisian, N., 3
Sarnoff, I., 265
Sarnoff, S., 265
Satir, Virginia, 211
Sauber, S. R., 520
Sauerman, T., 311
Saul, S., 346
Savage, H., 17
Savin-Williams, R. C., 311
Sawhill, I., 419
Sawin, L. L., 109
Scanzoni, J., 189, 198
Scarf, M., 194, 280, 457, 464
Scelfo, J., 502
Schacht, C., 195
Schackman, B. R., 245
Schalet, A. T., 229
Scharlach, Andrew, 464
Schellbarger, S., 101, 378
Schellhardt, T. P., 384
Schemo, D. J., 229
Schenck-Yglesias, C. G., 403
Schenkkan, Robert, 146
Scherreik, S., 173
Scheuble, L. K., 261
Schiffer, Claudia, 471
Schkade, D. A., 6
Schlefer, Meg, 546

Schmalz, J., 310
Schmidt, J. D., 476
Schmitt, J. P., 173, 314
Schneider, M., 135
Schneider, P., 150
Schoen, R., 509
Schoenborn, C. A., 525
Schoeni, R. F., 289, 291
Schram, V., 463
Schrof, J. M., 189, 199
Schvaneveldt, J., 81
Schwartz, J. L., A12
Schwartz, P., 173, 191–192, 278,
    313, 314
Schwartz, S. J., 560
Schwarz, J. C., 471
Seff, M. A., 101, 230
Seinfeld, Jerry, 287
Seitz, V., 407
Seligman, Martin, 2, 6, 7, 8, 414
Seltzer, J. A., 534
Selye, Hans, 482, 486
Selzer, J. A., 377
Senchak, M., 474
Senn, C., 471
Sennett, R., 189
Serovich, J. M., 519
Sessions, L. S., 166
Shaffer, S. M., 291
Shainberg, L. W., 238
Shakespeare, William, 133, 135
Shannon, J. D., 394
Shapiro, A. F., 392, 534
Shapiro, B. L., 471
Shapiro, L., 99
Sharma, A., 178
Sharp, D., 516
Sharpe, R., 430
Shaver, P., 129
Sheehan, E. P., 159
Sheen, Charlie, 287, 495
Sheffield, R., 357
Shellenbarger, S., 167, 374, 383,
    385, 427, 438
Shelton, B. A., 174, 508
Sheppard, A., 536
Sherman, L. W., 476
Shifrin, D. L., 221
Shiller, Yuri, 326–327
Shim, M., 253, 261
Shook, N. J., 469
Shore, W. B., 375
Shostak, A. B., 158
Shriver, J., 497, 512
Shulman, P., 141
Shultz-Jacob, Jennifer Lee, 357
Siegel, B., 486
Siegel, D. H., 360
Siegel, J. M., 465
Silsby, G., 48
Silver, M., 227–228
Silver, N., 197
Silverman, R. E., 262, 280,
    533–535, 547
Silverstein, Merrill, 404, 559
Simbey, Mapendo, 150
Simenauer, J., 158
Simon, C., 232
Simon, E., 459
Simon, Walter, 258
Simons, R. L., 395, 469–470
Simpson, J. A., 398
Skolnick, Arlene, 252
Slater, S., 81
Slon, Steve, 551
Small, S., 436

Smalley, David P., 280
Smalley, Marian, 280
Smeeding, T. M., 423
Smith, Anna Nicole, 192
Smith, C. S., 150
Smith, D., 568
Smith, Jamie Marie, 351
Smith, K. M., 110, 465
Smith, Russell, 498
Smith, S., 360
Smith, S. E., 197
Smith, S. L., 88–89
Smith, T. W., 195
Smock, P. J., 149, 171, 174, 497,
    529
Snipes, Wesley, 67, 92
Snowden, Lynn, 125
Snyder, M., 488
Sobieski, R., 466
Sok, E., 383
Sokhi, D. S., 204
Soldo, B. J., 454
Solomon, J. C., 480, 574
Solot, Dorian, 170, 175
Somers, M. D., 337
Song, E. Y., 230
Sontag, M. S., 79
Sontag, Susan, 463
Sorell, G. T., 297
Sorenson, E., 497, 530
Sorenson, S. B., 474
Soriano, C. S., 150
Sorkin, L., 372
Soukup, E., 326
South, S. J., 189, 200, 297, 510
Spanier, G., 149, 171, 549–550,
    561
Spears, Britany, 220, 495, 502
Spence, J., 109
Spencer, J., 19
Spice Girls, 220
Spindler, Amy, 232
Spock, Benjamin, 47
Sprecher, S., 140, 149, 151, 158,
    237
Sprey, J., 407
Spring, I., 382
Springen, K., 496
St. John, W., 160
Stacey, Judith, 318, 322
Stack, S., 174
Staeheli, Jean Coppock, 458, 541
Stains, Laurence Roy, 125
Stallones, L., 9
Stanley, Scott, 174
Staples, Robert, 50, 300, 314
Stark, E., 480, 526
Starks, Deborah, 263
Starrels, M. E., 100
Stauth, C., 4
Steele, B. E., 479
Steffens, S., 252
Stein, Peter, 297, 299
Stephens, B., 461
Stephens, M., Jr., 497, 510
Stepp, L. S., 345
Sternberg, D. P., 207
Sternberg, Robert J., 131–132,
    134, 202, 282–283
Stets, J. E., 471
Stevens, Guy, 374
Stevenson, B., 197
Stewart, A. J., 514
Stewart, J. H., 374, 376, 386, 399
Stewart, T., 311
Stiller, Ben, 251

Stinnett, Nick, 582
Stinson, K. M., 465
Stith, Sandra, 475
Stodgill, R., 220, 228, 229
Stolberg, S. G., A3
Stone, B., 126
Storch, Mindy, 499
Storrow, H. A., 462
Stossel, S., 6
Stout, F., 501
Stout, H., 500
Strasburger, V. C., 221
Straus, M. A., 374, 386, 399, 400,
    460, 472, 474
Strauss, Alicia, 336
Strauss, Doug, 336
Strauss, N., 148
Strekfuss, D., 89
Stroes, J., 404
Stroup, A. L., 497, 529
Strouse, J. S., 221
Stutzer, A., 265
Styron, W., 460–461
Suárez-Orozco, M., 290
Sue, D., 235
Sugarman, D. B., 474
Sugarman, S. D., 302
Sugrue, T. J., 379
Suler, John, 187
Sullivan, K., 161
Sumner, W. C., 550
Suomi, S. J., 390
Supancic, M., 508, 510
Surowiecki, J., 417
Surra, C. A., 156
Sussman, M., 513
Swayze, Patrick, 92
Sweeney, M. M., 511
Sweet, J. A., 569
Sweet, S., 472
Swisher, K., 475
Swoboda, F., 437
Symons, D., 97
Symons, Johnny, 318
Szabo, X. P., 462

T

Talbot, M., 497
Tannen, Deborah, 209–210
Taris, T. W., 228
Tasker, F. L., 320
Tatara, T., 481
Taylor, B. G., 477
Taylor, C. M., 524
Taylor, Elizabeth, 548
Taylor, R. L., 101
Teachman, J. D., 173, 456, 511,
    530
Teachout, T., 251
Terry, Cindy, 258
Terry-Humen, E., 227–228
Tesser, A., 190
Teti, D. M., 255
Thelen, M. H., 109
Therrien, M., 50
Thoennes, N., 121, 138
Thomas, D. S., 74
Thomas, K., 533
Thomas, William I., 74
Thompson, A., 457, 515
Thompson, C., 311
Thompson, E., 339
Thompson, L., 192, 428,
    549–550
Thompson, M. P., 478

Subject Index

Bondage/discipline-dominance/submission-
sadism-masochism (BDSM), 239
Bonding, 390–391
Books, 119, 251
Boomerang effect, 454
Boomerang Nation (Furman), 291
Boundaries, 561, 573–575
Breadth, of intimacy, 10
Breadwinner fathers, 394
Breaking up relationships, 176–179
Breast feeding, 345
Bridal shower, 259
Bride price, 150
Bulimia, 462–463
Bundling, 41

C

Calendar method of birth control, 346,
A10
Cannabis, 459
*Can't Buy My Love: How Advertising Changes
the Way We Think and Feel*
(Kilbourne), 37
Capitalist class, 419
Caretakers, 76, 129, 361, 464
Caring, in marriage, 279–280
Car insurance, for unmarried couples, 322
Case study method, 63
Catholicism, 43
Celibacy, 237
Cell phones, 186–187
Centennial Park Action Committee, 326
Ceremonial component of marriage, 12
Cervical caps, 346, A9
Cervical mucus method of birth control,
346, A10
Chicanos, 26. *See also* Hispanics (Latinos)
Child abuse and neglect, 477–480
Child care, 383
Child-care centers, 434
Child-centered culture, 47
Child custody, 503, 532–535
Child-free couples, 16, 407
Child-free marriages, 336, 340, 407
Childless marriages, 336
Child pornography, 238
Children. *See also* Adoption; Parenting;
Parents; Stepchildren
abuse and neglect of, 477–480
of adolescent parents, 376
adult, 402–404
child-free and childless marriages,
336–337
child support, 530
conflict about, 201
divorce and, 511, 535–539
foster children, 360–363
with gay parents, 320, 322–323
influences on, 385–388
in Native American families, 39–40
only child and multiple child marriages,
338–339
postponing having, 337–338
as a reason for marriage, 15, 67
of single parents, 303
status and rights of children, 370–375
of working mothers, 442
Children's allowance (government), 531
Child stealing/abduction, 535
Child support, 530–531
Child Support Enforcement Amendments,
531
China, 123
Chinese Americans, 27. *See also* Asian
Americans

Chlamydia, 243, A4
Chronic illness, 463–464
Circular reasoning, 57
Civil annulment, 502
Civil unions, 315–317, 498
Class
dating and, 154–155
designations in U.S., 419–421
fertility rates and, 341
gender socialization and, 101
marital success and, 278
parenting and, 379
Classified ads, 159
Clinical research, 62–63
Clitoral orgasm, A1
Closed adoptions, 360
Closed couples, 300, 313
Closed fields, 158
Closeness, 194
Coercive power, 190
Cognitive development theory of gender
differences, 98
Cohabitation
advantages and disadvantages, 174–
175
characteristics of people who live
together, 170
defined, 168
divorce and, 510
experience of, 172–174
family of, 16
ground rules for, 175
reasons for, 168–170
uncoupling and, 499
Co-housing, 324, 325
Coitus, 237
Coitus interruptus, A9
Collaborating conflict style, 202
Collaborative divorce, 521–522
College students
drug use, 459–460
living arrangements, 325
marriages, 167
relationships, 166–167
sexual values, 224
Colonial era, 38–44
Colpotomy, A15
Combination pill, A11
Comic strips, 89
Coming out, 309
Commercial sex, 238
Commitment
cohabitation and, 174
companionate love and, 124–125
engagement as, 166
homosexuals and, 314–315
marriage and, 279
triangular theory of love and, 132
working mothers, 432
Committed singles, 300
Common couple violence, 473
Common-law marriages, 13, 321
Common Sense Media, 387
Communal living arrangements, 325
Communes, 324–325
Communication
barriers to, 211–213
divorce and, 513
effective, 213–215
gender differences, 209–211
nonverbal communication, 206–209
parenting and, 398–399
popular culture and the media, 186–187
technology and, 21, 22, 211
Community divorce, 519
Community property, 503

Commuter marriages, 290
Compadrazgo, 43
Companionate family, 46
Companionate grandparents, 406
Companionate love, 123–125, 132
Companionate marriages, 274
Companionship, 152, 174, 254
Competing conflict style, 201
Compressed workweek, 439
Compromising conflict style, 202
Computers, effect on families, 22
Computers (in miscommunicating), 211
Conclusions, 56
Condoms, 344, 346, A6–A9, A9, A13
Conflict
defined, 195
divorce and, 514
intimacy and, 194–196
in parenting, 435–436
in popular culture and the media,
186–187
power and, 188–193
resolving, 202–205
sources of, 196–201
styles of, 201–202
Conflict-habituated marriages, 271–272
Conflict taboo, 195
Conflict theoretical perspective, 73, 80, 114,
246, 281, 540
Conjugal love, 133
Conservative feminism, 111
Consummate love, 132
Contempt, 212
Content analysis, 66
Continuity, as a benefit of families, 19
Continuous coverage system, 391
Contraception, 344–347, A8–A15
Control, conflict about, 200
Control groups, 65, 68
Controlled separation, 500–501
Convenience, cohabitation and, 169
Co-parental divorce, 518
Coping
by abused children, 386–387
adaptation *versus*, 484–488
defense reactions, 483–484
definitions, 484
good *versus* bad stressors, 482
strategies for, 484–488
by working mothers, 431
Copper-T IUD, A12
Co-provider families, 429–430
Corporal punishment, parenting and, 399
Corporate welfare, 426
Costs. *See* Finances
Counseling. *See* Family therapy and
counseling
Courtly love, 122
Courtship, 149–152
Covenant marriage, 261–262
Crib deaths, 466
Crises. *See also* Violence
coping strategies, 482–488
defined, 449
hardiness and, 451
predictable stressors of the family life
cycle, 453–454
psychological stress reactions, 448–451
stress and stressors, 448–449
unpredictable stressors of the family life
cycle, 454–466
Critical thinking, 52–59
Criticism, 212
Cross-cultural studies, 65
Cross-dressers, 92
Crude divorce rate, 504

H

Hallucinogens, 459
Hanging out, 166
Happiness
    contributors to, 7
    cultural well-being and, 6–7
    genetics and, 6
    having children and, 370
    levels of, 7
    money and, 6
    remarriages and, 555–557
    through love and intimacy, 2–7
    uncoupling and, 496–497
    unmarried singles, 297
    work and a sense of purpose, 414
Hardiness, 451
Hassles versus crises, 448–449
Hasty generalizations, 56–57
Hawthorne effect, 64
Head Start Programs, 434
Health issues, 322, 525
Hedonic adaptation, 6
Hedonism, 226
Hedonistic affairs, 457
Hepatitis B, 243, A3
Hermaphrodites, 94
Herpes, 243, A4
Heterogamy, 277
Heterosexism, 67
Heterosexuality defined, 305
Heterosexual singles, 296–303
Hidden agendas, in blended families, 567
Hierarchy of needs (Maslow), 2
Hispanics (Latinos). See also Race and
        ethnicity
    child poverty rate and, 373
    demographics, 26–27
    divorce and, 511
    families, 43–44
    fertility rates, 340
    gender socialization and, 101
    HIV/AIDS and, 244
    immigration and, 50
    interracial marriage, 257–258
    learning about sex from parents, 229
    parenting, 379
Historians, family, 404
Historical studies, 65–66
HIV/AIDS, 236, 237, 242–246, A3, A8
Holmes-Rahe Life Events Scale, 450
Homemaker role, 428
Home ownership, for unmarried couples,
        323
Homoeroticism, 309
Homogamy, 153, 277
Homophobia, 310
Homosexuality, 67, 244. See also Gay and
        lesbian relationships
Homosexuality defined, 305
Honesty, 213
Honeymoons, 258, 260
Hooking up, 166
Hormonal methods of birth control, 346,
        A9–A10, A12
Hormones, 97
Hostility, 212
Household production, 19
Household tasks, conflict about, 197
Househusbands, 429
Housework, cohabitation and, 173–174
How to Fall Out of Love (Phillips), 178
HPV (human papilloma virus), 243, A4
Human immunodeficiency virus (HIV). See
        HIV/AIDS
Human papilloma virus (HPV), 243, A4

Hypergamy, 155
Hypogamy, 155
Hysterotomy, A16

I

Identity bargaining, 266
Immature versus mature love, 139–141
Immigrants and immigration, 28, 44–45,
        49–52, 290
Implants for birth control, 346
Incest, 477
Income, 418, 510. See also Finances
Independence, 194, 266
Independent variables, 65
India, 123, 150
Individualism, 21
Induced abortion, A16, 348
Inductive arguments, 56
Industrialization, 44–45, 415
Industrial Revolution, 21, 44
Inequality, 77, 190. See also Equality
Inexperience, 223
Infant mortality rate, 372–373
Infatuation, 132
Infertility, 353–358
Infidelity, 456–458, 513, 515
Inflation, 422
Inflexibility versus flexibility, 58
Informal separation, 500
Informational power, 191
Inhalants, 459
Inhibited female orgasm, A2
Inhibited sexual desire (ISD), 240
Injections for birth control, 346
Insight-oriented therapy, 205
Instrumental role, 71, 91
Insurance for unmarried couples, 322
Integrative couples therapy, 204
Interaction, 74
Internal stressors, 452
International adoptions, 362
Internet
    cybersex affairs on, 457
    effect on families, 22
    e-mail, 187
    meeting online, 160–162
    online dating, 126
    online porn, 221, 238
Interracial dating, 154
Interracial marriage, 256–258
Intersexuals, 94
Interviewer bias, 62
Interviews, 62
Intimacy
    conflict and, 194–205
    dating as, 152
    defined, 10
    dimensions of, 10–12
    love as, 120, 121, 124–125, 130–134
    males and, 109
    power and, 188–193
Intimacy reduction affairs, 457
Intimate partner abuse, 472–476
Intrafamilial abuse, 480
Intrauterine device (IUD), A11, A12, A13
Intrauterine system (IUS), A12
Intrinsic marriages, 272–273, 274
Introduction services, 162–163
Intuition, 60–61
In vitro fertilization (IVF), 355
Involved fathers, 394
Iron John (Bly), 112
Irrelevant attack on opponent, 57
ISD (inhibited sexual desire), 240–241
IUD (intrauterine device), A11, A12, A13

IUS (intrauterine system), A12
IVF (in vitro fertilization), 355

J

Jealousy, 135–137
Job sharing, 439
Joined-at-the-hip relationships, 166–167
Joint biological-stepfamily, 558–559
Joint custody, 532
Joint legal custody, 532
Joint physical custody, 532
Joint tenancy with right of survivorship, 323
Jumping to conclusions, 56

K

Kaposi's sarcoma, 243
Kibbutzes, 325
Kidnapping, 535
Kin, 16–17
Kinship systems, 39, 42–43, 45
Kissing, 125, 235
Klein Grid, 307
Kyrgyzstan, forced marriages in, 150

L

Labor force, 415
Laissez-faire parenting, 396
Laparoscopy, A15
Laparotomy, A15
Latchkey children, 383
Latent functions, 71
Latinos. See Hispanics (Latinos)
LAT (living-apart-together) couples, 290
Learned helplessness, 475
Lee's six styles of love, 133–134
Legal issues, 12–13, 261, 321–322, 508,
        517
Legitimate power, 191
Leisure, 7, 416–417
Lesbian feminism, 111
Lesbian relationships, 127
Lesbians. See Homosexuality
Leveling, 213
LGBT (lesbian, gay, bisexual, and
        transgender (or transgendered)
        people, 305
Liberal feminism, 110
Life insurance, for unmarried couples, 322
Lifestyle choice, 301
Lifestyles, defined, 293
Lifestyle stage, 301
Linus blanket, cohabitation and, 169
Listening, conflict and, 204
Living-apart-together (LAT) couples, 290
Living wage laws, 423
Loneliness, divorce and, 524
Longitudinal studies, 66
Love. See also Intimacy
    appreciation and happiness and, 4, 5
    defining, 120–127
    falling out of, 178, 514
    immature versus mature, 139–141
    marriage and happiness and, 3
    money and, 413
    negative forms of, 135–138
    theories of the origins of, 128–134
Lower middle class, 420
Loyalty, conflict about, 199–200
Loyalty response, to deteriorating
        relationships, 177
Ludus, 133
Lunelle, A12
Lust, 124

Photo Credits